*new dictionary of the* history of ideas

# EDITORIAL BOARD

**Editor in Chief**

Maryanne Cline Horowitz, *Occidental College*

*University of California, Los Angeles*

**Associate Editors**

Jonathan Berkey, *Davidson College*

Zvi Ben-Dor Benite, *New York University*

Benjamin A. Elman, *Princeton University*

George Esenwein, *University of Florida, Gainesville*

Cary J. Nederman, *Texas A&M University*

Vassiliki Betty Smocovitis, *University of Florida, Gainesville*

Neferti Tadiar, *University of California, Santa Cruz*

Mary J. Weismantel, *Northwestern University*

Paul Tiyambe Zeleza, *Pennsylvania State University*

**Advisors**

Diane Apostolos-Cappadona, *Georgetown University*

Edwina Barvosa-Carter, *University of California, Santa Barbara*

Nupur Chaudhuri, *Texas Southern University*

Kostas Gavroglu, *University of Athens, Greece*

Donald R. Kelley, *Rutgers University*

Zine Magubane, *University of Illinois, Urbana-Champaign*

J. B. Schneewind, *Johns Hopkins University*

Blair Sullivan, *University of California, Los Angeles*

Reed Ueda, *Tufts University*

**Librarian Advisory Board**

Mary W. George, *Princeton University*

Suzy Szasz Palmer, *University of Louisville*

**Editorial Assistant**

Lisa Griffin

# new dictionary of the history of ideas

maryanne cline horowitz, editor in chief

volume 3

Game Theory to Lysenkoism

**CHARLES SCRIBNER'S SONS**

*An imprint of Thomson Gale, a part of The Thomson Corporation*

**GERMANNA COMMUNITY COLLEGE**
GERMANNA CENTER FOR ADVANCED TECHNOLOGY
18121 TECHNOLOGY DRIVE
CULPEPER, VA 22701

Detroit • New York • San Francisco • San Diego • New Haven, Conn. • Waterville, Maine • London • Munich

## New Dictionary of the History of Ideas
### Maryanne Cline Horowitz, Editor in Chief

©2005 Thomson Gale, a part of the Thomson Corporation.

Thomson and Star Logo are trademarks and Gale is a registered trademark used herein under license.

*For more information, contact*
Thomson Gale
27500 Drake Rd.
Farmington Hills, MI 48331-3535
Or you can visit our Internet site at
http://www.gale.com

ALL RIGHTS RESERVED
No part of this work covered by the copyright hereon may be reproduced or used in any form or by any means—graphic, electronic, or mechanical, including photocopying, recording, taping, Web distribution, or information storage retrieval systems—without the written permission of the publisher.

For permission to use material from this product, submit your request via Web at http://www.gale-edit.com/permissions, or you may download our Permissions Request form and submit your request by fax or mail to:

*Permissions Department*
Thomson Gale
27500 Drake Road
Farmington Hills, MI 48331-3535
Permissions Hotline:
248-699-8006 or 800-877-4253, ext. 8006
Fax: 248-699-8074 or 800-762-4058

Since this page cannot legibly accommodate all copyright notices, the acknowledgments constitute an extension of the copyright notice.

While every effort has been made to ensure the reliability of the information presented in this publication, Thomson Gale does not guarantee the accuracy of the data contained herein. Thomson Gale accepts no payment for listing; and inclusion in the publication of any organization, agency, institution, publication, service, or individual does not imply endorsement of the editors or publisher. Errors brought to the attention of the publisher and verified to the satisfaction of the publisher will be corrected in future editions.

LIBRARY OF CONGRESS CATALOGING-IN-PUBLICATION DATA

New dictionary of the history of ideas / edited by Maryanne Cline Horowitz.
    p. cm.
    Includes bibliographical references and index.
    ISBN 0-684-31377-4 (set hardcover : alk. paper) — ISBN 0-684-31378-2 (v. 1) — ISBN 0-684-31379-0 (v. 2) — ISBN 0-684-31380-4 (v. 3) — ISBN 0-684-31381-2 (v. 4) — ISBN 0-684-31382-0 (v. 5) — ISBN 0-684-31383-9 (v. 6) — ISBN 0-684-31452-5 (e-book)
    1. Civilization—History—Dictionaries. 2. Intellectual life—History—Dictionaries.
    I. Horowitz, Maryanne Cline, 1945–

CB9.N49 2005
903—dc22                                                    2004014731

This title is also available as an e-book.
ISBN 0-684-31452-5
Contact your Thomson Gale sales representative for ordering information.

Printed in the United States of America
10 9 8 7 6 5 4 3 2

# CONTENTS

# EDITORIAL AND PRODUCTION STAFF

**Project Editors**
Mark LaFlaur, Scot Peacock, Jennifer Wisinski

**Editorial Support**
Kelly Baiseley, Andrew Claps, Alja Collar, Mark Drouillard,
Kenneth Mondschein, Sarah Turner, Ken Wachsberger,
Rachel Widawsky, Christopher Verdesi

**Art Editor**
Scot Peacock

**Chief Manuscript Editor**
Georgia S. Maas

**Manuscript Editors**
Jonathan G. Aretakis, John Barclay, Sylvia Cannizzaro,
Melissa A. Dobson, Ted Gilley, Gretchen Gordon,
Ellen Hawley, Archibald Hobson, Elizabeth B. Inserra,
Jean Fortune Kaplan, Christine Kelley, John Krol,
Julia Penelope, Richard Rothschild, David E. Salamie,
Linda Sanders, Alan Thwaits, Jane Marie Todd

**Proofreaders**
Beth Fhaner, Carol Holmes, Melodie Monahan,
Laura Specht Patchkofsky, Hilary White

**Cartographer**
XNR Productions, Madison, Wisconsin

**Caption Writer**
Shannon Kelly

**Indexer**
Cynthia Crippen, AEIOU, Inc.

**Design**
Jennifer Wahi

**Imaging**
Dean Dauphinais, Lezlie Light, Mary Grimes

**Permissions**
Margaret Abendroth, Peggie Ashlevitz, Lori Hines

**Compositor**
GGS Information Services, York, Pennsylvania

**Manager, Composition**
Mary Beth Trimper

**Assistant Manager, Composition**
Evi Seoud

**Manufacturing**
Wendy Blurton

**Senior Development Editor**
Nathalie Duval

**Editorial Director**
John Fitzpatrick

**Publisher**
Frank Menchaca

# READER'S GUIDE

*This Reader's Guide was compiled by the editors to provide a systematic outline of the contents of the* New Dictionary of the History of Ideas, *thereby offering teachers, scholars, and the general reader a way to organize their reading according to their preferences. The Reader's Guide is divided into four sections: Communication of Ideas, Geographical Areas, Chronological Periods, and Liberal Arts Disciplines and Professions, as indicated in the outline below.*

## COMMUNICATION OF IDEAS

**Introduction to History of Communication of Ideas**

**Communication Media**

## GEOGRAPHICAL AREAS

**Global Entries**

**Africa**

**Asia**

**Europe**

**Middle East**

**North America**

**Latin and South America**

## CHRONOLOGICAL PERIODS

**Ancient**

**Dynastic (400 C.E.–1400 C.E.)**

**Early Modern (1400–1800 C.E.)**

**Modern (1800–1945)**

**Contemporary**

## LIBERAL ARTS DISCIPLINES AND PROFESSIONS

**Fine Arts**

**Humanities**

**Social Sciences**

**Sciences**

**Professions**

**Multidisciplinary Practices**

**Especially Interdisciplinary Entries**

## COMMUNICATION OF IDEAS

This category is the newest aspect of the *New Dictionary of the History of Ideas*; cultural studies, communications studies, and cultural history are moving the disciplines in this direction.

**Introduction to History of Communication of Ideas**

The following entries focus on the media humans have used to communicate with one another.

Absolute Music
Aesthetics: Asia
Architecture: Overview
Architecture: Asia
Arts: Overview
Astronomy, Pre-Columbian and Latin American
Bilingualism and Multilingualism
Borders, Borderlands, and Frontiers, Global
Calendar
Cinema
City, The: The City as a Cultural Center
City, The: The City as Political Center
Communication of Ideas: Africa and Its Influence
Communication of Ideas: Asia and Its Influence
Communication of Ideas: Europe and Its Influence
Communication of Ideas: Middle East and Abroad
Communication of Ideas: Orality and Advent of Writing
Communication of Ideas: Southeast Asia
Communication of Ideas: The Americas and Their Influence
Consumerism
Cultural Revivals
Cultural Studies
Dance
Diffusion, Cultural
Dress
Dualism
Education: Asia, Traditional and Modern
Education: Global Education
Emotions
Experiment
Garden
Gesture
Humor
Iconography
Images, Icons, and Idols
Japanese Philosophy, Japanese Thought
Language and Linguistics
Language, Linguistics, and Literacy
Learning and Memory, Contemporary Views
Mathematics
Media, History of
Metaphor
Migration: United States
Modernity: Africa
Museums
Music, Anthropology of

## Communication Media

This is a listing of the types of historical evidence the author used in writing the entry. While entries in the original Dictionary of the History of Ideas were to a great extent the history of texts, the entries in the New Dictionary of the History of Ideas are generally the cultural history of ideas, making use of the records of oral communication, visual communication, and communication through practices, as well as the history of texts, in order to show the impact of the idea on a wide variety of people.

### ORAL

The selective list below contains the entries that give the most coverage to historical examples of the oral transmission and transformation of ideas.

COMMUNICATION THROUGH HIGH TECHNOLOGY MEDIA (radio, television, film, computer, etc.)

## VISUAL

Each of the following entries in the *NDHI* either evocatively describes ideas, includes a visual image of an idea, or provides historical examples of societies visually transmitting and transforming ideas.

**New Dictionary of the History of Ideas**

## PRACTICES

Most of the entries in the *NDHI* discuss how specific societies habituated people to specific ideas. This selective list includes the entries on schools of thought and practice, religions, and political movements, as well as the entries on distinctive practices.

Socialism
Socialisms, African
Sophists, The
Sport
Stoicism
Subjectivism
Suicide
Superstition
Symbolism
Syncretism
Temperance
Terror
Theater and Performance
Time: Traditional and Utilitarian
Totalitarianism
Totems
Trade
Tradition
Tragedy and Comedy
Tribalism, Middle East
Untouchability: Overview
Untouchability: Menstrual Taboos
Untouchability: Taboos
Utilitarianism
Visual Order to Organizing Collections
Volunteerism, U.S.
Westernization: Africa
Westernization: Middle East
Westernization: Southeast Asia
Witchcraft
Witchcraft, African Studies of
Work
Yoga
Zionism

## TEXTUAL

Every entry in the *New Dictionary of the History of Ideas* used texts. The following is a list of entries that focused mainly on the history of a succession of texts. Each academic discipline has a succession of major authors with whom later practitioners of the discipline build upon and respond to creatively. The historian of a discipline—such as the history of political philosophy, literary history, or the history of science—considers the responses of thinkers and practitioners of a discipline to the major earlier texts in the discipline. In tracing the origin, development, and transformation of an idea, the historian of ideas considers thinkers' responses to texts from a variety of disciplines.

Agnosticism
Alchemy: Europe and the Middle East
Algebras
Altruism
America
Analytical Philosophy
Aristotelianism
Asceticism: Hindu and Buddhist Asceticism
Autobiography
Autonomy
Biography
Bureaucracy
Capitalism: Overview
Cartesianism
Casuistry

Causality
Censorship
Change
Chinese Thought
Civil Disobedience
Class
Communitarianism in African Thought
Conservatism
Continental Philosophy
Cosmology: Cosmology and Astronomy
Creolization, Caribbean
Crisis
Cycles
Death and Afterlife, Islamic Understanding of
Deism
Dialogue and Dialectics: Socratic
Dialogue and Dialectics: Talmudic
Eclecticism
Encyclopedism
Epistemology: Ancient
Epistemology: Early Modern
Equality: Gender Equality
Eschatology
Essentialism
Existentialism
Experiment
Falsifiability
Fatalism
Fetishism: Fetishism in Literature and Cultural Studies
Form, Metaphysical, in Ancient and Medieval Thought
Free Will, Determinism, and Predestination
General Will
Generation
Genius
Genre
Geometry
Gift, The
Globalization: Asia
Gnosticism
Good
Greek Science
Happiness and Pleasure in European Thought
Heaven and Hell
Hegelianism
Hermeneutics
Hierarchy and Order
Hinduism
Historical and Dialectical Materialism
Historicism
Historiography
History, Idea of
Humanism: Africa
Humanism: Chinese Conception of
Humanism: Renaissance
Humanity: Asian Thought
Human Rights: Overview
Idealism
Ideas, History of
Identity, Multiple: Overview
Identity: Identity of Persons
Imagination
Immortality and the Afterlife
Individualism
Intelligentsia
Jouissance

## GEOGRAPHICAL AREAS

### Global Entries

ENTRIES ON AT LEAST THREE GEOGRAPHIC AREAS OR A GLOBAL TOPIC

New Dictionary of the History of Ideas

**Latin and South America**

**New Dictionary of the History of Ideas**

## CHRONOLOGICAL PERIODS

This section is divided according to five periods in world history: Ancient, Dynastic, Early Modern, Modern, and Contemporary. Use this section together with the section on Geographical Areas.

### Ancient (before 400 C.E.)

ENTRIES FOCUSED ON THE PERIOD

ENTRIES WITH EXAMPLES FROM BEFORE 400 C.E.

Generally the examples in this category are from the ancient Middle East, Europe, or Asia.

**New Dictionary of the History of Ideas**

## Modern (1800–1945)
ENTRIES FOCUSED ON THE PERIOD

**New Dictionary of the History of Ideas**

Jihad
Liberation Theology
Liberty
Life
Linguistic Turn
Literary History
Logic and Philosophy of Mathematics, Modern
Maoism
Marxism: Overview
Marxism: Asia
Marxism: Latin America
Media, History of
Modernization
Modernization Theory
Nationalism: Overview
Nationalism: Africa
Nationalism: Cultural Nationalism
Nationalism: Middle East
Neocolonialism
Neoliberalism
Nuclear Age
Orientalism: African and Black Orientalism
Pan-Africanism
Pan-Arabism
Pan-Asianism
Pan-Islamism
Pan-Turkism
Paradigm
Parties, Political
Personhood in African Thought
Phenomenology
Philosophies: Feminist, Twentieth-Century
Poetry and Poetics
Populism: Latin America
Populism: United States
Positivism
Postcolonial Studies
Postcolonial Theory and Literature
Postmodernism
Pragmatism
Presentism
Privatization
Protest, Political
Psychoanalysis
Psychology and Psychiatry
Quantum
Queer Theory
Realism: Africa
Relativism
Relativity
Science Fiction
Segregation
Sexual Harassment
Sexuality: Sexual Orientation
Sociability in African Thought
Social Darwinism
Socialisms, African
Structuralism and Poststructuralism: Overview
Structuralism and Poststructuralism: Anthropology
Subjectivism
Technology
Terrorism, Middle East
Text/Textuality
Theater and Performance
Third Cinema

Third World
Totalitarianism
Virtual Reality
Virtue Ethics
War
Westernization: Africa
Westernization: Southeast Asia
Witchcraft
Womanism
Women and Femininity in U.S. Popular Culture
Women's Studies
Zionism

ENTRIES WITH EXAMPLES FROM THE PERIOD SINCE 1945 (especially since the 1970s)
Absolute Music
Aesthetics: Africa
Aesthetics: Asia
Aesthetics: Europe and the Americas
Africa, Idea of
Afrocentricity
Afropessimism
Agnosticism
Algebras
Alienation
Altruism
Ambiguity
America
Analytical Philosophy
Anarchism
Animism
Anthropology
Antifeminism
Anti-Semitism: Overview
Architecture: Overview
Architecture: Africa
Arts: Overview
Arts: Africa
Asceticism: Western Asceticism
Asian-American Ideas (Cultural Migration)
Assimilation
Atheism
Authenticity: Africa
Authoritarianism: Overview
Authoritarianism: East Asia
Authoritarianism: Latin America
Authority
Autobiography
Autonomy
Avant-Garde: Overview
Aztlán
Barbarism and Civilization
Beauty and Ugliness
Behaviorism
Bilingualism and Multilingualism
Biography
Biology
Body, The
Bushido
Calculation and Computation
Cannibalism
Capitalism: Overview
Cartesianism
Casuistry
Causality
Causation

## LIBERAL ARTS DISCIPLINES AND PROFESSIONS

This section is in accord with the university divisions of the Liberal Arts into Fine Arts, Humanities, Social Sciences, and Sciences and the graduate programs of the professions of Law, Medicine, and Engineering. The sample of Interdisciplinary Programs are listed under their most common university grouping. For example, Fine Arts includes Performance Arts; Social Sciences includes Women's Studies and Gender Studies, as well as Ethnic Studies; Sciences includes Ecology and Geology, as well as Computer Sciences; Humanities includes programs of Communication, Language, and Linguistics. Meanwhile, the growth of interdisciplinary programs reflects the increasing overlap between studies listed under the labels of Fine Arts, Humanities, Social Sciences, and Sciences. A discipline or interdisciplinary program only appears once, but an entry may appear under the several disciplines and interdisciplinary programs that influenced the scholarship of the article. Titles that appear in bold indicate entries that are especially suited as a introduction to the discipline.

Under the category Multidisciplinary Practices, there are entries on the many methods, techniques, theories, and approaches that have spread across the disciplines. The Multidisciplinary Practices help explain the contemporary trend of interdisciplinarity for which the history of ideas has long been known. At the end of this Reader's Guide is a listing of a number of entries that overlap three of the four divisions and a listing of entries that overlap all four divisions.

## Humanities

### COMMUNICATION, LANGUAGE, AND LINGUISTICS

## Social Sciences

**New Dictionary of the History of Ideas**

## Sciences

Creationism
Critical Race Theory
Death
Demography
Determinism
Development
Dystopia
Ecology
Emotions
Environmental Ethics
Environmental History
Epistemology: Early Modern
Equality: Racial Equality
Ethnohistory, U.S.
Eugenics
**Evolution**
Family: Modernist Anthropological Theory
Family: Family in Anthropology since 1980
Family Planning
Feminism: Overview
Game Theory
Garden
Gender: Overview
Gender: Gender in the Middle East
Gender in Art
Gender Studies: Anthropology
**Genetics: Contemporary**
**Genetics: History of**
Genocide
Gesture
Greek Science
Health and Disease
Heaven and Hell
History, Idea of
Humanism: Secular Humanism in the United States
Humanity: African Thought
Hygiene
Identity: Identity of Persons
Immortality and the Afterlife
Intentionality
Islamic Science
Jainism
Jouissance
Kinship
Learning and Memory, Contemporary Views
Life
Life Cycle: Adolescence
Life Cycle: Elders/Old Age
Lysenkoism
Machiavellism
Marriage and Fertility, European Views
Masks
Materialism in Eighteenth-Century European Thought
Mechanical Philosophy
Medicine: China
Medicine: Europe and the United States
Medicine: Islamic Medicine
Meme
Memory
Men and Masculinity
Mestizaje
Monarchy: Overview
Motherhood and Maternity
Musical Performance and Audiences
Natural History

Naturalism
Natural Theology
Nature
Naturphilosophie
Negritude
Organicism
Other, The, European Views of
Periodization of the Arts
Person, Idea of the
Perspective
Philosophies: Islamic
Philosophy of Mind: Ancient and Medieval
Phrenology
Population
Prehistory, Rise of
Probability
Progress, Idea of
Psychoanalysis
Psychology and Psychiatry
Punishment
Queer Theory
Religion: Indigenous Peoples' View, South America
Representation: Mental Representation
Science: East Asia
Science, History of
Sexuality: Overview
Sexuality: Sexual Orientation
Sociability in African Thought
Social Darwinism
Sport
State of Nature
Subjectivism
Superstition
Temperance
Terror
Text/Textuality
Totems
Untouchability: Menstrual Taboos
Utilitarianism
Victorianism
Visual Order to Organizing Collections
War and Peace in the Arts
Wildlife
Women and Femininity in U.S. Popular Culture
PHYSICAL SCIENCES
Agnosticism
Alchemy: China
Astrology: China
Astronomy, Pre-Columbian and Latin American
Calculation and Computation
Calendar
Causality
Causation
Causation in East Asian and Southeast Asian Philosophy
Change
Chemistry
Classification of Arts and Sciences, Early Modern
Computer Science
Consciousness: Overview
Consilience
Cosmology: Asia
Cosmology: Cosmology and Astronomy
Creationism
Cycles

**New Dictionary of the History of Ideas**

Computer Science
Creativity in the Arts and Sciences
Death
Demography
Determinism
Diversity
Environment
Environmental History
Eugenics
Feminism: Overview
Feminism: Third World U.S. Movement
Gay Studies
Gender: Overview
Gender Studies: Anthropology
Genetics: Contemporary
Genetics: History of
Greek Science
**Health and Disease**
Hinduism
Humanity: African Thought
Humor
Hygiene
Iconography
Islam: Sunni
Islamic Science
Life
Life Cycle: Elders/Old Age
Literary Criticism
Magic
Mathematics
**Medicine: China**
**Medicine: Europe and the United States**
**Medicine: India**
**Medicine: Islamic Medicine**
Meditation: Eastern Meditation
Miracles
Motherhood and Maternity
Music, Anthropology of
Mysticism: Chinese Mysticism
Narrative
Naturphilosophie
Philosophies: Feminist, Twentieth-Century
Philosophies: Islamic
Phrenology
Population
Privacy
Psychoanalysis
Psychology and Psychiatry
Pythagoreanism
Queer Theory
Religion: Africa
Religion: African Diaspora
Religion: East and Southeast Asia
Religion: Indigenous Peoples' View, South America
Ritual: Religion
Science: East Asia
Science, History of
Sexuality: Overview
Skepticism
Superstition
University: Overview
Untouchability: Menstrual Taboos
Utilitarianism
Victorianism
Visual Culture

Visual Order to Organizing Collections
Volunteerism, U.S.
Westernization: Africa
Witchcraft
Women and Femininity in U.S. Popular Culture
Yin and Yang

LAW

Abolitionism
African-American Ideas
Altruism
Anticolonialism: Africa
Anticolonialism: Latin America
Anticolonialism: Southeast Asia
Antifeminism
Anti-Semitism: Islamic Anti-Semitism
Apartheid
Asian-American Ideas (Cultural Migration)
Assimilation
Authoritarianism: Overview
Authoritarianism: East Asia
Barbarism and Civilization
Bioethics
Black Consciousness
Cannibalism
Capitalism: Overview
Capitalism: Africa
Casuistry
Censorship
Citizenship: Overview
Citizenship: Cultural Citizenship
Citizenship: Naturalization
City, The: The Islamic and Byzantine City
Civil Disobedience
Civil Society: Europe and the United States
Colonialism: Southeast Asia
Consciousness: Chinese Thought
Constitutionalism
Context
Corruption in Developed and Developing Countries
Creationism
Critical Race Theory
Cultural History
Cultural Revivals
Deism
Democracy
Democracy: Africa
Dialogue and Dialectics: Socratic
Dialogue and Dialectics: Talmudic
Dictatorship in Latin America
Discrimination
Diversity
Education: Islamic Education
Empire and Imperialism: Overview
Empire and Imperialism: Europe
Empire and Imperialism: United States
Environmental History
Equality: Overview
Equality: Racial Equality
Ethnicity and Race: Anthropology
Ethnicity and Race: Islamic Views
Europe, Idea of
Extirpation
Fallacy, Logical
Falsifiability
Family Planning

## Multidisciplinary Practices

The *New Dictionary of the History of Ideas* has many entries that discuss the methods by which scholars and researchers pursue knowledge. The entries below discuss approaches, methods, and practices that have influenced many disciplines.

ENTRIES ON MULTIDISCIPLINARY PRACTICES
THAT ORIGINATED IN ANCIENT TIMES

**Especially Interdisciplinary Entries**

The most interdisciplinary entries synthesized knowledge by using the methods and focusing on the topics of practitioners of several disciplines. Very few entries listed below are in only one division. Common pairs for the history of ideas are social sciences and humanities, social sciences and sciences, and humanities and sciences. In the early twenty-first century there is generally a recognition of the common overlap of the social sciences with the humanities; social scientists may take ethical and literary factors into consideration and humanists may incorporate societal contexts into their work. The presence of psychology in the sciences, as well as the quantitative nature of some social sciences work, creates an overlap of social sciences with sciences. Another interesting overlap is between humanities and sciences—topics that in antiquity were treated as philosophy or religion are now investigated by those following scientific methods.

# G

**GAME THEORY.** Game theory, the formal analysis of conflict and cooperation, has pervaded every area of economics and the study of business strategy in the past quarter-century and exerts increasing influence in evolutionary biology, international relations, and political science, where the rational-choice approach to politics has been highly controversial. In a strategic game, each player chooses a strategy (a rule specifying what action to take for each possible information set) to maximize his or her expected payoff, taking into account that each of the other players is also making a rational strategic choice. In contrast to economic theories of competitive equilibrium, the focus of game theory is on strategic interaction and on what information is available to a player to predict the actions that the other players will take.

## The Origins of Game Theory

Writings by several nineteenth-century economists, such as A. A. Cournot and Joseph Bertrand on duopoly and F. Y. Edgeworth on bilateral monopoly, and later work in the 1930s by F. Zeuthen on bargaining and H. von Stackelberg on oligopoly, were later reinterpreted in game-theoretic terms, sometimes in problematic ways (Leonard, 1994; Dimand and Dimand). Game theory emerged as a distinct subdiscipline of applied mathematics, economics, and social science with the publication in 1944 of *Theory of Games and Economic Behavior,* a work of more than six hundred pages written in Princeton by two Continental European emigrés, John von Neumann, a Hungarian mathematician and physicist who was a pioneer in fields from quantum mechanics to computers, and Oskar Morgenstern, a former director of the Austrian Institute for Economic Research. They built upon analyses of two-person, zero-sum games published in the 1920s.

In a series of notes from 1921 to 1927 (three of which were translated into English in *Econometrica* in 1953), the French mathematician and probability theorist Emile Borel developed the concept of a mixed strategy (assigning a probability to each feasible strategy rather than a pure strategy selecting with certainty a single action that the opponent could then predict) and showed that for some particular games with small numbers of possible pure strategies, rational choices by the two players would lead to a minimax solution. Each player would choose the mixed strategy that would minimize the maximum payoff that the other player could be sure of achieving. The young John von Neumann provided the first proof that this minimax solution held for all two-person, constant-sum games (strictly competitive games) in 1928, although the proof of the minimax theorem used by von Neumann and Morgenstern in 1944 was based on the first elementary (that is, nontopological) proof

of the existence of a minimax solution, proved by Borel's student Jean Ville in 1938 (Weintraub; Leonard, 1995; Dimand and Dimand). For games with variable sums and more players, where coalitions among players are possible, von Neumann and Morgenstern proposed a more general solution concept, the stable set, but could not prove its existence. In the 1960s, William Lucas proved by counterexample that existence of the stable set solution could not be proved because it was not true in general.

Although von Neumann's and Morgenstern's work was the subject of long and extensive review articles in economics journals, some of which predicted widespread and rapid application, game theory was developed in the 1950s primarily by A. W. Tucker and his students in Princeton's mathematics department (see Shubik's recollections in Weintraub) and at the RAND Corporation, a nonprofit corporation based in Santa Monica, California, whose only client was the U.S. Air Force (Nasar). Expecting that the theory of strategic games would be as relevant to military and naval strategy as contemporary developments in operations research were, the U.S. Office of Naval Research supported much of the basic research, and Morgenstern was named as an editor of the *Naval Research Logistics Quarterly.*

Much has been written about the influence of game theory and related forms of rational-choice theory such as systems analysis on nuclear strategy (although General Curtis LeMay complained that RAND stood for Research And No Development) and of how the Cold War context and military funding helped shape game theory and economics (Heims; Poundstone; Mirowski), mirrored by the shaping of similar mathematical techniques into "planometrics" on the other side of the Cold War (Campbell). Researchers in peace studies, publishing largely in the *Journal of Conflict Resolution* in the late 1950s and the 1960s, drew on Prisoner's Dilemma games to analyze the Cold War (see Schelling), while from 1965 to 1968 (while ratification of the Nuclear Non-Proliferation Treaty was pending) the U.S. Arms Control and Disarmament Agency sponsored important research on bargaining games with incomplete information and their application to arms races and disarmament (later declassified and published as Mayberry with Harsanyi, Scarf, and Selten; and Aumann and Maschler with Stearns).

## Nash Equilibrium, the Nash Bargaining Solution, and the Shapley Value

John Nash, the outstanding figure among the Princeton and RAND game theorists (Nasar; Giocoli), developed, in articles from his dissertation, both the Nash equilibrium for noncooperative games, where the players cannot make binding agreements enforced by an outside agency, and the Nash bargaining solution for cooperative games where such binding agreements are possible (Nash). Nash equilibrium, by far the most widely influential solution concept in game theory, applied to games with any number of players and with payoffs whose sum carried with the combination of strategies chosen by the players, while von Neumann's minimax solution was limited to two-person, constant-sum games. A Nash equilibrium is a strategy combination in which each player's chosen strategy is a best response to the strategies of the other players, so that no player can get a higher expected payoff by changing strategy as long as the strategies of the other players stay the same. No player has an incentive to be the first to deviate from a Nash equilibrium.

Nash proved the existence of equilibrium but not uniqueness: a game will have at least one strategy combination that is a Nash equilibrium, but it may have many or even an infinity of Nash equilibria (especially if the choice of action involves picking a value for a continuous variable). Cournot's 1838 analysis of duopoly has been interpreted in retrospect as a special case of Nash equilibrium, just as Harsanyi perceived the congruity of Zeuthen's 1930 discussion of bargaining and the Nash bargaining solution. Refinements of Nash equilibrium, which serve to rule out some of the possible equilibria, include the concept of a subgame perfect equilibrium (see Harsanyi and Selten), which is a Nash equilibrium both for an entire extended game (a game in which actions must be chosen at several decision nodes in a game tree) and for any game starting from any decision node in the game tree, including points that would never be reached in equilibrium, so that any threats to take certain actions if another player were to deviate from the equilibrium path would be credible (rational in terms of self-interest once that point in the game had been reached). A further refinement rules out some subgame perfect Nash equilibria by allowing for the possibility of a "trembling hand," that is, a small probability that an opposing player, although rational, may make mistakes (Harsanyi and Selten). Thomas Schelling has suggested that if there is some clue that would lead players to regard one Nash equilibrium as more likely than others, that equilibrium will be a focal point.

Nash equilibrium, with its refinements, remains at the heart of noncooperative game theory. Applied to the study of market structure by Martin Shubik (1959), this approach has come to dominate the field of industrial organization, as indicated by Jean Tirole (1988) in a book widely accepted as the standard economics textbook on industrial organization and as a model for subsequent texts. More recently, noncooperative game theory has found economic applications ranging from strategic trade policy in international trade to the credibility of anti-inflationary monetary policy and the design of auctions for broadcast frequencies. From economics, noncooperative game theory based on refinements of Nash equilibrium has spread to business school courses on business strategy (see Ghemawat, applying game theory in six Harvard Business School cases for MBA students). Some economists view business strategy as an application of game theory, with ideas flowing in one direction, rather than as a distinct field (Shapiro).

However, scholars of strategic management remain sharply divided over whether game theory provides useful insights or just a rationalization for any conceivable observed behavior (see the papers by Barney, Saloner, Camerer, and Postrel in Rumelt, Schendel, and Teece, especially Postrel's paper, which verifies Rumelt's Flaming Trousers Conjecture by constructing a game-theoretic model with a subgame perfect Bayesian Nash equilibrium in which bank presidents publicly set their pants on fire, a form of costly signaling that is profitable only for a bank that can get repeat business, that is, a high-quality bank).

Nash proposed the Nash bargaining solution for two-person cooperative games, that the players maximize the product of their gains over what each would receive at the threat point (the Nash equilibrium of the noncooperative game that they would play if they failed to reach agreement on how to divide the gains), and showed it to be the only solution possessing all of a particular set of intuitively appealing properties (efficiency, symmetry, independence of unit changes, independence of irrelevant alternatives). Feminist economists such as Marjorie McElroy and Notburga Ott have begun to apply bargaining models whose outcome depends critically on the threat point (the outcome of the noncooperative game that would be played if bargaining does not lead to agreement), as well as Prisoner's Dilemma games, to bargaining within the household (see Seiz for a survey).

Another influential solution concept for cooperative games, the Shapley value for n-person games (Shapley), allots to each player the average of that player's marginal contribution to the payoff each possible coalition would receive and, for a class of games with large numbers of players, coincides with the core of a market (the set of undominated imputations or allocations), yet another solution concept discovered by graduate students at Princeton in the early 1950s (in this case, Shapley and D. B. Gillies) and then rediscovered by Shubik in Edgeworth's 1881 analysis. There is a large literature in accounting applying the Shapley value to cost allocation (Roth and Verrecchia).

## Applications of Game Theory

Lloyd Shapley and Shubik (1954), two Princeton contemporaries of Nash, began the application of game theory to political science, drawing on Shapley's 1953 publication to devise an index for voting power in a committee system. William Riker and his students at the University of Rochester took the lead in recasting political science in terms of strategic interaction of rational, self-interested players (see Riker and Ordeshook; Shubik, 1984; Riker in Weintraub), and there is now a specialized market for game-theory textbooks for political science students (Morrow). Donald Green and Ian Shapiro (1994) criticize recent applications to politics of game theory and related forms of rational-choice theory as viewing political behavior as too exclusively rational and self-interested to the exclusion of ideologies, values, and social norms (see Friedman for the ensuing controversy).

Recasting Marxism in terms of rational choice and analyzing class struggle as a strategic game is especially controversial (Carver and Thomas). Conflict and cooperation (whether in the form of coalitions or contracts) are at the heart of law, as of politics. Douglas Baird, Robert Gertner, and Randal Picker (1994), among others, treat such legal topics as tort, procedure, and contracts as examples of strategic interaction, as the growing subdiscipline of law and economics increasingly reasons in terms of game theory. As a counterpart at a more "macro" level to game-theoretic analysis of political and legal conflict and cooperation, Andrew Schotter (1981) and Shubik (1984) propose a "mathematical institutional economics" to explain the evolution of social institutions such as contract law, money, trust, and customs, norms, and conventions ("the rules of the game") as the outcome of strategic interaction by rational agents. This approach shows promise, but has been received skeptically by economists such as Ronald Coase who rely on less mathematical neoclassical techniques to develop a "New Institutional Economics," and with even less enthusiasm by economists outside the neoclassical mainstream, such as Philip Mirowski. Going beyond the explanation of merely mundane institutions, Steven Brams (1983) uses game theory to explore questions of theology.

## Prisoner's Dilemma

Game theorists and social scientists have been fascinated by Prisoner's Dilemma, a two-by-two game (two players, each with two possible pure strategies) with a particular payoff matrix (Rapoport and Chammah; Poundstone). The game's nickname and the accompanying story were provided by A. W. Tucker. Suppose that two prisoners, accused of jointly committing a serious crime, are interrogated separately. The prosecutor has sufficient evidence to convict them of a lesser crime without any confession, but can get a conviction on the more serious charge only with a confession. If neither prisoner confesses, they will each be sentenced to two years for the lesser charge. If both confess, each will receive a sentence of five years. However, if only one prisoner confesses, that prisoner will be sentenced to only one year, while the other prisoner will get ten years. In the absence of any external authority to enforce an agreement to deny the charges, each player has a dominant strategy of confessing (given that the other player has denied the charges, one year is a lighter sentence than two years; given that the other player has confessed, five years is a lighter sentence than ten years). The unique Nash equilibrium is for both players to confess (defect from any agreement to cooperate) and receive sentences of five years, even though both would be better off if both denied the charges (cooperated).

This game has been used as an explanation of how individually rational behavior can lead to undesirable outcomes ranging from arms races to overuse of natural resources ("the tragedy of the commons," a generalization to more than two players). If the game is repeated a known finite number of times, however large, the predicted result is the same: both players will confess (defect) on the last play, since there would be no opportunity of future punishment for defection or reward for cooperation; therefore both will also confess (defect) on the next-to-last play, since the last play is determined, and so on, with mutual defection on each round as the only subgame perfect Nash equilibrium. However, the "folk theorem" states that for *infinitely* repeated games, even with discounting of future benefits or a constant probability of the game ending on any particular round (provided that the discount rate and the probability of the game ending on the next round are sufficiently small and that the dimensionality of payoffs allows for the possibility of retaliation), *any* sequence of actions can be rationalized as a subgame perfect Nash equilibrium. (The folk theorem owes its name to its untraceable origin.)

However, players do not generally behave in accordance with Nash's prediction. Frequent cooperation in one-shot or finitely repeated Prisoner's Dilemma has been observed ever since it was first played. The first Prisoner's Dilemma experiment, conducted at RAND by Merrill Flood and Melvin Drescher in January 1950, involved one hundred repetitions with two sophisticated players, the economist Armen Alchian from the University of California, Los Angeles, and the game theorist John Williams, head of RAND's mathematics department. Alchian and Williams succeeded in cooperating on sixty plays, and mutual defection, the Nash equilibrium, occurred only fourteen times (Poundstone, pp. 107–116). Robert Axelrod (1984) conducted a computer tournament for iterated Prisoner's Dilemma, finding that Rapoport's simple "tit for tat" strategy (cooperate on the first round, then do whatever the other player did on the previous round) yielded the highest payoff.

One way to explain the observed extent of cooperation in experimental games and in life is to recognize that humans are only boundedly rational, relying on rules of thumb and conventions, and making choices about what to know because information is costly to acquire and process. Assumptions about rationality in game theory, such as common knowledge, can be very strong: "An event is common knowledge among a group of agents if each one knows it, if each one knows the others know it, if each one knows that each one knows it, and so on . . . the limit of a potentially infinite chain of reasoning about knowledge" (Geanakoplos, p. 54). Ariel Rubinstein (1998) sketches techniques for explicitly incorporating computability constraints and the process of choice in models of procedural rationality. Alternatively, evolutionary game theory, surveyed by Larry Samuelson (2002), emphasizes adaptation and evolution to explain behavior, rather than fully conscious rational choice, returning to human behavior the extension of game theory to evolutionarily stable strategies for animal behavior (Maynard Smith; Dugatkin and Reeve).

## Conclusion

The award of the Royal Bank of Sweden Prize in Economic Science in Memory of Alfred Nobel to John Nash, John Harsanyi, and Reinhard Selten in 1994 recognized the impact of game theory (and a film biography of Nash, based on Nasar's 1998 book, subsequently won Academy Awards for best picture and best actor), while the multivolume *Handbook of Game Theory*, edited by Robert Aumann and Sergiu Hart (1992–2002), presents a comprehensive overview. Reflecting on what has been achieved, David Kreps concludes that

> Non-cooperative game theory . . . has brought a fairly flexible language to many issues, together with a collection of notions of "similarity" that has allowed economists to move insights from one context to another

and to probe the reach of these insights. But too often it, and in particular equilibrium analysis, gets taken too seriously at levels where its current behavioural assumptions are inappropriate. We (economic theorists and economists more broadly) need to keep a better sense of proportion about when and how to use it. And we (economic and game theorists) would do well to see what can be done about developing formally that senses of proportion. (pp. 184)

Strategic interaction has proved to be a powerful idea, and, although its application, especially beyond economics, remains controversial, it has proven fruitful in suggesting new perspectives and new ways of formalizing older insights.

*See also* **Economics; Mathematics; Probability; Rational Choice.**

BIBLIOGRAPHY

Aumann, Robert J., and Sergiu Hart, eds. *Handbook of Game Theory with Economic Applications.* 3 vols. Amsterdam: North-Holland, 1992–2002.

Aumann, Robert J., and Michael B. Maschler, with the collaboration of Richard E. Stearns. *Repeated Games with Incomplete Information.* Cambridge, Mass.: MIT Press, 1995.

Axelrod, Robert. *The Evolution of Cooperation.* New York: Basic Books, 1984.

Baird, Douglas, Robert H. Gertner, and Randal C. Picker. *Game Theory and the Law.* Cambridge, Mass.: Harvard University Press, 1994.

Brams, Steven J. *Superior Beings: If They Exist, How Would We Know? Game-Theoretic Implications of Omniscience, Omnipotence, Immortality, and Incomprehensibility.* New York: Springer-Verlag, 1983.

Campbell, Robert W. "Marx, Kantorovich, and Novozhilov: *Stoimost'* versus Reality." *Slavic Review* 20 (1961): 402–418.

Carver, Terrell, and Paul Thomas, eds. *Rational Choice Marxism.* Houndmills, U.K.: Macmillan, 1995.

Dimand, Mary Ann, and Robert W. Dimand. *The History of Game Theory,* Vol. 1: *From the Beginnings to 1945.* London and New York: Routledge, 1996.

Dugatkin, Lee Alan, and Hudson Kern Reeve, eds. *Game Theory and Animal Behavior.* New York: Oxford University Press, 1998.

Friedman, Jeffrey, ed. "Rational Choice Theory." *Critical Review* 9 (1995).

Geanakoplos, John. "Common Knowledge." *Journal of Economic Perspectives* 6 (1992): 53–82.

Ghemawat, Pankaj. *Games Businesses Play: Cases and Models.* Cambridge, Mass.: MIT Press, 1997.

Giocoli, Nicola. *Modeling Rational Agents: From Interwar Economics to Early Modern Game Theory.* Cheltenham, U.K., and Northampton, Mass.: Edward Elgar, 2003.

Green, Donald P., and Ian Shapiro. *Pathologies of Rational Choice Theory: A Critique of Applications in Political Science.* New Haven, Conn.: Yale University Press, 1994.

Harsanyi, John C., and Reinhard Selten. *A General Theory of Equilibrium Selection in Games.* Cambridge, Mass.: MIT Press, 1988.

Heims, Steve J. *John Von Neumann and Norbert Wiener: From Mathematics to the Technologies of Life and Death.* Cambridge, Mass.: MIT Press, 1980.

Kreps, David M. *Game Theory and Economic Modelling.* Oxford: Clarendon Press, 1990.

Leonard, Robert J. "From Parlor Games to Social Science: Von Neumann, Morgenstern, and the Creation of Game Theory, 1928–1944." *Journal of Economic Literature* 33 (1995): 730–761.

———. "Reading Cournot, Reading Nash: The Creation and Stabilisation of the Nash Equilibrium," *Economic Journal* 104 (1994): 492–511.

Mayberry, John P., with John C. Harsanyi, Herbert E. Scarf, and Reinhard Selten. *Game-Theoretic Models of Cooperation and Conflict.* Boulder, Colo.: Westview 1992.

Maynard Smith, John. *Evolution and the Theory of Games.* Cambridge, U.K.: Cambridge University Press, 1982.

Mirowski, Philip. *Machine Dreams: Economics Becomes a Cyborg Science.* Cambridge, U.K.: Cambridge University Press, 2002.

Morrow, James D. *Game Theory for Political Scientists.* Princeton, N.J.: Princeton University Press, 1994.

Nasar, Sylvia. *A Beautiful Mind: A Biography of John Forbes Nash, Jr., Winner of the Nobel Prize in Economics, 1994.* New York: Simon and Schuster, 1998.

Nash, John F., Jr. *Essays on Game Theory.* Cheltenham, U.K., and Brookfield, Vt.: Edward Elgar, 1996.

Poundstone, William. *Prisoner's Dilemma: John von Neumann, Game Theory, and the Puzzle of the Bomb.* New York: Doubleday, 1992.

Rapoport, Anatol, and Albert M. Chammah. *Prisoner's Dilemma: A Study in Conflict and Cooperation.* Ann Arbor: University of Michigan Press, 1965.

Riker, William H., and Peter C. Ordeshook. *An Introduction to Positive Political Theory.* Englewood Cliffs, N.J.: Prentice Hall, 1973.

Roth, A. E., and R. E. Verrecchia. "The Shapley Value as Applied to Cost Allocation: a Reinterpretation." *Journal of Accounting Research* 17 (1979): 295–303.

Rubinstein, Ariel. *Modeling Bounded Rationality.* Cambridge, Mass.: MIT Press, 1998.

Rumelt, Richard P., Dan E. Schendel, and David J. Teece, eds. *Fundamental Issues in Strategy: A Research Agenda.* Boston: Harvard Business School Press, 1994.

Samuelson, Larry. "Evolution and Game Theory." *Journal of Economic Perspectives* 16 (2002): 47–66.

Schelling, Thomas. *The Strategy of Conflict.* Cambridge, Mass.: Harvard University Press, 1960.

Schotter, Andrew. *The Economic Theory of Social Institutions.* Cambridge, U.K.: Cambridge University Press, 1981.

Seiz, Janet A. "Game Theory and Bargaining Models." In *The Elgar Companion to Feminist Economics,* edited by Janice Peterson and Margaret Lewis. Cheltenham, U.K., and Northampton, Mass.: Edward Elgar, 1999.

Shapiro, Carl. "The Theory of Business Strategy." *RAND Journal of Economics* 20 (1989): 125–137.

Shapley, Lloyd S. "A Value for n-Person Games." In Harold Kuhn and Albert W. Tucker, eds., *Contributions to the Theory of Games,* Vol. 2, *Annals of Mathematics Studies,* no. 28. Princeton, N.J.: Princeton University Press, 1953.

Shapley, Lloyd S., and Martin Shubik, "A Method for Evaluating the Distribution of Power in a Committee System." *American Political Science Review* 48 (1954): 787–792.

Shubik, Martin. *A Game-Theoretic Approach to Political Economy.* Vol. 2 of *Game Theory in the Social Sciences.* Cambridge, Mass.: MIT Press, 1984.

———. *Strategy and Market Structure: Competition, Oligopoly, and the Theory of Games.* New York: Wiley, 1959.

Tirole, Jean. *The Theory of Industrial Organization.* Cambridge, Mass.: MIT Press, 1988.

Von Neumann, John, and Oskar Morgenstern. *Theory of Games and Economic Behavior.* Princeton, N.J.: Princeton University Press, 1944; 3rd ed. 1953.

Weintraub, E. Roy, ed. *Toward a History of Game Theory.* Durham, N.C.: Duke University Press, 1992. Annual supplement to *History of Political Economy.*

*Robert W. Dimand*

**GARDEN.** The term *garden,* which is of Germanic origin, means "yard" or "enclosure" and denotes ways of organizing earth, water, plants and, sometimes, people, animals, and art (sculpture, architecture, theater, music, and poetry), the formal qualitities of which are determined as much by pleasure, artistry, or aesthetics as by convenience or necessity. This definition excludes arrangements of sacred space based on religious customs and sports, exclusions that are consistent with most societies.

Not all cultures have gardens. For many reasons, anthropologists and garden historians consider most small cultivated plots to be forms of agriculture, as opposed to gardens. Gardens presuppose agriculture but in addition embrace a cultural and psychological distance from agriculture expressed in aesthetics.

### Gardens in the History of Ideas

Gardens have the capability to give physical form to ideas either by being modeled on familiar ideas or by creating a new design that generates or evokes new ideas, or through a combination of the two. Gardens make abstract ideas concrete—visible, tangible, and kinesthetic. In so doing, gardens can communicate complex abstract ideas convincingly.

### Death

Gardens express ideas of victory over death in three ways. First, since their living components could die at any time (as a result of neglect or the whim of the owner or overwhelming natural forces), their mere existence represents a triumph over ill-will, chaos, and death; gardens signal that the world can be made right, especially through the use of human knowledge, skill, and spirit. Second, because gardens' biological materials inevitably grow, die, decay, and are then reconstituted to form life once again, they provide a powerful symbol of the cyclical aspect of life, negating death's apparent finality with a metaphorical triumph over death, fear, and hopelessness. This biological cycle implicit in the garden suggests a transmutation of death and an antidote to despair. Finally, depending on the culture, the form gardens are given reflects either (a) their triumph over the chaos found in nature, a chaos that is perceived as a constant threat to humanity—and in monotheistic cultures, a symbol of humanity's distance from God, or (b) the tremendous power of nature, of which humanity is a necessary part. In this manner, the garden's form reflects the innate hope that humans express by either taming or cooperating with nature. This hope, this expression, allows beholders to feel part of larger forces, bigger than their own short lives and limited powers. These three symbolic triumphs over death and fear are so compelling that exceptions, such as the "monster" sculptures in one part of the Boboli Garden at the Pitti Palace, are rare. Usually they are ironic: the agony of Christ in the garden of Gethsemane; the tortures of damnation in Hieronymous Bosch's painting *The Garden of Earthly Delights.*

### Time and Temporality

Related to death are the various ideas of time and temporality—the internal experiences of time. Gardens in seasonal climates reveal the cyclical experience of the seasons, and all gardens underscore the cycles of day and night. Through these cycles one becomes more aware of the passing of time, of recurrence and passing away forever. Gardens often utilize sundials, or poems, to highlight the awareness of a particular idea of time.

Poems and allusions of all kinds, as well as relics and historical artifacts, can also be used to make people aware of the past (or some idea of it) and of their collective or personal histories.

### Order and Plenty

The people of ancient Egypt understood that by controlling the Nile River and the agriculture dependent upon it, they might impose order on the primordial chaos that was always a potential threat. Egyptian garden paintings, the world's earliest, show geometry and symmetry as the formal indications of this valuable foundation of such order. These early images show rectangular pools filled with fish, ducks, and lotus surrounded by regularly spaced fruit trees—emblematic of an ideal of the good life as it exists around the world.

The idea of the garden as a place where order is imposed upon an inherently chaotic, disorderly, painful, and dangerous natural world is central to ancient Egyptian, Persian, Islamic, European, and European-American concepts of the garden. The noted landscape gardener Lancelot "Capability" Brown (1715–1783), famous for designs of gardens that looked liked natural landscape, considered his efforts as improvements on the natural state (as well as on the rigid and geometric designs of previous gardenists); even nineteenth-century Romantic-era gardens, which thrived on the appearance of disorder, were carefully planned.

Related to the idea of an order that provides for humanity—and to the idea of the garden as a triumph over death—is the idea of the garden as a site of never-ending bounty, never failing with the seasons. This idea is more common in India and the monotheistic Middle East, Europe, and America. Homer described the garden of Alcinous, king of the Phaeceans, in *The Odyssey* (book vii): "and verdant olives flourish round the year. / The balmy spirit of the western gale / eternal breathes on fruits untaught to fail." Chinese and especially Japanese gardens differ in being more likely to celebrate the different beauties of the several seasons.

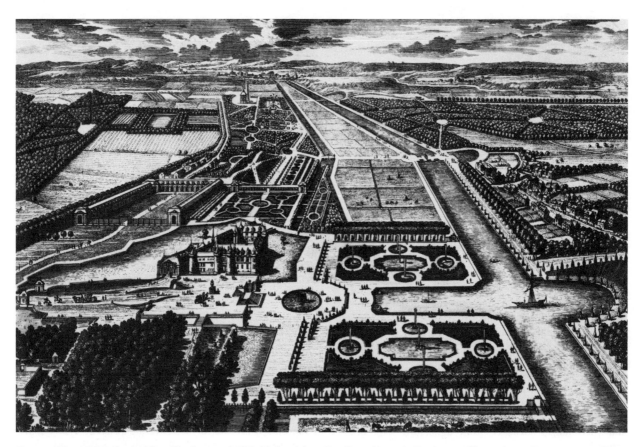

**France.** *Veue Generale de Chantilly du cote de l'Entrée* by Adam Perelle, 1650. A European villa garden. DUMBARTON OAKS, RESEARCH LIBRARY AND COLLECTION, WASHINGTON, D.C.

European villa gardens, of both the informal "pastoral" and the more formal French types, reflected instantiate the notion of the garden as a place of plenty by extolling the ideal of a close relationship to agriculture. Often this closeness was literal: gardens were situated within the larger farm, and might include (geometric) herb gardens, grape arbors, or symmetrically planted fruit groves; adjacent fields were actively cultivated.

### The Lost Home

Nebuchadnezzar (r. 605–562 B.C.E.), the Chaldean king of Babylon, introduced another persistent idea of the garden, that of the garden as a lost home. Nebuchadnezzar built the Hanging Gardens, one of the Seven Wonders of the ancient world, to comfort one of his wives, who missed "the meadows of her mountains, the green and hilly landscape of her youth" (Thacker, p. 16). A similar motivation prompted the creation of the Tuileries Gardens in Paris. The Qing emperor Kang Xi (1662–1723) built the Pi-shu shan-chuang at Rehe (Jehol) in China to emulate the Manchurian homelands. In the modern era, retirees in the deserts of the American Southwest, self-exiled from temperate climates, recreate the comforting lawns, maples, and flowers reminiscent of their previous homes. Homer used Odysseus's memories of his childhood in his garden with his father, who gave him fruit trees and taught him the names of the plants, to underscore the hero's longing for home.

The Hanging Gardens of Babylon were described by Diodorus Siculus:

Since the approach to the garden sloped like a hillside and the several parts of the structure rose from one another tier on tier . . . [it] resembled a theater . . . the uppermost gallery, which was fifty cubits high, bore the highest surface of the park . . . the roofs of the galleries were covered with beams of stone . . . sufficient for the roots of the largest trees; and the ground, when levelled off, was thickly planted with trees of every kind that . . . could give pleasure to the beholder . . . The galleries contained many royal lodgings; and there was one gallery which contained openings leading from the topmost surface and machines for supplying the garden with water. (Thacker, p. 17)

Admired by the ancient Greeks and Romans, they demonstrate several characteristics of gardens persisting to the early twenty-first century: the use of engineering and technology—often, paradoxically, to achieve a natural effect—and the attempt to make the garden a place of pleasure and sensuous delight; the integration of agriculture in the garden; and the integration of theater, poetry, and painting.

In terms of world history (not just garden design), the most far-reaching, if poignant, image of the garden as lost home is

**Italy: Ancient Rome.** Courtyard garden in Pompeii, with paintings of birds and flowers on the interior walls of the colonnade. MARA MILLER

found in the story of the Garden of Eden in the *Book of Genesis.*

## Garden as Paradise and Enclosure.

In 401 B.C.E., the Greek historian Xenophon, in his *Oeconomicus,* Book IV, introduced the idea of the pleasure garden (Persian, *paradeisos,* "enclosure") to Greece, based on gardens he had seen while fighting in Persia, and recommended its imitation. Xenophon's description of the Persian gardens was again popularized in 1692 by the Englishman William Temple in his influential *Essay upon the Gardens of Epicurs: Or, of Gardening, in the Year 1685* (1692):

> a paradise among them [the Persians] seems to have been a large Space of Ground, adorned and beautified with all Sorts of Trees, both of Fruits and of Forest, either found there before it was inclosed [*sic*], or planted after; either cultivated like Gardens, for Shades and for Walks, with Fountains or Streams, and all Sorts of Plants usual in the Climate, and pleasant to the Eye, the Smell, or the Taste; or else employed, like our Parks, for Inclosure [*sic*] and Harbour of all Sorts of Wild Beasts, as well as for the Pleasure of Riding and Walking: And so they were of more or less Extent, and of differing Entertainment, according to the several Humours of the

Princes that ordered and inclosed [*sic*] them.... (quoted in Hunt and Willis, pp. 96–97)

Enclosure is central to many types of gardens, including ancient Roman courtyards, which were surrounded by the house, Chinese and Korean coutyard gardens, and Japanese dry rock gardens (*karesansui*). Unlike the medieval European cloister gardens derived from them, Roman gardens often included mural paintings of gods and landscapes.

The Persian model of the garden as a paradise on earth later evolved into the Islamic *chahar-bagh,* an enclosed quadrangular garden with central perpendicular paths or canals dividing it into four equal sections. Later made famous in carpets and brought to India by the Mughals, *chahar-bagh*s, the most famous example of which is the Taj Mahal, reached Europe as the medieval *hortus conclusus,* or enclosed garden, as a result of the Crusades (1050–1150) and through Islamic gardens in Spain, Italy, and Sicily. Many twentieth-century rose gardens continue this form. Like its Islamic prototypes, the medieval garden was practical and symbolic, evoking the earthly and spiritual pleasures of the biblical Paradise and the Garden of Eden. Secular poetry such as the medieval French *Le Roman de la Rose,* purportedly composed during a dream in a rose garden, extended the *hortus conclusus* to include romantic love and Platonic ideals of fulfilment. Paintings and tapestries, too, especially the unicorn tapestries at Cluny

**Medieval France.** Bonnefont Cloister and Herb Garden, modeled after medieval gardens, The Cloisters, New York City. © GAIL MOONEY/CORBIS

and the Cloisters of the Metropolitan Museum of Art, showing unicorns and the "Lady in the Garden," take on various symbolic and allegorical readings.

The Garden of Eden, of course, is also a "lost home." Eden is described in *Genesis* as a kind of *chahar-bagh,* enclosed, divided into quarters by rivers meeting at right angles in the center, containing the Tree of the Knowledge of Good and Evil. Construed by Jews, Christians, and Muslims as an actual place from the human past, it was distinguished from Paradise, which was an ideal realm to be experienced by the righteous or the beloved of God in the future, and for Christians after their death or after the Second Coming. Eden as a prototype for European gardens was vastly expanded by the literary version John Milton presented in his epic *Paradise Lost* (1667) as a natural landscape (Hunt, p. 79).

The earliest East Asian depictions of the four Buddhist paradises show Buddhas and Bodhisattvas in palaces surrounded by fragrant trees and flowers, dancers, and musicians. As cave paintings at Dunhuang (China) show, the religious significance of lotus suggested using the visual image of the lotus floating in a pond; azure rectangles of water with pink blossoms began to appear, growing larger, eventually with buds showing souls reborn in paradise as babies. This inspired actual gardens, including the famous Buddhist garden at Anapchi, in Kyongju, Korea (674 C.E.).

The pond at Anapchi shows a second visual allusion to paradise, the Daoist Isles of the Immortals. Depicted here as actual islands, they are sometimes represented by rocks on an "ocean" of dry gravel. Originating with the Chinese emperor Wudi (141–87 B.C.E.), such depictions were originally intended to attract the Immortals themselves, in the hope they would share their secrets.

A number of Fujiwara-period (989–1185) Japanese gardens, starting with the Byodo-in's Phoenix Hall (a villa in Uji outside Kyoto), simulated the Mahayana Paradise described in a sutra that attested to women's ability to reach enlightenment (yieng-pruksawan). These gardens were designed to make paradise tangible and imaginable. Since the daughters of the Fujiwara clan were consistently married off to emperors, their eventual enlightenment was important both to their families and to the nation. The ability to visualize paradise was believed to facilitate enlightenment (legendary Queen Vaidehi's instruction by Buddha in meditation through visualization, including visualization of Paradise, was painted at Dunhuang). The construction of gardens as an aid to such visualization meant that the empresses would actually attain Paradise more easily.

**Garden as Rustic Retreat**

The Romans invented the idea of the villa—a home and farm in the countryside—which they believed provided a manner

**Korea.** Anapchi Garden in Kyongju, Unified Silla Period, 674 C.E. MARA MILLER

of living superior to that of city life. The villa achieves this goal both physically and spiritually or culturally by affording self-expression, self-cultivation, and self-definition. The garden became the setting and the occasion of this ideal, whereby emulating cultured and educated men one became more cultured and educated oneself. (Although the model is largely patriarchal, a few women have done the same: the Duchess Eleonora di Toledo [wife of Cosimo I] in the Boboli Garden, the Countess of Bedford at Moor-Park [Hertforshire], and Mildred Bliss at Dumbarton Oaks, designed by Beatrix Farrand).

The Roman pastoral ideal symbolized by the villa and its garden ideal was revived in Renaissance Italy and eighteenth-century England, whence it spread to America. It was based on models found in Vergil's *Aeneid* and *Georgics,* in the letters of Pliny the Younger, and in the architect Andrea Palladio's (1508–1580) books and buildings reinterpreting classical architecture. Pliny's celebratory descriptions of life in the country influenced literati in their creation of an image of a life worth living—and in their designs of gardens within which to live. The Greek and Roman forms of government presupposed politically active citizens, and the resuscitation of these models as an ideal form elicited from Europeans, Britons, and Americans active participation not only in governing but in reimagining the ways the world might be governed and how social intercourse could be encouraged; creating gardens as

representations of these emerging worldviews was part of the process of re-imaging.

The idea of the villa garden as a realm of personal cultivation in which one emulates historical role models is strikingly similar to one set of East Asian ideas of gardens, wherein gardens serve as places for contemplation, scholarship, artistic engagement, and social interaction with other literati. From the time of Wang Wei (699–c.760), East Asian paintings represent gardens of the literati as places of retreat from the corrupt world of everyday affairs, places that made possible the personal cultivation or "self-transformation" according to Buddhist, Confucian, and Daoist models. Paintings of the scholar Tao Yuanming (365–457), famous for his integrity, show a rustic fence and a few chrysanthemums depicting the garden whose tending was the pretext of his retirement.

Fruit-bearing trees and other forms of agriculture were important parts of Chinese villas and literati gardens of "retirement" (Clunas), a feature that also recalls Paradise and the notion of plenty.

In both Europe and East Asia, villa gardens as ideal realms eliciting personal cultivation coexist with the ideal of the rustic retreat, be it a shell-lined grotto or a humble thatched hut. Both remained vital for centuries, inspiring garden construction and permitting endless reformulation of intellecutal literati ideas and ideals.

**Korea.** The courtyard and garden of the Confucian Academy To-son Sowon (established 1574) were derived from Chinese influences. MARA MILLER

## Garden as Art

Gardens were often regarded as art, both in theory and as a result of intimate and intricate relations among gardens and other arts. Most famous is Horace Walpole's (1717–1797) theory of the interrelations of the "three arts," poetry, painting, and the garden, in his *History of the Modern Taste in Gardening* (1771–1780).

The inclusion of carved or handwritten poetic quotations is found frequently in Asian and European gardens of nearly all styles, and visiual allusions to well-known poems, legends, or stories provide the basis for garden vignettes, such as the flat angular "eight-plank" bridges alluding to the tales of Ise in Japanese gardens, as well as themes for garden "rooms" or motifs. Highly influential gardens have been designed—or described—by poets, most famously Murasaki Shikibu (d. c. 1014–1020), John Milton, Alexander Pope (1688–1744), Ishikawa Jozan (1583–1672), and Yuan Mei (eighteenth century).

Italian, French, German, and British formal gardens were used for theatrical entertainments and masques, sometimes in pavilions designed for the purpose (later gardens included shallow amphitheaters), while masques, operas, and other forms of early modern theater often had scenes set in a garden. Architecturally, gardens encompass—or are encompassed by—a house, palace, or temple. But formal gardens, English "natural" landscape gardens, European-American romantic gardens, and large Chinese gardens also incorporated small pavilions or "follies"; Japanese gardens often feature small rustic tea houses, or halls (later donated to temples). All have bridges both decorative and useful.

## Garden as Microcosm of Nature

East Asian thinking in many cases centered on the nature of the cosmos, the relation of yin and yang, the place of human beings in nature, and so on. These ideas were at once conceptual/intellectual, artistic, spiritual, and experiential/imaginative, designed to provide the scholar with an opportunity for contemplation of nature like that provided within the landscape itself. Miniature gardens assembled on trays (bonsai) presented the macrocosm in microcosm for the viewer to use to immerse himself in nature or contemplate the Dao.

Sixteenth-century European explorers returned home with exotic plants that were featured in the new scientific botanical gardens. The first botanic gardens were quartered geometric arrangements simulating the "four quarters of the world" with plants in the area allotted to their continent of origin. Twentieth-century botanic gardens specialized in the creation of miniature systems representing whole environments, either cultural (Japanese gardens) or biological, recreating specific biomes (tropical, desert) and capable of sustaining the plants (and sometimes animals) native to them. (The Denver and Brooklyn Botanic Gardens have both types.) In the twenty-first century zoos (formally known as "zoological gardens") have started re-creating the topography and native vegetation of the animals in their collections, thus becoming more like gardens.

## Garden as Microcosm of the State

In Han China (202 B.C.E.–220 C.E.) gardens such as Tu Yuan (Rabbit Park) were used to "extend the grandeur of the princely dwelling, to be a site for ceremonies and magic, and to continue the time-honored mold of a game park" (Morris, p. 13). The contemporary Chinese imperial garden described by Pere Attiret (1757) was designed to represent the country for the emperor, whose status forbade traveling freely.

From the sixteenth century, French gardens were used politically in myriad ways: "to impress foreigners with the power of the court, to stir the loyalty of Frenchmen and, after the political and religious crisis deepened in the second half of the sixteenth century, to subtly express the political policy of the state. The court festival, especially as it was masterminded by Catherine de Médicis, often provided an opportunity to bring together opposed factions, turning their 'real conflicts into a chivalrous pastime'" (Adams, p. 33). Versailles has been shown to be an elaborate four-dimensional demonstration of the power of Louis XIV; decision-making that went into the planning of its park was explicitly political (Berger). The British designed and interpreted gardens that were symbolic of the state and of political power. Such a connection was first drawn in Britain by Shakespeare in the gardener's speech in *Richard II* (act 3, scene 4).

**Mughal India.** *Jahangir and Prince Khurram Feasted by Nur Jahan,* c. 1617. Opaque watercolor and gold on paper. FREER GALLERY OF ART, SMITHSONIAN INSTITUTION, WASHINGTON, D.C.: GIFT OF CHARLES LANG FREER, F1907.258

**England.** View of the Elysian Fields, Stowe, which were first established in 1731. MARA MILLER

The propensity to use gardens to express political arguments and commitments, and to understand garden design in political terms, permitted the garden historian Walpole to associate French formal gardens with monarchy and tyranny, and "natural" growth and irregularity with the newly emerging opposition government (Chase; Miller, "Gardens as Political Discourse").

**Landscape**

The idea of the garden as a landscape is, in the early 2000s, most familiar as the natural landscape garden, or *jardin anglos-chinois,* an artistic bequest of the eighteenth-century British.

The garden as natural landscape rejecting artificiality and the symmetric knots of formal gardens is an extrapolation of Eden from *Paradise Lost* (1667). According to Haorace Walpole, Milton is responsible for popularizing in garden design the idea that "'only after the Fall did man have to invoke art to shore a damaged nature'" (Hunt and Willis, p. 79).

During the eighteenth century this account inspired new garden design in England. Since formal gardens exemplified monarchies, the specifics of Milton's description of Eden as a natural landscape rather than as a geometric formal garden (favored by kings) are a function of his intense interest in Puritan antimonarchical politics, adding to their persuasive force.

In 1692 William Temple introduced the Chinese term *sharawadgi,* of which the origin is undertermined (although he thought Chinese), to refer to beauty that imitated nature rather than relying on geometric pruning and symmetrical designes. Temple defined *sharawadgi* as that sort of oder "where Beauty shall be great, and strike the Eye, but without any Order or Disposition of Parts, that shall be commonly or easily observ'd" (Hunt and Willis, p. 98). For half a century Chinese "irregular" gardening principles, known also from Matteo Ripa's illustrations of Chinese gardens, were associated with antimonarchical (even Whig) politics, until Walpole reversed that association by comparing the Chinese gardens described by the French missionary to China Pere Attiret to French formal monarchical gardens.

In addition, visual appropriation of adjacent landscape was integral to gardens in Renaissance Italy, eighteenth-century Britain, and Muromachi, Momoyama, and Edo, Japan, where the term *shakkei,* or "borrowed scenery," was coined to describe it (Nitschke). In Japan, gardens have been imitating nature for nearly one thousand years, and the rules for such gardens were transmitted both orally and in writing (Slawson).

**Garden as Picture**

One variant of the garden as a landscape is the garden based on landscape painting (*Ut pictura hortus*). Christopher Hussey's landmark study *The Picturesque* demonstrated the

**Japan.** Landscape with figures by Unkoku Tjogan, Momoyama period (1573–1615). One of a pair of six-panel screens, ink on paper. AVERY BRUNDAGE COLLECTION, THE ASIAN ART MUSEUM OF SAN FRANCISCO

**Japan.** Daitoku-ji Temple in Kyoto. Dry rock garden of the landscape type inspired by Song Dynasty Chinese landscape painting. MARA MILLER

power of the garden, once it was modeled on painting, to make the "picturesque" a category that could be applied to all landscape—the principle upon which highway scenic overlooks are based. According to Walpole, the early English landscape gardens by William Kent were also designed based upon pictorial compositions. The idea of modeling a garden on a landscape painting has a lively history in East Asia as well, where it can be seen in the dry rock gardens of Daitoku-ji Temple in Kyoto, based on Song Chinese landscape paintings.

Artists have created many highly influential gardens, among them Wang Wei (690–c. 760), William Kent (1685–1748), and Claude Monet (1840–1926). Gardens such as those by Manet and Gertrude Jekyll (1843–1932) utilized an artist's sense of color. In all cultures with gardens, gardens present themselves as pictures, providing subject matter for painters; in East Asia they are particularly important philosophically.

## Contemporary Gardens

Contemporary gardens continue to express many of these ancient ideas. In the early twenty-first century, as throughout history, when gardeners adopt and adapt the designs and practices and materials of new technologies or foreign garden traditions, they also adopt—and perhaps change—the underlying ideas. When they use the large rocks of Japanese landscape gardens in a front yard in Colorado or a University grounds in Montreal, they usher in a different way of understanding nature, the relationship of the building to its environment, the meaning of being at home. When they cultivate domestic and public lands with native grasses or wildflowers, they visualize specific ideas of the meaning of that place and its place in the natural environment. When they plant the tops of their buildings with a "green roof," they present a new perception of the role of the building in its environment and of humanity's responsibility for that environment.

*See also* **Landscape in the Arts; Nature; Paradise on Earth; Wildlife.**

**BIBLIOGRAPHY**

Adams, William Howard. *The French Garden, 1500–1800.* New York: Braziller, 1979.

Berger, Robert W. *In the Garden of the Sun King: Studies on the Park of Versailles Under Louis XIV.* Washington, D.C.: Dumbarton Oaks Research Library and Collection, 1985.

Chambers, Douglas *The Planters of the English Landscape Garden: Botany, Trees, and the Georgics.* New Haven, Conn., and London: Yale University Press, 1993.

Chase, Isabella Wakelin Urban. *Horace Walpole: Gardenist. An Edition of Walpole's "The History of the Modern Taste in Gardening," with an Estimate of Walpole's Contribution to Landscape Architecture.* Princeton, N.J.: Princeton University Press, 1943.

Clunas, Craig. *Fruitful Sites: Garden Culture in Ming Dynasty China.* Durham, N.C.: Duke University Press, 1996.

du Prey, Pierre de la Ruffinière. *The Villas of Pliny from Antiquity to Posterity.* Chicago and London: University of Chicago Press, 1994.

Everett, Nigel. *The Tory View of Landscape.* New Haven, Conn.: Yale University Press, 1994.

Goody, Jack. *The Culture of Flowers.* Cambridge, U.K., and New York: Cambridge University Press, 1993.

Harvey, John. *Medieval Gardens.* London: B. T. Batsford, 1981.

Hunt, John Dixon, and Peter Willis, eds.. *The Genius of the Place: The English Landscape Garden 1620–1820.* London: Elek, 1975. Reprint, Cambridge, Mass.: MIT Press, 1988.

Hussey, Christopher. *The Picturesque.* London and New York: G. P. Putnam, 1927.

Itoh, Teiji. *Space and Illusion in the Japanese Garden.* Translated and adapted by Ralph Friedrich and Masajiro Shimamura. New York: Weatherhill, 1973.

Jashemski, Wilhelmina Mary Feemster. *The Gardens of Pompeii: Herculaneum and the Villas Destroyed by Vesuvius.* New Rochelle, N.Y.: Caratzas, 1979.

Lehrman, Jonas. *Earthly Paradise: Garden and Courtyard in Islam.* Berkeley and Los Angeles: University of California Press, 1980.

Marx, Leo. *The Machine in the Garden: Technology and the Pastoral Ideal in America.* Oxford: Oxford University Press, 1964.

Miller, Mara. *The Garden as an Art.* Albany: State University of New York Press, 1993.

——. "The Garden as Significant Form." *Journal of Speculative Philosophy* 2, no. 4 (1988): 267–287.

——. "Gardens as Political Discourse in the Age of Walpole." In vol. 5 of *Politics, Politeness, and Patriotism: Proceedings of the Folger Institute for the History of British Political Thought,* edited by Gordon Schochet, 263–280. Folger Shakespeare Library, 1993.

——. "Knot Gardens and the Genesis of the Scientific Attitude." *Comparative Civilizations Review* 18 (spring 1988): 58–90.

——. "The Lady in the Garden: Subjects and Objects in an Ideal World." In *Crossing the Bridge: Comparative Essays on Medieval European and Heian Japanese Women,* edited by Cynthia Ho and Barbara Stevenson. New York: Palgrave, 2000.

——. "The Politics of Garden Design: Perspective on the Walpole-Chambers Debate." In vol. 6 of *Empire and Revolutions: Proceedings of the Folger Institute for the History of British Political Thought,* edited by Gordon Schochet, 227–234. Washington, D.C.: Folger Shakespeare Library, 1993.

Morris, Edwin T. *The Gardens of China: History, Art, and Meanings.* New York: Scribners, 1983.

Nitschke, Gunter. *Japanese Gardens: Right Angle and Natural Form.* Cologne, Germany: Benedikt Taschen, 1993.

Pevsner, Nokolaus. *The Picturesque Garden and Its Influence Outside the British Isles.* Washington, D.C.: Dumbarton Oaks, Trustees for Harvard University, 1974.

Prest, John. *The Garden of Eden: The Botanic Garden and the Recreation of Paradise.* New Haven, Conn., and London: Yale University Press, 1981.

Quaintance, Richard E. "Walpole's Whig Interpretation of Landscaping History." *Studies in Eighteenth-Century Culture* 9 (1979): 285–300.

Sirén, Osvald. *China and Gardens of Europe of the Eighteenth Century.* New York: Ronald Press, 1951.

——. *Gardens of China.* New York: Ronald Press, 1949.

Slawson, David A. *Secret Teachings in the Art of Japanese Gardens: Design Principles, Aesthetic Values.* Tokyo: Kodansha, 1987.

Stein, Rolf A. *The World in Miniature: Container Gardens and Dwellings in Far Eastern Religious Thought.* Translated by Phyllis Brooks. Stanford, Calif.: Stanford University Press, 1990.

Thacker, Christopher. *The History of Gardens.* Berkeley and Los Angeles: University of California Press, 1979.

Yiengpruksawan, Mimi. "The Phoenix Hall at Uji and the Symmetries of Replication." *The Art Bulletin* 77 (1995): 647–672.

*Mara Miller*

## GAY STUDIES.

Gay studies in the early twenty-first century is a lively interdisciplinary field encompassing studies of literature, anthropology, sociology, psychology, the visual arts, indeed all fields in which nonheteronormative sexuality—and its institutionalized suppression—has become a point of politico-philosophical argument. It has two origins: a more recent starting point in twentieth-century liberal Western discourse, prompted by gay liberation and political and social movements on the one hand, and intellectual trends in literary theory and philosophy on the other, and the much older fact of same-sex love, a facet of human history that permeates and predates recorded civilization. Gay studies is today closely linked to notions of the democratic struggle for civil equality, because the sexual practices that are its focus have been the target of authoritarian forces as diverse as Judeo-Christianity, Puritanism, Neo-Confucianism, psychiatry, Nazism, Maoism, and McCarthyism, all of which have variously punished nonnormative sexual practices to promote conformist, repressive political structures. In other times and places, however, while sexuality was always subject to societal pressures to conform, patterns of repression and acceptance varied considerably.

### Premodern Traditions of Same-Sex Love in the West

Though classical Greek homosexuality became a romantic, wistful reference point for Victorian, Edwardian, and modern Anglo-American homoerotic literature, its relative cultural norms must not be conflated with bourgeois romance or twentieth-century sexual democracy. The early Stoics, for example, rationally argued for gender and sexual equality and removed conventional morality from the discussion of sex, and Zeno of Citium (c. 335–263 B.C.E.), father of the Stoics, "never resorted to a women, but always to boy-favorites," according to his biographer Antigonus of Carystus, quoted by Louis Crompton. A more typical example of ancient Greek attitudes toward sexuality can be found in Plato's Academy, founded circa 387 B.C.E. Here, convention dictated a bisexual model of intergenerational mentorship and pederasty, whereby men fulfilled social obligations for marital, procreative sex while erotically tutoring beardless, flowering adolescent boys. For two adult male citizens to form permanent relationships was infrequent and slightly transgressive; yet the taxonomy of love found in Plato's *Symposium,* the greatest text on Greek eros, finds mundane heterosexuality pedestrian in contrast to an idealized vision of male love. Nevertheless, in his ultimate work, the *Laws,* an elderly Plato ascetically renounces erotic life. The only documentation for Greek female homosexuality is found in the fragmentary verses of the poet Sappho (fl. c. 610–c. 580 B.C.E.), whose literary influence has nonetheless been significant.

Homosexuality was common during the Roman Empire, but in this period militarism and imperialism turned Platonic mentorship into hedonistic relations between imperialistic Roman masters and conquered, penetrated slaves—a possible source of contemporary formulaic oppositions of masculine-aggressive and feminine-passive sexual and gender roles. Juvenal satirized a widespread homosexuality perceived as base and undignified, but Roman literature elsewhere bustles with lively homoerotica, most obviously in Petronius's *Satyricon*, Ovid's *Metamorphoses*, and the verse of Catullus and Virgil. With the rise of Judeo-Christian morality, antihomosexual prohibitions such as the infamous passages in Leviticus 20:13 crept into Western thought, prompting the emperor Justinian, in 533 C.E., to make homosexuality a capital offense in his *Corpus juris civilis* (Body of civil law), thus foreshadowing the Christian animus toward homosexuality throughout Anglo-Saxon, medieval, and Renaissance times.

Until recently, the image in the West of homosexual life in the succeeding centuries was grim. In the Middle Ages, sodomites were burned along with witches (the origin of the epithet "faggot"); in the Renaissance Christopher Marlowe (1564–1593) was charged with espousing blasphemous (that is, homosexual) sentiments; and in 1644 the Puritans infamously banned all English theater, fearing licentiousness stemming from both the cross-dressed boys who played women's roles and the unladylike introduction of female actors in 1629. The Renaissance Neoplatonists abstracted Socratic male love into a purely intellectual bond, and in 1767 the first English rendition of Plato's *Symposium* was deliberately mistranslated to remove all elements of homosexuality.

More recent scholarship, however, has challenged this picture of unrelenting homophobia. Biblical revisionists now speculate that the Levitican prohibitions were more narrowly targeted than they appear, intended only to quash blasphemies and paganisms the Bible associated with sodomites (1 Kings 14:24), or to curb male prostitution and public bawdry. In the 1990s, scholars from the Conservative Judaic tradition interpreted homosexuality as no more sinful than not keeping kosher, breaking the Sabbath, or violating any of the other 613 Talmudic commandments. More controversially, John Boswell's landmark studies *Christianity, Social Tolerance, and Homosexuality* (1980) and *Same-Sex Unions in Premodern Europe* (1994) offer highly contested evidence that until the Middle Ages the Catholic and Eastern Orthodox Churches actually condoned homosexuality and sanctioned pseudomarital homosexual partnerships.

Similarly, a wealth of new studies of Renaissance and early modern Europe offer a far more complicated picture of gender and sexuality. Nevertheless, the insights from early gay and lesbian studies of the 1970s remain significant. These studies rejected the Augustinian split between mind and body, identified sexual orientation in terms of undeniable desire and not repressible behavior, and reclaimed male and female homosexuality as two sets of desire distinct from both heterosexual power structures and each other. Though by current standards insufficiently nuanced, this liberal platform offered a critique of Western Christian thinking that nevertheless provided an important outline of the interrelationship between homophobia and misogyny that remains a significant cultural inheritance. Within this paradigm, the female body was perceived mainly as a procreative vessel, and female pleasure was considered nearly irrelevant prior to the discoveries and theories of Sigmund Freud (1859–1939). Homosexuality, meanwhile, was reductively understood as a corruptive male sodomy that produces the passive, womanly, and thus powerless identities into which patriarchal men fear falling. Male homosexuals, exercising the power of Christian free will, could redeem themselves by mastering (or, in Freudian terms, sublimating) their desires, as Augustine suggests; disempowered women, however, officially had no desires to willfully redeem, though they were, paradoxically, still open to charges of sinful lust.

## Non-Western Traditions

Anthropologists have documented a wide range of attitudes toward sexuality in tribal and small-scale societies, which tend to be more egalitarian and to tolerate a far wider range of sexual behaviors, perhaps because where there are no significant forms of inherited wealth, sex can be more easily separated from procreation. Nevertheless, many small-scale societies developed elaborate forms of sexual identities and rituals, including "third sex" figures such as the Polynesian mahu and Native American "two-spirit person" (formerly referred to as "the berdache"), and the male–male semen ingestion rituals of Melanesia. None of these phenomena, still less others such as the cross-dressed performances common in shamanic ritual or the Indian phenomenon of the *hijra* (a broad category encompassing eunuchs and gender-ambiguous persons), are easily interpreted within Western notions of homosexuality and heterosexuality, but all of them attest to the rich variability of human sexual desire and gender performance.

In state-level societies characterized by hierarchies of class, wealth, and power, in contrast, patriarchy was the rule. Nevertheless, some forms of same-sex love were tolerated and even encouraged, often in hierarchical forms that allowed elite males to explore their desires through rarefied aesthetics of same-sex eroticism. In imperial China, for example, one finds homosexuality among the emperors of the Han dynasty (206 B.C.E.–220 C.E.), and the cross-dressing gender performance of Beijing and Cantonese opera, ranked among the most esteemed of all Chinese arts. Though Neo-Confucianists worried homosexuality would threaten family stability, an epicurean aesthetic of male love was routine among dynastic aristocrats, as the Ming dynasty (1368–1644 C.E.) anthology *Duan xiu pan* (Records of the cut sleeve) attests. In Japan, an intergenerational tradition of sexual mentoring—not too different from Plato's—was customary and honorable between older samurai (*nenja*) and adolescent initiates (*wakashu*), and during the Tokugawa period (1603–1867) bisexual "connoisseurs of boys" (*shōjin-zuki*) vied for the affections of young Kabuki actors, who typically doubled as male prostitutes, mainly for the merchant classes. Japan's bisexual ethos is present even in its greatest literary classic, *Tale of Genji* (early eleventh century), whose rakish hero sleeps with boys as well as women, while Ihara Saikaku, famous for *The Great Mirror of Male Love* (1687) and *The Life of a Sensuous Man* (1682), is arguably the world's first author of commercially produced homosexual and bisexual erotica.

## The Medicalized, Industrialized Nation-State

The French Revolution's republican ideologies prompted much of Europe to reexamine its anachronistic, antigay worldview: The Napoleonic Code in 1810, Bavaria in 1813, and Spain in 1822 all legalized consensual homosexuality. With the rise of nineteenth-century industrialism, however, homosexuality was no longer only a sinful offense to God, but a social offense to an emerging bourgeois state attempting to manufacture conformist, nationalistic, and procreative-cum-capitalistic values. Thus was the stage set for modernity's first gay-rights struggle. Under an umbrella of progressive medical science and the burgeoning discipline of psychology, early German gay-rights activists sought to debunk the 1851 Prussian penal code's antigay Paragraph 143, asserting that same-sex attraction was not a sin borne of Christian free will but an innate, genetic trait beyond one's control. In 1864 Karl Heinrich Ulrichs began publishing his multipart, pseudoscientific *Forschungen über das Rätsel der mannmännlichen Liebe* (Researches into the riddle of "manmanly" love), which theorized homosexuality as a natural mental "hermaphroditism" causing discontinuities between gender and sexual object choice. Continuing Ulrichs's notion of genetic abnormality, in 1869 Karl Westphal, a German physician, described a condition of "contrary" sexuality, of masculine women and effeminate men, a view later echoed by the German neuropsychiatrist Richard von Krafft-Ebing's *Psychopathia Sexualis* (1886; Sexual psychopathology). Though Westphal opposed punishment of homosexuality, he believed contrary sexuality could be remedied—unlike Ulrichs, who passionately pled for open tolerance. In English, Westphal's "contrary" sexuality became mistranslated as "inversion," a term popularized by Havelock Ellis's *Sexual Inversion* (1896), whose humanistic case studies argued that "inverts" should live as productive citizens, not be punished for received, arbitrary genetics. Perhaps more progressive was Karl Maria Benkert (creator of the word *homosexual*), who in 1869 published tracts that sought to undermine the Prussian penal code and rebuked Ulrichs's special pleadings, and instead advanced sexual egalitarianism based on French Revolutionary principles.

The most celebrated early gay scholar was the German-Jewish sexologist Magnus Hirschfeld (coiner of the term *transvestite*), who first argued for sexual broadmindedness in *Sappho und Sokrates* (1896) and *Jahrbuch für sexuelle Zwischenstufen* (1899–1923; Yearbook for intermediate sexual types) the world's first homosexually themed journal, which suggested that homosexuals constituted a "third," intermediate sex. In 1919 Hirschfeld founded his Institute for Sexual Science—eventually torched by the Nazis in 1933—and cowrote the screenplay for the world's first gay film, *Anders als die Andern* (Different from the others), which again pleads for homosexual tolerance on medical-genetic grounds. Hirschfeld, certainly, was marginal within the psychological community, and Freud's idea of an arrested latent stage, as coupled with an unresolved Oedipal complex, became the accepted model of homosexual identity until the contemporary gay-rights movement. Unlike Westphal and Krafft-Ebing, Freud viewed homosexuality not as an inborn de-

fect but as a commonplace neurosis no worse than any other, and in 1930 he signed a public statement calling for the repeal of Paragraph 175 (an 1871 revision of Paragraph 143), which the Nazis would soon use to persecute homosexuals.

Undoubtedly, the pathologization of homosexuality affected all spheres of contemporary art and culture: Homosexual or bisexual authors such as Nikolay Vasilyevich Gogol (1809–1852) and Leo Tolstoy (1828–1910) endured psychological torment because of their efforts to suppress their illicit desires, Marcel Proust (1871–1922) and Thomas Mann (1875–1955) framed their homosexualities as upper-class neurosis and decadence, and those who dared de-closet themselves risked the imprisonment Oscar Wilde (1854–1900) suffered, even if, occasionally, the romantic, private verse of an Arthur Rimbaud (1854–1891) or A. E. Housman (1859–1936) covertly legitimized a tender gay sensibility. When Radclyffe Hall's *The Well of Loneliness*—currently regarded as the first lesbian novel—first appeared in 1928, audiences were shocked that its tale of "sexual inversion" was presented in heroic, albeit tragic, terms. Immediately banned in Britain, it became the focus of notorious obscenity trials, and then a touchstone for early lesbian rights movements. Meanwhile, the nations of a rapidly modernizing Asia suppressed (or, in the case of Maoist China, erased) their millennia-old homosexual histories and blindly adopted Western medical prejudice. Japanese homosexuality would reappear (albeit with Western notions of shame attached) only in 1948 with Yukio Mishima's *Kamen no kokuhaku* (Confessions of a mask), and in the early twenty-first century consensual homosexuality remains illegal in communist China, whose memory-impaired leaders insist it is a decadent, Western illness.

Nevertheless, the antibourgeois anarchism that fueled the 1905 and 1917 Russian revolutions also birthed a tentative, fleeting acceptance of modern homosexuality, and the 1922 Bolshevik criminal code officially legalized consensual sodomy. Though a paranoid Joseph Stalin, the Soviet premier, would fully recriminalize homosexuality in 1933, the antibourgeois radicalism first witnessed in Russia still ignites much of modern and postmodern (homo)sexual discourse.

## Militancy and Visibility: The Assertion of Gay Identity

The contemporary gay-rights movement is usually traced to the riots that began on June 28, 1969, when patrons at Manhattan's Stonewall Inn refused to submit to the lewdness arrests gay men regularly endured at the time. There were, however, liberal precedents in Henry Gerber's short-lived Society for Human Rights (1924), the first gay-rights organization in the United States, and Communist Party leader Harry Hay's homophilic Mattachine Society (1950) and its sister lesbian organization, Daughters of Bilitis (1955). Meanwhile, under the nose of McCarthyism a contentious, frequently prosecuted homosexual subculture newly awakened through avant-garde filmmaker Kenneth Anger's *Fireworks* (1947), Allen Ginsberg's *Howl* (1956), William S. Burrough's *Naked Lunch* (1959), Christopher Isherwood's *A Single Man* (1964), and the gay-positive "physique" artistry of Bob Mizer, Bruce Bellas, and Tom of Finland. But it was Stonewall's unprecedented militant visibility politics that delivered gays and lesbians from the closet and into the mainstream.

The years following 1969 witnessed the Gay Liberation Front; *The Boys in the Band* (1970), Hollywood's first gay film; John Murphy's *Homosexual Liberation: A Personal View* (1971); *The Journal of Homosexuality* (1974); and (heterosexual) psychologist George Weinberg's *Society and the Healthy Homosexual* (1972), whose neologism *homophobia* identified public prejudice, not the homosexual, as neurotic. In 1973 the American Psychiatric Association—mainly to appease post-Stonewall politics—declassified homosexuality as a pathology in its *Diagnostic and Statistical Manual of Mental Disorders* (DSM), though the DSM-IV persists in recognizing a "gender identity disorder," implying that homosexual men and women are healthy only insofar as they respectively behave according to masculine-aggressive and feminine-passive gender stereotypes. In the 1970s and 1980s, psychiatry's patriarchal conservatism became a favorite target of lesbian feminists, most notably Monique Wittig, whose revolutionary declaration that lesbians were "not women" rejected Freud's mystifying construction of female sexuality and removed lesbians from the stifling female roles patriarchy had mandated.

In 1970 University of Nebraska professor Louis Crompton created academia's first gay studies class; in 1972 the first gay studies program in the United States was initiated at California State University, Sacramento. While initially gay studies sought to deconstruct the fallacious nineteenth-century medicalization of homosexuality (thus, the substitution of the nonstigmatic *gay*), and resist what Adrienne Rich would later call patriarchy's "compulsory heterosexuality," by the mid-1970s gay academics began turning to literature, resuscitating the tacitly recognized but largely unexamined homosexualities of authors whose canonical status could legitimize a tentative field susceptible to ridicule. The sexual orientations of Lord Byron, André Gide, Walt Whitman, and W. H. Auden were no longer incidental, but central to a critical literary approach to text, voice, subjectivity, and especially intentionality. Conservatives balked when gay scholars read Herman Melville's *Billy Budd* or Shakespearean sonnets as coded gay texts, but reader-response critics also argued that an author's sexuality was irrelevant, because all textual meaning is not received frozen from history but is an active, contemporary creation of a (sexually) empowered subjectivity. Nevertheless, a secondary gay canon emerged around definitively gay authors such as E. M. Forster, W. Somerset Maugham, Edward Carpenter, Jean Genet, and Gertrude Stein, and gay studies began intersecting with film studies to address the leftist gay cinemas of Pier Paolo Pasolini, Rosa von Praunheim, Rainer Werner Fassbinder, and Derek Jarman. But only in the late 1970s and early 1980s, under the guidance of lesbian feminism and multiculturalism, would once-Eurocentric gay academia fully embrace the likes of Audre Lorde, James Baldwin, Djuna Barnes, and Langston Hughes.

## From Gay Identity to Queer Theory

By the 1980s, gay studies came to a critical turning point. Its achievements were clear: A body of theory had emerged that legitimized nonreproductive sexualities, locating sexual desire in politically marginalized yet physically expressive bodies, and exploring how those bodies operated, or were operated upon, within repressive political climates. But if placing gay and les-

bian bodies in opposition to marital and economic norms offered the pleasures of subversion and righteous indignation, it also doomed them to permanent pariah status. Moreover, there was a growing awareness that gay studies, like the earlier disciplines it critiques, risked producing its own essentialized core gender identities, based upon a naturalized gay identity that still perceived anatomy and biology as inescapable. Missing from these formulations were the often polymorphous forms of gender identity and polyamorous quality of desire. The AIDS crisis, which took its toll throughout the 1980s to Reaganite-Thatcherite indifference, also fueled calls for a new, more radical politics. Queer theory responded by abandoning the neo-Marxism and social activism of gay rights, and built upon Michel Foucault's *The History of Sexuality* (1978–1984) and literary poststructuralism to argue that both sexuality and gender are social constructions produced within specific historical contexts. Queer social constructionism decouples sexuality from gender, abandoning any notion of sexual orientation as biologically determined. Male and female are no longer biological polarities but malleable constructs, and thus gender and sexuality (straight or gay) no longer automatically follow from one another. Sexual desire is not perceived as fixed and inherent in the body, but as a culturally created response that may or may not be related to a fixed social identity. Incorporating all categories of gay, lesbian, bisexual, transgender, transsexual, and even voluntary heterosexual desire, "queer," by having no definitive "Other" to mobilize against, represents everything and nothing, and posits a suprademocratic category through which identities—of class and race as well—can radically hybridize and transform.

The same intellectual ferment that began to define *gay* as retrogressive and *queer* as politically progressive inspired a new academic vocabulary. The word *homophobia*, for example, came under new scrutiny in the mid-1980s. Though it astutely characterized sexual bigotry as a passively received mass neurosis and not a moral choice, Weinberg's term was now seen as etymologically illogical, literally meaning a fear of sameness but figuratively suggesting a fear of otherness. Homophobia was replaced with *heterosexism*, emphasizing not a special "phobia" but a chauvinism as banally evil as sexism or racism. *Heteronormative*, popularized by queer theorist Michael Warner in the early 1990s, moves beyond heterosexism's critique of mere prejudice to challenge the ways patriarchy—especially the patriarchy implicit in late global capitalism—normalizes essential gender identity and punishes all nonheterosexual conduct. Perhaps most influential is Eve Kosofsky Sedgwick's neologism *homosocial*, introduced in *Between Men: English Literature and Male Homosocial Desire* (1985), which argues that heterosexual social institutions, particularly marriage, have historically used women to triangulate and transmit male bonds that, while not actually homosexual, transitively accrue ambiguous homoerotic meanings. After much overuse, however, the parameters of homosociality have become (perhaps deliberately) vague, and there is a tendency to overoptimistically describe all same-sex, homosocial institutions—schools, prisons, monasteries, and so on—as fertile breeding grounds for imagined or potential homosexualities, regardless of those environments' coercive or insular qualities.

More recently, theorists such as Gayatri Chakravorty Spivak have linked queer and postcolonial arguments to investigate how, even in the postmodern world of hybrids and multiple subjectivities, Asian and African nation-states continue to regulate sexual identity and suppress female agency in accordance with colonialist mentalities that they, in a postcolonial era, have failed to progress beyond, and often unwittingly internalize. Most radical has been Judith Butler, whose notion of "performativity," first introduced in *Gender Trouble* (1990) and later refined in *Bodies That Matter* (1993), maintains that gender is not simply a construct into which humans are historically delivered, but is a mask, a controllable, conscious act of mimicry, parody, and self-parody, as best represented in drag performance. After Butler, however, queer theory's drive to reimagine sexuality without boundaries or definitions seemed to reach an impasse. One emergent critique sees the elegant philosophical games and abstruse language of authors such as Butler and Spivak as elitist, and questioned whether such texts can be effective political tools for inspiring large-scale cultural change. Some authors even question the concept of Butlerian performativity, dismissing it as stylistic gamesmanship. While queer theorists might argue that questions of rhetoric and performance are key to sociopolitical norms and thus to their transformation, the critique of queer theory as elitist and jargon-filled has nonetheless been widely perceived as justified. Some gay scholars have, in response, recast queer theory in more populist terms, as does Warner in *The Trouble with Normal* (2000), in which he suggests that by seeking marriage rights, gays and lesbians misguidedly try to legitimatize their sexualities through an oppressively monogamous, proprietary, shame-based institution that forbids constructions of freer sexuality.

As national debates about gay marriage and civil rights continue, the gay identity politics queer postmodernism hoped to replace are making a resurgence. Recent years have seen a slightly less radical interpretation of queerness, which, lest it unintentionally reproduce an intolerant, authoritarian voice *within* queer communities, should also potentially include identity-based gay activism and oppositional lesbian feminism.

Indeed, as increased gay/queer visibility in film, television, and other popular media has only inflamed the fears of social conservatives, a diversified strategy of neopragmatic gay activism and utopian queer theory may be necessary to neutralize prejudices ingrained throughout the centuries.

*See also* **Cultural Studies; Gender; Protest, Political; Sexuality.**

BIBLIOGRAPHY

Boswell, John. *Christianity, Social Tolerance, and Homosexuality: Gay People in Western Europe from the Beginning of the Christian Era to the Fourteenth Century.* Chicago: University of Chicago Press, 1980.

Butler, Judith. *Bodies That Matter: On the Discursive Limits of "Sex."* New York: Routledge, 1993.

Crompton, Louis. *Homosexuality and Civilization.* Cambridge, Mass.: Harvard University Press, 2003.

Foucault, Michel. *The History of Sexuality,* Vol. 1: *An Introduction.* Translated by Robert Hurley. New York: Pantheon, 1978.

Hirschfeld, Magnus. *The Homosexuality of Men and Women.* Translated by Michael A. Lombardi-Nash. Amherst, N.Y.: Prometheus Books, 2000.

Murphy, John. *Homosexual Liberation: A Personal View.* New York: Praeger, 1971.

Rich, Adrienne. "Compulsory Heterosexuality and Lesbian Existence." *Signs: Journal of Women in Culture and Society* 5, no. 4 (1980): 631–660. Reprint, in her *Blood, Bread, and Poetry: Selected Prose, 1979–1985,* 23–75. New York: Norton, 1986.

Saikaku, Ihara. *The Great Mirror of Male Love.* Translated by Paul Gordon Schalow. Stanford, Calif.: Stanford University Press, 1990.

Sedgwick, Eve Kosofsky. *Epistemology of the Closet.* Berkeley and Los Angeles: University of California Press, 1990.

Ulrichs, Karl Heinrich. *The Riddle of "Man-Manly" Love: The Pioneering Work on Homosexuality.* 2 vols. Translated by Michael A. Lombardi-Nash. Buffalo, N.Y.: Prometheus Books, 1994. Collected works of Ulrichs.

Warner, Michael, ed. *Fear of a Queer Planet: Queer Politics and Social Theory.* Minneapolis: University of Minnesota Press, 1993.

Weinberg, George. *Society and the Healthy Homosexual.* New York: St. Martin's Press, 1972.

*Andrew Grossman*

# GENDER.

This entry includes two subentries:

*Overview*
*Gender in the Middle East*

## OVERVIEW

*Gender* is an old term in linguistic discourse used to designate whether nouns are masculine, feminine, or neuter. It was not normally used in the language of social or natural sciences or in sexology until 1955, when John Money adopted the term to serve as an umbrella concept to distinguish femininity, or womanliness, and masculinity, or manliness, from biological sex (male or female). Though the term was quickly adopted in studies of transvestism and transsexualism, it did not receive widespread circulation until 1972 in a book coauthored by Money and Anke Ehrhardt. Its popularity became firmly established in the 1980s as the feminist movement increasingly adopted the term *gender studies* as a replacement for *women's studies*. In a sense by using a new term to describe a variety of phenomena, Money opened up a whole new field of research since it implied that genitalia were not the only factor involved in being a man or a woman.

Money himself went on to develop a number of terms such as *gender identity* and *gender role* to categorize different aspects of one's identity. He also argued that the term *sex* should be used with a qualifier as in *genetic sex, hormonal sex,* or *external genitalia sex.* Gender was more inclusive since it entailed somatic and behavioral criteria on how one conducts oneself personally and socially, and how one is regarded legally. Sex belonged more to reproductive biology than to social sciences, romance, or nurture, whereas gender covered them all. The term was seized upon by an increasingly powerful feminist movement that was concerned with overcoming the biology-is-destiny argument that had been so long used to keep women in a subordinate status.

Gays and lesbians also found the term helpful in challenging traditional ideas. Since both the feminist and the gay and lesbian movements had well-organized constituencies, the research into gender had increasing political implications.

Popular adoption of the term, for example, was a major factor in the undermining of traditional Western ideas about dimorphic essentialism, that is, males and females are different and should display erotic sex and gender characteristics congruent with their sex because of their biological makeup or, in religious terms, their God-given nature had made it so. In simplistic terms, the first stage of a growing controversy was over whether nature or nurture was more important in forming individual development. Some of the early feminists argued that women's subordination to men had resulted from the dominance of the male, and if girls and boys were simply raised differently they would react differently. Boys, they argued, should be given dolls and girls trucks; girls should be encouraged to be more aggressive; and the role of males and females in society would change. There is undoubtedly an element of truth in such a belief, but it is much too simplistic. Still many of the differences were social and cultural, as demonstrated by the fact that once barriers were removed through equal opportunity legislation, women rapidly moved into fields formerly dominated by men and began to approach financial parity in salary and perquisites. Women athletes have also become increasingly important. As research progressed, important gender differences between the sexes were noted, but at the same time the issue also became much more complicated.

## Some Research on Gender Differences

Ann Constantinople, for example, questioned the assumption that masculinity was the opposite of femininity and suggested that the identification of masculine traits might be independent from rather than opposite to the identification of feminine traits. As new scales for masculinity and femininity were developed by researchers, they found wide variation in gender traits among individuals of the same biological sex, but interestingly they also found an almost compulsive pressure to conform put on those who varied too far from the norm. This was particularly noted to be the case in feminine boys. The wide spectrum of behaviors led to a greater emphasis on biological answers.

One theory developed by Bonnie Bullough (in a work coauthored with Vern Bullough) for the formation of gender identities and sexual preference held that there were at least three steps:

1. A genetic predisposition for a gender or cross-gender or cross-sexual identity, including high or low levels of activity and aggression.

2. Prenatal hormonal stimulation supported or countered the genetic predisposition, perhaps indelibly marking the neural pathways so the pattern that produced variant gender behavior con-

tinued after birth.

3. The socialization pattern shaped the specific manifestation of the predisposition.

It was not only social and natural scientists who entered the debate about the differences in gender behavior but scholars from the humanities and arts as well. One of the best known was Marjorie Garber, who attempted to escape the bipolar notions of male and female by advocating a third category, a way of describing alternative possibilities. Bipolar approaches, she held, create a "category crisis," a failure of definitional distinction, resulting in a border that becomes permeable and permits border crossing.

Research on homosexual men, for example, has found that a significant number were identified as feminine boys during their youth. Richard Green's longitudinal study of extremely effeminate boys, most of whom wished they had been born girls, found that 75 percent of his sample identified themselves as homosexual as adults although almost all of them had become less feminine in their behavior during their teens. The fact that not all of them came to identify as homosexual as adults emphasized the complexity of development although it was possible that some of them might at a later stage still identify as homosexual. Masculine-identified girls, or tomboys, have a lower proportion identifying as lesbians as adults perhaps because the pressure on them to conform was also less. Unfortunately, much less research has been done on tomboys than on feminine boys.

## Challenge to Bipolar Assumptions

Several strains of research seemed to be important in challenging traditional bipolar assumptions: genetic or biological research, the study of hermaphrodites, investigation of transsexuality, homosexuality, and bisexuality. The major subjects of Money's early studies were hermaphrodites. He was surprised to find that many who later were identified by chromosome analysis to have been raised in the wrong sex, preferred to remain in the sex in which they had been raised. This led him to posit that there was a critical stage in development where one's personal gender identity was set. While he was originally ambiguous on when this might happen, he eventually held that the age of two was critical. But such an assumption was difficult to prove.

Money felt he had found an ideal case in identical twin brothers, one of whom, while being circumcised at age seven months by an electric cautery gun, had his penis burned off. The parents, after considerable anguish, had the child's testicles removed and with Money as consultant and adviser, began raising the child as a girl at about twenty months. Initial follow-up articles pointed to a successful transition, and the case was widely used to emphasize the importance of social conditioning on sex identity. After the case disappeared from the literature, it turned out the "girl" had rebelled at her change in her teens, and after being finally told her story decided to become a boy. Such a change had been predicted by a critic of Money, Milton Diamond, and it was only through his long efforts to find the boy, who was then an adult male, that the

## GENDER STUDIES

The term *gender,* proposed by John Money in the 1950s, was immediately seized upon by scholars in a variety of disciplines, perhaps because it avoided the use of the term *sex,* a term many thought not suitable for public discourse, but the finite definition that Money and other scholars early used was quickly abandoned. Questions seeking to determine an individual's sex, even on government forms, no long asked for sex but for gender. Feminists particularly favored the use of the term and many programs that had started out as *women's studies* were renamed gender studies. By 2004, almost every American university had a program on gender studies and so did many high schools. Gay and lesbian studies became gay, lesbian and gender studies, or more often just gender studies. Gender studies are ubiquitous and not confined to the social and behavioral sciences, but appear in courses in literature and the humanities, and even in biology.

Gender studies deal with transvestism, transsexualism, bisexuality, as well as intersex, the original source of Money's classification. Vern Bullough, in his study of the history of sex research, predicted that gender would be the dominant theme of research upon sexuality in the first part of the twenty-first century and it certainly seems to be the case.

The advantage of using the term *gender studies* instead of *sexuality studies* is that gender in itself implies for a more variable interpretation of what being a woman or a man involves. Whether a person is an XX or an XY, there is much more to being a man or woman than chromosomes. Though males impregnate and females become impregnated, there is much more to gender than that. Some women are more masculine than a significant minority of men and some men are much more feminine than many women. Gender study data showing and explaining these differences and similarities have been growing as more and more disciplines enter the field. One of the interesting sequella of this is the increasing number of individuals who are calling themselves transgendered. Gender studies, in effect, have resulted in basic challenges on what a man or woman should be or could be.

In spite of the vast increase of publications on gender, there is still much that is not known. For example, the experiences of "Bruce" as told in John Colapinto's book *As Nature Made Him* and other similar stories have brought greater attention to biological components of variation as opposed to simply focusing on the effects of social settings or nurturing experiences on gender. The more we learn the more complicated the whole question of gender becomes. This seems to imply that gender studies will continue to increase since it offers such a rich field for research and perhaps even more radical changes in public behavior.

---

full story came out, much to the discredit of Money's theory. But the issue even here is complicated by the fact that another boy who also had a similar background, continued as an adult to live as a woman, although as a somewhat masculine-looking and -acting one. The two cases together emphasize that there might be strong biological factors involved.

Some adults very much want to belong to the opposite sex than that associated with their genitalia. This issue came to national attention through the Christine Jorgensen case in the 1950s. Jorgensen achieved worldwide notoriety by having her penis and testicles amputated, and through the administration of hormones successfully made a transition into a woman. What gender confusion could make a man want to be a woman? Whatever it was, surgery and hormones could make it possible, and Jorgensen's path to the opposite sex has since been taken by tens

of thousands of others, although there are somewhat fewer females who have undergone surgery to become males than of males to become females. There are also large numbers of transvestites who cross-dress and identity as women either for short periods or longer periods without benefit of sex-change surgery. Millions of people in the United States today identify as transgender, transsexual, homosexual, lesbian, or bisexual, and others like them exist all over the world and probably always have throughout human history. They represent one end of the continuum on gender development while the majority of the world lies elsewhere with many individual variations.

Some researchers like Diamond have argued that, in addition to chromosomes, prenatal hormones exert influence on neural pathways and the neural endocrine axis (the link between the hypothalamus, the pituitary gland, and other endocrine glands). These neural pathways control future hormonal production and consequently influence sexual behavior and gender identification. He holds that there are separate neural pathways for sexual identity as a male or female, for sexual object choice, for sexual patterns of maleness or femaleness, and for the sexual response patterns.

## Variations in Gender Behavior between and among the Sexes

Researchers (and perhaps common sense) have shown that the behavior pattern most associated with males is that of aggressiveness, and this has undoubtedly influenced gender characteristics in women, including the relative servitude that has marked their history as the subordinated sex. Aggressiveness, however, has varied levels in males, with some being much more aggressive than others. The same differential exists in females but at a lower scale. If this has any meaning politically, then the way to lessen its impact is by equal opportunity laws and regulations, a path that feminists and others have adopted in the United States and elsewhere.

When all the findings about gender are summarized, it seems that there is a wide variation in gender behavior between and among the sexes. Those societies that in the past had adopted strict dimorphic gender patterns will have more difficulty in changing to sexual equality than those that allow somewhat more ambiguity. In the United States and in much of the world, cross-gender behavior in the past was stigmatized and punished. Since the nineteenth century, when the medical model came into prominence as a means of diagnosing nonconforming sex and gender behavior, significant departures from a dimorphic model of masculinity and femininity were labeled as an illness. Similarly, sexual orientations other than exclusive heterosexuality were considered an illness until the American Psychiatric Association voted in 1973 to drop ordinary homosexuality from the upcoming edition of its *Diagnostic and Statistical Manual of Mental Disorders.*

## New Directions

In terms of research into sex and gender, the 1990s saw a shift in emphasis from societal factors, cultural molding, and nurture to physiological factors. Much of this research concentrated on the brain and on intrauterine developments. Boy babies as a group, for example, are more likely to spend more time looking at mechanical objects than do baby girls, who look longer at a human face. But there is also a tremendous amount of overlap and wide variation among individuals, and how society deals with this overlap is more a political and economic question than one science or social science can determine.

*See also* **Feminism: Overview; Sexuality: Overview.**

**BIBLIOGRAPHY**

American Psychiatric Association. *Diagnostic and Statistical Manual of Mental Disorders.* 3rd ed. Washington, D.C.: America Psychiatric Association, 1980.

Baron-Cohen, Simon. *The Essential Difference: The Truth about the Male and Female Brain.* New York: Perseus, 2003.

Bullough, Vern L. *Science in the Bedroom: A History of Sex Research.* New York: Basic Books, 1994.

Bullough, Vern L., and Bonnie Bullough. *Cross Dressing, Sex, and Gender.* Philadelphia: University of Pennsylvania Press, 1995.

Colapinto, John. *As Nature Made Him: The Boy Who Was Raised as a Girl.* New York: HarperCollins, 2000.

Constantinople, Ann. "Masculinity-Femininity: An Exception to a Famous Dictum." *Psychological Bulletin* 80 (1973): 389–407.

Diamond, Milton. "A Critical Evaluation of the Ontogeny of Human Sexual Behavior." *Quarterly Review of Biology* 40 (1965): 147–175.

———. "Human Sexual Development: Biological Foundations for Social Development." *Human Sexuality in Four Perspectives,* edited by Frank A. Beach. Baltimore: Johns Hopkins University Press, 1977.

Garber, Marjorie. *Vested Interests: Cross-Dressing and Cultural Anxiety.* New York: Routledge, 1992.

Green, Richard. *The "Sissy Boy Syndrome" and the Development of Homosexuality.* New Haven: Yale University Press, 1987.

Jones, Steven. *Y: The Descent of Men.* Boston: Houghton Mifflin, 2004.

Money, John. "Hermaphroditism, Gender, and Precocity in Hyper-Andrenocorticism: Psychologic Findings." *Bulletin of Johns Hopkins Hospital* 96 (1955): 253–254.

Money, John, and Anke A. Ehrhardt. *Man & Woman, Boy & Girl.* Baltimore: Johns Hopkins University Press, 1972.

Thorne, Barrie. *Girls and Boys in School: Together or Separate.* Reprint, New Brunswick, N.J.: Rutgers University Press, 1993.

*Vern L. Bullough*

## GENDER IN THE MIDDLE EAST

The term *gender* has no exact correlate in Middle Eastern sources, but instead is identified by scholars as a major analytical tool in the definition of differences between men and women. Many researchers in every discipline argue that gender has always been embedded in all societies, past and present. Scholars who study gender seek to question dominant, normative definitions of every society's assigned male and female roles. The gendered implications of religious and legal definitions, scripted as timeless injunctions, may be interrogated to reveal previously ignored multiple symbolic meanings. Thus, the interactive cultural categories of male and female, masculine and feminine, analyzed through the lens of gender, may be read as human interpretations and constructions rather than divine and eternal definitions. The study of the Middle East contextualizes the accepted readings assigned to both genders in all disciplines and documents them not as a process of consistent conformity, but rather as an outcome of internal contests over power and constructed meaning. The results of this research aims to historicize accepted truths and undermine those who seek to define them as forever divided into simple oppositional, binomial categories of male and female, right and wrong, sacred and profane.

## Origins

Feminist and women's studies in the 1960s and 1970s paved the foundation for the emergence of gender analysis in the

1980s. Women's studies and gender studies arose to combat the absence of documentation about women in all Western disciplines. Yet the focus on gender emphasizes the inextricable interaction between both sexes, while women's studies' singular focus does not. Documenting the experience of women led to the realization that it was necessary to deepen the exploration of the multiple meanings of male and female on symbolic and practical levels. Female scholars dominate this methodology, but men now contribute to the field. Gender studies draws theoretical inspiration from Western interdisciplinary sources but continues to refine such precedents, proving at once the importance of universal conceptual frameworks and the centrality of Middle Eastern context in their refinement. Proponents of gender studies support both academic intent and often an activist agenda for social change. Therefore, many intellectuals and religious leaders in Middle Eastern societies reject gender as an intrusive European and American construct.

Evidence of Islamic feminism in the Middle East does exist as the historical foundation for gender studies, but few scholars there connect this movement to the precedent of earlier challenges to male authority. In 1923, Huda Sha'rawi (d. 1947) founded the Egyptian Women's Union and called for equal rights for both women and men. She also publicly removed her veil as a denial of traditional strictures that she perceived as part of a corrupt, oppressive social hierarchy. Support for her reformist platform received public approbation from select secularist men and many upper-class Christian and Muslim women. Sha'rawi's example did not incite a mass movement in support of either feminism or, by extension, new definitions of male and female identity in the Middle East. Stiff opposition to such movements remains the norm.

In the late 1970s, Elizabeth Warnock Fernea and Basima Bezirgan edited a groundbreaking collection of documents designed to more accurately represent the complex history and multiple roles of Muslim women. These translated selections filled the need for English-speaking audiences to understand the women in this area in their own terms. The precedent-setting lives of early female historical figures were set alongside contemporary women's stories, poems, and recollections of resistance to colonial occupation. These selections drew in part upon previous works in the 1930s and 1940s by scholars such as Margaret Smith, who illuminated the importance of the early ascetic mystic, Rabi'a of Basra (c. 714–801 C.E.).

In the 1980s, women scholars in the Middle East took up the challenge raised by female coreligionists in the early twentieth century to oppose the assumed right of male authorities to define and control every aspect of their lives. They explicitly identified with Western feminist agendas and, as a result, their publications were condemned in their native lands. Fatima Mernissi's classic work, *The Veil and the Male Elite* (1987), argued that accepted male readings of the medieval Islamic past were deeply flawed and sexist when applied to the present. Although this work predated the emergence of gender studies, it, together with similar works, helped spur its birth. Ironically, Mernissi found the most receptive audience for her work outside the Middle East where feminists identified shared concerns. Support for her critique

of male dominance from scholars abroad fueled accusations in the Middle East that Mernissi had been co-opted by the enemies of Islam.

Since the 1990s, the struggle to apply gender inquiry to Middle Eastern societies has also been forcefully challenged by Muslim women in the United States. Many questioned the right of non-Muslims to speak on behalf of Middle Eastern men and women. In the wake of these protests, Western scholars of the Middle East display greater self-awareness as well as greater sensitivity to cultural differences. Muslim women seeking to better understand their place in Islamic society now increasingly invigorate public discussions of the gendered definitions of both sexes. In this process, Muslim women challenge long-standing precedents about cultural hierarchies and praxis. They claim the right to an active intellectual presence, which disrupts the assumption that Middle Eastern women are either silent or passive in their own societies.

## Anthropology, Literature, and History

Anthropological studies of gender contributed pioneering fieldwork that recorded definitions of masculine and feminine honor, sexuality, and self-representation through poetic expression in rural areas from Morocco to Iran. The documentation of unequal, gendered hierarchies of power demonstrated that women negotiated these structures in distinctly inventive ways. Erika Friedl's revealing observations of women in a rural Iranian village allowed the voices of these women to be heard without seeming intrusion. The gendered implications of their rich, lived experience in marriage, childbirth, and complex daily life emphasized their resilience. The support they lent one another often negated the poverty and isolation of their lives. Friedl's self-awareness of her role as observer, participant, and confidant questioned the boundaries between Middle Eastern women and their representation by outsiders.

Scholars of Middle Eastern literature differentiated between premodern works written by men about women and the emergence of women's writing about men, society, and themselves in the nineteenth and twentieth centuries. Medieval male writers devoted extensive amounts of energy to their definition of the feminine as the exact opposite of the masculine. These assertions received no recorded response by women in this period. In contrast, the emergence of women's writing in all genres of poetry, history, and social commentary emerged in full bloom in the nineteenth and twentieth centuries throughout the Middle East. These sources sought redefinition of women in tandem with new female definitions of men. Literary critics and historians, the latter informed by postmodern theoretical models and interests in the formation of modernity, examined magazines founded, edited, and written by women for upper- and middle-class women. Marilyn Booth's study of gender definitions replete in biographical collections authored by women captured the emergence of a new hierarchy of female exemplars, ranging from the Prophet's daughter, Fatima, to Joan of Arc. Booth's study deftly reconfigured gender at the intersection of Egyptian reaction to the British occupation and the emergence of nationalism.

Numerous studies now document gender in all periods of Middle Eastern history. Male articulations of the role of the Prophet's most controversial wife, Aisha bint Abi Bakr (614–678 C.E.), were dissected to yield new insights into the medieval construction of gender in politics, sexuality, and the sectarian division between Sunni and Shii Muslims. The importance of education, as taught to women by men and one another in the medieval period, also proved critical to a reexamination of literacy and intellectual achievement. Scholars of gender contradicted through archival research the traditional theory that Ottoman imperial decline was precipitated by meddlesome, royal women in the harem. In spheres of daily life presumed to have been exclusively masculine, the contributions of women's labor to the marketplace, silk production, and agriculture redefined the agency of nonelite women.

## Gender Politics: The Veil and the Koran

The issue of the veil, or modest Muslim attire for women, has, since the early twentieth century, been a vexed issue. This symbol also provoked debates about the gendered roles of women in a male-dominated society. Issues of power and female agency masked long-standing assumptions about the distinctions between men and women, which this clothing revealed. Human rationales for the veil were presumed to be supported by either divine Koranic injunction or oppressive male interpretation. Men and women in the Middle East often agreed upon the necessity for either doffing or donning the veil. The contentious, seemingly endless battle over the meaning of the veil has also been influenced by negative, misinformed reaction articulated in Western societies. Leila Ahmed's inquiry into the position of gender at the roots of these changes emphasized multiple discourses and agendas focused on the veil as articulated by secularists, nationalists, and Islamists.

Early feminist movements in the twentieth century based their platforms of equality in reinterpretations of the Koran. Opponents also focused on this source and the precedent of the prophet Muhammad's words about women. The struggle for exclusive interpretations of the truth served the purposes of those who defined both the subordination and liberation of women, respectively. Contests over power in society were scripted by adherents in each camp in terms of gender hierarchy. Historical transformations in the interpretation of the Koran in the Middle East were deftly documented by Barbara Freyer Stowasser. Many contemporary Muslim women in the Middle East and the United States now reject previous exclusive male commentaries and submit their own interpretations as equally valid. This position is demonstrated in the work of Amina Wadud, who powerfully argued, from within her faith, for the right of all Muslim women to engage the Koran directly and overwrite centuries of patriarchal domination. New readings by Muslim women implicitly recognize questions of gender in their desire to find revealed sources of more positive self-definition and religious participation. These directions have not met with a warm reception in the Middle East, where they remain a minority position.

## Gender and the Law

The study of Islamic law has always possessed a revered status in the Middle East. The law retained an exclusively masculine mystique because its educational and juristic institutions traditionally denied women access. Male legal interpretations of gender difference confined women to separate spheres because they were defined as intellectually deficient and dangerous to all men. Studies of gender as a factor in actual courtroom cases refuted the notion of female passivity when faced with male lawyers and judges. Judith Tucker's investigation of the preserved transcripts of women plaintiffs contradicted the assumption of a complete absence of female agency. She established the complicated relationship between gender and Islamic law in Ottoman Syria and Palestine. Women advanced their interests through their knowledge about the differences between Sunni law schools in family and inheritance law.

Women remain the objects of Islamic male legal decisions, which no longer offer recourse for question or dissent in much of the Middle East. Khaled Abou El Fadl documented the emergence of authoritarian control over women in this area. He asserted that those men who claim to speak for God in their decrees abuse the moral and religious bases of Islamic law. His book, *Speaking in God's Name: Islamic Law, Authority, and Women* (2001), focused, in part, on the example of the Saudi Arabian–based institute for legal opinions. These rulings continue to be spread not just in the Middle East, but worldwide through well-funded publications and Web sites. The highest level of Shii clerics in Iran also staunchly defend their singular capacity to interpret Islamic law for all adherents of the faith. They consistently embrace the ideal of a gender hierarchy in which women remain eternally subordinate. Gender differences based on male superiority are also articulated as divinely inspired.

## The Mainstream and the Margins

New centers founded by women in the Middle East incorporate gender in their research publications. In Egypt, scholars of the Women and Memory Forum publish a range of works dedicated to women and the recovery of their place in Islamic society. Every spectrum of ideological affiliation, from feminist to Islamist and positions in between, enriches the scholarship of this collective enterprise. Contributors to annual publications engage heated contemporary and historical problems from varied disciplinary perspectives. Familiarity with the concept of gender, whether applied or rejected, unites disparate ideological and scholarly affiliations.

In the early twenty-first century academic sites on the Internet link and inform scholars of gender and the Middle East around the world. H-Gender-MidEast, a source of announcements for specialists and nonspecialists, features information about conferences, research opportunities, and sources of both general and specialized information. Reviews of books in Western and Middle Eastern languages reach large, enthusiastic audiences. The web site, a collaborative effort based at the American University of Cairo and supported by the Humanities Network at Michigan State University, attempts to eradicate obvious geographical and cultural divisions. These collaborative initiatives equalize and embrace audiences from Western and Middle Eastern societies. H-Gender-MidEast promotes a forum for exchange and debate, which has helped refute the notion that the study of gender is an exclusively Western enterprise.

Senior female scholars now have the editorial power to incorporate gender within major, authoritative reference works on the Middle East. They select their authorities from the expertise of researchers found throughout the world. The definitive English-language *Encyclopaedia of the Qur'an* (2001), edited by Jane Dammen McAuliffe, includes a separate entry on gender's linguistic, legal, and thematic implications for the sacred text and its interpretation. Many other entries featured in this work are informed by gender, challenging the assumptions of older reference collections. The *Encyclopedia of Women and Islamic Cultures* (2003) locates both women's studies and gender studies at their point of Western inception, but underscores the importance of this methodology. This encyclopedia carefully maps the history of scholarly debate over conflicting responses to gender in an effort to avoid the appearance of Western bias and thus avoid the contentious identity politics of the 1990s. The goal of both these magisterial collections emphasizes inclusive rather than exclusive authorship and readership.

Female scholars of the Middle East founded the field of gender studies. They continue to predominate in this area of research. Their work has been acknowledged by male colleagues, who cite their pioneering studies but often appropriate the fruits of their research without mention of gender as a methodological category. This is true of scholars in the Middle East as well, who raise questions present in gender studies without acknowledging the discipline. Popular, accessible works of Middle Eastern studies now include obligatory chapters on women, but they frequently fail to differentiate between the materials they offer and the gendered interpretations that have led to their documentation. Students and the general public thus remain unaware that their understanding of male and female roles in Islamic societies is the product of a form of inquiry that often troubles and provokes male authorities in both Middle Eastern and Western societies. The reason for this marginalization of gender reveals that even scholarship mirrors contests over power and representation. Gender remains a charged category of analysis in process and practice everywhere.

*See also* **Feminism: Islamic Feminism; Islam; Women's Studies.**

**BIBLIOGRAPHY**

Abou El Fadl, Khaled. *Speaking in God's Name: Women, Authority, and Law.* Oxford: Oneworld Press, 2001.

Ahmed, Leila. *Women and Gender in Islam: Historical Roots of a Modern Debate.* New Haven, Conn.: Yale University Press, 1992.

Badran, Margot. "Gender." In *Encyclopaedia of the Qur'an,* edited by Jane Dammen McAuliffe. Vol. 2, 288–292. Leiden, Netherlands: Brill, 2001.

———. "Women Studies/Gender Studies." In *Encyclopedia of Women and Islamic Cultures,* edited by Suad Joseph. Vol. 1. Leiden, Netherlands: Brill, 2003.

Booth, Marilyn. *May Her Likes Be Multiplied: Biography and Gender Politics in Egypt.* Berkeley: University of California Press, 2001.

Fernea, Elizabeth Warnock, and Basima Qattan Bezirgan, eds. *Middle Eastern Muslim Women Speak.* Austin: University of Texas Press, 1977.

Friedl, Erika. *Women of Deh Koh: Lives in an Iranian Village.* Washington, D.C.: Smithsonian Institution Press, 1989.

Mernissi, Fatima. *The Veil and the Male Elite: A Feminist Interpretation of Women's Rights in Islam.* Translated by Mary Jo Lakeland. Cambridge, Mass.: Perseus Books, 1987.

Smith, Margaret. *Muslim Women Mystics: The Life and Work of Rābi'a and Other Women Mystics in Islam.* Reprint, New York: Oxford University Press, 2001.

Spellberg, D. A. *Politics, Gender, and the Islamic Past: The Legacy of 'A'isha bint Abi Bakr.* New York: Columbia University Press, 1994.

Stowasser, Barbara Freyer. *Women in the Qur'an, Traditions, and Interpretation.* New York: Oxford University Press, 1994.

Tucker, Judith. *In the House of the Law: Gender and Islamic Law in Ottoman Syria and Palestine.* Berkeley: University of California Press, 1998.

Wadud, Amina. *The Qur'an and Woman: Rereading the Sacred Text from a Women's Perspective.* Reprint, New York: Oxford University Press, 1999.

*D. A. Spellberg*

**GENDER IN ART.** *Gender,* other than a biological or physical determination of the sexes, is a cultural and social classification of masculinity and femininity. Gender presentations in art are the outcome of the cultural process of defining sexual and social identity. Pictorial art and literature, as means of expression through transformation and stylization, are the predominant media reflecting this cultural process.

While the term *gender* refers to both sexes, the concept of gender issues has been primarily driven by a movement of women's emancipation and the twentieth-century emergence of feminism, as women have sought to obtain the rights, privileges, and unique forms of expression that men have enjoyed historically in patriarchal societies where class, race, and sexuality were defined by the dominant gender. The emergence of feminist art and art history since the 1960s has not only resulted in a re-appreciation of the representation of the woman as a subject, creator, and receptor of pictorial art but also has inspired a broader examination of gender-related issues in art through the establishment of gay studies and men's studies, where questions of homosexuality, heterosexuality, masculinity, femininity, and indeed sex itself all pertain to the concept of *gender.* The understanding of gender in art is thus intrinsically linked to the method and perspective of contemporary gender research.

**From Antique through Classical Art**

Intellectual perceptions of masculinity and femininity have

**Terracotta relief of "The Queen of the Night," southern Iraq, c. 1800–1750 B.C.E.** In many male-dominated cultures, such as that of ancient Mesopotamia, strong female figures were often associated with seductiveness and the destructive sexual sway they held over men. BRITISH MUSEUM (NO. ANE 2003-7-18, 1), © JAMES DARLING/REUTERS/CORBIS

*Nativity and Adoration of the Shepherds* (gospel book; 1262) by T'oros Roslin. Tempera on parchment. During the Middle Ages depictions of the Virgin Mary symbolized contemporary notions of the feminine ideal—a mother devoted to the spiritual concepts of chastity, humility, piety, repentance, and salvation. THE WALTERS ART MUSEUM, BALTIMORE

been transformed into visual arts since antiquity. Female fertility and motherhood, as well as gender relationships, are prevalent themes in ancient depictions. One of the earliest pictorial examples of gender presentation is the faceless Paleolithic statuette *Venus of Willendorf* (c. 28,000–25,000 B.C.E.). This is a depiction of a female figure in a symbolic and conceptual context, representing feminine fertility. In a sculpture from Pakistan the figure of Hariti, the ancient Buddhist Indian goddess of childbirth and women healers, is presented surrounded by children. The exposed breast of Venus and Hariti's emphasized breast emerge as pictorial symbols of fertility and motherhood.

Gender representations in male-dominated cultures are often determined by notions of power and weakness, superiority and inferiority, benevolence and malevolence. This is exemplified in the figure of the Mesopotamian deity *Queen of the Night,* in an old Babylonian relief from around 1800 B.C.E. She might be as well the deity Ishtar, the Mesopotamian goddess of sexual love and war, or Ishtar's sister and rival, the goddess Ereshkigal, who ruled over the underworld. Other scholars believe the female figure represents the demoness Lilitu, known in Jewish tradition as Lilith. The nude female figure embodies a monolithic notion associated with women for ages and in diverse cultures, that of female sexual power and its asserted destructiveness.

Gender relations address both the intimate interactions and the social roles of men and women. An Egyptian relief of Tel el Amarna from around 1335 B.C.E. depicts the Egyptian royal couple Smenkhkare and his wife, Meritaten. His wife is depicted giving him flowers and expressing her affection yet at the same time illustrating her submissive marital position. While both figures have similar proportion and pictorial emphasis, the emperor's status is clearly designated.

In classical art, gender qualities associated with women are beauty, domesticity, and passivity and for males the contrary principles such as power, dominance, and social status. Antique art presentations of male nudity, such as in Greek sculpture, underline the physical perfection of the male body, representing superiority and civic authority. Yet domestic and everyday scenes depicting roles of men and women had less importance than symbolic representations of gender. In the antique world gender attributes served to emphasize and elevate the human and superhuman characteristics of gods, goddesses, and mythological figures. This becomes especially prominent in classical art. In ancient Greek depictions of Centauromachy (the mythological battle of the Centaurs with the Lapiths), notions of masculinity are transformed into battling figures that are half-man, half-animal. Goddesses such as Pallas Athena, Aphrodite, and Nike combine both male and female attributes to signify their dominance. Ro-

Sixteenth-century portrait *Simonetta Vespucci* by Piero di Cosimo (1462–1521). Italian Renaissance portraiture typically served to idealize the subject rather than serve as a realistic representation. The snake around the subject's neck symbolizes the dangers of temptation and lust. © BETTMANN/CORBIS

*Flora* (c. 1515–1520) by Tiziano Vecelli (Titian). Oil on canvas. Titian's painting of the goddess of spring, flowers, and fertility celebrated sexuality and asserted the beauty of the subject during a period when there was much criticism of works that celebrated female eroticism. © FRANCIS G. MAYER/CORBIS

man reliefs, sculptures, and coins, depicting emperors and empresses, often relate the figures to gods and goddesses, or they personify gender-specific virtues. Female figures in Roman art frequently represent virtues such as justice or piety or symbolize wisdom and victory.

## Middle Ages

During the Middle Ages, presentations of gender were sublimated mostly in depictions of biblical figures. Notably a single figure, that of the Virgin Mary, represented most of the attributes associated with the feminine in an idealized figure. Mary's role as Christ's mother in depictions such as T'oros Roslin's *Christ's Nativity and the Adoration of the Shepherds,* represents at the same time her physical burden as a spiritual concept of chastity, humility, piety, repentance, and salvation. The vast number of depictions of the Virgin Mary as well as her special spiritual importance has redefined other established female stereotypes in art since the Middle Ages. Furthermore, moralistic tendencies in the representations of gender relations can be found from the late Middle Ages onwards, as in the so-called *Weibermacht* (woman's power) depictions showing maltreatment of men at the hands of women. These depictions by male artists represent the polarity of viewing the female sex: idealization or misogynism.

## The Renaissance and the Baroque

Since the Renaissance, writers, intellectuals, and artists have been increasingly engaged with gender issues, particularly in discussing the social role of the feminine. The French phrase *querelle des femmes* (debate about women) referred to humanist discussions about womanhood and the female place in the contemporary culture of their day. Until then, following the Aristotelian approach, women were perceived as imperfect, created inferior to men. In his *De claris mulieribus* (Concerning famous women), Giovanni Boccaccio (1313–1375), the Italian Renaissance poet and writer, introduced women as powerful role models. Nevertheless, the virtues that Boccaccio saw women capable of achieving were established "male qualities" of the time.

One of the first to give voice to the autonomous virtues of women was the French poetess and historiographer Christine de Pisan (c. 1363–c. 1430). In her *Livre de la cité des dames* (c. 1404; Book of the city of the ladies) Pisan developed a comprehensive categorization of women's positions and functions as found in the society of her time. Others, like the Dutch writer Erasmus Desiderius of Rotterdam (1466?–1536), the Spanish humanist and philosopher Juan Luis Vives (1492–1540), and the German writer and philosopher Heinrich Cornelius Agrippa von Nettesheim (1486–1535), had laid the foundation for humanism's more progressed vision of women's role in society and culture.

Renaissance portraits of women intend to convey beauty—almost archetypical—and social role. The male was defined by attributes of profession and social statues. Female portraiture in Italian Renaissance art was not meant to be a direct representation of the individual. An example in premodern Italian portraiture is the bust of a nude woman by Piero di Cosimo (1462–1521). The moralistic implication is represented by a snake around the woman's neck to remind of the dangers of temptation and lust, traditionally know as the vice of *luxuria.*

Eroticism—the sublimation and stylization of sexual desire—depends on culture and social milieu. In art this relation is reflected in the sublimation of sexuality. Traditionally the key elements associating gender themes to visual issues have been female sexuality and nudity. Nudity and sexuality are the predominant aspects of gender themes in Renaissance and Baroque visual art. Sandro Botticelli's (1445–1510) painting *The Birth of Venus* from around the year 1485 has refined symbolism with the nude goddess of love being placed within the spiritual context of Renaissance philosophy. Erotic female presentations are central in the paintings by Titian (Tiziano Vecellio; 1488 or 1490–1576), as in his erotically charged painting of Flora, the goddess of spring, flowers, and fertility. The era also saw the emergence of female patronage in arts.

During the Renaissance and the Baroque Italian, female artists such as Lavinia Fontana (1552–1614) and Sofonisba Anguissola (1527–1625), offering a distinctive view of female artistic perspective at the time, promoted a more assertive image of the woman. This is most apparent when the woman becomes a violent figure as in Artemisia Gentileschi's painting *Judith Slaying Holofernes.* Gentileschi's heroines, struggling with the other sex and evoking strong empathy in the viewer, have become a focal point in gender studies of art history.

The Flemish Baroque artists Peter Paul Rubens (1577–1640) and Anthony van Dyck (1599–1641) depicted women with symbolic and allegorical references, emphasizing the sitters' high social status, as was popular in traditional Italian Renaissance portraiture during the fourteenth and fifteenth centuries (for example, van Dyck's *Venetia Stanley, Lady Digby, as Prudence,* 1633). Seventeenth-century Dutch portraits of women, however, express a new trend toward gender identity: men and women figures are not presented anymore as an ideal or a symbol but mostly in their realistic surroundings in a neutral manner (for example, Johannes Cornelisz Verspronck's *The Regentesses of the St. Elizabeth Hospital,* 1641). Rembrandt van Rijn's (1606–1669) depictions of his intimate partners Saskia van Uylenburgh and Hendrickje Stoffels suggest an authenticity that transcended traditional social gender conventions (see his *Saskia as Flora,* 1641). In popular seventeenth-century Dutch history paintings and genre scenes, sexuality is concealed in moralistic criticism. But in his presentation of the original sin (1638), Rembrandt transforms an archetypical presentation into a psychologically sensitive depiction of Adam and Eve as two insecure sinners.

### Eighteenth and Nineteenth Centuries

During the eighteenth and nineteenth centuries there was a gradual shift from an emphasis on gender to an emphasis on class. This change in visual art during the period of Louis XIV

*Adam and Eve,* **etching by Rembrandt van Rijn, 1638.** During the seventeenth century, Dutch renderings of the human figure became less idealized and more realistic, as can be seen in Rembrandt's depiction of an ordinary-looking Adam and Eve. REMBRANDT HARMENSZOON VAN RIJN, DUTCH, 1606–1669, *ADAM AND EVE,* 1638, ETCHING, 16.2 X 11.6 CM (IMAGE). GIFT OF THE MARJORIE BLUM KOLVER COLLECTION, HARRY MARIBEL BLUM FOUNDATION, 1987.247. REPRODUCTION, THE ART INSTITUTE OF CHICAGO

The growing appreciation of the necessity to redefine female social roles coexisted with such phenomena as male dominance, misogyny, and the witch hunt. In Renaissance and Baroque visual arts, mostly made by men, female figures appear less often than depictions of men, irrespective of whether they are the central figures or not. In addition to their outnumbering presentations, males are mostly depicted in dominant and central positions.

Since the Middle Ages demonology had been chiefly associated with femininity. The identification of women as more prone to witchcraft than men was based on traditional misogynist beliefs of what was perceived as basic female nature. Trials of witchcraft promoted discussions of gender issues and influenced the visual arts. In Renaissance graphic art, especially in northern Europe, female sorcery was a popular theme, as can be seen in engravings and woodcuts by Albrecht Dürer (1471–1528) and Hans Baldung Grien (1484–1545). In these works naked or partly nude, unsightly sorceresses are depicted in a variety of allegedly supernatural acts.

*A Roman Slave Market* (1867) by Jean-Léon Gérôme. Oil on canvas. Issues of male dominance, feminine submissiveness, and societal repression of women were frequently addressed in the works of nineteenth-century artists. THE WALTERS ART MUSEUM, BALTIMORE

(1638–1715) coincided with the emergence of a middle class in France. Increasing public appreciation was afforded women artists such as Rosalba Carriera (1675–1757), who was elected as a member of the male-dominated Académie Royale in 1720. Other significant female artists were Élisabeth Vigée-Lebrun (1755–1842), who was commissioned to portray Queen Marie Antoinette and later on became a member of the French academy, as well as Angelica Kauffmann (1741–1807), one of the founding members of the British Royal Academy.

Sexism and patriarchism were prevalent in the nineteenth century. In his painting *The Slave Market* the French artist Jean-Léon Gérôme (1824–1904) presents masculine dominance and male voyeurism in relation to female abuse. In Victorian English art, traditional binary gender distinctions prevailed (for example G.E. Hicks's *The Sinews of Old England,* 1757). Moralistic concepts of pure and modest womanhood, glorification of domestic life, and Christian ethics influenced gender visual imagery. In her painting *War* from

1883, Anna Lea Merritt highlights the Victorian ideal of female seclusion and spatial division of genders.

Such established gender types as the mother, the female as a lover or courtesan, and the femme fatale were often represented in Art Nouveau works by male artists such as the British illustrator Aubrey Beardsley (1872–1898) and the Austrian painter Gustav Klimt (1862–1918). Erotic gender identities and reprentation of traditional male roles, as in Klimt's painting *The Kiss,* show a gradual transition. Reciprocal roles and interchangeable gender identities manifest themselves in the art of Art Nouveau.

## Twentieth Century

The appearance of new fashion designs for women in the beginning of the twentieth century with its acknowledged elements designating traditional masculine features signaled a change in gender identity and the emergence of a cross-gender figure. This pertains to both new presentations on gender roles in society and culture. In the work of the Mexican artist Frida Kahlo (1907–1954), her masculine appearance in *Self-Portrait with Cropped Hair* testifies to a growing effort to legitimatize broader gender boundaries while being a statement of an assertive femininity. The work of the German female artist Käthe Kollwitz (1867–1945) explores the humanity of both male and female sexes and testifies to a growing social gender equality, combining both to create a powerful political statement.

Gender perceptions in the 1960s and 1970s were defined by the emergence of the feminist movement. Art of both genders became instruments of political and social change. In visual arts the pop art movement took issue with popular gender ideologies and icons such as beauty and eroticism by overamplifying them, as in multiple lithographed duplications of Marilyn Monroe's image by Andy Warhol. The American feminist artist Judy Chicago (b. 1939), in a 1979 installation titled *The Dinner Party,* questioned women's achievements and their social roles.

In visual art since the 1970s, physical appearance and gender distinctions blur. The photographers Cindy Sherman (b. 1954) and Nan Goldin (b. 1953) challenged and transformed stereotyped gender roles while exploring female identity, love, violence, and transgender identities. The feminist American artist Barbara Kruger (b. 1945) portrayed the female body as a battleground for gender dominance. The conceptual female artist Laurie Anderson (b. 1947) combined multimedia performance with music, poetry, and visual arts. Known for her unusual mix of music, art, and the spoken word, she ironically challenged gender stereotypes and male social dominance.

Another social development, the emergence of an open and confident gay and lesbian community, has redefined gender portrayals. Robert Mapplethorpe combined over-masculinized bodies and images of homosexuality with the stylized aestheticism of glamour photography. Lesbian visual art as it has emerged since the 1960s is multifaceted yet does not represent a cohesive stylistic movement. The artists reflect the experience of being a lesbian in patriarchal society. Lesbian artists such as Harmony Hammond (b. 1944) have been defining a homosexual iconography and terminology, individual and

sometimes reflecting stereotypes. This "queer" art has explored and broken down the conventions of traditional gender and sexual roles, as in John Kirby's *Self-Portrait* (1987), in which the artist presents himself in feminine underwear without concealing his masculine body.

## Gender and Art History

Feminist art history is closely related with the feminist movement. One of the earliest themes of feminist art historians was that of the male gaze and its consequence on visual art. The early feminist art historians documented works of women's art and the perception of the woman in male art and defined the history and methodologies of feminist art. In 1972 the scholarly study *Woman as Sex Object: Studies in Erotic Art, 1730–1970* was published by Thomas B. Hess and Linda Nochlin, the American art historian, introducing a feminist perspective to the field of art history and criticism. In the beginning of the 1980s, in *Old Mistresses: Women, Art and Ideology,* the British scholars Rozsika Parker and Griselda Pollock surveyed the place of women within the history of art. Subsequent feminist scholars such as Norma Broude and Mary D. Garrard have stated that feminist art history should not be confined to analysis of women artists alone and should not exclusively be the domain of female researchers. In the early 2000s, the focuses of gender studies in art history are gender identity, gender indistinctness, and cross-gender definitions as well as self-consciousness and perspectives on women looking at the other sex.

*See also* ***Aesthetics: Europe and the Americas; Gay Studies; Gender Studies: Anthropology; Humanity in the Arts; Men and Masculinity; Nude, The; Queer Theory; Sexuality: Overview; Women and Femininity in U.S. Popular Culture; Women's Studies.***

**BIBLIOGRAPHY**

Aldrich, Robert, and Garry Wotherspoon, eds. *Who's Who in Gay and Lesbian History.* London and New York: Routledge, 2002.

Broude, Norma, and Mary D. Garrard. *Feminism and Art History: Questioning the Litany.* New York: Harper and Row, 1982.

———, eds. *The Expanding Discourse: Feminism and Art History.* New York: Icon HarperCollins, 1992.

Butters, Ronald R., John M. Clum, and Michael Moon, eds. *Displacing Homophobia: Gay Male Perspectives in Literature and Culture.* Durham, N.C.: Duke University Press, 1989.

Chadwick, Whitney. *Women, Art, and Society.* London: Thames and Hudson, 1990.

Dotson, Edisol W. *Behold the Man: The Hype and Selling of Male Beauty in Media and Culture.* New York: Haworth Press, 1999.

Edwards, Tim. *Erotics and Politics: Gay Male Sexuality, Masculinity, and Feminism.* London and New York: Routledge, 1994.

Garrard, Mary D. *Artemisia Gentileschi: The Image of the Female Hero in Italian Baroque Art.* Princeton, N.J.: Princeton University Press, 1989.

Hammond, Harmony. *Lesbian Art in America: A Contemporary History.* New York: Rizzoli, 2000.

Hess, Thomas B., and Linda Nochlin. *Woman as Sex Object: Studies in Erotic Art, 1730–1970.* New York: Newsweek, 1972.

Jacobs, Fredrika H. *Defining the Renaissance Virtuosa: Women Artists and the Language of Art History and Criticism.* Cambridge, U.K., and New York: Cambridge University Press, 1997.

Maclean, Ian. *The Renaissance Notion of Woman: A Study in the Fortunes of Scholasticism and Medical Science in European Intellectual Life.* Cambridge, U.K.: Cambridge University Press, 1980.

Minton, Henry L. *Gay and Lesbian Studies.* New York: Haworth Press, 1992.

Parker, Rozsika, and Griselda Pollock. *Old Mistresses: Women, Art, and Ideology.* London: Routledge and Kegan Paul, 1981.

Perry, Gill, ed. *Gender and Art.* New Haven, Conn., and London: Yale University Press, 1999.

Russell, H. Diane, and Bernadine Barnes. *Eva/Ave: Woman in Renaissance and Baroque Prints.* Washington, D.C.: National Gallery of Art/Feminist Press at the City University of New York, 1990.

Tinagli, Paolo. *Women in Italian Renaissance Art: Gender, Representation, and Identity.* Manchester, U.K.: Manchester University Press, 1997.

*Anat Gilboa*

**GENDER STUDIES: ANTHROPOLOGY.** Gender studies in anthropology has a relatively short history, dating to the latter half of the twentieth century, but its prehistory can be discerned in the discipline's early concern with kinship and social reproduction. At the turn of the twentieth century, anthropologists focused their attentions mainly on small-scale societies in which kinship appeared to provide the organizing structure for production. What kinship studies revealed is that production and reproduction (both social and material) are mutually implicated processes, and that the relationship between these processes is sustained by principles of difference.

The evidence suggests that among the most powerful symbolic vehicles for both structuring and legitimating such differentiation around the world has been the representation of persons in gendered terms. Accordingly it has been the long and arduous project of gender studies to examine and explicate the ways in which gender difference is produced and subsequently naturalized, rendered in terms of iconic ideals, and incorporated in the bodily unconscious of human subjects. This not only has entailed considerations of the mechanisms for materializing sexual and gendered difference in ritual and other cultural practices, it has also required analyses of the political and economic structures of production within which they operate, the historical transformations to which they have been subject, and the relationships between gender and other discourses of difference at all levels, from household to state. More recently it has entailed recognition of the violences and excesses generated in and by systems of gendered difference, the possibilities for resistance that they facilitate, and the myriad forms in which desire, disavowal, attraction and revulsion, procreative energies and amity can appear across time and space.

**Kinship and/or Gender?**

In 1987 Jane Fishburne Collier and Sylvia Junko Yanagisako described their goal as putting gender "at the theoretical core of anthropology" by "calling into question the boundary between [the] two fields" of gender and kinship (p. 1). That kinship studies should have appeared as an autonomous field, distinct and

perhaps even resistant to the analysis of gender, was attributed largely to the particular conception of society espoused by the structural functionalists, led by A. R. Radcliffe-Brown. Like many feminist anthropologists, Collier and Yanagisako questioned the degree to which discussions of women's lives were relegated to considerations of the domestic sphere and to reproductive function. They repudiated assumptions (explicit or implicit) that the maternal-child relation is invariant across time and space, and they cast suspicion on the tendency to see historical change as a factor relevant only to political and economic systems in the public domain, while familial life was presumed to be constant and unchanging. Finally, they discerned in structural-functionalist writings an erroneous presumption that all societies have institutional functions that are comparable, even when the forms of their institutions differ.

Many of the questions articulated by Collier and Yanagisako generated productive new approaches to ethnography. In a companion essay in the same volume, they went on to pose another question which resurrected and refined one of Margaret Mead's (1901–1978) earlier challenges—namely, "What social and cultural processes cause men and women to *appear* different from each other?" (p. 15). In *Male and Female* (1949), Mead had observed that anatomical differences provide only the first point of identification for boys and girls, and noted that, from that moment on, children would compare themselves to others and in this fashion acquire a socially mediated sense of sexual selfhood based on traits and characteristics privileged or denigrated by their elders. Her own conception of sexual difference was indebted to Sigmund Freud's (1856–1939) analysis of sexuality in *Three Essays on the Theory of Sexuality* (1905) and retained his binary conception of sexual difference as based on biological antinomy. However, Mead disagreed with Freud's students and with his own postulation of a universally phallic stage in female development.

Against the backdrop of the Cold War and a burgeoning arms race, Mead's contribution to the ongoing tradition of gender studies is rooted in the denaturalizing comparativism that she embraced as the ground of critical anthropology: "If we recognize that we need every human gift and cannot afford to neglect any gift because of artificial barriers of sex or race or class or national origin, then one of the things we must know is where the assumed differences between the sexes are mere elaborations of unimportant differences that can be dealt with easily in this invention-conscious world" (p. 15). To this end Mead emphasized the extraordinary diversity of conceptions of ideal maleness and femaleness across cultures, and on this basis hypothesized the possibility that children might even disavow some of their "biological inheritance" in order to achieve a social ideal of masculinity or femininity (pp. 136–138). She thereby introduced a conception of maleness and femaleness as a social construction irreducible to the physiological basis in which it grounds itself. Nonetheless, the question of gender remained secondary to that of kinship, where it constituted an assumption rather than object of inquiry for several more decades.

Kinship theory in anthropology can be traced to Lewis Henry Morgan's treatise, *Systems of Consanguinity and Affinity of the Human Family* (1870), a work that would considerably influence Friedrich Engels, as well as both structuralist and Marxist anthropologists. Morgan argued that the family as an institution emerged only after a period of promiscuity and then incestuous cohabitation, and that it depended on the creation of a law of exogamy. Nearly a century later, Claude Lévi-Strauss (b. 1908) revived and revised Morgan's argument when he claimed that the incest taboo constituted the archetypal form of all law, and that it marked the threshold between nature and culture. Although he asserted that sexuality was the origin of sociality, insofar as sexual desire is an instinct that requires another person, it was the incest taboo that transformed consanguinity into alliance by rendering women as "the supreme gift" in his analysis.

### Rituals of Becoming: The Making of Sexual Difference

One of the primary assumptions of contemporary gender theory is the social construction of gender, but although this core idea is closely linked to the recognition that kinship and even parentage is not a biological matter but a social one and that descent is a mode of recognizing children rather than transmitting genetic material, the connection between the theorization of gender and kinship was not immediately obvious to anthropologists of the early twentieth century. Even Bronislaw Malinowski, who claimed that sex must be understood as but one moment in a vast system comprising love, eroticism, mythology, courtship, kinship, family life, economic and religious practices, and tribal structure, devoted little time to a consideration of how boys and girls come to assume the qualities that make them socially recognizable as such. For him, sexual and social maturation were inimitably linked, but his attention was narrowly focused on the transformation of willful desire between two persons—expressed most purely and freely by adolescents—into a relation capable of self-negation in parenting. Malinowski's most profound insight may have come in his argument that kinship is not so much a matter of sexual intercourse as it is a sublation of dyadic relations into triadic ones, of interpersonal intimacies into intergenerational dependencies. Yet, because his concern lay with the functional appropriation of individual facts for social ends and because his concept of function was so immediate, Malinowski never seems to have considered the difficulty of achieving what Margaret Mead would later term ideal maleness or femaleness.

For the majority of early writers on kinship, gender was the axiomatically binary ground on which kinship and marital exchange could be erected. In Western theoretical traditions, this axiomatic quality of binary gender differences naturalizes itself in biological metaphors to such an extent that gender difference collapses into sexual difference and appears as anatomically and/or genetically determined. Two main sources of critique inform the development of the social constructivist analysis of gender per se. The first is the vast literature on ritual and corporeal practice, from the archive of which anthropologists have assembled their cases for the relativity of somaticization and sexualization. The second is to be found in the reconsideration of earlier theoretical arguments about such practice, especially as developed in the 1970s and 1980s under

the influence and in the context of new social movements, especially feminism. This discussion begins with the consequences and potentialities of ritual theory for gender analysis.

In 1909 Arnold van Gennep undertook to formalize a theory of the rites associated with transitional stages of life and offered a tripartite model consisting of separation, liminality, and re-aggregation to explain their operations. Later elaborated by Victor Turner (1969) in a manner that highlighted the ambiguity and potential subversiveness of the interstitial phase, the notion of the ritual production of social status entailed a recognition that the bodily identity of a person is an inadequate determinant of her or his social identity. Indeed, Van Gennep made the brilliant observation that initiation rites work by overcoming the enormous chasm between biological puberty and what he termed "social puberty." Even more radically, he suggested that these rites do not so much mark puberty as they produce sexuality, removing people from an asexual state and birthing them as either male or female sexual subjects, who can then enter into legitimate sexual and especially reproductive relations with other adults. Van Gennep's radicalism has been mainly forgotten, but feminist anthropology has reclaimed his constructivist insight following a rapprochement with linguistic theory and dialectical materialism, the invention of "gender" as a category, and the emergence of a political project that has made the pursuit of resistance and other forms of counterhegemonic practice the goal of much comparativist work.

### Feminist Interventions: The Legacy of the Seventies

The first intervention of feminist anthropologists into the field of kinship studies and, thence, into anthropology more generally, consisted in the creation of a discursive object that would permit the simultaneous critique of existing theories and the reassessment of its empirical claims. That category was "gender," understood as "the constitutive element of social relationships based on perceived differences between the sexes" and as "a primary way of signifying relationships of power" (Scott, p. 42). Indeed "power and difference" became the crucial axes of gender analysis from the 1980s onward.

Feminists began by accusing early social theorists, but perhaps especially Claude Lévi-Strauss, of mistaking an ideological justification for the oppression of women with an ontology of the social. Because women are treated as commodities does not imply that their functioning as commodities is logically intrinsic to social life everywhere. Because women are frequently relegated to private or domestic domains does not mean that the social world is logically bifurcated along the axis of public and private or that these domains would have to be gendered when they were. And because sexual difference is the primary structure for differentiation of labor and structuring power in small-scale societies that lack a public sphere does not mean that, logically, gender must be a salient structural principle only in domestic spheres when these are encompassed by larger public ones. From these logical arguments emerged a series of questions regarding the universality and extremity of male dominance, the organization of domestic and public or political life, the relationship between political complexity and the status of women, the range of property systems through which women do or do not gain access to economic resources, and the more subterranean forms of power, value, renown, and influence that women exercise even in those contexts where formal authority is vested in male subjects. In essence, these questions and the energetic research that they spurred were driven by the pursuit of a counterexample. Evidence of equality or a different organizational imperative in one society would undermine claims for the universal virtue, necessity, or naturalness of particular inequalities everywhere else. Or so a generation of feminist scholars hoped. Their project was empiricist and comparativist, collaborative and emphatically political. Its result can be seen in the series of volumes they generated, including those edited by Michelle Rosaldo and Louise Lamphere (1974), Rayna Reiter (1975), Carol MacCormack and Marilyn Strathern (1980), Mona Etienne and Eleanor Leacock (1980), and Sherry Ortner and Harriett Whitehead (1981).

The contributors to these volumes arrived at various and oftentimes contradictory conclusions. Some of the writers included in Rosaldo and Lamphere's collection, notably Rosaldo, Nancy Chodorow, and Ortner, concluded that male dominance *is* universal, with Rosaldo attributing it to the division of labor and the distribution of authority across a violently enforced private/public divide, Chodorow locating women's exclusion from the public in their maternal function and the socialization of girls, and Ortner revising Lévi-Strauss's argument to claim that women are universally perceived as relatively close to nature and therefore thought to be in need of more vigorous regulatory oversight. Other writers, however, especially those influenced by Marxist thought and Friedrich Engels's *The Origin of the Family, Private Property, and the State*, differed. Karen Sacks and, later, Eleanor Leacock (1981) argued that not all societies are dominated by men and that egalitarianism prevails in those where private property, and the particular construction of women as private property, has not yet developed. In this case male dominance is a function of history and a relatively recent emergence. Still others, such as Peggy Sanday, asserted that male dominance is vitiated over time as technology and the transformation of production attenuates the advantages conferred by physical strength.

Such arguments stood or failed according to the persuasiveness with which the ethnographic evidence was adduced, and many of the writers later recanted or were persuaded by competing positions. One of the most lucid and sustained theoretical critiques to emerge from Rosaldo and Lamphere's 1974 volume was penned by Gayle Rubin under the title "The Traffic in Women: Notes Toward a 'Political Economy' of Sex." Rubin's essay commenced with a new category, that of the "sex/gender system." It was intended to overcome the prevalent dichotomy between sexual and economic systems and to prevent sexual relations from being reduced to reproductive function. As a formally empty category, the idea of a sex/gender system demanded ethnographic specification of the same sort that would distinguish between socialist or capitalist production. Rubin took Lévi-Strauss to task precisely for his lack of such differentiation, especially on the question of the traffic in women. Failing to differentiate between historically actual cases of women who are "given in marriage, taken in battle, exchanged for favors, sent as tribute, traded, bought

and sold" rendered the notion vacuous for Rubin, and she observed that men are also trafficked—for different purposes (p. 175). Michael Peletz would corroborate this assertion in 1996 with descriptions of the traffic in men by women in nineteenth-century Malay communities. It is, however, in her deconstruction of the concept of gender, as assumed in Lévi-Strauss's *The Elementary Structures of Kinship*, that Rubin made her most incisive intervention. Observing that the incest taboo as described by Lévi-Strauss is not merely a prohibition on incest but also on homosexuality and on sameness, one that orchestrates desire in terms of sexual difference, Rubin offered as counterexamples those instances in which same-sex relations are considered necessary for the production of adult gender (as in some parts of New Guinea) and those in which same-sex marriage is permitted (as among the Azande or the Dahomey), or where institutionalized transvestism is practiced (such as Native North America or India). Given these facts, she asserted, the taboo is not universal but merely the representation of a particular, if commonplace, ideology—for which, she admits, both Freud and Lévi-Strauss offer refined descriptions and unapologetic but illegitimate justifications.

## Materialism and Dialectical Analysis

Rubin began her essay by asserting that "there is no theory which accounts for the oppression of women . . . with anything like the explanatory power of the Marxist theory of class oppression" (p. 160). She concluded by calling for a new version of Engels's *The Origin of the Family*. Efforts to integrate gender analysis with class analysis and with more generally materialist concerns have taken a number of forms since Rubin's article was published. In general these have concerned the relationship between unremunerated housework and the reproduction of labor, the impact of colonialism and capitalist penetration on gender relations in local cultures, the new international division of labor, and the feminization of geopolitical regions.

Historically concerned with small-scale societies and undergirded by the assumption that the most elementary form of any social phenomenon reveals an essence that carries across other manifestations, Marxist anthropologists imagined the division of labor between men and women to be identical to the division between productive and reproductive functions. However, during the 1980s and beyond, questions of production and reproduction and of the status of women were increasingly reframed in terms of the colonial encompassment of indigenous economies and the new international distribution of labor. This led to studies of new logics of power, such as those by which class has displaced status as a rubric of social stratification in some places. It also generated analyses of new competitive relations between men and women as economic power became unified in a single (generalized) commodity form where previously it had been divided among regimes of value. In these contexts gender became the contested mechanism for regulating access to economic resources. A vast literature also developed in response to the emergence of transnational labor networks and the establishment of new manufacturing zones in the digitizing global economy of multinational finance. By attending to the gendered organization of value, and not merely the symbolic value (or lack thereof) accorded women (Weiner), it has become possible to speak of a "feminization of the global economy."

Materialist analyses of these latter processes, which take place in a transnational realm that exists both above and below the level of the nation-state, have perhaps inevitably privileged economic questions, but they have often stopped short of economic determinism. Dialectical analysis has been summoned here as a means of recognizing the degree to which indigenous forms of familial and social organization remain resilient or resistant in the face of encompassment by multinational capital, global finance, and other transnational forces. But a dialectical approach to the transformation of gender (or the sex/gender system) must actually redouble itself. For it not only entails the recognition that local life-worlds are transformed without being destroyed in the modern moment (hence it must examine the dialectics between the local, the global, and the emergence of transnationally comparable values like locality), it also requires a reading practice that seeks to comprehend, from two distinct locations or perspectives, the facts of these historical processes. Reading for resistance became a primary objective of much work in the field of gender studies during the last two decades of the twentieth century. Promising in many regards, it has nonetheless been weakened by a tendency to conflate the fact of social and structural specificity with an intentionalized and often strategic, or at least tactical, opposition to the forces of both foreignness and new inequity.

Resistance was the term by which gender studies sought to rescue itself from the absolutist pessimism of structuralist universalism as well as economic and cultural determinism. Under the influence of Clifford Geertz, American anthropological analysis of culture had tended to represent culture as a system of shared signs or symbols. Conceived as a theoretical refutation of the economic determinism that cruder forms of Marxism espoused, culturalism nonetheless reproduced its problematic negation of agency while also eviscerating any recognition of structural contradiction. Resistance conceived within the culturalist tradition thus came to be imagined as a possibility originating in the critical reading and interpretation of those signs and symbols that comprised cultural totalities. Ironically, the language of resistance permitted two distinct theoretical traditions to converge, those of the Italian Marxist Antonio Gramsci (1891–1937) and the French libertine philosopher Michel Foucault (1926–1984). It was a thematically and methodologically driven reading of Foucault's later writings on sexuality that informed the genealogical turn in gender studies and in anthropology more generally.

## Foucault and the Genealogy of Sexuality

Although Foucault's early writings attempted to excavate the sedimented structures of thought in a particular moment (and the discontinuous relations between moments), it was his development of a retrospective historiographical mode that made his writings on sexuality appear exemplary for historicist anthropologies concerned with the emergence of particular sex/gender systems. The first volume of *The History of Sexuality*, in particular, was quickly hailed for its demonstration of what the genealogical method could offer gender studies—although

many theorists mistook a mere reversal of chronology for Foucault's more radical demand that ontological thought be surrendered in favor of a negative concept of becoming.

Two main contributions were recognized. Firstly, Foucault argued that prohibition does not work to contain or repress that which it outlaws but rather cultivates its sanctioned objects in a new mode. The sexual repression of the Victorians, for example, did not so much eliminate an interest in sex as it permitted the extension of erotic pleasures into the domain of language, such that talking about sex—even in the form of denunciation—could be seen as one more incitement of sex, while making speech itself a scene of excitement. The second contribution lay in its analysis of the relationship between sexuality and political power in Western cultures.

At the end of *History of Sexuality*, Foucault described the emergence of a new political technology, one marked by power's investment in life, in the control and management of human beings as productive entities whose health and well-being it assiduously cultivated. Discourses on sexuality, and on so-called healthy sexuality, were coterminous for him with the displacement of centralized power by diffuse forms of discipline and control that saturated all dimensions of the life-world. Foucault described this new technology as one that entailed a "power over life" rather than a "right of death" and designated it as "biopower." From Europe's eighteenth century onward, biopower worked through the surveillance of sexual practice and by placing same-sex intimacies under increasingly violent prohibitions, as the demand for total productivity and intentionalized reproductivity intensified in the modern industrial era. In other contexts, he admitted, the organization of power over life might take other forms, and might structure subjectivity in terms other than those of sexuality, but his primary focus was the more familiar history of European modernity.

In Europe and elsewhere, Foucault's claim that homosexuality was a modern invention, the product of discourses upon normalcy and sexual health, scandalized many scholars and was initially misunderstood by many to imply the relatively recent appearance of same-sex intimacy. Foucault made no such claim; he was instead identifying a moment in which practice and identity were merged by virtue of new representational logics. This merging produced not same-sex intimacies but the figure, and henceforth, the felt experience, of the homosexual.

Although his exemplary case study came from the archives and entailed the story of an ambivalently sexed figure, Herculine Barbin, who was forced to assume a male identity by French medical and police authorities, feminists quickly observed that Foucault's analysis failed to distinguish between sexuality as it came to be configured for women and men. In other words, they argued that sexuality without consideration of gender could only reproduce the relative claim that the figure of maleness has on universality in Western philosophical discourse. Feminist writers were quick to observe, for example, that the prerogative of transvestism is often limited to members of one gender and suggested that the distribution of this prerogative might itself be indicative of power in the organization of local sex/gender systems. At the same time, however, many anthropologists, influenced by the burgeoning phenomenon of gay and lesbian studies, also saw in the tale of Barbin an exemplary ur-figure of modernity's sexualizing violence. A vast array of cross-cultural studies were devoted to excavating eras in other places where sex and gender was (or continues to be) organized according to less rigorously binary structures. And older reports of female husbands, institutionalized transvestism and androgyny, and legitimate same-sex intimacy were revisited with avidity.

The best of such work is assiduously historical, grounding itself in the meticulous scrutiny and translation of evidence from diverse archives and unofficial sources. However, much of the more ethnological comparativism has ignored Foucault's suggestion that biopower might be differently structured elsewhere and has sought analogues to European historical developments instead. As a result, it has borne a not inconsiderable resemblance to the oftentimes prurient studies of earlier sexology, especially when anthologized in collections devoted to the category of "third sex," "third gender," or comparative homosexualities. Historians, by contrast, have generated a series of supplementary histories that augment, clarify, or refute the suggestions made in Foucault's more programmatic moments, often bringing the same kind of analytic lens to the history of heterosexuality as he brought to homosexuality. And some anthropologists have attempted to understand the implications of Foucault's project for an analysis of institutional and discursive histories in the colonial context, paying particular attention to the organization of populations, institution of new educational systems, juridical rationalization, and forms of both public morality and sentiment that colonial regimes implemented.

Feminist critique of the masculinist bias in early Foucaultian analyses of sexuality has been followed by a bifurcation in the field and a proliferation of studies devoted to the analysis of masculinity and its relationship to systems of power, both within households and at the level of the state. These studies, whether overtly Foucaultian or not, consider the corporeal tactics and the ideological representations and values (such as machismo, honor, and valor) by which masculinity is cultivated in men, emphasizing the disjuncture between merely anatomical sex and social gender even when the two are conflated in local discourse (a 1998 study by Judith Halberstam extends this analysis in a consideration of what she terms "female masculinities"). The Foucaultian turn might thus be read as the process by which the feminist political slogan "the personal is the political" gets inverted, such that the political is understood as that which generates embodied persons. In any case, it generated a renewed theory of the importance of ritual in the constitution of sexual and gendered difference.

## Repeating Ritual: The Idea of Performativity
Feminism and gay studies, Foucault and the study of ritual, came together in the work of Judith Butler. In an eclectic theoretical blending of Foucault's discourse analysis, J. L. Austin's *How to Do Things with Words* (1962) linguistic pragmatics, and Hegelian dialectics tempered by Louis Althusser's notion

of interpolation, Butler demonstrated that the principle of reiteration (etymologically linked to rite and ritual) can be seen in the myriad gestures of daily life. Although her early work implied a degree of voluntarism not present in Austin's theory, Butler's later writings recognize that these gestures or "repeated acts" take place "within a highly rigid regulatory frame," and they produce, for Butler, gendered bodies not only as representations but as materialized and sensuously experienced entities. They do so in two senses. Repetition generates habitual forms that are recognized within the social world; and they subject persons to ideals but in a manner that leaves them relentlessly deficient. Transforming Althusser's notion of ideological hailing as that gesture by which power names and thereby summons a person in the terms that power confers, Butler suggests that all individuals are both hailed and made to bear the unconscious knowledge that they cannot, by definition, achieve the image that power gives to them as ideal. Compulsively enacting the forms that would demonstrate comformity to gender ideals, most train their bodies to become sexually legible. For some, however, a consciousness of the gap between ideal gender and materially actual difference can become the basis for resistance to the sex/gender system.

Butler's work reached anthropology in the wake of Pierre Bourdieu's "practice theory" (1977; see also Morris, 1995; Ortner, 1984) and was often read as the politically radical version of the French sociologist's reinvigorated structuralism. Bourdieu had analyzed what he termed the "doxa" of everyday life and suggested that architectural forms shape and constrain bodily gesture, inculcating dispositions that then cause people to act in ways that exteriorize the social structure. His description of this process in Kabyle villages suggested a necessary complementarity between men's and women's acts as the instruments for realizing a whole world otherwise divided between public and private domains. Bourdieu's notion of practice gave new life to Marcel Mauss's original assertion in 1968 that no bodily act, not even sex, is natural, and that the ideational or symbolic order of a given culture is something that exists in the body. This corporeal unconscious is never fully amenable to objectification in language and is actually dissipated in the moment that it becomes articulate. Unlike Bourdieu's vision of practice, which seemed incapable of explaining change, however, Butler provided a theory of how unconscious bodily sensitivities could become the basis of conscious opposition to the predominating sex/gender system.

Whether in response to Bourdieu or to Butler, the result was a proliferation of works broadly construed as anthropologies of the body. Many of these attempted to examine corporeal practices that appeared to be conspicuously implicated in the unequal distribution of power and the material constraint of women's sexual and sensual capacities. Many were also driven by the ambition to discover the different ways in which women interpreted these practices, so as to discover in them unexpected freedoms or self-experiences that differed from, and perhaps contradicted, the ideological representations of dominant discourse. Here the anthropology of the body met a globalizing feminist consciousness and a new politics of representation.

## Power, Representation, and Resistance: Lending Ears and Voices

Finding resistance in the interpretation of genital cutting—as, for example, freedom from desire, or in the experiences of factory workers possessed by spirits—as liberation from the monotonies of the assembly line may seem odd. Are these painful and debilitating experiences the ground of resistance? Or the symptoms of a system that makes women the handmaids of their own oppression? Can resistance be unconscious? And if so, is resistance a sign of agency?

In direct counterpoint to these readings of the subjectivity-less women in whose bodies the social world demonstrated its own violence and limitations there emerged in the 1980s another body of literature whose aims were to give expression to the conscious agencies of dominated women and other minorities, especially in the Global South.

Giving voice, or facilitating the self-expression of others—often through narrative forms that included biography and autobiography, fiction, poetry, and tokens of other expressive culture—became the commonplace gestures of well-intentioned anthropologists. These self-consciously feminist writers introduced a salutary counterbalance to those older texts in which the words of women, never mind their thoughts and experiences, were obliterated in generalizing and ostensibly gender-less statements about "the way things are." The felicitous result: the textured life-worlds of soap-opera-watching housewives in Egypt, of ambitious but marginalized poor women healers and middle-class merchants on the Indonesian periphery, of devout Pentecostals in South Africa and proudly political mothers in Argentina, all entered the canon of ethnography, irrevocably transforming it in a humanist direction.

Works in this oeuvre share a certain descriptive quality. They also share an ambition to translate, both literally and figuratively, the experiences of others. Ironically, perhaps, the instruments of that translation have been the concepts of gender—including men and women—and experience. For this new anthropology has made its claim on the basis of a presumptive capacity for readers to recognize, as the experience of women (or men), the representations provided by anthropologists.

In light of all the anthropological evidence that being female or male differs between cultural contexts, and after all the theoretical labor aimed at debunking the universalist presuppositions of structural functionalism and then structuralism, there remains in feminist anthropology an indissoluble commitment to the transcultural and transhistorical viability of woman as a category of infinite translatability. The same can be said of gender, which appears to be an empty category but which nonetheless works through the presumption that the social difference organized through reference to sexual difference is distinct from all other kinds of difference.

This presumption has been called into question by a number of minority writers from the Global South. They have insisted that there is no material referent for the abstract category of "woman," and that, to the contrary, those named as women are subjects whose lives are determined by complex webs of politico-economic and therefore discursive forces, whether

these be ones of race, class, location, or other principles. The implications of these claims for comparative gender studies have been enormous and deeply sobering, insofar as they suggest that there are not comparable communities of women whose experiences can be described and then compared. If some anthropologists ceded this point by advocating the self-representation of indigenous women (or by reading indigenous expressive forms as inherently self-representational), they did so in the face of an even more radical critique. The most acute proponent of that critique, Gayatri Chakravorty Spivak, argues that "subaltern women" cannot simply be ascribed or asked to inhabit the same kind of subjectivity that defines the position of white males in the European metropole. They cannot make themselves heard, except through a self-translation that rends them from their original location of invisibility and transforms them, through an ironically "enabling violence," into the kinds of beings whose speech is heard and recognized but only to the degree that it resembles that of its listeners.

Spivak's intervention made translation a question not only of technique but one determining the very possibility of gender studies. To be sure, translation had always been a question for comparative gender studies in anthropology, but it was defined much more narrowly. Originally it was recognized mainly in the comparative lexicons that anthropologists produced to demonstrate the relativity of kin terms (in places where men and women use different pronouns and kin terms). Since then it has been addressed through a variety of idioms, with silence and indirection often standing for women's incapacity to achieve or command a language of universal legibility. Conversely, silence and indirection have been read as indices of intentional resistance to dominant modes of communication (Gal). In a particularly innovative study of domestic intimacy in Sumatra, James T. Siegel demonstrated in 1969 how mistranslation, of the kind that lets women comprehend their treatment of men as patronizing indulgence (and hence indicative of their power) while also permitting men to read the same gestures as ones of deference (and hence testimony to their relative importance), actually facilitates gendered inequity and an odd kind of stability in Atchenese households. Siegel's writings offer an alternative theory of translation, one in which incommensurabilities in language and interpretation do not so much prohibit communication as they facilitate incompletely comprehended social relations, ones infused by power, which is dissimulated in the gaps between interlocutors. This does not make mistranslation a scene of resistance, any more than the translation of a subaltern woman's experiences into the representation of subalternity (for Western women readers) makes her an equal collaborator in global feminism. In very different ways, then, Siegel's and Spivak's insistence that power dissimulates itself in language and in claims to translational adequacy reveals the need for reflection upon the situation of speaking and reading. This problem is not mitigated by a recognition that globalization has brought about an increasing traffic in the terms and discourses emanating from the Anglo-American and European West.

Lexicalization and the transportation of idioms and concepts from one location to another—especially those concerning gender and sexuality, women's rights and human rights—do not guarantee that their meanings will be constant or comparable. Reflecting on the instability of the category "woman" across continents, languages, and power divides, and recognizing that anatomy does not obviate translational problems, contemporary writers have also reflected on the history and intensification of instabilities in the so-called biological being of women in the context of technological modernity.

### Redux: Sex, Kinship, and Agency in the Machine Age

Three main strands of thought have dominated the anthropological study of gender and technological modernity. The first of these, already discussed, concerns the organization of labor and the destructive or liberating effects of the commodity form and capitalism (industrial and financial) on the status of women, the organization of families, and the international division of labor. The second concerns the category of modernity itself and what it means for local life-worlds transformed by imperialism, colonialism, and multinational capital. Finally, analyses of gender and modernity have led to an interrogation of the consequences of new technological developments on reproductive possibilities, forms of kinship, the relationship between the pharmaceutical state and individual rights, bodily identity, and the transnational economy of suffering and its amelioration. It is the latter strand of thought—that which directly addresses the material conditions of mechanically dominated societies—that in the mid-1980s returned gender studies to its origins in kinship and the study of primitive society.

Donna Haraway's 1985 essay "A Manifesto for Cyborgs" threw down the gauntlet in this domain with its assertion that the corporeal and therefore sexualized body is not the discrete and encapsulated entity on which the fantasies of autonomous selfhood (and their attendant discourses of possessive individualism) are erected. Rather, they are discursively organized and technologically extended—opened and re-formed, as it were—by everything from drugs to plastic surgery, shoes to artificial joints. This recognition of the human body as a pliant material entity, the boundaries of which cannot be known in advance, resonated with anthropological accounts of ritual reform, such as those that marked gendered maturity or sexual transition through forms of scarification, genital cutting, and tattooing, among other practices.

These insights have been especially fruitful in the feminist study of Western scientific discourse, medical practice in the United States, and of medical representations more generally. Scholars have drawn attention to the violences and objectification that medicalization can entail. They have also revealed how the female form has been made to both figure and legitimate an invasive medical science whose invasiveness exceeds any possible utility.

Other writers have examined the ways in which economic logics enter and determine the conceptualization of bodies. Illustrative here is Emily Martin's (1994) argument that the contemporary concepts of bodily immunity and social epidemiology on which much AIDS research and prevention strategies have been based tends to valorize flexibility in a manner that mirrors contemporaneous economic logics. Bodies, in this sense,

reproduce what the economy produces, but at the level of representation. By contrast, Linda Singer (1993) argues that while an intimacy is to be discerned between economy and sexuality in the age of epidemic (mainly but not exclusively the age of AIDS), it lies in the logic of the panic. Such panic, when linked to sexuality, would permit the increased regulation of persons and populations, and it would do so in the very moment that sexuality would be valorized and, indeed, valued in the terms provided by late capitalism. Singer's early insistence that AIDS be conceived as a biopolitical economy and not merely as a disease was paradigmatic for other scholars who, in very different ways, attempted to map the geopolitics of life, illness, death, and healing, in examinations of the pharmaceutical state and the transnational traffic in gendered bodies, prostheses, and drugs.

In the 1990s there also emerged a less dystopic approach to the question of gender and technological modernity, one that manifests a distinctly American conception of private, rights-bearing subjects whose sense of personal agency and entitlement permits them to instrumentalize, if not fully control, the discourses and technologies afforded by contemporary science, especially medical science. Rayna Rapp's 1999 account of amniocentesis, and many of the essays in Faye Ginsburg and Rapp's 1995 collection on reproductive technologies, certainly evince the tendency of women's reproductive functions to be appropriated through new technologies, and they reveal the degree to which a vast medico-technological and pharmaceutical apparatus is brought to bear on women in the interest of securing their reproductive functions (often reducing women to such functions). At the same time, however, their accounts of women who are forced into difficult choices by knowledge about fetal health or viability is supplemented by the sense that these "choices" can also become the ground of new agencies.

A concern with choice is also evident in gay, lesbian, and queer studies, where the problem of kinship continues to provide an orienting point for theoretical explorations of identity formation and social status. In many cases, such as Kath Weston's 1991 study of gay and lesbian families, entitled *Families We Choose,* sexual alterity becomes the iconic representation of absolute agency and self-determining choice. Although some thinkers have repudiated this model and proposed a genetic basis for homosexuality, anthropological evidence contradicts such efforts, and suggests that the category of homosexuality is not fully translatable across cultures. Same-sex intimacy is variously accommodated in a range of sex/gender systems without ever cohering into a single identity structure. Here again translation emerges as a crucial issue for comparative sexuality studies.

Gay, lesbian, and queer transnational alliances that, like those of earlier humanist feminisms, have arisen in the interest of producing, recognizing, and securing rights for individuals engaged in same-sex intimacy around the world. Violent repudiations of "homosexuality" and the designation of it as a Western perversion have been associated with new assertions of cultural sovereignty throughout the world, although, as in parts of Western Europe and the Americas, such disavowals symptomatize modernity as much as they resist a globalization of sexual cultures. Just as Western labors to solicit gender solidarity were forced to confront the competing demands for sovereignty made by individuals and collectivities (in the name of sexual and individual rights or gender asymmetry and cultural rights), so gay, lesbian, and queer activism faces a comparably agonistic confrontation between the notions of collaboration across difference and solidarity based in identification. The terrain of this conflict is often the idea of family.

## Conclusions

It is important to recognize that kinship (and the family), as reconstrued by feminist gender studies since the 1970s, is not merely the particular locus of social production and reproduction. It is the symbol of sociality: an iconic form that stands for *something else,* just as the body can *stand for anything else,* as Margaret Mead recognized so many years ago. Similarly, it has been the project of gender studies to demonstrate how gender stands for and structures something else—namely, power and, therefore, difference.

In retrospect, then, it is necessary to understand gender studies not only as a discipline premised upon this fundamental axiom—that gender represents, and performatively constitutes, relations of power—but as a field whose own interests have been structured by other questions. Particularly in the United States but in the West more generally, gender studies has partaken of a general problematic, namely the opposition between choice and determination—a problematic central to the constitution of liberal democratic polities and their self-representation. Anthropologists, following Margaret Mead, referred to this opposition in terms of the "nature/nurture" binary, with "nature" being variously understood as comprised of anatomy, genetics, or mental structures. "Nurture" was the term applied to socially variable factors and has been widely equated with "environment." In culturalist discourse, this has lent an aura of voluntarism to social practice, which, because it is not natural, has appeared to be something to which individuals choose to accede. Notwithstanding structuralist efforts to demonstrate that the arbitrariness of social forms is precisely overcome by habit, convention, and history, a tendency to valorize individual choice has been omnipresent in gender studies and especially feminist anthropology. In this regard, studies of resistance can be seen as continuous with culturalism, albeit only insofar as they make social disadvantage or abjection a source of alienation from what history gives individuals as the natural form of society. The question of choice was, of course, differently conceived by Marxists, for whom history and the organization of production, rather than biology, constituted the primary sources of social determination.

Elizabeth Povinelli asserted in 2002 that sexuality is the discourse through which choice becomes the means of claiming Western subjecthood—compared to, for example, cultural descent, which makes a lack of choice, or submission to cultural law, the means of asserting subjecthood in many non-Western cultures, at least as they are represented to and for the West. This observation can be extended to include gender, sex, and sexuality. However, if conceptions of queer kinship privilege choice, many other analyses of gender and sexuality, and especially those grounding themselves in biologism, do not. The question is not whether sexuality is (always already) a discourse

of choice, but how and when gender or sexuality become the concept metaphors through which the questions of individual choice and social or natural determination get posed. A reflexive analysis of the conditions of possibility within which these questions emerge is, as Foucault rightly argued, prerequisite for any progress in the study of sociality.

*See also* **Family; Gay Studies; Kinship; Queer Theory; Sexuality; Structuralism and Poststructuralism: Anthropology; Women and Femininity in U.S. Popular Culture; Women's Studies.**

### BIBLIOGRAPHY

Abu-Lughod, Lila. "The Romance of Resistance: Tracing Transformations of Power through Bedouin Women." In *Beyond the Second Sex: New Directions in the Anthropology of Gender,* edited by Peggy Reeves Sanday and Ruth Gallagher Goodenough, 311–338. Philadelphia: University of Pennsylvania Press, 1990.

———. *Veiled Sentiments: Honor and Poetry in a Bedouin Society.* Cairo: American University of Cairo Press, 1986.

Barbin, Herculine. *Being the Recently Discovered Memoirs of a Nineteenth-Century French Hermaphrodite.* Introduction by Michel Foucault; translated by Richard McDougall. New York: Pantheon, 1980.

Bourdieu, Pierre. 1972. *Outline of a Theory of Practice.* Translated by Richard Nice. Cambridge and New York: Cambridge University Press, 1977.

Butler, Judith. *Bodies That Matter: On the Discursive Limits of "Sex."* New York: Routledge, 1993.

———. *Gender Trouble: Feminism and the Subversion of Identity.* New York: Routledge, 1990.

Chodorow, Nancy. "Family Structure and Feminine Personality." In *Woman, Culture, and Society,* edited by Michelle Zimbalist Rosaldo and Louise Lamphere, 43–66. Stanford, Calif.: Stanford University Press.

Collier, Jane Fishburne, and Sylvia Junko Yanagisako. "Introduction." In *Gender and Kinship: Essays toward a Unified Analysis,* edited by Jane Fishburne Collier and Sylvia Junko Yanagisako, 1–13. Stanford, Calif.: Stanford University Press, 1987.

Di Leonardo, Micaela. *Gender at the Crossroads of Knowledge: Feminist Anthropology in the Postmodern Era.* Berkeley: University of California, 1991.

Engels, Friedrich. *The Origin of the Family, Private Property, and the State.* New York: International Publishers, 1942.

Etienne, Mona, and Eleanor Leacock, eds. *Women and Colonization: Anthropological Perspectives.* New York: Praeger, 1980.

Foucault, Michel. *History of Sexuality.* 3 vols. Translated by Robert Hurley. New York: Vintage, 1986.

Freud, Sigmund. 1905. *Three Essays on the Theory of Sexuality.* Translated by James Strachey. New York: Basic Books, 1975.

Gal, Sue. "Between Speech and Silence: The Problematics of Research on Language and Gender." In *Gender at the Crossroads of Knowledge: Feminist Anthropology in the Postmodern Era,* edited by Micaela di Leonardo, 174–203. Berkeley: University of California Press, 1991.

Gennep, Arnold van. 1909. *The Rites of Passage.* Translated by Monika B. Vizedom and Gabrielle L. Caffee. Chicago: University of Chicago Press, 1960.

Ginsburg, Faye, and Rayna Rapp, eds. *Conceiving the New World Order: The Global Politics of Reproduction.* Berkeley: University of California Press, 1995.

Ginsburg, Faye, and Anna Lowenhaupt Tsing, eds. *Uncertain Terms: Negotiating Gender in American Culture.* Boston: Beacon, 1990.

Halberstam, Judith. *Female Masculinity.* Durham, N.C.: Duke University Press, 1998.

Haraway, Donna. "A Manifesto for Cyborgs: Science, Technology, and Socialist Feminism in the 1980s." *Socialist Review* 80, no. 2 (1985): 65–108.

Herdt, Gilbert. *Third Sex, Third Gender: Beyond Sexual Dimorphism in Culture and History.* New York: Zone, 1994.

Jordanova, Ludmilla. *Nature Displayed: Gender, Science, and Medicine, 1760–1820.* London and New York: Longman, 1999.

Katz, Jonathan Ned. *The Invention of Heterosexuality.* New York: Dutton, 1995.

Leacock, Eleanor Burke. *Myths of Male Dominance: Collected Essays on Women Cross-Culturally.* New York: Monthly Review Press, 1981.

Lévi-Strauss, Claude. *Elementary Structures of Kinship.* Rev. ed. Translated by James Harle Bell, John Richard von Sturmer, and Rodney Needham, editor. Boston: Beacon Press, 1969.

MacCormack, Carol P., and Marilyn Strathern, eds. *Nature, Culture, and Gender.* Cambridge and New York: Cambridge University Press, 1980.

Malinowski, Bronislaw. *Sex and Repression in Savage Society.* London: International Library of Psychology, Philosophy, and Scientific Method, 1927.

———. *The Sexual Life of Savages.* 3rd ed. Preface by Havelock Ellis, introduction by Annette Weiner. Boston: Beacon, 1987.

Martin, Emily. *Flexible Bodies: Tracking Immunity in American Culture from the Days of Polio to the Age of AIDS.* Boston: Beacon, 1994.

Mauss, Marcel. 1968. "Techniques of the Body." In *Incorporations,* edited by Jonathan Crary and Sanford Kwinter, 454–477. New York: Zone, 1992.

Mead, Margaret. *Male and Female: A Study of the Sexes in a Changing World.* New York: Morrow, 1949.

Mohanty, Chandra Talpade, Ann Russo, and Lourdes Torres. *Third World Women and the Politics of Feminism.* Bloomington: Indiana University Press, 1991.

Morgan, Lewis H. *Systems of Consanguinity and Affinity of the Human Family.* Smithsonian Contributions to Knowledge 17, no. 218. Washington, D.C.: Smithsonian Institute, 1870.

Morris, Rosalind C. "All Made Up: Performance Theory and the New Anthropology of Sex and Gender." *Annual Review of Anthropology* 24 (1995): 567–592.

Nash, June. "Aztec Women: The Transition from Status to Class in Empire and Colony." In *Women and Colonization,* edited by Mona Etienne and Eleanor Leacock, 134–148. New York: Praeger, 1980.

Ong, Aihwa. *Spirits of Resistance and Capitalist Discipline.* Albany: State University of New York Press, 1987.

Ortner, Sherry B. *Making Gender: The Politics and Erotics of Culture.* Boston: Beacon, 1996.

———. "Theory in Anthropology since the Sixties." *Comparative Studies in Society and History* 26, no. 1 (1984): 126–166.

Ortner, Sherry B., and Harriet Whitehead, eds. *Sexual Meanings: The Cultural Construction of Gender and Sexuality.* Cambridge and New York: Cambridge University Press, 1981.

Peletz, Michael G. *Reason and Passion: Representations of Gender in a Malay Society.* Berkeley: University of California Press, 1996.

Povinelli, Elizabeth A. "Notes on Gridlock: Intimacy, Genealogy, Sexuality." *Public Culture* 14, no. 1 (2002): 215–238.

Radcliffe-Brown, A. R. "Introduction." In *African Systems of Kinship and Marriage,* edited by A. R. Radcliffe-Brown and Daryll Forde. 1950. Reprint, Oxford: International African Institute and Oxford University Press, 1967.

Rapp, Rayna. *Testing Women, Testing the Fetus: The Social Impact of Amniocentesis in America.* New York: Routledge, 1999.

Reiter, Rayna R., ed. *Toward an Anthropology of Women.* New York: Monthly Review Press, 1975.

Rubin, Gayle. "The Traffic in Women: Notes toward a 'Political Economy' of Sex." In *Woman, Culture, and Society,* edited by Michelle Zimbalist Rosaldo and Louise Lamphere, 157–210. Stanford, Calif.: Stanford University Press, 1974.

Rosaldo, Michelle Zimbalist, and Louise Lamphere, eds. *Woman, Culture, and Society.* Stanford, Calif.: Stanford University Press, 1974.

Sacks, Karen. "Engels Revisited: Women, the Organization of Production, and Private Property." In *Toward an Anthropology of Women,* edited by Rayna R. Reiter, 211–234. New York: Monthly Review Press, 1975.

Sanday, Peggy. "Female Status in the Public Domain." In *Woman, Culture, and Society,* edited by Michelle Zimbalist Rosaldo and Louise Lamphere, 189–206. Stanford, Calif.: Stanford University Press, 1974.

Schneider, David M. *American Kinship: A Cultural Account.* Englewood Cliffs, N.J.: Prentice-Hall, 1968.

Scott, Joan. "Gender: A Useful Category of Historical Analysis." In her *Gender and the Politics of History,* 28–50. Rev. ed. New York: Columbia University Press, 1999.

Siegel, James T. *The Rope of God.* Berkeley: University of California Press, 1969.

Singer, Linda. *Erotic Welfare: Sexual Theory and Politics in the Age of Epidemic,* edited with an introduction by Judith Butler and Maureen MacGrogan. New York: Routledge, 1993.

Stoler, Ann Laura. *Carnal Knowledge and Imperial Power: Race and the Intimate in Colonial Rule.* Berkeley: University of California Press, 2002.

———. *Race and the Education of Desire: Foucault's History of Sexuality and the Colonial Order of Things.* Durham, N.C.: Duke University Press, 1995.

Strathern, Marilyn. *Reproducing the Future: Anthropology, Kinship, and the New Reproductive Technologies.* Manchester, U.K.: Manchester University Press, 1992.

Spivak, Gayatri Chakravorty. "Can the Subaltern Speak?" In *Marxism and the Interpretation of Culture,* edited by Cary Nelson and Lawrence Grossberg, 271–313. Urbana: University of Illinois, 1988.

Turner, Victor. *The Ritual Process: Structure and Anti-Structure.* Chicago: Aldine, 1969.

Weiner, Annette B. 1976. *Women of Value, Men of Renown: New Perspectives in Trobriand Exchange.* Austin: University of Texas Press, 1983.

Weston, Kath. *Families We Choose: Lesbians, Gays, Kinship.* New York: Columbia University Press, 1991.

Yanagisako, Sylvia Junko, and Jane Fishburne Collier. "Toward a Unified Analysis of Gender and Kinship." In their *Gender and Kinship: Essays toward a Unified Analysis,* 14–50. Stanford, Calif.: Stanford University Press, 1987.

*Rosalind C. Morris*

## JEAN-JACQUES ROUSSEAU

Jean-Jacques Rousseau (1712–1778), was born a "Citizen of Geneva," a title he used on many of his important works to suggest the challenge his thought posed to the regimes of his day. He ran away from his native city at sixteen, and led an unsettled life for the next dozen years, teaching himself a variety of subjects. He arrived in Paris in the early 1740s, hoping to make a name for himself as a composer and the inventor of a new system of musical notation. While his musical enterprises mostly failed, he became intimate with the circle of intellectuals who were soon involved in the *Encyclopédie*. He was commissioned to write the articles on music for the great compendium of enlightenment, but gained international celebrity with the publication of the *Discourse on the Sciences and Arts* (1751), in which he argued that the advancement of the sciences and arts had corrupted morals. He followed up the success of this first work with a series of increasingly provocative works published over the next decade: a well-received opera, *Le Devin du Village* (1752), a philosophical treatment of the historical development of human nature; the *Discourse on Inequality* (1755); a best-selling novel, *Julie* (1761); a pedagogical work, *Emile* (1762); and his political treatise, the *Social Contract* (1762). When the *Social Contract* and *Emile* were banned and burned both in Paris and his native Geneva, Rousseau fled Paris and lived essentially in exile for the rest of his life. During this time, apart from defenses of his works, he published his *Dictionary of Music* (1768), the first such lexicon, and wrote several autobiographical works published only posthumously, including the *Confessions,* usually considered the first modern autobiography, *Dialogues,* and *Reveries of the Solitary Walker.*

**GENERAL WILL.** *General will* (*volonté générale*) is inextricably associated with the philosophy of Jean-Jacques Rousseau (1712–1778). While Rousseau appropriated the general will from the theological debates of the late seventeenth and early eighteenth centuries, he made the concept his own with the political formulation he gave it in his *Du contrat social* (1762; On the social contract). Interpretations of the general will since Rousseau have largely been colored by views of the French Revolution (1789–1799) and of the role both thinker and concept played in the ideological justification of the Revolution and assessments of its inheritance.

### The General Will before Rousseau

The term *general will* originated in the debates over divine grace and providence nearly a century before Rousseau. The French philosopher Nicolas de Malebranche (1638–1715) first used the term in these debates to explain the divine governance of the realms of nature and grace through general laws as opposed to the notion that God operates through a continuous series of "particular wills." While the general will had little direct political bearing in these theological debates, the concept in its original usage did refer to the proper source and form of law.

The French political philosopher Montesquieu (1689–1755) was the first to give the general will a specifically political usage, doing so in one of the most important passages of his *De l'esprit des lois* (1748; On the spirit of the laws). In his discussion of the separation of powers, Montesquieu states that the "general will of the state" is located in the legislature but argues that the execution of the law must be placed in separate executive and judicial bodies. Uniting the legislative and executive functions in a single body would lead to tyranny since that body "can plunder the state through its general wills" in making law and then, in executing it, "destroy each citizen through its particular wills" (Montesquieu, I.6).

If Montesquieu put the general will on the political map, the most important influence on Rousseau's own development of the concept was the encyclopedist Denis Diderot (1713–1784). In the article "Droit naturel" (Natural right) for the *Encyclopédie* (1755), Diderot described the general will of all humanity as the source and rule for justice and morality. The right to decide the nature of the just and unjust must come from all humankind "because the good of all is the only passion it has. Particular wills are suspect . . . but the general will is always good" (p. 27). Using their reason and consulting the principles of right of all civilized nations, individuals should address the general will of humankind to consult their duties. Rousseau first responded to his then-friend's argument in his own article for the *Encyclopédie,* "Économie politique" (Political economy, 1755), conceived as a companion piece to Diderot's article. Rousseau rejected the conception of the general will as the will of all humanity, instead finding it in the legislative will of a free people in the state. "The first and most important maxim of legitimate or popular government—that is, one that has the good of the people as its object—is therefore . . . to follow the general will in all matters" ("Économie politique," pp. 247–248). He would develop these ideas in *Du contrat social.*

## Rousseau's General Will

Rousseau's *Du contrat social* was epoch-making in its argument that law legitimately comes only from the sovereign people legislating for itself: from the general will. Rousseau followed in the social contract tradition of Thomas Hobbes (1588–1679), John Locke (1632–1704), and others, but sought to find a form of political association in which naturally free individuals can join with others and yet remain as free as before. His solution was direct democratic self-legislation in which each citizen, as a member of the sovereign, makes laws that apply equally to all. "Each of us puts his person and all his power in common under the supreme direction of the general will; and in a body we receive each member as an indivisible part of the whole" (*Contrat social*, I.6). Rousseau pressed a radically voluntarist principle into service as the binding force of the political community. Although he recognized a "universal justice emanating from reason alone," he argued that this justice is ineffective for want of a natural sanction (*Contrat social*, II.6). Rousseau's general will was confined to the limits of the state.

"The general will is always right," claimed Rousseau. His statement has often been taken to imply a kind of mystical popular will in whose name the force of the state can be exercised. The general will is not something that transcends the state, but is the will of the citizens qua citizens in their capacity as members of the sovereign. Immediately after claiming that the general will is always right, Rousseau pointed to what he saw as the central problem of the state: "But it does not follow that the people's deliberations will always have the same rectitude" (*Contrat social*, II.3). The people may err in their deliberations for several reasons, but the rectitude of the general will is distorted most importantly by the natural tendency of individuals to consult the particular will they have qua individuals. "Indeed, each individual can, as a man, have a private will contrary to or differing from the general will he has as a citizen. His private interest can speak to him quite differently from the common interest." Such a person, Rousseau infamously concluded, "will be forced to be free." While this paradoxical statement has been interpreted as an authoritarian element in Rousseau's thought, less noticed is the continuation of the passage: "For this is the condition that, by giving each citizen to the fatherland, guarantees him against all personal dependence" (*Contrat social*, I.7). The mutual obligations of the political association ensure that the citizens are dependent only on the law of their own making, and not on the will of another individual (see Melzer). The law must come from everyone and apply equally to all. The general will is always directed toward the common justice and utility by virtue of its very generality: "the general will, to be truly such, should be general in its object as well as in its essence; that it should come from all to apply to all" (*Contrat social*, II.4). Proper civic education and favorably egalitarian conditions are necessary for the deliberations of the citizens to have the rectitude they require to make the general will triumph over particular interests. Self-legislation as part of the sovereign makes possible a new kind of freedom, a civil and moral freedom that transcends the natural freedom we have as individuals. Rousseau's general will inspired his followers with what they saw as a promise of revolutionary moral and political transformation.

## The General Will after Rousseau

A quarter century after the publication of Rousseau's political treatise, the French Revolution began, and the fortunes of the general will and the philosopher who gave the concept currency have been forever tied to the epochal event. Revolutionaries such as Maximilien de Robespierre (1758–1794) and the Abbé Sièyes (1748–1836) pressed the general will into service to legitimate their rule in the name of the nation. On the philosophic front, Immanuel Kant (1724–1804), Johann Fichte (1762–1814), and Georg Wilhelm Friedrich Hegel (1770–1831) appropriated and analyzed the concept itself as well as its seeming political instantiation. Kant's categorical imperative, although explicitly universal in scope, exhibits the direct influence of Rousseau's general will as self-legislation in the form of a generalizable law. Hegel associated the general will with the Terror and criticized what he saw as its one-sided subjectivity and arbitrary or absolute freedom. Later thinkers attempted to adapt the general will in less radical form. Grappling directly with the revolutionary inheritance, Benjamin Constant (1767–1830) criticized Rousseau's affinity for the liberty of the ancients, but still began his own *Principes de politique* (1815; Principles of politics) by stating: "Our present constitution formally recognizes the principle of the sovereignty of the people, that is, the supremacy of the general will over every particular will" (p. 310). The tension between the individual and the community that Rousseau tried to reconcile in his own way through the general will continues to dominate contemporary debates in political theory and practice.

*See also* **Authority; Enlightenment; Liberalism; Social Contract; State of Nature; Terror.**

### BIBLIOGRAPHY

PRIMARY SOURCES

Constant, Benjamin. *Principes de politique.* In *Écrits politiques.* Paris: Gallimard, 1997.

Diderot, Denis. "Droit Naturel." In *Oeuvres complètes,* vol. 7. Paris: Hermann, 1976. Originally published in vol. 5 of the *Encyclopédie.*

Montesquieu, Charles-Louis de Secondat, Baron de. *De l'esprit des lois.* In *Oeuvres complètes,* vol. 1. Paris: Gallimard, 1949–1951.

Rousseau, Jean-Jacques. *The Collected Writings of Rousseau.* Edited by Roger D. Masters and Christopher Kelly. Hanover, N.H.: University Press of New England, 1990–. 10 vols. to date. The standard edition of Rousseau's works in English translation.

———. *Oeuvres complètes.* Paris: Gallimard, 1959–1995. 5 vols. The standard critical edition of Rousseau's works. *Du contrat social* and *Économie politique* are included in vol. 3.

SECONDARY SOURCES

Keohane, Nannerl O. *Philosophy and the State in France: The Renaissance to the Enlightenment.* Princeton, N.J.: Princeton University Press, 1980.

Melzer, Arthur M. *The Natural Goodness of Man: On the System of Rousseau's Thought.* Chicago: University of Chicago Press, 1990.

Riley, Patrick. *The General Will before Rousseau: The Transformation of the Divine into the Civic.* Princeton, N.J.: Princeton University Press, 1986.

*John T. Scott*

**GENERATION.** In its most widely accepted modern sense, a *generation* is comprised of a group of people born around the same time and sharing certain formative experiences. The concept of generations has been used by social scientists, historians, and anthropologists to explain social change over time and to identify differences within social groups. The term has also been applied loosely to describe literary groups and genres, such as the metaphorical designation of "lost generation" applied by Gertrude Stein (1874–1946) to certain post–World War I writers and artists or the "lost generation" of British writers who literally disappeared in the trenches of the Western Front, or the Beat Generation of 1950s America. In the second half of the twentieth century, it was also deployed by advertisers and other producers of mass media–based popular culture (for example, Generation X) and entered into common usage as a way to identify and distinguish oneself or a particular group.

Early references to the significance of generations may be found in Western and non-Western classical texts and in both the Old and New Testaments of the Bible. Such references were mainly genealogical in nature yet also considered generations as a concept to chart change over time. Both Plato (c. 428–348 or 347 B.C.E.) and Aristotle (384–322 B.C.E.) recognized the significance of generational conflict as a motor of political change, with the former advocating that citizens older than ten years of age be expelled from the republic in order to facilitate the construction of the model society. Homer, in the *Iliad,* wrote that "as the leaves of the trees are born and perish, thus pass the ages of man." Herodotus (484–between 430 and 420 B.C.E.) used a scale of "a hundred years for each three generations" in recounting the succession of Egyptian kings and high priests, thus providing one of the earliest references to the common characterization of one generation spanning thirty years. The fourteenth-century Arab scholar Ibn Khaldun (1332–1406) also reflected extensively on the nature of familial, tribal, and dynastic ties and succession.

But it was not until the nineteenth century that European scholars attempted systematically to define the term and apply it to the study of human society. The first such important attempt was made by Auguste Comte (1798–1857). In *Cours de philosophie positive* (1830–1842; The course of positive philosophy), Comte proposed that social change is determined by generational change and in particular conflict between successive generations. As the members of a given generation age, their "instinct of social conservation" becomes stronger, which inevitably and necessarily brings them into conflict with the "normal attribute of youth"—innovation. Following Comte closely was John Stuart Mill (1806–1873), who argued that generational change and the process of a new "set" of people taking "possession of society" marked off one historical "age" from another. Around this time the German literary scholar Wilhelm Dilthey (1833–1911) suggested that the leading lights of German Romanticism, who were born at around the same time and shaped decisively in their young years by their social and intellectual milieu, represented a distinct and influential generation.

Most influential, however, was Karl Mannheim (1893–1947), who argued that two approaches to the study of generations had heretofore been dominant, neither of them satis-

factory. The "positivist" approach of Comte emphasized social change measured exclusively in fifteen-to-thirty-year life spans, which in Mannheim's view reduced history to "a chronological table." Conversely, the "Romantic-historical" school, represented by figures such as Dilthey, Wilhelm Pinder, and Martin Heidegger (1889–1976), emphasized the qualitative experience of the individual but downplayed or ignored the importance of social context (though Dilthey was not oblivious to this). Mannheim did not deny that the biological
life-death cycle produces "generations" but added that those born around the same time "share a common location in the historical dimension of the social process" and are thus formed by social experience, especially at a relatively young age. Change takes place as members of younger generations come into contact with members of older generations. Crucial for Mannheim was the rapidity in which the social context was changing, as not every generation comes to define itself as distinct. Hence periods of accelerated social change tended to produce more cohesive and distinctive generations. Yet Mannheim also noted that each generation can contain "a number of differentiated, antagonistic generation-units." He also called attention to the intersection of generation and class, though he did not attempt a theoretical reconciliation.

Another effort to theorize about generation was made by Jose Ortega y Gasset (1883–1955), who proposed that what constitutes a "generation" is not a select or large group of individuals but a "particular type of sensibility, an organic capacity for certain deeply rooted directions of thought" that places each generation on a "vital trajectory"; within the life span of each individual lies the basis for generational conflict and hence historical change. For Ortega, the years between one and fifteen are not marked by any political participation, whereas the following fifteen years are spent learning but also in passivity. From thirty to forty-five, the individual enters into conflict with the preceding generation—that is, those between forty-five and sixty and the possessors of power. In the final stage—sixty to seventy-five—the individual is a "survivor" who remains "outside of life" and a mere "witness." Gasset's ill-defined notions of "sensibility" and "vital trajectory" never attracted sustained critical attention from future scholars.

In 1949, one of Ortega's students, Julian Marias, summarized the various theories of generations, suggested new avenues of inquiry, and pointed out some of the shortcomings of the various conceptualizations. Marias argued that "generations" do not in fact exist but are purely social constructions, that the series of fifteen-year benchmarks proposed by Ortega and others is similarly arbitrary, that scholars had ignored women and were generally unclear on who gets included in a particular generation, and that theorizing on generations had not accounted for the rebel individual or "elite minorities" within generational groups. Marias himself did not advance a theory of generations of lasting influence, but his critique of previous characterizations pointed the way to more sophisticated interpretations.

In the postwar era, political scientists and sociologists, mainly in the United States and Germany, have produced the most extensive empirically based studies of generations. Political scientists have attempted to identify "political generations" as birth cohorts who share formative experiences and then go on to mobilize themselves for some kind of political action. The upheavals of the 1960s sparked considerable interest in the systematic study of generations in the United States, in large part because of the large role young people played in the civil rights, free speech, antiwar, and other protest and countercultural movements. While some scholars and much popular literature identified a "generational revolt" at the heart of the student protest movements, much evidence suggested that the rebellions, at least in the United States, were a response to the process of being socialized in a system that proclaimed liberal democratic values but did not live up to them in practice. Thus much of the student revolt was a confrontation with hypocrisy rather than parental values. The revolt produced a search for political and cultural models that could reconcile the perceived gulf in rhetoric and reality. Many young people become enamored of Third World revolutionaries, pioneered women's and gay liberation politics, focused on the environment, or experimented with countercultural lifestyles revolving around communal living, music, and experimentation with drugs.

Political scientists have also examined generational differences and political party loyalty in the United States. An influential study published in 1960, *The American Voter,* argued that younger American citizens were not as loyal to political parties as were their older compatriots. Further research confirmed that the high degree of party loyalty that had previously characterized American politics declined, at least among white voters, from 1952 to 1984. Some scholars argued for a "life-cycle thesis" while others pointed to the presence of distinct political generations in the postwar United States, thus suggesting that particular historical events account for the decline in partisanship.

Post-1980 scholarship on political generations has considered developments in the non-Western world. Ruth Cherrington's research on young intellectuals (the "reform generation") in 1980s China employed Mannheim's theoretical conceptualization to demonstrate that well-educated young people became disillusioned with the lack of political and economic change following the Cultural Revolution, the death of Mao Zedong and Chou Enlai, and certain educational and economic reforms that promised young people better lives and the possibilities of changing Chinese society. In the mid-1980s, this "reform generation" seems to have developed a distinct generational consciousness fueled by rising expectations, a sense of superiority vis-à-vis older generations, and a greater awareness of technological change and the world outside China. Largely though not exclusively as a result of this generational shift, a student movement and a prodemocracy movement emerged, culminating in the events of June 1989.

Historians have also studied generations with illuminating results, with the upheavals of the American and French revolutions, the failed revolutions of 1848, the American Civil War and reconstruction, the unifications of Germany and Italy, the defeat of Spain by the United States in 1898, and above all World War I and its aftermath providing particularly fertile fields of study. Robert Wohl examined how members of the "generation of 1914"—a select cohort of educated young British, French, Italian, Spanish, and German men who fought in the Great War or at least were altered irrevocably by its traumas—thought of themselves as representing a new generation freed from the stultifying past of bourgeois complacency and charged with the rejuvenation of their societies. Wohl sees this rejection of the past and desire to revitalize the society of the present as fueling many members of this self-proclaimed generation's enthusiasm for fascism. In modern Arab and Israeli political culture and thought there are several key historical concepts related to generations and associated with decisive defeats or victories: *Jil al-Nakba* (Generation of the Catastrophe), namely the generation that experienced the defeat of 1948; and *Jil al-Naqsa* (Generation of the Setback), the generation that experienced the defeat of 1967. In Israeli culture the term "dor tashach" (the generation of 1948) refers to the men and women who fought for and created the modern Jewish state.

The German historian Michael Wildt examined the generation of young men who formed the leadership cohort of the Nazi Reich Main Security Service of the SS (the Schutzstaffel) and became responsible for directing the early stages of the systematic assault on Europe's Jewish populations. Of the 221 individuals studied by Wildt, three quarters were born in and after 1900 and thus were too young to have fought in World War I yet old enough to have been shaped by the traumas of the postwar years and the accelerating radicalization of German political culture. Wildt noted that the Reich Main Security Office drew more than three quarters of its members from this *Kriegsjugendgeneration.* Well educated and in the prime of their lives when Hitler came to power in 1933, they were ideal matches for an institutional culture of the regime's ideological police, a culture that promoted both unwavering ideological fervor (further radicalized by war) and obedience along with modern rational bureaucratic organizational skills.

The generations theme has also been important for historians of modern immigration. Particularly influential was Marcus Lee Hansen's thesis that the second generation of the children of immigrants tends to strive for complete assimilation and shows little interest in parents' home cultures while the third generation becomes remarkably interested in "returning" to grandparents' cultural roots. Hansen's thesis was a broad generalization based largely on personal experience rather than empirical research, yet it influenced successive scholars of the immigrant experience, such as Nathan Glazer, Oscar Handlin, and many others. By the 1980s, however, scholars had demonstrated via local studies of ethnic and religious groups the weakness of Hansen's thesis. More recently, scholars of immigration have begun to consider "generations" as social constructions used, for instance, by immigrant-descended writers exploring the tensions between assimilation and identity. The concept of "generations," therefore, is not a satisfactory explanatory tool but merits study as a cultural construction.

Anthropologists have focused on generations principally in terms of genealogy, the structures of kinship, and aging. Yet they have also relied on the modern social-scientific conceptualization of a generation as a cohort of people who identify with each other based on common experiences. Cultural anthropology, however, has turned away from generalizations based on culture and has considered the importance of difference, local context, and structures of power and how these things influence conceptions of age, kinship, and gender. Cultural anthropologists have also recently addressed the kinship ties in gay and lesbian families. Some scholars have argued that gay and lesbian families are distinct from dominant conceptions of the "American family" in that they do not place a high value on biological ties in defining kinship. Others have argued that "motherhood" is central to womanhood in American culture, thus overriding any distinct "lesbian" identities.

That the conceptualization of a birth cohort shaped by social forces has become the standard approach to defining and analyzing a generation or generations is illustrated by recent popular and scholarly work on the "hip-hop generation." Journalists and scholars have sought to move beyond the pop culture industry to explore the relationship between hip-hop, black youth culture, and the persistence of political and economic inequality in the United States. Bakari Kitwana has employed Mannheim's basic framework in analyzing the cohort of black Americans born between 1965 and 1984 and has argued that hip-hop largely defines this cohort, the first to come of age in postsegregation America. Hip-hop culture has evolved beyond its original four core elements—graffiti, break dancing, DJing, and rap music—to encompass language, dress, attitude, and political and social activism that both draw and distinguish it from the experiences and values of the preceding generation.

Kitwana suggests that six factors have shaped this generation's worldview. One is rap music, which has given black youth culture unprecedented international visibility while providing the "medium" by which a common culture could be constructed. A second is the accelerated development of global capitalism in the 1980s and 1990s, which has led to increased income disparities that have hit black Americans disproportionately hard. Third is the persistence of segregation and inequality in wages and salaries, housing, electoral politics, and other segments of society. A fourth factor is widespread mistrust of and cynicism about the criminal justice system. A fifth involves the ways in which young blacks are portrayed in the mainstream media, particularly in reporting on crime. Finally, there is the reality of relatively high unemployment rates and rates of incarceration, gang activity, gun homicide, suicide, and AIDS. Kitwana suggests that the implications of these factors remain little studied or understood by scholars, journalists, or policy-makers. Further, he argues that an enormous divide exists between the hip-hop generation and the preceding generation, which was influenced decisively by the black Church and the civil rights and Black Power movements.

While "generation" as conceptualized by Mannheim continues to draw some interest from scholars and has become pervasive and scholarly popular points of reference, the main problem with the study of generations has been that the collective identity of any birth cohort is crosscut and shaped by multiple factors, thus greatly complicating empirical research and generalization. Sustained interest in some of these factors—above all class, race, ethnicity, gender, and the body—among social scientists, historians, literary scholars, and cultural anthropologists has not encouraged substantial new theoretical or empirical work on generations. Further, in the last decades of the twentieth century the influence of postmodern cultural theory, which challenged the validity of sweeping explanatory models or "metanarratives" that claim to explain social change—such as "generations"—contributed to the decline in scholarly work on the subject.

*See also* **Cycles; History, Idea of; Life Cycle.**

**BIBLIOGRAPHY**

Abramson, Paul R. "Generations and Political Change in the United States." *Research in Political Sociology* 4 (1989): 235–280.

Ajami, Fouad. *The Dream Palace of the Arabs: A Generation's Odyssey.* New York: Pantheon, 1998.

Campbell, Agnes. *The American Voter.* New York: Wiley, 1960.

Cherrington, Ruth. "Generational Issues in China: A Case Study of the 1980s Generation of Young Intellectuals." *British Journal of Sociology* 48 (1997): 302–320.

Comte, Auguste. *The Positive Philosophy.* With a new introduction by Abraham S. Blumberg. New York: AMS Press, 1974.

Dilthey, Wilhelm. *Über das Studium der Geschichte der Wissenschaft.* Leipzig: Teubner, 1924.

Eisenstadt, Shmuel. *From Generation to Generation: Age Groups and Social Structure.* Glencoe, Ill.: Free Press, 1956.

Elon, Amos. *The Israelis: Founders and Sons.* New York: Penguin, 1983.

Hansen, Marcus Lee. *The Immigrant in American History.* Edited with a foreword by Arthur M. Schlesinger. Cambridge, Mass.: Harvard University Press, 1940.

Hayden, Corinne P. "Gender, Genetics, and Generation: Reformulating Biology in Lesbian Kinship." *Cultural Anthropology* 10 (1995): 41–63.

Kitwana, Bakari. *The Hip Hop Generation: Young Blacks and the Crisis in African American Culture.* New York: Basic Civitas Books, 2002.

Kivisto, Peter, and Blanck, Dag, eds. *American Immigrants and Their Generations: Studies and Commentaries on the Hansen Thesis after Fifty Years.* Urbana: University of Illinois Press, 1990.

Mannheim, Karl. "The Problem of Generations." In his *Essays on the Sociology of Knowledge,* edited by Paul Kecskemeti. New York: Oxford University Press, 1952.

Marias, Julian. *Generations: A Historical Method.* Translated by Harold C. Raley. Mobile: University of Alabama Press, 1970.

Mill, John Stuart. *A System of Logic, Ratiocinative and Inductive: Being a Connected View of the Principles of Evidence and the Methods of Scientific Investigation.* Edited by J. M. Robson. Toronto: University of Toronto Press, 1978.

Ortega y Gasset, Jose. *The Modern Theme.* Translated by James Cleugh. New York: Norton, 1933.

Wildt, Michael. *Generation des Unbedingten: Das Führungskorps des Reichssicherheitshauptamtes.* Hamburg, Germany: Hamburger Edition, 2002.

Wohl, Robert. *The Generation of 1914.* Cambridge, Mass.: Harvard University Press, 1979.

*Steven P. Remy*

**New Dictionary of the History of Ideas**

# GENETICS.

The entry includes two subentries:

*History of*
*Contemporary*

## HISTORY OF

Genetics as a discipline is young, but the concept that forms its subject—inheritance—stretches back in time. The word has been formed from the adjective *genetic,* found in the sciences of the nineteenth and twentieth centuries—for example, biogenetic law, genetic affinity, genetic psychology—and meaning, according to the *Oxford English Dictionary,* "pertaining to, or having references to, origin." Not until 1906 was the noun *genetics* publicly proposed to cover those labors that, in the words of its author, William Bateson, "are devoted to the elucidation of the phenomena of heredity and variation: in other words to the physiology of descent, with implied bearing on the theoretical problems of the evolutionist and the systematist, and application to the practical problems of breeders, whether of animals or plants."

We begin, therefore, by commenting briefly on the long history of notions of heredity and variation, reflecting the while on the significance of cultural and economic factors that both drew attention to them and shaped them. Next we turn to the father figure of genetics, Gregor Mendel (1822–1884), and his introduction of the Mendelian experiment. With the rediscovery of his work in 1900 we explore the contribution of the early "Mendelians," the melding of Mendelian heredity with the theory of the chromosome, a synthesis that revealed a geography of heredity in the cell but did not answer the question, "What is the identity of the genetic material?" Only with the introduction of the Watson-Crick structure for DNA in 1953 was a window opened through which to glimpse the terrain that was to become "molecular genetics."

Heredity and variation are today considered as two sides of the same coin. Thus variation among sibs results from the varied commingling and expression of the hereditary determinants from two parents. Spontaneous changes in the hereditary material (mutations) give rise to variations, and these are inherited. In other words there is heredity, variation, and the heredity of variation, and they belong together. Prior to the latter half of the nineteenth century this conceptual framework did not exist. There still lingered relics of the ancient view of heredity as the result of the reproduction of the type, whereas any deviance from the type was ascribed to the effects of the mother's imagination, changed conditions of life, and so on. Moreover both heredity and variation were situated within the broad topic of "generation." This included the regeneration of lost and damaged organs, the development of the embryo from the fertilized egg, and all forms of reproduction, both sexual and asexual. But as attention directed to human heredity increased during the nineteenth century the subject of the transmission of hereditary characters began to acquire a separate conceptual status.

In the eighteenth century two rival conceptions of the phenomenon of inheritance were in play: the doctrine of preformation claimed that like generates like because the offspring are in some way already present in the germ and have only to unfold or "evolve" to yield offspring like the parents. A literal view of this doctrine was held by some who claimed that hidden miniatures of future generations must have existed from the time of creation, all nested one within another, like a set of Russian dolls, hence the term preexistence for this version of the doctrine. Procreation became, as it were, the act of revealing what had been created long before. Opposed to this was the doctrine of epigenesis, according to which the parts of the offspring are formed successively, and in the process the embryo undergoes a series of transformations. Support for this view came from descriptions of the development of the fertilized egg. Experimental support came also from the hybridization experiments of Joseph Kölreuter, who in 1766 described how he had succeeded in transforming one species of plant into another. How, he asked, was this possible if the offspring is already preformed? He also found that no matter which parent supplied the "male seed" (pollen) and which the female "seed" (ovules), the resulting hybrids were the same. How could these results be accounted for on the basis of any theory of preformation—whether, as the animalculists claimed, the preformed miniatures reside in the spermatozoa, or as the ovists urged, in the egg? A further difficulty arose for preformationists when nineteenth-century microscopists developed a cell theory according to which the fundamental unit of life is the cell, not some preformed rudiments of the organism.

These two resources—hybridization and the cell theory—were to form the basis for Gregor Mendel's research. Prior to his work, however, the study of hybridization had been carried out under different assumptions and in a much more limited manner. The number of hybrid offspring grown in an experiment was limited, and the prevalence of the effect of hybridization in diluting character differences supported the view that heredity is a blending process, like the mixing of ink and water. The conception of the organism too was generally holistic: that is, the type of the species acts as a whole, its "essential" characteristics—flower color, habit, leaf shape, and so on—being but expressions of the type. With this point of view, effective analysis of hereditary transmission is impossible.

## Gregor Johann Mendel

Raised on a farm in rural Heinzendorf in German-speaking Silesia, the young Johann, as he was christened, had an early education in the practical aspects of horticulture and agriculture before he left home to attend a gymnasium and at eighteen years of age entered the University of Olmütz. The stress of inadequate finances there led him to apply in 1843 to the Augustinian monastery in Brünn, the industrial and economic capital of Moravia. It was there that, supported by the wise and understanding abbot Cyril Napp, he was encouraged to institute experiments analyzing the phenomenon of hybridization. The subject was of concern to the monastery, with its extensive agricultural holdings in Moravia, a region known for its sheep and wine. Also thanks to the abbot, Mendel had spent two years at Vienna University, studying principally physics, botany, and zoology. There he had learned about the cell theory, according to which the organism is composed neither of a continuous fabric like lacework nor of a multitude of globules but of individual vesicles or *cells,* all formed by division of preexisting cells that can be traced back to the foundation cell or fertilized egg, this having arisen by fertilization of the egg cell by one pollen cell.

The experiments that led to his well-known theory began with the testing of thirty-four varieties of the edible pea (*Pisum*) followed by eight years of hybridization (1856–1863). Taking seven traits, he followed the hereditary transmission of each. The scale of the research was unprecedented, the size of his progeny populations being such that clear statistical regularities emerged. It was not just that he noted the separate behavior of the seven traits he studied, nor that there was a marked difference between the population sizes of those carrying the two contrasted characters, but that they approximated to the ratio 3:1. Thus for the trait seed color, Mendel harvested 6,022 green seeds and 2,001 yellow from his hybrid progeny, offering the most striking example among his seven traits of a 3:1 ratio. Further research revealed that two-thirds of the larger class did not breed true and the other third did. Thus the ratio 3:1 was really constituted of three classes in the ratio 1:2:1.

As a physicist trained in combinatorial mathematics this ratio reminded him of the binomial equation $(A + a)^2 = 1A^2 + 2Aa + 1a^2$. Using $A$ and $a$ to represent the potential carried in the pollen cell and in the egg cell, and knowing that $A$ obscures (is dominant over) $a$, this expansion appears as $3A + 1a$. Well-grounded in cytology, he suggested that the differing elements brought together in the hybrid remain together until the germ cells are formed. Then they separate and pass into separate germ cells. There result, he declared, "as many sorts of egg and pollen cells as there are combinations possible of formative elements." These claims—known as "germinal segregation" and the "independent assortment" of characters—he supported from his crossing of plants differing in two and in three traits. These two principles were later to be called Mendel's two laws.

Mendel's work did not meet with an enthusiastic response because it was opposed to several securely held beliefs. All the traits he included in the data concerned nonblending characters, but the consensus was that blending is the rule and that the agreed representation of heredity is in terms of fractions: one-half being from the two parents, one-quarter from the four grandparents, and so on, implying that no contribution is entirely lost but that there is a repeated dilution of differences in reproduction. Mendel's theory denied this, for in his theory, after segregation, the elements in question would either be present or absent in a given pollen cell or egg cell, and it would be a question of chance as to which elements finished up in the foundation cell of the offspring.

His paper was directed to two specific questions: First, whether hybridization can lead to the multiplication of species; and second, what part hybridization plays in the production of variation. On the first of these he was clear that *Pisum* does not yield constant hybrids—that is, hybrids that breed true, reproducing the hybrid form like a pure species. Therefore he insti-

tuted experiments with other species to test the general validity of his results. As to the second question, he explained how the variation following hybridization can be understood as the result of the recombination of independently transmitted characters brought together in the hybrid. Therefore he opposed those who, like Darwin, attributed such variation ultimately to the act of bringing together species that have been exposed to different conditions of life. Those who claimed, like Darwin, that cultivated plants are more variable than wild ones due to their changed conditions of life, he also strongly opposed.

## Rediscovery

In 1900 three European botanists, Hugo de Vries, Carl Correns, and Erik Tschermak, published the results of their experiments carried out in the 1890s that supported Mendel's experimental results and his conclusions. Although the first two had in fact seen Mendel's paper earlier, its significance had not struck them. Only later, when they had their own results, did they encounter his paper again and realize its importance. In England the Cambridge zoologist William Bateson teamed up with the Reverend William Wilks, secretary of the Royal Horticultural Society, and Maxwell Masters, chairman of the society's scientific committee, to spread the word about Mendel. Through this prestigious and influential society Bateson introduced Mendel's work to the English-speaking world, and the Reverend Wilks asked Charles Druery, a hybridist and fellow of the society, to translate Mendel's paper into English for its publication in the society's journal.

It was at the Royal Horticultural Society's Third International Conference on Hybridisation and Cross-breeding that Bateson introduced the term "genetics" to the audience gathered in London in 1906. When the conference proceedings appeared Wilks had renamed it *Report of the Third International Conference 1906 on Genetics: Hybridization.*

British biologists were for the most part unreceptive to Mendel's work. Karl Pearson, upholder of Galton's biometric tradition, was opposed. Darwinians like Alfred Russel Wallace were appalled, and the Oxford professor Edward B. Poulton reported the consensus he had found among eminent zoologists that Mendelian writings were "injurious to Biological Science, and a hindrance in the attempt to solve the problem of evolution." According to Pearson, the Mendelian theory was not conformable with the statistical data he was amassing on the relation between successive generations (the regression coefficients). It took the insight and persistence of the young Ronald Aylmer Fisher (1890–1962) to remove this roadblock to the integration of Mendelism and biometry. His solution of the problem finally appeared in 1918.

The biometricians' theory was ancestrian, meaning that the hereditary constitution of offspring was considered to be a collection of representations from the ancestors, the proportions of which are based on some form of the old fractional theory. This was formulated under the title "The Ancestral Law of Inheritance." Confining their attention to what is visible, the biometricians were not concerned with so-called hidden elements. As a positivist, Karl Pearson was particularly concerned not to invent or invoke unobservable entities like Mendelian factors. Mendelians, by contrast, were opening up the space between the hereditary determinant (Mendelian factor) and the observable character or characters for which it is responsible. Mendel's language of the transmission of characters was giving place to the Mendelians' growing reference to the transmission of factors.

Powerful opposition to the biometricians came not only from Bateson in England but from Wilhelm Johannsen in Denmark. He complained that the biometric approach was based on the assumption that the "personal qualities" of an individual "are the true heritable elements or traits." But this, he declared, "is the most naïve and oldest conception of heredity" and can be traced back to Hippocrates. It was, he claimed, borrowed from the legal language of inheritance and heirs to property. As such it includes not only long-standing possessions but what has been acquired by the testator in his or her lifetime. But in biology the evidence was against acquired characters being heritable, and the modern view of heredity was that the "sexual substances" in the egg and sperm determine the personal qualities of the individual, not the reverse. To banish these confusions Johannsen proposed a new language for heredity in the form of the "gene," "genotype," and "phenotype." "The gene," he explained, "is nothing but a very applicable little word, easily combined with others, and hence it may be useful as an expression for the 'unit-factors,' 'elements,' or 'allelomorphs' in the gametes, demonstrated by modern Mendelian researchers. A 'genotype' is the sum total of all the 'genes'" in a germ cell or fertilized egg. Avoiding speculation as to the nature of the gene, he felt that "the terms 'gene' and 'genotype' will prejudice nothing" (Johannsen, p. 133). But just as it took a long time for the term *genetics* to become generally established, so was the case for Johannsen's terms.

### The Chromosome Theory of Heredity

Meanwhile, in America a bridge between zoology and Mendelism was being constructed at Columbia University, New York City. There, Edward Beecher Wilson was promoting the search for parallels between Mendelian heredity and the theory of the chromosome. Subsequently the embryologist Thomas Hunt Morgan, studying the determination of sex and the hereditary transmission of mutations in the fruit fly (*Drosophila*), discovered what he called "sex-limited" inheritance, and in 1911 he associated it with a specific chromosome. This led in 1915 to his groundbreaking text *The Mechanism of Mendelian Heredity*, which he coauthored with the three young men working under him: Alfred Henry Sturtevant, Hermann Joseph Muller, and Calvin Bridges. Here the authors distanced themselves from any suggestion that the factorial hypothesis ("gene" hypothesis) can account for the embryological development of the hereditary characters. A whole mysterious world, they explained, lies between the factor and the character. So they challenged the claim that "until we know something of the reactions that transform the egg into the adult" our hereditary theories "must remain superficial." The Mendelian theory, they argued, does not explain development, nor does it pretend to. Yet "it stands as a scientific explanation of heredity, because it fulfills all the requirements of any causal explanation" (Morgan, p. 280).

Here the authors were seeking to separate genetics from embryology. At the same time, they were developing its relation with the cytologists' study of the chromosomes. This association had at first seemed improbable since many organisms were known to have very few chromosomes—*Pisum* has seven pairs, the fruit fly four, and the horse thread worm (*Parascaris*) only two. Assuming the Mendelian factors for the numerous hereditary factors are able to recombine in all possible combinations, as Mendel claimed, surely they could not be tied together on just a few chromosomes. Fortunately in 1909 F. A. Janssens in Belgium had observed "cross-over" patterns between chromosomes that he called "chiasmata," a discovery that gave Morgan the idea that chromosomes might exchange parts, thus permitting recombination. This insight was followed by Sturtevant's suggestion that the frequency of such recombinations between factors could be used as a measure of the distance separating them along the chromosome, and the mapping of genes became a reality. Already the simple picture of Mendelian heredity had been complicated by the discovery of interaction between factors, association of factors (linkage), and the determination of a character by many factors (polygenic inheritance). The latter brought blending heredity under the explanatory arm of Mendelian heredity. The degree of blending was determined by the number of genes involved. Ancestral inheritance was absorbed into Mendelian heredity. What had once been likened to fluids mixing was now attributed to a finite and fixed number of Mendelian factors.

### Culture of Heredity

Alongside the developing experimental tradition of the biologists, the nineteenth century saw increasing attention given to family histories (genealogy) and to population studies (biometry). Both owed their popularity to the growing concerns about human heredity. Was increasing urbanization affecting the quality of human heredity as evidenced by the increasing numbers of the insane, the tubercular, the alcoholic? Supporting this concern was the medical concept of a diathesis—that is, the predisposing to certain diseases, especially those chronic conditions like gout, epilepsy, asthma, tuberculosis, and cancer, that are often manifested later in life. Diatheses were judged to be features of a person's hereditary constitution. Although the tuberculous diathesis was not banished by Robert Koch's isolation of the tubercle bacillus in 1882, it did become transformed into the genetic susceptibility to the pathogen.

Genealogy became of special interest for several reasons. Many an aspiring family in Napoleonic Europe, wishing to claim the status of *majorat* (Napoleon I's substitute for aristocracy), needed to provide their family genealogies as evidence of the fraction of "blue blood" in their ancestry. In Jamaica the fractional theory was used to draw the line between those descended from mulattos who could and could not be considered white. Hence the classification: mulatto, half black; terceron, one-quarter; quateron, one-eighth; quinteron, one-sixteenth. In England, Francis Galton, concerned about what he saw as a growing mediocrity in urban populations, used genealogy to argue for the inheritance of what he called "genius"—exceptional ability that is inborn. Such he found in families like the Bachs, Bernoullis, and Darwins and thought to find especially among judges. In the early years of the twentieth century, with the advent of Mendelism, the hunt for pedigrees that exemplified Mendelian heredity was all the rage. Hereditary night blindness offered the most extensive pedigree, but many were the studies of the familial incidence of feeblemindedness, inebriation, epilepsy, pauperism, and criminality. Concerns about degeneration of the European races, and the felt need to apply science to the problem, provided a political climate in which Galton decided in 1904 he could launch his bid for the science he had earlier (1883) called "eugenics" and defined as "the science of improving the stock . . . which, especially in the case of man, takes cognizance of all the influences that tend in however remote a degree to give to the more suitable races or strains of blood, a better chance of prevailing speedily over the less suitable than they otherwise would have" (*Human Faculty*, p. 17).

The stark hereditarian leaning of Galton did not go unchallenged. His first book, *Hereditary Genius* (1869), received mixed reviews, the accuracy of his biographical data coming under fire. In Switzerland, Alphonse de Candolle argued persuasively for the effects of the educational, cultural, and political climate, rather than heredity, to account for the remarkably high representation of Swiss scientists among foreign members of the Royal Society and the Académie des Sciences. In this way de Candolle countered the emphasis Galton had placed on heredity in his work *English Men of Science* (1874). As for the enthusiasts for eugenics, both those in the biometric tradition of Galton and the experimental tradition of Mendel were for the most part supportive. One Mendelian who adopted a more cautious position was William Bateson. Though an elitist, he judged the scientific basis of many of the eugenists' claims inadequate and kept his group of coworkers at a distance from the eugenically inspired Mendel Society that had formed in England during the early years of Mendelism. As an hereditarian, of course, Bateson was concerned that those carrying harmful genes should be discouraged from bearing offspring. He was thus a supporter of negative eugenics. But as to positive eugenics—the encouraging of selected individuals to mate and have offspring—he was not clear what particular traits should be looked for.

## Fine Structure of the Gene

Morgan's introduction of the fruit fly to genetics revolutionized it because the fly's rapid life cycle and minute size enabled the scale of experimentation to be markedly increased. Contrast the whole year required between generations of peas and corn with the two weeks needed for the fruit fly. This meant that in a short time over a hundred characters had been studied and many mutants found. *Drosophila* became as a result the most prominent "model organism" of genetics. Bridges oversaw and maintained the growing stock of the mutant types and made them freely available internationally. The lab at Columbia, known as the "Fly Room," was an example of team effort, led by a genial, exuberant boss. Morgan had to undergo quite a conversion by his team, but the outcome was a giant step forward in genetics, crowned with the award of the Nobel Prize in 1933.

H. J. Muller was less close to Morgan than the others and did not long remain in the group. Their views on genetics dif-

fered. Whereas Morgan was happy to leave to one side the question of the material basis of the gene, Muller wanted to know the answer. His pioneer work on the production of mutations by X rays not only won him the Nobel Prize but offered him the hope of establishing the size of the gene. This approach was used by the brilliant Russian geneticist N. V. Timoféeff-Ressovsky, in Germany, to yield an estimate of the "sensitive volume" of the gene as that space needed by one thousand atoms, or about the size of an average protein. Unfortunately, as later work revealed, the methodology and interpretation of this experiment proved faulty.

*Drosophila* was by no means the only model organism for genetics. In addition to commercial cereal crops, poultry, mice, and yeast, the bread mold *Neurospora* figures prominently in the development of the field. Using this organism, George Beadle and Edward Tatum concluded that there is a 1:1 relation between a gene and a given enzyme, thus suggesting that the primary product of a gene is an enzyme. But for the fine structure analysis of the gene the model system that was to bring the analysis down to the molecular level was the viral infected colon bacillus (*Escherichia coli*). Here the bacterial virus (bacteriophage, or phage) has just one chromosome, and in mixed infections this chromosome can recombine with one from another, thus permitting recombination and making fine structure mapping possible. By 1957 Seymour Benzer had used this system to make an estimate of the likelihood of crossing-over between two mutants one DNA base apart in the bacteriophage T4 to be 1 in 10,000. His own analysis had then reached 1 in 20,000.

## Molecular Genetics

The period covering the first half of the twentieth century is often referred to as "classical genetics." Morgan had set the tone, treating the gene as an abstraction and the Mendelian analysis of experimental data as an algorithm. But as early as 1922 Muller had drawn the analogy between bacterial viruses and genes and glimpsed the possibility of grinding "genes in a mortar" and cooking them "in a beaker." There existed too a continuing concern during this period to identify gene products chemically, working with flower pigments in plants and eye pigments in insects. Nonetheless, the chemical constitution of the gene remained vague, and geneticists were content to assume it was a protein of a special kind: one that can both catalyze its own reproduction (autocatalysis) and provide an enzyme that catalyzes a quite different reaction in the general metabolism of the cell (heterocatalysis.)

The protein nature of the gene was called into question in 1944 when three Rockefeller scientists, Ostwald Avery, Colin MacLeod, and Maclyn McCarty, published their identification of the so-called transforming principle as deoxyribonucleic acid (DNA). This principle, obtained from dead bacterial cells of one strain, was shown to transfer a characteristic from that strain to another strain. This extract contained only the minutest traces of protein; the rest was DNA. Geneticists knew about this work, but the majority assumed that the DNA was acting as a mutagen, altering the genetic constitution of the recipient cell, not transferring a gene. Evidence from other quarters was needed to shift the status quo. It came from the cytochemists and the phage biologists. The former discovered the correlation between the quantity of DNA in the nucleus and the number of chromosomes. Germ cells had half the content of body cells. Cells containing multiple sets of chromosomes (polyploids) had correspondingly raised DNA content. The same was not true of protein.

Phage biologists did not achieve as clean a transfer of DNA in their work as had Avery in his, but they were able to separate the functions of the protein and the nucleic acid of the phage particle, assigning the protein to the task of attaching to the host and causing it to burst (lyse), whereas the nucleic acid finds its way into the host and is used to constitute the progeny phage particles. By 1952 Alfred Hershey and Martha Chase at Cold Spring Harbor Laboratory could show that 85 percent of the parental DNA is present in the progeny particles. This result had an impact because of the visual evidence previously provided by the electron microscope of the sperm-like particles and their "ghosts" empty, their DNA contents removed.

Making the case for DNA acting as the repository of the genetic specificities of the organism called for establishing the kind of structure DNA possesses that would permit it to function thus. Known to be a long-chain molecule, its backbone composed of sugar rings attached to one another by phosphate arms, it has only four kinds of side-groups attached to the sugars—the bases adenine, guanine, thymine, and cytosine. This contrasts unfavorably with the proteins, for they have twenty different amino acids that can be arranged in countless different sequences.

The proposal of the double-helical model of DNA by James Watson and Francis Crick in 1953 overcame this difficulty because their structure, a cylindrical one with the four kinds of bases packed inside the two helically entwined sugar-phosphate backbones, permits any kind of sequence of the bases. Moreover, these bases are paired by weak bonds across from one base to its opposite number, adenine with thymine, guanine with cytosine. Watson and Crick therefore visualized the duplication of the gene as the result of separating the two chains of the parent double helix and attaching free bases to those now unpaired in accordance with the above complementary relations.

The work of Rosalind Franklin and Maurice Wilkins in London had not only aided Watson and Crick in devising their proposed structure, but when published alongside it offered crucial support. Yet it was not until 1958 that evidence from quite different approaches was published confirming predictions made from the model. Only then did interest in the structure become widespread. In genetics the work of Sydney Brenner, Francis Crick, Leslie Barnett, and R. J. Watts-Tobin, using mutagenesis in bacteriophage to establish the general nature of the genetic code, was published in 1961. It marked a success in applying the genetic approach to questions at the molecular level, for they showed that the genetic message is composed of triplets of bases, read from a fixed starting point, in only one direction, and without commas between the triplets. Meanwhile biochemists had been establishing the identity of the amino acids coded by given triplet sequences of bases.

It was the physicist George Gamow who had first suggested a DNA code for the amino acids in proteins. He had hoped

the right code could be established by mathematical reasoning but had to accept that nature does not use the most mathematically elegant solution. The amino acid sequences being discovered in proteins showed no limitations on the permutations of nearest neighbors of the kinds required by these mathematical codes. Hence the need to turn to the biochemists and the geneticists to solve the problem. They attacked it with vigor, and by 1966 the full details of the code were established. But the major transformation of genetics came with the introduction in the 1970s of the techniques of recombinant DNA technology that made directed manipulation of the genetic material possible.

## The Molecular Gene

It has been remarked that molecularizing the gene, far from establishing it as a discrete entity, had the opposite effect, fragmenting and destroying it. True, ever since the 1930s there had been discussion of what was euphemistically called "position effect"—the idea that a gene defined by its function can suffer two distinct mutations and that even if one normal example of the two mutated sites is present in the cell, the gene will only function when both lie on the same chromosome. The neat coincidence between the gene defined by function, by location, and by mutation was broken in these cases. But unraveling the mystery of protein synthesis, in which the function of the genes is to specify which amino acids are to be incorporated into the protein and in what order, revealed further complexity. It turned out that the genetic message (messenger RNA) from many genes is cut into parts, some fragments being rejected (known as introns) and the remainder (exons) incorporated into the chain that is transcribed into a sequence of amino acids. Different parts of the same message may thus be incorporated into different gene products. To those working in the field, these complexities are par for the course. The word *gene* has not died and been buried, but the context in which it is used tells the informed listener in what sense to understand the term. The simple conception of the Mendelian factor or gene of classical genetics has surely suffered a major series of revisions. The simple picture of genes like beads on a string, though essential to get a hand-hold on the problem, has not survived. But the early claim of Richard Goldschmidt that any discreteness of the gene be dropped, and that the chromosome be considered one continuous developmental unit, has never been accepted. There are codons in the DNA for starting and terminating the genetic message. Genes are interspersed with non-coding regions in the DNA. But the relation between the DNA and the proteins around it is a subtle and dynamic one.

Since Johannsen introduced the term "gene" first in 1909 it has served as a flexible concept, suffering many revisions and acquiring many meanings. In the process the extreme hereditarian view of DNA as dictating the life of the cell has been undermined by the discovery of a hierarchy of interactions between DNA and proteins. Genetics has in truth found its place at the core of biology, and in doing so it has revealed a machinery of the cell more intricate and subtle than could ever have been imagined.

See also **Biology; Eugenics; Evolution; Genetics: Contemporary; Health and Disease; Hygiene; Life; Medicine: Europe and the United States.**

## BIBLIOGRAPHY

PRIMARY SOURCES

Bateson, William. "After Dinner Speech." In *Report of the Third International Conference 1906 on Genetics: Hybridisation (Cross-Breeding of Genera or Species, the Cross-Breeding of Varieties, and General Plant Breeding)*, edited by the Reverend W. Wilks, 91. London: Royal Horticultural Society, 1907.

Corcos, Alain F., and Floyd V. Monaghan. *Gregor Mendel's Experiments on Plant Hybrids: A Guided Study.* New Brunswick, N.J.: Rutgers University Press, 1993.

Crick, Francis. *What Mad Pursuit: A Personal View of Scientific Discovery.* New York: Basic Books, 1988. See especially chapter 8, "The Genetic Code."

Crick, Francis H. C., Leslie Barnett, Sydney Brenner, and R. J. Watts-Tobin. "General Nature of the Genetic Code for Proteins." *Nature* 192 (1962): 1227–1232.

De Candolle, Alphonse. *Histoire des sciences et des savants depuis deux siècles, d'après l'opinion des principales académies ou sociétés scientifique.* Edited by Bruno Latour. Paris: Fayard, 1987.

Galton, Francis. *Inquiries into Human Faculty and Its Development.* London: Macmillan, 1883. (Quotation taken from the slightly altered reprint, London: Dent; and New York: Dutton, 1908.)

Johannsen, Wilhelm. "The Genotype Conception of Heredity." *American Naturalist* 45 (1911): 329–363.

Stern, Curt, and Eva R. Sherwood. *The Origin of Genetics: A Mendel Source Book.* San Francisco: Freeman, 1966.

Watson, James D. *The Double Helix: A Personal Account of the Discovery of the Structure of DNA.* Edited by Gunther S. Stent. New York: Norton Critical Editions, 1980.

Wilkins, Maurice. *The Third Man of the Double Helix.* Oxford and New York: Oxford University Press, 2003.

SECONDARY SOURCES

Adams, Mark B., ed. *The Wellborn Science: Eugenics in Germany, France, Brazil, and Russia.* New York: Oxford University Press, 1990. See especially Adams's essay "Towards a Comparative History of Eugenics," 217–231.

Allen, Garland, E. *Thomas Hunt Morgan: The Man and His Science.* Princeton. N.J.: Princeton University Press, 1978.

Baxter, A., and John Farley. "Mendel and Meiosis." *Journal of the History of Biology* 12 (1979): 137–173.

Beurton, Peter J., Raphael Falk, and Hans-Jörg Rheinberger, eds. *The Concept of the Gene in Development and Evolution: Historical and Epistemological Perspectives.* Cambridge, U.K., and New York: Cambridge University Press, 2000. See especially the essay on Seymour Benzer by Frederick L. Holmes.

Brock, Thomas D. *The Emergence of Bacterial Genetics.* Cold Spring Harbor, N.Y.: Cold Spring Harbor Laboratory, 1990.

Chadarevian, Soraya de. "Sequences, Conformations, Information: Biochemists and Molecular Biologists in the 1950s." *Journal of the History of Biology* 29 (1996): 361–386.

Gillham, Nicholas. *A Life of Sir Francis Galton: From African Exploration to the Birth of Eugenics.* New York: Oxford University Press, 2001.

Henig, Robin Marantz. *The Monk in the Garden: The Lost and Found Genius of Gregor Mendel, the Father of Genetics.* Boston: Houghton Mifflin, 2000.

Kevles, Daniel J. *In the Name of Eugenics: Genetics and the Uses of Human Genetics.* Cambridge, Mass., and London: Harvard University Press, 1995.

Kohler, Robert. *The Lords of the Fly: Drosophila Genetics and the Experimental Life.* Chicago: University of Chicago Press, 1994.

Magnello, M. Eileen. "The Non-Correlation of Biometrics and Eugenics: Rival Forms of Laboratory Work in Karl Pearson's Career at University College London." *History of Science* 37 (1999): 79–106, 123–150.

Meijer, Onno G. "De Vries No Mendelian." *Annals of Science* 42 (1985): 89–232.

Morange, Michel. *A History of Molecular Biology.* Translated by Matthew Cobb. Cambridge, Mass., and London: Harvard University Press, 1998.

Olby, Robert. "Constitutional and Hereditary Disorders." In *Companion Encyclopedia of the History of Medicine,* edited by W. F. Bynum and Roy Porter, 412–437. London and New York: Routledge, 1993.

———. "The Dimensions of Controversy: The Biometric-Mendelian Debate." *British Society for the History of Science* 22 (1989): 299–320.

———. "Horticulture: The Font for the Baptism of Genetics." *Nature Reviews Genetics* 1 (2000): 65–70.

———. "The Monk in the Garden, by Robin M. Henig." *Perspectives in Biology and Medicine* 46 (2003): 142–145.

———. *The Path to the Double Helix.* London: Macmillan, 1974.

Orel, Vítezslav. *Gregor Mendel: The First Geneticist.* Translated by Stephen Finn. Oxford and New York: Oxford University Press, 1996.

Paul, Diane B. *Controlling Human Heredity: 1865 to the Present.* Atlantic Highlands, N.J.: Humanities Press, 1995.

Peters, James A. *Classic Papers in Genetics.* Englewood Cliffs, N.J.: Prentice Hall, 1959.

Pick, Daniel. *Faces of Degeneration. A European Disorder, c. 1848–c. 1918.* Cambridge, U.K., and New York: Cambridge University Press, 1989.

Pinto-Correia, Clara. *The Ovary of Eve: Egg and Sperm and Preformation.* Chicago and London: University of Chicago Press, 1997.

Roe, Shirley A. *Matter, Life, and Generation: Eighteenth Century Embryology and the Haller-Wolff Debate.* Cambridge, U.K., and New York: 1981.

Roll, Hansen. "The Crucial Experiment of Wilhelm Johannsen." *Biology and Philosophy* 4 (1989): 303–329.

Russell, Nicholas. *Like Engend'ring Like: Heredity and Animal Breeding in Early Modern England.* Cambridge, U.K., and New York: Cambridge University Press, 1986.

Wood, Roger J., and Vítezslav Orel. *Genetic Prehistory in Selective Breeding: A Prelude to Mendel.* Baltimore: Johns Hopkins University Press, 2003.

*Robert Olby*

## CONTEMPORARY

One of the most startling and disturbing revelations from the Nuremburg Trials following World War II was the extent of the atrocities committed by the Nazi government in the name of genetics. Massive sterilizations and euthanasia programs for those deemed genetically unfit ("lives not worth living" in Nazi phraseology) had raised ethical issues about the use and abuse of science and the complicity of scientists at a level equaled only by that of development of the atomic bomb. By the end of the war, participation of physicists in the development of such a massively destructive force had already brought moral and ethical issues to the fore in a painful way. In a similar way, biologists—geneticists in particular—who had participated in the worldwide eugenics movement between 1910 and 1940 faced the enormous ethical and moral consequences of their pursuits. The legacy for those in the genetics community continues to be felt in the twenty-first century. Since the end of World War II it has become impossible to maintain the conventional myth of science as an ivory tower pursuit "following truth wherever it may lead." In Germany, many geneticists sought out ways to work for the Nazi cause, whether in research on eugenics or other biological problems such as germ warfare. In other countries, especially the United States, where eugenicists had struggled for over fifteen years to enact state compulsory sterilization laws for the "genetically unfit," there was widespread excitement (and a little envy) at the ease and rapidity with which German eugenicists and race hygienists passed a national eugenic sterilization law in 1933, only months after taking power.

This entry focuses on the ethical and moral issues raised by genetic technology during the whole of the twentieth century. The issues divide chronologically between the first and second halves of the century, associated with different genetic theories and technologies in each time period. Between 1900 and 1950, the science of genetics emerged as a professional field with enormous practical (agricultural, medical) and sociopolitical (race improvement) implications. This was the era in which heredity assumed center stage among the life sciences, beginning in 1900 with the rediscovery of Mendel's paper on hybridization in peas, originally published in 1866. As Mendel's generalizations were shown to apply to an ever-widening group of organisms, including humans, hopes ran high that at long last biologists would be able to solve the persistent problems of animal and plant breeding as well as understand the basis of many human physical and mental diseases. The new science was viewed with great esteem, as it also represented one of the first areas of biology to incorporate many of the characteristics of the physical sciences: experimentation, quantification, prediction, and mathematical analysis. Almost immediately, especially after 1910, the new Mendelian genetics was applied by a group of social reformers known as eugenicists to the solution of many seemingly intractable societal problems, from tuberculosis to "feeblemindedness," manic-depressive alcoholism, criminality, pauperism, and sexual perversion.

In the second half of the twentieth century a new genetic technology, molecular genetics, deriving from elucidation of the molecular structure of DNA and the mechanisms of replication and protein synthesis, led to a revival of many of the same sorts of agricultural, medical, and social hopes that had inspired classical geneticists fifty years earlier. In both periods new and exciting work in the laboratory led to a view of genetics as a "magic bullet" that would solve a host of agricultural, medical, and so-

cial ills. The argument that in the early twenty-first century we are not in danger of falling into the errors of the past because "we now know so much more" has a certain validity, since we do in fact know a great deal more about genetic mechanisms and the genetic basis of many diseases than in the 1920s or 1930s. But it is also true that the *use* to which our knowledge—or our still partial knowledge—is put continues to confront the same social, ethical, and legal issues that were raised in the early twentieth century. Thus, an understanding of both the historical and philosophical underpinnings of genetics since that time will provide the basis for evaluating issues in the twenty-first century: What are valid claims for the genetic basis of various traits (Huntington's disease versus intelligence or criminality)? How should genetic information be used in the public and private spheres? What sorts of genetic information should be stored as parts of a person's medical record? Who should have access to that record and under what conditions? Should humans be cloned to supposedly replace lost loved ones? Should embryos be cloned solely for providing replacement organs? Should stem cells be cultivated for medical and genetic therapies? Many of the twenty-first century's issues involve technologies that could not have been imagined in the early twentieth century. Yet the experience of those who have enthusiastically embraced the genetic technology of the day (past or present) without consideration of the full social, moral, and ethical issues involved can serve as a somber reminder that science must always be understood and used in its social context as a guide for exploring current genetics.

## Eugenics and the Ethical Issues of Selective Breeding (1900–1945)

The term *eugenics,* derived from the Greek *eugenes,* was first coined by the English mathematician and geographer Francis Galton (1822–1911) in his book *Inquiries into Human Faculty and Its Development* (1883) to refer to one born "good in stock, hereditarily endowed with noble qualities." As an intellectual and social movement in the early twentieth century, eugenics came to mean, in the words of one of its strongest American supporters, Charles B. Davenport (1866–1944), "the improvement of the human race by better breeding." For both Galton and Davenport, better breeding implied improving the hereditary quality of the human species by using the known scientific principles of heredity and selective mating. Eugenics movements were prominent in many countries of Western Europe, Canada, Latin America, and Asia, though they were strongest and most long-lived in the United States, Britain, Scandinavia, and Germany (where eugenic principles became one of the cornerstones of the Nazi state). Although some eugenics movements (France, Brazil) were based on non-Mendelian concepts of heredity (most notably neo-Lamarckism, or the inheritance of acquired characteristics), the majority operated within the new Mendelian paradigm: genes were seen as discrete hereditary units, each controlling a specific adult trait (such as eye color, height, or skin color, the so-called unit-character hypothesis). Although laboratory geneticists recognized by 1920 that genes often interacted with one another (epistasis), or that most genes affected a number of traits (pleiotropy), among eugenicists the unit-character concept held sway, especially in the United States, well into the 1930s.

Unlike genetic research on laboratory organisms (mice, fruit flies, corn) eugenic research involved studying inheritance in an organism that could not be bred under controlled conditions and that had so few offspring that statistically significant results were hard to come by. As a result, eugenicists were forced to use the correlation and family pedigree methods of investigation. Correlation studies were based on choosing particular traits, such as height, that could be correlated between groups of known genetic relatedness, for example parents and offspring. Strong correlations (0.7 or higher out of a total 1.0) suggested a significant relationship, which eugenicists interpreted as demonstrating a strong genetic component. The problem with this method was that while it applied to groups, it did not provide any way of assessing the genetic influence in any individual case. Thus it was of little value in the long run for eugenical purposes, where the aim was to identify individuals who should be encouraged to breed (what was called positive eugenics) or discouraged or prevented from breeding (what was called negative eugenics). The alternative methodology, family pedigree studies, involved tracing a given trait (or traits) through numerous generations of a family line. The advantage of this method was that it provided data for a specific family, and if the family were large enough, some general predictions might be made for future reproductive decisions (especially for relatively clear-cut traits such as hemophilia or Huntington's disease). The disadvantage of the pedigree method is that reliable information on the traits was often difficult to come by, and families were often not large enough to provide statistically significant numbers. Where social and personality traits were concerned, both methods suffered from problems of defining clearly and objectively the conditions, especially complex ones such as "criminality," "alcoholism," or "feeblemindedness." In addition, neither method had any way to separate out the effects of environment (families share lifestyles, including diets, exercise, use of alcohol, and so on, as well as genes), and without knowing the details of both the genetic and environmental components, assessing the relative influence of each on the adult trait becomes exceedingly difficult. Such problems did not bother many eugenicists, however, who often made bold claims about the genetic basis of feeblemindedness (measured as scoring below 70 on the standard IQ tests of the day), alcoholism, criminality, even thalassophilia ("love of the sea").

Eugenicists did not restrict their efforts solely to research. Many were actively interested or engaged in various educational and political activities. Many wrote popular articles or gave public lectures, and there were eugenics societies in most major industrialized countries. There were several major international eugenics organizations, and three international congresses (in 1912 in London, 1921 and 1932 in New York). On the political front, eugenicists lobbied successfully in Britain for the Mental Deficiency Act (1913) and in the United States for immigration restriction based on eugenic claims and for passage of compulsory eugenic sterilization laws in over thirty states. Eugenical sterilization became a major international eugenics crusade, including in Canada, Germany, and the Scandinavian countries. It is ironic that Germany was one of the last countries to adopt eugenical sterilization—only after the Nazis came to power in 1933. By that time the United States was leading the world in the total number of eugeni-

cally based compulsory sterilizations (somewhere around thirty thousand). Germany ultimately sterilized over ten times that number before sterilization evolved into euthanasia. In all cases, however, one of the main (though not the only) argument for sterilization was to prevent the individual from passing on his or her defective genes to the next generation. (Other frequently cited reasons included the claim that, especially in the case of those with mental defects, even if the child were normal the parent would not be fit to raise him or her). In most countries, but especially in the United States and Germany, the rationale for sterilization (as opposed to segregation) was economic and social efficiency. It was argued that states (and countries) were spending millions of dollars a year to house defectives who "should never have been born." The rational and efficient procedure would be to sterilize the adult defective and, where possible, return him or her to society, or at least, if they remained incarcerated, to be sure reproduction was impossible. In Germany genetically defective or other nonproductive people were referred to as "useless eaters."

The ethical as well as legal dimensions of compulsory sterilization raised many questions both at the time and in subsequent years. The eugenical sterilization laws in countries other than Germany were aimed exclusively at institutionalized persons, including the mentally ill, paupers, criminals, and the mentally defective (in other words, those who were called "feebleminded" at the time). This group often represented the poorest and most vulnerable elements of society, those least able to defend themselves. All countries' sterilization laws specified some sort of due process by which the sterilization decision was made, allowed for a family member or someone else to appear on behalf of the patient, and had some provisions for appeal. In most cases that have been studied historically, however, it appears that the proceedings of such courts or due process committees were often perfunctory. Particularly vulnerable for sterilization were children brought up for sterilization in reformatories, as they entered puberty. In some cases sterilization was a condition for being released; in others as a condition for remaining in the institution (a particularly powerful threat for families unable or unwilling to deal with a retarded or recalcitrant child at home).

The ethical problems encountered with sterilization involve both biological and moral claims. On the biological side, the evidence that many of the traits for which people were sterilized (feeblemindedness, pauperism, criminality, sexual promiscuity, aggression) had a genetic basis was circumstantial at best, nonexistent at worst. Since the methods for determining human heredity could not effectively separate out genetic from environmental effects, the claims that individuals who came from families with various defects would automatically "pass on" these traits was biologically unsound. The moral questions that arose revolved around whether sterilization was a "cruel and unusual punishment," whether tampering with reproductive capacity involved the state superseding its proscribed powers, whether the state should decide who is "defective" or not, and whether having a child was a "right" (more or less the traditional view) or a "privilege" (the eugenical view). Religious groups, especially the Catholic Church, were among the strongest critics of eugenics, especially on the sterilization issue.

In 1930 a papal encyclical, "Casti connubii," specifically targeted eugenical sterilization as violating Catholic doctrine. After Nuremberg, the issue became even more clear with regard to the state's right to determine who should and who should not be parents. The line has remained a fuzzy one, however, since it is generally accepted that the state has the right to regulate matters of public health: on the grounds that reproducing defective offspring constituted a public health hazard, it was argued that eugenic sterilization fell under a public health aegis. In setting out the majority opinion in the well-known 1927 Supreme Court case of *Buck v. Bell,* which tested the constitutionality of Virginia's eugenical sterilization law, Chief Justice Oliver Wendell Holmes argued that compulsory sterilization of genetically defective individuals could be justified by the same public health principle that required compulsory vaccination. Eugenics stood for the right of the community to safeguard itself against certain wasteful expenditures over the automatic right of the individual to bring children into the world.

### DNA, Genomics, and the New Ethical Dilemmas

In many respects the genetic technology that has grown up around the elucidation of the molecular structure of DNA since 1953 has raised even more ethical and moral questions than its predecessor in the classical Mendelian era. The rapid and exciting development of molecular genetics in the period from 1953 to 1970 provided the basis for understanding aspects of genetics at the molecular level that had only been imagined by prewar geneticists. Understanding how DNA replicates itself and how genes control cell function by coding for proteins that serve both structural and catalytic (enzymatic) roles, the nature and universality of the genetic code itself, and the way in which genes are controlled (turned on and off during development) all suggested that soon human beings would be able to engineer organisms in almost any conceivable direction. Indeed, the term *genetic engineering* was coined during the 1960s and early 1970s to express the new hope and excitement held forth by the understanding of molecular mechanisms of heredity.

As with the rapid advances in Mendelian and chromosome genetics in the 1920s and 1930s, so with the advancement of molecular genetics; new genetic discoveries were being announced almost weekly. Although many theories of molecular genetics came and went, they were all subject to being tested and accepted or rejected. For example, initial claims about how transcription (forming messenger RNA from a DNA strand) and translation (using the messenger to synthesize a specific protein), based on work with prokaryotic (bacterial) systems, proved to have many differences from the same process in eukaryotic cells (as in all cells of higher organisms). Bacterial and viral chromosomes turned out to be organized quite differently from the chromosomes of the fruit fly or the human. The statement that "what is true for *E. coli* [a common bacterium used for molecular genetic research] is true for the elephant," as molecular biologist Jacques Monod put it, turned out to be not quite that simple. But yet there did appear to be an evolutionary unity among all forms of life on earth that was even more apparent at the molecular level than at the level of gross phenotype.

The application of the new genetics to practical concerns, both in agriculture and medicine, raised a number of social, political, and ethical issues, some of which overlapped with concerns from the classical era and some of which were quite new to the molecular era. At the agricultural level, one of the first great controversies to emerge concerned the technology for transferring genes from one organism to another. The common method for doing this was to use a bacterial or viral plasmid (a small chromosome-like element of DNA) as a "vector." An isolated segment of DNA from one type of organism could be inserted into the plasmid, which, because of its size, could be incorporated into another cell type and eventually integrated into the host cell's genome. This meant that the foreign, or transplant, DNA would subsequently be replicated every time the DNA of the host cell replicated. Characteristics such as insect, mold, and frost resistance could thus be genetically engineered by transferring DNA (genes) from a species that had one of these traits of great commercial value. The controversies arising from the appearance of this technology reached significant proportions in the early 1980s in Cambridge, Massachusetts, where much of the experimental work was being carried out by Harvard and Massachusetts Institute of Technology biologists. Fear that viral plastids could "get loose" into the community through the massive use of the new technology sparked a series of public meetings and calls for a moratorium on all genetic engineering until safeguards could be assured. A meeting of many of the leading biotechnological researchers at Asilomar, California, in 1975 brought to the fore a discussion of the potential hazards from inserting genes from one kind of organism into the genome of another. Although hailed as one of the boldest exercises in social responsibility by scientists since World War II, interestingly enough, the most dangerous use of the new biotechnology—that is, to create biological weapons—was discussed). Later guidelines incorporated into all grants funded by the National Institutes of Health were based on some of the early decisions among molecular biologists themselves.

Especially in the agricultural realm, the issue of "genetically modified organisms" (GMOs) became a matter of global concern in the 1980s and 1990s. Although the use of viral and bacterial plasmids turned out not to pose as serious a threat as originally thought, critics of biotechnology argued that GMOs could have altered metabolic characteristics in a way that could adversely affect the physiology of the consumer and of the environment at large. One such case became a cause célèbre in 1999 when it was found that corn genetically modified to contain a bacterial gene, Bt, that made the corn insect resistant, was killing off monarch butterflies in various localities in Britain where the corn was being planted. Indeed, as megacorporations such as Monsanto and others turned aggressively to exploiting the GMO market, many countries, especially those in the European Union and Africa, began to place restrictions on, or even ban, the sale or importation of GMOs within their borders. The issue was less the effect on a specific species such as the monarch butterfly than the fact that destruction of the monarch symbolized a major problem with GMOs: as a result of competitive pressure from rival companies they were often rushed onto the market without thorough testing. Long-standing distrust of corporate agribusiness, where quick profits have been seen as taking precedence over human health and the quality of the environment, has fueled much of the negative response to GMOs worldwide.

Equally as important has been the issue of using human subjects in genetic research. The problem of "informed consent," never something biologists routinely worried about prior to World War II (though some were scrupulous about informing their subjects about the nature of the research in which they were involved) became a central aspect of the ethics of all human subject research protocols from the 1970s onward. All universities and hospitals engaged in any sort of human genetics (or other) research now have internal review boards (IRBs) responsible for overseeing projects in which human subjects are involved. With regard to genetic information about individuals, the issue of consent is meant not only to insure that individual subjects understand the nature of the research of which they are a part, and to insure their safety, but also to place tight restrictions on who has access to the resulting information. A particular concern regarding genetic information about people in clinical studies is whether individual subjects could be identified from examining published or unpublished reports, notebooks, or other documents. Preserving anonymity has become a hallmark of all modern genetic research involving human subjects.

The question of accessibility of genetic information has had ramifications in another aspect of medicine as well as that of designing research protocols. As testing for genes known to be related to specific human genetic diseases, such as sickle-cell anemia, Huntington's disease, or cystic fibrosis (CF) has been made available to clinicians, two questions have loomed large, especially in the United States: the accuracy of the tests (that is, incidence of false positives) and the question of who should have access to the information. Fears that genetic information might lead to job or health care discrimination have surfaced throughout the United States as genetic screening programs have become more technically feasible and thus more frequently employed. Perhaps the more general concern is the potential for insurance companies to obtain, or even require, genetic testing of adults as the basis for medical coverage, or harkening back to what seems like an almost eugenic-like view of testing fetuses, with the threat of loss of coverage if a fetus with a known genetic defect is born. Medical insurance companies in the past have tried to classify genetic diseases as "prior conditions" that are thus exempt from coverage. Most of these attempts have not been carried through, but the threat is there and raises a host of legal as well as social and psychological concerns. As of 2004 a small number (seven) of states in the United States have passed legislation specifically prohibiting insurers from denying coverage to individuals based on genetic data.

**Human Behavior Genetics**
In the latter half of the twentieth century a field known as behavior genetics came to prominence, focusing largely on animal models (fruit flies, mice, honeybees, spiders). Specific behaviors, such as *Drosophila* mating dances, were observed to involve several different genetic components, a mutation in any one of which could alter the course and outcome of the mat-

ing response. Inevitably attempts were made to apply similar claims to complex human behavior—indeed, to many of the same behaviors that had been the subject of investigation by eugenicists a half century earlier. Starting the late 1960s an upsurge in claims about the genetic basis of traits such as IQ, alcoholism, schizophrenia, manic depression, criminality, violence, shyness, homosexuality, and more newly named traits such as attention deficit hyperactivity disorder (ADHD), obsessive-compulsive disorder (OCD) and "risk taking" became widespread in both clinical and popular literature. Many of these newer studies were carried out by psychologists and psychiatrists employing the more traditional methods of family, twin, or adoption studies, correlated with genetic markers, that is, marker regions of chromosomes or DNA. Many of these studies attracted controversy that threw doubts on much of the methodology on which the current human behavior genetics is based. Among the controversial studies were those published in 1969 by the Berkeley psychologist Arthur Jensen claiming that IQ is 80 percent heritable, based on data collected over a half century by the British psychologist Cyril Burt (later claimed to be spurious or even falsified); a study published in the late 1980s by the Minnesota psychologist Thomas Bouchard of identical twins raised apart, which claimed that traits such as liking John Wayne movies, having wives with the same names, or driving identical cars are genetic in origin (no similar results have been confirmed by other researchers); and a 1994 study by Dean Hamer that claimed to have found a genetic marker associated with homosexuality in thirty-three out of forty pairs of gay brothers but that could not be replicated by a separate lab study using a different study population.

The same methodological problems that confronted eugenicists has confronted many of these current theories: difficulty in defining behaviors in a clear manner; treating complex behaviors as if they were a single entity; the difficulty of separating out familial and cultural inheritance from biological inheritance; the problematic use of statistics, especially "heritability"; and difficulty in replicating the results of one study using a different population. As in the eugenic period, critics of hereditarian studies have argued that despite the uncertainty of the conclusions, the widespread dissemination of the results as positive outcomes serves the social function of distracting attention from social and economic reforms that might go a long way toward altering the prevalence of certain "problem" behaviors. As Thomas Hunt Morgan (1866–1945), the first Nobel laureate in genetics (1933) stated in 1925: "In the past we could have bred for greater resistance to cholera or disease; but it was quicker and more satisfactory to clean up the environment." Many fear that modern claims for a genetic basis of many social problems will serve as a smokescreen for "cleaning up the environment" by blaming societal problems on the "defective biology" of individuals.

**Cloning and Stem Cell Research**
With increased research in molecular genetics per se two related technologies have come to the fore as centers of ethical concern: cloning and research on embryonic stem cells. Cloning is the process of creating a new organism that is a carbon copy of an already existing organism. In one sense cloning

is not a new technology, since bacterial and all other asexually reproducing organisms reproduce in clones (a bacterial colony is a clone, as are tissue cultures that have been used for decades in biological research). What is new in the controversy about cloning in the twenty-first century is the prospect of producing a higher organism such as a mammal or human being from a single cell of an already existing adult organism. In 1997 Dolly the sheep became the most sensational and well-known example of a cloned organism. Dolly was produced by removing the nucleus from the egg cell of one female sheep and causing that enucleated cell to fuse with an adult cell from (with its nucleus intact) a different donor sheep. The new "hybrid" egg cell contained a full set of chromosomes from the donor and thus would develop into a genetic replica of the donor. While transplanting nuclei from one variety of animal to another had been accomplished with amphibians in the early 1950s, nothing of the sort had been accomplished with mammals until the mid-1990s. The advantage of cloning for agriculture is clear: the genetic composition of the offspring is completely predictable (which is not true in conventional breeding methods). The major biological question raised by Dolly was whether cloned organisms are as healthy and long-lived as ones produced by natural fertilization of an egg by a sperm. As it turned out, Dolly showed signs of early aging, a result perhaps of the fact that the donor cell came from a six-year-old ewe, who was already halfway through the sheep's natural life span. The chromosomes of mammals gradually shorten at the ends (telomeres) with aging, a process that is not completely understood but which appears to have important implications for cloning from already aging adult cells.

The leap from Dolly to cloning humans and other mammals (businesses sprang up offering to clone family pets, for example) was quick in coming. Among the ethical problems raised here was the expectation that by having an organism with the same genetic composition it was going to be a replica in every way of the adult from which the donor cell was taken. With humans or pets this meant to many people having a new individual with the same personality and behavioral traits as the donor. Such expectations were based on a simplistic understanding of genetics, especially with regard to complex characteristics such as behavior and personality. One of the important lessons of modern genetic research has been that genes do not unfold automatically into an adult trait. Genes interact with other genes and with the environment to produce a number of variant outcomes, so that a genetic clone would no more behave like its progenitor than any two organisms of the same species.

Cloning humans, of course, raises all sorts of other ethical issues, particularly those surrounding what has come to be known as fetal selection. What does it mean if parents want to control so completely all the physical and physiological, not to say psychological, characteristics of their children? Bioethicists raise the question of how far engineering human traits should be allowed to go. Would it be permissible to clone an embryo from a person who needs a kidney or liver transplant just to get an immunologically compatible organ? Is an embryo produced by cloning really a human being, since it has not been formed by union of egg and sperm? If the answer is yes, then should cloning and bringing the embryo to full term be allowed? Should we be able to clone a terminally ill child in order to provide a replacement? These are not simple questions, but as the technology becomes more certain and available (as it no doubt will) the social and ethical questions must be faced critically and squarely.

Stem cell research poses many of the same problems raised by cloning, but it has a more realistic and immediate medical application as well as some distinct ethical issues of its own. Stem cells are undifferentiated embryo-like cells that are found in various tissues of the adult body. Among the earliest recognized and prolific stem cells are those in bone marrow, but biologists have now found stem cells even in brain tissue that has previously been regarded as incapable of regeneration. What has attracted so much attention about stem cells is that for the most part they have retained the ability to differentiate into a variety of other specialized cells. This is particularly true of embryonic stem cells, which are the most totipotent (capable of differentiation into virtually all other body cell types) of all stem cells. Research into how to culture and deliver stem cells to specific tissues in individuals suffering from particular diseases (for example providing brain stem cells to a person with Alzheimer's or to someone who has suffered brain damage from a stroke) thus offers considerable potential for treating conditions that are now considered incurable. Creating embryos by cloning and growing them just long enough to harvest embryonic stem cells would provide the most ready source of totipotent cells. But many ethicists and religious leaders claim that such embryos *are* truly human beings and that to grow them only for stem cells, like growing them only for organs and tissues, would amount to murder. Issues like this surfaced after biologists began using existing embryonic stem cell lines for research (derived from frozen embryos left over from fertility clinics) with the result that U.S. President George W. Bush banned the production of any more embryos specifically for the purpose of culturing stem cells (an existing 1993 law had prevented the use of any tax dollars for research on human embryos). The questions of how a human life is defined, at what point in the biological life cycle does it become "human," and, regardless of how we define it, how to form humane social and legal policies regarding early human embryos as research objects are all issues about which there is a great deal of current disagreement. Biomedical researchers and many others think that early embryos (less that twelve weeks) should be available for research purposes, while many political conservatives and religious spokespeople oppose the use of *any* human embryo that has the capability of developing normally into a fetus. Many countries of Europe, especially England, have been more liberal with their policies regarding embryonic stem cell research, with the consequence that some U.S. researchers have either moved or have contemplated moving their laboratories abroad.

## Conclusion

New genetic technologies, whether those associated the classical genetics of the first half of the twentieth century or the molecular genetics and genomics of the second half, have always raised a wide variety of ethical issues within the larger society. Whether genetic knowledge is being used politically to place blame for social problems on "defective biology" or genetic engineering technologies are being used to produce "designer babies," geneticists have continually found themselves in the midst of highly controversial issues, ones that are often far more difficult and complex than those associated with other biomedical technologies. This may be in part a result of the long-standing, though mistaken, view that "genetics is destiny" and that knowing the genotype (genetic makeup) of an organism can lead to accurate predictions about its ultimate phenotype (that is, what actual traits will appear and in what form). But it is also in part due to Western society's optimistic faith that science and technology can provide answers to larger economic and social issues. This is an unrealistic view of what role scientific and technological information can play in human life. There is no question that knowing the science involved in any given area of biomedicine (especially human genetics) is critical for making social and political decisions. But it is never enough. Even if scientists could predict with complete accuracy the exact clinical effects that would characterize a fetus with Down's syndrome or Huntington's disease, the decision about how to respond to that knowledge would involve social, political, economic, and philosophical considerations that lie outside of the science itself. As much as anything else, consideration of the ethical and moral aspects of genetic technology should be a reminder that science itself is not, nor has it ever been, a magic bullet for the solution of social problems. Nowhere has that been demonstrated more clearly than in the history of genetics in the twentieth century.

*See also* **Behaviorism; Bioethics; Biology; Determinism; Eugenics; Genetics: History of; Health and Disease; Medicine: Europe and the United States; Nature.**

### BIBLIOGRAPHY

Allen, Garland E. "The Ideology of Elimination: American and German Eugenics, 1900–1945." In *Medicine and Medical Ethics in Nazi Germany: Origins, Practices, Legacies,* edited by Francis R. Nicosia and Jonathan Huener, 13–39. New York: Berghahn Books, 2002.

Goodman, Alan H., Deborah Heath and M. Susan Lindee. *Genetic Nature/Culture: Anthropology and Science beyond the Two-Culture Divide.* Berkeley: University of California Press, 2003.

Kevles, Daniel J. *In the Name of Eugenics.* New York: Knopf, 1985.

Maienschein, Jane. *Whose View of Life? Embryos, Cloning and Stem Cells.* Cambridge, Mass.: Harvard University Press, 2003.

Paul, Diane B. *Controlling Human Heredity, 1865 to the Present.* Atlantic Highlands, N.J.: Humanities Press, 1995.

Weir, Robert F., Susan C. Lawrence, and Evan Fales, eds. *Genes and Human Self-Knowledge: Historical and Philosophical Reflections on Modern Genetics.* Iowa City: University of Iowa Press, 1994.

*Garland E. Allen*

**GENIUS.** The notion of genius as it is known in the early twenty-first century emerged most fully during the eighteenth-century Enlightenment period. Although the idea of genius was around before the time of Immanuel Kant (1724–1804), Kant most clearly defined it in the late eighteenth century in his third critique, *The Critique of Judgment.* In fact, Kant's discussion still influences contemporary notions of genius. Kant opposed genius to a notion of *taste.* Genius, Kant says, is "the exemplary originality of the natural endowments of an individual in the free employment of his cognitive faculties" (p. 181). Genius is a natural human ability; it is not measurable or traceable, and the vagaries of language cannot adequately articulate it. Genius cannot define itself. Genius must, nonetheless, inspire imitation, so that the concept of the product of that genius may be derivatively articulated. Genius must inspire concept, but it cannot conceptualize.

To the function of taste is accorded the responsibility of conceptualizing the products of genius. Kant wrote that "taste, like judgment in general, is the discipline (or corrective) of genius. It severely clips its wings, and makes it orderly or polished; but at the same time it gives it guidance directing and controlling its flight, so that it may preserve its character of finality" (p. 183). Taste is a matter of judgment, a critical faculty that works in relation to genius. In contrast, genius is a matter of imagination. In Kant's model, taste and genius work together dialectically: taste shapes and guides genius, whereas genius creates fine art precisely by working free "from all guidance of rules" (p. 180). In Friedrich Nietzsche's (1844–1900) view, the genius is in fact a criminal, because he or she works outside conventional standards.

Kant's notion of genius is still quite viable in the academic institutions of the twenty-first century. Most English departments, for instance, continue to categorize their curricula according to "literature"—or the critical study of literature—and "creative writing." The underlying assumption of this organization is that creation of art is one thing, the critical assessment of art entirely another.

Genius, above all, was for the eighteenth century and even much of the nineteenth century *ahistorical:* although still considered human, the genius artist was not thought by eighteenth-century thinkers to be confined to social, political, or historical circumstances. The genius artist was judged to be so to the degree that she or he realized *universal* values or truths. An entirely Romantic notion, genius emerged contemporaneously with the idea of *the self,* the free and creatively self-sustaining individual of classical liberalism. The genius artist, like the self in classical liberalism, was thought to be a spontaneous creator, in a nearly divine sense. Seventeenth-century philosopher René Descartes (1596–1650) proved the veracity of his existence merely by asserting, "I think, therefore I am." It is this lionization of the human ability to reason from which the notion of genius gained its energy. If the human self is powerful enough to reason, then the human self is powerful enough to create *ex nihilo.*

## Genius in the Twentieth Century

Although much eighteenth-century thought about genius continues to be retained in academic institutions as well as in popular culture, late-twentieth-century critics returned to reconsider the category of genius in the light of contemporary critical trends. Literary criticism was dominated in the latter half of the twentieth century by poststructuralism, a critical school the major by-product of which is the critique of *discourse.* The meaning of any linguistic utterance always exceeds the utterance itself; there is always more meaning in any text than may be apprehended by simply understanding the words. This excess meaning, the poststructuralists say, is socially, historically, and politically determined and produced. With this critical apparatus, critics have reconsidered the category of genius of the eighteenth and nineteenth centuries as a *discursive* formation. That is, current critics see the notion of genius as an idea that was shaped, indeed constructed, by the social, political, and historical circumstances of the Enlightenment.

In addition to the poststructuralist idea that meaning is produced, the twentieth-century philosopher and critic Jacques Derrida (b. 1930), in his theory that is now called *deconstruction,* has pointed out that all of Western thinking is predicated on a system of binary oppositions, such as good and evil, man and woman, white and black. More important, Derrida argues that one component of these Western oppositions is always prioritized over the other. Good is always better than evil, white is always better than black, and man is always better than woman. Likewise, reason has always, for nearly the entire span of recorded Western history, been prioritized over feeling. Both Aristotle and Plato valued reason above emotion; these Aristotelian and Platonic ideas were revived by Renaissance thinkers in the fourteenth and fifteenth centuries. By the eighteenth century the priority of reason was fully entrenched. Western culture has not yet let it go. Derrida's principal contribution was to point out that all the prioritized components in Western oppositions tend to enjoy similar advantage. Reason, prioritized over emotion, is thus a predominantly male characteristic. Genius, with its divine ability to create, was on a par with the divine ability to reason; likewise, genius was associated with masculinity and with men's superior ability to reason. While Kant opposed genius to taste, this opposition did not obtain in the discursive formation of genius. Rather, genius, in its association with human power (of reason and creation), became notably opposed to sentiment.

But even before the poststructuralism of the latter part of the twentieth century, feminists were already beginning to ascertain the historical vicissitudes of genius. Virginia Woolf, in her remarkable 1929 book *A Room of One's Own,* conducts a lively thought experiment, imagining that Shakespeare had a sister named Judith and wondering what life would have been like for her. After considering all the social constraints placed on an Englishwoman of the sixteenth century, Woolf concludes that "a highly gifted girl who had tried to use her gift for poetry would have been so thwarted and hindered by other people, so tortured and pulled asunder by her own contrary instincts, that she must have lost her health and sanity to a certainty" (p. 49). Woolf points to the unevenness of history's representation of genius; she identifies the sociohistorical circumstances that determined which writers would be published and read, and what those writers would write about. And although Woolf wrote before Derrida, Derrida's critique of Western culture applies.

Woolf, however, does not identify genius itself as a discursive formation, because she still believes in it, and argues for the genius of women writers; but she does indicate the way in which women were not allowed to realize their genius until around the nineteenth century. While Woolf rightly identifies the exclusion of women writers from "high culture," she does not consider "genius" itself to be a discursively formed masculine category. For Woolf, poetry is the "high culture" into which women ought to be admitted. Although Woolf recognizes the gendering of genre, she fails to recognize the gender of genius. A deconstructive reading, by contrast, identifies genius as a prioritized oppositional category; moreover, the category of "high culture" is prioritized in its opposition to "popular culture."

In the late twentieth- and early twenty-first centuries critics have considered genius precisely through the critical lens of gender. Literary reviewers most often relegated women writers of the nineteenth century to the category of sentimentalism. In Derrida's register, genius was opposed to sentiment, with the concomitant prioritization of genius. In nineteenth-century evaluations of artists, genius and sentiment worked as a gender-determined opposition. Woolf is aware of this opposition in *A Room of One's Own.* She evaluates the novel as the likely genre for women writers such as Jane Austen and Emily Brontë because of the novel's propensity for feeling and sentiment. Yet Woolf wishes for women to realize their genius in *poetry*—she seems not to notice the genderedness of genius, as do late-twentieth-century critics. Historically, genius was, gender studies critics maintain, a territory mapped out for masculine writers. The categories of domesticity and sentiment emerged as a standard for evaluating women's writing that excluded women from the "high culture" of genius.

Queer theorists have taken this work in the gender of genius and explored the ways in which nineteenth-century constructions of genius actually crossed gender lines. The critic Gustavus Stadler has found that many male authors were consumptives and victims of affect, indulgences that the literary community was generally content to allow its genius writers. These afflictions were typically associated with the feminine gender; the degree to which male "geniuses" were afflicted with these tendencies suggests the way in which "genius" routinely crossed the gender divide in the nineteenth century. Stadler points out that, "It is on this queer turf [of genius], in which famous literary men become madwomen and dying girls enable women to become public authors, that the discourse of genius holds the most promise for disrupting and diversifying the assumptions about gender and sexuality that undergird our understanding of nineteenth-century American literature" (p. 662).

Critics have also noted the ways in which conventions and styles of writing were overtly gendered by nineteenth-century literary movers and shakers. For instance, Andrew Elfenbein has noted that women writers were considered poor writers if they engaged in "literary cross-dressing" (p. 931)—if, that is, they wrote in genres that were the reserved province of male writers, or wrote in a style usually thought of as masculine. In short, women were supposed to write about private life, domesticity, and matters exclusively feminine in concern. Some writers, however, did cross-dress, Elfenbein tells us, such as Mary Wollstonecraft, who thought that genius was a combination of masculine characteristics, such as logical thinking and intense concentration, with feminine qualities, such as emotionality and loss of control. Here in Wollstonecraft can be seen an attempt to deconstruct the traditional oppositions associated with nineteenth-century notions of genius.

*See also* **Creativity in the Arts and Sciences; Enlightenment; Person, Idea of the.**

### BIBLIOGRAPHY

PRIMARY SOURCES

Kant, Immanuel. *The Critique of Judgment.* Translated by James Creed Meredith. Oxford: Clarendon, 1952. The best translation in English.

Woolf, Virginia. *A Room of One's Own.* Foreword by Mary Gordon. San Diego, Calif.: Harcourt Brace Jovanovich, 1929.

SECONDARY SOURCES

Battersby, Christine. *Gender and Genius: Towards a Feminist Aesthetics.* Bloomington: Indiana University Press, 1989. Writers often refer to this text for a discussion of gender and genius.

Bromwich, David. *A Choice of Inheritance: Self and Community from Edmund Burke to Robert Frost.* Cambridge, Mass.: Harvard University Press, 1989. See especially "Reflections on the Word *Genius*," 20–42.

Elfenbein, Andrew. "Lesbianism and Romantic Genius: The Poetry of Anne Bannerman." *English Literary History* 63, no. 4 (1996): 929–957.

Murray, Penelope, ed. *Genius: The History of an Idea.* Oxford: Basil Blackwell, 1989. This volume is a comprehensive study of the history of genius from antiquity to postmodernism. It also examines the role of genius across several disciplines, from literature to psychiatry.

Stadler, Gustavus. "Louisa May Alcott's Queer Geniuses." *American Literature* 71, no. 4 (1999): 657–677.

*Valerie Holliday*

**GENOCIDE.** Mass slaughter of human beings by other human beings has been a recurrent phenomenon over the centuries, but until recently neither governments nor international legal specialists had sought to devise formal rules and institutions that could help prevent, or if necessary punish, the perpetrators of large-scale atrocities. Massacres that took place during and immediately after World War I, when Turks killed hundreds of thousands of Armenians, and the systematic annihilation of millions of Jews and hundreds of thousands of Gypsies (Roma) by Nazi Germany during World War II, gave rise to the concept of *genocide,* which is defined by *Merriam-Webster's Collegiate Dictionary* as "the deliberate and systematic destruction of a racial, political, or cultural group." Scholars have differed in their analyses of the concept, but the most widely accepted understanding of genocide pertains to the deliberate slaughter of vast numbers of human beings.

### Origins and Evolution of the Concept

The term *genocide* was coined in the mid-1940s by Raphael Lemkin (1900–1959), a lawyer of Polish Jewish origin who escaped from Poland after the Nazis occupied it in September 1939. Lemkin fled to Lithuania and then to Sweden before eventually reaching the United States in April 1941. In November 1944 he published a lengthy book, *Axis Rule in Occupied Europe,* which exhaustively documented the legal basis of the Nazis' policies of mass extermination, deportations, and slave labor. The book is best remembered nowadays for Lemkin's use of the new word *genocide.* He settled on that term after much deliberation and defined it as "a coordinated plan of different actions aiming at the destruction of essential foundations of the life of national groups, with the aim of annihilating the groups themselves." Because the word became indelibly associated with the Nazi Holocaust, it promptly gained wide currency as the standard by which to judge human destructiveness. Lemkin himself, however, never believed that the term should refer only to carnage and atrocities of the magnitude perpetrated by the Nazis against Jews. He wanted it to encompass all attempts to destroy cultural or ethnic identities, regardless of whether the perpetrators were seeking to exterminate every member of the targeted group.

From the time Lemkin's book appeared, the term genocide has stirred controversy both in the public arena and among scholars. Lawyers, scholars, and political leaders have differed over the scope and nature of the crimes involved. Some, like Lemkin, have sought as broad a definition as possible, not limiting it to large-scale killing. Others, including many prominent historians and political scientists, have advocated a more restrictive definition, focusing on clear-cut cases of mass slaughter and attempts at systematic extermination. Still others have questioned whether genocide necessarily requires the targeting of a specific cultural, ethnic, racial, or linguistic group. Scholars who express reservations about this last point have argued that if genocide depends on the targeting of a particular cultural or ethnic group, slaughters such as those perpetrated by the Khmer Rouge in Cambodia in 1977–1978—with a death toll as high as 1.5 million—would not be covered. By the same token, many of the atrocities committed in the Soviet Union under Joseph Stalin or in China under Mao Zedong would not be classed as genocide if the target had to be a specific ethnic or cultural group. Although Stalin did carry out mass deportations of nationalities in the 1930s and 1940s, most of his other violent abuses, affecting tens of millions of people, were not directed against ethnic groups per se. The same is true of most of the slaughters and systematic atrocities perpetrated in China under Mao. By excluding many of the worst abuses and crimes of the twentieth century, the requirement of a targeted cultural or ethnic group has arguably been the most controversial aspect of the concept of genocide.

To help fill these crucial gaps, Barbara Harff and Ted R. Gurr have argued that the concept of *politicide* should supplement genocide. Politicide, as Harff and Gurr define it, refers to the killing of groups of people who are targeted not because of shared ethnic or communal traits, but because of "their hierarchical position or political opposition to the regime and dominant groups" (p. 360). Similarly, Rudolph Rummel has suggested that the term *democide* could cover all intentional killing of unarmed civilians by governments. According to Rummel, democide includes the slaughter of cultural and ethnic groups, the massacring of politically marginal groups, and all other government-sponsored killing of unarmed civilians. The concept has come under criticism for being too amorphous, but Rummel has sought to refine it in a number of books. Although neither "politicide" nor "democide" has been widely adopted by other scholars, the coinage of these terms highlights the continuing dissatisfaction with the term *genocide*.

One other issue that has sparked occasional disagreement is whether genocide must be deliberate from the start. This question has been most often raised in analyses of devastating famines such as the one that occurred in southern regions of the Soviet Union in 1932–1933 or in Ireland in the 1840s. The Soviet famine, which killed as many as four million Ukrainians, a million Russians, and a million Kazakhs, resulted from policies adopted by Stalin to crush the Soviet peasantry and to force the collectivization of agriculture. Some scholars, such as Nicolas Werth and Andrea Gnaziosi, have argued that even if Stalin did not set out to kill so many people, the famines were the inevitable result of his policies. They also have pointed out that when Stalin learned that vast numbers of people were dying of starvation, he took steps to keep peasants from escaping the affected regions, thereby consigning them to certain death.

The Soviet famine has come up particularly often in discussions of genocide because of what some writers, such as Robert Conquest, perceive as the deliberate targeting of Ukrainians (though it should be noted that, proportionally, more Kazakhs than Ukrainians died in the famine). Other specialists such as Jean-Louis Margolin have argued that even when famines do not affect concentrated ethnic or cultural groups, the deaths may still amount to genocide. Among the examples cited by those who subscribe to this view are the terrible famines in China in the late 1950s that resulted from Mao's Great Leap Forward policies. Although Mao undoubtedly did not foresee that the Great Leap Forward would cause tens of millions of people to die of starvation, he failed to take any remedial action even when he became aware of the scale of the suffering. Hence, scholars such as Margolin have argued that the death toll during the Great Leap Forward should be added to the millions of other victims whom Mao deliberately set out to kill.

**The Genocide Convention**
Revelations at the end of World War II about the scale of the Nazi Holocaust spurred an effort within the newly created United Nations (UN) to set up an international legal convention that would prohibit genocide and require signatory governments to take all necessary steps to prevent or halt it. Although political leaders were initially slow in moving on the issue, Lemkin did his best to keep the issue on the UN's agenda. He repeatedly called on the world's governments to establish a legal framework that would apply to all acts of genocide, not just to those committed during interstate wars. In December 1946 the UN General Assembly unanimously

adopted a resolution denouncing genocide as "the denial of the right of existence of entire human groups" and describing it as "contrary to moral law and to the spirit and aims of the United Nations." The resolution also set up a committee to draft an international treaty that would formally outlaw genocide. The result, after protracted and often arduous negotiations, was the Convention on the Prevention and Punishment of the Crime of Genocide, which was approved by the UN General Assembly on a 55-to-0 vote in December 1948. The Genocide Convention was slated to enter into force after twenty of the fifty-five UN member-states that voted in favor of it submitted their formal instruments of ratification. Although some signatories of the convention, notably the United States, took many years before they ratified it, ratification by the twentieth country was completed in October 1950, allowing the convention to take effect in January 1951.

The Genocide Convention defines genocide as "acts committed with intent to destroy, in whole or in part, a national, ethnical, racial or religious group." In giving examples of the type of "acts" encompassed by this phrasing, the convention makes clear that genocide can occur even if no one has carried out (or intends to carry out) "mass killings." The definition in the convention is largely in keeping with Lemkin's own preference for the broadest possible scope. It also is in keeping with Lemkin's belief that genocide is targeted against an ethnic, religious, or racial group, and that the motives of the perpetrators are irrelevant. Although the convention stipulates that genocide is deliberate and purposeful (reflected in the phrase "intent to destroy") and includes "conspiracy to commit genocide" and "incitement to commit genocide" as well as the destruction itself, it does not require the signatories to determine why the perpetrators are seeking to wipe out the targeted group. Under the convention, genocide can occur irrespective of motive, in peacetime or in war.

The long delay in U.S. ratification of the Genocide Convention stemmed in part from domestic political maneuvering, but it also reflected continued disagreements among lawyers and politicians about the concept of genocide. Some U.S. senators were concerned, especially during the Korean War and the Vietnam War, that U.S. officials might come under frivolous accusations of genocide. Others worried that if the United States formally adhered to the convention, the government would be obligated to send military forces to distant countries to enforce it. Not until February 1986—nearly four decades after the convention was signed—did the U.S. Senate vote 83 to 11 in favor of ratification, albeit with a list of "reservations" in the resolution of ratification. It took another two years before Congress passed legislation that actually implemented the convention by making genocide a crime under U.S. law. Moreover, even after the ratification was approved (with reservations), U.S. officials and legislators continued to debate such matters as the scope of the convention and the means of enforcement. One of the ironies of the convention, as demonstrated during the mass killing in Rwanda in 1994, is that U.S. and other Western leaders have been reluctant to enforce it. As a result, they have refrained from using the term *genocide* to describe even flagrant instances of systematic killing and large-scale atrocities.

Some observers, notably Samantha Power in her prize-winning book on U.S. policy toward genocide in the twentieth century, have argued that U.S. leaders would be more inclined to enforce the convention if they knew they would be held accountable for failing to uphold it. Short of some action by Congress, however, there are few if any ways to ensure that presidents will faithfully implement the convention. Thus far, Congress has not tried to hold the president or other senior foreign policy officials accountable for preventing or punishing genocide. On the contrary, many in Congress have shared the executive branch's reluctance to send troops to enforce the Genocide Convention. (Although the convention was not invoked by the administration of U.S. president Bill Clinton when it decided to bomb Serbia in 1999 to curb human rights abuses in Kosovo, some specialists argued that the convention was in fact relevant. Yet, congressional support for even that limited use of force was meager.) Power maintains that the calculus of U.S. officials on this matter will not be altered unless they are held "publicly or professionally accountable for inaction" (p. 510).

## Persistent Controversies and Ambiguities

The concept of genocide has remained a source of disagreement not only in the political arena, but also among legal scholars, historians, and political scientists. Although most scholars accept the view that genocide is targeted against a particular group, many have sought to expand the criteria for identifying particular groups. Rather than limiting the potential victims to ethnic and cultural groups, scholars such as Helen Fein and Leo Kuper have argued that genocide can also be directed against political or socioeconomic groups. This broadening of the concept is in line with Harff's and Gurr's concept of politicide, but it departs from the criteria laid out in the Genocide Convention. Some specialists, however, find even the broader conception of targeted groups to be still insufficient. In particular, Rummel has argued that the requirement for victims to be members of a group is a fatal drawback for those who want to take account of the full range of government-sponsored killing of unarmed civilians. Most scholars readily agree that genocide, if conceived of as directed against groups, leaves out many instances of slaughter and atrocities, but they still find the concept a useful one for describing a particular form of extreme abuse.

Even as scholars have generally expanded the range of potential victims of genocide, they have tended to move in the opposite direction when discussing the nature and scale of acts that fit under the rubric of genocide. In recent years, relatively few historians and political scientists have used the expansive definition of acts of genocide laid out in the Genocide Convention (in accord with Lemkin's preferences). The trend in the 1990s and early twenty-first century has generally been toward a more restrictive definition—a definition that limits acts of genocide to intentional killing of particular groups. Steven T. Katz, for example, has argued that "the concept of genocide applies only when there is an actualized intent, however successfully carried out, to physically destroy an entire group (as such a group is defined by the perpetrators)" (p. viii), and Mark Kramer has defined genocide as "deliberate mass slaughter aimed at complete extermination." (p. 2). Although some

scholars continue to espouse a much broader definition of acts of genocide (a definition that would include such things as mass slavery, restrictions on cultural practices, discriminatory education policies, and limits on travel), the narrower conceptions have tended to win favor in the scholarly community.

Outside the scholarly community, however, genocide has remained an expansive concept. Many advocacy groups and nongovernmental organizations (NGOs), such as Human Rights Watch, Amnesty International, and Genocide Watch, have sought to broaden, not restrict, the definition of acts prohibited by the Genocide Convention. They also have tried to strengthen the means of enforcing the convention. These groups vigorously supported efforts in the 1990s to establish international criminal tribunals to investigate and prosecute mass atrocities committed in the former Yugoslavia and in Rwanda. They also strongly backed the ultimately successful campaign to set up an International Criminal Court (ICC), which was created under a statute signed in Rome in July 1998. Although the United States and China declined to take part in the ICC, enough other governments ratified the Rome Statute to enable the ICC to begin functioning in mid-2002.

The human rights NGOs have been less successful, however, in their attempts to persuade Western governments to enforce the Genocide Convention more rigorously. No governments adhering to the convention were willing to brand as genocide the mass atrocities committed in the late 1980s and early 1990s by the Iraqi leader, Saddam Hussein, against Kurds, marsh Arabs, and Iraqi Shiites. Nor were any Western governments willing to regard the mass killing in Bosnia-Hercegovina in the first half of the 1990s as genocide. Even during the slaughter of some 800,000 people (predominantly Tutsis) by Hutus in Rwanda in 1994, Western governments carefully refrained from using the term *genocide* to describe what was going on. Officials worried that the mere use of the term would obligate them to send troops to put an end to the killing.

The unwillingness of governments to invoke the Genocide Convention in response to the massacres in Rwanda in 1994 or to the systematic atrocities perpetrated by government-backed Arab militias in the Darfur region of western Sudan in 2004 underscored the limits of both the convention and the ICC. In the absence of a concerted effort by parties to the convention to enforce it, debates about the precise scope and nature of acts of genocide are largely irrelevant. The special international tribunals for the former Yugoslavia and Rwanda and the ICC have no means of enforcing their own rulings; instead, like all international organizations, they depend entirely on individual states for enforcement. The Genocide Convention, as Lemkin recognized from the outset, is little more than a paper document unless the signatories are willing to take concrete steps to prevent mass killing and to punish the perpetrators. In a few instances, states have sent military forces to put an end to egregious human rights abuses, as Vietnam did in Cambodia in 1978 and Tanzania did in Uganda in 1979. In both of these cases, the interventions were only partly motivated by humanitarian concerns, but there is no doubt that the actions, whatever their motive, did put an end to systematic atrocities. Nonetheless, these incidents were rare exceptions.

The most powerful countries, including the United States and other permanent members of the UN Security Council, have been averse to intervening abroad solely to uphold the Genocide Convention.

Despite the problems in enforcing the Genocide Convention, the document has had a notable influence on international politics. In large part through Lemkin's efforts and the widespread revulsion at the atrocities perpetrated by Nazi Germany, the convention not only attached a permanent stigma to the crime of genocide, but also helped ensure that governments could not simply brush it aside as an "internal affair" of a sovereign state. The convention made clear that unless a government lived up to certain minimum standards of conduct vis-à-vis its own citizens, that government could potentially be removed and punished by other states. No longer would sovereignty be an insuperable barrier against international action. Moving from this principle to concrete enforcement has not yet been practical, but the establishment of the principle itself has been a crucial step on the road toward more effective international responses to genocide.

See also **Human Rights; International Order; Race and Racism; State, The; War.**

**BIBLIOGRAPHY**

Chalk, Frank, and Kurt Jonassohn. *The History and Sociology of Genocide: Analyses and Case Studies.* New Haven, Conn.: Yale University Press, 1990.

Fein, Helen. *Genocide: A Sociological Perspective.* London and Newbury Park, Calif.: Sage Publications, 1993.

Gellately, Robert, and Ben Kiernan, eds. *The Specter of Genocide: Mass Murder in Historical Perspective.* New York: Cambridge University Press, 2003.

Harff, Barbara, and Ted R. Gurr. "Toward Empirical Theory of Genocides and Politicides: Identification and Measurement of Cases since 1945." *International Studies Quarterly,* 37, no. 3 (September 1988): 359–371.

Katz, Steven T. *The Holocaust in Historical Context.* Vol. 1: *The Holocaust and Mass Death Before the Modern Age.* New York: Oxford University Press, 1994.

Kramer, Mark. "Introduction." In *Redrawing Nations: Ethnic Cleansing in East-Central Europe, 1944–1948,* edited by Philipp Ther and Ana Siljak, 1–42. Lanham, Md.: Rowan and Littlefield, 2001.

Kuper, Leo. *Genocide: Its Political Use in the Twentieth Century.* New Haven, Conn.: Yale University Press, 1982.

Lemkin, Raphael. *Axis Rule in Occupied Europe: Laws of Occupation, Analysis of Government, Proposals for Redress.* Washington, D.C.: Carnegie Endowment for International Peace, 1944.

Power, Samantha. *"A Problem from Hell": America and the Age of Genocide.* New York: Basic Books, 2002.

Rummel, R. J. *Death by Government.* New Brunswick, N.J.: Transaction Books, 1994.

*Mark Kramer*

**GENRE.** Genre is the division and grouping of texts on the basis of formal, thematic, or stylistic criteria. Texts may be produced, it can be argued, in compliance with or against the strictures of an established and identifiable genre, though it is equally feasible to impose a genre identity upon a work in retrospect, thus attributing to it further possibilities of meaning or, conversely, limiting its potential signification. Paradoxically, genre is conceptually located both within and outside of an individual text; it is a tool that may be employed with equal facility by author, reader, and critic. It is, equally paradoxically, both an instrument of restriction and a mode of liberation.

As a system of division, genre lacks universally accepted boundaries. It is, perhaps, most obviously vested in the formal distinctions between narrative (or prose), drama, and poetry (or verse), though there are some critics who would distinguish these three broad, recurrent identities as "modes," reserving the distinction of genre for what are essentially a work's technically distinguishable or thematically organized components—the sonnet within lyric or poetry, the novel and the gothic within prose fiction, tragedy within drama, and so on. Confusingly, other critics have been known to use the term *mode* to indicate a recognized textual tendency within one of the three broad genres. These already unstable boundaries may be further confused through an adaptation of the terminology of the German critic Karl Viëtor (1892–1951), under which genre distinctions, such as the romance and the pastoral, that occur across cultures may be labeled (somewhat misleadingly) as "universals."

On the one hand—and to adopt, for the purposes of argument, what is admittedly an extreme position—the regulated and regularized conventions of genre represent a restriction on what *may* be produced and what *ought* to be consumed. The conventions of genre, in this respect, hold the potential of functioning as instruments of a restrictive conservatism of generation and reception which may both discourage innovation at the level of the individual text and exclude noncompliant examples from the canon. To write within a culturally accepted or approved genre is thus both to aspire to inclusion within a community of letters and to align the text (and, possibly, its creator) with implications and identities that are often as much social as they are literary. The same might be said for other cultural practices in which genre is the primary mode of division—art, music, and cinema providing obvious parallels. These issues of production, interpretation, imposition, and definition apply as much in these visual and aural media as they do in oral and written textuality. For the sake of clarity and accessibility, the contentions of this essay are illustrated primarily with the oral and written text.

Conversely, however, the conventions and requirements of genre may function more as developmental departure-points than as blockades restricting innovation. They may enhance or supplement rather than concretize the existing borders of a genre, evolving and expanding in order to comprehend the novelty of texts that take issue with their own heritage. Although such innovation within genre may easily be taken as evidence of the artistic and cultural vitality of the context out of which any particular genre arises, it may equally proclaim the final limit of toleration, the point at which a genre may be seen to divide internally into subgenres or even, at the extreme, to fragment into new extrageneric divisions, often distinctly named in order to proclaim the finality and totality of separation. Drama may embrace within its bounds both tragedy and comedy, and may exhibit sufficient flexibility for all concerned to comprehend such a hybrid as tragicomedy. However, purists concerned with the study of the gothic novel, a literary genre whose origins lie in the eighteenth century, may find it considerably less easy to accept the existence of a subgenre proclaiming itself "gothic science fiction," even though the antecedent of such a concept might arguably include that quintessential "first-wave" gothic novel, Mary Shelley's *Frankenstein* (1818), published at the close of the period commonly designated as the "first wave" of gothic writing. In short, the degree to which the title of genre is awarded to a broader or narrower field of artistic production, and the extent to which that distinction is accepted, reflects the debate between the interested parties in authorship, reception, and culture more generally.

Genres, in common with the texts that sustain and promulgate them, thus exist in relationship to other bodies and other institutions, textual as well as organizational. Equally, genres exist and are modified and negotiated in debates among literary critics, as well as in the critical function and content of the artistic work itself. The relationships between genres may be complementary or oppositional, and may vary between the two across a period of cultural history. Fixity is not an invariable feature of internal genre identity and, equally, the complementary or combative relationships that pertain between genres are themselves fluid. The literary critic Jonathan Culler suggests that "the function of genre conventions is essentially to establish a contract between writer and reader" (p. 147). From Culler's observation that this contract serves in part to "make certain relevant expectations operative," it is logical to suggest that such a contract always retains the potential for renegotiation, given the constant revision of genre standards and components. Culler, however, appears to disregard the presence in such contractual renegotiations of a third party, namely the publishing and marketing industries. Indeed, it is this commercial activity, which, by way of evocative series titles and cover blurbs, has both popularized the notion of genre in the public imagination and, in the case of some popular genres, most notably the historical novel and gothic traditions, has reduced the dynamics of production to little more than stylistic repetition. This has been a risk associated with genre from its origins in classical writing.

## Classical Origins

The distinction that underpins the three broad divisions of genre have their origins in the rigid formalities and hierarchies of classical thought. Book 3 of Plato's *Republic* (c. 380 B.C.E.) is preoccupied with the effective censoring of writing deemed inappropriate to the dignity of the projected Republic and its guardians. Though this activity finds its parallel in Aristotle's later consideration of "decorum," or the proper relationship of style to subject matter, Plato's dialogue is most influential in its systematization of genre, albeit in a vision premised upon the perception of narrative voice through direct speech, rather than a more protracted encounter with technique in itself, as the primary item of definition. Plato's division, contained for the most

part within what are traditionally numbered paragraphs 392–396 of Book 3, contends that "any poem or story deals with things past, present or future" by way of "either simple narrative, or representation, or a mixture of both" (p. 131). The division here is based upon the relative positions of the poet allegedly speaking as himself ("narrative") and the imitative function whereby the speech or manner of another person is imitated in an act of "representation." Using Homer's *Iliad* as an example, the dialogue further develops the presence of a hybrid form in which passages of narration alternate with those of representation, the poet speaking first "in his own person" and then "in the person of Chryses" (p. 131). Notably, the later genre distinction between "poetry [and] drama" is ignored in this early classification, the "styles" of narration being the only distinction permitted to those engaged in the act of creation.

The most influential classical formulation of discrete and persistent genre criteria based upon a perceived difference in media as much as on the condition of narrative voice and subject matter is in Aristotle's undated treatise *On the Art of Poetry* (also known as *The Poetics*), though it is apparent that the work may have had limited currency from antiquity until its rediscovery during the Renaissance. The treatise is committed to a hierarchical differentiation of poetry, Aristotle's introductory history of poetic writing acknowledging an early division of art into "two channels": a "serious-minded" tradition preoccupied with "noble actions and the doings of noble persons" (p. 35) and a more invective, trivial form that charted the dealings of the "meaner sort of people" (p. 36). Three different methods of distinguishing the essential nature of a work are outlined in the *Poetics,* these being the medium (effectively the verse or rhythmic form) through which a work may imitate reality; the "object of imitation" (how a character is represented or exaggerated—in Aristotle's contention, specifically in moral terms); and finally (and in continuation of the Platonic model), the "manner of imitation" or difference between representation and narration (pp. 32–34).

The hierarchical model exercises itself within the *Poetics* through the distinction between the qualities of tragedy, comedy, and epic. Comedy, it is suggested, is a "low" form, in that it is a projection of the ridiculous or of that which is painful to perceive, though this is undertaken in such a manner as not to cause pain to the audience. One would add to this the assumption that such a form would be unlikely to provoke deep thought or self-reflection, though developments in the satirical tradition of Roman literature might well achieve this. In Aristotle's understanding, Greek epic and tragedy, in contrast to comedy, do provoke introspection, both laying claim to be "a reflection, in dignified verse, of serious actions" (p. 38)—though Aristotle eventually concludes the tragic to be the more effective and thus the most prestigious of the two.

Epic differs from tragedy also through formal conventions. According to Aristotle, epic, alone, conventionally "keeps to a single metre and is in narrative form" (p. 38). The two are dissimilar, again, in the scope of their respective temporal coverage, the epic being restricted by "no limits in its time of action" where tragedy was traditionally associated with "a complete action" played out during a period of around twenty-four hours (pp. 45, 38). There is considerably more at stake in this genre distinction than the convention of "fear and pity" (p. 48), which has been at times simplistically used as the defining icon of tragedy. Different meters distinguish the various forms considered by Aristotle, the iambic, for example being derived from an association with the "iamb" or lampoon, where heroic hexameter "is the right metre for epic" (p. 67). Stage tragedy employed choral song in lyric meters, with spoken exchanges delivered in tetrameters or iambic trimeters. The notion of "decorum" or appropriateness is rigid in this vision of genre: the "dignified verse" of epic or tragedy being reserved only for those forms, the diction of the latter being modified still further through "the use of expanded, abbreviated and altered forms of words" to "raise the diction above the commonplace" (pp. 63, 65). Contorted language in comedy would, by contrast, prototypically lead to confusion rather than to the thought-provoking—and ultimately fatal—riddle posed by the Sphinx, or indeed those posed by Teiresias to Oedipus in Sophocles' *Oedipus the King*. Inappropriate usage, in this respect, would challenge audience expectation, were not the classical institutions of literature so rigid in their discouragement of such experimentation.

Aristotle's preoccupation with tragedy in the *Poetics* has left a corresponding deficiency in the criticism of the lyric, comedy, and, to a considerably lesser extent, epic—criticism of the latter being inevitably colored by the explicit partial congruence with tragedy as well as through Aristotle's discrete pronouncements upon epic stylistics. In consequence, subsequent critics have addressed this imbalance not merely by considering those genre areas specifically but also by developing further the Platonic and Aristotelian canons of genre beyond their apparent boundaries of lyric, comedy, and epic. This expansion and clarification is in many ways retrospective, based as it is in part upon an observation of recurrent textual preoccupations rather than any universally accepted criteria for generation. In contrast to the specific denominations of Platonic and Aristotelian criticism, such developments are frequently termed "classical divisions" or "the classical genres," gaining a certain value—as alleged origins, as touchstones for subsequent work—in consequence.

Access to the specifics of these "classical" genres—and to the vagueness that often surrounds them—might be most conveniently made through what has effectively become a genre in modern criticism itself, the critical handbook marketed at undergraduate readers. Writing in 2002, John Peck and Martin Coyle inform the student reader that "the main generic division today is into poetry, drama and the novel, but in earlier times the major genres were recognised as epic, tragedy, lyric, comedy and satire" (p. 1). Ross Murfin and Supryia M. Ray, writing in 1997, concur, though they offer "pastoral" as an equal to the five "classical" genres. What is apparent, again, is the lack of consensus among critics.

Notable also, however, is the particular valorization of satire as a discrete genre, rather than in its more traditional status in Greek criticism as an element in comedy. Claimed as a uniquely Roman tradition by Quintilian, satire was in Aristotelian terms little more than a base ancestor of comedy or a mere component of that lesser genre. Although its inclu-

sion in a modern tabulation of genres may reflect the acknowledgment of the parallel status of Roman art alongside Greek, it may arguably also be associated with the enhanced status enjoyed by satirical writing in the modern world. The pastoral or "bucolic" genre similarly enjoyed a classical reputation as a component of epic, lyric, or tragedy, though its potential as a discrete genre was established by the Greek poet Theocritus (third century B.C.E.), its conventions being further developed and popularized by the Roman poet Virgil (70–19 B.C.E.). Again, though classical antecedents are undoubtedly important in the establishment of pastoral as a discrete genre, it must be acknowledged that its status in the contemporary critical field is enhanced by the influence of pastoral stylistics upon individual writers from William Shakespeare to Thomas Hardy, and its contribution to literary and critical movements from the Romanticism of the eighteenth and nineteenth centuries to late-twentieth-century ecocriticism. Genre, as it were, may be valued as much for the texts it has inspired indirectly as for its direct generational capacity as a literary matrix.

## Renaissance, Neoclassical, and Romantic Conceptions

The Age of Reason, as has so often been asserted, was an age characterized for many by a commitment to individual and social order, supported by the adoption of taxonomies and systems conducive to the maintenance of that order. It should come as no surprise, therefore, to perceive the continued presence of genre, particularly as a limiting agent in literary culture, for a significant part of this period, albeit with limited acceptance in some quarters toward the close of the eighteenth century.

The persistence of genre in the Age of Reason is a logical continuation of the revival of classical thought, and indeed, of renewed reverence for the classical texts of Greek and Roman antiquity, during the Renaissance period of the fifteenth and sixteenth centuries. The Renaissance brought a revival of interest in the writings of Aristotle in particular, and already-established notions of decorum—the relationship of form to subject matter or occasion—were in many respects confirmed for the purposes of the present by the antecedent of classical thought. The association, for example, of the sonnet as a form particularly suitable for amorous verse was effectively concretized in the courtly writings of the Renaissance period, the essay also coming to parallel (and subsequently to eclipse, albeit later, in the eighteenth century) the Socratic dialogue as the appropriate medium for philosophical and literary speculation. The broader genres of classical thought thus began to fragment into distinct stylistic identities that held the potential of eventual development into genres (or at least subgenres) in their own right. The pastoral also reappeared in the form of eclogues (short poems, not necessarily in dialogue form) in the Latin and vernacular tongues, in many cases under the influence of the Italian poet Petrarch (1304–1374) and his imitators, following a period of neglect during the Middle Ages.

This is not to say that the Renaissance was simply an age of revival, devoid of genre development and speculation. Developing from a medieval and early Renaissance tradition of chivalric, and at times fantastic, storytelling, the romance became an established literary form from the fifteenth century, and in England at least was considered predominantly a prose genre. In this context, the romance is a genre of adventure or experience, describing events and actions often fanciful or exaggerated, though which may be frequently utilized as a vehicle for personal or social exploration. The Renaissance genre of romance—and, by implication, its medieval antecedents in the depiction of Arthurian and classical heroes—itself enters into introspection in the early seventeenth century with the publication of Miguel de Cervantes' *Don Quixote* (1605–1615), which mocks not merely the style of romance but its aspirations toward an idealized and meaningful life. Significantly, the romance, with its pretensions of the fantastic and its recollections of a recent, spectacular past, became unfashionable as neoclassical thought gained aesthetic ascendancy, returning to an enhanced position only with the rise of gothicism and Romanticism in the second half of the eighteenth century.

The Renaissance is the period also, perhaps unsurprisingly, of the rise as a distinct tendency within prose fiction of the picaresque, or novel of roguery. Growing from literary origins in sixteenth-century Spain, the picaresque evolved into a prose genre closely aligned to the romance by the early eighteenth century. The generic distinction, it must be noted, was applied in retrospect from the nineteenth century, though such tales of illicit love and scandal had been often distinguished in England from the mid-seventeenth century through the term *novel.* Despite this precedent, extended (and often episodic) picaresque works were frequently prefaced on their title pages by grandiose distinctions, such as "history" or "expedition"— applied to Henry Fielding's *Tom Jones* (1749) and Tobias Smollett's *Humphry Clinker* (1771), respectively—these niceties adding a pretension of factuality to tantalize, or trap, the potential reader. As in the classical period, any discrete genre exists in relation to other literary forms, and the relative status of one might be accreted to another through the appropriation of a signifier such as a recurrent device in titling or structure. Order, as it were, implies hierarchy and stratification as much as control and regularity: such falsehoods as those on the title pages of *Tom Jones* and *Humphry Clinker* effectively resist the alleged control exercised by the neoclassical preoccupations of the Age of Reason.

It would be overly simplistic to structure the rise of Romanticism from the last quarter of the eighteenth century as being little more than a reaction to the spiritual, political, and literary strictures allegedly imposed by the Age of Reason. Indeed, the movement proposed little more than an alternative aesthetic rather than an end to conventionalism and formulaic production through genre. In its engagement with outmoded or discarded forms of spirituality and its addressing of demotic identities, Romanticism maintained a restrictive convention of decorum, albeit one at odds with neoclassicism's reverence of Greek and Roman stylistics. Demotic and elaborately archaized forms of poetry were particularly celebrated in the presentation of uncanny events and scenes of pathos, the latter at times developing many of the sentimental attributes previously associated with the pastoral. The ballad, in particular, became a major and distinctive vehicle by which poetry might be directed away from the lofty forms and heroic subject matter of classicism and

neoclassicism toward an often emotional evocation of the language and social environment of common people. Again, the association of form with subject matter or voice is an agent in the fragmentation of larger genre identities.

Romantic writers were often influenced to a greater or lesser degree by the gothic, which flourished in its first wave from the mid-eighteenth century to the early nineteenth. In terms of genre, however, the importance of the gothic lies not in its predominantly supernatural subject matter or commitment to depictions of the grotesque and excessive, but to its aesthetics and conventions being applied across prose, poetry, and drama. The rise of the gothic arguably marks the distinctive transition from a conception of genre based primarily upon formal differentiation to one where conventions of subject matter predominate. Decorum may no longer impose singularity: the poetic ballad may be as suitable a medium for gothic description as the prose novel. The same ballad, again, might hold the potential of being viewed as a product not merely of gothic stylistics but, recalling the parallel influence of Romanticism, as a representation of demotic or folk culture, also. Though such possibilities had been hinted at by earlier literary developments— the novel of sensibility had retained some affinity with sentimental poetry, for example—the gothic was arguably the most influential force in this blurring of generic boundaries essentially inimical to the rigid hierarchies of Enlightenment thought.

In addition to this, the shift in perception that placed subject-matter convention over form encouraged a new interest in satire, itself a form of literary production that blurs genre boundaries through its intertextual dynamic between allusion and satiric comedy. In gothic, the novelistic mockeries of Thomas Love Peacock (1785–1866) and Jane Austen (1775–1817) inform a long tradition of acute observation and wry comment, which underpins the twentieth-century cinematic satires of *Young Frankenstein* (1974) and *The Rocky Horror Picture Show* (1975). Modern gothic, it might be added, is cinematic as well as theatrical, poetic, and novelistic in its compass.

## Twentieth-Century Perceptions

Although the gothic, with Romanticism, effectively crossed and revised the boundaries between the three major genre fields of prose, poetry, and drama, this lead was not readily taken up with any effectiveness by another major transgenre movement until the rise of modernism. Instead, critical attention across the nineteenth century became preoccupied with the increasing specialization within the three major genres, a process alternatively of subdivision or fragmentation that might lead, depending on perspective, to subgenres or genres in their own right. Such changes are not necessarily evolutionary—the grotesque social awareness of Charles Dickens (1812–1870), for example, does not lead seamlessly to the politicized naturalism of Émile Zola (1840–1902). Critics in both the nineteenth and twentieth centuries have, however, attempted at times to appropriate a model of evolution (and in the case of Max Nordau, of decadence) to the act of criticism, associating changes in taste and genre with the perceived development or regression of the social and cultural standards that form the text's content. To do this is again to engage with the exclusive powers of genre: the decadent fiction of the nineteenth-century *fin de siècle,* for example, may have been critically rejected upon formal grounds, though the institutions of the dominant culture are more likely to have taken issue with its subject matter. The sense of decorum here does not stop conventionally at associating one set of formal criteria as being appropriate to the depiction of a specific issue or subject. In the context of the nineteenth-century *fin de siècle,* the debate on decorum of preoccupied with whether *any* form should be associated with the matter depicted by the authors deemed decadent. "Decadence" thus becomes effectively another genre engaged in defining works, often in conventional form, that fall outside the cannons of taste.

It is clear, though, that genre was enhanced (whether as internal division or fragmentation outward is irrelevant here) by the rise of a mass publishing and distribution industry in the nineteenth century, and through public consciousness of a world made considerably more complex through social change, empire, and technology. It is this context that maintains the novel as a convenient physical form for distribution and consumption, but that prefaces that demarcation with conditions generated out of the context of the day. Thus, the term *novel* progressively functions only as the mantissa of a variable concept conditioned by its prefix. In the United Kingdom, the century was to see the rise and fall of "condition of England" novels in the 1840s, the "new woman" novel of gender assertiveness in the 1890s, and the "problem novel" of sexual manners in the early 1900s. Such specialisms may lay claim to distinctiveness of subject matter, some enjoying a discrete and highly conventionalized decorum of form in addition. Audiences, again, often became equally specialized and well-versed in the conventions of the genre, their demand for works both stimulating production and potentially blocking its development beyond existing boundaries. Notably, many of the minor genres of the century were short lived, their currency being determined as much by fashion and the topicality of current affairs as by literary taste.

There remains, however, a perceptible difference between the stylistically and overtly literary production and the merely prosaic act of communication, and this distinction came to preoccupy the systematic scrutiny of fiction undertaken by Russian formalist critics during the first three decades of the twentieth century. Abandoning the social contexts of art in favor of a return to structural and formal issues, the movement produced a number of significant concepts pertinent to the issues of genre and genre formation. Among these was Roman Jakobson's conceptualization of a literary type by way of "the dominant," "the focusing element of a work of art," which "rules, determines and transforms the remaining components" (p. 82). The dominant, as Jakobson subsequently clarifies, may be external to the work, a component of the stylistic canon of the poetic school or age. The parallels to earlier notions of genre are obvious here, though it is worth adding a note of caution to Jakobson's assertion by way of a reference to Jurij Tynjanov's observation that the foregrounding of "dominant" elements necessarily implies the deformation of components elsewhere in the text. It may equally imply the overlooking of components in the drive to define a genre by its most prominent—or most fashionable—feature.

This deformation, though, is not immutable. Evolution, or a change of emphasis in the definition of a genre by the hierarchy of its components, may determine how a body of texts is defined across a historical period. Citing the example of the novel, Tynjanov notes that where once it was distinguished by its commitment to a narrative of "love intrigue," the genre has subsequently become defined by "its size and the nature of its plot development" (p. 73). Tynjanov's definition appears here to treat of the broadest category of novel, rejecting the generic fragmentations so popular in the nineteenth century, though elsewhere Jakobson acknowledges the importance of "transitional genres"—exemplified by "letters, diaries, notebooks, travelogues"—which are "extraliterary and extrapoetical" or supplementary to the canonical genres of literature (p. 86). Again, these might well be defined as genres within their own right under an alternative critical viewpoint. Emphasis, and interpretation, remains in the eye of the perceiver.

Jakobson's contention—which appears orthodox across Russian formalist thought—that genre is as much a hierarchy and system of values as verse does have important implications for generic change. Changes in the hierarchy of poetic devices within a genre affect how that genre may be defined. Generic evolution is not so much a question of the disappearance of certain elements but of a shift in the relationship of dominant to muted, a change of emphasis rather than a change of content. Russian formalism demands that an approach to genre be based upon a consciousness of its status as a system, and of the relationship of the text to elements within that system as well as those that might be deemed "extraliterary"—for the moment, at least.

This systematic approach also informs the influential work of both Northrop Frye and Tzvetan Todorov, two major theoreticians of genre brought into effective dialogue through the publication of Todorov's *The Fantastic: A Structural Approach to a Literary Genre* (1970). As Todorov observes, Frye formulates in his *Anatomy of Criticism* (1957) a theoretical rather than historical model of genre. It is apparent that in part this model draws upon Aristotelian concepts not merely of division, but also of presentation. Decorum is, thus, again a limiting factor. The primary demarcations envisaged by Frye are, conventionally, drama (poetry or prose to be performed), lyric (poetry to be sung), epic (poetry to be recited) and prose that may simply be read. The first three are, essentially, performative, and the texts they produce remain within their respective genre definitions even when presented in the form of the printed page. These three genres are further associated with what Frye terms the *epos,* a convention of addressing an audience based upon oral presentation. Frye refines his fourth genre area, that of prose, by moving quickly to a consideration of "fiction," "the genre of the printed page" or, alternately, "the genre that addresses a reader through a book" (p. 248) rather than in expectation of oral performance.

This demarcation, though, may be compromised by the conventions of writing itself, so that prose fiction may assume a connection with the *epos,* or oral address, according to Frye, simply by making "some attempt to preserve the convention of recitation and a listening audience" (p. 248). Further confusion may also occur through Frye's generalization that fiction is continuous and the *epos* conventionally episodic. As he admits, under both of these criteria the works of Charles Dickens are wholly fiction when published in volume form, though they will—because Victorian serials were conventionally read aloud to family gatherings—have been touched by the *epos* in their earlier incarnation in periodical form. Further, when Dickens began to undertake public reading tours, during which his works were first arranged and then declaimed by the author to an audience, "the genre changed wholly to *epos*" (Frye, p. 249). Though at first sight conventionally rigid, Frye's demarcations become somewhat permeable as the relationship between text and reader (or audience) becomes acknowledged as mutable rather than fixed.

One might also point out here briefly Frye's consideration of "archetypes" or recurrent acts of communication and their implications for genre. Although, Frye observes, "certain common images," such as "the sea or the forest," may connect "one poem with another" (p. 99), creating a perceptible unity between them, the works of an author might equally be recalled to the coherence of an oeuvre through that writer's "preoccupation with two or three archetypes" (p. 268). Taken to an extreme, there appears to be little conceptual difference between an oeuvre and genre by this definition, particularly where questions of *epos* and audience are themselves apparently questionable. Both are adequate modes of division, but little more—and the adequacy of genre as an effective container of certain liminal forms (which Frye himself demonstrates as being far more diverse than the transitional genres associated with Jakobson) appears far from convincing in the detail of his model. Frye's model is far from conclusive, and indeed far from comprehensive given its often conflicting complexity. He should, though, be credited with a consideration that might profitably inform all attempts to improve, define, or use genre. As Frye asserts, genre distinctions are not practical but rather "among the ways in which literary works are *ideally* presented, whatever the actualities are" (p. 247).

The first chapter of *The Fantastic* is for much of its length a response to *Anatomy of Criticism*, its focus being directed in particular to the perceived incoherence and lack of specificity in of Frye's tabulation of genre. Although the subsequent nine chapters of *The Fantastic* demonstrate Todorov's thought through the exposition of a single genre and its internal structures and tensions, much of that thought encloses the polemical content of the first chapter. Like Frye and the earlier formalists, Todorov asserts the individual text to be the product of convention, a reworking of what has already been achieved in literature rather than an emotive or unique form of self-expression. The individual text is thus not valued in its own right but rather becomes the basic resource in a deductive process from which a hypothesis or generalization regarding "a principle operative in a number of texts" (Todorov, p. 3) may be projected. Such distinctions are not adequate for the formulation of universal laws, though they are appropriate for smaller (and implicitly more coherent) theoretical units—generic identities such as the fantastic, through which Todorov explicates his theory.

Central to Todorov's model of genre is the statement that "*every* work modifies the sum of possible works" (p. 6). This is not a new idea: it has a precedent in the Russian formalist definition of the literary by way of defamiliarization and innovation. Todorov, however, does not dismiss the noninnovative work as being merely prosaic or unliterary, thus compromising its position within genre. Rather, he considers such productions as being effectively within genre, albeit as (dependent upon audience context) "so-called 'popular' or 'mass' literature in the one case; in the other that of the academic exercise or unoriginal experiment" (p. 6). The innovative text, though, permits a statement to be made in criticism about the context of genre through its own evocation of fiction, just as genre itself facilitates commentary upon the text. Again, this is not original: Jakobson suggests in "The Dominant" how a reader may be aware of "two orders," namely "the traditional canon and the artistic novelty as a deviation from that canon" (p. 87). *Canon,* in this context, functions as an effective synonym for *genre*. A problem arises, however, with regard to the comparative prestige that is associated, in Russian formalism and elsewhere, with the iconoclastic text. Canon, like genre, is traditionally the standard to be emulated and maintained, lest the individual text be dismissed or suppressed. Modern criticism, however, has inverted that hierarchy, the generic or canonical context being relegated to the status of a starting point, the prestige going to each successive departure from a seemingly devalued standard that yet paradoxically holds its value as a reference point to be exceeded. If a text does not challenge an accepted norm it is, on the one hand either "popular" or "unoriginal," though on the other it is conservatively "generic." It is, in effect, unstable, locked into a conceptual position where more than one perception may formulate its definition, its acceptance or rejection.

### The Future of Genre

Todorov's contention that "any description of a text . . . is a description of genre" (p. 7) may thus set the tone for the future of genre considerations. The awareness that characterizes the reading process as much as it does the writing activity in postmodernity has irrevocably changed the relationship between text and audience, in the same way as it has disrupted that which has previously pertained between text and genre. Jonathan Culler, quoting the critic Gérard Genette, asserts that literature, "like any other activity of the mind[,] is based on conventions of which, with some exceptions, it is not aware" (p. 116). Even at the time of its publication in 1975 this was an extraordinary—and, indeed, outmoded—statement. Genre awareness—in this case, of the discrete form of the novel in the nineteenth and twentieth centuries, and of literary theory as a context for the writing of postmodern fiction—surely informs not merely the writing of, but also critical acclamation for, John Fowles's seminal *The French Lieutenant's Woman* in 1969. Similar assumptions might be made about equally self-consciously "literary" or "theoretical" works such as Muriel Spark's *The Driver's Seat* (1970) and Robert Coover's *The Public Burning* (1977). The reader versed in such things is no longer positioned as a passive spectator, his or her only prerogative being to respond in a predictable manner to customary genre signals or to concur in the rejection of texts that breach decorum. Though some readers may maintain such standards, the postmodern reader is allegedly well informed, and capable of rejecting the orthodox rather than the heterodox in textuality. The author, too, is aware, and the text is the emblem of that awareness by its own evocation of questions of theory, reception, and, inevitably, genre. Metafiction—self-conscious, self-referential, and reciprocally intimate to the generalizations that organize textuality at all levels—is the logical outcome of the cultural preoccupation with genre.

In the late twentieth century, fiction in the form of metafiction became a commentary not merely upon other texts (through intertextuality), nor indeed solely upon the internal workings of the fictional artifact itself (through the laying bare of device). To expand upon Todorov's contention above, a statement made within or demonstrated by the workings of an individual text is, equally, a statement about genre and, consequently, the limitations and the liberties associated with genre. The reader's recognition not merely of the genre context but also of the development of that context is crucial to such experiments, which are, perversely, both anti-genre and yet genre-dependent for their effect. Genre, in its function as reference point within the very texts that seek to signal their departure from its structures is, at the start of the twenty-first century, possibly as much as a conceptual ideal as Frye suggested it was in the late 1950s.

*See also* **Literary Criticism; Narrative; Postmodernism.**

**BIBLIOGRAPHY**
Anonymous. "Satire." In *The Oxford Companion to Classical Literature,* edited by M. C. Howatson, 507. Oxford: Oxford University Press, 1997.
Anonymous. "Tragedy." In *The Oxford Companion to Classical Literature,* edited by M. C. Howatson, 575–578. Oxford: Oxford University Press, 1997.
Aristotle. *On the Art of Poetry.* In *Classical Literary Criticism,* translated by T. S. Dorsch, 31–75. Harmondsworth, U.K.: Penguin, 1979.
Culler, Jonathan. *Structuralist Poetics: Structuralism, Linguistics, and the Study of Literature.* Ithaca, N.Y.: Cornell University Press, 1975.
Currie, Mark, ed. *Metafiction.* London and New York: Longman, 1995.
Dubrow, Heather. *Genre.* London and New York: Methuen, 1982.
Frye, Northrop. *Anatomy of Criticism: Four Essays.* Princeton, N.J.: Princeton University Press, 1957.
Howatson, M. C., ed. *The Oxford Companion to Classical Literature.* Oxford: Oxford University Press, 1997.
Jakobson, Roman. "The Dominant." 1935. In *Readings in Russian Poetics: Formalist and Structuralist Views,* edited by Ladislav Matejka and Krystyna Pomorska, 82–87. Ann Arbor: Michigan Slavic Publications, 1978.
Keating, Peter. *The Haunted Study: A Social History of the English Novel, 1875–1914.* London: Secker and Warburg, 1989.
Murfin, Ross, and Supryia M. Ray. *The Bedford Glossary of Critical and Literary Terms.* Boston: Bedford Books, 1997.
Peck, John, and Martin Coyle. *Literary Terms and Criticism.* 3rd ed. Basingstoke, U.K.: Palgrave, 2002.
Perry, Anne. *The Twisted Root.* New York: Ballantine, 1999.
Plato. *The Republic.* Translated by H. D. P. Lee. Harmondsworth, U.K.: Penguin, 1968.
Punter, David. *The Gothic Tradition.* Vol. 1 of *The Literature of Terror: A History of Gothic Fictions from 1765 to the Present Day.* 2nd ed. London and New York: Longman, 1996.
Seed, David. "Gothic Science Fiction." In *The Handbook to Gothic Literature,* edited by Marie Mulvey-Roberts, 272. Basingstoke, U.K.: Macmillan, 1998.
Shklovsky, Victor. "Art as Technique." 1917. In *Russian Formalist Criticism: Four Essays,* translated by Lee T. Lemon and Marion J. Reis, 3–24. Lincoln: University of Nebraska Press, 1965.
Sophocles. *Oedipus the King.* In *The Theban Plays,* translated by E. F. Watling, 23–68. Harmondsworth, U.K.: Penguin, 1967.
Todorov, Tzvetan. *The Fantastic: A Structural Approach to a Literary Genre,* translated by Richard Howard. Ithaca, N.Y.: Cornell University Press, 1975.
Tynjanov, Jurij. "On Literary Evolution." 1927. In *Readings in Russian Poetics: Formalist and Structuralist Views,* edited by Ladislav Matejka and Krystyna Pomorska, 66–78. Ann Arbor: Michigan Slavic Publications, 1978.

*William Hughes*

**GEOGRAPHY.** Only relatively recently accepted as a subject of study by universities, geography has been characterized as a Cinderella among the disciplines. It was not one of the traditional liberal arts, and it appeared in its modern form in the curriculum of universities in the nineteenth and twentieth centuries; it still remains a small component, and is sometimes not present at all, in institutions of higher learning. Part of the reason for this is that society, and even geographers themselves, are not sure of the nature of geography. Geographers are only rarely members of national academies of science, or of the humanities, falling between the stools with the social or so-called soft sciences.

## The Nature of Geography

In his seminal studies on the methodology of the subject, Richard Hartshorne (1899–1992) proposed the following definition: "Geography is concerned to provide an accurate, orderly, and rational description of the variable character of the earth's surface" (Hartshorne, p. 21). Understandably this characterization has not been universally accepted, and others have suggested terms such as "areal differentiation," and "spatial interaction" as better expressing the core of geography. It has been seen as more akin to history than to the systematic sciences (physics, chemistry, biology, geology, meteorology, etc.) in that it has no body of material peculiar to itself, but rather adopts a point of view. But subjects studied by some geographers, such as map projections, are highly "scientific."

In France the alliance between geography and history—"geohistory"—extends from Jean Bodin to Montesquieu to Jules Michelet to the *Annales* school, especially Lucien Febvre, *A Geographical Introduction to History,* and Fernand Braudel and their followers. In Germany geography was an auxiliary science in the encyclopedia of history, or *Historik,* as taught in the universities from the eighteenth century; and there are parallels in other national traditions.

If geography is Cinderella, its Prince Charming is cartography and, by extension, remote sensing of the environment. Maps and related images of the Earth have a wide appeal to collectors and others and are used professionally in several disciplines. But preeminently, they are the tools of geographers so that their study is often confused with the reality of the Earth itself, as expressed in the old tag "Geography is about maps."

Maps may help in an understanding of the "reality" of geography, but are not "reality" themselves, consisting, as they do, of conventional symbols. Humankind, since prehistoric times, has been concerned with the local environment, as evidenced in maps made before the written record. The subject came into focus in the later classical period as exemplified by the *Geography* of Strabo (63 B.C.E.–c. 24 C.E.), a verbal description of the then-known world, and the similarly titled *Geographia* of Ptolemy (second century C.E.), containing instructions for map-making, of essentially the same area of Eurasia and North Africa described earlier by Strabo. The Greeks from the time of Plato (427–348 or 247 B.C.E.) appear to have accepted the idea of the Earth as a perfect sphere, which, apparently, was not a part of early Babylonian, Egyptian, or Chinese cosmography. Although Buddhism spread from India to China and Japan (after 400 B.C.E.), and following the establishment of Buddhism there, priests returned to India to seek their religious roots and wrote about their travels, this geographical lore did not enter the mainstream of thought in translation until comparatively recent times. The same is largely true of Islam following the death of Muhammad (570–632 C.E.), in spite of close contact between this religion and Christianity in the Mediterranean and elsewhere over many centuries. Thus the travels of "Sinbad the Sailor" and more scientific geographies were available only in translation as relatively late additions to European literature and in this sense are considered to be "nonhistorical" in the West. Even the accounts of Marco Polo (1254–1324) of his travels from Venice to Cathay (China) and return were at first disbelieved.

This article need not go into detail concerning the remarkably accurate measurement of the circumference of the Earth by Eratosthenes (third century B.C.E.), or its rejection by others (including Ptolemy), until the later Renaissance and the scientific revolution in Europe, of the fifteenth to seventeenth centuries. At that time Ptolemy's *Geographia* was "rediscovered" and translated from Greek into Latin and formed the basis of much of the study of geography in this era. It was in turn criticized, improved upon, and superseded during the period of European ascendancy in science and global discovery when half the coasts of the world were "discovered" and charted. The dichotomy represented by the conceptions of the Greeks—Strabo on the one hand and Ptolemy on the other—continued into the Enlightenment period through the writings of, for example, Bernhard Varen (Varenius, 1622–1650) in regional geography, or chorography, and in the ideas of Edmond Halley (1656–1742), who, in addition to his work in astronomy, laid the foundations of physical, thematic mapping, with representations of winds, tides, and Earth magnetism with isogones (lines of equal magnetic variation) delineated on published charts. More than a century later, the polymath

Alexander von Humboldt (1769–1859), well trained in the natural and physical sciences, attempted to give unity to geography, while still considering the Earth in relation to the cosmos (*Kosmos* is the title of his greatest work). It was Humboldt's contemporary Carl Ritter (1779–1859) who, similarly, emphasized the unity of the field, but with a person-centered (even teleological) approach to human/land relationships, following Immanuel Kant (1724–1804) and others. But the division between physical and human geography continued and increased in the nineteenth and in the first half of the twentieth century in France, Britain, the United States, and areas influenced by these countries. That this is still the case is evidenced by recent multiauthored volumes titled, respectively, *Horizons in Physical Geography* (1987) and *Human Geography: An Essential Anthology* (1996). Accordingly, it is necessary to recognize recent trends in these major, separate divisions of geography; this article will later cite attempts at reconciliation between these two disparate streams, and others.

## Geographical Determinism

A concept that retarded the acceptance of geography as a serious academic endeavor until quite recently was geographical determinism. Although stemming from earlier work by the German geographer and ethnographer Friedrich Ratzel (1844–1904), with adherents in other European countries, the high priestess of this cult in the United States was Ellen C. Semple (1863–1932); another American espouser of "determinism" was Ellsworth Huntington (1876–1947). In its extreme expression the theory asserts that the work of humans is controlled or "determined" by geographical conditions: climate, landforms, and the like. This idea was opposed by the scientifically trained English scholar Eva G. R. Taylor (1879–1966) and others in Britain, France, and elsewhere. The debate continued throughout the twentieth century, but has few adherents in the early 2000s. An alternative to determinism was proposed, namely possibilism, which suggests that humans have a number of possibilities from which to select. Possibilism apparently owed its origin to the French geographer Paul Vidal de la Blache (1845–1918), who, with his followers, never accepted the concept of determinism. At this time most of the world, including North America, was influenced by European ideas so that traditional, indigenous geographies became subsumed under colonial and other European ideology. Thus India, under British rule, became one of the best studied and surveyed areas in the world. China, Japan, and Korea resisted this cultural hegemony, but eventually accepted it.

## Military and Public Geography

If geography has had a mixed reception in research universities, its ideas and practitioners have been embraced by both the military and the public sectors. Thus Napoléon Bonaparte (1769–1821) not only developed strategy based on knowledge of geography but also sponsored a translation of Strabo's *Geography*. Following the Napoleonic Wars there was a great interest in geographical exploration worldwide, especially the interiors of the continents (little known at the time), and geographical societies were founded in major cities. Furthermore, instruction in geography has been part of the training in service academies ever since. There is, understandably, an increased interest in geographical intelligence during times of war in all of the military services—navy, army, and air forces—which engage in so-called defense studies and mapping. Thus during World War II the British Royal Navy, Naval Intelligence Division, commissioned a series of handbooks on the geography of various areas that were later declassified and made available to general libraries. This was also true of maps made by the U.S. Army Map Service and of charts, the work of various hydrographic services together with coastal studies in the form of navigational pilot books. The role of air forces is well-known in not only providing the means for aerial reconnaissance but also in sponsoring aeronautical chart series at "geographical" scales. Thus map coverage of the Earth on the scale of 1:1,000,000, begun through the efforts of Albrecht Penck (1858–1945) as the International Map of the World (IMW), was completed at this scale by the maps of the U.S. Aeronautical Chart and Information Service during World War II. Ironically the United States had not officially cooperated with the IMW, but the private American Geographical Society of New York mapped all of Latin America at this scale. Furthermore, as a result of wartime experience, many returning veterans in several countries during this period made careers in applied or theoretical geography, some founding or working in geography departments, which were established in many colleges and universities in the 1940s and 1950s. These personnel are now mostly retired, or deceased, and later wars did not produce a similar great expansion in academic geography. In fact some of the then newly created departments, especially in the United States, were merged with other instructional units, renamed, or terminated. This is attributable to a number of causes, not least the abandonment of the geography department at Harvard University during the presidency of the scientist James Conant (1893–1978). The Harvard precedent was followed by other, even public, institutions that formerly had strong departments of geography. These universities often have splendid map collections, which find little use among students and faculty not geographically "literate."

Just as geography is essential to the military establishment, so it is valued in the public, civilian sector. Thus, that most fundamental of human geographical distributions, population itself, is of the greatest interest to census bureaus of various countries and internationally, with the United Nations having a vital concern with demography. Similarly, topographic and land use data of various scales is essential to the effective administration of urban and rural areas in the form of maps and reports. Thomas Jefferson (1743–1826), who also sponsored geographical exploration and wrote an important geographical treatise, well understood this, and he initiated the United States Public Land Survey, passed into law as the Land Ordinance of 1785 and first applied in Ohio. Subsequently rectilinear surveys expanded over three-quarters of the United States, which became the public domain, thereby transforming the American landscape and producing a torrent of cadastral maps, plat books, and county atlases in the nineteenth century, and beyond. Also, between World War I and World

War II, the detailed Land Utilisation Survey of Britain was conducted under the direction of L. Dudley Stamp (1889–1966), and it has had a profound effect on the economic life of that area (despite its title, Scotland was not covered). The idea was to make a record of existing land uses and to plan for the future. By 1940 the survey was essentially complete and proved of enormous value to Britain as it expanded its agricultural production during World War II. The concept was adopted by other, especially densely settled, countries and gave rise to the formation of the Commission of the International Geographical Union (IGU) on land use.

The remarkable expansion and improvement of highways of all kinds during this period led to the production of road data, published by government highway departments, automobile clubs, or oil and tire companies in many countries, becoming perhaps the most commonly available geographical source material worldwide. To a lesser or greater degree all government departments from foreign offices to small municipalities require geographical data, and more personnel are needed to process this information than are trained in existing educational institutions. However, the great success of geography in these applied fields has not been matched by similar success in theoretical realms in recent years, which will be the subject of most of the remainder of this essay.

**Geographical Theories**

Both Kant in Königsberg and Isaac Newton (1642–1727) at Cambridge University in England taught what might be called geography today, but they are not remembered for that activity. Newton also postulated that the Earth is an oblate (polar flattened) spheroid before it was proved by geophysical methods. This and other findings were to be of practical use in the development of detailed topographic maps in the nineteenth and twentieth centuries and especially during the space age in the second half of the twentieth century and the first years of the twenty-first century. Among the greatest contributions to science have been understanding of the shape, size, and motions of the planet Earth and of its place in the Universe. Although other societies and cultures such as the Chinese and Indian probably recognized the "curved" surface of the Earth, a full realization of the figure, mass, and movements of this planet is essentially a triumph of Western thought. This has become almost universally accepted so that Eurocentrism, as well as Sino-, Indo-, and other "centrisms" are dead, or dying.

This article has stressed the duality of the subject between physical and human, and theoretical and applied aspects, and needs now to detail a further division, that between systematic and regional geography. Some scholars will take a physical entity, such as vegetation or soils, or a cultural feature, such as urbanization or transportation, and discuss it with little or no reference to other topics. Contrasting with this is regional geography, in which the worker attempts to characterize an assemblage of features such as landforms, rivers, roads, soils, human population, and settlements to demonstrate how they are related, or "interact." Of course, the choice of what factors are most significant in a given area is of critical importance. Some assert that it is easier to analyze than to synthesize, and that regional geography is "the highest form of the geographer's craft."

## The Limits in Geography

What are the limits of the focus in the study of geography? It is usually assumed that geography is concerned with the surface or "shell" of the Earth, but workers do not specify how deep or high this sphere of interest to geographers extends. With some prescience Hartshorne wrote before 1966, "Man has for the first time projected his world of action beyond the [Earth's] atmosphere . . . and may soon be expected to extend that range to the moon" (Hartshorne, p. 24). This prediction was shortly realized when the United States, through its Apollo 11 mission of July 1969, landed two astronauts on the Earth's natural satellite, and images were taken of the Earth from the Moon. Further, rocks from the lunar surface were collected for the study of which the term *geology* was employed. Subsequently, many artificial satellites, both with humans aboard and unmanned, have been launched so that we now have a much greater understanding of the "blue planet" Earth, from above. Considering that the first aerial photographs of parts of the Earth were taken from a balloon in 1858, and that the science of photogrammetry—making maps from overlapping vertical air photographs—was developed in the first half of the twentieth century, progress has been remarkable. This was largely accomplished in European and North American countries, which assisted other areas that benefited from this technology.

Another realm of the Earth that has been seriously investigated is the ocean depths, made possible by modern technology—sonar or echo sounding. The oceans, the greater part of the surface of the Earth, have, of course, long interested maritime nations but until recently this interest had been confined to the surface, coastal limits, and other shallow areas—or to speculation. The most remarkable example of the latter is the postulation by the German meteorologist and physicist Alfred Wegener (1880–1930), who proposed that at an earlier period the continent(s) consisted of a single or, at most, two major land masses that had subsequently drifted apart. At the time of his death, not enough evidence was forthcoming to prove Wegener's theory of "continental displacement," or "continental drift" as it was later termed. Sonic sounding now permits continuous traces, or profiles, to be made across the ocean floor by ships in progress, which, in aggregate, provide a true three-dimensional image, making possible the charting of the ocean basins. This process has revealed an assemblage of "forms" as varied as those on land areas above sea level, including profound depths greater than the highest mountains on Earth. Most important, it has given validity to Wegener's theory, through identification of mid-ocean ridges, from which apparently the continents spread for the most part laterally. Other forms of evidence support this fundamental, and now widely accepted but hitherto controversial, theory.

The two examples given above illustrate how the Earth's surface or limits have been vastly enlarged in the past half century, and they also suggest that geographers who are concerned with the Earth as the "home" of humankind must come to terms with this increased realm. Geography, however, remains a very divided subject searching for a core. As indicated above, a few women geographers in the past have made signal contributions to the subject. However, as in many other studies, often women geographers became editors, school teachers, and librarians, in spite of the tradition of the intrepid Victorian lady traveler. Until quite recently women were often "excused" from field work in geography departments, considered a necessary part of the curriculum for males. Now that they constitute about one-half of the enrollment in colleges and universities, and owing to changing mores, women are now making an impact on the subject at the research level. This is expected to continue and expand, since previously, half of the human in human (and physical) geography had been excluded. The closeness of the female to Mother Nature, it is speculated, gives women an advantage in geography that is now being realized, understood, and, to a greater extent than previously, appreciated.

Just as women and their special points of view have not been an important part of geography in the past, so, it is argued, have the interests and aspirations of the proletariat not been included. An attempt to address this lacuna has been through what has been called in its extreme form (and comparable to feminist geography) Marxist or, more acceptably, socialist geography. Notable proponents of feminist geography are Cindi Katz and Janice Monk; and of Marxist and Socialist geography, Massimo Quaino and David Harvey. Marxist and socialist practitioners assert, with considerable justification, that geography has been a white male, Eurocentric (even imperialistic) study, with the protection of the "establishment" in mind. This conservative view is being challenged by new graduates of "red-brick" universities, particularly, recalling their working-class roots. This concern also extends to various, often ethnic, minorities who were not previously part of the geographical equation. How far this development will redress past inequities and affect the future direction of the discipline may depend on further recruitment of university students from the underclasses and those concerned with their welfare.

The wide range of topics investigated by geographers will not be elaborated here, but it is suggested by the indexes of textbooks in physical and human geography where they are later treated in varying degrees of detail. Methods mentioned earlier, including field work, interpretation of aerial photographs, and individual images from space are of course still available, but other methods have been added recently: continuous surveillance and imaging of the Earth, since 1972, through the Earth Resources Technology Satellite (ERTS) and its successor, Landsat; and new computer programs, especially ARC/INFO, introduced in 1982.

## Geographical Models

Before treating computer graphics and geographical information systems (GIS), which purists consider only tools, mention should be made of the criticism of academic geography as being mere description, with a lack of theories. Traditionalists would argue that all places on the Earth are different, that therefore description of these variations represents reality, and that geographers need only address themselves to the "real" world. These practitioners often reject models, two of the most successful of which in geography have been Central Place Theory in human geography, and the Köppen system of world climates in physical geography, which are examined, as examples, below.

Central Place Theory arose from studies of the distribution of settlements in the eighteenth century in Germany where it was postulated that places of varying size and function on a "uniform plain" would be arranged in hexagonal hierarchies. This has proved to be essentially the case, for example, on the delta of the Nile in Egypt, and elsewhere, as demonstrated by cartography and remote sensing. An elaboration of this is in the location of functional areas within cities, as exemplified by the case of Chicago. However, critics have observed that both concentric and sector patterns are evident in Chicago and that what obtains in a relatively modern city in the American Midwest does not necessarily apply to European and especially Asian cities. Chicago, with its location on the shores of one of the Great Lakes, is unique because of its special geographical setting and other factors.

More successful has been the Köppen system of climatic classification, which also had its origins in Europe, through the work of Wladimir Köppen (1846–1940) in the nineteenth and twentieth centuries. When long-term information was available from weather stations worldwide, it was observed that patterns were repeated in separate, but expected locations around the globe. Thus, to take one example, between approximately 30° and 40° latitude on the west coasts of all the continents, a Mediterranean climate was recognized. This climatic type is characterized by having high-sun (summer) drought and almost all of its precipitation in the low-sun (winter) months, the opposite of what would be expected. Thus in addition to the type example in Europe and the Middle East, it was found that California in the northern hemisphere, and Central Chile, Southwest Africa, and Southwest Australia in the southern, have "Mediterranean" climates. On the basis of climatic similarities, scholars have attempted to refine the Köppen system so that six major, and a total of sixteen, subtypes are now recognized globally. Being based to some extent on "native" vegetation, and not altogether on climate, critics consider the Köppen system to be a technical grouping rather than a true classification. Nevertheless, the Köppen system has proved to be a powerful teaching device that has not been superseded by other classifications. Although largely similar, each of the geographically separated Mediterranean areas have differences owing to local factors but, in comparison with other areas, they are more alike than different. This is also true of the other subtypes of the Köppen climatic classification. Critics assert that all places on Earth have some, if only minor, differences and thus cannot be classified.

The two examples of theoretical geography given above, with their origins in the past, have been fine-tuned and have become part of the curricula of geography departments, more than most other theories in a field that has been characterized as more empirical than theoretical. Since the mid-1970s, two developments have revolutionized geography—the computer and space exploration—as much as any previous advances.

## Computers and Space Exploration

Before the computer, proto-quantitative geography was developed with the aid of various calculating machines, but it was only after Herman Hollerith (1860–1929) combined punched cards with the then-recent electromagnetic inventions that it became possible to count and classify in a much shorter time and with greater detail and precision than by any previous methods. But through the 1950s the machines required to perform these operations remained expensive, large, and clumsy. A turning point occurred in 1982 with the introduction of ARC/INFO, a geographical information software package that combines traditional automated systems with advanced spatial data-based handling capability. This is accomplished by combining a series of layers each with a different theme: relief, roads, political boundaries, settlements, and so on—the desideratum of the regional geographer. Specifically, ARC/INFO uses both vector (line) and raster (tabular) storage; transformations can be undertaken and questions asked concerning numbers, distance, addresses, and so forth. The utility of such a system to those who are concerned with geographical distributions is enormous, as is time saved by these procedures. Maps can be made using the system and simulated, three-dimensional representations produced. It can also be animated to show, for example, population change through time. The machines on which these procedures can be accomplished have been incredibly reduced in size, price, and availability.

Equally as remarkable as the widespread utility of the computer to geography have been the space programs of various countries and consortia. As in the case of the computer, space technology did not arrive fully developed without a period of gestation, partly alluded to above in the references to aerial photography. A breakthrough similar to that of the computer was made when German rocket scientists joined the incipient United States space program, and that of the Soviet Union, following World War II. Prior to this, around 1910, the Germans had used rockets fitted with cameras to image small areas of the Earth. The range of these missiles was increased in World War II when, as Vergeltungswaffe 2 (V-2) rockets, they were used for military purposes. From 1960, the Television and Infra-Red Observation Satellite (TIROS), a series of unmanned satellites, was launched in the United States, and demonstrated the ability to gather weather data from above Earth's cloud layers, the first important use of the new technology. Meanwhile the Soviets launched the Synchronously Programmed User Terminal and Network Interface (Sputnik) in 1957, imaged the previously unseen side of the Moon in 1959, and put a human in space in 1961. The next year marked the first manned space flight by the United States, which soon began a series of missions imaging the Earth from space—Gemini (1965–1966), and Apollo (1968–1969), with handheld cameras loaded with color and, later, color infrared (CIR) film, which had been perfected during World War II. As mentioned above, it was the Apollo 11 mission in 1969 that landed humans on the Moon. Subsequently, nonphotographic systems were also used so that the term "Remote Sensing of the Environment" was coined to replace air photo interpretation, which was included in the definition.

The next development was continuous, extensive surveillance of the planet Earth, first accomplished by the Earth Resources Technology Satellite (ERTS) in 1972. Another similar satellite was launched in 1975, and the program was renamed Land Remote Sensing Satellite (Landsat). Since that time, the surface of the Earth (except the polar regions that the system does not cover) has been scanned by Landsat every nine days. By international agreement Landsat imagery, which is telemetered to the Earth in at least four multispectral bands, is available to users in any part of the world. The French Satellite Pour l'Observation de la Terre (SPOT) and various Russian satellite programs produce very high quality images but, unlike Landsat, do not have continuous satellite coverage of the Earth. However, other countries and consortia (such as the European Space Center) make contributions to existing programs, as in the case of Britain and Australia. At the time of writing China has successfully launched an extraterrestrial satellite, recalling the early interest of the Chinese in gunpowder and rockets, and the United States has an operating imaging system on Mars.

## Summary and Conclusion

An attempt to bring the subject together, after a long hiatus, is *Geography: A Modern Synthesis* by Peter Haggett. This is suggested by the titles of a selection of chapters of his book: "The Fertile Planet"; "Environment Risks and Uncertainties"; "Ecosystems and Environmental Regions"; "Resources and Conservation"; "Spatial Diffusion"; "Toward a Regional Convergence"; and "Outer Space, Inner Space." Analysis may give partial answers, but syntheses is essential to provide cohesion to the reality that is geography. The holistic view of the Earth as seen from space should be imperative for geography as a unified discipline, concerned with ecosystems on a fragile planet.

As indicated above, in recent decades the study of geography has suffered a decline in institutions of higher learning in the United States, and it is opined that there will only be improvement by the re-establishment of the subject in high schools. The abysmal ignorance of most Americans about the world, which may be a legacy of isolationism, contrasts with the situation in other (even so-called Third World) countries where geography is taught at all levels. In those colleges and universities in the United States where the subject continues to be taught it is often necessary to recruit faculty worldwide. If wars in the Middle East and elsewhere are not enough to goad Americans into giving more attention to the subject, then perhaps increasing dependence on resources from overseas will provide the impetus to achieve this end.

*See also* **Demography; Maps and the Ideas They Express.**

### BIBLIOGRAPHY

Agnew, John, David N. Livingstone, and Alisdair Rogers, eds. *Human Geography: An Essential Anthology.* Oxford and Cambridge, Mass.: Blackwell, 1996. See especially: David Harvey, "On the Present Condition of Geography"; J. B. Harley, "Deconstructing the Map"; Yi Fu Tuan, "Space and Place"; Torsten Hagerstrand, "Diorama, Path and Project"; and Stan Openshaw, "A View of the GIS Crisis in Geography."

Clark, Michael J., Kenneth J. Gregory, and Angela M. Gurnell, eds. *Horizons in Physical Geography.* Basingstoke and London: Macmillan Education, 1987. See especially: Roger G. Barry, "Perspectives on the Atmosphere"; Keith M. Clayton, "Per-

spectives on the Geosphere"; and Richard J. Chorley, "Perspectives on the Hydrosphere."

Cosgrove, Denis. *Apollo's Eye: A Cartographic Genealogy of the Earth in the Western Imagination.* Baltimore and London: John Hopkins University Press, 2001.

Diamond, Jared. *Guns, Germs, and Steel: The Fates of Human Societies.* New York: Norton, 1999.

Entrikin, J. Nicholas, and Stanley D. Brunn, eds. *Reflections on Richard Hartshorne's "The Nature of Geography."* Washington, D.C.: Association of American Geographers, 1989.

Haggett, Peter. *Geography: A Modern Synthesis.* 2nd ed. New York: Harper and Row, 1975.

Hartshorne, Richard. *Perspective on the Nature of Geography.* Chicago: Published by Rand McNally and Company as Monograph No. 1, 1959.

——. *The Nature of Geography: A Critical Survey of Current Thought in the Light of the Past.* Lancaster, Pa.: The Association, 1939. Reprint: Westport, Conn.: Greenwood Press, 1976.

Harvey, David. *Spaces of the Capital: Towards a Critical Geography.* Edinburgh: Edinburgh University Press, 2001.

Katz, Cindi, and Janis Monk, eds. *Full Circles: Geographies of Women over the Life Course.* London and New York: Routledge, 1993.

Lewis, Martin W., and Karen E. Wilgen. *The Myth of Continents: A Critique of Metageography.* Berkeley and Los Angeles: University of California Press, 1997.

Livingston, David N., and Charles W. J. Withers, eds. *Geography and Enlightenment.* Chicago: University of Chicago Press, 1999.

Quaino, Massimo. *Geography and Marxism.* Translated by Alan Braley. Totowa, N.J.: Barnes and Noble, 1982.

Romm, James S. *The Edges of the Earth in Ancient Thought: Geography, Exploration, and Fiction.* Princeton, N.J.: Princeton University Press, 1992.

Spate, O. H. K. "Toynbee and Huntington: A Study in Determinism." *Geographical Journal* 118 (1952): 406–428.

Thrower, Norman J. W. *Maps and Civilization: Cartography in Culture and Society.* 2nd ed. Chicago and London: University of Chicago Press, 1999.

*Norman J. W. Thrower*

**GEOMETRY.** While the origins of geometry are likely to remain a matter of pure speculation, the elaborate written cultures of ancient Egypt and Babylon provide a wealth of information about the uses of geometry. Area and volume measurements abound in work connected with taxation, the provision of cities, and large-scale building works. Sometimes the Babylonians' evidence (which survives because they wrote on durable clay tablets) spills over into purer matters, and reveals methods for finding the areas of circles, and an impressive calculation of the length of the diagonal of a unit square. The so-called Pythagorean Theorem for right-angled triangles was used to find sides and diagonals of rectangles, and approximate methods for finding square roots. Other tablets display a cut-and-paste method for dealing with questions that could be formulated as quadratic equations—the origins of the method of completing the square—that depends for its validity on a certain amount of elementary geometry.

## Antiquity and the Middle Ages

Unfortunately there is little evidence of the transmission of geometrical knowledge from either Egypt or Babylonia to the emerging Greek culture. Significantly, the Greeks seem to have been interested in .proof, and the nature of mathematical knowledge, in a way that these other cultures were not. Plato's dialogues display these features in a dramatic way. In the *Meno,* for example, Plato has Socrates ask a slave boy about the diagonal of a square. What Socrates elicits is a comparison between the square of the diagonal and the square on the side; not a numerical answer, and not an approximation to $\sqrt{2}$, but an argument accompanied by a proof.

The advent of proof permitted an important discovery: $\sqrt{2}$ is what we would call an irrational number: there are no integers $p$ and $q$ such that $\sqrt{2} = p/q$. Historians used to present this discovery as momentous. Allegedly the mathematics of earlier, Pythagorean, times was based on the idea that everything could be counted, any two lengths could be regarded as multiples of a common measure. The incommensurability of the side and diagonal of a square put an end to that belief and caused a crisis in Greek mathematics. In the late twentieth century, however, historians retreated from this position. The only evidence for it is very late, and no contemporaneous evidence suggests a crisis. Rather, as Plato's dialogues suggest, there might have been surprise and excitement. The slave boy, after all, gave an acceptable answer. The existence of incommensurable pairs of lengths greatly complicated the theory of proportion, which is attributed to Eudoxus of Cnidus (c. 400–c. 350 B.C.E.) and presented in books 5 and 6 of Euclid's (fl. c. 300 B.C.E.) *Elements,* but again there is no suggestion of a crisis.

***The paradoxes of Zeno.*** Further evidence of the sophistication of Greek thought is found in Zeno of Elea's (c. 495–c. 430 B.C.E.) paradoxes, which survive only in the form of a somewhat hostile account by Aristotle (384–322 B.C.E.). Zeno aimed to show that the analysis of motion led inevitably to contradictions. Achilles may never catch a tortoise, because each time he runs to where the tortoise was it is still ahead, committing Zeno to an infinite chase. Indeed, by a somewhat similar argument he cannot get started. An arrow cannot move in an instant; therefore, it is at rest in every instant of its flight and therefore always at rest. Whatever Zeno's intention in proclaiming them, his paradoxes testify to a deep-seated interest in logical reasoning, and they continued to attract interest.

***The notion of proof.*** Much of Greek mathematics would be impossible without good notions of proof. The simplest form of proof was proof by showing, in which arrangements of pebbles were used to show such results as the sum of two odd numbers is even. Zeno's paradoxes display another form of reasoning, called *reductio ad absurdum,* in which a proposition is refuted by showing that it leads logically to a self-contradiction or other evident impossibility. This method was used extensively by Archimedes in his estimation of areas and volumes, and also earlier by Euclid in his *Elements,* for example when he showed that there are infinitely many prime numbers. For, if there are not, then there are only finitely many prime numbers, $p_1, p_2, \ldots,$ $p_n$ say, in which case the number $p_1 p_2 \ldots p_n + 1$ is larger than

any of these, so it cannot be prime, and yet it is divisible by none of them, so it must be prime.

Proofs in geometry turn approximate estimates based on a finite number of cases into certain knowledge. For example, the assumptions made at the start of Euclid's *Elements,* including the parallel postulate as described below, permitted Euclid to prove that the angle sum of a triangle is exactly two right angles by exhibiting a suitable pair of parallel lines, to prove Pythagoras's theorem by moving areas around, and, ultimately, to show that there are exactly five regular solids.

***Euclid's* Elements *and the axiomatization of geometry.*** The most impressive form of proof, however, in Greek mathematics is the axiomatic method, developed at length in Euclid's *Elements.* The aim, not perfectly honored but impressively so, was to state definitions of the fundamental terms, gives rules for what may be said about them, and then to derive truths successively from this base of assumptions (the axioms). The result is that later propositions in each book of the *Elements* depend in an elaborate, tree-like way, on the earlier ones, and confidence in these results depends on the transparency of the proofs and the quality of the original axioms.

***Apollonius and Archimedes.*** One of the intellectual high points of Greek mathematics is undoubtedly Apollonius of Perga's (c. 262–c. 190 B.C.E.) theory of conic sections. It is forbiddingly austere, but it goes a long way to creating a unified theory of all (nondegenerate) plane sections of a cone: the ellipse, parabola, and hyperbola. The names derive from the way their construction is shown to produce an area that falls short, is equal to, or exceeds another area (compare the terms for figures of speech: elliptical, or of few words; a parable is exact, hyperbole an exaggeration). The comparisons of areas yield a proportion, which is modernized as the equation of the curves, and Apollonius shows in some detail how the equation may be simplified by suitable geometric choices and how properties of the conic sections may be obtained, such as the focal properties of conics and the construction of tangents.

Archimedes (c. 287–212 B.C.E.), a near contemporary of Apollonius, has earned a reputation as the greatest of the Greek geometers not only for the brilliance of his achievements, but also perhaps because they are easier to admire. He found volumes of sections of cones and various solid figures, he was the first to show that the constant ($\pi$) that enters the formulas for

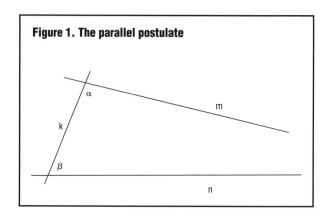

**Figure 1. The parallel postulate**

the circumference and the area of a circle is in fact the same, and he also made a number of practical and mechanical discoveries. He also left a unique account, known as the Method, of how he came to some of his discoveries by heuristic means, regarding areas as made up of lines that could be moved around. A tenth-century copy of this account was discovered in 1906 in a monastery in Istanbul. It was then lost again, but reappeared in 1998, when it was put on auction and sold for the surprisingly small sum of $2.2 million.

***Arabic and Islamic work on geometry.*** Islamic scholars did much more than simply transmit Greek ideas to the later West, as some accounts have suggested. They far surpassed all previous cultures in geometric design. They also produced the most penetrating analyses of the single most obvious weakness in all of Euclid's *Elements*: the parallel postulate. Euclid had assumed that if two lines *m* and *n* cross a third, *k*, and the angles $\alpha$ and $\beta$ the lines *m* and *n* make with *k* are less than two right angles on one side of the line (in the figure $\alpha + \beta < 2$ right angles) then the lines will meet on that side of the line if they are produced sufficiently far (see fig. 1).

Unlike all Euclid's other assumptions, the parallel postulate makes claims about what happens arbitrarily far away and so could be false. However, very few theorems can be proved unless the parallel postulate is known, so mathematicians were in a quandary. Greek and still more Islamic commentators took the view that it would be better to drop the parallel postulate from the list of axioms, and to derive it instead from the other axioms as a theorem.

Remarkably, from Thabit ibn Qurrah (c. 836–901) to Nasir ad-Din at-Tusi (1201–1274), they all failed. To give just one example, Ibn al-Haytham (Alhazen; 965–1039) assumed that if a segment of fixed length and perpendicular to a given line moves with one endpoint on the line then the other end point draws a straight line, parallel to the given line. Certainly, the parallel postulate follows as a theorem if one may make this assumption, and the parallel postulate implies it, but this only invites the question: how can the assumption itself be proved, or is it merely an alternative assumption to the parallel postulate? Some years later, Omar Khayyám (1048?–?1131) objected to the assumption on just these grounds, arguing that it was an illegitimate use of motion in geometry to attempt to define a curve this way, still more to assume that the curve so produced was a straight line.

## Modern Era

Significant Western interest in mathematics ebbed for a long time during and after the Roman Empire, before flowing at times in the Middle Ages. Only in the sixteenth century did a continual process of growth begin, aided by the rediscovery of Greek and Arabic texts and the publication of editions of Euclid's *Elements* and the works of Apollonius and Archimedes. At the same time, the discovery of the method of single-focused perspective transformed first architecture and then the practice of painting, where it produced a dramatically heightened realism. The technique proved eminently teachable, although few painters apart from Piero della Francesca (c. 1420–1492) also understood the mathematics involved.

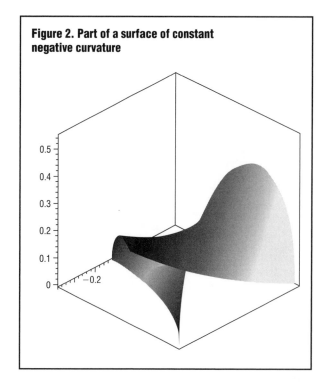

**Figure 2. Part of a surface of constant negative curvature**

***Analytic and projective geometry.*** Girard Desargues (1591–1661) brought together projective ideas from both architecture and painting to create the first fully unified theory of conic sections (all nondegenerate conic sections are projections of a circle). This theory naturally highlights those aspects that are projective (such as tangency questions) and it led directly or indirectly to a number of novel discoveries over the next century before it petered out. It was then rediscovered by Gaspard Monge (1746–1818) and Jean-Victor Poncelet (1788–1867) at the time of the French Revolution. In the form of simple horizontal and vertical projections it became the core technique of descriptive geometry or engineering drawing, a mainstay of French mathematical education throughout the nineteenth century, and, of course, it is still in use in the early twenty-first century.

Poncelet's breakthrough at the start of the nineteenth century was to see that, for many geometric properties a curve is equivalent to any of its "shadows" (its images under central projection). His own way of doing this was not found to be acceptable by later mathematicians, but Michel Chasles (1793–1880) in France and August Ferdinand Möbius (1790–1868) and Julius Plücker (1801–1868) in Germany all independently found more rigorous ways of making his insight work, and the resulting subject of projective geometry became the fundamental geometry of the nineteenth century. Although the details remained obscure for some time, the key point was that projective geometry discussed geometric properties of figures that do not involve the concept of distance. Any theorem in projective geometry is true in Euclidean geometry, but not vice versa, and so projective geometry is more basic than Euclidean geometry.

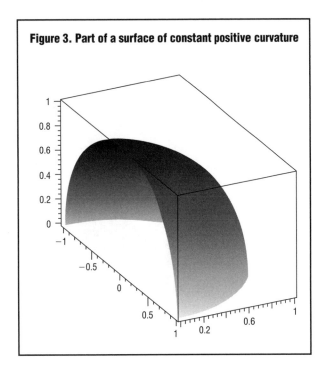

**Figure 3. Part of a surface of constant positive curvature**

point) is a measure of the best fitting sphere, plane, or saddle at that point (see figs. 2 and 3).

Gauss found that this quantity is intrinsic: it can be determined by measurements taken in the surface itself without reference to the ambient Euclidean space. This property was so unexpected Gauss called the result an exceptional theorem.

***Gaussian curvature and the emergence of non-Euclidean geometries.*** After Gauss's death it emerged that he, alone of the mathematicians of his time, had had some sympathy with efforts to show that Euclidean geometry was not the only possible geometry of space, and indeed his astronomer friends Friedrich Wilhelm Bessel (1784–1846) and Heinrich Wilhelm Matthäus Olbers (1758–1840) had also inclined that way. This leads back to the question of the parallel postulate.

Around 1830 János Bolyai (1802–1860) in present-day Hungary and Nicolai Ivanovich Lobachevsky (1792–1856) in remote Kazan in Russia, wrote down and published detailed accounts of what a geometry would look like in which the parallel postulate was false and the angle sum of a triangle is always less than two right angles (reprinted in English translation in Bonola, 1912). Although independent, their work is remarkably similar and can be described together. They studied geometry in two and three dimensions, and found formulas for triangles in the plane analogous to the formulas of spherical trigonometry for triangles on the sphere. These new formulas showed that small regions of the new geometry differed only slightly from small regions of the Euclidean plane, thus explaining why the new geometry had not been noticed hitherto, but they also showed what many a previous defence of the parallel postulate had hinted at—that the new geometry was different from Euclidean geometry in many respects.

Such was the novelty of Bolyai's and Lobachevsky's work that few read it and the published responses to it were extreme in their hostility. Most people instinctively found it incoherent; they "knew" it was wrong but were not willing to find out where. Gauss, however, wrote to Bolyai to say that he agreed with János's presentation but implying that he knew it all already (a claim for which there is little surviving evidence). János was so enraged he never published again. In 1840 Gauss nominated Lobachevsky to the Göttingen Academy of Sciences, but did nothing else to promote the new geometry. The result was that both men died without getting the acclaim their discoveries undoubtedly merited.

***Riemann's generalization for spaces of higher dimensions.***
The hegemony of Euclidean geometry came to an end not with the discoveries of Bolyai and Lobachevsky, but in stages, starting with Riemann's wholly novel approach to geometry that severely undercut it. Bernhard Riemann (1826–1866) was a student of mathematics at the University of Göttingen in the mid-1850s. In his postdoctoral thesis he set out the view that geometry was the study of any "space" of points upon which one could talk about lengths, and he indicated a variety of ways in which the techniques of the calculus could do such service. This is a rather natural and elementary idea, the problems come in spelling out the details in any useful way.

Desargues's contemporary, René Descartes (1596–1650) was much more successful with a work that was ruthlessly modern in its approach, and entirely eclipsed earlier attempts. Descartes took contemporary algebra, rewrote it in simpler notation, and proceeded to solve geometric problems by recasting them in algebraic terms and solving them by algebraic means, then reinterpreting the solution in geometric terms. Typically, the algebraic solution will be a single equation between two unknowns. Descartes interpreted this as defining a curve, and gave an elaborate discussion of how, given an equation, the corresponding curve can be drawn. He published his ideas as an appendix (entitled *La géométrie*) to a longer philosophical work in 1637.

Descartes did not explain the more elementary parts of his approach. This was done by a number of Dutch scholars who came after him, and the study of geometry by means of algebra (Cartesian, analytic, or coordinate geometry) was swiftly established. It took about a century for mathematicians to decide that the algebraic equation was an acceptable answer to a geometric problem, and to drop Descartes's search for geometric constructions, but the idea that geometric figures are naturally and fruitfully described by algebra has remained central to much of mathematics ever since.

***Differential geometry.*** Differential geometry, on the other hand, began as the study of curves and surfaces where the calculus is allowed. It is connected to such questions as: when a map of the earth's surface (assumed to be a sphere) is made on a plane, what geometric properties can be preserved? The decisive reformulation of the early nineteenth century came when Carl Friedrich Gauss (1777–1855) investigated the curvature of surfaces in space. The curvature of a surface at a point (and generally the curvature of a surface varies from point to

Riemann concentrated on intrinsic properties of the space, such as Gauss's idea of the curvature of a surface, and he noted that there would be different geometries on spaces with different intrinsic properties. That includes spaces of different dimensions, and also spaces of dimension two, say, but different curvatures. What it does not do is say that Euclidean space of some dimension is the source of geometric concepts, thus Euclidean geometry is overthrown.

Riemann's thesis was published posthumously in 1867, just in time to resolve the doubts of an Italian mathematician, Eugenio Beltrami (1835–1899), who had come to some of the same ideas. He immediately published his reworking of the geometry of Bolyai and Lobachevsky as the geometry of a surface of constant negative curvature, of which he had a description in a disc of unit (Euclidean) radius. Beltrami's map and Riemann's philosophy of geometry convinced mathematicians, but not all philosophers, of the validity of non-Euclidean geometry, as the Bolyai-Lobachevsky geometry became known.

## Twentieth Century

There, curiously, Riemann's ideas remained for more than a generation. There was some interest in novel three-dimensional geometries, almost none in geometries, in Riemann's sense, of higher dimensions, except to show that mechanics could be done in such a setting, and in simplifying the formidable algebraic complexity of the subject (today handled by means of the tensor calculus). The decisive change came with the work of Albert Einstein (1879–1955).

Einstein's special theory of relativity of 1905 was a thorough reworking of the mathematics of motion, and at first Einstein was unsympathetic to the geometrical reworking given to his ideas by Hermann Minkowski (1864–1909) in 1908. But when Einstein started to think of a general theory of relativity that would find an equivalence between forces and accelerations, he found the ideas of Riemannian differential geometry invaluable. The theory he came to in 1915 formulated gravitation as a change in the metric of space-time. On this theory, matter changes the shape of space, which is how it exerts its attractive force.

### Felix Klein's Erlangen program.

By the 1870s, projective geometry had established itself as the fundamental geometry, with Euclidean geometry as a special case, along with some other geometries not described in this essay. The young German mathematician Felix Klein (1849–1925) then proposed to unify the subject, by treating projective geometry as the main geometry, and deriving the other geometries as special cases. Every geometry Klein was interested in, most strikingly non-Euclidean geometry, was defined on projective space or a subset of it, and the relevant geometric properties were those kept invariant by the action of a suitable subgroup of the group of all projective transformations. This view, called the Erlangen Program, after the university where Klein first published it, has remained the orthodoxy since the 1890s, when Klein republished it, but in its day the novelty was the explicit introduction of the then-novel concept of a group, and the shift of attention from properties of figures to the idea that these properties are geometric precisely because they are invariant under the appropriate group of transformations.

### Italians, Hilbert, and the axiomatization of geometry.

Klein's geometries do not include many of the geometries Riemann had pointed toward. It included only those that have large groups of transformations, which, however, is most of those of interest in physics and much of mathematics for a long time, including, it was to transpire, Einstein's special theory of relativity. The first step beyond what Klein had done, and for that matter Riemann, was proposed by David Hilbert (1862–1943), starting in 1899, although a number of Italian geometers had had similar ideas in the decade before.

Hilbert was insistent that theorems in geometry should only use the properties of objects that entered into their definitions, and to this end he formulated elementary geometry carefully in terms of five families of axioms. What distinguished his work from his Italian predecessors was his insistence that there was an interesting new branch of mathematics to be explored, which studied axiom systems. It would aim at showing the independence of certain axioms from others, and establishing what sorts of axioms were needed to deduce particular results. Whereas the Italian mathematicians had mostly aimed at axiomatizing projective and perhaps Euclidean geometry once and for all, Hilbert saw the axiomatic method as both creative and of wide applicability. He even indicated ways in which it could work in mathematical physics.

By 1915, the axiomatization of geometry had begun to spread to other branches of mathematics as well, with a consequent improvement in the standards of formal proof, and Einstein's general theory of relativity had similarly improved the ideas about the applications of geometry.

*See also* **Cosmology: Cosmology and Astronomy; Greek Science; Islamic Science; Mathematics; Physics; Relativity.**

BIBLIOGRAPHY

Berggren, J. Len. *Episodes in the Mathematics of Medieval Islam.* New York: Springer-Verlag, 1986.

Bonola, R. *History of Non-Euclidean Geometry.* Translated by H. S. Carslaw, preface by F. Enriques. Chicago: Open Court, 1912.

Bos, Henk. J. M. *Redefining Geometrical Exactness: Descartes' Transformation of the Early Modern Concept of Construction.* New York: Springer-Verlag, 2001.

Field, Judith V., and Jeremy J. Gray, eds. *The Geometrical Work of Girard Desargues.* New York: Springer-Verlag, 1987.

Fowler, David H. *The Mathematics of Plato's Academy: A New Reconstruction.* 2nd ed. Oxford: Clarendon, 1999.

Gray, Jeremy J. *The Hilbert Challenge.* Oxford: Oxford University Press, 2000.

———. *Ideas of Space: Euclidean, Non-Euclidean, and Relativistic.* 2nd edition. Oxford: Oxford University Press, 1989.

Hilbert, David. *Foundations of Geometry.* 10th English edition, translation of the second German edition by L. Unger. Chicago: Open Court, 1971.

Høyrup, Jens. *Lengths, Widths, Surfaces: A Portrait of Old Babylonian Algebra and Its Kin.* New York: Springer-Verlag, 2002.

Jaouiche, K. *La théorie des parallèles en pays d'Islam: Contributions à la préhistoire des géométries non-euclidiennes.* Paris: Vrin, 1986.

Robson, Eleanor. "Neither Sherlock Holmes nor Babylon: A Reassessment of Plimpton 322." *Historia Mathematica* 28 (2001): 167–206.

Salmon, Wesley C., ed. *Zeno's Paradoxes.* Indianapolis: Bobbs-Merrill, 1970.

*Jeremy Gray*

**GESTURE.** The concept of gesture suffers to some extent from insufficiently defined and imprecisely drawn outlines of what we understand by this term. The *Oxford English Dictionary* defines gesture as any "significant movement of limb or body"; Merriam Webster's *Collegiate Dictionary* defines it as "any movement of the body, or part of the body, that expresses or emphasizes an idea, sentiment or attitude." However varied the definitions may be, they always contain the same element: a gesture is a combination of a body movement (or a bodily posture) and a meaning. It is generally assumed (and borne out by social practice) that this combination is understood by the outside spectator, and hence functions as a means of communication.

Taking the concept in its broadest sense, gestures can be roughly divided into two major types. One type consists of conventionalized body movements or limited actions, such as pointing with the hand and the outstretched index finger, or shaking hands. These movements have a firmly established, "timeless" meaning. They are consciously performed, and since their meaning is instantly and clearly understood, they play a significant part in everyday communication, and have a role in the arts.

The other group of gestures consists of body movements made without conscious intention, often even without a person's being aware of performing them. Nevertheless, they can clearly convey some meaning, and are thus understood as communicating some message. Blushing is interpreted as a sign of shame; going pale is understood as a sign of sudden fear. Though in fact it is sometimes hard to tell such gestures from symptoms in medicine, the study of gestures must also consider such "natural" occurrences.

Conventionalized body movements in particular play an important and often highly visible part in many domains of social life. Both their shapes and meanings have been preserved for many ages. One thinks, for example, of the religious sphere. The gestures of kneeling and folding the hands in prayer are in no need of explanation in the Western world, nor are the movements of the priest officiating at Mass, especially in the elevation of the host and in other religious rituals. In different parts of the world, with various religions and rituals, equivalent gestures, even if somewhat dissimilar in their execution, have been developed for worship and are instantly understood.

The military is another domain in which the shape of at least some body movements is given much attention. Of individual military gestures, gait and the salute instantly come to mind. Military education explicitly cultivates certain modes of body movement, seeing such performance as expressing an overall spirit.

Highly conventionalized gestures are not found only in special fields; they abound in all domains of established social life.

When a witness stands up in court and raises his hand to take an oath, or when a man lifts his hat to greet an acquaintance on the street, he is performing a highly conventional gesture that has a long history.

Some conventional gestures have become so fully crystallized in themselves, and what they convey has become so deeply engraved in our minds, that they could be detached from the figure performing them. One example of such an independent gesture, detached, as it were, from the person making it, is the movement of making the sign of the cross; another is a hand with outstretched index finger pointing in a direction.

Conventional gestures have often been defined as a universal language, and the question of whether gesture language has, or does not have, a grammar, has occupied scholars. The most developed codification of gestures is found in the sign language of the deaf. Other attempts at linguistic codification of gestures are known from history, a well-known example being that of the Cistercian monks who, abstaining from speech as part of their ascetic life, developed a sign language and even prepared a dictionary of the most frequently performed body movements that replaced spoken words.

### The Study of Gestures

The interpretation of gestures, their origin, and the long history of gesticulation, has attracted the attention of students whose discussions, even if intermittent, have shed interesting

**Sculpture relief depicting the goddess Tyche of Palmyra.** Throughout history, from ancient civilization to contemporary times, works of art have frequently incorporated gestures to convey mood and concept.

***Christ before Caiaphas*** (1304–1306) by Giotto di Bondone. Fresco. Gestures have long been a part of religious ritual and imagery. Many gestures of this genre, though they may differ from faith to faith, are universally recognizable. THE ART ARCHIVE/SCROVEGNI CHAPEL PADUA/DAGLI ORTI (A)

light on the problems that emerge in the study of gestures. In recent decades, concern with the human body and its manifold manifestations has attracted increasing attention to gestures, both conventional and spontaneous.

Reflections on gestures, however fragmentary, are found in the literature of early history. In the Bible, prayer gestures are described as self-evident: "And when ye spread forth your hands, . . . when ye make many prayers" (Isaiah 1:15). Reflections on specific gestures are scattered throughout the literature

of classical antiquity, especially in texts on physiognomics and rhetorics, but references to gesticulation are also found in other writings. Homer abounds in allusions to gestures and expressive movements, as may be seen for instance in his reference to mourning (*The Iliad,* 18:23–27).

In Roman civilization the "eloquence of the body" (*eloquentia corporis*) commanded a great deal of attention. Two categories of professionals in particular, orators and actors, studied gesture intensively. Bodily gestures follow movements of the

**Coin depicting Roman Emperor Domitian at surrender of Germany.** Distinctive gestures have been a component of military organization since ancient times. Ritualized gestures are frequently seen as a method of fostering unity among soldiers.

**Supplicating barbarian. Bronze figurine.** Gesture and physicality commanded a great deal of attention in ancient Roman culture. Gestures in stage productions of the period were often broad and eloquent.

soul. Cicero compared man's body, face, and voice to the strings of a harp: "They sound just as the soul's motion strikes them" (*De oratore* 3.216). And Quintilian says simply: "Gesticulation obeys our mind" (*Institutio oratoria* XI, chap. 3, 65). The most detailed and careful description of gestures that survives from ancient literature is found in Quintilian (XI, chap. 3). Since he saw gesticulation as part of the delivery of a speech, he included a discussion of gestures in his teaching of oratory. The Roman stage was another place for the formalization of gestures. As stock types were preferred on the stage, gestures were basic and strictly codified. Broad gestures, such as shaking the head or slapping the thigh in anger, were typical of slaves.

In antiquity, another field of knowledge pertaining to our subject was defined and flourished: physiognomics, the reading of character from the structure and movement of body and face. The literary legacy of ancient physiognomics influenced thought in modern times. The works of the Renaissance scholar Giambattista della Porta, the great French artist Charles Le Brun (around 1700), and the Swiss scholar Johann Lavater in the eighteenth century are ample testimony to this influence in the culture of Europe.

In the Middle Ages, especially in the earlier part of the period, codified gestures seem to have played a particularly important part in legal transactions. Since most people could not read or write, documents were frequented validated through the use of prescribed gestures. A richly illuminated late medieval manuscript, the *Sachsenspiegel*, gives us some inkling of the variety and role of conventional gestures in the legal and political life of the time.

In Renaissance culture, which gave so much thought and attention to the comportment of people (especially the nobility) and to their education, the problem of gesture was approached from a new point of view. The concern was with how the educated should behave in their bodily presentation, and how the child and young person should be taught so that, as an adult, he or she would behave in a proper manner. Some of the central figures in Renaissance culture, such as Baldassare Castiglione, author of *The Courtier*, and Desiderius Erasmus, devoted much attention to proper gesticulation. Erasmus wrote a little book on the education of children (*Institutio principis Christiani* [1516; *Education of a Christian Prince*]) which in the sixteenth century alone went through eighty editions in Latin, and was certainly a factor in forming habits of movement and views of gesture.

In spite of this long history, however, it is safe to say that the critical, scientific study of gestures is a product of the nineteenth century. It was also then that the major approaches to the interpretation of gesture crystallized. Reduced to basic distinctions, two lines of thought emerge. One of them may be called universal language (or universalizing), the other particularistic (or particularizing).

The notion of gesture as a universal language is based upon the assumption that all people and societies in all ages make

**930**

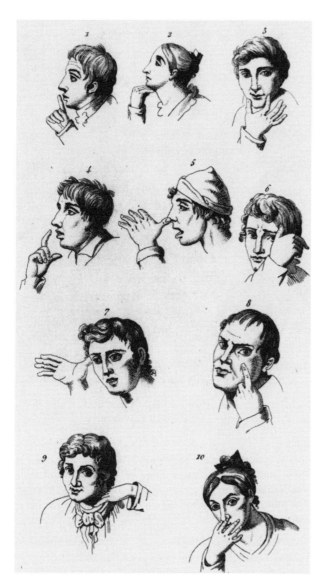

*Crucifixion of Christ* (1515) by Matthias Grunewald. **From the Isenheim Altarpiece, oil on wood.** During the Renaissance, much emphasis was placed on bodily comportment and gesticulation, a trend readily apparent in creations by artists of the period. PHOTO CREDIT: ERICH LESSING/ART RESOURCE, NY

**Illustration of hand and facial gestures.** Comprehensive study and classification of gestures did not properly begin until the nineteenth century. Early pioneers in the field were Charles Darwin and Wilhelm Wundt.

essentially the same gestures under similar conditions and as a response to similar situations. This interpretation was put forward in explicit and systematic form for the first time by Charles Darwin in his *The Expression of the Emotions in Man and Animals* (1872). In this work Darwin devoted a great deal of attention, both in particular observations and in comprehensive classification, to gestures of the body and the face. Summing up his ideas, he says that he has "endeavored to show in considerable detail that all the chief expressions exhibited by man are the same throughout the world."

When we consider Darwin's work within the earlier prevailing tradition of interpreting human gestures, two features stand out. First, Darwin's observations are exclusively observations of

*Melencolia I* (1514) by Albrecht Dürer. Line engraving. A gesture does not always require movement to be understood. Often, the positioning of the body is enough to indicate mood or meaning. THE GRANGER COLLECTION, NEW YORK

*Quarrel in Naples,* **by Andrea de Jorio.** In 1832 de Jorio published a study of the gestures of his fellow Neapolitans. He sought to understand how ancient gestures were manifested in contemporary society as a means to interpret the body movements in classical plays.

nature, that is, observations of the behavior of living creatures; he excludes literary texts or pictorial representations. The cultural artifact is beyond the scope of his study. In the introduction he even explicitly states that the artistic representation of figures dominated by an emotion (suffering) follows principles differing from those of nature, and are therefore misleading as materials for the student of natural reality. Second, an idea permeating Darwin's study is that there is a continuity from the bodily behavior and gesticulation of some kinds of beasts to the gestures commonly performed by human beings. While there are some gestures that are characteristic only of man, most of the expressive movements are found, to some degree, in certain classes of animals.

One of the many examples that Darwin adduces is the facial expression of rage. The physiognomic changes undergone by a human in the grip of rage, and the typical gestures he or she performs in this condition, have occupied the human mind in all ages; already in antiquity books were being written on the subject—for example, Seneca's *De ira.* In art the features of an angry man's face have been firmly established. Darwin finds the physiognomic contortions of the angry human face also in beasts, in such expressions as snarling and prominently exhibiting the teeth. "Considering how seldom the teeth are used by men in fighting," he says, the "retraction of the lips and the uncovering of the teeth during paroxysms of rage, as if to bite" are remarkable. In this facial gesture the memory survives of our ancestors, the higher primates, that still really fight with their teeth. This theory further supports the doctrine of the universality of gesture language.

The influential German scholar Wilhelm Wundt, who in 1900 published the first volume of his *Völkerpsychologie,* which contains an extensive discussion of gesture, claimed that primordial speech was a kind of gesticulation that "mirrored the soul."

In modern kinesics, the systematic study of the relationship between nonlinguistic body motions and communication, and related fields of study (especially some branches of linguistics), communicating gestures are regarded as a kind of language, possibly even the predecessor of spoken language in general. Students have compiled dictionaries of expressive body movements. Of particular interest are collections of such movements performed by aboriginals. In the background of these scientific studies one finds the idea of gesture as a universal language.

The other, altogether different interpretation of the origin of gestures sees individual modes of behavior, as they developed in small groups living under specific conditions, as the true origin of, and the force shaping, our expressive movements. The first text of modern gesture study presented this view. *La mimica degli antichi investigata nel gestire napoletano,* written by Andrea de Jorio, a cleric from Naples with wide intellectual interests, was published in 1832. In this work, which may be considered the birth certificate of the modern discussion of gestures, the author devotes his main efforts to the observation and description of the actual gestural behavior of Neapolitans of his day. The northern nations, de Jorio believes, are restrained in gesture; southerners, especially people living in and around Naples, have rich gesticulation. His motive, however (as he explicitly states it), was not to study the habits of contemporary Neapolitans. He wanted to contribute to a better understanding of the plays of antiquity. De Jorio believed that there was a long and continuous tradition leading directly from some of the ancient communities to people in the Naples area in the early nineteenth century. In this tradition gestures were transmitted through the ages, and if we look at people in Naples we can, therefore, grasp what ancient poets meant when in their plays they alluded to body movements. Gestures, then, do not have a universal origin, but emerge from specific conditions prevailing in individual societies. Gestures are inherited from such particular traditions and remain in use for ages.

In the middle of the twentieth century this trend of thought received a classic formulation from the French anthropologist Marcel Mauss. His most influential study of the subject, "Les techniques du corps," reverberates in the study of gesture to this day. Mauss describes his approach as "descriptive ethnology" and focuses on the specific forms of gesticulation in specific societies. Based on heritage and tradition, we continue to perform gestures in the form we inherited from former generations and as they were shaped by education and experience. He focuses on social and cultural differences rather than a supposed common origin and universal validity. Mauss believed that he could identify a girl educated in a convent by her comportment and way of walking: she will walk with her hands closed into fists.

Another view of the particular interpretation of gestures is the influential concept of the body and its manifestations as formulated by the anthropologist Mary Douglas in which she perceives the body as a symbol of social relations. As social relations change, the body and its movements—the gestures we make—manifest these changes.

## Gestures in the Arts

Gestures play a significant part in the arts, particularly in the performing and visual arts, as the history of these arts makes clear. In antiquity, especially in the Roman period, a particular category of theater play emerged, the pantomime. (*Pantomimus* meant both the play and the actor performing it.) The main characteristic of the pantomime was that it replaced the spoken text with a wide range of gestures, including dance. We know that whole tragedies were performed without the actor uttering even a single word, using instead a highly developed system of postures and gestures. In the sixth century C.E. Cassiodorus still characterizes the activity of the pantomime actor by describing his "speaking hands," his fingers that are similar to tongues, and his "loud sounding silence."

The origin of the pantomime is believed to have been the Dionysian feast in Egypt inaugurated during the rule of the Ptolemies. The multinational, and hence also multilingual, composition of society and army in the Roman Empire probably favored an art form that did not rely on a specific language and thus evaded linguistic limitations. The pantomime reached a peak of popularity in the imperial period in Rome. Pantomime actors, quite a few of whom are known to us by name, seem to have been idols of Roman society. When the emperor Augustus exiled a famous pantomime player, Pylades, from Italy, the reaction of popular audiences in the

capital was so powerful that the ruler had to cancel his edict and bring the banished actor back to Rome. The pantomime as a particular genre had a long life, and in the course of centuries many fathers of the church, among them Tertullian, Clement of Alexandria, and Minucius Felix, violently condemned such performances. In the year 305 the Church Council of Elvira decided that a pantomime actor who wanted to convert to Christianity had to give up his profession.

In the Middle Ages the pantomime did not persist as an independent genre, but the gesticulation of the actors in a medieval performance (which took place in a church or town square) was pronounced and exaggerated, often even grotesque. A good deal of the effect these plays had on their audiences was achieved by means of expressive body movement. Grotesque gesticulation plays a major part from medieval plays to performances of the commedia dell'arte. In modern times the performance based largely on body movements has had a long and eventful history. The recent inheritors of this tradition are the modern ballet and, more rarely, actual pantomime performances.

Since the time of the Egyptian and Mesopotamian cultures, the representation of gestures in painting and sculpture has been a central means of conveying moods, ideas, and even more conceptual messages. The great artists of all centuries, especially since the Renaissance—among them Leonardo da Vinci, Michelangelo, Gian Lorenzo Bernini, Rembrandt, and up to some works by Picasso—created classic formulations of gestural motifs that have impressed themselves profoundly on the modern cultural memory.

*See also* **Anthropology; Body, The; Cultural Studies; Theater and Performance.**

### BIBLIOGRAPHY
Barasch, Moshe. *Giotto and the Language of Gesture.* Cambridge, U.K.: Cambridge University Press, 1987.
Bremmer, Jan, and Herman Roodenburg, eds. *A Cultural History of Gesture.* Ithaca, N.Y.: Cornell University Press, 1992. Includes a useful bibliography.
Brilliant, Richard. *Gesture and Rank in Roman Art: The Use of Gestures to Denote Status in Roman Sculpture and Coinage.* New Haven, Conn.: Academy, 1963.
Darwin, Charles. *The Expression of Emotions in Man and Animals.* London: F. Pinter, 1983. First published in 1872.
Douglas, Mary. *Natural Symbols: Explorations in Cosmology.* New York: Pantheon, 1970.
Jorio, Andrea de. *La mimica degli antichi investigata nel gestire napoletano.* Naples, 1832. English translation published as *Gesture in Naples and Gesture in Classical Antiquity,* edited by Adam Kendon. Bloomington: Indiana University Press, 2000.
Kendon, Adam, ed. *Nonverbal Communication, Interaction, and Gesture.* The Hague: Mouton, 1981.
Mauss, Marcel. "Les techniques du corps." *Journal de psychologie normale et pathologique* 39 (1935): 271–293. English translation appears in Mauss, *Sociology and Psychology,* 97–123. London: Routledge, 1979.
Schmitt, Jean-Claude. *La raison des gestes dans l'Occident médiéval.* Paris: Gallimard, 1990.
Sittl, Karl. *Die Gebärden der Griechen und Römer.* Leipzig: Teubner, 1890.

*Moshe Barasch*

GERMANNA COMMUNITY COLLEGE
GERMANNA CENTER FOR ADVANCED TECHNOLOGY
18121 TECHNOLOGY DRIVE
CULPEPER, VA 22701

**Jewish family in Nazi ghetto, Lublin, Poland, c. 1941.** Although the term *ghetto* has evolved to serve as a name for any poor urban neighborhood, it was originally used in the sixteenth century to denote an area in which Jews were forced to live. AP/WIDE WORLD PHOTOS

**GHETTO.** The name of a district in sixteenth-century Venice where Jews were required to live, *ghetto* came to be the name for any segregated Jewish quarter. The name was applied (1) to compulsorily segregated Jewish residential districts in Europe between 1516 and 1870; (2) to urban areas of first settlement of Jewish immigrants and their distinctive culture after about 1880; and (3) from 1940 to 1944, to rigidly segregated districts in German-occupied European cities where the occupiers imprisoned Jews before methodically murdering them.

As a striking historical example of recurring policies of marginalization and demonization, *ghetto* was also applied to phenomena of Western history unconnected with Jews. In the nineteenth century, the term came to refer to (1) urban concentrations of distinctive businesses, classes, and ethnic groups. In the twentieth century in the United States, the term was applied to ethnic neighborhoods, particularly to (2) black neighborhoods in northern cities. Other urban areas have been called "the hippie ghetto," "Pakistani ghettos in the (English) midlands," and "the golden ghetto." Before the Enlightenment, mention of the ghetto was meant to arouse re-

vulsion at the inhabitants; afterward, its mention could also be meant to evoke indignation at the infliction of shame and suffering.

### Jewish Urban Quarters before the Ghetto
Diaspora Jews in late antiquity and the European Middle Ages lived together voluntarily, for security and communal convenience, in urban neighborhoods that were called *Judengasse,* in German-speaking countries; *giudecca, Judaica, juiverie, carrière,* or *judería* in Romance-speaking countries; and, in Muslim countries, equivalents of Harat-al-Yahud, "the Jewish quarter." Besides these voluntary Jewish enclaves, in which non-Jews also lived, medieval governments occasionally attracted Jews to settle in undeveloped regions by reserving special areas for them. These voluntary Jewish districts were usually walled and gated.

A different form of restricted residence that affected millions of Jews was the Russian Pale of Settlement, covering four hundred thousand square miles between the Baltic and Black seas, defined in 1791 and abolished after the 1917 revolution. Between 1772 and 1795, Russia, which had no Jews, annexed Polish territory with a large Jewish population. It restricted Jewish residence to some of the annexed territory, which Czar Nicholas I (reigned 1835–1855) gave the name "Pale of Settlement." In the course of the nineteenth century, Jews, who were a minority in these territories, were expelled from villages and compelled to live in towns and cities, and were limited to certain occupations. These regulations, which by 1897 applied to nearly five million Jews, became onerous at a time when restrictions on other population groups were relaxed. Pauperization, legal restrictions, and hostility in the pale provoked mass Jewish emigration, which flowed to the ghettos in other countries.

### Establishment of Ghettos
To control heresy, the Roman Catholic Church tried at times to separate Jews from Christians. Separation became a widespread policy from 1300 to 1600, when England, France, Spain, and Portugal expelled Jews, and many German and Italian cities enacted strict controls on those who were allowed to remain. Venice first permitted Jews to residence in 1513 and in 1516 required them to settle in the *ghetto nuovo,* the "new foundry" district, which it encouraged Christians to leave. The city later allowed Jewish settlement in other districts, the *ghetto vecchio* and the *nuovissimo ghetto.*

In 1555, as part of Counter-Reformation policy, Pope Paul IV (reigned 1555–1559) restricted Jewish residence in papal territories to segregated quarters, which by 1562 were called "ghettos." Through the eighteenth century they were established in western and central Europe. "Ghetto" conventionally evoked a forbidding image of impoverished Jews who lived locked behind walls from dusk to dawn in crowded, narrow streets, under their own authorities. During the French revolutionary wars, Napoleon Bonaparte (1769–1821) abolished ghettos and granted citizenship to Jews; this became permanent during the nineteenth century. The last ghetto, in Rome, was abolished in 1870.

GERMANNA COMMUNITY COLLEGE
CENTER FOR ADVANCED TECHNOLOGY
18121 TECHNOLOGY DRIVE
CULPEPER, VA 22701

## Ghetto as Metaphor for Slum

The image of the ghetto was applied to a variety of situations. The *Oxford English Dictionary* records *ghetto* as referring in 1887 to a neighborhood of book dealers. In 1903, Jack London compared the ghetto to the misery of slums inflicted on workers—only a small percentage of them Jews—by the unrestrained operation of laissez-faire economics:

> At one time the nations of Europe confined the undesirable Jews in city ghettos. But today the dominant economic class, by less arbitrary but nonetheless rigorous methods, has confined the undesirable yet necessary workers into ghettos of remarkable meanness and vastness. East London is such a ghetto, where the rich and the powerful do not dwell, and the traveler cometh not, and where two million workers swarm, procreate, and die.

The areas of first settlement by the mass immigration of Russian and Polish Jews to the United States, between 1880 and 1924, were called ghettos. Some earlier settlers considered these immigrants—like those from Italy, Poland, Scandinavia, and Asia—threats to American morality, hygiene, economics, and race. The immigrant "ghetto slums" lasted for a generation or two, until most inhabitants moved away or became invisible by learning English and adopting the manners and clothing of the country.

## Black Ghettos

Large numbers of black Americans in search of economic and social opportunities also arrived in northern cities in waves of internal migration during World War I, World War II, and the 1950s. They often first settled in immigrant neighborhoods, and the terms *ghetto* and *slum* came to refer to visible poor black neighborhoods that did not disappear through assimilation. Sociologist Kenneth Clark wrote:

> America has contributed to the concept of the ghetto the restriction of persons to a special area and the limiting of their freedom of choice on the basis of skin color. The dark ghetto's invisible walls have been erected by the white society, by those who have power, both to confine those who have no power and to perpetuate their powerlessness. . . . The objective dimensions of the American urban ghettoes are overcrowded and deteriorated housing, high infant mortality, crime, and disease. The subjective dimensions are resentment, hostility, despair, apathy, self-depreciation, and its ironic companion, compensatory grandiose behavior.

Many social scientists later discarded the ghetto metaphor because it carried misleading expectations that the underclass in the inner city would also disappear automatically.

## Nazi Ghettos

Between 1939 and 1944, Nazi racial ideology was put into operation in German-occupied Europe. The occupiers separated Jews from other subject peoples and imprisoned them in more than one thousand ghettos, which the Germans did not consistently give that name. The Germans ruled through governing councils that they selected. The occupiers allowed disease to spread widely and imposed both substarvation rations and the death penalty for smuggling food.

Hans Frank, chief of the Generalgouvernement of Poland, summarized the policy in August 1942 when he stated that if the Jews did not die of starvation, other measures would need to be taken. The Germans liquidated all the ghettos, and sent the survivors to extermination camps. Under these conditions, the Jews' attempts to preserve normal communal life and to demonstrate their productivity qualify as resistance, but the desperate armed uprising by the last inhabitants of the ghetto in Warsaw, in April and May 1943, added an unprecedented association to the term *ghetto*.

*See also* **Anti-Semitism; Ethnicity and Race; Genocide; Resistance; Segregation.**

**BIBLIOGRAPHY**

Clark, Kenneth B. *Dark Ghetto: Dilemmas of Social Power.* New York, Evanston, Ill., and London: Harper and Row, 1965.

"Ghettos." In *The Holocaust Encyclopedia,* edited by Walter Laqueur, 259–265. New Haven, Conn., and London: Yale University Press, 2001.

Gutman, Yisrael. *The Jews of Warsaw, 1939–1943: Ghetto, Underground, Revolt.* Bloomington: Indiana University Press, 1982.

London, Jack. *The People of the Abyss.* London and Sterling, Va.: Pluto Press, 2001. Originally published in 1903.

Ravid, Benjamin C. I. "From Geographical Realia to Historiographical Symbol: The Odyssey of the Word Ghetto." In *Essential Papers on Jewish Culture in Renaissance and Baroque Italy,* edited by David B. Ruderman, 373–385. New York: New York University Press, 1992.

Slutsky, Yehuda. "Pale of Settlement." In *Encyclopedia Judaica,* columns 24–28. Jerusalem: Encyclopedia Judaica, 1971.

Ward, David. *Poverty, Ethnicity, and the American City, 1840–1925: Changing Conceptions of the Slum and the Ghetto.* Cambridge, U.K., and New York: Cambridge University Press, 1989.

Wirth, Louis. *The Ghetto.* New Brunswick, N.J.: Transaction, 1998. Originally published in 1928.

*Arthur M. Lesley*

**GIFT, THE.** Reflection on gifts and their paradoxes goes back to the Bible, where humans are reminded that everything they have is a gift from God, for which they must be grateful and which should inspire them to give to others. Yet the Scriptures also condemn gifts, as those to judges, which corrupt or harm. Greek literary texts describe a wide range of gift practices, from the honorable gifts among warriors to the strategic hospitality to foreigners, but also warn of ambiguities, as in the saying "the gifts of enemies are not gifts."

Aristotle's (384–322 B.C.E.) *Nichomachean Ethics* embedded gifts and benefits in his discussion of the virtue of liberality, the forms of friendship, and the varieties of just distribution. Here, too, there were good gifts and bad: the liberal person gave "to the right people the right amounts and at the right time," the prodigal person bestowed gifts on flatterers and other wrong people, and received from bad sources as well. Aristotle saw giving-and-taking and buying-and-selling as versions of the exchange and reciprocity that held society together, but giving-and-taking was his preferred model. Humans "give a prominent place to the temple of the Graces—to promote the requital of services; for this is characteristic of grace—we should serve in return one who has shown grace to us, and should another time take the initiative in showing it" (bk. 4, ch. 1, pp. 1120a 25–26; bk. 5, ch. 5, pp. 1133a1–5). Giving-and-taking had a utilitarian element to it, but it also drew on feelings of gratitude.

Gratitude is a central theme of Seneca's (4 B.C.E.–65 C.E.) *On Benefits,* the other great gift-text of classical times. Gratitude was a "natural" response to a gift, benefit, or kindness, and this would generate further generosity in the recipient. The ungrateful person was detestable. Seneca explored all the fine points of giving and receiving, including between persons of unequal status. Of return on the gift, there should ideally be no expectation by the donor: "to bestow a favor in hope to receive another is a contemptible and base usury" (bk. 1, chap. 6, p. 6). Even more than Aristotle, Seneca contrasted the rules for gifts with the rules for sales and loans, especially in regard to the time for rewarding a benefit: the person who "requited a kindness with too much haste hath not the mind of a grateful man, but of a debtor" (bk. 4, chap. 40, p. 178).

Biblical, classical, and patristic texts nourished the Christian writing on gifts during the medieval period, even while thinkers responded to new socioeconomic relations and political and religious institutions. Gift subjects flowed into diverse channels: writings on the church as an object of charitable donation and an instrument for dispensing charity; on the Mass as a heartfelt sacrifice to God; on the virtue of charity and the vice of avarice; on various kinds of poverty and the meaning of alms; on the importance of hospitality, both ecclesiastical and feudal. Similarly, in the fifteenth, sixteenth, and seventeenth centuries, giving-and-taking themes clustered around diverse subjects: the liberality of the nobleman and noblewoman and the ordering of their obligations; the gifts of kings and queens, and whom they should reward; charitable donations to the poor, and how they should be organized; gifts of parents to children, and how they should be decided. At the same time, gifts were quarreled about and denounced as wrongful. The gifts that were omnipresent in the quest for favor in the political life of early modern polities were condemned as "corruption," especially when they went to judges, and the word *bribe* became part of parlance in English. Sermons warned against alms to the "undeserving poor" among the beggars and vagabonds, now identified more sharply than ever before. Meanwhile, the Protestant Reformation and Catholic Counter-Reformation of the sixteenth and seventeenth centuries offered alternate concepts of the meaning of sacrifice and of how gratitude for God's gifts should express itself in human behavior.

Disparate though this writing was, it was still linked by the common belief in the necessity for gratitude: the world was a gift from God, for which one should be grateful and be moved to generosity. The three Graces were often depicted in emblem books, with the message of reciprocity repeated.

The notion of a single realm of gift, as something to generalize about beyond the movement of gifts in diverse places and forms, emerged only after the idea of the economy or of the political economy. By the mid-eighteenth century, as colonial markets and European markets expanded and fields of social thought sought "scientific" systematization, tracts on trade had names such as *Tableau Oeconomique* or *Inquiry into the Principles of Political Oeconomy*. Gifts had little role in these texts, not because gifts had ceased to exist, but because the new theories left little room for them. Whatever he had said about sympathy in his early *Theory of Moral Sentiments,* Adam Smith's (1723–1790) *Wealth of Nations* (1776) is based on persons seeking their own advantage as they sell and buy goods on the market. Harmony came from the pursuit of self-interest, not through the alliance of gift-giving generating more gifts. Jeremy Bentham (1748–1832) allowed a prudently limited benevolence in his calculus of morals, as in the pleasure of giving a friend something for nothing, but a person could enjoy the same pleasure from a gain through exchange.

Interestingly enough, when Karl Marx (1818–1883) came to criticize political economy, he too left little space for gift relations. Linen, silk, paper, watches, and other useful things become "commodities" when they are put into exchange under the capitalist mode of production. The human labor that went into preparing them and gives them their true value is hidden in capitalist exchange. Instead the things themselves are assigned value: commodities are "fetishized," that is, the social relations of labor are transmuted into relations between things exchanged on the market. Marx made no analysis of what happened to things and the perception of things when they passed as gifts. His countermodels were patriarchal peasant production, where things stayed within the family (he did not discuss their internal distribution), and the performance of services and payments in kind under the "personal dependence" of feudal society. Charity and other gift forms were presumably among the "idyllic" relations and illusions torn up by the "naked self-interest" of capitalism. Even his image of a future society, where the means of production were held in common, stressed "free individuals" and "free development for each" rather than patterns of sharing.

Other critics of political economy, especially in late nineteenth-century Germany, found in gift-giving an alternate approach. By the time the French sociologist Marcel Mauss (1872–1950) began his great work on the gift, he could draw on historical studies such as Richard Meyer's *Zur Geschichte des Schenkens* (1898, *On the History of Gift-Giving)* and on anthropological studies, notably Bronislaw Malinowski's (1884–1942) description of the circular exchange among the Trobriand Islanders and Franz Boas's (1858–1942) account of the potlatch among the Kwakiutl on America's Northwest coast. When it appeared in 1925 Mauss called his book *Essai sur le Don (Essay on the Gift: The Form and Reason for Exchange in Archaic Societies)*. With his phrase *the gift,* Mauss committed himself to the search for a common pattern or mode of behavior, under which one could group the diverse forms of gifts, including sacrifice. Exchange and contract in "archaic societies," he explained, are carried on in the form of gifts: "In theory [the gifts] are voluntary, in reality given and returned obligatorily"; "apparently free and disinterested, [they are] nevertheless constrained and self-interested" (p. 3). Every gift produces a return gift in a chain of events that brings about many things: goods are exchanged and redistributed in societies that do not have separate commercial markets; peace is maintained and sometimes alliance and friendship; and status is confirmed or competed for in rival display. Mauss asked what beliefs impelled people in these societies to keep the gift moving: to give presents, to receive presents, to reciprocate presents. His answer drew upon the *hau* or "spirit of things" of the Maori people, an idea of embeddedment rather different from Marx's fetishization of commodities. In the former, the given object carries with it something of the giver, stressing the personal bond created through gifts; in the latter, the displaced symbolism conceals the personal relation of work and oppression in capitalism.

In his historical treatment of the gift economy, Mauss was something of an evolutionist. As markets and formal contracts advanced and legal systems distinguished between persons and things, so the total gift economy contracted. Still, as an independent socialist, he saw evidence for the gift ethos in his own day and hoped it would expand.

In the years since Mauss's book appeared, anthropologists, economists, historians, and philosophers have reflected on his argument and the gift more generally. Discussion has circled around two subjects: the relation of gifts to markets and the character of reciprocity. In his *Great Transformation* of 1944 and subsequent essays in the next twenty years, the economist Karl Polanyi (1886–1964) argued that until capitalist markets and the profit motive took hold in the eighteenth century, goods and services moved by gifts or redistribution. Personal relations and obligations took precedence, and money exchange, while present, was limited by regulation and convention. Once in place, the capitalist mode simply swept away competing forms of exchange and mentalities. But he did not see this as an inevitable historical stage, and hoped that postcolonial societies might take a different path.

If some writers continued to hold to the older evolutionary scheme, an important strand of current research and interpretation in both anthropology and history has discarded it altogether. Instead, gift forms and commercial market forms are seen as permanent and significant parts of the social landscape, albeit in shifting relations to each other. So anthropologist Maurice Godelier (b. 1934) has maintained even for Western societies, while Nicholas Thomas has described objects in Oceanic societies as "entangled" in both gift and market meanings, and Serge Latouche has shown how exchange in African communities operates "between the gift and the market." Historical studies have described crossovers between gift practices and commercial practices in both early modern and modern periods in Europe, and have identified some growth in gift forms, especially in the political and international sphere, even while market mentalities expanded. These views have required a reexamination of what transactions can be called gifts, and, as Serge Latouche has urged, the rejection of a simple *homo donator* (Man the Giver), as narrowly conceived as a *homo oecomicus* (Economic Man).

Studies on the cultural possibilities in gift reciprocity have addressed such challenges and have led to images more complex than Mauss's gift/return-gift, with its psychology of "in theory, voluntary, in reality, obligatory." The anthropologist Marshall Sahlins (b. 1930) suggested a "spectrum of reciprocities," with "generalized reciprocity" at one end, involving free and unstinting giving with little thought of return, and "negative reciprocity" at the other, as in trying to get something for nothing. Annette Weiner (1933–1997), going back to Malinowski's Trobriand Islands and especially to their women, broadened the time span in gift relations from a circular model to one lasting over the life cycle and across the generations.

Historical studies have drawn upon these patterns, but have also added new ways of thinking about gift exchange. At one end of the scale, medieval and early modern Christian discourse sometimes constructed human gifts to God in terms of reciprocity, other times in gratuitous terms. At the other end of the scale, concern about the bad gift, the gift that "corrupts," has a long history, expressed already in the Bible. "Bribes" were a recognized danger of gift systems in medieval and early modern political life, and provide a helpful perspective on contemporary political "corruption."

Writing of gift economies after World War II, Georges Bataille (1897–1962) noted both the grand excess in nature and human life, which must be expended "in gift-giving . . . without reciprocation" (pp. 37–38) and the use of gifts on the international scale to compel loyalty in the Cold War. Jacques Derrida (b. 1930) has dismissed the true gift and gratuitousness as logically impossible, but most commentators welcome the paradoxes and ambiguities in gift relations, and find them relevant to an age of globalization and its discontents.

*See also* **Anthropology; Economics; Poverty; Utilitarianism; Wealth.**

### BIBLIOGRAPHY

Algazi, Gadi, Valentin Groebner, and Bernhard Jussen, eds. *Negotiating the Gift: Pre-Modern Figurations of Exchange.* Göttingen, Germany: Vandenhoeck and Ruprecht, 2003.

Aristotle. "Nicomachean Ethics." In *The Basic Works of Aristotle,* edited by Richard McKeon. New York: Random House, 1941.

Bataille, Georges. *The Accursed Share: An Essay on General Economy.* Translated by Robert Hurley. New York: Zone Books, 1988–1991. Published in French in 1947.

Bentham, Jeremy. *An Introduction to the The Principles of Morals and Legislation.* 1789. Oxford: Clarendon, 1996.

Caillé, Alain. *Don, intérêt et désintéressement: Bourdieu, Mauss, Platon et quelques autres* (Gift, interest, and selflessness: Bourdieu, Mauss, Plato and others). Paris: La Découverte/MAUSS, 1994.

Carrier, James G. *Gifts and Commodities: Exchange and Western Capitalism since 1700.* London and New York: Routledge, 1995.

Clavero, Bartolomé. *La grâce du don: Anthropologie catholique de l'économie moderne* (The grace of the gift: Catholic anthropology and early modern economy). Translated from the Spanish by Jean- Frédéric Schaub. Paris: Albin Michel, 1996.

Davis, Natalie Zemon. *The Gift in Sixteenth-Century France.* Madison: University of Wisconsin Press; Oxford: Oxford University Press, 2000.

Derrida, Jacques. *Donner le temps* (Given time). Paris: Éditions Galilée, 1991.

Godbout, Jacques T. *Le don, la dette et l'identité: Homo donator versus homo oeconomicus* (Gift, debt and identity: Homo donator versus homo oeconomicus). Montréal: Éditions du Boréal, 2000.

Godelier, Maurice. *L'énigme du don* (The enigma of the gift). Paris: Fayard, 1996.

Groebner, Valentin. *Liquid Assets, Dangerous Gifts: Presents and Politics at the End of the Middle Ages.* Translated by Pamela E. Selwyn. Philadelphia: University of Pennsylvania Press, 2002.

Hénaff, Marcel. *Le prix de la verité: Le don, l'argent, la philosophie* (The price of truth: gift, money, philosophy). Paris: Éditions du Seuil, 2002.

Hirschman, Albert O. *The Passions and the Interests. Political Arguments for Capitalism before Its Triumph.* Princeton, N. J.: Princeton University Press, 1977.

Hyde, Lewis. *The Gift: Imagination and the Erotic Life of Property.* New York: Vintage Books, 1983.

Latouche, Serge. *L'autre Afrique: Entre don et marché* (The other Africa: Between gift and market). Paris: Albin Michel, 1998.

Malinowski, Bronislaw. *Argonauts of the Western Pacific: An Account of Native Enterprise and Adventure in the Archipelagoes of Melanesian New Guinea.* 1922. London: Routledge and Kegan Paul, 1964.

Marx, Karl. *Capital: A Critique of Political Economy.* Translated by Samuel Moore and Edward Aveling; edited by Frederick Engels. New York: Modern Library, 1906.

Mauss, Marcel. *The Gift: The Form and Reason for Exchange in Archaic Societies.* Translated by W. D. Halls. New York and London: W. W. Norton, 1990. The best translation of Mauss's 1925 *Essai sur le Don.*

Nagel, Thomas. *The Possibility of Altruism.* Oxford: Clarendon, 1979.

Noonan, John T. *Bribes.* New York: Macmillan, 1984.

Peck, Linda Levy. *Court Patronage and Corruption in Early Stuart England.* London and Boston: Unwin Hyman, 1990.

Polanyi, Karl. *The Great Transformation. The Political and Economic Origins of Our Time.* New York: Rinehart, 1944.

———. *Primitive, Archaic and Modern Economies; Essays of Karl Polanyi.* Edited by George Dalton. Boston: Beacon Press, 1968.

Sahlins, Marshall. *Stone Age Economics.* Chicago: Aldine, 1972.

Seneca. *On Benefits.* Translated by Thomas Lodge. London: Aldine House, 1899.

Smith, Adam. *An Inquiry into the Nature and Causes of the Wealth of Nations.* 1776. Edited by R. H. Campbell and A. S. Skinner. Oxford: Clarendon, 1976.

Thomas, Nicholas. *Entangled Objects: Exchange, Material Culture, and Colonialism in the Pacific.* Cambridge, Mass.: Harvard University Press, 1991.

Titmuss, Richard. *The Gift Relationship: From Human Blood to Social Policy.* New York: Vintage Books, 1972.

Wacquet, Jean-Claude. *Corruption: Ethics and Power in Florence, 1600–1770.* Translated by Linda McCall. University Park: Pennsylvania State University Press, 1991.

Weiner, Annette B. *Inalienable Possessions: The Paradox of Keeping-While-Giving.* Berkeley and Los Angeles: University of California Press, 1992.

———. *Women of Value, Men of Renown: New Perspectives in Trobriand Exchange.* Austin: University of Texas Press, 1976.

*Natalie Zemon Davis*

# GLOBALIZATION.

The entry includes three subentries:

*Africa*
*Asia*
*General*

## AFRICA

Globalization represents a process of rapid intensification of broad economic, political, and cultural interconnectedness among the different actors in the global system. The process is qualitatively different from the global expansion of product markets that is inherent to the capitalist socioeconomic system and emerges during certain epochs of capitalism under conditions of political and economic hegemony and a balance of power among social classes that is decisively tilted in favor of capital at the global level. A confluence of these two conditions, which are not always present in the capitalist system, sets in motion a vision of capitalism that aims to integrate national economies into a single economic space through various institutional arrangements and policy instruments crafted along the liberal ideology.

## Old Globalization versus New Globalization

There is little agreement on whether globalization is new or old. Some observers contend that the unfolding global order is entirely new. Others claim that it is not fundamentally different from the order that prevailed in the nineteenth century roughly between 1840 and 1914 under the political and economic hegemony of Great Britain. In any case, globalization has emerged since the closing decades of the twentieth century after an interlude of roughly seventy-five years that were characterized by the episodes of the welfare state system and socialism, two social systems characterized by the relative ascendancy of working-class influence in global politics and the absence of a hegemonic power and a hegemonic ideology.

Old globalization incorporated countries outside of western Europe and North America largely through imperialism and often through direct colonialism. The rise of powers that were able to challenge British hegemony by the end of the nineteenth century culminated in World War I and brought old globalization to an end.

Like old globalization, new globalization is projected by a new political and economic hegemony and the ascendancy in the power of capital relative to other social classes. Views on the nature of the new hegemony vary widely. One view is that the United States sets the rules of the new global order and represents the new hegemonic power. Another view is that the new hegemony is a collective hegemony dominated by the advanced countries led by the United States, which has largely co-opted lesser powers. A third view contends that the new hegemony is composed of a decentralized transnational political elite. Despite these differences, there is a consensus that a hegemonic political, economic, and ideological order has emerged in the post–Cold War global system.

Unlike old globalization, new globalization has unfolded without direct colonialism. Instead it utilizes institutional arrangements and policy instruments as globalizing mechanisms. In the African context, as in many other developing countries, these mechanisms include retrenchment of state involvement in economic activity and institutional changes, such as privatization, and liberalization of trade and capital mobility. These policies are encapsulated in the package of reforms known as structural adjustment programs.

## Globalization's Implications for Africa

Incorporation of African economies into the global capitalist system produced profound changes on African societies. New globalization has also begun to impact African societies in significant ways. The literature on Africa's incorporation, however, has not drawn a distinction between the continent's incorporation into the capitalist system and its incorporation under globalization. The lack of distinction may be due to the fact that, despite their differences, both types of incorporations have been painful to the continent. The distinction, however, has to be made, as there are significant differences.

At least four different phases of Africa's incorporation into the global capitalist system can be identified. The first phase took place prior to the era of colonization roughly between the middle of the fifteenth century and the middle of the nineteenth century. This phase itself had at least two stages, including the early commercial incorporation and the pillage of Africa during the era of slave trade, when roughly 22 million slaves were exported out of Africa between 1500 and 1890 (Ogot, p. 43). The second phase of incorporation took place during the period of direct colonial domination roughly between 1884 and 1960. The pillage that took place during the era of the slave trade was devastating for African societies, but it did not produce the broad fundamental changes in African political and economic systems, culture, and institutions that old globalization's incorporation of the continent through colonialism did. Africa's present political map, economic structures, and its place in the global division of labor were all formed during this phase to best serve the interests of European powers.

The third phase of Africa's incorporation took place during the three decades between the beginning of its decolonization in the early 1960s and the end of the Cold War in 1991. Due to many factors, decolonization did not give African countries the level of sovereignty necessary for determining their own terms of integration with the global system. Nevertheless, decolonization meant a marked loosening of the monopolistic grip on African economies by European colonial powers, resulting in some diversification of the trading partners of African countries. The Cold War rivalry between the superpowers and the welfare state ideology of compromise between social classes that prevailed during the Cold War era also allowed African states to expand public services, such as education and health care, to their populations and to initiate some level of industrialization behind protectionist policies. Despite these benefits, the Cold War context of decolonization subjected African countries to ideological cleavage and fre-

quent external intervention from both ideological camps. Civil wars in the Congo, Mozambique, Angola, and Ethiopia are the most obvious examples. Many of the post-decolonization African political elite were also co-opted in order to preserve the old economic structures, fragmenting postcolonial African political systems.

The fourth phase of Africa's incorporation corresponds with the advent of new globalization and represents significant reduction of the limited sovereignty African countries mustered at the time of decolonization and modification of the Cold War era terms of incorporation of African economies into the global system. As noted, with new globalization, retrenchment of state involvement in economic activity, along with policies of liberalization that foster openness of the economy, has become a condition for integration with the global economy for African economies as well as for those of other developing countries.

African perspectives on globalization are diverse but mostly apprehensive. Many African leaders are publicly critical of it but few have dared to oppose its implementation. African leftist scholars are highly critical of globalization. Even scholars of the liberal persuasion, who are sympathetic to globalization, are critical of the rigid conditionalities international financial institutions impose on African countries. A 2003 survey by the Pew Research Center, however, shows that 58 percent of Nigerians, 46 percent of Kenyans, 44 percent of Ugandans, and 41 percent of South Africans view globalization very positively. At the same time, the survey shows that more than 80 percent of African respondents view globalization as a serious threat to African traditions.

Proponents argue that globalization promotes economic growth and diversification and by so doing fosters political stability, gender equality, and cultural development in African societies. Economic diversification, for example, is expected to accelerate the absorption of women into the modern economy, which has a strong positive gender equity effect. Economic prosperity is also expected to promote cultural development by expanding leisure opportunities for the population. Proponents contend that openness and liberalization of trade allow local opportunity costs of resources to be reflected more accurately. Decontrolling interest rates also raises rates and thereby encourages savings and the adoption of appropriate technology. Liberalization of capital mobility is also expected to stimulate foreign investment, and it is anticipated that privatization of banks will allow banks to allocate funds to finance private investments in industry.

However, each of these policies can also produce adverse results depending on the prevailing conditions. Lifting protectionist policies can, for example, lead to loss of revenue and the destruction of potentially competitive local infant industry by cheap imports. Higher interest rates and tight credit may also hurt industry, which tends to have higher working capital needs, while privatization of banks may discourage investments in industry, which tends to have longer duration and higher risks. Deregulation of capital mobility may also destabilize monetary systems, as has occurred in several developing economies.

In contrast to the optimism of proponents, the adverse impacts of liberalization have been severe in many African countries. According to the United Nations Development Programme (UNDP, 2002), for instance, twenty-two sub-Saharan African countries had lower per capita incomes in 2000 than they did in the period between 1975 and 1985. Industries of a number of African countries have also suffered significant losses due to cheap imports. The textile industries of Nigeria, Mozambique, Malawi, and Tanzania, for example, have been devastated by cheap imports triggered by premature and indiscriminate free trade. Beyond the identified examples, the overall picture of Africa's industry since the implementation of liberalization policies beginning in the middle of the 1980s has been rather grim. Average annual growth rates of value added in industry in sub-Saharan Africa have declined from 2.2 percent for the 1975–1984 period to 1.7 percent for the 1985–1989 period and to 1.3 percent for the 1990–2000 period. Annual average gross national savings as percentage of GDP have also declined from 20.6 percent in 1975–1984 to 15.7 percent in 1985–1989 and to 12.8 percent in 1990–2000 (World Bank, 2002).

Another globalizing mechanism promoted through the structural adjustment programs is retrenchment of public expenditures to reduce budgetary deficits. This policy is intended to restrain the growth of money supply and thereby lead to stable prices and a climate conducive for investment. Obviously unrestricted budgetary deficits are unsustainable as they are likely to lead to economic instability undermining the development process. However, in the African case, where the level of human development and development of infrastructure is extremely low, retrenchment of public expenditures is likely to limit investments in human development and development of infrastructure, curtailing the long-term prospects for overall development of African countries. With a human development index of less than 0.500 for 2000, sub-Saharan Africa ranks the lowest of all geographical regions in terms of human development (UNDP, 2002). All twenty-four countries at the bottom of the index and thirty out of the thirty-four countries at the bottom of the index are in sub-Saharan Africa. The number of the destitute—people living on less than one U.S. dollar per day—has also increased from 241 million in 1990 to 329 million in 2000. Many sub-Saharan African countries have also retrenched their expenditures on public services since adopting adjustment mechanisms. Public expenditure on education has, for example, declined from 4.5 percent of GDP in 1992 to 3.3 percent in 1999 (World Commission on the Social Dimension of Globalization, 2004).

The globalization mechanisms also fail to address some of the serious external constraints African countries face, including the ever-increasing debt burden, Africa's limited access to the markets of developed countries, the paltry foreign investment flows to Africa, and the continent's persistent unfavorable terms of trade, which have declined from 0.6 for the 1974–1984 period to −3.8 for the 1985–1989 years and to −0.5 for 1990–2000 (World Bank, 2002). Sub-Saharan Africa's total external debt service payments (long-term loans and International Monetary Fund credit) have averaged $11.643 million annually for the years 1990–2000. Farming subsidies in rich countries have also made it difficult for African countries to compete in the markets of rich countries. Even more damaging to African countries is that subsidized agricultural exports from rich countries are driving small farmers out of business.

In the absence of the expected growth and economic diversification, retrenchment of public expenditures and state involvement in the economy is likely to lead to perpetuation and exacerbation of gross inequalities that are rampant in the continent, including gender inequalities. Transformation of the subsistence sector, which is essential for internal integration of the economy, is also likely to be adversely affected by state disengagement. Regional and ethnic inequalities in access to public services are also likely to linger without active state engagement, fueling internal conflicts. Cultural fragmentation is also more likely than cultural development to take place.

Globalization certainly is not the only culprit for these problems. Many factors, including poor governance and widespread political unrest, along with poor infrastructure, eroding educational systems and human capital, and lack of diversification of the economy have contributed to Africa's economic ills. Such domestic factors in fact prevent African countries from taking advantage of some of the limited opportunities globalization creates. However, the hegemonic ideology of globalization blocks the search for alternative development strategies that may address these factors and undermines the limited autonomy that African states were able to muster at the time of their decolonization. New globalization has thus integrated African economies in terms of ideology and policy, but in terms of participation in global production it has perpetuated their relegation to the peripheral margins of the global capitalist system as suppliers of primary commodities.

*See also* **Africa, Idea of; Afropessimism; Anticolonialism: Africa; Capitalism: Africa; Colonialism: Africa; Development; Postcolonial Studies; Socialisms, African; Westernization: Africa.**

**BIBLIOGRAPHY**

Ake, Claude. "The New World Order: A View from Africa." In *Whose World Order? Uneven Globalization and the End of the Cold War,* edited by Hans-Henrik Holm and Georg Sørensen, 19–42. Boulder: Westview Press, 1995.

Amin, Samir. *Delinking: Towards a Polycentric World.* London: Zed Books 1985.

Bienefeld, Manfred. "The New World Order: Echoes of New Imperialism." *Third World Quarterly* 15, no. 1 (1994): 31–48.

Duncan, Alex, and John Howell. "Assessing the Impact of Structural Adjustment." In *Structural Adjustment and the African Farmer,* edited by Alex Duncan and John Howell, 1–13. London: Overseas Development Institute/James Currey/Heinemann, 1992.

Ogot. B. A. *General History of Africa: Africa from the Sixteenth to the Eighteenth Century.* Abridged ed. Paris: UNESCO, 1999.

Petras, James, and Henry Veltmeyer. *Globalization Unmasked: Imperialism in the Twenty-first Century.* Halifax, N.S.: Fernwood/Zed Books, 2001.

Pew Research Center. "Globalization with Few Discontents?" 3 June 2003.

Sachs, Jeffrey. "International Economies: Unlocking the Mysteries of Globalization." *Foreign Policy* 110 (spring 1998): 97–111.

United Nations Economic Commission for Africa. *African Alternative Framework to Structural Adjustment Programmes for Socio-Economic Recovery and Transformation.* Addis Ababa: The Commission, 1991.

UNDP. *Human Development Report 2002.* New York and Oxford: Oxford University Press, 2002.

Wood, Ellen Meiksins. "Capitalist Change and Generational Shifts." *Monthly Review* 5, no. 5 (October 1998): 1–10.

World Bank. *African Development Indicators 2002.* Washington, D.C.: World Bank, 2002.

———. *World Development Indicators 2001.* Washington, D.C.: World Bank, 2001.

World Commission on the Social Dimension of Globalization. *A Fair Globalization: Creating Opportunities for All.* Geneva: ILO, 24 February 2004.

*Kidane Mengisteab*

## ASIA

Globalization is a far-ranging topic. It has as many perspectives as commentators. Western views of globalization often focus on economics and politics, while Eastern views often focus on philosophy and culture. Two Canadian scholars, Marshall McLuhan and Harold Innis, seem to bridge both East and West in their studies.

### Asian Views of Globalization

In the early 1960s the Canadian communications pioneer Marshall McLuhan (1911–1980) was one of the first scholars to seriously consider globalization. His perspective was shaped by a multicultural Canadian environment. From the inception, globalization was a concept intertwining both Eastern and Western civilizations. Impressed by another Canadian, the historian Harold Innis (1894–1952), McLuhan began a study of both Asian and Western societies that spanned the entirety of his academic career. Innis had recognized that technology was changing the face of modern nation-states. The direction was clearly set. Space was overcoming time. In making a case for the wisdom of the past, Innis embarked on a discussion of ancient cultures, including Greece, Egypt, and especially China. Decades later McLuhan followed this lead. At first Innis recognized that China had a time-biased civilization. It created mammoth temples and statues that stood the test of the ages. China later invented paper, ink, and books. The motivation was spatial. While temples and statues would last for millennia, their accessibility was restricted. Scrolls and books could be transported easily but were limited by physical structure and duration. They were space-biased. For thousands of years, China managed to reinvigorate its civilization through a finely tuned combination of temporal and spatial communications alongside oral and written traditions. The oral tradition assisted Buddhism in gaining popularity during its migration from India, while the written tradition helped solidify the reverence for Confu-

cianism. Printing accommodated both: popular literature for Buddhists and classical texts for Confucians. These yin-yang polarities of writing and speaking had worldwide implications. As well the import of Chinese paper accelerated the influence of the Greeks, Persians, and Arabians throughout Europe. As such, Innis and McLuhan highlight positive functions of an archaic Chinese form of globalization.

While Chinese paper and goods encouraged the trade with the Western world, it also set the stage for a clash of civilizations and belief systems. The technological revolutions of the Western world with its infatuation for space and property ownership would eventually annihilate the East's sacredness of time and its philosophical wisdom. As Innis writes, "The oral tradition implies the spirit but writing and printing are inherently materialistic" (p. 130). Taking a cue from China, Innis maintained that a harmony of time and space was necessary for a healthy society or a healthy world. Nevertheless, the West shunned religion and the oral tradition that it represented in favor of reason and the written tradition that legitimized it. When the equilibrium of time/space and oral/written fell out of kilter, the West colonized the very civilizations that initially helped fashion its communicative modes.

### The Global Village

McLuhan went one step further than Innis. While the mechanical world extended bodies in space, the electric and electronic technologies "extended our central nervous system itself in a global embrace, abolishing both space and time as far as our planet is concerned" (1964, p. 19). Hence we have the expression "the global village." But this village was not as harmonious as those ancient societies of time/space concordance. McLuhan maintains, "The global village is at once as wide as the planet and as small as the little town where everybody is maliciously engaged in poking his nose into everybody else's business" (quoted in Benedetti and DeHart, p. 40). Globalization is a two-edged sword that extends Western knowledge everywhere but threatens the wisdoms of the Eastern world. According to McLuhan, the world needs a combination of both Western and Eastern knowledge. The West operates by way of visual space as a linear, quantitative mode of perception, while the East operates by way of acoustic space as a holistic, qualitative mode of perception. Because both worlds are constantly colliding, we need a mutual understanding in order to foster peace (see McLuhan and Powers).

McLuhan encapsulates Western visual space as a "mind's eye" that connects abstract figures with definitive boundaries and is "homogenous (uniform everywhere), and static (qualitatively unchangeable)" (McLuhan and Powers, p. 45). Eastern acoustic space as a "mind's ear" encompasses both preliterate and postliterate cultures. It is nonhomogenous and discontinuous. As McLuhan relates: "Its resonant and interpenetrating processes are simultaneously related with centers everywhere and boundaries nowhere. Like music . . . acoustic space requires neither proof nor explanation but is made manifest through its cultural content" (p. 45). Hence visual and acoustic spaces are "bicultural." They are at the same time incompatible (like history and eternity) and compatible (like science and art). According to McLuhan, the East utilizes both visual and acoustic space. As he writes, "A Westerner, for example, arranges flowers in space; the Chinese and Japanese harmonize the space between the flowers" (pp. 62–63). Manipulating the discontinuous space, the Asians fill the void with imagination. In this sense, the overly logical Western world could learn from the East.

For McLuhan, Rudyard Kipling's famous expression "East is East, and West is West" was obsolete. It gave way to James Joyce: "The west shall shake the East awake . . . while ye have the night for morn" (quoted in McLuhan and Fiore, p. 143). Innis and McLuhan were two of the first thinkers in the West to recognize the importance of East Asia in the formation of concepts of globalization.

### Definitions of Globalization: West and East

Globalization is itself an equivocal term. There are as many definitions of globalization as there are interpreters. Globalization is not as value laden as "cultural imperialism" or "orientalism." The latter two terms are more prone to views of domination, especially by the West over the East. The following definitions are neutral. David Jary and Julia Jary define globalization in *HarperCollins Dictionary of Sociology* as: "a multifaceted process in which the world is becoming more and more interconnected and communication is becoming instantaneous" (p. 249). This includes: "(a) the transformation of the spatial arrangement and organization of social relations involving 'action at a distance,' a stretching of social relations and transactions (and power) . . . ; (b) the increasing extensity, intensity, velocity and impact of global social relations . . . ; (c) the creation of new networks and nodes—the 'network society' . . . ; (d) a dialectic between the global and the local" (p. 249). Unlike imperialism or orientalism, globalization is rather open-ended. The "have" nations do not automatically overshadow the "have not" nations. Tim O'Sullivan and colleagues define globalization as "the growth and acceleration of economic and cultural networks which operate on a worldwide scale and basis. Globalization is strongly linked with debates about 'world culture,' and emerged as a critical concept in the late 1980s. The term refers to the whole complex of flows and processes which have increasingly transcended national boundaries in the last twenty years" (p. 130).

In China, there is a distinction between internationalization (*guojihua*) and globalization (*quanqiuhua*). Internationalization refers to trading with wealthy nations, such as the United States or Germany. This is generally considered good for China's world development. Globalization refers literally to matters of change in the entire world, such as ecological considerations and appropriate responses. McLuhan's term "global village" (*quanqiucun*) entered Chinese-English dictionaries in the early 1980s possibly because of China's keen interest in friendly relations with Canada and Canadian thinkers. By contrast, in Japan, internationalization (*kokusaika*) is a heavily laden term that is either extremely good or bad, depending on one's national allegiance; globalization (*gurobarizeshon* or *gurobaruka*) is a term that conjures up fears of falling behind, especially as Japan seems to recede into an economic sunset in the wake of China's emergence as a world force. On the one hand, globalization for Japan means that the goddess Amaterasu is backing

into her cave, a time in Shinto legend when the world falls into darkness. On the other hand, globalization for China means the awakening of a sleeping dragon or a time of renewal, revitalization, and resurrection.

### Globalization in Classical China

While the term *globalization* is relatively new in China, its concept is not. China has participated in globalization for thousands of years. For the most part, the history of China involves open-ended relations with the world. As a Middle Kingdom (*zhongguo*), China reached across the globe in exploration with the express purpose of exchanging ideas, technology, and goods. In the preface to a book on Eastern and Western cultures, Jeff Yang writes, "America was Asian before it was American; the ancestors of the continent's original inhabitants were Siberians who made the long, cold journey across the Bering Strait some 11,000 years ago" (Yang et al., introduction). Yang goes on to state that "the Chinese have their own pre-Columbus discovery myth: they claim that Hui Shen, a Buddhist monk living in the fifth century C.E., sailed to Mexico, lived there for 40 years, and returned to tell the tale." While these examples are legendary, they do point to Zheng He, a Yunnan Muslim explorer from the Ming dynasty who traveled to India and Africa on seven voyages between 1405 and 1433. With hundreds of vessels and thousands of sailors, the expeditions were not "colonizing." Rather, they were "diplomatic." As John Fairbank relates, "They exchanged gifts, enrolled tributaries, and brought back geographic information and scientific curiosities" (p. 138). Jacques Gernet argues that the expeditions followed well-established trade routes of the eleventh century that continued uninterrupted for several hundred years. In explaining the differences between Mongol military conquest and Ming explorations, Gernet writes that "it was no longer a question of undertaking mere conquests for the sake of economic exploitation but of securing the recognition of the power and prestige of the Ming empire in South-East Asia and the Indian Ocean" (p. 401).

The Ming voyages were curtailed in 1433 and their records destroyed in 1479. Nevertheless, China was far out front of any other nation in the age of exploration. It was a half century ahead of the Portuguese traveling to the Gold Coast of Africa or of Columbus arriving in the West Indies. Although highly speculative, Gavin Menzies even proposes that Zheng He made a voyage to North America in 1421 in gigantic junks almost five hundred feet long.

As early as the Qin Dynasty (221 B.C.E.), China utilized the Silk Roads to India as two-way streets of communications, commerce, and culture. Along the trade routes, goods such as tea and silk came from China, while hundreds of Buddhist religions came from India. The Silk Roads stretched from Chang'an, the capital of the Western Han dynasty through Dunhuang, the Tarim Basin, Kashgar, and the Pamir Mountains all the way to Antioch on the Mediterranean Sea. Other routes moved to Hanoi in Vietnam through to Indonesia, the Malay Peninsula, and the Indian Ocean, which facilitated sea commerce to the Roman Orient. In 139 B.C.E. Emperor Han Wudi sent his envoy Zhang Qian to the edges of the Hellenistic world in Bactria, from whence Zhang Qian returned with information on the distant Roman world. Bringing silk and bamboo to the West, he came back with pearls, linen, and horses from central Asia. In 104, 102, and 42 B.C.E. Chinese armies defeated the Turkic nomad Xiongnu alongside captive Roman soldiers in the former Greek kingdom of Sogdiana. Describing further Roman contact, Ann Paludan writes, "In A.D. 122 jugglers from Da Qin (Rome) arrived [in China] from the south and were followed in 166 by a group of merchants claiming to be ambassadors from the Roman emperor Antun (Marcus Aurelius Antoninus)" (p. 56). Attesting to the early interaction between Eastern and Western civilizations, anyone visiting the Confucian homes in China's Anhui Province notices similarities with Roman houses, especially the open courtyard designs, entrances, and interior chambers.

## Globalization in Modern China

According to Liu Kang, China in the early twenty-first century has a multifaceted view of globalization that stands in between two significant historical events: the disintegration of Soviet-led communism and a rapidly expanding transnational capitalism. For China, the challenge of globalization is to withstand the wholesale commodification of Western-style capitalism while still entering the world system as a prominent player with its own unique socialist values. In the late twentieth and early twenty-first centuries China has engaged in debates in "nationalism, postmodernism, and neo-humanism, and a 'discursive hybridity' that blends neo-conservatism and radicalism" (Liu, p. 165). The results are necessarily fragmented and unevenly displayed. Yet they seem to congeal into a new global Chinese intellectual strategy.

Part of China's response to the overwhelming compulsion toward Western modernity is to embrace its own past, much of which was suspended during a century of hot and cold wars. In this sense, China once again becomes a "cloud water" (*yunshui*) or a shape shifter that metamorphoses to fit the times. The "cloud water" is a Buddhist term of old that referred to young, novice monks who gathered around a master like wandering clouds; alternatively it is like a vagabond Daoist priest, changing his shape like water.

In October 1994 China celebrated both the overthrow of the Qing dynasty and the 2,545th anniversary of Confucius's birth. This celebration was remarkable for its unique assembly of both scholarly and political figures. Participants included Gu Mu, a former politburo member and vice premier who was acknowledged as the engineer of Deng Xiaoping's economic modernization program. Others included Li Ruihuan, chair of the Chinese People's Political Consultative Congress; Zhou Nan, an important Beijing representative in Hong Kong; Lee Kuan Yew, former founding prime minister of Singapore; and Jiang Zemin, president of China. Li's inaugural speech praised the ancient Confucian philosopher Mencius for his advice to rulers to listen to the people. Gu Mu's talk was especially important for outlining China's philosophy in a global age, both at home and abroad. The essence of this strategy was to transform China's culture by adapting to Western style on the outside while retaining Eastern essence on the inside. Gu Mu relates, "Culture serves both as the emblem of the level of civilization of a nation or a country and the guidance for its political and economic life" (quoted in de Bary and Tu, p. xii).

In adhering to Confucian ideals of "harmony-making for prosperity" and "harmony above all," China would attempt to merge Eastern and Western views of nation, patriotism, science, and democracy.

## Philosophy Returns to China

Since this mandate, China's attitude to globalization relies on the primacy of cultural exchanges with the rest of the world alongside a reemergence and reappraisal of both classical Eastern and Western philosophy. Mutual topics of exchange include the self and society, rights and rites in Confucian ritual, and Chinese law and human rights in global perspective.

The Twelfth International Conference on Chinese Philosophy met in July 2001 in Beijing, where nearly four hundred leading world scholars gathered to debate issues around globalization in terms of the practicality of ancient and contemporary theories. As a significant moment in Chinese history, it announced the return home of Chinese philosophy. China once again became the center of its own philosophy that had been marginalized during the twentieth century. The conference was hosted by the Chinese government under the supervision of Fang Keli, director of the Graduate School of the Chinese Academy of Social Sciences and president of the International Society for Chinese Philosophy (ISCP). The ISCP, founded in 1975 by Cheng Chung-Ying, is one of the best examples of China's program for globalization based on an international community of inquirers who engage in the comparison of Eastern and Western philosophy, religion, and culture. In 1993 the ISCP was the first international conference of top-ranking scholars of Chinese philosophy acknowledged and accepted by the Beijing government. Not only does Chinese philosophy play a leading role in the revitalization of traditions and the renewal of Chinese civilization, but it also adapts to and learns from Western thought. Hence it is the cornerstone of global strategies. As Cheng writes, "Chinese philosophy can contribute to a global ethics of virtue and right, a global metaphysics of the dao and God, a global epistemology of naturalization and transcendence, a global political philosophy of justice and harmony, a global aesthetics of genius and refinement, a global logic of communication and understanding, and a global science of human well-being and liberation" (p. 404).

In an attempt to rediscover core human values in this global context, the works of Jürgen Habermas (1929– ), Jacques Derrida (1930–), Hans-Georg Gadamer (1900–2002), and Martin Heidegger (1889–1976) have come to the forefront in China as well as the three ancient teachings of Confucianism, Daoism, and Buddhism.

## Habermas and Derrida in China

In April 2001 Habermas toured China, speaking on various topics, including globalization and communicative rationality. China is intrigued with his Weberian-inspired views on value rationality and instrumental (purposive) rationality, that is, in the relationship between the ends themselves and the means to ends in both economic and social actions. What distinguishes Habermas from Max Weber is a focus on the universality of communicative action within internationally sensitive lifeworlds. In debate with Habermas, Tong Shijun, a leading philosopher, characterizes China's discourse on modernity as composed of several stages: (1) the early twentieth century creation of science and democracy, (2) the later twentieth century socialist model, and (3) the early-twenty-first century discussion on market economies and legal systems (p. 82). Tong utilizes an ancient Chinese polarity of *ti* (substance, body, ground) and *yong* (function, use, manifestation) to compare with Habermas: *ti* as value rationality and *yong* as instrumental rationality. The relation between an object and its movement, the nature of a thing and its expression, a moral principle and its application is the connection of *ti* and *yong*. Closely related to these pairings are *dao* (way) and *qi* (instrument). In the nineteenth century Qing bureaucrats referred to the slogan "Chinese learning as *ti* or substance and Western learning as *yong* or function" (Tong, p. 82). These pairings might neatly compare with Gu Mu's dictum for Chinese views of globalization: Eastern on the inside and Western on the outside. In dialogue with Western thinkers such as Habermas, the Chinese pairings help grapple with everyday interactive decisions of the lifeworld over and against the global compulsions of economic, political, social, and philosophical systems.

In September 2001 Derrida completed a similar tour. Chinese intellectuals discussed his "specters of Marx" theory that still holds transformational possibilities. Although Chinese Marxist scholars primarily view globalization as an economic moment in the continuing internationalization of capitalist modes of production, they are also concerned with cultural consequences. Derrida's multicultural approach to law, language, and society might help the Chinese form a New International that addresses the homogenization of global economics by way of a participatory response of cultural difference and diversity. China can be in globalization without completely being of globalization. Chinese scholars look for universal value in globalization beyond obvious hegemonic implications. Derrida agrees that there are many confusing debates around globalization because of "a certain transparence and with the appearance of liberal exchange" (Zhang Ning, p. 160), while forms of monopoly march forward. China's awareness of these trends and continued participation in the discourse on globalization can profit from European philosophers (including postmodernists) as a complement to North American thinkers.

### Gadamer in China

In June 2002 the Gadamer translator Richard Palmer explained hermeneutics to China in his lecture tour. As a close associate and student of Gadamer, Palmer offered the first comprehensive outline on hermeneutics for a North American audience and did the same for China three decades later. In recovering its ancient world, China wishes to employ exegetical strategies for regenerating universal claims from both Eastern and Western classics in a search for new humanist values to suit a global age. Palmer argues that, like Confucius, Gadamer was an educator who valued the virtues of classical traditions, poetry, and art. Like Confucius, he pursued harmony through a "fusion of horizons." Drawing upon the corpus of Heidegger's work, Gadamer's "truth" and "method" were aimed at disclosing the ontological experiences of everyday life along the way to things as they are. Somewhat following Heidegger,

Gadamer's *Zeitlichkeit* (timeliness) speaks to the power of language in revealing the universal truth of a text. The essence of ancient time can be recovered in the simultaneity or contemporaneity of today. Gadamer's emphasis on phronesis (the Greek term for practical wisdom) as an ethical judgment implies a facility for selecting the virtuous. This is similar to Confucius, who emphasizes the care of doing what is right. Part of the understanding of both thinkers involves *applicatio* (application) as the proper fit of understanding and daily use. Gadamer's hermeneutics can be collected into one major concept, that of *wirkungsgeschichtliches Bewusstsein* (consciousness in which history is always working). This is similar to Heidegger's hermeneutic circle, where one must already understand in order to understand. Gadamer's emphasis on openness in *Gespräch* (conversation) and respect for interlocutors is a crucial platform for China's global dialogues, as he demonstrated in an *Auseinandersetzung* (debate) with Habermas, Derrida, and others in the late twentieth century and early twenty-first century.

### Heidegger in China

While Gadamer's rhythmic style of thinking parallels Confucius in many ways, Heidegger's reclusive mountain life parallels the Daoist and Buddhist perspectives that he revered. In lectures at Beidaihe, Beijing, Shanghai, and Wuhu in Anhui Province in the summers of 2001 and 2002, Jay Goulding, accompanying Cheng Chung-Ying and Palmer, explained the interactions between Heidegger's hermeneutic phenomenology and ancient Chinese philosophy (see Goulding, forthcoming). Not only are the Chinese embracing a hermeneutics of disclosure but they are also concerned with the phenomenological shaping of appearances in a global lifeworld. The Chinese word for phenomenology is *xianxiangxue*. It means literally the study of the manifestation of appearance or that which shines forth through the present. Those appearances are philosophical, cultural, religious, economic, political, and psychological all wrapped together. As the number one Western philosopher in China in the early twenty-first century, Heidegger's shift from rational, logical prose styles of writing to poetry seems to follow the shift from Confucian logic to Daoist and Buddhist philosophy and meditation. An early translator of Daoist and Buddhist classics in North America, Chang Chung-yuan, writes, "It was after Heidegger's *Being and Time,* however, that he made a complete change from complexity to simplicity, from an analytical approach to a direct, intuitive one, from highly technical, philosophical expressions to common, simple language, from book-form presentation to plain, simple dialogue, such as in his 'Conversation of a Country Path'" (p. 246). This shift continues forward from *Dichtung* (poetry) to *Lichtung* (the clearing). The clearing is an imaginative opening for the simultaneous revelation and concealment of being. It is a place for the renewal of society and thought. For Heidegger, wood paths can lead either to a clearing or to a dead end. The Chinese word for Lichtung is *chengming* (the clearing); it captures both Heidegger's luminosity and the Daoist cultivation of clarity and stillness.

What China gains from the above thinkers, especially Gadamer and Heidegger, is the idea of an authentic person comporting himself or herself toward the truth. This form of authenticity is similar to the Confucian *junzi* (a gentle and upright scholar) and the Daoist *zhenren* (a true and sincere person). In all three, there is an ability to change with the times while retaining principles, a valuable talent in a global age.

## Globalization in Classical Japan

Japan holds a different view of globalization than China. Its position, however, is inextricably interwoven with China's fate. Much of the early history of Japan was peppered with samurai clan warfare. Consequently it was occupied with an inward-looking gaze, while China enjoyed an outward-looking gaze. By the Tang dynasty (618–907 C.E.), periods of disunity in China came to a close and the spread of Chinese culture throughout Asia flourished. By the sixth century Confucianism and Buddhism flooded into Japan through Korea. The effect of Chinese models of government, culture, and philosophy influenced Japan for more than a millennium throughout the Nara, Heian, Kamakura, and Ashikaga periods. In the sixteenth century Portuguese and Dutch traders appeared in Japan with muskets and Bibles. This changed the course of Japanese history in terms of warfare, religion, and relationships with the newly developing global trade networks. At the end of the Muromachi Bakufu, another period of fierce clan "provincial" warfare, a triumvirate of unifiers emerged: Oda Nobunaga (1534–1582), Toyotomi Hideyoshi (1536–1598), and Tokugawa Ieyasu (1542–1616). These three *daimyo* (great names) were open to Western influences as far as it could advance their cause. Oda, for instance, supported the Jesuits in an attempt to disrupt Buddhist alliances against him. Likewise Toyotomi encouraged Jesuit trade while sending out his own commercial ships (vermilion seal ships) to ports in the Philippines and Siam. In 1570 Omura Sumitada, a prominent *daimymo* (samurai lord) who converted to Christianity, opened Nagasaki to Portuguese trade, later yielding it to the Jesuits as a territorial possession.

After the deaths of Oda and Toyotomi, Tokugawa ended another century of conflict at the battle of Sekigahara in 1600 that marked the beginning of the Tokugawa Shogunate. Lasting until 1868, the Tokugawa peace undertook a policy of *sakoku* (closed country) or national seclusion that officially saw the banning of Christianity, the revival of Shinto, and the suspicion of foreign philosophies, including China's. However, Japan was not as secluded as it pretended. Although frowned upon by the shogunate, the newly developed town cultures of Edo, Osaka, and Kyoto continued to see an influx of Western and Asian traders. This culture was known as the *ukiyo* (the Floating World) that included tea houses, baths, brothels, and theaters. As a compendium of Eastern and Western cultural trends, the Floating World left a lasting mark on both sides of the Pacific. Popular among the townsfolk were paintings, poetry, literature, puppet plays, and *kabuki* theater that were in turn exported to Europe. Unofficially Chinese junks continued to arrive at a welcoming Nagasaki port. Marius Jansen reports on Tokugawa's false image of isolation and its true indebtedness to China:

> Chinese influence rose to a peak in the Tokugawa years. The rising tide of literacy meant that more Japanese could read and write Chinese. The production of poetry in Chinese, something expected of every educated

person, was so great that it may have exceeded the amount of verse composed in Japanese. (p. 4)

Various Chinatowns populated the coast from the Kii Peninsula to Kyushu and in Yamaguchi, Matsuyama, Kawagoe, and Odawara. In 1853 U.S. admiral Matthew Perry's "black ships" arrived in Japan from the United States, followed in 1856 by Townsend Harris, the first American consul. The resulting trade treaties effectively ended Tokugawa's seclusion policy as it entered a new global age. While the Meiji Restoration (1868–1911) oscillated between cries of expelling the barbarians and returning to ancient wisdom, it witnessed a wave of scholars and youth leaving for North America. On the home front, Tokyo and Yokohama saw the introduction of railroads, telegraph, steamships, and other Western inventions that continued up until World War I.

## Globalization in Modern Japan

Following World War II, Japan's inventive role in communication technologies enhanced global perspectives on Japan itself. The exportation of cultural artifacts from Tokugawa's era sees a parallel in the technological products of computers, VCRs, and videocassette tapes in the early twenty-first century. Not only these technologies but their contents are part of Japan's changing role in globalization. Koichi Iwabuchi describes Japan's ironic return to Asia after a long hiatus following defeat in World War II:

> Japan and Asia tend to be discussed and perceived within Japan as two separate geographies, whose inherent contradiction is unquestioned. Japan is unequivocally located in a geography called 'Asia,' but it no less unambiguously exists outside a cultural imaginary of 'Asia' in Japanese mental maps. (p. 7)

Iwabuchi maintains that "the West" became a positive role model for Japanese culture, while "Asia" receded into a negative mystical hallucination. He writes: "In prewar Japan, Japanization was articulated in the term *kominka,* which means 'the assimilation of ethnic others (such as Ainu, Okinawans, Taiwanese, and Koreans) into a Japanese imperial citizenship under the Emperor's benevolence.' Japanization also referred to the indigenization and domestication of foreign (Western) culture. The famous slogan *'wakon yosai'* (Japanese spirit, Western technologies) exemplifies the latter usage" (Iwabuchi, p. 9). In a global context, Japanization involves the adaptation of both American and Asian products, customs, and idea systems to a Japanese cultural landscape. With the end of the Cold War and the emergence of economy and culture under a revitalized Chinese aegis, Japan once again searches for an identity within Asia.

Japanese popular culture illustrates a response to American influences. With an inundation of American cultural icons, Japan responds defensively with the global going local or the global in the local. A typical case of this is the Japanese *anime* (animated cartoons) of Miyazaki Hayao. Although overwhelmed with the Western-style action of sword and sorcery on the surface, Miyazaki plummets to the depth of Chinese and ancient Japanese philosophy, religion, and folklore. *Princess Mononoke* (*Mononoke hime*) is an epic-style film of individual dueling and massive battle scenes that appeals to Western audiences. Yet it also explores relationships between Shinto, Buddhism, and Confucianism against a backdrop of *Nihonshoki* (Chronicle of Japan) and *Kojiki* (Record of ancient matters) that are Japanese equivalents of Greek and Roman myths. Similarly *Spirited Away* (*Sen to chihiro no kamikakushi*) is an American dreamscape of a child's day at an amusement park. Yet it also explores relationships between Shinto and Confucian interpretations of a Buddhist hell. Rather than be overrun by Western sensibilities alone, Japan recycles them into the themes of the ancient Asian world. Looking for the roots of Japanese philosophy and culture in the Chinese world is a trend of scholarship encouraged by the Japanese government in the last decade.

## Western Thinkers in Japan

Concerning the reception of Western philosophers of global issues, Japan's reaction is somewhat more guarded than China's. Heidegger is an exception. His work is still read with excitement because of the early contact with renowned Japanese scholars such as Kuki Shuzo and Nishitani Keiji. Heidegger's compassion for mutual understanding of Eastern and Western life in a global context is foremost in these thinkers. Attesting to his popularity, Japan has attempted more translations of Heidegger's 1927 magnum opus, *Sein und Zeit* (English trans. *Being and Time,* 1962), and probably published more secondary sources than any other nation.

Habermas and Derrida have received varied responses. Since Japanese discussion of premodern and modern societies began in the nineteenth century, much of Habermas's debates with postmodern thinkers such as Jean-François Lyotard are considered outdated. Naoki Sakai sees Habermas's position on global communicative rationality as obsolete. Habermas's "Occidental rationalism" juxtaposes Western reason to Eastern myth in a naive way. While the West might need the East as a "mirror" for its own clarification, "Habermas obviously does not ask if the mirror may be extremely obscure" (p. 96). Instead, Sakai echoes Iwabuchi in arguing that "it is understandable that the discursive object called Japan has presented a heterogeneous instance that could not be easily integrated into the global configuration organized according to the pairing of the modern and the premodern" (p. 97).

In regard to Derrida, the Japanese have maintained that their society has no structure, and therefore deconstruction is not possible. Japan is so much a product of globalization's hyper-accelerated consumption that the very space of such academic talk is already swallowed up. Hence, the transcriptions of Derrida's conversations would be consumed (and forgotten) in one week. From a Japanese perspective, Japan is caught in something like a McLuhanesque series of conundrums between the negativities of mass consumption and the liberating powers of media knowledge.

*See also* **Communication of Ideas; Confucianism; Empire and Imperialism: Asia; Orientalism.**

## BIBLIOGRAPHY

Benedetti, Paul, and Nancy DeHart, eds. *Forward through the Rearview Mirror: Reflections on and by Marshall McLuhan.* Toronto: Prentice-Hall Canada, 1996.

Chang Chung-yuan. "Commentary on J. Glenn Gray's 'Splendor of the Simple.'" *Philosophy East and West* 20, no. 3 (July 1970): 241–246.

Cheng Chun-Ying. "An Onto-Hermeneutic Interpretation of Twentieth-Century Chinese Philosophy: Identity and Vision." In *Contemporary Chinese Philosophy,* edited by Cheng Chung-Ying and Nicholas Bunnin, 365–404. London and Malden, Mass.: Blackwell, 2002.

Craig, Timothy J., and Richard King, eds. *Global Goes Local: Popular Culture in Asia.* Vancouver: University of British Columbia Press, 2002.

De Bary, William Theodore. "Preface." In *Confucianism and Human Rights,* edited by William Theodore de Bary and Tu Weiming. New York: Columbia University Press, 1998.

De Bary, William Theodore, and Tu Weiming, eds. *Confucianism and Human Rights.* New York: Columbia University Press, 1998.

Dirlik, Arif, and Xudong Zhang, eds. *Postmodernism and China.* Durham, N.C.: Duke University Press, 2000.

Fairbank, John King. *China: A New History.* Cambridge, Mass.: Belknap Press of Harvard University Press, 1992. Enlarged ed., with Merle Goldman, 1998.

Gadamer, Hans-Georg. *Gadamer in Conversation: Reflections and Commentary.* Edited and translated by Richard E. Palmer. New Haven, Conn.: Yale University Press, 2001.

Gernet, Jacques. *A History of Chinese Civilization.* 2nd ed. Translated by J. R. Foster and Charles Hartman. Cambridge, U.K., and New York: Cambridge University Press, 1996.

Goulding, Jay. "Li Chenyang, the Tao Encounters the West: Explorations in Comparative Philosophy." *Dao: A Journal of Comparative Philosophy* 2, no. 1 (winter 2002): 166–171.

———. *Visceral Manifestation and the East Asian Communicative Body.* Cresskill, N.J.: Hampton Press, forthcoming.

Heidegger, Martin. *Being and Time.* 1927. Reprint, translated by John Macquarrie and Edward Robinson. New York: Harper and Row, 1962.

Hirth, Friedrich. *China and the Roman Orient: Researches into Their Ancient and Mediaeval Relations as Represented in Old Chinese Records.* Shanghai and Hong Kong: Kelly and Walsh, 1885. Reprint, Chicago: Ares Publishers, 1975.

Innis, Harold A. *The Bias of Communication.* Toronto: University of Toronto Press, 1951.

Ivy, Marilyn. "Critical Texts, Mass Artifacts: The Consumption of Knowledge in Postmodern Japan." In *Postmodernism and Japan,* edited by Masao Miyoshi and H. D. Harootunian, 21–46. Durham, N.C.: Duke University Press, 1989.

———. *Discourses of the Vanishing: Modernity, Phantasm, Japan.* Chicago: University of Chicago Press, 1995.

Iwabuchi, Koichi. *Recentering Globalization: Popular Culture and Japanese Transnationalism.* Durham, N.C.: Duke University Press, 2002.

Jameson, Fredric, and Masao Miyoshi, eds. *The Cultures of Globalization.* Durham, N.C.: Duke University Press, 1998.

Jansen, Marius B. *China in the Tokugawa World.* Cambridge, Mass.: Harvard University Press, 1992.

Jary, David, and Julia Jary. *The HarperCollins Dictionary of Sociology.* 3rd ed. Glasgow: HarperCollins, 2000.

Li, Anshan. *A History of Chinese Overseas in Africa.* Beijing: Chinese Overseas Publishing House, 2000.

Li, Chenyang. *The Tao Encounters the West: Explorations in Comparative Philosophy*. Albany: State University of New York Press, 1999.

Liu, Kang. "Is There an Alternative to (Capitalist) Globalization? The Debate about Modernity in China." In his *The Cultures of Globalization*. Durham, N.C.: Duke University Press, 1998.

McLuhan, Marshall, *Understanding Media: The Extensions of Man*. New York: Signet Books, 1964.

McLuhan, Marshall, and Quentin Fiore. *The Medium Is the Massage: An Inventory of Effects*. New York: Bantam Books, 1967.

McLuhan, Marshall, and Bruce R. Powers. *The Global Village: Transformations in World Life and Media in the 21st Century*. New York: Oxford University Press, 1989.

Menzies, Gavin. *1421: The Year China Discovered America*. New York: William Morrow, 2003.

Miyoshi, Masao, and H. D. Harootunian, eds. *Postmodernism and Japan*. Durham, N.C.: Duke University Press, 1989.

Morley, David, and Kevin Robins. *Spaces of Identity: Global Media, Electronic Landscapes, and Cultural Boundaries*. New York: Routledge, 1995.

O'Sullivan, Tim, et al. *Key Concepts in Communication and Cultural Studies*. 2nd ed. New York: Routledge, 1994.

Palmer, Richard E. *Hermeneutics*. Evanston, Ill.: Northwestern University Press, 1969.

———. "Seven Key Terms in the Philosophy of Hans-Georg Gadamer." Lecture presented at Anhui Normal University, Wuhu China, 22–24 June 2002.

Paludan, Ann. *Chronicle of the Chinese Emperors: The Reign-by-Reign Record of the Rulers of Imperial China*. London: Thames and Hudson, 1998.

Parkes, Graham. "Translator's Preface." In *Heidegger's Hidden Sources: East Asian Influences on His Work*, by Reinhard May. Translated by Graham Parkes. New York: Routledge, 1996.

Said, Edward W. *Culture and Imperialism*. New York: Knopf, 1993.

Sakai, Naoki. "Modernity and Its Critique: The Problem of Universalism and Particularism." In *Postmodernism and Japan*, edited by Masao Miyoshi and H. D. Harootunian. Durham, N.C.: Duke University Press, 1989.

Tanaka, Stefan. *Japan's Orient: Rendering Pasts into History*. Berkeley: University of California Press, 1993.

Tong, Shijun. "Habermas and Chinese Discourse of Modernity." *Dao: A Journal of Comparative Philosophy* 1, no. 1 (winter 2001): 81–106.

Varley, Paul. *Japanese Culture*. 4th ed. Honolulu: University of Hawai'i Press, 2000.

Wang, Jing. *High Culture Fever: Politics, Aesthetics, and Ideology in Deng's China*. Berkeley: University of California Press, 1996.

Wilson, Rob, and Wimal Dissanayake, eds. *Global/Local: Cultural Production and the Transnational Imaginary*. Durham, N.C.: Duke University Press, 1996.

Xu Shi Gu, executive ed. *A New English-Chinese Dictionary*. 2nd ed. Beijing and New York: Commercial Press and John Wiley and Sons, 1984.

Yang, Jeff, et al. *Eastern Standard Time: A Guide to Asian Influence on American Culture from Astro Boy to Zen Buddhism*. New York: Houghton Mifflin, 1997.

Zhang Dainian. *Key Concepts in Chinese Philosophy*. Translated and edited by Edmund Ryden. New Haven, Conn., and Beijing: Yale University and Foreign Language Press, 2002.

Zhang Ning. "Jacques Derrida's First Visit to China: A Summary of His Lectures and Seminars." *Dao: A Journal of Comparative Philosophy* 2, no. 1 (winter 2002): 141–162.

*Jay Goulding*

## GENERAL

Globalization is a complex and controversial concept. There is little agreement in the literature on what it is, whether it is or is not taking place, whether it is new or old, and if it is good or bad. In its narrower conception, globalization signifies a process of intensification of economic, political, and cultural interconnectedness among the various actors in the global system. In the economic arena, where globalization is pursued more systematically, it represents a process of integration of national economies with the aim of making the global economy develop the capacity to work as a unit.

### Conceptualizing Globalization

The process of intensification of interconnectedness, however, does not come about without certain underlying socioeconomic conditions and policy mechanisms. Globalization, thus, needs to be understood not merely in terms of greater interconnectedness or of creating a single global economic space but also in terms of the underlying context that has made it possible, as well as the institutional arrangements and policy instruments that serve as mechanisms for promoting it. A brief examination of some of the most important changes that have precipitated globalization over the last two or more decades helps shed some light on what constitutes globalization's broader conception.

One major change in the global system that facilitated globalization was the reconfiguration of the distribution of power at the global level and the emergence of the United States as the sole superpower following the collapse of the Soviet Union. This reconfiguration of the distribution of power has largely eliminated (at least for now) the contest among competing powers for global dominance and leadership. It would be unlikely for the global system to move in the direction of forming a single economic space when there are contending superpowers. From this angle, the view that globalization is essentially a U.S.-dominated global system seems to be compelling. This view also implies that globalization emerges from a single, unchallenged configuration of power and that the process would be reversible if another center of power should emerge to counteract the hegemony of the United States.

Another underlying factor that facilitated globalization is the restoration of the global hegemony of capitalism and of the market system following the collapse of the Soviet economic system. Contending economic systems and visions would be incompatible with the process of creating a single economic space. The rise to prominence of the neoliberal ideology and the absence of a serious competition between different economic visions has created a conducive environment for globalization.

With the establishment of the identified underlying conditions, various policy instruments, crafted along the lines of neoliberal doctrine, have been developed to serve as mechanisms of globalization. New multilateral institutions have also been created and older ones have been retooled to promote and manage globalization mechanisms. The World Trade Organization (WTO), the International Monetary Fund (IMF), and the World Bank are among the key institutions. Policy mechanisms crafted along the lines of the neoliberal ideology have also been developed to foster globalization. Such mechanisms include the retrenchment of state involvement in economic activity (including its regulatory measures) and institutional changes such as privatization, restriction of trade barriers, and liberalization of capital mobility. These mechanisms have been promoted in much of the developing world through the IMF and World Bank–sponsored structural adjustment programs.

Two main reasons may help us explain why globalization entails homogenization of economic policy along neoliberal lines. The first is that it would be almost impossible to conceive of an integration of national economies into a single space dominated by a hegemonic power where states are unrestrained from exercising their own power to unilaterally design economic policies in a manner that corresponds to their specific circumstances. Another explanation is that the identified underlying changes represent a shift in the balance of power among social classes in favor of capital at the global level. This shift, in conjunction with U.S. hegemony, has created a condition for the consolidation of capital's vision of the global economic system. The vision entails liberalization of trade and the flow of capital and the deregulation of labor markets in line with the interests of big capital. Liberalization of the flow of capital across borders, together with advances in communication technology, have, in turn, reinforced the surge in the power of capital by giving it the power of mobility. By contrast, labor's ability to organize and to maintain collective bargaining has been weakened by deregulation of the labor market (and capital mobility) and by technological advances, which either replace labor or reorganize work.

In light of the identified underlying changes and the globalizing mechanisms, globalization can be defined more comprehensively as a process of intensification of interconnectedness among national economies with the vision of creating a single economic space, largely corresponding with the interests of capital, and spearheaded by a hegemonic power and promoted through various institutional arrangements and policy instruments.

## Is Globalization New?

There are lingering questions as to whether or not globalization is new. Some consider it to be not only new but revolutionary. Others, such as Kenneth Waltz, dispute the claim that global interconnectedness has intensified, noting that the current global system has not even attained the level of integration that existed during the pre–World War I era. Waltz also contends that governments now intervene much more than they did in the pre–World War I era. The points raised in this argument are valid. However, they do not repudiate the fact that capitalism has now resumed a vigorous pace of global integration that was interrupted during the interwar period (1918–1939) and during much of the Cold War era, when

the Keynesian welfare state system was predominant in the Western world and the socialist system prevailed in the East. The levels of integration of the global system of production and state disengagement from economic activity may not yet have exceeded the levels of 1910, but they are rapidly intensifying and are likely to soon surpass the levels of 1910 if globalization continues at its present pace.

The welfare state system that predominated since the interwar years of the last century has also declined notably and a new vision of global order, crafted along the lines of the intellectual tradition of Friedrich Hayek and Milton Friedman, has emerged. In Hayek's view, for instance, concerns of social inequality are mere vestiges of the bygone era of primitive communalism that need to be weeded out and replaced by individual freedom and responsibility, irrespective of the problems of inequality and poverty. There has also been a surge in the perception that national economies have converged into a single space of global economy and that there is only one appropriate form of social organization. A single world economy is far from being a reality. However, there has emerged a powerful advocacy for such a perspective.

In any case, as Kevin O'Rourke and Jeffrey Williamson point out, in historical terms the liberal order that globalization represents is not new, as it was the predominant order in the nineteenth century, roughly between 1840 and 1914. However, globalization represents a significant departure from the global order that prevailed between the outbreak of World War I and the end of the Cold War.

There is also controversy over the factors that promote globalization. Some view globalization as largely driven by technology. Needless to say, technological advances have facilitated the intensification of interconnectedness. It is not likely, however, that technological changes, by themselves, would bring about globalization without a corresponding ideological homogenization or the growing disengagement of the state from economic activity that is currently underway. It is not clear, for example, that capital mobility would come about as a result of technological changes alone, although advances in communication technology, along with the deregulation of capital flows, have enhanced capital mobility.

Others contend that globalization is shaped by market forces. However, an economic system cannot be realized without a corresponding political system, and globalization is shaped by the acquiescence (if not active support) of governments, especially the U.S. hegemonic power and other advanced countries, as Thomas Friedman notes. Adherents of the market forces argument claim that globalization is forced upon governments and that these governments cannot stand in the way of globalization without incurring severe costs. Powerful capital interests are certainly in a position to punish governments that adopt fiscal and monetary policies that adversely impact their goals. The government of South Africa, for example, can be punished by capital flight if it insists on implementing its agenda of social reform outlined in its Reconstruction and Development Program. However, the masses of South Africa are likely to sustain heavier costs if the government abandons its mandate for social reforms in order to comply with the demands of globalization. Faced with such a dilemma, governments in developing countries have generally selected the side of capital, largely because of the pressure they face from governments in advanced countries and the multilateral agents of globalization.

Capital has now succeeded in capturing the attention of most governments. It is unlikely that the global economic order projected by globalization would be possible in an environment in which labor is organized enough to counterbalance the influence of capital on governments. Powerful countries such as the United States are not helpless against globalization. They can prevent it if they choose to do so or if the balance of power among social classes within the powerful countries changes. The demise of nineteenth-century globalization, due primarily to political forces, as O'Rourke and Williamson note, also indicates that globalization does not come and go merely as a result of market forces or technological change. The view that the state has facilitated (if not authored) globalization is thus compelling. Yet there is little doubt that changes in economic forces and advances in technology, along with changes in government policies reflecting changes in the balance of power among social classes, have all contributed to making globalization possible.

**Implications of Globalization**

Views on the positive or negative impact of globalization are also highly polarized. Proponents credit globalization with promoting global prosperity, peace, stability, and democracy. Critics, however, attribute to globalization a long list of societal ills, including rising inequality and poverty, environmental mismanagement, and the narrowing of the scope of democracy. Some even view it as a veil for imperialist domination of the developing world. The global cultural interconnectedness that has expanded with the rise of economic interconnectedness is also often viewed as Western cultural imperialism. Some, however, reject this view. Anthony Giddens, for example, claims that global economic and cultural influences are mutual since, as the West is increasingly influenced by the rest of the world, "reverse colonialism" has become more common. Others contend that, along with economic boundaries, cultural boundaries are coming down and culture without space is emerging. Claims of cultural hybridization or cultural deterritorialization, however, grossly understate the disparity in the levels of influence reflected in the imbalance of the control of capital, technology, and media outlets between the advanced West and the developing world.

Proponents of globalization assert that there is a strong positive relationship between the "openness" attained by reducing the allocating and regulatory roles of states and success in industrial development and socioeconomic transformation in those states. Others show that the claim is at best contentious. There is also strong historical evidence that countries that have successfully industrialized did so behind protectionist policies and strong state involvement in their economies. The Dutch Golden Age of the seventeenth century, for example, was perpetuated by strong state involvement in the importation of raw materials and exportation of manufactured goods. During the eighteenth century, Britain stimulated industrialization,

especially in the area of textiles, not only by imposing tariffs on imports from India and China but also by outlawing the wearing of some imported items. In the nineteenth century, countries like France, Germany, and the United States, in an effort to develop national industries, counteracted British hegemony through nationalist economic strategies that included protective tariffs and credit facilities from state banks. In the twentieth century Japan, South Korea, and Taiwan promoted industrialization through a number of state-instituted policy measures, including land reform, targeting of investments and credits to selected industries, and the protection of young industries, and by providing extensive support for marketing and research facilities.

With regard to the relationship between globalization and democracy, opponents argue that globalization reduces democracy to mere electoral contestations with little of substance determined by popular vote. They note that the more limited the role of the state, the more the sphere of public decisions narrows, resulting in hollow democracy. For proponents such as Hayek (1978), Samuel Brittan (1977), and Hutt (1979), only market democracy constitutes genuine democracy, and state involvement in economic activity—as in the welfare state system—represents the transfer of control from the people and market democracy to politicians and coercive interest groups.

Despite the polarization of views, globalization appears to present gains and opportunities to some and losses and challenges to others both within and among countries. Generally, the more advanced economies, which have the ability to compete in open markets, face opportunities, while those less able to compete, such as sub-Saharan African countries, face challenges. Globalization's economic vision, including deregulation of labor and the retrenchment of the welfare state, has also increased inequality and relative (if not absolute) poverty. Various aspects of workers' rights have been rolled back in order to bolster the bottom line of corporations. The plight of the masses in low-income countries, such as those in sub-Saharan Africa, where governments have been unable or unwilling to provide their populations with even the most basic protection from the brunt of the structural adjustment programs, has been particularly severe.

The impact of globalization on democracy also has been both positive and negative. Globalization has contributed to the spread of democracy but it has also limited the scope of democracy by narrowing the sphere of public decisions. The argument that market democracy is more genuine (and less exclusive) is not convincing. Market democracy, in which voting rests on a base of purchasing power, is inherently oligarchic in an economic system that is characterized by inequality—as capitalism is.

**Conclusion**

According to the foregoing analysis, globalization is not merely an intensification of global interconnectedness brought about by market forces and technological change. Rather, it is a worldview shaped by capital and hegemonic power that aspires to establish a global system in line with the interests of capital. Capitalism, as a market-oriented system of production, has an inherent globalizing tendency. However, capitalism is not always characterized by the level of adherence to the liberal principles that globalization represents. In E. M. Wood's penetrating analysis, globalization represents a new phase of capitalism that is more universal, more unchallenged, more pure, and more unadulterated, than ever before.

The financial crises affecting different countries have shaken the confidence of the advocates of globalization. The World Bank, for example, in stark contrast to the minimalist state dictum it advocated in the 1980s, in the early twenty-first century recognizes the importance of the role of the state in protecting and correcting markets. There also has been a growing realization that unfettered financial flows, especially from advanced countries to emerging markets, can create profound instability. Some proponents of globalization have even admitted that Keynes's skepticism about financial mobility may still be relevant today. The September 11, 2001, terrorist attacks on the United States also (temporarily, at least) raised questions about the wisdom of supporting globalization. Yet despite notable setbacks and shaken confidence, the advocacy for globalization remains strong.

*See also* **Capitalism; Economics; Hegemony; Human Rights; Modernization; Neoliberalism; Technology; Third World.**

**BIBLIOGRAPHY**

Bienefeld, Manfred. "The New World Order: Echoes of a New Imperialism." *Third World Quarterly* 15, no. 1 (1994): 31–48.

Brittan, Samuel. "Can Democracy Manage an Economy." In *The End of the Keynesian Era,* edited by Robert Skidelski. New York: Holmes and Meier, 1977.

Castells, Manuel. *End of Millennium.* Malden, Mass.: Blackwell, 1998.

Edwards, Sebastian. "Openness, Trade Liberalization, and Growth in Developing Countries." *Journal of Economic Literature* 31, no. 3 (September 1993): 1358–1393.

Friedman, Thomas L. *The Lexus and the Olive Tree.* New York: Farrar, Straus, and Giroux, 1999.

Giddens, Anthony. *Runaway World: How Globalization Is Reshaping Our Lives.* New York: Routledge, 2000.

Hayek, F. A. *Law, Legislation, and Liberty: A New Statement of the Liberal Principles of Justice and Political Economy.* Vol. 1. Chicago: University of Chicago Press, 1973.

———. "The Miscarriage of the Democratic Ideal." *Encounter* 50, no. 3 (1978): 14–17.

Hutt, W. H. *The Keynesian Episode: A Reassessment.* Indianapolis: Liberty Press, 1979.

Krugman, Paul. "Dutch Tulips and Emerging Markets." *Foreign Affairs* (July–August 1995): 28–44.

O'Rourke, Kevin, and Jeffrey G. Williamson. *Globalization and History: The Evolution of the Nineteenth Century Atlantic Economy.* Cambridge, Mass.: MIT Press, 2000.

Panitch, Leo. "Rethinking the Role of the State." In *Globalization: Critical Reflections,* edited by James H. Mittelman. Boulder, Colo.: Lynne Rienner, 1996.

Petras, James, and Henry Veltmeyer. *Globalization Unmasked: Imperialism in the Twenty-first Century.* Halifax, Nova Scotia: Fernwood, and New York: Zed Books, 2001.

Sachs, Jeffrey, and Andrew Warner. "Economic Reform and the Process of Global Integration." *Brookings Papers on Economic Activity* 1 (1995): 1–118.

Skidelsky, Robert, ed. *The End of the Keynesian Era.* New York: Holmes and Meier, 1977.

Stiglitz, Joseph, and Lyn Squire. "International Development: Is It Possible?" *Foreign Policy* (spring 1998): 138–151.

Waltz, Kenneth N. "Globalization and Governance." *PS: Political Science and Politics* 32 (December 1999): 693–700.

Wertheim, Wim F. "The State and the Dialectics of Emancipation." *Development and Change* 23, no. 3 (July 1992): 257–281.

Wood, Ellen Meiksins. "Capitalist Change and Generational Shifts." *Monthly Review* 50, no. 5 (October 1998): 1–10.

World Bank. *World Development Indicators 1997.* Washington D.C.: The World Bank, 1997.

*Kidane Mengisteab*

**GNOSTICISM.** Gnosticism is a modern category used for defining a set of second- and third-century C.E. schools of thought and trends that have in common gnosis, a peculiar form of revealed knowledge that leads to salvation, having in itself both its value and its basis. In opposition to faith, gnosis takes root in the experience, generally human, of perceiving a division, a split between the self and the world, between the self and God, and between the self as a founding reality and the empirical ego. As global and absolute knowledge, gnosis aims at overcoming these dichotomies, recovering the individual's threatened integrity and restoring the lost unity of being.

Gnostic forms of knowledge leading to salvation are present in several religious traditions, theistic or not, such as Hinduism, Buddhism, Hebrew kabbalah, or Islamic esoteric traditions. However, in the Gnosticism of the second century C.E. a complex historical reality occurred, characterized by specific identity features, demonstrated by the fact that the holders of gnosis called themselves *gnostikoi.*

The plurality of available sources, from the Nag Hammadi texts to the writings of those fathers of the church, the so-called heresiologists who fought against Gnosticism as a heresy, makes difficult a reconstruction both of its origins and its history. The use of the category "Gnosticism" has been criticized because it provides an overview that hides the complexity of ancient historical reality by imposing an alleged unity to phenomena that were very different. However, this category is a legitimate interpretative historical tool, the only one that grasps the distinctive and unifying feature of schools of thought and movements otherwise different and at times controversial.

### Overview

The Nag Hammadi texts are dated no earlier than the second century C.E. The heresiological texts support this dating. The integrated study of these sources leads to an unavoidable conclusion: based on earlier texts that defended the existence of a Gnostic myth—either pre-Christian or contemporary with the origins of Christianity, and probably of Jewish origin—the phenomenon of Gnosticism arose and became established during the second century C.E. in large Hellenistic cities such as Alexandria. It was linked to Scholastic forms of transmission based on esoteric background of a special knowledge, and was deeply bound with the history of the formation of Christianity as a religion.

Besides a first, less well known stage during which, according to the heresiological texts, figures such as Saturninus, Menander, Basilides and, toward the middle of the century, Marcion and Valentinus followed one another, a second stage took place in the second half of the century, mastered by the Valentinian school of thought. Through the contribution of some Nag Hammadi texts, a tradition of sage philosophy also clearly stands out, deeply influenced by the coeval Platonic schools, and audaciously reinterpreting the Christian theological heritage using the background of doctrinal myths intended to go into the mystery of God's eternal genesis as well as the bond that unites the individual Gnostic to the world of the divine fullness, the pleroma. Beside this Christian Gnostic school of thought, Nag Hammadi texts disclose the existence of a plurality of groups and deeply diversified Gnostic trends tenuously tied to the nascent Christianity of the second half of the second century.

Some scholars supposed the existence of a real Sethian group, so named by the common mythical ancestor, the Seth in Genesis (Gen. 4:25) who became, in the Gnostic myth, the celestial founder of the Gnostics, a select group of divine origin predestined to salvation despite all the attempts at subjugation by the wicked Demiurge and its archons. It is impossible to apprehend from these mythological stories, taking place in the rarefied and impenetrable atmosphere of the pleroma of divine life, precise and convincing sociological indications. Nowadays the dominant trend is to look independently into each of the different texts once attributed to the alleged Sethians, trying to reconstitute the ideology and the course of the groups who used them, by a thorough editorial analysis.

The Gnostic communities reserved a special place for women: the possession of gnosis eliminated normal power hierarchies, favoring, in an ascetic background, a spiritual equality. This explains the privileged role played in certain texts by female figures such as Mary Magdalene. However, one must not draw sociological conclusions from the role played by figures of female savers present in certain Gnostic texts.

***Mythology and doctrine.*** The subject of the Gnostic revelation is the ontological Self, the true spiritual reality, consubstantial with (of the same substance as) the divine. Communicated by a revealer–savior and guaranteed by an esoteric tradition, this gnosis is often associated with instruction that has as a subject the communication of a mythical story. It aims at answering the questions related to existence arising from a radically pessimistic conception of the world as created by a god or a wicked demiurge in opposition to the good, absolutely transcendent God—unknown and unknowable except through Gnostic enlightenment. The Gnostic mythology narrates the events of that Gnostic god, describing his divine origin, expressing and explaining the causes for the oblivion that is his prison, and showing in the end the way back, which brings salvation.

The variegated world of Gnostic mythology is formed starting from this dualistic vision, opposing, in some ways, the pleroma, or world of light and fullness, to our world of darkness, in others, the pneuma, or spiritual reality, to the psychophysical compound created by the Demiurge. The Gnostic myths share the story that, originally, the divine world experienced a perfect fullness, which, through an "accident" within the life itself of the pleroma (in its best-known version it is represented as a mistake committed by Sophia, the last of the aeons emanated by the primordial androgyne), gave way to a world of lack and emptiness, whose master is the Demiurge.

This mythology contains a theogony narrating the unknown God's "eternal birth," which makes it possible for the Gnostic in its turn to be born again reviving his new life; a cosmogony that presents the antibiblical Gnostic version of the genesis of this cosmos, the seat of evil and prison of the Gnostic; an anthropogony, according to which the Demiurge creates the psychophysical compound into which he then (Gnostic reinterpretation of Gen. 2:7) unconsciously insufflates the spiritual principle inherited by his mother, the pleromatic Sophia; and, finally, an eschatology, according to which the world is destined to destruction and only the spiritual dimension will survive, returning then to pleroma.

***Influence and global reach.*** In the Western tradition of thought, Gnosticism experienced historical revivals, from Manichaeism to the medieval Catharism. Generally these were internal dualistic forms within the Christian area, which retained the cosmic pessimism and the conception of a second wicked god creator. Beginning in the Renaissance, the Christian esoteric traditions occupied the privileged place of transmission and retention of Gnostic forms of thought. Fundamental is the work of Jakob Böhme (1575–1624), whose theosophy, phenomenologically akin to that of Gnosticism, is marked by the absence of dualism and whose work fed the subsequent fortunes of Gnosticism. Leaving out of consideration, as devoid of historic importance, the attempts of neognostic churches to revitalize ancient Gnosticism, the next important Gnostic revival was early German Romanticism, with its insistence on totality and absolute knowledge, as well as pessimistic and nihilistic hints. It provided twentieth-century culture—in forms that are sometimes difficult to investigate—themes at times tied to the pessimistic side of Gnosticism, at times to its optimistic side. These themes seem to be spread in heterogeneous sectors of our culture, from the depth psychology referring to Carl Gustav Jung (1875–1961), to Gnostic themes appearing in new forms of religiousness. However, a more precise identification and interpretation looks difficult, in the absence of a clear sociological basis of specific worship forms and, in general terms, because of the difficulty inherent in defining a modern Gnosticism.

*See also* ***Agnosticism; Christianity; Evil; Heresy and Apostasy; Knowledge; Manichaeism; Mysticism; Myth; Nihilism; Philosophy of Religion; Platonism; Sage Philosophy; Scholasticism.***

**BIBLIOGRAPHY**

PRIMARY SOURCES
Robinson, James M., ed. *The Nag Hammadi Library in English.* San Francisco: Harper and Row, 1988.

SECONDARY SOURCES

Faivre, Antoine. *Theosophy, Imagination, Tradition: Studies in Western Esotericism*. Albany: State University of New York Press, 2000. Fundamental collection of studies, with an excellent bibliography.

Filoramo, Giovanni. *A History of Gnosticism*. Oxford: Blackwell, 1990.

King, K. L. *Images of the Feminine in Gnosticism*. Philadelphia: Fortress, 1988. Exemplary study of gender.

Scholer, David M. *Nag Hammadi Bibliography, 1948–1969*. Leiden: Brill, 1971. Vol. 2: *Nag Hammadi Bibliography, 1970–1994*. Leiden: Brill, 1997.

Turner, John D., and Anne McGuire, eds. *The Nag Hammadi Library after Fifty Years*. Leiden, New York, and Cologne, 1997. Important critical balance.

*Giovanni Filoramo*

**GOD.** *See* **Religion;** *see also specific religions by name.*

**GOOD.** Philosophical accounts of "the good" are, broadly speaking, accounts of what it is to be an *object of value—* especially of moral value. A systematic study of these accounts is aided by such distinctions as the following.

### Moral versus Nonmoral Good

There is an important difference between "moral" and other types of value (e.g., aesthetic, economic, or informational). One might say, broadly, that the nonmoral good is what we find "attractive," what is apt to serve as enjoyment; whereas the moral good is that which pertains more narrowly to moral virtue or moral rules. Hence at the very beginning of his *Foundation of the Metaphysics of Morals* (1785), the German philosopher Immanuel Kant (1724–1804) distinguishes "the good will" (the will that acts on the basis of the moral law) as what possesses the highest moral value. In comparison, all other things—even such good qualities as courage and intelligence—have, in Kant's doctrine, at best a kind of relative moral goodness: they are morally good only insofar as they are guided by a good will.

### Intrinsic and Merely Instrumental Good

Another important difference, first clearly enunciated by Aristotle (384–322 B.C.E.), is that between what is "intrinsically good" (good in itself) and what is "instrumentally good" (good as a means to some other end). So, for instance, from the perspective of philosophical utilitarianism (the views, most prominently, of the nineteenth-century British thinkers Jeremy Bentham and John Stuart Mill), pleasure is the sole (intrinsic) good; other things, including money, health, and even such "virtues" as philosophers have traditionally recognized (honesty, generosity, integrity) are good merely as means to that end. By contrast, for Aristotle himself, the virtues would be both means to what he regards as the supreme end (*eudaimonia*— i.e., "happiness" or "well-being") but also *part* of that supreme good and thus, to that extent, ends in themselves.

Some have questioned, however (see Korsgaard), whether there might not be *two* differences here: good as a means versus good as an end; "intrinsic" versus "extrinsic" good. The difference between each pair is perhaps clearest in such cases as this. Someone might hold that the good of a beautiful sunset is "extrinsic," that it is grounded in something outside itself—say, human modes of perception and aesthetic response—but still *resist* holding that this sunset is good merely as a means to something else—for example, the enjoyment of those happening to see it.

### Subjective versus Objective Accounts

Another pervasive difference would involve "subjective" versus "objective" conceptions of the good. At its crudest, a subjective view would simply identify the good for a given person as

---

### TELEOLOGICAL VERSUS CONSEQUENTIALIST VIEWS OF THE GOOD

There are actually two major, competing, nondeontological traditions of the good. One, running from Aristotle to the pragmatic naturalism of American philosophers such as John Dewey (1859–1952) and Ralph Barton Perry (1876–1957) in the first half of the twentieth century, is "teleological"—that is, it construes the good in terms of the fulfillment of such ends as are natural or proper to a creature. Thus the good is conceived as internal or immanent. By contrast, the consequentialist holds that the good is some quantity to be maximized (produced in or by our acts). Against the teleological conception, the consequentialist may object that teleology stands in need of some standard of value (like that provided by utilitarianism) to distinguish between good and bad tendencies in us. Against consequentialism, the teleologist may object that a merely external standard (such as utilitarianism offers) need not provide a compelling reason or motive of action.

---

> ## STOIC AND EPICUREAN VISIONS OF "THE GOOD LIFE"
>
> Ancient Greek philosophy—especially in the "Hellenistic" period following Aristotle (384–322 B.C.E.)—aimed to provide not merely accounts of such abstractions from life as "the good" or the "virtuous" but more concrete guidance as to how the good life was to be achieved. In this regard, two schools stand out. The Stoics taught a rigorous adherence to virtue, duty, and honor. These, they reasoned, were subject to our control and attainable through correct discipline of the will; thus attained, they would be a source of happiness regardless of one's external circumstances. The followers of Epicurus (341–270 B.C.E.), like the Stoics, warned against such emotional attachments as could easily threaten one's peace of mind but, unlike the Stoics, identified the goal of life (and the purpose for avoiding such attachments) as pleasure—not the extremes of sensual pleasure, but pleasures moderate in intensity and apt to endure (to be attained through self-sufficiency, simplicity of life, and friendship).

what that person "prefers" or "desires." This appears to be the working conception of "the good" employed in economic theory. A number of views, especially in the empiricist tradition, tend toward this conception. For the "positivist" school, because value judgments are not scientifically verifiable, they can amount to no more than expressions of what one likes or desires. For an important strain in eighteenth-century British thought (the Scots Adam Smith and David Hume being perhaps its most important representatives), the good is understood in terms of one's preferences under ideal (e.g., personally disinterested, emotionally calm) circumstances.

At the other extreme, views in the tradition of Plato (c. 428–348 or 347 B.C.E.) construe "the good" as a kind of object of abstract contemplation. This object, then, is not constituted by our preferences or desires; it exists as an objective feature of the universe—according to Plato's analogy in the *Republic,* like the sun shedding light on all other things.

There is a related point of difference between subjective and objective views. In the former, the good is fundamentally an object of noncognitive attitudes such as desire or will. If, however, the good is conceived as an object existing independently of the human mind, it is natural to construe it as primarily an object of knowledge. Critics of the objective view—most prominently Hume—claim that it cannot account for the "action-guiding" nature of values and moral discourse generally. Mere contemplation of an object does not necessarily affect one's desires and will; but recognition that something is good surely does have this effect. For their part, defenders of an objective view have often replied that a subjective conception cannot account for genuine moral disagreement. They point out that a subjective account of a moral disagreement (in which person A says "x is good" while B says that "x is not good") will imply that it is merely a case of A saying "I

desire x" and B saying "I don't desire x"—which is no real disagreement.

## Aristotle, Platonism, and Christianity
We may notice how Aristotle's conception of the good partakes of both elements of this dichotomy between objective and subject conceptions. For Aristotle, the good is identified in the first instance as what one "aims at" in any given activity—in a word, "the end" (*telos*) of that activity. Thus the end of running might be health or winning races. Ultimately, though, we arrive at the aforementioned "happiness" (*eudaimonia*) as the final good (end) for human beings. This end, however, is not a mere subjective preference. It depends, in Aristotle's account, ultimately on our natural purpose or function as rational creatures. At the same time, however, it is not a Platonic object, existing separate and apart from humanity or human tendencies.

This difference between Aristotle's "teleological" and Plato's more "metaphysical" conception of the good is important in understanding the good as it figures in Western religious thought. One important strain in Christian thought draws on a Platonic conception of the good as residing in a distinct object accessible to human knowledge yet quite remote from ordinary, this-worldly experiences. A more "Aristotelian" strain of Christianity, most clearly represented in the thought of Saint Thomas Aquinas (1225–1274), accepts Aristotle's conception of the good as happiness but construes this "final end" as including our spiritual as well as our physical, social, and intellectual ends as humans. So in this conception more than in the Platonic, secular and otherworldly goods are seen as complementary; the spiritual is seen as completing or "perfecting" nature—rather than as standing in stark Platonic opposition to it.

## The Good of the Whole: Leibniz, Whitehead, and Spinoza

If the good is somehow objective, one will want to inquire as to the elements or proper analysis of this object. Even G. E. Moore (1873–1958), who argued that goodness was a simple, indefinable property (see below), held that we could say something about the nature of the good as a kind of "organic unity." In this vein, one finds something of a consensus among those philosophers who have addressed this particular concern (including even the diverse pair of metaphysicians Gottfried Leibniz [1646–1716], the seventeenth-century German rationalist, and Alfred North Whitehead [1861–1941], the twentieth-century British mathematician): that the good must involve a kind of maximum of both complexity and organic unity. Such a conception has an important bearing both on questions of environmental or ecological value and on the traditional theological problem of evil.

Environmentalists (especially of the more radical variety) are concerned to uphold the intrinsic (or noninstrumental) value of nature, but this raises important questions of whether or how everything in nature (for example, a solitary gnat) has such value. Here the Leibniz-Whitehead vision of unity in complexity can be helpful in understanding the value, for instance, of living organisms—indeed, of nature as a whole. Theologically, such a conception may be employed to justify apparent evil as part of a desirable ordered complex unity. In Whitehead's theodicy, all evil is the result of a lack of unity (yielding disharmony and ultimately pain) or a lack of complexity (ultimately yielding boredom).

Quite a different metaphysical vision is offered by Baruch Spinoza (1632–1677), the seventeenth-century Dutch thinker. For Spinoza, such an ordered complexity is strictly neither good nor bad; thus, since he identifies this whole with God, God is beyond such attributes. Still, according to Spinoza, in the contemplation and especially in the understanding of this whole there lies a kind of supreme good for humankind.

## The Good in Metaethics

Especially during the first half of the twentieth century, for philosophers in the Anglo-American "tradition," metaethics (an analysis of the distinctive *language* of moral discourse) tended to replace direct ethical and metaphysical argument. Thus in his *Principia Ethica* (1903), G. E. Moore argued for the indefinability of the term *good* and against attempts to construe "good" naturalistically. Moore pointed out in his famous "open question test" that one might significantly ask whether, say, pleasure is good, but not whether "good is good" (thus arguing that goodness could not be defined as or identified with such natural qualities as pleasure). The next-generation Oxford moral philosopher R. M. Hare (1919–2002) explained Moore's results by claiming that that ascribing "goodness" to an object is not describing it at all but performing a different type of linguistic act, one of "commending." Still, a third highly influential British metaethicist, Philippa Foot, advanced a form of naturalism with affinities to Aristotle. Foot was especially critical of an apparent consequence of Hare's "nondescriptive" account: that one could call literally anything good as long as one was performing an act of commending it.

## The Right and the Good

Modern ethical theory is defined largely by its distinction between "the good" as a morally positive goal to be achieved through our acts, and "the right" as a set of rules or moral norms *constraining* our pursuit of the good. In contemporary parlance, the "consequentialist" takes the good as primary, treating "right acts" as those productive of the most good. The contrasting view, that of deontology, takes the right as primary, as defined independently of the good, and as forbidding even acts productive of the most good when these violate such fundamental moral rules as the prohibitions against killing, theft, and lying.

A consequentialist may be a utilitarian (identifying pleasure as the sole good; pain as the sole evil), may advocate some other form of naturalism (e.g., equating the good with evolutionary fitness, as did such nineteenth-century Social Darwinists as Herbert Spencer), or (like G. E. Moore) may reject a naturalistic account of the good altogether. Deontologists, in turn, may be distinguished according to whether they take the aforementioned constraints to be absolute (as does Kant, who treats lying, for instance, as wrong even to save a life) or merely having some independent force—that is, *sometimes* able to override considerations of doing good (as does W. D. Ross [1877–1971], an early twentieth-century British moral theorist).

In philosophy since the mid–twentieth century, perhaps the most significant employment and development of these ideas is in John Rawls's *A Theory of Justice* (1971). In Rawls's view, the principles of justice state norms capable of overriding merely utilitarian considerations. These norms, as in the contract tradition of such early modern political philosophers as Thomas Hobbes, John Locke, and Jean-Jacques Rousseau, are conceived as being chosen by appropriately situated individuals out of their own self-interest. But clearly such individuals must have some notion of "what is good" (beyond the bare abstraction of "my good"). Accordingly, Rawls distinguishes a "thin conception" of the good required in the "original position" (the situation of choice) from a fuller conception, one resulting from the choices they make.

## Virtues, Perfectionism, and the Good Life

The moral virtues might be characterized, roughly, as those qualities apt to be productive of moral good. Yet there is an important difference between consequentialist and virtue ethics. This pertains not only to the split between teleology and consequentialism just described but also to two factors distinctive of virtue ethics and going back to Aristotle. First, virtue ethics rejects the supposed distinction between the strictly "moral" in a Kantian sense and what is more broadly of personal value. The four cardinal virtues of Greek thought (courage, wisdom, temperance, justice) illustrate this, as only the last of these is "moral" in a Kantian sense. The second difference is that virtue ethics tends to focus on qualities of an *agent* as opposed to those of an act. Thus the right act is seen in terms of what the best sort of person (the virtuous agent) would do.

These features of virtue ethics, carried far enough, may lead to quite a different moral conception in which the good is understood in terms of the achievements of those relatively few truly good (or "great") individuals. In modern philosophy, this tendency is perhaps most clearly realized in Friedrich Nietzsche's (1844–1900) figure in *Thus Spake Zarathustra* (1883–1891) of the *Übermensch* ("overman," or superman), whose self-mastery, creativity, and other virtues transcend the mediocrity of the common run of humankind. It is also presaged in Aristotle's conception of the "great-souled man"—who "thinks he deserves and actually does deserve great things" (*Nicomachean Ethics,* book 4). More broadly, a perfectionist conception of the good understands value in terms of an individual's realization of such qualities, talents, and skills as might represent "the best in him or her." Hence, like the novelist Ayn Rand (*The Fountainhead,* 1943), the perfectionist upholds the value of individuality and stands in extreme opposition to what is termed *communitarianism* in contemporary political philosophy.

*See also* **Evil; Moral Sense; Virtue Ethics.**

**BIBLIOGRAPHY**

Aristotle. *Nicomachean Ethics.* Translated with an introduction by David Ross, revised by J. L. Ackrill and J. O. Urmson. Oxford and New York: Oxford University Press, 1998.

Cahn, Steven, and Peter Markie, eds. *Ethics: History, Theory, and Contemporary Issues.* 2nd ed. New York: Oxford University Press, 2001.

Gibbard, Allan. *Wise Choices, Apt Feelings: A Theory of Normative Judgment.* Cambridge, Mass.: Harvard University Press, 1990.

Kant, Immanuel. *Foundations of the Metaphysic of Morals.* Translated by Lewis White Beck, critical essays edited by Robert Paul Wolff. Indianapolis: Bobbs-Merrill, 1969.

Korsgaard, Christine. "Two Distinctions in Goodness." *Philosophical Review* 92 (1983): 169–195.

Leopold, Aldo. *A Sand County Almanac.* Enlarged ed. New York: Oxford University Press, 1966.

MacIntyre, Alasdair. *A Short History of Ethics.* New York: Macmillan, 1966.

Mill, John Stuart. *Utilitarianism.* Edited by Roger Crisp. Oxford and New York: Oxford University Press, 1998.

Naess, Arne. "Self-Realization in Mixed Communities of Humans, Bears, Sheep, and Wolves." *Inquiry* 22 (1979): 231–242.

Pepper, Stephen C. *The Sources of Value.* Berkeley: University of California Press, 1958.

Ralston, Holmes, III. *Environmental Ethics: Duties to and Values in the Natural World.* Philadelphia: Temple University Press, 1988.

Scanlon, T. M. *What We Owe to Each Other.* Cambridge, Mass.: Harvard University Press, 1998.

Scheffler, Samuel. *The Rejection of Consequentialism: A Philosophical Investigation of the Considerations Underlying Rival Moral Conceptions.* Rev. ed. New York: Oxford University Press, 1994.

Singer, Peter, ed. *A Companion to Ethics.* Oxford and Cambridge, Mass.: Blackwell Reference, 1991.

*James A. Montmarquet*

**GOVERNMENT.** *See* **Political Science.**

**GREEK SCIENCE.** The activities characterized as Greek science cover a wide range of practices and theories that do not correspond to modern science in a simple or meaningful way. The boundaries between disciplines were fluid in the ancient period and the definition of subjects and methodologies were discussed vigorously. Hence, it is often futile to try to draw firm boundaries between subjects such as philosophy, medical theory, mathematics, technology, astrology, and astronomy. Rival theories were discussed and challenged to produce a wide range of competing theories and methodologies. Indeed, an important characteristic of much Greek scientific thought is that it is self reflexive and often concerned with "second order" problems such as what constitutes a good theory or a persuasive proof.

**Early Cosmology**

Thales, Anaximander, and Anaximenes (sixth century B.C.E.)— all from Miletus—are often identified as the earliest Greek philosophers and cosmologists. This identification is partly due to Aristotle (384–322 B.C.E.), who presented them as "forerunners" for his own physical theories. Aristotle is also the main source for their work, so his accounts must be treated with care as they are frequently colored by his theories. More generally, because so little is known about them, the Milesians have proved a malleable material to later thinkers in search of a Greek origin for their discipline.

The Milesians dealt both with natural phenomena, such as earthquakes and lightning, and with the structure of the cosmos, for instance how the earth is supported. Their explanations refer to the physical properties of things, but often rely on reasoning rather than observation. Thales supposedly argued that the earth is supported by water, while Anaximander stated that the earth rests in the middle of the cosmos, because it has no more reason to go in one direction than another. Aristotle identified a fundamental physical entity in each of the thinkers' theories: water, the boundless, and air, respectively. It is unlikely, however, that all the Milesians used these entities as material building blocks of the cosmos in the way that Aristotle envisaged.

The theories of the Milesians are often contrasted with mythological accounts found in Hesiod and Homer. However, while the Milesians do not refer to actions of the gods in their cosmologies, their theories owe much to earlier Greek and near-Eastern myths and their explanations are speculative.

The Milesians were followed by an array of thinkers criticizing and developing their thoughts. Among these were the Atomists, who argued for an infinte cosmos consisting of atoms and the void, and governed only by material interaction.

**Plato**

Plato's (427–347 B.C.E.) main interest was with morals and he distanced himself from the material forms of explanation found in the Milesians and the Atomists. In the *Timaeus* he gives an account of the cosmos based on theology, in which the world is created by a divine craftsman. With this image he clearly demonstrates his commitment to design and an ordered and purposeful universe.

According to the account in the *Timaeus,* the Earth lies at the center of the cosmos and consists of atomic elements shaped like regular solids; geometry is thus built into the system at the most basic level. The cosmos has a soul and is itself a living being. After the creation a little soul was left over and human souls consist of remnants of the world soul. Studying the geometrical regularities exhibited by the movements of the stars and planets improves the human soul, because they mirror the world soul. According to Plato, astronomy should not be studied for its usefulness or in order to understand the physical world. Rather Plato recommends in the *Republic* that astronomy is studied to direct the mind toward an unchanging reality of which the sensible world is but a faint image.

Because of Plato's lack of interest in the sensible world he has often been seen as an enemy of science. However, this view must be tempered not least because of his emphasis on the fundamental role of mathematics. Plato also founded the Academy, which drew many eminent mathematicians and philosophers, among them Plato's most famous student, Aristotle.

## Aristotle

The works of Aristotle are of special interest in the history of science, not just because of his physical theories and their immense influence, but also because of his profound interest in how we should organize and understand our knowledge of nature. In *Posterior Analytics,* Aristotle offers the first technical definition of knowledge, *episteme,* as an organized body of deductive arguments. Although Aristotle did not himself adhere to his own rigirous requirements for presenting knowledge, the idea of establishing strict conditions for what counts as knowledge and for its presentation was highly influential.

Aristotle's *Physics* sets out a program for how to study nature. He argued that to know about a thing or a phenomenon one has to consider its four causes: first the *material* cause, which asks what something is made of; second the *formal* cause, which concerns its shape or organization; third the *efficient* cause, which is the agent or "origin of change" that produced the thing; and last the *final* cause, which is the "end" or purpose of something. For Aristotle nature is directed toward the best. The teleology in Aristotle's approach to nature is particularly evident in his thoroughly researched biological treatises where functional explanations play an important role.

In Aristotle's account of the cosmos, all matter on earth consists of combinations of four elements: earth, water, fire, and air. Each of the elements has a natural direction of motion: downward for the former two, and upward for the latter. Thus the Earth is situated in the center of the universe, while air and fire move outward toward the heavens. The cosmos is divided into two distinct spheres. The terrestrial sphere is characterized by change, force, and the movements of the four elements. The celestial on the other hand is unchanging, and the heavenly bodies are made of a fifth element, ether, which moves in perfect circles, thus accounting for the regular circular motions of stars and planets.

In general Aristotle's work is characterized by a lack of dogmatism and a willingness to adopt new methods to deal with the problem at hand. Later Aristotelianism produced influential systematic accounts of Aristotle's work, but these do not reflect the breadth of Aristotle's interests and approaches.

## Mathematics

The early history of advanced geometry is little known, but hotly debated. The deductive-axiomatic method typical of Greek geometry appears to have developed in both mathematics and philosophy and it was probably practiced by Eudoxus in the late fourth century B.C.E. The first complete axiomatic work that has been preserved, however, is Euclid's (c. 325–270 B.C.E.) *Elements.* Euclid presents geometry as a deductively ordered sequence of propositions derived from a set of indemonstrables. It is known to contain material from earlier mathematicians and its aim was probably to systematize known material rather than to present original work.

With Archimedes (287–212 B.C.E.) the geometrical approach is developed and extended. Archimedes used the axiomatic method to explore new areas such as curvilinear figures; in *Plane Equilibria* and *On Floating Bodies* he also made the physical phenomena of statics and hydrostatics accessible to mathematical analysis. While Archimedes' work presents a series of rigorous geometrical proofs, he shows, in the *Method,* how many of the results were first found through a mechanical method.

Late antiquity was dominated by a mathematical tradition based on commentaries, which produced new classifications, systematizations, and definitions based on earlier work. Despite the dependence on earlier work, the treatises of mathematicians such as Pappus (fl. 320 C.E.) and Proclus (410–485 C.E.) cannot be described as merely derivative.

At any time, the community of advanced practitioners was probably very small. Mathematics as a whole, however, was not a minority pursuit or isolated from the world. Mathematics included disciplines such as optics, mechanics, harmonics, and astronomy, and professions such as builders, astrologers, land measurers, tax collectors, and traders used and displayed mathematical knowledge for a variety of purposes.

## Mechanics and Technology

It is often claimed that technology and science were completely separate activities in the ancient world, and that technology was marginalized and played a minor role in ancient society. This view, however, collapses when considering the relationship between mechanics and technology. Practical expertise, *techne,* however, often had to fight against associations with simple manual labor.

The discipline of mechanics in the ancient periods was concerned with the construction of machines, but it is uncertain to what extent the machines described were actually built. At times they were treated as mathematical objects and at times described as real machines. The earliest preserved mechanical treatise, *Mechanical Problems,* was written by a member of the Aristotelian school and answers an array of questions with reference to the principle of the lever. Later mechanical writers from Alexandria, such as Philo of Byzantium (c. 200 B.C.E.) and Hero of Alexandria (first century B.C.E.), wrote a large number of works on mechanical topics ranging from the construction of automatic theaters and mirror devices for temples to techniques for land measurement, lifting, and catapult construction. The mechanical treatises combined practical claims to efficacy with mathematical treatments demonstrating a close relationship between geometry, technology, and physics in this field.

While many of the devices described in mechanical treatises may have been pure invention, others were based on real machines. Technological invention and skill played important roles in construction work, land measurement, entertainment, and catapult construction. Catapults were becoming widespread in warfare from the fourth century B.C.E. and were central in sieges; and mechanical automata were used to induce wonder, for instance in religious processions. Images of instruments on gravestones and on wall paintings also testify that technology was part of society at a multitude of levels.

## Astronomy

The use of the rising and setting of stars to mark seasons is described in literature from the sixth century and some Mesopotamian data were known in Greece certainly by the fifth century. In the fourth century Greek astronomy begins to focus on producing geometrical models of planetary movements based on uniform circular motion. The first known geometrical model of planetary motion is associated with Eudoxus (late fourth century), who also played a central role in the axiomatization of mathematics. Though his model was geometrically sophisticated, it deviated from observed facts in many respects, thus revealing an important aspect of early Greek astronomy; that it was concerned with producing geometrical models of planetary motion rather than with describing the physical cosmos.

The mathematical models were made more complex by the introductions of epicycles (a circle whose center moves on the circumference of another circle) and eccentric models (placing the earth off the center). Such techniques were used by Aristarchus of Samos (c. 280 B.C.E.), famous for proposing a heliocentric model of the world as well as the standard geocentric one, and were developed by Hipparchus of Nicea (fl. late second century) who began to use models to predict astronomical events.

Only little is known about the achievements of these writers as their work was eclipsed by Claudius Ptolemy's (c. 100–170 C.E.) great oeuvre on astronomy, the *Syntaxis* (often known under its Arabic title *Almagest*). Here, Ptolemy derives models for the planets, Sun, and Moon from first principles, using geometrical methods and observed data. In much of his work, Ptolemy mixed a geometrical approach with observation and an interest in physical mechanisms, carefully combining the rhetorical powers of mathematical precision with the status of Aristotelian physics. Ptolemy also wrote an important work on astrology, the *Tetrabiblos,* and in general astrological traditions flourished in the ancient Greek world.

## Medicine

Disease and its causes occupied a prominent place in Greek culture and thinking. It played central roles, for example in Homer's epic poems, in histories and in tragedies, and there exists evidence for a plurality of competitive practices ranging from inscriptions at temples to literary material with close ties to philosophy.

The main source on early medicine is a collection of medical treatises known as the *Hippocratic corpus,* which derives from many authors mainly from the fifth and fourth centuries. It is difficult to characterize this diverse collection of works, but the majority of the Hippocratic doctors were committed to explaining health and disease as physical phenomena. Authors recommend systematic approaches to diagnosis through close observation of symptoms and offered dietary regimes to maintain health. The treatise *On the Nature of Man* influentially described health as a balance between the humors: blood, yellow and black bile, and phlegm.

In Alexandria in the Hellenistic period anatomy and physiology changed through the work of Herophilus (c. 335–280 B.C.E.) and Erasistratos (c. 304–250 B.C.E.), who unusually for the Greek world based their work on human dissection. Later in this period different medical schools also emerged, which vigorously debated the relative merits of theory and practice in medicine; these debates are known mainly through Galen's somewhat biased accounts of them.

Galen of Pergamum (probably 130–200 C.E.) shaped subsequent medical theory up until the renaissance and a vast number of his works has been preserved. Galen drew on material from many previous authorities, but explicitly attempted to reconcile the theories of the Hippocratics (for example, on the humors) with those of Plato (such as the tripartite division of the soul). He famously stated that the best doctor is also a philosopher and recommended demonstrative knowledge in medicine. He also, however, emphasized that a doctor must be good with his hands and he describes both surgery and dissections of animals in great detail.

*See also* **Cosmology; Geometry; Islamic Science; Physics; Science; Science, History of.**

BIBLIOGRAPHY

Aristotle. *The Complete Works of Aristotle: The Revised Oxford Translation,* edited by J. Barnes. Princeton, N.J.: Princeton University Press, 1984.

Cuomo, Serafina. *Ancient Mathematics.* London: Routledge, 2001. Accessible account of ancient mathematics and mechanics in its historical context.

Evans, James. *The History and Practice of Ancient Astronomy.* New York: Oxford University Press, 1998. Covers both theories and instrumentation.

Heath, Thomas, L. *A History of Greek Mathematics.* 2 vols. Oxford: Clarendon, 1921. Comprehensive study of Greek mathematics focusing on the mathematical content.

Kirk, G. S., J. E. Raven, and M. Schofield. *The Presocratic Philosophers: A Critical History with a Selection of Texts.* 2nd rev. ed. Cambridge, U.K.: Cambridge University Press, 1982. Main collection of fragments from the earliest Greek philosophers with commentary.

Lloyd, Geoffrey E. R. *Aristotelian Explorations.* Cambridge, U.K.: Cambridge University Press, 1996. Discussions of a number of issues in Aristotle's thought.

Lloyd, Geoffery E. R., ed. *The Hippocratic Writings.* Harmondsworth, U.K.: Penguin, 1995. Translations with a general introduction.

Marsden, E. W. *Greek and Roman Artillery.* 2 vols. Oxford: Clarendon, 1971. Detailed account of the development of Greek and Roman artillery with translations of ancient texts on artillery-construction.

Netz, Reviel. *The Shaping of Deduction in Greek Mathematics: A Study in Cognitive History.* Cambridge, U.K.: Cambridge University Press, 1999. Important study of the development and characteristics of Greek deductive mathematics.

Nutton, Vivian. *Ancient Medicine.* London: Routledge, 2004. Accessible account covering the whole period.

Plato. *Complete Works.* Edited by J. M. Cooper. Indianapolis: Hackett, 1997.

Toomer, G. J., ed. and trans. *Ptolemy's Almagest.* Rev. ed. Princeton, N.J.: Princeton University Press, 1998. Commentary and translation.

Vlastos, Gregory. *Plato's Universe.* Oxford: Clarendon, 1975. Plato's theory of the cosmos.

Von Staden, Heinrich. *Herophilus: The Art of Medicine in Early Alexandria.* Cambridge, U.K.: Cambridge University Press, 1989. Translations with interpretive essays and an introduction on Alexandrian medicine.

*Karin Tybjerg*

# H

**HAGIOGRAPHY.**   *See* **Biography.**

## HAPPINESS AND PLEASURE IN EUROPEAN THOUGHT.

Most contemporary understandings of happiness are hedonic: happiness is a state of feeling most precisely defined by the subject of the feeling. Happiness in this sense is subjective and can be of brief duration. Ancient discussions of happiness, however, revolve around the Greek term *eudaimonia,* and while this word is commonly translated as "happiness," it has a different meaning and scope than hedonic understandings of happiness.

Aristotle (384–322 B.C.E.) gives the earliest complete discussion of *eudaimonia* in the *Nicomachean Ethics* where he says *eudaimonia* is the one final overall good we aim at. *Eudaimonia* is complete, self-sufficient, and most choice-worthy; it applies to the life as a whole, not to a transitory and subjective sensory state, and so functions like a "life plan." The specification of *eudaimonia* as the final end for an individual is necessarily thin in Aristotle, corresponding to a general notion of one's life going well. Aristotle—while recognizing disagreement about what constitutes living well—adds substance to *eudaimonia* by stating in *Nicomachean Ethics* 1.7 that this highest human good is an "activity of the soul in conformity with virtue," thus linking *eudaimonia* with his theory of the virtues. *Eudaimonia,* then, is ultimately located in the *bios theoretikos* ("contemplative life") and hence highly dependent on a teleological biology.

Linking *eudaimonia* with an individual's final end produced two broad categories of commentary on the eudaimonistic tradition. Some critics argue that eudaimonistic focus on the *bios theoretikos* divorces one's own happiness from broader ethical or moral considerations, and so conclude that the eudaimonistic tradition had no conception of genuine moral virtues. Most current readers of the eudaimonistic tradition, however, see no conflict between the pursuit of individual happiness and external considerations, hence eudaimonism can encompass ethical and altruistic components.

### The Hellenistic Era
Hellenistic thinkers agree with Aristotle that *eudaimonia* is the final end for humans but differ in their description of what happiness consists. The broadest school of Hellenistic philosophy, the Stoics, held that happiness consisted in a disposition to restrict one's will and achieve a state of *ataraxia,* or tranquility. This means that one must reduce one's desires as nearly as possible to those that can be satisfied autonomously;

these turn out to be largely internally regulated. Maintaining *ataraxia* against external vicissitudes allows impassivity in the face of changing fortune and an eudaimonistic life. *Eudaimonia* for the Stoics was similar in this sense to the beliefs of classical thinkers: it held that happiness was a way in which one lived as opposed to a subjective emotional state.

One notable exception in Hellenistic thinking on happiness is Epicurean philosophy. While the Epicureans held similar views on the place of happiness in a human life, their views on what happiness was came closest in the ancient world to hedonic conceptions of happiness. But there is an important distinction to be kept in mind in making this comparison. While Epicurus (341–270 B.C.E.) held that happiness consisted in staving off unpleasant sensations, he said one does this by keeping one's needs simple and easily satisfied. The reason for this was that Epicurus held that pleasures are largely products of the mind, and that consequently people can find greater pleasure through the mind than by pursuing things that most people mistakenly believe to be greater pleasures.

### The Medieval View
Medieval discussions of happiness link discussions of happiness with proximity to or contemplation of the divine. Saint Augustine of Hippo (354–430 C.E.) follows the Greeks in emphasizing that all men desire happiness but makes a distinction between fleeting forms of happiness found in earthly existence and true happiness, which is found in the divine. Most human beings mistake hedonic forms of happiness for true happiness, which comes only from proximity to God. Thomas Aquinas (c. 1224–1274) agrees, following Aristotle's discussion of final ends, adding that happiness consists in the operation of speculative rather than practical intellect, which in turn leads one to the divine.

### Modern Views on Happiness
In the modern epoch, the notion of happiness has narrowed considerably. Immanuel Kant (1724–1804) plays a principal role in this development in his *Groundwork of the Metaphysics of Morals.* There, he establishes his deontological moral theory, which has no room for happiness since moral actions are undertaken out of a sense of duty rather than from a psychological state or feeling. In this view, any "moral" system based on happiness amounts to hedonism, which cannot possibly provide the groundwork for morality. As such, the importance of happiness in ancient virtue ethics gets severely undercut.

### Act Utilitarianism
In some ways, then, Kant's deontological system opens the door for defenses of happiness, and consequentialism emerged

in this role. Of course, happiness in the consequentialist accounts is treated much more vaguely than it was in the virtue ethics accounts. Utilitarianism, especially as promoted by Jeremy Bentham (1748–1832), provides a counterview to both the virtue ethicists and the deontologists. Bentham's version of utilitarianism establishes it as a hedonistic view in which the maximization of pleasure and the minimization of pain are classified as good. On the face of it, Bentham appears to be reviving the ancient Epicurean view, especially since, like the Epicureans, Bentham contends that humans naturally seek pleasure and avoid pain. But Epicurean hedonism differs from Benthamite hedonism insofar as the Epicureans grounded their view in *ataraxia,* which corresponds quite well with the ancient view of happiness or *eudaimonia.* Bentham's hedonism contains no such ground. Instead, what makes an action good is not its effect on the psychological state of the actor but rather the consequences of the action for the (narrow) happiness of the actor. An action is good if its consequences are good (i.e., if the action maximizes pleasure and minimizes pain).

## Rule Utilitarianism

This "act utilitarianism" has been criticized because it only seems to consider the consequences of an act for the actor and therefore leaves aside the consequences of an action for others. As a result, John Stuart Mill (1806–1873) and John Austin (1790–1859) proposed a system of "rule utilitarianism" in which actions would be deemed moral based upon their adherence to a specific rule of conduct that has the best overall consequences. Of course some, principally David Lyons (b. 1935), have argued that rule utilitarianism amounts to the same thing as act utilitarianism since it would simply suggest that the same sorts of acts be followed as in act utilitarianism. The only apparent difference between the two systems is that they follow different methods in order to arrive at the same place.

## John Rawls

In more recent years, philosophers have returned in some ways to views of happiness that are quite similar to that of the virtue ethicists. John Rawls (1921–2002), in *A Theory of Justice* (1971), provides the best example. Consciously drawing on Aristotle, Rawls claims that "a person's good is determined by what is for him the most rational long-term plan of life given reasonably favorable circumstances. A man is happy when he is more or less successfully in the way of carrying out this plan" (pp. 92–93). The favorable circumstances to which Rawls refers are found in his "primary goods," a notion that links up well with the importance of "external goods" in Aristotle's system. Primary goods, like Aristotle's external goods, are the "necessary means" to achieving "one's system of ends" (p. 93). As such, at least among certain philosophers the view of happiness has refocused on the virtue ethics' position. Still, this is a far cry from saying what Aristotle was able to say in the *Nicomachean Ethics,* namely, that the identification of *eudaimonia* (or happiness) as the final good for humans was a platitude. We have surely not gotten back to this position on happiness.

*See also* **Emotions; Epicureanism; Stoicism; Utilitarianism.**

BIBLIOGRAPHY

Annas, Julia. *The Morality of Happiness.* Oxford, U.K., and New York: Oxford University Press, 1993.

Austin, Jean. "Pleasure and Happiness." *Philosophy* 43 (1968): 51–62.

Austin, John. *The Province of Jurisprudence Determined.* Amherst, N.Y.: Prometheus Books, 2000.

Cooper, John M. *Reason and Human Good in Aristotle.* Cambridge, Mass.: Harvard University Press, 1975.

Dongan, Alan. *The Theory of Morality.* Chicago: Chicago University Press, 1977.

Irwin, Terence. *Aristotle's First Principles.* Oxford, U.K.: Clarendon Press, 1988.

Kant, Immanuel. *Groundwork of the Metaphysics of Morals.* Translated by Mary Gregor. Cambridge, U.K., and New York: Cambridge University Press, 1998.

Kenny, Anthony. "Happiness." *Proceedings of the Aristotelian Society* 66 (1965–1966): 87–102.

Long, A. A. *Hellenistic Philosophy: Stoics, Epicureans, Sceptics.* 2nd ed. Berkeley: University of California Press, 1986.

Lyons, David. *Forms and Limits of Utilitarianism.* Oxford, U.K.: Clarendon Press, 1965.

Mill, John Stuart. *Utilitarianism.* 2nd ed. Edited by George Sher. Indianapolis: Hackett, 2002.

Montague, R. "Happiness." *Proceedings of the Aristotelian Society* 67 (1967): 87–102.

Nussbaum, Martha C. *The Fragility of Goodness: Luck and Ethics in Greek Tragedy and Philosophy.* Cambridge, U.K., and New York: Cambridge University Press, 1986.

Rawls, John. *A Theory of Justice.* Cambridge, Mass.: The Belknap Press of Harvard University Press, 1971.

Ring, M. "Aristotle and the Concept of Happiness" In *The Greeks and the Good Life: Proceedings of the Ninth Annual Philosophy Symposium, California State University, Fullerton,* edited by D. J. Depew, 69–90. Indianapolis: Hackett, 1980.

Tuck, Richard. *Natural Rights Theories: Their Origin and Development.* Cambridge, U.K., and New York: Cambridge University Press, 1979.

Wike, Victoria S. "The Role of Happiness in Kant's Groundwork." *The Journal of Value Inquiry* (1987): 73–78.

Williams, Bernard. *Ethics and the Limits of Philosophy.* Cambridge, Mass.: Harvard University Press, 1985.

*Tim Duvall*
*Jeffrey Miller*

**HARMONY.** *Harmony* is derived from the classical Greek *harmonia* (meaning a joint between the planks of a ship or a joining of those planks). From the beginning, the term was also used in its current metaphorical sense, that of a combination of parts or related things to form a consistent whole or an agreement.

## Harmony in Ancient Greek Writings on Music

In ancient Greek writings on the subject of music, harmony (also known as "harmonics") was the study of the formation of melody. This study began with the elements of melody—the individual notes—and continued with the specification of appropriate ways in which pairs of notes, a higher and a lower,

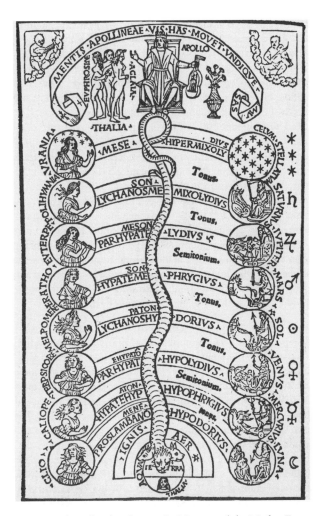

**Diagram of Apollo, the planets, the Muses, and the Modes. From *Practica musicae* (1496) by Franchino Gaffurio.** The philosopher Plato believed the universe was constructed and arranged based on harmonic principals that closely resembled Pythagorean numerical theory. APOLLO PRESIDING OVER THE MUSIC OF THE SPHERES, FROM 'PRACTICA MUSICAE' BY FRANCHINO GAFFURIO, FIRST PUBLISHED IN 1496 IN 'REVUE D'HISTOIRE DU THEATRE,' 1959 (WOODCUT) (B/W PHOTO), ITALIAN SCHOOL (15TH CENTURY)/BIBLIOTHEQUE DES ARTS DECORATIFS, PARIS, FRANCE, CREDIT: ARCHIVES CHARMET/WWW.BRIDGEMAN.CO.UK

could be combined successively into melodic intervals. (The simultaneous combination of notes was not a part of classical Greek musical practice.) These melodic intervals were in turn combined into a variety of complex scalar systems, the defining structures of complete melodies. In general terms, classical Greek harmonics falls into two traditions: the Aristoxenian and the Pythagorean.

***Aristoxenian harmonics.*** To Aristoxenus (c. 375–300 B.C.E.), a prolific writer on a variety of philosophical and historical subjects and the son of a musician, harmonics was the study of music as we hear it. Its task was to arrive at an understanding of the musical sounds that the human ear hears as pleasing or melodic through a systematic analysis of the perceived phenomena. The definition of "melodic" must concern itself only with the sounded elements of music—the notes, described exactly as they are heard by the ear, namely, as different pitches on a melodic continuum; furthermore, the general rules that govern melodic structure must not be derived from any abstract principles. However, Aristoxenus, to support his phenomenalist argument for the existence of certain melodic combinations of notes that have an "affinity" with one another, makes an analogy to a related property of speech: "And yet the order which relates to the melodic and unmelodic is similar to that concerned with the combination of letters in speech: from a given set of letters a syllable is not generated in just any way, but in some ways and not in others" (Barker, p. 153).

***Pythagorean harmonics.*** By contrast, Pythagorean harmonics, the set of beliefs about music attributed to the contemporary followers of Pythagoras of Samos (c. 580–c. 500 B.C.E.) and his intellectual heirs in the fourth and third centuries B.C.E., was centered on the discovery that the fundamental melodic intervals of the octave, the fifth, and the fourth could be produced by the lengths of the two sections of a stretched string in the simple and elegant mathematical ratios of 2:1, 3:2, and 4:3, respectively. The Pythagoreans took this musical discovery as an affirmation of their belief in the mathematical nature of reality and argued that certain musical intervals are pleasing to the ear because of their underlying structure, not for any reason having to do with musical sound considered only as an audible phenomenon. Within Pythagorean harmonics, all subsequent combinations of tones into scalar systems were generated from these basic ratios, including 9:8, the mathematical ratio associated with a musical whole tone. To the Pythagoreans, these scalar constructions—the Pythagorean system of intonation—were musical embodiments of a cosmic scalar relationship among the planets governed by their distances from the earth and their revolutionary speed: the harmony of the spheres. (This idea may have had Mesopotamian roots; see Kilmer, "Mesopotamia.")

## Plato's Harmonic Cosmology

None of the writings produced by Pythagoras or his contemporaries are extant (see Burkert for a discussion of the authenticity of information about fifth- and sixth-century B.C.E. Pythagoreans), but the impact that the simplicity and exactness of the Pythagorean proportions had on the philosopher Plato (428–348 or 347 B.C.E.) is revealed most clearly in his late dialogue *Timaeus,* in which Timaeus, a man trained in Pythagorean doctrine, describes the origin and nature of the physical world. Central to this cosmological drama is the Demiurge, a kind of primary arranger, who begins with formless matter in a primitive state of chaos. He proceeds by using a fixed set of numbers to construct the soul of the world as a mixture of metaphysical oppositions (indivisible and divisible existence, indivisible and divisible sameness and difference). Successive lengths of primary material are mixed in the ratios 2:1, 3:2, 4:3, and 9:8, that is, exactly the Pythagorean harmonic ratios (*Timaeus* 35–36, pp. 64–73). Thus the world's soul is constructed as a harmony of opposites permeated by number in which the formative principles of Platonic cosmology are identical to those of Pythagorean harmonic theory. In a following section, Plato turns to the construction of the physical universe as an "eternal image, moving according to number" (*Timaeus* 37D, pp. 76–77). The seven celestial bodies—the Moon, Mercury, Venus, the Sun, Mars, Saturn, and Jupiter—are created and placed in orbits about the earth determined by these same harmonic ratios. According to this model, the sun is located at the midpoint of a seven-note scale of revolving bodies; the whole thing is contained within an outer starry sphere that sets the limits of the universe. In his *Republic,* written some thirty years before the *Timaeus,* Plato had used striking imagery rather than mathematical relationships to describe his harmonic universe of planetary spheres: "And on the upper surface of each circle is a siren, who goes round with them, hymning a single tone or note. Together they form the concord of a single harmony [musical scale]" ("The Myth of Er," *Republic* 617B, pp. 502–505).

## Neoplatonic Speculative Harmony

At some point Plato's sirens were replaced by Muses, possibly in the lost commentary on the *Republic* by the Neoplatonist Porphyry (c. 234–c. 305). A unique passage transmitting the "musical" version of Plato's image is found in the first book of Martianus Capella's fifth-century Neoplatonic treatise, *De nuptiis Philologiae et Mercurii* (On the marriage of Philology and Mercury). Martianus describes the Muses arriving at their celestial locations:

> The upper planets and the sevenfold spheres produced together the clear harmonies of a certain sweet melody in a sound even more pleasant than usual, undoubtedly because they knew that the Muses were approaching. Passing through all the spheres one by one, each Muse stopped when she recognized the pitch that was familiar to her. Urania occupied the most distant sphere of the starry universe, which was carried along resonating an acute clear tone. Polymnia took the circle of Saturn; Euterpe that of Jupiter. Erato, once she had entered the sphere, sang the pitch of Mars. Melpone took the middle orbit where the sun makes the sky beautiful with his flaming light. Terpsichore was united with the gold of Venus. Calliope took possession of the sphere of Mercury, and Clio the innermost circle . . . on the moon, which resonated a deep pitch in a harsher tone. (Martianus Capella, *De nuptiis,* book 1, pp. 12–13)

Later in the treatise, Martianus describes Philology's traveling from earth through the heavenly bodies to the outermost sphere, giving the length of each leg of her journey in terms of a specific musical interval and indicating that the entire musical distance is equal to six whole tones, or an octave. Thus he presents an explicit working-out of the Platonic cosmological parallel between the ordering of the universe and the harmonic organization of a musical scale.

## Continuation of the Pythagorean-Platonic Tradition in Music

Pythagorean–Platonic musical mathematics was transmitted to scholars during the Latin Middle Ages principally through the following texts: Calcidius's late-fourth-century Latin translation of most of the *Timaeus* (up to *Timaeus* 53c) and his accompanying commentary on that text; Macrobius's fifth-century commentary on Cicero's *Somnium Scipionis* (Scipio's dream); Martianus Capella's *De nuptiis philologiae et Mercurii,* quoted above; book 2 of Cassiodorus's sixth-century *Institutiones divinarum et humanum litterarum* (Institutions); book 3 of Isidore of Seville's sixth-century *Etymologiae* (Etymologies); and finally the extremely important work of Boethius (c. 480–c. 524), *De institutione musica* (The fundaments of music), a learned statement of the Neopythagorean and Neoplatonic traditions in music probably based on the work of the Greek writers Nicomachus of Gerasa (fl. c. 100 C.E.) and Ptolemy (2nd century C.E.). After affirming the correctness of Plato's assertion that the soul of the universe is joined according to musical concord (Boethius, book 1, chapter 1), Boethius formulates an evocative triadic version of the tradition (Boethius, book 1, chapter 2): *musica mundana* (cosmic music), the principle of the universe controlling planetary motion, seasons, and elemental combinations; *musica humana* (human music), the integrating force between body and soul; and *musica instrumentalis* (instrumental music), the music produced by string, wind, and percussion instruments.

By about the middle of the ninth century, during the Carolingian era, writers on the subject of music began to produce treatises that contained large excerpts from the writers cited above, but that attempted to place the Pythagorean–Platonic harmonic tradition within a Christian framework and adapt it to the current need to codify and regulate the performance of liturgical chant within the mass and the holy office. For example, Aurelian of Réôme in his *Musica disciplina* (The discipline of music), written around the middle of the ninth century, justifies the classification of liturgical chant into eight different modes by referring to the seven planetary orbits plus the outer starry sphere (now referred to as the Zodiac), exactly as laid out in Plato. Referring to his Latin authorities (Boethius, Cassiodorus, Isidore), he writes that "the whole theory of the art of music consists of numbers . . . Music has to do with numbers that are abstract, mobile, and in proportion" (Aurelian, *Musica disciplina,* chapter 8, pp. 22–23).

The last truly original and complete statement of Pythagorean-Platonic speculative harmony was given in the Renaissance by the German astronomer and writer on music Johannes Kepler (1571–1630), who in his treatise *Harmonice mundi* (The harmony of the world) posits a world created by God in accordance with the archetypal harmonies represented in the principal musical consonances. The tradition, however, is clearly implicit in subsequent works, such as *Die Welt als Wille und Vorstellung* (The world as will and representation) by Arthur Schopenhauer (1788–1860*),* and explicit in the work of the twentieth-century Swiss aesthetician Hans Kayser (1891–1964). Kayser's principal contribution was a harmonic theory, informed by a close reading of Kepler's *Harmonice mundi,* according to which the measurement of the intervallic properties of sound could also serve as an exact measurement of feeling. Finally, late-twentieth-century "superstring theory," a cosmic physical theory that, in principle, is capable of describing all physical phenomena, is clearly Pythagorean in essence and scope:

> Music has long since provided the metaphors of choice for those puzzling over questions of cosmic concern.

From the ancient Pythagorean "music of the spheres" to the "harmonies of nature" that have guided inquiry through the ages we have collectively sought the song of nature in the gentle wanderings of celestial bodies and the riotous fulminations of subatomic particles. With the discovery of superstring theory, musical metaphors take on a startling reality, for the theory suggests that the microscopic landscape is suffused with tiny strings whose vibrational patterns orchestrate the evolution of the cosmos. The winds of change, according to superstring theory, gust through an aeolian universe. (Greene, p. 135)

## Harmony as the Organizing Principle of Western Music

In a significant departure from its original meaning in Greek music theory as the melodic or horizontal combination of two different notes, the term *harmony,* beginning with the two-voice polyphony of the Middle Ages, came to refer to the simultaneous or vertical combination of two or more notes, as well as the horizontal or linear relationships between the complex sounds thus produced. The primary subjects of harmonic analysis are relationships between notes, properties of chords, consonance and dissonance, and tonality and key. Since the Middle Ages, the study of harmony has developed in two basic areas: speculative or theoretical harmony and practical harmony.

*Speculative or theoretical harmony.* The theoretical study of harmony developed directly from ancient mathematical speculations on the foundation and structure of music, in particular, Pythagorean, Platonic, and Neoplatonic theory. At least through the seventeenth century, mathematical relationships were generally considered to be the formative principles of musical phenomena. Then in the eighteenth century, Jean-Philippe Rameau (1683–1764), in a series of treatises inspired by the acoustical research of Joseph Sauveur (1653–1716), broke with the Pythagorean–Platonic tradition and attempted to discover a strict scientific basis for musical sound through a consideration of the physical principles observable in the natural harmonic series, consisting of a principle tone generated by a vibrating body (*corps sonore*) at a particular frequency and the integral multiples of that tone that are known as its harmonics or overtones. Although this "natural" theory—which can be viewed as a continuation of the Aristoxenian or phenomenalist tradition of harmonic analysis—was intuitively more appealing as a basis for the generation of musical intervals and chords than the proportional divisions of a stretched string offered by the purely mathematical tradition, Rameau's analysis failed to provide a complete systematic explanation of all commonly used chords and chordal progressions.

In the mid-nineteenth century, Moritz Hauptmann (1792–1868), in *Die Natur der Harmonie und der Metrik* (The nature of harmony and meter), turned away from both the mathematical tradition and the type of physical explanation proposed by Rameau to argue—probably following Hegelian philosophical doctrine—that the universal principles underlying music must be identical to those of human thought: unity,

opposition, and reunion or higher unity. In recent years, in addition to theoretical investigations of the physical properties of musical sound, empirical studies of musical perception and cognition have produced information of a comparative nature about different musical styles and cultures in an effort to demonstrate the existence of universally perceived harmonic properties, such as scalar organization of tones and tonal centers (see, for example, Krumhansl, *Cognitive Foundations*).

*Practical harmony.* The study of practical harmony, rather than having the aim of producing speculative theories about musical phenomena, is intended to educate musical practicians: composers, performers, educators, and amateurs. Its history largely coincides with that of harmonic tonality, the Western music of the "common practice" period, approximately 1600 through 1910. From the beginning, practical harmony, or harmonic practice, has included topics such as rules for the composition of counterpoint; techniques of improvisation; and the vertical and horizontal analysis of chordal structures and chordal progressions, the so-called Roman numeral analysis of tonal music. Throughout much of the twentieth century, following the nineteenth-century consolidation of the canon of music within the Western "classical" tradition (that is, "art music" rather than "popular music"), textbooks on harmonic practice tended to concentrate on the analysis of the musical structures at work in the compositions of Bach, Beethoven, Brahms, and other composers of this repertory (see, for example, Piston, *Harmony*). This approach, however, produces somewhat chaotic results when applied to the extremely chromatic, and therefore not strictly tonal, music of the late nineteenth century. Musicologist Jean-Jacques Nattiez, for example, cites thirty-three different functional harmonic analyses of one particular chord—the famous "*Tristan* chord," F–B–D♯–G♯—which occurs in the opening measure of the prelude to Richard Wagner's opera *Tristan und Isolde* (Nattiez, chapter 9). A significant late-twentieth-century development has been the loosening of the distinction between classical and popular music and the inclusion of largely diatonic, rather than chromatic, musical idioms—such as folk music, jazz, blues, and rock and roll—within contemporary textbooks on harmonic practice.

*See also* **Composition, Musical; Mathematics; Musicology; Platonism; Pythagoreanism.**

### BIBLIOGRAPHY

PRIMARY SOURCES

Aurelian of Réôme. *Musica disciplina.* Translated by Joseph Ponte. Colorado Springs: Colorado College Music Press, 1968.

Boethius. *De institutione musica.* Translated, with introduction and notes, by Calvin M. Bower. Edited by Claude V. Palisca. New Haven: Yale University Press, 1989.

Martianus Capella. *De nuptiis Philologiae et Mercurii.* Edited by James Willis. Leipzig: B. G. Teubner, 1983.

Plato. *Republic, Books 6–10.* Translated by Paul Shorey. Loeb Classical Library no. 276 (*Plato,* vol. VI). Cambridge, Mass., and London: Harvard University Press, 1935. Reprint, 2000.

Plato. *Timaeus.* Translated by R. G. Bury. In Loeb Classical Library no. 234 (*Plato,* vol. IX). Cambridge, Mass. and London: Harvard University Press, 1942. Reprint, 1989.

SECONDARY SOURCES

Barker, Andrew, ed. *Greek Musical Writings.* Vol. 2: *Harmonic and Acoustic Theory.* Cambridge, U.K., and New York: Cambridge University Press, 1990.

Burkert, Walter. *Lore and Science in Ancient Pythagoreanism.* Translated by E. L. Minar. Cambridge, Mass.: Harvard University Press, 1972.

Godwin, Joscelyn, ed. *Harmony of the Spheres: A Sourcebook of the Pythagorean Tradition in Music.* Rochester, Vt.: Inner Traditions International, 1993.

Greene, Brian. *The Elegant Universe: Superstrings, Hidden Dimensions, and the Quest for the Ultimate Theory.* New York and London: W. W. Norton, 1999.

Kilmer, Anne Draffkorn. "Mesopotamia." In *The New Grove Dictionary of Music and Musicians,* edited by Stanley Sadie and John Tyrrell, vol. 16, pp. 480–487. London: Macmillan, 2001.

Krumhansl, Carol L. *Cognitive Foundations of Musical Pitch.* Oxford Psychology Series No. 17. New York and Oxford: Oxford University Press, 1990.

Mathiesen, Thomas J. *Apollo's Lyre: Greek Music and Music Theory in Antiquity and the Middle Ages.* Lincoln: University of Nebraska Press, 1999.

Nattiez, Jean–Jacques. *Music and Discourse: Toward a Semiology of Music.* Translated by Carolyn Abbate. Princeton: Princeton University Press, 1990.

Nolan, Catherine. "Music Theory and Mathematics." In *The Cambridge History of Western Music Theory,* edited by Thomas Christensen, pp. 272–304. Cambridge, U.K., and New York: Cambridge University Press, 2002.

Piston, Walter. *Harmony.* 5th ed. Revised and expanded by Mark De Voto. New York and London: W. W. Norton, 1987.

Stephenson, Bruce. *The Music of the Heavens: Kepler's Harmonic Astronomy.* Princeton: Princeton University Press, 1994.

*Blair Sullivan*

**HATE.** As a concept, hate has several interrelated dimensions. It attempts to provide historical, psychological, and sociocultural depth to the forms of hostility and animosity that the term *hate* ostensibly defines, and to make the idea clear in terms of its linguistic usages. As such, it faces obstacles that often appear insuperable. Nonetheless, "hate crimes"—criminal acts and behaviors motivated by hate—have been added to the repertoire of statutory codes of criminal justice jurisdictions throughout the world. The laws help to illuminate the social and political dynamics of racial and xenophobic ethnic hostility as well as gender discrimination.

Hatreds based on identities, lifestyles, cultural values, and tastes appear to have historic continuity and keep simmering across generations. Hate crimes reflect a reservoir of biases and angry memories widely shared within groups that nurse grievances whose origins are often blurred or obscured by time but that retain, nevertheless, a need for revenge and retribution. These antagonisms can act as a flash point for violent behavior in times of economic deprivation or during the stresses that accompany profound demographic transitions in a community that experiences the impact of forced immigration.

Indeed, crimes precipitated by hate involve some of our deepest and darkest instincts. Although moral and ethical principles are basic to the understanding of the problem and instrumental in its resolution, it should not be supposed that effective coping with this particular negative human potential has been achieved.

## Hate Mongering

Saying hateful things is facilitated by the standard discourse of most cultures, which usually furnishes speakers with a rich vocabulary of words and colloquial expressions that can demean, denigrate, mortify, insult, instigate, and arouse violent behavior. Even mass media outlets appear to have been polarized along political–ideological cleavages in which extremist fringes (on the right or left) disseminate pernicious ideas and caricatures, all under the guise of free speech.

## International Scope of Hate Crimes

In April 2002, the United Nations Centre for International Crime Prevention issued a paper on "Preventing Hate Crimes: International Strategies and Practice." The document suggested that most countries are concerned about hate crime, but that there are important differences in the kinds of behavior that may be included under the rubric "hate crime."

European nations, including Germany and the United Kingdom, emphasize primarily crimes where a racial motive is apparent. Hateful speech also falls under hate crime definitions in these states. French law refers to hate crime in terms of racism, intolerance, and xenophobia. By contrast, in Germany, the expression "hate crime" is rarely used. Instead, "politically motivated violence," "xenophobic criminality," and "right- or left-wing extremism" are more common indicators of hate crimes. Australia refers to the idea of "racial vilification" as its criminal conceptualization of a hate crime. The legal terminology of Canada and the United States tends to be more inclusive by citing as hate crimes acts against those of a particular religious affiliation, ethnic and racial background, sexual orientation, age, gender, and, more recently, disability or physical impairment.

The United States Hate Crime Statistics Act of 1990 (HCSA) defines hate crimes as "crimes that manifest evidence of prejudice based on race, religion, sexual orientation, or ethnicity, including, where appropriate, the crimes of murder, non-negligent manslaughter, forcible rape, aggravated and simple assault, intimidation, arson, and destruction, damage, or vandalism of property." The act has also been amended to include physical disability.

In determining whether a hate crime has been committed, the qualifier "hate" must convey a distinctive sense about the underlying dynamics promoting this behavior, showing that behind the crime is an aversion for the victim or a morbid attraction to a potential victim precisely because of his or her perceived individual and social attributes. Thus, what seem to distinguish hate crimes from other crimes are the motives that drive violent, destructive behavior against others or their property. However, proving that hate is the prime motive in committing a criminal act can be very difficult, and in consequence

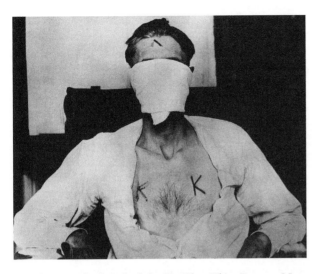

**Man bearing the brand of the Ku Klux Klan, Boston, Mass-achusetts, 1924.** The origins of the Ku Klux Klan—also known as the Invisible Empire—can be found during the period imme-diately following the American Civil War, when the group formed to oppose the Reconstruction government and espouse white su-premacy. © HULTON-DEUTSCH COLLECTION/CORBIS

many such offenses go unrecorded or are not prosecuted as hate crimes for lack of a strong, convincing body of evidence.

### New Perspectives
With the end of the forty-five years of the Cold War (1945–1991), the major powers that were left standing dismantled their empires, leaving in their wake a bevy of new states and nations striving to establish their sovereignty. Another legacy of the colonial period is the abiding hatred and bitter resent-ment of former colonies, many of which are mired in tribal-ism, warlordism, and an unremitting fear of "others."

In the new world of the twenty-first century the phenom-enon of hate crimes is a cultural artifact of a particular kind, however etiolated by social and psychological theories. To un-derstand hate crimes in this context of new and swarming states, it is essential to consider how they have come into his-torical being, in what ways their meanings have changed over time, and why, today, they command emotional legitimacy. It appears that hate crimes are the distillation of complex racial, ethnic, and political-historical forces. These elements are fur-ther defined and formulated into legal and/or criminal categories, and concomitantly into statutory law, becoming "modular." Hence, they are capable of being transplanted, with varying degrees of applicability, to a variety of social terrains, and to merge and be merged with a correspondingly broad class of legal and criminal codes.

A forerunner of modern hate crime legislation was the American civil rights movement of the 1950s and 1960s, which brought about profound changes in American jurisprudence concerned with hate-related violations of individual rights. The movement's ethical and legal courage bequeathed to the world new standards of decency in behavior and attitude expressed in hate crime law.

The terrorist attacks of September 11, 2001, and subse-quent terrorist actions around the globe have made it clear that, despite the significant advances societies have attained in humane treatment of their members, there still lurks a world-view as treacherous as the Nazi insanity of the twentieth century. Unbridled terrorist violence, with its conjoining fanaticisms, steps across moral thresholds accepted by most of the world. Simply put, there are groups who are skilled in the use of chem-ical weapons, ballistic devices, and biological weapons that can correctly be classified as weapons of mass destruction, who are prepared to kill randomly. In viewing these two notions, ter-rorism and hate, as folded into each other, it is quickly sensed that more than a political point is being made. Gratuitous ha-tred is painfully evident.

These terrorists make no effort to justify the bloodshed be-yond perfunctory claims of imperialist colonialism, Zionist re-pressions, and American-led interventions into non-Christian societies.

Hate crimes will probably continue to occur because, re-gardless of the actual inequality and exploitation that may pre-vail in every country, the state/nation itself, at any point in time, is ultimately conceived as a deep, horizontal comrade-ship. It is this fraternity that makes criminal behavior driven by hate possible.

*See also* **Empire and Imperialism; Human Rights; Prejudice; Terror.**

**BIBLIOGRAPHY**
Jacobs, James, and Kimberly Potter. *Hate Crimes: Criminal Law and Identity Politics.* Oxford: Oxford University Press, 1998.
Kelly, Robert, and Jess Maghan, eds. *Hate Crime: The Global Pol-itics of Polarization.* Carbondale: Southern Illinois University Press, 1998.
"Preventing Hate Crimes: International Strategies and Practice." United Nations Centre for International Crime Prevention, 2002.
Public Law 101-275, 104STAT. 140: Hate Crime Statistics Act. Washington, D.C.: U.S. Government Printing Office, 1990.
Title VII of the Civil Rights Act of 1964 as amended by the Equal Employment Opportunity Act of 1972, Statutory Provisions, section 14:55. Washington, D.C.: U.S. Government Printing Office.

*Jess Maghan*

**HEALTH AND DISEASE.** Health and disease seem at first glance to be obvious and opposing concepts. We are ei-ther healthy or suffering from some disease. In practice, how-ever, health and disease are neither clearly defined nor mutually exclusive. Asthmatics and diabetics have won Olympic gold medals, and amputees can live to a ripe old age. "Healthy" people in their eighties cannot do things they could easily have done half a century before; they may still be able to perform tasks they could not have as healthy infants. Conditions that would be perceived as a disease in one society might be con-sidered perfectly normal in another.

**New Dictionary of the History of Ideas**

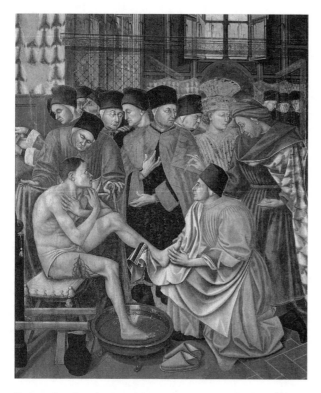

**Fresco showing doctor giving treatment to sick man with cut on leg (1443) by Domenico di Bartolo.** Due to the strong influence of religion during the Middle Ages, illness was often blamed on supernatural forces or sins committed by the sick person. © THE ART ARCHIVE/SANTA MARIA DELLA SCALA HOSPITAL SIENA/ DAGLI ORTI (A)

Health is a more problematic and conditional state than is disease, and it is generally less visible historically. It is less likely to be noticed by the individual or commented on by healers or philosophers. Often, health is simply the default mode, the condition to which people revert after they recover from some illness. Illness is of course not the same as disease. The former is a subjective experience, suffered by a person; the latter is more objective, in that others, especially medical practitioners, share in its conceptualization. The diagnosis, or naming, of the disease generally presupposes some notion of its cause. There may be different frameworks of putative causation operating between patients and their healers. The patient may believe he or she fell ill because of exposure to the cold or consumption of the wrong kind of food. The doctor may have other ideas. For most of human history, however, doctors and patients shared similar causative cosmologies. With the rise of modern biomedicine, the potential divergence of the explanatory frameworks increased. This separation of the conceptual worlds of doctor and patient is part of the power, and the problems, of modern medicine.

More constant are the normative dimensions of health and disease. Health, however conceived, has positive qualities, disease negative ones. Aesthetics plays a large part in contemporary judgments on these matters. Sumo wrestlers and weight lifters are perceived as healthy, even if their life expectancies

may be less than those of ninety-pound weaklings. Straight teeth are considered healthier than crooked ones. Plump women in some cultures are considered healthier than their leaner sisters; in other times and places, the reverse is the case. Sunbathing is a relatively recent phenomenon among the lighter skinned races; malignant melanoma has caused a reevaluation of the relative merits of the aesthetic and the medical.

All of these examples point to the complexity and historical contingency of perceptions of health and disease. Following Alexander Pope's dictum, "this long disease, my life," this essay will use disease as the standard and assume that notions of health are somehow implicit in the historical perception of disease.

## Beginnings

In preliterate societies, disease was often assumed to be the product of one of two opposing occurrences: object intrusion or spirit loss. The intrusion of some foreign object was invoked to explain diseases marked by pain, restlessness, and other acute symptoms. Spirit loss resulted in wasting, lethargy, and other signs of debility. These grand divisions, corresponding very roughly to "noisy" (acute) diseases and "quiet" (chronic) ones, recur throughout history. In preliterate societies, the explanations were embedded within magico-religious frameworks, and the remote causes of disease might be witchcraft, malevolent spirits, or individual transgression of some cultural taboo. Healing was often a communal affair, and the principal healer generally combined the offices of priest and doctor. While the conceptual framework was religious or magical or both, the steps toward healing, or disease prevention, rationally followed the assigned causes. Notions of health generally incorporated aspects of fecundity or potency and are reflected in famous prehistoric works of art.

Literate Near Eastern communities in Egypt, Mesopotamia, and elsewhere developed medical systems that indissolubly mixed the religious and the medical, and the priest-physician was a central figure in them all. Myths of a golden age, when disease did not exist, were common, as was the tacit assumption that individual transgression could be implicated as the root cause of disease.

Three great systems of medicine with great staying power developed in the centuries before the Common Era. These arose in Greece, India, and China. Modern Western biomedicine can be traced to the work of Hippocrates and his followers. The ayurvedic system in India developed autonomously, as did Chinese medicine. The latter two systems still have many followers and have been more impervious to change than has Hippocratic medicine. There are a few, probably incidental, commonalties in the three systems. In each of them, bodily fluids (humors) and spirits (pneuma) were more important than the solid parts in determining health and disease. Longevity was a more explicit goal of health than was fertility or potency. Notions of balance were central to each system.

There are also important differences. The Chinese associated health with plumpness (Buddha is always depicted as rotund), whereas Greek sculptures of idealized athletes show the

**Shaman attending to a sick child, Ladakh, India.** In many early cultures, ministering to the sick was the purview of religious leaders called shamans. These healers attempted to cure the illnesses of community members through spiritual possession. © CHRIS LISLE/CORBIS

taut muscular development that Western values still identify with health and vitality. The Chinese polar principles of yin and yang have no obvious parallels in Western thought. The three Indian humors (*dosa*) of wind, bile, and phlegm cannot be equated to the four humors of Greek medicine.

The series of treatises written between the fifth and second centuries B.C.E. by Hippocrates and his followers provide the touchstone of modern Western biomedicine. So powerful is this legacy that both the dominant scientific biomedicine and the alternative Western medical cosmologies, such as homeopathy, naturopathy, osteopathy, chiropractic, and hydropathy, all claim descent from this "father" of Western medicine. The Hippocratics naturalized disease, making it part of ordinary human existence, rather than the result of supernatural forces. They also reinforced the notion of health as a balance of the four humors, disease occurring when one or more of the humors was in excess or deficiency.

Greek humoralism was one of the most powerful explanatory systems ever devised within medicine. It was linked to Greek natural philosophy (the four humors having their counterparts in the four elements, air, earth, fire, and water) and contained a framework that made good sense of the human life cycle, individual temperament, and the role of the environment in health and disease. One Hippocratic treatise, *Airs, Waters, Places,* is simultaneously a subtle treatise on environmental medicine and a foundation document on the formative role of place and topography on human culture.

The Hippocratics always insisted that the physician was the servant of nature. Through their important doctrine of the healing power of nature *(vis medicatrix naturae),* they interpreted the phenomena of the bedside—sweating, vomiting, diarrhea, jaundice, productive coughs—as evidence that the body was trying to rid itself of its excessive humors or to restore defective or deficient ones. Disease was for them an individual

affair, based on the person's stage in the life cycle, normal temperament, sex, occupation, and other individualized factors. They elaborated a system of hygiene, advice to the individual on how he or she might preserve health and achieve longevity, through diet, exercise, and mode of living. Humoral medicine made no sharp distinction between mental and bodily disorder, explicating melancholy, mania, and hysteria along identical lines as fevers, cancer, or chronic wasting diseases such as phthisis.

Hippocratic humoralism was by no means the only medical system developed during the Mediterranean antiquity, but it was the most influential one, especially after Galen (c. 129–c. 199/216) identified with it and consolidated and extended its nuances. Hippocrates and Galen enjoyed positions of unrivalled prestige for more than a millennium. Galen's monotheism and philosophical bent especially appealed to elite physicians after Christianity became the dominant religion of the West. The otherworldly dimension of Christianity during the medieval period meant that bodily health and disease could be devalued, in pursuit of the eternal felicity of the other world, but medical orthodoxy still operated within the humoral framework. Both religion and magic also offered important alternative interpretations, and both cause and cure of disease could be sought in the realms of the supernatural. Holy shrines and pilgrimages became part of the simultaneous expiation of sin and restoration of health. Several of the seven deadly sins (gluttony and sloth, for example) were also intertwined with causative explanations of disease. Indeed, sloth (also called acedia) was actually medicalized into a diagnostic category and seemed to be especially common among monks who found it difficult to leave their warm beds for early-morning prayers.

**Early Modern Concepts**
The early modern period witnessed great changes in physical science, with the decline of Aristotelianism and the mechanization of the world picture during the period dubbed the scientific revolution. Notions of health and disease reflected some of these developments, although continuities are also obvious. Manuals of health and longevity became popular, as health became a desirable goal in societies now concerned with investigating the wider world and the stars above. As always, health was generally associated with moderation, especially through the regulation of what were called the six "nonnaturals": air, food and drink, sleep and wakefulness, retentions and excretions, motion and rest, and the affections of the mind. An Italian nobleman, Luigi Cornaro (c. 1463–1566), wrote in his old age a treatise on hygiene, based on his own experience of moderate living. It was widely translated and remained in print for several centuries. Although the explanatory framework would differ today, Cornaro's treatise is filled with advice that would not be out of place in a contemporary lifestyle medical manual.

There was much continuity in advice manuals on health for a long time after Cornaro, but ideas about the causes and mechanisms of disease began to change. Hippocratic humoralism had much staying power, but doctors such as Paracelsus (1493–1541) and Jan Baptista van Helmont (1579–1644) elaborated new medical systems. Van Helmont linked physiological function in both health and disease with a vital power that he identified with the *archeus,* a principle he associated with each organ. It had the effect of separating the disease from the body of the individual sufferer, as the *archeus* had some sort of independent existence. Van Helmont inclined toward chemical explanations of disease, but other doctors leaned toward mechanical models of both normal and pathological functions, following in the wake of the triumphant natural philosophers such as Galileo Galilei (1564–1642) and Isaac Newton (1642–1727). Iatrochemists and iatromechanists, as they were called, vied with each other for theoretical dominance from the late seventeenth century.

In the midst of all these theoretical concerns, one clinician remained true to Hippocratic humoralism. Thomas Sydenham (1624–1689), the "English Hippocrates," approached clinical medicine without much concern for the newfangled chemistry or mechanical physiology. He left superb descriptions of a number of diseases, including gout, smallpox, and hysteria, insisting that medicine was an empirical affair, ultimately based on careful observation and the trial-and-error use of remedies. One such remedy, Peruvian bark (which contains quinine), so impressed him in its capacity to extirpate "agues" (malarial fevers), that he came to believe that diseases could be classified in the same way that naturalists classified plants and animals. Nosology, or disease classification, became a preoccupation among eighteenth-century physicians. It came to be based primarily on symptoms, and the number of disease categories multiplied. Sydenham's remarks on the specificity of diseases came into their own in the late nineteenth century, when germ theorists began to identify the disease with the germ that was proposed as its causative agent.

Hippocratic humoralism gradually lost its persuasiveness during the eighteenth century, as doctors turned to the blood, nervous system, or glands as the primary foci of disease causation. At the same time, pathologists such as Giovanni Morgagni (1682–1771) began to note consistent patterns of structural changes in the bodies of patients they autopsied and to attempt to correlate these changes in the organs and tissues with the diseases they had diagnosed and the symptoms that the patient had suffered from during life. This clinico-pathological correlation became the basis of the hospital medicine that flourished in Paris after the French Revolution.

## The Modern Period

In order better to follow the course of disease in the living, French clinicians routinized systematic physical examinations of their patients. Jean Corvisart (1755–1821) developed percussion, tapping on the thorax and abdomen, to demarcate enlarged organs, collections of fluid, or tumors, and René Laennec [1781–1826] invented the stethoscope in 1816. Paris itself became a world center of medical education, and foreign students exported the French way of doing things throughout the Western world. French medicine was based primarily on the diseases of the organs, such as the heart, lungs, or liver. The development of better microscopes in the 1820s encouraged doctors to push pathological analysis into the tissues (a concept popularized by the French clinician M. F. X. Bichat [1771–1802]), and by the late 1830s, cell theories had been

elaborated by German scientists such as Matthias Jakob Schleiden (1804–1881), for plants, and Theodor Schwann (1810–1882), for all living organisms. Rudolf Virchow's (1821–1902) *Cellular Pathology* (1858) put the cell at the heart of medical reasoning.

At about the same time, the work of microbiologists such as Louis Pasteur (1822–1895) and Robert Koch (1843–1910) showed the causative importance of bacteria and other microorganisms in a host of diseases. The germ theory of disease had dramatic practical spin-offs for medicine and public health, but it also separated the "disease" (the microorganism) and the victim of disease. Without the tubercle bacillus, there could be no tuberculosis. For some doctors, the disease could now be equated with its causative organism.

The germ theory was never without problems. Many clinicians considered germs as either incidental to or the result of disease, rather than its cause. Enthusiastic researchers found germs for many diseases, such as pellagra and cancer, which subsequent investigations would disprove. Some social activists complained that obsession with germs deflected concern from other factors that also influenced health, such as housing or inequalities of wealth. Why two individuals exposed to the same germ might have completely different reactions highlighted important host-parasite interactions. The range of agents causally associated with disease has been extended from the bacteria to include worms, plasmodia, amoebas, viruses, and, more recently, prions. Always, anomalies have driven researchers back to the bedside, community, or laboratory.

Since the mid-nineteenth century, the thrust of biomedical levels of disease explanation has been toward ever more minute categories: intracellular elements, chemicals, and molecules with known compositions and structures. Molecular biology is the preeminent science of the present day, created just before, but reaching powerful maturity after, the elucidation of the structure of DNA in 1953 by James Watson and Francis Crick. The biological importance of DNA had been recognized before Watson and Crick's work, but understanding its structure provided a model of how this long-chained molecule, found in the chromosomes of the cell's nucleus, controlled the inherited continuity that is characteristic of living organisms.

Modern biomedical research has revealed many of the mechanisms of disease at the molecular level. The first "molecular disease," sickle-cell anemia, was identified by Linus Pauling in 1949 as the result of a minor structural (but large functional) change in the hemoglobin molecule. Molecular medicine has progressed rapidly since the mid-twentieth century, with the Human Genome Project offering the prospect of much greater knowledge about the role of genetic factors in health and disease. Genetic information also creates a host of ethical problems, such as confidentiality, insurance premiums, employability, and advice on parenthood. Critics argue that it is eugenics in new dress; advocates insist that the knowledge itself is neutral and its use is a matter for society to sort out.

By the twenty-first century the concept of disease had been diluted, as we have all been medicalized. Acts, desires, and choices that in previous generations would have been conceptualized within moral, religious, or legal frameworks could now be attributed to disease. Eating disorders, suicide, many forms of criminality or deviancy, stress, and many other "facts" of modern life are often included within disease categories. Homosexuality has been a normal stage of the life cycle, a sin, a crime, a disease, and a life choice in different periods within Western society. "Mental" diseases continue to carry a moral burden.

If modern medicine has been expansionist in the field of disease, it has been less successful in assimilating health into its orbit. The more we know, the more prevalent disease, or potential disease, seems to be. Orthodox medical advice about health is largely statistical in its foundations and behavioral, not medical, in its recommendations. The Hippocratic injunction to moderation is still at the heart of Western medicine. What is "normal"—that is, healthy—is often based on epidemiological surveys, actuarial information, and cultural values. Despite the enormous power of modern biomedicine, health and disease still have important cultural, aesthetic, and moral dimensions to them.

*See also* **Biology; Eugenics; Hygiene; Medicine; Psychology and Psychiatry; Scientific Revolution.**

BIBLIOGRAPHY

Canguilhem, Georges. *On the Normal and the Pathological.* Dordrecht, Netherlands, and London: Reidel, 1978.

Caplan, Arthur L., Tristram H. Engelhardt, and James J. McCartney, eds. *Concepts of Health and Disease: Interdisciplinary Perspectives.* Reading, Mass.: Addison-Wesley, 1981.

Conrad, Lawrence I., et al. *The Western Medical Tradition: 800 B.C.–1800 A.D.* Cambridge, U.K.: Cambridge University Press, 1995.

Cooter, Roger, and John Pickstone, eds. *Medicine in the Twentieth Century.* Amsterdam: Harwood, 2000.

Faber, Knud H. *Nosography: The Evolution of Clinical Medicine in Modern Times.* Rev. ed. New York: Hoeber, 1930. Reprint, New York: AMS, 1978.

Gerhardt, Uta. *Ideas about Illness: An Intellectual and Political History of Medical Sociology.* New York: New York University Press, 1989.

Gilman, Sander L. *Health and Illness: Images of Difference.* London: Reaktion, 1995.

King, Lester S. *Medical Thinking: A Historical Preface.* Princeton, N.J.: Princeton University Press, 1982.

Kiple, Kenneth F., ed. *The Cambridge World History of Human Disease.* Cambridge, U.K.: Cambridge University Press, 1993.

Kuriyama, Shigehisa. *The Expressiveness of the Body and the Divergence of Greek and Chinese Medicine.* New York: Zone Books, 1999.

Rosenberg, Charles E., and Janet Golden, eds. *Framing Disease: Studies in Cultural History.* New Brunswick, N.J.: Rutgers University Press, 1992.

Temkin, Owsei. *The Double Face of Janus and Other Essays in the History of Medicine.* Baltimore: Johns Hopkins University Press, 1977.

*W. F. Bynum*

**HEAVEN AND HELL.**   Aspects of heaven and hell cross religious traditions. Paradise can be a city, a palace, a court, a garden, a vision of God, a mystical diagram, or an ineffable concept. Physical, indeed sexual, terms and images express the soul's union with God. In Hell, fires, dragons, serpents, stench, cacophony, torturers, and their paraphernalia abound. Christian, Islamic, Zoroastrian, and Japanese sources test souls on a sword-edged bridge to paradise over a fiery stream or feculent abyss, the voracious hell. Unbelievers fall to torment below. Many voyagers observe these worlds: Enoch, Wiraz, Muhammad, Paul, Dante, and various bodhisattvas throughout time. Overlapping with religious images are the secular hells of war, poverty, and disease and their inverted counterparts in bliss, the paradises of resorts, wealth, luxury, and sexual pleasure. Transcending these, most religions insist that heaven and hell—or their approximate counterparts—are out of all proportion to our experience of time, joy, distress, or understanding. Analysis can only approximate their positions. Furthermore, each religion produced many schools of thought, and no one position stands for all.

No postmortem fate is possible without the notion that some aspect of the person survives death. That inner core, the heart, soul, spirit, or atman, is sometimes perceived first as one's self-knowledge; sometimes in the experience of ghosts, the personalities of the dead. The term "porous death" refers to an idea of death in which the dead return to haunt the living and the living may visit the dead, for example, in dreams or visions. By contrast, "neutral death" refers to an idea in which the living banish all the dead, whether good or evil, to a distant enclosure that is neither heaven nor hell. The ancient Babylonian land of the dead (*Arallu*), the Jewish Sheol (the Grave), and the Greek Hades (particularly in Homer) are morally neutral.

In "moral death," reward follows a good life; punishment, an evil one. Moral death has two main varieties, cyclical and linear. In some linear systems, retribution is eternal; in others, destruction awaits the wicked. In the cyclical concept, postmortem pleasure and pain vary over eons as the person awaits promotion or demotion in eventual rebirths. (Cultures that oppose spirit to flesh call this process reincarnation.) Both linear and cyclical concepts of moral death are of great antiquity and emerge first in Egypt and India, respectively.

## Egypt

In ancient Egypt, texts inscribed on the inner walls of the pyramids and coffins or on papyrus scrolls like the *Book of the Dead,* which began to circulate in the sixteenth century B.C.E, make the dead testify to their own moral character. One image weighs the heart against a standard of justice. A monster devours those who flunk. Images from the *Book of Gates* (c. 1320 B.C.E.) show the fate of those who oppose the sun god, Re, as he plumbs the underworld at night and ascends at dawn each day. These enemies of rebirth and of Osiris, the god who is its symbol, are dispatched into ovens and destroyed—not punished forever. The god's friends move beyond judgment to the same occupations they had when alive: cultivating fields, reaping bounteous harvests. These contrasting fates presuppose a distinction between good and evil.

***Dante and Virgil in Hell*** (1822) **by Eugène Delacroix. Oil on canvas.** Dante's version of hell is multileveled in structure, with different categories of sinners confined to a particular level. The inhabitants suffer excruciating physical torments specific to the crimes they have committed. ERICH LESSING/ART RESOURCE, NY

### Zoroastrianism

The prophet Zoroaster (Zarathustra) understood the cosmos as divided in enduring conflict between good and evil, truth and the lie, darkness and light (but not body and soul or spirit and flesh). After nine thousand years, a purging cataclysm separates the opposing forces and subordinates evil to good. At this time, the eternal community of good prevails in light and annihilates the community of the lie. *The Book of the Righteous Wiraz* fixes the Cinvat Bridge between hell and heaven. Only the saved can cross it. The morally neutral inhabit the heavens of the sun, moon, and stars. Above them paradisaical gardens of perpetual radiance welcome the faithful. Beneath the bridge, condemned by their own deeds, which appear dramatically before them personified as aggressive hags, the wicked endure graphically described tortures. They beg for the nine thousand years to end. When it does, their punishment proves temporary.

### Hinduism

Other consequences of moral difference emerged in India. Early on, in the *Rig Veda*, Yama, the first man to die, now a god, rules the dead from "the highest heaven" (10:14). The soul or self (atman) carries with it the moral qualities and blemishes of all its lives. Determined by its own actions (karma), it moves through cycles (samsara) of births, deaths, and rebirths, making all life the result of one's past lives. Life in the world becomes a temporary hell (or purgatory) that creates a yearning for release (*moksha*). In the Hinduism closest to the *Upanishads,* release occurs only when one understands the unity of the self or soul and the cosmos. Then the individual soul transcends itself and becomes its true atman as it blends in glory into the unity of the cosmos and attains Brahman. Brahman is Hinduism's highest reality, but it is not synonymous with the heavens, which are below, part of changeable samsara.

Later, after Hinduism adopted a savior figure active in multiple forms, or avatars, the *Bhagavad Gita* distinguished among the dead persons, who become either like gods or like demons. "The fate of a god is release (*moksha*); the fate of a demon is bondage." For the arrogant there is a downward spiral of rebirth into successive wombs of demons. "[This] is how men of evil karma fall down into hells." The *Markandeya Purana* characterizes seven hells administered by Yama, each with its own name: The Terrible Hell, the Great Terrible, Cutting-off, Unsupported, Sword-leaf-forest, and the Hot-pot hells. The reborn progress through lives as "worms, insects, moths, beasts of prey, mosquitoes . . . elephants, trees, untouchable women, finally up through the castes as Servant, Commoner, Warrior, Priest." Meritorious people enjoy celestial garlands, gems, singing, dancing, nymphs, rebirth into royal and noble families, "the very best pleasures." Yet there is a "great misery even in heaven" at the thought of a fall, since the heavens are also subject to samsara (chapters 10–12). Only *moksha* is perfect release.

## Buddhism

Siddhartha Gautama, the Buddha, modified the Hindu tradition he inherited. The two religions share a belief that karma determines each life and assigns a series of experiences that can include various heavens or hells or rebirth as humans. Though even in Hinduism "atman" and "self" are not synonymous, the Buddha repudiated any association between them as a misguided psychological crutch that might multiply illicit cravings for property, offspring, or fame and so impede the emptiness required for nirvana. The goal instead is detachment from all desire. The human being is not an individual but a variable combination of five aspects of personhood: form, sensations, perceptions, volitions, and consciousness. Since emptiness alone attains nirvana, those addicted to a self are reborn. The "Wheel of Life" charts the fates of persons reborn into any of six realms as humans, gods, titans, animals, ghosts, and denizens of hell. Even the realms of light, residences of the gods, like the Hindu heavens, are painful, since they are less than nirvana, that is, they still participate in samsara. As Edward Conze paraphrases "Nanda the Fair," attributed to Ashvaghosha: "The sojourn in Paradise is only temporary, and . . . the day must come when the deities fall to earth and wail in deep distress."

Mahayana (or Great Vehicle) Buddhism proposed four heavenly Buddhas in their own paradises at the cardinal points of the compass surrounding the historic Buddha in the center. Mystical diagrams called mandalas chart this cosmos. Each Buddha takes an active role in saving his devotees. Helpful in this effort and mitigating the distinction between the cycle of rebirths and salvation are the bodhisattvas, saintly creatures so charitable as to refuse enlightenment for themselves until they have helped all sentient beings from the six realms. Their concern for the dead may reflect very ancient Chinese cults in which care for graves and offerings for ancestors were central to piety. Later, in *The Tibetan Book of the Dead,* Yama instructs the recently deceased as he judges them by the image of their souls in the Mirror of Karma. "Apart from one's own hallucinations, in reality there are no such things existing outside oneself as Lord of Death, or god, or demon." One's inner life is all.

## Ancient Greek Religion

Aspects of moral death entered Greek religion from Persia and Egypt. Legends of Pythagoras in the underworld and the Eleusinian mysteries bring this change. The distinction between swamps for outsiders and Elysium for initiates of the mysteries parallels a shift from Homer's neutral Hades to Plato's punitive Tartarus. In the Myth of Er, which concludes

Plato's *Republic,* heaven preserves the righteous from further reincarnations, and Tartarus imprisons "the incurable" forever. The majority are reincarnated. In his version of moral death, therefore, Plato combined linear and cyclical time. In mythology, heroes the gods engendered with humans could, by apotheosis, attain eternal life among the Olympians. Like Hercules, they become constellations in the physical heavens.

## Etruscans and Romans

Archaeological evidence from before Roman dominance preserves Etruscan tombs modeled on homes, an indigenous tradition projecting earthly existence into the afterlife. Roman popular religion preserves not the dwelling, but the familial tie. The divine *manes* (parents and ancestors) rewarded piety (respect for family, divinities, and the state) with active intercession and a "better option" among the dead. Despite its formal state cult based on the Olympian pantheon, Roman religion had no central authority, hence no orthodoxy. Virgil incorporates a Platonic system in Book VI of the *Aeneid,* but only literati knew this cyclical, moral afterlife. Worship of the emperor was a small part of this complex whole, though it gained heaven for Christian martyrs executed for spurning it.

## Judaism

Moral death entered the Hebrew Bible gradually and late. Judaism's neutral otherworld (Sheol) draws the scorn of Job, because the wicked and the just "lie down alike in the dust" (21:26). Jeremiah begins to distinguish a separate fate for those who worshipped false gods. In Ge-hinnom (Gehenna), a ravine outside Jerusalem, he says, the dead lie unburied, their bones exposed to the sun and the stars whom they wrongly worshipped (7:30–8:2, 19:7). Their evil loyalties should determine their evil fates, which should never end. Isaiah (14:15) imagines the wicked king of Babylon not merely in Sheol, but reviled in the depths of the Pit. Psalm 73 identifies moral categories: the false dispatched "far from thee" and the loyal "near God." These images of place follow from the idea of paradise as the Garden of Eden, where God set Adam and Eve, but from which he banished them. Return to *gan eden,* which Christians would call "the Earthly Paradise," is physical yet also beyond time: an eternally blissful state. The most recent book of the Hebrew Bible articulates moral death clearly. Daniel (12:2) proclaims resurrection and assignment either to "everlasting life" or "everlasting contempt."

Postbiblical Judaism offered great latitude on these matters. Though all pray for "a portion in the world to come," the Talmudic sages left open the questions of how God renders judgment, where his justice parts from his mercy, and how long sinners remain in Gehenna. The tenth-century Sa'adia Gaon argues for eternal reward and punishment. Around 1200, Moses Maimonides regarded these as childish ideas that students should outgrow. In contrast to tolerance concerning the otherworld, the Talmud and subsequent speculation insist on the resurrection of the flesh.

## Christianity

The New Testament of the Christian Bible promises the faithful eternal life. The blessed inherit "the kingdom prepared for you from the foundation of the world" (Matt. 25:34) or "the marriage supper of the Lamb" (Rev. 19:9), a kingdom of light, host to "armies . . . upon white horses, clothed in fine linen" (Rev. 19:14). It is also a court that renders judgment on the physically resurrected dead, where the elect are witnesses (Rev. 20, passim). Paul proclaims a collective view: a God who in the end will be "all in all" or everything to everyone (1 Cor. 15:28). "The Kingdom of God," by far the most frequent name for heaven in the Bible, Luke declares, is *entos humōn*, "within you" or "among you," depending on the translation. "Heaven," therefore, covers a physical place where the divine King holds court, a communal bond, and an internal condition. For the wicked, the Christian Scriptures threaten those who neglect the helpless with "everlasting fire, prepared for the devil and his angels" (Matt. 25:41) and "the lake of fire and brimstone, where . . . [the wicked] shall be tormented day and night for ever and ever" (Rev. 20:10). Unbelievers are "condemned already" (John 3:18).

Christians debated whether hell is eternal. Origen of Alexandria (185?–254?) opposed eternal punishment: divine action must be curative. Souls expiate their sins through repeated reincarnations. Restoration (*apokatastasis*) makes the end like the beginning, evoking Paul's phrase "all in all." Though condemned twice by Justinian, this tradition remains influential in Eastern Christianity. Rejecting Origen's cycles of reincarnation, Augustine (354–430) defended a hell that, because it afflicts the body physically, causes the spirit "fruitless repentance." Despite his opinion that hell wracks flesh, Augustine considered the reprobates' severest torment to be exile from God. Conversely, heaven is eternal life in God's presence, the communion of the elect, true peace, and endless bliss.

A late-fourth-century apocryphal vision, the Apocalypse of Saint Paul, relates Paul's visit "up to the third heaven" (2 Cor. 12:2–3). There he tours the Land of Promise. He sees the four rivers of paradise running with milk, honey, wine, and oil. He meets major figures from the Hebrew Bible: the patriarchs, Moses, Lot, Job, Noah, David, the prophets, and finally the Virgin Mary. Twelve walls surround Christ's golden city. In hell he sees rivers of fire, demons slashing victims' entrails, stonings, worm infestations, hangings, dismemberments, carcasses roasted on spits, and inmates gnawing their own bodies. In the center of this chaos is a covered well within which the punishments are seven times harsher. Seeing these, Paul sighs; Jesus hears. Christ visits this pit, chastises the inmates, then grants them amnesty every Sunday. For all its gore, this text aspires to mitigate hell.

Building on the idea of exile and its associated alienation, allegorical and psychological interpretations multiplied. Though he describes many gruesome physical torments in the *Inferno*, Dante identifies hell's essence while describing souls encased in flames: "Each one swathes himself in that which makes him burn" (26.48). The reformer Martin Luther put the afterlife in a psychological context, too, when he declared in 1517, "Hell, Purgatory, and Heaven appear to differ as despair, almost despair, and peace of mind differ." Of his own spiritual rebirth he said, "I felt that I was altogether born again and had entered paradise itself through open gates."

If faith is the way to heaven, hell begins even before death, when the faithless soul endures isolation and disorientation. As Luther put it, "Everyone carries his own hell with him wherever he is." Though earlier theology anticipates the statement, Calvin appears the first (1534) to say "Hell is not a place but a condition." In 1999, Pope John Paul II declared heaven "complete intimacy with the Father," partnership "in his heavenly glorification," the "blessed community of all who are perfectly incorporated into Christ." Hell he called "the ultimate consequence of sin itself, which turns against the person who committed it." This definition of hell emphasizes the alienating, self-reflexive character of freely chosen exclusion, whereas heaven embraces a longed-for community wholly dedicated to the divine. Invoking the scriptural letter, Evangelicals resist allegorical interpretations.

## Islam

The Koran abounds in references to "the Fire," "the Burning," and "the Gardens beneath which rivers flow." Beyond the Koran, many hadith (sayings) and other, later records of oral traditions develop Islamic eschatology. The account of Muhammad's Ascension, which retraces the Prophet's progress from hell to paradise, resembles Asian and European accounts in organization and vividness. In the late eighth century, the Sufi mystic Rabi'ah of Basra claimed that neither fear of hell nor hope for heaven befit the pious soul: "O God! if I worship Thee in fear of Hell, burn me in Hell; and if I worship Thee in hope of Paradise, exclude me from Paradise; but if I worship Thee for Thine own sake, withhold not Thine everlasting beauty!"

*See also* **Buddhism; Christianity; Death; Death and Afterlife, Islamic Understanding of; Heaven and Hell (Asian Focus); Hinduism; Immortality and the Afterlife; Judaism; Platonism.**

### BIBLIOGRAPHY

Bernstein, Alan E. *The Formation of Hell: Death and Retribution in the Ancient and Early Christian Worlds.* Ithaca, N.Y.: Cornell University Press, 1993.

Conze, Edward, ed. *Buddhist Scriptures.* London: Penguin, 1959.

Eliade, Mircea. *A History of Religious Ideas.* 3 vols. Translated by Willard R. Trask. Chicago: University of Chicago Press, 1978–1985.

Gardiner, Eileen, ed. *Visions of Heaven and Hell before Dante.* New York: Italica Press, 1989.

King, Charles. "The Living and the Dead: Ancient Roman Conceptions of the Afterlife." Ph.D. diss., University of Chicago, 1998.

McDannell, Colleen, and Bernhard Lang. *Heaven: A History.* New Haven, Conn.: Yale University Press, 1988.

O'Flaherty, Wendy Doniger, ed., with Daniel Gold, David Haberman, and David Shulman. *Textual Sources for the Study of Hinduism.* Chicago: University of Chicago Press, 1990.

Russell, Jeffrey Burton. *A History of Heaven: The Singing Silence.* Princeton, N.J.: Princeton University Press, 1997.

Smith, Jane Idleman, and Yvonne Yazbeck Haddad. *The Islamic Understanding of Death and Resurrection.* Albany: State University of New York Press, 1981.

Wright, J. Edward. *The Early History of Heaven.* New York: Oxford University Press, 2000.

Zaleski, Carol. *Otherworld Journeys: Accounts of Near-Death Experience in Medieval and Modern Times.* New York: Oxford University Press, 1987.

*Alan E. Bernstein*

**HEAVEN AND HELL (ASIAN FOCUS).** The ideas on heaven and hell are closely associated with human imagination about the afterlife in Asian civilizations. The images of heaven and hell, however, vary greatly in different regions such as in the southern, central, and eastern parts of the Asian continent, and they have changed significantly throughout history. There is no such thing as a unique Asian mind or a collective Asian concept of heaven and hell, and therefore we should not simplify or twist the historical evidence available to us in order to create a clear statement of the Asian idea of heaven and hell for the convenience of a Western audience. Instead, we should examine the two related concepts in their original historical and regional contexts and focus on both textual and material evidence to discuss the compositions and historical changes of heaven and hell in Asian cultures.

## Heaven

Mainly as an ideal place for the afterlife, heaven was described as a mysterious island in the ocean or a palace on the top of mountain or a multilayered structure in the sky. In different regions and times, people have different ideas about the location and appearance of heaven.

*South Asia.* Various heavens, seven in total and one above the other, are recorded in the Pali literature, some of the earliest written information on heaven preserved in South Asia. Thirty-three heavens, again one above the other, are also described in ancient Sanskrit texts. These ideas about heaven were adopted in the sixth century B.C.E. by the historical Buddha, who, in turn, developed a more systematic and elaborate vision of heaven that we see in the surviving Buddhist scriptures. From the Buddhist perspective, the most important heaven is Sukhavati or the Western Paradise, the land of bliss. The master of the Western Paradise is Buddha Amitabha and the residents of the land are all holy beings. At the opposite location is the Eastern Paradise of Buddha Bhaisajya-guru or the Healing Buddha. This horizontal placement of the Western and Eastern Paradises is supplemented by a vertical structure consisting of thirty-three heavens in the sky. Beautiful and comfortable, all Buddhist heavens are occupied by holy beings such as the Buddhas and Bodhisattvas and are ready to accept the reborn souls of the virtuous Buddhist devotees. In early Buddhist iconography, heaven is depicted as a part of the narrative representation of Siddhartha Gautama Buddha's (the historical Buddha, c. 563–483 B.C.E.) life; it is shown as a small house located on the top of a pagoda-like ladder. The Tushita Heaven of Bodhisattva Maitreya is also depicted as a frame-like house. The number of pictorial representations of heaven in ancient Indian Buddhist art, however, seems to be very small. The scarcity and simplicity of heaven images in ancient Indian art suggest that the motif of paradise in India was far less popular than in East Asian countries.

*East Asia.* Before the introduction of Buddhism into China around the first century C.E., heaven and paradise were considered two different concepts. Heaven is up in the sky, and from there deceased ancestors provide legitimacy to the living rulers or send mythical signs celebrating or criticizing the rulers' behavior. Paradise is a livable place located either in the Eastern Sea or on the top of the Kunlun Mountains in the west. In the early thoughts of Daoism, an indigenous religion that began in China at almost the same time as Buddhism in South Asia, the islands of immortality float in the sea in the east. The lucky ones might obtain elixirs from the immortals on the islands and live forever. The most influential local paradise before the introduction of Buddhism is the paradise of the Queen Mother of the West, located on the top of the Kunlun Mountains in the remote west of China. The islands of immortality in the Eastern Sea and the Queen Mother's paradise on the Kunlun Mountains in the west also form a horizontal orientation. During the Qin-Han period (third century B.C.E. to third century C.E.), heaven (or the sky) and paradise (place for the afterlife) are shown in totally different visual forms: the former is perceived as an astronomical entity and depicted as a star map, and the latter is understood as a place and depicted as a remote mount where the deceased could meet the Queen Mother. When Buddhist ideas of heaven-paradise entered China in the first century C.E., they provided a great stimulation to the Chinese imagination regarding the afterlife and fundamentally changed the vision of heaven throughout East Asia. Thousands of pictures of the Buddhist paradise were created in medieval China and Japan to serve as aids in visualization by religious practitioners and to satisfy the need of ordinary devotees to accumulate merits and prepare for the future entrance into paradise. The most popular visual pattern of Buddhist paradise in East Asia consists of four basic elements: the holy icons of the Buddha and Bodhisattvas, the palatial buildings in which devotees could imagine themselves living, large water ponds in which devotees could imagine themselves being reborn, and musicians and dancers who could entertain the devotees. In most cases, the visual details are created according to local and contemporary customs and somehow reflect the historical conditions of that time. The local visions of Buddhist paradise created in various regions in Asia can certainly help us understand the diversity of heaven images and provide us with critical evidence to understand the histories and cultures of Asia.

## Hell

While Buddhist heaven is designed for the holy beings and prepared for the virtuous devotees who will live pure and happy lives there upon their deaths, a painful underground hell is imagined as a place to imprison the souls of those who do not behave well in their lifetime. Heaven and hell, therefore, form a system of reward and punishment according to religious and social disciplines. In addition to its primary function as a place for punishment, hell is also one of the six states of existence (e.g., gods, men, monsters, hell, hungry ghosts, and animals). The six states of existence are interchangeable through the process of rebirth, and no state is permanent. The six states of existence are also described as six paths of rebirth and visually represented as a wheel, which is divided into six radiating panels in

Buddhist art. Ten courts of justice, supervised by the ten kings of hell, are set up on the way to hell to clarify the sinners' specific evil deeds and to decide the level or type of punishment. The most evil sinner is sent to Avici, the deepest and most painful section of hell. The tortures in hell include hot and cold treatments such as being thrown into fire, dipped into boiling oil, drinking hot liquid copper, or staying in a frozen cave of ice. In some local versions, a specific means of punishment is created to target a certain crime. An old woman who badmouths a neighbor, for instance, might be punished by having her tongue cut off by an executioner in hell as we can see in stone carvings at Dazu, Sichuan province, in southwestern China.

## Conclusion

Heaven and hell are not only religious ideas but also philosophical, social, and political concepts in Asia. The visual forms of heaven and hell are mostly local products with identifiable regional features and could be better understood in local historical context.

*See also* **Buddhism; Death; Death and Afterlife, Islamic Understanding of; Heaven and Hell; Immortality and the Afterlife; Religion: East and Southeast Asia.**

**BIBLIOGRAPHY**

Gómez, O. Luis, trans. *The Land of Bliss: The Paradise of the Buddha of Measureless Light.* Honolulu: University of Hawaii Press, 1996.

Law, Bimala C. *Heaven and Hell in Buddhist Perspective.* Reprint, Varanasi, India: Bhartiya Publishing House, reprint, 1973.

Loewe, Michael. *Ways to Paradise: The Chinese Quest for Immortality.* London and Boston: Allen and Unwin, 1979.

Qiang, Ning. *Art, Religion, and Politics in Medieval China: The Dunhuang Cave of the Zhai Family.* Honolulu: University of Hawaii Press, 2004.

Soothill, William Edward, and Lewis Hodous, comps. *A Dictionary of Chinese Buddhist Terms.* Reprint, Taiwan: Buddha-Light Publishing House, 1979.

Teiser, Stephen F. *The Ghost Festival in Medieval China.* Princeton: Princeton University Press, 1988.

———. *The Scripture on the Ten Kings and the Making of Purgatory in Medieval Chinese Buddhism.* Honululu: University of Hawaii Press, 1994.

Wu, Hung, and Ning Qiang. "Paradise Images in Early Chinese Art." In *The Flowering of a Foreign Faith: New Studies in Chinese Buddhist Art,* edited by Janet Baker, 54–67. New Delhi: Marg Publication, 1998.

*Ning Qiang*

# HEDONISM IN EUROPEAN THOUGHT.

Hedonism is a modern word derived from the Greek *hedone,* or "pleasure." As a philosophical position, moral hedonism justifies pleasure as a good, or even the good. Its history can be traced back to Hellenistic philosophy.

Ancient ethics can be defined as a response to the question: "What is a good life?" The first reply to such a question is "happiness" (*eudaimonia*). This starting point is common to Plato (c. 428–348 or 347 B.C.E.) and Aristotle (384–322 B.C.E.), to Epicureanism and Stoicism, but then the competition about the proper definition of "happiness" begins. What is happiness? And here, with the variety of meanings of *eudaimonia,* the discrepancy among philosophical traditions unfolds. Yet, at the point where the disagreement begins, we find a remarkable consensus about what usually comes to mind as the most obvious candidate. It is pleasure.

Now, for Plato, Aristotle, and the Stoics, *hedone* is both the first and the worst candidate. Only the Epicureans, after the Cyrenaics, accept it fully as the condition of a good life. The claim that pleasure is a value, even the criterion for moral worth, lies at the core of hedonism and its tradition.

Of all the philosophers who reject the value of pleasure, the most radical is Plato. He endorses the archaic vision of delight as oblivion, carelessness, and selfishness; worse still, except in the enjoyment of knowledge, pleasure cannot truly be, because desire is insatiable.

Whereas, for Plato, pleasure is unlimited, irrational, incompatible with virtue, especially justice, for Epicurus (341–270 B.C.E.), pleasure is rational. It is a state of well being, made possible by the avoidance of pain, both physical and psychological, and by the satisfaction of desires, which are necessary, natural, and measured. For Epicurus, you calculate the amount of pleasure gained from an action, a passion, or a habit. You weigh the consequences, you make an optimal decision, choosing between an intense excitement, for which you will have to pay later, and a renouncement that will prevent predictable anxieties. This evaluation requires a constant use of prudence (*phronesis*), the moral and intellectual ability to anticipate the consequences of your choices in the long run. Pleasure is thus compatible with virtue. It is even virtue's essential goal, since, in order to be healthy and tranquil, you need to be thoughtful, cautious, and wise in all deeds. To the same end, you also have to manage the people around you, your beloved, your friends, your fellow citizens; and in view of that, you have to act beautifully (*kalos*) and justly (*honeste*).

Justice is nothing else than what is useful (*sympheron*) to avoid reciprocal harm within a community. Natural law is the acknowledgment of what successfully serves individuals in order not to injure each other. Pleasure is not ecstatic and excessive, and therefore it is not destructive. It is, on the contrary, beneficial and peaceful, thus it is vital. It is not shortsighted and self-centered; it is clairvoyant and inevitably generous. The Epicurean shift in the ethics of pleasure, intended as a person's best interest, is innovative. It is the original source of utilitarianism and of the transformation of the passions into reasonable calculations, a critical turn in the emergence of modernity.

During antiquity, Epicurus's thought was little known in Greece, yet became influential in Italy, where its simplicity fascinated the Roman elite. Philosophically, it was constantly under attack. Its novelty—its candid acknowledgment that human beings are equipped for honest pleasure and entitled to it—appeared always suspicious. Cicero was particularly contemptuous of it, precisely because of the conflation of *honestas* and *voluptas* (pleasure). The Epicureans couple the two, he claims, something which is to be deplored since the latter obscures—not to say pollutes—the full splendor of the former. The dialogue *De finibus bonorum et malorum* revolves around the disaster of such a disfiguration. Cicero argues that virtue and pleasure must be distinct and opposed to each other. When it comes to morality, the skeptical Cicero speaks a language with Stoic accents and sets the stage of a paradigmatic controversy about hedonism, which will constantly reemerge in modern philosophy.

On one side of this debate stand the Stoics, with their theory of virtue as the exercise of reason, the eradication of passions, and a complete detachment from any contingency. Following the principle of Platonic ethics, the Stoics fight against any form of instrumentality to which the good might be made subservient. To say that virtues are conducive to pleasure, and that pleasure should be their end, would be to degrade them to the level of means; this would be contradictory to the idea of *honestum,* as that which should be attained for its intrinsic, absolute value. On the other side are the Epicureans, for whom the good life results from a constant assessment of profits and losses, contingent to what can be expected, from the environment and in the foreseeable future. Virtue is connected to pleasure for an ethical and psychological reason. Evil is not simply done: it is not conducive to pleasure because evil is also felt by the one doing evil. Mistakes cause emotional disturbance. Vices are sources of endless worries, fears, and anxiety, whereas pleasure consists, above all, in a sensation of relief, from any kind of unsettling feelings. It is for the sake of tranquility and in one's best interest to avoid wickedness, envy, lust, violence, and all other flawed behaviors for the life of those who cultivate these passions is nothing but distress (*intercapedo molestiae*). By contrast, the *honestum* and the *iustum* (justice) set the mind to rest and results in ataraxy, a peaceful, as well as a virtuous, experience. It follows from a rational choice not to be anguished, but that means, of course, that the value of all the virtues depends upon their utility to that end. "Pleasure" is the name of their instrumentality.

In the fifteenth century, Lorenzo Valla and other humanists revived this debate about the possibility of a *honesta voluptas* and of a voluptuous excellence. The most important statement about the value of Epicurus's wisdom, however, is to be found in Erasmus' *Colloquium familiare,* entitled *Epicureus* (1533). This dialogue in defense of *vera voluptas* (pleasure in truth) offers a fervid celebration of the Garden, certainly inspired by Lorenzo Valla. Following a traditional line of argument that reverts to Torquatus, the Epicurean character in Cicero's *De finibus bonorum ac malorum,* a Mister Pleasure, Hedonius, takes up the defense of what can be an authentic and fine form of hedonism, against an incredulous Spudaeus (Earnest). There is no virtue without pleasure, Hedonius claims, and no true pleasure without virtue. This morality is compatible with Christian theology, because the calculation of pleasure is the perfect means to reach the end of afterlife bliss.

Even more, a virtuous existence is already exquisitely agreeable. Epicurus "puts the happiness of man in pleasure" and considers that a life is the happiest if it contains the maximum

of pleasure and the minimum possible of sadness. "What could be said, that would be more saintly [*sanctius*] than this sentence?" asks Mister Pleasure. Indeed, nobody is more Epicurean than the Christians who lead a pious life (*Christiani pie viventes*): here are the most Epicurean people. True pleasure has nothing to do with sensuality and luxury, but with the fruition of true goods (*vera bona*), he argues. Now such enjoyment is possible only in a healthy and pious soul, because only a virtuous existence makes humanity happy, by reconciling God, the source of the highest good (*summi boni fons*) with man. The origin of that *fruitio* (fruition) and thus of *voluptas,* is God, more precisely the absolute goodness of God, the *summum bonum* that flows, so to speak, into the various forms of goodness accessible on Earth. Erasmus' praise of the Epicurean/Christian pleasure could not offer a more consistent resonance to the morality presented by Raphael Hythlodeus and the Utopians in Thomas More's *Utopia* (1515). With their insights about *voluptas,* those virtuous pagans, untouched by the Revelation, have found a kind of pre-Christian wisdom.

The defense of honest pleasure, against the recurrent misunderstandings of Epicurean ethics, continues along the same lines and with the same anti-Stoic arguments through the works of Pierre Gassendi to culminate in the "apology of Volupté," to be found in the *Encyclopédie* by Denis Didérot (1713–1784) and Jean Le Rond d'Alembert (1717–1783). After the eighteenth century, it is in the language of utilitarianism, therefore in terms of maximized advantage or best interest, that this ethic continued to flourish. In the early twenty-first century hedonism lost all philosophical dignity, to become a lifestyle, good only for literature and advertising.

*See also* **Altruism; Epicureanism; Happiness and Pleasure in European Thought; Utilitarianism.**

**BIBLIOGRAPHY**

Gosling, J. C. B. *Pleasure and Desire: The Case for Hedonism Reviewed.* Oxford: Clarendon, 1969.

Mitsis, Phillip. *Epicurus' Ethical Theory: The Pleasures of Invulnerability.* Ithaca, N.Y.: Cornell University Press, 1988.

Rosenbaum, Stephen E. "Epicurus on Pleasure and the Complete Life." *The Monist* 73 (1990): 21–41.

Rudebusch, George. *Socrates, Pleasure, and Value.* New York: Oxford University Press, 1999.

Vaughan, Frederick. *The Tradition of Political Hedonism: From Hobbes to J. S. Mill.* New York: Fordham University Press, 1982.

*Giulia Sissa*

**HEGELIANISM.** Given the complexity of his thought, it is not surprising that Hegel's philosophy has been interpreted in a number of different and often opposed ways. As such, while many philosophical movements might be described as "Hegelian," there is no univocal sense of this term, nor any unanimity about what the proper interpretation of Hegel's idealism involves. Perhaps because of these interpretive difficulties, the appeal of Hegelianism in its various guises has waxed and waned in the two centuries following Hegel's own work.

At first glance, Hegel's philosophy presents a seemingly thoroughgoing idealism, in which the world is explained as a manifestation or determination of Absolute Spirit. The *Logic,* for example, begins with an exploration of Being and dialectically derives from it the particularity of the world. But while there is some truth to viewing Hegel's idealism in such metaphysical terms, the system he develops is far more complicated and subtle than the initial appearance might suggest. Rather, Hegel is concerned to answer a question that had been posed by Kant: How can people find certainty in their knowledge of the world? Another central feature of Hegel's position involves the claim that rationality cannot be understood apart from history: thought matures in a dialectical process that, for Hegel, reveals the development of reason's own capacities in various social and historical epochs. This emphasis on the historical nature of reason stands as a hallmark of much of what can be called "Hegelianism."

Although the bulk of Hegel's philosophical work was done in the early part of the 1800s, its influence was not forcibly felt in Germany until 1818, when he was appointed to a position in Berlin. His lectures there—on topics ranging from history to aesthetics—attracted an enormous amount of attention, especially among students interested in social and political reform. Hegel himself was not especially active politically, but even before his death in 1831, a heated debate broke out between his more conservative interpreters—the "Old Guard"—and the more socially oriented and reform-minded "Young Hegelians." At issue was whether Hegel's famous assertion that "the actual is the rational" expressed a factual claim about contemporary Prussia as the culmination of the dialectic of Spirit, or whether it stood as a call to arms to lead society to greater heights. Where the Old, or Right, Hegelians focused mostly on the religious aspects of the Absolute in the service of justifying a conservative Prussian state, the Young, or Left, Hegelians were far more inspired by what they saw as the radical implications of Hegel's political thought. For the Left Hegelians, notably Ludwig Feuerbach and Bruno Bauer, the *Philosophy of Right* provides a blueprint for the reform of European politics, with an emphasis on free markets and participatory democracy. The Left Hegelians also embraced a humanist project: Feuerbach, Bauer, and Strauss, for example, all offered historicist accounts of Christianity, and attempted to show that religion must be understood as a social rather than a divine phenomenon. The force of the Left Hegelian movement, however, was thwarted in 1841 by the appointment of the aging Friedrich Schelling to Hegel's former chair in Berlin in an attempt to quash the threat of reformist Hegelianism.

By the end of the 1850s, Hegel's influence had begun to fade, and indeed the neo-Kantian movement—guided by the motto "Back to Kant!"—arose largely in response to a perceived lassitude in Hegelianism. For these thinkers, philosophy required a recovery from what became known as "Hegelian bankruptcy," which was induced by an overemphasis on the metaphysical trappings of Hegel's system.

## Marxist Hegelianism
Despite Hegel's waning influence in the middle of the nineteenth century, the Left Hegelian movement did produce one lasting effect in Marxism. Like the other Left Hegelians, Marx's reception of Hegel was not free of substantial criticism. The most overt aspect of Hegel's influence on Marx is the so-called "dialectical method" by which theoretical and social entities are said to inherently generate their opposites. Marx and his followers make frequent use of this method, though in many cases it assumes the coarse and popular triad of "thesis-antithesis-synthesis," which was never used by Hegel himself. Marx's main criticism of Hegel is directed at the latter's idealism, which Marx aimed to replace by his own "dialectical materialism." Hegel's social and historical philosophies also exercised considerable influence over Marx. This may seem odd at first sight since Hegel was *the* bourgeois philosopher par excellence. Yet Hegel's intellectual integrity compelled him to uncover the unavoidable abuse of the poor in the ideal society and state he envisaged in his *Philosophy of Right,* and this latent social criticism was adopted and radically intensified by Marx. Marx and Hegel also share the view of humanity as product of society and history as well as the view of human history as a series of dialectical developments whose final end is the realization of freedom. Marx, however, rejects the quietist implications of Hegel's philosophy of history, according to which one cannot comprehend a period and act in it simultaneously since, according to Hegel, philosophical understanding of a period comes only once this period has already passed.

In spite of the sharp decline of Hegelianism at the second half of the nineteenth century, Marx considered himself a pupil of Hegel till his very last days. The importance of Hegel for the understanding of Marx was a matter of dispute among Marx's followers. While Lenin argued that Marx cannot be understood without the background of Hegel's *Logic,* the more common Marxist attitude seems content with mere lip service to Hegel's dialectical method. In 1923, following the discovery of Marx's early manuscripts, two important works by George Lukács and Karl Korsch attempted to reassert the importance of Hegel for Marxist philosophy, but this approach was strongly rejected by the official international communist movement (Third International), while nonorthodox Marxists of the Frankfurt School (most notably Theodor Adorno and Max Horkheimer) related to it more sympathetically. French structuralist Marxism tended to be hostile to the association of Marxism with Hegel's thought.

## Hegel in France
From its very inception, existentialism has been in an intense dialogue with Hegel's heritage. Kierkegaard, for example, considered his own thought as a rebellion against the effacement of individuality in Hegel's grand system. Twentieth-century French existentialism was much more sympathetic to Hegel. The crucial event in the development of twentieth-century French reception of Hegel was a series of lectures on Hegel's *Phenomenology* given by the Russian émigré, Alexandre Kojève, at the École Pratique des Hautes Études between 1933 and 1939 (the lectures were edited and published in 1947). Among the participants in these seminars were Maurice Merleau-Ponty, Simone de Beauvoir, Jean-Paul Sartre, Georges Bataille, Alexandre Koyré, Emmanuel Levinas, Eric Weil, and Jacques Lacan. Through this extraordinary group of intellectuals Kojève's reading of Hegel became extremely influential.

For Kojève, the key text for understanding the *Phenomenology* was the famous dialectic of master and slave. Kojève's reading, which is significantly indebted to both Marx and Heidegger, centers upon the human struggle for recognition by the other and the emergence of human culture [*Bildung*] from the life and consciousness of the slave. Another influential interpretation of Hegel was suggested by Jean Hyppolite, who attempted to reconcile the humanistic spirit of the *Phenomenology* with the rigorous and individual-effacing *Logic*.

Postmodern French philosophy engaged with Hegel and his grand logical and historical narratives as part of the main stream of Western metaphysics, whose undermining was one of the main aims of deconstructionist thought. In contemporary French thought, Jean-Luc Nancy seems to present the most interesting attempt to revive the philosophical dialogue with Hegel.

## Hegel and Anglo-American Philosophy

During the second half of the nineteenth century, Hegel's ideas began exercising considerable influence on several British and American philosophers, notably Edward Caird, F. H. Bradley, Bernard Bosanquet, and John McTaggart. For them, Hegel provided the vantage point from which they could criticize the empiricism and metaphysical atomism of the utilitarians. Both Russell and Moore also began in this tradition, and their break from—and response to—it in the early 1900s marks the beginning of Anglophone "analytic" philosophy.

Despite continued interest in Hegel's thought, the main stream of Anglo-American philosophy in the twentieth century tended to be hostile to Hegel because of his opaque style of writing and his alleged willingness to compromise the absoluteness of the law of noncontradiction. Popper's view of Hegel as one of the sources of modern totalitarianism and nationalism was also very influential in the Anglo-American world (though it is now known that unlike Kant, Hegel was despised by the Nazis).

In the last two decades of the twentieth century, the animosity toward Hegel among "analytic" philosophers abated. Works by Charles Taylor, H. S. Harris, Terry Pinkard, and Robert Pippin, among others, have helped to revive interest in Hegel's thought, and many of these efforts have attempted to present a "critical" rather than metaphysical interpretation of Hegel. Pippin, for example, develops an account of Hegel's idealism that stresses its indebtedness to Kant while noting the ways in which Hegel's emphasis on history and society advance Kant's critical project. Also, in recent works both John McDowell and Robert Brandom have begun the process of what McDowell calls the "domestication" of Hegel's idealism in the service of developing an alternative to naturalist accounts of cognition and intentionality.

*See also* **Continental Philosophy; Existentialism; Phenomenology; Philosophy.**

### BIBLIOGRAPHY

Beiser, Frederick C., ed. *The Cambridge Companion to Hegel.* Cambridge, U.K.: Cambridge University Press, 1993. Includes a detailed and categorized bibliography.

Hegel, G. W. F. *Elements of the Philosophy of Right.* Edited by Allen W. Wood and translated by H. B. Nisbet. Cambridge, U.K.: Cambridge University Press, 1991.

——. *The Encyclopedia Logic, with the Zusätze: Part I of the Encyclopaedia of Philosophical Sciences with the Zusätze.* Translated by T. F. Geraets, W. A. Suchting, and H. S. Harris. Indianapolis: Hackett, 1991.

——. *Gesammelte Werke—Kritische Ausgabe.* Deutsche Forschungsgemeinschaft im Verbindung mit Rheinische-westfälischen Akademie der Wissenschaften. Hamburg, Germany: Felix Meiner Verlag, 1968– . The critical edition of Hegel's works. New volumes are published every few years.

——. *Phenomenology of Spirit.* Translated by A. V. Miller. Oxford: Clarendon 1977.

Hyppolite, Jean. *Genesis and Structure of Hegel's* Phenomenology of Spirit. Translated by Samuel Cherniak and John Heckman. Evanston, Ill.: Northwestern University Press, 1974.

Kojève, Alexandre. *Introduction to the Reading of Hegel: Lectures on the* Phenomenology of Spirit. Assembled by Raymond Queneau, edited by Allan Bloom, and translated by James H. Nichols, Jr. Ithaca, N.Y.: Cornell University Press, 1969. An abridged translation of the French text.

Nancy, Jean-Luc. *Hegel: The Restlessness of the Negative.* Translated by Jason Smith and Steven Miller. Minneapolis: University of Minnesota Press, 2002.

Pippin, Robert. *Hegel's Idealism: The Satisfactions of Self-Consciousness.* Cambridge, U.K.: Cambridge University Press, 1989.

*Yitzhak Y. Melamed*
*Peter Thielke*

**HEGEMONY.** Hegemony, from the Greek *hegemón* (guide, ruler, leader) and *hegemonia* (rule, leadership), denotes the preeminent influence a state, social class, group, or individual exercises over others. Today it is especially associated with the Italian Marxist and revolutionary Antonio Gramsci (1891–1937), for whom it is the core and organizing concept of his social and political ideas. More recently hegemony has gained wide currency in social and political thought, international politics, as well as in cultural and literary studies.

In ancient Greek usage, one meaning of a *hegemón* is leader of a consensual alliance of the military forces of different *poleis.* Another, and more important, sense of *hegemón* refers to a *polis* at the head of an alliance consisting of a number of *poleis* that come together freely in order to address a common military threat. Here hegemony is a system of alliances in which a state exercises power and leadership over mutually consenting states. Herodotus (484–c. 420 B.C.E.) in his *Histories* describes the war of the Greeks against the Persians in terms of such an alliance. Thucydides (460/455–c. 401 B.C.E.), in his *History of the Peloponnesian War,* often uses the term in both senses of a military and political alliance. He notes that the Delian League, originally a voluntary alliance of states under the leadership of Athens established to confront the Persian threat against the common interests of the members, gradually turned into an Athenian Empire in which allies became subjects serving only Athenian self-interest. Thucydides cites this transformation as the primary reason for the Peloponnesian War.

In effect, in ancient Greece an alliance in which a hegemonic state assumes predominant military and political leadership is characterized by four fundamental structural elements. The first is a duality in structure: the *hegemón* on one side and its allies on the other. The second factor is the lack of a common citizenship. Individuals were citizens only of their own *polis*. And the third characteristic was that membership in the alliance was fluid—that is, different *poleis* entered or left it according to the strategic and political dynamics of the international environment. A fourth element, historically but not necessarily conceptually linked to the other three, is the tendency of a hegemonic alliance to transform itself into the imperial rule of the leading state.

Aristotle (384–322 B.C.E.) and Isocrates (436–338 B.C.E.) also employ hegemony to distinguish imperial from hegemonic rule. In the *Politics,* Aristotle distinguishes two types of rule, despotic and political (or constitutional). The first describes government over unequals in the interest of the ruler, and the second is rule among equals in the interest of the ruled. He uses the term *hegemony* when talking about the leadership of equals in the interest of all, and *despotism* when discussing the domination of others in the ruler's self-interest. It is to be noted that Aristotle's use of hegemony is closely related to his classification of governments in which legitimate and illegitimate types are differentiated according to whether they are law-abiding and pursue the common good.

Isocrates, in such works as *The Panegyricus* and *On the Peace,* laments the transformation of the Delian League into the Athenian Empire, attributing Athens's fall to its despotic rule over Greeks. He establishes a distinction not unlike Aristotle's: hegemony is leadership exercised over free and consenting allies, and despotism is the exercise of domination or force. Isocrates links the exercise of hegemony with the dissemination of moral/intellectual as well as cultural and aesthetic ideas. Athens is the natural hegemonic leader because she is the school of Hellas, the teacher and guide of Hellenes and, through them, the world.

Athens as the cultural and moral center of Greece (also proclaimed by Pericles in his Funeral Oration) points to another important meaning of hegemony: namely, as the ruling or guiding principle or idea. Thus Isocrates, following the rhetorician Gorgias (c. 485–c. 380 B.C.E.), proclaimed the supremacy of reason and discourse. Thus too rhetoric and public speech were deemed central to political and social life, and opposing discourses and narratives competed for recognition and preeminence. Moreover, Greek political thought generally struggled with the relation between power and knowledge. Without knowledge, power is reduced to mindless violence and coercion, purposeless and unpredictable. And without power, knowledge is ineffectual. Greek thinkers tried to reconcile or synthesize power and knowledge in order to construct a stable and just political order. Hegemony as a ruling principle expresses this ambition to empower knowledge and to educate power.

Macedon and Rome put an end to these political and conceptual distinctions. The rise of Stoicism and Epicureanism, the triumph of Christianity, combined with the Germanic invasions, inaugurated a new civilization wherein the classical emphasis on political and public action, with its concomitant distinctions between free rule and despotism, hegemony and empire, ceased to have meaning. The rise of the Italian city-states, the coming of the Reformation, and the rise of English and Dutch republican radicalism, as well as the social, economic, and cultural/intellectual changes that paralleled these events, once again placed at center stage political and conceptual issues dealing with liberty and domination, constitutional and despotic government, state independence and imperialism.

Hegemony, however, both as a term and a concept, did not regain currency until the nineteenth century. Since then, with important exceptions and under the rubric of hegemonism, it was generally applied to the international sphere in which a state exercises overwhelming power over others and thus comes to dominate them.

In Europe during the latter half of the nineteenth century, the rise of working-class and peasant parties and movements, combined with socialist, anarchist, and Marxist critiques of liberalism and capitalism, challenged the existing sociopolitical order and questioned the legitimacy of its moral/intellectual claims to liberty and equality. In Germany, controversies within the working-class movement and its Social Democratic Party centered around the mechanics of capitalism and appropriate strategies (reform or revolution) for its overthrow. In Russia the term *hegemony* was made current by socialists such as George V. Plekhanov (1855?–1918), Paul B. Akselrod (1850–1928), Leon Trotsky (1879–1940), and Vladimir I. Lenin (1870–1924), and it referred to the leading role of the working class in a system of alliances directed against the prevailing order. During the first decade of the twentieth century, Lenin and the Bolsheviks, in their competition with Mensheviks and socialist revolutionaries for the favor of workers and peasants, devised a revolutionary strategy in which the proletariat would assume a hegemonic role and lead the peasantry and oppressed national minorities to the overthrow of tsarism and the institution of a socialist sociopolitical order. Here hegemony is seen as an alliance of social forces in which the working class plays a preeminent role. The Bolshevik seizure of power in 1917, the dissolution of the Constituent Assembly in 1918, and the consequent imposition of party dictatorship revealed the authoritarian character of Soviet communism, which exposed the rhetoric of hegemony and democratic alliances as mere instrumental formulas masking domination and terror.

It is with Antonio Gramsci, especially in his prison writings collected in the *Prison Notebooks* (1929–1935), that hegemony acquired conceptual coherence and theoretical significance. In his thought, hegemony became more than a synonym for preeminent power or a term used ad hoc to refer to asymmetrical power relations. Like Lenin, he criticized the economic determinism of Marxist thought and emphasized the use of reason and will to change economic, social, and political structures. Unlike Lenin, he developed a more nuanced and more articulated theory of state and society. His notion of hegemony regarded state and society and their interrelationships as based on the formulation and dissemination of cultural, ideological, and moral/intellectual systems of value and belief. Thus the state is not pure force and violence, nor is it merely the dictatorship of one class over another. Returning to Hegel's notion of history and politics as the products of humanity's reflexive activity in the world, Gramsci understood hegemony as the historical unfolding and its articulation within concrete societies of a conscious and disciplined human subjectivity.

Both Lenin and Gramsci identified the formation of a conscious historical subject as the fundamental problem of revolutionary Marxism: though the economic and structural conditions were present, the working class, the actor assigned to carry out the revolution, was culturally and politically ill prepared to organize it and construct a new order. In Russia, Lenin and the Bolshevik Party gave history a push and manufactured the revolution in the name of the workers and peasants, a strategy that failed in more advanced countries. Attempting to understand this failure, especially the victory of fascism in Italy, Gramsci focused on the differences between the West and Russia regarding the nature, structure, and purpose of state and society. Gramsci contrasts the sociopolitical order confronting Lenin's Bolsheviks in Russia and that faced by the communists in the West. The differences in social and political structures between the East and the West require different methods and strategy in order to overcome liberal capitalism. Gramsci notes that in Russia the "State was everything" and civil society "primordial" and weak, while in the West civil society was strong and resilient, such that there was a "proper relation" between state and civil society.

Gramsci radically changes both the Marxist conceptions of state and society and their interrelationship. Civil society is the sphere of liberty, where consent and persuasion are generated. Yet it is also the sphere of cultural, ideological, religious, and economic conflict, where this conflict is defined by the contest of voluntary and secondary associations such as trade unions, political parties, sects and churches, schools and universities, civic organizations, and interest groups of various kinds. Civil society in the West has developed massive and complex structures of social and political institutions that together legitimate and render stable the prevailing order. The interwoven and multiple layers of complex associations of modern democracy render revolution impossible in the West. Gramsci opposes civil society to political society and hegemony to dictatorship. The latter means the juridical, administrative, and military apparatus of government and represents force and coercion. It is also the classical liberal understanding of the state, what nineteenth-century Europeans called the "nightwatchman" state. The two spheres, while analytically distinct, mutually penetrate and reinforce each other. In fact, one presupposes the other. Hence Gramsci sees what he calls the "integral state" as "civil society plus political society." Hence too, in Gramsci (as in Hobbes and Locke), one cannot have a viable civil society without a viable government.

Hegemony is intimately linked to civil society. The strength and viability of civil society (i.e., the degree of complexity and articulation of social, economic, and cultural groups) is directly related to the degree of hegemonic power. Within both state and society, hegemony is seen as the generation and organization of consent—namely, the formation of a "conception of the world" and its dissemination throughout the people. Such a conception (an "ideology" or a system of beliefs) is always opposed to different conceptions of the world. These are constantly in conflict, in a "battle" against each other, and the hegemonic conception is one that has been transformed into the generalized habits and customs of the people. A counterconception, or a counterhegemony, is constantly generated, even if only embryonically, to challenge the prevailing one. Intellectuals generate and disseminate these values and ideas, yet the latter cannot become politically and historically significant without their proliferation throughout the people. Hence, in modern society, especially democracies, the battle over opposing values and competing *Weltanschauungen* underlines the crucial role played by the people, especially in the form of public opinion.

What Gramsci looks at is the ways in which minority elite opinion (of intellectuals and opinion makers generally) is transformed into the people's or the majority's opinion and, in turn, the ways in which the two kinds of opinion interact and mutually affect one another. These concerns are reflected in his analyses of popular culture and its relation to high culture, in his discussion of the role played in modern society by newspapers, journals, and mass media generally, and in his inquiry into the historical and social bases of myth, folklore, and religion. The focus on popular culture and its relation to elite culture reflects Gramsci's original radical project: to discover within capitalist society a subordinate group (called "subaltern" by Gramsci) potentially able to become hegemonic. The purpose, character, and direction of Gramsci's hegemony is to understand why power structures are stable and persist over time and simultaneously to uncover within this structure subaltern groups, cultures, and ideas capable of hegemonic development.

Thus the hegemonic and the subaltern are intimately related, such that each is defined by the other. A group is hegemonic to the extent that it formulates a coherent system of knowledge and an articulated conception of the world that, once disseminated throughout the population, have become the way of life and the way of thinking of the entire society. Similarly, a group is subaltern to the extent that its ways of thinking and its consciousness are "disaggregated," fragmented and "discontinuous," such that it is incapable of autonomous action. It is in the opposition between the hegemonic and the subaltern that a sociopolitical and sociocultural space opens up for the autonomous development of the latter. Hegemony was developed by Gramsci to identify within the preexisting order groups capable of opposition, both cultural and political, and capable of presenting an alternative to the structure of power and to its system of beliefs. The movement from the subaltern to the hegemonic is the movement from fragmentation to political and cultural coherence, and is what describes the formation of a group capable of self-government and thus capable of rule. In this sense, every hegemony generates a counterhegemony, in which opposing conceptions of the world, and opposing systems of knowledge, confront each other in a struggle to construct and to transform reality.

Gramsci's emphasis on culture, its generation, proliferation, and transmission, led him to inquire into the reciprocal ways that language and power influence each other. Language formation and use construct ways of looking at the natural and social world. Language not merely expresses or reflects reality, but, more important, organizes and structures the world. There is a reciprocal relation between a hegemonic ruling group and the language it uses to define itself and to establish its supremacy. A subordinate group aspiring to preeminence must devise a language capable of understanding and capturing the reality it seeks to master. Languages, therefore, are either hegemonic or subaltern, and if the latter, potentially hegemonic.

In effect, hegemony is a complex and highly articulated concept and operates at various levels. First, in the manner of the ancient Greeks, it is a free and consensual alliance of groups that share similar interests and perhaps similar values, under the leadership of that group that manages to represent and pursue the interests and aims of the associated groups. Gramsci expresses this relationship in the polarity domination/leadership: leadership is exercised over allied groups, and domination ("even with armed force") over antagonistic groups. Second, hegemony may refer to the formation of an equilibrium between force and consent, such that force does not prevail "too much" over consent. Third, hegemonic power is power generated by values and beliefs, by moral/intellectual ideas through which the world is organized and perceived and through which the world acquires meaning. In this case hegemonic takes the sense of ruling principle or organizing idea. It explains the strength and resilience of the existing liberal capitalist system and the ability of its ruling groups to attain and maintain the allegiance of subordinate groups. Fourth, hegemony refers to a group equal to or capable of rule and self-rule—and capable of extending its view of the world throughout society. It describes the process by which a subordinate group acquires the ideological, institutional, and political means to formulate its own hegemonic conception of the world and oppose it to that espoused by the existing ruling group.

Hegemony, originally developed by Gramsci to unpack the complex of economic, political, and cultural sources of power in order to discover within the existing system the germs for revolutionary transformation, has been appropriated, either selectively or more rigorously, by a diverse number of intellectual discourses and academic disciplines. In international politics and political science, it is used variously either to describe an imperial system of domination, a voluntary alliance under a leading state, or simply to refer to the noncoercive, nonmilitary elements of power. In anthropology, it refers to the power and structural characteristics that underlie culture in its broadest sense. In sociolinguistics, the interaction between sociopolitical power and the emergence and development of languages (natural and specialized, local and dialectal) is stressed. In literary and cultural studies, popular forms of narratives and art as well as folk traditions and beliefs are analyzed. The polarity between the hegemonic and the subaltern has become central to fields of inquiry ranging from colonial and neocolonial studies to philosophy of language, to the study of rhetoric, and to the philosophy and sociology of education.

Such a polarity uncovers the power and class relationships that underlie fields of knowledge and the cognitive and methodological constructions developed to understand and to capture the material and the sociocultural reality. Since the

hegemonic and the subaltern presuppose each other, understanding of a given reality means inquiring into the ways in which a dominant hegemony interacts with a subordinate culture, as well as the manner in which elite and mass mutually penetrate, oppose, or reinforce each other. Since the relation between hegemony and subalternity is fluid and changing, and since the subaltern is potentially hegemonic, contemporary uses of hegemony in various fields and disciplines articulate, and reflect, a political contest among competing interpretations and opposing values. Precisely because hegemony was developed as methodological concept to investigate established sociopolitical reality, it is also a political and social tool useful in the "battle" to generate differing views of the world and competing models of knowledge.

*See also* **Civil Society; International Order; Leadership.**

### BIBLIOGRAPHY

Adamson, Walter L. *Hegemony and Revolution: A Study of Antonio Gramsci's Political and Cultural Theory.* Berkeley: University of California Press, 1980.

Anderson, Perry. "The Antinomies of Antonio Gramsci." *New Left Review* 100 (1976): 7–78.

Buttigieg, Joseph A. "Introduction." In Antonio Gramsci, *Prison Notebooks,* vol. 1, edited by Joseph A. Buttigieg, and translated by Joseph A. Buttigieg and Antonio Callari. New York: Columbia University Press, 1993, pp. 1–64.

———. "Philology and Politics: Returning to the Text of Antonio Gramsci." *Boundary* 2, no. 21 (1994): 98–138.

Davidson, Alastair. *Antonio Gramsci: Towards an Intellectual Biography.* London: Merlin Press, 1977.

Ehrenberg, Victor. *The Greek State.* New York: W. W. Norton, 1960.

Finocchiaro, Maurice A. *Gramsci and the History of Dialectical Thought.* Cambridge, U.K.: Cambridge University Press, 1988.

Fontana, Benedetto. "*Logos* and *Kratos:* Gramsci and the Ancients on Hegemony." *Journal of the History of Ideas* 61 (2000): 305–326.

Gill, Stephen, ed. *Gramsci, Historical Materialism and International Relations.* Cambridge, U.K.: Cambridge University Press, 1993.

Gramsci, Antonio. *Further Selections from the Prison Notebooks.* Translated and edited by Derek Boothman. Minneapolis: University of Minnesota Press, 1995.

———. *Selections from Cultural Writings.* Edited by David Forgacs and Geoffrey Nowell-Smith and translated by William Boelhower. Cambridge, Mass.: Harvard University Press, 1985.

———. *Selections from the Prison Notebooks of Antonio Gramsci.* Edited and translated by Quintin Hoare and Geoffrey Nowell-Smith. New York: International Publishers, 1971.

James, Martin, ed. *Antonio Gramsci: Critical Assessments of Political Philosophers.* 4 vols. London: Routledge, 2001.

Sassoon, Anne Showstack. *Gramsci and Contemporary Politics: Beyond Pessimism of the Intellect.* London and New York: Routledge, 2000.

Sinclair, T. A. *A History of Greek Political Thought.* Cleveland, Ohio: World, 1968.

Wolf, Eric. *Envisioning Power: Ideologies of Dominance and Crisis.* Berkeley: University of California Press, 1999.

*Benedetto Fontana*

**HELL.** *See* **Heaven and Hell.**

**HERESY AND APOSTASY.** *Heresy* is derived from a Greek word literally meaning "a choice." St. Irenaeus (c. 120 to 140–c. 200 to 203) defined heresy as deviation from the standard of sound doctrine. This definition provided a model for subsequent conceptions of heresy. Referring to the Greek word, St. Jerome (c. 347–419 or 420) wrote that each one chooses the rule that one judges to be the best. So, he continued, "anyone who understands Scripture in a way other than the Holy Spirit, which dictated how Scripture should be written, demands would be called heretic, even if he is not excluded from the Church, and derives from the work of the flesh because he chooses the worst." The voluntary choice of a carnal meaning leads a reader of Scripture to shape a doctrine that contradicts the teaching of the church, thereby falling into heresy. Heresy, then, was a departure from the unity of the faith, while believing to subscribe to the Christian faith. The reverse side of it is the church's assertion of doctrinal authority. Heresy, denial or doubt of any defined doctrine, is sharply distinguished from apostasy, which denotes deliberate abandonment of the Christian faith itself. Hence, in a Christian context, heretics do not include the people of other faiths like the Jews and the Muslims, although they were not immune from religious persecution along with Christian heretics. The distinction between schism and heresy, on the other hand, is not as clear, since both concepts denote the separation from unity; indeed, the schism between the Western and Eastern Churches generated the accusation by both churches of the other being heretical rather than schismatic.

### Early Christianity

The earliest form of Christian heresy originates in Jewish sectarianism. The teachings of the Gnostic master Simon of Samaria, which combined Jewish teaching with some Christian doctrines, appear in the early catalogue of heretics, and Eusebius of Caesarea (c. 260–c. 339) recorded him as the prime author of every kind of heresy. Perhaps the most prominent of heresies is Arianism, which claimed that Christ was mere creation, thereby rejecting the eternity of the Son of God. The Arian view, despite official condemnation by Alexander, patriarch of Alexandria (St. Alexander; c. 250–328), continued to spread until the emperor Constantine's (ruled 306–337) call for unity at the Council of Nicaea (325). Among other early Christian heresies were Manichaeism and Donatism. Manichaeism was a Gnostic dualistic doctrine influenced by St. Paul's teaching, whilst Donatism was a schismatic group in the African church dissenting from the appointment of Caecillian as bishop of Carthage. Faced by the Donatist controversy, St. Augustine of Hippo (354–430), a Manichaean before his spiritual conversion, was a powerful proponent of the use of state punishment for the leaders of heresy. For Augustine, it is not only right for the public authority to use compulsive measures to punish wrongdoers, since in so doing they are acting on behalf of God. It is also an act of charity that is intended to correct and reform those who are punished.

In the twelfth century, speculative theologians like Peter Abelard and St. Bernard of Clairvaux viewed heretics as the

**Engraving showing Protestants being burned at the stake by Roman Catholics (1546).** During the rule of Pope Innocent III (1198–1216), the practice of accusing people of heresy began to be replaced with inquisitions. The typical sentence for those found guilty was excommunication. A later inquisition in Spain, however, led to the execution of thousands of suspected heretics. © BETTMANN/CORBIS

product of pride and the aspiration for fame. But heresy was not only the concern of doctrinal theology but also of canon law. Once Gratian of Bologna produced the *Decretum* (c. 1140), the juristic concept of heresy was established: the essential feature of heresy was considered pertinacity or obstinacy. Heresy was reduced to repeated refusals to submit to doctrinal correction by ecclesiastical authority. Heresy, therefore, required the church's authority to declare it; typically, it was maintained that the authority to declare heresy rested with the pope. This juristic idea of heresy pervaded the practice of inquisition and censure, which was triggered by the rise of popular heretical movements such as Cathars and Waldensians. The Cathars are a loosely identified group of heretics who embraced dualism: a belief that there are two powers in the universe, good and omnipotent God and its opponent Devil. Catharism, which increased its influence rapidly in Western Europe in the twelfth century, did not constitute a theologically coherent unity. The Albigensians, a rigorous branch of the Cathars who were mainly based in Southern France, were condemned by successive councils including the Fourth Lateran Council (1215).

Faced by the rapid and widespread proliferation of popular heresy, Pope Innocent III (ruled 1198–1216) recognized the urgent need for the efficient prosecution of heretics; therefore, he replaced the hitherto widely practiced accusatorial procedure with inquisitorial practice, thereby curtailing the presumption of innocence. This "persecuting" culture penetrated the academic community from the late thirteenth century onward; the bishop of Paris, Stephen Tempier's condemnation of 219 propositions (1277) restricted academic freedom and opened the way to the condemnation of the idiosyncratic teachings of thinkers like Peter John Olivi, Jean de Pouilly, and Thomas Waleys. Peter Olivi's teaching of *usus pauper*—the rigorous practice of poverty that rejects ownership and restricts use of the goods—attracted a number of followers constituting the Spiritual Franciscans, a significant heretical group of the "non-conformist" friars.

Heresy, however, was not a problem that could be observed among theologians and lay believers alone. Heretical ecclesiastics, including the pope, were an ecclesiological dilemma that troubled theologians and canonists alike, and the classical solution to this problem was that a heretical pope would be ipso facto deposed. However, this argument is, in practical terms, insignificant because no one is supposed to be superior to the pope in the ecclesiastical order. In his involvement with the dispute between the Avignon papacy and the Friars Minor, the Franciscan William of Ockham (c. 1285–c. 1347) propounded an extensive discourse on heresy with special reference to papal heresy. In it he redefined heresy as deliberate rejection of the truth of Christian doctrine manifested in the Bible and other doctrinal sources. Thus, Ockham reduced heresy to an interpretative category of theological enquiry into doctrinal texts, thereby rejecting the juristic idea of heresy as repeated disobedience to ecclesiastical authority. This implied that the discovery of heresy requires no ecclesiastical authority. This cognitive perspective on heresy was also evident in the polemical writings of the Italian political philosopher Marsilius of Padua (c. 1280–c. 1343), who proposed that the detection of heresy should be entrusted to the experts of Scripture rather than the holders of the ecclesiastical office.

The Oxford philosopher John Wycliffe's (c. 1330–1384) rejection of the scriptural foundations of religious life—papal authority and the mendicant orders in particular—and his attack on the doctrine of transubstantiation inspired the popular heretical movement of Lollardy. The Lollards were the loyal heir of Wycliffe's teaching of *sola scriptura*; the doctrinal appeal to the Bible alone was an antithesis to the contemporary practice of Roman Catholic Christianity. The influence of Wycliffe's teaching reached beyond England; in Bohemia, Jan Hus (1372 or 1373–1415) assimilated the Wycliffite reformative ecclesiology, which resulted in his official condemnation and execution at the Council of Constance (1414–1418)

### Non-Christian Heresy

Heresy is not an idea known to Christian civilization alone. The Islamic concept equivalent to heresy may be *bid'a*, meaning literally "deviation": the counterconcept of *sunna*, meaning the tradition established by Muhammad. Unlike heresy, *bid'a* does not always have negative denotation; departure from the tradition may be tolerated as innovation, and the extreme deviation alone may be subject to condemnation. *Zandaqa*—the idea that rejects the existence or omnipotence of God, as in Zoroastrianism and Manichaeism—exemplifies Islamic heresy. The Islamic concept equivalent to apostasy is called *irtidat* or *ridda*, which is according to the Koran subject to death penalty or life imprisonment.

Heresy seems to be an idea whose application is overwhelmingly confined to monotheistic religions. While occasional attempts have been made to regularize the teachings of Confucianism, and thus to create a division between orthodoxy

and heresy, these have not succeeded for long. The revealed word of a single god implies heterodoxy in a way that the assumptions about supernatural belief in other religions do not.

*See also* **Christianity; Ecumenism; Islam; Manichaeism; Orthodoxy; Religion; Toleration.**

**BIBLIOGRAPHY**

Jeanjean, Benoît. *Saint Jérome et l'hérésie.* Paris: Institut d'Études Augustiniennes, 1999.

Lambert, Malcolm. *Medieval Heresy: Popular Movements from the Gregorian Reform to the Reformation.* Oxford: Blackwell, 2002.

Laursen, John Christian, ed. *Histories of Heresy in Early Modern Europe: For, against, and beyond Persecution and Toleration.* New York: Palgrave, 2002.

Leff, Gordon. *Heresy in the Later Middle Ages.* 2 vols. Manchester: Manchester University Press, 1967.

Moore, R. I. *The Formation of a Persecuting Society: Power and Deviance in Western Europe, 950–1250.* Oxford: Blackwell, 1987.

Pelikan, Jaroslav. *The Christian Tradition: A History of the Development of Doctrine.* 5 vols. Chicago: University of Chicago Press, 1971–1989.

*Takashi Shogimen*

**HERMENEUTICS.** Traditionally understood as the art of interpretation (*ars hermeneutica*) that provided rules for the interpretation of sacred texts, hermeneutics today serves to characterize a broad current in contemporary continental philosophy that deals with the issues of interpretation and stresses the historical and linguistic nature of our world-experience. Since this characterization is also valid for contemporary thinking as a whole, the boundaries of hermeneutics are difficult to delineate with pinpoint accuracy. In contemporary thought it is mostly associated with the thinking of Hans-Georg Gadamer (1900–2002), who continues the hermeneutic tradition of thinkers such as Wilhelm Dilthey (1833–1911) and Martin Heidegger (1889–1976). All three authors unfolded a distinct philosophical understanding of hermeneutics (that is, interpretation theory) that drew on the more ancient tradition of hermeneutics. Since their thinking is a radicalization of and reaction to this older conception, it is with it that one must start.

### The Art of Interpretation of Sacred Texts

Originally, hermeneutics was developed as an auxiliary discipline in the fields that deal with the interpretation of canonical texts, i.e. texts that contain authoritative meaning such as sacred or judicial texts. Hermeneutic rules were especially required when one was confronted with ambiguous passages (*ambigua*) of Scripture. Some of the most influential treatises in this regard were St. Augustine of Hippo's *De doctrina Christiana* (427) and Philipp Melanchthon's *Rhetoric* (1519). Since most of these rules had to do with the nature of language, the major thinkers of the hermeneutic tradition up until the nineteenth century borrowed their guidelines from the then still very lively tradition of rhetoric, for example, the requirement that ambiguous passages should be understood within their context, a rule that later gave rise to the notion of a "hermeneutical circle" according to which the parts of a text should be comprehended out of the whole in which they stand, such as the whole of a book and its intent (*scopus*), of a literary genre, and of the work and life of an author. Supplying such rules, hermeneutics enjoyed a normative or regulatory function for the interpretation of canonical texts. A specific hermeneutics was developed for the Bible (*hermeneutica sacra*), for law (*hermeneutica juris*), and for classical texts (*hermeneutica profana*).

The German theologian Friedrich Schleiermacher (1768–1834) is a foremost example of this tradition, but also an author who points to a more philosophical understanding of hermeneutics in at least two ways. First, at the beginning of his lectures on hermeneutics, published posthumously by his pupil Friedrich Lücke (1791–1855) in 1838, he complains that there are many special hermeneutics and that hermeneutics does not yet exist as a general or universal discipline, i.e. as an art (*Kunst, Kunstlehre*) of understanding itself that would establish binding rules for all forms of interpretation. Second, Schleiermacher further laments that hermeneutics has hitherto only consisted of a vague collection of dislocated guidelines. Hermeneutical rules, he urges in *Hemeneutics and Criticism,* should become "more of a method" (*mehr Methode*). A more rigorous methodology of understanding could enable the interpreter to understand the authors as well or even better than they understood themselves.

## Hermeneutics as the Methodological Basis of the Human Sciences

Most familiar with the thinking and life of Schleiermacher, of whom he was the biographer, Dilthey devoted his lifework to the challenge of a foundation of the human sciences (*Geisteswissenschaften*). Whereas the exact sciences had already received, in the wake of Immanuel Kant's *Critique of Pure Reason,* a philosophical base and a methodology guaranteeing the validity of their knowledge, the human sciences still lacked such a foundation. Under the motto of a "critique of historical reason," Dilthey sought a logical, epistemological, and methodological foundation for the human sciences. Without such a foundation, their own scientific legitimacy could be called into question: is everything in the human sciences merely subjective, historically relative, and, as we tend to say, but with a touch of derision, a mere matter of interpretation? If these areas of our knowledge are to entertain any scientific credibility, Dilthey argued, they need to rest on a sound methodology.

In some of his later texts (most notably in his essay "The Rise of Hermeneutics," 1900), Dilthey sought such a methodical basis for the humanities in hermeneutics, the old discipline of text interpretation that could receive renewed actuality in light of this new challenge. Hermeneutics could serve as the bedrock of all human sciences and could thus be called upon to fulfill a need that arises out of the emergence of historical conscience and threatens the validity of historical knowledge. Even if it remains largely programmatic in his later texts, the idea that hermeneutics could serve as a universal foundation of the human sciences bestowed upon hermeneutics a

philosophical relevance and visibility that it never really enjoyed before Dilthey. Up to this day, important thinkers such as Emilio Betti and E. D. Hirsch look to hermeneutics to deliver a methodical foundation for the truth claim of the humanities, the literary, and the juridical disciplines. According to them, a hermeneutics that would relinquish this task would miss the point about what hermeneutics is all about.

Life articulates itself, Dilthey says, in manifold forms of expression (*Ausdruck*) that our understanding seeks to penetrate by recreating the inner life experience (*Erlebnis*) out of which they sprang. Dilthey's far-reaching intuition is that interpretation and understanding are not processes that occur simply in the human sciences but that they are constitutive of our quest for orientation. The notion that historical life is as such hermeneutical and interpretatory to the core was buttressed by Friedrich Nietzsche's contemporaneous reflections on the interpretatory nature of our world-experience. "There are no facts, only interpretations," wrote Nietzsche in Fragment 481 of *The Will to Power.* This first glimpse of the potential universality of the "hermeneutic universe" appeared to call into question Dilthey's dream of a methodical foundation of the human sciences, but it raised a new hermeneutics task.

## Heidegger's Hermeneutics of Existence

Seizing upon this idea that life is intrinsically interpretative, the early Heidegger spoke of a "hermeneutical intuition" as early as 1919. His teacher Edmund Husserl (1859–1938) had reinstated the urgency and legitimacy of primal "intuition" in philosophy. But Heidegger revealed himself a reader of Dilthey when he stressed that every intuition is hermeneutical. Understanding is not a cognitive inquiry that the human sciences would methodically refine, it is our primary means of orientation in the world. Our factual life is involved in this world ("being there": *Dasein,* as he would later put it) by ways of understanding. Relying here on the German expression *sich auf etwas verstehen,* which means "to know one's way about," "to be able," Heidegger puts a new twist on the notion of understanding by viewing it less as an intellectual undertaking than as an ability. It is more akin to a "know-how." Understanding is not primarily the reconstruction of the meaning of an expression (as in classical hermeneutics and Dilthey); it always entails the projecting, and self-projecting, of a possibility of my own existence. There is no understanding without projection or anticipations.

We are factually (*faktisch*) thrown into existence as finite beings, in a world that we will never fully master. This anxiety for one's own being is for Heidegger the source of understanding. Because we are overwhelmed by existence and confronted with our mortality, we project ourselves in ways of intelligibility and reason that help us keep things in check for a while. Every mode of understanding is related to this "being there" (*Dasein*) in this overwhelming world. A momentous shift in the focus of hermeneutics has silently taken place in the work of Heidegger from texts or a certain type of science to existence itself and its quest of understanding.

This rising program was carried over in Heidegger's main work *Being and Time* (1927), but with some slight modifications

(Grondin, 2003). While it remained obvious that human facticity is forgetful of itself and its interpretatory nature, and possibilities, the focus shifted to the question of Being as such. The primary theme of hermeneutics was less the immediate facticity of our Being in this world than the fact that the presuppositions of the understanding of Being remain hidden in a tradition that needs to be reopened (or "destroyed," as Heidegger puts it). Such a hermeneutics still aims at a self-awakening of existence, but it does so by promising to sort out the fundamental structures of our understanding of being.

These structures are temporal in nature (hence the title *Being and Time*) and have everything to do with the inauthentic or authentic carrying through of our existence. Heidegger's later philosophy, while relinquishing the notion of hermeneutics as such, nevertheless radicalized this idea by claiming that our understanding of Being is brought about by the event of an overbearing history of Being that commands all our interpretations. Postmodern readings of Heidegger (Michel Foucault, Gianni Vattimo, Richard Rorty, Jacques Derrida) drew relativistic conclusions out of this shift of hermeneutics toward the history of Being. Hence, the tendency in recent debates to amalgamate hermeneutics and postmodernism, a tendency that the hermeneutics of Gadamer seems both to encourage and to combat.

## Gadamer's Hermeneutics of the Event of Understanding

Hans-Georg Gadamer's project is strongly influenced by Heidegger, but in his masterpiece *Truth and Method* (1960) his starting point is undoubtedly provided by Dilthey's hermeneutical inquiry on the methodology of the human sciences. While taking anew the dialogue with the human sciences and the open question of their claim to truth, Gadamer calls into question Dilthey's premise according to which the experience of truth in the humanities depends on method. In seeking a methodological foundation that alone could guarantee their scientific or objective status, Dilthey sought to keep the humanities to the model of the exact sciences and would thus have forfeited the specificity of the humanities, where the involvement of the interpreter whose understanding is constitutive of the experience of meaning: the texts that we interpret are texts that say something to us and that are always understood in some way out of our questions and "prejudices." The implication of the interpreter in the "event" of meaning, as Gadamer likes to put it, can only be deemed detrimental from the model of objectivity heralded by the natural sciences. Instead of this outdated notion of objectivity, the human sciences would do well to understand their contribution to knowledge out of the somewhat forgotten tradition of humanism and the importance it bestowed upon the notion of *Bildung* (formation and education). The humanities do not seek to master an object that stands at a distance (as with the exact sciences), but their aim is rather to develop and form the human spirit. The truth one experiences in the encounter with major texts and history is one that transforms us, taking us up in the event of meaning itself.

Gadamer finds the most revealing model for this type of understanding in the experience of art since we are always involved by the presentation of an art work, which Gadamer understands as the revelation of the truth or the essence of something, so that a play reveals something about the meaning of existence, just as a portrait reveals the true essence of someone. Yet it is a truth-experience in which we partake in that it can only unfold through a process of interpretation. For Gadamer hermeneutics is to be understood, first and foremost, out of the arts we call the "arts of interpretation" or the "performative arts": just as a piece of music must be interpreted by the violinist (that is, never arbitrarily, but with a leeway that has to be filled by the virtuosity of interpretation), a drama by the actors or the ballet by the dancers, a book must be interpreted through the process of reading and a picture must be contemplated by the eye of the beholder. It is only in this presentation (*Darstellung* or *Vollzug*) of a meaning to someone, a performance which is always an interpretation, that meaning comes to be realized. One notices here that "interpretation" refers both to the interpretation of a work of art by the performers and to the "spectators" who attend the performance and must also "interpret" the piece.

The difference between the two forms of interpretation is less important for Gadamer than the fact that the experience of meaning, and the truth experience it brings out, essentially requires the productive implication of the interpreter. The same holds for the interpretation of a text or a historical event, even in the scientific context of the human sciences. The point is that interpretation is not the simple recreation of a meaning that always remains the same and can be methodically verified, nor, for that matter, the subjective, and potentially relativistic, bestowing of meaning upon an objective reality (because the reality to be understood can only be reached through a renewed attempt of understanding). In other words, to claim that interpretation is relativistic on the grounds that it implies the subjectivity of the interpreter is to miss the point of what the humanities and the experience of meaning are all about.

The objectivistic model of the exact sciences is ill-equipped to do justice to this experience of meaning. Distance, methodical verification, and independence from the observer, Gadamer concludes, are not the sole conditions of knowledge. When we understand, we do not only follow a methodical procedure but we are "taken up " as the art experience illustrates, by the meaning that "seizes" us, as it were. The instrumental sounding idea of procedure is somewhat suspect for Gadamer, for understanding is more of an event than a procedure. "Understanding and Event" is indeed one of the original titles Gadamer thought about for his major work, before settling on "Truth and Method," which underlines the very same point that truth is not only a matter of method and can never be entirely detached from our concerns.

But these concerns come to us from a tradition and a history that are more often than not opaque to consciousness. Every understanding stands in the stream of a *Wirkungsgeschichte* or "effective history," in which the horizons of the past and the present coalesce. Understanding thus entails a "fusion of horizons" between the past and the present, that is, between the interpreter, with all the history silently at work in his understanding, and his or her object. This fusion is not to be viewed as an autonomous operation of subjectivity but as an event of tradition (*Überlieferungsgeschehen*) in the course of which a meaning from the past is somehow applied to the present.

This leads *Truth and Method* to suggest that the best model for the humanities was perhaps offered by disciplines that had been traditionally preoccupied with the questions of interpretation such as juridical and theological hermeneutics, insofar as the meaning that is to be understood in these fields is one that has to be applied to a given situation. In the same way a judge has to creatively apply a text of law to a particular case and a preacher has to apply a text of Scripture to the situation of his or her congregation, every act of understanding involves an effort of "application" of what is understood to the present. Gadamer does not mean by this that one first has to understand a meaning, of a text or a historical event and then apply it to a given situation by bestowing new "relevance" upon it. His idea is rather that every understanding is at its root an application of meaning, where our experience and background are brought to bear. This "application" is, by no means, a conscious procedure. It always happens in the course of understanding to the extent that interpretation brings into play the situation and "prejudices" of the interpreter that are less "his" or "hers" than the ones carved by the effective history in which we all stand.

Gadamer expands on this idea by comparing understanding to a process of translation. "I understand something" means that I can translate it into my own words, thus applying it to my situation. Any meaning I can relate to is one that is translated into a meaning I can articulate. It is not only important to underline the obvious fact that translation always implies an act of interpretation (a translator is also called in English an *interpreter*) but even more to stress that this interpretation is by no means arbitrary: it is bound by the meaning it seeks to render, but it can only do so by translating it into a language where it can speak anew. What occurs in the process of translation is thus a fusion of horizons between the foreign meaning and its interpretation-translation in a new language, horizon, and situation, where the meaning resonates.

*Truth and Method* draws on this insight to highlight the fundamentally linguistic nature of understanding. Understanding is always an act of developing something into words, and I only understand to the extent that I seek (and find) words to express this understanding. Understanding is not a process that could be separated from its linguistic unfolding: to think, to understand, is to seek words for that which strives to be understood. There is a crucial fusion between the process of interpretation and its linguistic formulation. It will not be the only fusion of horizons that will interest Gadamer in his hermeneutics of language. His thesis goes even further: not only is the process (*Vollzug*) of interpreting (*interpretare*) linguistically oriented, what it seeks to understand (the *interpretandum*) is also language. Language also determines the object (*Gegenstand*) of understanding itself. In the end there occurs a fusion between the "process" of understanding and its "object" in the sense that no object (*Gegenstand*) can be separated from the attempt (*Vollzug*) to understand it. Gadamer's famous phrase to express this fusion between the object and the process of understanding itself is: "Being that can be understood is language."

This simple, yet enigmatic dictum can be read in two quite different directions: it can mean that every experience of Being is mediated by language, and thus by a historical and cultural horizon (negatively put: "there is no experience of Being without an historical understanding or language"). This would seem to draw Gadamer into the "relativistic camp." It is striking to note, however, that Gadamer always resisted this merely relativistic appropriation of his thought. This has been overlooked by postmodern readers of Gadamer, but in his dictum "Being that can be understood is language," the stress can also be put on Being itself. What Gadamer hopes to say by this is that the effort of understanding is in a way ordained to the language of the things themselves. A difficult and unpalatable notion for postmodernism, to be sure, but one that is essential to Gadamer's hermeneutics: language is not only the subjective, say, contingent translation of meaning, it is also the event by which Being itself comes to light. Our language is not only "our" language, it is also the language of Being itself, the way in which Being presents itself in our understanding. This is why, when one speaks and interprets, one cannot say everything one fancies. One is bound by something like the language of the thing. What is this language? Difficult to say since we can only approach it through *our* language, and the language of tradition, but it is nevertheless the instance that resists too unilateral or too violent readings of this Being. It is this language of Being that I seek to understand, and to the extent that understanding succeeds, a fusion of horizons has happened, a fusion between Being and understanding, an event I do not master, but in which I partake.

**Gadamer and His Critics**

The history of hermeneutics after Gadamer can be read as a history of the debates provoked by *Truth and Method*. Some of the first responses to Gadamer were sparked by the methodological notion of hermeneutics that prevailed in the tradition of Dilthey. After all, it had been the dominant conception of hermeneutics until Gadamer (with the sole, albeit very peculiar, exception of Heidegger's "hermeneutics of existence" that had left behind the older hermeneutic tradition which had been concerned with text interpretation and the human sciences). Since Gadamer, in spite of his Heideggerian roots, took his starting point in Dilthey's inquiry on the truth claim of the humanities, he was often seen and criticized from this tradition. Emilio Betti, the Italian jurist who had published a voluminous *General Theory of Interpretation* (in Italian) in 1955, which was intended as a methodical foundation of the humanities in the Dilthey tradition, vigorously criticized Gadamer's seeming rejection of the methodological paradigm. If Gadamer's own "method" for the humanities consisted in saying that one just has to follow one's own prejudices, it had to be condemned as a perversion of the very idea of hermeneutics. Betti, who was followed in this regard by E. D. Hirsch in America, opposed the relativistic idea that interpretation always entails an essential element of application to the present. Surely, texts do acquire different meanings or relevance in the course of their reception, but one has to distinguish the actuality or significance (*Bedeutsamkeit*) thus garnered from the original meaning (*Bedeutung*) of the texts, that is, the meaning of the text in the mind of its author (*mens auctoris*), which remains the focus of hermeneutics.

Coming from the Frankfurt School, Jürgen Habermas hailed, for his part, this element of application in understanding, claiming that knowledge is always guided by some interests. This hermeneutical insight, he believed, could help free the social sciences, spearheaded by psychoanalysis and the critique of ideology, from an all too objectivistic understanding of knowledge and science. Hermeneutics teaches us that our understanding and practices are always motivated and linguistically articulated. It is Gadamer's too strong reliance on tradition and the importance of authority in understanding that Habermas opposed. He faulted it for being "conservative"; but Habermas's lasting point, that language can also transcend its own limits, followed an idea that he discovered in Gadamer but turned against him. When Gadamer said that our experience of the world was linguistical, he also stressed, for Habermas, that it is open to self-correction, that is, that it could, to some extent, overcome its own limitations by seeking better expressions or dissolving its own rigidity and was thus open to any meaning that could be understood. Habermas and Karl-Otto Apel drew from this self-transcendence of language the important notion of a linguistic or communicative rationality, which is laden with universalistic assumptions that can form the basis of an ethical theory.

Paul Ricoeur tried to build a bridge—a most hermeneutical task and virtue in itself—between Habermas and Gadamer, by claiming both authors had stressed different but complementary elements in the tension that is inherent to understanding: whereas Gadamer underlined the belongingness of the interpreter to his object and his tradition, Habermas took heed of the reflective distance toward it. Understanding, viewed as application, does not only have to appropriate naively its subject matter, it can stand at a critical distance from it—a distance that is already given by the fact that the *interpretandum* is an objectified text. This notion of a hermeneutics that seeks to decipher objectivations came mainly from Dilthey, but Ricoeur used it in a productive manner in his decisive confrontations with psychoanalysis (Sigmund Freud) and structuralism (Claude Lévi-Strauss). He linked them to a "hermeneutics of suspicion" that is most useful in that it can help us get rid of superstition and false understanding. But such a hermeneutics can only be conducted in the hope of a better and more critical understanding of understanding. A "hermeneutics of trust" thus remains the ultimate focus of his work: the meaning we seek to understand is one that helps us better understand our world and ourselves. We interpret because we are open to the truths that can be gained from the objectivations of meaning in the grand myths, texts, and narratives of mankind, in which the temporal and tragic aspects of our human condition are expressed. Ricoeur drew far-reaching ethical conclusions from this hermeneutics of trust that has learned from the school of suspicion.

Betti, Hirsch, Habermas (and, to a certain extent, Ricoeur) all faulted Gadamer and hermeneutics for being too "relativistic" (i.e., too reliant on tradition). Postmodernism went, to some degree, in an opposite direction: it welcomed Gadamer's alleged "relativism" but only believed it did not go far enough. Gadamer would have been somewhat inconsequential in not acknowledging fully the relativistic consequences of his hermeneutics.

To understand this shift in the hermeneutical debates, it is important to observe that authors such as Heidegger (especially the later Heidegger) and Nietzsche play a paramount role for postmodernist thinkers. One thinks, in this regard, of the Nietzsche who said that there are no facts, only interpretations, or of the Heidegger who claimed that our understanding was framed by the history of Being. The postmodernists lumped this Nietzschean-Heideggerian outlook together with Gadamer's seeming critique of scientific objectivity, his stress on the prejudices of interpretation, and his insistence on the linguistic nature of understanding. Stressing these elements, hermeneutics, they believed, jettisoned the idea of an objective truth. There is no such thing given the interpretatory and linguistic nature of our experience. This lead Gianni Vattimo to "nihilistic" consequences and Richard Rorty to a renewed form of pragmatism: some interpretations are more useful or amenable than others, but none can per se be claimed to be "closer" to the Truth. In the name of tolerance and mutual understanding, one has to accept the plurality of interpretations; it is only the notion that there is only one valid one that is harmful.

Jacques Derrida can also be seen in the "postmodern" tradition, since he too depends heavily on the later Heidegger and Nietzsche, stresses the linguistical nature of our experience, and also urges a "deconstructive" attitude toward the tradition of metaphysics that governs our thinking, an attitude that Paul Ricoeur would classify in the "hermeneutics of suspicion." But his deconstruction does not directly take the direction of the pragmatist tradition of Rorty or the nihilism of Vattimo. Despite the Heideggerian origins of his notion of deconstruction and his pan-linguisticism, Derrida does not identify himself with the tradition of hermeneutics. His "deconstruction" is indeed distrustful of any form of hermeneutics: every understanding, he contends, would involve or hide a form of "appropriation" of the other and its otherness. In his discussion with Gadamer in 1981, he challenged Gadamer's rather commonplace assumption that understanding implies the goodwill to understand the other. What about this will? asked Derrida. Is it not chained to the will to dominate that is emblematic of our metaphysical and Western philosophical tradition? Hence Derrida's mistrust of the hermeneutical drive to understand the other and of the hermeneutic claim to universality. Gadamer was touched by this criticism to the extent that he claimed that understanding implied some form of application, which can indeed be read as a form of appropriation. This is perhaps the reason why, in his later writings, he more readily underlined the open nature of the hermeneutical experience. "The soul of hermeneutics," he then said, "is that the other can be right."

*See also* **Modernity; Postmodernism; Relativism.**

BIBLIOGRAPHY

Bernstein, Richard J. *Beyond Objectivism and Relativism: Science, Hermeneutics, and Praxis.* Philadelphia: University of Pennsylvania Press, 1983. Sees in the hermeneutical rehabilitation of common sense a parallel to pragmatism and a corrective to the bugbear of relativism.

Betti, Emilio. "Hermeneutics as the General Methodology of the *Geisteswissenschaften.*" 1962. Reprinted in *Contemporary*

*Hermeneutics: Hermeneutics as Method, Philosophy, and Critique,* edited by Josef Bleicher. London and Boston: Routledge and Kegan Paul, 1980. Polemical defense of a methodology of interpretation against Gadamer.

Bleicher, Josef, ed. *Contemporary Hermeneutics: Hermeneutics as Method, Philosophy and Critique.* London and Boston: Routledge and Kegan Paul, 1980. Best collection of essays by Betti, Gadamer, Habermas, Apel.

Caputo, John D. *Radical Hermeneutics: Repetition, Deconstruction and the Hermeneutic Project.* Bloomington: Indiana University Press, 1987. Postmodern, Derridian reading and critique of hermeneutics.

Dilthey, Wilhelm. "The Rise of Hermeneutics." In his *Hermeneutics and the Study of History,* edited by Rudolf A. Makkreel and Frithjof Rodi, 235–258. Vol. 4. Princeton, N.J.: Princeton University Press, 1996. Seminal study on the significance of hermeneutics for Dilthey.

Dostal, Robert J., ed. *The Cambridge Companion to Gadamer.* Cambridge, U.K., and New York: Cambridge University Press, 2002. Authoritative collection of essays on Gadamer, with good biographical and bibliographical material.

Gadamer, Hans-Georg. *Philosophical Hermeneutics.* Translated by David E. Linge. Berkeley: University of California Press, 1976. Studies that complete Gadamer's opus magnum.

———. *Truth and Method.* Translation revised by Joel Weinsheimer and Donald G. Marshall. New York: Crossroad, 1989. The bible of contemporary hermeneutics.

Grondin, Jean. *Introduction to Philosophical Hermeneutics.* Translated by Joel Weinsheimer. New Haven: Yale University Press, 1994. History of the hermeneutic tradition from antiquity to the present from the vantage point of the inner word.

———. *Le tournant herméneutique de la phénoménologie.* Paris: PUF, 2003. A study of the different conceptions of hermeneutics espoused by Heidegger, Gadamer and Derrida.

Habermas, Jürgen. "The Hermeneutic Claim to Universality." In *Contemporary Hermeneutics: Hermeneutics as Method, Philosophy, and Critique,* edited by Josef Bleicher. London and Boston: Routledge and Kegan Paul, 1980. A famous critique of Gadamer inspired by ideology critique and psychoanalysis.

———. "A Review of Gadamer's Truth and Method". In *Understanding and Social Inquiry,* edited and translated by Fred R. Dallmayr and Thomas A. McCarthy. Notre Dame, Ind.: University of Notre Dame Press, 1977.

Heidegger, Martin. *Being and Time.* Translated by John Macquarrie and Edward Robinson. New York: Harper, 1962. Heidegger's main work, based on a hermeneutics of existence.

———. *Ontology: The Hermeneutics of Facticity.* 1923. Translated by John van Buren. Bloomington: Indiana University Press, 1999. Seminal text of Heidegger's early hermeneutic conception.

Hirsch, E. D., Jr. *Validity in Interpretation.* New Haven: Yale University Press, 1967. Defends a methodical conception of hermeneutics against Gadamer.

Michelfelder, Diane P., and Richard E. Palmer, eds. *Dialogue and Deconstruction. The Gadamer-Derrida Encounter.* Albany: State University of New York Press, 1989. Contains the basic texts of the famous encounter between Derrida and Gadamer.

Palmer, Richard E. *Hermeneutics. Interpretation Theory in Schleiermacher, Dilthey, Heidegger, and Gadamer.* Evanston, Ill.: Northwestern University Press, 1969. Ground-breaking and clear presentation of the major figures of the hermeneutic tradition.

Ricoeur, Paul. *Hermeneutics and the Human Sciences: Essays on Language, Action, and Interpretation,* edited and translated by John B. Thomson. Cambridge, U.K., and New York: Cambridge University Press, 1981.

———. *From Text to Action. Essays in Hermeneutics.* Translated by Kathleen Blamey and John B. Thompson. Evanston, Ill.: Northwestern University Press, 1991. Both books document the hermeneutic itinerary of a major hermeneutic thinker of our time.

Rorty, Richard. "Being That Can Be Understood Is Language." *London Review of Books,* 16 March 2000, 23–25. A tribute to Gadamer's alleged linguistic relativism.

———. *Philosophy and the Mirror of Nature.* Princeton, N.J.: Princeton University Press, 1979. Hermeneutics presented as the outcome of philosophy, out of the tradition of American pragmatism.

Schleiermacher, Friedrich. *Hemeneutics and Criticism and Other Writings.* Edited and translated by Andrew Bowie. New York: Cambridge University Press, 1998. Classical texts of the founder of modern-day hermeneutics.

Vattimo, Gianni. *Beyond Interpretation: The Meaning of Hermeneutics for Philosophy.* Translated by David Webb. Cambridge, U.K., and New York: Polity Press, 1997.

———. *The End of Modernity: Nihilism and Hermeneutics in Postmodern Culture.* Translated by Jon R. Snyder. Baltimore: John Hopkins University Press, 1988. Both volumes testify to the postmodern appropriation of hermeneutics.

*Jean Grondin*

# HIERARCHY AND ORDER.

Hierarchy (Greek *hierarchia*; from *hieros,* sacred + *archein,* rule) is a kind of order, supposing existence of higher (or more sacred) and lower (less sacred) levels of reality. Order, in its turn, is a linkage of fundamentally different elements by means of general laws, so that the whole is greater than a simple arithmetical sum of its parts. Since order presupposes difference, it often takes the form of hierarchy. The place of an element in the hierarchical order is determined by the same laws of the whole, which are constitutive of the order itself.

## Uncreated Cosmos

The understanding of the universe as a hierarchical order came into being in early antiquity and is reflected in mythological conceptions. Ancient Greek mythology and philosophy put forth this idea in the conception of Cosmos as being opposite to Chaos. The Cosmos (meaning "beautiful" in its most ancient definition) is sculpturally organized by the laws of beauty and as such is similar to that of a beautiful human body. So, according to Platonic thought, the order of the Cosmos is similar to the order of the human being. The Cosmos is not created by any god, which means there is both a complex dialectic of Cosmos and Chaos and the idea of hierarchical primacy of the Cosmos over all other things, including gods and human beings. The last idea is expressed in mythology by the concept of destiny, which defines the exact place of any thing in the order of the Cosmos. Neither god nor man can escape from destiny, which is why, for example, Oedipus is doomed to be blinded and Juno, the wife and sister of the supreme Roman god Jupiter, cannot affect the life of Aeneas, who was destined to be the founder of Rome.

The dialectic of Cosmos and Chaos is one of the most puzzling questions in Greek philosophy. In mythology this dialectic is described as a birth of the hierarchy of gods out of primitive Chaos. According to Hesiod's *Theogony*, "Verily at the first Chaos came to be, but next wide-bosomed Earth, the ever-sure foundations of all" (line 116). This "coming to be," however, is described in pre-Socratic philosophy as a complex process of the circulation of Chaos and Cosmos. According to the Greek philosopher Heracleitus (c. 540–c. 480 B.C.E.), fire, which is the basis of the world, flares up and dies out at times. The extinction of fire is interpreted as the birth of the world order and the worldwide conflagration is the death of the Cosmos. According to Empedocles (c. 490–430 B.C.E.), another pre-Socratic philosopher, the Cosmos is organized through the struggle of two constitutive forces, Love (*Philia*) and Strife (*Oikos*). This struggle gives birth to four stages of the world's development, the first of which is Chaos (constituted by the absolute predominance of Strife) and the last being absolute unity of everything in the form of a sphere (which is organized by predominant Love).

In the Platonic tradition, the material Cosmos is just a shadow of the order of ideas (*kosmos noēticos*). Ideas, being hierarchically primary to material things—understood by Plato as forms (*eidoi*), reasons (*logoi*), and exemplars (*paradeigmai*) of things—are themselves organized in hierarchical order. The idea of the Good (*ta kalon*), being the most general of all ideas (*eidos tōn eidōn*), is on the very top of this hierarchy. Things are striving for their prototypes and this striving, by the same token, is responsible for the maintenance of the world's order. However, the very nature of the relations between the realm of ideas, which is situated in some beyond-celestial place (*hyprauranios topos*), and the world of things is problematic in the context of Platonic doctrine and was described differently in variants of Platonism. For Plato, a Master (*Demiourgos*) was responsible for creating the world, and the nature of the striving of things to their ideas is described as an activity of the World's Soul. The Roman philosopher Plotinus (205–270 C.E.), the father of Neoplatonism, described the creation of the world order as the process of emanation of the One (*to hen*), and the Cosmos is meant to be a reference point for the self-conscious existence of the Soul. However, another problem arises in both Platonic traditions: the question of obvious defects in the world's order. Namely, if the ideal Cosmos is good (because the most general idea is the idea of the Good), who is responsible for the origin of evil? According to Plato, it is a result of imperfect reflection of ideas in matter. Matter is described as a pure potency of existence. As such, it is actually nothing (*mēon*), while it has potential to be something. It follows that if evil is a result of the materiality of things, it can be described as nothing as well, that is, as a defect of reflection. Influenced by the Gnostics of the second century C.E., who had explained existence of evil by the imperfection or even wickedness of God the Creator (*Demiourgos*), Plotinus described the origin of evil as a result of the error made by the Soul in valuing its expressions in physical Cosmos over the contemplation of the divine Forms.

## Created Order

Christian thought shares the Neoplatonic understanding of order as two actual orders: the lower one is the order of the material world and higher one is the structure of the ideal Cosmos. The difference, however, is that the order of material things was now considered a created one. The realm of the Forms or ideas transforms into the content of Divine Logos, the Word of God, pre-existing the world. The origin of the universal order is described as creation out of nothing (*creatio ex nihilo*). However, the understanding of this formula in Christian thought is quite different. Some philosophers consider the process of creation as the creation out of some existing nothing (so, according to Russian philosopher Sergey Nikolaevich Bulgakov (1871–1944), the levels of the order should range from nothingness to the highest hierarchy of Trinity). Others understand it as the assertion that God did not need anything for the creation of the world (Anselm of Canterbury, 1033 or 1034–1109). Finally, some thinkers believe that creation out of nothing means creation of the world out of God's nature. Thus, for John Scotus Erigena (c. 810–c. 877) uncreated and creating nature (God) descends through created and creating nature (the ideas or primordial causes) into created and not creating nature (numeric things). These three natures, forming the order of the Universe, will be united in the end of the world into the form of uncreated and not creating nature.

This shift from emanation to creation meant that: (1) neither God, nor matter created by God can be responsible for the existence of the evil. Evil is described as a result of man's free will; (2) God is understood as both immanent to the world (because God is present in it) and transcendent (because God exists in eternity and the world is created); (3) God is a guarantee for the maintenance of the world's order; and (4) that a human being is able to overcome the laws of the Cosmos and be united with God again in deification (Gk. *theosis*, Lat. *deificatio*).

One of the teachings of order, transitional from the ancient to the Christian understanding, was a doctrine of Origen of Alexandria (185?–254?), a near contemporary of Plotinus (205–270). In *De Principiis* he describes the world's order as a set of parallel worlds, which are the places for the fallen souls, created by God in eternity. Being eternal, the souls can proceed from one world to another and, thus, with the lapse of time, all of them (including the soul of Satan) will be united with God. The present world's order will come to an end, and the condition of *apokatastasis* (restoration of all things) will be established. However, in eternity, some souls will misuse their free will again, a new Fall will ensue, and a new world will be created. This conception obviously has some elements of ancient teaching on the circulation of Cosmos and Chaos.

In the fifth century, St. Augustine of Hippo (354–430) in the West and Dionysius the Areopagite (Pseudo-Dionysius) in the Christian East constructed the foundations for mature Christian doctrine of order and hierarchy. Augustine in his early treatise *De ordine* (On order) asserted that nothing could be out of the order of created things. What seems to us to be evil also exists in the framework of order. So, if there were no hangmen, robbery would fill the earth, and if there were no prostitutes, debauchery would flourish. The origin of evil lies in the free will of the human being, but God uses what is worst in the best possible way. Once evil has been created, God included it in God's order, which is good as a whole. This means that nothing is absolutely evil and God does not leave the world unattended after its creation. Rather the process of creation can be described as a continuous holding of things into being (*creatio continua*). Ideas became the content of God's Logos (Word), by which God has created all things. These ideas are exemplars for material things and were also created by God in God's Word. Thus, the problem of the relations between ideas and material things has been solved through the conception of creation, and the problem of evil has been solved both through the notion of the Fall, which had been caused by the misuse of free will, given by God to human beings, and through the notion of continuous creation of the world. The last notion became the main basis of Gottfried Wilhelm Leibniz's (1646–1716) theodicy, interpreting the world as the best of all possible worlds. Indeed, according to Leibniz, this world is the best exactly because God uses the worst things in the best possible way.

Pseudo-Dionysius considered evil things as belonging to the realm of non-being. Indeed, according to him, everything that is connected with God, who is the Being and the Good, exists and is a good thing. That means that everything which exists is good. Evil is privation and lack of goodness in good things, and, thus, exists in the good as in its substance. In other words, evil things are evil only because they are less good than the others. This conception is quite Neoplatonic, but it does not constitute Docetism, that is, a heresy based upon the doctrine of the fundamental evilness of the matter. The connection of all things with God is described in Pseudo-Dionysius's doctrine as the presence of God in all things, described as *theophanias* (God's appearances). That means, in its turn, that the universe is united with God by virtue of the presence of God's energies (*dynames*) in this world. This conception was implemented in Pseudo-Dionysius's well-known ideas of celestial and ecclesiastical hierarchies. In *The Celestial Hierarchy,* Pseudo-Dionysius distinguishes three groups of three angelic orders (*taksis*). The first consists of Seraphim, Cherubim, and Thrones, the second of Dominions, Virtues, and Powers, and the third of Principalities, Archangels, and Angels. Those nine angelic orders deliver information from God to human beings. The higher orders are responsible for purification (Gk. *katharsis,* Lat. *purificatio*), illumination (Gk. *phōtismos,* Lat. *illuminatio*) and deification (Gk. *theosis,* Lat. *deificatio*) of the lower ones. Purification, illumination, and deification are also the stages of human mystical experience. Ecclesiastical hierarchy (described by Pseudo-Dionysius in his *Ecclesiastical Hierarchy*) consists of two triple groups, reflecting the structure of celestial hierarchy. One group is of hierarchs, priests, and deacons and the other consists of monks, believers, and catechumens. The place of the highest order is occupied not by human beings, but by sacraments, uniting heaven and earth. This is the order of Eucharist, Baptism, and Anointing. By means of these two hierarchies, according to Dionysius, God communicates with human beings and enables them also to be purified, illuminated, and perfected.

Ideally, the order of the society in medieval thought corresponded with the order of the universe. God was considered to be the single source of power both in theocratic society and in the universe as a whole. This picture, however,

was complicated first by struggle between spiritual and temporal powers and secondly by opposition between the aspiration for one great Christian empire and the complex system of feudal rights. The theories of political order in the middle ages ranged from ideas of the bull *unam sanctam* of Pope Boniface VIII (1235–1303), asserting absolute power of the pope, to Marsilius of Padua's (c. 1275–c. 1342) functionalist doctrine of an autonomous and independent state.

Human society, existing in history, represents a developing image of the eternal divine order and follows God's providential plan. This plan was often described as a divinely ordered sequence of four world empires, engaged in a conflict that would eventually lead to the last great empire. According to St. Augustine's *De civitate dei,* this fifth kingdom is a spiritual one, constituted by love for God. An idea still present in some millenarist doctrines can be found in the thoughts of Joachim of Fiore (c. 1132-1202) who saw the whole world history as a tripartite process, the successive ages of God representing God the Father, God the Son, and God the Holy Spirit.

Platonic, Aristotelian, and Christian concepts of hierarchy and order were fused in a theory known as the Great Chain of Being, which dominated cosmology from the Middle Ages to the dawn of modernity. The idea was that the universe consists of an immense or even infinite number of links, ranging hierarchically from the lowest being (or nothingness) through every possible grade to the highest, most perfect Being (*ens perfectissimum*). The levels of perfection were described differently: according to a Renaissance vision, for instance, they were constituted by different proportions of matter and spirit in different things. That is why alchemists of the Renaissance believed that lower lead could be transformed to higher gold, if someone could learn the method for adding some spirit to the mix. The idea of the Great Chain of Being reached its culmination in the doctrines of Benedict de (Baruch) Spinoza (1632–1677) and Leibniz. For them the chain has every possible degree of perfection and, therefore, is complete. The perfection of the whole, by the same token, does suppose existence of imperfect things. This idea formed a new basis for theodicy. According to Leibniz, the differences in perfection are infinitesimal and, therefore, the universe is a continuum. Imperfect things are caused, contingent, and dependent, the most perfect God is self-caused (*causa sui*). Because nothingness is on the bottom of the chain, more perfection means more being. That is why both Spinoza and Leibniz were inclined to accept Anselm of Canterbury's ontological argument for God's existence, based on the thought that the very idea of the most perfect being had to be the idea of being in existence.

## Nonwestern and New Conceptions

Conceptions of order and hierarchy are by no means occidental ones. Ancient Chinese philosophers, discussing the world's order, used the term *dao* (way, guide). They usually spoke of three main species of *dao* (and, consequently, of three orders): human (social) *dao, tian* (natural or heavenly) *dao,* and great *dao.* The first is a way or guide for human behavior; the second is similar to the laws of nature, which cause things to happen reliably; the third comprises everything which has happened, is happening, or will happen in the world. It is obvious, therefore, that both human *dao* and *tian dao* are parts of the great *dao*. It is great *dao* that is responsible for the order of things in the world.

However, because the concept of *dao* is rather vague, there are different interpretations of this order, ranging from anarchist and pluralist doctrines to hierarchical and authoritarian interpretations. It is possible to say that philosophical doctrines of Daoism lean toward pluralism, skepticism, poltical equality, and freedom. Religious mysticism, on the other hand, often claims some direct access to a single correct dao, forming a basis for esoteric, hierarchical and authoritarian thought. The most prominent representatives of philosophical Daoism were Laozi (c. 604–c. 531 B.C.E.), author of *Dao De Jing,* and Zhuangzi (c. 369–c. 286 B.C.E), who created a mature form of philosophical Daoism.

In the Indian Buddhist tradition, the main cause of the order in the world is human will, attaching human being to the world and dragging the world into an endless circle of suffering, the true essence of the world's order. The main point of Buddhist ethics is to stop the suffering through quitting the will and achieving the highest possible mental state, that of *nirvana.*

Scholars of African religious traditions show that African religious philosophy, such as Yoruba belief, implies a complex hierarchy in the world, created by the supreme god Oludomare, described as the omnipotent creator of all good and bad things. The numerous gods, created by Oludomare, form a hierarchy of mediators between him and the world. The most striking feature of Yoruba belief, distinguishing this religion from Judeo-Christian tradition, is that Oludomare is perceived as responsible for both good and evil, using both good and bad in the process of ensuring justice. Moreover, the world is ordered in a way that implies immediate punishment for sinful deeds of the people.

One Eastern Christian doctrine of hierarchy and order can be found in the Russian philosophy of All-Unity, which flourished at the end of the nineteenth century. The main idea of this tradition is that the world can be reunited with God through the efforts of human beings and by uniting the things with the prototypes that exist in Divine Wisdom (Sophia). For the founder of this tradition, Vladimir Solovyev (1853–1900), Sophia is a world in its ideal, true being and is created in eternity by eternal Logos. Sergey Bulgakov, who worked in the first half of the twentieth century, considered Sophia as God's fourth hypostasis. Sophiology enabled these philosophers to understand the order of the universe as potential all-unity, already existed in Divine Sophia.

Contemporary theories of order are not so numerous. The crisis of the idea of the Great Chain of Being, caused both by the rise of natural science and by the crisis of religious consciousness, led to nonhierarchical understandings of order. The order becomes a characteristic feature of various systems. The Brussels school in natural science (Prigogine and Stengers) considers order as a spontaneous result of the process of self-organization in open systems, exchanging energy with their environment. Society and biological systems, according to

Prigogine, are such self-organizing systems and cannot be described in terms of the old mechanical paradigm of science.

Contemporary postmodern and poststructuralist authors criticize "western logocentric tradition" for its attempts to find order, hierarchy and meaning in all things. They argue for the existence of many differences, which are so chaotic in their relations to each other that they exclude any possibility of organized oppositions. As a result, the unordered chaos does not allow for the contrast of differences, and differences are no longer perceived as such. Gilles Deleuze (1925-1995), in his quest for "difference in itself," rejects the old Platonic and Hegelian tradition, which understands the difference in reference to self-identical objects, and which, in turn, makes the difference an element of hierarchical structure. Difference-in-itself, on the contrary, does not imply order at all, and various differences, remaining in "formless chaos," does not form any structure.

*See also* **Christianity; Cosmology; Daoism; Harmony; Neoplatonism; Platonism; Society.**

**BIBLIOGRAPHY**

Armstrong, A. H., trans. *Plotinus: The Enneads.* 7 vols. Cambridge, Mass.: Harvard University Press, 1966–1988.
Cooper, John M., ed. *Plato: Complete Works.* Indianapolis: Hackett Publishing, 1997.
Crouzel, Henri. *Origen: The Life and Thought of the First Great Theologian.* Translated by A. S. Worrall. San Francisco: Harper and Row, 1989.
Ferguson, Everett, ed. *Encyclopedia of Early Christianity.* New York: Garland, 1990.
Garber, Daniel, and Roger Ariew, trans. *Discourse on Metaphysics and Other Essays.* Indianapolis: Hackett, 1991.
Lovejoy, Arthur O. *The Great Chain of Being: A Study of the History of an Idea.* Reprint, Cambridge, Mass.: Harvard University Press, 1970.
Luibheid, Colm, trans. *Pseudo-Dionysius: The Complete Works.* New York: Paulist Press, 1987.
Origen of Alexandria. *On First Principles* [De Principiis]. In *The Ante-Nicene Fathers,* vol. 4. Reprint, Grand Rapids, Mich.: Eerdmans, 1979.
Prigogine, Ilya, and Isabelle Stengers. *Order Out of Chaos: Man's New Dialogue with Nature.* London: Heinemann, 1984.
Shirley, Samuel, trans. *Baruch Spinoza: The Ethics; Treatise on the Emendation of the Intellect; Selected Letters.* Edited by Seymour Feldman. Indianapolis: Hackett, 1992.
Solovyev, Vladimir. *Lectures on Godmanhood.* London: Dennis Dobson, 1948.
Taliaferro, R. C., trans. *Saint Augustine: The Immortality of the Soul and Other Works.* Washington, D.C.: Catholic University of America Press, 1950.

*Maxim Khomiakov*

**HINDUISM.** Hinduism, the religion of nearly one billion people mostly of South Asian provenance or descent, is notoriously difficult to define or even to describe with accuracy and comprehensiveness. Like all complex and ancient religious traditions, it is problematic to speak about Hinduism as if it were one monolithic religion rather than merely a label for many different traditions. The conglomeration of religious traditions sheltered under this umbrella incorporates a bewildering array of texts, beliefs, practices, and sects—so disparate a collection that some modern scholars have questioned the legitimacy of artificially unifying them. According to these scholars, one cannot really speak about a single Hinduism but at best only a variety of Hinduisms.

## Defining Hinduism

The word *Hinduism* itself derives from one of the principal rivers of South Asia, the Indus, and was probably first used by the ancient Persians to designate the people and territory of the northwestern portion of the subcontinent. As a name for a religion (at first inclusive of what is now differentiated as Hinduism, Jainism, and Buddhism), it probably owes its origin to the Muslim invaders of the early part of the second millennium C.E., and as a discrete (but still enormously variegated) Indian religion, *Hinduism* was the term the British gave in the nineteenth century to all those in India who were neither Muslim nor Christian.

Diversity—historical, cultural, linguistic, doctrinal, and sectarian—is descriptive of all world religions also designated by a unitary label, including Christianity, Judaism, Buddhism, and Islam. Hinduism may be an extreme example, but it is hardly unique in this regard. And as is true in other religions, in Hinduism conceptual unity can be identified within this diversity. Some scholars have identified a set of key concepts or beliefs they regard as distinctively Hindu, including the beliefs in karma and rebirth; the impermanent and fundamentally suffering nature of the world (samsara); and the possibility of liberation from suffering and rebirth and the attainment of a permanent state of bliss (*moksha*). None of these beliefs, however, belongs exclusively to Hinduism. Buddhism, Jainism, and other "non-Hindu" Indian religions also hold these doctrines. Other observers content themselves with the notion that Hinduism is distinguished by religious methods and practices that may be categorized under three broad headings or paths: the way of action or ritual (*karma marga*), the way of knowledge or wisdom (*jnana marga*), and of devotion (*bhakti marga*).

Still others argue that what is truly distinctive of Hinduism is its social structure—the caste system—and the religious ideology that underlies it, especially the notion of the superiority and spiritual purity of the Brahman castes. Indeed, some scholars use the term *Brahmanism* (or *Brahminism*) as synonymous with *Hinduism* to emphasize the notion that the essence of this religion is its belief in caste hierarchy, with the Brahmans at the top. But although it is true that caste and Brahman privilege are ancient and enduring features of Indian society, it is not clear that a religion is defined by the social structure it promotes, nor is caste confined to "Hinduism"—there are Muslim, Christian, Sikh, and Parsi castes as well as Hindu ones.

Perhaps the most promising way to envision the underlying unity of Hinduism is to concentrate on the way Hindu traditions understand and use scriptural authority to legitimate a variegated set of beliefs and practices. Hinduism can thus be understood as a unified and continuous religious tradition in terms of the particular sources and strategies used to establish, legitimate, and maintain its religious authority. The most common way Hindus of various sorts do this is to appeal to the authority of the Veda, the most ancient and most universally acknowledged of Hinduism's sacred texts. Hinduism, then, might be envisaged as the label for those traditions that legitimate themselves through the authority of the Veda. Traditions that deny the sacrality and authority of the Veda and posit alternative sources of such authority (those traditions called Buddhist, Muslim, Christian, Sikh, and so on) are, for this reason, not Hindu. Although the subject matter of the Vedic texts is not always, or even usually, of importance to any given Hindu sect or tradition, the legitimating authority of the Veda has been one, and perhaps the only, mark of orthodoxy in the long history of this complex group of Indic traditions.

Hinduism has had an incalculable impact on Indian society. Indeed, some modern religious nationalists in India would argue that Indian and Hindu culture and history are synonymous, although this turns a blind eye to the enormous contribution of Muslims and others who are, under virtually any definition, not Hindus. Nevertheless, in virtually all areas of Indian society and culture, including social structure, art, music, architecture, literature, and government, Hinduism has left its imprint, such that India cannot really be understood without some understanding of its majority religion.

## Historical Overview

Most scholars trace the earliest origins of Hinduism to two different sources. The first of these is the Indus Valley civilization, which dates back to the third millennium B.C.E. and reaches its high point around 2000 B.C.E. The characteristics of this civilization remain somewhat elusive, since the inscriptions on the artifacts that have been recovered remain undeciphered. Nevertheless, on the basis of both large-scale and small-scale remains, scholars have postulated that certain features of later Hinduism may have their earliest foundations and expressions in the Indus Valley civilization. These features include the emphasis on ritual purity, the worship of a goddess figure connected to fertility, and the sacrality of certain animals and trees. The most famous of the depictions found on seals dug up at the various archeological sites is what has been called proto-Shiva. A horned figure, surrounded by animals and sitting in what appears to be a yogic position with an erect phallus, seems to indicate a possible connection to the later Hindu deity who is similarly conceptualized and symbolically represented.

The second root of Hinduism is the Aryans or Indo-Europeans who, it is thought, began to enter the Indic subcontinent from the northwest in several migratory waves beginning sometime in the second millennium B.C.E. The South Asian branch of the far-flung Indo-European peoples is associated with the Vedic period of Indian history. Named after the texts called the Vedas (or, collectively, the Veda), which are written in Sanskrit, this historical epoch is known to us almost entirely on the basis of those ancient texts. The Vedas depict a religion entirely oriented to the performance of and philosophical speculations concerning fire sacrifice. Sacrifices, or *yajna*s, were offered to the pantheon of deities located in one or another of the three worlds of sky, atmosphere, and earth; some of the gods of the later Hindu pantheon were already worshipped in the Vedic era. Sacrifices to the gods were performed with oblations of cakes made of grain but also with animals (goats, rams, bulls, stallions, and, at least theoretically, human males) and with the apparently intoxicating juices from the plant known as soma.

The basic assumption of the Vedic sacrifice was that if the gods were pleased through such offerings, the cosmos would be put into order and beneficial results would be procured by the sacrificer. These results included prosperity of all sorts, worldly success and fame, long life, and a place in heaven after death. As time went on, it seems as though the sacrifice took on power of its own, apart from the will and favor of the gods. If the ritual was performed correctly by the Brahman priests, who knew all the rules of the sacrifice, results would occur automatically.

Also over time, an increasing emphasis seems to have been put not only on the simple performance of the ritual but also on mystical knowledge of the hidden meanings of or connections between the sacrifice, the cosmos, and the individual. These speculations reached their apogee in the middle centuries of the first millennium B.C.E. as is recorded in the texts known as the Upanishads. Mystical knowledge or wisdom (*jnana*) in these texts supersedes ritual action (karma) as the way to attain the highest goal, now conceived of not as a place in heaven but rather as the realization of one's true nature, expressed in the equation between one's true self (*atman*) and the underlying cosmic unity (*brahman*).

The Upanishads are also associated with a world-renunciatory movement of the middle centuries of the first millennium B.C.E. that also brought Buddhism and Jainism into being. For the renouncers, ascetics, and mystics of this period, the Vedic sacrifice was regarded as, at best, of lesser importance than practices associated with self-discipline, meditation, yoga, and renunciation of ritual and worldly pursuits. Action, or *karma,* especially when motivated by desire, was seen as problematic in that it was supposed to result in repeated, and potentially endless, rebirth. The world was seen as a place of suffering and imprisonment, and a new goal, release from this wheel of birth, death, and rebirth, was posited.

As a result both of challenges within the tradition (the world-renouncing strains that were manifest in the Upanishads) and without (the heterodox traditions of Buddhism, Jainism, and other new religions), Hinduism was reformulated. Texts dating to around 400 B.C.E. and those produced subsequently over the course of several centuries reflect characteristic and definitive shifts in the religion. Among these was a sense of orthodoxy, which can be seen both in the way the Vedas were now understood as revealed, or *shruti,* and in the religio-social importance given to caste and the hierarchically superior place of the Brahmans. Especially important was the concept of *dharma,* or religious duty, and the reinstatement of religious value to worldly life. From this time on, Hinduism has harbored within itself both an emphasis on doing one's duty in the world and the importance of renouncing the world.

By the early centuries of the first millennium C.E. can be seen the earliest manifestations of another development within the increasingly variegated mix of traditions collectively called Hinduism. This was the rise of a new form of theistic religion called the *bhakti* movement, which brought with it the rise to supreme importance of the major deities of the Hindu pantheon, especially Vishnu (in all his incarnations, including Krishna and Rama), Shiva, and the various forms of the Goddess. The first temples where such deities were worshipped date to this period, as do Sanskrit and Tamil texts that center on one or another of these principal divinities. From this time forth, in addition to the notion (dating to the Upanishads) that the divine is "without qualities" (*nirguna*), one finds within Hinduism the conceptualization of God "with qualities" (*saguna*) and the representation of the divine in the form of images.

Dating also to this period is another widespread and influential movement that would add yet another ingredient to Hinduism. This movement, itself varied in its beliefs and practices, has been called Tantrism. Originating perhaps in the peripheral areas of northwest and northeast India, Tantric ideas and practices probably date to the fifth century C.E. or before, although most of the texts in which the distinctive doctrines of this strain within Hinduism appear are several centuries later. With an emphasis on radical and unconventional methods (including, in some cases, ritual sex) for attaining liberation in the present lifetime, and with an array of deities—almost always including a goddess figure—often depicted in quite horrific forms, the Tantric movement was always esoteric and controversial. Nevertheless, by the medieval period and in subsequent centuries Tantrism influenced all forms of Hinduism. It has been noted that the pantheon of present-day Hinduism is largely made up of Tantric deities. Tantrism also left its imprint on the temples, iconography, and rituals of the more mainstream Hinduism.

The mainstream—by which is usually meant the elite, Sanskritic tradition of orthodox or Brahmanic Hinduism—was philosophically systematized beginning in the early centuries of the first millennium C.E. into six schools. Perhaps the most influential of these is Vedanta and its greatest teacher was Shankara (c. 800 C.E.). Based on a particular reading of the earliest Upanishads, the Vedanta philosophy in all its forms (and there are several) argues for some version of monism and regards the phenomenal world of experience as fundamentally illusory. The philosophical schools of Yoga and Samkhya, by way of contrast, envision a kind of dualism between matter and spirit and see the goal of the religious quest as the isolation of the pure spirit. Other and less influential of the philosophical schools emphasize analysis of Vedic ritual and ritual speech (Mimamsa), logic and methods of argumentation (Nyaya), and a theory of atomism (Vaisheshika).

The second millennium C.E. saw the further development of *bhakti,* or devotional, forms of Hinduism, especially among poet-saints, who composed often ecstatic songs and poems in the vernacular languages of India. These poet-saints sometimes included women and members of the lower castes, and in general the devotional movement became more and more the religion of the Hindu masses. As Muslim influence and eventually rule was established in north India, syncretistic devotional figures and groups emerged. The *bhakti* of a saint like Kabir (1440–1518), for example, was heavily influenced by Islamic monotheism, iconoclasm, and other concepts.

The European impact on Hinduism came primarily in the form of British imperialism and colonialism. Modern Hinduism, especially as it is conceptualized by the educated elite of India, was shaped by the interactions and dialectical relations between outside influences and rising nationalist aspirations. Nineteenth-century reformers such as Rammohan Roy, Dayananda Sarasvati, and Vivekananda created what has sometimes been called Neo-Hinduism in an effort to modernize and respond to the challenges of Western colonialism while retaining pride in the traditions of ancient Hinduism. The reforming impulse put into motion by these leaders and others has also sometimes been labeled the back-to-the-Vedas movement because of its emphasis on returning to the ancient past's purity to validate innovations such as rights for women, opposition to image worship, and caste reform.

In the twentieth century, two different and contrasting influences have exerted influence on the shape of Hinduism. On the one hand, Mohandas Gandhi (1869–1948; the Mahatma, or Great Soul) put forward an inclusive, tolerant Hinduism that picked up one strand of the ancient past: the non-violence and self-control of the world-renouncers. On the other hand, the twentieth century also saw the rise of an often militant form of Hindu nationalism that emphasized an exclusivist Hinduism and valorized powerful Hindu kings of the past and divine ruler-warriors like the god Rama.

### Sacred Texts and Sects

The Veda are earliest texts of Hinduism. Written in Sanskrit and for millennia preserved only orally, the oldest portion of the Veda—the Rig Veda, composed about 1200 B.C.E. or before—is also among the oldest known texts of the Indo-European world.

The Vedas are entirely centered on the performance of and speculations surrounding the ancient religion of the Aryans in India, the cult of fire sacrifice. Each of the four Vedas—the Rig, Yajur, Sama, and Atharva—consists of a Samhita (collection of hymns, verses, and chants), a Brahmana (in which the mythical origins, contexts, and meanings of the ritual are explained), an Aranyaka (a forest text, where the more esoteric and secret significances of the rites are detailed), and an Upanishad (comprised of mystical speculations and philosophical ruminations). The Samhitas of the four Vedas are correlated to the functions of the four main priests of the Vedic sacrifice and were composed and preserved by these priests for ritual use. Each of the four Vedas has several recensions due to the varying practices of different ritual schools; some of these recensions have survived—completely or in fragments—and many have not.

The Veda is traditionally thought to be unauthored (either by a god or humans); rather, it is believed to exist eternally in the form of sound. Ancient sages are said to have heard it (or

part of it) and then recited it to others. The Veda was, and continues to be, memorized syllable by syllable and transmitted orally by means of an intricate method of recitation. Although ancient India had a writing system by the middle of the first millennium B.C.E., it was only in relatively recent times that the oral Veda was written down.

Hinduism traditionally accorded the Vedic texts the status of revelation, or *shruti*. All the other sacred texts of Hinduism, no matter the esteem in which they are held by their adherents, are technically classified not as revelation but only as traditional or remembered (*smriti*). The *smriti* texts are admittedly authored by great teachers of the past.

The earliest of the traditional texts are collectively known as the Vedangas or limbs of the Veda. Composed mainly from about 700 B.C.E. to about 200 C.E., these works were technical treatises written in the shorthand, aphoristic form called the *sutra*. The Vedangas make up the six sciences necessary for the correct and exact performance of the Vedic rituals: *vyakarana* (the study of grammar, linguistics, and philology); *nirukta* (etymology); *chanda* (the explanation and practice of verse meters); *shiksha* (the study of faultless pronunciation); and *jyotisha* (the science of astronomy and astrology). The sixth limb of the Veda is the Kalpa Sutras, manuals in which the rules for performing the various types of Vedic sacrifice are given. The Shrauta Sutras lay out the rules for performing the most elaborate of these sacrifices, and the Grhya Sutras detail the protocol for executing the simpler rites of the domestic ceremonial performed by the householder himself. Also included are the Shulba Sutras, in which geometrical rules are laid out for the proper construction of the sacred space and altars of the Vedic ritual.

The last component of a Kalpa Sutra (and again, different versions of these texts were composed and preserved by a variety of ritual schools) is the Dharma Sutra (also known as the Dharma Shastra, or Teaching, or the Dharma Smriti). These encyclopedic texts extend the rules governing human activity, which were previously confined to the ritual sphere, to nearly every aspect of daily life, and especially concentrate on the specific obligations or duties (*dharma*) one has as a member of a particular social class or caste at various stages of life.

The *sutra* form was also favored by the authors of several other important texts. The Mimamsa Sutras, attributed to Jaimini and dated at about 200 B.C.E., is the root text of the philosophical school of Mimamsa, or enquiry into the cosmic and moral significance of the Vedic sacrifice. The Yoga Sutras of Patanjali (c. 200–300 C.E.) are the first systematic presentation of the practice and theory of yoga, or psycho-physical discipline. And the Vedanta Sutras of the great teacher Shankara (c. early ninth century C.E.), which are actually commentaries on an earlier text, form the most important enunciation of the highly influential Hindu philosophical tradition known as Advaita Vedanta, which teaches an absolute monistic doctrine of the oneness of all being.

Among the most popular and best-known of the Hindu scriptures are the two great epics *The Mahabharata* and *The Ramayana*. Both of these enormous works (*The Mahabharata* is a collection of over 100,000 stanzas and *The Ramayana* is about one-fourth of that) were composed, in various recensions, over a period of almost a thousand years between approximately 400 B.C.E. and approximately 400 C.E. Both consist of a heterogeneous assortment of material—mythology, pseudo-historical lore, folktales, teachings concerning religious duty, the meaning of life, and salvation—but both also relate narratives that have come to be regarded as the backbone of the Indian cultural heritage.

*The Mahabharata* claims to be divinely inspired and all-encompassing. The text tells the story of a legendary battle for rule over India fought between two sides of the same family. After many twists and turns in the plot, the warring parties meet at the battlefield for the climactic battle. It is at this point in the story that perhaps the single most popular Hindu text and one of the world's greatest religious works is found. *The Bhagavad Gita,* or Song of the Lord, is a discussion of duty and faith conducted by one of the warriors, Arjuna, and his charioteer, Krishna—who is, the reader learns in the course of the text, God in human form.

*The Ramayana,* attributed to the seer Valmiki, is the story of Rama, the Prince of Ayodhya: his birth and childhood, his marriage to Sita, his unjust banishment and exile into the wilderness, Sita's abduction by the wicked Ravana, Rama's battle with and defeat of Ravana and his rescue of Sita, and Rama's triumphant return to Ayodhya as king. Whereas the characters in *The Mahabharata* tend to be flawed in various ways, Rama and Sita are widely regarded as ideals of obedience, loyalty, fidelity, strength, courage, and heroism. Both of the great Hindu epics were traditionally recited by bards at the courts of kings but were also often recited or dramatically enacted for the masses as religious performance and popular entertainment. Both have also been made into television serials and videotapes, thus metamorphosing into a somewhat different kind of sacred text.

Beginning in the early middle centuries of the Common Era, Sanskrit texts that codified the worldviews, doctrines, and practices of the various Hindu theistic sects were composed. Chief among these are the Puranas (Stories of antiquity). Centering on one or another of the principal deities of sectarian Hinduism—Vishnu, Shiva, or the Goddess—these texts are traditionally said to comprise five topics: the creation of the world, the dissolution of the world, the ages of the world, genealogies, and the history of dynasties. In actuality, however, the Puranas are as encyclopedic as the epics, replete with all sorts of myths, legends, didactic passages on religious duty and salvation, ritual instructions for temple and image worship, and tales about holy places and pilgrimage sites. Early-twenty-first-century scholarship has indicated that most, if not all, of the Puranas were composed under the auspices of one or another ruler of particular Hindu kingdoms by priests associated with the dominant sect of the region.

Other sectarian texts are known by different names. The 108 sacred texts of the Vaishnava sect known as the Pancaratras are designated Samhitas (collection of hymns, verses, and chants) or Agamas; certain sects worshipping the god Shiva have also produced texts called Agamas; and sects worshipping

one or another form of the goddess have composed Tantras—sectarian treatises that are similar in content and purpose to the Puranas but tend to be more purely theological in their orientation and to specify ritual practices to be followed in the temple and at home.

Whereas all the literature discussed above is in Sanskrit, the sacred texts of what might be called popular Hinduism were composed in one or another of the vernacular languages of South Asia. Among the most important of these are the Tamil works of the poet-saints who served as figureheads for the devotional, and often ecstatic and emotional, movements that began in South India as early as the seventh century C.E. Led by the devotees of Vishnu known as the Alvars and the worshippers of Shiva called the Nayanmars, the devotional movement became popular and spread throughout India. The poems and songs of later Hindu saints of north India—Kabir, Caitanya (1485–1533), Surdas (1485–1563), Mirabai (sixteenth century), and others—also depict the longing for God and the bliss of union with the divine in simple yet moving terms.

## Principal Beliefs

While it is difficult to list doctrines that *all* Hindus and Hindu traditions would accept, there is a group of core beliefs that come close to being universally shared by all those called "Hindu."

*Karma and Rebirth.* The original meaning of the word *karma* is "work," and the earliest application of the term in Vedic texts is "ritual action or labor"—that is, correctly and precisely executed activity that will have a salutary effect on the participants of the ritual and on the universe as a whole. Rituals beginning with the *samskaras*, rites of passage performed at critical junctures in the life of a youth, had as their purpose to repair the imperfections of birth. Ritual work thus also consisted of the construction of a religiously viable self, and while Vedic fire sacrifices tended to be eclipsed by other forms of religious practice in later Hinduism, the performance of the *samskaras* has continued to the present day and is done for much the same reason. Finally, already in the Vedic period, ritual work was also the means for creating a desirable afterlife for oneself. A divine, or heavenly, self is "born out of the sacrifice"—that is, it is the product of one's ritual résumé, of the work one has done throughout one's lifetime.

The notion that one's own ritual acts (for in Vedic times these were the only acts that really mattered) had consequences—in the future as well as the present—is one of the possible sources for a doctrine that was to have huge implications for the Hindu religious worldview: the notion that all actions produced fruit, good or bad, that determined the quality of one's life. This causal and moral law of karma first appears in the early Upanishads and also features as a prominent doctrine in the new religions that arose in India at this time, Buddhism and Jainism. From this time forward, the nature of one's actions—and the attitude with which actions were performed—was believed to have determinative consequences over one's future, both in this lifetime and in future rebirths.

This concept of a "law of karma"—whereby good acts result in good results, bad in bad—extends the Vedic notion of consequential action from the confines of the ritual to the whole of life. Just as in the Vedic period one's future life is the product of one's activity, here too one's rebirth is directly correlated to actions performed in this life. But the law of karma also presupposes a series of past lives; the deeds done in those lives determine the circumstances of one's present existence. And the theory assumes future lives, not just in heavens or hells but in this world or any of a potentially infinite number of world systems. Finally, it presupposes that one may be reborn in any of these locales as any number of entities, ranging from gods to inanimate objects; good karma obviously would entail a better rebirth, bad karma results in a worse existence.

***Dharma and the Varnashrama Dharma system.*** Another key concept of Hinduism, and one that is closely connected to those of karma and rebirth, is dharma, a multivalent term that includes within its semantic range religion or righteousness, but also duty. Doing one's dharma means not only remaining ethical but also assuming the duties that are proper to the class or caste one is born into (due to one's past karma), and to the stage of life one is presently in. Performing one's own duty (*svadharma*), as it has been assigned to by birth and by the stage of life, has traditionally been an important Hindu ideal: "Your own duty done imperfectly is better than another man's done well. It is better to die in one's own duty; another man's duty is perilous" (*Bhagavad Gita*, 3.35).

The doctrine of *svadharma*, backed up by the concepts of karma and rebirth, underlies one of the most important and enduring institutions of Hindu India, the caste system. Inequalities in the present life are regarded as a result of differing past karma, and the inequalities of a projected future will reflect the rewards and punishments of actions done in the present: "Now people here whose behavior is pleasant can expect to enter a pleasant womb, like that of a woman of the Brahman [the priestly class], the Ksatriya [the warrior class], of the Vaisya [agriculturalist and trader] class. But people of foul behavior can expect to enter a foul womb, like that of a dog, a pig, or an outcaste woman" (Chandogya Upanishad, 5.10.7).

From the time of the Veda onward, the four basic classes of Hindu society—Brahmans, Kshatriyas, Vaishyas, and Shudras (servants)—were assigned specific roles and functions and urged not to deviate from such in-born duties. The naturalness of this arrangement—or even its divine sanction—was asserted in part by integrating the origins of the social classes within stories about the cosmos's origins. The most famous of the texts in which the social classes are depicted as part of the original creation is Rig Veda 10.90, which tells of the universe originating from a primordial sacrifice of God, here called the Cosmic Man. From that sacrifice and dismemberment, the various elements of the cosmos came into being: the worlds, the sun and moon, the seasons, the various types of supernatural beings, the animals, and so forth. The social classes originated then, brought forth from the parts of the body of the creator god: "When they divided the Cosmic Man, into how many parts did they apportion him? What do they call his mouth, his two arms and thighs and feet? His mouth became the Brahmin; his arms were made into the Kshatriya; his thighs

the Vaishya; and from his feet the Shudras were born" (Rig Veda, 10.90.11–12).

Such is the basic outline of the caste system: four principal classes, each with its own assigned occupation, hierarchically ranked (and correlated with the appropriate body part of the creator god). At the top is the class whose job concerns the religious sphere; the Brahman priest is, according to the texts (not coincidentally composed by members of this class), to be regarded as a kind of human god. The Kshatriyas are to be rulers and warriors and engage in the activities appropriate to their birth. As for the commoners, they are to pursue occupations concerned with wealth and prosperity, tending to livestock and trade. The servants' duties and occupations are straightforward: to humbly serve members of the higher classes and hope for a better rebirth. Finally, there are the occupations of those who live below this hierarchy, the so-called untouchables, who are below even the servants.

Dharma, or proper duty, is thus differentiated according to class and caste but also according to stage of life. The first stage in the ideal structure laid out in Hindu texts is that of a student. A young boy is given over to a teacher, or guru, with whom he lives and serves for a period of many years while studying the sacred Veda under the teacher's guidance. The lifestyle assigned to this stage of life is one of austerity, asceticism, and discipline. Among the other duties laid out for those in the student stage of life are chastity, study of the sacred texts, and obedience to the teacher.

The next stage of life, that of the householder, begins when the student leaves his teacher's home, marries, and takes up his proper profession. In the householder stage of life, he properly pursues not only dharma (used here in the specific sense of religious duties) but also the human ends of *artha*—private gain, understood as material prosperity, self-interest, political advantage, and in general getting ahead in the world—and *kama* or pleasure. The householder is charged with supporting not just his household but also other community members through alms and other gifts to those in other stages of life.

After having raised a family as a householder, a man may enter the third stage of life as what is called a forest-dweller. This stage is characterized by ascetic practices and gradual detachment from the world, including the renunciation of cultivated food (he should live on food that grows in the jungle) and of "all possessions":

> After he has lived in the householder's stage of life in accordance with the rules in this way, a twice-born Vedic graduate should live in the forest, properly restrained and with his sensory powers conquered. . . . When a householder sees that he is wrinkled and gray, and (when he sees) the children of his children, then he should take himself to the wilderness. Renouncing all food cultivated in the village and all possessions, he should hand his wife over to his sons and go to the forest—or take her along . . . . He should eat vegetables that grow on land or in water, flowers, roots, and fruits, the products of pure trees, and the oils from fruits. . . . He should

not eat anything grown from land tilled with a plough, even if someone has thrown it out, nor roots and fruits grown in a village, even if he is in distress [from hunger]. (Manu, 6.1–3, 13, 16)

The final stage of life is that of the world-renouncer, who continues and furthers the ascetic practices of the forest-dweller. In this stage, the wandering hermit should live entirely detached from the things of this world, alone and without companionship, perfectly content and in a state of equanimity. He should beg but once a day, and not be "addicted to food," hope for lots of alms, or be disappointed should he receive nothing:

He should always go all alone, with no companion, to achieve success; realizing that success is for the man who is alone, he neither deserts nor is deserted. The hermit should have no fire and no home, but should go to a village to get food, silent, indifferent, unwavering and deep in concentration. A skull-bowl, the roots of trees, poor clothing, no companionship, and equanimity to everything—this is the distinguishing mark of one who is freed. He should not welcome dying, nor should he welcome living, but wait for the right time as a servant waits for orders. . . . He should live here on earth seated in ecstatic contemplation of the soul, indifferent, without any carnal desires, with the soul as his only companion and happiness as his goal. . . . He should go begging once a day and not be eager to get a great quantity, for an ascetic who is addicted to food becomes attached to sensory objects, too. . . . He should not be sad when he does not get anything nor delighted when he gets something, but take only what will daily sustain his vital breath, transcending any attachment to material things. (Manu, 6.42-45; 49; 55; 57)

***Samsara, liberation, and the ways to attain liberation.*** Yet another central concept in Hinduism is the notion that perpetual birth, death, and rebirth occur not just at the level of human beings but of the universe as a whole. The Sanskrit name for this theory is *samsara,* a word that literally means to wander or pass through a series of states or conditions. Samsara describes the beginningless and endless cycle of cosmic or universal death and rebirth; all of phenomenal existence is transient, ever-changing, and cyclical. Correlative to this understanding of the world is belief in the fundamentally illusory nature of the world of appearances—a concept known in Hinduism as *maya.* It is because one is ignorant of reality's true nature that one perceives a world of differentiation and change; and it is through our own ignorance that we suffer and produce karma.

Samsara is contrasted to an unconditioned, eternal, and transcendent state that is equated with freedom or liberation from such ignorance, transience, suffering, and rebirth. All Hindu traditions posit an alternative to karma and rebirth and the wheel of samsara. This state of release, freedom, or liberation from karma and rebirth is called *moksha.* To obtain this liberation, most Hindu traditions believe that one must find a way to stop the workings of karma and the ignorant desire

that motivates ordinary action. Among the various groups of world-renouncers that have arisen in the history of Hinduism, a kind of pessimism surrounds the value of worldly life. Release from the wheel of phenomenal existence among these groups often entails eliminating desire through ascetic practices and renouncing the world of ordinary activity:

On knowing him [the true self], one becomes an ascetic. Desiring him only as their home, mendicants wander forth. Verily, because they know this, the ancients desired not offspring, saying: "What shall we do with offspring, we whose is this Soul, this world?" They, verily, rising above the desire for sons and the desire for wealth and the desire for worlds, lived the life of a mendicant. For the desire for sons is the desire for wealth, and the desire for wealth is the desire for worlds; for both these are desires. (Brhadaranyaka Upanishad, 4.4.22)

Another strategy for eliminating karma and its bonds to samsara was the development of the discipline called yoga. Yoga was intended to calm the mind and body, obtain equanimity and tranquility, by ceasing to act ("curbing his movements," as the text below states) and focusing the mind:

When he keeps his body straight, with the three sections erect, and draws the senses together with the mind into his heart, a wise man shall cross all the frightful rivers. . . . Compressing his breaths in here and curbing his movements, a man should exhale through one nostril when his breath is exhausted. A wise man should keep his mind vigilantly under control, just as he would that wagon yoked to unruly horses. (Svetesvatara Upanishad, 2.8–9)

Yet another method to final liberation within the traditions that comprise Hinduism is the development of wisdom, or *jnana.* The path of wisdom requires, first and foremost, that one understand properly the nature of the universe. In the monistic philosophy first encountered in the Upanishads and later forming one of the principal schools of Hindu philosophy, *jnana* means penetrating the illusory appearance of the world as differentiated, and attaining a mystical wisdom of the unitary true nature of the universe and all that is in it. Attaining such transformative wisdom is itself equated with *moksha,* or liberation—liberation from ignorance, and also liberation from karma.

True knowledge is the knowledge of the true self's unity and identity (the *atman*) with the cosmic One, the *brahman.* Both the real self (which is not the individual ego but one's changeless true nature) and the cosmic One are depicted as unborn, unchanging, and therefore not affected by karma: "Verily, he is the great, unborn Soul, who is this [person] consisting of knowledge among the senses. In the space within the heart lies the ruler of all, the lord of all, the king of all. He does not become greater by good action nor inferior by bad action" (Brhadaranyaka Upanisad, 4.4.22). Wisdom acts as a kind of fire that burns up the individual's accumulated past karma, and uproots desire, which is the very source of karma and the rebirths it provokes.

Another strand within the Hindu tradition also accepts the necessity for wisdom and self-discipline to attain the final goal but denies that action can simply be avoided or somehow arrested. The point is not to renounce society and duty but rather to attain a desireless state within the world of activity. Although upholding the doctrine of duty, or *svadharma, The Bhagavad Gita* also teaches that such actions should be performed without desire. Since desire is the root cause of karma, desireless action in accordance with one's dharma will have no karmic consequences. Such a person is said to be truly wise, like the world-renouncers, but unlike them does not abandon action but rather performs it in the right way.

Also in *The Bhagavad Gita* are found the earliest expressions in the Sanskrit texts of what would become an enormously influential movement in Hinduism, that of devotion to a personalized deity. The theistic strains within Hinduism emphasize a different method to liberation, that of *bhakti,* or devotion to and faith in God. In the *Gita,* desireless action is also represented as sacrificial action, with the karmic fruits of all acts being given up to God. It is, finally, devotion, or *bhakti,* to Krishna that the *Gita* teaches is the way to salvation:

Whatever you do—what you take, what you offer, what you give, what penances you perform—do as an offering to me, Arjuna! You will be freed from the bonds of action, from the fruit of fortune and misfortune; armed with the discipline of renunciation, your self liberated, you will join me. (*Bhagavad Gita,* 9.27–28)

The devotionalistic wings of Hinduism, with their array of deities, each one regarded by devotees as supreme, all assume that it is by God's grace that suffering can be overcome and salvation made possible. In some of its forms, the *bhakti* movement seems to have attracted many low caste followers and others who had been left out or diminished by caste-oriented Hinduism. The movement's emphasis on simple devotion, humility, and the power of God's grace to redeem even the sinner had obvious appeal, and the power attributed to *bhakti* to short-circuit the karmic process is often said to be enormous and unfathomable. The *bhakti* movement also reinterpreted a long-standing Hindu belief that desire was the product of ignorance and the root of karma, rebirth, and suffering. For in devotionalistic traditions, longing for God—often portrayed in erotic terms—and the pain of separation from the object of desire become the emotional means for ratcheting up one's devotion to fever pitch. At the same time, most devotionalistic cults eschewed the goal of merging with or achieving identity with the object of their devotion, for that would preclude the bliss of remaining distinct while basking in God's love.

The set of traditions collectively termed Tantrism likewise reworked desire from its conceptualization as the ultimate source of human suffering into a religious tool. Esoteric tantric groups gained notoriety for their radical and transgressive methods, often arguing that the best way to attain liberation from suffering and its causes was not to renounce but rather to confront them and, under ritual conditions, engage in practices that for the uninitiated would result in the most disastrous karmic ends. Through various meditative and ritual techniques, the tantric practitioner could practice what others prohibited and could eradicate desire by means of desire.

For some tantric groups, methods to liberation included antisocial ascetic practices such as eschewing clothing and ordinary hygiene, meditating in cemeteries, carrying human skulls as begging bowls, practices involving human corpses, and the worship of deities in gruesome, terrifying forms. For others, it has meant engaging in ritualized sex and exchange of bodily fluids, or rituals that call for the ingestion of otherwise prohibited substances. In all cases, the purpose of such antinomian behavior seems to have been in one way or another to transcend the world of dualities (including pure/impure, good/bad) and achieve the liberation from samsara all Hindu groups posit as the highest goal.

For most Hindus, however, final liberation seems to be out of reach in this life. The vast majority, past and present, simply try to live virtuously and obtain, as a result, a pleasant life here on earth and a better rebirth in the future. From Vedic times to the present, rituals such as sacrifice and the worship service known as *puja* (performed either in the temple or at home), whereby one ritually honors the deity in the form of an image, had pleasing the gods as their goal in the hopes that the gods would protect and aid the worshipper. Festivals, pilgrimages, and lifecycle rituals are also popular among ordinary Hindus, as they are among religious practitioners the world over. Although religious virtuosi may follow the various methods laid out to attain the highest ends of Hinduism, the vast majority of Hindus content themselves with more modest goals.

*See also* **Buddhism; Christianity; Islam; Jainism; Judaism; Religion.**

**BIBLIOGRAPHY**

Embree, Ainslie T., ed. *Sources of Indian Tradition.* Vol. 1: *From the Beginning to 1800.* 2nd ed. New York: Columbia University Press, 1988.

Herman, A. L. *A Brief Introduction to Hinduism: Religion, Philosophy, and Ways of Liberation.* Boulder, Colo.: Westview, 1991.

Hopkins, Thomas J. *The Hindu Religious Tradition.* Encino, Calif.: Dickenson, 1971.

Kinsley, David R. *Hinduism: A Cultural Perspective.* 2nd ed. Englewood Cliffs, N.J.: Prentice Hall, 1993.

Klostermaier, Klaus K. *A Survey of Hinduism.* Albany: State University of New York Press, 1989.

*The Laws of Manu.* Translated by Wendy Doniger, with Brian K. Smith. London, New York: Penguin Books, 1991.

*Brian Smith*

# HISTORICAL AND DIALECTICAL MATERIALISM.

Historical and dialectical materialism are doctrines in the philosophy of history and in metaphysics, respectively. They were developed within the Marxist tradition and refer to ideas found in the works of Karl Marx (1818–1883). However, neither term

**Friedrich Engels (1820–1895).** Engels, a friend and collaborator of Karl Marx, believed that the concept of private property was to blame for all the problems of society. He authored several publications espousing scientific socialism, including the *Communist Manifesto* which he cowrote with Marx.

was used or endorsed by him explicitly, and the relationship between those doctrines and his writings has always been problematic. In recent years scholarship has clarified these questions considerably. While in the later twentieth century dialectical materialism all but faded away, historical materialism has had a remarkable revival in an "analytical" form.

## Engels and Marxism

Marx's friend and sometime collaborator Friedrich Engels (1820–1895) coined the term *materialist conception of history* (later shortened to historical materialism). In a review (1859) of the first published version of Marx's critique of contemporary economic science, Engels strove to introduce Marx to the public as a powerful intellect and polymathic systematizer. In his short narrative, Engels simplified a selection of Marx's ideas and presented them in a doctrinal form. In Engels's account Marx was said to have a method coincident with both Hegelian philosophy and contemporary physical science. On the latter point Engels identified Marx with a mechanistic materialism of matter-in-motion, and on the former with "dialectical" thought that was said to mirror this ontological universal. Engels repeated those views much more famously in his *Anti-Dühring* (1878; excerpted as *Socialism: Utopian and Scientific,* 1880) and *Ludwig Feuerbach and the End of Classical German Philosophy* (1886).

Marxism as a comprehensive worldview, allegedly based on these twin pillars of materialism, was developed only after

Engels's death. This doctrine was said to be applicable to human history and to unify philosophical with scientific thinking. It attracted numerous adherents in the intellectual world and drew millions into political movements. This process was abetted by even simpler versions, such as those by Georgi Plekhanov, V. I. Lenin, Nikolai Bukharin, Joseph Stalin, and Mao Zedong. Further millions learned this kind of Marxism from anti-Marxists pursuing an opposing politics. However, Marx and Engels were by no means completely known quantities because further works from both appeared posthumously during the twentieth century, and the complete works are not yet published in full. Engels's notebooks on "dialectics" were published in 1927 as *Dialectics of Nature,* and were said to account for nature in a way consistent with the work that he had left on history (summarized as historical materialism) and on thought itself (a vastly simplified reworking of Hegelian logic). Dialectical materialism (or "dialectics" or *diamat*) was thus said by the 1930s to be the master doctrine of Marxism, summarized into three laws: transformation of quantity into quality, interpenetration of opposites, and negation of the negation. Overall it was a doctrine of "becoming" rather than "being" in a fixed and static sense, and one that emphasized development and progress through contradictions, whether in logical relations or in political struggles. Historical materialism was a specially interesting instance of this overall view, given its directly political character.

## Economics, History, and Materialism

The political character of historical materialism derives from its narrative history of civilization, and the special role assigned to "relations of production" and technological change within it. Matter-in-motion does not figure in this account, except as an unacknowledged ontological presumption. Rather the materialism operative in the doctrine is transformed metaphorically into a selective focus on the human activities ordinarily termed "economic," that is, the production, consumption, distribution, and exchange of the "material" means of life. Linking those activities with materialism played on the material qualities of economic goods, associating them in turn with what is basic and indispensable for human life. This doctrine further suggests that the economic activities associated with goods of this kind are more real and therefore have more explanatory power than anything else, particularly "mere" ideas or thoughts. Religion, utopianism, "good intentions," morality, and moralizing were commonly cited by Marxists as "superstructural," as opposed to the material "foundation" or "basis" in economic activities regarded as "determining." The base/superstructure distinction is itself a metaphor derived from Marx's own preface to his *A Contribution to the Critique of Political Economy* (1859), the occasion for Engels's original systematizing review.

In the *Preface* Marx offers a periodization of history in successive "modes of production." These were evidently based on composites of technology together with legal and property systems: Asiatic, ancient, feudal, and modern. Since some of these were coincident with others in the world at large, the schema does not represent a strict diachronic account of history, nor is it the case that all transitions were necessarily progressive. What is clear is that Marx regarded modern commercial and

**Karl Marx (1818–1883).** Marx strove to organize a movement of the working class predicated on the principles of communism. He believed that society was headed for eventual economic collapse and an overthrow of the capitalist ruling class. ARCHIVE PHOTOS

capital-accumulating societies as distinctly different from previous economic and political systems because they were so much more productive of goods and services and so continuously innovative. Moreover they seemed to him to be a prelude to a comprehensive economic collapse and a political struggle between contending socioeconomic classes. From that would come a vastly different society, which he variously termed communism or socialism. Alternatively, he wrote (with Engels) in the *Communist Manifesto* (1848), the result would be a "common ruin."

Marx's *Preface* also contained certain passages that were commonly interpreted as causal claims relevant to the social and political changes marking a transition, for example, from feudalism to capitalism: "At a certain stage of their development the material productive forces of society come into contradiction with the already existing relations of production. . . . From forms of development of the productive forces these relations turn into their fetters. Then an epoch of social revolution commences."

Technological innovations, and the introduction of "free" wage-labor and individualized "private" property, were the important elements through which this massive change was effected. Marx's conception was thus an ambitious attempt to recast history in terms of economic systems and economic

changes (rather than reigns, religions, empires, etc.). It also aimed to identify the most crucial changes in modern life and politics with the economic changes around and through which revolutionary political forces gathered, ushering in constitutional, liberal democratic, and "bourgeois" forms of government. Whether these phrases fit the "dialectics" espoused by Engels, who late in life supplemented this with a notion of "determinism in the last instance," or whether they fit instead some non-dialectical explanatory model favored by other writers, has been a recurrent issue within and about the Marxist tradition.

## Analytical Marxism and the Future

In the 1970s a group of self-styled "analytical Marxists" revitalized historical materialism by redefining it as a doctrine of historical explanation, but excising all aspects of "dialectics." The main historical theorist of the group was G. A. Cohen, who developed a reworded version of Marx's own views. He attempted to edit them stringently to fit what could be empirically demonstrated in history as true, and to relocate his views on forces and relations of production, base, and superstructure, within a functional understanding of explanation. Ultimately Cohen concluded that his attempt to rework Marx's conceptions and phrases in what he termed the most favorable light proved the theory a failure. In terms of contemporary historiography and philosophy, however, this had the effect of liberating Marx's ideas about history and progress from any indissoluble connection with an overarching "dialectical" doctrine.

Contemporary Hegelians are unlikely to be much interested in Engels's attempt to marry dialectical thought with matter-in-motion materialism, since the latter has little purchase in philosophy, history, or social science, and the former is very naive and banal, particularly compared with later idealist, phenomenological, and poststructural appropriations of Hegel. Historical materialism, however, has a brighter future, in so far as Marx's own enigmatic and ambiguous writings on history and politics will prove a source of continuing inspiration.

*See also* ***History, Idea of; Marxism; Socialism.***

**BIBLIOGRAPHY**

PRIMARY SOURCES

Engels, Friedrich. *Anti-Dühring.* In *Karl Marx and Frederick Engels: Collected Works.* Vol. 25. London: Lawrence and Wishart, 1987.

———. *Dialectics of Nature.* In *Karl Marx and Frederick Engels: Collected Works.* Vol. 25. London: Lawrence and Wishart, 1987.

———. *Ludwig Feuerbach and the End of Classical German Philosophy.* In *Karl Marx and Frederick Engels: Collected Works.* Vol. 26. London: Lawrence and Wishart, 1990.

———. *Review of Marx: A Contribution to the Critique of Political Economy.* In *Karl Marx and Frederick Engels: Collected Works.* Vol. 16. London: Lawrence and Wishart, 1980.

———. *Socialism: Utopian and Scientific.* In *Karl Marx and Frederick Engels: Collected Works.* Vol. 24. London: Lawrence and Wishart, 1989.

Marx, Karl. *Manifesto of the Communist Party* (with Friedrich Engels). In *Marx: Later Political Writings,* edited and translated by Terrell Carver. Cambridge, U.K., and New York: Cambridge University Press, 1996. Reprint, 2002.

———. "Preface to *A Contribution to the Critique of Political Economy.*" In *Marx: Later Political Writings,* edited and translated by Terrell Carver. Cambridge, U.K.: Cambridge University Press, 1996. Reprint, 2002.

SECONDARY SOURCES

Carver, Terrell. *Marx's Social Theory.* Oxford and New York: Oxford University Press, 1982.

Cohen, G. A. *Karl Marx's Theory of History: A Defence.* Oxford: Oxford University Press, 2000.

Giddens, Anthony. *A Contemporary Critique of Historical Materialism.* 2 vols. Cambridge, U.K.: Polity, 1985.

Jordan, Z. A. *The Evolution of Dialectical Materialism: A Philosophical and Sociological Analysis.* New York: St. Martin's, 1967.

Kolakowski, Leszek. *Main Currents of Marxism: Its Rise, Growth, and Dissolution.* Translated by P. S. Falla. 3 vols. Oxford: Oxford University Press, 1978.

Ruben, David-Hillel. *Marxism and Materialism: A Study in Marxist Theory of Knowledge.* Rev. ed. Brighton, U.K.: Harvester, 1979.

Wetter, Gustav A. *Dialectical Materialism: A Historical and Systematic Survey of Philosophy in the Soviet Union.* Translated by Peter Heath. London: Routledge and Kegan Paul, 1958.

Wilde, Lawrence. *Marx and Contradiction.* Aldershot, U.K., and Brookfield, Vt.: Avebury, 1989.

*Terrell Carver*

**HISTORICISM.** Historicism (German *Historismus,* French *historisme,* Italian *storicismo*) is a term of Romantic origins associated first with the German Historical Schools and then more generally with historical method as applied to all the arts and sciences and to human life. "Historicism" appeared first in a fragment of Novalis, who contrasted it with other methods (chemical, mathematical, artistic, etc.) and associated it with "the system of confusion." Contemporaneously Friedrich Schlegel associated *Historismus* with the modern science of philology. The word was occasionally used in philosophical polemics, and again the usage seems pejorative since it was opposed to academic philosophy and, especially, unhistorical Kantian idealism. Felix Dahn argued that "historicism is above all a methodological moment, not a speculative principle . . . ; its goal is [not philosophy but] life"; Christlieb Julius Braniss opposed it to the reductionist and deterministic philosophy of naturalism; and in 1879 Karl Werner applied the phrase "philosophical historicism" to the work of Giambattista Vico, a connection later endorsed by Benedetto Croce, Friedrich Meinecke, Erich Auerbach, and others. And in 1895 Lord Acton pointed to "that influence for which the depressing names historicism and historical-mindedness have been devised"—"all things," for him, including law, theology, science, and philosophy itself.

By the later nineteenth century historicism had acquired a largely pejorative meaning because of its associations with relativism and the threats posed to the assumptions and values of philosophy, theology, and economics, which represented three of the absolutes of Western culture, namely, reason, religion, and the free market. The attack began in the newly professionalized field of economics, especially in 1883 by Karl Menger's liberal assault on "the errors of historicism," that is, the irrational methods of Gustav Schmoller and other members of the so-called younger historical school of economics. In a sense this war of methods *(Methodenstreit)* recapitulated the struggles between the historical and philosophical schools in the nineteenth century, but now with the weaponry of modern positivism and quantitative techniques. Liberal rejection of historicism, indeed of historical method in any sense, has persisted in many areas of social sciences, as well as in the humanities, as in Russian formalism, structural linguistics, and the New Criticism.

**The Errors of Historicism**

In theology the errors of historicism were equally offensive. In the prewar years, religious controversies raged around the various forms of "modernism," which had been denounced in Pope Pius IX's "Syllabus of Errors" of 1864, accompanied by a whole list of other secularizing "-isms." Positivism, psychologism, and historicism all posed threats not only to traditional moral values but also to the validity of both reason and revelation. The historicizing of Christianity was the avowed aim of the historical school of religion *(religionsgeschichtliche Schule)* headed by Weber's friend Ernst Troeltsch, whose classic work, *Die Soziallehren der christlichen Kitchen und Gruppen* (1912; *The Social Teachings of the Christian Churches*), marked the intersection of the socioeconomic and theological problematics of historicism; and it, too, was carried on with heavy anxiety about questions of traditional norms and the elimination of metaphysical and metahistorical absolutes.

Philosophers had worried about the threat of history since the later eighteenth century, and their anxieties resurfaced in the early twentieth century as a "crisis of historicism." In 1910 Edmund Husserl denounced historicism as the enemy of "philosophy as a rigorous science." Martin Heidegger, following Friedrich Nietzsche's famous critique of "the use and abuse of history," contrasted it with true historicity *(Geschichtlichkeit)* grounded in contemporary existence. Like Braniss, Troeltsch opposed "historicism" to "naturalism" and traced this war of methods back to the seventeenth century with special reference to Vico's attack on Cartesianism; and he celebrated historicism for removing the "dead hand" of dogma while at the same time fearing the threat it posed to philosophical and moral tradition. Following Troeltsch, Karl Heussi distinguished between "history for the sake of history" *(l'histoire pour l'histoire),* relativism, radical evolutionism, and speculative philosophy of history, and analyzed them all under the rubric "the crisis of historicism."

Historicism represented a problem for all the human sciences and, for Karl Mannheim, a complete *Weltanschauung* beyond the level of conscious reflection or ideology, so that history itself was caught in its net. It served the modern dynamic world as "timeless reason" had served a more static world. As a counterpart to the older faith in reason, now itself historicized, historicism also needed to be the object of critical theory. Yet it was not absolute but only bound to assumptions of spatial, temporal, and material conditions that had undercut universalist conceptions. The virtue of historicism for Mannheim was that it set dynamism at the center of its conceptualizations instead of relativizing it as in "the old static system," and so made it "the Archimedean lever" for the modern worldview and life experience, that is, made it in effect the condition of human, historical, and indeed philosophical understanding.

Croce, following Vico and Hegel, thought that the Germans had not pushed historicism far enough. He rejected the claims of modern social science, such as those of Max Weber and Émile Durkheim, to universal status, regarding them all as open to contingency and subject to historical conditions. So were human values, and Croce had no fear that relativism was a major threat, since for him historicism was "a logical principle . . . , the very category of logic." In Germany historicism was the reigning condition of contemporary thought and life—and according to Croce's famous aphorism, "every true history is contemporary history." Indeed philosophy itself was "absolute historicism," so that historicism was not the source of the intellectual crisis of the twentieth century but rather its potential solution. Croce's views and prejudices were carried over into the Anglophone world by R. G. Collingwood, who translated his work and followed his interpretation of historiographical tradition and who turned back to the classical view of history as a form of "inquiry" into human behavior, proceeding through the interpretation of evidence and aiming ultimately at "human self-knowledge."

The best known interpretation was Friedrich Meinecke's *Die Entstehung des Historismus* (1936; *Historicism: The Rise of a New Historical Outlook),* which offered a comprehensive map of European historical thought since the seventeenth century and gave systematic form to the Rankean principles of individuality and development. He granted a place for cultural history—as in Vico, Voltaire, Wallace K. Ferguson, Johann Joachim Winckelmann, and Johann Gottfried von Herder—and indeed he ended with a detailed assessment of Goethe, "Herder's pupil," down to the breakthrough of the fundamental ideas, though not its "full evolution." Yet he also includes the arch-naturalist Gottfried Wilhelm von Leibniz in his curious canon and so tends to overlook the linguistic and literary—and indeed in many ways antiphilosophical—orientation of historicism as it emerged in the age of Romanticism, neglecting the contributions of the historical schools (Reinhold Niebuhr, J. G. Eichhorn, Friedrich von Savigny, Jakob Grimm, Wilhelm Roscher, et al.) and the scholarly tradition as a whole. By reducing historicism to a philosophical doctrine, Meinecke violates the original impulse; for in general historicism is not a concept but an attitude, not a theory but a scholarly practice, not a system of explanation but a mode of interpretation; and it was part of an effort not to make history into a philosophical doctrine but rather to transform it into a foundational discipline to which philosophy itself would be subject. In this sense historicism penetrated even into Russia.

The later semantic history of historicism has become increasingly muddled because of misappropriations of the word

for philosophical or ideological but quite un- or even antihistorical purposes, beginning with Karl Popper's *Poverty of Historicism* (1957), which identifies historicism with naive biological determinism (precisely the opposite of the view of Braniss) and a total innocence of history, experience, and even common sense. Another instance is the book of Maurice Mandelbaum, who writes in *History, Man, and Reason,* "Historicism is a belief that an adequate understanding of the nature of any phenomenon and an adequate assessment of its value are to be gained through considering it in terms of the place which it occupied and the role which it played within a process of development," and Michael Gillespie, who thinks historians go "critically astray" in tracing the source of historicism to the attitudes associated with historical scholarship, especially that of early modern Europe. On the contrary, historicism was and is an alternative to conventional philosophy and scientific naturalism, and it flourished in the rich soil of literary and antiquarian learning and the teachings of the historical schools. In fact historicism is positioned in opposition to the scientisms that evade questions of point of view, perspective, cultural context, and the necessity of interpretation in posing questions about a past that is not only a "foreign country" but also largely inaccessible except through traces and testimonies that happen to have survived and that must be expressed in the language and conditions of the present—a present that is itself on its way soon to becoming a past.

## The New Historicism
The so-called new historicism, popularized since 1980, goes back at least to 1942, when Croce wrote that "The New Historicism accepts, extends, and applies Vico's principle that men know only what they do." The newer New Historicism, though avoiding philosophical claims, likewise turns, as Vico had done, to cultural forms, especially literature and art, to reveal underlying interests and power structures and to penetrate to inarticulate levels and marginal groups of society. In general, this New Historicism was part of the linguistic and textualist turn taken by history and the human sciences, including philosophy, in the past generation; and so were the closely allied innovationist movements that call themselves "the new cultural history" and "a new philosophy of history." Despite attempts to deprecate the Old Historicism on ideological as well as methodological and terminological grounds, the New Historicism shared or inherited some of the same assumptions and goals and in a long perspective forms part of the same story.

*See also* **Historiography; History, Idea of.**

BIBLIOGRAPHY
Bambach, Charles R. *Heidegger, Dilthey, and the Crisis of Historicism.* Ithaca, N.Y.: Cornell University Press, 1995).
Croce, Benedetto. *History as the Story of Liberty.* Translated by Sylvia Sprigge. New York: W. W. Norton, 1941.
———. *History, Its Theory and Practice.* Translated by Douglas Ainslie. New York, 1960.
Heussi, Karl. *Die Krisis des Historismus.* Tübingen: Mohr, 1932.
Iggers, Georg G. *The German Conception of History: The National Tradition of Historical Thought from Herder to the Present.* Middletown, Conn.: Wesleyan University Press, 1983.

Mannheim, Karl. "Historicism." In *Essays on the Sociology of Knowledge.* Translated by Paul Kecskemeti. London: Routledge and Kegan Paul, 1952.

Meinecke, Friedrich. *Historism: The Rise of a New Historical Outlook.* Translated by J. E. Anderson. London: Herder and Herder, 1972.

Popper, Karl. *The Poverty of Historicism.* Boston: Beacon Press, 1957.

Roberts, David. *Benedetto Croce and the Uses of Historicism.* Berkeley: University of California Press, 1987.

Thaden, Edward C. *The Rise of Historicism in Russia.* New York: Peter Lang, 1999.

Thomas, Brook. *The New Historicism and Other Old-Fashioned Topics.* Princeton: Princeton University Press, 1991.

Troeltsch, Ernst. *Historismus und seine Probleme.* Tübingen, 1922.

———. *The Social Teaching of the Christian Churches.* Translated by Olive Wyon. New York: Harper, 1960.

*Donald R. Kelley*

**HISTORY, ECONOMIC.**   Economic history emerged in the late nineteenth century as an academic field devoted to the study of past economic phenomena and processes. Since then it has undergone significant changes in terms of its thematic and theoretical concerns, analytical methodologies and language, and the spatial and temporal scales in which it is framed. Distinctive national and regional approaches and traditions can be identified that reflect the different and changing social systems and ideologies across the world as well as the diverse forms of training and disciplinary affiliations of the economic historians themselves.

### The Emergence of Economic History

As an academic discipline, economic history first emerged in Western Europe and North America, specifically, in Britain, Germany, and the United States. Although publications that, more or less, incorporated economic history go back to the eighteenth century, the phrase "economic history" apparently first appeared in a book title in the work of a German scholar, Von Inama-Sternegg, published in 1877 and 1879, *Über die quellen der deutschen wirtschaftsgeschichte* and *Deutsche Wirtschaftsgeschichte,* covering the Middle Ages. The first academic appointment in economic history was made at Harvard University in 1892 and went to a British scholar, William Ashley. The work of the early economic historians focused on either general economic development or specific sectors and processes, especially agriculture, commerce, and industrialization.

But the emerging field exhibited different regional and national tendencies. Although neoclassical models dominated, Marxist perspectives had a lot more appeal to European economic historians, especially in Germany, than to those in America. German historical economists mainly saw economic development in terms of stages and they emphasized the inductive rather than the deductive method. In Britain, the political economists who turned to economic history stressed issues of distribution, especially prices and wages. For their part, American economic historians showed a strong preference for quantitative approaches. Their studies increasingly focused on business history and business cycles, thanks in part to the relative abundance of statistics from census data and governmental and private agencies. In fact, the subsequent growth of economic history in these countries and elsewhere in the world was tied to the increasing capacity and needs of governments to produce and consume statistical data. Also critical was the expansion of, and rising disciplinary specialization in, the universities, the improvement of library collections and archives, the establishment of economic history societies and journals, and the production of large-scale surveys and other bibliographic resources.

Many of the pioneer economic historians were men, but the field also included some remarkable women, such as Eileen Power in Britain, who was at the center of the Economic History Society and the London School of Economics until her death in 1940, and Katherine Coman in the United States, who published an influential economic history text, *Industrial History of the United States,* in 1905. Unfortunately, the important contributions of these women were ignored as the discipline became more male dominated, particularly after World War II, as the concerns and constituencies of the discipline narrowed, although corrective studies have appeared in more recent years.

### Economic History in Asia, Latin America, and Africa

By the 1940s economic history had become an established discipline not only in Western Europe and North America, but also in other parts of the world. In Japan, Tokuzo Fukuda, who studied in Germany and tried to apply the German theory of economic stages to Japan, published the first treatise on Japanese economic history in 1900. In the next few decades, besides economic stage theory, Japanese economic history was dominated by historical materialism. Analytical focus shifted from commercial activities to rural and local economic history, whereas externally much attention was paid to the economic history of England, seen as the classical homeland of capitalism (see, for example, Komatsu). In China, which became officially communist from 1949, the Marxist approaches became even more pervasive, although Marx's notion of the "Asiatic mode of production" was disavowed. Chinese economic historians were preoccupied with two issues: first, the question of transition from "feudalism" to "capitalism," and second, the contradictory but ultimately destructive impact of Western imperialism on China's economy.

For formerly colonized regions and countries the question of imperialism and the challenges of internalizing their economic history loomed large, affecting everything from periodization to the themes and theories selected for analysis. In India, for example, economic historiography, which began to flourish following independence in 1947, had to grapple with the validity of the division between "ancient India" and "modern India," designating the periods before and after European conquest, a periodization based largely on political events rather than on economic processes. In the early postindependence years, Indian economic historians, notwithstanding differences in the topics or periods of focus, displayed two main tendencies: first, a nationalist orientation in which the stable and productive character of early Indian economic and social institutions were emphasized and by implication at least the destructive impact of British rule was indicted, and second, a spatial concentration on the economic history of North India at the expense of other regions.

Periodization proved even more problematic for Latin American economic history, given the region's complex histories of European and African settlement and relations with the indigenous peoples. The region's economic historians, whether those influenced by neoclassical models of international trade, Marxist categories and stages of development, or dependency perspectives on underdevelopment and unequal exchange, largely took an external view of the region's economies as indicated by the preponderance of studies on the export sector. The emphasis on export rather than on the domestic economy began to shift in the mid-1950s, but there was continued concentration on the "modern" sector to the neglect of the "traditional" one.

The development of African economic history was a post-independence phenomenon, in which scholars grappled with various sets of generalizations made about African economic history. Geographically, the "Africa" discussed was largely confined to "sub-Saharan" Africa; thematically, there was excessive focus on trade and exchange systems, especially external trade, rather than on domestic production. Historically, the precolonial period was depicted as a static "traditional" backdrop to changes introduced by colonialism. Theoretically, there was the ubiquitous use of dichotomous models, in which change was often depicted as the abrupt substitution of one ideal type by its opposite—"traditional–modern" societies, "subsistence–market" economies, or "formal–informal" sectors. Various approaches vied for analytical preeminence, including neoclassical development theory, and dependency and Marxist paradigms.

## The Rise of Cliometrics or the New Economic History

At the turn of the 1960s a "new economic history," sometimes referred to as *cliometrics* or *econometric history,* emerged in the United States. The new approach involved the systematic application of economic theory and quantitative methods to economic history. It was facilitated by the existence of a large stock of quantitative data produced by various agencies, advances in computer technology that fostered the collection of large historical samples, and a new generation of economic historians keen to apply statistical and mathematical models and counterfactual arguments for more precise measurements of economic developments and relationships. The need for economic and statistical skills meant that cliometricians were increasingly recruited from economics rather than from history departments, and they tended to concentrate on topics with measurable variables and more recent historical periods on which adequate quantitative data was available. One effect was that fewer economic historians were located in history departments, whereas in economics departments their distinctiveness apparently dwindled.

Prominent among the new economic historians were Robert Fogel and Douglas North, who won the Nobel Prize for Economics in 1993. Initially, they both focused on the effects of changes in the price of transportation—Fogel on the railroads and North on shipping—and on the economic impact of slavery on the American South. In both cases and on many other topics their results challenged and sometimes overturned conventional historiographical wisdom. For example, it was demonstrated that the economic impact of the railroads was minimal and the alleged stagnation of the antebellum South was a myth. Fogel later turned his attention to the complex connections between nutrition, health, and productivity, and North concentrated on studying the role of institutions and organizations in economic growth.

Cliometric history had its critics in the American academy. Some charged that because of its hypothetical models, which could not be verified, and "antiempiricistic" and "antipositivistic" methods, it was not history but "quasihistory" (Redlich). But unlike the situation in Europe, where Fogel lamented the new economic history was not initially practiced, it became increasingly dominant among American economic historians. However, the frontier of cliometrics did expand beyond the United States. Writing in 1978 Donald McCloskey enthused, "Cliometrics has at least begun in the histories of Canada, Mexico, Brazil, Australia, Japan, China, India, Russia, West Africa, Israel, Italy, France, Central Europe, the Low Countries, Scandinavia, Ireland, and England" (p. 25). In an extensive survey, Nicholas Crafts provided interested examples in cliometric history ranging from unemployment in interwar Britain to comparisons between Britain and the United States centered on the Habakkuk debate on technological progress, the Kuznets curve on patterns of income distribution, and demographic transitions.

Nevertheless, cliometrics moored firmly in neoclassical principles remained predominantly an American school and preoccupation. The distinguished British economic historian A. K. Cairncross implored the cliometricians to bear in mind constantly "the contrast between the sharp outlines of their concepts and the fuzziness of real life categories and between the certainties of their conceptual relationships and the uncertainties of the data" (p. 178). He concluded that in his view "there is scope for econometric methods of analysis, complete with models and counterfactuals, in some but not by any means all situations that economic historians encounter" (p. 180). From the 1990s, the call for a reunion between the old qualitative and the new quantitative economic history, between narrative and statistics, words and numbers, became louder. One prominent pioneer called for a "post–New Economic History" and urged his fellow economic historians to reintegrate themselves with other historians by changing their methods: "Historians are the synthesizers of social science. Our goal should be to help them to incorporate our insights into their developing syntheses. To do this we must make our models adaptable, more portable, and more human" (Sutch, pp. 277–278).

In an extensive review and prognosis of European economic and social history, Charles Tilly and colleagues proclaimed,

As we peer into the futures of economic and social history, our most general message is quite simple: *it is time to de-economize economic history and re-economize social history.* The de-economization of economic history should include the analysis of rights, power, coercion, state action, and related "institutional" factors; it does not entail the abandonment of economic analysis, but its broadening from a single-minded application of free-market models. The re-economization of social history should include new treatments of the interdependence among different forms of production and reproduction, both material, biological, and social. It should challenge the surprising recent tendency either to treat the three as separate spheres or to reduce all of them to artifacts of discourse. In this limited but crucial sense, we call for the revival of materialist social and economic history [italics in original]. (p. 647)

## Late-Twentieth-Century Developments in Economic History

Economic theory and economic history have increasingly had to deal with new intellectual currents in economics, principally feminist economics, environmental economics, and the new institutional economics. Feminist economists have sought to liberate neoclassical economics from its positivist Cartesian trap, to broaden its analytical and thematic scope from a preoccupation with the rational choices of individual economic man, and to study how humans, both men and women, in interaction with each other and the environment, provide for their own needs and survival. They have tried to infuse gender in both macroeconomics and microeconomics, to strip neoclassical economics of its universalism and timelessness, as well as its normative and prescriptive certainties, to challenge stylized facts and dichotomies, and to make women and gender relations in all economic activities visible, by grounding economic analysis in concrete societies and histories that are invariably marked by inequalities, discrimination, exploitation, and struggle inscribed by the social and spatial constructions and hierarchies of gender, class, and place.

Environmental economics evolved out of diverse intellectual and ideological roots in the 1970s and 1980s in the context of growing concerns for sustainable development. Environmental economists seek to analyze the impact of economic activity on the environment and the influence of the environment on economic activity and human welfare by reformulating familiar neoclassical concepts, and occasionally inventing new, "greener" ones. And so they talk of the need to internalize externalities, that is, to account for the environmental effects of economic activity, to incorporate environmental factors in social cost–benefit analysis. They see environmental "resources" and "services" as "commodities" with consumptive, nonconsumptive, existence and bequest values, and discuss the preservation of natural environments in terms of their value as collective or public goods, and their expected utility or option value for future generations. A series of sophisticated methods and techniques has been devised to give monetary values to the environmental "commodities" and to measure the costs of environmental damage and degradation, and the impacts of market and policy failures and of investment projects and programs.

A key premise of the new institutional economics is that institutions matter, that economic change and development are products of both the institutional environment and the institutional arrangement. Studies inspired by the institutional perspective range from those that focus on the broad range of factors that have shaped the institutional environment, including the state, culture, and ideology, to those that concentrate on specific institutional arrangements, such as how changing regimes of property rights and transaction costs affect each other and economic performance. There is a lively debate on what constitutes an institution. Institutions are said to exist as a means to reduce transaction and information costs so that markets can operate efficiently, and markets themselves are regarded as institutions that interact with other social, political, and cultural institutions in the process of economic growth and change.

These new approaches offered opportunities for economic history to gain new analytical models and insights. They were welcomed by economic historians who believe that historical economic phenomena and processes are inseparable from cultural, political, social institutions, and the physical environments in which they occur, and the hierarchies and struggles inscribed by gender, class, and other social markers. Thus, economic history became increasingly more interdisciplinary.

Interdisciplinarity had long characterized economic history in the global South thanks to the paucity of statistical data and the pressing demands of development. According to Anthony Hopkins, a renowned economic historian of West Africa, African economic historians have always had a generous definition of economic history, one which embraces anthropology and political history as well as economics, which can be attributed to the youthfulness of the subject, the fortunate failure of any one school of thought to impose its dominance, and the diversity of evidence.

Economic historians of other regions appear to be moving in this direction. Readings on European economic history suggest growing interest in reconnecting economic, social, and political history. Before econometric history spread from the United States in the 1960s and specialization led to fragmentation of the discipline, one writer recalls, "few people then doubted that economic history included social history." (Barker, p. 25). Now the discipline seems to be returning to some of its roots and using new sources, including oral sources, which "can fill many gaps and much enrich our understanding of ordinary folk's social conditions and personal priorities" (Barker, p. 27).

The winds of change seem to be blowing even to the United States, as several commentators have noted. In a major intervention on the development of the American economy during the late nineteenth century, when corporate capitalism rose to prominence, James Livingston makes a compelling argument for bringing social analysis into American economic history:

At a higher level of argument it . . . follows that economic events are explicable only by reference to the social relations within which they appear—by reference, that is, to historically specific contexts of production and exchange. . . . We can see that the social and cultural context of economic change is not what the new economic historians have assumed it to be—an "exogenous factor" that can safely be ignored in building quantitative models of economic behavior and growth. (p.71)

Similar trends are apparent in Asian economic historiography. In China, for example, social and economic historians have been developing new paradigms, divorced from Western neoclassical models and communist models, both of which were based on simplistic dualisms and shared a vision of the benefits of commercialization (Huang, pp. 335–336).

A survey of the Eleventh International Economic History Congress held in 1994 confirms these developments toward the broadening of economic history. It shows that only one session was devoted to cliometrics and that the new economic history papers altogether accounted for about 20 percent of the whole congress program and were mainly given by North American scholars. Most of the papers took into account the role played by noneconomic factors and reflected "the influence of other kinds of histories, in particular social history, and other social sciences such as sociology, management and organization studies, and political science" (Subacchi, p. 607).

See also **Capitalism; Communism; Economics; Historiography; Marxism.**

**BIBLIOGRAPHY**

Barker, Theodore C. "What Is Economic History?" *History Today* February (1985): 25–27.

Berg, Maxine. "The First Women Economic Historians." *Economic History Review* 45, no. 2 (1992): 308–329.

Cairncross, A. K. "In Praise of Economic History." *Economic History Review* New Series 42, no. 2 (1987): 173–185.

Cochran, Thomas C. "Economic History, Old and New." *American Historical Review* 74, no. 5 (1969): 1571–1572.

Cole, Arthur H. "Economic History in the United States: Formative Years of a Discipline." *Journal of Economic Perspectives* 28, no. 4 (1968): 556–589.

Coleman, D. C. "History, Economic History and the Numbers Game." *Historical Journal* 38, no. 3 (1995): 635–646.

Crafts, Nicholas F. R. "Cliometrics, 1971–1986: A Survey." *Journal of Applied Econometrics* 2, no. 3 (1987): 171–192.

Elson, Diane. "Gender Analysis and Economics in the Context of Africa." In *Engendering African Social Sciences,* edited by Ayesha Imam, Amina Mama, and Fatou Sow, 153–189. Dakar: Codesria Book Series, 1997.

Feuerwerker, Albert. "China's Modern Economic History in Communist Chinese Historiography." *China Quarterly* 22 (1965): 31–61.

Fogel, Robert W. "The New Economic History. 1. Its Findings and Methods." *Economic History Review* New Series, 19, no. 3 (1966): 642–656.

Furubotn, Eirik, and Rudolf Richter, eds. *Institutions and Economic Theory: Contributions of the New Institutional Economics.* Ann Arbor: University of Michigan Press, 1998.

Goldin, Claudia. "Cliometrics and the Nobel." *Journal of Economic Perspectives* 9, no. 2 (1995): 191–208.

Gras, Norman S. B. "The Rise and Development of Economic History." *Economic History Review* 1, no. 1 (1927): 12–34.

Hopkins, Anthony G. "African Economic History: The First Twenty-five Years." *Journal of African History* 30 (1989): 157–163.

Huang, Philip C. "The Paradigmatic Crisis in Chinese Studies: Paradoxes in Social and Economic History." *Modern China* 17, no. 3 (1991): 299–341.

Komatsu, Y. "The Study of Economic History in Japan." *Economic History Review* New Series 14, no. 1 (1961): 115–121.

Livingston, James. "The Social Analysis of Economic History and Theory: Conjectures of Late Nineteenth-Century American Development." *American Historical Review* 92 (1987): 69–95.

McCloskey, Donald N. "The Achievements of the Cliometric School." *Journal of Economic History* 38, no. 1 (1978): 13–28.

McGreevey, William Paul, and Robson B. Tyrer. "Recent Research on the Economic History of Latin America." *Latin American Research Review* 3, no. 2 (1968): 89–117.

Morris, David, and Burton Stein. "The Economic History of India: A Bibliographic Essay." *Journal of Economic History* 21, no. 2 (1961): 179–207.

Rawski, Thomas G., et al. *Economics and the Historian.* Berkeley: University of California Press, 1996.

Redlich, Fritz. "'New' and Traditional Approaches to Economic History and Their Interdependence." *Journal of Economic History* 25, no. 4 (1965): 480–495.

Subacchi, Paola. "Meta-Economic History: A Survey of the Eleventh International Economic History Congress." *Economic History Review* New Series 48, no. 3 (1995): 602–611.

Sutch, Richard. "All Things Reconsidered: The Life-Cycle Perspective and the Third Task of Economic History." *Journal of Economic History* 51, no. 2 (1991): 271–288.

Tisdell, Clem. *Environmental Economics: Policies for Environmental Management and Sustainable Development.* Aldershot, U.K.: Edward Elgar, 1993.

Zeleza, Paul Tiyambe. *A Modern Economic History of Africa.* Vol. 1: *The Nineteenth Century.* Dakar, Senegal: Codesria, 1993.

*Paul Tiyambe Zeleza*

**HISTORY, IDEA OF.** "History" began, with Herodotus (5th century B.C.E.), as a form of empirical inquiry and has had an adventurous semantic career since its early Greek coinage. It has come to refer not only to procedures of investigation but also to speculations about the past. From the very beginning there was confusion between history as what happened in the past and history as memory and description of human events and, on a further level, conjectures about their larger meaning. The definition of history ranged from the study of particulars to philosophical reflection, and the idea of history had a corresponding range of reference both in theory and in practice. For Herodotus, history was intended not only to cast light on the customs of the "barbarians" but also to explain the causes of the wars with the Persians.

For the Romans history was designed, as with Livy (59 B.C.E.–17 C.E.), not only to celebrate national traditions but also, as with Cicero (106–43 B.C.E.), to furnish moral lessons for careful readers; and in both models the political-nationalist and the moral-exemplarist modes of historical writing entered into alliance with rhetoric and its apparatus of persuasion and inspiration as manifested in "art of history" (*ars historica*). At its best, history was, in the words of Dionysius of Halicarnassus (fl. c. 20 B.C.E.), "philosophy teaching by example." These motives were all preserved in the conception of history of Christian authors, with the addition of an overarching providential design inherited from Judaism, which itself arose in the context of Near Eastern—and for Western authors "barbarian"—religions. Not that the idea of history in some sense was limited to the classical and Judeo-Christian traditions, but the writings of other cultures remained outside the Western sphere until the early modern period.

The key to the conceptualization of history is the effort to essentialize the past, first in a Herodotean or Thucydidean narrative, and then in more rational, conjectural, philosophical, and religious ways. The "past" became (in Arnold Toynbee's phrase) an "intelligible field of study," and anthropomorphism as well as religious beliefs and ethnic prejudices came into play in the interpretation of the results of historical inquiry. In the West this meant above all the biblical framework and history as the "grand design of god," which posited human experience in time as a pilgrimage under the laws of providence. From St. Augustine of Hippo (354–430) to Gotthold Ephraim Lessing (1729–1781) history was seen as the "education of the human race," whether on the way to a final judgment or to an earthly destiny represented as progress, destiny, or a cyclical trajectory. To be ignorant of history, in the often-cited words of Cicero, was always to remain a child. This line of thought was pursued within the framework of a "world history," which transcended the parochial biblical story, which was extended by "conjectural" methods in the eighteenth century, which, in the work especially of Johann Gottfried von Herder (1744–1803) and Georg Wilhelm Friedrich Hegel (1770–1831), eventuated in the genre of the "philosophy of history," which was given a more secular and "scientific" twist by Auguste Comte (1798–1857) and Karl Marx (1818–1883) and their followers, and which today is preserved in attempts at global history.

## Controversies and Models

Ancient notions of history were revived in the Renaissance and not only adapted to modern conditions but also subjected to critical scrutiny, focusing on the question of whether history was an art or a "science," a question debated by historians down to the past century, notably in the famous exchange between George Macaulay Trevelyan (1876–1962) and John Bagnell Bury (1861–1927). In the sixteenth century history was in effect promoted from the level of art to that of science, especially in the work of Jean Bodin (1530–1596) and his followers on the "method" of history, although his primary aim was to place historical knowledge in the service of the sciences of law and society. Yet history retained its relations with philosophy, especially as a fulfillment of the ancient Greek motto of self-knowledge. "Know thyself," quoted Bodin's disciple Pierre Droit de Gaillard in another "method" of history. "Now this knowledge depends upon history, sacred as well as profane, universal as well as particular." Such was one of the essential elements of historical study down to the famous work on the "idea of history" by Robin George Collingwood (1889–1943). Another contemporaneous French scholar, Henri de la Popelinière, likewise carried on Bodin's project by writing not only a history of history but also a discussion of the "idea of perfect history" (*l'idée de l'histoire accomplie; historia perfecta*), which followed Bodin's ideas but preserved the autonomy of the discipline of history.

Another central theme of the theory of history begins with Aristotle's (384–322 B.C.E.) famous and debate-inspiring contrast between poetry and history, which maintains that the latter stands in relation to philosophy as the particular to the general, and indeed this distinction was maintained not only by early modern scholars but also in the contrast made in the later nineteenth century by Wilhelm Windelband (1848–1915) and Heinrich Rickert (1863–1936) between sciences that were "idiographic," treating particulars, and those that were "nomothetic," seeking general laws. German "historicism" as defined by Friedrich Meinecke (1862–1954) was a view that likewise set history apart from philosophy through the principle of "individuality" (as well as development). Among the manifestations of individuality and vulgar empiricism were the isolation of particular "facts" and "events," which came under fire from more sophisticated views of historical knowledge.

In the early modern period, history, following the usage of "natural history," was defined especially as the knowledge of particulars (*singulorum notitia, particularis cognitio*), but increasingly it was also connected with the dimension of time and chronology, which, with geography, was regarded as one of the "eyes" of history. Here the central question was the form taken by the temporal process: where did it begin, and where was it headed? Was it continuous, filled with crises or revolutionary breaks, or perhaps cyclical? How could historians move back into that "foreign country" that is the past? Was ordinary memory, supported by reason, sufficient for such explorations, or was imagination required as well? Or did history require assistance from neighboring disciplines in the human sciences? All these questions and more have given substance, shape, and direction to the idea of history in modern times.

## Hermeneutical Principles

In the nineteenth century the competing paradigms for historical interpretation were the natural-science model and cultural history inclining toward art and aesthetics, the first represented especially by Leopold von Ranke (1795–1886) and Theodor Mommsen (1817–1903) and the second by Jules Michelet (1798–1874) and Jacob Burckhardt (1818–1897)—and both represented in the famous exchange between Bury and Trevelyan. In general, historians have taken two paths to disciplinary science, one based on brute empiricism and reliance on primary sources and the other, under the influence of positivism, seeking general laws, as notoriously did Henry Thomas Buckle (1821–1862) and Hippolyte Taine (1828–1893). In this mode history was represented as a physical process that followed set patterns, a view that was reinforced by the analogy of Darwinian evolution. It was in this context, too, that the ideal of objectivity—history *sub specie aeternitatis*—was defended against the idea of history as a subjective literary art, to the extent indeed that the term "literary" became a pejorative term for scientific and professional historians following the quest of Ranke for history "as it actually happened."

Yet historians had long been aware that history had to be written from a particular "point of view" (*Sehepunkt*), and this hermeneutical insight, first expressed by Johann Martin Chladenius (1710–1759), was taught by the classical historian, and Ranke's colleague, Johann Gustav Droysen (1808–1884), for whom history was indeed partial insight and not "objective knowledge." For Droysen history was, as it had been for Herodotus, a matter of endless inquiry—"not," alluding to John the Baptist, "'the light and the truth' but a search therefor, a sermon thereupon, a consecration thereto." This was especially appropriate for art history, which was the model chosen by Jacob Burckhardt, for whom "History is actually the most unscientific of all the sciences" (1979, p. 21). Burckhardt rejected the "bogus objectivity" of Ranke for the subjectivity that arose in the Renaissance and Reformation. As he wrote about his own classic study of the civilization of the Renaissance in Italy, "To each eye, perhaps, the outlines of a given civilization present a different picture, [so that] it is unavoidable that individual judgment and feeling should tell every moment both on the writer and on the reader" (1950, p. 1). The result was a principle of relativism that applied to the study of history itself, for "each age has a new and different way of looking at the more remote periods of the past" (1998, p. 7).

## Many Ideas

One of the results of this is that to understand what the "idea of history" is, it is necessary to trace what it has been, and such indeed was the practice of Benedetto Croce (1866–1952) and his disciple Collingwood, for whom historical understanding had to be not a search for general or logical causes but a concern for individual motives—a kind of contemporary reenactment of past events in the fashion of Agatha Christie's sleuth, Hercule Poirot, and along the lines of modern hermeneutics. In any case Collingwood concludes his review of the "idea of history" (1946) by reducing it, in modern terms, to the Greek view that history was a unique form of inquiry into human behavior, proceeding through the interpretation of evidence, aiming at self-knowledge. One of the dangers of this view was the "Whig interpretation of history," denounced by Herbert Butterfield in 1931, but there seems no avoiding this sort of parochialism in a general sense.

In the twentieth century the idea of history took a number of forms, beginning with the old scientific ideal, encouraged by interdisciplinary studies and especially the methods and aims of the social sciences. One example of this was Marxist history, in which economic conditions and class struggle furnished the motor and revolution the goal of historical change, but in fact many political, social, and economic conditions have in their own ways preserved the search for the mechanisms of cause and effect underlying the historical process. This applies also to the adjacent field of the philosophy and theology of history, which has continued in the old Hegelian form, but which has diverged as well into the modern tradition of analytical philosophy, which is traceable back at least to F. H. Bradley's *Presuppositions of Critical History* (1874), but which became a major project in the third quarter of the twentieth century, when philosophers of history focused on published historical

accounts and the examination of propositions and explanations with little or no attention to problems of research and heuristics but with great interest in the propositional analysis of stable terms and in assigning of causes and determining the "covering laws" to be extracted from the discourse of historians. Yet this abstractive focus on the "logic" of historical inquiry in the style of F. H. Bradley, Maurice Mandelbaum, William Dray, and Morton White seems to have run its course, or at least outlived its usefulness for historians.

## Current Approaches

In many ways contemporary ideas of history have been reshaped and redirected in the wake of the linguistic and cultural turns taken by historical investigation and interpretation in the past century. With the decline of Marxist ideology and the rise of an anthropological model, historians have shifted from social to cultural matters, from the search for underlying causes to the human condition over time. Cultural history rejects the reductionism of economic and political history, gives up the "noble dream" of objectivity, the privileging of particular causes, recognizes the fundamental role of imagination in historical reconstruction, and, no longer aspiring to rigorous explanation, turns instead to what Clifford Geertz and Charles Taylor have called "interpretive social science." For cultural historians, following the lead of anthropology, nothing human was alien to their inquiries, so that their aim indeed became, in the words of Fernand Braudel, "the history of everything." Life around the clock, around the globe, from cradle to grave, and including the secrets of private life and sexuality: these have been the horizons of what has been trumpeted as the "new cultural history"; and the postmodern rejection of "grand narratives" has reinforced this move toward microhistory, multiple points of view, and loss of historiographical focus.

Yet the contemporary idea of history has in other ways lowered its sights, especially by shifting from a natural science to a linguistic model and so from a concern with primary sources to literary criticism of secondary, published and usually classic, narratives of key texts and questions of historiography. In a sense this shift, most conspicuously exemplified in the work of Hayden White and his followers, represents a return to the ancient rhetorical tradition of historical writing (and reading). To read history out of a text or to read history as a text: in either case we are impelled to shift from history as past reality (*res gestae*) to history as a phenomenon of literature (*rerum gestae narratio*)—from context to text. According to this shift of perspective, illustrated by the "New Historicism" of recent vintage, history is not a bygone process to be explained but a field of written accounts whose meaning can only be represented through the interpretation of traces, mainly linguistic traces. History is not rational but commemorative and imaginative; and there is no Archimedean point from which to view, still less to move, humanity in its passage. We may pose questions, but we cannot link cause and effect in any rigorous way. We may tell many stories, true as well as probable, about the past; but we cannot tell *the* story, the whole truth, the metanarrative, as scientific, philosophical, and theological historians used to do and, in some quarters, are still doing. This is the critical perspective from which the idea of history has encountered various deconstructionist, poststructuralist, and postmodernist views of the human sciences that have changed the way many historians write if not the way they think.

Such are some of the conditions of the modern idea, or ideas, of history. As Michael Oakeshott long ago and Croce longer ago argued, history is not a thing of the past; and as the authors of the old *artes historicae* also taught, writing and reading history is a thing of the present. So are the remnants and relics of the past on which historical interpretation is based and the "contexts" that historians try to reconstruct from their own standpoints. The result is to qualify some of the key elements of our received ideas of history. There can be no single account of an essentialized "past" but only multiple stories that select, arrange, and interpret surviving records, testimony, and artifacts from particular points of view; nor can there be "facts" outside of human interpretations of its remains and uncertain human memory—no objects outside a human subject. A philosopher has written that we cannot speak the truth because "words cannot mimic the way the world is." How much less can historians speak the truth of the way the world *was*—and its languages *were*? History cannot "speak" except through human ventriloquism, and (to invoke Jean-François Lyotard's postmodernist criticism) there can be no "metanarrative" that captures the "nature and destiny of man." Such metanarratives we have, of course—they have founded all sorts of ideologies and utopias—but as frameworks for the story of humanity they all sooner or later come to grief. The idea of history has in many ways become globalized. Yet it remains a human—time- and culture-bound—creation, whose technologically enhanced future is as uncertain as its past has been controversial and irregular; and its history will continue to be rewritten.

*See also* **Cycles; Hegelianism; Historiography; Marxism; Periodization; Prehistory, Rise of.**

### BIBLIOGRAPHY

Ankersmit, Frank, and Hans Kellner, eds. *A New Philosophy of History*. Chicago: University of Chicago Press, 1995.

Bodin, Jean. *Method for the Easy Comprehension of History*. Translated by Beatrice Reynolds. New York: Columbia University Press, 1945.

Burckhardt, Jacob. *The Civilization of the Renaissance in Italy*. Translated by S. G. C. Middlemore. New York: Phaidon, 1950.

———. *The Greeks and Greek Civilization*. New York: St. Martin's Press, 1998.

———. *Reflections on History*. Indianapolis: Liberty Classics, 1979.

Burke, Peter, ed. *New Perspectives on Historical Writing*. University Park: Pennsylvania State University Press, 1992.

Butterfield, Herbert. *The Whig Interpretation of History*. New York: AMS, 1978.

Certeau, Michel de. *The Writing of History*. Translated by Tom Conley. New York: Columbia University Press, 1988.

Collingwood, Robin G. *The Idea of History*. Oxford: Clarendon, 1946.

Croce, Benedetto. *History: Its Theory and Practice*. Translated by Douglas Ainslie. New York: Russell and Russell, 1960.

Green, Anna, and Kathleen Troup, eds. *The Houses of History*. New York: New York University Press, 1999.

Kelley, Donald R. *Faces of History: Historical Inquiry from Herodotus to Herder*. New Haven, Conn.: Yale University Press, 1998.

———. *Fortunes of History: Historical Inquiry from Herder to Huizinga*. New Haven, Conn.: Yale University Press, 2003.

———. "The Theory of History." In *Cambridge History of Renaissance Philosophy*, edited by Charles B. Schmitt et al., 746–762. Cambridge, U.K.: Cambridge University Press, 1988.

Kelley, Donald R., ed. *Versions of History: From Antiquity to the Enlightenment*. New Haven, Conn.: Yale University Press, 1991.

Koselleck, Reinhart. *Futures Past*. Translated by Keith Tribe. Cambridge, Mass.: MIT Press, 1985.

Kramer, Lloyd, and Sarah Maza, eds. *A Companion to Western Historical Thought*. Malden, Mass.: Blackwell, 2002.

Le Goff, Jacques, and Pierre Nora, eds. *Constructing the Past*. New York: Cambridge University Press, 1985.

Lowenthal, David. *The Past Is a Foreign Country*. New York: Cambridge University Press, 1985.

Mandelbaum, Maurice. *History, Man, and Reason*. Baltimore: Johns Hopkins University Press, 1971.

Meinecke, Friedrich. *Historism*. Translated by J. E. Anderson. New York: Herder and Herder, 1972.

Patrides, C. A. *The Grand Design of God*. London: Routledge and Kegan Paul, 1972.

Smith, Bonnie. *The Gender of History*. Cambridge, Mass.: Harvard University Press, 1998.

Stern, Fritz, ed. *The Varieties of History*. New York: Vintage, 1972.

White, Hayden. *Metahistory*. Baltimore: Johns Hopkins University Press, 1973.

White, Morton. *Foundations of Historical Knowledge*. New York: Harper and Row, 1965.

*Donald R. Kelley*

**HONOR.** Codes of honor are all-pervasive in human societies, but the modern study of honor as an academic formulation originated in the Mediterranean region, and especially in the work of anthropologists working in Spain and Greece. Julio Caro Baroja, J. G Peristiany, and Julian Pitt-Rivers wrote some of the seminal and most influential works on the concept of honor. They placed the honor complex in the Mediterranean world and based their work primarily on rural societies. Since those early works, the use of honor as a framework to study different cultures, especially those of Latin America with their Mediterranean roots, has become almost ubiquitous. Furthermore, the initial categories of analysis used in honor studies have been considerably refined and expanded.

The early model of Mediterranean honor as a catchall framework soon became the target of criticism by later scholars dissatisfied by a model based on peasant and rural sources, whose conceptions of honor cannot be transferred and applied willy-nilly to other times and places. Modern honor studies, although retaining these frameworks as a very useful starting point, take into account regional and temporal variations in the notion of honor, especially when applied to extremely diverse societies far distant from the Mediterranean.

## Early Conceptualizations of Honor

For these early scholars, honor was a brittle value—one that could not be rescued if harmed. They emphasized honor as a framework for social hierarchy and as an attribute that people were both born with (status) and attained or retained through proper behavior (virtue). More recently Frank Henderson Stewart has criticized this way of formulating honor. In his model, honor retains its dual characteristic of having both inner and outer manifestations, but more emphasis is placed on the interconnection between the two. Key to this argument is the notion that honor must be conceived as a right—the inherent right to be treated with respect. As such, the bipartite aspect of honor—as conceived by most scholars—becomes linked to inner values and outer respect.

Another way of approaching honor in a somewhat dualistic manner is to emphasize its inverse quality, that of shame. For instance, Ramón Gutiérrez's influential study of gender and sexuality in colonial New Mexico depends heavily on this model. Although honor represents the ability to hold one's head up high in public, there is a strong element of shame that feeds the system. The conduct that must be observed and respected in order to be respectable is reinforced because of sentiments of shame. Women, in particular, were expected to mediate their behavior based on their sense of shame. This could be translated into their body movements and contacts outside of the home and the ways in which they covered their bodies outside the walls of their house.

Much of this notion of honor comes from historical studies of the Mediterranean region but also from literary sources. In particular, plays of Golden Age Spain, as well as other nations, presented honor dramas in which the battle over honor was marked by seductions, betrayals, and many battles over reputation. Some scholars found these representations of honor quite persuasive and made an extrapolation from these literary sources to the societies that they were studying. More recent scholarship has been highly critical of such attitudes, citing the lack of any link between the types of behavior presented on stage and page and that found in the more mundane documents produced by individuals. These authors have pointed out that many of the groups not covered within the literary codes of honor actually viewed themselves as possessors of honor, and that, in contrast to literary representations of honor, there are many historical examples of lost honor being reparable.

## Public Expressions of Honor

The literature on honor and shame is closely connected to the study of public and private realms. Honor was a quality that was expressed in public, and contested there: insults and slights enacted in the public sphere could be construed as attacks on the public persona or reputation of a person, and thus on his honor. Thus, societies where honor was perceived as an important value were marked by violent outbursts particularly between men who protected their social reputation with duels for the elite and more informal fights—usually knife fights—for plebeians. Yet, despite what the early scholars of honor would have one believe, the courts were also a valid venue for the reparation of honor. Members of the elite in particular often used

litigation to defend their honor against public insults, as did women, to a surprising degree. Colonial Latin American court records have revealed many cases in which women sought to regain lost honor by having a seducer condemned as a rapist or forced to marry his victim—and sometimes both.

Honor was codified in such written forms as genealogies, titles of nobility, or coats of arms. In the Spanish world, public office, admission to universities, and most good marriages could only be obtained with the presentation of a kind of genealogy called a *limpieza de sangre* (purity of blood lines). Such a family tree certified that the party in question did not have any ancestors who were illegitimate, heretical, non-Catholic or newly converted, convicts, or who had held base employment. Titles of nobility also provided a strong case for the possession of honor as did coats of arms, which were, in a sense, a physical manifestation of one's honor. Other externals included the type of clothes one wore, the entourage, horses and carriages, and the body's bearing. In the Latin American context, *pureza de sangre* has been much discussed as an antecedent to later racial hierarchies; the combination of lineage and birth with elements of deportment and social reputation—and codes of honor—in this earlier concept can be seen to have influenced later ideas about race, in which individual behavior and family reputation are similarly emphasized in addition to purely physical attributes.

The public nature of honor was also expressed tangibly, through such bodily attitudes as doffing hats, bowing, curtsying, and lowering the eyes. Conversely, turning one's back or refusing to remove headgear could be construed as an attack on honor. The hierarchies of honor and its distribution were also made material through processions. These often religious, but also political, events placed people in an order that reflected their levels in society and thus represented the rankings of honor both to the general population and also to this smaller group.

## Honor and Gender

There were alternate types of morality based on gender. Male morality had little to do with prudent sexuality. In fact, men enhanced their honor at times by seducing women. In seventeenth-century Spain there was even a fashion in the upper circles of trying to seduce nuns. On the other hand, women protected family honor by remaining virginal until marriage or the taking of order and then remaining chaste within the bounds of their status. Straying from this model of sexual purity not only besmirched the honor of the woman in question but also that of any man considered responsible for her conduct—usually husbands, brothers, or fathers.

To be honorable, a woman had to demonstrate her chastity. Traditional studies of honor systems understood this female imperative as passive, in contrast to the active role of the patriarch as defender of female honor. More recent scholarship has found that women took a more active role, from actual physical violence to hidden pregnancies and "adoptions" of illegitimate children. Ann Twinam has shown that illegitimacy could be overcome in colonial Spanish America through a bureaucratic process, and other scholars have demonstrated how stains on honor were often overlooked particularly for the elite. For plebeian women, such exemptions were not available. The establishment of foundling homes was a response to these women's predicaments, both to protect their reputations and to rescue their babies from infanticide.

## Honor and Violence

Historians have been fascinated by the violence associated with the defense of honor, and especially with the duel. The ritualized nature of duels made this violence acceptable in elite male contexts, an acceptance that plebeians and women in general could not reproduce. In a larger sense, dueling has been analyzed as an example of the relationship between forms of social mediation and levels of violence within particular different societies, with some historians looking especially to the theories of civilization of Norbert Elias in order to understand the evolution of duels and social violence as a central part of honor culture.

Much of the scholarship on dueling has focused on the reasons for its gradual abandonment. Historians have found that while governments often tried to legislate dueling out of existence, other factors such as a generalized social disapproval, changing weaponry (from swords to pistols), and new understandings of honor were stronger factors. Even after duels had disappeared, however, the culture surrounding them privileged certain members of society.

Insults have proven a particularly useful source for historians interested in the workings of honor in past societies. Insults are linked to violence as they precede or provoke it, but they also constitute a type of verbal assault in their own right. Most often, these words only came to light when litigation ensued. Legal codes recognized insults as cause for restitution because they harmed the individual, attacking their honor and their ability to function in their own community.

## Honor and Space

Systems of honor also affected the way people conceived of spaces. The places in which insults were bandied have been productively analyzed to reveal the spatial framework of honor. Anthropologist Beverly Chiñas's study of Mexican Zapotec women added a gendered dimension: women acted covertly to manipulate men's movements, either preventing men who nursed a sense of insult against one another from meeting in public spaces—or putting them on a collision course. More generally, the dichotomy of public and private shaped honor for women, whose presence inside the home was honorable and outside the home was dangerous and dishonorable; codes of conduct and particularly dress were drastically affected by this dichotomy as well. For men, in contrast, absence from the public sphere might be considered questionable.

A more complex analysis of honor and space comes from the historians Elizabeth Cohen and Thomas Cohen, who showed how the house in sixteenth-century Rome became symbolic of the human body. Seating at public events and the relative arrangement in terms of height or distance from the most honorable point in the room became a concrete manifestation of the ideas of honor made concrete in spatial terms.

## Non-Elite Honor

Early twenty-first century scholarship has taken issue with the notion that slaves had no claim to honor. An earlier formulation held that the very purpose of the slave in the social scheme was to be "dishonored," and so to provide their owners, and indeed all free people, with enhanced status in contrast to the slave's abasement. In fact, however, studies have shown that the Africans who became part of slave society worked within the honor system and absorbed its values. Thus slaves often made claims on honor, and also used their honorable status—as married persons, for example—to make claims for justice.

Plebeians, too, once thought to be outside the reach of codes of honor, regularly made claims to honor and defended this status quite vigorously. Although plebeian men and women could not produce illustrious genealogies, they were very much aware of their status as derived from the legitimacy of their relationships. They also derived status from relative affluence within the ranks of plebeians. Finally, the external reputation for honorable conduct was extremely important to plebeians because it was their way of assuring credit. Small loans between market women or artisans were only possible for those whose conduct was unblemished and thus honorable.

## Honor and the State

One early-twenty-first-century development in the study of honor has been a changing appreciation for its role in the development of the modern state during the nineteenth and twentieth centuries. Earlier studies either focused on traditional societies or rural communities portrayed as isolated from modernity, or premodern state societies such as the European *ancien régime*. More recently, however, historians have used a more dynamic concept of honor to study such nineteenth-century phenomena as the integration of qualities associated with honor into the definition of citizenship. Instead of the family, the state becomes the guardian of honor, and begins to intervene in and exert control over individual struggles regarding honor, as in the attempts to stop the practice of dueling, discussed above. Similarly, the nation-state became much more involved in controlling the individual morality of women, particularly in campaigns about prostitution, but also as an arbiter of virginity and morality more generally. Men too began to feel more pressure to assume the role of income-earning head of household rather than simply inheriting the mantle of patriarchy, and honor began to be more entwined with both military or state service.

## Conclusion

Honor seems to be a value or social system that is so basic as to exist—under many other names—in most societies. Honor as a framework to understand past social dynamics has been diffused widely, from China to African slave societies to the more traditional Mediterranean cultures. Yet this very diffusion of honor as an analytical framework has attracted some criticism. Because of its seductive appeal, honor has perhaps been used in an ahistorical and sometimes facile manner. Thus it is important to balance the wide-ranging applicability of honor as an analytical framework and its aptness for the study of diverse historical circumstances.

*See also* **Citizenship; Gender; Honor, Middle Eastern Notions of; Identity; Machismo.**

**BIBLIOGRAPHY**

Caro Baroja, Julio. *La ciudad y el campo.* Madrid: Alfaguara, 1966.

Chiñas, Beverly. *The Isthmus Zapotecs: Women's Roles in Cultural Context.* New York: Holt, Rinehart, and Winston, 1973.

Cohen, Elizabeth S., and Thomas V. Cohen. "Open and Shut: The Social Meanings of the Cinquecento Roman House." *Studies in the Decorative Arts* 9, no. 1 (fall–winter 2001): 61–84.

Elias, Norbert. *Power and Civility.* Translated by Edmund Jephcott. New York: Pantheon Books, 1982.

Gowing, Laura. *Domestic Dangers: Women, Words, and Sex in Early Modern London.* Oxford and New York: Clarendon, 1996.

Gutiérrez, Ramón A. *When Jesus Came, the Corn Mothers Went Away: Marriage, Sexuality, and Power in New Mexico, 1500–1846.* Stanford, Calif.: Stanford University Press, 1991.

Johnson, Lyman L., and Sonya Lipsett-Rivera, eds. *The Faces of Honor: Sex, Shame and Violence in Colonial Latin America.* Albuquerque: University of New Mexico Press, 1998.

Miller, William Ian. *Humiliation and Other Essays on Honor, Social Discomfort, and Violence.* Ithaca, N.Y.: Cornell University Press, 1993.

Peristiany, J. G., ed. *Honour and Shame: The Values of Mediterranean Society.* London: Weidenfeld and Nicolson, 1966.

Peristiany, J. G., and Julian Pitt-Rivers, eds. *Honor and Grace in Anthropology.* Cambridge, U.K., and New York: Cambridge University Press, 1992.

Pitt-Rivers, Julian. *The Fate of Shechem; or, The Politics of Sex. Essays in the Anthropology of the Mediterranean.* Cambridge, U.K.: Cambridge University Press, 1977.

Reddy, William M. *The Invisible Code: Honor and Sentiment in Postrevolutionary France, 1815–1848.* Berkeley: University of California Press, 1997.

Stewart, Frank Henderson. *Honor.* Chicago: University of Chicago Press, 1994.

Twinam, Ann. *Public Lives, Private Secrets: Gender, Honor, Sexuality, and Illegitimacy in Colonial Spanish America.* Stanford, Calif.: Stanford University Press, 1999.

Wyatt-Brown, Bertram. *Southern Honor: Ethics and Behavior in the Old South.* New York: Oxford University Press, 1982.

*Sonya Lipsett-Rivera*

# HONOR: MIDDLE EASTERN NOTIONS OF.

Ancient and modern Arabs, as well as other ethnic groups of Muslim and Mediterranean peoples, adopted ideas of honor that reinforce the ties of an individual to his or her tribal clan or extended family. One type of honor, *sharaf,* applies to men and is attained through maintenance of a family's reputation, hospitality, generosity, chivalry, bravery, piety, and, sometimes, nobility or political power. Another variant of honor, *irdh* in Arabic (*irz* in Turkish), pertains to women, or more specifically, to the sexual use of their bodies, their virginity, or their chaste behavior. The honor of the clan was besmirched if unmarried women did not remain virgins, and if married women were unfaithful. Men were to maintain their clan's honor by punishing their errant women if they brought shame on the group, thus maintaining the patrilineal nature of lineage

and society. Scholars have termed this concept and resultant or related behavior the honor/shame dynamic. Lila Abu Lughod, in her study of the Awlad'Ali Bedouin, shows the complexities of this dynamic, for being humble and exhibiting "shame," *hashham,* can paradoxically demonstrate pride and honor.

Historically, honor has been closely connected to the institution of marriage. Women's honor corresponded to men's lineage rights, because the ultimate violation of *irdh* took place if a woman, unmarried or married, gave birth to an illegitimate child. Yet since a man's honor required legitimate male offspring to carry on his lineage, a wife's infertility could provide a man with an argument for taking a second wife, since polygamy is sanctioned by Islam, and outlawed in the early twenty-first century only in the Muslim countries of Tunisia and Turkey. Many groups continue to believe that family honor is maintained through endogamous marriages, often of cousins. While this tendency may be subsiding in larger cosompolitan centers, men in Bedouin society are frequently required to marry relatives whether or not they form a romantic attachment with them, and this also provides a rationale for polygamy.

Beyond marriage, many customs in the Middle East have developed to display or protect honor. Various articles of dress, which varied tremendously by geographic area, group, and subclimate, often identified membership in a particular tribe, or occupation, and thus demonstrated the honor of that group—for example, the urban notables or wealthy town dwellers of Moroccan cities. The custom of female as well as male circumcision was also related to the notion of honor. Male circumcision was and is practiced by Jews and Muslims in the region, but is not thought by most scholars to affect male sexual functions. Female circumcision, however, which involves removal, or partial removal, of the clitoris and sometimes the labia, as well as infibulation, and is found in North and Western Africa, the Nile valley, and among the Bedouin of the Sinai peninsula and the Negev, is clearly related to sexual honor. The custom predates the monotheistic religions, but is now considered by some to be "Islamic" and a marker of cultural purity and family honor since it may render girls less susceptible to sexual stimulation. Families still believe the custom to confer honor and purity on girls and that, if uncircumcised, they will be unwanted as marriage partners.

Clan or family honor was a strong factor in the pervasive system of tribal law governing revenge or monetary compensation, termed *dhiya* (blood payment), for murder or severe bodily injury. The act of revenge, or the sum paid in its place, restored "honor" to male family members who must avenge crimes involving their relatives. By making payment, or enacting revenge, a lengthier feud could be avoided. The system of compensation or revenge was incorporated into Islamic law, although modern civil penal codes since the nineteenth century have substituted state punishments or incarceration in most nations.

Mediation of conflicts by respected and honorable individuals in rural or urban settings derives in part from tribal norms, wherein the precise technique of choosing mediators and the method of mediation is customary. Similarly, some parties may seek refuge from avengers in the homes of honorable or prestigious clan members. Honor is often connected with status, prestige, noble lineage, and reputation.

Notions of honor have affected literary conventions, and also religious and political ideas. In classic Islamic literature, women's honor was seen to be protected when references to the beloved were made with the masculine verbal forms and pronouns in Arabic. The notion of courtly love, *hubb'udhri,* manifested ideals of honor, for this love was unrequited, indeed often undeclared, and so brought no shame upon the beloved. This ideal encircled the Mediterranean and was not restricted to Muslim countries.

Notions of honor have interacted with other ideals such as respect for piety, pious learning, and reverence for the prophet Muhammad, his family or descendents, other holy men and women, religious scholars, or the dedicated leaders of the Sufi orders. Such individuals believed to uphold the honor of the community through their devotion to piety, good works, and their ability to intercede for ordinary Muslims. In the Mediterranean and Middle East, similar beliefs concerning the honor of and respect for holy sites, connected with Christian saints and martyrs, or religious figures in Judaism, cause people to associate honor with a sacred landscape.

There is a popular belief that urbanization, modernization, materialism, the sedentarization of tribal peoples, incursions of tourism, and Western influences are eroding the traditional honor of individuals and groups. Hospitality is a revered aspect of honor to many groups in the region, expressed through a code of behavior toward strangers as well as neighbors or relatives. Festivities mounted by families for weddings and other celebrations are an extension of their honor. Couples also regard failures to supply material goods stipulated by marriage agreements as breaches of the other side's honor. Thus, honor is an increasingly expensive commodity, and not merely a philosophical "good."

Problems may be experienced where tourists violate, by their presence or conduct, norms of gender segregation, or where tribal members are economically impelled to serve as guides, or otherwise work in tourist-related services. Many women who have donned the head covering or dress referred to as *hijab,* or Islamic dress, perceive themselves to be upholding their honor, just as much as their piety or religiosity, since so many of them work in mixed-gender settings, or travel to work on public transportation.

Historically, and in the modern era, honor is also claimed by the rulers and ruling classes. In some cases, the noble or honorable lineage of particular rulers, such as the Hashemites of Jordan, or the rulers of Morocco, is attributed to their historical derivations and descent from the Prophet, and for the Hashemites as the former administrators of the holy cities of Mecca and Medina.

Presidents of modern countries are accorded a large degree of pomp and circumstance, and in the Middle East this is culturally expressed in terms of their honorable status and not

**Iranian women, Tehran, 1979.** Many Islamic women wear garments that conceal most of their body to show their piety and to uphold their honor. The Arabic concept of *irdh,* which addresses the acceptable behavior of women, disavows women who are not virgins at marriage or who are unfaithful. © CHRISTINE SPENGLER/CORBIS

merely the fact of their political power. Similarly, the elite politicians of many Mediterranean and Middle Eastern countries have held open houses, through which they have both claimed honor and granted political favors to their supporters.

Paradoxically, while honor accrued to those with power, tribal mores tended to elevate individuals. Politically, this construction of honor has been interpreted as a form of integrity, often in the face of an overwhelmingly corrupt milieu. Even beyond the Arab regions, such honorable integrity is, in the early twenty-first century, a part of a modernist, Islamist ideal for men that Fariba Adelkhah terms *javanmard.*

Honor has proved problematic for certain marginal elements in society. The honor of professional entertainers in Muslim and Mediterranean society has often been questioned; for females, because their bodies or voices were displayed in public; and for males, because their patrons might expect to dictate their choice of performance. Thus superior entertainers would uphold "honor" by demonstrating adherence to their own aesthetics and choice of repertoire.

*See also* **Feminism: Islamic Feminism; Gender: Gender in the Middle East; Sexuality: Islamic Views.**

**BIBLIOGRAPHY**

Abu-Lughod, Lila. *Veiled Sentiments: Honor and Poetry in a Bedouin Society.* Berkeley: University of California Press, 1986.

Adelkhah, Fariba. *Being Modern in Iran.* Translated by Jonathan Derrick. New York: Columbia University Press, 2000.

Altorki, Soraya. *Women in Saudi Arabia: Ideology and Behavior among the Elite.* New York: Columbia University Press, 1986.

Ginat, Joseph. *Blood Disputes among Bedouin and Rural Arabs in Israel: Revenge, Mediation, Outcasting, and Family Honor.* Pittsburgh: University of Pittsburgh, 1987.

al-Krenawi, Alean, and John R. Graham. "Culturally Sensitive Social Work Practice with Arab Clients in Mental Health Settings." *Health and Social Work* 25, no 1 (2000): 9–22.

Lavie, Smadar. *The Poetics of Military Occupation: Mzeina Allegories of Bedouin Identity under Israeli and Egyptian Rule.* Berkeley: University of California Press, 1990.

Zuhur, Sherifa. "Building a Man on Stage: Masculinity, Romance and Peformance according to Farid al-Atrash." *Men and Masculinities* 5, no. 3 (January 2003): Special Issue, "Islamic Masculinities," edited by Lahoucine Ouzgane, 275–294.

———. *Criminal Law, Women and Issues of Gender, Sex and Sexuality in the Middle East, North Africa, and the Islamic World.* Istanbul: Women for Women's Human Rights, 2004.

———. *Revealing Reveiling: Islamist Gender Ideology in Contemporary Egypt.* Albany: State University of New York Press, 1992.

*Sherifa Zuhur*

**HUMAN CAPITAL.**    Human capital refers to the knowledge, skills, and capabilities of individuals that generate economic output. Human capital averages about two-thirds of the total value of the capital of most economies, which includes land, machinery, and other physical assets as well as the skills and talents of people. The value of human capital is often apparent after physical destruction, as during World War II—many of the German and Japanese cities that were bombed intensely were able to recover 80 to 90 percent of their previous levels of production within months.

More than two centuries ago, Adam Smith observed in *Wealth of Nations* (1776) that an educated man must earn more than "common labor" to "replace to him the whole expense of his education." Human capital was first discussed extensively by two Nobel Prize–winning economists, Theodore Schultz (1979) and Gary Becker (1992), to explain how any personal decision to sacrifice today for a return tomorrow can be analyzed in the same way that a business considers an investment decision, such as whether to buy new machinery. A nation's stock of human capital and thus its economic growth potential could be increased, they reasoned, if governments reduced the cost and increased the benefits of schooling, the human capital embodied in individuals.

Human capital is rented in the labor market rather than "sold." Individuals exchange effort for reward, and acquire human capital in the expectation that their incomes will be higher. Human capital takes time to acquire, and the basic model of human capital acquisition compares the income stream from going to school with that of going to work immediately. The costs of going to school include the direct costs, in the form of tuition and books, as well as the indirect costs, the forgone earnings that could have been received from working. The benefits of more schooling are higher earnings in the future.

### Costs and Benefits
These costs and benefits must be brought to a single point in time so that the present value of the higher average lifetime earnings with more schooling and the lower average earnings with less schooling can be compared. A rational individual chooses the education and work profile that maximizes the present value of lifetime earnings.

This investment approach to education yields several important predictions about behavior. First, most people will get some education, and most students will be young, because the early years of education have few direct costs, and there are no forgone earnings because most societies prohibit children from working; younger people also have a longer period over which they can recoup their educational investment in the form of higher earnings. The analysis gets more interesting when young people reach the age at which they can work, sixteen or eighteen in most industrial countries, and twelve to fifteen in many developing countries. Youth in industrial countries tend to stay in school because the direct costs are often low and the forgone earnings may be low (working as a teen is often at the minimum wage), while earnings with a college education can be significantly higher. The interest rate used to compare future and present earnings is also important; if this interest rate is low because of subsidized loans, more people will choose to get more education.

Second, government policies shape individual decisions about how much human capital to acquire by affecting the cost of schooling and the payoff from work. Social attitudes also play a role, encouraging young people to stay in school, or to go to college with friends in industrial countries, but in developing countries often encouraging children to help support the family as soon as possible. More forward-looking people, those most able to sacrifice now for future returns, are likely to get the most education, such as those willing to undergo rigorous and time-consuming medical education.

In the United States a combination of higher lifetime earnings, government policies, and social attitudes has increased the percentage of high school graduates who go to college. In 1960, about 45 percent of all high school graduates enrolled in college in the following twelve months, 54 percent of men and 38 percent of women. By 1980, 49 percent of high school graduates enrolled in college: men dropped to 47 percent, and women rose to 52 percent. In 1999, the most recent data available, 63 percent of high school graduates enrolled in college, 61 percent of men and 64 percent of women. Most studies find that men are more present-oriented to immediate earnings opportunities than women, explaining why more women are in college.

The average earnings of college-educated persons are higher than the earnings of high school graduates, and rose in the late twentieth century. In 1979, male college graduates earned 33 percent more than high school graduates, the so-called college earnings premium, and female college graduates earned 41 percent. By 2000, these college earnings premiums rose to 84 percent for men and 67 percent for women, in part because the real earnings of those with less education fell as a result of globalization, which reduced the wages of many high school graduates employed in manufacturing.

Education is generally a good investment: the private rate of return to a college education ranges from 12 to 40 percent in most countries, more than the return on investments in stocks and bonds. Around the world, the rate of return to primary school education was estimated to be 29 percent in the early 1990s, 18 percent for secondary schooling, and 20 percent for higher education. In developing African countries, these rates were 39, 19, and 20 percent, respectively, while in the industrial countries that are members of the Organisation for Economic Co-Operation and Development (OECD), the rates were 22, 12, and 12 percent, respectively. The high rate of return on primary education suggests that countries should subsidize it most.

It is very hard to compute average rates of return for higher levels of education because it is likely that the most capable individuals go to college, so that colleges transmit knowledge that increase productivity and also serve as screening institutions for employers seeking the best workers; some economists argue that the screening role is more important than the productivity-increasing role. On the other hand, the private rate of return to a college education may be higher if more highly educated individuals have both higher incomes as well as more fringe benefits and better or more prestigious jobs. The social rate of return may be even higher than the private rate if highly educated individuals provide more leadership and commit fewer crimes.

Any personal investment that raises productivity in the future can add to an individual's human capital, including on-the-job training and migration. A job that offers training, for example, may have lower earnings but still be attractive because a person knows that, after completing the military, aviation, or stockbroker course, earnings will rise. On-the-job training that makes the person more useful to the employer who provided it is called job-specific training, while training that transmits general skills that make the trained individual useful to many employers is called general training. Employers are more likely to pay for specific than general training. Employers do a great deal of training; by some estimates, U.S. employers spend almost as much on training as is spent at colleges and universities.

### Migration of Human Capital

If people truly are the "wealth of a nation," should developing countries worry about a "brain drain" if their doctors, nurses, and scientists migrate to richer countries? The answer depends on the 3 R's of recruitment, remittances, and returns. Recruitment deals with who migrates abroad: Are the emigrants employed managers whose exit leads to layoffs, or unemployed workers who have jobs and earnings abroad but would have been unemployed at home? Remittances are the monies sent home by migrants abroad: Are they significant, and fuel for investment and job creation, or small and not used to speed development? Returns refers to whether migrants return to their countries of origin: Do they return after education or a period of employment abroad with enhanced skills, or do they return only to visit and retire?

During the 1990s the migration of highly skilled workers from developing to more developed countries increased, reflecting more foreign students as well as aging populations able to pay for more doctors and nurses and the internet-related economic boom. International organizations are exploring ways in which the more developed countries could replenish

the human capital they take from the developing world via migration, perhaps by contributing to or backing loans to improve their educational systems. If the human capital that migrates is not replenished, global inequalities may increase.

*See also* **Education; Globalization; Social Capital.**

BIBLIOGRAPHY

Becker, Gary S. *Human Capital. A Theoretical and Empirical Analysis, with Special Reference to Education.* New York: National Bureau of Economic Research, 1964.

Blaug, Mark. "The Empirical Status of Human Capital Theory: A Slightly Jaundiced Survey." *Journal of Economic Literature* 14 (September 1976): 827–855.

Mincer, Jacob. *Schooling, Experience, and Earnings.* New York: Columbia University Press, 1974.

Organisation for Economic Co-Operation and Development. *Human Capital Investment: An International Comparison.* Paris: OECD, 1998.

Psacharopoulos, George. "Returns to Investment in Education: A Global Update." *World Development* 22, no. 9 (1994): 1325–1343.

Smith, Adam. *An Inquiry into the Nature and Causes of the Wealth of Nations.* Dublin: Whitestone, 1776.

*Philip L. Martin*

## HUMAN RIGHTS.

This entry includes two subentries:

*Overview*
*Women's Rights*

### OVERVIEW

The idea of human rights posits that human beings, regardless of extrinsic differences in circumstance (nationality, class, religion) or physical condition (race, gender, age), possess a basic and absolute dignity that must be respected by governments and other people. Sometimes these rights claims have been grounded in systems of positive law, sometimes in conceptions of human nature or divine creation. Most scholars who study moral and political ideas on a global basis agree that the concept of human rights is Western in origin, although it has spread throughout the world in recent times. The United Nations Universal Declaration of Human Rights of 1948 and other proclamations that have followed from it establish that such rights pertain across the globe regardless of cultural, religious, social, or political differences. In this sense, the very idea of human rights stands logically opposed to moral relativism of any sort. Depending on one's perspective, this hallmark of rights is either a shortcoming or an advantage.

### Stoicism and Roman Jurisprudence

The assertion of the modernity of human rights theory must be qualified by the recognition that many of its characteristic elements were present in and elaborated by earlier theorists. For instance, scholars have found in Aristotle (384–322 B.C.E.) the logical rudiments of a rights theory, albeit imperfectly articulated and applied. More directly influential were the teachings of the Hellenistic Stoic philosophers. Starting with the founder of the school, Zeno of Citium (c. 335–c. 263 B.C.E.), the Stoics held that human beings were subject to a basic law of nature, the dictates of which were accessible to all equally by application of their reason. Of course, most human beings submitted to their passions rather than to reason, meaning that the vast majority were unhappy as well as vicious. The Roman author Cicero (106–43 B.C.E.), while not the Stoic sage that he was once thought to be, extended the doctrine of natural law to cover a basic guarantee of justice for all human beings equally and without differentiation. In his *De officiis* (44 B.C.E.; On duties), Cicero articulated the principle that people have a duty to secure justice for all members of the human race, regardless of their nationality or ethnicity.

The thinking of Cicero and others influenced by the Stoics led to what might be considered the earliest coherent expression of the language of human rights. The language of *ius* ("right") emerged quite soon after the foundation of the Roman Republic, mainly to denote a form of divine judgment. In later Roman times, *ius* constituted the basis of valid or obligatory Roman law, such that persons were fundamentally bearers of rights derived from and fixed by law. At the same time, Roman law drew a clear and enduring distinction between *ius naturale* and *ius civile*: the latter pertained to specific legal and social systems and might be variable, whereas the former comprised general rules or principles of equity with which all legal codes—regardless of time or place—were expected to comply. Thus, *ius naturale* captures one fundamental element of human rights: the universality of such rights that cannot be overridden by appeal to particular contexts or cultural conditions.

### Christianity and Medieval Contributions

Roman legal concepts and terminology carried over into the Christian era in Europe, albeit with important changes and additions. Medieval canon (church) lawyers and Scholastic philosophers insisted that God endowed human beings with basic rights regarding themselves and those goods they required to preserve their divinely created lives. Some recent scholars, most notably Brian Tierney (1997), have identified in the work of twelfth- and thirteenth-century canonists a consistent distinction between "subjective" and "objective" rights. The former resemble modern "natural rights" to life, liberty, and estate, while the latter are moral duties imposed by God regarding fellow human beings. The canonistic texts generally do not support the presence of a rigid and thoroughly examined separation between "subjective" and "objective" components of *iura* (rights), and no canonist developed a complete theoretical argument on the basis of the distinction. Yet, there is certainly evidence that church lawyers sometimes sought to develop a principle of human rights compatible with human freedom, a connection also central to an encompassing human rights theory.

Many attempts have been made to identify the "first" theorist of human or natural rights in the Middle Ages. The Scholastic philosophers/theologians Jean de Paris (c. 1255–1306), William of Ockham (c. 1285–?1349), and Jean Gerson (1363–1429) have been among the candidates. Several participants in the fourteenth-century controversy between the papacy and the members of the spiritual wing of the Franciscan order over the status of voluntary ecclesiastical poverty also moved the debate about the humanness of property ownership in the direction of a theory of rights. Yet, in each instance, some of the elements central to a fully "subjective" or individualistic doctrine of human rights associated with modern thought are absent.

It is perhaps best to examine the development of the theory of human rights as an incremental process. Various thinkers contributed important dimensions to its history without necessarily enunciating the idea in its final form or perhaps even appreciating the wider significance of their particular contributions. One such source may be found in the work of a group of theologians of a Thomist orientation working at the University of Paris in the later fifteenth and early sixteenth centuries, most prominently Konrad Summenhart (c. 1455–1502), John Mair (1469–1550), and Jacques Almain (c. 1480–1515). In a number of writings, these authors equated *ius* with *dominium* (lordship or ownership), which was understood to reside in people naturally and to license in them the power or faculty of acquiring those objects necessary for self-preservation. Their argument was as much theological as legal or philosophical: just as God enjoyed ultimate ownership of the earth and the rest of his creations by virtue of his will, so human beings, in whom God's image resided, could claim dominion over themselves and their property.

### Modern Natural Rights

Arguably, the idea of human rights culminated in the natural rights theories that characterize modern legal and political thought. The idea of natural rights may be contrasted with earlier teachings about natural law that were grounded in more robust principles of reason and natural or divine teleology. Many important thinkers of early modern Europe subscribed to a version of natural law without endorsing a doctrine of human rights. Central to the concept of natural rights is the view that each and every human being enjoys a complete and exclusive dominion over his or her mental and bodily facilities and the fruits thereof in the form of personal property. Thus, a human rights theory entails a conception of private ownership grounded in the subjective status of the individual human being. The rights arising from such human subjectivity are both inalienable and imprescriptible, in the sense that any attempt to renounce or extinguish them would constitute the cessation of one's personhood. Thus, for example, human rights theory renders incoherent arguments for slavery based on alleged human inequalities of intellect or physique.

Consequently, an important feature of the fully developed idea of natural rights is its direct and immediate political bearing. Given that natural rights may not be curtailed or eliminated without the denial to a person of his or her very humanity, any government that attempts to suppress them has no claim to the obedience of its citizens. Natural rights always take precedence over artificial communal or public rights that might be imposed by political institutions. In this way, the doctrine of natural rights circumscribes political power and may even generate a defense of resistance to or revolt against systems of government that violate the rights of persons.

One of the epochal moments that posed a challenge to the doctrine of human rights was the European encounter with the Americas. While the Roman Church had long experience with questions arising from the legal status of "infidels," the discovery of entire civilizations that had experience neither of European culture nor of Christian religion—in conjunction with the fact that they were rich in natural and mineral resources—created a severe intellectual crisis, especially in the Iberian world. Some thinkers were willing, on slender evidence, to equate the inhabitants of the Indies with Aristotelian "barbarians" or "slaves by nature." But Bartolomé de Las Casas (1474–1566), a member of the Spanish conquering class in the New World who experienced a profound change of heart, produced a voluminous body of writings that argued in favor of the "rights" of indigenous peoples. Las Casas drew on canonistic and civil legal literature, as well as scholastic and humanistic political discourse, to develop a polemical case that the inhabitants of Central and South America enjoyed an unfettered right (individually and collectively) to live unmolested by Europeans and to resist with force those who would kill or enslave them. Las Casas's clear invocation of human rights suggests that a watershed had been reached.

## The Reformation and Its Aftermath

At nearly the same time that Las Casas was grappling with Spanish imperialism, the idea of human rights also received refinement and application in the context of the religious Reformation. On the Protestant side, rights theory became a major element of late-sixteenth-century Huguenot efforts to ground their justification of resistance to governments that imposed doctrinal conformity on religious dissenters. While the earliest generations of Reformers had looked toward duty to God in order to justify acts of political disobedience, a noticeable change in language and concepts occurred in the wake of the St. Bartholomew Day's Massacre of 1572. In this vein, Théodore de Bèze (1519–1605) and Philippe de Mornay (1549–1623), as well as a large body of anonymous texts, argued for a condition of human liberty—a privilege of nature whose rightful withdrawal is impossible—that precedes the creation of political society. Therefore, any subsequent government must result from, and must be consonant with, the basic natural state of humanity. Those who would use political power to deny to human beings the exercise of their liberty—including the freedom of conscience to dissent from the established Roman Church—may properly and licitly be challenged with forms of resistance to their tyranny. The Huguenots stopped short, however, of advocating popular rebellion. Instead, they looked to "intermediary magistrates" as the appropriate instigators of resistance to tyrannical conduct. Hence, for sixteenth-century Reformers, the idea of human rights became a stimulus for a religio-political movement that directly opposed forms of religious intolerance and suppression of dissent.

The Counter-Reformation produced its own version of human rights theory that developed out of the language and concepts pioneered by the Parisian theologians Mair and Almain. This is especially evident in the work of the "Second Scholastic" thinkers associated with the School of Salamanca, such as

Francisco Vitoria (1486?–1546), Domingo de Soto (1494–1560), and Francisco Suárez (1548–1617). Vitoria had been trained in Paris and returned to Spain to spread the ideas to which he had been exposed there. Although Vitoria himself wrote nothing, leaving only lecture summaries, his students and their intellectual progeny produced some of the fullest and most enthusiastic elaborations of human rights (Las Casas, for example, was influenced by him). In particular, Vitoria and de Soto explored the complexities of rights theories, moving away from the traditional Thomistic conception of rights as objective duties required by reason. Vitoria's work seems to have contained two differing conceptions of subjective human rights—one connected with individual *dominium,* the other defined in relation to communal law. Each position involved notable limitations and flaws, which led de Soto to attempt to resolve them into a coherent formulation of rights that incorporated both public and private dimensions. Suárez added further to the theory by identifying *ius* with self-preservation and drawing from this some, albeit limited, political implications. He held that a human right existed to resist extreme forms of tyranny, construed as those circumstances in which the survival of the community as a whole was endangered. Otherwise, the misbehavior of government was to be tolerated, lest communal destruction result from acts of disobedience and resistance.

While the School of Salamanca remained steeped in the neo-Aristotelian doctrines of the later Middle Ages, other thinkers attempted to replace this framework with a paradigm for human rights rooted purely in legal principles. Especially celebrated in this regard were Hugo Grotius (1583–1645) and John Selden (1584–1654). Grotius proposed that rights should be grounded solely on the universality of the propriety of human self-preservation, thereby placing self-interest at the center of a human system. He reasoned that human beings enjoy *dominium* over those goods that are immediately necessary in order to preserve themselves: rightful private ownership is directly licensed as a human right. Moreover, he attacked the Aristotelian doctrine of the naturalism of political society. Instead, for Grotius social order must be voluntary, and the only reason that people would join civil society would be for self-protection. As a consequence, the individual does not surrender human rights by entering into a communal arrangement and, indeed, may resist a direct attack on those rights by a magistrate. While Selden enunciated a sustained critique of Grotius, he ultimately embraced an account of human rights derived from his adversary. Selden devalued reason in sense of a moral force with the power to bind and compel the actions of individuals. Rather, he stressed that human rights are directly correlated to natural liberty, such that the only basis for individual obligation is free assent to contracts and compacts, which, once agreed to, must be maintained without exception. For Selden, in contrast to Grotius, natural liberty itself could be renounced by a valid act of human will.

## The Classic Theories: Hobbes and Locke

Selden's best-known adherent was Thomas Hobbes (1588–1679), who developed the insights of the former into a powerful individualist theory of human rights. In his major works, culminating in *Leviathan* (1651), Hobbes ascribed to all human beings natural liberty as well as equality, on the basis of which they are licensed to undertake whatever actions might be necessary to preserve themselves from their fellow creatures. Such self-preservation constituted the indispensable core of human rights. Adopting an extreme position against the Aristotelian teaching of political naturalism, Hobbes maintained that the exercise of one's natural liberty leads directly to unceasing conflict and unremitting fear, inasmuch as nature confers on each individual the right to possess everything and imposes no limitation on one's freedom to enjoy this right. Unalloyed nature yields a state of chaos and warfare and, as a result, a "nasty, brutish, and short" life, the avoidance of which leads human beings to authorize a single sovereign ruler in order to maintain peace. The exchange of natural freedom for government-imposed order, constructed through a social compact, requires renunciation of all claims on rights that humans possess by nature (except, of course, for the right of self-preservation itself) and voluntary submission to any dictate imposed by the sovereign. In this way, Hobbes seconds Selden's defense of absolute government, yet upholds the basic right to self-preservation. Moreover, under the terms of Hobbes's absolute sovereignty, subjects are still deemed to retain the right to choose for themselves concerning any and all matters about which the ruler has not explicitly legislated.

John Locke (1632–1704) crystallized the preceding conceptions of human rights into the quintessential statement of the modern idea. He began his major work on political theory, the *Two Treatises of Government* (written c. 1680; published 1689), by postulating the divinely granted human rights of individuals, understood in terms of the absolute right to preserve one's life and to lay claim to the goods one requires for survival. Arguing against the patriarchal doctrine of Sir Robert Filmer (1588–1653), Locke insists that no natural basis—neither paternity nor descent—justifies the submission of one person to another. Rather, all people are deemed sufficiently rational, as well as free and equal, in their natural condition that they can govern themselves according to a basic cognizance of moral (natural) law, and, thus, will generally respect the rights of others. In contrast to Hobbes, Locke maintains that the condition of perfect natural liberty does not represent a state of war. In the state of nature, human beings can enjoy unimpeded rights to acquire private property, the ownership of which is asserted on the basis of the admixture of their labor (the natural talents and industry of their bodies) with the physical world. Indeed, Locke's state of nature resembles nothing so much as a fully functioning commercial society, which has introduced a system of exchange relations and money, all perfectly consonant with the recognition of the human rights of individuals.

On Locke's account, then, there is no pressing necessity for people living in the state of nature to eschew this condition for formalized communal life. Hence, should they choose to enter into bonds of civil society by means of a contract, the sole reason that they do so is to avoid the "inconveniences" and inefficiency of the pre-civil world. This does not require parties to the contract to surrender any of their human rights. Indeed, the only government worthy of authorization is that which strictly upholds and protects the rights that persons possess by

nature. According to Locke, any magistrate that systematically denies to his subjects the exercise of their natural rights to their life, liberty, and estate is tyrannical and unworthy of obedience. Locke closes the *Second Treatise* with a discussion of the dissolution of government. In his view, a regime that systematically violates human rights places itself in a state of war with the members of civil society, who severally and individually may renounce allegiance to it and may vote to establish a new government. Some have viewed Locke as justifying revolution on the basis of human rights, but his actual point seems to be less extreme: the retention of one's human rights in civil society affords one the ability to protect oneself from those (whether housebreakers or magistrates) who would try to take one's property or limit one's proper sphere of liberty. Locke's resistance theory represents a chastened, but nonetheless genuine, defense of human rights.

## Reception of the Classic Theories

Locke's theory, then, stated an integrated position that drew on many of the earlier strands of human rights thought. In turn, the eighteenth century would see the extension, refinement, and, in some respects, radicalization of the fundamentals of the Lockean doctrine. Locke's language was adopted, for instance, by both theorists and polemicists who sought to halt Europe's complicity in the global slave trade. Likewise, defenders of the equal rights of women to political and social power, such as Mary Wollstonecraft (1759–1797), framed their ideas in the language of rights. Critics of natural nobility and other claims to inborn human inequality invoked the universality of rights as the basis of their assertion of the equal worth and dignity of all people, regardless of birth, class, or occupation. Among the most famous of these was Thomas Paine (1737–1809), whose treatise on *The Rights of Man* (1789) was read and admired on both sides of the Atlantic. Of course, Lockean natural rights theory received its share of criticism during the eighteenth century as well, whether from communalist democrats such as Jean-Jacques Rousseau (1712–1778) or from more individualistic proponents of political economy such as Adam Smith (1723–1790).

Yet, in general, the 1700s may well be regarded as the "century of human rights." The American Declaration of Independence (1776), written by Thomas Jefferson (1743–1826), reaffirmed the "self-evidential" character of human rights. The elaboration of the Lockean stance during the eighteenth century perhaps enjoyed its European apotheosis in the post-Revolutionary French Declaration of the Rights of Man and the Citizen (1789). The declaration, which forms perhaps the major source for all later declarations of human rights, proclaims that the aim of civil life was "the preservation of the natural and imprescriptible rights of man"—they nearly included woman, too—including political, economic, social, religious, and cultural rights as well as resistance to tyranny.

## Critique and Disuse

The spread of rights language in political discourse was countered at the dawn of the nineteenth century by criticisms of the intellectual foundations of rights theory. Most famously, the major exponent of the utilitarian school, Jeremy Bentham

(1748–1832), denounced the doctrine of natural rights as "simply nonsense," adding that the conjunction of natural *and* inalienable rights was "nonsense upon stilts." Bentham's objection was at once political and philosophical. Having witnessed the violent consequences of appeals to absolute rights during the French Revolution and its aftermath, Bentham was appalled by the abuse of rights talk in order to justify coercive restrictions and individual "leveling." While sympathetic to democratic reforms, and no friend of conservative values, Bentham believed that legality constituted the only viable means of securing human liberty. Moreover, Bentham found the metaphysics (whether religious or naturalistic) that supported eighteenth-century conceptions of human rights to be hopelessly outdated and even intellectually dangerous, inasmuch as such doctrines could be as easily invoked to inhibit individual calculations of utility as to realize them.

From a very different perspective, social conservatives also strongly condemned the idea of rights. Most famously, Edmund Burke's (1729–1797) *Reflections on the Revolution in France* (1790) pointed out the political terror implicit in the invocation of metaphysically abstract human rights as the foundation of social and political order. Such rights could readily be employed to ruthlessly suppress existing institutions (the church, class status, governmental units) that constituted the sources of human identity and solidarity, which Burke took to be the real or concrete basis of human rights. As bearers of abstract rights, but without a context in which to exercise them, Burke expected that the masses would turn to an authoritarian figure who would direct them. In the rise of Napoleon Bonaparte (1769–1821), his expectations were accurately realized.

On the political left, suspicion of human rights was also rife among socialists, communists, and anarchists. Pierre-Joseph Proudhon (1809–1865) regarded rights to be the theory, and private ownership the practice, of theft. For Karl Marx (1818–1883) and many of his followers, "rights" were necessarily "bourgeois rights," that is, an ideological superstructure that bolstered and justified the appropriation of the surplus labor of the proletariat by the economically dominant capitalist class. In Marx's view, the rights posited in capitalist society—economic rights to property ownership and to sell one's labor as well as minimal political rights—are partial and cannot be historically distinguished from the interests of capital. By starting with an abstract and unhistorical concept, appeals to human rights thus necessarily covered over and legitimized the base structures of human domination.

**Twentieth-Century Developments**

Despite the critiques of philosophers and activists, the idea of human rights remains one of the most compelling, salient, and popular political doctrines of recent times. Impetus was given to this by the 1948 U.N. Universal Declaration of Human Rights and the many other attendant international and multinational agreements that have reinforced the notion that human beings as morally dignified persons are bearers of rights. The declaration offered a more robust version of what constitutes basic human rights than did most previous statements and theories. In addition to personal, political, legal, and economic rights, the framers of the declaration included a full set

of social rights that they regarded as essential to a minimum level of human flourishing. These included social welfare, public education, workplace protections, and an assured living standard—in sum, the way of life to which European social democracies aspire. It is an open question whether such human rights are really more a matter of social justice than fundamental moral dignity.

Stripped of theological and metaphysical connotations, rights in the post–World War II era again became intellectually respectable among certain legal and political theorists. Some thinkers interpreted rights in a positivistic fashion, namely, a "right" properly connotes a power that an individual might reasonably expect to have vindicated by the judicial system in a particular political system. Thus, it is meaningless to assert one's "right to free speech" in an authoritarian regime or to claim a "right to same-sex marriage" in a society that has constitutionally prohibited such unions. Hence, in the positivist interpretation, the appeal to human rights cannot be deployed as the grounds for social criticism or civil disobedience.

Likewise, the analytical school of philosophy that has predominated in the English-speaking world from the middle of the twentieth century has shown an interest primarily in examining the various contexts in which rights language is asserted. Perhaps the best-known figures on this score are H. L. A. Hart (1907–1992) and A. I. Melden (1910–1991), for whom the assertion of a right is the ground of a claim, in others, an appeal to a fundamental or irreducible principle. That such grounds are not always recognized, or that they are on occasion overridden, does nothing to contradict the linguistic observation that when a person appeals to a right he or she is affirming a precept that is deemed antecedent to, rather than created or authorized by, law. Analytical theory, of course, takes this to be a point about the use of human language or logic, not about an idea that must be rooted in metaphysical truths.

One finds an analogous, if more extreme, attitude toward rights arising from postmetaphysical schools of philosophy such as poststructuralism, multiculturalism, and neopragmatism. In the view of adherents to these antifoundationalist approaches, the very attempt to impose a universal category such as "human rights" takes on authoritarian overtones. From the inherent rights perspective, Muslim women who wear traditional headdress and garb must be oppressed by their religious and patriarchal society and are in need of liberation to dress however they wish. Such a claim, for postmetaphysical theorists, reveals the inherent secular, individualistic and, ultimately, paternalistic biases of human rights doctrines.

The denial of an extraconventional grounding to rights has, however, been challenged since the late twentieth century by neonatural law theorists such as John Finnis, Germaine Grisez, and Robert George. For these thinkers, appeal to rights without some theological or metaphysical foundations is incoherent. Robert Nozick's (1938–2002) influential *Anarchy, State, and Utopia* (1974) sought to reclaim for libertarian political thought the Lockean version of natural rights theory, albeit in a modified form that circumvented the metaphysical issues implicit in Locke. The politician Tom Campbell and others attempt to capture rights language for the political in order to support progressive causes in the realms of workers' organization, indigenous peoples, and the environment. While some liberal feminists also invoke rights language, there remains skepticism about the gendered history of the promulgation of human rights that makes it difficult for many academic feminists to include rights in their intellectual arsenal.

In comparison with lingering ambivalence among contemporary thinkers concerning the assertion of human rights, popular social and legal discourse in the Western world is permeated with declarations of personal and group rights. In a famous attack on the current prevalence of rights talk, Mary Ann Glendon (b. 1938) points out the corrosive effects of constant appeals to rights. Citizens who constantly seek "their" own rights tend to think of their fellows as obstacles to fulfillment rather than partners or persons with whom they share important qualities. In this quasi-Hobbesian world in which everyone primarily seeks his or her own rights, all are ultimately frustrated in their ability to attain what they believe is rightfully "theirs."

*See also* **Abolitionism; Authority; Citizenship; Class; Communism; Conservatism; Constitutionalism; Democracy; Enlightenment; Equality; Feminism; Hierarchy and Order; Human Capital; Justice; Law; Liberalism; Liberty; Person, Idea of the; Power; Property; Protest, Political; Resistance; Responsibility; Revolution; Social Contract; Society; Sovereignty; Totalitarianism; Utilitarianism.**

## BIBLIOGRAPHY

PRIMARY SOURCES

Burke, Edmund. *Reflections on the Revolution in France.* Edited by J. G. A. Pocock. Indianapolis: Hackett, 1987.

*The Cambridge Translations of Medieval Philosophical Texts.* Vol. 2: *Ethics and Political Philosophy,* edited by Arthur S. McGrade, John Kilcullen, and Matthew Kempshall. Cambridge, U.K.: Cambridge University Press, 2001.

Cicero, Marcus Tullius. *On Duties.* edited by M. T. Griffin and E. M. Atkins. Cambridge, U.K.: Cambridge University Press, 1991.

Hobbes, Thomas. *Leviathan.* Edited by Edwin Curley. Indianapolis: Hackett, 1994.

Las Casas, Bartolomé de. *In Defense of the Indians.* Translated by Stafford Poole. DeKalb: Northern Illinois University Press, 1974.

Locke, John. *Two Treatises of Government.* Edited by Peter Laslett. Cambridge, U.K.: Cambridge University Press, 1988.

Paine, Thomas. *Rights of Man.* Edited by Henry Collins. Harmondsworth, U.K.: Penguin, 1969.

Vitoria, Francesco de. *Political Writings.* Edited by Anthony Pagden and Jeremy Lawrance. Cambridge, U.K.: Cambridge University Press, 1991.

SECONDARY SOURCES

Brett, Annabel S. *Liberty, Right, and Nature: Individual Rights in Later Scholastic Thought.* Cambridge, U.K.: Cambridge University Press, 1997.

Finnis, John. *Natural Law and Natural Rights.* Oxford: Clarendon, 1980.

Glendon, Mary Ann. *Rights Talk: The Impoverishment of Political Discourse.* New York: Free Press, 1991.

Haakonssen, Knud. *Natural Law and Moral Philosophy: From Grotius to the Scottish Enlightenment.* Cambridge, U.K.: Cambridge University Press, 1996.

Melden, A. I., ed. *Human Rights.* Belmont, Calif.: Wadsworth, 1970.

Miller, Fred D., Jr. *Nature, Justice, and Rights in Aristotle's Politics.* Oxford: Clarendon, 1995.

Nozick, Robert. *Anarchy, State, and Utopia.* New York: Basic Books, 1974.

Tierney, Brian. *The Idea of Natural Rights: Studies on Natural Rights, Natural Law, and Church Law, 1150–1625.* Atlanta, Ga.: Scholars Press, 1997.

Tuck, Richard. *Natural Rights Theories: Their Origin and Development.* Cambridge, U.K.: Cambridge University Press, 1981.

Waldron, Jeremy, ed. *Theories of Rights.* Oxford: Oxford University Press, 1984.

*Cary J. Nederman*

## WOMEN'S RIGHTS

The Universal Declaration of Human Rights, adopted by the General Assembly of the United Nations (U.N.) on 10 December 1948, provided the most detailed outline of the human rights and fundamental freedoms of individuals in the modern era. Furthermore, it was a milestone in that these rights and freedoms applied to every person around the world. The language of the document was, however, gender neutral, meaning that it did not specify the unique rights of women. Throughout the modern human rights era, the debate continues as to whether or not this document and others like it truly encapsulate the needs and views of non-Westerners. Efforts to address the human rights of women have likewise been plagued by such disagreements. Nonetheless, by the turn of the twenty-first century much progress had been achieved, while more work remained to be done to advance the rights of women around the world.

### U.N. Decade for Women and World Conferences on Women

The Commission on the Status of Women (CSW), established in 1946 by the U.N. Economic and Social Council to promote the rights of women in political, economic, civil, social, and educational fields, successfully lobbied the U.N. General Assembly to designate 1975 the International Women's Year. The highlight of the year was the first World Conference on Women, held in Mexico City, which recommended a U.N. Decade for Women (1976–1985). The decade sought to address the needs of women in what were then known as the first, second, and third worlds with a tripartite theme of equality, peace, and development by making recommendations for action at local, national, and international levels.

Midway through the Decade for Women, in 1980, the World Conference of the U.N. Decade for Women was held in Copenhagen. A world conference was held in Nairobi in 1985 to review the achievements of the Decade for Women and to create a ten-year action plan for the advancement of women. The resulting document, *Forward-Looking Strategies*

| Landmark events for the advancement of women within the United Nations system | |
| --- | --- |
| **Year** | **Landmark Events for the Advancement of Women within the UN** |
| 1946 | Establishment of the Commission on the Status of Women and the Branch for the Advancement of Women |
| 1948 | Adoption of the Universal Declaration of Human Rights |
| 1953 | Adoption of the Convention on the Political Rights of Women |
| 1957 | Adoption of the Convention on the Nationality of Married Women |
| 1962 | Adoption of the Convention on Consent to Marriage, Minimum Age for Marriage and Registration of Marriages |
| 1967 | Approval of the Declaration on the Elimination of All Forms of Discrimination against Women |
| 1975 | International Women's Year, International Women's Day (8 March), World Conference of the International Women's Year (Mexico City) |
| 1976–85 | United Nations Decade for Women |
| 1979 | Adoption of the Convention on the Elimination of All Forms of Discrimination against Women |
| 1980 | World Conference of the United Nations Decade for Women (Copenhagen) |
| 1985 | World Conference to Review and Appraise the Achievements of the United Nations Decade for Women (Nairobi) |
| 1995 | Fourth World Conference on Women (Beijing) |
| 2000 | Beijing+5 (New York) |

SOURCE: Courtesy of the author

*for the Advancement of Women to the Year 2000,* served as a benchmark to measure improvements in women's conditions. Despite having begun with divergent goals, the U.N. Decade for Women succeeded in finding common ground between activists in the North and the South hemispheres and further legitimized activities to promote women's rights within the U.N. system and beyond. Aimed at accelerating implementation of the Nairobi agreement, the Platform for Action, approved at the Fourth World Conference on Women, held in Beijing in 1995, called for strategic action in twelve critical areas of concern, including women and poverty, education and training, women's health, and violence against women. Given the focus on human rights, population, and social development at world conferences in Vienna (1993), Cairo (1994), and Copenhagen (1995), respectively, increased attention was given to the issue of equality at Beijing. Implementation of the agreements made at Nairobi and Beijing and initiatives for the future were assessed at a special session of the General Assembly, commonly referred to as Beijing +5, held in New York in 2000.

## Women in the U.N. System
Women's issues are addressed by many agencies and bodies of the United Nations, several of which focus exclusively on the rights of women. Among them are the Division for the Advancement of Women (DAW) and the U.N. Development Fund for Women (UNIFEM). Other U.N. agencies have developed their own gender divisions such as the Bureau for Gender Equality of the International Labour Organization (ILO). These divisions strive to achieve the United Nations' goal of gender mainstreaming—a strategy to make gender perspectives and gender equality central to all activities of the United Nations including policy development, research, and program implementation. Despite the extensive institutionalization of gender mainstreaming throughout the United Nations, some have argued for the continued need for women-specific activities and enhanced efforts to draw more men into these processes.

## Nongovernmental Organizations
Nongovernmental organizations (NGOs) having consultative status with the United Nations have regularly influenced in-

ternational policies concerning women. With the growth in numbers and diversity of NGOs since the 1970s, a new breed of women's NGOs and networks has emerged. At each of the major world conferences on women, representatives from these NGOs participated in parallel NGO forums. Their involvement in the preparatory processes of other international conferences has ensured the inclusion of women's issues on international agendas, particularly those impacting women in developing countries and those incorporating a multiplicity of feminist perspectives.

## International Treaties and Women's Rights
While a few other international treaties have addressed the rights of women, the Convention on the Elimination of All Forms of Discrimination against Women (CEDAW) surpasses these other treaties in terms of its scope and in its monitoring capabilities. This "international bill of rights for women" was officially adopted by the U.N. General Assembly in December 1979 and entered into force two years later. By ratifying CEDAW, states pledge to end discrimination against women in all forms and must submit regular reports on the status of implementation of the convention to the U.N. Committee on the Elimination of Discrimination against Women. It is one of the most widely accepted international human rights treaties in existence, although a number of countries have submitted reservations to key articles of the agreement on cultural and religious grounds. For example, several Muslim countries have submitted reservations against articles deemed to run counter to Islamic law.

## Major Issues in the Human Rights of Women
The scope of issues falling under the heading of the human rights of women has expanded greatly since the 1970s, with poverty and violence being two major areas that have been addressed.

***Women and poverty.*** According to the United Nations, of the world's 1.3 billion poor people, it is estimated that 70 percent are women. To blame is a complex web of factors including external debt, structural adjustment policies, and globalization. Ester Boserup's pivotal 1970 book *Woman's Role in Economic Development* first brought to light women's role in the process of development. Since then, the field has experienced a range of policy approaches (welfare, equity, antipoverty, efficiency, and empowerment), which reflect the changing debates on the topic and expanded participation of women from the Southern Hemisphere. Development has been a key issue in several international conferences and declarations and has been incorporated into the intersectoral work of several U.N. agencies.

In the late twentieth century, the topic evolved into discussions of gender and macroeconomics and women and poverty. Multiple actors, including governments, multilateral financial and development institutions, and national and international nongovernmental organizations and women's groups, have been urged to provide women economic opportunities, autonomy and resources, access to education and support services, and equal participation in decision-making processes. Despite several decades' worth of efforts to improve the lot of poor women, in the early years of the twenty-first century the gap between the world's rich and poor continued to expand unceasingly.

***Violence against women.*** Women and girls are often victims of violence because of their sex. Thanks in large part to the efforts of transnational networks, the topic of violence against women finally gained U.N. attention in the mid-1980s. It has since garnered enormous notice in a wide range of areas of concern including domestic violence, sexual assault and abuse, sexual harassment and trafficking in women, as well as prenatal sex selection in favor of male babies, female infanticide, female genital mutilation, forced prostitution, dowry-related violence, battering, and marital rape. In the late twentieth and early twenty-first centuries, there has been a surge in violence against women in situations of armed conflict, in particular murder, systematic rape, sexual slavery, and forced pregnancy.

The Declaration on the Elimination of Violence against Women, adopted by the U.N. General Assembly in 1993, and the Beijing Platform for Action are the most comprehensive international policy statements to address gender-based violence. The U.N. General Assembly established at UNIFEM the Trust Fund in Support of Actions to Eliminate Violence against Women with the aim of identifying and supporting inventive projects to prevent and eliminate gender-based violence. Among other suggestions, governments and other national bodies are urged to enact and enforce legislation against the perpetrators of practices and acts of violence against women, to promote the modification of social and cultural patterns that condone violence, and to ameliorate institutional mechanisms for the reporting of violence. With increased attention to the issue, violence against women is bound to appear to get worse before it improves due to an increase in the reporting of violence and an ever expanding number of acts subsumed in the definition of violence.

Women have long strived to expand modern notions of human rights to move beyond Western, liberal conceptions based on the rights of *man* meaning males. Those from the South in particular have struggled to ensure that the human rights of women take into consideration their unique needs and concerns. With the help of national governments and national and international organizations, including human rights and women's rights networks, the U.N. system has become instrumental in identi-

fying and addressing the human rights of women as being unique from those of men. Though progress has been achieved, much work remains for the full realization of equality between the sexes.

*See also* **Equality: Gender Equality; Feminism; Gender.**

**BIBLIOGRAPHY**

Agosín, Marjorie. *Women, Gender, and Human Rights: A Global Perspective.* New Brunswick, N.J:. Rutgers University Press, 2001.

Askin, Kelly D., and Dorean M. Koenig, eds. *Women and International Human Rights Law.* Ardsley, N.Y.: Transnational, 1999.

Benedek, Wolfgang, Esther M. Kisaakye, and Gerd Oberleitner, eds. *The Human Rights of Women: International Instruments and African Experiences.* London and New York: Zed Books, 2002.

Chen, Martha Alter. "Engendering World Conferences: The International Women's Movement and the U.N." In *NGOs, the U.N. and Global Governance,* edited by Thomas G. Weiss and Leon Gordenker. Boulder, Colo.: Lynne Rienner, 1996.

Cook, Rebecca J., ed. *Human Rights of Women: National and International Perspectives.* Philadelphia: University of Pennsylvania Press, 1994.

Kerr, Joanna, ed. *Ours by Right: Women's Rights as Human Rights.* London and Atlantic Highlands, N.J.: Zed Books, 1993.

Lockwood, Carol Elizabeth, et al., eds. *The International Human Rights of Women: Instruments of Change.* Washington, D.C.: American Bar Association, 1998.

Peters, Julie, and Andrea Wolper, eds. *Women's Rights, Human Rights: International Feminist Perspectives.* New York: Routledge, 1995.

Pietilä Hilkka, and Jeanne Vickers. *Making Women Matter: The Role of the United Nations.* Rev. ed. London and Atlantic Highlands, N.J.: Zed Books, 1994.

Sen, Gita. *Development, Crises, and Alternative Visions: Third World Women's Perspectives.* New York: Monthly Review Press, 1987.

United Nations. *The United Nations and the Advancement of Women, 1945–1996.* Rev. ed. New York: Department of Public Information, United Nations, 1996.

Walter, Lynn, ed. *Women's Rights: A Global View.* Westport, Conn.: Greenwood Press, 2001.

*Christine Min Wotipka*

# HUMANISM.

This entry includes five subentries:

*Africa*
*Chinese Conception of*
*Europe and the Middle East*
*Renaissance*
*Secular Humanism in the United States*

## AFRICA

A common misconception of African humanism is that it is a set of values brought into, instead of emerging from, communities on the African continent. This prejudice is due primarily to the influence of modern European humanism, which is premised upon a secular naturalism as the only model of humanism. The modern European humanist tradition, which treats Christianity as the model of all religion, is critical of Christianity because it claims that Christianity discourages human beings from focusing on the value of human action on Earth beyond concerns for redemption from original sin in an afterlife. If we define humanism as a value system that places priority on the welfare, worth, and dignity of human beings, we should also consider those traditions in which human beings do not seek redemption in an afterlife because, for them, punishment or redemption exists only on Earth. Consequently, their tendency is to place great weight on human action and human subjects. The focus on earthly actions is a key feature of many African religions and, consequently, African humanism.

## Indigenous Foundations

Despite the presence of many indigenous ethnic groups in Africa, there is much similarity in the cosmologies that ground their religious practices, especially those of people south of the Sahara. A major reason for this commonality is that many of them are descended from a set of communities along the ancient lakes and plains of the Sahara-Sahelian region of northern Africa that subsequently dried up, becoming desert. The cosmologies of these groups tend to have a concomitant ontology, or conception of being, and a system of values, in which greater reality and value are afforded to things of the past. Thus, the Creator, being first, has the greatest ontological weight, and whoever is brought into being closer in time to the moment of the origin of the world is afforded greater weight. This view gives one's ancestors greater ontological weight and value than their descendants. Also, one's past actions are of greater ontological weight than one's present actions. (One's future actions are of no ontological weight since they have not yet occurred.) Indigenous African systems affirm that human beings negotiate their affairs with the understanding that they cannot change the past (although they can be informed by it, especially through ancestors), are entirely responsible for the present, and must take responsibility for their future. This form of humanism does not require the rejection of religion, but may exist alongside it. As Kwame Gyekye observed in his classic study of Akan humanism among the Asante of Ghana, for example:

> In Akan religious thought the Supreme Being is not conceived as a terrible being who ought to be feared because he can cast one into eternal hellfire. (The Supreme Being is believed to punish evildoers only in this world.) Again, in spite of Akan belief in immortality, their conception of the hereafter does not include hopes of a happier, more blessed life beyond the grave. Western humanism sees religion as impeding the concentration of human energies on building the good society. In Akan thought this tension between supernaturalism and humanism does not appear; for the Akan, religion is not seen as hindering the pursuit of one's interests in this world . . . Akan humanism is the consequence not only of a belief in the existence of a Supreme Being and other supernatural entities, but, more importantly I think, of

a desire to utilize the munificence and powers of such entities for the promotion of human welfare and happiness. (pp. 144–145)

## Muslim Humanism in North Africa

Ibn Rushd (1126–1198), known by his Latin name Averroës, was a North African philosopher whose work came to prominence in Cordoba, Spain. He was a pioneer in African Muslim thought, and his influence includes commentaries on Aristotle that affected European scholasticism and the struggles to transform it. Rushd argued for the secularization of political life and the dominance of reason. For this position, he was widely rejected in the Muslim world, save for a small set of followers. The debate over these ideas, however, continued in the question of the role of modernity in the Muslim world. Among the many scholars who took up this issue was the Egyptian-born Imam Muhammad Abdou (1849–1905), who argued for freeing thought from convention and who presented a political theory of citizen rights for social justice, rather than blind obedience to the religious state. Zaki Naguib Mahmoud (1905–1993) defended the dominance of reason through logical positivism in science and based his form of humanism on secular naturalism. Abdel-Rahman Badawi (1917–2002), also Egyptian born, presented his atheistic existential philosophy as a more radical humanism for the Muslim world by comparing it with Sufism. In both Sufism and his philosophy, he argued, the human subject is prioritized. The writings of the Algerian novelist and historian Assia Djebar (1936–) has brought a new dimension to the question of subjectivity and the impact of physical and historical limits. In her historical work, Djebar examines the emergence of women revolutionaries under extraordinary repressive circumstances and, in her novels, how reclamation of their voices and bodies exemplify liberation for women.

## "Modern" African Humanism

Beyond the indigenous models of humanism there has arisen what may be called modern African humanism, which emerged from African responses to conquest, colonization, and the various slave trades along the African coasts. These forms usually involve engagements with Christian, liberal, and republican (domination-free) values, or with values that emerged as a result of engagement with various Muslim empires in the Middle Ages, whose impact continues to be felt today. We should bear in mind that much of eastern Africa is also populated by Semitic peoples, and that their Coptic and Abyssinian (or Ethiopian) Christianity has left a legacy that is as old as its European, Roman, and Greek counterparts.

Many modern African humanists address a problem raised in early medieval African Christian philosophy in the thought of St. Augustine of Hippo (354–430): the problem of theodicy, which involves accounting for the presence of evil in a universe ruled by an omnipotent, omniscient, and benevolent god or God. It is a problem also found in the thought of the Ethiopian Christian philosopher Zara Yacob (1599–1696). St. Augustine argued that human beings are responsible for evil because such actions are a necessary possibility of freedom. He also argued that human beings have limited knowledge of God's ultimate will or God's justice—the literal meaning of theodicy, *theo* (god) and *dikē* (justice). The modern African faced the same problem when he or she looked at such evils as the slave trade and colonialism. Wilhelm Amo (1703–1756) and Ottobah Cugoano (b. c. 1757), both from Ghana, wrote treatises calling for the abolition of the slave trade. These authors argued that human beings are responsible for their actions, and that Europeans faced the negative moral consequences of the slave trade. Although couched in a Christian context, their work included reflections on the humanity of African peoples that have become a feature of modern African humanistic thought—namely, its concern with philosophical anthropology.

## Secular Humanism in Africa

In the twentieth century, a form of secular humanism emerged in Africa primarily through the efforts of the Senegalese intellectuals Cheikh Anta Diop (1923–1986) and Léopold Sédar Senghor (1906–2001). Diop advocated a strong historicist humanism that focused on the achievements of ancient Africans as the first Homo sapiens, arguing that they laid the groundwork for the cultural life of the species. Although secular, the familiar theme of ancestral value is echoed in his work. Senghor is best known as a co-founder, with the Martinican poet Aimé Césaire (b. 1913) of the negritude movement, which focused on the creative potential of black consciousness. Whereas Diop represented the historicist tradition of African secular humanism, Senghor is the father of the poeticizing tradition. He defended the humanity of black Africans primarily through literature, although his thought also included reflections on music. Senghor argued that African value systems were more properly humanistic than European ones because the African models affirmed that the passionate or emotional side of a person carries the same value and legitimacy as the rational, analytic side. In Ghana, the secular humanist tradition also took hold through the thought of Kwame Nkrumah (1909–1972), who in 1946 offered what he called *consciencism,* or critical material consciousness. For Nkrumah, African humanism was a call for explicitly political responses to social problems.

The most famous formulation of secular humanism to emerge on the African continent came, however, by way of the thought of Frantz Fanon (1925–1961), a Martinican expatriate in Algeria. Fanon diagnosed a sick modern world premised upon human actions, wherein the tasks faced by contemporary Africans must be to build up their material infrastructure (based on national consciousness) and thereby transform negative cultural symbols into positive ones that could set humanity aright. The secular humanist tradition continued along historicist and poeticizing lines, and with political allegiances of the Marxist (and, occasionally, liberal) variety through such writers and political leaders as Almicar Cabral and Julius Nyerye until the emergence of leaders in the struggle against apartheid in South Africa took center stage.

The two most influential formulations of secular humanism to emerge focused on the question of consciousness. The first was Stephen Bantu Biko (1946–1977), who developed a theory of black consciousness that drew upon the political dimension of racial oppression. *Black,* for Biko, designated a form of oppression that could be faced by an East Indian, an East Asian, or a colored (in Africa, a person of mixed race, for example of

indigenous and Afrikaaner parents) as well as an indigenous African. The second was Noël C. Manganyi, advisor to the vice-chancellor and principal of the University of Pretoria. Manganyi is a psychologist whose writings during the apartheid years were of an existential phenomenological variety, with many similarities to Fanon and Jean-Paul Sartre. There have, however, also been highly political Christian humanist responses in the South African context that should be considered, the most noted representative of which is the Nobel Peace Prize laureate Bishop Desmond Tutu, whose leadership in forming South Africa's Peace and Reconciliation Commission exemplifies what might be called the Christian liberal tradition.

## Recent African Humanisms

The last quarter of the twentieth century was marked by the emergence of African academic intellectuals as chief spokespersons for secular African humanism. Many of these writers present their case from the disciplinary perspectives of philosophy, political theory, and political economy (especially as critics of development studies), and many of them, save, for example, Kwame Gyekye (Ghana), Manganyi (South Africa), Mbogo P. More (South Africa), and Samir Amin (Senegal), are expatriates living in North America and Europe. They include, among others, V. Y. Mudimbe (Congo/Zaire), Ato Sekyi-Otu (Ghana), Kwasi Wiredu (Ghana), K. Anthony Appiah (United Kingdom/ Ghana), Nkiru Nzegwu (Nigeria), Oyeronke Oyewumi (Nigeria), D. A. Masolo (Kenya), Tsenay Serequeberhan (Eritrea), Teodros Kiros (Ethiopia), Albert Mosley (Senegal), Souleyman Bachir Diagne (Senegal), Elias Bongmba (Cameroon), and Samuel Imbo (Kenya). To this academic group can be added East Indian and white Africans such as Mahmood Mandani (Uganda), John and Jean Comaroff, David Theo Goldberg, and Neil Lazarus (all from South Africa). This stage of African secular humanism is marked by such themes as postmodern skeptical humanism, liberal cosmopolitanism, New Left Marxism, and African feminism.

The poeticist-humanist tradition has continued through many novelists and dramatists such as Wole Soyinka (Nigeria), Chinua Achebe (Nigeria), Ngugi wa Thiong'o (Kenya), Ama Ata Aidoo (Ghana), Ayi Kwei Armah (Ghana), and white authors, the best known of whom are the South African Nobel laureates Nadine Gordimer and John Coetzee. There is also the emergence of a form of musical poeticist humanism that has been part of the rise of "world music," whose artists come from all parts of Africa and represent nearly all its traditions. They serve as critical commentators on Africa's contemporary condition. Perhaps the most famous of such artists was the Nigerian Fela Anikulapo-Kuti (1938–1997).

*See also* **Africa, Idea of; African-American Ideas; Black Consciousness; Humanity: African Thought; Negritude; Philosophies: African.**

### BIBLIOGRAPHY

Comaroff, John, and Jean Comaroff. *Of Revelation and Revolution.* 2 vols. Chicago: University of Chicago Press, 1997.
———. "On Personhood: An Anthropological Perspective from Africa." *Social Identities* 7, no. 2 (2001): 267–283.

Eze, Emmanuel Chukwudi, ed. *African Philosophy: An Anthology.* Oxford: Blackwell, 1998.

Gyekye, Kwame. *An Essay on African Philosophical Thought: The Akan Conceptual Scheme.* Rev. ed. Philadelphia: Temple University Press, 1995.

Hallen, Barry. *A Short History of African Philosophy.* Bloomington: Indiana University Press, 2002.

Henry, Paget. "African and Afro-Caribbean Existential Philosophies." In *Existence in Black: An Anthology of Black Existential Philosophy,* edited by Lewis R. Gordon, 11–36. New York: Routledge, 1997.

———. *Caliban's Reason: Introducing Afro-Caribbean Philosophy.* New York: Routledge, 2000.

Kopytoff, Igor, ed. *The African Frontier: The Reproduction of Traditional African Societies.* Bloomington: Indiana University Press, 1987.

Masolo, D. A. *African Philosophy in Search of Identity.* Bloomington: Indiana University Press, 1994.

Mbiti, John. *African Religions and Philosophy.* 2nd rev. and enl. ed. Oxford: Heinemann, 1990.

Wiredu, Kwasi, ed. *A Companion to African Philosophy.* Malden, Mass.: Blackwell, 2004.

*Lewis R. Gordon*

## CHINESE CONCEPTION OF

The dominant Chinese conception of humanism is the Confucian theory of *ren.* The term *ren* has been translated in various ways, including as "benevolence," "goodness," "virtue," "humanity," "humanness," and "being authoritative." These different translations indicate the complexity of this Confucian theory.

In introducing *ren* as the central notion of his philosophy, Confucius (551–479 B.C.E.) takes it both as a general ethical quality and as a particular one. As a particular ethical quality, the term means "to love one's fellow men" (*Analects,* 12:22). "Benevolence" is an appropriate translation for capturing this sense of love and affection. *Ren* as benevolence is distinguished from other particular virtues, such as courage and knowledge, and can be conceived independently of them. More often, however, *ren* refers to a general dispositional state that embraces particular character traits such as knowledge, courage, filial piety, loyalty, respectfulness, tolerance, trustworthiness in word, and generosity. In this sense, *ren* is a virtue in its entirety or in its inclusiveness and has also been reasonably rendered or referred to as "virtue" or "complete virtue."

*Ren* as the dispositional state is based on what a human being is. Both the *Doctrine of the Mean* (chap. 20) and *Mencius* (7a: 16)—two texts that have been grouped together with the *Analects* (plus the *Great Learning*) as the four core Confucian classics—include the formula "Ren zhe ren ye," literally "to be *ren* is to be a man." This means that *ren* is the quality that makes a person a true person. It is for this reason that many translators choose "humanity" or "humanness" to render this term. Such a translation is essentially correct, and it effectively points out that the Confucian theory of *ren* is a form of humanism. Nevertheless, it is important to keep in mind that, while both "humanity" and "humaneness" can refer to the inborn characteristic of a person, the notion of *ren,* although

based on the special human characteristic, is a cultivated disposition, that is, humanity or humanness in its cultivated form. The theory of *ren,* then, is the combination of humanism and virtue ethics.

Confucius calls a person who possesses the character of *ren, junzi* (variously translated as "the gentleman," "the profound person," or "the exemplary person"). This term literally means "the lord's son" and refers to the aristocrats or feudal princes. Confucius shifts its meaning to "the man possessing noble human qualities." By doing so, he emphasizes that the good quality of human beings is not limited to one special class but is related to the humanity that all humans share in common. Simply put, because *ren* is what makes a person a person, *junzi,* a person of *ren,* is one who has fulfilled and manifested what is genuinely human.

### Underlying Beliefs

Understanding what is genuinely human in the Confucian theory of *ren* requires knowing *ren*'s underlying metaphysical and psychological beliefs. According to ancient Chinese belief, Heaven (*tian,* literally meaning "sky") has an impersonal ordering force. Heaven is said to have its *dao* (literally, "path" or "road," usually translated as "way," meaning the characteristic mode of existence or action of a thing). Everything in the world has its own *dao,* or way, as well. Each particular thing's *dao* is related to the *dao* of Heaven in the way that the *dao* of each thing is the individualization of the *dao* of Heaven in that thing. If everything follows its imparted or natural *dao,* the *dao* prevails in the whole world and the world is a harmonious and integrated organism. Following this, the human *dao* is thought to be the *dao* of Heaven as individualized in a human life. It is the *dao* in accordance with which one should lead one's life. If one can live in accordance with the human *dao,* one also embodies the *dao* of Heaven. Such a life is meaningful and authentic. In Chinese intellectual history, it was Confucius who first raised the following question: Where is the *dao* of Heaven as individualized in a human life, that is, the way (*dao*) of being a human? From Confucius on, it became the common task for classical Chinese philosophers to find and establish the *dao.* Chinese philosophical schools in the classical period offered competing accounts of what *dao* is.

Human *dao,* the individualization of the *dao* of Heaven in human beings, is called *de* (related to the verb "to get"). A person who acquires the *dao* of Heaven is a person of *de.* The term appears in the ancient oracle bone inscriptions, referring to the psychic power that an individual possesses to influence and attract other people and even the surrounding environment. In particular, *de* means the power that rulers hold that enables them to command others without appealing to physical force. Because the exertion of such power is associated with desirable attributes such as kindness and dutifulness, *de* comes to be used to refer to these attributes or qualities as well, and hence it is usually translated into English as "virtue."

The *Analects* has this *dao/de* (way/virtue) framework at its core in its discussion of what a human being is, as in the following passage: "How can a man be said either to have anything or not to have anything who fails to hold on to virtue

[*de*] with all his might or to believe in the *dao* with all his heart[?]" (19:2). Both *dao* and *de*, however, are formal concepts. When Confucius sets out to reflect systematically upon what human *dao* or *de* is, that is, the way of being a human, he must provide a substantive specification of its content.

The theory of *ren* is a specification of what Confucius thinks human *de* or human *dao* is. (This explains why both *de* and *ren* in the *Analects* can be translated as "virtue." *De* is a formal conception of virtue, whereas *ren* is Confucius's understanding of what it is in a substantial sense). Hence, Confucius's theory of *ren*, that is, his humanism, is about the *dao*, or way, of being a human, and in his pursuit of human *dao*, he appeals to *ren* (the virtuous disposition that makes a human being a true human being).

### Achieving *Ren*

How, then, does one achieve *ren?* Confucius's first reply is that to achieve *ren* is "to return to *li*" (*Analects*, 12:1). *Li* refers to the traditional ritual and cultural practices, fully developed in China's early Zhou dynasty (founded in the eleventh century B.C.E.). Its core is a humane social hierarchy modeled on family relationships. "Let the ruler a ruler, the subject a subject, the father a father, the son a son" (12:11). "To return to *li*" means to be shaped or transformed by traditional values. Moreover, to be a person of *ren* also involves an emotional aspect. According to Confucius, to be *ren* means to "love your fellow men" (12:22). The love is based on one's filial love for parents and brothers and is extended to all human beings (1:2, 1:6). Furthermore, *ren* involves an intellectual aspect: "The Master said, 'In his dealings with the world the gentleman is not invariably for or against anything. He is on the side of what is appropriate [*yi*]'" (4:10). This intellectual aspect enables a Confucian agent to avoid following traditional values blindly.

The cultivation of *ren* is not an isolated process. The path toward human realization goes through family, community, tradition, state, and even the whole world. To promote human realization, the Confucian school teaches, in addition to the classics that record traditional values, six arts in its curriculum: ritual, music, archery, charioteering, calligraphy, and arithmetic. To a great extent, this corresponds to the Renaissance *studia humanitatis*.

Because Confucius's ethics has a metaphysical basis—that *ren* is the manifestation of Heaven's *dao* in a human being—it presupposes that humans must have the root of *de* or *ren* in their original nature that comes from Heaven. Confucius himself holds that humans have a natural potential for becoming good: "Is *ren* really far away? No sooner do I desire it than it is here" (*Analects*, 7:30). Nevertheless, although everyone has the root of *ren*, it is through learning and practice that one can manifest and actualize it. Thus, Confucius says that "men are close to one another by nature [*xing*]. They diverge as a result of repeated practice" (17:2).

### The Beliefs of Mencius

Mencius (c. 371–c. 289 B.C.E.), the most influential Confucian after Confucius, focuses on a specification of what this natural basis of *ren* is. Mencius is known for his view that *xing*

(usually translated as "nature" or "human nature") is good. He believes that in everyone's natural endowment there is an organ called *xin* (heart/mind) that carries with it four inborn seeds (*duan*) for moral behavior: the heart of compassion (also called "the unbearable mind"), the sense of shame and disgust, the sense of compliance and respect, and the sense of right and wrong. These seeds are not infused into people from outside, but were there from the beginning (*Mencius*, 6a/6). Human beings do not have to learn or work in order to get them; in fact, they have them just as they have four limbs (2a/6). When these seeds grow and become mature, they turn into four major virtues: benevolence, dutifulness, observance of propriety, and wisdom. These are not four independent virtues, but four different aspects of the general virtue of *ren*.

When Mencius says that human nature is good, he does not mean that everything that is inborn is good. He is fully aware that human nature itself is a complex, inclusive not only of elements that are good but also of elements that are either morally neutral or have little moral value. When he says that *xing* (human nature) is good, he refers only to one part of this complex, the part that is composed of the four seeds and the flourishing of which makes a noble person (*junzi*).

Mencius singles out this part from the complex of human nature because it is the part that makes a human being a human being, and because it distinguishes human beings from other animals (*Mencius*, 2a/6). Although humans have these inborn seeds, the seeds are fragile and it takes great human effort to make them grow. A person who completely casts away these seeds is not much different from the beasts (6a/8). A person who preserves and develops these seeds becomes an excellent person (4b/19). It is the four seeds that form the characteristic feature of being a human, and to be a person of *ren* is to actualize these seeds.

Because *ren* has such a natural basis that is imparted from the *dao* of Heaven, the actualization of *ren* is not just a moral ideal, but a state in which one is unified with Heaven. This state is called *cheng* ("self-completion," also translated as "sincerity" or "creativity"), in which one completely actualizes one's humanity, one's self-understanding, and Heaven, and in which one can help other people fulfill their humanity. *Cheng* is an ever-renewing and ceaseless process of self-understanding and creativity. In this way, a person becomes a counterpart of Heaven and Earth, or a participant in their creative activity, in the sense that as Heaven and Earth help things in the world grow and flourish, persons of *ren* fulfill others as well as themselves.

To sum up, Confucian humanism pursues a desirable kind of humanity and involves features such as a belief in the goodness of human nature, confidence in the power of education and self-cultivation in actualizing human goodness, an emphasis on traditional community and family values, the requirement of altruist love and affection, and a strong belief in the organismic unity of man and nature. This Confucian human ideal was further elaborated by subsequent Confucians in different dynasties, most notably by the Neo-Confucianism of the Song-Ming period (960–1644). In coping with the challenge from Buddhism, Neo-Confucianism sought to provide a more solid and detailed cosmological basis for Confucian humanism.

## Contemporary Revival of Confucianism

In the second half of the twentieth century, there was a revival of Confucianism, both in East Asia and in the United States, called "New Confucianism," or "The Third Epoch of Confucian Humanism." The revival of Confucianism was greatly encouraged and promoted in the 1970s and 1980s by the industrial success of the states located in the circle of Confucian culture. Led by Tu Wei-ming, Confucian scholars explored the relationship between Confucian humanism and the East Asian entrepreneurial spirit and argued that Confucianism provided an alternative view of Enlightenment rationalism and modern Western liberalism. They further maintained that Confucianism, the main concern of which is the well-being of humanity, can answer many serious challenges in the contemporary world community, and that Confucian values should be universalized.

The contemporary value of Confucian humanism can also be appreciated from its similarity to the virtue ethics of the Greek philosopher Aristotle (384–322 B.C.E.). Aristotelian virtue ethics, which has seen its own revival within contemporary ethics, is attractive for two main reasons. First, it concerns the goodness of the agent's whole life rather than focusing on moral acts, as modern Western ethics does; second, its consideration is centered on the character and virtue that a person must have in order to live happily or to flourish, rather than contending that the task of ethics is to formulate rules and principles to govern moral acts. The Confucian humanist ethics shares these two features. Its main concern is to find the human *dao*, that is, the path a person's life should take, and this *dao* is through the cultivation of *ren*, the virtuous disposition based on humanity. Indeed, the Confucian view that *ren* is what makes a human being a true human being is similar to Aristotle's definition of human virtue (*areté*) as the excellent performance of human function as a rational animal, although Confucians emphasize not only rationality but also emotion and human relationality. It is in elaborating the notion of *ren* that Confucianism reflects and discusses issues such as human nature and its fulfillment, the role of social custom and traditions, moral character and cultivation, emotion, habituation and education, the mode of moral reasoning, family, friendship, the role of ethics in politics, and so on. These are precisely Aristotle's main concerns in his exposition of virtue. To a great extent, Aristotelian ethics is taken as a model by contemporary virtue ethics precisely because these important ethical concerns have been left out or at least marginalized in dominant modern moral theories. A virtue ethics approach to Confucianism can help bring out the contemporary significance of Confucian humanism.

*See also* **Chinese Thought; Consciousness: Chinese Thought; Virtue Ethics.**

BIBLIOGRAPHY

Chan, Wing-tsit. "The Evolution of the Confucian Concept *Jen*." *Philosophy East and West* 4, no. 4 (1955): 295–319.

Confucius. *The Analects.* Translated by D. C. Lau. Hong Kong: Chinese University Press, 1979.

Graham, A. C. *Disputers of the Tao: Philosophical Argument in Ancient China.* La Salle, Ill.: Open Court, 1989.

Mencius. *Mencius.* Translated by D. C. Lau. Hong Kong: Chinese University Press, 1984.

Tu, Wei-ming. "The Third Epoch of Confucian Humanism." In his *Way, Learning, and Politics: Essays on the Confucian Intellectual,* 141–159. Albany: State University of New York Press, 1993.

*Jiyuan Yu*

## EUROPE AND THE MIDDLE EAST

The introduction of the term *humanism* is commonly attributed to the German pedagogical theorist F. J. Niethammer's 1808 book, which promoted reading of the ancient classics among secondary students as a counterweight to scientific and technological training. The word soon enjoyed wide currency in many European languages, in part because the much earlier Italian term *umanista* was already used to describe a person committed to the production or study of the artifacts of human culture. In turn, humanism contains echoes of the much earlier Latin ideal of *humanitas,* humanity or humaneness.

The application of the term *humanism* has been widely disputed. Some scholars, most notably Paul Oskar Kristeller, insist that it should be employed strictly to denote the intellectual and literary movement associated with Renaissance Italy, and especially Florence, during the fifteenth century and spreading thereafter to the rest of Europe. Others apply a less rigorous definition that permits a broader field of use, both culturally and chronologically. Joel L. Kramer has isolated three features that are germane to a capacious conception of humanism: the common kinship and unity of humankind; an emphasis on *paideia*, or the shaping of human mental and moral capacities through literary and philosophical education; and the recognition of *philanthropia*, that is, humane love or love of humanity. An even more general account of humanism permits its application to any position that ascribes intrinsic value to the activity of human beings or to their pursuit of happiness in a human way apart from extra-human considerations. All these ideas of humanism offer useful filters and standards on the basis of which to understand its history. The more capacious constructions of humanism may be best, however, because they enable scholars to find bases of comparative analysis between world cultures across time.

### The Greek "Discovery" of Human Nature

The earliest philosophers of ancient Greece directed their attention almost exclusively toward the nature of the cosmos and of metaphysical being. During the course of the fifth century B.C.E., this orientation began to change. The reasons are myriad. Certainly, Greek expeditions (mainly for commercial purposes) throughout the Mediterranean region led to encounters with cultures and social systems that were organized differently than the Hellenic city-state (*polis*), and these encounters led philosophers to reflect on the ways in which human beings lived—their *nomoi*, meaning conventions or ways of life as well as laws. The rise of medical science, especially the school on the island of Cos that is associated with Hippocrates, highlighted the problems posed by a specifically human sort of nature (*physis*), separate and distinct from the sorts of substance that pertained to *psyche* (soul or mind).

The first group of thinkers to address conceptual problems of the human condition were the Sophists (from the Greek word for *wise men*), a term applied to a loose affiliation of teachers and writers who mingled in Athens during the second half of the fifth century B.C.E.. Although divided on most issues of philosophical import, and thus not strictly speaking a school of thought, the Sophists were united in directing their interest toward humanity, and in particular toward the moral, political, and epistemic questions arising from human life. Perhaps the most famous of these thinkers was Protagoras of Abdera (c. 490–c. 420 B.C.E.), whose name is associated with the principle that "man is the measure of all things." Although his doctrines must be pieced together from fragmentary sources, Protagoras seems to have embraced a *polis*-centered form of moral and political relativism and a subjectivist epistemology that endowed human beings with the capacity to fashion their own conditions of life and forms of fulfillment. It is perhaps not surprising that Protagoras was reputedly a counselor to the famous Athenian democratic leader Pericles.

Socrates (469–399 B.C.E.) also advanced important humanist themes. While distancing himself from the Sophists, whom he regarded as charlatans, Socrates asserted that virtue was a form of knowledge, and that knowledge was teachable if the correct method (namely the question-and-answer technique of Socratic dialectic) was employed. Even those who might be considered too benighted to know anything—such as a simple adolescent slave, for example—could be shown to possess knowledge of sophisticated abstract concepts. Hence, all human beings were for Socrates capable of knowing goodness and of acting in accordance with it, since this knowledge was imprinted on each and every human soul and could be recovered by means of self-reflection.

A further manifestation of humanistic ideals came from the Hellenistic philosophical school of Stoicism, which appeared in the fourth century B.C.E.. The Stoics upheld a cosmopolitan doctrine of universal human reason and rejected particularistic attachments to place and culture in preference to a generalized care for humanity. This doctrine became popular among Roman thinkers such as Marcus Tullius Cicero (106–43 B.C.E.), who posited a general "bond" in human society, among persons who are connected through speech and reason, and from which arose the moral and material fruits of civilized human conduct. The aspirations toward *humanitas* and *philanthropia* crystallized in the Hellenistic and early Roman periods.

## Tenth-Century Islamic Humanism
In the tenth century C.E., a group of philosophically inclined men with literary training who were associated with the Abbasid dynasty participated in an Islamic renaissance centered in Baghdad. Joel L. Kraemer has claimed for this group of thinkers the mantle of humanism on the grounds that they subscribed to an intellectual agenda that privileged the wisdom of the ancient Greeks, upheld the ideal of "urbanity," and endorsed ideas such as individualism, cosmopolitanism, and secularism, which are commonly embraced by humanists.

Although this humanist movement exercised a limited influence on later Islamic philosophy, it seems to have enjoyed a wide following among both scholars and courtly scribes. In turn, these figures were patronized by some of the most powerful political officials of the Muslim world at the time. Hence, the Islamic humanist revival ought not to be viewed as a tangential or marginal phenomenon in medieval Arabic civilization. Indeed, it helps explain the more advanced state of learning in the East than in the Christian West throughout the Middle Ages.

## Twelfth-Century Renaissance Humanism
Christianity, with its orientation toward otherworldly existence and its potential for asceticism and extreme self-renunciation, may seem to be at odds with humanism, yet scholars have repeatedly held that forms of humanism flourished during the European Middle Ages in spite of countervailing tendencies within the Christian faith. In particular, the twelfth century witnessed a renewed interest in human ideals and aspirations not dissimilar to that which had occurred in the Islamic East a couple of centuries earlier.

The humanism of what is called the twelfth-century Renaissance had several facets. One, highlighted by Charles Homer Haskins, whose 1927 book drew attention to this Renaissance, is its similarity to the literary humanism that typified the fifteenth-century Renaissance. Many texts dating to Latin antiquity began to circulate for the first time in centuries, and Latin translations of both classical Greek authors and Arabic commentaries made their first appearance in Europe. Moreover, the revival of interest in classical rhetoric, and in the art of persuasive writing (particularly in the form of letters), emphasized the importance of developing an accomplished literary style and urbane expression.

More recently, Richard Southern has emphasized a second aspect of medieval humanism, which stresses its scholastic base. According to this view, the humanist elements in twelfth-century thought derived from a recognition of human dignity and of the concomitant dignity of nature, both of which were seen as intelligible and capable of being accessed by human beings through the application of reason. The truth that authors sought was, therefore, nothing less than a comprehensive knowledge of the operation of the universe in which humanity itself constituted the noblest (if still flawed, because fallen) of God's creations. This scholastic humanism embraced an optimistic confidence that the acquisition of truth about divine creation was not only possible but constituted a demonstration of religious devotion.

A third facet of twelfth-century humanism was the valorization of human life, which stood in contrast to the despairing, antihumanist orientation of thinkers who devalued and disparaged all forms of earthly existence. This conception of humanism was more minimalist and circumscribed than either the literary or scholastic varieties, inasmuch as it placed heavy weight on the centrality of God to human life. Yet by opposing those who denigrated the worth of all earthly human achievements, this self-consciously Christian humanism upheld the view that works of virtue and intellect could be found even among those who had not accepted (or who had lived before the time of) Christianity and endorsed the idea that although ultimate human beatitude occurred only within the confines of religious salvation, a measure of human happiness could be found in the temporal realm through the pursuit of human (and humane) goals. This definition acknowledged the existence of a human path to happiness that all human beings sought and could know. Happiness was not given to the human race but was something that had to be earned by exertion, and human beings could be fooled or mistaken about the correct sources of happiness—for example, by confusing pleasure with true satisfaction. Hence, happy human existence embraced both active and reflective dimensions: One must do the good (virtue) as well as know the good (wisdom) in order to flourish. Thus, although non-Christians were unable to achieve ultimate salvation, their earthly lives could still have merit. Moreover, in matters of happiness pertaining to the present life, humans could learn equally from the deeds and writings of infidels and from those of believers. Christian authorities would certainly guide humans toward happiness (eternal as well as temporal), but they could usefully be supplemented by studying the acts and ideas of worthy pagans, which also contributed toward instilling in humanity the virtue and wisdom that produced the measure of earthly fulfillment of which humans were capable. This account of humanism, then, can comport with both the literary and scholastic ideas of humanism already discussed.

Christian humanism continued to resonate into the Renaissance, when many of the Italian humanists and their northern successors privileged human dignity because of humanity's creation "in the image and likeness of God."

## Modern Humanism

The humanists of medieval and Renaissance Europe—and indeed of Greek antiquity and Islam—were driven by spiritual, moral, and cultural ideals and values. In the eighteenth century, another form of humanism, one that adopted a more materialistic stance concerning human perfectibility, emerged. The Enlightenment stressed that the application of human reason, unimpeded by the state or by religious authority, could alone produce human progress in the sense of improved conditions of life for the whole human race. Immanuel Kant's (1724–1804) plea in his essay "What Is Enlightenment?" for the release of the human intellect from its condition of tutelage into the full flower of its maturity captured this demand for the freeing of the human mind. The French philosophes, such as Voltaire (1694–1778) and Denis Diderot (1713–1784), may have spearheaded this position, but it echoed throughout the Western hemisphere during the late eighteenth and early nineteenth centuries—in Great Britain (David Hume, Jeremy Bentham), Germany (Immanuel Kant, G. E. Lessing, Moses Mendelssohn), and North America (Benjamin Franklin, Thomas Jefferson). Whereas the Enlightenment version of humanism was more scientific than literary in its orientation, its demand for an anthropocentric perspective on human affairs, encouragement of creative enterprise, and advocacy of social and political reform marked it as a clear successor to earlier forms of humanistic thought.

The question of what impeded the realization of the humanist project became crucial for humanism in the nineteenth century. For the philosopher Ludwig Feuerbach (1804–1872),

it was religion that stood in the way of human fulfillment. Although other humanists had questioned whether religious institutions or monotheistic beliefs were compatible with humanism, Feuerbach attacked religion per se. Adapting the Hegelian dialectical method to a materialist metaphysic, Feuerbach asserted that the supposedly divine object of worship was itself something human, a purely mundane creation. Until human beings realized that they had abased themselves before a fictitious deity that represented nothing more than the sum of humanity's creative and intellectual potential, they would live under conditions of extreme self-alienation and immiseration.

Although he drew on many elements of Feuerbach's analysis, Karl Marx (1808–1883) found his conclusion that the elimination of religious faith would herald the beginning of human happiness far too idealistic. In his writings dating from the early 1840s, Marx claimed that mere atheism constituted "theoretical humanism." He asserted, by contrast, that communism was "practical humanism" or a truly "radical" humanism. Marx meant by this that the sources of inhumanity were not products merely of the human mind but also of the distribution of property into private hands and of an economic system that forced the vast mass of humankind to toil under conditions of extreme alienation. Communism, which he saw as social ownership of the means of production, would yield the material conditions under which all of humanity could flourish in a free and creative manner.

Humanism in more recent times has been manifested in a number of different movements. In addition to "secular humanism" in the United States, existentialism has been trumpeted as a form of humanist philosophy, inasmuch as it holds that individual human freedom constitutes the source of all authentic human values. For the existentialist, the failure to choose by submitting to the value systems of others (whether churches, nations, or political movements) is a dehumanizing force. In Eastern Europe during the 1950s and 1960s, and in recognition of the rediscovery of Marx's early writings, many socialists reinterpreted their philosophy as a form of humanism, emphasizing the subjective consequences of economic and political oppression. This not only generated a reinvigorated critique of the alienated state of capitalist society but also became a stimulus for communist regimes to loosen their grip on their populations.

*See also* **Classicism; Existentialism; Humanity; Marxism; Renaissance; Secularization and Secularism.**

**BIBLIOGRAPHY**

Feuerbach, Ludwig. *The Essence of Christianity.* Translated by George Eliot. New York: Harper, 1957.

Fromm, Erich, ed. *Socialist Humanism.* New York: Doubleday, 1965.

Haskins, Charles Homer. *The Renaissance of the Twelfth Century.* Cambridge, Mass.: Harvard University Press, 1927.

Jaeger, Werner. *Paideia: The Ideals of Greek Culture.* 2nd ed., 3 vols. Translated by Gilbert Highet. New York: Oxford University Press, 1945.

Kerford, G. B. *The Sophistic Movement.* Cambridge, U.K.: Cambridge University Press, 1981.

Kraemer, Joel L. *Humanism in the Renaissance of Islam: The Cultural Revival during the Buyid Age.* 2nd ed. Leiden, Netherlands: Brill, 1992.

Kristeller, Paul Oskar. *Renaissance Thought: The Classic, Scholastic, and Humanist Strains.* New York: Harper and Row, 1961.

Marx, Karl. *Early Writings.* Translated by T. B. Bottomore. New York: McGraw-Hill, 1964.

Sartre, Jean-Paul. *Existentialism and Humanism.* Translated by Philip Mariet. Brooklyn, N.Y.: Haskell House, 1977.

Southern, R. W. *Scholastic Humanism and the Unification of Europe.* 2 vols. Cambridge, Mass.: Blackwell, 1995–2001.

Trinkaus, Charles. *In Our Image and Likeness: Humanity and Divinity in Italian Humanist Thought.* 2 vols. Chicago: University of Chicago Press, 1970.

Versényi, Laszlo. *Socratic Humanism.* New Haven, Conn.: Yale University Press, 1963.

Walsh, Gerald. G. *Medieval Humanism.* New York: Macmillan, 1942.

*Cary J. Nederman*

## RENAISSANCE

In the mid-twentieth century, Paul Oskar Kristeller (1905–1999) established the understanding of Renaissance humanism accepted by all scholars in the field. Humanists or *umanisti* were practitioners of the *studia humanitatis* or liberal arts: grammar, poetry, rhetoric, history, and moral philosophy. Their origins are traceable to the notaries who worked for courts and cities in medieval Italy writing letters and preparing legal documents. The practice of these notaries was, from 1100, influenced by the *ars dictaminis* or manuals of letter writing emanating from France. Italian notaries subsequently began to write manuals of their own; their innovation was to abandon medieval Latin style and to emulate the Latin style of classical Roman writers. They focused particularly on the rhetoricians (most notably Cicero from the 1380s), whose interests as public lay intellectuals most closely matched their own.

### Spread of Humanism

Humanism first achieved public visibility through Francesco Petrarca (Petrarch; 1304–1374) whose achievements impressed his humanist contemporaries. His immediate disciples were Giovanni Boccaccio (1313–1375) and Coluccio Salutati (1331–1406), both Florentines. Salutati, as chancellor (chief administrative officer) of the city from 1375 until his death, did much to encourage the growth of humanism, especially employing humanists and bringing Manuel Chrysoloras (c. 1353–1415) to Florence, where he taught Greek for three years (1397–1400) and left behind a group of scholars competent to continue Greek studies on their own. From its center in Florence, humanism spread rapidly throughout Italy during the fifteenth century and established itself as the most defining intellectual movement of the Renaissance (1350–1600). Its spread always involved the establishment of schools. Three influential pedagogues were Gasparino Barzizza (1360–1430), the most outstanding scholar of Cicero in his generation, who taught in Venice, Bologna, and Padua; Vittorino da Feltre (1378–1446), a student of Barzizza's who taught in Padua and Venice and established a school in Mantua; and Guarino da Verona (Guarino Veronese; 1374–1460), who taught in Venice,

Verona, and Florence, and established a school in Ferrara. All three had illustrious students, some of whom became rulers of city-states, others reputable scholars and teachers.

During the second half of the fifteenth century the movement also established itself in Spain, France, Germany, the Low Countries, and England, as well as in eastern Europe as far as Prague, Vienna, and Budapest. But during the second generation of its expansion outside Italy, the Reformation in Germany and then elsewhere absorbed a good deal of humanist energy. The influence of humanism on the religious disputes of the sixteenth century was great, in large part because the Bible and the church fathers came so centrally into play. But its influence extended to other areas as well: to art, politics, philosophy, medicine, law, and mathematics. Humanism began to merge into other intellectual movements after 1600, though its program of education remained central in western Europe and the United States until the twentieth century.

### Development of the *Studia humanitatis*

The classical texts of Greece and Rome were the basis of humanist education, the purpose of which was to teach students to read, write, and speak well in Latin by using classical sources. The earliest of many humanist treatises on education was Pierpaolo Vergerio's (c. 1369–1444) *De ingenuis moribus et liberalibus studiis* (1403; The character and studies befitting a free-born youth); he is the first to describe in print the *studia humanitatis* as the best course of study for an emerging nonclerical elite, both in private letters and in public life. Leonardo Bruni (c. 1370–1444) wrote a parallel treatise (as a letter) for girls (*De studiis et litteris*; [1524, The study of literature]). Grammar for each of them meant a thorough knowledge of Latin, enabling a student to read the historians, rhetoricians, poets, and moral philosophers (Bruni especially includes the church fathers among these) of classical Latin antiquity. Although Vergerio also includes arithmetic and geometry in his curriculum, Bruni eliminates these as well as rhetoric from the education of women, for whom these subjects have no practical use, since all are related to public vocations not open to women. Later humanists not only wrote educational treatises (Maffeo Vegio, Enea Silvio Piccolomini, Battista Guarini, Erasmus, and Juan Luis Vives among them) but also produced texts designed to help students master Latin, most notable among these Lorenzo Valla's (1407–1457) *Elegantiae linguae latinae* (1437, pub. 1471; Elegances of the Latin language) and a number of works by Desiderius Erasmus (1466?–1536), including *De ratione studii ac legendi interpretandique auctores* (1511; On the method of study and of reading and interpreting authors), *De conscribendis epistolis* (1522; On the writing of letters), *De pueris statim ac liberaliter instituendis declamatio* (1529; A declamation on the subject of liberal education for children), and the *Colloquia familiaria* (1518–1533; Colloquies).

Under the heading of grammar, the humanist emendations of texts and the development of methods of textual study and their literary and historical critique should also be included. A method for doing so was put forth by Angelo Poliziano (1454–1494) in his *Miscellaneorum centuria prima* (1480; Miscellanies), marking the real beginning of modern methods of textual research. The most famous attack on a forged text was Lorenzo Valla's *De falso credita et ementita Constantini donatione declamatio* (1440; Falsely believed and fictitious Donation of Constantine), in which he proved on philological and historical grounds that the Donation was an eighth-century forgery.

***Rhetoric.*** In the Middle Ages, Cicero was known as a philosopher, but his orations and his major theoretical works on oratory were entirely unknown. Petrarch made the earliest discovery of a Ciceronian oration, *Pro Archia poeta* (In defense of the poet Archias), extolling the value of poetry and literature. Gian Francesco Poggio Bracciolini (1380–1459) discovered ten additional orations of Cicero and a complete copy of Quintilian (which provides the step by step education of an orator), and Cicero's *De institutione oratoria* (On the education of the orator). In 1421 Gerardo Landriani discovered in Lodi Cicero's other major oratorical treatises: *Brutus* (his history of rhetoric), *Orator* (the ideal orator), and *De oratore* (the ingredients of a great orator). Thus Cicero the orator became known again for the first time in a thousand years.

The Greek tradition was recovered more slowly. George of Trebizond (1396–1473) made the first humanist translation of Aristotle's *Rhetoric* into Latin. But it was not until the following century that the Greek rhetorical tradition was made as fully available as is now known. Aldus Manutius published *Rhetores graeci* (1508) comprising ninety manuscripts, and including the works of Plato, Aristotle, Hermogenes, Aphthonius, Demosthenes, Isocrates, Aeschines, and other Attic orators.

Humanists also wrote treatises on rhetoric and aids to teaching it. George of Trebizond wrote the first comprehensive rhetoric of the Renaissance, *Rhetoricorum libri V* (1434), in which illustrations from both Greek and Latin traditions were included. In the next century Philipp Melanchthon's (1497–1560) *Institutiones rhetoricae* (1521; Training in rhetoric) extended the humanistic rhetorical art to Protestant Germany, while Cypriano Soarez's *De arte rhetorica libri tres ex Aristotele, Cicerone, et Quintiliano deprompti* (1562; Three books on the art of rhetoric drawn from Aristotle, Cicero, and Quintilian) circulated in Jesuit schools throughout the world and was continuously reprinted into the eighteenth century. Among the many practical treatises Erasmus wrote to teach rhetoric was *De duplici copia verborum ac rerum* (1512, rev. 1514, 1534; Copia of words and ideas), offering many ideas and ways to amplify ideas.

Humanists used their rhetorical models to attack scholastic philosophy and the central position given to logic in it. Valla, in his *Disputationes dialecticae* (1439), claimed that the logicians had created fictitious abstractions and categories; he did away with the abstractions and most of the categories and made logic a subdivision of invention, one of the five parts of rhetoric. Rodolphus Agricola (Roelof Huysman; 1443 or 1444–1485) studied in Italy and in later years published *De inventione dialectica* (1479, pub. 1515; On dialectical invention; 47 editions by 1562, all in northern Europe). It is not clear whether he knew Valla's earlier work, but he sought to substitute a logic based on topics for one based on terms, and the probabilities of dialectic and rhetoric for the certitude of the syllogism. Agricola's views were taken up by Johannes

Sturm (1507–1589) who propagated them in Paris (1528–1535) and Strasbourg (1538 ff.). While in Paris he taught Petrus Ramus (Pierre de La Ramée; 1515–1572), who attacked Aristotelian logic in his *Aristotelicae animadversiones* (1543; Aristotelian animadversions) and developed a topics logic following Agricola, emphasizing rules of natural reasoning. He was enormously popular between 1575 and 1600, and in Puritan New England during the seventeenth century.

***History.*** Latin historians were known during the Middle Ages, but humanists began the scholarly study of their texts by annotating and emending manuscripts of the classical Roman historians (notably Livy, Tacitus, Suetonius, Caesar, Sallust, and Velleius Paterculus), and once printing became established in the late 1460s the Roman historians were among the most popular texts printed. The Greek historians were less known, but between 1400 and 1450 many Greek manuscripts were brought from Constantinople to Italy, and a cadre of humanists trained in Greek began to translate them. Plutarch's *Lives* were particularly popular as comparative biographies, and Polybius's discussion of the various forms of constitutions attracted much interest. Humanists began at once to translate these texts into Latin. Niccolò Perotti translated Polybius 1–5, and Valla translated Herodotus and Thucydides.

Erasmus published editions of a number of the church fathers and the first Greek edition of the New Testament (1516, expanded and republished in 1519, 1522, 1527, and 1535) placing in a parallel column his own translation of it into Latin, and adding annotations as well. In separate volumes he published paraphrases. Martin Luther (1483–1546) used Erasmus's first edition in his lectures on Romans in 1516. Cardinal Jiménez de Cisneros (1436–1517) founded the University of Alcalá de Henares in 1499 (opened 1508) to promote study of the biblical languages. His first large project was publication of the Bible in its original languages, which was accomplished between 1513 and 1517 in six volumes, though a delay until 1520 in gaining papal approval prevented publication of the New Testament; hence Erasmus's Greek Bible was the first to appear.

Humanists were prolific writers of history. They regarded it as a branch of moral philosophy ("moral philosophy taught by example"), but over time the lessons they drew became increasingly complex. Bruni's history of Florence, modeled on Livy, was one of the earliest and most famous humanist histories, extolling the liberty and virtue of Florence, triumphant over Milanese attempts to conquer the city. By the end of the century, histories of Florence by Niccolò Machiavelli (1469–1527) and Francesco Guicciardini (1483–1540), written in Italian rather than in Latin, were much more grim in evaluations of human character, behavior, and judgment—and much more fully grounded in documentary evidence. Flavio Biondo (1392–1463) wrote the first history of medieval Italy, making use of archaeological information; but a history covering much the same period by Carlo Sigonio (ca. 1522–1584) a century later used archives to make a great advance in detail and precision over what Biondo was able to achieve.

Historical writing developed in important ways also in France. Paolo Emilio (d. 1529), who returned from Italy to France with Charles VIII in 1498, abandoned the medieval chronicle tradition. Guillaume Budé (1467–1530) wrote the first extensive humanist study of Justinian's Digest. In the next generation Jacques Cujas (1522–1590) introduced the *mos gallicus docendi,* the French or historical method of teaching Roman law based on the awareness that the law was specific to a given society, changed over time, and was not universal. The *mos italicus,* to which the French method was opposed, sought to clarify the universal principles exemplified in the law and continued to be practiced in Italy. Cujas inspired a group of historians to study the French past in the same way; Jacques Auguste de Thou (1553–1617) went further and tried to incorporate the histories of the various European states into one history, a "universal" or "perfect" history.

***Poetry and poetics.*** Humanists wrote a great deal of Latin poetry, virtually all of which faded into obscurity with the rise of the vernaculars. Petrarch's Italian lyric poetry and the sonnet form he created, however, exercised enormous influence on Renaissance Italian, French, and English poets. In the sixteenth century Ariosto and Tasso, who created the most influential narrative poems in Italian (see below) were trained as humanists and wrote poetry in Latin as well as Italian, but self-consciously turned against Latin and, in Ariosto's case, became critical of humanist education.

Humanist texts on literary theory, on the other hand, exercised great influence. Aristotle's *Poetics* was published in a new Latin translation from Greek in 1498; the Greek text was published in 1508. After a lag of a generation humanists began to write commentaries on it, most notably Ludovico Castelvetro (*Poetica di Aristotele vulgarizzata;* 1570). But they also wrote treatises on their own poetics, most famously Julius Caesar Scaliger, *Poetices libri septem* (1561; Seven books on the art of poetry) and Francesco Patrizi, *Della poetica* (1586; On the art of poetry). Philip Sidney's *Defence of Poesie* (1583, pub. 1595) was much influenced by the Italian tradition and skillfully blended Horace and Aristotle. These works led to various literary debates, among them the importance of Aristotle's unities of time, place, and plot. Ludovico Ariosto's (1474–1533) *Orlando furioso* (1516, 1532) did not honor them, while Torquato Tasso's (1544–1595) later *Gerusalemme liberata* (1581) was regarded as having done so, setting off a debate in favor of one or the other.

***Moral philosophy.*** Humanists were not "school" philosophers, but they recovered many texts that belonged to various schools, including most of Plato, Greek Stoicism (Epictetus), Epicureanism (Lucretius), and Skepticism (Sextus Empiricus). Platonism became a strong presence through the Platonic "Academy" in Florence under Marsilio Ficino (1433–1499), who translated Plato and Platonists (including Plotinus) into Latin, making them available in that language for the first time in more than a thousand years. The translation of Sextus Empiricus into Latin (1563) was the major source behind Michel de Montaigne's (1533–1592) pyrrhonian stance in his "Apology for Raymond Sebond" (1575).

Humanists used these and other texts to reflect on moral issues. Is happiness, the supreme good, achievable in this life? Petrarch said no and criticized Aristotle for having believed otherwise; many humanists agreed with him, as did Valla in his *De voluptate* (1434; On pleasure), in which he argued that

while Epicurus was right to argue for the superiority of pleasure over virtue, the supreme pleasure was achievable only through Christian faith in life after death. Ficino, on the other hand, believed enjoyment of God was possible in this life. Isotta Nogarola (1418–1466), one of a dozen or so women humanists in fifteenth-century Italy, wrote a dialogue, together with a Venetian humanist, Ludovico Foscarini, on the relative responsibility of Adam and Eve for the Fall; Nogarola defended Eve, Foscarini Adam.

The relative merits of men and women was another important topic. The starting point for this discussion was Boccaccio's *De claris mulieribus* (1361; Famous women), portraits of mostly classical (and excluding Christian) women, which provided many of the examples used by Christine de Pizan (1364–c. 1430) in building her city of ladies (*Le livre de la cité des dames,* 1405; The book of the city of ladies). Thus a humanist text led to a new chapter in the debate about women (the *querelle des femmes*), new because de Pisan was the first woman to respond directly to male misogynistic treatises. The most important humanist text in this debate, was Baldassare Castiglione's (1478–1529) *Il cortegiano* (1528; Book of the courtier,), written in Italian, book 3 of which summed up the *querelle* to that point and influenced later writing in the genre. Several women writers from Venice wrote important texts in Italian on the theme in the seventeenth century: Moderata Fonte (1555–1592), *Il merito delle donne* (pub. 1600; The worth of women); Lucrezia Marinella (1571–1653), *La nobiltà et eccellenza delle donne, co' difetti et mancamenti de gli huomini* (1600, 2nd ed., 1601; The nobility and excellence of women and the defects and vices of men); and Arcangela Tarabotti (1604–1652), *Tirannia paterna* (pub. 1654; Paternal tyranny). Marie le Jars de Gournay wrote an important text in French, *Égalité des hommes et des femmes* (1622; Equality of men and women) on the same subject.

The "mirror of princes" literature sought to describe the perfect prince and the education that would produce one; Erasmus's *Institutio principis Christiani* (1516; Education of a Christian prince) is a notable example. Others sought to describe the perfect courtier or gentleman; the most enduring of these has been Castiglione's *Il cortegiano,* which portrays both the perfect male (Book 1) and the perfect female (Book 3) courtier; Sir Thomas Elyot's (c. 1490?–1546) *Boke Named the Governour* (1531) is an English counterpart. Much debated were the relative merits of the contemplative and active life, with most opting for the latter. The relation between intellect and will was also much discussed, the latter being much more strongly supported by humanists skeptical of the power of reason to know and do the good. A related topic was the power of fate and fortune over human life. On none of these issues did humanists speak with a single voice; they explored all sides of questions and took various positions.

In three cases humanist moral philosophical texts achieved greatness: Erasmus's *Encomium moriae* (1511; Praise of folly; rev. 1512, 1514, 1516), François Rabelais's (c. 1494–1553) *Gargantua and Pantagruel* (1532–1556), and Montaigne's *Essais* (1580, 1588, 1595). The first, written in Latin, is an oration of praise spoken by a goddess, Folly, who praises folly as wise, an oxymoron that becomes transformed in the "Christian fool," whose divine wisdom is folly to all the world. Though unique as a text, its spirit is visible in Rabelais, whose book celebrates the violation of boundaries, and in nothing more than in providing serious commentary and in the next breath undoing all he had just said. The *Tiers Livre* (1546) does this throughout on the question of marriage and is a central text in the *querelle des femmes*. Montaigne's *Essays* is filled with quotations and allusions from classical authors, as if all of humanist scholarship had been poured into him, but it is all employed to explore his own consciousness and distill his experience in a new "essay" form, which he invented.

## Political Implications of Renaissance Humanism

Leonardo Bruni, who later followed Salutati as chancellor of Florence (1427–1444), was the first to use an ancient Greek model (Aelius Aristides' *Panathenaicus*) to compose a panegyric (*Laudatio florentinae urbis,* 1403–1404; Panegyric to the city of Florence). This has turned out to be a very important text, since Hans Baron (1900–1988) made much use of it in developing his theory that "civic humanism" first emerged in Florence as a result of the struggle for Florentine liberty (1389–1402) against the tyrant of Milan, Gian Galeazzo Visconti. According to Baron, this struggle led to a new awareness on the part of Florentine humanists of their citizenship in a republic, which they (and most notably Bruni) began to defend. This change meant, Baron argued, that the humanists had to bring their classical studies and civic commitment into harmony. Initially rejecting Machiavelli as a civic humanist, Baron subsequently included him, arguing that his *Discourses on Livy,* which supported a republican view of government, superceded his earlier *Prince,* supporting authoritarian rule. Because of Florence's central place in Renaissance culture, Baron contended that civic humanism influenced all of Europe and lay behind the growth of western democracy into the nineteenth century. This thesis has been among the most hotly contested in Renaissance humanist studies ever since it was propounded in 1956. If any consensus has emerged out of this debate it is that civic humanism is recognizable as a humanist option, but that its appearance cannot be neatly tied to the one event to which Baron links it; the allegiances of humanists were complicated, beginning with those of Bruni, on whom no critical biography has yet been written.

A significant debate took place in Spain in 1550–1551 between a humanistically trained lawyer and cleric, shortly after the Spanish conquest in the New World, over the question of whether Christians had a right to enslave the natives in the New World; Bartolomé de Las Casas (1474–1566), a Dominican (and the first person to be ordained in the New World), challenged that right as unchristian, and Juan Ginés de Sepúlveda (1490?–1572 or 1573) defended it on the basis of Aristotle's view that some are born to be natural slaves.

Humanists contributed two classics to political literature: Machiavelli's *Prince* (1513, pub. 1532) and Thomas More's *Utopia* (1516). Machiavelli was the first to describe politics as a struggle for power, which may well be incompatible with morality and religion. More presents a vision of how politics might remain moral, which should always be its aim. Both texts have created very large literatures ever since they were first published.

*See also* **Philosophy, Moral; Poetry and Poetics; Reformation; Renaissance; Rhetoric.**

## BIBLIOGRAPHY

PRIMARY SOURCES

Astell, Mary. *The First English Feminist: Reflections on Marriage and Other Writings.* Edited by Bridget Hill. New York: St. Martin's Press, 1986.

Boccaccio, Giovanni. *Famous Women.* Edited and translated by Virginia Brown. The I Tatti Renaissance Library. Cambridge, Mass.: Harvard University Press, 2001.

Henderson, Katherine Usher, and Barbara F. McManus. *Half Humankind: Contexts and Texts of the Controversy about Women in England, 1540–1640.* Urbana: University of Illinois Press, 1985.

King, Margaret L., and Albert Rabil, Jr., eds. *Her Immaculate Hand: Selected Works by and about the Women Humanists of Quattrocento Italy.* 2nd ed. Asheville, N.C.: Pegagus Press, 1997. Separate volumes devoted to the writings of three of the writers included in this volume have appeared in "The Other Voice" series (below): Laura Cereta, Cassandra Fedele, and Isotta Nogarola.

"The Other Voice in Early Modern Europe," a project in the textual recovery of continental European women's writings, c. 1400–1700, edited by Margaret L. King and Albert Rabil Jr. and published by the University of Chicago Press. Sixty-eight volumes have been approved for publication, and as of the end of 2003, twenty-five had been published, translated from French, Italian, Latin, and Spanish. Published texts include those by Moderata Fonte, Marie le Jars de Gournay, Lucrezia Marinella, Isotta Nogarola, Anna Maria van Schurman, and Arcangela Tarabotti, some of whom are mentioned in the body of this essay.

SECONDARY SOURCES

Baron, Hans. *The Crisis of the Early Italian Renaissance.* 2 vols. in one. Princeton, N.J.: Princeton University Press, 1966.

———. *In Search of Florentine Civic Humanism: Essays on the Transition from Medieval to Modern Thought.* 2 vols. Princeton, N.J.: Princeton University Press, 1988. See, in conjunction with both entries, James Hankins, "The 'Baron Thesis' after Forty Years and Some Recent Studies of Leonardo Bruni," *Journal of the History of Ideas* 56 (1995): 309–339; and AHR Forum on the Baron thesis, with commentary by Ronald Witt, John Najemy, Craig Kallendorf, and Werner Gundersheimer, *The American Historical Review* 101 (1996): 107–144. See further, Mark Jurdjevic, "Civic Humanism and the Rise of the Medici," *Renaissance Quarterly* 52 (1999): 994–1020, which argues convincingly why and how civic humanists could support the Medici regime in Florence after 1434.

Eden, Kathy. *Hermeneutics and the Rhetorical Tradition: Chapters in the Ancient Legacy and Its Humanist Reception.* New Haven, Conn.: Yale University Press, 1997.

Garin, Eugenio. *Italian Humanism: Philosophy and Civic Life in the Renaissance.* Translated by Peter Munz. New York: Harper and Row, 1965. His thesis concerning the conjunction of these three elements (humanism, philosophy, civic life).

Kekewich, Lucille, ed. *The Renaissance in Europe: A Cultural Enquiry.* Vol. 1: *The Impact of Humanism.* New Haven, Conn., and London: Yale University Press in association with The Open University, 2000. There are two additional volumes on other aspects of Renaissance culture art and politics), plus two

King, Margaret L. *Venetian Humanism in an Age of Patrician Dominance.* Princeton, N.J.: Princeton University Press, 1986.

———. *Women of the Renaissance.* Chicago: University of Chicago Press, 1991.

Kraye, Jill, ed. *The Cambridge Companion to Renaissance Humanism.* Cambridge: Cambridge University Press, 1996.

Kristeller, Paul O. *Renaissance Thought: The Classic, Scholastic, and Humanist Strains.* New York: Harper and Brothers, 1961.

———. *Renaissance Thought II: Papers on Humanism and the Arts.* New York: Harper and Row, 1965. These two short books are the best statements of Kristeller's thesis regarding humanism, its difference from other movements in Renaissance Italy, and its diffusion.

Nauert, Charles G., Jr. *Humanism and the Culture of Renaissance Europe.* Cambridge, U.K.: Cambridge University Press, 1995. The best of the recent book-length treatments of humanism designed for students and general readers.

Rabil, Albert, Jr., ed. *Renaissance Humanism: Foundations, Forms, and Legacy.* 3 vols. Philadelphia: University of Pennsylvania Press, 1988. Paperback edition with corrections 1992. The most comprehensive contemporary treatment of the subject in one source.

Rummel, Erika. *The Humanist-Scholastic Debate in the Renaissance and Reformation.* Cambridge, Mass.: Harvard University Press, 1995.

Trinkaus, Charles. *In Our Image and Likeness: Humanity and Divinity in Italian Humanist Thought.* 2 vols. Chicago: University of Chicago Press, 1970. Demonstrates in great detail the religious and theological interests of Italian humanists.

Witt, Ronald G. *In the Footsteps of the Ancients: The Origins of Humanism from Lovato to Bruni.* Boston: Brill, 2000. The emergence of humanism from the 1240s until just after 1400 in Italy; the second volume in a two-volume study of the historical background of humanism. The first volume (forthcoming) will cover developments in the earlier Middle Ages up to the 1240s (outlined in Rabil, ed., above, 1.29–70). Witt's thesis refines but does not alter Kristeller's paradigm.

*Albert Rabil Jr.*

## SECULAR HUMANISM IN THE UNITED STATES

The philosophy and ideology of secular humanism has its roots in Enlightenment thought and is based in large part on the Western tradition of liberalism and notions about the status and role of science in the modern world. At base it is a non-theistic belief system that upholds the prime importance of rationality, human autonomy, and democracy. The term *secular humanism* has come to be widely used in the United States to indicate both an explicitly worked-out humanistic worldview as well as a more ambiguous irreligious or nonreligious secularism with which it is often confused.

### Influences on Humanism

The groundwork for modern humanism was laid during the Enlightenment by those philosophers who sought to purge religion of most of its superstitious elements and replace them with a deistic or atheistic rationalism. Thomas Paine's *Age of Reason* (1794–1796), which argues for a religion based on a belief that the world was created by a rational God, was one of the most important such works in this period.

In the nineteenth century, two major influences were important. First, at an institutional level, the Unitarian Church came into existence and by century's end had developed a commitment to toleration and a disavowal of any type of creedalism. This development, combined with the Unitarians' progressive, liberal ideology, created a framework that would accept the kind of religious radicalism that humanists came to espouse in the early twentieth century. The fact that humanism came to be institutionalized in the Unitarian Church would be both fortunate and problematic.

One of the most significant intellectual transformations of the nineteenth century was the widespread acceptance of a developmental view of the past. This revolution in thought had a profound effect on modern religious history. Although many people found ways to reconcile biological evolution and traditional religion, naturalistic evolution gave ammunition to critics of Christianity who branded it as intellectually stagnant and naïve. More important, however, developmentalism also made it possible to see human history as in flux; indeed when applied to religious history, it had the effect of relativizing religion. Humanism drew on both aspects of evolutionary thinking.

### Religious Humanism

Humanism as a distinct intellectual movement arose in early-twentieth-century America among self-described religious humanists. It arose first among radical theologians, especially Unitarian clergymen, who saw religious humanism as anything but an irreligious movement; although these men entirely rejected the "God language" of their colleagues, they felt it essential to retain the institution of religion. Religion was a historical construction, they believed, which developed and changed over time to accommodate new social forms, and it would have to remake itself dramatically in order to continue to exist in the modern world. Already many Protestant modernist theologians were arguing that traditional religion was outdated, based as it was on views of God as a king or lord over creation, and that religion must change and embrace a democratic ethos. The humanists went further, rejecting all discussion of God as unjustified in a scientific age. And yet, they argued, religion itself was not defunct; it fulfilled certain social and psychological urges of human beings. The challenge for moderns was to find ways to integrate current scientific knowledge and democratic social values with the institutions of religion. This is largely what early religious humanism was designed to do.

### Progress and Science

Liberal theologians were not the sole architects of twentieth-century humanism. These religionists were also joined by a number of well-respected academic philosophers in the Deweyan tradition, who were either fellow pragmatists or scientific naturalists. The influential Columbia University school of philosophy as well as a number of professors in mid-Western universities actively participated in the humanist movement.

Humanists by and large rejected teleology even as many other early-twentieth-century thinkers, philosophers and religionists alike, embraced it. No deity, the humanists argued, was responsible for the direction of the cosmos, nor did nature and human history have a direction apart from human effort and human will. Mankind, they said, should not look outside of humanity for assistance to their problems; our fate was entirely in our own hands. Although some thinkers who espoused these ideas came to be called futilitarians because of the somewhat pessimistic outlook that this notion of "man alone in the cosmos" seemed to connote, most humanists were not pessimistic. Indeed, one might characterize the humanist movement as driven by a powerful optimism concerning the ability of human beings to make their own future.

One reason that humanists remained optimistic about human progress in the face of an impersonal cosmos was that they held great faith in the ability of human beings to learn and apply their knowledge in rational and ethical ways. Scientific knowledge and technological control of nature gave human beings the power to identify problems and find solutions to them. Democracy and respect for human rights gave people the ethical framework within which to apply this knowledge. As a result, humanists have not been averse to considering technologies that claim to offer solutions to major social issues even when those technologies might otherwise challenge core beliefs about human nature and freedom. In recent years, for example, humanists have advocated psychological conditioning and genetic engineering as solutions to social problems. These ideas have not been unanimously or uncritically accepted by all who consider themselves humanists, but in general, scientific faith and technological optimism lie at the root of humanist thought, in contrast to a more skeptical and restrained approach to science and technology typical among more traditional religionists.

## Humanism in American Culture

In the last third of the twentieth century, American humanism went through a variety of transitions, and the movement diversified and grew, although still remaining quite small in absolute terms. It was in this period that the term *secular humanism* came into currency, popularized by conservative Christians who saw humanism as a nascent secular religion. These religious conservatives argued that the extensive secularization of America in the second half of the century was largely a result of the influence of secular humanists in control of American social and cultural institutions.

They portrayed the issue as a constitutional problem. Since the late 1940s the federal judiciary had issued a series of landmark rulings strictly enforcing church-state separation and removing traditional religious influence on public institutions. This was especially true for public schools, where morning prayer and religious instruction were banned. At the same time, secular modernity strongly influenced those same institutions, and ideas opposed to traditional religious tenets were introduced. Evolution and sex education, for example, were integrated into the school curriculum. These changes seemed to many Christian critics to be tantamount to the establishment of a competing religion, which they identified with humanism.

The existence of the American Humanist Association (AHA), which was founded by Unitarian and Ethical Culture ministers, gave fodder to the critics' charges that humanism was a religion in its own right. A 1933 document, "A Humanist Manifesto," published by some of these early humanists and signed by such notable scholars as John Dewey, was frequently cited as evidence of the religious dogma of humanism. By tying this "religion without God" to secularization in general, the conservative Christians argued that the government was in many ways abetting the establishment of a humanist religion in flagrant violation of the First Amendment. And indeed, similar arguments underlay court challenges to the teaching of evolution in the public schools in this same period. This argument proved ineffective in Supreme Court battles in the United States, but it was effective in marshaling grassroots political support among conservative religious activists. Humanists for their part attacked the rise of Christian fundamentalism and defended their stance as truly secular; in fact, many humanists in the 1970s and 1980s explicitly rejected the "religious humanist" label as misleading.

In contrast to the first two-thirds of the twentieth century, the decades after 1970 were not a comfortable time for humanists, who found their ideas under attack not only by conservative Christians but also in other areas of popular and elite culture. Humanists declaimed against the irrationality of superstitions and paranormal beliefs such as UFOs, haunted houses, and many alternative medical practices. Furthermore, they worried about growing irrationalism in the academy as postmodern philosophy gained popularity. In all of these arenas, it appeared to humanists that rational thought and scientific authority were endangered. Because of their long-held views that democracy and fundamental human rights were inseparable from modern, rational, scientific thought, humanists also worried about growing authoritarian tendencies and the decline of political liberalism.

The philosophy of humanism at the beginning of the twenty-first century is fostered by several membership organizations in North America, many of which publish nationally circulated magazines and newsletters; there is a successful publishing house directed by a major humanist leader; and the various organizations collaborate to support an institute for training humanist leaders. The movement is small but has established a stable and influential presence in American culture.

*See also* **Religion and the State: United States; Secularization and Secularism.**

BIBLIOGRAPHY

Dewey, John. *A Common Faith.* New Haven, Conn.: Yale University Press, 1934.

Ehrenfeld, David W. *The Arrogance of Humanism.* New York: Oxford University Press, 1978.

Kurtz, Paul, ed. *The Humanist Alternative: Some Definitions of Humanism.* Buffalo, N.Y.: Prometheus Books, 1973.

LaHaye, Tim. *The Battle for the Mind.* Old Tappan, N.J.: Revell, 1980.

Lamont, Corliss. *The Philosophy of Humanism.* 7th ed. New York: Continuum, 1990.

Meyer, Donald H. "Secular Transcendence: The American Religious Humanists." *American Quarterly* 5 (winter 1982): 524–542.

Radest, Howard B. *The Devil and Secular Humanism: The Children of the Enlightenment.* New York: Praeger, 1990.

*Stephen Weldon*

# HUMANITY.

This entry includes three subentries:

*African Thought*
*Asian Thought*
*European Thought*

## AFRICAN THOUGHT

While reason tells us that it is obvious to anyone, irrespective of his or her background, that humans are bipedal, featherless creatures, other characteristics we attribute to humans are not always so obvious. Also, while we all appear to assume that humans are creatures who have minds, in contrast to other creatures, it is not quite obvious what is meant by "mind" or what happens at death to the elements that constitute the essential elements we attribute to humanness. Less obvious still are the social characteristics that we consider primary to humans. Questions regarding human nature, personhood, or the self continue to form the core of metaphysical inquiries. As a result, there are not only multiple constitutive views about human nature, but also questions about whether humans, like other beings, can be said to have an ideal or perfect nature that they already have or aspire to have under certain circumstances. These nonobvious ideas about how we think of the essence of humankind define the differences and similarities in the various beliefs that make up various traditions throughout the world, whether they are cultural traditions passed down from one generation to the next, or intellectual ones shaped by a combination of inherited beliefs with systematic conceptual accounts. Yet, despite these differences, all such beliefs are compatible with the wider thesis that underlies them, namely that all natural kinds have essences.

There are variations in African beliefs as well as in contemporary African philosophical thought regarding how these essences are endowed in humans. Some believe that humans acquire much of what defines the course of their life from a deity or that deity's emissaries, thus adopting a fairly deterministic view of human nature. The Yoruba people of West Africa believe that the human person, *èníyàn,* is constituted of several elements, supreme among which is *orí,* the determinant of destiny. The others are *ara, okán,* and *emí.* The god *Olodumare* delegates tasks to his emissaries, the lower divinities under him called *orisas,* and they oversee the various elements that are then "assembled to construct" selves, the *èníyàan,* with their individual identities. According to Segun Gbadegesin, a Yoruba-born philosopher who has explicated many of these matters, "Ara is the physico-material part of the human being [and] includes the external and internal components" (1991, p. 28).

Because *èníyàn* denotes personhood beyond mere biological identity and selfhood, the Yoruba rebuke selfish people by saying that their views stop at their *ara,* meaning that they ignore what really matters, namely their higher value as *èníyàn.* It would therefore appear that *ara* refers to the material or physical individuality of every person. Also physical is *okán,* the element believed to be responsible for the organistic functions of the body, like pumping and circulating blood throughout the system. But it also has attributes that are not entirely physical, because, according to Gbadegesin (p. 32), the Yoruba make references to people keeping their inner thoughts in their *okán.* Again, although it is believed to be material in nature, it is also regarded as the element responsible for the emotional and mental states and functions of a person and indicates his or her conscious identity. In other words, "it is that from which thought originates" (Gbadegesin, p. 30). Emotional qualities such as bravery, love, hate, joy, sadness, and cowardice are attributed to *okán.* *Emí* is believed to be the life principle or vital spirit; it turns *èníyàn* on (to life). Legend has it that the chief divinity *Orìsà-nlá* molded the body and then put *emí* into it to make it fully functional—speaking, walking, eating, and even thinking—although one thinks with *okán,* the mind, but without *emí,* even *okán* would not perform its thinking function. *Emí,* however, is also a kind of private consciousness: when one puts his or her mind (*okán*) on some idea, it is *emí* that pictures the idea; it "looks" at it through *okán.* *Emí* does not require rest like the *ara,* the body. It is tirelessly always at work; thus, it is what travels and speaks to other people when *ara,* the body, is asleep. It is the dreamer. It is the conscious self. Yet, in the Yoruba modes of thought, all these human functions, including the decision-making activities of *emí,* are predestined by *orí,* the determinant of everyone's path in life. The Yoruba teach that, in life, humans are constantly striving to attain the good, because their *emí* learns about what is good and is drawn to it. If, however, the desires of *emí* are in contrast with the selection of their *orí,* their striving will be to no avail, as they will be destined to be controlled by the dictates of the superior element, the *orí.* By this token, in the Yoruba conceptual scheme *orí* is regarded as the most important aspect of life, for all endeavors of a person's life depend on this element and must be relied on to lead one through the complexities of life. People may not pay attention to the little things that occur in the course of their everyday life experiences, but significant ones, such as big fortunes or calamities, will often raise questions about fate. In this regard, ignorance of the future, that shield that the French social philosopher Jean-Jacques Rousseau (1712–1778) called "the veil of ignorance," allows us to act as if we were free agents capable, so we believe, of creating the world—in terms of influencing history—by our false sense of freedom. It is this sense of false freedom that makes us agents generally, and moral agents in particular. Evidently, it can be a difficult task trying to reconcile the roles played by all the elements in the ensemble of *èníyàn,* the plurally constituted self. What is clear is that there is an attempt to understand and account for all the characteristics exhibited by being human, both functionally and by constitution.

We gather from Chinua Achebe's fiction, *Things Fall Apart,* that, like the Yoruba, the Igbo, also of West Africa, believe that human destiny is controlled by one's chosen *Chi.* For them, however, life is made much less deterministic by human amnesia, which makes us forget the dictates of *Chi* we chose before birth, and so we strive to attain goals in life as if we were free. The amnesia accounts for human courage and diligence in setting and pursuing goals, making life worthwhile until constant and inexplicable failure drives one to seek divinatory counseling and explanation.

The above examples indicate other interesting characteristics of Africans' conceptualization of human nature. Among these is the view of human agency and responsibility, namely, that there are two levels at which we perform in the process of executing those matters that pertain to our specific kind. On the surface, we are free enough for our consciousness to deliberate and execute its duties according to the rules and principles demanded by the various circumstances of human experience, including the acquisition and application of knowledge appropriate to different domains. Yet, both collectively and individually, and unknown to us in specific terms, we are bound by some type of predestination; what we do is actually regulated by and is in line with the dictates of our inner nature as bestowed on us by the divinities. This consideration raises the question of whether humans act freely or are predestined to act the way we do. As Achebe indicates in the novel, questions of this nature arise in those instances when we realize that, despite our unfailing diligence and self-application to tasks, either all or a significant portion of our actions yield negative results. We also observe that others succeed with far less effort where we fail, despite what we reckon to be great and right effort. We are then led to infer that we have a fate that runs contrary to our desires and aspirations. It is this that leads Igbo people to infer that their *Chi* has a different and unalterable destiny for them.

African thought oscillates between these two metaphysical views about human action. The Luo of Kenya, a people who are deeply monistic in their metaphysics of things and of humans, laugh at the idea of predestination, especially when this is attributed to some distant deity beyond time and the world. In their view, most human efforts, if well executed, should yield their intended results. The failure of people's aspirations and goals is the result of either of two causes: one's own lapses, or the actions of another, ill-intentioned person who knowingly and clandestinely undermines other people's plans. Such a person is a *jajuok,* one who is morally crooked and so wishes others ill, going out of his or her way to see that those they do not like or are jealous of do not succeed in their endeavors.

A major question and the source of a major difference among African philosophers concerns whether the ideas about the various elements in human nature as just described do actually articulate multiple substances which, together in some kind of union or relation with each other, make up personhood. Contrary to the preceding pluralist claims, other African philosophers opine that such names are no more than mere conceptual distinctions of the different functions of an otherwise singular and physical constitution of the person.

This view, championed principally by the Ghanaian philosopher Kwasi Wiredu, contends that such names as *èmí, okán,* and so on, as used in Yoruba belief, and arguably present in

the conceptual schemes of several other African communities, are no more than indications of different functions of the same complex material body. This physicalist view proposes that, in African conceptions, for anything to be claimed to exist, it must occupy space; hence nothing can be claimed to be a separate entity that, in conjunction with others, makes up personhood unless all of them, like the body, can be shown to either actually occupy or be capable of occupying a physical space distinct from the body with which they are believed to be in union.

According to Wiredu, it would be ridiculous, among the Akan of Ghana, to think or imagine a clear-cut dualism, à la René Descartes (1596–1650), that posits mind and body as distinct from each other in such a way that one can operate independently of the other. Thus, the claim, "I think therefore I am," turns out to be logically untenable for the Akan. To be sure, mind is not physical in the same measure as the body is, so it is neither an appendage of the body nor identical with it, but it is a functional (responsive) property of the specifically human body by means of which it learns cognitively to respond to its surroundings. The body manifests it in the instance of perception of both self and the external world, although its objects and contents are ordered and given shape gradually through communication. It is brought into existence by the functions of the body while its objects and contents are given order through communication. Thus, mind is a quasi-physical thing, just as the glow in a light bulb is the physical property of the type and arrangement of energy-conducting wires.

The body, at least the human body, is a complex organ that responds to different stimuli to produce different "things." In Wiredu's view, the fault of claiming the constituents of personhood to be separate entities is not with the belief systems in which these ideas are found; rather, it is the failure to analyze the ideas received from tradition critically and sufficiently, a failure probably attributable to currents of cultural influences, such as Christianity, on both African scholars drawn into it and on foreign Africanists who read African worlds through the lenses of Western conceptual categories. Dualism originates from ancient Egyptian worldviews, from their belief that there is something divinely permanent and indestructible about human nature that, by ordinary everyday evidence, is also significantly physical.

Dualism was also clearly present in Greek thought by the fifth century B.C.E., before it became a pertinent issue in the systematic approach of the Socratic period. Later Egyptian thinkers of the Greco-Roman era helped to infuse Christian teachings with it, together with the doctrines of immortality and resurrection. These were assimilated, joining other dogmatic pillars of the Christian faith. According to Wiredu, the concepts of mind and body in African thought are not expressed as the polarized material-spiritual opposition found in Western thought. Rather, many African beliefs appear to indicate a quasi-physical conception not only of the mind, but also of the afterlife. The ancient Egyptian concepts of the afterlife clearly expected those who died to return to this life physically. According to this expectation, the dead wander away into the world of sunset *in order to* rise again one day, and African beliefs in the continuous "social" engagement between the dead and the living is an extension of this quasi-physical conception of personhood. Its foreignness to the Western Christian theory of the afterlife continues to indicate a sort of mystery within the system because of its incongruence with the clear Cartesian dualist principle to which Christian teaching tends to cling. The African influence on the Christian aspiration was never cleanly attained, and several "mysteries" considered crucial to Christian faith resulted from the failed merger of African beliefs with non-African aspirations (Masolo, 2004).

As a constituting element of human nature, mind, too, is a function of the social nature of humans. Mind draws its origin from and depends on communication. It is the human capacity to process meanings that are the core and formal object of communication: that is, the cognitive responsiveness of the human organism to its social surroundings and through society—from which the individual learns the theoretical and practical meanings—to the rest of the surrounding world in which such meanings are tested and applied. Perhaps emphasis on the social dimension of human nature separates African thought most significantly from other traditions. At both the personal and social levels, African thought reflects considerations and maxims that view the individual as socially embedded. Not only is mind, such a significant part of individual selfhood, considered to be socially generated, but its operations, like the determination of what is true and what is good, are played out in the social realm, thus defining knowledge, both cognitive and moral, as inherently social enterprises. In *Cultural Universals and Particulars,* Wiredu describes mind in the Akan conceptual scheme as "primarily the capacity to think thoughts, feel emotions, construct arguments, imagine things, perceive objects and situations, dream dreams of both night and day and so on" (1996, p. 126).

Like the Akan, the Luo think of mind as part of the biological functioning specific to humans. Mind is powered by *chuny,* the sustainer of biological life that all living things share, including plants. The human *chuny* is no greater than, nor superior to, that of a cornstalk or of a flower; they only perform different things in each case. Thus, in humans, *chuny* is the seat of thought, meditation, and imagination, but the acts take place in the head. Even the instinctive reactions of a dog are coordinated in its head by *chuny.* At death, the *chuny* stops or, as the Luo literally put it, disconnects its flow, and so all the animal operations cease and plants wither. In every case, it is said that the *chuny* has disconnected (*chunye ochot*). Because *chuny* is the center of everything, when it is broken, such as happens at death, or when the core of an argument (*chuny wach*) is shattered by a counterposition, total disintegration occurs.

In these Akan and Luo metaphysical examples, personhood emerges in the course of an individual human being's learning to respond to and participate in the social world of handling meanings through which the operations of mind are shaped in an ascending degree of complexity. But it is in African social theory that the communalist nature of personhood has been best articulated. Modern African politics, as

well as the more established indigenous political orders and systems of defining and managing kinship systems, emphasize every person's responsibility for the communal good as the end that everyone seeks, even when they may differ in their separate "ways" to it. Thus, although the immediate postindependence ideology dubbed "African socialism" has waned as the guiding ideological and moral norm for political and socioeconomic orders, the communalistic spirit that it reflected continues to drive Africans' value judgments. Sometimes such judgments are made spontaneously in response to needs of others in family circles, at other times they are consciously applied as political strategies for implementing public policy and programs. Thus, communalism continues to be present in the political and socioeconomic practices at various levels of society, despite the individualistic challenges it faces from capitalist economy and values.

If human nature is communally cultivated over time by enabling individuals to develop and to use their specifically human capacities within given sociocultural contexts, then it is reasonable to expect that the sustenance and improvement of the human condition will require no less than the provisions and circumstances that enable its attainment. Indeed, the idea of human rights agrees with and reasserts this expectation by stipulating, in effect, that every person deserves those provisions and conditions necessary for the quality of life commensurate with the moral status of humans. There appears to be, in the 1948 U.N. Declaration of Human Rights, a hidden argument that the social nature of human life makes it imperative that the attainment and sustenance of those human rights be the result of active commitment by all. Thus, not only does every person have the right to life, but he or she also has the right to a quality of life that enables him or her, both as an individual and as a member of a group, to exercise the characteristics of his or her humanity fully, namely, to be able to perform, have, or enjoy those things that human beings perform and pursue to have or to become by virtue of being members of the species.

Understandably, the specifics and measures of these will, in diverse manners, be culturally determined and allowed under the guidance of right reason. Although philosophers no longer concur that reason, in its instrumental sense, is what distinguishes humans from other entities in the world, it is at least plausible to claim that the freedom of having and expressing one's opinion is still characteristically human. And, because such ideals are what every human being requires, they turn out to be the common goods that can be effectively realized only by reciprocal (intersubjective) recognition and respect among us. They are the foundations of the humane treatment of others as a social, if not a moral, ideal.

Ultimately, it is not difficult to see why the observance of human rights for all is important. Africans have borne witness to sufferings and other forms of humiliation associated with the denial of their human rights. Not only did colonialism strip Africans of their civil and political freedoms, it also tried to obliterate their historical identity by trying to destroy everything they had created in terms of material, intellectual, and religious traditions. As if these colonial calamities had not caused enough suffering, African people have, since independence, been subjected to civil wars and cycles of violence perpetrated on them by their own leaders and neighbors, resulting in the denationalization of millions constrained to live in refugee camps and other forms of makeshift settlements abroad. It is easy, therefore, to see how the postcolonial African state has been mired in contradictions. Ironically, not only did such leaders and other perpetrators of African genocide violate fundamental (common or universal) human rights of their victims, they violated, in the name of ethnic and personal interests, those very rights considered in African communalist thought to be most basic to the concept of humanity. Lessons from such experiences drive home the idea that the practice of mutual recognition and respect is likely to allow everyone to become, in turn, an active and competent participant in the production and consumption of the material, as well as the cognitive, moral, sociopolitical, economic, and aesthetic values on which specifically human life is based. Human beings can, therefore, be regarded as living an acceptable level of human life only if: they are accorded moral dignity and respect; they live a life of reasonable social and political freedom under adequate and appropriate social and political protection; they have the necessary means to live a life free of degrading or dehumanizing poverty; and they live a life that allows them free and reasonable cultural expression. To unduly deny, interrupt, or interfere with any of these rights with respect to other persons, groups, or nations, is to deny them their basic human rights, viewed as those rights every human being can claim as necessary for the expression of his or her humanity.

*See also* **Authenticity: Africa; Colonialism: Africa; Communication of Ideas: Africa and Its Influence; Communitarianism in African Thought; Person, Idea of the; Personhood in African Thought; Philosophies: African; Religion: Africa.**

BIBLIOGRAPHY

Achebe, Chinua. *Things Fall Apart.* Oxford: Heinemann, 1996.

Gbadegesin, Segun. *African Philosophy: Traditional Yoruba Philosophy and Contemporary African Realities.* New York: Peter Lang, 1991.

Gyekye, Kwame. *An Essay on African Philosophical Thought: The Akan Conceptual Scheme.* 2nd rev. ed. Philadelphia: Temple University Press. 1995.

———. *Tradition and Modernity: Philosophical Reflections on the African Experience.* New York and Oxford: Oxford University Press, 1997.

Hallen, Barry. *The Good, the Bad, and the Beautiful: Discourse about Values in an Yoruba Culture.* Bloomington: Indiana University Press, 2000.

Hallen, Barry, and J. O. Sodipo. *Knowledge, Belief, and Witchcraft: Analytic Experiments in African Philosophy.* 2nd ed. Stanford, Calif.: Stanford University Press, 1997.

Karp, Ivan, and D. A. Masolo, eds. *African Philosophy as Cultural Inquiry.* Bloomington: Indiana University Press, 2000.

Masolo, D. A. "African Philosophers in the Greco-Roman Era." In *A Companion to African Philosophy,* edited by Kwasi Wiredu. Malden, Mass.: Blackwell, 2004.

———. "The Concept of the Person in Luo Modes of Thought." In *African Philosophy: New and Traditional Perspectives,* edited by Lee M. Brown. Oxford: Oxford University Press, 2004.

Wiredu, Kwasi. *Cultural Universals and Particulars: An African Perspective.* Bloomington: Indiana University Press, 1996.

———. *Philosophy and an African Culture.* Cambridge, U.K.: Cambridge University Press, 1980.

Wiredu, Kwasi, and Kwame Gyekye, eds. *Person and Community: Ghanaian Philosophical Studies, I.* Washington D.C.: Council for Research in Values and Philosophy, 1992.

*D. A. Masolo*

## ASIAN THOUGHT

Philosophy in East Asia generally avoids abstract metaphysical speculation and focuses on practical questions. Discussions of human nature tend to be related to concerns about social problems and how to solve them. This practical orientation can be seen in the thought of Confucius (Kong fuzi, 551–479 B.C.E.), China's most influential philosopher, who lived during a time of social strife and whose life was dedicated to reforming China and returning it to the paradigms of the past as he understood them.

Confucius's study of ancient Chinese classics led him to believe that during the reigns of the "sage kings" Yao and Shun, China had been well governed and harmony had prevailed throughout their realms. This was accomplished not through harsh punishments or excessive regulations, but by the moral force of their personalities and their attention to social rituals. They are extolled as examples of "noble men" (*junzi*), who embodied the best of human virtues and whose good qualities prompted others to strive for moral excellence themselves. Confucius believed that the presence of such people in a society is the key to social harmony and that all men have the capacity to become perfect exemplars of virtue. He was, however, a product of his time, and his writings indicate that he did not view women as having the same capacities as men. All of his students and close associates were men, and the few instances of mentions of women indicate that he mainly saw them as wives and supporters of men striving to perfect themselves.

For Confucius, education is the key to moral development. Although humans have the capacity to become "noble men," only those who study diligently and actively pursue this ideal are able to reach it. He urged his students to study the classics in order to discern for themselves the eternal paradigms that guide sages. A true sage, in his conception, is one who has learned to discipline his mind and body, whose outward comportment is always appropriate and whose thoughts are oriented toward the betterment of society. Such a person is resolute in the pursuit of virtue but not rigid, learned but not boastful, deeply moral without being moralistic, courageous but not reckless, and always strives to practice what is right in any given situation.

### Human Nature: Good or Evil?

One of the enduring questions of East Asian philosophy concerns how human nature should be construed: Are humans by nature good or evil? Is morality natural to humans, or must they be taught (or coerced) to do what is right? Confucius never directly answered these questions, but the perfectibility of humanity is a dominant theme in his philosophy, and he clearly thought that humans (or at least male humans) possess the capacity for perfection, although they must consciously strive to actualize it. Mencius (Mengzi, c. 371–c. 289 B.C.E.), the most prominent thinker in the tradition after Confucius, asserted that human nature is good, and believed that people are naturally inclined toward virtue. Unfortunately, the negative elements of society tend to corrupt most people, and only a few are able to overcome them. He compared the tendency toward goodness to Ox Mountain, a hill that was once forested. The trees were cut down in order to make a place for cows to graze, but tree shoots continue to crop up there. The cows chew them, and so the trees never reach maturity, but the potential for tree growth is always present. In the same way, humans have the capacity to pursue sagehood, but most become corrupted and fail to actualize this potential.

According to Mencius, the path to perfection begins with cultivation of the heart/mind (*xin*), an innate faculty that allows us to discriminate between right and wrong. It operates in harmony with "vital energy" (*qi*), a universal force that pervades all phenomena and that promotes both personal morality and social harmony. Those who cultivate their heart/mind through study and practice of morality increase the power of their vital energy, which becomes a "flood-like *qi*" (*haoran qi*) in sages. As a strong wind bends grass, flood-like *qi* prompts those who encounter sages to emulate their example.

After Mencius, the notion that human nature is basically good was widely accepted by Confucians, but many of their rivals held other positions. The Legalists, for example, contended that human nature is evil and that unless people are regulated by laws and punishments they will go astray. Society only functions harmoniously when the populace fears the apparatus of state control, and the Legalists counseled rulers to keep their subjects in line by publicly inflicting harsh punishments on those who transgress the laws and by maintaining a powerful and pervasive police force and a network of spies.

A rival position was propounded by Mozi (c. 470–c. 391 B.C.E.), who advocated a philosophy of "universal love" (*jianai*). He contended that China's problems stemmed from a lack of shared benevolence, and he urged people to recognize that if everyone were to practice love of everyone else, the entire society would benefit. When people pursue their self-interest at the expense of others, everyone suffers, and so he taught that the most rational course of action for individuals is to contribute to the common good so that everyone might prosper.

Responding to Mozi, Confucians characterized his ideas as impracticable. First, Confucians believed that people naturally have deeper feelings for those who are close to them and that it is appropriate to favor them. Second, an appeal to pursue morality out of self-interest is bound to fail because those who are moral for selfish reasons will soon realize that while the whole society may benefit from universal love, an individual who takes advantage of the situation might well profit more than others. Only a universal code of morality will make people behave in a truly moral way.

In responding to the Legalists, the Confucians stated that in their version of society people become morally degenerate. They live according to society's expectations and will only be moral as long as there is a credible threat of punishment. They will not develop a moral sense, which is only possible for people who feel shame when they transgress the moral code. Shame keeps the noble man on track even when there is no one to punish or disapprove of immoral behavior.

Another alternative view of human nature was propounded by the Daoists. Laozi (571?–480? B.C.E) the most prominent of the early Daoist thinkers, held that humans at birth are like uncarved blocks of wood (*pu*) and that as they get older, society molds and shapes them. While the Confucians believed that this process is desirable and that education is the key to attaining human perfection, Laozi contended that it brutalizes people and creates the seeds of social turmoil and negative behavior. Trees need no education to grow in accordance with the rhythms of nature, nor does water need to study the classics in order to flow toward its lowest point. Like all the things of the world, humans are born with an innate sense of right and wrong, which accords with the movement of the *dao*, an impersonal, universal force that pervades all phenomena and regulates how things grow and develop.

In the ideal Daoist society, people do not waste their time with education and moral training; rather, the Daoist ruler works to keep his subjects ignorant so that they remain happy with their simple lives. He ensures that they have enough to eat and he avoids conflicts with neighboring states so that the people are not disturbed by wars or overburdened with taxes. In the perfect society, according to Laozi, the people will be so content in their rural villages that even if they hear the cocks crowing in a neighboring town they have no interest in visiting because they have everything they need at home.

## Revival of the Tradition
During most of Chinese history Confucianism was the dominant philosophy and the basis of the state cult, but significant numbers of Chinese intellectuals rejected it in favor of Daoism and later Buddhism. Following centuries of decline, the Confucian tradition was revived in the Song dynasty (960–1279), when a new movement generally referred to as Neo-Confucianism (*xing li xue*, "learning of nature and principle" in Chinese) began among Chinese literati. Many of them had been Buddhists and Daoists, and they often incorporated elements of these systems into their philosophies. During this time the new Confucians initiated educational and political reforms, wrote new histories, and edited classical texts. At the same time, new evolutionary cosmologies and systems of humanistic ethics were devised, and a vigorous defense of Confucianism was mounted.

The Neo-Confucians dismissed Daoism as impracticable and unsuited to the real needs of Chinese society, while Buddhism was characterized as un-Chinese because of its emphasis on monasticism (which they claimed leads people to ignore their filial duties). In addition, the Buddhist doctrine of "emptiness" (Sanskrit, *sunyata*; Chinese, *kong*) was used as an example of the "nihilism" of Buddhism, while Confucianism was described as practical and world-affirming. Moreover, because Buddhist monastics are not supposed to work for a living and are required to subsist on alms, they were characterized as social parasites.

At the same time, aspects of society that had been neglected by Confucius and early Confucians were addressed by thinkers of this period. A number of books regarding the proper conduct of women were composed—mostly by men, although a few were written by women. A central concern was women's education. Early Confucians had generally held that women should be illiterate because their mental capacities are inferior to those of men and education is irrelevant to their primary duties within the domestic sphere. The Neo-Confucians accepted the inferior status of women and the notion that their main roles in the society should be as wives and mothers, but some contended that they would be more effective in raising and training their children if they had at least rudimentary knowledge of the classics and the philosophies of Confucianism.

One of the earliest writers to espouse this theme was Ban Zhao (c. 79–8 B.C.E.), whose *Admonitions for Women* (*Nujie*) is a set of instructions regarding the "way of wives" (*fudao*). She accepts the traditional hierarchy of Chinese society, in which wives are subservient to their husbands, and their primary sphere of activity is within the home and family. She advises her readers to be humble and thrifty, to serve their husbands and families to the best of their abilities, but she also holds that success in women's work requires a solid education.

Other female Confucian writers echoed these sentiments while acknowledging the secondary place of women in society. But just as Confucian officials had a duty to remonstrate with wayward or corrupt rulers even at the risk of imprisonment or death, women were allotted the role of moral compass for their husbands. In Madam Cheng's *Classic of Filial Piety for Women* (*Nu Xiaojing*), for example, women are told to be humble and obedient, but service to their husbands also requires that they correct them when they transgress Confucian morality. In Madam Cheng's vision, the virtue, humility, and filiality of their wives should serve as salutary examples for husbands, whose own conduct will be uplifted by that of their spouses. In the fifteenth century, Empress Xu (the third wife of the third Ming emperor, Yongle) expanded the potential role of women in Chinese society, arguing that all humans possess the same capacity for sagehood and that even women can aspire to the supreme goal of Confucianism. In her *Instructions for the Inner Quarters* (*Neixun*), she contends that women play a central role in the regulation of the state, which begins with well-trained children and well-regulated families. She accepts the notion that the home is the primary sphere of women's activities, but in her system it is the basis for proper functioning of the whole society, and women are not merely adjuncts to their husbands, but rather complementary partners in the task of promoting social harmony and order.

## Zhu Xi and the Study of Principle

The most influential thinker of Neo-Confucianism was Zhu Xi (1130–1200), who wrote new commentaries on most of the Confucian classics and whose school became the orthodox tradition in China and Korea. Zhu emphasized the "learning of principle" (*lixue*). The term "principle" (*li*) appears in the classics, where it refers to a standard or pattern. Zhu contended that there is a principle that underlies all existence and that this can be discerned through studying phenomena. There is one principle, but it is manifested variously in the things of the universe. The myriad phenomena are in a state of constant flux, but all changes are determined by the universal principle. The force behind change is vital energy, which is the means by which principle is manifested. Both principle and vital energy influence each other, and they are central to the proper functioning of both the natural world and human society. Sages regulate and control their vital energy and act in accordance with principle, and thus they are able to manifest human-heartedness, filiality, and righteousness.

In common with the mainstream of the Confucian tradition, Zhu believed that education is the key to both moral behavior and sagehood. His approach is referred to as "investigation of things" (*kewu*), which involves beginning with what is known and then proceeding to understand the mysterious. Because everything manifests principle, as one investigates things, one progressively comes to understand the nature and elaborations of principle, and this in turn leads to improved wisdom and morality.

Zhu's main opponent was Wang Yangming (1472–1528), who rejected the notion of the exhaustive study of things as a waste of time. He agreed with Zhu that principle is manifested in all phenomena, but held that the human faculty of the heart/mind allows people to discern it directly without an exhaustive study of things. Because humans are innately endowed with the capacity for sagehood, all that is necessary is to engage in introspection using the heart/mind, and through this they can comprehend principle directly.

## The Spread of Confucianism

Although Wang's school was widely influential, Zhu's tradition became the state orthodoxy in China, and it was also imported to Korea and Japan. By the fourth century C.E., Confucianism was well-established in Korea, and during the Koryu dynasty (918–1392) a number of Confucian academies were built. Although Buddhism was the official state ideology, the government instituted a system of civil examinations that followed the Chinese Confucian model.

During the Yi dynasty (1392–1910), Confucianism replaced Buddhism as the state ideology, and Zhu Xi's school became dominant. Korean Confucians generally emphasized the study of human nature and principle (*songnihak*) and "learning of the way" (*tohak*). Following Zhu's lead, Korean Confucians focused on the concepts of principle, vital energy, and heart/mind. The most influential Korean Neo-Confucian, T'oegye (the literary name of Yi Hwang, 1501–1570), was primarily concerned with practical questions of how Confucian ideas should be manifested in human activity.

After Confucianism became the state ideology, the main emphasis of the tradition was textual study, which over time became mostly arid and unoriginal. In the seventeenth and eighteenth centuries, a new school arose in Korea, which came to be known as the "Practical Learning" (Silhak). Its proponents criticized the scholastic Confucians for focusing on words and ignoring practical concerns. Chung Mong-ju (1337–1392), the founder of the movement, stated that "the way of Confucianism lies in the ordinary affairs of daily life. Even in sexual relations and in eating and drinking there is a meaningful principle." The main focus of this school was on how to improve society and directly help the people, and its adherents characterized traditional Confucians as being overly concerned with empty academic study that had no practical use.

The Yi dynasty ended with the Japanese invasion and annexation of Korea in 1911. During the occupation, Confucianism declined due to lack of state support, and when the Japanese were expelled after World War II, the new government decided not to support Confucian institutions, which continued their decline. In the early twenty-first century most of the remaining Confucian academies are museums, but there is still one Confucian university, the Songgyun'gwan in Seoul, and a few traditional scholars (mostly elderly) who continue to uphold the tradition. Their numbers are dwindling, however, and there are few young Koreans who are interested in undertaking the extensive training required of traditional Confucians.

Despite its modern travails, Confucianism continues to be widely influential in East Asia, and its philosophies and moral codes are a core element of the culture of China, Korea, and Japan. In the early 2000s the Confucian educational system that once dominated the intellectual life of East Asia is a thing of the past, and the great Confucian academies are merely historical monuments, but Confucian ideas about human nature, morality, and good governance still influence the way people in the region see themselves and their societies.

See also **Confucianism; Daoism.**

BIBLIOGRAPHY

Ames, Roger T., ed. *Self as Person in Asian Theory and Practice.* Albany: State University of New York Press, 1994.

Csikszentmihalyi, Mark, and Philip J. Ivanhoe. *Religious and Philosophical Aspects of the Laozi.* Albany: State University of New York Press, 1999.

De Bary, Wm. Theodore, and JaHyun Kim Haboush, eds. *The Rise of Neo-Confucianism in Korea.* New York: Columbia University Press, 1985.

Hall, David L., and Roger T. Ames. *Thinking Through Confucius.* Albany: State University of New York Press, 1987.

Ko, Dorothy. *Teachers of the Inner Chambers: Women and Culture in Seventeenth-Century China.* Stanford, Calif.: Stanford University Press, 1994.

Kohn, Livia. *Early Chinese Mysticism: Philosophy and Soteriology in the Daoist Tradition.* Princeton, N.J.: Princeton University Press, 1992.

Mann, Susa, and Yu-Yin Cheng, ed. *Under Confucian Eyes: Writings on Gender in Chinese History.* Berkeley: University of California Press, 2001.

Schwartz, Benjamin. *The World of Thought in Ancient China.* Cambridge, Mass.: Belknap Press, 1985.

Yao, Xinzhong. *An Introduction to Confucianism.* Cambridge, U.K., and New York: Cambridge University Press, 2000.

*John Powers*

## EUROPEAN THOUGHT

Studies of European views of *man* and of the *dignity of man* have been central to the history of ideas, and books continue to be published discussing Western or European views of *man*. Meanwhile, women, lower-class men, and people of color have delved into the scholarship to determine if a thinker's text intended *man* (*homme* in French) to be generic as in the Hebrew *adam*, Greek *anthropos*, or Latin *homo sapiens*; or whether the intention or application was narrowed by sex, rank, class, nationality, or ethnic/racial construct. Of course the androcentric *man* does emphasize the male in implying *humanity*. Feminist scholarship, with precedents in medieval and early modern women authors, has sought out instances wherein *man* androcentrically included *woman* and the *dignity of man* the *dignity of man and woman*. Likewise, with precedents in the sixteenth-century debates between Bartolomé de Las Casas (1474–1566) and Juan Ginés de Sepúlveda (1490–1572 or 1573) on the humanity of indigenous peoples of the Americas, as well as in the eighteenth- and nineteenth-century movements against the trade and enslavement of Africans, scholars have explored the documents that did expand inclusively the "natural rights of man." *Humanity* as a term for the human species has begun to be utilized to replace *man* in discussion of texts that meant by *man* all humans. The history of the idea of *humanity* (or philosophical anthropology as Charles Trinkaus labeled it in his *"In Our Image and Likeness": Humanity and Divinity in Italian Humanist Thought*, 1970) is then a sequel to previous scholarship on the history of the idea of generic man, *anthropos*.

### Universalism versus Particularism

A guiding universalist principle might be that if an idea about *man* is valid, or if an international law is fair, then it applies to all of *humanity*. In the postcolonial era, those opposing false universalism—which intentionally misleads the oppressed—have targeted especially European ideas about *man* that were meant to apply only to elite European males and white feminists' ideas about women that exploit or ignore women of color. Global feminist critiques, as by Chandra Talpade Mohanty, deconstructed the Eurocentric generalizations about "Third World women" and "First World women." Historical and legal scholarship by necessity covers a spectrum from universalist to particularist, exposing in their wake examples of false universalism. Lynn Hunt's *The French Revolution and Human Rights* (1996) applies universalism in exploration of origins of human rights in the natural rights document "The Declaration of the Rights of Man and Citizen" (1789) and applies particularism in exposing the policy debates among French Revolution deputies about citizenship rights of the poor and the propertied, the Jews, free blacks and slaves, and women.

In updating the "Universal Declaration of Human Rights" (United Nations, 1948) by the "Beijing Declaration and

Platform of Action" (United Nations Fourth World Conference on Women, 1995), women planned to realize generic human rights by considering the particularities of women's situations: socioeconomic conditions such as regional poverty and obstacles to women's paid employment; political situations such as men leaving women out of decision making; and bodily factors such as control over health, especially one's own fertility. Emerging is an idea of humanity that recognizes difference.

## Essentialism versus Choice

Ancient Greek philosophers from the fifth century B.C.E. onward speculated on the essence of human nature, and Aristotle's views came to dominate in medieval universities. In his four-part theory of causation (material, efficient, teleological, and formal causes), Aristotle (384–322 B.C.E.) defined human nature by the end (the *telos*) and the form, the fully developed human being; his ideal human was the free, self-governing man who ruled over household and shared community rule in a democratic state. As he noted that a black parent and white parent could mate and produce a child of either color, he viewed all human peoples as the same species. Proposing that all human seeds strive for their full development, which he viewed as male, he thought that women were defective males, but alas the same species. Aristotle's view contrasted with his teacher Plato (c. 428–348 or 347 B.C.E.), who in the *Republic* taught that the only difference between men and women is that one begets within the other; in order to have the best women available and trained to be philosopher-kings, Plato proposed a communal mating and child-rearing system in the guardian class. Throughout the Middle Ages the text of Plato most available was the *Timaeus,* which suggests that men who misbehave are reincarnated as women; as a result, Renaissance male commentators tended to read the *Republic* with the misogynist preconception from the *Timaeus.* When the *Republic* was discussed in the Renaissance, there was mockery of Plato's description of women exercising in the nude as men did in Greece. Nevertheless, in a treatise defending the dignity of female humanity, "La nobilita et l'eccellenza delle done, co'diffettie mancamenti de gli huomoni" (1600; The nobility and excellence of women and the defects and vices of men) Lucretia Marinella (1571–1653) handled the arguments of Aristotle and Plato with aplomb; and the twentieth-century daycare, as proposed in Vladimir Ilyich Lenin's *State and Revolution* (1917) or as established by many employers by the early twenty-first century, applied Plato's distinction between birth mother and the child caregiver to release parents' talents for the good of the community.

Renaissance humanists were knowledgeable in the debates of ancient Greek philosophers on the essence of human nature and the highest good, but they viewed the essence and highest good within the biblical framework of the Creator God. Giovanni Pico della Mirandola (1463–1494) in his *Oration,* in stating God's words to androgynous "adam" (before woman was separated), broke with a fixed essence for human nature by emphasizing freedom of will as the essence of human nature. He suggested that humans may choose to lower themselves in imitating animal behavior or raise themselves in imitation of angelic behavior. Pico poses as the highest goal to attempt in one's lifetime to contemplate God, a viewpoint compatible with his teacher Marsilio Ficino's (1433–1499) proof that the striving to contemplate God in this life suggests that there must be an afterlife where the goal can be achieved (texts in *Renaissance Philosophy of Man,* 1948).

The rejection of "essences" awaited atheist Jean-Paul Sartre's "Existentialism Is a Humanism" (1946), wherein he declares that there is no essential human nature, but that all persons must choose their own natures. He rejects the essentialist human nature of Denis Diderot, Voltaire, and Immanuel Kant, and follows Martin Heidegger in proclaiming that existence precedes essence. Like Pico, Sartre emphasizes the freedom of the will; unlike Pico, Sartre leaves it up to persons to determine the universalist image of humanity that they believe is best for molding themselves. In dialogue with Sartre, Simone de Beauvoir in the *Second Sex* (1949) elaborated on the complexities of a woman's existence and the challenges of defining her own essence when woman is seen as "the other" by men and has internalized men's viewpoints. Peoples of Africa and India, freeing themselves from the "otherness" of European colonial rule, extended the discourse to their own definitions of essence in establishing political independence. A diversity of feminists questioned whether there was any common essence to womanhood, and emphasized differences. Sartre's viewpoint of each individual defining an essence as best for humanity gave way to self-definitions particularized to national, religious, and racial communal norms, as well as to self-definitions expressive of multiple identities and of personal individuality.

## Potential for Good or for Evil

While the Homeric religion of the ancient Greeks suggested that the gods and goddesses played with human events, the ancient Greek philosophers after Socrates (c. 470–399 B.C.E.) analyzed the parts of the human psyche to gain control over human conduct, and debated the highest good (*eudaimonia*). The Platonic Academy under Plato sought contemplation of the Forms such as Justice, Truth, and Beauty. Criticized not only by the Aristotelian Lyceum, but also by the Epicureans who proposed pleasure as highest good, and the Stoics who proposed virtue and the highest good, the Academy in its skeptical stage during the second century B.C.E. sought tranquility from doubt. Marcus Tullius Cicero (106–43 B.C.E.) passed on the heritage of the Hellenistic debates in numerous Latin dialogues wherein he proposed to fellow Romans of the Republic his goal of *studia humanitatis,* the studies appropriate to a free citizen. The particular set of disciplines constituting the humanities education have changed over the centuries but retain Cicero's educational goal to develop natural potentiality of humanity. Influenced by Greek Stoic imagery of notions imprinted on the mind, Cicero described the positive potential in human nature as the rudimentary beginnings of intelligence, right reason, or common notions that the mind naturally develops. Lucius Annaeus Seneca's (4 B.C.E.?–65 C.E.) *Epistles* passed down to medieval Christians the identification of common notions with seeds of virtue and knowledge. In this optimistic view of human nature, right reason is an internal access to natural law, and humans know to seek good and flee evil.

> While born of a noble Florentine family of modest means, Dante around 1310 in his *Convivio* (*The Banquet*) establishes a clear-cut precedent for a tracing of nobility only to virtue:
>
> > Let not those men who are of the Uberti of Florence, nor those of the Visconti of Milan say "Because I am of such a family or race, I am Noble," for the Divine seed falls not into a race of men, that is into a family; but it falls into individual persons, and, as will be proved below, the family does not make individual persons Noble, but the individual persons make the family Noble. (*The Banquet*, book 4, ch. 20, trans. Sayer, p. 238 in A. Smith-Palmer, *The Ideal of the Gentleman*, p. 172)
>
> Yet Dante in *Paradiso* also expresses pride in meeting his twelfth-century noble ancestor Cacciguida. Note the use of *race* in premodern Europe for a family line or lineage, especially for the distinction between those families of highest social rank and other people. It was in the eighteenth century that race came to be an anthropological term to distinguish body types encountered in different continents. In the early twenty-first century, many scholars viewed much previous discussion of race as pseudoscience and studied instead the "racial constructs" of particular cultures.

In contrast to the Greco-Roman tradition, wherein ethics and law developed without a heavy interference from religion, Hebrew scriptures provided a divinely revealed law code, on which rabbinical discussion ensued in the Babylonian Talmud. A basic premise of Judaism is that the created world of God is good and that humanity in particular is very good: "created in the image of God, male and female" (Gen. 1:26). Psalm one compares a righteous man to "a tree . . . that bringeth forth its fruit in its season," and the prophet Jeremiah holds man responsible for bringing forth sweet good deeds (Jer. 2:21).

St. Augustine of Hippo (354–430) reinterpreted Genesis in his development of the doctrine of original sin, a sin Augustine viewed as committed by Adam and passed down to offspring through male concupiscence in sexual intercourse. While through baptism, a Christian overcomes some original sin inherited from Adam through the grace of the new Adam, Jesus, humans are stained nevertheless and must be alert to temptations. In his *Summa Theologiae*, St. Thomas Aquinas (c. 1224–1274) utilizes the phrase "seeds of virtue and knowledge" to explicate the basis of natural law within human nature, and Thomism vied with Augustinianism. During the Italian Renaissance, a prosperous middle class rising into the nobility argued that nobility was based not on the "seed of lineage" but on the "seed of virtue." The further optimism concerning potentialities of human free will of the Renaissance neo-Platonists Ficino and Pico della Mirandola helped bring about a reemphasis on Augustinian original sin through Martin Luther (1483–1546) and John Calvin (1509–1564) and among Catholic Jansenists.

More radical than the Protestant and Catholic Reformations were the secular authors who attempted to describe human nature independently from the Judeo-Christian tradition. Niccolò Machiavelli (1469–1527) used ancient models to write about history and politics, and proposed autonomous principles governing the success of a new prince over the unruly human nature of his population. The Enlightenment thinkers sought to define human nature within a pregovernment ancient state of nature suggested by Cicero's description of the origins of government in the common notions of community. Following Machiavelli's negative view of human nature, Thomas Hobbes (1588–1679) suggested a war of each against all. In contrast, John Locke (1632–1704) transformed the natural law into natural rights within human nature, and a philosophical tradition developed that attributed ills of humankind to social arrangements. Jean-Jacques Rousseau (1712–1778) culminated this tradition in looking back to a golden age before inequality became so severe, and suggesting that human communities might make a new social contract, which would provide equality to male citizens. In the nineteenth century utilitarians worked out arrangements for the greatest good of the greatest number; utopian socialists developed schemes for community ownership of property; and Karl Marx (1818–1883) and Friedrich Engels (1820–1895) developed a historical theory for revolutionary change to result ultimately in such peaceful relations of humanity that the government would wither away. Twentieth-century behaviorist psychologists continued the nurture versus nature debate on the side of the malleability of humanity, while the testing industry attempted to measure more and more precisely the variations in abilities among students.

The beats of Igor Stravinsky's *Rites of Spring* (1913), as well as Expressionist art, evoke the transformation of views of human nature by authors exploring the irrational in antiquity as well as in modern clashes of world cultures. Friedrich Nietzsche (1844–1900) followed Machiavelli in criticizing the feminine weakness of Christianity and seeking to revive the masculine warrior courage of the Romans. Nietzsche provided an image of a human greater than ordinary for whom ordinary morality was too limiting. Such a person might transcend moral convention. Sigmund Freud (1856–1939) suggested that sexuality pervaded the human psyche. Humanity was driven by the sexuality and aggression of the id; the ego tried to control the id under guidance from the parentally socialized superego. These psychological explorations suggested a more sinister side of human nature, evident in the European colonial competitions in Africa and in the developments of totalitarian regimes in Europe.

Twentieth-century authors had to contend with the realization of the nightmare of two world wars fought on European soil. A revival of Augustinian notions of original sin developed within Catholic and Protestant theologians, yet the Second Vatican Council, 1962–1965, in its ecumenical discussions, did affirm "that God does not deny the possibility of salvation to all men of good will" (reaffirmed by Pope John Paul II, *The Splendor of Truth*, pp. 6–7). Most European theorists of human nature, absorbed in witnessing the atrocities of their times, concluded negatively on human nature. Yet in July 1944, Anne Frank, hoping the Nazis would not find her Jewish residence in Amsterdam, wrote "It's really a wonder that I haven't dropped all my ideals. . . . Yet I keep them, because in spite of everything I still believe that people are really good at heart" (p. 287).

*See also* **Class; Essentialism; Evil; Existentialism; Feminism; Free Will, Determinism, and Predestination; Good; Humanism; Race and Racism; Stoicism; Universalism.**

**BIBLIOGRAPHY**

PRIMARY SOURCES

Frank, Anne. *The Diary of a Young Girl.* Translated by B. A. Mooyarrt-Doubleday. New York: Doubleday, 1967.

Fromm, Eric, and Ramón Xirau, eds. *The Nature of Man: Readings.* New York: Macmillan, 1968.

Osborne, Martha Lee, ed. *Woman in Western Thought.* New York: Random House, 1979.

Palmer, Abram Smythe. *The Ideal of a Gentleman; or, A Mirror for Gentlefolks: A Portrayal in Literature from the Earliest Times.* London: Routledge, 1908.

SECONDARY SOURCES

Cassirer, Ernest, et al., eds. *Renaissance Philosophy of Man.* Chicago: University of Chicago Press, 1948.

Horowitz, Maryanne Cline. *Seeds of Virtue and Knowledge.* Princeton, N.J.: Princeton University Press, 1998.

Horowitz, Maryanne Cline, ed. *Race, Class, and Gender in Nineteenth-Century Culture.* Rochester, N.Y.: University of Rochester Press, 1991.

———, ed. *Race, Gender, and Rank: Early Modern Ideas of Humanity.* Rochester, N.Y.: University of Rochester Press, 1992.

John Paul II. *The Splendor of Truth.* Washington, D.C.: U.S. Catholic Conference, 1993.

Mohantry, Chandra Talpade. "Under Western Eyes: Feminist Scholarship and Colonial Discourses." In *Feminist Theory: A Reader,* edited by Wendy Kolmar and Frances Bartkowski. London: Mayfield, 2000.

Nussbaum, Martha. "In Defense of Universal Values." In *Controversies in Feminism,* edited by James P. Sterba. Lanham, Md.: Rowman and Littlefield, 2001.

Passmore, John. *The Perfectibility of Man.* 3rd ed. Indianapolis, Ind.: Liberty Fund, 2000.

Richards, Graham. *"Race", Racism, and Psychology: Towards a Reflexive History.* New York: Routledge, 1997.

Sassi, Maria Michela. *The Science of Man in Ancient Greece.* Translated by Paul Tucker. Chicago: University of Chicago Press, 2001.

Trigg, Roger. *Ideas of Human Nature: An Historical Introduction.* 2nd ed. Malden, Mass.: Blackwell, 1999.

Tuana, Nancy. *The Less Noble Sex: Scientific, Religious, and Philosophical Conceptions of Woman's Nature.* Bloomington: Indiana University Press, 1993.

Winston, Andrew S., ed. *Defining Difference: Race and Racism in the History of Psychology.* Washington, D.C.: American Psychological Association, 2004.

*Maryanne Cline Horowitz*

**HUMANITY IN THE ARTS.** Four sculpted images of the male figure loom before the viewer. These four works span a period of almost 2,500 years, are fabricated from a variety of media, and range from naturalistic to realistic to abstract presentations. Perceived through the eyes of art historians they have been described as "the classic nude," "a prime force," "in

**Idealized male figure.** Zeus (or Poseidon) from Cape Artemisium (c. 460 B.C.E.). Bronze. © ERICH LESSING/ART RESOURCE, NY

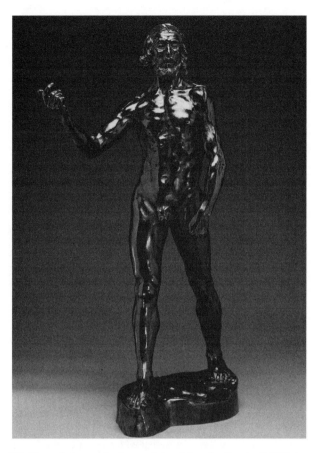

**Vitality of the male form.** *Saint John the Baptist* (1879) by Auguste Rodin. Bronze. © CHRISTIE'S IMAGES/CORBIS

motion," and "*pars pro toto,* or the part which stands for the whole." However, when seen through the eyes of cultural historians, these same four sculptures are characterized with such diverse adjectives as "heroic," "fragmented," "ethereal," or "earthly" and described as "ideal," "cultic," "tragic," or "ambiguous," as symbolic of cultural attitudes toward the body, the human person, and thereby of humanity. Yet all four provide sufficient visual information to be deemed male, figural, and most especially, human—not divine, animal, or object.

The classical principles of the human form as an expression of the idea of humanity, especially that of the athlete, as the "temple of the gods," is reflected in the idealized male figure in *Zeus* (or *Posideon*) (c. 460 B.C.E.). He stands with his left leg bent slightly at the knee and his left foot planted firmly upon the earth as his right foot springs forward slightly, providing both a sense of motion and a gesture of transcendence. As his muscular right arm bends at the elbow to propel his energies through his right hand, this athlete apparently prepares to hurl a javelin. His left arm extends outward to direct his sight and the projected path of his weapon. Balanced according to the classical proportions between head and torso and then between head and legs and arms, his handsome body, through its posture and gestures, voices the cultural attitude of the perfection of the human form as a nexus of humanity and divinity, of immanence and transcendence.

The otherwise distinctive presentation of the male body with shortened extremities, diminutive hands, enlarged feet, elongated torso, protruding belly, and protracted phallus on the otherwise untitled Baluban sculpture *Male Figure* (probably nineteenth century), might at first glance appear as a "primitive" distortion of the human image. However, prolonged observation proffers the indigenous perspective on the human, if not simply the male, body. The widespread stance of this man is echoed in the extension of his hips and buttocks and balanced by his broad shoulders. His bare feet, which appear initially to be too large for his legs, are entrenched firmly and flatly on the earth and support his dense male body. Whether simply by weight or symbolic values, his distended belly and penis sag downward toward the earth. His undersize hands clutch the outermost perimeter of swollen belly, emphasizing simultaneously the abdominal protuberance and enhanced navel and his long genital. Gesture, posture, and bodily attributes turn the viewer's eye not upward toward this figure's enlarged head or dramatically incised facial features but rather downward toward the earth. The visual connectives denote the sympathetic magic with the fertility of the earth and two distinctive traits of the African ethos: its earth-centeredness and the centrality of the human body in the indistinguishable unity of art, life, and spirituality, even to the conclusion that dance is Africa's primal and primary art.

The sinewy musculature of the life-size bronze rendering in Auguste Rodin's *St. John the Baptist* (1879) evokes simultaneously a response of awe at the sculptor's craftsmanship and marvel at the handsomeness of the human body. Captured at mid-stride, the bronze body of this male figure pulsates with the connections between muscle, sinew, skin, and respiration. Like the figure of Zeus, this St. John has one foot flat on the ground and the other slightly elevated to accentuate the internal and external motion of a walker. He gestures welcome with his right hand while his left hand turns the viewer's attention to the earth as he signifies immanence as a direction toward transcendence. No matter how long or great the distance from which we look, it is the torso of St. John that captures the viewer's attention. The careful detailing of his rib cage, including the intimate relationships between flesh and muscle, muscle and bone, capture our attention, enabling the viewer to recognize the artistic, medical, and technical advances that separate Zeus from St. John while also highlighting the commonalities between these two visual renditions of the male figure, especially as a representation of the idea of humanity.

The greater visual divide is the artistic move in the early twentieth century to abstractions leading to Constantin Brancusi's *Torso of a Young Man* (1924). As with his three sculpted predecessors, this bronze sculpture captures the essence of being male and human despite the absence of a full representational and physical body, an individualized face, or symbolic gestures. Rather, the energies emanating from this carefully composed abstracted torso and its initial point of division into two lower limbs simultaneously references humanity and maleness. The sculptor has carefully placed his piece on an orchestrated base that affects our seeing of it as a torso, as human, as male—not simply as three interconnected brass cylinders. Nonetheless, these four variations in sculptural

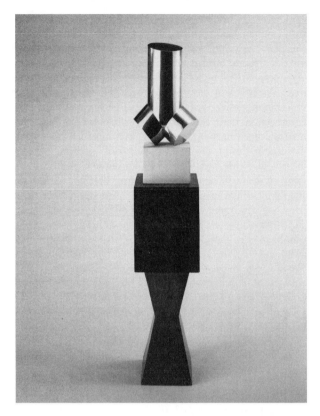

**The essence of maleness.** *Torso of a Young Man* (1924) by Constantin Brancusi. Polished bronze on stone and wood base. HIRSHHORN MUSEUM AND SCULPTURE GARDEN, SMITHSONIAN INSTITUTION, GIFT OF JOSEPH H. HIRSHHORN, 1966. PHOTO BY LEE STALSWORTH. © 2004 ARTISTS RIGHTS SOCIETY (ARS), NEW YORK/ADAGP, PARIS

styles and forms enable the viewer to see the essence of the male figure and, more generically, humanity. The focus in this visual essay is the modes and means by which sculpture relays the idea(s) of humanity across historical and cultural boundaries. The methodology is comparative but not chronological, as the concerns here are the visual transmission of an idea and the visual critique of a universal ideal. This procedure will then create a recognition of this idea not by the chronological sequence of stylistic developments in sculpture but rather through the transmission of key elements in both universal and regional conceptions of being human.

**Toward a Definition of the Idea of Humanity**
The primary definitions of *humanity* in the *Oxford English Dictionary* include "The quality or condition of being human, manhood; the human faculties or attributes collectively; human nature; man in the abstract." As a plural, *humanities*, the *OED* continues, "Human attributes; traits or touches of human nature or feeling; points that concern mankind, or appeal to human sensibilities." Further, in connection with the word *humane, humanity* is defined as "The character or quality of being humane; behaviour or disposition towards others such as befits a human being." This examination of the idea of humanity through the sculpted image incorporates these

three characteristics of being human in representational, figural, or abstract forms; in the expression of sensibilities and sensitivities; and in depictions of modes of behavior and interactions with others. The duality within the phrase "humanity in the arts" is exemplified by the artistic recognition of the existence in nature of the human body, and further of the potential symbolic and evocative patterns of human forms, gestures, and postures.

In his 1954 Andrew W. Mellon Lecture in the Fine Arts, the art historian Herbert Read focused his attention on the problematic of *The Art of Sculpture* (1956). Through detailed analyses of sculptures from varied cultures and time periods, Read proposed that more than 90 percent of all sculpture is of the human body, thereby naming the close association between sculpture and humanity. More than forty years later, another art historian, Tom Flynn, pronounced that the history of the sculpture was the history of the body (1998). The close associations between sculpture and humanity are confirmed in classical myths such as the stories of Deucalion and Pyrrha and of Pygmalion. Further recognition of this affinity in Western culture is found in the Second Commandment, as biblical and art historical scholars have argued over the centuries as to the meaning of the terms *graven image* and *idol.* Clearly, early Western monotheism emphasized the negative connectives between idolatry, graven images, and sculpture even unto the almost complete absence of sculpted images in Christianity until the Middle Ages. The visual and emotive realities are obvious: the encounter with either a life-size or monumental sculpture is similar to that with another human being.

The often-missed irony is that the majority, if not all, of the world's religions, including Christianity, incorporate within their narratives of origins a story of the creation of humanity. Western monotheistic traditions premise their univocal foundation toward human nature and, thereby, humanity, on *Genesis,* especially 1:26–27. The operative principles are that humanity is fashioned as both men and women and in the image of God, implying both a parity of the sexes and a scriptural anthropology. Each of the monotheistic traditions, however, reads these and ensuing passages with distinct theological eyes so that the original story becomes layered with scriptural, theological, and societal meanings.

For example, Judaism encodes the categories of men and women with cultural, societal, and scriptural definitions to affirm its distinctiveness within the larger cultures in which it existed. Christianity affirms *Genesis* 1:26–27 with the Incarnation of Jesus as the Christ (*John* 1:14) and the later theological theses including the fourth-century patristic texts of Augustine and Jerome. The early Christian understanding of humanity is, of course, complicated by the dogmatizing of Christology in the face of heresies, controversies, and debates. The fourth-century transformation of Christianity into the Imperial Church simultaneously transformed the social order toward that of the Byzantine court, thus resulting in fewer roles for women in liturgical ceremonies, sacramental rites, and church life. Analogous modifications occurred throughout the history of Christianity in its multiple public formations. Koranic teachings reaffirm and oftentimes enhance the Genesis

**A symbol of fertility.** *Chac Mool, the Rain Spirit* from Chichén Itzá (948–1697). Limestone. THE ART ARCHIVE/NATIONAL ANTHROPOLOGICAL MUSEUM MEXICO/DAGLI ORTI

narrative in light of the then contemporary cultural, legal, and societal situations of Islam.

Nonwestern cultures, however, do not necessarily either frame or discuss the idea of humanity within this same, or similar, structural boundaries, interpretive narratives, or visualizing processes. Nevertheless, the reality exists that there is a universal foundation that privileges the relationship between humanity and the religious as evidenced in scriptural or spiritual texts and visual evidence with regional and religious variations, that is, indigenous traditions, Buddhism, Confucianism, Daoism, Hinduism, and so on.

As an example of the cross-cultural and transhistorical scope of the discussion of the idea of humanity in sculpture, consider this revisiting of one of Herbert Read's comparisons between

a *Chac Mool, the Rain Spirit* from Chichén Itzá (948–1697) and the twentieth-century sculpture by Henry Moore of a *Reclining Woman* (1929). The parallels are not one-for-one between these two images, as if Moore had seen and had been highly influenced by the Aztec work; rather, the similarities are in the potential affinities and differences in the understandings of humanity. From that perspective, we see two figures resting on the ground: the one more geometric and angular in form, the other curved and rotund even unto her "squared" right shoulder and thigh. The Chac Mool rests his lower back and buttocks on the ground, raises his legs, which are bent at the knees, but has his feet flat on the ground as did the Baluban man. His torso is elevated almost as if leaning against a series of pillows as he twists his head to acknowledge any approaching supplicants. Typically Mesoamerican art emphasizes a strong connection between fertility and death, thereby the natural order of the life cycle. The Chac Mool, as both a rain spirit and a male figure who connects so clearly to the earth, affirms the empathy between the rain that encourages the fertility of the earth and the male semen that signifies human fertility.

Moore's female figure reposes more naturally than her geometrically compact Aztec ancestor. She is a supine configuration of intersecting curves and lines as her body rests on the ground and her shoulders twist upward with her left arm raised to support her head, which turns to face the viewer. Continuing the Western cultural and religious fascination with the affinities between the female and the earth, this twentieth-century depiction accentuates her hips and thighs and positions her legs to underscore the genital area. The commonalities between these two images encompass the universality and ahistoricity of "natural" placements in which the human body can be positioned, the representation of gender and thereby of power, and a consideration of the original function as opposed to the sanctification such works of art receive by being installed in museums.

The form, shape, posture, gesture, and costume conferred upon the human body by sculptors in different cultures, historical periods, and religious commitments allow researchers to see and critique the embedded inscriptions of gender, class, identity, and power. Body types vary not simply from geographic region to geographic region but also from cultural categories that transmute according to prevailing economic, political, religious, and social attitudes. Sculptures such as the Baluban *Male Figure,* the Aztec *Chac Mool,* and the Greek *Zeus (Poseidon)* invite comparisons in relation to their varying centers of gravity, which define their physical postures and their internal spiritual nexuses. Analyses of their comparative expressions of mass, weight, and volume coordinate projections of natural versus ideal body types, symbolic patterns of the human body especially with regard to divinity and the sacred, and nutritional and medical factors that reveal information about class, race, and gender.

## The Task of the Sculpted Body for the Idea of Humanity

The critical question voiced by the art historian Moshe Barasch—"What tasks is the human figure made to fulfill in painting and sculpture, and how has it been employed by artists and understood by the viewer in varying periods?"—affects the interpretation(s) and valuing of the idea of humanity. Expressive of a diverse spectrum of religious values and cultural attitudes, the imaging of the human body has been instrumental in fertility rites, magical ceremonies, cult objects and rituals, idolatry, natural medicine, social advancement, intellectual achievement, and sacred correspondence. One of the significant components in the artistic renderings of humanity has been in the social and cultural constructions of gender, that is, what distinguishes the categories "feminine" and "masculine" in modes of behavior, demeanor, dress, and meaning. Biology determines sex, while society, from its privileged coordination of culture, economics, politics, and religion, conditions definitions of and attitudes toward gender.

**An androgynous deity.** *Kuan-yin* (China, 960–1279). © FOTO WETTSTEIN & KAUF; MUSEUM REITBERG ZÜRICH

Post-1960s scholarship, which introduced and incorporated the inclusion of the marginalized—that is, those previously neglected groups such as racial and ethnic minorities, the economically impoverished, and women—has prompted reevaluations of the canons and categorizations of Western history. Commensurately, this new scholarship critiqued and questioned the traditional litany of the distinctions between "East" and "West" from cultural, philosophic, and religious perspectives. Differing cultures define particularized patterns and structures for identical realities such as gender, as evidenced in the classical Mediterranean *Aphrodite of Knidos* (350 B.C.E) the Indian *Rukmini* (tenth century), and the Chinese *Kuan-yin* (or Guanyin, 960–1279). Ostensibly these three images depict female bodies with some regional distinctions apparent, such as the small, almost adolescent breasts but thickened waist, wide hips, and heavy thighs on the Greco-Roman goddess of love as opposed to the narrowed waist and globular breasts on the Hindu deity of fertility or the wispy waist and prepubescent chest of the Buddhist purveyor of mercy and compassion. All three representations correspond to the principle of the human form as the vehicle through which the divine is expressed or manifested. All three interconnect in their gestural signs, which communicate the empathy between the feminine and fertility and the earth—from Aphrodite's right hand denoting female modesty, the site of generation, and sexual pleasure, to Rukmini's voluptuous display of her feminine attributes, to Kuan-yin's earthbound posture and right-handed gesture pointing toward the earth.

However, there is a disconnect here despite the ostensibly feminine presence of these three deities. For upon careful examination of physical characteristics there is the question of recognize that Western culture, and thereby Western scholarship, has traditionally been preoccupied with order and clarity. Gender distinctions and their ensuant visualizations may be more subtly rendered and understood in non-Western cultures and defy normative Western iconographic patterns, thereby proffering wider horizons for defining and evaluating universalized ideas of humanity.

The human body, whether male, female, androgynous, or hermaphrodite, is a carrier of meaning and values inscribed with subjective associations and objective perceptions, stylistic variations, and institutional identifiers. One of the most significant of those "inscribers" is religion. The enigma of religious art—the question of what makes art religious beyond the labeling of an image as religious—is a consideration in the visual comparison of the idea of humanity in Gian Bernini's seventeenth-century sculptures of *Apollo and Daphne* (1622–1634) and *The Ecstasy of Saint Teresa* (1645–1652). Each of these works is a "group" as opposed to an individual sculpture, that is, there is more than one person represented; in the former it is a mythological couple and in the latter an angel paired with the female mystic. So the dynamics of interaction between individuals becomes central to the ways that such sculptures project internally the idea of humanity. The Baroque characteristics of theatrical drama of the moment, of an upward swirling movement, and of theatrical lighting combine with a reaffirmed sense of the spirituality of the body to fashion an aesthetic that reflects the changing Counter-Reformation attitudes toward the human and the human body in opposition to the harmony, balance, order, and anthropocentricism of the Renaissance.

Bernini's two works challenge the viewer to consider the importance of posture, dress, and narrative in the projection of the idea of humanity through the vehicle of the human body in sculpture. Daphne appears almost completely uncovered, a nude female in the classic sense of the term as she gracefully swivels her body away from the clutches of her pursuer, the similarly minimally clad Apollo. The upward gyrations of her escape are transformed into an elegant series of curvilinear swirls of what appears to be drapery suggestively covering her pubic area and her left leg while skimming the inner edge of her right leg. Close observation, however, reveals that this drapery is the initiation of the trunk of the laurel tree that will enclose her and thereby protect her from Apollo. Her upraised arms curve into what had been her hands, which have transmogrified into laurel tree branches. Although both the running figure of Apollo and that of the metamorphosing Daphne are clearly modeled upon classical prototypes, Bernini's bodies lack the muscular weight and tension found in the classical Greek *Zeus* (*Poseidon*) or the classical Greco-Roman *Aphrodite of Knidos*. Despite the time factor—more than a century of cultural, medical, political, scientific, social, and theological advances—Bernini's figures appear softer to the eye, as if they were almost weightless and thus able to float off from the earth as opposed to the earthbound realistic renderings of the human body as muscled and monumental, characterized by the Renaissance. Further, this characterization of Apollo is that of a soft beautiful youth who hovers between masculinity and androgyny. Although the theme is secular, the ethereal quality

**The allusion of spirituality in a classically inspired work.** *Apollo and Daphne* (1622–1624) by Gian Bernini. Marble. © BETTMANN/CORBIS

the gender ambiguity of Kuan-yin, who appears to be more androgynous than specifically male or female. Historians of religion, especially those specializing in Eastern religions, have debated the reasons for and the historical route of the transformation of the Indian Buddhist male bodhisattva Avalokiteshvara into the androgynous Chinese Buddhist bodhisattva Kuan-yin, who becomes ultimately the Japanese Buddhist female bodhisattva Kwannon. The present issue is not an attempt to unravel this religio-historical conundrum but rather to raise the question of cultural perceptions of gender and thereby of humanity. For by whatever name this deity is identified and by whatever anthropomorphic form configured, the fundamental questions of identification relate first to the fact that this is the deity of mercy and compassion—virtues that cultural conditioning may categorize as feminine or masculine—and second to cultural disparities in attitudes toward gender, meaning that the gestures, postures, and modes of behavior one culture (say, southern Europe) names as "male" and "female" are opposite to those of the Indian subcontinent or the Far East. Both in terms of artistic creation and scholarly interpretation, it is necessary to

**Reverential or voyeuristic?** *The Ecstasy of Saint Teresa* (1645–1652) by Gian Bernini. Altar of Cornaro Chapel, Church of Santa Maria della Vittoria, Rome. THE ART ARCHIVE/ALBUM/JOSEPH MARTIN

of the sculpted bodies of Apollo and Daphne direct the viewer to consider the spiritual implications of this "chase."

Bernini's rendering of the bodily presence of the Carmelite mystic Teresa of Avila is almost bodiless as she sinks backward onto the rocky ledge (or cloud?) that is poised immediately beneath her. The lassitude of her body might suggest either a weightlessness caused by faint or trance or that graceful litheness of a ballerina as she "floats through the air." The vitality of this sculptured figure is the dramatic energy released by the swirls of drapery that envelope her while the elasticity of her protruding left hand and foot effect the *pars pro toto* of her swooned body. The tight whirling and spinning of the angel's robes contrast with the looser delicate layering of cloth that swallows the mystic's limp body. As opposed to the "in unison" posture of the two standing figures in Bernini's earlier work, the male angel stands erect as he looks down upon the supine figure of the female saint. The interrelationships thereby shift from one of physical or gender parity to one of dominance or empowerment. The visibly insubstantial nature of the saint's body creates an aura of spiritual apprehension.

The presence and signification of the familiar form of the angel as divine messenger directs the viewer to contemplate this work as religious art. The question becomes how an individual without a culturally trained Western eye or knowledge of Christianity would see these images. Is the attitude toward the body as corruptible, redeemed, or mystical unique to Christianity, Western culture, or even to this singular sculptor? The normative reading has been that this sculpture is a visualization of the sacramentalism of the human body in a moment of agapic love as appropriate to the Tridentine teachings of Roman Catholicism. Nonetheless, criticisms of this same image identify it as a secular, almost voyeuristic, depiction of female orgasm. The lens, then, through which images are seen ordains the method and mode of interpretation, as does the receptivity of the viewer, as discussed in the relatively new category of response theory (see Freedberg). Thus revisiting Barasch's question, it may now be paraphrased as: "What tasks is the human figure made to fulfill in painting and sculpture, and how has *the viewer understood that image*?"

## Comparative Studies in World Cultures

Through a series of categories—the authority of the male figure, the human as divine revelation, maternity, and abstraction of anxiety and uncertainty—comparisons of selected images from differing historical cultures are contrasted in a bifurcated effort to identify the process of the visual transmission of ideas and to encourage thinking about the meaning, function, intentionality, and reception of the body as the idea of humanity. The curious, if not ironic, fact that the human body is a product of the natural order, however one comes to understand that body, is shaped by social reality and cultural and religious values.

***The authority of the male figure.*** The male figure, which is identified as normative in defining power and authority, or so feminist scholars in the late twentieth century would assert, can serve as a locus for consideration of the relationship between the function of images and the idea of humanity. Referencing

**The human form interpreted as symbols of power and authority.** *King Men-kau-Ra between the goddess Hathor and the Goddess of the Nome of Diospolis Parva* (Egypt, IV Dynasty, 2800 B.C.E.). Schist. © ROGER WOOD/CORBIS

the classical Greek statue of *Zeus* (*Poseidon*) (460 B.C.E.) as a particularly fine example of the visualization of the classical principles of harmony and order through the human figure, the handsomeness of this human form becomes quickened by muscular tensions, especially in his arms, legs, and torso, and the intimations of respiration. This sculpted rendition of male energy and movement can be read as expressive of ideal form, creation and fertility, kingship and military power, guardian and athlete, and prevalent social and cultural order. A figure of extraordinary vitality, *Zeus* (*Poseidon*) visually attests to the "Western" principle of entrancement with the beauty of the human figure, especially as the revelation of the imaged forms of the gods and goddesses. Muscular structure, movement (whether internal or external), and the ability to connote emotion through facial expression, gesture, or pose, are among the sculptor's tools in transmitting the idea of humanity. This sculpture is called by the name of a god, but he is in the form of a human being.

By contrast, the classical Egyptian carved relief of *King Men-kau-Ra between the goddess Hathor and the Goddess of the Nome of Diospolis Parvis* (IV Dynasty, 2800 B.C.E.) is more formal in presentation and interrelationships among the three figures than the group interaction in either of Bernini's works. This is a sculpture of hieratic art in which the depictions of the human body do not visualize the canon of beauty through harmony and order; rather, this is an envisioning of social structures and of the body more as a symbol than an organic composition. The conception of bodily forms, while identifiably male and female even by twenty-first-century Western standards—physical attributes such as breasts, distinctive hairstyles, and social positioning (female behind the male, the male in the leadership slot)—are evident beyond the static geometric and linear emphases. Here the "ideal body" mirrors the social constructs of authority, power, and sovereignty as much through the weightiness of forms as through individual postures.

The straight-backed, almost stiff bearing of all three personages voices their class and role in their cultural world as they affirm, not challenge, the received situation in daily life. Both the king and the goddesses display their bodies without a sense of shame or rejection. Extraordinary delicacy and dexterity was required to carve the diaphanous garments on the two goddesses and the pleated kilt of manhood on the king. The bodily proportions of both the male and female figures are realistic, neither elongated nor disjointed. However, the smooth formation of the torsos and extremities unto the visual lack of muscle-skin-bone-respiration provides us with the reverse situation of *Zeus* (*Poseidon*), for Men-kau-Ra is a human being in the form of a god.

***The human as divine revelation.*** Perhaps the fundamental connector between Eastern and Western cultures, especially in terms of religious values and the arts, is the human figure as the signifier of the hypothetical image of divinity. The classical Greek tradition advocated the idealization of the human form as a reflection of divine beauty, a philosophic and artistic legacy operative throughout the evolution of Western culture, which affirmed the dignity of humanity. Christianity inherited this principle but was oftentimes antagonistic to it and vacillated in its attitudes toward the human as graced by the Incarnation, as matter in need of redemption, as the vehicle of innocence, and as the purveyor of sin and lust, especially in terms of women. Commensurately the Eastern attitude, despite its religious and cultural variations, affirmed an abstracted relationship between humanity and the supernatural. This is to say that the human body, either wholly or in part, signified an aspect or character of the mystical ideal so that nakedness/nudity, especially in the Indian subcontinent, connoted the sensuality of the fertility spirits, postures, and gestures, while in Chinese art, nakedness/nudity served a didactic function, especially in terms of ethical behavior. More generically, however, the distortion of a specific body part or its total abstraction signified its embodiment of spiritual ideals.

Variations in body types do not necessarily signal distinctive attitudes toward the idea of humanity but more likely than not reflect the actuality of the global assortment of climatic, meterological, agricultural, and dietary differences not simply between East and West but also North and South, intracontinental as well as intercontinental. So for example, there is an identifiable "northern European body type" which can be distinguished from a "southern European body type." The latter is premised upon the Greek ideal of beauty and proposes that whether male or female, the torso is distinguished by two equal

triangles with the base of one running the width of the hips with the intersecting side angles converging toward the waist to meet the tip of the other triangle, which expands as its inverted base crosses the span of the shoulders. This visual sensation of a mathematically balanced harmony is extended through a geometric progression of the size of the head to a grouping of four heads to the length of the torso and extremities, respectively. This "southern body," which basks regularly in the sun and its warmth, also benefits from the regularity of fresh crops and is thereby comfortable in its skin, wearing lighter and perhaps revealing clothing not for sexual enticement but for physical ease and climatic comfort.

Conversely, the "northern body" displays less proportionate relationships between shoulder and waist, waist and hip, head and torso, and torso and limbs. Rather one sees in works of art and other visual documentation men and women with narrowed shoulders, elongated torsos, protruding abdomens, slender hips, and spindly extremities. Like the huddled masses, they cover themselves with layers of heavy clothing to protect their bodies from the almost perpetual cold and damp weather. Further, this "northern body" is not regularly sustained by the availability of fresh fruits and vegetables; rather the normal diet consisted of salted and preserved meats, pickled vegetables, dark breads, and beer. Similar variations in body types and sizes can be distinguished throughout world cultures, as can the ideal of beauty and the definition of the exotic. Thereby the recognition of the fundamental roles of nature and natural elements in the formation of the human body must not be ignored, and attitudes toward humanity extend beyond what we identify as normative but created influences: culture, economics, politics, religion, and society.

A further consideration to be discussed is posture and stance. How individuals perceive themselves and others and how they are viewed by others is dependent upon a variety of factors including physical position. So whether standing or seated, an individual figure projects differing attitudes toward herself and others, as well as reflecting societal status, class distinctions, and hierarchical values. Similarly the element of dress, or lack thereof in the instance of sculptured figures, also places an interpretive value on the human person and her identity. Gestures, whether digital, hand, or facial, communicate more than emotions, sensitivities, or feelings. Ideas including cultural, religious, and social values can be exchanged or taught through gesturing. All aspects of the human body, then, can safely be said to contribute to the idea of humanity in world cultures, as individual regional groups develop specific forms of body and gestural language and attitudes toward gender, body types, and dress within the more universal categorizations of sex and stages of physical maturation.

One of those universals is the body as a nexus for humanity and divinity. For example, consider the following four sculptures: the figure of Christ from *The Pentecost* (c. 1132), *Standing Buddha* (first century), *The Maitreya of the Koryuji Temple* (seventh century) and *Shiva Nataraja, Lord of the Dance* (eleventh century). These are four different renderings of the divine through the human figure in standing, seated, praying, and dancing postures; clothed, draped, and partially

**Poised between heaven and earth.** *Christ of the Pentecost* (detail from *The Pentecost*, c. 1132), tympanum in the narthex of the Cathedral de la Madeleine, Vézelay. THE ART ARCHIVE/DAGLI ORTI

**Simultaneously human and divine.** *Standing Buddha* (1st century C.E.), Takht-i- Bahi, northwest Pakistan. Schist. HIP/SCALA/ART RESOURCE, NY

clothed forms; and with or without halos. Each communicates simultaneously the nobility and the simplicity of being human and male and yet also configured in some way divine.

The twelfth-century Christ of *The Pentecost* tympanum is an elegantly rendered, seated but nonetheless kinetic figure. This particular image is identified iconographically as a *Majestas* (or *Maiestas*) *Domini,* or Lord's Majesty, in which the Resurrected Christ, denoted by his cruciform nimbus, is depicted as the ruler (and judge) of the universe, surrounded by the tetramorphs (Ezekiel 1:4–28; Revelation). His bodily form is ethereal, with elongated torso and limbs and enlarged hands and feet. This is not a depiction premised upon the Greek ideal; rather this is a mystical rendering of the "Word made flesh" who is emphatically contoured against the large mandorla that encases him as a sign of his divinity. The refined drapery is highlighted by the variations between thin and thick reticulations in the folds and pleats. At certain places the drapery highlights the naturalness of his humanity, such as the almost sheer covering over his legs, particularly the protrusion of his right knee, while in other places the heavy layers of fabric, such as that over his arms, resembles wings. Throughout, the curvature of these draped layers of fabric create dynamic, musically organized circles, arcs, and curves that express extraordinary vitality. Thereby, although seated, this male form is enlivened yet hesitates between a state of vibrant motion and calm stillness. This is a Christ caught, if you will, between heaven and earth, between humanity and divinity, between materiality and

spirituality. This is not a Christ who would be known or understood by early Christians who affirmed his Incarnation but envisioned him only symbolically.

By contrast the first-century C.E. *Standing Buddha* radiates serenity, calm, and stillness. His skillfully delineated garment swirls leisurely around his almost pillar-like form. Such an image of the Buddha was influenced by the Greco-Roman models of both sculpted figures and costume. Like the Christ figure, this Buddha is also missing a hand—the former his left hand, the latter his right hand. Ostensibly such selective destruction is the result of an act of iconoclasm that is often religiously inspired when the "images" provoke too much of an aura of reality and threaten the status quo of a religion or political group. Whereas the Christ communicated ethereality and the perceived ability to float away from the cathedral wall and upward to the heavens, this Gandharan Buddha is solidly placed on the ground, although the viewer does not see how firmly, as his feet have either been excised purposively or removed by a natural disaster. This is an image of the eternal, divine Buddha, not the moral teacher of the earliest Buddhist tradition. He is simultaneously regal and humble, human and divine, solid yet spiritual. Despite the refinement, spirituality, and disciplined strength, this Buddha image communicates the

**The dancer as godly creator and destroyer.** *Shiva Nataraja, Lord of the Dance* (Chola period, 11th century). Copper. *NATARAJA: SHIVA AS KING OF DANCE.* SOUTH INDIA, CHOLA DYNASTY, 11TH CENTURY. BRONZE, 111.5 X 101.65 CM © THE CLEVELAND MUSEUM OF ART, 2002. PURCHASE FROM THE J. H. WADE FUND, 1930.331

gravitas of humanity as refined aristocracy, particularly when contrasted with the Christ figure.

*The Maitreya of the Koryuji Temple* is a elegantly aligned figuration of the Japanese Buddhist principles of silence, calm, and compassion that lead toward enlightenment. Although a male form, this Maitreya is an asexual androgyne with soft and delicate hands and fingers that gesture teachings on wisdom and compassion. His slender body almost defies the weight of his enlarged head and thickened neck as it tilts forward in a meditation posture. His slight frame—small, gentle bones with minimal to no musculature—is revealed by his naked torso. His legs are covered by a loosely pleated drape as they intertwine into a yoga position with the soles of his feet turned outward to the sky and away from the earth. As with images of the human form in other historical time periods, cultures, and media, this Maitreya privileges the symbolic nature of the body over portraiture, emblem, or realism. The delicacy and fragility of this bodhisattva portends the ideals of spiritual wisdom and compassion, especially as expressed through love. Another commonality between Eastern and Western religious art in the utilization of the human body is that of the portrayal of love, especially divine love, in which men are characterized by a softening of their otherwise hard-edged masculinity. Thus John the Beloved Disciple (also known as John the Evangelist) is rendered as a soft, delicate, almost fragile but youthful male figure verging for some viewers on androgyny or femininity.

The ecstasy of the so-called Dancing Shiva professes the fundamental essence of rhythmic movement as both a primordial human act and a signifier of divine energies. The Hindu tradition characterizes Shiva, like the other deities, through a multiplicity of forms such as the Lord of the Dance who creates and destroys in one conflated activity. The child at his feet is the representative of the new: life, year, creation. However, for the new to emerge the old must be destroyed in the choreography of the life cycle. This is the image of an anthropomorphic deity who defies traditional categories of description as he balances the world on one foot. That foot, however, is symbolically naked and absolutely flat on the ground or the resting child. The contorted postures of his bent knees, elevated left leg, swaggered buttocks, wispy waist, dramatically stiff neck and head, and ceremoniously gesturing four arms and hands are coordinated to presuppose the appearance of a circle, particularly a flaming circle, as the symbol of eternity. Curiously, if the Christ from *The Pentecost* were placed next to the *Shiva Nataraja* one is brought to silence by the visual parallels and counterpoints. The extension of Shiva's outer arms is identical to that of Christ, although the hand gestures differ significantly: Shiva is holding objects such as a cymbal and a lotus in his hands, while the remaining right hand of Christ is empty as it turns palm out to the viewer; presumably he held a book, Bible, or orb in his left hand. The dramatic swag of the hips is visually parallel, although Christ's two enlarged bare feet rest flat on the edge of the mandorla while Shiva's enlarged feet are positioned differently. The right foot rests flatly and firmly on the offered child, while his right leg is elevated high above his bent left knee. Although further visual comparisons could be made here, what becomes significant is the difference: the ethereality of Christ causes a viewer to wonder if he won't just float away, while the gravitas of Shiva leaves him earthbound.

***Maternity.*** The universal category of maternity is something "more" than the iconographic convention of Mother and Child in either religious or secular art. This image is a confirmation initially of the limitless importance and nature of fertility and secondarily of the survival of both the species and of individual human beings. Found in all forms of religious and secular art within world cultures, the presentation of women with their children is simultaneously ahistorical and historicized. If the faces, costuming, or relationships depicted are identifiable then this pairing can be interpreted as individualized, portraiture, and historical; if unidentifiable or universalized as types, depictions of the mother and child are categorized as ahistorical, symbolic, and culturally or socially relevant. For example, consider the contrasts and commonalities between a twelfth-century Byzantine-style *Virgin and Child* (late eleventh to early twelfth century), a Gothic *Virgin and Child* (fourteenth century), an Indian *Mother and Child* (eleventh century), Michelangelo's *Vatican Pietà* (1498–1500), and Stephen De Staebler's *Pietà* (1988).

The Byzantine-styled *Virgin and Child* projects a vision of clear demarcations as to the theological and social definitions of maternity. The rigid, almost stiff posture of this standing female figure is emphasized, if not highlighted, by the tightly draped and pleated fabric of her dress and mantle, which cover

**Naturalized rendering of the divine mother and child.** *Virgin and Child* (14th century; Cathedral de Notre-Dame, Paris). GIRAUDON/ART RESOURCE, NY

**Formalized depiction of maternity.** *Virgin and Child* (Byzantine; 11th–12th century). Ivory. VICTORIA & ALBERT MUSEUM, LONDON/ART RESOURCE, NY

the disproportionate frame of her androgynous body. Her feminine attributes are visible only in her softened but anonymous facial features, her conveyance of a child, and in the gentle emotion expressed in their mutual hand gestures. The

normative convention—in Byzantine and in Western medieval and Renaissance art—of depicting the Christ Child as a miniature adult heightens the hieratic posture and authority communicated by this ivory sculpture. The visual moment of naturalness is found solely in the forward positioning of her left leg as the mother shifts her imagined body weight to accommodate that of her child. The unnaturalness of these figures may be exacerbated by the then dominant Christian antagonism both to sculpture and to the artistic rendering of natural bodies.

The elegant form of the Gothic *Virgin and Child* creates the impression of quiet motion through the interconnecting linear and curvilinear relationships of the loosely pleated layers of fabric of her garments with the *S*-shaped curve of her body. Exhibiting a very natural swayed posture for a mother who hoists her child on either her protruding hip or twisting upper body, this depiction of the Virgin offers a visual and societal counterpoint to the Byzantine portrayal. The legal status and rights of women, albeit women of class, expanded at this time in history, as evidenced by the way in which this Gothic queen, whose elaborate crown replaces the simple mantle of her Byzantine counterpart, holds forth the symbol of her country with her right hand and the body of her son with her

**Mother as creator and nurturer.** *Mother and Child* (11th century). Statue from Kajuraho, Madhya Pradesh, India. Chandella dynasty. BORROMEO/ART RESOURCE, NY

**The maternal life force.** *Pieta* (1988) by Stephen De Staebler. Bronze. PHOTO BY SCOTT MCCUE; COURTESY OF STEPHEN DE STAEBLER

left hand. He offers his mother a round object, apparently an apple or an orb but in either case an object, a piece of property for her to hold and to own. The softened female form of this Virgin, despite her postural exaggeration and that of her child, approach a regularized vision of the human form.

As a contrast, or perhaps a confirmation, of the universality of maternity as an idea and a visual expression of the idea of humanity, consider an eleventh-century Indian sculpture of *Mother and Child*. The normative "Eastern" approach to the softened and voluptuous body of the female figure is evident even without the exaggerated turns of the neck and abdomen. The intersecting curves and arches of this woman's body both nurture and commune with the rounded figure of her child, whom she holds before her with a firm right hand, placing the child in a position for maternal examination as her solidly balanced left hand draws the child near to her rotund breasts. This mother figure, like her Indian contemporaries, is dressed both for bodily display and for comfort. Her minimized clothing emphasizes the biologically female characteristics of full lactating breasts, an abdominal swell, and swaying hips in coordination with the soft and delicate expression of maternal love and compassion.

Although this Indian mother, like her Byzantine-styled and Gothic counterparts, is depicted standing, she communes directly with her child, from the bend of their heads to the physicality of their connections—the child's hands on her

breasts, legs akimbo across the mother's abdomen, the mother silently extending her pelvic region forward to support her child—so that the emphasis here is on maternal kinetics as opposed to religious, societal, or ritual significance. Fertility and survival fuse in this visual metaphor for human creation as the sacred merges with the secular into a potent motif that transcends geographic borders, economic classes, and religious divisions to express fundamental human and moral values.

Michelangelo amplifies the mother and child relationship and the nature of maternity in his first presentation of the *Pietà,* a Christian iconographic motif signaling the singular mourning of the mother for her dead child. This is a moment of great intimacy and emotion, which Michelangelo elevates to the higher levels of spiritual significance. Here the now seated mother encompasses the limp body of her deceased son in her lap. The varying circular, linear, arched, and swirled drapery that enfolds her body and her head turns initial attention away from both the size and symbolic meaning of her form. The sculptor skillfully creates a series of internal relationships between these two figures so that our sense in seeing this *Pietà* is first of the beauty of the human figures and the placid presentation of emotion.

**Emotional presentation of mother and child relationship.** *Pietà* (1498–1500) by Michelangelo. Marble. © Bettmann/Corbis

**Anguished humanity.** *Figure of a Man* (1947) by Alberto Giacometti. Bronze. DIGITAL IMAGE © THE MUSEUM OF MODERN ART/LICENSED BY SCALA/ART RESOURCE, NY. © 2004 ARTISTS RIGHTS SOCIETY (ARS), NEW YORK/ADAGP, PARIS

**The imperfections of humanity.** *Archangel* (1987) by Stephen De Staebler. Bronze. PHOTO BY SCOTT MCCUE; COURTESY OF STEPHEN DE STAEBLER

However, careful viewing results in the recognition of the circuit of visual games Michelangelo has created within this one sculpture. There is the Neoplatonic philosophic emphasis on the beauty of form and thereby of a retrieval of the classical Greek tenet of the spiritual valuing of the body. This formal beauty, in fact, is of religio-philosophical importance for Renaissance Christianity and a distraction from the more important internal visual "game." The mother's body is greatly out of proportion to the relationship of an adult male body to that of an adult female body. Attentive viewing moves us beyond the theological reading that Mary's ample body signifies *mater ecclesia* (mother church) to a recognition that the interrelationship between mother and son is actually that of mother with her youthful child. Further, she attends not to the viewer as her Byzantine and Gothic ancestresses did but rather to the sighting of the life force within her son's body—respiration. Given the Renaissance fascination with and knowledge of human anatomy and medicine, this sighting of Christ's diaphragm is more than a visual centering point; it is emblematic of the merged valuation of art, life, religion, and science.

Stephen De Staebler's late-twentieth-century *Pietà* provides a counterpoint to these four sculptures of the universal of maternity. Manifesting a modern recognition of the fragmenta-

tion and fragility of the human body with the eternal dynamic of spirituality, this pairing of figures is abstracted to their fundamental essences. Removing all pretense or social conventions of costume and decoration, as well as any historicized identity by "erasing" identifiable facial features on both the mother and her child, De Staebler recognizes the universal truth of maternity as a life force defiant against disaster, war, and limitations. The child is fused to the mother through her heart as well as her body, as signaled in the positioning of his head emergent from her breast. This abstraction, however, visually reaffirms the natural postural relationships between mothers and children as evidenced in the four sculptures here examined as well as in everyday situations. This mother strides forward on elevated toes as her fragmented body appears poised to levitate above the restrictions of human finitude and guilt, of life and death, despite the scientific and medical advances of the twentieth century; and yet she remains conjoined to the earth, whose contours and surface textures parallel those of this same figuration.

Among the most powerful symbolic pairs in world art and iconography, the stylization, exaggeration, postures, or body types in renderings of the mother and child relate as much to the historical and political time periods in which they are

EXCERPTS FROM SIR HERBERT READ

We are immediately struck by the surprising fact that at least nine-tenths of all the sculpture ever carved is devoted to one subject— the human body.

Only by conceiving an *image* of the body can we situate ourselves in the external world.

SOURCE: Herbert Read, *The Art of Sculpture,* 1956, pp. 25, 29.

Man is the product of the attributes of heaven and earth, by the interaction of the dual forces of nature, the union of the animal and intelligent souls, and the finest subtile matter of the five elements.

Therefore man is the heart and mind of heaven and earth, and the visible embodiment of the five elements. He lives in the enjoyment of all flavours, the discriminating of all notes of harmony, and the enrobing of all colours.

SOURCE: "The Nature of the Universe and Man" from the Li Ki. *The World Bible,* New York, 1939, pp. 492–493.

created as to the religious or secular values they signify. Whether African, Oceanic, Mesoamerican, pre-Columbian, prehistoric, or modern, this universal expression of the idea of humanity confirms visually the enduring meaning of fertility, survival, and love through maternity.

***Abstraction of anxiety and uncertainty.*** The final universal category for the idea of humanity through sculpture is that of the abstraction of anxiety and uncertainty as recorded in Brancusi's *Torso of a Young Man* (early twentieth century), Alberto Giacometti's *Figure of a Man* (1947), and Stephen De Staebler's *Archangel* (1987). Despite the diversity of styles and artistic movements identified as twentieth-century sculpture, the common descriptor is the term *abstract,* which is derived from the Latin *ab stracto,* "to take the essence from." These three modern, thereby abstract sculptures simplify the traditional detailing and characteristics of the human figure in calculated departures from the philosophy, spirituality, and politics of the classical ideal. Economic but elegant employment of lines and curves analyze the essence of the structure and geometry of the human form while never denigrating the native spirituality of the idea of humanity.

Beginning with Brancusi's elemental torso, the human body is depicted as a fragment symbolic of the whole. Such a fragmenting of the body is often interpreted as a disruption, a sign of the philosophic and religious distress of the early twentieth century and a cause for anxiety. However, given the influences on Western culture and art of *le primitif,* especially the influence of Africa and Oceania in the late 1800s and early 1900s, of "the East" at midcentury, and of "the marginalized" from the late 1960s, the tendency toward abstracting expressed here, first through Brancusi and finally by De Staebler, signifies a retrieval of the fundamental native symbolic valuing communicated through the image of humanity. How humanity is configured—radical simplification, emotional expression, organic forms, geometric structures, or ideal beauty—is as dependent upon cultural attitudes, social mores, and religious values as on the realities of climate, nutrition, economics, and the prevailing conventions of art.

In contrast to Brancusi, Giacometti appears to return to figuration. However, it is not the classic ideal but rather an elongated and disproportionate figure that connotes the anguish and distress of World War II, existentialism, and the recognition of human finitude and frailty. Nonetheless the spindly distentions of this man's arms create a curious mixture of identifying gesticulations in his right hand and transcendence through his left hand, almost as if he were the reincarnation in minimalist terms of the Christ figure at the Last Judgment. The distortions in Giacometti's figure are, however, no less calculated than those in Michelangelo's sculptures. The geometrically progressive nature of the relationships of head to torso and torso to extremities combine with the fundamental human characteristic of gestural communication to project the sense of a "real person."

De Staebler's *Archangel* may initially be perceived as disjunctive, as the angelic form merges with the human in what appears to be a visual fragment. However, just as cultural and philosophic shifts occur throughout cultural history, the viewer's mode of "reading" images moves from that of a sequential narrative to a gradual absorption of shifting concepts of truth and fiction. Reflective of midcentury societal and religious critiques, De Staebler's figures are a re-visioning of the idea of humanity, no longer premised on the philosophic ideals of classical Greece but rather upon the realities of human frailty, including variations in body types, illness, and the process of aging. Although Western artists have recognized that the idea of humanity, like the human form, can be deduced from the most minimized detail, it was sculptures such as De Staebler's *Archangel* that challenged late-twentieth-century viewers to ponder the meaning of being human and to rejoice in the spirituality of humanity despite its imperfections.

## Scholarship on Humanity through Sculpture
There is no central or classic study of the theme of the idea of humanity either in the arts or more specifically in sculpture.

For the student of art who wishes to trace the dramatic changes that have taken place in the rendering of man, it is the cultural image of the human body that will remain in the foreground. The student of art will always be concerned with how man sees himself, and how he documents this vision in painting and sculpture. The process of perceiving and imaging the human body is to some degree made up of social and cultural components.

SOURCE: Moshe Barasch, *Imago Hominis: Studies in the Language of Art,* 1994, p. 11.

However, there are classic studies such as Herbert Read's *The Art of Sculpture* (1956) and Tom Flynn's *The Body in Three Dimensions* (1998) that consider the chronological development of sculpture in Western culture in relation to artistic presentation of and cultural attitudes toward the body. Kenneth Clark's masterful *The Nude: A Study in Ideal Form* (1956) is a carefully argued art historical analysis of the cultural concepts of the naked and the nude with a subtext that the body is a conveyor of cultural and religious values. The art historian Moshe Barasch expands the boundaries of Read, Flynn, and Clark to include gestures, postures, and philosophic attitudes toward the body as transmitter of culture and values in his collected essays published as *Imago Hominis: Studies in the Language of Art* (1991). The now classic texts of Margaret Walters's *The Male Nude* (1978) and Bernard Rudofsky's *The Unfashionable Human Body* (1971) are specialized studies that initiated a series of critical questions related to the body and gender well in advance of scholarly interest in the marginalized. A variety of intriguing texts including Linda Nochlin's *The Body in Pieces: The Fragment as a Metaphor of Modernity* (1994), Marcia R. Pointon's *Naked Authority: The Body in Western Painting* (1990), and Margaret R. Miles's *Carnal Knowing: Female Nakedness and Religious Meaning in the Christian West* (1989) provide a feminist lens through which to analyze and critique the depiction of the human form in the visual arts. Similarly Caroline Walker Bynum's *The Resurrection of the Body in Western Christianity* (1995) and Bram Dijkstra's *Idols of Perversity: Fantasies of Feminine Evil in Fin-de-Siècle Culture* (1986) provide specialized studies of theological, cultural, and philosophic depictions of specific engendered renderings of humanity in the arts. The reality of both the interdisciplinary motif and methodology for the study of the idea of humanity through sculpture has been privileged by Western scholars within the frame of Western cultural history. The three singular exceptions, simultaneously the only culturally comparative works on a closely identified theme, are the exhibition and catalog for *In Her Image: The Great Goddess in Indian Asia and the Madonna in Christian Culture* by Rebecca P. Gowen, Gerald J. Larson, and Pratapaditya Pal (1980); the exhibition and catalog for *The Human Image* edited by J. C. N. King (2000); and several special issues of *P Art and Culture Magazine,* which is published in Turkey.

See also **Buddhism; Christianity: Overview; Classicism; Dress; Gender in Art; Gender: Overview; Gesture; Hinduism; Men and Masculinity; Motherhood and Maternity.**

BIBLIOGRAPHY

Adler, Kathleen, and Marcia Pointon, eds. *The Body Imaged: The Human Form and Visual Culture since the Renaissance.* Cambridge, U.K., and New York: Cambridge University Press, 1993.

Arscott, Caroline, and Katie Scott, eds. *Manifestations of Venus: Art and Sexuality.* Manchester, U.K.: Manchester University Press, 2000.

Barasch, Moshe. *Imago Hominis: Studies in the Language of Art.* Vienna: IRSA, 1991.

Baring, Anne, and Cashford, Jules. *The Myth of the Goddess: Evolution of an Image.* London: Penguin, 1993.

Bernal, Martin. *Black Athena: The Afro-Asiatic Roots of Classical Civilisation.* London: Vintage, 1991.

Blundell, Sue. *Women in Ancient Greece.* London: British Museum Press, 1995.

Bowie, Theodore, and Cornelia V. Christenson, eds. *Studies in Erotic Art.* New York: Basic Books, 1970.

Broude, Norma, and Mary D. Garrard, eds. *The Expanding Discourse: Feminism and Art History.* New York: Icon Harper-Collins, 1992.

———. *Feminism and Art History: Questioning the Litany.* New York: Harper and Row, 1982.

Bynum, Caroline Walker. *The Resurrection of the Body in Western Christianity, 200–1336.* New York: Columbia University Press, 1995.

Carson, Fiona, and Claire Pajaczkowska, eds. *Feminist Visual Culture.* New York: Routledge, 2001.

Clark, Kenneth. 1956. *The Nude: A Study in Ideal Form.* Princeton, N.J.: Princeton University Press, 1984.

Dijkstra, Bram. *Idols of Perversity: Fantasies of Feminine Evil in Fin-de-Siècle Culture.* New York: Oxford University Press, 1986.

Dutton, Kenneth R. *The Perfectible Body: The Western Ideal of Physical Perfection.* London: Cassell, 1995.

Feher, Michel, Ramona Naddaff, and Nadia Tazi, eds. *Fragments for a History of the Human Body.* 3 vols. New York: Zone Books, 1989.

Freedberg, David. *The Power of Images: Studies in the History and Theory of Response.* Chicago: University of Chicago Press, 1989.

Flynn, Tom. *The Body in Three Dimensions.* New York: Harry N. Abrams, 1998. Published in the U.K. as *The Body in Sculpture.* London: Weidenfield and Nicolson, 1998.

Gowen, Rebecca, Gerald J. Larson, and Pratapaditya Pal, eds. *In Her Image: The Great Goddess in Indian Asia and the Madonna in Christian Culture.* Santa Barbara: UCSB Art Museum, University of California, Santa Barbara, 1980. Exhibition catalog.

Hollander, Anne. *Seeing through Clothes.* New York: Viking Press, 1978.

Kemp, Martin, and Marina Wallace. *Spectacular Bodies: The Art and Science of the Human Body from Leonardo to Now.* Berkeley: University of California Press, 2000. Exhibition catalog.

King, J. C. N., ed. *The Human Image.* London: British Museum Press, 2000. Exhibition catalog.

Kristeva, Julia. *Powers of Horror: An Essay on Abjection.* Translated by Leon S. Roudiez. New York: Columbia University Press, 1982.

Lucie-Smith, Edward. *Sexuality in Western Art.* New York: Thames and Hudson, 1991.

Mellor, Philip A., and Chris Shilling. *Re-Forming the Body: Religion, Community, and Modernity.* London: Thousand Oaks, 1997.

Miles, Margaret R. *Carnal Knowing: Female Nakedness and Religious Meaning in the Christian West.* Boston: Beacon, 1989.

Mullins, Edwin. *The Painted Witch: How Western Artists Have Viewed the Sexuality of Women.* London: Secker and Warburg, 1985.

Nochlin, Linda. *The Body in Pieces: The Fragment as a Metaphor of Modernity.* London: Thames and Hudson, 1994.

Paglia, Camille. *Sexual Personae: Art and Decadence from Nefertiti to Emily Dickinson.* New Haven, Conn.: Yale University Press, 1990.

Perry, Gill, ed. *Gender and Art.* New Haven, Conn.: Yale University Press, 1999.

Pointon, Marcia R. *Naked Authority: The Body in Western Painting, 1830–1908.* Cambridge, U.K.: Cambridge University Press, 1990.

Read, Herbert. *The Art of Sculpture.* New York: Pantheon, 1956.

Rudofsky, Bernard. *The Unfashionable Human Body.* Garden City, N.Y.: Doubleday, 1971.

Saunders, Gill. *The Nude: A New Perspective.* New York: Harper and Row, 1989.

Sennett, Richard. *Flesh and Stone: The Body and the City in Western Civilisation.* London: Faber, 1994.

Shilling, Chris. *The Body and Social Theory.* London: Thousand Oaks, 1993.

Smith, Alison. *The Victorian Nude: Sexuality, Morality, and Art.* Manchester: Manchester University Press, 1996.

———, ed. *Exposed: The Victorian Nude.* London: Tate, 2001. Exhibition catalog.

Steinberg, Leo. *The Sexuality of Christ in Renaissance Art and in Modern Oblivion.* 2nd rev. ed. Chicago: University of Chicago Press, 1996.

Suleiman, Susan Rubin, ed. *The Female Body in Western Culture: Contemporary Perspectives.* Cambridge: Harvard University Press, 1986.

Üster, Celâl, ed. "Nude in Art." *P Art and Culture Magazine* 9 (spring 2003): 1–132. Special issue.

Vernant, Jean-Pierre. *Mortals and Immortals: Collected Essays,* edited by Froma I. Zeitlin. Princeton, N.J.: Princeton University Press, 1991.

Walters, Margaret. *The Nude Male.* London: Penguin, 1979.

*Diane Apostolos-Cappadona*

# HUMOR.

Humor is such an integral part of the human psyche that philosophers and other intellectuals have long been fascinated with its origins in and its effects on the human brain. Several early theorists have provided subject matter for continuing observation and debate. The Greek word *chumoi* means "juices," and the ancient Greeks used the word, from which we get the English *humor* (as well as *humid*), to refer to the bodily fluids of blood, phlegm, yellow bile, and black bile. The amount of these fluids and how they happened to be mixed in a person's body was assumed to determine that person's disposition or temperament. When authors, playwrights, and comedy performers create eccentric characters, they are going back to this old idea of some people being extremely bilious, phlegmatic, sanguine, or jaundiced.

Related to this idea of bodily fluids is a belief that humor is good for one's health as reflected in the Book of Proverbs: "A merry heart doeth good like a medicine; but a broken spirit drieth the bones" (17:22). In 1979 Norman Cousins, a talented writer and former editor of the *Saturday Review,* popularized the wish-fulfilling idea that laughter could reduce pain and release healing chemicals into people's bodies. While the idea caught the fancy of the general public on a worldwide scale, the twenty-first century's thoughtful researchers are asking questions about possible confusions between causes and effects. For example, even if well-documented evidence could be collected to show that people with a sense of humor live longer, it might be that they have a sense of humor because they are healthy and things are going well. Along the same lines, it might be that hospital patients who are pleasant and find things to laugh about will get well faster than grumpy patients because their pleasant personalities attract a broader support group and make doctors and nurses more willing to spend time with them.

## Release or Relief Theory

The subjects that people joke about are likely to be things that make them feel unsure or uncomfortable, as with questions about religion, politics, sex, and ethnic differences. People joke about these subjects as a way of releasing feelings of tension and also as a way of sending up trial balloons. If they say something that does not go over well, they can backtrack and hide behind the cliché, "I was only kidding."

At a 1984 humor conference held at Arizona State University, Robert Priest, a psychologist at West Point, reported on his Moderate Intergroup Conflict Humor (MICH) theory. He agreed that for people to be inspired to create a joke they must feel some tension, but he argued that joking will relieve only moderate levels of tension. If groups or individuals are feeling strong—rather than moderate—levels of tension, they will feel frustrated rather than satisfied by jokes. He illustrated his point by showing how history is filled with jokes about the so-called battle of the sexes, but in the late 1970s and the 1980s, as the feminist movement developed and hostilities between men and women increased, sexist joking was no longer viewed as humor. Instead, it was viewed as aggression, and those who told sexist jokes were taken to court and punished for creating hostile workplaces.

A related way of explaining this idea that people need some distance from a problem before they can find humor in it is the statement that "tragedy plus time equals humor." James Thurber has been credited with this observation, but many people, including Steve Allen and Bob Hope, have commented on the idea. After the September 11, 2001, tragedy, it was a topic of general public discussion when comedy clubs and late-night comedians took time off.

"THERE ARE ESSENTIALLY FOUR BASIC FORMS FOR A JOKE — THE CONCEALING OF KNOWLEDGE LATER REVEALED, THE SUBSTITUTION OF ONE CONCEPT FOR ANOTHER, AN UNEXPECTED CONCLUSION TO A LOGICAL PROGRESSION, AND SLIPPING ON A BANANA PEEL."

**Cartoon, "The Meaning of Humor," by Sidney Harris.** One theory of humor posits that statements or situations become funny when what occurs is not what was expected, as is frequently the case with physical humor. COURTESY OF SIDNEY HARRIS

## Superiority Theory

Conflicts over the censorship of humor go back at least to the fifth century B.C.E., when Plato expressed the idea in his *Republic* that jokes and humorous incidents should be removed from stories about the gods before they are presented to young people. Plato's idea was that if children were amused by the gods, they would feel themselves superior and hence would lose respect.

Several centuries later the English philosopher Thomas Hobbes spelled out more clearly the idea that humor is an expression of superiority. In his 1651 *Leviathan,* he defined humor as "the sudden glory arising from the sudden conception of some eminency in ourselves, by comparison with the infirmity of others." In the seventeenth century Blaise Pascal, a French scientist and philosopher, proposed, "Nothing produces laughter more than a surprising disproportion between that which one expects and that which one sees." In 1750 the Scottish philosopher Frances Hutcheson further developed what has come to be known as the incongruity theory. In his *Reflections upon Laughter,* Hutcheson pointed out that people do not go to asylums to laugh at the "inferior" beings, nor do they laugh at animals except when they resemble human beings. Even when someone slips on a banana peel, observers laugh not because they feel superior but because of the incongruity between expectations and reality.

## Incongruity Theory

In 1790 the German philosopher Immanuel Kant in *The Critique of Judgment* focused on the requirement of surprise when he claimed that laughter is an emotion that arises from a strained expectation suddenly reduced to nothing. William Hazlitt, in his 1819 *Lectures on the Comic Writers,* credited laughter as coming from the incongruity that results when one idea disconnects or is bumped up against another feeling. Arthur Schopenhauer agreed in 1844, when he explained in *The World as Will and Idea* that laughter is a way of acknowledging an incongruity between the conceptions that listeners or viewers hold in their minds and what happens to upset their expectations.

The incongruity theory is especially powerful in explaining humor across different genres, including accidental humor and humor in nature. Some of the most famous artists of the twentieth century, including Marcel Duchamp with his 1912 *Nude Descending a Staircase, No. 2,* surprised and amused (and sometimes offended) the public by breaking with the expectation that an artist's job was to faithfully re-create items as seen by the human eye. Playful dance companies and playful musicians startle audiences by suddenly changing their patterns, as did Franz Joseph Haydn (1732–1809) in his Symphony no. 94, also known as the *Surprise Symphony.* Haydn interspersed fortissimo chords into soft repetitive sequences to wake up slumbering audiences. Designers of theme-park hotels and of much of the community art that decorates modern American cities play with surprise and incongruity. Even comedians who tell stories in sets of three (two to establish a pattern and one to break it) are relying on surprise and incongruity.

Scatological humor is incongruous in that it "unmasks" people as it reminds them of their animal nature. This was one of the ideas expressed by Sigmund Freud in his 1905 *Jokes and Their Relation to the Unconscious.* Freud viewed the jokes that people told as a window to their minds. He thought that jokes were more likely to come from the id or subconscious, while people's other communications come from the superego, where they are refined by a public consciousness. Freud's work with jokes and his belief that humor is basically tendentious and hostile is not as respected as is his other work because modern critics, especially feminists, point out that the source of his jokes (his patients) were far from being a typical sample. Other critics reject the idea that jokes are formed in the subconscious in the same way that dreams are.

The one concept that the general public recognizes from Freud's work is that of the Freudian slip. These are verbal mistakes that people make, which Freud said revealed what they really wanted. In actual conversations, Freudian slips may or may not reveal inner desires. Sometimes they are simply pronunciation or spelling errors, as with the examples that Richard Lederer collected for his popular *Anguished English* (1987). On the other hand, when creative writers put Freudian slips into the mouths of their characters, their intention is to communicate something about the speaker's personality. Norman Lear was a master at this when in the popular television show *All in the Family* (1971–1979) he had Archie Bunker reveal his lack of education and his xenophobic tendencies with such phrases as "Blackberry Finn," "pushy imported ricans," "welfare incipients," and "the immaculate connection."

## Wit, or Derisive Humor

The French philosopher Henri Bergson in his *Le rire* (*Laughter,* 1911) made the point that wit or derisive humor is a universal corrective for deviancy in the social order. He softened the idea of overt hostility by saying that the creators of wit undergo "a momentary anesthesia of the heart" as they poke fun at the actions of someone. According to Bergson's point of view, wit is a tool of satire in that its purpose is to bring about change. Such thinkers and writers as Ambrose Bierce, H. L. Mencken, Ogden Nash, Dorothy Parker, Will Rogers, Carl Sandburg, George Bernard Shaw, Mark Twain, Artemus Ward, and Oscar Wilde used their wit to focus attention on the kinds of behavior they thought inappropriate or damaging to society as a whole. Most of the twenty-first century's editorial cartoonists and late-night comedians use wit for similar purposes as they criticize changing social, sexual, religious, and political mores.

John Simon in *Paradigms Lost* describes wit as "aggressive, often destructive (though one hopes, in a good cause), and almost always directed at others." He compares it to humor, which he describes as "basically good natured and often directed toward oneself, if only by subsumption under the heading 'general human foolishness'" (p. 72).

Simon's description of self-deprecating humor as being "basically good natured" is important in understanding why members of ethnic groups can tell jokes about themselves but get offended when someone from outside the group tells the same joke. When a person is inside a group and clearly identifies with that group, then the telling of a joke about the group usually falls under the category of good-natured encouragement for group members to think about changing their ways. Henry Spalding in his *Joys of Jewish Humor* (1985) says that many Jewish jokes come in the form of "honey-coated barbs" at the people and things loved most by Jews. While they verbally attack their family and friends as well as their own religion, they do it with a great sense of affection. A joke teller from outside of a group has little or no influence on group beliefs and actions and so by telling such jokes is cementing negative stereotypes rather than bringing about changes.

Christie Davies, who has collected and studied jokes across different cultures, as has the cultural anthropologist Alan Dundes, explains that there is great satisfaction in assigning a negative trait to someone outside of one's own group. Placing negative traits far away from oneself is satisfying because it frees the joke tellers from having to think about whether these characteristics are pertinent to their personalities. The comedy writer Max Shulman, in a 1982 talk at Arizona State University, said something similar when he explained that if one of his stories makes a reader say, "I know someone like that," the reader is amused and laughs. But if the story is so on target that the reader says, "Oh, no, that's me!" the reader is not amused.

## Other Views

While scholars still believe in theories of superiority and hostility and of surprise and incongruity, the twenty-first century's mass media provides the world with so many different kinds of humor that few scholars try to make observations about all humor. Instead, they study humor to gain insights into their particular areas of expertise. For example, in *They Used to Call Me Snow White . . . but I Drifted: Women's Strategic Use of Humor* (1991), the feminist scholar Regina Barreca uses examples of women's humor to illustrate how a group's humor is shaped as well as evaluated according to the roles that the members play in society. Henry Louis Gates did something similar in *The Signifying Monkey: A Theory of Afro-American Literary Criticism* (1988) by showing how African-American slaves developed double entendre trickster signifiers because they were denied the use of normal and private communication.

For obvious reasons, performers, comedians, public speakers, and advertisers are interested in the features or the characteristics of humor. They want to know what makes people laugh so that they can create and re-create such situations. Rhetoricians and teachers of writing are also interested. Mary Ann Rishel, a professor in the Department of Writing at Ithaca College, teaches a class in comedy writing and has authored a book on the subject. Her idea is not to prepare students to move to Hollywood or New York to join comedy writing teams. Instead, she wants to use the pleasures of humor to help students develop the skills needed for most kinds of writing: originality of vision, a keen eye for observation, the inclusion of telling details, and most importantly, succinctness.

The historian Joseph Boskin collects joke cycles, what he calls comic zeitgeists, and uses their popularity as data for revealing Americans' preoccupations and attitudes. He concludes his book *Rebellious Laughter* (1997) with "Tattered Dreams," a chapter about how "the roseate years of expansion" (p. 180) that followed World War II collided with such technological failures as the meltdown at the Three Mile Island nuclear plant in Pennsylvania, the radioactive explosion at Chernobyl, the loss of the *Challenger* space shuttle, and such oil spills as that of the *Exxon Valdez.* These catastrophes "overwhelmed sensibilities from the late 1970s into the 1990s," and the jokes were as extreme as the events (Boskin, p. 181). They offered "the specter of a totally irrational universe," where the only defense was to engage in what has been labeled "a hellish laughter" (Boskin, p. 190).

Modern literary critics often focus on this kind of humor as they work with deconstructionism, postmodernism, and magical realism. They have long defined *satire* (which often includes elements of irony and wit) as humor designed for the specific purpose of convincing readers and viewers of the need for some kind of action or a change in attitude and beliefs. On the other hand, black humor or dark humor (also referred to as gallows humor, absurd humor, existentialism, and film noir) illustrates the futility of looking for easy and neat answers to the tragedies of life. In such humor, the lines between fantasy and reality and between tragedy and comedy keep shifting. People laugh because they do not know what else to do. The laughter is itself a testament to the strength of the human spirit in showing that people can laugh in spite of bewilderment, death, and chaos.

Linguists, especially computer programmers working with artificial intelligence and translation, study jokes because their abbreviated scripts leave listeners to fill in the mundane details that "go without saying." Many jokes provide an even greater challenge for computers because they are designed to lead listeners to interpret the story along mundane lines, but then comes the climax or the punch line, which makes listeners laugh in surprise as they realize they have been led "down the garden path." The linguist Victor Raskin at Purdue University is working to program computers with the ability to bring in a myriad of cultural references while simultaneously testing possible interpretations so as to arrive at the one that is "funny." In his book *Semantic Mechanisms of Humor* (1985) Raskin distinguishes between what he calls bona fide scripts and joke scripts. Joke scripts differ from stereotypes in that a stereotype is an idea that many people seriously believe in and act on, while joke or comic scripts are more literary than sociological or political. They are amusing ideas that serve as the nucleus for folklore. New Englanders do not really believe that French-speaking Canadians are stupid, nor do the British think that the Irish are dirty, nor does the world at large think that Italians are cowards, yet extensive joke scripts circle around these and many other groups. The fact that joke scripts develop rather haphazardly out of the history of particular countries helps to explain why people from different cultures have a hard time catching on to each other's jokes, many of which are variations on old themes or examples of one's expectations being suddenly violated.

The idea of looking at the creation and reception of humor to trace the intellectual (as opposed to the emotional) paths that humor takes through the brain is fairly new. Arthur Koestler in *The Act of Creation* (1964) claims that for people to think in new and creative ways, they must engage in bisociative thinking so as to bring concepts together in original ways. The "Ah!" kind occurs when people have an emotional reaction as they create or recognize artistic originality. The "Aha!" kind occurs when they bring divergent concepts together into scientific discoveries, while the "Ha Ha!" kind occurs with the comic recognition of ridiculous situations.

As indicated by these examples, the humor research of the future is likely to focus on particular kinds of humor as created and received by individuals in particular situations. And as the world grows smaller and people are forced to communicate with and adapt to people with different customs and beliefs, there will probably be increased interest in understanding both the bonding and the out-bonding as well as the release of frustration that comes when people laugh together.

*See also* **Dream; Mind; Philosophy; Tragedy and Comedy.**

**BIBLIOGRAPHY**
Barreca, Regina. *They Used to Call Me Snow White—but I Drifted: Women's Strategic Use of Humor.* New York: Viking, 1991.
Bergson, Henri. *Laughter: An Essay on the Meaning of the Comic.* Translated by Cloudesley Brereton and Fred Rothwell. New York: Macmillan, 1911.
Boskin, Joseph. *Rebellious Laughter: People's Humor in American Culture.* Syracuse, N.Y.: Syracuse University Press, 1997.
Cousins, Norman. *Anatomy of an Illness as Perceived by the Patient: Reflections on Healing and Regeneration.* New York: W.W. Norton, 1979.
Davies, Christie. *Ethnic Humor around the World: A Comparative Analysis.* Bloomington: Indiana University Press, 1990.
Freud, Sigmund. *Jokes and Their Relation to the Unconscious.* Translated and edited by James Strachey. New York: W.W. Norton, 1960.
Gates, Henry Louis, Jr. *The Signifying Monkey: A Theory of Afro-American Literary Criticism.* New York: Oxford University Press, 1988.
Koestler, Arthur. *The Act of Creation.* New York: Macmillan, 1964.
Lederer, Richard. *Anguished English: An Anthology of Accidental Assaults upon Our Language.* Charleston, S.C.: Wyrick, 1987.
Morreall, John, ed. *The Philosophy of Laughter and Humor.* Albany: State University of New York Press, 1987.
Nilsen, Alleen Pace, and Don L. F. Nilsen. *Encyclopedia of Twentieth-Century American Humor.* Phoenix, Ariz.: Oryx Press/Greenwood, 2000.
Raskin, Victor. *Semantic Mechanisms of Humor.* Dordrecht, Netherlands: Reidel, 1985.
Rishel, Mary Ann. *Writing Humor: Creativity and the Comic Mind.* Detroit: Wayne State University Press, 2002.
Simon, John. *Paradigms Lost: Reflections on Literacy and Its Decline.* New York: Potter/Crown, 1980.
Spalding, Henry D. *Joys of Jewish Humor.* New York: Jonathan David, 1985.

*Alleen Pace Nilsen*
*Don L. F. Nilsen*

**HYGIENE.** *Hygiene* is defined in current English dictionaries as "the science of health." This definition, though formally correct, hides a long history of change in the word's use, from its holistic classical meaning of "individual regimens to preserve health" to its nineteenth-century connotations of "social medicine" (including lethal eugenics programs), to its current limited construal as "personal cleanliness" or "germ removal." For more than 2,500 years of use in many different lands, concepts of hygiene have been integral to personal identity, shaping sense of self through boundary maintenance and spirituality.

**The Ancient World, c. 500 B.C.E.–200 C.E.**
In Greek mythology Hygeia was one of the daughters of Aesculapius, a renowned healer and demigod; she was considered the goddess of health. The Greek word *hygiene hygieinē* meant "sound, healthy, or strong," and was possibly related to the Sanskrit *ugias,* or "strength." In the works of Greek physicians, from Hippocrates (460–c. 377 B.C.E.) onward, hygiene was that branch of medicine dedicated to the "art of health," distinguished by Galen (129–c. 199 C.E.) from its other arm, therapeutics, or the treatment of disease. The Greeks understood the world to be composed of four elements—earth, air, fire, and water—and, analogously, understood life to be controlled by the four principles of hot and cold, wet and dry, which corresponded to the four "humors" that composed the body: yellow and black bile, blood, and phlegm. The body was understood holistically as a dynamic state of interaction between these four principles, whose imbalance could cause disease. The goal of hygienic practice was to achieve qualitative and humoral balance within the body, and thus for each person to live out their allotted lifespan.

**Volk und Rasse**

September 1936        Heft 9

J. F. Lehmanns Verlag München · Einzelheft RM. 70

**Cover of September 1936 issue of *Volk und Rasse* (Folk and Race).** This issue of *Volk und Rasse*, a Nazi anthropological and genetics journal, attempted to link physical strength, athleticism, and race. The ultimate expression of Nazi racial theories was a policy of euthanasia, a precursor to the genocide of the Holocaust. COURTESY OF THE LEO BAECK INSTITUTE, NEW YORK

Hygienic instruction was tailored to each individual's constitution, itself the result of humoral activity, and to their environmental and personal circumstances, such as age, sex, status, and relations with others. Proper hygiene included regulations concerning sexual activity, sleeping and waking, bathing, exercise (a central activity for freeborn Greeks), and above all, diet. Dietary regimens were extremely detailed as to when it was or was not appropriate to eat particular kinds of animals or grains and considered food very carefully in all its cooked and raw states, discussing strategies such as boiling, grilling, roasting, and breading that would moisten, dry, heat, and bind. Because food was considered to have such powers in altering a person's internal humoral balance, the distinction between hygiene and therapeutics was blurred, as the same foods could be prescribed to cure disease as well as maintain health. Although the Greek physicians regarded their work as purely empirical, in contrast to superstitious medical practices such as appeasing angry gods, their texts clearly equated healthy

practices with the moral order of their culture: a hygienic person went with his fellows to the gymnasium, was abstemious with alcohol, and had only acceptable sexual relations.

The Greeks' conception of the body as an organic whole integrated into its environment, and their regimen-based methods of preserving health by achieving harmony within the body, were remarkably similar to health systems that apparently coincidentally evolved in India and China. Though their explanatory frameworks differ from the Greeks and from each other, both Indian Ayurvedic medicine and traditional Chinese medicine have longevity and prolonged states of health as their goal, and both discuss which substances, qualities, and actions are life-enhancing and which are not. Because of these similarities, the word *hygiene* is sometimes inaccurately used to refer to these traditions in English-language medical histories of these peoples.

### The Middle Ages and Renaissance, 200–1700 C.E.

European medical writing all but ceased as academic study disintegrated with the Roman Empire. Academic medicine owed its revival in the ninth century C.E. to the enthusiasm of Muslim scholars, who, having established an empire from Persia to Spain, translated and extended the classical medical corpus, particularly the works of Galen. The concept of *hygiene* was revitalized, particularly as it could readily absorb the Islamic belief that the spiritual unity of the cosmos was the basis for all medical practice and the cleansing and purification rituals that surrounded prayer. New texts of regimens for health were produced by such renowned physicians as Abu Bakr Muhammad ibn Zakariya ar-Razi (Rhazes; c. 865–between 923 and 935 C.E.) and Avicenna (Ibn Sina; 980–1037 C.E).

These Islamic physicians followed Galen's successors in considering the six "nonnaturals" (that is, factors external to the body) as the canonical categories that composed hygiene: air (or "environment"), food and drink, sleeping and waking, movement and rest, retention and evacuation (including ejaculation), and mental-emotions ("passions of the soul"). Regimens and advice books were structured around these categories. While regimens were widely respected, in practice, as in the classical period, many people blended them with the incantations, rituals, and charms of popular medicine, just as the notion of spiritual harmony integral to Islamic hygiene coexisted with religious notions of disease as a test or punishment.

European enthusiasm for hygiene returned with the upsurge in medical writing that marked the Renaissance, and handbooks were produced for a much wider audience. For example, in England between 1456 and 1604, 115 out of 392 editions of books on medicine and regimen were issued in the vernacular. However, these works contained an increasing diversity of thought that left the content of hygienic practice unfixed, further blurred the distinction between hygiene and therapeutics, and, under the influence of nascent sciences and the growing authority of mathematics, assigned and calculated degrees to humoral balance. Emphases and goals were shifting. For example, although exercise had largely dropped out of hygienic manuals in the medieval period, there was a renewed emphasis on regimens of movement in the Renaissance; and practitioners now aimed higher than the Galenic allotment of years,

**Health propaganda poster, c. 1940s.** As civilization progressed during the twentieth century into expanded industrialization, frequent overcrowding, and two world wars, health risks increased. As a result, governments instituted programs aimed at encouraging citizens to practice good hygiene for a healthier society. © K.J. HISTORICAL/CORBIS

wishing instead to preserve their youth and achieve an unlimited longevity.

Personal hygiene also became more clearly equated with the health of the soul as it was reinterpreted through Christian belief and practice. Thus classical hygienic prescriptions on diet became condemnations of the "sins" of gluttony and drunkenness. Self-help and an increasing asceticism (all-cold regimens were popular) were the twin characteristics of hygiene at this time. The works of social theorists John Locke (1632–1704) and John Wesley (1703–1791, founder of Methodism) emphasized "hardening" regimens and sobriety. These clearly moralistic ideas about hygiene fueled criticisms of "civilization" by Jean-Jacques Rousseau (1712–1778) and others, who suggested that compared with the "noble savages" of the "new" world, Europeans were being devitalized by nervous diseases brought on by overeating and drinking, failure to exercise, late rising, and tight lacing. Hygienic regimens were to aid in maintaining European identity in the face of dissolution.

### Hygiene and Public Health, 1700–1945

The concept of hygiene underwent immense changes during and after the eighteenth century. As the use of dissection and

the microscope became increasingly common for the new medical sciences of anatomy, physiology, and pathology, Galenic theories were quickly discarded. Many physicians began to treat traditional hygiene as at best a branch of education rather than an area of medicine, at worst a form of folklore. However the status of hygienic study was defended by Paris professor of medicine Jean Noel Hallé (1754–1822), who argued that the subject of hygiene had two facets: the individual, in which the physician would consider such factors as age, sex, temperament, habits, profession, poverty, and travel; and the social, in which the physician would consider climate, location, occupations, customs, laws, and governments, as they affected health. This transference of many of the ideas incorporated in traditional hygiene to the level of the public and the population was reflective of a general growing interest in "state science," literally "statistiks." This referred to the collection of numerical data about the composition, strengths, and weakness of a *population* on the grounds that the economic and political strength of a nation were directly proportional to the health of its citizens. (Indeed, the concept *population* may be said to have been produced by these new measurement techniques.) As Hallé wrote, the hygienist must become counsel and spiritual guide to the legislator, intervening in those areas where an individual had little control.

The concept of "public hygiene" increased in importance as European societies experienced the devastating epidemics of cholera, typhoid, smallpox, and plague that struck as a result of war, colonization, and industrialization. Acting on the statistical relationship between mortality rates and living conditions, the primary government response was in terms of "sanitation," the removal of environmental pollution by garbage and nightsoil collection services, building ventilation devices in houses, and limiting industrial refuse. This environmental focus in public-health strategies reflected the popularity of the miasmatic theory of disease transmission, which conceived disease as the airy product of refuse, decay, and smell. It also shaped, and was shaped by, an increasing social preoccupation with cleanliness, possibly attributable to the transmission of the eighteenth-century French aristocracy's mannerly culture, a new kind of hygienic regimen that was distinguished from its predecessors by its cleansing rituals, from nose-blowing to bathing. *Hygiene* was partially distinguished from *sanitation* (though the two terms were interchangeable) by its focus on the social and moral health of society, the ultimate aim of sanitation. As Benjamin Ward Richardson (1828–1896) captured in his utopian tale *Hygeia: A City of Health,* it was felt that the mere fact of living in uncrowded conditions and enjoying regular bathing would result in the moral and spiritual uplift and pursuit of self-improvement among the great unwashed who were filling the fever-decimated hospitals, prisons, shipping vessels, and factories of the day.

Thus hygiene became a central technique of social government in the nineteenth and early twentieth centuries; indeed this could well be termed the Hygienic Era in honor of the proliferation of societies and subjects devoted to hygiene, each of which connected individuals to projects in governing society. In domestic hygiene, maternal hygiene, tropical hygiene, international hygiene, industrial hygiene, sex hygiene, moral

## RACIAL HYGIENE

In the hygienic era, national populations were conceptualized as biological entities, that is, as races. Encompassing much more than skin color, the notion of race reflected social characteristics (such as courage or honesty) as well as physical ones (such as longevity and intelligence) that were considered to be hereditary. Races were thought about in Darwinian terms as organisms that could evolve or degenerate, win or become extinct, according to changes in their membership and in competition with others. Accordingly, at the beginning of the twentieth century many Western physicians and social reformers were concerned that their race would "degenerate" and become devitalized by the reproduction of "unfit" specimens, that is, those with undesirable physical and social characteristics thought to be heritable, including insanity, alcoholism, Down's syndrome, epilepsy, criminality, and poor eyesight. As new tests for fitness, such as the Binet IQ test, were developed and distributed across populations, ever increasing numbers of such "unfit" were discovered and anxieties worsened.

Racial hygienists sought to improve their racial stock by encouraging the propagation of the fit, sterilizing the unfit, and forbidding racial "dilution" by intermarriage. These policies were written into law in most Western countries in one form or another, such as in the antimiscegenation and sterilization laws passed in a majority of the United States, which by 1941 had caused 36,000 individuals to have been compulsorily sterilized. The ultimate expression of these ideas was of course found in Nazi Germany, where euthanasia of "unfit" children and of the inmates of psychiatric institutions was carried out in the 1930s, a precursor to the horrors of the mass genocide of Jews, Gypsies, and others designated unfit during World War II.

In the aftermath of war, many racial hygiene associations, where couples had been encouraged to seek medical testing and confirmation of fitness before marrying, gradually became planned parenthood organizations with different social goals in mind.

---

hygiene, and many other arenas of hygiene, governments sought to regulate their citizens' movements, interactions, choices, habits, and thoughts. As public-health measures proliferated, from establishing house, city, or national-border based quarantines to building "lock hospitals" for prostitutes with venereal disease, "lines of hygiene" became literally lines of rule, and conversely, lines of rule were manifest through hygienic regulations. This was most obvious in the colonial world, where the containment, education, and/or exclusion of nonwhites (predominantly ethnic populations and immigrant laborers) were often managed medically by quarantines or isolation measures directed at their supposedly diseased bodies and unhygienic habits.

Population hygiene or health was now clearly predicated on notions of purity and pollution as Western cultures struggled to imaginatively maintain the boundaries of their bodies and identities against the incursions of various "others," from viruses to Chinese gold-seekers. Domestic hygiene aimed at excluding dirt, and equivalently moral hygiene aimed at excluding evil. Indeed, practices and instruments of hygiene, such as the minutely detailed bodily training given to those with tuberculosis or inactive typhoid bacteria about how to prevent their illness from spreading to others, produced identities. Hygienic practice marked who was white or nonwhite,

citizen or alien, clean or contaminated, a good wife and mother or an impure one. By World War I, proper hygiene was regarded as a duty that all citizens owed their society. The widespread acceptance of the germ theory of disease in the 1890s encouraged this trend by focusing public-health measures away from the general environment and much more on personal practices, as the ordinary actions of apparently healthy people were now revealed to be the mechanisms that transmitted illness. With the sudden explosion of antibacterial soaps, powders for clothing, tissues, and face masks—beards were shaved and skirts lifted as Americans worried they harbored germs—came a renewed obsession with domestic and bodily cleanliness as the markers of healthiness and moral and civic responsibility.

In the late twentieth century, the concept of hygiene lost its prewar obsessions with purity and its heavy moral agenda. *Hygiene* in the twenty-first century refers virtually solely to personal cleanliness, and more particularly to personal habits that minimize exposure to germs. For the past century this has been its global definition also, as since the nineteenth century the practices of personal hygiene have been relentlessly proselytized in developing nations, not only by anxious colonizing Europeans, but also by indigenous cultures as they replaced traditional knowledges with Western medicine. (For example, the Japanese Private Association of Hygiene was founded in

1883, a decade after the new Medical Constitution of Japan, which formally declared that Western medicine would be the only legal practice in the nation, was passed.) Many physician-historians regard the spread of such personal hygiene practices as having been, and continuing to be, directly responsible for saving millions of lives, and point to the sharp downward slide in incidence of once-devastating epidemic diseases as evidence for this contention. They are not wrong—but ideas about hygiene have produced and continue to produce identities and politics that colonize other social worlds, as well as healthy bodies.

*See also* **Biology; Eugenics; Health and Disease; Medicine.**

### BIBLIOGRAPHY

PRIMARY SOURCES

Galen. *A Translation of Galen's Hygiene (De sanitate tuenda).* Translated by Robert Montraville Greene. Springfield, Ill.: Thomas, 1951.

Richardson, Benjamin Ward. *Hygeia: A City of Health.* London: Macmillan, 1876.

SECONDARY SOURCES

Armstrong, David. "Public Health Spaces and the Fabrication of Identity." *Sociology* 27 (1993): 393–403.

Bashford, Alison. *Imperial Hygiene: A Critical History of Colonial-ism, Nationalism, and Public Health.* New York: Palgrave Macmillan, 2003.

Hamarneh, Sami Khalaf. *Health Sciences in Early Islam: Collected Papers.* San Antonio, Tex.: Zahra, 1983.

Mikkeli, Heikki. *Hygiene in the Early Modern Medical Tradition.* Helsinki: Finnish Academy of Science and Letters, 1999.

Proctor, Robert. *Racial Hygiene: Medicine under the Nazis.* Cambridge, Mass.: Harvard University Press, 1988.

Tomes, Nancy. *The Gospel of Germs: Men, Women, and the Microbe in American Life.* Cambridge, Mass.: Harvard University Press, 1998.

Vigarello, Georges. *Concepts of Cleanliness: Changing Attitudes in France since the Middle Ages.* Cambridge, U.K.: Cambridge University Press, 1988.

Wear, Andrew. "History of Personal Hygiene." In *The Companion Encyclopedia of the History of Medicine,* edited by William F. Bynum and Roy Porter. Vol. 2. London and New York: Routledge, 1993.

Yamamoto Shun Ichi. "Introduction of the Western Concept and Practice of Hygiene to Japan during the Nineteenth Century." In *The History of Hygiene: Proceedings of the Twelfth International Symposium on the Comparative History of Medicine, East and West,* edited by Yosio Kawakita, Shizu Sakai, and Yasuo Otsuka. Susono-shi, Shizuoka, Japan: Ishiyabe EuroAmerica Inc., 1987.

*Claire Hooker*

# I

**ICONOGRAPHY.** Iconography is the description, classification, and interpretation of the subject matter of a work of art. Derived from the Greek words *eikon,* meaning image or icon, and *graphia,* meaning description, writing, or sketch, the word *iconography* is one of the least understood, most abused, and most flexible terms in the English language. Its primary purpose is to understand and explicate the meaning behind what is represented. Simply described, it is by definition closely related to the equally complex but more abstract term *iconology,* traditionally understood as a more advanced (and secondary) phase in visual definition. Iconology has been described as "the description, classification, or analysis of meaning or symbolism in the visual arts that takes into account the tradition of pictorial motifs and their historical, cultural, and social meaning" (Baca, p. 89). Whereas these two terms were historically distinct, with the latter usually seen as the ultimate aim of all iconographic research, it is clear that modern usage has lessened their division. They have, to a certain extent, become interchangeable.

As a subject iconography is as old as the first image created by humans, but as a concept in the history of ideas its documented study first dates from the end of the sixteenth century. Although iconography is still largely the province of the art historian, in whose discipline it was first used and with which it became irretrievably linked, it is clear that this is no longer true. Within that discipline its purpose has changed significantly from its prime association with the representational; iconography is now used to support new fields of research at the crossroads of disciplinary studies. Increasingly iconography is being applied to the nonvisual and to studies using textual, aural, or verbal material, which has extended its meaning. Within the field of popular research and computerization, studies have shown that iconography is the most widely used field of inquiry apart from that of artist or maker.

Iconography can work on many levels, from the simply descriptive to the cultural and symbolic, and may be applied to the wider relational framework of content. The easiest of these is undoubtedly the descriptive, where the multivalent nature of images causes the greatest problems (Eliade, p. 15). Even though most art-historical research is underpinned in one form or another by iconography, this study will deal only with the historical development of the concept, the methodology used in its classification, and some modern trends and not with research such as that by Johannes Molanus in *De picturis et imaginibus sacris* (1570), which uses an iconographical approach but does not deal with the idea itself.

*Madonna of Mercy* (1445–1462) from the *Polyptych of the Madonna della Misericordia* by Piero della Francesca. **Mixed technique on panel.** By the early twentieth century, systemization in the field of iconography was underway. Categories such as origin and artist could be cross-referenced with broader subject headings such as Christian art or landscapes. © ALINARI ARCHIVES/CORBIS

## Historical Development

Italy at the end of the sixteenth century provided the first scholarly studies in iconographical classification, all of which appeared within twenty-five years of each other. These include Andrea Alciati's *Emblematum liber* (Augsburg, 1531), Pierio Valeriano's *Hieroglyphica* (Basel, 1556), and Vincenzo Cartari's

**Black Madonna and Child. Haitian.** As the field of iconography has grown in importance, studies have grown broader and deeper, addressing such once-neglected issues as gender, race, and color. PHOTO CREDIT: NICOLAS SAPIEHA/ART RESOURCE, NY

*Le imagini, con la spositione de i dei de gli antichi* (Venice, 1556). All of these were superseded by what is now seen as the first study to deal with the theory of iconography, Cesare Ripa's

*Iconologia* (c. 1555–1622), a slightly ironic publication in that it was initially published without any image whatsoever (not until the third edition in 1603 were woodcuts included). Ripa's study formed the basis for much subsequent research and is one of the most comprehensive iconographic manuals for the student of personifications. It was thanks to the success of his study (and the inclusion of images in subsequent editions) that Ripa's original focus on his subject matter, as documented by the textual, was lost.

Images came to assume a greater role with the consequent and irretrievable association of what was then called iconology and art history. Ripa's initial conceptualizations of what could be represented were removed from its meaning, and iconology came to assume an association with what was there rather than what could be there. Iconology came to deal in visual fact, not theory, and began to take on humanistic associations. From the mid-seventeenth century onward, iconology was synonymous with the study of visual matter, with a slight emphasis initially on religious themes (which was later extended to the secular). It was also around this time that iconography, the now more widely used of these two terms, came into use with its specific reference to visual (usually portraits) rather than textual material. Over time it was a word that came to be applied to specific generic types of subject matter—not only portraits but medical and scientific material as well. Although the term *ichnography* (the art or process of drawings), yet a third variant, had been in use since the late fifteenth century or early sixteenth century, it became popular at the beginning of the seventeenth century for its particular reference to architectural subjects. The primary position occupied by Ripa throughout the eighteenth and nineteenth centuries was never seriously threatened despite the appearance of a series of other iconographical dictionaries, encyclopedias, and studies, such as those by Giovanni Pietro Bellori (1672), Jacob Spon (1679), Giuseppe Kurtzböck (1735), Honoré Lacombe de Prézel

---

### CESARE RIPA (FL. 1593)

Little is known of Ripa apart from the fact that he was probably born in Perugia between 1555 and 1560 and is next recorded in the service of Cardinal Antonio Maria Salviati, for whom he acted as controller of the household in Rome. His *Iconologia* was first published in 1593 to great acclaim and included descriptions of over 1,250 personifications ranging from *Abondanza* (I, 1 Abundance) to *Zelo* (V, 417 Zealousness), each of which is described in detail as a manual for writers, artists, and illustrators of the period. The personifications are always described in terms of human forms with their attributes and poses clearly delineated. This dictionary of visual imagery is highly subjective; Ripa not only drew widely on existing representations but, when such precedents did not exist, created structures showing how they should be depicted. The modern iconographic research into nonvisual material is very much in keeping with Ripa's focus, which was intended to encompass all of the arts, visual and otherwise.

---

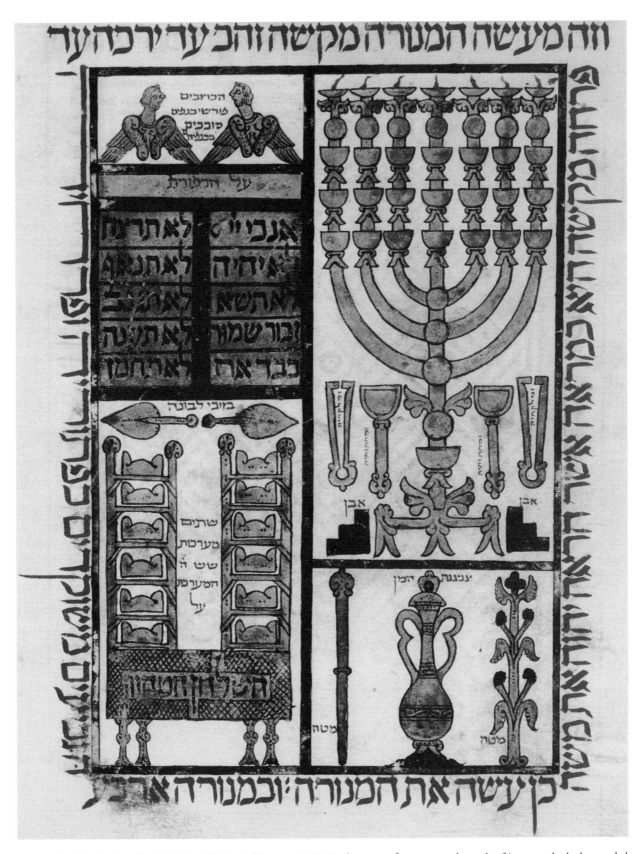

**Manuscript illumination depicting Jewish ritual objects, c. 1300.** By the twenty-first century, the study of iconography had expanded from primarily Western art forms and moved into other realms such as Islamic and Jewish art. © ARCHIVO ICONOGRAFICO, S.A./COR-BIS

***Welcoming Descent of Amida Buddha,* eighteenth century.**
Many iconographers of the twentieth century believed that the
subtextual evaluation of a work of art could exemplify the religious persuasion of a society. © CHRISTIE'S IMAGES/CORBIS

(1756), Jean-Charles Delafosse (1768), Johann J. Winckelmann
(1717–1768), Friedrich Rehberg (1794), August Stöber (1807),
Adolphe-Napoléon Didron (1806–1867), Josef Strzygowski
(1885), and Henry Spencer Ashbee (1895).

The nineteenth century saw the organized beginnings of
large-scale iconographical studies. This was what could be
called the age of theory in art history, in which iconography
was to assume a pivotal and dominant role and extend its tenets
into other fields. One of the most important interdisciplinary
approaches was that developed out of textual studies by a group
of French scholars, including Fernand Cabrol (1855–1937),
Charles Cahier (1807–1882), François-René de Chateaubriand
(1768–1848), Adolphe-Napoléon Didron (1806–1867), Émile

Mâle (1862–1954), Albert Marignan (fl. nineteenth century),
Xavier Barbier de Montault (1830–1901), and Walter Pater
(1839–1894). These studies were formative in the establishment and development of iconography as a modern interdisciplinary tool. If the works by these scholars were largely
iconographical (with occasional forays into iconology), they
nevertheless defined the parameters of future research.

Prior to this time, the focus of iconographical studies had
been largely on style. However, a new emphasis on content,
based on the concept of beauty personified in the Christian
ideas embedded in medieval art, emerged with the publication
of Chateaubriand's *Génie du Christianisme* in 1802. In it, he
balanced neoclassicism and rationalism against the concept of
genius and spirit as represented by the world of medieval art.
If Chateaubriand justified the study of art in all its forms from
a slightly conceptual stance, it was Didron who actually enforced a more comprehensive iconographical approach. They
were the first art historical iconographers of medieval art,
which at that stage was still in its infancy and which culminated in Mâle's *L'art religieux du XIIIe siècle en France: Étude
sur l'iconographie du Moyen Age* (trans., *Religious Art in France,
the Thirteenth Century: A Study of Medieval Iconography and
Its Sources*), first published in 1898. Mâle's nationalistic stance
may be seen as a subjective aside (a factor of the post–World
War I period) and not one that was to influence future iconographical studies. On the other hand, he is the first art historian to be either criticized or credited with the fact that
iconography became irrevocably text-driven. The association
between text and image is a characteristic that has both hindered and promoted research since then and is an element
whose relationship is still not clearly defined.

The twentieth century brought about a major reevaluation
of the meaning of such terms and an even wider application
of the practice. Resulting largely from the establishment of art
history as a formal discipline in universities and the improvement of photographic reproductions, along with the greater
availability of images and an increase in publications, iconography and iconology came into common usage and were applied to large-scale collections. The establishment for the first
time of art historical photographic archives, such as the Witt
Library (Courtauld Institute of Art), the Index of Christian
Art (Princeton University), and the Frick Art Reference Library, meant that relatively large-scale visual resources were
available for the study of particular themes and subjects.

The organization of the many large photo archives created
at the start of the century used subject matter or iconography
as a point of access. One of the best-known archives, the Index of Christian Art, founded in 1917 at Princeton University, was also one of the earliest to use a thematic approach
developed by Erwin Panofsky (1892–1968). This archive was
undoubtedly to provide the impetus for what is considered the
most innovative and insightful approach into the psychology
of iconographical perception created by Panofsky, who was not
only a friend of the founder but also one of the most ardent
users and supporters of the Index.

It was in the first few decades of the twentieth century that
the value of iconography was analyzed for the first time in hu-

## ÉMILE MÂLE (1862–1954)

Mâle was the first art historian to deal exclusively with medieval iconography, albeit largely with French medieval material. A student of literature at the École normale supérieure in Paris until 1886, his first appointment was as professor of rhetoric at the university at St.Étienne. His reputation was established once he accepted the position of chair in the Department of Medieval Archaeology at the Sorbonne, Paris, in 1908. His studies largely focused on the French origins of both Romanesque and Gothic sculpture and were conducted from a strongly nationalistic and religious perspective. His major work, *L'art religieux du XIIe siècle en France,* was published in 1922 and was the first in a series of similarly titled studies that evaluated the entire medieval period as a progressive movement, from a stylistic and iconographical stance. Named director of the École français de Rome in 1923, Mâle was criticized both during his lifetime and afterward for his tendency to view iconography as a finite concept and for his unwillingness to see beyond his own period or area of expertise.

## ERWIN PANOFSKY (1892–1968)

Born in Hanover, Panofsky received his Ph.D. in 1914 from the University of Freiburg. He is recognized as one of the most influential scholars of the twentieth century, not only for his academic studies but for his analysis of the methodologies of iconographic analysis and interpretation, which culminated in *Studies in Iconology* (1939). Before assuming part-time teaching duties at New York University in 1931, he taught at the Universities of Munich, Berlin, and Hamburg (1926–1933), where he was strongly influenced by Aby Warburg and what was then known as iconographical analysis. After the Nazis came to power, Panofsky left Germany for good and took up teaching in New York. In 1935, at the invitation of his friend Charles Rufus Morey, Panofsky transferred to the newly established Institute for Advanced Study at Princeton University, where he remained until his death in 1968. His writings are characterized by a rare erudition and range. A humanist in the broadest sense, Panofsky wrote on such diverse topics as Gothic scholasticism, Albrecht Dürer, German sculpture, and Suger and the Abbey of St. Denis as well as Mozart, the cinema, and the detective story.

manistic terms. Typical of such studies were those by Charles Rufus Morey (1877–1955), who saw iconography as a linchpin in understanding the broader context of any art-historical work. Iconography could therefore be used to determine date, style, and the broader sociocultural position of the work and was no longer limited to subject matter. This movement was ultimately to lead to a certain degree of stagnation in a number of studies prior to the 1930s in which iconography was a slave to the determination of date and origin. It was Morey who was responsible for bringing Erwin Panofsky to Princeton's Institute for Advanced Study. It is difficult not to acknowledge the influence the index must have had on Panofsky's theories, considering that the work undertaken in the archive had been under way some twenty years before his work (*Studies in Iconology: Humanistic Themes in the Art of the Renaissance,* 1939) was published. Morey, like Panofsky, was a firm believer in the theory that iconography could be "read" like a text—a practice that continues in most cataloging systems. Though he is generally seen as the father of iconography, Panofsky's theories (see sidebar) have been sharply criticized in the late twentieth century, but his work is pivotal in understanding the methodology of subject analysis and would influence the role that iconography was to assume to the end of the twentieth century and beyond.

If Panofsky is seen as the scholar whose work culminated in the best-known study, Aby Warburg (1866–1929), a like-minded scholar, was also instrumental in promoting iconographical research methods. Panofksy was also preceded by some notable iconographers, mostly on the other side of the Atlantic (with the exception of Meyer Schapiro [1905–1996], who, although born in Lithuania, lived in the United States), whose theories paralleled his own. Among these were Fritz Saxl (1890–1948) and Edgar Wind (1900–1971) of the Warburg Institute. All German by birth and training, they saw a need to evaluate the work from an interdisciplinary perspective in which its true meaning could be elucidated not just in relation to its immediate context but in its broader value, thus revealing "the basic attitude of a nation, a period, a class, a religious or philosophical persuasion" (Panofsky, 1939, p. 7). Panofsky's theories are very much the product of the art-historical milieu in which he lived and worked, a world in which art history was termed *Kunstgeschichte als Geistesgeschichte* (art history as the history of ideas; see Dvořák), and of course his Kantian philosophy. The German philosopher Immanuel Kant (1724–1804) was a major influence in Panofsky's formulation of a number of theories, such as "Copernican Revolution," in which he argues that it is the image or representation that makes the object possible instead of the opposite. Kant's belief that the human brain played an active role in perception and was not just a passive recipient influenced Panofsky's structure as to how the brain perceived images and structured iconography. It was at this stage that the terms *iconography* and *iconology* were revised, with iconography redefined as the basic stage of interpretation and iconology seen as the more advanced stage of interpretation.

Iconography was to develop slowly yet consistently through the rest of the twentieth century until a period of critical self-examination in art history brought about some new developments. The whole discipline—not just iconography or Panofsky's theories—came under criticism and revision in the 1960s and 1970s. The relevance of iconography in art-historical studies was questioned, mainly by iconographers, and relegated to a secondary position by some factions within the discipline. Iconography, like Panofsky's theories, was seen as resistant to change and too self-contained within its own parameters. Now that this period of self-examination seems to have abated, the relevance of iconography to what is called the "new art history" has once again been accepted as one of the fundamental tenets of the discipline. The implications for its understanding have also been extended into previously under-researched fields, such as reception, color, gender, and ethnography.

## Methodology

If Ripa was among the first iconographical theoreticians to realize the importance of structure and systematization in this field, others did not follow his path until the beginning of the

**Detail of *Durga Slaying the Buffalo Demon*. Relief sculpture, Mahabalipuram, Tamil Nadu, India.** Although the study of iconography is not limited to the visual arts, and indeed can be applied to textual or verbal material, it is still considered primarily the purview of the art historian. © GIAN BERTO VANNI/CORBIS

twentieth century. Informal, loosely defined, and independent structures were developed at the end of the nineteenth century with many scholarly studies in which related concepts and themes were grouped together, and significant and dominant subjects were discovered with the amassing of large bodies of visual data. It was from such studies that the twin applications of methodology to cataloging and interpretation developed. The former, albeit on a less-developed basis, was in place prior to Panofsky's work.

The need to organize large visual collections using meaningful and practical guidelines led not only to the creation of formal principles but was directly responsible for Panofsky's work, which could only have emerged with such a platform in place. This work was initially undertaken in the photo archives that developed at the start of the century. It must be remembered that because no guidelines existed for the handling of such material, the organizational principles in use largely emulated those of the traditional book library—a policy that has caused some difficulties. The primary cataloging principle in visual collections was organization on a national basis (French, Italian, Spanish). This was followed by the maker's name (Fragonard, Giotto, Goya). The output was iconographically subdivided (portraits, male, landscapes, still life, abstract), depending on the complexity of the artist's output. Such subject headings could also form the primary access point to the material, as in the case of the Index of Christian Art or the Rijksbureau Voor Kunsthistorische Documentatie in The Hague.

Whereas such structures were broadly similar in their construction and could include any number of themes (usually referred to as subject headings), there were no existing principles or guidelines with which to determine terminology or structure. This was to change with Panofsky's pioneering study, which provided a framework for interpreting and understanding iconography and iconology. His threefold division of interpretation and understanding also examined the psychology and mental processes involved in creative work:

1. The first level is a description of the factual (or expressional), termed the "pre-iconographic description," in which uninterpreted subjects are enumerated. This level does not require any indepth knowledge of either the work or its context, apart from the ability to recognize what is represented.

2. The secondary level, iconographical analysis, involves an understanding of the subject matter. It "constitutes the world of images, stories and allegories" (Panofsky 1939, p. 14) and requires an analysis of the pre-iconographic material, which can be derived only from a familiarity with and knowledge of the themes and concepts represented. The recognition of such themes can be based on external sources (such as textual material) and may be extensive, but it is usually acquired from familiarization with the material.

3. The third or iconographical level is the most complicated of the three and involves an understanding of the intrinsic meaning or content, constituting the world of "symbolical values." This level requires "a familiarity with the essential tendencies of the human mind" and attempts to place the deeper meaning of the work (if it exists) within the realm of the conscious. Such deeper meanings cannot be immediately recognized.

Why Panofsky completely reversed the use of existing terminology remains a mystery, but it was probably to accommodate his structure, which in itself is slightly unsatisfactory because of its inability to formulate a satisfactory term for the first level. The three divisions are clearly structured as a paper system, but in reality the speed with which the human mind culturally contextualizes subjects at a pre-iconographic level slightly blurs the three divisions. Considering the cultural associations everyone possesses, and which must be applied at a conscious or subconscious level, it is difficult to disentangle the various levels into coherent thought processes. Nevertheless, Panofsky's legacy was to influence art-historical studies for many generations. His pioneering work, even in the early twenty-first century, forms the basic principle for iconographical analysis. In Roland Barthes's (1973) semiological system, the terminology and structure of "sign," "signifier," and "signified" was influenced by, and is remarkably similar to, Panofsky's.

Panofsky's theories were also to provide an ordered framework for developing methodologies in subject classification. Even in the early twenty-first century, whether in computerized or manual format, most classification systems structure a tripartite division that, although slightly out of sync with Panofsky's system, nevertheless mirrors it in essence. Such structures differ from Panofsky's in their relationship to user needs.

1. The first of these is usually the broad level descriptor or general subject heading, such as portrait or landscape—an iconographic descriptor at its broadest.

2. The second is the pre-iconographic description of the work—the generic elements in the work, such as bridge, lake, table, and so forth.

3. The third level is the specifics of the work—for example, an identified person's name, the name of a battle or of a bridge—an amalgam of the iconographical and iconological.

Most cataloging systems fail to address iconological analysis, leaving such work to scholarly researchers. One of the basic requirements for iconographic classification is consistency and standardization, and it was this factor that led one of Panofsky's colleagues, Henri van de Waal (1910–1972), the next great iconographer of the postwar period, to discuss with Panofsky in 1948 the principles of iconographical analysis. Their discussions resulted in what is now the most widely used iconographical system in the world, ICONCLASS. This alphanumeric system, published between 1973 and 1985, divides what can be represented into nine divisions, with further subdivisions to the specific. For example, 73C14 is the code for the Burial of St. John the Baptist and is based on the divisions:

7: Subjects drawn from the Bible

73: Subjects drawn from the New Testament

73C: The public life of Christ from baptism until the Passion

73C1: Story of John the Baptist

73C14: Burial of John the Baptist

Systems may appear in natural language or coded (as in ICONCLASS) and use the construction of subject headings, thesaurus-based terms, or free text descriptions.

## CHARLES RUFUS MOREY (1877–1955)

Chairman of the Department of Art and Archaeology at Princeton University, Morey was a historian of early Christian art whose primary field of study was the iconography of Italian art of the pre-700 period. Apart from his scholarly studies, which ranged from research on gold-glass mosaics to early Latin manuscripts and iconographical motifs of the origins of early Christian art, he is best remembered for founding the Index of Christian Art in 1917. As an iconographer he realized that the major obstacle to understanding the development of particular themes and subjects lay in the lack of available knowledge. It was this that led to his establishment of the world's largest iconographically organized archive of medieval art. Morey's studies, while now slightly outdated, demonstrate his belief that the full understanding of a work of art depends on the use of iconography in a contextualized manner. A close friend of Panofsky, Morey believed that iconography was an organic entity that was constantly developing and that could be understood only in relation to what was known at any one time.

With the advent of computerization to art history (and the computer's application to iconographical studies in particular), such systems have proliferated, highlighting the popularity of subject analysis but also increasing the visual material available for scholarly research which has, in many ways, brought about a renewal of interest in iconography. However, no matter how structured or developed the classification system, the inherent difficulties and, ultimately, the impossible task of describing the visual with the verbal remain.

### Trends and Developments

Computerization and its application to art history has been the most dominant factor in the popular renewal of interest in iconography. User studies have shown the popularity of accessing subject matter in such venues as museum and gallery databases. There has been a similar renewed interest in scholarly research. Iconography is developing along twin tracks whereby the traditional is being refined with a greater need for detail and new needs are being created with the opening up of new fields. Large-scale iconographical projects have developed in art history with specializations, such as mythology, music, classical and legal material, medicine, and costume, to name just a few. Up to the end of the twentieth century, iconographical studies were largely concerned with Western art and the representational but must now encompass the abstract, stylized, non-Western, and nonrepresentational.

Generalities will no longer suffice; more detail is required that reflects the study of minutiae now demanded by scholarship. With such details, specific iconographic subfields, which had hitherto been neglected or treated only in passing, have assumed greater importance. Among these are such issues as gender, race, gesture, color, and politics. A number of these concepts have developed in response to new art-

historical concerns. With the opening up of art history into new fields of research, we have also moved into non-Western art and an iconography that was never extensively researched. Islamic, Judaic, Chinese, and Indian art forms are now being studied from an iconographical and iconological perspective; consequently there is a need to develop a suitable terminology and to apply different approaches that theories such as Panofsky's cannot encompass. Whereas in the past iconographical studies dealt largely with classical, medieval, or religious subjects, the whole field of study has opened significantly and now reflects a number of disciplines, not just the more classically oriented. Iconography is responding to a widening field of scholarship. In all of these developments, and especially in its associations with other disciplines, the humanistic background of iconographical research is being reinforced and extended.

If iconography has changed, so has the way in which it is used. We have moved beyond iconographical interpretation into issues of reception that, in many ways, are an extension of Panofsky's cultural contextualization. Now, however, there is greater focus on the specific work (and what we can learn from it) than on the national or cultural contexts and their relationship to subject matter, which was Panofsky's premise for understanding iconology. We are now attempting to understand not just the hidden meaning behind a specific theme or motif but also how subjects are received and understood by the viewer. The new focus of iconography demands that viewers transpose themselves to the period of creation and reception and operate at a spiritual level that moves beyond the work of art itself. It is disappointing that the majority of iconographical studies fails to consider form and function—factors

## HENRI VAN DE WAAL (1910–1972)

Born in Rotterdam, van de Waal began his studies in 1929 at the University of Leiden, which was to be his academic home for the rest of his career. He received his Ph.D. in 1940 for a study on the seventeenth-century Batavian revolt. As a writer he is best known for his iconological study on three centuries of representing Dutch national history, *Drie eeuwen vaderlandsche geschieduitbeelding 1500–1800: Een iconologische studie* (The Hague, 1952), which, although ready for the printer in 1942, was not published until 1952 as the typescript was destroyed by the Germans during the occupation of the Netherlands. While interned in a prisoner of war camp, he began to formulate his theories on structuring a system for iconographic classification that eventually was called ICONCLASS and was published between 1973 and 1985. After the war van de Waal was named director of the University of Leiden's print room and was later made professor of art history there. His classification system is based on Panofsky's pre-iconographic and iconographic levels with nothing iconological in the structure. Factually based, it merges form and content and is now the most widely used iconographical classification system in the world.

that are pivotal to understanding the meaning of any work holistically.

Despite the application of the term to disciplines other than the visual, iconography remains very much within the province of the art-historical world. Its popular use in relation to textual, musical, political, religious, theatrical, or dramatic studies, to name just a few of the disciplines to which it has been applied, is nearly always based on visual material within those fields. Its use is therefore less clearly defined in such fields although, as a concept, there seems no reason why it should not be applied even at all three of Panofsky's levels. Iconography still remains highly dependent on the need to find a textual support for its subject matter—a characteristic that has impeded research. The overriding need to find a textual basis, even where none may exist, has created an unreal association between the verbal and the visual. Iconographical scholarship, especially that of the medieval period, has looked for sources for the visual among a variety of documents, from the legal to the poetic, when no visual relationship may exist. But even if still text-driven, iconography has fortunately moved away from the need to find the earliest example of whatever theme or subject is being studied.

Chronological or developmental stages in the history of a motif are no longer seen as being of paramount importance. There have been some trends to extend iconographical significance to reflect an even wider application beyond what has hitherto been defined. Terms such as *aboutness* or *relatedness* denote concepts and ideas beyond the iconological. Brought about largely through the application of computers to iconographical studies, such terms reflect the need to extend meaning to the absolute. Unsatisfactory in meaning and application, they attempt to extend the iconological significance of a work

to what are perceived to be broader, yet related, iconological concepts that, like the terms themselves, are highly subjective and may not be supported by factual evidence. If iconology was believed to have separated art from form and content, this new direction threatens to put such relationships even further into the background.

*See also* **Aesthetics; Arts; Classification of Arts and Sciences, Early Modern; Context; Hierarchy and Order; Interdisciplinarity; Language and Linguistics; Logic; Symbolism; Visual Culture; Visual Order to Organizing Collections.**

**BIBLIOGRAPHY**

Baca, Murtha, ed. *An Introduction to Art Image Access: Issues, Tools, Standards, Strategies.* Los Angeles: Getty Research Institute, 2002.

Barthes, Roland. *Mythologies.* Selected and translated from the French by Annette Lavers. New York: Hill and Wang, 1972.

Bazin, Germain. *Histoire de l'histoire de l'art: De Vasari à nos jours.* Paris: A. Michel, 1986.

Beilmann, M. "Hans Van De Waal (1910–1972)." In *Altmeister Moderner Kunstgeschichte,* edited by Heinrich Dilly. Berlin: D. Reimer, 1990.

Bialostocki, Jan. "Iconografia e Iconologia." In *Enciclopedia universale dell'arte,* vol. 7. Venice: Istituto per la collaborazione culturale, 1962.

———. *Stil und Ikonographie: Studien zur Kunstwissenschaft.* Cologne, Germany: DuMont, 1981.

Bolvig, Axel, and Phillip Lindley, eds. *History and Images: Towards a New Iconology.* Turnhout, Belgium: Brepols, 2003.

Cassidy, Brendan, ed. *Iconography at the Crossroads: Papers from the Colloquium Sponsored by the Index of Christian Art, Princeton University, 23–24 March 1990.* Princeton, N.J.: Princeton University Department of Art and Archaeology, 1993.

Dvořák, Max. *The History of Art as the History of Ideas.* Translated by John Hardy. London and Boston: Routledge and Kegan Paul, 1984.

Eliade, Mircea. *Images and Symbols: Studies in Religious Symbolism.* Translated by Philip Mairet. New York: Sheed and Ward, 1961.

*Émile Mâle: Le symbolisme chrétien: Exposition.* Vichy, France: La Bibliothèque, 1983.

Ferretti, Silvia. *Cassirer, Panofsky, and Warburg: Symbol, Art, and History.* Translated by Richard Pierce. New Haven, Conn.: Yale University Press, 1989.

Foskett, Antony Charles. *The Subject Approach to Information.* London: Bingley; Hamden, Conn.: Linnet, 1981.

Friedman, John B., and Jessica M. Wegmann. *Medieval Iconography: A Research Guide.* New York: Garland, 1998.

Heckscher, William. "The Genesis of Iconology." In *Stil und Überlieferung in der Kunst des Abendlandes,* 239–262. Berlin: Gebr. Mann, 1967.

Heidt Heller, Renate. *Erwin Panofsky: Kunsttheorie u. Einzelwerk.* Cologne and Vienna: Böhlau, 1977.

Holly, Michael Ann. *Panofsky and the Foundations of Art History.* Ithaca, N.Y.: Cornell University Press, 1984.

———. "The Origin and Development of Erwin Panofsky's Theories of Art." Ph.D. diss., Cornell University, 1981.

Hourihane, Colum, ed. *Insights and Interpretations: Studies in Celebration of the Eighty-Fifth Anniversary of the Index of Christian Art.* Princeton, N.J.: Princeton University Press, 2002.

Kaemmerling, Ekkehard, ed. *Ikonographie und Ikonologie: Theorien, Entwicklung, Probleme.* Bd. 1: *Bildende Kunst als Zeichensystem.* Cologne: DuMont, 1979.

Lavin, Irving, ed. *Meaning in the Visual Arts: Views from the Outside: A Centennial Commemoration of Erwin Panofsky 1892–1968.* Princeton, N.J.: Princeton University Institute for Advanced Study, 1995.

Lavin, Marilyn. *The Eye of the Tiger: The Founding and Development of the Department of Art and Archaeology, Princeton University, 1883–1923.* Princeton, N.J.: Princeton University Press, 1983.

Meiss, Millard, ed. *De artibus opuscula XL: Essays in Honor of Erwin Panofsky.* New York: New York University, 1961.

Molanus, Johannes. *Traité des saintes images: De picturis et imaginibus sacris.* Paris: Cerf, 1996.

Panofsky, Erwin. *Meaning in the Visual Arts: Papers in and on Art History.* Garden City, N.Y.: Doubleday, 1955.

———. *Studies in Iconology: Humanistic Themes in the Art of the Renaissance.* New York: Oxford University Press, 1939.

Porter, A. Kingsley. "Spain or Toulouse? and Other Questions." *Art Bulletin* 7 (1924): 4.

Ripa, Caesare. *Iconologia.* Edited by Piero Buscaroli. 2 vols. Turin, Italy: Fògola, 1986.

Smyth, Craig Hugh, and Peter Lukehart, eds. *The Early Years of Art History in the United States.* Princeton, N.J.: Princeton University Department of Art and Archaeology, 1993.

Straten, Roelof van. *An Introduction to Iconography.* Translated by Patricia de Man. Langhorne, Pa.: Gordon and Breach, 1993.

Waal, Henri van de. *ICONCLASS, an Iconographic Classification System.* Completed and edited by L. D. Couprie et al. Amsterdam: n.p., 1985.

*Colum Hourihane*

**IDEALISM.** The term *idealism* in its broadest sense denotes the philosophical position that ideas (mental or spiritual

entities) are primary and lie at the very foundation of reality, knowledge, and morality, while non-ideal entities (such as physical or material things) are secondary and perhaps even illusory. Strands of idealistic thought can be found in ancient and medieval philosophy, but modern idealism begins in the wake of René Descartes (1596–1650), whose method of doubt problematized the relation of the mind (or spirit or ideas) to the material world and thus raised questions about how ideas "inside" the mind can be known to interact with or correspond to any material, extended thing "outside" the mind.

## Early Modern Idealism: Leibniz and Berkeley

The idealism of Gottfried Wilhem Leibniz (1646–1716) arose largely in response to questions raised by Descartes about the relation between mental substances and physical substances. According to Leibniz, real substances do not and cannot interact, because to be a substance is to be independent of the influences of other substances (but no finite substance is altogether independent of God, who is the ground and cause of all finite substances, including ourselves). Furthermore, Leibniz argued that every genuine substance must be utterly non-composite or simple (i.e., not made of parts), because the ongoing unity and existence of any being made of parts depends on causes outside of the being itself (and such dependence contradicts the very definition of substance). Accordingly Leibniz held that no genuine substance can be material, because matter is essentially composite, which means that matter cannot be substantially or independently real. Leibniz thus concluded that substances must be percipient, or have perceptions, because the only way in which a substance can be utterly simple and yet reflect diversity within itself is through the undivided activity of perception. Leibniz's idealism can be summed up in the proposition that "to be is to be a substance, and to be a substance is to be percipient." For Leibniz, the real world is simply the totality of all such non-interacting ("windowless") and percipient substances (called "monads"), and our experience of the material world is to be explained idealistically: to be a substance is to be percipient, and the perceptions belonging to any one substance accurately reflect the states of all other substances, not because there is any real interaction among substances but because God has ordained a "pre-established harmony" among all finite substances and their perceptions.

If modern philosophy is divided into two main schools of thought—"rationalism" and "empiricism"—then Leibniz is a "rationalist" idealist, while George Berkeley (1685–1753) is an "empiricist" idealist. Berkeley began with John Locke's empiricist premise that the mind does not possess innate ideas but acquires ideas only through sensory experience. Like Locke, Berkeley also held that the mind has immediate or direct perception only of its own ideas. But unlike Locke, Berkeley denied that the mind's immediate perception of its own ideas can give it indirect knowledge of material things outside of it. Berkeley further insisted that "an idea can be like nothing but an idea" (*Principles,* part 1, section 8), and so we can never know whether the immaterial ideas in our minds resemble or accurately depict material things outside of our minds. Furthermore, Berkeley argued, there is something self-contradictory in the proposition that objects of perception can exist without being perceived. In order to avoid skeptical or altogether absurd conclusions, Berkeley argued, one must abandon belief in the independent existence of material things and become an idealist or "immaterialist." For Berkeley, the ideas that we have of sensible things are not *caused* in us by independently existing material things; rather, these ideas simply *are* the sensible things themselves. But sensible things have continued existence—even when we finite minds are not perceiving them—because they continue to exist in the mind of God, whose perception of things not only causes the sensible things to exist but also from time to time causes them to be perceived by us. Thus for Berkeley, our perception of sensible things is nothing other than our perception of ideas in God, and sensible things have an orderly, predictable, and enduring existence because of the wisdom and goodness of God. For Berkeley, then, the immaterialist view of reality not only refutes skepticism but also provides indirect theoretical support for theism. Far from seeking to reduce the real world to the status of "mere" ideas, the real aim of Berkeley's immaterialism is to elevate "mere" ideas to the status of the real world.

### Kant's Transcendental Idealism

Immanuel Kant (1724–1804) famously wrote that his "transcendental idealism" arose in response to the radical skepticism of David Hume (1711–1776; see *Prolegomena*, p. 260). Unlike Berkeley, Hume doubted not only the independent existence of material objects but even the objective validity of concepts that still remained central to Berkeley's immaterialist system, such as the concepts of causality and God. Kant recognized that these and other metaphysical concepts could be neither verified nor falsified by recourse to experience alone; however, Kant did not simply reject metaphysics (as Hume had done) but sought to determine the legitimacy and scope of metaphysics by asking the prior question of what reason might justifiably claim to know a priori (that is, independent of all experience).

For Kant, the question of the legitimacy and scope of metaphysics is intimately linked to the question of the possibility of "synthetic *apriori* judgments." As synthetic, such judgments extend our knowledge beyond our mere concepts of things, and as a priori, they have necessary and universal validity. Prior to Kant, the empiricists had argued that all synthetic judgments must be a posteriori (that is, based on experience), while Leibniz and Leibnizians had argued that even seemingly synthetic judgments are not really synthetic, because all the predicates belonging to any particular thing can in principle be discovered through an analysis of the mere concept of the thing. The Leibnizian option was unacceptable to Kant, because it entailed that human sensibility is not essentially different from (but is simply a confused form of) human understanding, and thus that human knowing is different in degree, but not in kind, from divine knowing. The empiricist option was unacceptable because, for Kant, judgments based on experience (a posteriori judgments) could never yield knowledge about what is necessarily and universally the case. Against both sides, Kant argued that synthetic a priori knowledge is possible for us, because we possess a kind of sensibility (or intuition) that is not

merely empirical (a posteriori) but a priori. More specifically, we possess the a priori forms of intuition—space and time—where space is the form of all outer sense, and time is the form of all inner sense. For Kant, no object can be given to us (and thus we can have no access to objects beyond our mere concepts), except through the a priori forms of space and time, which are the "subjective conditions" of our own mode of intuiting things. Kant also argued that we possess a priori concepts or "categories" of the understanding which—like the a priori forms of intuition—are not derived from experience but rather which make our experience of objects possible in the first place. Indeed, Kant argues, there would be no such thing as "objects" for us if we did not make judgments applying our own a priori concepts (or categories) to the sensible manifold that is intuited by us through our own a priori forms of space and time. Kant concludes that the "objects" we know through the a priori forms of intuition and categories of the understanding are not "things-in-themselves" (they are not things as they might exist apart from our own a priori conditions of knowing) but only appearances.

Kant's denial that we can have knowledge of "things-in-themselves" is not meant to imply that the empirical objects of ordinary experience (what Kant calls appearances) are "unreal" or merely illusory. For Kant, the objects of ordinary experience are certainly real, for "the real" is simply that which exercises some degree of influence on our sensibility (*Critique*, A 165; B 208). But while objects of ordinary experience are empirically real, Kant insists that they are "transcendentally ideal" (and not transcendentally real), which is to say that they are not to be identified with anything beyond—or anything that transcends—the bounds of possible experience or the a priori subjective conditions that make such experience possible in the first place. Simultaneously embracing both "transcendental idealism" and "empirical realism," Kant claims to have shown how we are justified in making synthetic a priori knowledge claims and in employing concepts that are neither derived from nor verified through experience. But just as Kant's transcendental idealism entails the distinction between things-in-themselves and appearances, it also entails a distinction between the legitimate and illegitimate employment of pure (a priori) reason. For Kant, we can legitimately pursue a limited "metaphysics of experience," and we can legitimately make synthetic a priori knowledge claims about objects of possible experience. For example, the concept of "causality" (even though "pure" and underived from experience) remains objectively valid when applied to things that can be intuited by us under the a priori conditions of space and time. But Kant also argues that we cannot legitimately pursue metaphysics or make synthetic a priori claims regarding objects that transcend all possible experience. Furthermore, he argues that the attempt to make knowledge claims about the non-sensible objects of traditional metaphysics (for example, God, the soul, and the world as a whole) inevitably leads reason into illusion and self-contradiction. But while we cannot obtain objectively valid theoretical knowledge of such non-sensible objects, our *ideas* regarding such objects (for example, our idea of God) may continue to play a legitimate role in guiding our search for complete knowledge in our theoretical pursuits and the complete good in our moral pursuits.

## Idealism, from Kant to Fichte and Schelling

In the years following its public promulgation, Kant's transcendental idealist philosophy was the object of widespread excitement but also much critical scrutiny. Three interrelated problems (or perceived problems) would prove to be significant for the subsequent development of German idealism. First, critics argued that Kant failed to derive or "deduce" the forms of intuition and the categories of the understanding in a systematic and rigorous way, and as a result his critical system could claim only contingent or inductive (as opposed to universal and necessary) validity for itself. Second, critics claimed that Kant's inadequate derivation of the forms of intuition and categories of the understanding committed him to a series of unacceptable dualisms, all of them rooted (directly or indirectly) in the dualism between sensibility and understanding (for example, the dualisms between intuitions and concepts, activity and passivity, receptivity and spontaneity, the a priori and a posteriori, knowledge and belief, theoretical reason and practical reason). Third, critics argued, Kant's strict separation of sensibility and understanding made it impossible for him to account for the receptive character of human knowing except by reference to "things-in-themselves" that allegedly exist apart from the human knower and thus render the activity of human knowing finite, dependent, and passive; but this postulation of things-in-themselves contradicts the spirit of Kant's own transcendental idealism, according to which we cannot know anything about things-in-themselves, including what role—if any—they play in rendering human knowing finite, dependent, and passive.

In the midst of ongoing debates about Kant's transcendental idealism, the young Johann Gottlieb Fichte (1762–1814) became convinced that the Kantian system was essentially correct but stood in need of a more systematic formulation and rigorous defense. First, Fichte argued that it was wrong to think of the "faculty of thinking" or the "mind" or the "self" as if these terms referred to a substrate that underlies our mental operations and persists even in the absence of actual cognitive activity. To think of the self in this way, he claimed, is to regard it as an unknown "thing in itself" that has existence even apart from its being known, and such a view is inimical to transcendental idealism. Fichte went on to argue that the self is nothing other than the free, uncoerced activity of "self-positing" or "self-awareness" and that this very activity can serve as the single, foundational principle from which one could rigorously derive all the other conditions of synthetic a priori knowing, including even the self's apparent dependence on things outside of it. More specifically, Fichte argued that the self would have no occasion to reflect back on itself, and thus it could never even *be* a self if it did not also take itself to be finite and partly determined by a "not-self" outside of it. In other words, Fichte held that even the apparent dependence of human knowing on supposedly independent, unknowable things-in-themselves could be explained on the basis of the necessary conditions of the self's own activity of self-positing. He went on to assert that the not-self, without which the self could not even *be* a self, must ultimately be understood as another free self, thereby arguing for the necessity of belief in other selves (or intersubjectivity) as a condition of the possibility of the self's own self-positing. In practical philosophy,

Fichte also took a step beyond Kant, arguing that the idea of God is necessary for our moral purposes but also that this idea in fact signified nothing other than the moral order of the world itself.

Friedrich Wilhelm Joseph Schelling (1775–1854) was an early follower of Fichte but eventually distanced himself from the Fichtean claim that a properly critical philosophy can begin only with the activity of the self-positing self. By 1799 Schelling was arguing (along with Fichte) that one could derive the not-self (or "nature") from the self-positing activity of the self, but also (against Fichte) that one could equally derive the self-positing activity of the self from the not-self (or "nature"). In subsequent years Schelling departed even farther from Fichte, explicitly rejecting the Fichtean claim that the distinction between subject and object (self and not-self) is a distinction that can be made only by and within subjectivity itself. In effect Schelling argued that Fichte was right to relativize Kant's rigid distinction between subject and object (or correlatively, between understanding and sensibility, or concepts and intuitions) but wrong to achieve such relativization by locating the distinction within subjectivity alone. For Schelling, the distinction between subject and object is not merely subjective but arises only from within an "absolute identity" that is neither subject nor object but both at once. Furthermore, Schelling held, this absolute identity cannot be discursively demonstrated or conceptually articulated (because demonstration and conceptualization already presuppose a subject-object split) but can only be apprehended immediately in an intellectual intuition or (according to Schelling's later thought) an aesthetic intuition. According to Fichte, Schelling's appeal to immediate intuition and his claim that unconscious nature is continuous with and provides the conditions for the emergence of conscious subjectivity could only signal a return to pre-critical, pre-Kantian metaphysics. But Schelling insisted that his "identity philosophy" incorporated the truths of transcendental idealism, while also moving beyond Kant's and Fichte's "subjective idealisms" to a more comprehensive and satisfactory "absolute idealism." This absolute idealism, Schelling argued, did not uncritically presuppose any dualisms between subject and object, freedom and nature, or human agency and God, but rather explained all such dualisms as mere moments within the absolute's own process of internal self-differentiation.

## Hegelian Idealism and Its Aftermath

In 1801 the virtually unknown Georg Wilhelm Friedrich Hegel (1770–1831) published a short book entitled *The Difference between Fichte's and Schelling's System of Philosophy,* in which he argued that Schelling had rightly criticized Fichte's "subjective idealism." But by 1807, with the publication of his *Phenomenology of Spirit,* Hegel had begun to criticize Schelling for reasons that were to become determinative for the development of his own version of absolute idealism. First of all, Hegel argued against Schelling that the pathway to a truly "scientific" absolute idealism could not be based merely on an immediate intuition (whether intellectual or aesthetic) but instead had to be conceptually articulated and discursively mediated. Indeed Hegel referred to his own *Phenomenology* as the "ladder" by means of which readers could be led discursively from the standpoint of ordinary consciousness to that scientific consciousness or "absolute knowing" (see *Phenomenology,* p. 14). Second, and contrary to what might be implied by Schelling's insistence on immediate intuition, Hegel argued that the discursive pathway to absolute idealism is not external to, but constitutes an integral part of, the very truth of absolute idealism. For Hegel, then, Schelling was correct to claim that previous expressions of the subject-object identity within the absolute (for example, in nature and in earlier forms of philosophy) contained the conditions of the emergence of the subjectivity that eventually grasps the truth of absolute idealism; however, Schelling was wrong to hold that his being correct about this could be ascertained through an immediate intuition. For Hegel, quite simply, one could not know that absolute idealism is true if one did not conceptually recollect the previous forms of thought leading up to it. Because of this, Hegel also held that previous forms of thought do not lead just accidentally or haphazardly to his own thought but rather find their necessary consummation only within his absolute idealism. Third, Hegel agreed with Schelling that a true idealism must not simply presuppose the traditional dualisms of subject and object, freedom and nature, or human agency and God (thus Hegel held that our own coming-to-be conscious of the truth of absolute idealism is not essentially separable from God's own coming-to-be God). But because of his commitment to conceptual rigor and discursive articulation, Hegel went on to argue that the denial of these traditional dualisms required the development of a new and "dialectical" logic, one that would demonstrate how all finite things reflect within themselves the fundamental yet contradictory identity-in-difference of Being and Nothing (*Logic,* p. 85). All things are in themselves contradictory, Hegel argued, and so Kant was wrong to try to eliminate or contain such contradiction by introducing his distinction between appearances and things-in-themselves (*Logic,* p. 237).

Hegel's idealism represents the most systematic and comprehensive version of post-Kantian idealism, for it contained within itself not only a new dialectical logic but also very detailed philosophies of nature, history, art, law, and religion. Not long after Hegel's death, however, his idealistic philosophy became the object of a sustained materialist critique and transformation, primarily at the hands of Ludwig Feuerbach (1804–1872), Karl Marx (1818–1883), and Friedrich Engels (1820–1895). Most famously, Marx and Engels sought to transform Hegel's dialectical idealism into a form of "dialectical materialism." They agreed with Hegel that existing reality is fundamentally dialectical and in contradiction with itself, but against Hegel they argued that reality's basic contradictions are rooted not in merely conceptual determinations (such as the identity-in-difference of Being and Nothing) but rather in the material conditions underlying all forms of precommunist social and economic organization. They went on to assert that systems such as Hegel's tended to perpetuate the destructive contradictions at work in precommunist society insofar as these systems tended to regard such contradictions as merely ideal and—worse still—as necessary to the proper unfolding of the history of thought. But just as Hegel had argued that a recollective conceptual journey through incomplete forms of thought is necessary to the very truth of absolute idealism, so

too Marx and Engels argued that an actual material journey through incomplete forms of social organization (feudalism, mercantilism, and capitalism) is necessary to emergence of the truly just communist society that is yet to be. In spite of this materialist critique, Hegelian idealism enjoyed an energetic revival in Anglo-American philosophy during the late nineteenth and early twentieth centuries. The three most important post-Hegelian British idealists were Thomas Hill Green (1836–1882), Francis Herbert Bradley (1846–1924), and Bernard Bosanquet (1848–1923), while their most important American counterpart was Josiah Royce (1855–1916).

*See also* **Empiricism; Epistemology; Hegelianism; Marxism; Rationalism.**

## BIBLIOGRAPHY

### PRIMARY SOURCES

Berkeley, George. *A Treatise Concerning the Principles of Human Knowledge.* Edited by Jonathan Dancy. Oxford: Oxford University Press, 1998.

Fichte, Johann Gottlieb. *Early Philosophical Writings.* Translated and edited by Daniel Breazeale. Ithaca, N.Y.: Cornell University Press, 1988.

———. *Science of Knowledge.* Translated by Peter Heath and John Lachs. New York: Cambridge University Press, 1982. Parenthetical citations refer to the pagination of Fichte's *Gesamtausgabe,* edited by I. H. Fichte, which is also indicated in the margins of this English translation.

Hegel, Georg Wilhelm Friedrich. *The Difference between Fichte's and Schelling's System of Philosophy.* Translated by H. S. Harris and Walter Cerf. Albany: State University of New York Press, 1977.

———. *Phenomenology of Spirit.* Translated by A. V. Miller. New York: Oxford University Press, 1977.

———. *Science of Logic.* Translated by A. V. Miller. New York: Humanities Press, 1976.

Kant, Immanuel. *Critique of Pure Reason.* Translated by Paul Guyer and Allen Wood. New York: Cambridge University Press, 1997. Parenthetical citations refer to the A and/or B pagination of the Akademie edition, which is also indicated in the margins of this English translation.

———. *Prolegomena to Any Future Metaphysics That Will Be Able to Come Forward as Science.* New ed, translated by Paul Carus and revised by James W. Ellington. Indianapolis: Hackett, 1977. Parenthetical citations refer to the pagination of the Akademie edition, which is also indicated in the margins of this English translation.

Leibniz, Gottfried Wilhelm. *Philosophical Essays.* Translated by Roger Ariew and Daniel Garber. Indianapolis: Hackett, 1989. The views described in this entry are to be found especially in Leibniz's "Monadology" and "Discourse on Metaphysics."

Marx, Karl. *Selected Writings.* Edited by David McClellan. Oxford: Oxford University Press, 1977.

Schelling, Friedrich Wilhelm Joseph. *System of Transcendental Idealism.* Translated by Peter Heath. Charlottesville: University of Virginia Press, 1978.

### SECONDARY SOURCES

Ameriks, Karl, ed. *Cambridge Companion to German Idealism.* Cambridge, U.K., and New York: Cambridge University Press, 2000.

Baur, Michael, and Daniel O. Dahlstrom, eds. *The Emergence of German Idealism.* Washington, D.C.: Catholic University of America Press, 1999.

Beiser, Frederick C. *The Fate of Reason: German Philosophy from Kant to Fichte.* Cambridge, Mass.: Harvard University Press, 1987.

———. *German Idealism: The Struggle against Subjectivism, 1781–1801.* Cambridge, Mass.: Harvard University Press, 2002.

Harris, H. S. *Hegel's Development.* Vol. 1: *Toward the Sunlight (1770–1801).* Vol. 2: *Night Thoughts (Jena 1801–1806).* Oxford: Clarendon, 1972, 1983.

Hylton, Peter. *Russell, Idealism, and the Emergence of Analytic Philosophy.* Oxford: Clarendon, 1990.

Neuhouser, Frederick. *Fichte's Theory of Subjectivity.* Cambridge, U.K., and New York: Cambridge University Press, 1990.

Pinkard, Terry. *German Philosophy 1760–1860.* Cambridge, U.K., and New York: Cambridge University Press, 2002.

Pippin, Robert B. *Hegel's Idealism: The Satisfactions of Self-Consciousness.* Cambridge, U.K., and New York: Cambridge University Press, 1989.

Taylor, Charles. *Hegel.* Cambridge, U.K., and New York: Cambridge University Press, 1975.

*Michael Baur*

# IDEAS, HISTORY OF.

The "history of ideas," phrase and concept, goes back almost three centuries to the work of J. J. Brucker (1696–1770) and Giambattista Vico (1668–1744) in the early eighteenth century, followed in the nineteenth century by Victor Cousin (1792–1867) and his eclectic and "spiritualist" philosophy. The story begins with Brucker's *Historia doctrina de ideis* (1723), which surveyed the Platonic doctrine, and Vico's criticism, which rejected the idea of a Greek monopoly on ideas. For Vico philosophy was joined to religion in a larger and older tradition of wisdom and theology, "queen of the sciences," which, he wrote, "took its start not when the philosophers began to reflect [*riflettere*] on human ideas" (as, he added, in the "erudite and scholarly little book" recently published by Brucker) "but rather when the first men began to think humanly." Thus the history of ideas began not with Plato but with myth and poetry, and this poetic wisdom was the basis not only for Plato's theory of ideas but also for Vico's "history of ideas," which was one face of his "New Science." Victor Cousin and his followers also took a broad view of the history of ideas, from antiquity down to modern times.

The history of ideas was given new life in the twentieth century, especially under the guidance of Arthur O. Lovejoy (1873–1962), one of the leading American philosophers of this time. Even before Lovejoy the phrase had been applied to a series of volumes published by the philosophy department of Columbia University between 1918 and 1935, which were devoted to "a field . . . in which it appears that ideas have a history and that their history is influenced by contact with lines of experience not commonly called philosophical." Lovejoy was more deliberate in applying the phrase to what he regarded as a new discipline distinct from the history of philosophy and the "new history," championed by James Harvey Robinson

(1863–1936) and his followers. The History of Ideas Club at the Johns Hopkins University (where Lovejoy taught), which began meeting from 1923, was the scene of papers given by many distinguished scholars. The classic work in the field that since 1919 Lovejoy had been calling the "history of ideas" was his William James lectures in Harvard, which were published in 1936 as *The Great Chain of Being.*

In the history of philosophy, according to Lovejoy, "is to be found the common seed-plot, the locus of initial manifestation in writing, of the greater number of the more fundamental and pervasive ideas, and especially of the ruling preconceptions, which manifest themselves in other regions of intellectual history" (p. 8). Yet Lovejoy also aspired to make the history of ideas an interdisciplinary enterprise, accommodating also literature, the arts, and the natural and social sciences. Nor were Lovejoy's "unit-ideas" limited to formal concepts, for he also wanted to accommodate "implicit or incompletely explicit assumptions or more or less unconscious mental *habits,* operating in the thought of an individual or a generation"; "dialectical motives," or methodological assumptions (nominalist or "organismic," for example) also inexpressible in propositions; metaphysical pathos (which awakened particular moods, for example); and ideas associated with particular sacred words and phrases intelligible through semantic analysis. All of these "ideas," which were regarded as the expression of whole groups and ages, were interpreted mainly by literary texts, especially poetry, from several national traditions, in keeping with the international and interdisciplinary thrust of Lovejoy's agenda.

In Lovejoy's program the history of ideas extended its sway over no fewer than twelve fields of study, beginning with the history of philosophy and including the history of science, religion, the arts, language, literature, comparative literature, folklore, economic, political, and social history, and the sociology of knowledge. These fields were all disciplinary traditions in themselves; the novelty was treating them in an interdisciplinary and synthetic way for larger purposes. For Lovejoy (writing in the dark year 1940) the final task of the history of ideas was "the gravest and most fundamental of our questions, 'What's the matter with man?'"

Lovejoy's colleague George Boas (1891–1980) expanded on the idealist implications of his methods. For Boas ideas are basic meanings that lie behind—and that evolve independently of—words. "The history of ideas is not confined to historical semantics," he wrote and "a dictionary aims only to give the meaning of words, not of ideas, and sometimes a single idea may have two names" (1969, p. 11). Yet these are assumptions that cannot be expressed or communicated except through words and historical semantics—a paradox that neither Lovejoy nor Boas resolved, or chose to confront. As they acknowledged, "The history of any idea, or complex of ideas, is best presented through the citation of the *ipsissima verba* of the writers who have expressed it."

Lovejoy's agenda found an institutional basis when the *Journal of the History of Ideas* (*JHI*) was founded in 1940, the first issue being prefaced by his "reflections," which suggested the orientation of this periodical more or less down to the present, especially in terms of "influences"—classical on modern thought, philosophical ideas and scientific discoveries on all areas of study, other pervasive ideas such as evolution, progress, primitivism, and various ideas of human nature, on historical understanding. This program was also reflected in the old *Dictionary of the History of Ideas,* edited in 1968 by Philip P. Wiener, first editor of the *JHI* (and succeeded, if not replaced, by the present work).

The history of ideas had counterparts in other European traditions, including German *Ideengeschichte, Geistesgeschichte,* and especially *Begriffsgeschichte,* and French *mentalités.* In the later twentieth century all of these approaches were affected by the "linguistic turn," which shifted attention from unproblematized "ideas" to language and discourse, since ideas, as Jorge Luis Borges (1889–1986) wrote, "are not, like marble, everlasting," and as Ludwig Wittgenstein (1889–1951) put it, "The limits of my language mean the limits of my world." Not that Lovejoy was unaware of such problems, for long before he had pointed out "the role of semantic shifts, ambiguities, and confusions, in the history of thought and taste," and he remarked that "nearly all of the great catchwords have been equivocal—or rather, multivocal." For this reason Lovejoy took pains to distinguish the varied meanings behind keywords such as *nature, progress, perfectibility, romanticism,* and *pragmatism,* as well as more inflammatory terms of ideological debate.

In the later twentieth century the history of ideas was invaded and shaken by a number of intellectual movements, including hermeneutics, reception theory, psych-history (and -biography), deconstruction, poststructuralism, constructivism, the new historicism, cultural materialism, the new cultural history, Derridean textualism, and various efforts of the "social history of ideas." Following the Nietzschean notion of "the interpretive character of all that happens" and the impact of literary theory, the history of ideas in its classic, spiritualist form also entered into decline, being superseded (except among philosophers) by intellectual history and deeper concerns of language and historical context as well as material culture.

One line of post-Marxian criticism was launched by Michel Foucault, who rejected a number of unreflective rubrics such as tradition, influence, development and evolution, spirit, pregiven unities and links, and especially the notion of the self-conscious agent, the "sovereign subject," and "authorial presence," which underlie the imaginary vehicle of "ideas." In the course of his intellectual iteration Foucault shifted from ideas to "discourse," from history to "archaeology," then to Nietzschean "genealogy," from development to "rupture," and from spirit or mentality to "episteme" and so to dismantle the history of ideas and to unmask the ideological surface of past and present culture. In his "grammatology" Jacques Derrida carried the critique of ideas beyond language to the world of textuality and intertextuality as the ultimate context of historicity and civil society. In the wake of such "litero-philosophy" many recent intellectual historians, including Hayden White, Dominick LaCapra, Hans Kellner, Roger Chartier, and Frank Ankersmit have distanced themselves from the old tradition of the history of ideas, though without entirely abandoning it.

Intellectual history can no longer be studied without attention to these warnings about unexamined premises of the human sciences. Yet "ideas" remain an essential shorthand for history as well as philosophy and other human sciences, and the history of ideas continues in channels both new and old, with methodological debates recurring across the range of interdisciplinary studies. And the critical pursuit of the history of ideas, or intellectual history, continues not only among historians of culture but also among scholars in the history of philosophy, literature, art, science, and the human sciences.

*See also* **Cultural History; Enlightenment; Historicism; Humanism; Language, Linguistics, and Literacy; Philosophy: Relations to Other Intellectual Realms; Science, History of; Tradition.**

BIBLIOGRAPHY

Boas, George. *The History of Ideas: An Introduction.* New York: Scribners, 1969.

Boas, George, et al. *Studies in Intellectual History.* Baltimore: Johns Hopkins Press, 1953. Includes studies by Arthur O. Lovejoy, George Boas, Harold Cherniss, Ludwig Edelstein, Leo Spitzer, Gilbert Chinard, Philip Wiener, Dorothy Stimson, Erich Auerbach, Carl Becker, Charles Beard, Niels Bohr, John von Neumann, Hans Baron, Owen Lattimore, Lionel Venturi, Samuel E. Morison, Americo Castro, Charles Singleton, Hajo Holborn, Don Cameron Allen, Basel Willey, Alexandre Koyré, and Eric Vogelin.

Foucault, Michel. *The Archeology of Knowledge.* Translated by A. M. Sheridan Smith. New York: Pantheon, 1972.

Kelley, Donald R. *The Descent of Ideas: The History of Intellectual History.* Aldershot, U.K., and Burlington, Vt.: Ashgate, 2002.

———. "Intellectual and Cultural History: The Inside and the Outside." *History of the Human Sciences* 15 (2002): 1–19.

———. "What Is Happening to the History of Ideas?" *Journal of the History of Ideas* 51 (1990): 3–25.

Kelley, Donald R., ed. *The History of Ideas: Canon and Variations.* Rochester, N.Y.: University of Rochester Press, 1990.

LaCapra, Dominick, and Steven L. Kaplan, eds. *Modern European Intellectual History: Reappraisals and New Perspectives.* Ithaca, N.Y.: Cornell University Press, 1982.

Lovejoy, Arthur O. *Essays in the History of Ideas* Baltimore: John Hopkins Press, 1948.

———. *The Great Chain of Being: A Study of the History of an Idea.* Cambridge, Mass.: Harvard University Press, 1936.

Lovejoy, Arthur O., and George Boas. *Primitivism and Related Ideas in Antiquity.* Baltimore: John Hopkins Press, 1935.

*Studies in the History of Ideas.* Edited by the Department of Philosophy of Columbia University. 3 vols. New York: Columbia University Press, 1918, 1925, 1935. Includes papers by John Dewey, Frederick Woodbridge, John Hermann Randall, Richard McKeon, Sidney Hook, Herbert Schneider, and Ernest Nagel.

Tobey, Jeremy L. *The History of Ideas: A Bibliographical Introduction.* Santa Barbara, Calif.: Clio, 1975–1977.

Wiener, Philip P., ed. *Dictionary of the History of Ideas.* 6 vols. New York: Scribners, 1968.

Wilson, Daniel J. *Arthur O. Lovejoy and the Quest for Intelligibility.* Chapel Hill: University of North Carolina Press, 1980.

*Donald R. Kelley*

# IDENTITY.

This entry includes two subentries.

*Identity of Persons*
*Personal and Social Identity*

## IDENTITY OF PERSONS

General problems about identity had been discussed long before the early modern period, but the problem of personal identity in the form in which it is so widely discussed today has its origin in John Locke's (1632–1704) chapter "Of Identity and Diversity," which he added to the second edition of his *Essay Concerning Human Understanding* (1694). Indeed, most early twenty-first-century views on the issue were anticipated in the seventeenth and eighteenth centuries.

## Seventeenth Century

A standard topic in medieval philosophy was the search for a principle of individuation—that is, the question about what it is that makes an individual (object or person) the individual it is and distinguishes it from all other individuals of the same kind. Indeed, the medieval disputes formed a major part of the background for the early modern discussions about the issue. But from about the middle of the seventeenth century onward most philosophers (for example, Thomas Hobbes, Robert Boyle, Locke) neglected the issue of individuation and focused on identity over time instead—that is, on the question about the requirements for an individual's remaining the same over time, although that individual may have undergone some change. Also, there was a marked shift in the discussions away from a primarily ontological to a more subjective treatment of the topic. Our concepts of those things whose identity is in question came to be regarded as crucial for dealing with problems of individuation and identity. In Locke this move is connected to his view that we cannot know the real essences of substances. For Locke the question of how much a thing can change without losing its identity can be answered only with respect to "nominal essences"—that is, with respect to our abstract or "sortal" ideas of those beings whose identity is under consideration.

Early modern philosophers considered the issue of the identity of persons over time to be of special importance, as it is central to theological issues such as the doctrine of life after death and related moral questions. But for most of those thinkers (such as René Descartes) who believed that the soul is an immaterial substance, there was no real problem of personal identity at all. They argued that personal identity consists in the identity of a mental substance or soul and that the identity of the mental substance is a direct consequence of its immaterial nature; it is because of its immateriality that the mind is not subject to change and remains the same through time.

Locke's account marked a decisive break with both the Cartesian and Scholastic positions, which identified either the soul or the man (or human being) with the person as a *res* whose individuality and identity is constituted independently of and prior to consciousness. Locke treated the special problem of personal identity in accordance with his general theory of identity. Therefore, he argued that we need to be clear about the concept of person in order to be able to determine what constitutes the identity of persons. And to be clear about the concept of person, we have to distinguish it from those of thinking substance or spirit, and of man or human being because each of these concepts carries with it different identity-criteria. The identity of the self as man (or human being) consists in the identity of the same organic body. As we do not know the real nature of the soul as substance, personal identity is accounted for in terms of what we know about the self through inner experience or consciousness uniting thoughts and actions. To consider the self as a person is to consider the self with regard to all those thoughts and actions of which it is conscious. Through consciousness we link present with past thoughts and actions, thereby constituting our personal identity. Only with respect to our personal identity are we morally and legally responsible for past actions. This is why Locke said that "person" is a "forensic" term.

Locke's theory aroused controversy soon after its first publication and inspired critics and defenders throughout the eighteenth century. One standard objection was the charge of circularity, urging that consciousness presupposes personal identity and therefore cannot constitute personal identity (John Sergeant, Joseph Butler). However, this charge presupposes the very thing Locke challenged, namely that the person is an object, thing, or substance to which consciousness relates as to an already individuated being. Another standard objection was that Locke's theory is inconsistent with the transitivity of identity because consciousness is not transitive (George Berkeley, Thomas Reid). In Germany, Locke's most important contemporary critic, Gottfried Wilhelm Leibniz (1646–1716), distinguished between the metaphysical identity of the self (as immaterial substance), which is secured a priori by its intrinsic nature or "complete notion," and the moral identity of the self (as person), which is constituted by consciousness (*Nouveaux Essais,* 1704). However, while Locke argued for keeping personal and substantial identity separate, Leibniz maintained that the (personal) identity required for morality could be preserved only by the metaphysical identity of the self as immaterial soul. Through Christian von Wolff (1679–1754), Leibnizian theory dominated philosophy at German universities until about the middle of the eighteenth century.

## Eighteenth Century

In eighteenth-century Britain, the most important treatment of the topic is by David Hume (1711–1776) in a famous section of his *Treatise of Human Nature* (1739). Hume rejects the traditional Cartesian view, arguing that through inner experience one can identify only a variety (a "bundle") of distinct perceptions; there is no experiential evidence of a soul that remains the same through time. Hume recognizes, however, that we nevertheless have a "natural propension" to ascribe unity and identity to the self. He argues that the idea of a unitary and identical mind is to the result of the imagination's connecting successive ideas in such a way as to create the belief that there is an identical self to which all these ideas belong. In the appendix to the *Treatise* Hume reflects critically on his own discussion of personal identity, relating the problem to his earlier explanation of "the principle of connexion" that "makes us attribute" identity to the mind. But Hume still holds that inner experience and observation reveal only collections or "bundles" of perceptions and that we nevertheless have a "natural propension" to ascribe identity to the self. Hume has mostly been read as reducing the self to its experiences or perceptions and as denying the existence of an essential self beyond the perceptions; but this reading has been criticized in recent commentary. While most eighteenth-century materialist thinkers simply adopted the Lockean view about personal identity, some (Michael Hissmann, Thomas Cooper) started from a Humean position but explicitly argued, unlike Hume, that there is no such a thing as personal identity at all.

Immanuel Kant's (1724–1804) approach, however, is different in kind from previous theories, as he was not concerned with empirical personal identity. Although Kant commented on empirical questions in some places, he did so in the light of his important distinction between empirical and what he calls "pure" or "transcendental" self-consciousness, or apperception, in the *Critique of Pure Reason* (1781). Unity and identity of self-consciousness are required for any thought to be possible at all. The identity of transcendental self-consciousness is "original" because it "precedes a priori all my determinate thought." Empirical consciousness, by contrast, "is in itself diverse and without relation to the identity of the subject." Kant makes use of this distinction in his critique of traditional rationalist metaphysics of the self or soul, known as "rational psychology." Its aim, according to Kant, is to show by way of a priori reasoning that (among other things) the self is a simple substance or soul and numerically identical at different points of time. But he argues that even the substantiality of the soul could not be inferred from the consciousness that I am the subject of all my thoughts. For knowledge of objects, including knowledge of the self as object, requires experience. In his moral philosophy Kant distinguished moral personality from both the empirical and the transcendental self and attempted to show that the idea of moral-practical freedom of the self has objective reality. In German idealism, too, the issue of empirical personal identity through time was not a major concern. However, both Kantian and empiricist examinations of consciousness and identity continued to appear simultaneously with the speculations of the idealists.

## Twentieth and Twenty-First Centuries

In the twentieth and early twenty-first centuries the issue of personal identity has continued to be a major theme especially in Anglo-American analytical philosophy. The debate is mainly between those who favor bodily continuity and those who favor psychological continuity as constituting personal identity. There is, however, considerable variety within the two main positions. Thus, some proponents of the psychological continuity view assign special importance to some rather than other psychological relations (such as memory). Since the 1970s the debate has focused on a revival of reductionist accounts of personal identity according to which selves are nothing over and above people's bodies and their mental lives. For Derek Parfit the common-sense view that regards personal identity as significant is mistaken. Rather, what matters are psychological

relations that are normally but not necessarily connected with the personal identity relation. By arguing that personal identity is not "what matters" Parfit undermines notions, such as responsibility, that presuppose personal identity. The debate about Parfit's reductionism has also sparked off a revival of Kantian arguments about identity. It is argued that the subject should be regarded primarily as an agent and not as a mere locus of experience, and that this emphasis on the concept of agency leads to nonreductionist conclusions about personal identity: the identity of the self as agent is a necessity of practical reason. Another important feature of recent debates in the reductionist context is the introduction of a four-dimensional view of persons. On this view, which goes back to Willard van Orman Quine (1953), persons (as well as physical objects) are extended not only in space but also in time and thus can be said to have temporal parts. That is to say, at one point of time only part of me exists, in the same way in which the parts of my body exist only in their respective spatial regions. The four-dimensionalist view has been criticized from within the analytical tradition as conceptually incoherent and as inconsistent with our common-sense way of talking and thinking about things and persons.

Feminist philosophers have argued that analytical philosophers' reliance on a distinction between psychological and bodily continuity is in effect "marginalizing the body," and they promote instead a view according to which selves are embodied, discontinuous, malleable, and socially constructed beings (James, pp. 31–32). The most influential account of personal identity in Continental philosophy has been developed by Paul Ricoeur in terms of the notion of narrativity. According to this account, our personal identity is not given to us or constituted metaphysically prior to or independently of our activity of making sense of our own self by telling ourselves a story about our own lives. Only this narrative links actions into one and the same person. The view according to which a person creates his or her identity by forming an autobiographical narrative has recently been taken up in analytical discussions.

*See also* **Identity: Personal and Social Identity; Responsibility; Society.**

### BIBLIOGRAPHY

James, Susan. "Feminism in Philosophy of Mind: The Question of Personal Identity." In *The Cambridge Companion to Feminism in Philosophy,* edited by Miranda Fricker and Jennifer Hornsby. Cambridge, U.K.: Cambridge University Press, 2000.

Korsgaard, Christine. "Personal Identity and the Unity of Agency: A Kantian Response to Parfit." *Philosophy and Public Affairs* 18 (1989): 101–132.

Martin, Raymond, and John Barresi, eds. *Personal Identity.* Oxford: Blackwell, 2002.

Noonan, Harold. *Personal Identity.* 2nd ed. London: Routledge, 2003.

Oderberg, David S. *The Metaphysics of Identity over Time.* New York: St. Martin's Press, 1993.

Parfit, Derek. *Reasons and Persons.* Oxford: Clarendon, 1984.

Quine, Willard van Orman. "Identity, Ostension, and Hypostasis." In his *From a Logical Point of View: Nine Logico-Philosophical Essays.* 2nd ed. rev. New York: Harper and Row, 1963.

Ricoeur, Paul. *Oneself As Another.* Translated by Kathleen Blamey. Chicago and London: University of Chicago Press, 1992.

Thiel, Udo. "Individuation." In *The Cambridge History of Seventeenth-Century Philosophy,* edited by Daniel Garber and Michael Ayers. Cambridge, U.K.: Cambridge University Press, 1998.

———. "Personal Identity." In *The Cambridge History of Seventeenth-Century Philosophy,* edited by Daniel Garber and Michael Ayers. Cambridge, U.K.: Cambridge University Press, 1998.

———. "Self-Consciousness and Personal Identity." In *The Cambridge History of Eighteenth-Century Philosophy,* edited by K. Haakonssen. Cambridge, U.K.: Cambridge University Press, 2005.

*Udo Thiel*

## PERSONAL AND SOCIAL IDENTITY

Although identity has deeps roots in social psychology, sociology, bridges between them (e.g., symbolic interactionism), and related disciplines, the explicit distinction between personal and social identity, within social psychology at least, can be traced to J. C. Turner's seminal article "Towards a Cognitive Redefinition of the Group" (1982). This formed the basis for self-categorization theory (SCT), in which personal and social identity is most explicitly articulated.

The concept of social identity had been developed earlier in social identity theory (SIT), a theory of intergroup relations that attempted to define a level of self-definition (social identity), that corresponded to the level of analysis of intergroup behavior in intergroup contexts. To this end Henri Tajfel conceived of an interpersonal-intergroup continuum that captured the range of situations relevant to behavior as individuals versus group members. In intergroup contexts the social identity corresponding to membership of the relevant group or social category structured perception, being, and behavior. Tajfel defined social identity as "that part of an individual's self-concept which derives from his membership of a social group (or groups), together with the value and emotional significance attached to this" (p. 63). This was an important step in showing that being and behavior did not always reflect a fixed or individual self, but that self-definition varies with social context, becoming defined at the group level in intergroup contexts. As such, SIT represented an important and welcome shift from the individualistic and essentialist analyses of intergroup relations (discrimination, prejudice, intergroup conflict) that had gone before (for instance, in terms of the authoritarian personality, frustration-aggression, and so forth). The notion that in intergroup contexts individuals see others, and indeed themselves, primarily (and in extreme cases, purely) as representatives of the salient social categories at play—a process later labeled "depersonalization" by self-categorization theory—is an important and lasting contribution of SIT.

Strictly speaking, however, social identity theory continued to conceive of social identity as part of "the" self-concept (as the quote from Tajfel suggests) and this has also tended to be how approaches to the self within social psychology generally viewed social identity or the "collective self." The contribution

of self-categorization theory (SCT) was to address the issue of levels of self more directly and make an explicit distinction between personal and social (read "group level") identity, or levels of self-categorization. Although SIT had talked of interpersonal contexts, it did not refer to personal identity as such, but only to individual level behavior. Many subsequent writers and researchers have however (erroneously) attributed the notion of personal identity to social identity theory. Although it may have been there in spirit, if not in explicit form, Tajfel's interests lay primarily in developing the concept of social identity, so he bracketed this off from more general issues of self and self theory.

The consequence of the personal/social identity distinction of SCT was threefold. First it disputed the notion of a unitary or fixed self-structure ("the" self concept). Second, it explicitly avoided the privileging of either personal or group identity (group identity does not have to be nested within a more general individual self-concept), seeing them as dependent on context (an interactionist position). Third, just as there may be multiple social identities or group self-categorizations corresponding to situated group memberships, in principle there may also be multiple "personal" identities corresponding to the range of situations, roles, and relationships in which individuals find themselves.

This last point has rarely been stated and is perhaps least generally understood. Even among users of SCT, personal identity is still widely seen as a unitary construct, the global sum of the individual's characteristics, at least those residual characteristics not tied to particular group memberships. However, this more unitary conceptualization of personal identity is difficult to distinguish from more essentialist notions of personality, which treat the individual's makeup as relatively fixed, stable, and insensitive to context. From the perspective of self-categorization theory at least, there is no reason why the contextual sensitivity of group identity should not apply equally to personal identity, making personal identities just as multiple in principle (if not more so, given the limited range of social categories) than social qua group identities. From this analysis there is also a strong sense in which both social and personal identities are "social" to the degree that they may be constructed and constituted in situ by the local comparative context.

### Contextualism, Interactionism

The idea that personal and group identity can be seen in a radically contextualist and antiessentialist way was presaged by the ideas of the sociologist Georg Simmel. From a traditional self-theory perspective one might conceive of the individual self as being defined by a list of traits, as well as behaviors, roles, group memberships, and so forth. At one level it might be tempting to define "personality traits" as part of personal identity, and group memberships as part of social identity. However, following Simmel (and SCT), this would again depend on the social context. The trait intelligence could be a personal property (especially where it distinguishes the individual from other individuals), however it could also form the basis for a (situated) group identity (for example, in distinguishing intellectuals from "philistines"). Similarly, a group membership label (such as a chess player or a Scot) may be seen as a feature of personal identity when there is no systematic grouping of people with these features in common in the current social context. In an interpersonal or intragroup context (for instance, a cruise party) these group labels become features that allow individuals to see themselves as individually distinct from others, helping to define personal identity. However, when the characteristics are shared with others, and used to differentiate from an outgroup, they become group defining features of social identity.

This analysis also points to the mechanism by which social identity (but also personal identity) becomes salient. Previously, following social identity theory, social identity was regarded as being salient in intergroup contexts (such as during intergroup conflict) although this rather begs the question of what counts as an intergroup context. SCT offered a cognitive/perceptual analysis of identity salience based on Jerome Bruner's notion "perceptual readiness" (or "accessibility") and "fit" applied to categorization processes generally. Following Penelope Oakes, who further developed Bruner's concept, one source of category salience is, therefore, the degree to which a group is socially differentiated from another in terms of its attributes. For example, a group that is sociable but not intellectual would differ from a group that is intellectual and unsociable. The social comparison would be high in comparative fit (or *meta-contrast,* to use Turner's term) and the social category should become salient. If these group differences are associated with known stereotypes, then the social categorization would also display high "normative" fit, further enhancing the salience of group differences. For example, a group of hairdressers (sociable but not intellectual) differs from a group of chess players (intellectual but not sociable), in an expected way (stereotypically).

Importantly, as Simmel's analysis also suggests, both identities and their contents (self- or ingroup stereotypes) are highly context sensitive. Whether an Asian woman categorizes herself (or is categorized by others as such) as Asian or female may depend on the outgroup present (males or Caucasians, for example). Whether psychology students see themselves as sociable or intellectual may vary depending on whether they compare themselves with physics students or school leavers.

Social stereotypes (as shared constructs about groups) are ostensibly less applicable to the mechanisms in which personal identity (and relevant content) is made salient, but the comparative principle remains the same. A personal identity and its particular contents will become salient through differentiating comparisons with others in the social frame of reference (individuals may see themselves as powerful and competent in comparison with their younger siblings, but the opposite in comparison with a university professor).

### Commitment, Culture, and the Relation between Personal and Social Identity
This analysis also starts to reveal the close relationship between personal and social identities. From the perspective of self-categorization theory, similar processes apply in activating personal and social identities but at a different level of analysis or

abstraction. Self-categorization theory distinguishes subordinate (interpersonal), intermediate (intergroup), and superordinate (supragroup or interspecies) levels of analysis. The principle of "functional antagonism" states that any given level of categorization, to the extent that it becomes salient, will inhibit other competing identities. This is seen as controversial in certain respects, suggesting that people cannot simultaneously countenance more than one identity, seemingly ruling out dual or compound identities. However, this is less problematic when salience is conceived as a relatively automatic and ephemeral process that can shift quickly with comparative context, and be overridden by conscious awareness and strategic processes. Moreover, in principle there is no limit on the complexity or idiosyncrasy of identities, and SCT explicitly eschews the sociologistic assumption that the imposed social categories (those that the researcher or experimenter prescribes or might assume are operative) are the ones that are genuinely psychologically relevant for the participant in research. This is an empirically contingent question.

This analysis suggests that context largely determines the activation of personal or social identity. It also suggests a somewhat divorced relationship between personal and social identity, enhanced by the functional antagonism metaphor. However, there are likely to be strong individual differences and individual inputs into this process, which is consistent with SCT as an interactionist theory in the sense of person-situation interaction. One important factor that is likely to determine the activation of levels of identity, and specific social identities is the concept of commitment. At the group level, commitment refers to the degree of identification with a particular group, and high identification is likely to enhance the accessibility of that self-categorization, even when the consequences of embracing this identity is negative or threatening. This is important because it is precisely when the group is threatened that it most needs its group members to support it. It is also important, however, to see group identification in a dynamic way, as an outcome of, as well as an input into, group process; otherwise, the metatheory reduces back to the individualism of personality theories.

Just as commitment to group identities can affect the social identities that are activated and used, so commitment to personal identity (or identities) can be argued to do the same. Indeed some have argued that there is a "motivational primacy" that generally favors personal identity over group identity, and, more contingently, others have argued that the personal self or identity is inherent to Western societies. The motivational primacy debate has argued that the individual self is more basic than the collective self because of evidence that people switch to a social identity when the personal identity is threatened, but not vice versa. However, this research can be criticized on a number of levels. First, the research tends to pit a *generalized* individual self against *specific* social identities, confounding comparisons. Second, as the response of high identifiers faced with threat to their group identities has shown, lack of switching when threatened can be read as evidence of commitment, and not that the identity is secondary. Some research that attempts to calibrate the general importance of personal versus social identities, although at odds with the contextualist spirit of SCT, also provides evidence that the general priority given to personal identity compared to social identity in Western countries, is not true of all categorizations and cultures.

This point serves as a reminder that there is much cross-cultural work that sheds important light on the personal-social identity distinction and the complex and contingent relation between them. Although SCT has the most explicit and perhaps radical analysis of the personal versus social identity distinction it is not the only theoretical framework or research program to address this distinction, although the terminology is not always identical. Many researchers refer to the individual versus collective self or the private versus collective self. In particular, researchers interested in cultural differences in social relations and the self, particularly between individualist and collectivist cultures, have been keen to emphasize forms of selfhood that are less individualistic, less grounded in the Cartesian notions of the preformed individual self, as separate, independent, egoistic, and so forth. However, these approaches do not always distinguish between the personal and social identity, so much as blur the boundary between the two, suggesting that in collectivist cultures the connection of the individual (qua personal identity), is much more chronically bound up with and connected to the group (the family, work relations, and other social networks). It is not clear, therefore, that the personal-social identity distinction of self-categorization theory has quite the same analytic resonance in say, Chinese culture.

In the tradition of social cognition research some of these approaches see personal and social identities as separate cognitive structures (as representing different stores or "baskets" to use the analogy of D. Trafimow et al.). This argument forms a challenge for SCT, which argues that the content of these two levels of identity is difficult to pin down because they are so context-dependent and dynamic.

## Caveats, Criticism, and Extensions

One criticism that is sometimes leveled at the self-categorization analysis of group identities in particular (but by implication also personal identity) is its cognitive and perceptual focus, and a consequent neglect of motivational and affective processes. Second, constructionist themes that recognize individual and collective activity around defining identities and bringing them to life are also relatively neglected. It is worth pausing to consider these issues.

The (individual) self-literature identifies a series of self-motives or needs (such as self-evaluation and self-enhancement, but also accuracy motives, such as self-verification) that can be evoked to complement and question a purely perceptualist reading of personal and social identity. Self-motives such as accuracy and self-verification are well captured by the emphasis in SCT on social reality as a basis for social perception and stereotyping. Self-evaluation and self-enhancement motives are less clearly apparent in SCT although enhancement and positive distinctiveness motives at the group level are well addressed in social identity theory. SIT proposes that, at least to the extent that people internalize their social identities and identify with the group to some degree, that they will strive for a positive group distinctiveness in which their own group is seen as distinct and better than a comparison group.

This idea has been operationalized as the self-esteem hypothesis, which has generated much research but remains somewhat controversial because it is not clear whether the positive group distinctiveness premise can or should be reduced to the more individualistic concept of self-esteem. Social identity theory does predict that groups will tend to differentiate themselves most strongly from similar outgroups in order to gain or maintain group distinctiveness. This raises potentially interesting conflicts with SCT, which seems to imply intergroup differentiation resulting from group difference (i.e., comparative fit, meta-contrast).

Marilynn Brewer's optimal distinctiveness theory (ODT) is another theoretical approach to personal and group identity that addresses distinctiveness motives. ODT defines distinctiveness here in terms of relative group size rather than in relation to the similarity of out groups as in SIT. It argues that distinctive groups simultaneously address the need to be included and to differentiate oneself from others, with the result that relatively small (distinctive) groups are best placed to address both these needs.

Whereas social identity theory and optimal distinctiveness theories provide a motivational dimension to group being behavior, primarily around distinctiveness processes, intergroup emotion theory (IET) attempts to introduce a more differentiated analysis of the emotional relations between groups that colors the nature of intergroup relations and the specific behaviors (or *action tendencies,* to use the language of emotion theorists) evoked by particular intergroup relationships (i.e., governed by an appraisal or status or power differences). As such, once again there is an attempt to extend the analysis of emotion operating at the interpersonal level (and this relation to personal identity) to the intergroup level as applied to social identity. This analysis suggests that as members of groups, individuals have emotional reactions to other people in terms of their group memberships. This analysis has been helpful in informing the subtly different forms of discrimination and prejudice that can occur, in terms of anger, contempt, envy, schadenfreude, and so forth.

Another criticism that can be leveled at the cognitive-perceptual emphasis of SCT, but also many related approaches to group identity within social psychology, is the danger of reifying social categories (and thus self-categorizations). Even though social categories are seen as radically tied to context and comparison in SCT, there seems little room for the agents (individuals and indeed groups) in determining categorizations that appear to predefine comparisons. The agency of individuals in helping to construct and shape identities, to negotiate these in context, and to change their position and meaning through collective struggle is not always captured through the perceptualist prism of theorizing. Once again, this is more clearly addressed in social identity theory, which was conceived as a theory of social change, and indeed where Tajfel conceived of social identity (in addition to the substantive definition offered earlier) as an intervening variable in the process of social change.

However, it could be argued that the nature of social identity—as being transformed as well as being transformative—is not fully acknowledged or theorized in the social identity approach. This is perhaps not so surprising because self-categorization theorists in particular have tended to define their project in opposition to radical versions of social constructionism, which, in line with postmodernist thinking, seem to question the social reality that is such a strong basis of the social identity approach. However, some theorists in the SIT/SCT tradition have tried to show that social categories and social identities are not givens but are often contested and fought over, especially in contexts of political conflict and struggle. This can then radically transform the meaning of social identities, and indeed can have implications for personal identity (one's sense of oneself abstracted from the group context). In other words, it is possible to think of social and personal identities not just as descriptive statements of comparative content in the status quo ("being"), but prescriptive attempts to change one's context and indeed the meaning of self or identity ("becoming"), that themselves become transformed through social action.

*See also* **Identity: Identity of Persons; Identity, Multiple; Person, Idea of the.**

**BIBLIOGRAPHY**

Brewer, Marilynn B. "The Social Self: On Being the Same and Different at the Same Time." *Personality and Social Psychology Bulletin* 17 (1991): 475–482.

Bruner, Jerome S. "On Perceptual Readiness." *Psychological Review* 64 (1957): 123–152.

Oakes, Penelope J. "The Salience of Social Categories." In *Rediscovering the Social Group,* edited by John C. Turner et al. New York: Blackwell, 1987.

Sedikides, Constantine, and Marilynn B. Brewer, eds. *Individual Self, Relational Self, Collective Self: Partners, Opponents, or Strangers?* Philadelphia: Psychology Press, 2001.

Simmel, Georg. *The Web of Group Affiliations.* Glencoe, Ill.: Free Press, 1955.

Simon, B. "Self and Group in Modern Society: Ten Theses on the Individual Self and the Collective Self." In *The Social Psychology of Stereotyping and Group Life,* edited by Russell Spears et al., 318–335. Cambridge, Mass.: Blackwell, 1997.

Spears, Russell. "The Interaction between the Individual and the Collective Self: Self-Categorization in Context." In *Individual Self, Relational Self, Collective Self: Partners, Opponents, or Strangers?,* edited by Constantine Sedikides and Marilynn B. Brewer, 171–198. Philadelphia: Psychology Press, 2001.

Tajfel, Henri. "Social Psychology of Intergroup Relations." *Annual Review of Psychology* 33 (1982): 1–39.

Tajfel, Henri, ed. *Differentiation between Social Groups: Studies in the Social Psychology of Intergroup Relations.* London: Academic Press, 1978.

Tajfel, Henri, and Turner, J. C. "The Social Identity Theory of Intergroup Behavior." In *Psychology of Intergroup Relations,* edited by Stephen Worchel and William G. Austin, 7–24. Chicago: Nelson Hall, 1986.

Trafimow, D., H. C. Triandis, and Sharon G. Goto. "Some Tests of the Distinction Between the Private Self and the Collective Self." *Journal of Personality and Social Psychology* 60 (1991): 649–655.

Turner, J. C. "Towards a Cognitive Redefinition of the Group." In *Social Identity and Intergroup Relations,* edited by Henri Tajfel, 15–40. New York: Cambridge University Press, 1982.

*Russell Spears*

# IDENTITY, MULTIPLE.

This entry includes three subentries:

*Overview*
*Asian-Americans*
*Jewish Multiple Identity*

## OVERVIEW

Within Western thought the subject—that is, the self as a thinking, feeling, psycho-physiological entity—has been traditionally defined as a centered consciousness, characterized and unified by one self-defining identity. Within this tradition, a centered subjectivity was long thought to exist and function independently of the social contexts surrounding it, without significant influence from those contexts. Later, the centered subject came to be regarded as socially constructed in and through social contexts, yet still rendered whole by a single self-defining identity or identity-grounding element that would center the subject in any and all circumstances.

Multiple identity, on the other hand, is one specific conceptualization of the more general idea that the subject is not centered, but instead decentered and multiple. Such a decentered subjectivity can encompass many different, perhaps even contradictory, identities, and is not necessarily centered by one self-defining or "true" identity. Rather, since identities are socially constructed and constructing, their specific number and character are a function of the various forms of socialization that forge the subject over time, as well as of the lifeworlds in which he or she participates. Consequently, the multiple identities of a subject (both social and personal) are relevant to and engaged in specific social milieux and are manifest in a context-dependent manner. Since subjects engage different and multiple identities in response to the social contexts in which they find themselves at a given moment, no one identity is a priori or necessarily more central, self-defining, or true than any other.

### The Critique of the Subject

The idea of a decentered subjectivity composed of multiple, socially constructed and context-dependent identities began to emerge during the late nineteenth and early twentieth centuries in the writings of a variety of thinkers including William James (1842–1910), Sigmund Freud (1856–1939), and the critical theorists Max Horkheimer (1895–1973) and Theodor Adorno (1903–1969). These and other thinkers initiated a widespread reevaluation of the philosophy of the subject in the West, and during the twentieth century the "critique of the subject" was debated across a wide array of academic disciplines. Over time the general idea of a decentered multiple subject gained increasingly wide acceptance. With this shift, more specific conceptualizations of it, such as mestiza consciousness and

*Los das Fridas* (*Me Twice,* 1939) by Frida Kahlo. Kahlo's painting illustrates her feeling of being divided between the pull of tradi-tional values and her more worldly, progressive persona. Many contemporary Mexican-Americans struggle with issues of identity in re-lation to cultural dichotomies. PHOTOGRAPH BY BOB SCHALKWIJK. COPYRIGHT © 2004 BANCO DE MEXICO DIEGO RIVERA & FRIDA KAHLO MUSEUMS TRUST. AV. CINCO DE MAYO NO. 2, COL. CENTRO, DEL. CUAUHTEMOC 06059, MEXICO, D.F.

multiple identity, emerged to attempt to integrate the multi-plicity, diversity, and contradiction into the philosophical un-derstandings of the subject and identity. Such theoretical formulations have generated new philosophical questions, ques-tions that still remain matters of inquiry and debate.

***Early modern conceptions of the subject.*** Early modern conceptions of a centered subjectivity can be traced in part to Cartesian dualism in which the mind and its thinking essence were seen as functioning independently of the body and the material world (René Descartes; *Discourse on Method,* 1637; and *Meditations,* 1641). The writings of Immanuel Kant (1724–1804) also oriented modern thought on the subject. On traditional readings of his philosophy, Kant defined the self as a fully self-transparent, self-conscious, self-consistent, and transcendent free will—what is commonly understood as an autonomous ego. For Kant, the autonomy of the subject depended on the self-legislation of the will (i.e., on living by rules that one gives to oneself). Thus the Kantian subject possessed free will only to the extent that the social dynamics surrounding the self did not dictate its thoughts and actions. Ideally, therefore, this Kantian noumenal or transcendental self was guided or centered by a consistent, rational set of universal principles that the subject held independent of, perhaps even despite, its surroundings. In this sense, the Kantian subject could be described as unencumbered (not socially constructed or embedded), centered (as a single psychic entity made whole by its orientation to the universal principles of right), and unitary (internally consistent, with uniformity and conformity toward its centering elements).

### Modernist critiques of the centered subject.
Critiques of the Kantian account of the subject emerged from a variety of quarters, on a range of grounds. Often referred to collectively as the "critique of the subject," these criticisms are not, as is sometimes thought, limited to postmodernist critiques of the Enlightenment project. On the contrary, modernist thinkers who endorsed many Enlightenment principles were among the earliest to reject the Kantian account of the subject. The writings of Max Horkheimer and Theodor Adorno, for example, fall into this category. Like others in the Frankfurt School and Critical Theory tradition, Horkheimer and Adorno retained the Enlightenment's commitment to rational reflection as a critical means to social justice and social transformation. Yet, they also rejected the exclusionary logic of Enlightenment reason.

In their critique of Enlightenment reason and the conception of the unencumbered, centered, and unitary subject, Horkheimer and Adorno contend in the *Dialectic of Enlightenment* (1947) that the "Enlightenment behaves toward things as a dictator toward men. He knows them in so far as he can manipulate them [and] . . . [i]n the metamorphosis the nature of things, as a substratum of domination, is revealed as always the same" (p. 9). For Horkheimer and Adorno, this logic of identity—this logic of "same" within the Enlightenment tradition and its conceptions of the "unity of the subject" and "its correlate, the unity of nature" (p. 10) homogenized and manipulated the self and nature through a denial of the multiplicity and chaos inherent in both. They argued that by using a logic of identity to mask the unruly multiplicity of the self and nature and by vilifying that multiplicity as unreason, Enlightenment thought ultimately distorted and concealed the very human subjectivity that it sought to advance and protect. Extending this argument to his critique of the Kantian subject, Adorno stressed in *Negative Dialectics* that a viable account of the self must attend to the connections between ethical action and the "nonidentity" of the self. For Adorno, the diversity, multiplicity, and nonidentity of the self distinguishes it from the social forces that form it, for "[w]hatever stirs in a man contradicts his unity" (p. 277).

### Freudian and psychoanalytic critiques of the subject.
Horkheimer and Adorno's critiques of the centered subject were not unrelated to those of Sigmund Freud who, like Horkheimer and Adorno, remained committed to various aspects of the Enlightenment project while nonetheless rejecting the Enlightenment conception of the centered, unified subject. Freud's theory of the unconscious differentiated the self into the ego, id, and superego, and divided it also into the conscious and unconscious. This differentiation rejects the idea

that the subject is centered by a single, fully self-conscious, self-transparent, or self-defining identity and ego. Freud, in short, "decentered" the self by theorizing its fundamentally divided character. Later, Jacques Lacan (1901–1981) influentially echoed and extended Freud's critique of the centered, unitary, and unencumbered autonomous ego. Lacan stressed that by asserting the ego's mastery of the world through its separation from the world, the idea of a unified ego served as a shield from reality. This comforting shield—the fantasy of ego—imposed a false unity and rigidity onto the self that hid the more multiple and fragmented character of subjectivity.

### Postmodernist and poststructuralist influences.
Freudian and Critical Theory critiques of the subject represent attempts to usefully amend, rather than abandon all aspects of the Enlightenment project. Such critiques decentered the subject by regarding it as divided in character. They also insisted on its multiplicity and its chaos, thus rejecting the idea of the subject as a uniform or self-consistent whole. In addition, postmodernist and poststructuralist critiques of centered subjectivity have been advanced within a wide variety of scholarly fields. These critiques of the subject have often been combined with more general rejection of the Enlightenment project with its insistence on universal truth, reason, necessary human progress, and in particular the tendency of Enlightenment thought to privilege a white male European worldview as the universal standard of truth and rationality.

Among the earliest and most influential of these critiques of the centered subject were those of Friedrich Nietzsche (1844–1900), who related the "chaos in oneself" to the process of self-remaking, a self-overcoming that he took to be the key to escaping the homogenizing morality of the West's religious and Enlightenment traditions (1966). For Nietzsche, subjectivity is characterized by diversity—and it is the subject that can secure human freedom and excellence over time.

## The Linguistic Turn and the Social Construction of the Subject
Deep shifts in language philosophy are also among the converging intellectual currents that have fostered a rethinking of the subject as decentered and multiple. Wittgensteinian language philosophy, as well as the works of postmodernist and poststructuralist thinkers such as Jacques Derrida (b. 1930) and Michel Foucault (1926–1984), insist on the centrality of language as the necessary and primary medium of thought and action. With this in view, the formation of social relations and groups, cultural norms and practices, and ultimately the formation of subjectivity itself, is seen as a function of language-mediated processes. This linguistic turn has challenged past philosophical dependence on "universal truths" and "essential" or "natural" characteristics in favor of the ongoing social construction of the self and society as specificities in time and place.

In this way, the linguistic turn contributed significantly to the reconfiguration of the subject by casting it as something formed by, embedded in, and cogenerating of complex sets of language-mediated social dynamics. In turn, this view of subjectivity suggests, by extension, that where the subject and its identities are formed in and through multiple and diverse social dynamics, and that the subject will, likewise, become multiple and diverse in character. Still further, to argue that the subject is entirely and *only* a product of language-mediated social construction suggests that there is nothing else constitutive of subjectivity beyond what is socially given to it in and through the linguistic, and partially material, processes of social construction. So divergent from Western tradition is this last point that is has been, and at times remains, a matter of particular controversy.

***Feminist, ethnic, and postcolonial formulations of multiple identity.*** In addition to the philosophical traditions discussed above, the idea of a decentered and multiple subject enjoys wide currency in Ethnic Studies, as well as feminist and postcolonial thought. Collated here under the term "multiple identity," specific conceptualizations of a decentered and multiple subjectivity in these scholarly domains utilize a wide diversity of terminology and varying theoretical formulations, yet often display broad similarities. The tradition is long. W. E. B. Du Bois (1868–1963) first linked the experience of multiple identity to the history of interracial conflict in *The Souls of Black Folk,* published in 1903. Calling it a state of "double consciousness" Du Bois described black subjectivity as something in which "[o]ne ever feels his twoness—an American, a Negro; two souls, two thoughts, two unreconciled strivings; two warring ideals in one dark body, whose dogged strength alone keeps it from being torn asunder" (p. 17).

For Du Bois, this grappling with the identity contradictions of double consciousness replicate, within the microcosm of the subject, the large-scale societal and political struggles of blacks against their subordination by whites. Du Bois highlighted how these struggles profoundly shaped the formation of the black subject—the very souls of blacks—because in the social context of America, racial subordination barred black men and women from understanding themselves through the lens of their own ethnic group alone. Rather the subordination of blacks "only lets him [the black man or woman] see himself through the revelation of the other world" (p. 16); the "white world" with its norms of racial privilege and exclusion against which the "black world" is constructed. Du Bois wrote, "it is a peculiar sensation, this double-consciousness, this sense of always looking at one's self through the eyes of others, of measuring one's soul by the tape of a world that looks on in amused contempt and pity" (pp. 16–17).

Du Bois's idea of double consciousness still resonates at times in the works of contemporary black thinkers and in writings on racism in America. In addition, postcolonial thinkers have extended similar logic to the formation of subjectivity in the context of colonial oppression. Developing conceptions of "hybridity," for example, postcolonial theorists such as Homi Bhabha have focused on the way that colonial and postcolonial dynamics have contributed to the politicized and diverse social construction of specific subjectivities resulting in multiple and often contradictory forms of identification.

The idea of a decentered and multiple subject also finds favorable expression in a wide array of works by feminist thinkers. Over the past twenty years many feminist theorists working from various perspectives have stressed the "fragmentation" of the subject and the ability of subjects to live in "multiple subject positions." Among them, Latina feminist thinkers Gloria Anzaldúa (1924–2004) and María Lugones have developed the concept of "mestiza consciousness," which describes the conditions that forge multiple identities and the experiences of living them in everyday life. Their particular formulation has been taken up by other philosophers to help address the philosophical questions that yet remain with respect to decentered subjectivity.

## New Philosophical Challenges

The breadth of scholarship utilizing some formulation of multiple identity has firmly established its place in contemporary Western thought. However, many philosophical and practical questions regarding decentered multiple subjectivity remain to be fully theorized, and the general rethinking of the subject, which began more than a century ago, is still perhaps best thought of as an ongoing project. For example, some commentators continue to conflate the idea of a decentered and multiple subject with the clinical manifestations of a rare and controversial psychological disorder called Dissociative Identity Disorder. Close scrutiny of the clinical evidence indicates that there is little overlap between philosophical theories of a decentered subjectivity and such disorders. Yet, the use of imprecise terms such as "fragmented" and "multiple" continues to invite such comparisons, and to muddy the waters.

Such issues have justified calls for more detailed theories of decentered subjectivity. Feminist theorists Jessica Benjamin and Jane Flax (both with a background in clinical psychology) some time ago stressed that existence of disorders involving extremely severe fragmentation (i.e., a nearly total lack of interconnection) among identities, although very rare, makes it essential to distinguish such ailments from new theoretical frameworks through more precise theorizing of the decentered multiple subject. They have thus challenged theorists to identify exactly what elements make a decentered and multiple subjectivity hang together as a functional psycho-physiological unit. If the decentered subject is not centered by a single identity, what specifically is the relationship among the subject's different identities? Is there something that makes multiple identities cohere as a subjectivity, and if so, what does that coherence, if any, hinge on?

Similar questions are also posed by the work of those philosophers who accept the idea of a socially embedded or "situated" and constructed subject, but who continue to reject the idea of a fully decentered and multiple subjectivity. From such a perspective, the socially constructed subject remains centered by some dimension that, once it is produced through linguistically mediated processes, stands as a self-defining and self-centering element that is not context dependent, but instead consistently centers the subject within all of the various social contexts that it enters. Among those who take this general approach, the precise element that is thought to center the subject differs widely. Some regard the situated self as centered by a self-defining self-narrative. Others center and unify the constructed subject with a single identity or a single moral orientation that guides the self. Still others see the subject as centered through a procedure of "choosing" the subject, which renders some element as a central or true identity. A very few others continue to hold the view that there is some centering element of subjectivity that is prelinguistic.

Recognizing the need for further clarity, a number of feminist philosophers have persisted in highlighting the subject's multiplicity and complexity by working to further refine our understanding of the relationship among the multiple identities within a decentered subjectivity. One promising approach to this can be found in Latina feminist philosophy, and particularly in the work of María Lugones. Lugones has drawn upon and extends the work of Gloria Anzaldúa, whose conception of "mestiza consciousness" has been one of the most widely influential accounts of a decentered and multiple subjectivity to date. In brief, in *Borderlands/La Frontera: The New Mestiza,* Gloria Anzaldúa theorizes "mestiza consciousness" as arising from the social construction of subjectivity in and through different sets of social relations including, but not limited to, relations of class, ethnicity, race, gender, sexuality, nationality, religion, region, language community, and subculture. Living thus embedded in a multitude of conflicting social relations of culture, class, and sexuality, Anzaldúa's *mestiza* gains a multiple or "dual identity" with which the subject lives in multiple lifeworlds. Similar to Du Bois's double consciousness, Anzaldúa describes, as an example, how Mexican Americans are often constructed by and identify (at least partly) with both Mexican and Anglo American cultures—often struggling with the prevailing hierarchies between those two cultural systems. The result is a Chicano/a subjectivity with multiple identities produced within the interplay two interrelated cultures.

Such multiple identities are different, distinct, and sometimes even contradictory. Yet, they can also intersect in ways associated with the societal level dynamics that constructed those identities, including perhaps relations of subordination and privilege, conflict, contradiction, and differentials of power, access, and voice. The multiple identities constructed in and through these elements are often related in ways that mirror those constructing elements. The mestiza is forced by these dynamics (as components of identity formation and identity performance) to engage with the conflicting worldviews and complexities that comprise her multiple identities. Anzaldúa's mestiza thus moves among and negotiates her multiple identities at times by shifting among them, at other times by syncretizing competing perspectives into positions greater that than the "severed parts" from which they were forged. The ability to negotiate, to move between, or to syncretize the different value systems of her multiple identities is what Anzaldúa calls *la Facultad.*

Working with Anzaldúa's conception of mestiza consciousness, María Lugones emphasizes in "Purity, Impurity, and Separation" (1994) that the multiple identities that make up mestiza consciousness are not entirely fragmented but rather are interconnected and mutually conditioning even as they remain distinct (a point consistent with the common feminist emphasis on the intersection of race, class, and gender). Like Anzaldúa, Lugones stresses the complexity of the social relations in which the subject is embedded and constructed. She underscores in still stronger terms than Anzaldúa however, how these social relations of subordination and privilege intersect.

Philosopher Cheshire Calhoun has applied Lugones's work on mestiza consciousness to theorize exactly how a decentered subjectivity that engages multiple identities in a context dependent manner can possess agency and act with integrity toward the sometimes competing moral and political value systems that inhere in those multiple identities. Diana Meyers has also employed Lugones's approach to the intersection of multiple identities. Calling it "intersectional identity," Meyers has argued that Lugones's model of subjectivity offers an important basis from which to generate a new conception of autonomy that departs from the Enlightenment tradition and integrates key feminist tenets.

## Implications of Multiple Identity

If full conceptualization of multiple identity is still a philosophical work in progress, then even more wide open are conclusions as to its practical implications. For many, the consequences are not yet fully apparent. Others suggest that the implications of concepts such as multiple identity are generally negative, particularly with respect to how the subject can function in contexts calling for moral and political judgment. Critical of the idea of decentered subjectivity, Alasdair MacIntyre has claimed, "[t]his divided self has to be characterized negatively, by what it lacks. It is not only without any standpoint from which it can pass critical judgments on the standards governing its various roles, but it must also lack those virtues of integrity and constancy that are prerequisites for exercising the powers of moral agency" (pp. 324–325). Others find the idea of multiple identity useful for the purposes of critique, but useless for producing or theorizing political or social transformation.

In contrast, advocates of various models of multiple identity often have high hopes for its social and political relevance. Scholars across disciplines have long contended that decentered multiple subjectivity is not only a practical reality, but potentially an enormously positive factor in broad-scale political interactions, particularly in the midst of deepening social diversity. Some political theorists have suggested that a decentered, multiply constituted, contradictory self is highly conducive to democratic politics. Bonnie Honig, for example, suggests that the internal conflict and struggle within a decentered self harbors important potential for democratic practices. For Honig,

> decentered subjects . . . have the power to energize their social democracies, while pressing upon them claims to justice, fairness, fidelity and ethicality on behalf of those differences to which social democratic regimes tend to become deaf in their eagerness to administer to represented identities that are established, stable, and familiar. (p. 273)

The range of issues for which multiple identity is of possible significance is wide. Iris Marion Young, Yen Le Espiritu and others have connected multiple identity with social group diversity, the dynamics of political coalition building, political participation, and group politics. Others have underscored the role of multiple identity in political identification and in transnational politics, and Paul Barry Clarke has argued that the multiplicity of the subject is a necessary characteristic of the ideal citizen within deeply diverse democratic regimes. Sociologist Mary Romero has argued that paying attention to the lived experience of multiple identity can better illuminate the power relations affecting Latinos within American society. Other scholars addressing the dynamics of mixed race/ethnic heritage, diverse ethnic identification, and the American mixed-race movement contend that multiple identity may play a role in breaking down the politicized dichotomies of race in America. The complexities of multiple identity are also relevant to new legal approaches to social conflict such as Critical Race Theory.

Articulating her own hopes for its broad implications, Gloria Anzaldúa has argued that in practice the multiple identities of mestiza consciousness can better position the subject for social and political critique and for bridging social cleavages of race, sex, and gender in a manner that could "bring us to the end of rape, of violence, of war" (p. 80). While such expectations may prove overly optimistic, the ultimate validity of these and other assessments of multiple identity need to be explored through additional research and theorizing. The intriguing possibility that important social and political implications could be derived from thinking of the subject as decentered and multiple will no doubt foster further development of the ideas surrounding multiple identity.

*See also* **Critical Race Theory; Democracy; Identity: Personal and Social Identity; Mestizaje; Universalism.**

**BIBLIOGRAPHY**
Adorno, Theodor. *Negative Dialectics.* Translated by E. B. Ashton. New York: Continuum, 1990. Reprint of 1973 translation.
Anzaldúa, Gloria. *Borderlands—La Frontera: The New Mestiza.* San Francisco: Spinster/Aunt Lute Books, 1987.
Benhabib, Seyla. *Situating the Self: Gender, Community, and Postmodernism in Contemporary Ethics.* New York: Routledge, 1992.
Benjamin, Jessica. "The Shadow of the Other (Subject): Intersubjectivity and Feminist Theory." *Constellations* 1, no. 2 (1994): 231–254.
Butler, Judith. *Gender Trouble: Feminism and the Subversion of Identity.* New York: Routledge, 1990.
Du Bois, W. E. B. *The Souls of Black Folks.* Greenwich, Conn.: Fawcett, 1961.
Espiritu, Yen Le. "The Intersection of Race, Ethnicity, and Class: The Multiple Identities of Second-Generation Filipinos." *Identities* 1, no. 2–3 (1994): 249–273.
Honig, Bonnie. "Difference, Dilemmas, and the Politics of Home." In *Democracy and Difference: Contesting the Boundaries of the Political,* edited by Seyla Benhabib, 237–277. Princeton, N.J.: Princeton University Press, 1996.
Horkheimer, Max, and Theodor W. Adorno. *Dialectic of Enlightenment.* New York: Continuum, 1991.
Lugones, María. "Purity, Impurity, and Separation." *Signs* 19 (1994): 458–479.
MacIntyre, Alasdair. "Social Structures and their Threats to Moral Agency." *Philosophy* 74 (1999): 311–329.
Meyers, Diana. T. "Intersectional Identity and the Authentic Self? Opposites Attract." In *Relational Autonomy,* edited by Catriona Mackenzie and Natalie Stoljar, 151–180. New York: Oxford University Press, 2000.
Ricoeur, Paul. *Oneself As Another.* Chicago: Chicago University Press, 1992.
Romero, Mary. "Life as the Maid's Daughter: An Exploration of the Everyday Boundaries of Race, Class, and Gender." In *Challenging Fronteras: Structuring Latina and Latino Lives in the U.S.,* edited by Mary Romero, Pierrette Hondagneu-Sotelo, and Vilma Ortiz, 195–209. New York: Routledge, 1997.
Taylor, Charles. *Sources of the Self: The Making of the Modern Identity.* Cambridge, Mass.: Harvard University Press, 1989.
Zack, Naomi. *American Mixed Race: The Culture of Microdiversity.* Lanham, Md.: Rowman and Littlefield, 1995.

*Edwina Barvosa-Carter*

## ASIAN-AMERICANS

Although Filipinos lived in the United States in the sixteenth century, the first large Asian group in the modern era arrived in the United States in the nineteenth century. Since then two inclinations have simultaneously characterized how Asian-Americans' ethnic identity has been viewed. One tendency has been to look at their identity either in terms of a collective panethnic identity as "Asian-Americans" or an ethnic-specific identity, such as "Filipino-American."

The second tendency is rooted in the fact that ethnic identity is both a concept applied to a cultural group (a group that shares assumptions about the world and ways of interpreting and interacting) and a sense of connection created by that group. That tendency has been for exogenous views (that is, perspectives of those outside Asian-American communities) to differ from endogenous views (that is, perspectives within Asian-American communities) about the meaning and significance of ethnicity. Both tendencies have arisen because, like race, a concept rooted in ideology more than morphology, ethnicity is not simply a direct reflection of what exists; it is a concept created for various uses.

### Endogenous and Exogenous Perspectives

The designation of nineteenth- and twentieth-century Asian immigrants as "Asians" was not a label Asians brought to the United States. By the beginning of the twentieth century, most Asian immigrants were either Chinese, Japanese, Korean, or Filipino, and they self-identified either in ethnic-specific terms or even more precisely (for example, in terms of a Chinese province). By helping immigrants find work and deal with racism, ethnic-specific loan associations, churches, and other formal and informal organizations reinforced an endogenous ethnic-specific identity.

Nevertheless, collective identities were quickly imposed exogenously (by white Americans). Occasionally panethnic identities were actively protested, as in the case of Japan's opposition to segregated, so-called Oriental schools, where all California Asians were to be educated. Usually, however, Asian-Americans had no say, and exogenous panethnic identities dominated.

The impulse for this exogenous emphasis on a collective identity sprang from the categorization of various Asian groups as from one, nonwhite race. For centuries the West viewed nonwhite races generally as "Others"—"not us" and more specifically "nonwhite." It viewed Asians, in particular, as alike in their fundamental and extreme contrast to Westerners. Once Asian-Americans were classified as a racial Other, additional distinctions between them were usually dismissed as irrelevant. Prohibitions against naturalized citizenship and entry into unions as well as other actions designed to restrict Asian-Americans' socioeconomic mobility and political power put Asians into similar socioeconomic circumstances, which further reinforced beliefs about their similarity.

Gradually, though, suspicion and fear of the racial "Other" and differences in the power and foreign policy of Asian countries spurred exogenous efforts to make ethnic-specific distinctions, often mirroring differences in the immigrants' nationality. These changing perceptions produced an array of classifications by the Census Bureau which, at various times, categorized Asian-Americans as nonwhite, Other, Oriental, or in ethnic-specific terms.

Reflecting public concerns, the Census Bureau has long focused more attention on distinguishing between nonwhite than between white Americans. Accordingly, at a time when U.S. relations with Asian countries varied widely, the 1930 census distinguished between white, "Negro," Hindu, Indian, Chinese, Filipino, Korean, Japanese, and all others—which was, Sharon Lee points out in "Racial Classification in the U.S. Census: 1890–1990" (1993), a striking number of distinctions between Asians then constituting less than 0.25 percent of the U.S. population and at a time when the United States had basically stopped further immigration of Asians.

Fear of the racial Other, coupled with a belief in white racial supremacy, led to preemptive efforts to undermine a coalescing of Asian workers under a panethnic identity. Asian workers on white-owned Hawaiian plantations, for instance, were residentially segregated and paid on ethnic-specific pay scales. Similarly Asian-Americans were pitted against other minorities, as in the case of Filipinos replacing striking African-American railroad workers; doing so promoted and sustained the economic superiority of white Americans while undermining the development of a collective identity and political mobilization with other minorities.

Throughout the nineteenth century and much of the twentieth century, the white American public viewed Asian-Americans as inferior, all-alike Others. This view was created from portrayals established for self-serving purposes. Much as portrayals of enslaved African-Americans were self-serving reflections of the slaveholders' desire to minimize contradictions between their self-concept as good Christians and their treatment of the enslaved, self-serving characterizations of Asian-Americans were created by plantation owners paying Asians less per hour than white workers, by missionaries reporting the reasons they failed to convert Asians, and by competing workers. Because of the belief that Asians were homogeneous Others, portrayals of the first Chinese immigrants (as sneaky, for example) were extended to subsequently immigrating Asian groups, such as the Japanese and Koreans. Much like musical, television, and movie depictions do now, popular magazine serial and minstrel show depictions of almost interchangeable Chinese, Japanese, or Filipinos propagated an identity as homogenous Others.

In the early 2000s dominant exogenous views of Asian-Americans still emphasized Otherness. In a world divided into mutually exclusive and oppositional East versus West and in a country typically imagined as either white or black, Asian-Americans are usually classified as essentially Asian and foreign (which is the reason Asian-Americans are never said to have "all-American good looks").

The culture forming the supposed basis of their ethnic identity has been exogenously depicted as Oriental—a mystic, unchanging, centuries-old, anachronistic if not mythical culture supposedly deeply ingrained in the twenty-first century's Asian-Americans, who have been only superficially influenced by experiences in the United States. Explanations of European-Americans' behaviors in the early twenty-first century typically bypass reference to three-hundred-year-old influences on Western culture as too far removed from current motives to be pertinent; but caricatures of Asian-Americans in terms of 2,500-year-old Confucian thought—gross equation of Asian-American cultures to a vague Orientalized past—are commonplace. Yet for many U.S.-born Asian-Americans, a sense of connection to ethnic ancestors in Asian countries is a stretch of the imagination; Orientalization is a fiction akin to feeling connected to Adam and Eve and eclipses the ethnic identities Asian-Americans actually create.

Orientalizing portrayals also oversimplify. The varied cultural backgrounds of Chinese-Americans—with ancestors from Cambodia, Hong Kong, Laos, the People's Republic of China, Taiwan, Thailand, and Vietnam as well as differences in socioeconomic status and acculturation—expose the faulty assumption that an Asian-American group, much less Asian-Americans generally, can be defined in terms of a single (much less Orientalized) culture. Because their ancestors came at different times in history, various Asian-American groups are not creating and redefining an ethnic identity from the same experiences in America.

Nevertheless, inaccurate exogenous portrayals still dominate because Asian-Americans' perspectives are usually unsought. Representations of Asian-Americans' lives are either absent (for example, in the curriculum) or distorted (for example, by mass media), resulting in caricatures that racially marginalize Asian-Americans as foreign, out-of-step, ancillary, and irrelevant.

**Panethnic Identity**

Although Asian-Americans initially saw themselves in ethnic-specific terms, they gradually developed a panethnic identity. Endogenous panethnic Asian-American identities first developed in Hawaii before World War II. Ethnic-specific strikes by Asian farm laborers were only partially effective. Seeing that exploitative plantation owners were pitting them against each other and that their unfair wages and poor living conditions were linked, the workers organized powerful panethnic, islandwide strikes whose success reinforced a panethnic identity. Panethnic identities developed further as the second Asian generation in Hawaii reached voting age: Asians and native Hawaiians formed voting blocs to unseat racist politicians.

After World War II, foreign relations among Asian countries were no longer undercutting pan-Asian-American relations as they had earlier. Spurred by the civil rights movement, a panethnic identity, with its potential for increased political voice about community concerns, began to develop in the 1960s on the U.S. mainland.

A collective identity as "Asian-Americans" was not difficult to form then. Groups were never asked to abandon an ethnic-specific identity. Due to restrictions on the immigration of Asians, 79 percent of Asian-Americans just before the 1965 Hart-Celler Immigration Act were either Chinese- or Japanese-Americans who shared many similarities as U.S.-born descendants of immigrants who came before a series of racist immigration laws essentially stopped Asian immigration and experienced similar race-based discrimination. Their political affiliations were not as varied as now among Asian/Pacific Islanders. In addition they were frequently seen as almost interchangeable by non-Asian-Americans in terms of racial and cultural Otherness, education and crime levels, and the tendency to avoid bumptiousness.

"Asian/Pacific Islander," a modern panethnic label, encompasses roughly thirty groups, including many, such as Thai, Burmese, and Samoans, who were not in the United States in the nineteenth century. The 1965 Immigration Act, the first to drop racial criteria, resulted in an increase in Asian immigration and a panethnic population that includes more cultures and more varied cultures than ever. In this sense, Asian-Americans' panethnicity has expanded.

Nevertheless, ethnic-specific identities still predominate. A panethnic identity that subsumes varied cultures and ancestral nationalities can be difficult to sustain, partly because it downplays endogenously apparent cultural and social differences. The varied groups now do not share many of the historically similar experiences of the pre-1965 Asian-American population. Even though asserting a panethnic identity might enable Asian-Americans to expand and mobilize resources, strengthen their political voice, and elicit more responsiveness from society, it can also exaggerate tendencies to direct hostile feelings about one Asian-American group to Asian-Americans generally.

Much like their counterparts centuries ago, immigrants arrive now with an ethnic-specific identity, reinvigorating the tendency to sustain such identities. However, the immigrants find that in addition to being considered, for example, Koreans, they are viewed as Korean-Americans, Asians, Asian-Americans, and Asian/Pacific Islanders.

After being longtime U.S. residents, they may add a panethnic identity, as do some U.S.-born Asian-Americans. However, those who do not usually do not oppose a panethnic identity; they do not see its usefulness.

The term *Asian-American* is both older and more widely used than *Asian/Pacific Islander,* but both are part of a never-ending process of creating and challenging identities. Even the issue of who should be included in the panethnic identity is questioned. For example, the Census Bureau, reflecting input from scholars, classifies East Indians as Asian, but the public often rejects their inclusion as Asian-Americans on the grounds that they do not seem to be the same race, much less the same ethnicity, as other Asian-Americans.

Grouping Asian-Americans and Pacific Islanders is also contested. On the one hand, inclusion of Pacific Islanders may make their political voice louder to the larger society than it would have been otherwise; on the other hand, distinguishing the groups would more accurately reflect differences in cultural background, identity, and social needs and might produce more focus on their concerns. For Pacific Islanders, as for many Southeast Asians, panethnic stereotypes (such as the inaccurate model minority stereotype) have sometimes caused society to overlook their needs and exclude them from equal-opportunity programs.

## The Ongoing Creation of Identities

Whether a panethnic identity is invoked sometimes depends on the context. Accordingly a young Korean-American man might think of himself as Korean when with his grandparents, Korean-American while at a Korean-American church, and Asian-American when thinking about whom to casually date. Selectively porous and elastic ethnic boundaries create multiple, simultaneous identities.

Those multiple forms of ethnic identity are created in the context of other identities, such as socioeconomic status, residential region, gender, and degree of acculturation or multinational identity, which add to the complexity and change the meaning, relevance, and significance of ethnic identity. Ethnicity for Korean-Americans in Los Angeles's Koreatown has a different meaning than it does for Korean-Americans in Bismarck, North Dakota; a wealthy Chinese-American man and a poor Filipina-American picture bride experience their ethnicity differently.

The consequences of ethnicity create meanings. For example, when the mid-nineteenth-century Foreign Miner's tax (as high as 98 percent of income) was applied only to Chinese miners, the meaning of being (a miner who was) Chinese was that one would be subjected to unfair taxes. In the early twenty-first century some young Asian-Americans see their ethnicity as a way of consciously connecting with their parents; a few see it as a passport to gang membership; still others see it as a source of self-esteem.

Adding to the complexity, *ethnicity,* like *culture,* is often used as a sugarcoated code word for *race.* Using *ethnicity* in this way makes events seem to be innocent reflections of ethnic differences rather than racial bias or socioeconomic opportunities, promotes the impression that racism is irrelevant to the lives of Asian-Americans, and deflates attempts to change racial inequities.

Compounding the complexity and changing meaning of ethnic identity is the difference between the ethnic identity of Asian-Americans and European-Americans, both as an attributed concept and as a choice individuals make when identifying themselves. European-Americans' ethnic identity is regarded as largely irrelevant—to the point that many do not even know their full ethnic background.

Ethnic identifications of Asian-Americans occur more often than for European-Americans because they are perceived as more relevant to the former. Indeed experience has shown that when Asian-Americans identify themselves simply as "Americans," that identification is commonly rejected as inadequate. Despite America's purported embrace of ethnic diversity, so-called hyphenated Americans (such as Chinese-Americans or Asian-Americans) frequently find that a hyphenated identity is sometimes objectionable as well. As the historian James Loewen pointed out in his book *Lies My Teacher Told Me* (1995), racists like Woodrow Wilson interpreted the hyphenation as a sign of treachery. Others claim the hyphenated term, which places ethnicity first, makes ethnicity more important than nationality. (Actually in the term *Asian-American, Asian* is just an adjective modifying the more important noun, *American.*) In the face of such criticism and misunderstanding, people struggle to create an ethnic identity.

Contrary to most assumptions, ethnicity is "not a way of looking back at the [country from which ancestors came; rather it is] a way of being American" (Greeley, p. 32). In that spirit, Japanese-Americans rarely learn the intricacies of a Japanese tea ceremony; instead, they have created ways of being American with a nod toward their background. As Fukiko Uba Odanaka recounted (in a personal communication), in the 1930s, when Japanese-Americans were not allowed on school teams, she and some friends created female basketball teams paralleling teams created for young Japanese-American males in the early twenty-first century. Since then organizational sponsors have seen thousands of Japanese-American boys and girls play in basketball leagues, which have become a central cultural activity among West Coast Japanese-Americans. The leagues create cohesion while giving youngsters who go to schools that have few Japanese-Americans the opportunity to learn Japanese-American values and interaction styles. Rather than being an unambiguous demographic indicator of ancestry, ethnic identity has many contrary, complex, changing meanings, and its created significance changes accordingly.

*See also* **Critical Race Theory; Cultural Revivals; Loyalties, Dual; Race and Racism: Reception of Asians to the United States.**

**BIBLIOGRAPHY**

Andersen, Margaret L., and Patricia Hill Collins. *Race, Class, and Gender: An Anthology.* 4th ed. Belmont, Calif.: Wadsworth, 2001.

Ferrante, Joan, and Prince Browne Jr. *The Social Construction of Race and Ethnicity in the United States.* 2nd ed. Upper Saddle River, N.J.: Prentice Hall, 2001.

Fong, Timothy P., and Larry H. Shinagawa. *Asian-Americans: Experiences and Perspectives.* Upper Saddle River, N.J.: Prentice Hall, 2000.

Greeley, Andrew M. "The Ethnic Miracle." *Public Interest* 45 (fall 1976): 20–36.

Lee, Sharon. "Racial Classification in the U.S. Census, 1890–1990." *Ethnic and Racial Studies* 16, no. 1 (1993): 75–94.

Loewen, James W. *Lies My Teacher Told Me: Everything Your American History Textbook Got Wrong.* New York: Simon and Schuster, 1995.

Okihiro, Gary Y. *The Columbia Guide to Asian American History.* New York: Columbia University Press, 2001.

Omi, Michael, and Howard Winant. *Racial Formation in the United States from the 1960s to the 1990s.* 2nd ed. New York: Routledge, 1994.

Tuan, Mia. *Forever Foreigners or Honorary Whites? The Asian Ethnic Experience Today.* New Brunswick, N.J.: Rutgers University Press, 1998.

Uba, Laura. *Asian-Americans: Personality Patterns, Identity, and Mental Health.* New York: Guilford, 1994.

———. *A Postmodern Psychology of Asian Americans: Creating Knowledge of a Racial Minority.* Albany: State University of New York Press, 2002.

Williams-Léon, Teresa, and Cynthia L. Nakashima. *The Sum of Our Parts: Mixed-Heritage Asian Americans.* Philadelphia: Temple University Press, 2001.

*Laura Uba*

## JEWISH MULTIPLE IDENTITY

As a collective that has lived and created its history for the most part not merely in diaspora but among a vast array of "host" peoples, Jewry across the generations has been powerfully marked by the need to negotiate, on the one hand, elements of identity understood to be shared with all Jews at all times and places and, on the other hand, cultural motifs and practices shared with their non-Jewish neighbors.

### Sephardim and Ashkenazim

The medieval Jewish view divided the world between Edom (Christendom) and Ishmael (the realm of Islam), and the Jewish world was likewise bifurcated (for example, by Maimonides) into *Galut Edom* (Jews under the cross) and *Galut Ishmael* (Jews under the crescent). More broadly, and continuing throughout roughly the second Christian millennium, most of the Jews of the world have generally been understood to belong to two major subgroups. One group is called *Sephardim,* a term derived from the Hebrew name of Spain. The term originally denoted only Iberian Jews, but after the expulsion of Jews from the Iberian Peninsula in 1492, it was colloquially expanded to include all the Jewish communities of the circum-Mediterranean, Middle East, and North Africa. The second group is known as *Ashkenazim.* This term is derived from the Hebrew word designating the German lands and was used to describe virtually all the Jewish communities of northern, western, and eastern Europe, who shared the Yiddish idiom until the modern era. Until the nineteenth century, the former group was more numerous, but the Ashkenazi population increased dramatically in the modern era. Since the establishment of the state of Israel, however, scholars and activists have worked to promote the collective identity and cultural heritage of Arabic-speaking Jews as distinguished, on the one hand, from the "true" Sephardim (Ladino-speaking communities that trace their origin to Iberia) and, on the other, from the largely secular Ashkenazim who founded the central Zionist institutions. It is also understood in the early twenty-first century that the bifurcation of Jewishness into Sephardic and Ashkenazic identities occluded the stubborn persistence of Jewish communal identities in widely scattered parts of the world such as Ethiopia, India, and China, and of nonrabbinic Jewish groups, most notably the Karaites.

## Fundaments and Contingencies

Understandably, what is emphasized in the religious liturgy, in traditional literature, and in contemporary collective memory are the supposedly "constant" marks of Jewish identity: study and adherence to the laws of the Bible and (especially) the Talmud and other rabbinic glosses and codices; observance of the weekly Sabbath and the festivals that mark the annual (lunar) calendar; solidarity with Jews in distant places, especially those whose safety is threatened at any particular time; and a shared understanding that Zion is both the origin and the eschatological destination of all Jews everywhere.

Continuity of Jewish identity in diaspora can be traced not only to the existence of these texts and rituals as a "portable homeland" but also to policing of the bounds of identity from within (through autonomously governing communal structures) and without (through social discrimination and restrictive legislation enacted by Christian and Muslim religious and secular officials). Moreover, any Jew in the premodern world who strayed too far from competence in Jewish culture risked a painful loss of status. Hence the story of the village Jew so illiterate that his fellow congregants mocked him as "Zalmen the goy [gentile]." When the rabbi admonished them not to be so cruel, they complied but in a way that dug even deeper, calling him instead "Zalmen the Yid [Jew]."

However, the tradition also acknowledges that Jewish ability to identify as, if not necessarily empathize with, non-Jews is also of value to the Jewish community and its survival. The story recited by Jewish communities each year on the festival of Purim is exemplary here: The emperor Ahasuerus in ancient Persia holds a contest to find the most beautiful woman in the kingdom and make her his queen, and the Jewish girl Esther is selected. Throughout the selection process and the beginning of her reign, she conceals from the emperor the fact of her Jewish birth, only revealing it as she denounces the author of a plot to kill all the Jews of the empire. A clear moral of this story is that at certain times, an individual's pretending not to be Jewish can benefit the entire community.

## Questions of Gender

Jewishness is often implicitly conflated with maleness since participation in ritual and in textual study was often limited to males. Indeed, like most group identities, especially perhaps in the West, Jewishness is explicitly patriarchal. However, for centuries Jewishness as an identity transmitted at birth has been determined matrilineally. The contribution of women to the transmission and constant renewal of Jewishness is often articulated only in response to feminist critiques of traditional sexism, but there should be no question that women's role as educators and shapers of the sensibilities of new Jewish generations has always been indispensable.

## Modernity and Beyond

Under the pressures of modern secularizing and state-building tendencies, the unique mix of a sense of core unity and adaptive

flexibility that sustained Jewish diasporic communities for millennia was massively weakened. Among both Jews and non-Jews, the collective identity of autonomous communities came to be seen as inimical to modernity. Debates raged for decades as to whether Jewish identity was primarily religious, national, or racial; and movements for reform, the establishment of a Jewish nation-state (in Palestine or elsewhere), and the elimination of Jewish difference through intermarriage and assimilation were promoted accordingly. From the Enlightenment until the rise of European fascism, it was commonly believed that it was possible for Jews to identify both with their co-religionists everywhere and with fellow citizens of their countries of residence.

Since World War II, it has been a commonplace that the twin pillars of shared Jewish identity are the memory of Nazi genocide and identification with the Jewish state of Israel. However, since the last decades of the twentieth century these emphases have been countered, or at least balanced, by a renewed engagement with the Jewish textual tradition and by a reinvention of the liturgical and ritual tradition, both placing more emphasis than ever before on the goal of making women equal participants in Jewish identity. These phenomena, along with the dramatic regeneration of Orthodox Jewish communities, demonstrate the continued vitality of Jewish capacities for the negotiation of multiple Jewish and human identities.

*See also* **Diasporas: Jewish Diaspora; Judaism.**

BIBLIOGRAPHY
Biale, David, ed. *Cultures of the Jews: A New History.* New York: Schocken, 2002.
Gilman, Sander L. *Jewish Self-Hatred: Anti-Semitism and the Hidden Language of the Jews.* Baltimore and London: Johns Hopkins University Press, 1983.
Goldberg, David Theo, and Michael Krausz, eds. *Jewish Identity.* Philadelphia: Temple University Press, 1993.
Zimmels, H. J. *Ashkenazim and Sephardim: Their Relations, Differences, and Problems as Reflected in the Rabbinical Responsa.* Hoboken, N.J.: Ktav, 1996.

*Jonathan Boyarin*

**IMAGES, ICONS, AND IDOLS.** Placing the words *images, icons,* and *idols* together as the subject of an entry that seeks to articulate the perspective of world culture suggests their intimate relationship. Such a grouping also demands that an emphasis be placed on the particular role biblical religions have had in the development and use of the last two terms, the ideas of "icon" and "idol" that play off each other and highlight a central idea of the "image" in the three traditions— Judaism, Christianity, and Islam—commonly characterized as monotheistic. While all three terms have come to be used by scholars in their analysis of many cultures, the terms *icon* and *idol* have a specific and central place in the discourse on images in the cultural history and the history of ideas in the West. The notion of idol and idolatry was carried to many parts of the world with the Christian and Muslim mission movements and entered local vocabularies through this means.

## Sacred Image

The representation of gods, saints, and heroes, of mythic events and of formative historical events, has been a widespread phenomenon in the history of religion. Conventional notions suggest that some religions, for example Islam and prophetic Judaism, are aniconic, meaning that they are against the use of idols or images. At the iconic end of the spectrum we find Mahayana Buddhism and Hinduism, traditions in which images articulate, order, and fill the sacred spaces of both temple and home. Scholars who adopt such a schematic approach place Protestantism, Vedaism, and ancient Buddhism toward the aniconic end of the scale and Roman Catholicism, Eastern Orthodoxy, and the religions of ancient Egypt, Greece, and Rome toward the iconic end.

The historical study of religion, however, has shown that the understanding and use of images have been complex and have shifted in emphasis in various periods. Hinduism and its daughter Buddhism both appear to have started out without the use of images and grew into iconic faiths over many generations. The phenomenological study of religion shows that the veneration of images by a devout woman or man may vary, even dramatically, from what is said about the importance of the image or even about its sacred character. Theravada Buddhists, for example, may say that the image of the Buddha is simply a "representation" and that the historical Buddha died like any other person and is therefore obviously not present in any way in the image. Yet, they bow with reverence and make offerings to statues of the Buddha even if they encounter them in unexpected places far outside the traditional environment of the sacred. In a given tradition at any given moment, one often finds that the attitude toward images runs a remarkable spectrum of belief. Among Orthodox Christians entering a church for the Divine Liturgy on a Sunday morning, there will be many who take candles to the front of the church and offer them in memory as they pause to pray before the icons. Some will speak of the icon as miraculous while their neighbor will note its pedagogical role as a visual scripture or hagiography and others will say the icon is a "window of divine grace" or, in the case of the icon of Jesus Christ, an "embodiment of God" and witness to the Incarnation.

The image may also be understood as divine. Stilpo, a fourth-century-B.C.E. citizen of Athens, was banished for teaching that the Greek sculptor Phidias's statue of Athena was not a goddess, and the ninth-century South Indian mystic Andal is said to have married an image of Vishnu and miraculously been absorbed into the God's embrace. Images may become divine when they are initiated in and through a ritual. When images arrive for installation in Hindu temples they are initiated through the ritual of *prana partista,* and the "breath of God enters them" never to be removed. In ancient Egypt the high priest would enter the temple chamber in the morning ritual and take the statue of the god from its resting place, clean, clothe, and feed the deity and then retire from this most holy place until the following morning.

Perhaps one of the most widespread practices is the use of images as a focus for veneration with a clear sense that they function as a reminder of the deity's characteristics, inviting one to offer both one's struggles and joys, concerns and thankfulness, through prayer, meditation, or devotion. For the devotees the image is a way of engaging the holy. This, of course, makes the image sacred but not in and of itself a deity.

## Icon as Revelation

While the Greek word for image, *eikōn,* has entered the common vocabulary of the English speaking world as *icon* and is applied to everything from pictures identifying computer programs to symbols from archaic cultures, it is in the Orthodox Christian tradition that iconography has received its highest articulation and where it occupies a central place in the life of worship. Holy icons are central to Orthodox theology and worship and developed over the better part of a millennium into a distinct form of liturgical art. In devout Orthodox households, whether in New York City or Romanian villages, one finds the "beautiful corner" with its icon of Christ and the Theotokos ("Birth-giver of God," or Virgin Mary) and various other icons adorned with linen drapery. A vigil lamp or candle may burn in front of the icons. In Orthodox churches the whole space is often completely decorated with icons, painted in fresco or secco, arranged according to a canonical program. The iconostasis bridging the nave and the altar area of the church holds various key icons both on the screen itself and on its various doors. The axis of the iconographic program in the church is formed by the large painting or mosaic of Christ the "All Ruler" (*Pantocrator*) in the central dome and the Theotokos in the apse of the church. The porch is also painted, and in some Orthodox churches, particularly in Romania, the exterior of the church is covered with frescoes of saints, biblical and other sacred narratives, and occasionally images of pagan luminaries from Socrates to Petrarch.

An icon table close to the entrance or inside the church will hold the icon appropriate to the feast or saint's day according to the liturgical calendar. When the faithful enter the church they customarily venerate the image, making the sign of the cross and often lighting a candle as they pray for the living and the dead.

This highly articulated tradition of icon use is the result of generations of theological reflection in the Christian East. It was largely taken for granted until various Byzantine emperors initiated two iconoclastic periods, 730–787 and 813–843. During these periods an attempt, largely successful, led to the destruction of all images in churches in the empire.

The iconoclasts were not enemies of art but rather took exception to the presence of all images of Christ, the Theotokos, and saints in the church. The emperors at the forefront of this movement continued to promote imperial imagery on coins and banners throughout the empire. A striking parallel may be found in both the Soviet Union and the United States of America, where iconoclastic cultures have flourished along with the extravagant use of images of political figures in public places.

The controversy during this period was essentially dogmatic and centered on the heart of the Orthodox theological proclamation of the incarnation of God in Jesus Christ. It was rooted in the persistence of Hellenistic spiritualism represented by Origen (?185–?254) and Christian forms of Neoplatonic thought seeking a return to pre-Christian notions of the separation of the spirit and matter. The followers of the iconoclastic movement saw the image as an obstacle to prayer and the spiritual life because the image was made out of "crude matter" and because its emphasis on the human body failed to privilege and grant the elevated place rightfully belonging to the spirit. This movement denied the Gospel witness to the incarnation of God in Jesus Christ as a restoration of all human beings to the divine image proclaimed in the Genesis account of creation.

This state-sponsored iconoclasm (literally "image smashing") was countered by John of Damascus (c. 675–749), Germanus I, patriarch of Constantinople (c. 634–c. 732), and Theodore Studites (759–826), who marshaled scripture and theological thinking in favor of the use of icons in Christian worship. John of Damascus argued that God was the first and original image-maker of the universe and that the son of God was the living image of God in his very nature. Since Paul in the Epistle to the Colossians had written, "He is the image of the invisible God" (Col. 1:15), the worship of the icon of Jesus Christ was not idolatrous, because, in the oft-quoted formula of Saint Basil of Caesarea (c. 329–379) in *De Spiritu Sancto* (On the Holy Spirit), "The honor paid to the image [the Son] passes over to the prototype [the Father]." The Orthodox doctrine of the veneration of icons calls the faithful, not to a veneration of art or images in general, but to the veneration of the image of a person whose life has been sanctified and who has come to union with God through divine grace. It is a realization of Christ's words in the Gospel, "The kingdom of God is within you" (Luke 17:21). The icon expresses the Gospel precisely because it is a manifestation of the human nature having recovered its fullness in the divine life. It represents the patristic formula "God became man so that man might become God."

Orthodox iconography centers on the human person and its canons require that all that is depicted be rooted in the human story shown from the perspective of the human being's recovery of holiness. Icons are not "art" in the usual sense but liturgical aids to prayer orienting the mind and heart of the faithful to the kingdom of God, fulfilling Christ's words, "The glory which thou has given me I have given to them" (John 17:22).

The Orthodox veneration of images was called for by the revelation of the enfleshment of God. While the early Christian thinkers agreed that the God of the Hebrew Bible could not be portrayed, they went on to argue that since Christ is the incarnation of God and had taken on the fullness of human nature, it would be a denial of the Incarnation to refuse to portray Christ in images. Sacred images are a conjoining of the human and divine spheres and serve as indicators and vehicles of the kingdom of God, of all creation transfigured in Christ. The apologists for the icon used the arguments of earlier church fathers who had written on the Scriptures and sacraments and deployed these in favor of images. The biblical texts have long been talked about as a network of types, pointers,

and connections to the presence of the "Word made flesh" in Jesus Christ. These arguments received their official sanction by the Seventh Ecumenical Council at Nicaea in 787 and the icons were restored to the church permanently in 843 following a second series of iconoclast emperors.

## Idol and Idolatry

The English word *idol* is a translation of the Greek word for "image," *eidōlon*. The word *idolatry* combines *eidōlon* with the Greek word for "adoration," *latreia*. The concept of idols and idolatry is central to the biblical narrative and to Jewish, Christian, and Islamic tradition. The richest home of this concept is in the Hebrew Scriptures, where we find the prophets engaged in a running polemic against the pagan worship of aspects of creation rather than of the Creator, and against the erecting, under Canaanite influence, images to Yahweh. The prophets address the predilection of the children of Israel to create images of divine beings in order to worship them, turning away from the proper worship of the "one Lord of all history." The second commandment of the Decalogue (Exod. 20:4–6; Deut. 5:8–10; cf. Lev. 26:1; Deut. 4:15–23) prohibits the making of images of anything "in the heavens above, or the earth below, or the waters beneath the earth." This commandment passes into the Christian New Testament and on to the strict monotheism of Islam, where the concept forms one of the Five Pillars of the faith.

The word *eidōlon* is used seventy times in the Greek Septuagint to translate sixteen different Hebrew words, while the Latin Vulgate uses *idolum* 112 times and its corollary *simulacrum* thirty-two times to translate fifteen Hebrew words. The Hebrew Bible uses thirty different nouns in references to idols and names forty-four pagan deities throughout its various narratives. While the word *idol* or *idolatry* is not found in the Gospels, *eidōlon* appears in many of the Epistles of the Apostle Paul and in the book of Revelation. The Bible's preoccupation with idolatry rests on the notion that the many images of deities that have flourished in human culture are false, images in "word and stone," and that those who follow after them are engaged in a fantasy at best. In the writings of the Apostle Paul the word *idol* takes on the connotation of deception that is the work of demons who deceive the human mind and heart about their proper nature.

The polemic against idolatry continues in an unbroken stream in the Christian tradition in both the Greek and Latin apologists and church fathers. Saint Justin (c.100–c.165) in his first *Apology* speaks of the error in creating human forms to replicate the divine, the lack of soul in base substance, and of how artisans and thieves use such objects to deprive people of their money. Clement of Alexandria (c. 150–between 211 and 215) wrote his *Protreptikos* to persuade those who worshiped the embodiment of pagan mythic figures of the origin of such cultic practice. Partly inspired by Plato, Clement argues that such images are the result of the deification of human beings created by artists to honor kings. The gravity of such worship, Clement argued, is that it replaces the human compulsion to worship the true God with invented demons that are at best mere wood and stone and at worst excite the human passions.

## To See Her Face

I had met the local Hindu priest on two occasions in the 1970s. He had walked me through his plans for a new temple to serve the eclectic community of people with roots in India who had come to live in Edmonton, Alberta, Canada, and discussed how he planned to shape the sanctum sanctorum to accommodate the various devotions of a mixed community of Shaivites and Vaishnavites. Now we sat together in his home just to the right of his shrine to the Shakti, the Feminine Divine Energy and manifestation of Shiva, the deity that had captured his attention many years ago and come to shape his personal devotion. It was my first time in his home and our conversation had moved from his own spiritual formation in Ludhiana, India, through the trauma of the stillbirth of his first child and his entering the Shi Ramakrishna mission in England seeking solace for the loss of this child. He spoke of growing up under the influence of the Arya Samaj movement, of its iconoclasm as well as its place in the Vedic renaissance in India in the nineteenth century and how he came to devote himself to the ritual life centered

on *murti,* the image of deities. He had talked affectionately about the worship of deities at some length and then, rather abruptly, turned to speak about the goal of the Hindu life: to finally come to worship the formless form, the Eternal Absolute beyond embodiment. This, he told me, would finally lead to *moksha,* the liberation that is the final release from the cycle of rebirth. After he had spoken for a considerable time on the formless form, distinguishing it from what he called "idol worship," I said to him that while this was a powerful idea I did not quite understand how it sat with his deep and faithful devotion to the beautiful embodiment of Shakti, a devotion he offered to her each morning and evening. What does the formless form have to do with her who is so beautifully formed and who has so completely won your affections? Tears filled his eyes. "In this life, in this round, all I hope for is just once to see her face. Just once to truly glimpse her beauty."

SOURCE: From the author's field notes.

When the Visigoths under Alaric conquered Rome on 24 August 410 C.E. the pagan subjects of the city accused their Christian neighbors of bringing the event about by destroying the worship of the gods. The Christians had chased away the divine protectors of the ancient and glorious city. Saint Augustine (354–430) was called upon to answer this charge in what proved to be the last great apologetic work against paganism, *The City of God.* He begins with a critique of the Roman gods and the mythology that had shaped the identity of Romans for centuries and then examines the arguments of Varro, Cicero, Seneca, Euhemerus, Apuleius, and Plato. Augustine argues that idols are not neutral inventions but are harmful precisely because they are created out of the heart and mind, a manifestation of human aspiration, ambition, and illusion. In his works *On Christian Doctrine* and *On True Religion* he continues his substantial psychoanalysis of how the demonic, born of the human mind, takes on a character of its own. Idols are not without power for they receive life and force from the invisible numen born of their origin in human misunderstanding. While idols are false gods and as such not gods, they represent the enormous struggle in the human heart and mind to apprehend the truth about human nature, creation, and the divine.

The great controversies such as iconoclasm and the Protestant Reformation illustrate the struggle within the church over

what constitutes idolatry. In the sixteenth and seventeenth centuries various Protestant theologians accused Roman Catholicism of replacing the proper worship of the divine with the idolatrous worship of Mary and the saints. The worship of idols has remained a perennial concern in various denominations of the Christian church as they expanded into Africa, Asia, and North America.

### Islam and Shirk

Muslims around the world, both in the mosque and in their daily prayers, chant the creedal statement: "God is most great. There is no god but Allah. Muhammad is the Prophet of God." The Koran constantly speaks of God as the One, Al-Wahid, and the Prophet Muhammad's singular passion was to root out idolatry and the indigenous forms of polytheism in the Arab communities of his day. For Muhammad and for faithful Muslims ever since, the heavens and the earth are established on what we read in sura 112 of the Koran, "Say: He is God alone: God the eternal. He begetteth not, and he is not begotten; and there is none like unto him."

In the religious world of Islam any association of other beings with God or of any human attribute with what belongs to God alone is the gravest of sins. *Shirk,* this type of grave sin, finds its polar opposite in *tawhid,* the declaration central to Muslim belief and prayer of the unity of God, a unity declared in faith and lived out in private and public life.

Muhammad inherited the opposition to idolatry from the Judeo-Christian tradition and saw Abraham as the prototype of the faith in one God. Abraham's firstborn son Ishmael faithfully followed in his father's footsteps in his rejection of local idols. Considerable attention is given in the Koran to Abraham's destruction of idols and Moses' attempt to call his people back to the worship of the one God (sura 26:69–83; 21:53/52–70; 25:3–5/4; 7:134/138). The propensity to associate a god or gods with God represents the gravest human struggle and Islamic law is clear and absolute about its many dangers and manifestations.

Idolaters are to be shunned and Muslims are called to fight against them (sura 9:36). One must never marry an idol worshiper and one must protect children from their influence. Idolatry is an insult to God for only God is the creator of the world and God is beyond image or representation.

In the last half of the twentieth century, archaeological work at the third-century Jewish synagogue at Dura Europos in eastern Syria helped us appreciate that the absolute prohibition of images in the law of Moses did not deter Jews contemporary with early Christianity from painting sacred images in their places of worship. Carl Kraeling argues that the Dura synagogue was one of the finest synagogues in ancient Judaism and that its decorative paintings are a forerunner of Byzantine art. While this discovery has demanded that scholars of *image, icon,* and *idol* become more complex in their application of these terms, it remains the case that the cultural history and history of ideas in the West, in Jewish, Christian, and Muslim circles, has been significantly shaped by the debate on the nature and meaning of images. This debate continues in the contemporary Protestant church considering what decorative program to adopt, as it does periodically in public discussion when an art gallery or a film shows images of Jesus Christ, the Virgin Mary, or a prophet that deconstruct some of the public's expectations.

*See also* **Iconography; Orthopraxy; Religion; Sacred Places; Sacred Texts.**

**BIBLIOGRAPHY**

Augustine, Saint, Bishop of Hippo. *The City of God against the Pagans.* Translated and edited by R. W. Dyson. Cambridge, U.K.: Cambridge University Press, 1998.

Basil, Saint, Bishop of Caesarea. *On the Holy Spirit.* Translated by David Anderson. Crestwood, N.Y.: New York: St. Vladimir's Seminary Press, 1980.

Belting, Hans. *Likeness and Presence: A History of the Image before the Era of Art.* Translated by Edmund Jephcott. Chicago and London: University of Chicago Press, 1994.

Coomaraswamy, A. K. *Coomaraswamy.* Edited by Roger Lipsey. Princeton, N.J.: Princeton University Press, 1977.

Daniélou, Alain. *Hindu Polytheism.* New York: Bollingen Foundation, distributed by Pantheon, 1964.

Eliade, Mircea. *Images and Symbols: Studies in Religious Symbolism.* Translated by Philip Mairet. New York: Sheed and Ward, 1961.

Florovsky, George. "Origen, Eusebius, and the Iconoclastic Controversy." *Church History* 19 (1950): 77–96.

Goblet d'Alviella, Eugène. "Les origins de l'idolatrie." In his *Croyances, rites, institutions.* Vol. 2. Paris: P. Geuthner, 1911.

Grabar, André. *Early Christian Art: From the Rise of Christianity to the Death of Theodosius.* Translated by Stuart Gilbert and James Emmons. New York: Odyssey, 1969.

Grabar, Oleg. *The Formation of Islamic Art.* New Haven, Conn.: Yale University Press, 1973.

John of Damascus, Saint. *On the Divine Images: Three Apologies against Those Who Attack the Divine Images.* Crestwood, N.Y.: New York: St. Vladimir's Seminary Press, 1980.

Kraeling, Carl H. *The Synagogue.* 2nd ed. New York: KTAV, 1979.

Lossky, Vladimir. *In the Image and Likeness of God.* Edited by John H. Erickson and Thomas E. Bird. Repr. Crestwood, N.Y.: Saint Vladimir's Seminary Press, 1985.

Moore, Albert C. *Iconography of Religions: An Introduction.* Philadelphia: Fortress, 1977.

Nicephorus, Saint, Patriarch of Constantinople. *Discours contre les iconoclastes.* Translated by Marie-José Mondzain-Baudinet. Paris: Klincksieck, 1989.

Ricoeur, Paul. *The Rule of Metaphor: Multi-Disciplinary Studies of the Creation of Meaning in Language.* Translated by Robert Czerny, with Kathleen McLaughlin and John Costello. Toronto and Buffalo, N.Y.: University of Toronto Press, 1978.

Theodore Studites, Saint. *On the Holy Icons.* Translated by Catharine P. Roth. Crestwood, N.Y.: St. Vladimir's Seminary Press, 1981.

Trubetskoi, Evgenii Nikolaevich. *Icons: Theology in Color.* Translated by Gertrude Vahar. New York: Saint Vladimir's Seminary Press, 1973.

Ward, Keith. *Images of Eternity: Concepts of God in Five Religious Traditions.* London: Darton, Longman, and Todd, 1987.

*David J. Goa*

**IMAGINATION.** The idea of imagination is sometimes thought of as a product of the Enlightenment. However, although it only came to full flower in the seventeenth, eighteenth, and nineteenth centuries, its roots are much more ancient.

**Biblical Beginnings**

Given the stern admonition of the second commandment of the Decalogue against the making of images of anything "in the heavens above, or the earth below, or the waters beneath the earth" (Exodus 20:4; Deuteronomy 5:8), it is ironic that the idea of *imagination* probably found its earliest expression in the first chapter of Genesis. In the biblical accounts of creation, two different words are used: in the first account, *bara,* implying *creatio ex nihilo* (Genesis 1:27); in the second, *yatsar,* by which man is created from the dust of the earth (Genesis 2:7). The first power is reserved to God alone; the second—the power to reshape existing matter—is shared with humankind. Thus the Hebrew word for imagination comes to be *yetser,* the ability to share in the divine creative power.

For humankind, however, *yetser* is not always used for good: "the imagination of man's heart is evil from his youth" (Genesis 8: 21; and see Genesis 6: 5). Thus the rabbinical tradition came to distinguish between the evil imagination (*yetser hara*), often associated with sexual desire, and the good imagination (*yetser hatov*), which "opens up history to an I-Thou dialogue between man and his Creator" (Kearney, p. 47).

## Non-Western Traditions

The Sufi tradition of Islam offers an analogue of imagination in the concept of *barzakh*, referring to "the whole intermediate realm between the spiritual and the corporeal." Since this world of imagination is "closer to the World of Light" than the corporeal world (Chittick, p. 14), it can give valid knowledge of higher reality. In the Buddhist tradition there is no systematic view of imagination; the Sanskrit word for it is *prtibha* ("poetic genius"), but it is not given much emphasis in Buddhist thought. Hinduism, on the other hand, offers in the Vedic tradition a highly developed view of imagination as both the transcendent power by which the gods create and sustain the harmony of the universe, and the human faculty by which the human artist, priest, or sage recognizes and celebrates this harmony. It is, in short, the imagination that "joins the human spirit with ultimate reality itself" (Mahoney, p. 2).

## Ancient Greece

In the ancient Greek tradition, too, the idea of imagination is closely bound up with divine power and prerogatives. In the pre-philosophical era it is most dramatically expressed in the myth of Prometheus, whose theft of fire from heaven brought the creative energy of the gods to humankind. It is only in the work of Plato and Aristotle, however, that the idea is brought to some level of conceptual clarity. Although Plato's earliest dialogues espouse a firm idealism inherited from Parmenides, by the time of the *Republic* he has begun to see the need to bring together the material, phenomenal world and the world of ideas. The imagination (*phantasia* or *eikasia*), if used in aid of reason can attain to, and even express, universal ideas. By the time of the *Phaedrus* and the *Timaeus,* Plato sees that imaginative representation "recalls to mind those eternal forms of Beauty which are the innate possessions of the soul and the objects of its contemplation" (Bundy, p. 58). Aristotle's more pragmatic approach shifts the focus from metaphysical foundations to form and function, from objective to subjective. Thus imitation (*mimesis*) is for him an inductive and psychological process rather than a divinely inspired intuition. It was his emphasis rather than Plato's that was to predominate in the Western tradition until the eighteenth century.

## Medieval and Renaissance Views

There are wide divergences in medieval views of imagination. Although one finds in such synthetic thinkers as St. Augustine of Hippo (354–430) and St. Thomas Aquinas (1225–1274) (and later in the poetry of Dante [1265–1321]) attempts to reconcile the idealism of Plato and the Neoplatonists with the more psychological approach of Aristotle, it is the latter that generally finds favor among faculty-oriented Scholastic philosophers. For all this, though, a Platonic undercurrent often remains—as in Aquinas and in the Jewish philosopher Moses ben Maimon (Maimonides; 1135–1204)—to explain the intrinsic relationship between the material world and the

transcendent, the human and the divine. Arab philosophers of the period, notably Avicenna (Ibn Sina; 980–1037), tend to give priority to imagination over intellect in achieving true knowledge, while the Western tradition invariably insists that imagination must remain under the control of intellect. However, imagination (*imaginatio* and *phantasia* are used synonymously in Aquinas) is crucial for most of the medieval Scholastics as a means of expressing the analogical relationship between the sensible world and transcendent reality.

In the Renaissance, the *Vita nuova* and *Divina commedia* of Dante and *De imaginatione sive phantasia* of Giovanni Pico della Mirandola (1463–1494) may fairly be taken as representative. All three draw heavily from Scholastic philosophy, and although Dante is, like his master Aquinas, an Aristotelian, both are more deeply interested in the possibilities of vision than in the epistemological process itself. Thus, in part through them, the Platonic tradition continues into succeeding generations, with such theorists as Sir Philip Sidney (1554–1586) in his *Apology for Poetry.* Even as he strongly emphasizes the teaching role of poetry in achieving "virtuous action," using Plato's ideas for a moral purpose, Sidney keeps alive the Platonic emphasis on imaginative vision.

## The Enlightenment

If the European Enlightenment did not invent the idea of imagination, it certainly brought it to its fullest articulation, broadening its reach to include not only literature and the arts, along with philosophy and theology, but also political and social theory and even science. It became during the eighteenth century, in short, a crucial tool in virtually every area of intellectual life.

Until this time, intellectual inquiry had tended to focus on humankind's relationship with God, with nature, and with others. Thinkers like Thomas Hobbes (1588–1679), however, began to look inward, to consider the processes of human perception, the psychological dimensions of human experience, bringing to bear the empirical method that was to become increasingly important throughout the eighteenth century. Imagination for Hobbes was an active, creative faculty, not a mere passive receiver of impressions; it is the power that shapes our thoughts and sense impressions into unity, even into a coherent view of the world. Even John Locke (1632–1704), however much he might deplore imagination as "illusory," emphasized the unifying activity of the mind; later, David Hume (1711–1776), for all his skepticism, viewed the imagination as the power that brought together thought and feeling. Clearly the way was being paved for later thinkers like Coleridge, who would see imagination as the unifying power in human perception and creativity.

Even as Hobbes pushed forward the "Aristotelian" dimensions of imagination, probing the processes of the mind, his contemporary Shaftesbury (Anthony Ashley Cooper, 3rd Earl of Shaftesbury, 1671–1713) emphasized the Platonic heritage. Standing in the line of sixteenth-century Cambridge Platonists like Henry More and Ralph Cudworth, he also returned to the works of Plato and his Neoplatonic successors. While Hobbes focused on empirical knowledge, Shaftesbury was

**Engraving by Gustave Doré for Dante's *Paridiso*, 1868.** Although Dante subscribed to Aristotle's belief that imagination was a physical process rather than a spiritual one, in his works he nonetheless preferred to explore the vast and often mystical possibilities of inner vision. © BETTMANN/CORBIS interested in the human grasp of the ideal and of spiritual reality. The result, at least for British intellectual history, was a richly balanced legacy for the Romantic thinkers who followed.

But the influence of Hobbes and Shaftesbury, along with that of other English and Scottish philosophers, reached far beyond England. Shaftesbury was introduced into Germany by Gottfried Wilhelm von Leibniz (1646–1716) and remained a lasting influence there throughout the eighteenth century, while the empiricist psychology of Hobbes, Locke, and others was eagerly welcomed in the German universities.

The two great thinkers on imagination in Germany are Johannes Nikolaus Tetens (1736–1807) and Immanuel Kant (1724–1804), who "stand like two colossi in their concepts of imagination" (Engell, p. 118). The contribution of Tetens, under the influence of the Scottish philosopher Alexander Gerard (1728–1795), was to widen the scope of imagination to make it central in all human perception, from the immediacy of sense perception to the complex creative act of the artist, thus laying the groundwork for what would later become Coleridge's distinction between primary and secondary imagination. Tetens was also insistent, as later Romantic theorists would be, that imagination is as crucial for the scientist and the philosopher as for the poet or painter.

Kant's role in the development of the idea of imagination, under the influence of Tetens, was to synthesize two currents of thought, reflecting the ancient tension between Platonic and Aristotelian views of the world: an idealist strain deriving from such thinkers as Leibniz, Christian von Wolff (1679–1754), Shaftesbury, Baruch Spinoza (1632–1677), and Friedrich Jacobi (1743–1819), and the more empirical line of Hobbes, Locke, Hume, and other British empiricists (see Engell, p. 128–29). Although he never clarified his thought to his own (or indeed to anyone else's) satisfaction, Kant's more transcendentalist analysis of imagination in the second edition of the *Critique of Pure Reason* and later in the *Critique of Judgment* is centrally important for the emerging Romantic period, in that Kant never lost sight of the role of objective perception even as he emphasized the formative and productive power of the human mind. Although he will use different terms for it (*Einbildungskraft, Phantasie*) and although the balance shifts throughout his life, imagination in Kant brings together with considerable success the sensible and the ideal worlds, the empirical and the transcendent.

## Romanticism

Friedrich Wilhelm Joseph von Schelling (1775–1854), looking back at Kant's work a generation later, judged that Kant, by failing to demonstrate the validity of human perception, had left a dichotomy between the human mind and external reality. His own *Naturphilosophie* was meant to heal that rupture, and imagination played a central role in his endeavor. It was crucial for Schelling that imagination was both human and divine. God possesses imagination in its fullness, and the divine imagination (*die göttliche Einbildungskraft*) is "the generating power of the universe" (Engell, p. 304). The human imagination shares in this faculty, though on a lower level: ordinary mortals in the power to perceive unity in the multiplicity

of our experience; the creative genius in the ability to create new unity out of existing things. Imagination is not apart from nature, it is present as a power in nature from the beginning of creation. Here the distinction between *natura naturata* and *natura naturans,* inherited from the medieval Scholastics, is important. *Natura naturata* is the created sensible object, whether it be a natural being or the product of a human creative act—a poem or painting or piece of music. The *natura naturans* is the active power of imagination itself, a quickening spirit giving life and energy to all being, including the human mind; it is, in effect, God present as an active force in the world. Thus imagination, as the *natura naturans,* is the living link not only between the human mind and the external world but between the created world and the transcendent.

The Romantic poet and thinker Samuel Taylor Coleridge (1772–1834), although he wrote no single treatise on the imagination, is arguably the central figure in its modern development. He drew heavily on most of the major work that preceded him, including the biblical, classical, and medieval sources, as well as the most important thinkers of the century before him such as Leibniz, Tetens, and Kant and contemporaries like Schelling. Coleridge offered no system to support his view of imagination, but the insights and arguments scattered throughout his works finally yield a coherent and important perspective. His most influential work of literary theory and criticism is his *Biographia Literaria* (1817), in which he both acknowledges his debts to such thinkers as Kant and Schelling and at times diverges significantly from them. His *locus classicus* on imagination (chapter 13) distinguishes between primary and secondary imagination, and between imagination and fancy. Primary imagination is "the living Power and prime Agent of all human Perception, and as a repetition in the finite mind of the eternal act of creation in the infinite I AM." The secondary is "an echo of the former, co-existing with the conscious will"; it "dissolves, diffuses, dissipates, in order to re-create." The lesser faculty of fancy is only a "mode of Memory," dealing with "fixities and definites," with sensible realities rather than with "ideas." This view of imagination is clearly similar to Schelling's: primary imagination is the faculty by which all human beings shape their experience of the world into meaningful perception; secondary imagination is the artist's ability to create new shapes and meaning out of existing material. It is also similar in its strong affirmation of the relationship between the human and divine imaginations: the human creative act participates in the infinite creative act of God, from which it derives its power.

Coleridge's view of imagination is intimately related to his conception of *idea* and *symbol*. An idea is a suprasensible reality incarnated in sense images; it is the product of all the human faculties—reason, understanding, sense—working under the unifying power of the imagination. An idea "cannot be conveyed but by a symbol" (chapter 9), which is a product of the imagination. As Coleridge writes in the *Statesman's Manual* (1816), symbols are "the living educts of the Imagination; of that reconciling and mediatory power, which incorporating the Reason in Images of the Sense . . . gives birth to a system of symbols, harmonious in themselves, and consubstantial with

**Illustration of Urizen by William Blake from the *The First Book of Urizen* (copy B; 1795).** Blake's illustrated verse, through which he created his own personal mythology, often dealt with mystical themes and advocated the power of the imagination. THE PIERPONT MORGAN LIBRARY, NEW YORK. PML 63139

the truths, of which they are the conductors." Coleridge's conception differs significantly from Kant's, in that the ideas thus incarnated, including such ideas as God and immortality, are not merely regulative (as in Kant) but are truly constitutive of reality.

Other important Romantic explorations of imagination include the prophetic poetry of William Blake (1757–1827) and the *Defence of Poetry* of Percy Bysshe Shelley (1792–1822), both of which affirm the transcendent reach of imagination, and so are generally congruent with Coleridge and William Hazlitt's (1778–1830) essays and the letters of John Keats (1795–1821), which offer a more secular view but still affirm the unifying power of imagination.

## Twentieth Century

The transcendentalist view of imagination that came to full flower in the early nineteenth century was seriously questioned by existentialist philosophers like Søren Kierkegaard (1813–1855), Friedrich Nietzsche (1844–1900), Martin Heidegger (1889–1971), and Jean-Paul Sartre (1905–1980). For them, the humanist values implicit in the Romantic idea of imagination as affirmative and redemptive were no longer tenable

in a modern world of violence and inhumanity. Negation and angst replaced the affirmations of humanism. In their wake, postmodernist thinkers like Jacques Lacan (1901–1981), Michel Foucault (1926–1984), and Jacques Derrida (b. 1930) further undermined the Romantic idea of imagination by questioning or denying a valid relationship between image and reality. As Derrida put it, there is no "*hors-texte.*"

For all this, however, there have remained strong and serious countervailing voices—philosophers like Hans-Georg Gadamer and Emmanuel Levinas, theorists like Paul Riceour and Walter Ong, critics such as George Steiner and Geoffrey Hartman, who affirm (in Ong's phrase) the "presence of the Word" and the possibilities of transcendence. Most important of all, artists still create in poetry, in paint, in music, in drama, and in film, and there continue to be those who reflect on this creative work and affirm its human value and the unifying power of the imagination that shaped it. Given its long history and its continuing force, the idea of imagination seems likely to endure.

*See also* **Creativity in the Arts and Sciences; Existentialism; Kantianism; Metaphysics; Naturphilosophie; Neoplatonism; Philosophy of Mind; Platonism; Romanticism in Literature and Politics; Scholasticism.**

### BIBLIOGRAPHY

Abrams, M. H. *The Mirror and the Lamp: Romantic Theory and the Critical Tradition.* London: Oxford University Press, 1953.

Bantly, Francisca Cho. *Embracing Illusion: Truth and Fiction in The Dream of the Nine Clouds.* Albany: State University of New York Press, 1996. Although there is no formal concept of imagination in Buddhism, chapter one articulates helpfully the Buddhist "ontology of illusion."

Barth, J. Robert. *The Symbolic Imagination: Coleridge and the Romantic Tradition.* 2nd ed. Bronx, N.Y.: Fordham University Press, 2001.

Bate, Walter Jackson. *From Classic to Romantic: Premises of Taste in Eighteenth-Century England.* Cambridge, Mass: Harvard University Press, 1946.

Bundy, Murray Wright. *The Theory of Imagination in Classical and Mediaeval Thought.* Urbana: University of Illinois Press, 1927.

Chittick, William C. *The Sufi Path of Knowledge: Ibn al-'Arabi's Metaphysics of Imagination.* Albany: State University of New York Press, 1989. A clear and useful study of the imagination in Islam.

Engell, James. *The Creative Imagination: Enlightenment to Romanticism.* Cambridge, Mass.: Harvard University Press, 1981. The definitive study of imagination during the period of its fullest development.

Kearney, Richard. *The Wake of Imagination: Toward a Postmodern Culture.* London and New York: Routledge, 1988. A comprehensive survey and analysis of the idea of imagination from the Hebrew scriptures to postmodernism.

Mahony, William K. *The Artful Universe: An Introduction to the Vedic Religious Imagination.* Albany: State University of New York Press, 1998. A thorough study of imagination in the Hindu tradition.

McFarland, Thomas. *Originality and Imagination.* Baltimore: Johns Hopkins University Press, 1985.

Todorov, Tzvetan. *Theories of the Symbol.* Translated by Catherine Porter. Ithaca, N.Y.: Cornell University Press, 1982.

Tracy, David. *The Analogical Imagination: Christian Theology and the Culture of Pluralism.* New York: Crossroad, 1981.

Warnock, Mary. *Imagination.* Berkeley: University of California Press, 1976.

Wellek, René. *Immanuel Kant in England, 1793–1838.* Princeton: Princeton University Press, 1931.

*J. Robert Barth*

## IMMORTALITY AND THE AFTERLIFE.

Modern thinkers often begin their discussions of immortality and the afterlife with Plato, (c. 428–348 or 347 B.C.E.) which makes sense given that his *Republic* is one of the most influential works in Western philosophy. However, his view on immortality is not as straightforward as some take it to be. Book X of the *Republic* contains the Myth of Er, which puts forward the view that souls exist in separation from the body after death and that when separated from bodies, souls are omnipotent. This allows Plato to provide some footing for the view that knowledge is merely recollection of what we already know, a view discussed in his dialogue *Meno*. But as with his teacher, Socrates (c. 470–399 B.C.E.), Plato's "views" are not always consistent.

Indeed, in the early twenty-first century, Nicholas Smith has argued that Plato's views in the *Republic* seem to be intended to provoke thought rather than to set forth consistent views. As such, we should not be surprised that in Plato's work another "view" of immortality can be found. Plato's *Symposium* offers this alternative view. Here Plato's Socrates recounts Diotima's speech on true love, which puts forth the notion of being pregnant in body and in soul. This latter pregnancy gives birth to wisdom as its offspring (*Symposium* 208e1–209a4), which is immortal. This view is strikingly similar to Aristotle's in *De Anima* (430a23–24, 408b13–29, 413b24–27), where he argues that while the soul does not survive the death of the body, the active intellect does. He argues that active intellect is eternal and immortal; it produces ideas and in so doing reproduces itself in much the same way that the body produces physical offspring and in so doing reproduces itself. In this way, modern thinkers may be overreading Plato's view on immortality. The death of the individual involves the cessation of function for that individual, but the life of that person does not end if he or she has produced offspring, if that person has been pregnant in body or soul.

Early Judaic tradition held very similar views of immortality. These views held that immortality was reached through the survival of one's children and people (though there were vague references to a netherworld known as Sheol). The first emergence of a notion of bodily resurrection did not come until the Jews encountered the Greeks, who began to make successful incursions into the Middle East in the late fourth century B.C.E. Then righteous Jews killed in battle were promised bodily resurrection (Isa. 27:19), which helps to explain the prohibitions on cremation and the various rituals of Jewish burial (Moed Katan 3:5, Deut. 21:24, Amos 2:1). Of course, the statement at Genesis 3:19 that the body begins with dust and ends as dust runs counter to the view of bodily resurrection, but this reflects the earlier view that bodily resurrection does not occur.

The basis of Christianity, of course, is bodily resurrection. Paul's first letter to the Corinthians states this view very clearly: "Now if Christ is preached as raised from the dead, how can some of you say that there is no resurrection of the dead?" (1 Cor. 15:12). However, this central teaching of Christianity is not necessarily so obvious to contemporary Christians. Contemporary Christians, according to Oscar Cullman, tend to confuse the Christian teaching of bodily resurrection with the Platonic/Aristotelian view of the immortal soul (or part of the soul). For Cullman, the doctrine of the immortality of the soul depends upon the resurrection of the dead. The immortality of the soul view cannot be held without the bodily resurrection view.

Strictly speaking, then, for Christianity the soul is not immortal. It dies with the body and is resurrected at the end of time. Hence the connections drawn between any presumed body/soul duality in Plato or Aristotle and the Christian view of afterlife via resurrection must be faulty. Connections between immortality of soul and other religious views, however, are quite strong. Indeed, discussions of the transmigration of souls (or reincarnation) significantly predate Plato. Empedocles of Acragas, who was born in the early fifth century B.C.E., was known to have said: "For I have already been once a boy and a girl, a bush and a bird, and a leaping journeying fish" (Kirk, Raven, and Schofield, p. 319). Xenophanes reports that Pythagoras held similar views, leading to an argument against mistreating any living thing as it may contain the soul of a loved one (p. 219). Herodotus claims that the first people to postulate "the doctrine that the soul of man is immortal" were the Egyptians (p. 219). It is not clear, however, that the Egyptians really were the origin of the immortal soul view, and it is even less likely that they originated a view of reincarnation. Beliefs in the transmigration of souls probably originated in the East and eventually made their way to the Greeks, Romans, Egyptians, and so on.

For Hindus, for example, life on earth is characterized by a cycle of birth, death, and rebirth, a cycle that ends only once spiritual enlightenment is attained. The type of rebirth one can expect is based on the quality of one's "karma." Karma is caused by the actions of a person and it is good when it is objective or unattached to the interests or benefit of the actor. This is then grounded in "dharma," which means the path of righteousness or duty or obligation or virtue or many other similar notions. The word *dharma* itself comes from Sanskrit and means to sustain or to hold. In this way, dharma is understood to be the sustenance of the universe, and good karma then becomes acting in accord with the cosmos. Righteousness, understood as selflessness, is the order of the cosmos, and release from the cycle of birth, death, and rebirth comes as a result of communing with this order. The views of Buddhism and Sikhism are very similar, even incorporating some of the same principles (e.g., karma and dharma), though at times in subtly different ways.

Interestingly, some modern philosophers have developed views that rather closely follow Eastern views of karma and dharma, though no direct connection seems to exist. Immanuel Kant, for example, claims that for an action to be moral, it must be undertaken from a motive that is exclusive of the interests of the actor—a motive of duty or obligation to act according to a self-willed universal law. This position closely resembles karmic action grounded in dharma but, interestingly, it carries with it no connection to the divine, immortality, or an afterlife. Other philosophers in the Western tradition, however, have tried to compel good action by highlighting its consequences for the actor. John Locke's view of the state of nature, for example, depends upon the view that good actions on earth will be rewarded with good consequences in the afterlife, while evil actions will be divinely punished.

In more recent times, we have become rather incredulous toward such arguments. John Hick spoke about this in his 1977 Ingersoll Lecture on the Immortality of Man. He argued that many of his "thoughtful theological contemporaries" felt "that talk of an afterlife is not only too improbable factually, but also too morally and religiously dubious, to constitute a proper branch of Christian belief" (p. 2). As a result of the takeover of scientific reasoning, we have found it increasingly difficult to fathom a "belief in a post-mortem life" (p. 2). Indeed, cognitive science has made it difficult for us to conceive of a mind/brain duality, much less a soul/body duality, which means that the notion of the personality living beyond the death of the body becomes unfathomable to the modern scientific mind/brain. And so even some Christian theologians (such as Wolfhart Pannenberg and Gordon Kaufman) have argued that modern science makes belief in the idea of the immortality of the soul "untenable" (Pannenberg, 1970, 1968; Kaufman). Hick vehemently disagrees with such views, arguing in part that they cannot possibly be consistent with a Christian viewpoint (or, indeed, any other viewpoint that contains a belief in divine consciousness) because the belief in God depends upon a belief in a divine consciousness that is separate from any sort of embodiment.

These same theologians, Hick reports, have also argued that the afterlife principle, while problematic in factual terms, is actually damaging in moral terms. Here Hick is not referring to the Marxian view that a promise of immortality allows people to become inured to their misery here on earth as they count on eternal splendor in the afterlife (and a similar perspective can be found with respect to beliefs in reincarnation). Rather, he calls attention to the idea "that the concern for personal immortality (whether by the resurrection of the body or the immortality of the soul) is a selfish and thus a basically irreligious concern" (p. 5). We might say, then, that the problem with the belief in personal immortality is that it causes us to focus on selfish concerns rather than on selfless ones. Indeed, the Hindu or the Sikh or the Buddhist might raise just such an objection, since good karma relies on selfless actions.

In fact this is precisely the point Hick makes. He says that the problem does not lie with the principle of the afterlife but instead with the way we think about the afterlife. Drawing on the many similarities between Christianity, Judaism, Islam, Hinduism, and Buddhism, Hick concludes that the Christian view of the afterlife is too limited because it encourages us to

think that we have one mortal life in which to get things right and that failing to do so will lead to eternal damnation of the self. This is a view that is too individualized to cohere with Christian tenets (as well as the tenets of the other major religions). It makes more sense to rely on the basic principles of the world's major religions regarding (1) the potentialities of the human spirit (e.g., as child of God in Judeo-Christian tradition, as a potential Buddha capable of liberation in nirvana, as in communion with Brahman and thus a liberated soul while still on earth); (2) the realization that attaining deeper human potential "is not a matter of perpetuating but rather of transcending our present self-enclosed individual existence" (e.g., Jesus' teaching of love of others before self, Judaism's obedience to the Torah, Islam's submission of the ego to Allah's will, etc.); (3) the present conscious ego, which "must voluntarily relinquish its own self-centered existence" and the purpose of all the world's major religions, which "is to carry men and women through this momentous choice" (Hick, pp. 6–8).

Given these connections, Hick encourages Christianity to consider the possibility that this mortal life is not our only mortal life. Rather, since the goal is to actualize the potentiality of the human spirit to transcend its self-enclosed existence, Christian religion needs to incorporate the idea that mortal life was intended by God to engage a learning process leading it toward the goal of self-transcendence, and until this is accomplished, mortal life and death must continue for each individual consciousness. This view is strikingly familiar, since it seems to be an argument for reincarnation. But Hick's view differs from the Eastern view insofar as it postulates the idea that our different mortal lives occur in different worlds (perhaps even different dimensions?) until we make the proper "momentous" choice, a choice that will depend in part on the conditions in which the mortal life is lived.

This raises an interesting point. Perhaps our current world provides a terrible context for those of us currently living our mortal lives. Living in a world that valorizes individual choice in a social and economic environment that lauds competition between individuals for scarce resources and rewards because such competition makes our production more efficient, we may be in perhaps the worst milieu for the encouragement of self-transcendence. Hick's argument, then, seems to require that religion actually play a part in altering the mortal context, so that we might become capable of the self-transcendence that the major religions support. The implications of this are staggering, though not especially surprising given that many have argued that religion's cousin, philosophy, ought to play just such a role (Aristotle and Marx come immediately to mind). What is surprising is that few, if any, contemporary philosophers would make such an argument, in spite of the fact that this is a role to which philosophy (before the death of metaphysics) seems particularly well suited.

*See also* **Buddhism; Christianity; Death; Heaven and Hell; Hinduism; Judaism; Platonism.**

**BIBLIOGRAPHY**

Ackrill, J. L., ed. *A New Aristotle Reader.* Princeton, N.J.: Princeton University, 1987.

Cobb, John B., Jr. "The Resurrection of the Soul." *Harvard Theological Review* 80 (1987): 213–227.

Cooper, John M., ed. *Plato: Complete Works.* Indianapolis: Hackett, 1997.

Cullman, Oscar. "Immortality of the Soul or Resurrection of the Dead?" *Theologische Zeitschrift* 2 (1956): 126ff.

Hick, John. "Present and Future Life." *Harvard Theological Review* 71 (1978): 1–15.

Kant, Immanuel. *Ethical Philosophy: The Complete Texts of Grounding for the Metaphysics of Morals, and Metaphysical Principles of Virtue, Part II of the Metaphysics of Morals.* Translated by James W. Ellington; introduction by Warner A. Wick. Indianapolis: Hackett, 1983.

Kaufman, Gordon D. *Systematic Theology: A Historicist Perspective.* New York: Scribners, 1978.

Kirk, G. S., J. E. Raven, and M. Schofield. *The Presocratic Philosophers: A Critical History with a Selection of Texts.* 2nd ed. Cambridge, U.K., and New York: Cambridge University Press, 1983.

Moltmann, Jürgen. "Resurrection as Hope." *Harvard Theological Review* 61 (1968): 129–147.

Pannenberg, Wolfhart. *Jesus—God and Man.* Translated by Lewis L. Wilkins and Duane A. Priebe. London: S.C.M. Press, 1968.

———. *What Is Man? Contemporary Anthropology in Theological Perspective.* Translated by Duane A. Priebe. Philadelphia: Fortress Press, 1970.

Smith, Nicholas D. "Images, Education, and Paradox in Plato's *Republic.*" In *Recognition, Remembrance, and Reality: New Essays on Plato's Epistemology and Metaphysics,* supplement to *Apeiron* 33 (2000): 126–140.

*Tim Duvall*

**IMPERIALISM.** *See* **Empire and Imperialism.**

**IMPRESSIONISM.** Impressionism was an artistic movement that originated in France in the 1860s and 1870s. In 1874, painters including Claude Monet, Camille Pissarro, Auguste Renoir, Alfred Sisley, Berthe Morisot, Edgar Degas, Armand Guillaumin, and Paul Cézanne participated in the first of eight independent Impressionist exhibitions held until 1886. They were eventually joined by Gustave Caillebotte and the American Mary Cassatt. Closely identified with the Impressionists was Edouard Manet, whose controversial works of the 1860s led the mostly younger Impressionists to consider him their leader, even though he refused to exhibit in their shows. The painter Frédéric Bazille was also associated with the group but was killed during the Franco-Prussian War, before he could join in the exhibitions he helped conceive.

## Impressionist Practice and Purpose
Impressionism transformed the Western conception of landscape painting from timeless and nostalgic idealizations of distant places to accurate and brilliantly colored representations of existing, often familiar sites seen at specific moments. Responding to calls for modernity and naturalism—to reflect the environments of contemporary (French) humanity—the

Impressionists recorded their peers at both work and play. Although today we take for granted the practice of painting on the spot directly from observation, in the nineteenth century that commitment was controversial. It was inseparable from debates over the role of modern subjects in art (as opposed to classical ones), accompanied by pejorative comparisons to photography, which was considered mechanical, hence noncreative. Impressionist practices were also fraught with political connotations, conditioned by the new prosperity and related democratic aspirations. With their views of specifically contemporary activities, whether in Parisian cafés, on beaches or in flowery fields, or of the economic life on waterways, railways, and boulevards, the Impressionists made their paintings sensitive and inclusive reflections of modernity.

The name Impressionism was coined, following the first Impressionist exhibition, by a satirical critic named Louis Leroy. He made fun of Monet's *Impression: Sunrise* (1873, Musée Marmottan, Paris) a sketch-like view of the harbor of the painter's native Le Havre: "*Impression*: I was sure of it. I was telling myself, since I'm so impressed, there must be an impression in it. And what freedom, what ease in handling! A sketch for wallpaper is more finished than that there seascape!" Another name, Intransigents, though eventually abandoned, referred to a broader revolutionary significance. Following the Paris Commune (1871) by just a few years, the Impressionists elicited memories of radical politics because of their independent movement and their free and broken brushwork, which challenged the official art salons' monopoly on public exhibitions and defied the traditional craft of academic art, which taught careful draftsmanship and polished finishing.

Although there are wide variations in Impressionist style, especially when comparing the relatively traditional handling of Degas (*A Carriage at the Races,* 1869, Museum of Fine Arts, Boston) to the fragmented brushstrokes of color that Monet and Renoir (*La Grenouillère,* 1869, Nationalmuseum, Stockholm) developed side by side on the banks of the river Seine, the artists shared a commitment to the representation of modern life based on exacting observation of their own world. For those like Monet, Pissarro (*Red Roofs,* 1877, National Gallery, London), and Sisley (*The Bridge at Villeneuve-la-Garenne,* 1872, Metropolitan Museum of Art, New York), who painted primarily landscapes, working out of doors or *en plein air,* was an important step away from the artifices of the studio. Their more urban colleagues Manet (*A Bar at the Folies Bergère,* 1883, Courtauld Institute, London) and Degas surveyed the dance halls and the Opéra, as well as shops and boulevards for scenes of pleasure and material consumption, while the female Impressionists, Morisot (*The Cradle,* 1872, Musée d'Orsay, Paris) and Cassatt (*Little Girl in a Blue Armchair,* 1878, National Gallery of Art, Washington, D.C.), given the limitations of their access to the primarily male public world, developed a flair for domestic scenes.

For many, modernity was exemplified by countryside locations and sporting activities (Caillebotte, *Rowers on the Yerre River,* 1877, private collection). But Monet, Guillaumin (*Bridge over the Marne at Nogent,* 1871, Metropolitan Museum of Art, New York), Pissarro, and Cézanne (in his early years) included

***Impression: Sunrise* (1873) by Claude Monet. Oil on canvas.** Monet was arguably the most well-known of the Impressionists, and his painting technique became the hallmark of the movement. The term *Impressionist* was coined by a skeptical art critic reviewing Monet's *Impression: Sunrise.* © 1999 ARTISTS RIGHTS SOCIETY (ARS), NEW YORK / ADAGP, PARIS. REPRODUCED BY PERMISSION OF THE ARTISTS RIGHTS SOCIETY, INC.

as a counterpart to leisure scenes evidence of the productivity, infrastructure, and technologies that underlay French progress in the new industrial age. Indeed, the poet Charles Baudelaire, while lamenting the loss of taste occasioned by the rise of the bourgeoisie, urged modern artists to somehow capture the essence of their world, which for him was one of constant change, including the flow of crowded commercial avenues and socializing at sidewalk cafés. In addition, the productive processes and speed associated with factories and train travel were as much a part of the landscape of modern vision as were ladies on beaches and promenades among poppy fields. The liberal art critic Jules Castagnary actually called for a modern landscape that would reflect contemporary progress built on democratic change.

### Neo-Impressionism and Beyond

Implicit in the word *impression* are two ostensibly opposed concepts: that of the rapid glance or instinctive judgment and that of the exact imprint, as in a photographic impression. Hence Impressionism could appear to some, such as Leroy, a shoddy

and unskilled practice, whereas to others the intuition that light is the basis of vision, and color its medium in art, was scientifically true. In addition, Impressionism's commitment to direct observation and its evocation of progressive change are generally associated with the spirit of positivism, a contemporary philosophy developed by Auguste Comte and applied to art by his disciple and specialist in the psychology of perception, Hippolyte Taine. Comte's quasireligion of progress based on scientific attitudes was followed by Taine's deterministic theories on the history of art. Their ideas might be stated as the relationship between art and its immediate physical and social environment, expressed through the empirical perceptions of the talented individual. Their follower, the novelist Émile Zola, a childhood friend of Cézanne, through whom he met the Impressionists, wrote famously that "art is no more nor less than a corner of nature seen through a temperament."

The association between these ideas and Impressionism can be gauged by the neo-Impressionist critique of their achievement. Certain artists of the next generation, especially Georges Seurat (*Sunday Afternoon on the Island of La Grande Jatte,* 1886,

Art Institute of Chicago), according to the critic Félix Féneon, sought to make Impressionism more socially responsible and democratic by developing a collective technique accessible to all. Seurat's dot-dash or pointillist method reduced the labor of painting to a repeatable formula, while at the same time creating the sensation of duration over time rather than a spontaneously grasped instant. On both grounds, neo-Impressionism claimed greater objectivity, thus challenging the individualist basis of Impressionist naturalism in favor of a shared and more permanent, hence more classical, vision. Through Seurat's eyes, then, Impressionism celebrated merely momentary, superficial pleasures and casual, intuitive craft rather than the mental and physical concentration derived from rational calculation and rigorous effort. This moralizing argument fit a political critique of bourgeois society that came to be associated with avant-garde painting of both the Right and the Left after Impressionism.

By contrast, while adhering always to the Impressionist model of painting directly from the motif with dabs of color, Paul Cézanne also managed to transcend the Impressionist sense of moment to produce what he called "a more lasting art, like that of the museums" (*Montagne Sainte-Victoire*, c. 1882, Metropolitan Museum of Art, New York). In ways more fruitful than Seurat, his increasing abstraction led toward future styles of the twentieth century, especially Cubism.

In the other arts, however, Impressionism's impact was limited. The sensitive, mobile surfaces of Auguste Rodin's bronze sculptures caught the light in ways associated with Impressionism. Claude Debussy's music came to be called Impressionist because it challenged past styles and evoked certain motifs in nature associated with Impressionist painting. In the literature of Henry James, the term refers to the literal naturalism of settings described in so much detail that it both overwhelms and yet concentrates our anticipation of the narrative.

In painting, almost every country had its Impressionist school; the British and the American, with their direct ties to Monet's circle, were the strongest. In later art, the abstract expressionism of artists like Jackson Pollock has been traced to Claude Monet's late *Water Lilies,* and the contemporary painter Joan Mitchell, who spent much time near Monet's former residence in Giverny, has been called an "abstract Impressionist." However, perhaps the greatest legacy of Impressionism is that it is the most popular style for so many amateur art colonies and Sunday painters, who celebrate both nature and leisure while working hard to develop their personal techniques.

After all the memoirs, biographies, and correspondence written by the painters and their contemporaries, Impressionism studies began in earnest with John Rewald, who used such documents to trace the Impressionist painters almost day by day and site by site. Interpretations of their art, however, remained within the legend of revolutionary aesthetic innovation and celebration of its seminal step toward modernist departures from literal representation.

The first writer to take seriously the social dimension to Impressionism's significance was Meyer Schapiro in his lectures at Columbia University and in a few short articles. He

was followed by Robert L. Herbert, whose disciples in particular have stressed the relationship between the artists and the history and significance of places they inhabited. At the same time, the social art historian T. J. Clark has focused on Impressionist paintings as documents of the changing physical environment and its social implications. Feminist scholars led by Linda Nochlin have focused on the female Impressionists as well as on the role of women as subjects of the male Impressionist gaze. Finally, a number of younger scholars have explored the relationship between Impressionism and politics.

*See also* **Arts; Modernism; Nature; Visual Culture.**

BIBLIOGRAPHY
Berson, Ruth. *The New Painting: Impressionism 1874-1886: Documents.* 2 vols. San Francisco: Fine Arts Museums of San Francisco, 1996.
Brettell, Richard. *Impression: Painting Quickly in France, 1860-1890.* New Haven and London: Yale University Press, 2000.
Callen, Anthea. *Techniques of the Impressionists.* London: Orbis, 1982.
Clark, Timothy J. *The Painting of Modern Life: Paris in the Art of Manet and His Followers.* Princeton: Princeton University Press, 1984.
Herbert, Robert L. *Impressionism: Art, Leisure and Parisian Society.* New Haven and London: Yale University Press, 1988.
Moffet, Charles S. *The New Painting: Impressionism 1874–1886.* San Francisco: Fine Arts Museums of San Francisco, 1986.
Rewald, John. *A History of Impressionism.* 4th revised ed. New York: Museum of Modern Art, 1973.
Rubin, James H. *Impressionism.* London: Phaidon, 1999.
Tinterow, Gary, and Henri Loyrette. *Origins of Impressionism.* New York: The Metropolitan Museum of Art, 1994.

*James H. Rubin*

**INDIGENISMO.** The term *indigenismo* encompasses a diverse array of intellectual production concerning the indigenous peoples of Latin America. The twentieth century in particular witnessed an explosion of literary, critical, and visual work on the figure of the Indian. It should be made clear from the outset that the term, although most closely associated with Mexico and Guatemala and especially with the Andean region during the first half of the twentieth century, is applicable to Latin America's diverse nations and histories, including those not typically viewed as influenced by indigenismo. This broad geographical and historical scope stems from the wide appeal of indigenismo's central, self-declared objective: the defense and vindication of the continent's indigenous peoples. This objective distinguishes indigenismo from idyllic and idealized representations of the Indian with which Latin American cultural history is rife, as evidenced by, for example, Romanticism-inflected Indianist works of the nineteenth century. Indianism tended to portray the Indian in a sentimental light and did not address the social plight of indigenous peoples in modern Latin America. *Cumandá* (1879) by Ecuador's Juan León Mera (1832–1894) illustrates Indianism's tendency to portray the Indians as part of an idealized past and thus to ignore their contemporary presence.

Though extraordinary, the life of José Carlos Mariátegui (1894–1930) illustrates the contradictions that riddle indigenismo. Impoverished mestizos from the provinces, the young Mariátegui and his family emigrated to Lima, Peru's capital city, in hopes of bettering their social condition. Having dropped out of grade school in order to work, the crippled Mariátegui rose to prominence within the growing journalism industry with virtually no formal education. He did not turn his full attention to the problem of the Indian until his return from Europe in 1923, when he famously stated that his exile had allowed him to see Peru for the first time. This vision, filtered through his study of Marxism, led to his groundbreaking *Siete ensayos de interpretación de la realidad peruana* (1928; reprint. Mexico: Era, 1993), in which he declared:

la literatura indigenista no puede darnos una versión rigurosamente verista del indio. Tiene que idealizarlo y estilizarlo. Tampoco puede darnos su propia ánima. Es todavía una literatura de mestizos. Por eso se llama indigenista y no indígena. Una literatura indígena, si debe venir, vendrá en su tiempo. Cuando los propios indios estén en grado de producirla. [indigenista literature cannot give us a rigorously truthful version of the Indian. It has to idealize and stylize him. Nor can it give us his own soul. It is still a literature made by mestizos. That is why it is called indigenista and not indigenous. An indigenous literature, if it is to come, will come when it is ready. When the Indians themselves have the capacity to produce it.] (p. 306)

Conscious of his place within this dynamic, Mariátegui facilitated the forging of an indigenous voice through his publication of *Labor*, (1928–1929) a paper for the working class, and through his encouragement of indigenous self-organization.

In contrast to Indianism, indigenismo defines itself through its critical stance vis-à-vis the dominant society that exploits and debases indigenous peoples and their cultures. Clearly, this perspective has not been unique to modernity. Indigenismo finds foundational antecedents in the accounts of figures such as Bartolomé de las Casas (1474–1566) and el Inca Garcilaso de la Vega (1539–1616), who, respectively, denounced the ills visited upon Indians by the Spanish colonizers and praised the integrity and complexity of the Inca Empire in the face of accusations of its barbarity. Other sympathetic works on the Indian can be found in the eighteenth and nineteenth centuries, including Clorinda Matto de Turner's (1854–1909) *Aves sin nido* (1889; Birds without a nest) and Narciso Aréstegui's (1818–1892) *El Padre Horán* (1848). The critic Efraín Kristal considered the latter to be the first indigenista work. These works evidence the outrage typical of indigenista works as well as their authors' willingness to challenge such structures of authority as the church and the government. Thus, the vindication of the Indian through the indictment of social and political institutions was already in place at least as early as the mid-nineteenth century. Later indigenistas were equally in debt to figures such as Manuel González Prada (1848–1918) who was the first, in works such as "Discurso en el Politeama" (1888; Speech in the Politeama), to call for social revolt in order to rectify the abuses committed against the indigenous peoples.

**The 1920s and 1930s**

While indigenismo should and must be contextualized among the many discourses on the Indian produced during the colonial and Republican periods, its defining moment occurs with the explosion of voices on indigenous matters in the 1920s and 1930s. The movement's seminal novels, such as Alcides

Arguedas's (1879–1946) *Raza de bronce* (1919; Bronze race), Jorge Icaza's (1906–1978) *Huasipungo* (1934), and Ciro Alegría's (1909–1967) *El mundo es ancho y ajeno* (1941; Broad and alien is the world), should nevertheless not overshadow the significant and arguably as important critical and scholarly production on the Indian in the same period. Works such as José Carlos Mariátegui's (1894–1930) *Siete ensayos de interpretación de la realidad peruana* (1928; Seven interpretative essays on Peruvian reality), Pío Jaramillo Alvarado's (1884–1968) *El indio ecuatoriano* (1936; The Ecuadorian Indian), Hildebrando Castro Pozo's (1890–1945) *Nuestra comunidad indígena* (1924; Our indigenous community), and José Vasconcelos's (1882–1959) *Indología* (1926) purported to study "the indigenous question" in a scientific light. These critical works, perhaps more so than their aesthetic counterparts, reveal the ways in which the importation and acquisition of foreign theoretical models fomented new perspectives on the indigenous problem and thereby offered novel solutions. Marxism, for example, played a central role in giving the defense of the Indian a distinctly revolutionary flavor. On the whole, novelistic, poetic, and critical discourses on the Indian had a profound impact on social and political movements, such as the APRA (Alianza Popular Revolucionaria Americana) in Peru and the Mexican Revolution, which sought to challenge the standing political and social order. A full study of the impact of the indigenista project on Latin American politics remains to be carried out. It should also be noted that the indigenistas were generally not progressive in terms of gender and that in fact most indigenismo is rife with stereotypical representations of femininity and masculinity.

The Uruguayan critic Angel Rama has presented the most compelling analysis of the social dynamics behind the effervescence of indigenismo in the 1920s and 1930s. In his seminal *Transculturación narrativa en América Latina* (1982; Narrative transculturation in Latin America), largely concerned with the problem of representing autochthony in the region, Rama argues that the indigenismo of this period is in fact a product of the rise of the mestizo middle classes to power. In Rama's scheme of things, indigenismo is a kind of Trojan horse that, while addressing authentic social concerns regarding the Indian, nevertheless makes inroads against the dominant land-owning oligarchies to the benefit of mestizos—persons of mixed European and American Indian ancestry—and not especially the indigenous peoples. This observation reveals a crucial feature of indigenismo that has been taken for granted by most criticism, although notably not that of Mariátegui and his interlocutor Luis Alberto Sánchez (1900–1994). It demonstrates that while indigenismo claims to speak of the Indian's plight, it is in fact a phenomenon that occurs almost entirely within the majority mestizo culture of the continent. In the end, then, indigenismo benefits what Rama calls *mesticismo,* or the empowerment of the mestizo.

This observation rests primarily on the cultural and social heterogeneity that undergirds indigenismo. Indigenismo's mode of production reiterates the paradox at the center of the indigenistas' intellectual production: through its expression in the dominant language and culture, it tends to exclude those very subjects it represents. As such, indigenismo should be viewed less as a window on the indigenous people of Latin America and more as a complex example of how intellectuals have imagined alterity, or otherness, in the continent. Indigenista production can and must be read against the grain, as it certainly provides a vast and detailed portrait of the urban mestizo middle classes at the beginning and throughout much of the twentieth century. Indeed, the more recent writers in the indigenistra tradition, including Rosario Castellanos (1925–1974), Miguel Angel Asturias (1899–1974), and José María Arguedas (1911–1969), have since 1950 transformed the indigenista vision into one that increasingly considers the role of indigenous culture in relation to mestizo society.

*See also* **Mestizaje.**

BIBLIOGRAPHY

Aquézolo Castro, Manuel, ed. *La polémica del indigenismo.* Lima: Mosca Azul, 1976.

Cornejo Polar, Antonio. *Literatura y sociedad en el Perú: La novela indigenista.* Lima: Lasontay, 1980.

Kristal, Efraín. *The Andes Viewed from the City: Literary and Political Discourse on the Indian in Peru (1848–1930).* New York: Lang, 1987.

Mariátegui, José Carlos. *Seven Interpretive Essays on Peruvian Reality.* Translated by Marjory Urquidi. Austin: University of Texas Press, 1971.

Rama, Angel. *Transculturación narrativa en América Latina.* Hanover, N.H.: Ediciones del Norte, 1982.

*Jorge Coronado*

**INDIVIDUALISM.** Individualism endorses the principle that the ends or purposes of the human individual possess dignity and worth that take precedence over communal, metaphysical, cosmological, or religious priorities. While individualism may appeal to certain metaphysical or epistemological schools of thought such as nominalism or empiricism, it will be treated here as primarily a moral and/or political doctrine. Individualism is commonly seen by both its proponents and opponents to be the creation of the modern Western world, a development of Enlightenment liberal values.

The term *individualism* was first coined in the nineteenth century, initially around 1820 in French, and then quickly spread to the other European languages. In its origins, the term's connotations were pejorative: Joseph de Maistre (1753–1821) equated "individualism" with the "infinite fragmentation of all doctrines," and Félicité Robert de Lamennais (1782–1854) treated it as indistinguishable from anarchy. The language of individualism was picked up and widely spread by the followers of Claude-Henri Saint-Simon (1760–1825). In Germany, England, and the United States, however, the negative overtones were soon stripped away. In Germany individualism became closely associated with the aspirations of Romanticism, in England, with utilitarianism and laissez-faire economics, and in America with the core political and social values of democracy and capitalism.

Concentration on the linguistic diffusion of individualism overlooks the fact that many cultures outside the Atlantic world at many times before the nineteenth century have promulgated doctrines that were individualistic in inclination. Moreover, it should not be forgotten that many who champion individualism count tendencies inherent in modernity itself among the chief threats to the individual. Thus, a full study of the history of individualism requires a survey of a broad range of thinkers and writings.

### Ancient Sources

The major schools of classical Indian religion and philosophy generally upheld the doctrine of karma, the idea that an individual's status in the present life is a function of one's deeds in previous lives. This entailed not only that the soul was separable from the body—indeed, any body—but that it had a specific identity that transcended even corporeal death. Karma thus implied deep individual responsibility for one's actions and a system of assigning merit and demerit in the future depending on how one lives one's life in the present. That moral judgment is embedded in dharma—a universalistic system of absolute moral duties—is irrelevant. It still remains central to Indian thought that individual deeds are the wellspring of the moral system. For many Indian schools, and especially for Buddhists and Jainists, spiritual purification and eventual union with the Ultimate stem solely from the personal efforts of the individual. The right path is laid out, but it is up to the individual to follow it.

China produced doctrines that echoed the Indian emphasis on the individual. Confucius (551–479 B.C.E.) challenged both egalitarianism and hierarchical naturalism as explanations of human character. Although people are born with equal capacities, only some achieve superior moral standing because the individual's moral qualities are dependent on practice and education. Confucius's follower Meng-Tzu (c. 371–298 B.C.E.; romanized as Mencius) elaborated this position by stipulating that environment and instruction are insufficient as explanations for why only some individuals attain superiority; in his view many simply "throw themselves away," choosing not to adopt the path to righteousness, beneficence, and wisdom. Attainment of superiority thus rests in part on something like self-determination. Daoism, particularly Neo-Daoism, also evinced respect for individuality. The Daoist belief that each thing possessed its own nature could be interpreted not merely to pertain to natural species or types but to individual characters. According to the Daoist Chuang Tzu (fourth century B.C.E.), the freedom and peace of the spirit occur solely through knowledge of one's own inner nature, a position that, in turn, requires equal recognition and respect on the part of each person for the nature of one's fellow creatures. This focus on the nature of the individual was crystallized in the Neo-Daoist concentration on the particularity of human natures.

Self-knowledge was also the path to one's individuality for the Greek philosopher Socrates (469–399 B.C.E.), who sought to live by what he claimed as his personal motto, "Know yourself." Accordingly, he maintained that virtue and other forms of knowledge cannot be taught or communicated directly from one person to another. Rather, each individual must discover what is true for him- or herself. But if wisdom is incommunicable, the philosopher may still question other human beings in order to prod them to realize the falsity that they embrace and to stimulate them in the process of self-questioning that yields self-knowledge. In Plato's *Apology* Socrates describes himself as a "gadfly" who annoys fellow Athenian citizens with his difficult and embarrassing questions and reveals their ignorance. Socrates' trial and death at the hands of the Athenian democracy has often been held up as a noble self-sacrifice in the cause of individualism against the conformity of the masses.

Socrates was not alone among Greek thinkers in proposing a version of individualism. Democritus (c. 460–c. 370 B.C.E.) emphasized the atomic nature of all matter and, thus, licensed a conception of humanity that emphasized the discrete character of individual creatures. In turn, this theory of individuation has been shown by recent scholars to have direct political overtones that favored the Athenian democracy. The Sophist Protagoras of Abdera (c. 485–420 B.C.E.) upheld the doctrine that "man is the measure," which he interpreted as a moral principle, as well as an epistemological one, that supported the individual as the source and standard of human virtue.

### Revealed Religion
Christianity contributed doctrines of the freedom of the will and personal salvation that added a further dimension to human individuality. Created as equal persons in God's image, human beings enjoy inherent dignity by virtue of the divine flame that burns within their souls. Christian moral teaching replaced status, race, gender, occupation, and all other markers of social difference with one's individual orientation toward God as the determinant of the ultimate disposition of one's soul. While Judaism had conveyed some overtones of personal salvation, the dominant relation with God was conditioned by the divine covenant with the Jewish people as a whole. In contrast, Jesus' message was directed to all people who were open to his words and treated them as individuals capable of receiving divine grace and blessing. Every person, as one of God's created, could, through individual effort and renunciation of worldly concerns, render him- or herself worthy for salvation.

The implicit individualism of early Christian moral theology was reinforced by later thinkers such as St. Augustine of Hippo (354–430 C.E.). According to Augustine, all human beings possess the capacity to choose between good and evil and to choose to accept or to turn away from the divine will. Of course, the objects between which one chooses are not of equal worth. Rejecting God by preferring one's own desires yields dissatisfaction and unhappiness in one's earthly life as well as the misery of eternal damnation, whereas submitting to God properly expresses one's divinely granted freedom, the correct use of the will with which human beings have been endowed. Nevertheless, it remains up to the individual (even up to the moment preceding death) to decide whether to submit to or renounce God's offering. The individual is the final and ultimate source of the destiny of his or her own soul.

Islam did not entirely share Christianity's affinity for personal freedom of the will, emphasizing instead a strict adherence to religious law, namely, *shari'a*. Yet the Koran did uphold human freedom, so Muslim teaching maintained that it was the individual, not God, who was responsible for sin. Likewise, the Koran offered a vision of personal salvation that was far more embodied and carnal than Christianity's. Thus Islam, too, adopted important elements of individualism.

Despite the common perception of medieval Europe as monolithic and hostile to expressions of individualism, the period did much to extend the idea of human individuality. In law, the concept of human beings with personal rights and liberties was expressed in both secular and religious documents. In public life, the principle of individual consent to the imposition of political power (captured in the ubiquitous phrase "What touches all must be approved by all") was articulated. In moral philosophy and theology, the conception of the rational will, which defined the individual as the primary unit of analysis, was elevated to axiomatic status. Regardless of the institutional and ecclesiastical barriers to individualism, scholars have repeatedly looked to Latin Christian Europe as a source for individualism.

### The Reformation and the Aftermath
These medieval tendencies came to fruition during the sixteenth and seventeenth centuries, so that individualism in the modern world deserves to be understood as a culmination of far earlier intellectual trends. The Reformation brought not only a challenge in practice to the unity of the Christian Church but also a transformation of important theological categories. Martin Luther (1483–1546) insisted on the unique presence of God alone in the conscience of believers, with the implication that the faithful Christian is responsible directly and immediately to God. The consequence of this teaching— while perhaps recognized only fleetingly by Luther and his

followers—was that salvation did not depend on submission to the authority of the priesthood or the church. Nor did it fall to the secular power, to which pertained the control of bodies and behavior, to discipline the souls of subjects. Thus, whether intentionally or not, Luther opened the door to claims of public respect for liberty of conscience and eventually individual freedom of worship.

In the generation after Luther, inferences about personal freedom of religion were deduced by reforming thinkers. Sebastian Castellion (1515–1563) published pseudonymously a treatise entitled *De haereticis, an sint persequendi* (On heretics, whether they are to be persecuted) in response to John Calvin's organization of the burning of a fellow Christian theologian for heresy at Geneva. Castellion argued that Christian belief must be held with sincere conviction. Hence, clerics and magistrates must refrain from persecution of convinced Christians who cling to doctrines that do not coincide with official teachings. Castellion maintained that the individual Christian's duties extend to forbearance of the free and honest faith of one's fellows even in the face of disagreements of understanding and interpretation.

In the seventeenth century, the individualism implicit in confessional pluralism would become more pronounced. For instance, Baruch Spinoza (1632–1677) claimed a broad application for the right to liberty of thought and belief without interference from a sovereign power's (or a church's) determination of the truth or falsity of one's ideas. Pierre Bayle (1647–1706) asserted that all forms of persecution (innocuous as well as harsh) of religious diversity encourage hypocrisy and erode social order. An erring conscience, if it be held in good faith, deserves as much protection as a correct one—a principle that Bayle extended even to atheists.

John Locke (1632–1704) proposed liberty of individual conscience as justified in the case of most Christian (and perhaps some non-Christian) rites. For Locke, the role of the magistrate should be confined to the maintenance of public tranquility and the defense of individual rights rather than the care of the soul. Hence, Locke's *Letter concerning Toleration* (1690) defended a vision of the church as a purely voluntary association that a believer was free, according to conscience, to enter or leave at will. Locke crystallized a key Reformation shift: the idea that one's religious confession is a matter of individual choice rather than institutional imposition.

The evolving acceptance of individualism paralleled changes in other European cultural, social, and political practices and attitudes. The invention of the printing press and movable type in the mid-fifteenth century immeasurably enhanced the ability of individuals to spread their ideas and made it possible for a larger public to access the written word. Demands were heard for freedom of the press (literally and figuratively) from censorship by clerical and secular authorities alike. While republican values that promoted civic virtue over personal choice retained a hold on public discourse, political liberty in geographically extensive regimes with monarchic institutions tended to be conceived in terms of individual freedom rather than civic populism. Hence, it is at this time and place that the origins of the bundle of individualist doctrines known as liberalism are found.

## Liberalism and Individualism

Thomas Hobbes (1588–1679) generally is identified as the most important direct antecedent of modern individualist philosophy. In his *Leviathan* (1651), Hobbes ascribed to all individuals natural liberty (as well as equality) on the basis of which they are licensed to undertake whatever actions are necessary in order to preserve themselves from their fellow creatures. Hobbes believed that the exercise of such natural liberty logically leads to unceasing conflict and unremitting fear so long as no single sovereign ruler exists to maintain peace. The exchange of chaotic natural freedom for government-imposed order requires renunciation of all freedoms that humans possess by nature (except, of course, self-preservation) and voluntary submission to any dictate imposed by the sovereign. Yet, even under the terms of Hobbes's absolute sovereignty, individuals are deemed to remain at liberty to choose for themselves concerning any and all matters about which the ruler has not explicitly legislated.

Locke begins his mature political theory in the *Second Treatise of Government* (1689) with the postulation of the divinely granted liberty of all individuals, understood in terms of the absolute right to preserve one's life and to lay claim to the goods one requires for survival. Arguing against the patriarchal doctrine of Sir Robert Filmer (1588–1653), Locke insists that no natural basis—neither paternity nor descent—justifies the submission of one person to another. Rather, each individual is the proprietor of his or her (divinely endowed) physical and mental talents, abilities, and energies. The individual thus constitutes the basic unit of social and political analysis for Locke, who is sometimes considered the proponent of the doctrine of "possessive individualism" par excellence.

In contrast to Hobbes, Locke maintains that the natural condition of individual proprietorship can be maintained tranquilly because human beings are deemed sufficiently rational that they can and do generally constrain their free action under the terms of the laws of nature. Hence, should people choose to enter into formal bonds of civil society and authorize a government in order to avoid the "inconveniences" and inefficiency of the precivil world, the only rule worthy of consent is that which strictly upholds and protects the liberty they naturally possess. According to Locke, any government that systematically denies to its subjects the exercise of their God-given liberty (as Hobbes's sovereign would do) is tyrannical and cannot expect obedience.

## Individualism and Modern Society

The eighteenth and nineteenth centuries witnessed an emerging role for the individual that culminated in the appearance of the language of individualism. One strand in the intensified interest in the individual was the rise of capitalism as an economic system that emphasized the individual both as the holder of self-interest and as the foundation of all legal rights. Perhaps the most famous early advocate of economic individualism was Adam Smith (1723–1790). Although Smith is sometimes labeled the first great economist of capitalism, he preferred to describe his system in terms of "natural liberty," arguing that the welfare of society is best served when every individual seeks his or her own advantage without reference to any overarching scheme of goodness or justice. When individuals are left to their own devices, Smith held, the ensuing system possesses an inherently self-adjusting quality that will ensure the maximum satisfaction of individual desires.

The apotheosis of individualism may be found in the utilitarian doctrine, formulated most clearly by Jeremy Bentham (1748–1832), that social policy should promote the greatest good for the greatest number of people. This idea rested on the principle that all individual estimations of utility deserve equal treatment and respect in comparison with all others. Hence, no person could claim that his or her calculation of happiness counted for any more or less than another's. A truly democratic society should treat the wishes and desires of each of its individual members with the same dignity, without regard for moral judgments concerning the content of those aims. Bentham elaborates the basic insight of Smith to cover the full range of political and social programs and institutions.

Although liberalism could seem to take individualism for granted, the extreme egalitarianism of the utilitarian position, coupled with the events of the French Revolution (1789–1799), made many thinkers (including those of a liberal stripe) nervous. Edmund Burke (1729–1797) was concerned that the spread of democratic equality and the breakdown of the organic social order would lead to the fragmentation of persons into atomized individuals lacking any sense of identity or place. He scorned the individual's "private stock of reason" in comparison with the wisdom of history, fearing that the glorification of individuality presaged the crumbling of regard for the tradition-bearers of social authority, such as the monarchy, the nobility, and the church. Under such circumstances, Burke predicted (presciently, as it turns out) that authoritarian forms of government would step into the breach and provide an artificial identity for individuals as a remedy for their extreme alienation.

The French social commentator Alexis de Tocqueville (1805–1859) similarly believed that an excess of democratic equality bred individualistic isolation in which people retreat from public life into families and small groups of interested combines. The unavoidable results of individualism are egoism, the suppression of all virtues, and the concession of political deliberation to the "tyranny of the majority"—conclusions reached on the basis of his observations of American as well as French modes of democracy. In Tocqueville's view, America's avoidance of the corrosive effects of individualism (at least in the early nineteenth century) stemmed from its valorization of liberty over equality as the basis of social relations. Note that true liberty is not, for Tocqueville, individualistic.

Karl Marx (1818–1883) occupies an interesting position in the history of individualism. Although Marx is commonly regarded as a holistic social thinker, he in fact repeatedly asserted that individual self-realization was the standard against which social relations should be judged. In his early writings, he condemned capitalism for the alienating and dehumanizing impact that it exercised on individual workers, while in the *Communist Manifesto* (1848) he called for a system of equitable distribution of the fruits of labor on the grounds that the precondition of the liberty of each is the liberty of all. Like his predecessor Jean-Jacques Rousseau (1712–1778) and his contemporaries, such as the anarchist Jean-Pierre Proudhon (1809–1865) and the utopian Charles Fourier (1772–1837), Marx believed that communal equality constituted the necessary prerequisite for the flourishing of free individuals.

John Stuart Mill (1806–1873) shared some elements of nineteenth-century skepticism about mass democratic society, but his writings crystallized the understanding of individualism still widely shared in Western societies. According to Mill's important essay "On Liberty" (1859), the interests of humanity are "progressive," in the Enlightenment sense that human beings seek material and moral improvement. Mill holds that the societies that are most likely to promote this goal—societies that he terms "civilized"—share the common factor of defending and promoting individual liberty. Individualism—understood as experimentation with lifestyles and ideas—challenges uncritically received sureties and broadens the basis of human knowledge. Borrowing from Tocqueville, Mill admits that democratic society contains the potential to dampen or even forbid many expressions of personal liberty that stand at odds with mass tastes or beliefs. In contrast to Tocqueville, however, Mill maintains that individualism stands on the side of liberty, not equality. A free society supports individualism.

The trend toward the foregrounding of the individual continued in the work of Friedrich Nietzsche (1844–1900). Nietzsche reviled the "herd mentality" of modern mass society, which espouses conformity and mediocrity as the highest aspirations of humanity. He proposed, instead, that an individual might attain the "transvaluation of values," by which he meant that one could generate authentically for one's self the unique principles that would guide oneself and oneself alone. Principles of this higher sort cannot be imposed or taught by one to another. Rather, the authentic individual must discover in a radically individualized way those precepts that realize his or her own valuation. Nietzsche drew no explicit political theory from this because politics, as the realm of imposition of coercive authority over others (the "will to power"), was incompatible with the deep individualism that he advocated.

**Persisting Debate**

The twentieth and early twenty-first centuries have witnessed the spread around the globe of a culture that valorizes the human individual. Expressions of this individualism have been, however, extremely diverse. The philosophical and literary school of existentialism found a vast audience among both intellectuals and popular audiences during the middle of the twentieth century. The existentialists—the best known of whom were Martin Heidegger (1889–1976) and Jean-Paul Sartre (1905–1980)—proclaimed the radically individualistic situation of human beings. In particular they focused on the profound nothingness of death—the one element of human existence that each person necessarily experiences uniquely and individually, since no one can die another person's death—as a way of clarifying the condition of human Being. Positing the nonexistence of God, existentialism asserts that each individual must *create* meaning in his or her life through acts of personal will.

Dependence on other people or institutions—priests, philosophers, governments, or even family and friends—for meaning leads to inauthentic forms of existence. Because death cannot be escaped, inauthenticity ultimately reveals itself in the confrontation with one's own mortality. Each and every individual must eventually face the question, "Why do *I* exist?" And only in the deeds one freely performs does an authentic response arise.

Under the growing influence of economic thought, individualism has also been promoted under the guise of the logic of market relations. Libertarians such as Friedrich von Hayek (1899–1992), Robert Nozick (1938–2002), and, more popularly, Ayn Rand (1905–1982) proposed schemes of society that radically limited the power of the state and permitted broad scope for individual choice in all spheres of life. Each adopted a different starting point for these doctrines: for Hayek it was a quasi-utilitarian model of laissez-faire economics, for Nozick Lockean natural rights theory, and for Rand an original philosophical system that she called "objectivism." Yet, each thinker proposed that governmental regulation of the individual, and thus constraint on free choice and autonomy, amounted to a denial of authentic humanity.

In its avowedly neoclassic turn against Keynsian welfare economics, recent economic thought reinforces much of the individualism of the libertarian school (Hayek, of course, is well known as a leading economist as well as a political philosopher). Neoclassic economics holds that growth and efficiency within markets depends on the maximization of individual rational satisfaction. When political institutions (or presumably any other extrinsic factors) impinge on choice by limiting options or regulating competition, the perfect flow of information that the free market produces is impeded and inefficiency is introduced. The salient assumption of this economic theory is that individuals are rational satisficers or mazimizers; that is, they are the best (indeed, the only legitimate) source of decisions about what is best for themselves. Neoclassic economics, broadly construed, embraces rational egoism and hedonism as the only psychological premises that comport with the principles of free markets. The economic model has in turn been appropriated by other social sciences, such as political science, under the name of "public choice" or "rational choice" theory.

Of course, individualism remains a controversial idea. No less than Saint-Simon and his followers, modern communitarians worry about the socially corrosive effects of individualism, as evinced by rising levels of crime, political alienation, and unrestricted consumerism. In a widely acclaimed recent empirical analysis of social capital in America, Robert D. Putnam (b. 1940) has argued that the phenomena Tocqueville once identified as bulwarks against social decay in American democracy—in particular, local-level voluntary associations and community-based activities—are increasingly disappearing. Americans are "bowling alone" (to employ Putnam's own central image of rampant individualism) rather than joining leagues or social clubs to pursue common interests. Leaving aside its empirical dimensions, Putnam's provocative thesis raises for communitarians the specter of whether a social order composed of monadic units can sustain the values of democratic politics.

See also **Alienation; Free Will, Determinism, and Predestination; Identity; Person, Idea of the; Personhood in African Thought; Responsibility; Society; State, The; Utilitarianism; Utopia.**

BIBLIOGRAPHY

Black, Anthony. "Society and the Individual from the Middle Ages to Rousseau: Jurisprudence and Constitutional Theory." *History of Political Thought* 1 (1980): 145–166.

Coleman, Janet, ed. *The Individual in Political Theory and Practice.* New York: Oxford University Press, 1996.

Engelmann, Stephen G. *Imagining Interest in Political Thought: Origins of Economic Rationality.* Durham, N.C.: Duke University Press, 2003.

Farrar, Cynthia. *The Origins of Democratic Thinking: The Invention of Politics in Classical Athens.* Cambridge, U.K.: Cambridge University Press, 1988.

Hobbes, Thomas. *Leviathan.* Edited by Edwin Curley. Indianapolis: Hackett, 1984.

Locke, John. *Letter concerning Toleration in Focus.* Edited by John P. Horton and Susan Mendus. London: Routledge, 1991.

———. *Two Treatises of Government.* Edited by Peter Laslett. Cambridge, U.K.: Cambridge University Press, 1988.

Lukes, Steven. *Individualism.* Oxford: Oxford University Press, 1973.

Macfarlane, Alan. *The Origins of English Individualism: The Family, Property, and Social Transition.* Oxford: Blackwell, 1978.

Macpherson, C. B. *The Political Theory of Possessive Individualism, Hobbes to Locke.* Oxford: Oxford University Press, 1962.

Marx, Karl. *The Marx-Engels Reader.* Edited by Robert C. Tucker. New York: Norton, 1978.

Mill, John Stuart. *On Liberty in Focus.* Edited by John Gray and G. W. Smith. London: Routledge, 1991.

Plato. *The Apology of Socrates.* In *Five Dialogues,* translated by G. M. A. Grube. Indianapolis: Hackett, 1981.

Putnam, Robert D. *Bowling Alone.* Cambridge, Mass.: Harvard University Press, 2000.

Tocqueville, Alexis de. *Democracy in America.* Edited by J. P. Mayer. New York: Harper, 1969.

*Cary J. Nederman*

**INTELLECTUALS.** *See* **Intelligentsia.**

**INTELLIGENCE, ARTIFICIAL.** *See* **Computer Science.**

**INTELLIGENTSIA.** An abundance of studies on the subject of intellectuals has focused on societal differences and disparate issues, and featured a wide array of eras, cultures, and practices. A comparison by Raymond Williams between the French tradition of the intellectual engaged in public issues and the more reserved role ascribed to his or her English counterpart attests to this difference among societies. It has become customary to associate intellectual activity with the ideas of modernity and universality that arose during the Enlightenment.

However, the nature, configuration, and functions of that activity have evolved considerably since the eighteenth century, covering a range of subjects that are as diverse as the intelligentsia's areas of influence, forms of expression, and objects and goals. As the scholar and critic Edward Said (1935–2003) observed:

> The proliferation of intellectuals has extended even into the very large number of fields in which intellectuals—possibly following on [Antonio] Gramsci's pioneering suggestions in *The Prison Notebooks,* which almost for the first time saw intellectuals, and not social classes, as pivotal to the working of modern society—have become the object of study. . . . There are thousands of different histories and sociologies of intellectuals available, as well as endless accounts of intellectuals and nationalism, and power, and tradition, and revolution, and on and on. Each region of the world has produced its intellectuals and each of those formations is debated and argued over with fiery passion. There has been no major revolution in modern history without intellectuals; conversely, there has been no major counter-revolution without intellectuals. (p. 8)

## Intelligentsia and Society

Although the intellectual world's diversity and multiplicity have been recognized, the question of the precise nature of intellectual activity continues to be debated. The early-twenty-first-century controversy over scientific research in France provides an excellent example with which to consider the question of the intelligentsia within the particular context of globalization. In this conflict, the parties involved are, on one side, researchers who have accused the French government of taking an anti-intellectual stance in making budget cuts and putting severe limits on scientific research, and, on the other, government policy makers who label such protestors as ideologues. And, in the debate that seems to have developed ever since the Dreyfus affair—an event that is commonly associated with the coining of the word *intellectual* and that pitted artists, journalists, and other intellectuals against the two most powerful institutions in French society, the army and the government—the polarization of the Left (progressives and liberals) and the Right (conservatives and reactionaries) has taken shape in the public arena with new intellectual figures (here considered as actors) and focusing on intelligence (conceived of as a resource). Some intellectuals who are opposed to this polarization have denied an identification with the role of the intellectual and any relationship to government that that implies The principal promoter of this middle path, Alain Finkielkraut, justifies his position in refusing to be defined as an intellectual, saying that intellectuals in the early-twenty-first-century "only enter the public arena to accuse the guilty." He takes issue with the petition denouncing "the war on intellectualism" launched against the French government by the magazine *Les Inrockuptibles.*

In contrast to Finkielkraut, Said insists on the rebellious role of the intellectual, as one who questions more than he or she sanctions—"The intellectual as exile and marginal, as amateur, and as the author of a language that tries the truth to power." Said also noted that, in English, "the word 'intellectual' was [usually associated with] 'ivory tower' and 'sneer.'" The negative connotations of the term are underlined by Raymond Williams in *Keywords: A Vocabulary of Culture and Society.* Until the middle of the twentieth century, unfavorable uses of *intellectual, intellectualism,* and *intelligentsia* were dominant in English, and, according to Said, "it is clear that such uses persist" (pp. xiv, x).

The contemporary controversy over the identity and goals of the intellectual, by way of the references and history that the controversy summons up, emphasizes questions about the nature and political economy of intelligence in its relationship to society and the public arena. Two questions in particular recur repeatedly in this debate. The first is whether or not intellectual work and activist intervention are compatible, and if the intellectual has a duty to declare a position for or against the important issues of the day. The second is whether or not the intellectual has the means and legitimacy to intervene in the public debate. The arguments triggered by the negative assessment by researchers and cultural figures of the politics of the French government are not new. On the contrary, they are part of a long tradition that has shaped the function, role, representation, and actions of intellectuals in contemporary society, in their variety, their clashing and changing trajectories, and the conflicts that they bring or incite.

The controversies involve political, cultural, and moral questions as much as they do issues relating to the influence of language, traditions, and historical conditions on intellectual intervention. More precisely, it is a question of determining whether, in taking positions, the intellectual must make clear his or her relative independence, or take a position aligned with a political party, church, or cultural group. Should the intellectual express support for a universalist tradition disdainful of all local cultural roots and all references to a particular place, belief, or community? If one accepts that every intellectual has a particular audience and belongs to a particular culture, what establishes him or her as an intellectual is the ability to think and act independently from them. The possibility of moving between sticking to what is familiar (staying within one's historical community) and being open-minded (embracing the universalist tradition), speaking out in public or retreating to the ivory tower, seems to have contributed to the identity of the intellectual and the utilization of intelligence in all human societies.

Of course, styles, grammars, and degrees of prolificness are not all similar as marks or emblems, even if the historical path of the West has become established as the metanarrative and the inescapable point of reference with respect to human universality. Despite this, whether in agreement with the Western model or dissenting from it, different practices have flourished since the opening of the world to European imperialism, addressing Western hegemony in light of particular aspects of dominated societies (colonial and postcolonial) or peripheral societies (China and Japan, for example), striving to create alternative visions. The emergence of these new voices, the diversification of intellectual horizons, whether colonial or postcolonial or embracing non-European nationalisms, and the cultural, ethnic, religious, and racial emphases that distinguish human societies, continue to give rise to an extraordinary metamorphosis in intellectual identity. As a result, the most basic intellectual foundations and the assumption of a fixed point around which everything revolved have been called into question. Whereas the philosophical ideas of the Enlightenment seemed to have succeeded in dividing rational intelligence from feelings, personal life from public life, the twentieth and twenty-first centuries have seen configurations of greater complexity, a diversity of intellectual vehicles, sources, and individuals and groups who declare themselves to be (or are regarded as) intellectuals.

## Definitions

Edward Said's *Representations of the Intellectual: The 1993 Reith Lectures* offers an excellent starting point for defining this type. Among the supporting materials on which Said relies are two well-known books, *Quaderni del carcere* (1947; *Prison Notebooks*) by Antonio Gramsci (1891-1937) and *La trahison des clercs* (1927; *The Treason of the Intellectuals*) by Julien Benda (1867–1956). These texts were written in different circumstances but with identical concerns, relating to the appearance of theories and practices that contradict or threaten the transcendent values of truth, justice, and humanity. After comparing Benda and Gramsci—who "clash fundamentally" over the issue of who qualifies as an intellectual (for Benda, it is a small group of clerks chosen in a draconian manner; for Gramsci, all individuals are intellectuals, even if not all perform such a function in society)—Said proposes a simple definition of *intellectual*: "An individual endowed with a faculty for representing, embodying, articulating a message, an attitude, philosophy, or opinion to, as well as for, a public" (p. 9). The intellectual's vocation is manifested in the consummate art of representation through words, writing, teaching, and participation in the media, including radio, television, and the press.

It is not disputed that the mission of the intellectual is to advance human knowledge and freedom. It is the differences in thoughts and beliefs that are important and often irreconcilable in determining who should be in command of this task, to what ends, and with what means. But who are these intellectuals whose nature is revealed by the role that they play or that society assigns them? Gramsci made a distinction between two types: on the one hand, the traditional intellectuals, priests, teachers, administrators, who ensure the cohesion of the hegemonic culture, while renewing, generation after generation, these traditional roles; and on the other hand, the "organic" intellectuals who, while a part of civil society, maintain a sometimes strained relationship with it. They are in the service of the social classes or enterprises that organize them and mobilize them to defend particular interests. They are, to borrow a phrase from the French philosopher Jean-Paul Sartre, engaged in society.

Benda was concerned with a category that he identified as a small group of erudite people, guardians of an irreproachable morality: a "conscience of humanity" responsible for1118 administering the empire of justice and truth that transcends the world in which they live. In Benda's vision, intellectuals have the responsibility of denouncing corruption, defending the weak, and defying oppressive authority. In this sense, they are agents of a mission that, if betrayed, has harmful effects on society. The values that they try to secure and preserve, because they apply to all peoples and nations, carry a seal of universality, for they are transcendent, transhistorical, transnational, and transcultural.

In the early twentieth century, Gramsci and Benda traced the spread of intellectualism and the identifying elements that marked the intellectual; the definitions in use at the beginning of the twenty-first century are variations based on their ideas, to which have been added a consideration of the emergence and consolidation of power, of wealth, and of the ascendance of new professions engaged in intellectual pursuits. In effect, in the early twenty-first century the term *intellectual* is applied to all activities connected with the production and circulation of knowledge as described by Gramsci; as noted by Said, "broadcasters, academic professionals, computer analysts, sports and media lawyers, management consultants, policy experts, government advisers, authors of specialized market reports, and indeed the whole field of modern mass journalism itself . . . have vindicated Gramsci's vision" (p. 7). Located there is the creative tension present at the heart of the mission and the demands of the intellectual, caught between the rebellion against and constant questioning of the hegemonic culture and support for the latter in order to ensure "order and continuity in public life" (p. 27).

Régis Debray has provided an excellent history of the intellectuals in modern France. Debray's discussion is divided into three historical periods: Between 1880 and 1930, the figure of the intellectual was solidly attached to institutions, none more so than the university; as professionals devoted to teaching and research, intellectuals found in these institutions effective protection against the church and its power. Between 1930 and 1968, the university lost its privileged place in the intellectual firmament, at least in the representation of the intellectual figure; in that function it was superseded by publishing houses, in which intellectuals and publishers formed "a new spiritual family," as Debray aptly described the relationship, citing such "family" members as Sartre, André Gide, Simone de Beauvoir, the Gallimards, and André Malraux. After 1968 this spiritual family broke up; intellectual engagement in the political sphere and the public arena took a new turn and created new idioms. Mao Zedong's China replaced the USSR as the ne plus ultra of socialism. Discourses and practices took to the fields or factories before moving on to editorial offices or radio and television production, government ministries, literary or film work. Debray strongly criticized this transformation, which enlarged intellectuals' sphere of influence while at the same time endangering their authority, for their reliance on their peers gave way to a search for a captive audience: "By extending the reception area, the mass media have reduced the sources of intellectual legitimacy, with wider concentric circles that are less demanding and therefore more easily won over. . . . The mass media have broken down the closure of the traditional intelligentsia, together with its evaluative norms and its scale of values" (pp. 71, 81).

Even though the history related by Debray applies to France, from his study one can draw the general conclusion that the power and legitimacy of intellectuals derive as much from the institutions with which they are affiliated and from the influence that they are able to exert as a result as they do to their individual authority. For example, describing the situation of intellectuals in the United States, Alvin Gouldner emphasizes the considerable increase in the areas of expertise that one could categorize as "intellectual" and the development of a culture of critical discourse for each of those categories. Beyond those identified by Said and Debray, he cites such late-twentieth-century additions as military strategist and international lawyer, which, like publisher and writer, utilize a specialized vocabulary that is shared only with peers of these disciplines. The French philosopher and social critic Michel Foucault (1926–1984), commenting on this enlargement of the intellectual sphere to include new kinds of practitioners, pondered the consequences of replacing the universalist intellectual—the kind that Benda and Gramsci had been concerned with—by the specialist, whose expertise justified his or her intervention in other spheres, the public arena in particular.

## Challenges to Traditional Discourse

The studies outlined above emphasized the transformations of the intellectual sphere, the diversification of its principal practitioners, and changes in vocabulary, kinds of expertise, and institutional configurations or means of representation. Challenging the universality of the West's historical path (as much through racial as sexual distinctions) opened a space in which to deploy other narrations and different forms of intellectual engagement. Feminist, civil rights, and colonialist and postcolonialist social movements that have arisen in opposition to Western conceptions of universality and modernity have striven to set precise goals for intellectuals. The questions that preoccupy thinkers, in Africa as in Asia, are whether or not there will be, on the one hand, changes to accepted bodies of knowledge and the traditional role of indigenous intellectuals, and, on the other hand, the nativization of modern Western procedures and forms of learning and intellectual intervention in societies where Western modes of reference have been imposed. For Africa and the black diaspora, there are two excellent texts: Frantz Fanon's *Les damnés de la terre* (1961; *The Wretched of the Earth*) and Robin Kelley's *Freedom Dreams: The Black Radical Imagination*. The latter succinctly captures the assault by newcomers on the universalist metanarrative:

> Social movements generate new knowledge, new theories, new questions. The most radical ideas often grow out of a concrete intellectual engagement with the problems of aggrieved populations confronting systems of oppression. For example, the academic study of race has been inextricably intertwined with political struggles. Just as imperialism, colonialism, and post-Reconstruction redemption politics created the intellectual ground for Social Darwinism and other manifestations of scientific racism, the struggle against racism generated cultural relativist and social constructionist scholarship on race. The great work of W. E. B. Dubois, Franz Boas, Olivier Cox, and many others were invariably shaped by social

movements as well as social crises such as the proliferation of lynching and the rise of fascism. Similarly, gender analysis was brought to us by the feminist movement, not only by the individual genius of the Grimke sisters or Anna Julia Cooper, Simone de Beauvoir, or Audre Lorde. Thinking gender and the possibility of transformation evolved largely in relationship to social struggle. (p. 9)

Kelley is interested in the connections between intellectual practices and social movements, whereas Fanon is concerned with the mission of the colonized intellectual in the context of the struggle for national independence and social revolution. He shows how the man or woman of culture—the intellectual—in this context, using historical sources, strives to systematically counter the thesis of the barbarism of precolonial societies in order to re-create a community, his nation and state. Fanon shrewdly presents the different phases in the maturing of the nationalist intellectual, who begins by assimilating the colonial culture of his masters and ends with revolutionary combat, through which he or she is transformed into a guide of the people, producing a body of intellectual work that furthers revolutionary nationalist goals. Between these two poles, there is an intermediate phase of discovery of the self—a creative moment when the intellectual celebrates his or her people, history, and legends reinterpreted through the prism of an aesthetic and a worldview borrowed from the West. More sophisticated than the rigid orthodoxy of Fanon is the relatively soulful approach of Paul Robeson (1898–1976), which has given rise to a plan of liberation that takes into account emotion (exemplified by the West African poet Léopold Sédar Senghor) and poetic knowledge (as seen in the West Indian poet Aimé Césaire). Robeson transformed the idea of Western modernity by subverting the rationalist ideas of the Enlightenment in order to restore Negro spirituality to the portrait of European civilization. In an article from 1936, "Primitives," Robeson—who, according to Kelley, blamed the Enlightenment for the rise of fascism—wrote that the Enlightenment's focus on rationality and intellect removed spirituality from European civilization and, in doing so, led to its ultimate failure. Robeson believed that to save Western civilization, spirituality and art needed to be restored to a central position in social life and that American Negroes, who knew Western culture yet retained the "core cultural values of their ancestral homeland," were uniquely qualified to do so.

Another noteworthy branch of later intellectual history is that of Chinese intellectuals who, at the beginning of the twentieth century, tried to respond to the challenges of Western modernity. At the forefront of this mission was a group who went under the name the May Fourth Movement. "In May Fourth discourse," observe Leo Ou-fan Lee and Merle Goldman in their introduction to *An Intellectual History of Modern China*, "The modern intellectual stands in privileged position vis-à-vis Chinese society and the Chinese people—as the former's moral conscience and reformist advocate and the latter's voice. Despite the May Fourth's revolutionary nature, the intellectual elite position vis-à-vis society resonated with that of their literati ancestors. Like them, they saw themselves as the rejuvenators of Chinese culture, which they believed was the key to China's salvation" (p. 4). Thus, Lee and Goldman point out that the balancing act noted in the West and in nationalist and postcolonial traditions also occurred in China from the beginning of the twentieth century up to the changing ideologies of the Chinese Revolution under various figures, a role pioneered by intellectuals during the Cultural Revolution (1966–1976). The reforms of the 1980s and the opening up of China to certain forms of capitalist production seem to have had similar overall effects on intellectuals there as in the rest of the world, namely enlargement and diversification of the kinds of intellectual activity being practiced. According to Lee and Goldman, "Chinese intellectuals at the end of the twentieth century had turned themselves into scholars, technocrats, cultural producers, business people, and entertainers, but they were no longer social prophets, the agents of national salvation, or visionary leaders of change as they had been throughout most Chinese history and even into the Mao era until Mao brutally suppressed them" (p. 8).

## Response to Orthodoxy

There are numerous examples throughout the world that show, in the diversity of intellectual approaches, appropriations, and rejections of Enlightenment rationality, acute tendencies toward fragmentation. Today, conflicts of unprecedented violence have resulted from intellectual, philosophical, and religious constructions stemming from narrow-minded orthodoxies. In setting off ethnic and religious subsets of the public sphere, customs and codes have been installed forbidding rebellion, questioning, and dissent. One could therefore take up the invitation to reflection and to critical dialogue offered by the Iranian philosopher Abdolkarim Soroush. In an interview with Farish Noor, Soroush commented on renewing and rebuilding intellectual engagement at the beginning of the twenty-first century. Although his particular concern is Muslim intellectuals, his message is of universal significance:

> Modern Muslim intellectuals are, in a sense, a hybrid species. They emerged in the liminal space between modern ideas and traditional thought. We have seen the emergence of such figures in many Muslim countries that have experienced the effects of colonization and the introduction of a plural economic and educational system. They have their feet planted in their local traditions as well as the broader world of the modern age. As such, they are comfortable in both, handicapped by neither. The modern Muslim intellectual is one who is not daunted by the task of delving into his or her religious knowledge for critical answers and solutions to the present. Such intellectuals are better able to do so because they are not the product of a traditional educational system, which is narrow and rigid. They are not bound by traditional norms and rules of religious discursive activity, because they are not really part of that particular narrow tradition. Unlike the traditional ulama [learned men], who never go beyond the texts that they read, the modern intellectual will be able to read deeper into the text in a critical, imaginative manner.

*See also* **Education; University.**

## BIBLIOGRAPHY

Benda, Julien. *The Treason of the Intellectuals.* Translated by Richard Aldington. New York: Norton, 1969.

Césaire, Aimé. "Poetry and Knowledge." In *Refusal of the Shadow: Surrealism and the Caribbean,* edited by Michael Richardson; translated by Krzysztof Fijalkowski and Michael Richardson. London and New York: Verson, 1996.

Chakrabarty, Dipesh. *Habitations of Modernity: Essays in the Wake of Subaltern Studies.* Chicago: University of Chicago Press, 2002.

Debray, Régis. *Teachers, Writers, Celebrities: The Intellectuals of Modern France.* Translated by David Macey. London: NLB, 1981.

Fanon, Frantz. *The Wretched of the Earth.* Translated by Constance Farrington. New York: Grove, 1965.

Gouldner, Alvin W. *The Future of Intellectuals and the Rise of the New Class: A Frame of Reference, Theses, Conjectures, Arguments, and an Historical Perspective on the Role of Intellectuals and Intelligentsia in the International Class Contest of the Modern Era.* New York: Seabury, 1979.

Gramsci, Antonio. *Selections from the Prison Notebooks of Antonio Gramsci.* Edited and translated by Quintin Hoare and Geoffrey Nowell Smith. New York: International, 1972.

Halter, Marek. "Les Amis Intellectuels de Jean Pierre Raffarin." *Le Monde Week End,* 14–15 March 2004, p. 1.

Kelley, Robin D. G. *Freedom Dreams: The Black Radical Imagination.* Boston: Beacon, 2002.

Maclean, Ian, Alan Montefiore, and Peter Winch, eds. *The Political Responsibility of Intellectuals.* Cambridge, U.K., and New York: Cambridge University Press, 1990. See especially the essay by Ernest Gellner, "La trahison de la trahison des clercs."

Noor, Farish A., ed. "The Responsibilities of the Muslim Intellectual in the 21st Century: Interview with Abdolkarim Soroush." In his *New Voices of Islam.* Leiden, Netherlands: ISIM, 2002.

Ory, Pascal, and Jean-François Sirinelli. *Les Intellectuels en France, de l'Affaire Dreyfus à nos jours.* Paris: A. Colin, 1986.

Ou-fan Lee, Leo, and Merle Goldman, "Introduction: The Intellectual History of Modern China." In *An Intellectual History of Modern China,* edited by Merle Goldman and Leo Ou-fan Lee. Cambridge, U.K., and New York: Cambridge University Press, 2002.

Said, Edward W. *Representations of the Intellectual: The 1993 Reith Lectures.* New York: Pantheon, 1994.

Schalk, David L. *War and the Ivory Tower: Algeria and Vietnam.* New York: Oxford University Press, 1991.

Williams, Raymond. *Keywords: A Vocabulary of Culture and Society.* Rev. ed. New York: Oxford University Press, 1985.

*Mamadou Diouf*

**INTENTIONALITY.** Intentionality is that feature of many mental states by which they are *directed at* or *about* or *of* objects and states of affairs in the world. So, for example, if I have a belief, it must be a belief that such and such is the case. If I have a desire, it must be the desire that such and such should be the case. If I have an intention, it must be the intention that I do something. *Intentionality* is a technical term not to be confused with the ordinary English words *intend* and *intentional.* Intending in the sense of intending to do something is just one kind of intentionality, along with hunger, thirst, belief, desire, fear, hope, pride, shame, love, hate, perception, memory, and so on.

## *Intentionality* and Its History

The concept of "intentionality" in this modern sense was reintroduced into philosophy by Franz Brentano (1874), who took the notion from the medieval scholastics. Brentano used the German expression *Intentionalität,* derived from the medieval Latin *intentio,* which meant what we nowadays call an intension or concept and which comes from the classical Latin *tendere,* meaning to aim at something. Brentano thought that intentionality was "the mark of the mental," and because he thought that intentionality could not be reduced to anything physical, dualism seemed to follow; a world of intentional phenomena, the mind, is distinct from the world of physical phenomena.

Edmund Husserl (1900), a student of Brentano and the inventor of phenomenology, made the investigation of intentionality his main philosophical project. Husserl's method was to suspend the assumption that there is a real world on the other side of our mental acts (this suspension he called the *époche,* or phenomenological reduction) and examine the structure of and thus the intentionality of the acts themselves (this structure he called the *noema,* plural *noemata*). In Anglo-American philosophy, the topic of intentionality was introduced in large part by Roderick Chisholm (1957). Chisholm was influenced by Brentano and attempted to produce a linguistic criterion of intentionality. In addition to his writings on the subject, he edited a collection of works by Brentano, Husserl, and others (Chisholm, 1960) and conducted a lengthy published correspondence on the topic with Wilfrid Sellars (Chisholm and Sellars, 1958).

## Two Mistaken Theories of Intentionality

In his early work, Brentano thought that every intentional state must have an intentional object. If, for example, I believe that the mail carrier arrives at 11 A.M., then it seems that the object of my belief is the mail carrier. But what is the intentional object when a child believes that Santa Claus comes on Christmas Eve? There is no such person as Santa Claus, so what is the child's belief directed at? Brentano thought that to provide an intentional object in such cases, we have to postulate it inside the intentional state itself. Brentano called this mode of existence "intentional inexistence." This is an error. The statement, "Santa Claus comes on Christmas Eve" has a meaning but does not thereby succeed in referring to Santa Claus because there is no such thing to refer to; and likewise the belief that Santa Claus comes on Christmas Eve has an intentional content but does not have an intentional object. Brentano was confusing intentional content with intentional object. By definition every intentional state has an intentional content but not every intentional state has an intentional object. An intentional state has an intentional object only if something fits or satisfies the intentional content.

A second error is to suppose that there is some essential connection between intentionality with a "t" and intensionality with an "s." Intensionality with an "s" is a property of sentences by which they fail certain tests for extensionality. The most famous test is called "Leibnitz's law" or the "substitutability of identicals." If two expressions refer to the same object, then one can be substituted for the other, without loss or change of truth value. Thus, if *a* equals *b,* and *a* has property *F,* then *b* has property *F.* But for some sentences about intentional states, this law does not hold. So, for example:

1. Sam believes that Caesar crossed the Rubicon; and

2. Caesar is identical with Mark Anthony's best friend;

do not imply that:

3. Sam believes that Mark Anthony's best friend crossed the Rubicon;

because Sam might not know or might disbelieve that Caesar is Mark Anthony's best friend. The sentence about the intentional state is intensional with an "s" but it does not follow from this that the state itself is intensional with an "s." Chisholm and others have tried to make the intensionality of sentences about intentional states into a criterion of intentionality and thus make intentionality seem to be a linguistic phenomenon. But the effort failed. There are intensional sentences that do not report intentionality and reports of intentionality that are not intensional. For example, 4 is intensional but not about intentionality:

4. Necessarily, 9 is greater than 7;

5. The number of planets equals 9.

But it does not follow that:

6. Necessarily the number of planets is greater than 7.

Sentence 7 is about intentionality but is not intensional.

7. Sam saw the Eiffel Tower; and

8. The Eiffel Tower is the tallest iron structure in Paris.

do imply:

9. Sam saw the tallest iron structure in Paris;

even if Sam does not know the truth of 8.

If intensionality is not a sure test for intentionality, what then is the relation between them? Sam's belief that Caesar crossed the Rubicon represents the state of affairs that Caesar crossed the Rubicon. But the report of Sam's belief does not represent that state of affairs; rather it reports what is going on in Sam's head. The report is a representation of a representation. So the truth of the report requires that the way that Sam represents Caesar be truly reported, and hence substitution fails, for the substitution of a different representation may not truly report what is in Sam's head (Searle, 1983).

## The Relation of Intentionality to Consciousness

Every intentional state is mental, but not every conscious mental state is intentional. For example, one may have feelings of anxiety that do not have any intentional content. One is not anxious about any particular thing; one just has a general undirected feeling of anxiety. Such a state is conscious and therefore mental without being intentional. If Brentano was wrong that intentionality is the mark of the mental, this leads to the larger question: What exactly is the relation between intentionality and consciousness? The answer is that there is a very heavy overlap but the two are not coextensive. At any given point in my life, many of my intentional states are unconscious. For example, I can believe that in 2004 George W. Bush was president even when I am not thinking about it or when I am asleep. And many of my conscious states are not intentional, as, for example, the undirected anxiety that I mentioned above.

There does, however, seem to be a close connection between intentionality and consciousness in the following respect: Whenever someone has an intentional state that is unconscious, as when one is sound asleep, we understand it as that particular intentional state only in virtue of the fact that it is the kind of thing that can become conscious. A person might be unable to bring intentionality to consciousness because of being asleep or because of brain damage or repression, for example; but our understanding of an intentional state as a mental state is dependent on our being able to conceive of that state as occurring in consciousness.

## The Irreducibility of Intentionality

For philosophers who reject dualism, intentionality, like consciousness, has always been an embarrassment. How is it possible in a purely physical world, in a world composed of physical particles in fields of force, that there could be such a thing as mental aboutness or directedness? Many philosophers think it is impossible, and they have made various efforts to reduce intentionality to some materialist basis or to eliminate it altogether. Hence in the *behaviorist* period in the philosophy of mind, many philosophers (e.g., Ryle, 1949) felt that having a state of belief or desire was simply a matter of being disposed to behave in certain ways under certain stimulus conditions. Later on, *functionalist* theories of mind (e.g., Armstrong, 1993) tried to analyze intentional states in terms of causal relations to input stimuli and external behavior. A more recent variation on functionalism is to try to identify intentional states with computational states. The idea of *computationalism* is that the brain is a digital computer and the intentional states are just states of the computer program (Crane, 2003).

All of these efforts fail because they try to reduce intentionality to something else. But it is not something else. I believe the way to avoid dualism while recognizing the reality and irreducibility of intentionality is to recognize that intentionality is a biological phenomenon like growth or photosynthesis or digestion. If we ask the question in the abstract: How can an animal have a belief about some distant object? that may seem like an extremely difficult question, but if we ask the more directly biological question: How is it possible for an animal to see anything or to feel hungry or thirsty or frightened? then it does not seem so difficult. We can build more sophisticated forms of intentionality, such as belief and desire and imagination, on the more biological basic forms such as perception and intentional action.

## The Structure of Intentionality

Four concepts are essential for understanding the structure and functioning of intentionality (Searle, 1983). First, the distinction between intentional content and psychological mode; second, the notion of direction of fit; third, the notions of conditions of satisfaction; and fourth, the holistic network of intentionality.

***The distinction between intentional content and psychological mode.*** Every intentional state consists of an intentional content in a certain psychological mode. You can see this clearly by keeping intentional content constant while varying the mode. Thus, I can *believe* that you will leave the room, *wish* that you will leave the room, and *wonder whether* you will leave the room. In each case the state consists of a *propositional content,* which we will represent by the variable *p,* in a certain psychological mode, which we will represent with an *M.* The structure, then, of these intentional states is *M(p).* Because the contents of these intentional states are entire propositions, they are sometimes called, following Bertrand Russell, "propositional attitudes." Not all intentional states have an entire proposition as their content, as one might simply admire George Washington, or love Sally Smith. Here the intentionality is directed at an object, but it does not have a whole propositional content. Its form is not *M(p)* but *M(n).*

***Direction of fit.*** The propositional content of the intentional state will relate to reality in different ways depending on the mode in which that content is presented. Thus beliefs, like statements, are supposed to be true, and they are true in virtue of the fact that they accurately represent some state of affairs in the world. They have what we can call the *mind-to-world direction of fit,* or *responsibility of fitting.* Desires and intentions, on the other hand, are not designed to represent how things are in fact but how we would like them to be or how we intend to make them be. Such intentional states have the *world-to-mind direction of fit* or *the world-to-mind responsibility for fitting.* Some intentional states take the preexisting fit for granted. Thus, for example, if I am sorry that I offended you or I am glad for your good fortune, in each case I take for granted the truth of the proposition that I offended you or that you have had good fortune, and I have an attitude about the state of affairs represented.

***Conditions of satisfaction.*** Where the intentional state does have a direction of fit, such as belief, desire, perception, or intention, we can say that the intentional state is a representation of its conditions of satisfaction. Just as the belief will be satisfied if and only if it is true, so the desire will be satisfied if and only if it is fulfilled, and the intention will be satisfied if and only if it is carried out.

***The network of intentionality.*** Intentional states do not come to us in isolated atoms but as part of a holistic network of intentionality. This is perhaps most obvious in the case of the emotions. In order, for example, that someone be angry at another person, he or she must have a set of beliefs and desires. He or she will typically believe the other person has done some harm, will desire that the harm had not been done, will desire to harm, or express disapproval of the person at whom he or she is angry, and so on. Intentional states do not come to us individually and do not function in an atomistic form, but rather one has one intentional state only in relation to other intentional states. This holistic network is essential even for the functioning of simple beliefs.

So, for example, one can believe that in 2004 George W. Bush was president of the United States only if one has a rather large number of other beliefs. One must believe at least a certain number of things such as that the United States is a republic, that it elects presidents, that its president serves for a certain number of years, that presidents have certain powers and responsibilities, and so on. One way to describe this feature is to say that any intentional state functions, it determines its conditions of satisfaction, only in relation to a network of other intentional states. Most philosophers today accept some form of holism as opposed to atomism. A controversial extension of holism is the view that the whole network functions only against a background of taken-for-granted abilities and presuppositions that are not themselves intentional (Searle, 1983).

### The Determination of Intentional Content
Parallel to the question of how intentionality is possible at all is the question: How is it possible that intentional states have the particular content that they do? What makes my belief that in 2004 George W. Bush was president about George W. Bush, for example, and not about his brother, Jeb, or his father, George H. W. Bush, also named "George Bush," or about anything else?

There are two common answers to this in contemporary philosophy: a traditional answer called internalism, according to which the contents of the head are sufficient to fix intentional content; and a relatively recent answer (from the 1970s) called externalism, according to which the contents of the head are not sufficient. Some outside causal (Putnam, 1975) or social (Burge, 1979) relations not represented in the heads of intentional agents are also essential. The argument for externalism is always that two agents might have the same thing in their head and yet have different intentional contents. For example two agents might have the same thing in their heads associated with the word *water*, but if one agent had a causal history originating with $H_2O$ and the other had a history originating in some different but perceptually similar chemical, they would have different contents associated with the word even though the brains states were identical.

The reply given to this by the internalists is that in such cases the intentional content is determined indexically by indicating relations to the head or heads in question. By *water*, each person means the type of substance that he is familiar with or that his community has baptized as *water*. The situation is exactly like identical twins, each of whom thinks, "I am

hungry." The contents in their heads may be of exactly the same type, but they determine different intentional contents, because the same indexical expression "I" refers to different people. It refers to whoever utters or thinks it. On this view there is nothing external about indexical intentional content. Type identical intentional contents may have different conditions of satisfaction because of internal indexical content. The dispute between externalism and internalism is very much alive.

### Intentional Causation
Explanations of human behavior rely essentially on the causal functioning of intentionality. When we say "Jones voted for the Republicans because he wanted lower taxes and believed the Republican candidate would produce lower taxes," we are giving a causal explanation in terms of the intentionality of desire and belief. This form of causal explanation is important not only in practical affairs but also in theoretical accounts of human behavior in the social sciences such as sociology, political science, and economics.

Such disciplines necessarily use an intentionalistic explanatory apparatus that is in several ways quite different from that of the natural sciences. First, in explanations appealing to intentional causation, the intentional content in the explanation must match the intentional content that is actually functioning causally in the mind of the agent. So the explanation, Jones "wanted lower taxes" must match Jones's desire: "I want lower taxes," and this content functions causally. This is quite unlike physics, where the content of the explanation reports a cause, such as gravity, but the content as content does not function causally. Second, explanations using intentional causation are subject to constraints of rationality in a way that physical forces are not. And third, typical intentionalistic explanations allow for free will in a way that is unlike explanations in classical physics. When I say the ball fell because of the force of gravity, the explanation is deterministic in the sense that given the forces acting on it, there is no other way the ball could have behaved. But if I say Jones voted for the Republicans because he wanted lower taxes, the explanation is not deterministic in form. It does not imply that Jones could not have acted otherwise in that situation.

Intentionality, along with consciousness, is the main problem in contemporary philosophy of mind, and under the name *information processing*, it is the main topic of cognitive science.

*See also* **Causation; Consciousness; Philosophy.**

**BIBLIOGRAPHY**
Armstrong, D. M. *A Materialist Theory of the Mind.* London: Routledge, 1993.
Brentano, Franz Clemens. *Psychologie vom empirischen Standpunkt.* Leipzig: Dunker and Humblot, 1874. Published in English as *Psychology from an Empirical Standpoint.* London: Routledge and Kegan Paul, 1973. Excerpted in Chalmers, 2002.
Burge, T. "Individualism and the Mental." In *Midwest Studies in Philosophy.* Vol. 4. Edited by P. French, T. Uehling, and H. Wettstein. Minneapolis: University of Minnesota Press, 1979. Reprinted in Rosenthal, 1991.

Chalmers, David J. *The Philosophy of Mind: Classical and Con-temporary Readings.* Oxford: Oxford University Press, 2002.

Chisholm, R. *Perceiving: A Philosophical Study.* Ithaca, N.Y.: Cornell University Press, 1957. Excerpted in Chalmers, 2002, and Rosenthal, 1991.

———, ed. *Realism and the Background of Phenomenology.* Glencoe, Ill.: Free Press, 1960.

Chisholm, R., and W. Sellars. "Intentionality and the Mental." In *Minnesota Studies in the Philosophy of Science.* Vol. 2. Edited by H. Feigl, M. Scriven, and G. Maxwell. Minneapolis: University of Minnesota Press, 1958.

Crane, Tim. *The Mechanical Mind: A Philosophical Introduction to Minds, Machines, and Mental Representation.* 2nd ed. London: Routledge, 2003.

Dreyfus, Hubert, ed., in collaboration with Harrison Hall. *Husserl, Intentionality, and Cognitive Science.* Cambridge, Mass.: MIT Press, 1982.

Husserl, Edmund. *Logische Untersuchungen.* 2 vols. Halle: Max Niemayer, 1900. Published in English as *Logical Investigations.* Translated by J. N. Findlay. London: Routledge and Kegan Paul, 1970.

Putnam, Hilary. "The Meaning of 'Meaning.'" In *Mind, Language, and Reality.* Vol. 2 of *Philosophical Papers.* Cambridge, U.K.: Cambridge University Press, 1975. Excerpted in Chalmers, 2002.

O'Connor, Timothy, and David Robb, eds. *Philosophy of Mind: Contemporary Readings.* London: Routledge, 2003.

Rosenthal, David M., ed. *The Nature of Mind.* New York: Oxford University Press, 1991.

Ryle, Gilbert. *The Concept of Mind.* London: Hutchinson, 1949.

Searle, John R. *Intentionality: An Essay in the Philosophy of Mind.* Cambridge, U.K.: Cambridge University Press, 1983.

———. "Minds, Brains and Programs." *Behavioral and Brain Sciences,* 3 (1980): 3. Reprinted in Rosenthal, 1991, and O'Connor and Robb, 2003.

———. *The Rediscovery of the Mind.* Cambridge, Mass.: MIT Press, 1992.

*John R. Searle*

## INTERCESSION IN MIDDLE EASTERN SOCIETY.

The notion of intercession (*shafa'a*) is present within Muslim religious tradition as well as Muslim and Middle Eastern social and political culture. Intercession implies a special intervention or act of patronage providing favors, power, victory, or, in the religious variety, redemption from the terrible fate of sinners. Although there have been some objections, historic and modern, to this idea, it is frequently ascribed to the prophet Muhammad, his family, and the angels, as well as other Muslim holy men and women. For instance, the relics of the imam Husayn, the Prophet's grandson, are visited by the Shia in Damascus, and three famous pious women—Sayyida Zaynab, Sayyida Ruqayya, and Sayyida Nafisa—function as the patron saints of the city of Cairo. Pilgrims' prayers and entreaties call for intercession and blessing. Such visitations or requests of holy figures are made throughout the Muslim world, the Middle East, and North Africa. Intercession is also sought from certain key Sufi leaders and poets via ritual, recitation, or visitations.

The primary aim of Prophetic intercession is to save Muslim sinners on the Day of Judgment when all souls will be considered, and former earthly status, wealth, or power will be meaningless. His intercession, confirmed in the Koran (17:29), could prevent the believer from slipping off the Straight Path, a bridge spanning Hell. The traditions that ascribe the potential for intercession to the prophet Muhammad emphasize his exemplary nature.

According to one, humankind sought an intercessor on the Day of Judgment from among the prophets. Each was asked, and all but Jesus believed that they had themselves sinned, and all of the prophets but Muhammad replied that they feared for themselves. Yet God told Muhammad, who is the only human to have been forgiven his sins, that he might ask what he willed, and so may intercede on behalf of the Muslim community. *Shafa'a* is thus an aspect of Muhammad's "grace." In addition, various traditions relate the Prophet's miraculous night journey (*isra*) and ascension to heaven (*mi'raj*) that established his relationship with the chain of prophecy, and during which he interceded with God to reduce the number of daily prayers required of Muslims from fifty to five. Even non-Muslims recognized the Prophet's rights of intercession, according to another tradition about a Jewish tribe who called for intercession in the name of the Prophet before a major battle and were subsequently victorious over their foes.

All four Sunni Muslim legal schools agreed that the Prophet could intercede for sinners, although Muslims must strive to cleave to the Straight Path on their own. Muhammad's intercession, in other words, is intended for sinners, not the pious. Related practices, like the uttering of the *salawat sharifa,* the phrase usually translated as "bless him and grant him peace," at every mention of the Prophet's name is believed to obtain the blessing of angels and might aid intercession.

In Shii Islam, the concept of *shafa'a* and its correlate, *tawassul* (attainment of an objective or achievement of purpose), is extended to the family of the Prophet, the *ahl al-bayt.* The Prophet is supposed to have said to his daughter Fatima that on the Day of Judgment she would intercede for women, and he for men, and furthermore that every person who had wept over the tragic death of Husayn would be taken by the hand and led into Paradise. Many other traditions including several ascribed to Ja'far al-Sadiq (Muhammad's great-great-great-grandson and the sixth Shii imam) prescribe weeping and mourning on Ashura, the day of remembrance of Husayn's death, and state that paradise is the reward for those who weep. Consequently, in Shiism, martyrdom is also linked to the notions of intercession and redemption.

In both Sunni and Shii Islam, the notion of intercession is related to other practices in which the prophet Muhammad is venerated, such as the celebration of his birthday, and to the literature and poetry written in his praise. A thirteenth-century poet, Muhammad al-Busiri, a member of the Shadhiliyya mystic order, refers constantly to *shafa'a* in his famous poem known as "al-Burda":

Our Prophet, who commands and prohibits and not a single one

Is more truthful than he is saying No or Yes;
And he is the beloved for whose intercession one hopes
In every horror and hazardous undertaking. (Schimmel, p. 185)

In Suleyman Chelebi's *mevlut* (c. 1400) a chorus begins each line with "Welcome" as in "Welcome O intercessor of the worlds," and each refrain proclaims "If you want to be rescued from Hellfire / Utter the blessings over him with love and [longing] pain." (Schimmel, p. 155). Similar references occur in countless lyrics for the Prophet and songs celebrating the hajj or pilgrimage. The concept is closely entwined with the emotional entreaties of the Sufi *dhikr,* or ceremony of remembrance, and their *inshad* (sung poetry).

The early Islamic philosophical school known as the Mu'tazila disputed the idea of Prophetic intercession because they believed that it diminished the absolute justice of God. And although the medieval jurist and polemicist Ibn Taymiyya accepted the traditions concerning Prophetic intercession, his spiritual descendants in the modern world, the Wahhabiyya of Saudi Arabia, have disputed the notions of *shafa'a* and *tawassul,* as have other modernizing reformers. Some hold that granting such powers to the Prophet or other holy figures is akin to the polytheistic practices of the pre-Islamic period. The Wahhabis interpret the Koran (2:25) to mean that because only God can grant permission for intercession, this will only be gained by a monotheist, and that the devotion to dead saints is misguided. Such reformers also object to the use of amulets or jewelry with Koranic inscriptions (or for the Shia, sometimes the image of 'Ali and the prophet Muhammad). Believers wear and bestow such items on each other in the hopes that they will confer *baraka* ("blessing"), similar to the charismatic blessing of a dead saint.

The Prophet's intercession is described as being connected to his *baraka* and is described as being made of divine light itself. Similarly, the *baraka* of the other Muslim holy figures is sought and thought to bring about this light-infused intercession, whether through the action of the believer at a visitation to a holy place, such as an Imamzadeh for the Shia, or in the use of language that creates an emotional bridge to the *baraka* of a text and its author.

Intercession in Middle Eastern societies is not limited to the religious sphere. Other social and political practices reflect the reliance on intercession of the powerful in Muslim and even in non-Muslim Middle Eastern societies. In the social sphere, powerful or prestigious figures have served as mediators for conflicts, interceding for each party until resolution was achieved. In political life, the concept of intercession led to the dominance of particular elites, in what was known as the politics of patronage in the nineteenth and twentieth centuries as well as during earlier periods.

The *zu'ama* (literally chieftains, elite leaders) of Lebanon, or urban Syria, as well as politicians in Egypt and elsewhere sponsored clients and expected their political loyalty in return for favors. It was important for the less socially and politically powerful to locate patrons, obtain their "influence," or find an intermediary (a *wasta* or "link") who could do so. This has lent an aura of corruption, fatalism, and violence to the political process, as people doubted that anything could be accomplished without such an intermediary. It is not unreasonable to speak of a parallel between the temporal and religious reliance on intercession. On a psychological level, the strength or efficacy of one's connections can contribute to feelings of security. Some argue that such dependence has obstructed populist tendencies and democratization. Intercession has been a major factor in social and political life, even where mass parties have been established, as in Egypt, Iraq, or Syria, cementing the cultural belief that the strength of one's connections was invariably more significant than talent, merit, or energy.

*See also* **Islam.**

**BIBLIOGRAPHY**
Ayoub, Mahmoud. *Redemptive Suffering in Islam: A Study of the Devotional Aspects of 'Ashura in Twelver Shi'ism.* The Hague: Mouton de Gruyter, 1978.
Gilsenan, Michael. *Lords of the Lebanese Marches: Violence and Narrative in an Arab Society.* Berkeley: University of California Press, 1996.
———. *Saint and Sufi in Modern Egypt: An Essay in the Sociology of Religion.* Oxford: Clarendon, 1973.
Nasr, Seyyed Hossein, Hamid Dabashi, and Seyyed Vali Reza Nasr, eds. *Shi'ism: Doctrines, Thought and Spirituality.* Albany: State University of New York Press, 1988.
Reeves, Edward B. *The Hidden Government: Ritual, Clientelism, and Legitimation in Northern Egypt.* Salt Lake City: University of Utah Press, 1990.
Schimmel, Annemarie. *And Muhammad Is His Messenger: The Veneration of the Prophet in Islamic Piety.* Chapel Hill: University of North Carolina Press, 1985.
Waugh, Earl H. *The Munshidiin of Egypt: Their World and Their Song.* Columbia: University of South Carolina Press, 1989.

*Sherifa Zuhur*

**INTERDISCIPLINARITY.** The development of innovative and creative ideas in the academy is taking place in the early 2000s largely across departmental and disciplinary divides. Intradisciplinary practice tends to be microfocused and piecemeal. Innovation proceeds intradisciplinarily, where it proceeds at all, mostly in small if not minute increments. Departmental institutionalization itself has been transforming, prompted by interdisciplinary practice. This is the case whether one considers the sciences or humanities, technology development or the arts, or the social or applied sciences. Universities continue to organize themselves around discrete departments of mathematics, physics, biology, or computer science, schools of engineering, and professional colleges, to be sure. Science research, however, tends to occur collectively and collaboratively. Laboratories (for example, in bioinformatics or in nanoscience) require teams of researchers with more or less wide-ranging field training, methodologies, techniques, and technological expertise. Experiments, discoveries, and research outcomes in the sciences may be attributed to the individual lab as much as to the traditional disciplines or departmental structures. Departments profit too from the results of these interdisciplinary research labs (not least from the external grant funding they generate). Hiring in the sciences consequently is often made between multiple departments and increasingly with interdisciplinary research goals in mind.

Where the sciences have been largely fearless in leading, the social sciences and the humanities have tended to follow, if for their own reasons. Schools or colleges of constitutively interdisciplinary applied social science programs have become increasingly popular, often supplemented by resident historians or philosophers or, increasingly, cultural analysts. A similar mutually constitutive relationship has been unfolding in U.S. universities between core humanities departments and interdisciplinary humanistic inquiry.

While interdisciplinarity has become de rigueur, at least rhetorically, more widespread acknowledgment and institutional credit nevertheless has been much slower in the making. An interdisciplinary model, humanistic or social scientific or more compellingly erosive of that divide, requires a shift from largely contained and constrained, field-specific themes and methods to problem- or issue-based objects of analysis, more or less unbounded questions, and multifaceted methodologies. This latter disposition likewise tends to be less figured around national imaginaries or boundaries than has largely been the case in many humanistic fields in the past. It concerns itself consequently more with contact, flows of ideas, and cultural intersections than with the cultural heritage of nationally defined and fixed products.

This newly emergent model accordingly can be considered an intellectual byproduct of globalization. Social thinking and the humanities as a result have been transformed in unexpected and unpredictable ways. For example, the renaissance of classical studies in the early twenty-first century has flowed from the merging of traditional linguistic and historical studies of specifically located areas in the ancient world with archaeology enhanced by new techniques of digital imaging and an expansive political geography. These interactive developments have transformed the map of the ancient world by asking questions posed by critical race theory, gender studies, or postcolonial theory in addition to the more traditional interrogations of objects, texts, and images from the period in question. Similarly, the latter-day emergence of oceanic or regional studies is a function not only of the implosion of area studies but also of the perceived limits of disciplinary determinations in the face of complex thematic and problem-driven research foci.

## Humanities and Social Sciences

The humanities have characteristically taken themselves as revealing what it is to be human and humane, just as the social sciences have long reproduced what they have presupposed as normative models of psychology, sociality, governmentality, even historicality. Together they have purported to teach what it means to be rational and reasoned, cultured and moral, social and political, learned and worldly. The institutional history of what has been conceived as "the humanities," and perhaps of social thinking more broadly, has always been

deeply inflected with, if it was not founded on, dominant class and ethnonational determination. It has been a difficult revelation, then, that prior to at least World War II, and really well into the 1970s, the dominant trends in the humanities and social sciences throughout the Anglo-European academy as well as in universities worldwide that are founded on the Anglo-European (and more recently American) model(s)—and often part of a colonial project—for the most part were little more than expressions of European culture, society, and governance.

Even this way of putting it is misleading, for it was not European culture, sociality, and political structure in some broad articulation that was taken to represent intellectual, moral, cultural, and political superiority. Rather, it was the sociocultural articulation of historical layers and tissues of connection between dominant national configurations within the European orbit. Philosophy and classics, English, Romance languages (principally French and Italian) and German, and even history not only embody their own particular histories; they are taken, even—one could say especially—in their dominant ethnonational articulation, to represent the march of history as such. The "best that had been thought and written" had a distinct and delimited geolinguistic and intellectual range. Anything—and the intellectual life of anywhere beyond the English, French, and German, prompted by earlier influences of the Italian and Greek—was either rendered invisible or arrogantly dismissed as exotic, quaint, or simply inferior.

## Creating Disciplines

The definitions and elaborations of the terms of the human, the humane, and the humanistic were the stuff principally of the dominant disciplines in the humanities—philosophy and classics, national languages and literatures, history, and art history. The terms of the psychological, social, political, and cultural, by extension, were the domain of the social sciences. The prevailing objects of analysis in the humanities accordingly were conceptual, linguistic, artifactual, or textual; those in the social sciences were largely empirical (at least in the broad sense, both quantitative and qualitative). In both cases, objects and methods of analysis were distinctly disciplinarily driven and far from universal, as they more often than not assumed themselves to be. By the middle of the twentieth century, these disciplines tended to be self-contained and self-referential, methodologically streamlined, if not singular. Disciplinary training consisted of analytical, epistemological, and methodological apprenticeship. This included the ability not only to apply the analytic apparatus and methodology thought properly constitutive of the discipline but also to determine what was considered, from inside the discipline, to be the right questions to ask. This after all was what it meant to acquire (a) discipline.

Intellectual hegemony within the humanities and social sciences was never complete nor was it ever completely stable. Intellectual resistances, for example, emerged in the 1930s, complementing the political ones. Entangled intellectual and political countermovements ebbed and flowed between the 1930s and 1960s. Intellectual diversification within and across the academy was boosted by the growing class, ethnic, racial, and gendered diversification of those entering at least the American university in the wake of World War II, bolstered initially by the GI Bill and then by the rising tide of middle-class aspirations. These developments unleashed novel interests and demands for different knowledges and new forms of representation that cut across the traditional epistemological organization known as disciplines. It is this rich mix that has come to be recognized as "interdisciplinarity."

Often implicitly, sometimes overtly, this emerging interdisciplinarity assumed humanistic configuration from its inception, even when not specifically noted as such. The University of Chicago's influential "Great Books" program insisted that any understanding of basic human problems had to be informed by "a select number of classic ancient and modern texts" independent of their disciplinary origin. What discipline, precisely, is responsible for the standard Great Books syllabus that includes Aristotle and Aquinas, Shakespeare, Tolstoy, Hegel, and Freud? Chicago's Committee on Social Thought, while proposed primarily by social scientists in 1941, singles out contributions that would ordinarily be called "humanities" as the basis and preparation for serious intellectual work. In fact, this humanistic basis for inquiry is so much a given that it is not even labeled as such.

Many scholars working in the academy in the intervening decades have reached for new constructs that could encompass the intellectual and social energies, interests, and problematics of their day while providing foundations that are both historically and culturally expansive. This imperative toward humanistic interdisciplinarity recalls the nineteenth century, when, as Lisa Lattuca argues, many intellectuals insisted on more expansive forms of inquiry not organized along the strict(ly) disciplinary lines being routinized, regularized, and institutionalized by college administrators concerned to develop "coherent and integrated courses of study." And yet nineteenth-century versions, while precursors, are really "predisciplinary," to use William Newell's term, not really amounting to interdisciplinarities (Lattuca, pp. 5–6). The disposition was perhaps there, though not quite yet the thick institutionalization of disciplines to which interdisciplinarity is a response, a resistance, a need, a challenge. Graduate and professional education and certification at the end of the nineteenth century also helped to create disciplinary boundaries, structures, and institutional bureaucracies that concretized intellectual borders. These developments served over time to transform complicated and interwoven histories of ideas (the blurred boundaries between science, anthropology, philosophy, and literature, for example) into discrete "departments" with specialized training and networks of professional affiliation (including learned societies and journals) along with the criteria of credentializing to which they gave rise and which in turn further reified disciplinary determinations.

## Toward Interdisciplinarity

The new material and human arrangements brought about by globalization, long-standing processes dramatically intensified and speeded up since the end of World War II, have contributed substantially to the changing intellectual borders of disciplines. This has prompted perhaps the increasing emphasis on the "social" rather than the "science" of many social scientists, the turn to ethnography by a growing number of humanists, and the appreciation of affective aesthetic and expressive forms by many in both the humanities and the social sciences. The interdisciplinarity to which this points is not some other word for "pluralism" but rather is emerging as a result of the difficult, entangled, and ongoing problems that demonstrate the need to find better interpretive tools and complex models of cultural and human exchange and new arrangements of knowledge. As with any paradigm shift, these new structures of thinking about novel and emergent global arrangements inevitably illuminate ancillary areas of inquiry—including many different configurations of premodern studies that have taken on new focus and energy by contact with postcolonial and global theory. If culture is the traditional site of the humanities, humanities has traditionally restricted culture to its national delimitations. By contrast, contemporary interdisciplinary humanities takes up culture as a critical diagnostic for comprehending life in the wake of globalization. It registers the contradictions and complexes of globalization, offering horizons for understanding through reflection and interpretation. It denaturalizes sedimented ways of knowing by offering novel categories of analysis and comprehension and new catalogs of cultural archive.

This broadened frame, in turn, has begun to erode the wider boundaries between the humanities and social sciences just as newly emerging questions have begun to soften the traditionally hard lines between the sciences, technology, the humanities, the social sciences, and even the arts. The National Science Foundation in the United States, for instance, is insisting in the early 2000s that proposals for engineering new digital technologies demonstrate their constitutive human and community benefits, a mandate that in turn is driving new collaborative engagements between technologists, humanists, social scientists, lawyers, and artists to mutually transformative effect.

Disciplinarity, then, is an institutional creation, forged out of specific histories, in specific places. It has offered an anchor in the face of increasing epistemological dubitability as disciplinary influences and effects have traveled, circulating between metropolitan and colonial sites. What has come to be marked as interdisciplinary practice prompts objects of analysis more diffuse and multiplicitous, more fully prompted than those disciplinarily driven. These objects of analysis are less likely (at least thus far) to be implied by the histories of their intellectual practice and range. Rather, interdisciplinary objects of analysis in social, cultural, and humanistic thinking tend to be concerns identified as abundant in social and cultural life in various geopolitical sites. That the objects and modes of analysis can no longer simply be said to be fueled by the extension of European interests and assumptions is indicative as much of the shift in intellectual dispositions as it is a function of dramatic developments in globalized arrangements of capital and, consequently, of persons. Interdisciplinary practice that has become such an index of contemporary thinking is marked accordingly by the appeal of multiple methodologies and by broader scope and styles of question.

## Models for Interdisciplinarity

There has been a good deal of what one might call the mantric recourse to interdisciplinarity as something that ought to be done in the humanities and theoretical social sciences. And yet the seminal work on conceiving the nature and scope of interdisciplinary work confirms the extensive representational power of the sciences. The natural sciences especially, complemented by the empirical social sciences, have provided the dominant model for the nature of interdisciplinarity. This has been at once liberating and delimiting. In some instances science interdisciplinarity has been robust. Information science and policy and genomic research, policy, and ethics offer two good examples. But there are other models of interdisciplinarity not well served by the model of science. The report of the Gulbenkian Commission on the Restructuring of the Social Sciences, "Open the Social Sciences" (1996), rightly points out that the humanities in some formations may be far more interdisciplinary in fact than the empirical social sciences. Jeffrey Sachs rightly insists in a *New York Times Magazine* interview discussing his commitment to "sustainable development" that interdisciplinarity is the only way to solve world problems. The need, he asserts, is "to focus not on the disciplines but on the problems and to bring together five main areas in an intensive dialogue: the earth sciences, ecological science, engineering, public health, and the social sciences with a heavy dose of economics" (Sachs, p. 45). Jeffrey Sachs notwithstanding, economics is hardly the model of interdisciplinarity that one should strive to emulate. Political economy, for instance, has suffered in the shadow of its more positivistic cousin. There are practices and ways of thinking about interdisciplinarity, and so models for it are not narrowly reducible to the prevailing conceptions in the sciences and empirical social sciences.

While some scientists embrace a vigorous interdisciplinary perspective, it is not unusual to find scientists referring both conceptually and in their exemplification of interdisciplinary practice exclusively to the sciences—biology, chemistry, the cognitive sciences, and so forth. Humanists often speak with equal and equally intense insularity: interdisciplinarity all too often is delimited to literature and history, with a grudging nod perhaps to anthropology or a facile invocation of sociology or political economy. It is important, then, to pay attention to the fact that there are different conceptions, models, and practices of interdisciplinary venture. Of particular interest are the robust senses of interdisciplinarity across the more traditional divides between the humanities, the sciences, the applied sciences and technology, the arts, and the social sciences.

These shifts are evidenced by the fact that the regime of interdisciplinarity has occasioned tremendous changes in habits of reading. Under the *ancien régime* of robust disciplinarity, reading was driven mostly from *within* the discipline. This included who and what one read (or at least professed to have read) and discussed within seminars and colloquia, at departmental affairs, in oral dissertations, and so on. A scholar was socialized into and by the disciplinary bounds of reading and through conversation around and about these sets of readings. It is revealing to notice that in the late twentieth century this boundedness of reading broke down rather dramatically. Twenty-first-century scholars read with little, or far less,

attention to disciplinary constraint and concern, more readily drawing on work that speaks to the problematics and themes with which they are concerned. Work in literature might readily draw on historical studies, obviously, but also on reading from women's or critical gender or race studies, from visual studies, art history, and philosophy traditionally conceived, as well as from sociology or politics or anthropology. The history and philosophy of science are no longer the only endeavors in the humanities to engage with the sciences, as the distinctions between nature and culture and the social and biological increasingly blur, and one looks for new languages of representation and novel vocabularies of reference. Science and technology studies are the natural outgrowth of this convergence of interests. The first generation of digital humanities that has focused almost exclusively on digital collections of cultural heritage, important as they have been, are now leading to more robust, mutually transformative engagements between engineering, information technology, humanities, and the arts.

***Obstacles to pedagogy.*** One obstacle to vigorous interdisciplinary pedagogy concerns methodological and epistemological considerations. There is, of course, the pedagogical tension between the clean slate proposed by John Locke (1632–1704) and the historicality associated with the legacy of Wihelm Dilthey (1833–1911). It is difficult to train students in interdisciplinary modes of analysis and thought when they have yet to grasp the intellectual histories, historically prevailing questions, and thematics prompting the interdisciplinary disposition to begin with. It is no doubt easier to introduce rigorous interdisciplinary modalities in teaching at the graduate level than at the undergraduate level, notwithstanding the consideration that less-formed minds tend to be more open to new possibilities. And a good part of the restraint on interdisciplinary pedagogy has to do with the fact that teaching in universities and colleges tends so largely to be ordered around disciplinarily organized departments with relatively few possibilities provided for recognized and credited cross-disciplinary pedagogical partnerships.

There are various ways to sharpen the contrast between disciplinarity and interdisciplinarity. One of course is methodological. But there are also deep epistemological distinctions. Disciplines produce knowledge according to different criteria than does interdisciplinary practice, and they credentialize that knowledge on different grounds. There does seem to be a contrast between the positive sciences, broadly conceived, as engaging in the practice of "looking for" and the humanities, for which "thinking about" or reflection, for want of better terms, is the driving modality. Disciplinarity, relatedly, is often thought to produce so-called positive knowledge through constraint and boundedness, a "knowing that," to use Gilbert Ryle's (1900–1976) term, in contrast to a "knowing how." Interdisciplinarity, no doubt, can sometimes be as limited and specialized as any disciplinary project, if one is simply bringing to bear different methodologies on one highly focused question or problem (a commonplace of multidisciplinary experiment in the sciences). The sort of robust interdisciplinarity for which we are making an argument here concerns ways of combining different methodologies and approaches in seeking new yet still systematic ways to address large and complex problems not susceptible to analysis (or solution) from a single perspective.

The humanities often embrace affective aspects of intelligence, such as imagination, play, improvisation, and serendipity, as much as they embrace conventional rationalist forms of inquiry, such as logic, analysis, deconstruction, and critique. They value aesthetics as much as politics. The romance of these artful aspects, after all, revealing of one of the two major humanistic traditions, prompts a loosening of disciplinary bounds, further softening entrenched lines between humanities and the arts.

Mark Gibson and Alec McHoul talk relatedly of the constitutive incompleteness of disciplines. In large part a product of disciplinary boundedness, insularity, self-containment, and (often productive) delimitations, this constitutive incompleteness suggests epistemological partiality on the part of disciplines, both a necessarily incomplete and a relatedly one-sided knowledge of the object in question. From within the boundaries one knows an object as no more than the discipline would have it. Epistemological curiosity, if not the epistemological drive to complete knowledge, to know it all, so to speak, suggests too an epistemological push or ontological pull beyond disciplinary boundaries. This dispositive draw—the "need" of the knowing subject, qua knowledge, to know it all, the "necessity" of the object to be known—conjures or points to the beyond that might critically be called interdisciplinarities.

Less grandiosely, Kenneth Wissoker has suggested that interdisciplinarity varies by discipline: questions asked of an object of analysis, methods considered legitimate, and the conceptual apparatus deemed appropriate vary from one discipline to another, and so the practice of interdisciplinarity prompted from different disciplinary sites will vary accordingly. Interdisciplinarity prompted or practiced from within disciplines is likely to look different from interdisciplinarities the starting points for which are, say, problem- or issue-promoted (where the problem or issue is not simply discipline-specific).

## Interdisciplinarity as a Critical Project
This raises the question whether it is possible to think of interdisciplinarity as cast adrift from any particular discipline, not simply the view from nowhere but from the point of transience, migration, betweenness. Is there an interdisciplinary practice not fixed or bounded by the disciplines but prompted from those spaces and gaps and interstices the disciplines inevitably fail to exhaust, their blind spots, even in their overlap? But what then is the force of the "*inter*" in interdisciplinarity (as opposed to focusing on the disciplines to which interdisciplinarity is a contrast)? What happens in the intellectual, conceptual, methodological spaces between disciplines? What is suggested here is a redirected focus for interdisciplinarity, from the disciplines between which there is exchange to the exchange to which the disciplines contribute and themselves change as they do.

Conceived thus, it may be asked whether interdisciplinarity is, or should be, committed first and foremost to a critical project. The preceding line of argument suggests it is. If so, a prime feature of such a critical project would be antireductionism. Very often reductionism and disciplinarity are bound up with each other, predicated thus always on its object of critique. Disciplines by definition are reductive. To know an object through or via the discipline is to know it reduced to the parameters determined by disciplinary constraints, conceptual, methodological, or theoretical. If knowledge through disciplines is perspectival in this way, interdisciplinarity seeks to pluralize the sources, perspectives, dispositions, and determinations of knowledge. If disciplinary knowledge seeks objectivity through constraint, interdisciplinarity seeks knowledge through relationalities.

To learn a discipline, it might be said, is to learn a language. It is not enough simply to learn the vocabulary, though that surely is necessary. This means that keen attention also must be paid—especially—to what could be called the syntax and semantics of the discipline, and to the cultures it conjures and projects. Approached in this way, the contrast between disciplinarity and interdisciplinarity may begin to be discerned. To become fluent interdisciplinarily is not simply to learn more than one language, to multiply the syntactical and semantic structures and cultures known. Rather, it means to assume a different, if related (even derivative), mode of speaking, to inhabit a different culture, and in that inhabitation to see differently. It is in more than an idle sense to learn—to inhabit—a creole culture (and perhaps to be treated as creoles so often have).

It follows from all of this that there is not simply a singular correct or proper (form of) interdisciplinarity. There are, in short, interdisciplinarities rather than one interdisciplinary model or method. Were interdisciplinarity to become the currency of the academy, as Marjorie Garber has warned, it would tend to the conventional, to devolve into its own kind of disciplinarity. Heterogenizing the practices and their institutional arrangements encourages, by contrast, renewed possibilities, promotes institutional settings sustaining rather than delimiting robust knowledge promotion, even invites a more heterogeneous inhabitation of the academy. Such interdisciplinary institutional arrangements would come and go, transact and transform in vigorous relation to the vicissitudes of the problematics—the objects of study and analysis—for which they exist and serve to illuminate. Such robust interdisciplinarities are seen as relational, flexible and transformative, self-confident and open-ended, suggestive and servicing, rather than deterministic and delimiting. Historically grounded without being historicist, they are heterogeneous and not reductionistic in assumption and scope, pluralizing and radically nonessentializing, facing heterogeneous worlds with curiosity, generosity, and sensitivity rather than with narrow introspection and incessant denial. Such robust interdisciplinarities, vigorous without being arrogant, engaged without being imperialistic, look to make connections across every area of the university—including the sciences, engineering, and the professional schools in their reach.

*See also **Cultural Studies; Science; Technology; University.***

**BIBLIOGRAPHY**
Garber, Marjorie. *Academic Instincts.* Princeton, N.J.: Princeton University Press, 2001.
Gibson, Mark, and McHoul Alec. "Interdisciplinarity." In *A Companion to Cultural Studies,* edited by Toby Miller, 23–35. Oxford: Blackwell, 2001.

INTERNAL COLONIALISM

Klein, Julie Thompson. *Crossing Boundaries: Knowledge, Disciplinarities, and Interdisciplinarities.* Charlottesville: University of Virginia Press, 1996.

———. *Interdisciplinarity: History, Theory, and Practice.* Detroit: Wayne State University Press, 1990.

Lattuca, Lisa R. *Creating Interdisciplinarity: Interdisciplinary Research and Teaching among College and University Faculty.* Nashville: Vanderbilt University Press, 2001.

Sachs, Jeffrey. "Poor Man's Economist: Questions for Jeffrey Sachs." *New York Times Magazine,* 12 December 2002, 45.

Wissoker, Kenneth. "Negotiating a Passage between Disciplinary Borders." *Chronicle of Higher Education,* 14 April 2000, 4–6.

*David Theo Goldberg*
*Cathy N. Davidson*

**INTERNAL COLONIALISM.** The term *internal colonialism* defines a condition of oppression or subordination, often of one ethnic group over another (as in the subordination of Mexicans in the United States at the conclusion of the U.S.-Mexican War of 1846–1848). Some view the term as a contraposition to the claim that all people in the United States "are immigrants." For example, *immigrant* does not describe accurately the lives of people of Mexican origin living in the territory known today as the southwestern United States. Many residents of what is now New Mexico and Texas trace their ancestry back to the 1600s. For them, the term *immigrant* does not reflect their history or relationship to the United States and it mischaracterizes the place of native-born Mexican-origin peoples. Moreover, in relation to other ethnic groups, immigrant status fails to reflect accurately the histories of African slave descendants, nor does it do justice to relocated and disrupted Native peoples.

Because the general claim that all Americans are of immigrant stock is problematic, the nature of Mexicans' status in the United States must be supplemented with other terms or concepts. For Mexicans, or Chicanos and Chicanas, as their descendants are termed today, the term *internal colonialism* is applied by social scientists and others to understand the historical and cultural conditions or experiences that were a direct result of the actions of governments. Because of the conditions in the 1840s, many Mexicans and Native peoples suddenly found themselves residents, though not citizens, of a new government and its structures. In view of the fact that these people had been "colonized" by a contiguous power, that is, the larger and more prosperous United States, and they owned or lived on land considered highly desirable, Chicana and Chicano scholars, as well as others sensitive to the history of this ethnic group, began to apply the term *internal colonialism* to describe how people were locked into certain jobs, how the economy that developed particularly in the Southwest relied on an organized system of subordinator and subordinated.

Other scholars have more recently differentiated the ways in which workers in the Southwest differ from one region to another, and a more nuanced understanding of differences and similarities is therefore achieved. An example would be how urban people and rural people differed during any period, or

how men's and women's values changed, and not always in tandem. While internal colonialism might help explain various features of a lived experience, in a period of hostile warfare between two nations, for example, it cannot explain all aspects of culture, politics, or philosophies and religions.

At times, internal colonialism is set against colonialism, with the latter viewed as older and more authoritarian, that is, more rigid in structure and organization. In the early twenty-first century, however, the fact of colonization itself is rarely questioned; that is, it is assumed that Mexican-origin and to some extent indigenous/Native peoples were colonized by a nation-state still in its formative years (beginning in the Southwest around 1803 and extending up to the time of the war's outbreak in 1846). It might be useful to think of internal colonialism as less organized than colonialism in its reach, but its impact was felt by people across a spectrum of classes and social locations. Even wealthy merchants of Mexican origin in Santa Fe were forced to accept a new authority in the form of judges, military officials, and federal appointees in a newly-imposed court system after 1848. Before long, internal colonialism assured their subordination. For women, the same applied. No longer able to bring lawsuits, retain property in their own names, or retain their family names or lands, women suffered a diminishment in their status as well.

Colonized from within by a government or power greater than that which had once existed would be another way to approach how useful internal colonialism is to nonimmigrant, Mexican-origin people of the Southwest and far West. The United States brought Protestant, English-based institutions, as well as schools and businesses, when it created a pathway toward California. Accompanying the movement of goods, products, and English-speaking people were racial ideologies, political orientations, and doctrines that specified why Mexicans and Native Americans could not hold public office, travel freely, own businesses, or live their lives independent of wages earned working for others. The concept of "manifest destiny" decreed that people of the white, Anglo "race" were superior to Mexicans and Indians. The legal codes developed in the United States and forcibly applied to all the colonized territory that had once belonged to Mexico, along with the violence of lynchings and deportations that continued into the twentieth century, conveyed an important message about internal colonialism. The fear and terror evidenced in actions against Mexicans based on their race, for example, lynchings that would number more than 500 between 1850 and 1920, reveal the way internal colonialism operated on what was essentially a "frontier" territory.

To understand the significance of this concept means more than just debating whether it explains fully how racism and oppression operated; it means taking seriously the history of exclusion and its enforcement among ethnic groups or races judged to be inferior to white, Anglo-Saxon, and European-origin peoples. In that sense, the phrase and idea of internal colonialism are useful for unraveling the history of the Southwestern and Western United States. Scholars in the early twenty-first century recommend consideration as well about colonialism or transnational capital movement, that is, global capitalism, and not just focus on internal colonialism; but the everyday, lived experiences of many ethnic groups that can be understood through a deeper comprehension of internal colonialism. Although the term does not explain racial or gender relations fully, it introduces the idea that politics and economics worked together to displace and replace residents of a territory and then continued this practice as immigrants began repopulating the former Mexican north after the war with Mexico had long since ended.

The demographic reclamation of the same territory proceeding in the early twenty-first century in a process of immigration and migration is ironic to the extent that what the United States most disliked, that is, people of color determining their own futures, is an ongoing process and consequence of these earlier wars and the displacements they introduced, whether social, religious, political, or economic. Internal colonialism thus continues to fuel a much larger, global issue, that of the mass movement of people toward industrial capitalist centers or toward the developed urban nation-state. Because the impact of these currents is so strong in such places as Los Angeles, Phoenix, Houston, and the Southern United States as well as in the Midwest (where people of Mexican origin now reside in record numbers), defining the operations of internal colonialism is useful. Local and global developments demand it.

*See also* **Assimilation; Colonialism; Identity, Multiple; Loyalties, Dual; Migration.**

BIBLIOGRAPHY

Almaguer, Thomás. *Racial Fault Lines: The Historical Origins of White Supremacy in California.* Berkeley: University of California Press, 1994.

Barrera, Mario. *Race and Class in the Southwest: A Theory of Racial Inequality.* Notre Dame, Ind.: University of Notre Dame Press, 1979.

Blauner, Robert. *Racial Oppression in America.* New York: Harper and Row, 1972.

Hechter, Michael. *Internal Colonialism: The Celtic Fringe in British National Development.* With a new introduction and appendix by the author. New Brunswick, N.J.: Transaction Publishers, 1999.

Montejano, David. *Anglos and Mexicans in the Making of Texas, 1836–1986.* Austin: University of Texas Press, 1987.

*Deena J. González*

**INTERNATIONAL ORDER.** The image of a peaceful, orderly world where men and nations resolve their differences without war, where the lion lies down with the lamb, has haunted humankind for millennia. Roman law expressed the gulf between the ideal and the reality concisely by contrasting the condition of man living under the *ius naturale,* the natural law, a world of peace and harmony, with the human condition as it actually was under the *ius gentium,* the law of nations, a condition that included war and conflict. The very creation of government at the lowest level was the beginning of efforts to create order at least within a small area, to establish an order within which people could live peacefully with one another by accepting a set of rules that shaped their relations with one another. At the next level, there is the need to create rules that enable neighboring societies to get along with one another. At the ultimate level, there was the desire to create a peaceful world order that would bring all the nations of the world into a peaceful, harmonious relationship.

In the history of the Western world, there is a long tradition of attempts to create some kind of international order. One of the major obstacles to the creation of such an order stemmed from the fact that ancient political thought identified the small, independent city-state as the ideal environment for the development of the human personality. The freedom associated in theory with life in the city-state, however, posed a threat to order because of the wars among these states. On the other hand, there were empires, powerful states consisting of a ruling group dominating a number of conquered societies and maintaining order but at a price that the Greeks would not accept.

From a modern perspective, the Greek world, violent and even chaotic as it often was, was superior to the orderly Persian world because it was associated with freedom, democracy, and creativity. Yet the golden age of Athens ended in a disastrous war, and the age of creativity and democracy died with it. A lesson that the Greek experience might teach is that empires last longer and maintain an orderly world longer than small city-states can, but they do so at a price that many would deem too high.

### The Greek and Roman World

The Greek world did produce one solution to the tension between freedom and order, that is between city-state and empire, when Philip of Macedon (d. 336 B.C.E.) and his son, Alexander the Great (d. 323 B.C.E), created a great empire stretching from Greece to the Indus Valley. At the core of that empire were the Greek city-states that Philip had conquered and united. He saw himself as bringing the Greek world to the fullest stage of development, creating a unified world order under Greek leadership. According to his biographer Arrian (second century C.E.) writing several centuries later, Alexander aimed at creating an empire that brought peace to the regions he had conquered but that would be administered by the Greeks. The goal was to create a *cosmos polis,* a world community in which all the members shared the sense of unity and brotherhood that the members of a traditional city-state shared. If Alexander had lived, he might have created a vast peaceful and orderly world community under a single imperial ruler. His early death, however, destroyed any possibility that such a community would actually be created. In the years after Alexander the Great's death, one school of Greek philosophers, the Stoics, followers of Zeno of Citium (c. 335–c. 263 B.C.E.), did develop the concept of mankind as forming a single community. This concept flourished subsequently among the Romans and, apparently, even helped shape the Christian notion of mankind as ultimately forming a single community.

The most extensive example of a stable international order in the ancient Western world was the Roman Empire. In the course of its history, first as the Roman Republic expanding to bring all of Italy south of the Po River under a single government and then in a series of wars, first against the Carthaginians in the West and then against the Macedonians and Greeks in the East, the Romans brought the entire Mediterranean basin under their control. By the time of the first emperor, Augustus (r. 27 B.C.E.–14 C.E.), Roman jurisdiction ran from northern England to the Syrian Desert and from the Rhine River south to the Atlas Mountains and the Sahara. The network of roads that the Romans constructed enabled them to keep the peace within the empire by dispatching troops rapidly when rebellion arose among the conquered peoples.

The Roman imperial order, the Pax Romana, succeeded because it relied not simply on Roman troops but on the Roman ability to obtain the cooperation of the leaders of the societies that they conquered. The peace treaty signed at the end of a war with Rome often held out to the leading men among the conquered people the possibility of Roman citizenship, that is membership in the ruling elite of the Roman world, to those who accepted the new order. This practice gave many of the conquered peoples a vested interest in keeping the peace. At the same time, the Romans generally abstained from interfering in the internal affairs of the states that they conquered, thus reducing possible points of conflict.

The gradual decline of the Roman Empire in the West beginning in the fourth century meant the end of the Pax Romana. Any possibility of a stable international order was lost as the Roman government collapsed and new populations moved into the lands that the Romans once ruled. The Carolingian Empire of the eighth and ninth centuries was a failed attempt to restore the peaceful order of the ancient Roman imperial world on Christian principles. In reality, however, there was no longer any possibility of a single dominant power exercising jurisdiction over a large region.

## The Medieval Christian Conception of International Order

As a series of small kingdoms emerged in Europe out of the ruins of the Carolingian world, a new conception of international order emerged, the notion that there is a natural right order of the world that human understanding could comprehend. This new approach conceived of human society as hierarchical, with lesser societies subordinate to higher ones. Recognition of the natural right order and the acceptance of a society's place within that order was the key to international harmony. To a great extent those who saw the world in these terms differed only on the issue of who would head the hierarchical structure and mediate international conflicts, the Holy Roman Emperor or the pope. Supporters of the imperial position argued that the Christian Roman emperor was the true *dominus mundi,* the Lord of the World, and the kings of Europe were rulers of what were in effect provinces of the empire. The other view was that the pope as the spiritual head of Christian society was the head of an international society and that he was the ultimate regulator of international order. These competing views about the leadership of Christian society provided one of the fundamental elements of the medieval church-state conflict.

By the thirteenth century, the papal vision of a Christian world order came to dominate, because the emperors could not impose their claim to suzerainty over the kings of Europe. Increasingly kings claimed that within their own kingdoms they possessed the powers attributed to the emperor in the empire, that is they were claiming to be sovereign and therefore not subject to any other temporal ruler. They could not, however, claim exemption from papal jurisdiction. The papal legal system, the canon law, operated throughout the entire Western Christian world, and the pope acted as the *judex omnium,* the judge of all Christians, even emperors and kings. With regard to international order, the papal approach assumed that all serious issues fell under the jurisdiction of the canon law so that international conflicts, clearly among the most serious of issues, should be brought to the papal court for adjudication. One consequence of the papal conception of the world was that several thirteenth-century popes intervened in conflicts between Christian kings in order to prevent wars and to keep the peace. Another aspect of medieval thought on international order concerned Christian relations with non-Christian societies, especially Muslim societies. The emergence of Islam in seventh-century Arabia led to the creation of the Dar al-Islam ("the abode of Islam"), a Muslim cultural and social order that contended with Christendom militarily and spiritually for the next thousand years along a line that stretched from eastern Europe, through the Near East, and across North Africa and into Spain. Was it possible for Christians to live at peace with such neighbors? In practice, throughout the Middle Ages, Christians and Muslims engaged in trade throughout the Mediterranean, demonstrating that peaceful relations were possible under some conditions. Furthermore, until the eleventh century, Christian pilgrims were generally able to go on pilgrimage to the Holy Land and visit the places associated with the life of Christ, even though Palestine had been in Muslim hands since the fall of Jerusalem in 638.

The call for a crusade to free the Holy Land in 1095 was a crucial turning point in relations between Christians and Muslims, because Christians claimed the right to regain possession of Christian lands previously conquered by the Muslims as well as the right to protect themselves against advancing Muslim armies. The crusade was also seen as a means for developing a peaceful Christian world by diverting the violent to the frontier with the Muslims. At the same time, however, the crusaders also contributed to the deepening split within the Christian world between the Latin Church of Europe and the Greek Church of the Byzantine Empire. They did this by refusing to restore the lands they conquered from the Muslims to Byzantine control and by imposing the Latin ritual and Latin bishops on the Christian peoples of the East, peoples that adhered to versions of Christianity deemed heretical by the papacy.

In the mid-thirteenth century, Pope Innocent IV (r. 1243–1254), a leading canon lawyer, outlined a kind of world legal order under papal direction. He argued that the pope was the ultimate judge of all humankind, judging men and women according to the law to which they were subject. Thus, the pope judged Christians according to the canon law, Jews according to the Law of Moses, and all other people by the terms of the natural law that is accessible to all rational human beings. Such a vision was impossible to realize even within Christian Europe, but the canon lawyers may have been the first thinkers to conceive of all humankind as ultimately forming a community with a universal legal order and therefore the first thinkers to suggest the possibility of a formal set of rules to regulate international relations. Subsequently, a leading ecclesiastical thinker, Nicholas of Cusa (1401–1464), published his *De Concordantia Catholica,* an outline of the medieval Christian conception of an orderly world, a world in which every kingdom and principality, Christian and non-Christian, functioned within its proper place.

A second medieval approach to the problem of international order appeared in the *De Monarchia* of the poet Dante Alighieri (1265–1321). Like the ecclesiastical conception of world order, Dante conceived of mankind as a single community but under the jurisdiction of the Holy Roman Emperor who was, according to Roman Law, the *dominus mundi,* the Lord of the World. Dante's primary interest was in regulating relations among the European states in order to end the constant round of wars.

During the Middle Ages, discussions of world order did not progress beyond the theoretical level. These theories assumed that humankind potentially formed a single human community subject to enforceable universal legal standards and functionally organized in a hierarchically constructed system under papal or imperial leadership. Such theories were based on a limited knowledge of the actual geography of the earth and its inhabitants. Around 1500, two events radically undermined these medieval theories of world order: the voyages of Columbus and the Protestant Reformation. Columbus's voyages revealed to Europeans for the first time the vastness of the sea and the diversity of the earth's population. The Protestant Reformers rejected the papacy and the entire ecclesiastical structure that the popes headed and therefore rejected the hierarchical conception of world order associated with it. These developments reshaped discussions of world order, dividing discussion into several distinct topics. These included: order among the nations of Europe; access to and jurisdiction over the sea; and the rights of the peoples of the New World in the face of European expansion.

## The New World in the European International Order
The initial attempt to create a stable international order after Columbus's first voyage came in the form of three papal bulls that Pope Alexander VI (1492–1503) issued in 1493. These bulls, known by the opening words of the first of them, *Inter caetera,* divided the world along a line from the North Pole to the South Pole one hundred leagues west of the Azores and the Cape Verde Islands. To the east of that line, the pope granted the Portuguese complete jurisdiction, authorizing them to occupy lands held by the Muslim enemies of the Christian world and to support missionary efforts among the newly encountered peoples. In order to support these efforts, the Portuguese were granted a monopoly of trade with the peoples of these lands and of the route to Asia by way of circumnavigating Africa. The Spanish were granted the same privileges west of the line, guaranteeing them a monopoly of what was then

believed to be the westward route to Asia. No other Christian could enter these regions without the express permission of the ruler to whom the region was assigned.

*Inter caetera* was only the latest in a series of bulls going back to 1420 that had sought to regulate relations between the Portuguese and the Spanish as they expanded out into the Atlantic, seeking a route to Asia. During the fifteenth century, these two kingdoms had fought a series of wars that spilled over into the Atlantic, where both kingdoms laid claim to various island chains. In the course of settling these disputes, a series of popes had issued bulls regulating relations between these kingdoms in the Atlantic, assigning responsibility for specific islands to each kingdom and making each ruler responsible for Christianizing the peoples encountered there. *Inter caetera* did the same thing on a larger scale. Alexander VI's bulls also provided a justification for the European conquest of the New World. If the inhabitants interfered with Europeans who came peacefully to trade or to preach the Christian faith or if they engaged in practices that violated the natural law, European rulers had the right to send in troops to protect the merchants and missionaries and to punish violations of the natural law.

The Catholic position on world order received its fullest exposition in the works of a number of Spanish theologians, philosophers, and lawyers in the sixteenth and seventeenth centuries. The most famous of these authors were Francisco Vitoria O. P. (1486–1546) and Francisco Suarez S. J. (1548–1617). Vitoria approached the problem of international order from a position that we would now associate with human rights. That is, did the Europeans have the legal right to conquer and occupy the Americas, or did the inhabitants of the New World have legal right to their lands and did they have the right to govern themselves free of outside intervention? Finally, even if the inhabitants of the New World did have rights, were they subject to the natural law and could their violations of that law justify their conquest?

By challenging the papacy's conception of a hierarchically constructed Christendom, Protestant Reformers provided a basis for reconsidering the nature of international order. In the first place, the religious wars of the Reformation spelled the end of both papal and imperial claims to some form of leadership of European and even world society. The Peace of Westphalia (1648) ending 150 years of German wars of religion had no role for the pope and reduced the imperial office to a ghost of its former self. The notion of a unified Christendom ended, replaced by a group of what came to be identified as sovereign nation-states. These states rejected any notion of overlordship, papal or imperial, in their own internal affairs. Peace among the states of Europe would be achieved by political arrangements that the participating governments made among themselves. The key to such arrangements was the balance of power, that is, alliance networks designed to prevent any one country from dominating Europe.

## International Order and the Law of the Sea
The second area of concern was jurisdiction over the seas. Could the sea be owned or, at the very least, could anyone

assert jurisdiction over the sea in order to prevent others from entering as Alexander VI had asserted in *Inter caetera*? The debate about possession of the sea drew the most attention from European scholars, because the discovery of the size and extent of the world's oceans significantly changed the nature of the debate about world order. Instead of armies of foot soldiers conquering new lands, the new empires of the early modern world, with the exception of Spain, were primarily concerned with trade and not with the acquisition of large amounts of territory. They were seaborne empires. Alexander VI's allocation of spheres of responsibility to the Portuguese and Spanish, if accepted by all European rulers, would have blocked overseas expansion except for those whom these two nations allowed into the regions allotted to them. The early years of the seventeenth century saw the publication of a number of legal treatises on the law of the sea. The Portuguese scholar Serafim de Freitas (c. 1570–1633) wrote a lengthy treatise on the legitimacy of Portuguese claims to monopoly of trade in the Indian Ocean on the basis of the papal grant. John Selden (1584–1684), an English scholar, argued that although the pope had no right to allot the seas to specific Christian monarchs, various European states had long-standing claims to possess parts of the sea. The most important work on the topic of the sea was Hugo Grotius's (1583–1645) *Mare liberum* (The freedom of the seas; 1609). Obviously defending Dutch claims to the right to travel anywhere in the peaceful pursuit of trade, Grotius argued that the seas were open to all and that no ruler had the right to exclude anyone from any sea.

### International Order and Sovereign Nation-States

Like Alexander VI, Grotius's goal was to reduce the conflicts among the various European nations that were beginning to assemble overseas empires but without recourse to a universal ruler such as the pope or the Holy Roman Emperor. His *De iure belli ac pacis* (Concerning the law of war and peace; 1625) was a lengthy analysis of the causes of war that ultimately proposed rules for international relations that would not end all wars but, if followed, reduce their number. Increasingly, the issues associated with international order and dealt with in terms of international law came to focus almost exclusively on relations among European nations to the exclusion of any participation by other nations in the creation of international order. The building blocks of this international order were the sovereign nation-states that were developing in Europe and were expected to work in concert to maintain that order. Grotius's work marked a withdrawal from the conception of all mankind forming a single community subject to the terms of the natural law under the leadership of emperor or pope.

During the seventeenth and eighteenth centuries a number of important European thinkers developed theories of international law designed to mitigate if not end the horrors of war. These theorists, Samuel Pufendorf (1632–1694), Emmerich de Vattel (1714–1767), Immanuel Kant (1724–1804), to name only the most famous, sought to create an international order that did not depend on belief in God but on a purely rational analysis of the human situation in keeping with the secular rationalism of the Enlightenment.

During the nineteenth century a new stage of thinking and practice regarding international order developed. At the Congress of Vienna (1814–1815) the major powers, England, Prussia, Russia, Austria (later joined by France), formed the Quadruple Alliance and claimed responsibility for maintaining peace in Europe. Seeing the possibility of revolutions influenced by French revolutionary thought as the greatest threat to peace, these countries asserted the right to restore rulers ousted by revolutionary means as a way of stabilizing European politics. A series of congresses between 1818 and 1822 settled peacefully disputes that might otherwise have led to war, but these efforts faded after 1822 when the English withdrew from participation. Toward the end of the nineteenth century, however, Otto von Bismarck, the German chancellor, sponsored a conference in Berlin (1884–1885) to regulate European entry into Africa so that the rush to obtain African land did not lead to wars among the competing European states. This was the last gasp of the European congress system for regulating international affairs.

### International Order in the Twentieth Century

In 1898, Tsar Nicholas II of Russia called for a meeting of the leaders of nations in order to develop a process for peacefully resolving international disputes. For the first time, the nations considered suitable for inclusion within the international legal order included non-European states such as the United States and Japan. Representatives of twenty-six nations met the next year at The Hague and signed an agreement promising to seek peaceful resolution of conflicts and established the International Court of Arbitration as a vehicle for achieving this. They also entered into an agreement regarding the laws of war. In 1907 there was a second meeting to discuss other issues. One of the fears motivating this interest in peaceful resolution of interstate conflicts was the growth of alliance networks that eventually divided Europe into two major blocs, one headed by Germany, the other led by France and England. Because of these alliance networks, what might have been a conflict between two states could escalate into a large-scale war as the countries involved called upon their allies to support them, something that did occur in August 1914. The weakness of the Hague meetings was that recourse to the court established there relied on the willingness of the parties to take that route rather than war. The court lacked any power to force states to come before it or, for that matter, to enforce any decisions it might reach.

During the twentieth century, the theory and the practice of international order attempted to reconcile several conflicting issues. The first of these dealt with the tension between a desire to incorporate all the nations of the earth into a single coherent system for the settlement of international disputes and a recognition of the fact that a few nations dominated international affairs militarily and politically. A second conflict arose from the desire to enforce adherence to internationally recognized standards of state behavior even in internal matters while recognizing the sovereign status of every state. Finally, there was the difficulty of determining generally acceptable standards of state behavior in a world composed of states with quite different cultural traditions.

The most famous twentieth-century approach to world order came out of the Versailles Peace Conference after World War I. President Woodrow Wilson, whose 14 Points outlined what he believed to be the causes of the war and what he saw as the steps necessary to prevent such a war from occurring again, proposed as the key to world peace a League of Nations that would be open to all states throughout the world and would be capable of enforcing peace. Although egalitarian at the level of the General Assembly in which each member state had one vote, at the highest level there was a council composed of representatives of the five great powers—France, England, Italy, Japan, and the United States—supplemented by representatives of four other powers elected by the General Assembly. Wilson's plans for an international order were frustrated by the national interests of the various countries involved, by the refusal of the U.S. Senate to vote in support of membership in the League, and by the refusal to admit Germany and Russia. This meant that three of the most powerful countries in the world were outside of the orderly world network that the League of Nations was supposed to create.

During the 1920s, there were various attempts to create a peaceful international order by executing treaties that would bind nations to seek peaceful solutions to conflicts. Germany, for example, signed a series of treaties that bound it to accept the borders established at the end of World War I and to accept arbitration in those cases where there were conflicts with neighboring countries. The Kellogg-Briand Pact (1927) bound signatories to use arbitration to settle disputes, and, in 1930, the major naval powers signed a treaty in London to regulate the size of navies and regulating submarine warfare. These treaties and others entered into during the 1920s suggested to some observers that a legally based international order was coming into being. No means were created, however, for enforcing adherence to these treaties.

In addition to resolving conflicts among European nations, the post–World War I era saw the development of efforts to regulate relations among the nations of the rest of the world and to assist in the development of these nations. Former German colonies in Africa were assigned to various European powers. Other areas, lost to the collapsing Ottoman Empire, Syria and Iraq, for example, became independent states but under the supervision of France and England, respectively. These arrangements were made under the direction or mandate of the League of Nations and were expected to end once these countries had become fully developed modern states and therefore capable of participation in the network of states that controlled international order.

The experience of the 1930s, however, demonstrated that international order, especially where it concerned the interests of the major nations, could not be secured without the use of force. The failure of the French to secure support for the occupation of the Ruhr in 1923 marked the last attempt to use force to ensure German adherence to the terms of the Versailles Treaty. When Adolf Hitler repudiated the treaty's limitations on the size of the German armed forces in 1935, the League of Nations took no steps to enforce adherence to the treaty. Likewise, there was no forceful reaction the following year when the Germans reoccupied the demilitarized Rhineland in violation of the treaty.

The efforts at establishing international order that were made after World War II were designed to avoid the problems associated with the post–World War I settlement. The United Nations (UN), formally created in October 1945, was established to maintain the unity of the countries that won the war. Like the League of Nations, the United Nations consisted of two houses, the General Assembly where each nation had one vote and the Security Council that consisted of five permanent members and six elected by the General Assembly. Membership in the UN grew rapidly from the initial 51 members to more than 160 in 2003. Some saw the UN as paving the way for a world government that would maintain world order, but there were a number of forces that worked against such an outcome, above all, the division of the world into two large political blocs identified with the North Atlantic Treaty Organization (NATO) and the Warsaw Pact. These two large military and political blocs in turn not only confronted one another directly, they also competed for support from the so-called Third World nations of Asia and Africa. To a great extent, world order in the post–World War II era was created by the tension between the two great power blocs.

In the face of increasing demands for independence and self-government, a number of new states emerged. Decolonization, as this process was termed, was expected to lead to the creation of new sovereign states that would easily fit into the state-based international order that was being constructed under the aegis of the United Nations. The UN was actively involved in efforts to resolve border disputes generated by the collapse of the colonial empires, Some of these interventions succeeded in avoiding war by partitioning the disputed territory between the two claimants and then using troops from neutral countries as a permanent buffer between the conflicting groups.

The demolition of the Berlin Wall in 1989 marked the end of the division of the world into two large blocs and generated a great deal of discussion of what some termed a New World Order. In political terms, this meant the victory of Western liberal, capitalistic democracy; in practice, it meant uncontested American world leadership. Francis Fukuyama's *The End of History and the Last Man* (1992) articulated the view that with the fall of the Berlin Wall, the "end point of mankind's ideological evolution" had been reached, as liberal democracy survived the greatest challenge it had ever faced. One implication of this argument was that as all the nations of the world adopted the liberal democratic and capitalistic way of life, a stable, orderly world of political order composed of nation-states along European lines would emerge. In reality, of course, this has not happened. In contrast to the vision of a peaceful international order that Fukuyama presented, Samuel Huntington has argued that the twenty-first century will see conflict not between nation-states but between cultural blocs with different conceptions of international order.

The beginning of the twenty-first century reveals several kinds of development relevant to the formation of a peaceful world order. The first of these is the unchallenged role of the

United States in world affairs. President George W. Bush asserted American responsibility for maintaining a terrorist-free international order and a willingness to act alone if necessary. Detractors increasingly labeled the United States an empire with all of the negative meanings attached to that term. At one level, the expansion of the European Union is a response to American power, unifying European states into a bloc capable of playing a significant role in the international order.

There is also renewed emphasis on humankind as forming a world community subject to universally applicable and enforceable standards of humanitarian behavior. In some cases, UN judgments are enforced by troops of member nations operating under the UN flag. In other cases, however, elements of this development operate separately from the United Nations. The establishment of an International Criminal Court at The Hague in 1998 is one sign of an effort to enforce universal standards outside of the UN framework. This court deals not with states but with individual officials, military and civilian, whose actions violated international standards and follows in the steps of the war crimes trials held at Nuremberg and Tokyo at the end of World War II.

The current trend is toward some form of international order that enforces adherence to standards of behavior through a legal and institutional structure that includes all humankind, a somewhat hierarchical structure that reflects the realities of political power. The power and leadership role of the United States is recognized, but these are restrained by the existence of the United Nations and the international legal order. Furthermore, the sovereignty of states, a fundamental element of international law since the seventeenth century, has been undermined as the United Nations has issued documents on human rights. These documents charge the UN with defending the rights of citizens when their rulers oppress them, even authorizing humanitarian intervention under UN auspices to protect the citizens from their own government. It remains to be seen, however, whether these various elements of international order will coalesce into a formal, permanent structure providing both order and freedom for all humanity.

*See also* **Christianity; Empire and Imperialism; Hierarchy and Order; Nationalism; Peace; War.**

**BIBLIOGRAPHY**

PRIMARY SOURCES

Brown, Chris, Terry Nardin, and Nicholas Rengger, eds. *International Relations in Political Thought: Texts from the Ancient Greeks to the First World War.* Cambridge, U.K., and New York: Cambridge University Press, 2002.

Office of the United Nations High Commissioner. *Human Rights: A Compilation of International Instruments.* Vol. 1, part 2: *Universal Instruments.* New York: United Nations, 1993.

Scott, James Brown, ed. *Classics of International Law.* 22 vols. Washington, D.C: Carnegie Endowment for International Peace, 1911–1950. Many of the leading writers on international law are represented in this series, which was reprinted by Oceana Publications in 1964.

SECONDARY SOURCES

Bull, Hedley. *The Anarchical Society: A Study of Order in World Politics.* New York: Columbia University Press, 1977.

Bull, Hedley, Benedict Kingsbury, and Adam Roberts, eds. *Hugo Grotius and International Relations.* Oxford: Clarendon, 1990.

Fukuyama, Francis. *The End of History and the Last Man.* New York: Free Press, 1992.

Huntington, Samuel P. *The Clash of Civilizations and the Remaking of World Order.* New York: Simon and Schuster, 1996.

Jackson, Robert H. *Quasi-States: Sovereignty, International relations and the Third World.* Cambridge, U.K., and New York: Cambridge University Press, 1990.

Keene, Edward. *Beyond the Anarchical Society: Grotius, Colonialism and Order in World Politics.* Cambridge, U.K., and New York: Cambridge University Press, 2002.

Kissinger, Henry A. *A World Restored; Metternich, Castlereagh, and the Problems of Peace, 1812–22.* Boston: Houghton Mifflin, 1957.

Muldoon, James. *Popes, Lawyers, and Infidels: The Church and the Non-Christian World, 1250–1550.* Philadelphia: University of Pennsylvania Press, 1979.

Murphy, Cornelius F., Jr. *Theories of World Governance: A Study in the History of Ideas.* Washington, D.C.: Catholic University of America Press, 1999.

Sewell, Sarah B., and Carl Kaysen. *The United States and the International Criminal Court: National Security and International Law.* Lanham, Md.: Rowman and Littlefield, 2000.

Tuck, Richard. *The Rights of War and Peace: Political Thought and the International Order from Grotius to Kant.* Oxford and New York: Oxford University Press, 1999.

*James Muldoon*

**INTERPRETATION.** The problem of interpretation is as old as the written record, even as old as the capacity for human beings to disagree fundamentally. It was raised by Plato. It marked many a conflict in early Christendom. From the Middle Ages to early modernity, cultural texts proliferated. Interpretation was the task of those who were in charge of biblical exegeses and of those who judged a text's originality, authenticity, and truthfulness. As interpretation became an increasingly prominent feature of the modern conundrum, questions about a work's truth and authenticity also prompted the development of philological methods of analysis. Toward the end of the eighteenth century, however, the older concerns for religious authenticity began to give way to a modern hermeneutics that raised new questions about making historical interpretations. In this period Kantian philosophy championed the centrality of the human subject as the foundational problem for all cognition. In addition, the problem of art and the role, function, and purpose of the artist, the concern for the "inner life" (*kultur*) (Elias), and the rise of modern selfhood (Taylor) began to affect the study of meaning. By the nineteenth century, philological approaches gave way to a reflexive concern for how epistemology, and more specifically, history, was to be conceptualized, approached, and thus interpreted. This new impulse marked the rise of modern hermeneutics and gave it a special role in understanding how the problem of interpretation is grappled with in the twenty-first century.

The rise of modern hermeneutics is often attributed to the writings of Friedrich Schleiermacher (1768–1834). Moving beyond philology, exegeses, and art criticism, he posed a new challenge: to understand culture and lived experience. Schleiermacher asked how a denizen of one historical era might understand the meaningful experience of a life or cultural text from another. He shifted hermeneutics toward the problem of experience within a context and argued that a viable interpretation had to proceed through an identification with the subject under study. In doing so, he posed the problem of historical hermeneutics—the challenge of understanding the meaning held by historically situated actors. Thus, with Schleiermacher, the new conditions placed in context took precedence over the ritual incantation of dogma, received truths, and essences. The concerns of the modern social sciences and humanities owe much to the rise of a historically reflexive hermeneutics.

In the nineteenth century, Wilhelm Dilthey (1833–1911) expanded *methodological hermeneutics,* which sought to produce systematic and scientific interpretations by situating a text in the context of its production. According to Dilthey, all manner of cultural texts—poetry, the spoken word, art, human action—are meaningful expressions with "mental contents" and human intentionality, and thus worthy of understanding (*verstehen*) through critical study. Meanings are also the product of historical constraint; the content and values of cultural texts reflect the period and location of the subject. Understanding thus involves the methodological construction of the *hermeneutical circle*—the connections that lead from the analysis of a cultural text to the author's life and the historical context in which the author is located, and then back to the cultural work.

In the twentieth century, Martin Heidegger (1889–1976) and Hans-Georg Gadamer (1900–2002) championed a *philosophical hermeneutics* by shifting concerns toward an understanding of existential meaning, in which being in the world can be grasped as a direct and unmediated condition of authenticity and subjectivity. One's knowledge and experience constitute a present horizon, which is the fundamental ground on which understanding takes place. This horizon, however, can be extended through exposure to the discourses of others, thus bringing one's own views into relief. It is through language as the core of human activity that subjects share their subjectivity, the basis of traditions, and their evaluation. Understanding has a potentially dynamic quality: it can proceed from one horizon to an emergent horizon, but is nonetheless bound to the traditions embedded in history.

Later, Jürgen Habermas (1929– ) challenged Gadamer's relativism by arguing for a self-reflexive *critical hermeneutics* that aims at a comprehensive reconstruction of the social world. Gadamer had claimed a universality for hermeneutics; no form of knowledge can escape the limitations of interpretation and its ties to deeper traditions. Habermas rejected this constraint on interpretation and argued that the human communication process contains transcendental elements. We are not trapped in nature or history because we can know and thus transform our language. In the structure of language, autonomy

and responsibility are posited for us. By overcoming the systematic distortions, the legacies of history and tradition that are embedded in language, we are able to envision an emancipated society whose members' autonomy and mutual responsibility can be realized through the development of nonauthoritarian dialogue and reciprocity.

The issues opened up by modern hermeneutics shaped the way interpretation is conceptualized, approached, and carried out in interdisciplinary studies. Indeed, the boundaries between the social sciences and the humanities have never been so porous as they are in the twenty-first century. Just as literary studies influence anthropology and cultural studies, literary theory reaches toward social theories. The convergence and confluence of questions and issues is more characteristic than the maintenance of disciplinary boundaries. With the rise of modern hermeneutics, the problem of interpretation took on a social and historical dimension, which allowed this new concern with meaning to be assimilated by anthropology, literary studies, and later, cultural studies, reception and audience studies, and aspects of feminist theory. By tracking the history of interpretation, we gain an appreciation for the interdisciplinary developments of interpretive theorizing in the twenty-first century.

## The Hermeneutic and Interpretive Impulse in the Rise of Social Studies

Karl Marx (1818–1883) did not address the problems defined by Dilthey, but his approach to the problem of historicism was in some ways continuous with historicist hermeneutics. Marx's theories also had a major impact on social scientific approaches to the study and interpretation of history. Georg Wilhelm Friedrich Hegel (1770–1831), the nineteenth-century German idealist philosopher whose views Marx modified, saw history as the unfolding manifestation of the human spirit. According to Hegel, the human spirit will eventually reach a truly revolutionary stage in which it will be able to see through itself for the first time. This radical philosophical view of spirit developing a consciousness of itself was transformed by Marx into sociological language. Knowledge and consciousness can be socially constituted and grounded only in a distinct human subject. But such a reflexive and revolutionary consciousness will not develop in just any subject. The subject and the knowledge for this development has to be special—that is, specially located in history. For Marx, this historical process can be realized only through the embodied consciousness of a human subject whose social and historical location provides it with the privilege to achieve such awareness. This subject is the *proletariat*—the social class within modern capitalism that embodies the historical forces that will provide it with the capacity to see itself as an object produced by history (Marx and Engels). In this manner, Marx turned the problem of epistemology (the problem of knowledge) into a historicist sociology. All forms of knowledge are expressions of human activity and practice, and such knowledge can be grasped only as manifestations of the historical conditions in which they take their social form. In essence, culture, ideology, ethics, religion—the entire enterprise of knowledge making—is a reflection of the historical mode of human production, a process ultimately rooted in human labor. This history remains unseen, ungrasped, misunderstood, misrepresented by ideology. Thus estrangement or alienation—the inability to see the underlying reality—characterizes human history and can be overcome only by the historical rise of a human subject situated in ways that enable this kind of critical consciousness to take hold.

Much criticism has been leveled at how Marx privileged economic and material aspects at the expense of the cultural realm. Certainly, the problem of culture was not a central concern for Marx. Culture was relegated to the "superstructure" where ideas, values, ethics, and ideology circulated as fictitious echoes and reflections of the "real" activity of labor and the materialist dimensions of the class struggle. Yet Marx's views are crucial to the modern enterprise of interpretation, especially in the idea that subjects, actors, and texts cannot exist as autonomous entities or things in themselves, but are rather fundamentally immersed in social and historical contexts. In this manner, Marx's sociology, notwithstanding trenchant criticism, consistently challenged interpreters to understand that practices and texts are inseparable from social and historical conditions. The implications for interpretation were profoundly expanded. The most discrete activity was to be connected to the broader material, social, and historical formation. Whether it be a specific tool or element of technology, a cultural ritual, a poem, a scientific treatise, or a social institution under examination, the interpretive task is to understand the element in relation to a social totality (mode of production). Marx's seminal view—the historicist view of all things in the human world—remains a vibrant aspect of twenty-first century interpretation.

In contrast to Marx's theories, the sociology of Émile Durkheim (1858–1917) marked the rise of the cultural approach to the social sciences in which the study of symbolic production is central. For Durkheim, the underlying phenomenon to be interpreted is *solidarity*. Only through *representations* is human solidarity and society made visible and open to sociological interpretation. Thus, when cultural and religious solidarity is violated, the preeminent indicator of the collective response is repressive/penal law. Punishment expiates the sense of violation. In Durkheim's sociology the realm of cultural life is brought into view and interpreted through the study of symbolic and semiotic practices that express the underlying cultural cohesion but also govern and maintain it. This makes Durkheimian sociology a fundamentally interpretive enterprise. The social and cultural realm can be grasped only through symbolic production, because it is instantiated in and organized through it. Although Durkheim insisted on a social reality instantiated through routine cultural practices that sociology was to ascertain, his major contribution to modern cultural interpretation was his emphasis on the formal study of representations.

The hermeneutic insistence on identifying with the inner logic of a socially embedded subject also shares some traits with what the Scottish moralists David Hume (1711–1776) and Adam Smith (1723–1790) called human "sympathy" (A. Smith). It is in Max Weber (1864–1920), however, that historical hermeneutics finds a direct link to sociology. For Weber, the primary challenge for sociological interpretation is to decipher the modes of meaning and the forms of rationality characteristic of social activity. These forms of organized meaning ultimately have a cultural dimension, but for Weber the task was to grasp them as modes of *rationality*. The formulation and interpretation of modes of rationality provide the sociological keys to understanding the everyday practices of individuals engaged in organized activity. Drawing on the ideas of Dilthey and Heinrich Rickert (Hughes), Weber argued for a sociology that places interpretation at its core. According to Weber, "interpretive sociology considers the individual and his action as the basic unit, as its 'atom.'. . . The individual. . . is the upper limit and the sole carrier of meaningful conduct. . . . Such concepts as 'state,' 'association,' 'feudalism,' and the like, designate certain categories of human interaction. Hence it is the task of sociology to reduce these concepts to 'understandable' action, that is without exception, to the actions of participating individual men" (Gerth and Mills, p. 55). Weber synthesized both earlier hermeneutic currents as well as Marxian historicism. Yet he did not share Marx's faith in a notion of history that operates inexorably and fatefully to create a privileged subject (the proletariat) and instead placed the emphasis on the underlying rationality that makes every cultural formation a sociologically interpretable phenomenon.

With the work of Karl Mannheim (1893–1947), the problem of interpretation took a formidable turn toward the "sociology of knowledge." Mannheim shared the concerns of Dilthey, Marx, and Edmund Husserl, who insisted that the act of knowing and interpreting is always bound to social conditions. Thus, for Mannheim all knowledge was *partial* knowledge. Because of social context, a group can achieve a certain interest-based quality of understanding and generate in turn knowledge and truth claims based on views from its vantage point. These claims, however, can be understood (sociologically) only as elements in a *pluralist* arena of competing views, which are also *relative* to their location, social position, and point of view. The interpretation of a cultural expression thus hinges not only on the intrinsic meanings held by actors and subjects but also on a comprehension of the limits imposed by the location and conditions of the subject's social origins. Consistent with pluralist and relativist aspects of Franz Boas's anthropological writings, Mannheim's sociology of knowledge insisted that cultural views—statements, beliefs, values, literary productions, and so forth—always bear the stamp of their context.

## The Interdisciplinary Challenges of Interpretation

The determinant importance of the social and cultural context that runs from hermeneutics to classic social theory, and certainly from Dilthey to Mannheim, and which shapes as well the way we understand values and meanings held by social actors and the social and cultural texts they produce, continues as part of the formidable framework even within twenty-first century theories of interpretation. This is especially true for the historical importance granted to the context in which cultural texts emerge and are read, appropriated, used, and interpreted and to the limitations such a context imposes. Yet new issues and tensions within interpretive theories have taken hold. They may not represent a serious rupture in relation to earlier paradigms, however, or a revolutionary upheaval in intellect, but may merely be a difference in analytical emphasis.

The work of Michel Foucault (1926–1984), whose intellectual profile cuts across the social sciences and the humanities, had a major impact on interpretation. In a move as profound as Marx's positing of the concept of *mode of production,* Foucault insisted that what is at play in the realm of history and human affairs is the construction of discursive regimes that govern every enterprise of knowledge making. In this regard, knowledge and power remain inextricably coupled and constitute the most productive dimensions of human activity. Foucault questioned the very modern category of knowledge and the assumption that knowledge is the product of neutral tools of investigation. According to him, the production of all knowledge is carried out in the constitutive effectivity of the discursive forms that make the knowledge enterprise possible. Thus there is no escape from the forms and modes of discourse; they condition and shape what becomes knowledge. In this regard, Foucault's views undermine the notion that rationality has a universal, transcendental, and foundational status allowing it to claim the transcendental privilege of ascertaining truth. Because of the conditions of discourse, the idea of Truth as a reality to be grasped "out there" through the deployment of the discursive schemas of language must give way to the study of what discourse actually produces—"truth effects." This antifoundational approach conditions every act of interpretation, casting it into the position of a continual reflection on its very capacity to frame the problem of meaning. The task set by Foucault is to comprehend the *idea* of truth and the constructive effects such an idea has on the forms and organizations of social and historical life. He argued that epistemology must be replaced by a genealogy of knowledge forms. Like Mannheim's sociology of knowledge, the study of discursive forms can yield an understanding of what Foucault called *epistemes* (Mannheim used the term *Weltanschauung,* or "worldview")—a horizon of historicity that represents the cumulative frameworks of knowledge production but is also open to historical ruptures and the ensuing transformations. Likewise, Foucault's insistence on discursive forms as the principal arena for social and historical analysis has links to French sociology's emphasis on representations.

Foucault's influence can be seen in the way cultural interpretation has taken on new perspectives and issues. In the early twentieth century, the problem of culture was largely seen as the prerogative of anthropologists. In the twenty-first century, however, every discipline within the social sciences and the humanities takes culture as a major concern. It is worth noting that within anthropology, the very notion of culture as a set of practices that exist "out there" and can be studied objectively by the social scientist has given way somewhat to a more reflexive notion of culture as a peculiarly problematic intellectual construction. Anthropologists are no longer solely interested in studying the culture of others; they also want to study and interpret culture. This additional interest has its roots in Claude Lévi-Strauss's insistence (drawing from Ferdinand de Saussure, who in turn drew from Durkheim) that culture operates like language and should therefore be studied similarly. The so-called linguistic turn was fully evident in the late 1970s in the work of the anthropologist Clifford Geertz (1926– ) who, though not influenced by Foucault, nonetheless recast culture primarily as the construction of narratives. The anthropological shift from a concern with a "culture out there" to a preoccupation with the *constitutive* power of narrative and discursive forms is noteworthy in the work of James Clifford and George Marcus, among others, who emphasize the narrative dimension of *writing* social science and view cultural interpretation as inextricably tied to the act of inscription. As cultural texts, writings in the social sciences do not so much "discover" the social as construct narratives that in turn condition the social world.

In the wake of Foucault's views, literary theory has converged with social theory around the problem of historical interpretation. This can be seen in the theories affiliated with New Historicism which, in keeping with historicist hermeneutics and the sociology of knowledge, argues that formalist, text-centered approaches to literature need to be replaced by methods that include the social and political circumstances of their production (Greenblatt; Gallagher; Mitchell). In a synthesis of Marx and Foucault, literature is conceptualized not as a distinct category of human production to be studied as an isolated phenomenon but as a historically embedded form. As a situated cultural product, literature can reveal the ideological contours of its conditions of production. A literary work can therefore mean different things to different people who do not share the same context. The shift in the problem of interpretation toward the social conditions that govern cultural appropriation has also influenced the study of the uses of literature and cultural texts. Reader-response theory (Tompkins), theories of interpretive communities (Fish), and reception theory (Holub) do not begin with the presumption that texts have meanings but instead emphasize the social and subjective dimensions of how texts are read and appropriated, an approach that resembles the "uses and gratifications" approach in mass media studies. Texts are thus subordinated to readers and audiences and the social frameworks and dispositions they bring to the act of interpreting cultural texts.

New Historicism is sometimes criticized for conflating history and text and for projecting contemporary issues onto situations from the past. History is not necessarily the cause and source of a literary work; instead, the ties between history and text are reduced to a dialectically recursive problem. The text is interpreted as product and production, end and source of history. In this regard, New Historicism reflects the influence Louis Althusser's structuralist theories of ideological reproduction have had on literary theory and his insistence that all cultural production is "structured in dominance." Contemporary theoretical problems are also sometimes "read back" into a historical context where they may not apply, as when modern social categories are used as analytical devices for interpreting subjects in a quite different historical epoch. Althusserian theories of ideological reproduction can be seen in the important subcultural studies carried out within the field of British cultural studies that emerged in England in the late 1970s and early 1980s. Paul Willis's ethnographic work exemplified the desire to restore a subject-sympathetic analysis of participants in the rich world of subcultures, especially youth subcultures. While this approach privileged the voices and views of his subjects, thus giving the study of a subculture a more human dimension, the subjects of his study—working-class youth—struggle for a sense of self, autonomy, and dignity only to contribute culturally and unwittingly to their own domination.

The attention to subjects is mired in the constraints of history and social location. But subject-centered interpretive theory also has its redemptive impulses. From the 1970s on, much historical work has retrieved the social lives of various groups hitherto ignored by historiography. Some aspects of feminist theories of interpretation exemplify this retrievalist impulse. While the larger horizon of feminist theory, in its analysis of society and history, has mainly addressed the subjugation of women, there are attempts to recast the narrative of perpetual domination by highlighting subjects in ways that emphasize their capacity for critical resistance. This approach to locating and interpreting critical subjectivity moves toward a revisionist feminist epistemology that begins with a *situated knower* who has *situated knowledge* that reflects her perspectives (D. Smith). Known as "standpoint theory," this view has similarities to Mannheim's sociology of knowledge, but the conceptual framework shares more with the ideas of the cultural theorist Georg Lukács (1885–1971). It was Lukács who argued that a subject's location in society and history provides a "standpoint" that can give epistemological ground to the critical study of consciousness. As a Marxist, Lukács had a historically privileged subject in mind—the proletariat. In early feminist standpoint theory, the privileged historical category shifted from class to gender, and the problem of a gendered subject's knowledge was itself a gendered historical formation (D. Smith; Harstock). The attempt to establish a single feminist standpoint, however, has given way to postmodern theory's pluralist concerns and the acknowledgment of multiple, epistemologically informative situated standpoints (Harding; Collins; Alarcon; Sandoval).

Twenty-first century theories of interpretation reflect significant cross-disciplinary reflection. Although there is merit in approaching the problem of interpretation from distinct disciplines, it is apparent that the boundaries that divide the disciplines *within* the humanities and the social sciences, and the divisions that occur *between* the humanities and the social sciences, are obfuscatory. Interpretation has become the core problem within the study of culture; and culture, in turn, has come to occupy a vast area traversing every discipline within the humanities and the social sciences. For these reasons, the problem of interpretation will quite likely continue to be one of the more formidable, persistent, and challenging issues of intellectual inquiry well into the future.

*See also* **Cultural Studies; Hermeneutics; Interdisciplinarity.**

## BIBLIOGRAPHY

Alarcon, Norma. "The Theoretical Subject(s) of This Bridge Called My Back and Anglo-American Feminism." In *The Postmodern Turn,* edited by Steven Seidman, 40–52. Cambridge, U.K.: Cambridge University Press, 1997.

Althusser, Louis. "Ideology and Ideological State Apparatuses." In his *Lenin and Philosophy and Other Essays,* translated by Ben Brewster. New York: Monthly Review Press, 1971.

Clifford, James, and George E. Marcus, eds. *Writing Culture: The Poetics and Politics of Ethnography.* Berkeley: University of California Press, 1986.

Collins, Patricia Hill. *Black Feminist Thought: Knowledge, Consciousness, and the Politics of Empowerment.* Boston: Unwin Hyman, 1990.

Dilthey, W. "The Rise of Hermeneutics." Translated by T. Hall. In *Critical Sociology: Selected Readings,* edited by P. Connerton, 104–116. Harmondsworth, U.K.: Penguin, 1976. Excerpted from W. Dilthey, "Die Entstehung der Hermeneutik" (1900), in his *Gesammelte Schriften,* 317–320, 323–331. Leipzig: B.G. Teubner, 1923.

Durkheim, Émile. *The Division of Labor in Society.* Translated by George Simpson. New York: Free Press, 1933.

———. *The Elementary Forms of the Religious Life.* Translated by Joseph Ward Swain. London: Allen and Unwin, 1915.

Elias, Norbert. *The Civilizing Process.* 1939. Vol. 1. Translated by Edmund Jephcoot. New York: Urizen Books, 1978.

Fish, Stanley. *Is There a Text in This Class? The Authority of Interpretive Communities.* Cambridge, Mass.: Harvard University Press, 1980.

Foucault, Michel. *The Archaeology of Knowledge.* Translated by A. M. Sheridan. New York: Harper and Row, 1972.

———. *Discipline and Punish: The Birth of the Prison.* Translated by Alan Sheridan. New York: Vintage Books, 1979.

———. *The History of Sexuality.* Translated by Robert Hurley. New York: Vintage Books, 1980.

Gallagher, Catherine. *The Industrial Reformation of English Fiction: Social Discourse and Narrative Form, 1832–1867.* Chicago: University of Chicago Press, 1985.

Geertz, Clifford. *The Interpretation of Cultures: Selected Essays.* New York: Basic Books, 1973.

Gerth, H. H., and C. Wright Mills, eds. and trans. *From Max Weber: Essays in Sociology.* New York: Oxford University Press, 1946.

Greenblatt, Stephen. *Renaissance Self-fashioning: From More to Shakespeare.* Chicago: University of Chicago Press, 1980.

Habermas, Jürgen. *Knowledge and Human Interests.* Translated by Jeremy J. Shapiro. Boston: Beacon Press, 1971.

Harding, Sandra. *Is Science Multicultural? Postcolonialisms, Feminisms, and Epistemologies.* Bloomington: Indiana University Press, 1998.

Harstock, Nancy. "The Feminist Standpoint: Developing the Ground for a Specifically Feminist Historical Materialism." In *Feminism and Methodology: Social Science Issues,* edited by Sandra Harding. Bloomington: Indiana University Press, 1987.

Holub, Robert C. *Reception Theory: A Critical Introduction.* London: Methuen, 1984.

Hughes, H. Stuart. *Consciousness and Society: The Reorientation of European Social Thought, 1890–1930.* New York: Vintage Books, 1958.

Lukács, Georg. *History and Class Consciousness.* Translated by Rodney Livingstone. Cambridge, Mass.: MIT Press, 1971.

Mannheim, Karl. *Ideology and Utopia: An Introduction to the Sociology of Knowledge.* Translated by Louis Wirth and Edward Shils. New York: Harcourt, Brace, 1936.

Marx, Karl, and Frederick Engels. *Basic Writings on Politics and Philosophy.* Edited by Lewis S. Feuer. New York: Doubleday, 1959.

Mitchell, W. J. T., ed. *The Politics of Interpretation*. Chicago: University of Chicago Press, 1983.

Sandoval, Chela. *Methodology of the Oppressed*. Minneapolis: University of Minnesota Press, 2000.

Schleiermacher, Friedrich. *Hermeneutics and Criticism and Other Writings*. Translated and edited by Andrew Bowie. New York: Cambridge University Press, 1998.

Smith, Adam. 1759. *The Theory of Moral Sentiments*. Edited by Knud Haakonssen. New York: Cambridge University Press, 2002.

Smith, Dorothy E. *The Everyday World as Problematic: A Feminist Sociology*. Boston: Northeastern University Press, 1987.

Taylor, Charles. *Sources of the Self: The Making of the Modern Identity*. Cambridge, Mass.: Harvard University Press, 1989.

Tompkins, Jane P., ed. *Reader-Response Criticism: From Formalism to Post-Structuralism*. Baltimore: Johns Hopkins University Press, 1980.

Willis, Paul. *Learning to Labor: How Working Class Kids Get Working Class Jobs*. New York: Columbia University Press, 1981.

*Jon Cruz*

# ISLAM.

This entry includes four subentries:

*Africa*
*Shii*
*Southeast Asia*
*Sunni*

## AFRICA

It was the long, drawn-out confrontation of the seventh century C.E. between the emerging Islamic caliphate and the declining Roman Empire over the Mediterranean African shores, and the subsequent breakdown of the empire, that created favorable conditions for the establishment of the two earliest Islamic frontier provinces in North Africa: Egypt and Tunisia. But the establishment of these two provinces did not, by itself, lead to immediate large settlements of immigrant Muslims, or to dramatic transformations in African communities. Yet, barely six hundred years after the death of the prophet Muhammad, various African communities and chieftains had either adopted Islam as a court religion or incorporated Muslim practices into their religious systems. Grasping the cultures and structures of these Islamized and Islamizing communities is indispensable to understanding the development of Islam in Africa. However, space does not permit a detailed examination of each of these communities. For our purposes it is sufficient to identify the major frontier communities through which Islam made inroads into Africa, to give a brief summary of the main controversies in Islamic philosophical outlook, to examine the types of African social forces that appropriated it, and to make a few observations that seem relevant for an understanding of the current signs of regeneration of Islam in modern Africa.

### Muslim Frontier Communities

After striking its roots in Egypt and in the far West, Islam was carried into the fringes of black Africa by indigenous tribesmen.

Through the foundation of trading centers, the movement of populations, and the affiliation with local ruling elites, Muslim influence in the interior of the region was strongly felt. In their eleventh-century search for gold, Berber nomadic tribesmen reached the area of upper Niger, which was inhabited by the Mande-speaking peoples (Malinke). Following their ruler, a sizable number of them embraced Islam. With the favorable political environment and the flourishing trans-Sahara trade, a Muslim community also flourished and became an important link between the older Islamic world north of the Sahara and the African interior southwards as far as the fringes of the forest. It was under this Islamic influence that the medieval empires of Ghana, Mali, and Songhay had functioned and prospered. Throughout the fourteenth century, a number of competent Muslim chiefs were able to create a considerable domestic power base and to cultivate strong relations with the older Muslim world, especially Egypt, Morocco, and Arabia.

Like the Berber in the north, the Christian Nubians of the Nile resisted the Muslim-Arab invasion and delayed the advance of Islam for centuries, although an Islamic state had been securely established in adjacent Egypt since the seventh century. It was only through persuasion and trade that Arab tribesmen and merchants were able to penetrate far beyond Aswan, which was used, like al-Qurawan in Maghrib, as a frontier garrison to protect the Muslims against the raids of the Nubians and the Beja. Although there was no deliberate policy of spreading Islam to the south, the gradual settlements and intermarriages between the Arabs and Nubians began a process of Arabization and Islamization that laid the foundations for the subsequent institutionalization of Islam. The discoveries of significant gold mines in the eastern region, and the intensive traffic caused by the religious pilgrimage known as the hajj, led to the rise of the Red Sea ports and to the flourishing of Muslim communities within them.

Apart from gold mines, the east African coast, which comprises what are today Eritrea, Ethiopia, Djibouti, and Somalia, had experienced constant exposure to Islamic influence since the seventh century. Persian and Arab traders were active in the region for centuries, and through them Islam infiltrated the area through the Red Sea ports of Badi, Aidab, and Suakin. Consequently a string of Muslim enclaves and settlements arose and extended from the Gulf of Aden to Mozambique. However, a variety of factors halted the advance of these communities into the hinterland (present-day Kenya, Tanzania, Uganda, Rwanda, and Burundi), and it was not until the nineteenth century that their Islamic influence reached Malawi and the Congo basin.

Searching for ivory, some pioneering Arab merchants from the east coast of Africa, especially Zanzibar, ended up within these central African regions. Trade in ivory had, however, become inseparable from the slave trade in which those Arabs were involved as intermediaries between indigenous slave traders and Europeans. But trade in ivory and slaves brought Africans, Arabs, and the European colonial powers to loggerheads. The Arabs' presence in central Africa was eventually broken during the European scramble for Africa, which had negative effects on the advance of Islam in that region.

Interestingly, the same institution of slavery that hampered the advance of Islam in central Africa generated numerous incentives to Islamic conversion in southern Africa. Between the late seventeenth and early nineteenth centuries, European colonialists, mainly Dutch, brought tens of thousands of slaves from Madagascar, the Indian subcontinent, and the Indonesian archipelago into South Africa. Although Christians, these European slaves did not evangelize among their slaves—such a practice would have held out the promise of legal and social equality. Discouraged from becoming Christians, some slaves turned to Islam and, together with exiled Muslim imams and political prisoners who were expelled from the same region, laid the foundations for an alternative Islamic culture and community.

Looking at the relatively rapid growth of Islam in African public life, one might think that Islam was an ideology of the rulers, or even a royal religion, as indeed some scholars have thought. Overemphasizing the role of tribal chiefs and traders, some scholars have also maintained that the spread of Islam was due not so much to a recognition on the part of the converts of the intrinsic qualities of the faith as to the desire for fame and wealth.

Traders and chiefs were important external agents of Islamization, but their efforts would have made little headway without two important internal factors: the self-propagating system of rituals that bind the individual worshipers and the scholar-led, mass-oriented Sufi brotherhoods that bridge the gap between government and society. If we are to understand the deeper Islamic influence in Africa, we must look beyond political institutions and ideologies into the Islamic system of worship, the centers of learning, and the social structures they stimulate.

Islam was not introduced to the common people as either theology or law but as a system of worship. After uttering the *Shihada* (a public declaration of faith) and learning to perform the obligatory rituals, a person would normally be designated a Muslim regardless of the adequacy of his knowledge about the theological and ethical implications of the faith. Simple as they may appear to be, these pillars of worship would ultimately bring in the other parts of the Islamic system, that is, the social and moral, and the political. The hajj, which entails an annual journey to Mecca, is a case in point. African pilgrims used to take the trans-Sahara route from central Africa to Tripoli or Egypt, or, alternatively, travel from the Chad region through Darfur, crossing modern-day Sudan to Massawa or Sawakin at the Red Sea. Such annual, collective spiritual journeys were instrumental in educating African Muslims and deepening their Islamic consciousness. The hajj would, necessarily, expose them to other peoples and cultures and give them prestige and influence in their own local communities. Upon completing his hajj and returning home, a person would usually be more committed to Islam and acquire, in the eyes of other believers, a kind of mystical aura; he might even become a focus of spiritual attraction. Through him and through his fellow travelers, new ideas would be introduced and new attitudes would be established. But before we can understand how Islam transformed ideas and attitudes, we must briefly examine the wider Islamic philosophical outlook.

## Islamic Philosophy

Islamic philosophy flowered as a later development of Islamic thought. It was preceded by the *kalam* (disputation) science, the discipline of confirming the Muslim creed and defending it against subversive factions. It originated in the theological controversies of the eighth century over God's unity and attributes. Like the Jewish scripture, the Koran also emphasizes the unity of God, the resurrection of the dead, and the accountability of man. But it is the first article—the unity of God—that has come to occupy a central place in Muslim philosophical and theological thinking.

The earliest problematic question dealt with the relationship between God and his attributes, that is, whether God is one without division or quality, or one in essence but multiple in attributes. Debating this issue brought in some of the centuries-old ontological and epistemological questions, such as: What is the nature of God's existence? Does God, for instance, exist as a concept in one's mind, or does he also exist in an extra-mental (or supernatural) reality? And in any case, what is the relationship between God and man, and between God and the world, and how can a human being know him and understand his commands?

The debate could have continued peacefully had not the Mu'tazilites, who took an extreme rationalist position, resorted to force. Converting the Abbasid caliph al-Ma'mun to their cause, they gained a hold on the highest positions in the caliphate and used that power to impose their views. The Islamic world at large was shocked by the way they treated their opponents, especially Ahmad ibn Hanbal (780–855), an eminent scholar and founder of one of the four schools of Islamic law, who was subjected to flogging and imprisonment because of his opposition to the Mu'tazilites' views on the nature of God's speech.

Distancing themselves from the repulsive Mu'tazilite politics and extreme interpretations, most jurists took a middle position, making an honest effort to keep close to the Koranic and Sunna texts *bila kaifa*, that is, without asking a "how" question. Their aim was to shift the debate from theology to jurisprudence and law. Rather than focusing on God's attributes and essence, attention should be directed, they argued, to man's behavior and actions in compliance (or lack thereof) with God's law. But when al-Ash'ari (c. 873–935) dramatically broke away from the Mu'tazilites, returned to the moderate position of the people of the *Sunna*, and, thus, dealt the death blow to Mu'tazilism, followers of the orthodox schools of law lent him their support. The Ash'arite school became the theological representative of the mainstream Sunni Muslims.

With the rise of Ash'arism some theological issues lost their appeal, though new ones have emerged, for instance, concerning the question of perception as an independent source of knowledge in contrast to revelation. Like the Mu'tazilites before them, most of the Ash'arite scholars argued that perception is a source of knowledge. None of them, however, maintained (as did the ancient Geek materialists and modern crude Western empiricists) that perception is the only source of knowledge. According to Ash'arism, knowledge that is derived from the senses is legitimate, but it must be subordinated to the revealed truth, if certainty is to be attained.

In this view, revelation has an epistemological as well as a social function. In addition to illuminating the wider picture of oneself, the world, human existence, and ultimate human ends, it also serves to free the individual from irrational fear of natural forces, and instills in him a tendency to attempt a systematic understanding of these forces and their impact on human life. The revealed vision, moreover, liberates the individual from subordination to the ego and ethnocentrism and the dehumanization of the other that hinders rational argument and understanding.

But this balance between the revealed vision and the inquisitive mind has not always been maintained. In contrast to the Sunnis, who struggle to maintain a distinction between God and humans, the Shia contend that the distance that separates God from human souls is the source of all evil. Engulfed in matter, and cut off from their origins, human souls have no hope of being saved except through knowledge (*irfan*). But the redeeming knowledge, wherein God reveals himself and his divine designs, is attainable only through the guardians whom God assigns to accompany the prophets. Prophets bring the outer (*zahir*) divine command, whereas the guardians initiate people into the *batin*, or inner commands.

Borrowing this element of *batin*, the Sufis, on the other hand, developed a slightly different theory of knowledge. For them, understanding the divine sources of Islam rests neither in holy guardians nor in language, but on the "people of reality" (*ahl al-haqiqa*). They maintained that the Koran includes certain divine secrets and subtleties (*asrar wa lata'if*) that only the people of reality—Sufis—are capable of understanding.

It was mainly due to such tendencies of *batini* (esoteric) interpretations that a barrier of mistrust developed among Shia, Sufi, and Sunni jurists in Islamic history. Instead of debating the nature of God's attributes, the new questions for debate asked what it means for a term to have a specific meaning, and how one can know that a statement is true. These questions led eventually to the evolution of the philosophy of language, mysticism, logic, and jurisprudence as new Islamic disciplines. Opposing these Shia and Sufi trends of interpretation, most Sunni jurists resorted to the tradition of the Prophet and classic Arabic usage of language, employing the first as an explicit code of conduct and the second as an objective code of meaning. Both were meant to restrict extreme tendencies of interpretation.

Closely related to these debates was the issue of the source of moral knowledge and obligation. Conceiving God as the ultimately wise and just Being, the Mu'tazilites refused to establish a relation between God and evil. Endowed with a free will, they argued, humans are the authors of their own actions and ought to be rewarded or punished accordingly. Moral judgment and knowledge, in their view, stems from human reason, which can independently distinguish between good and bad.

For Sunni scholars, it was all very well to emphasize a person's capacity to reason. What they found objectionable,

however, was the assertion that human reason is the sole criterion of truth and behavior, or that by following the dictates of reason alone one can be virtuous and attain happiness. This tinge of Aristotelian rationalism was thought to be irreconcilable with Islam's sources of guidance, reason, and revelation.

It is curious, however, that the Mu'tazilites' philosophical method, as well as some of the unresolved problems they left behind, have become, despite their political defeat, an important source of intellectual ferment in Muslim thought. Some of the issues they raised persisted and were pursued, with more moderation, by other eminent linguists, commentators, and philosophers. And most of those—Ibn Tufayl, Ibn Rushd and Ibn Khaldun, among others—appeared in the Muslim West (North Africa and medieval Spain) and not in the East, as might be assumed.

## Indigenous Vehicles of Islamization

The political movements and philosophical trends that prevailed in the older Islamic world did not immediately sway African Muslims. Even the process of linguistic and ethnic Arabization, in which the indigenous peoples acquired Arabic as their language and connected themselves in the Arab tribal system, did not take hold immediately, nor did it proceed equally in all regions. Nevertheless, it must be recognized that the level of Arabization that took place had a huge impact in transmitting the new Islamic outlook—words, ideas, and behavior usually being interconnected.

Similar to the performance of hajj that we have mentioned earlier, learning the Arabic language (and writing in it) had also become an important instrument for linking the fledgling African religious elites, especially in the relatively stable mosque-colleges that emerged in the western, eastern, and central regions of the continent, enriching and authenticating a genuine Islamic civilization. In some of these mosque-colleges, works of al-Muhasibi, the famous Sufi of Baghdad (c. 751–857), and al-Ghazali (1058–1111), the Sufi and Ash'ari theologian, were required readings. It should also be noted that the traditional rift between the *ulama* (doctors of law) and the Sufis, which prevailed in the older Muslim regions, had been mitigated in these new African centers of learning. Along the eastern coast and the Nile, the Arabized and Islamized Nubians, Beja, and Somalis developed, since the fourteenth century, indigenous Sufi brotherhoods that succeeded in blending law with Sufism. Maliki and Shafi'i jurists did, in some cases, embrace Sufism.

The traditional Islamic principle affirming that the *ulama* are the heirs of the prophets had nearly been actualized in the African situation. African Muslim *ulama* had truly become the points of intersection of religious and political ideas, activism, ethnicity, and intellectualism. The groups that coalesced around the *ulama* would usually become the indigenous vehicles through which Islam acquired its significance as a basis of political power and resource mobilization. The reasons for this are not hard to find.

The scholar serves mainly as a spiritual mentor who helps the people, through sessions of recitation and meditation, to relate to God. Demands for spiritual help necessitate close contact and regular sessions with the scholar during which certain litanies (*dhikr*) are chanted, thus sharing in the blessing of the Koran and the Prophet. In these ways the scholar shapes individual behavior. Moreover, the *ulama* would naturally, as scholars, investigate, describe, analyze, and explain, but as citizens most of them would be deeply embedded in the social and political structures of their communities. Their scholarship would not be disconnected from their social and political activities and commitments. This is what gave some of them particular force, encouraging political groups and movements to identify with them and with their ideas.

To make this clearer we may take the example of Muhammad ibn Sahnun, of the Qairawan mosque-college, who was responsible for the promotion of Malikism in Africa. The Qairawan, where he and his disciples taught, became the citadel of Sunnism. Some of their works (for example, the *Mudawana,* the *Risala,* and the *Mukhtasar*) have become important sources of Islamic thought and have had the greatest influence on African Muslim communities. The Maliki trend took a more serious turn when Ibn Tumart (c. 1080–1130), a Berber from South Morocco (Masmuda tribes), and one of his Zenati followers and successors, Abd-al-Mumin, mobilized their followers and founded the greatest empire in the Muslim West that ruled from 1147 to 1269.

It is therefore reasonable to contend that most Islamic social and political movements that had a significant impact on African communities were the outgrowth of a type of *ulama*-tribal alliance. The rise of Shiism in North and West Africa; the expansion of Malikism and the Sufi brotherhoods; and the revolutionary (jihadist) movements are prominent examples of the crucial role of the *ulama*-tribal alliances.

But Islam was not alone in shaping African communities or determining their future development. By the end of the nineteenth century, the entire African continent (with the exception of Ethiopia and Liberia) was shared out among the European colonial powers. In line with the secular modernization begun by the colonialists, Arabic was replaced by French in West Africa, and by English in Central, East, and South Africa. These and similar drastic colonial policies not only undermined the centuries-old Islamic educational system (and the religious elites that relied on it) but ushered in a new, westernized African elite that wielded enormous power out of its connections with the colonial state and/or the Christian missionaries.

With the internalization of secular values, and the incorporation of African communities into the international economy, older bases of legitimacy were challenged and new value systems and ideologies began to compete for people's minds. That cultural and economic experience, as well as the fractured, postcolonial social structures that remain, constitute the major challenge to African Muslims today. Whether this apparently complete secular modernization process will continue to strangle Muslim communities—thus provoking an imminent counterinsurgence of Islamic fundamentalism and providing it with needed resources of resistance—or manage to break these communities' cultural isolation and revive a wider

meaning of human existence that Islam itself impresses on its believers, remains to be seen.

*See also* **Africa, Idea of; Colonialism: Africa; Communication of Ideas: Africa and Its Influence; Education: Islamic Education; Islam: Shii; Islam: Sunni; Philosophies: Islamic; Philosophy of Religion; Religion: Africa.**

**BIBLIOGRAPHY**

Hamdun, Said. *Ibn Battuta in Black Africa.* Princeton, N.J.: Markus Weiner, 1994.

Harbeson, John W., and Donald Rothchild, eds. *Africa in World Politics: Post–Cold War Challenges.* Boulder, Colo.: Westview, 1995.

Klein, Martin A. *Islam and Imperialism in Senegal: Sine-Saloum.* Stanford, Calif.: Stanford University Press, 1968.

Levtzion, Nehemiah, and Randall Pouwels, eds. *The History of Islam in Africa.* Athens: Ohio University Press, 2000.

Lewis, I. M., ed. *Islam in Tropical Africa.* Oxford: Oxford University Press, 1966.

Saad, Elias N. *Social History of Timbuktu: The Role of Muslim Scholars and Notables, 1400–1900.* Cambridge, U.K.: Cambridge University Press, 1983.

Sells, Michael, ed. and trans. *Early Islamic Mysticism.* New York: Paulist Press, 1996.

Sulaiman, Ibraheem. *A Revolution in History: The Jihad of Usman Dan Fodio.* New York: Mansell, 1986.

Watt, W. Montgomery. *Islamic Philosophy and Theology: An Extended Survey.* Edinburgh: Edinburgh University Press, 1962.

*Eltigani Abdelgadir Hamid*

## SHII

Shiis, representing the largest sectarian division of Islam after Sunnism, make up roughly one-tenth of the world population of Muslims. The label Shia, which originally referred to the "partisans" of 'Ali, the Prophet Muhammad's cousin and son-in-law, designates various groups in Islamic history united by a belief that the leader of the Muslim community, termed *caliph* or *imam*, should be a member of the Prophet Muhammad's family (*ahl al-bayt*). The Shia first formed an identifiable movement in Islamic history during the First Civil War (*fitna*), which tore the Muslim Community apart between 656 and 661 C.E. According to Shii doctrine, 'Ali was meant to assume leadership of the Community upon the Prophet's death in 632, the Prophet having explicitly designated him as his successor, but the jealousy and ambition of his enemies prevented him as a succession of three other leaders, Abu Bakr (632–634), 'Umar (634–644), and 'Uthman (644–656), were chosen instead. The Shiis are divided into several sects according to the historical line of imams they accept as legitimate, the most important being the Twelvers, Zaydis, and Ismailis.

A common misconception, based on the fact that Iran is today predominantly Shii, holds that Iran is the historic "homeland" of Shii Islam. However, the truth is that Medina and southern Iraq are the original centers of Shii Islam, which spread from there to other areas in the Muslim world. The heyday of the Shiis was in the tenth and eleventh centuries, when dynasties representing the three main Shii sects, Twelvers, Zaydis, and Ismailis, succeeded in conquering most of the Muslim world. For over a century, the Fatimids (Ismaili) controlled Egypt, Syria, the Hijaz, Tunisia, and for a time Sicily. The Hamdanids and other lesser Twelver dynasties controlled northern Syria and Iraq, the Buwayhids (Zaydis/Twelvers) controlled much of Iran and Iraq, Zaydi dynasties controlled areas around the Caspian and Yemen, and the Qaramitah controlled eastern Arabia. Between the eighth and the fifteenth centuries, Shiis in Iran formed the majority in a number of smaller towns such as Qum, Kashan, Aveh, and Sabzevar, and a significant minority in certain major cities such as Rayy and Nishapur. Altogether, though, they probably represented no more than 20 percent of the Iranian population. This situation changed after 1501, when Shah Ismail I conquered the city of Tabriz, founded the Safavid dynasty, and declared Twelver Shiism the religion of the empire. The Safavids (1501–1736) promoted Shii Islam through patronage and propaganda, and over the next several centuries, most Iranians converted. Conversely, former Shiite populations have either disappeared or dwindled in a number of areas, particularly following the fall of the Fatimids and other Shiite dynasties of the tenth, eleventh, and twelfth centuries, and regular persecution by subsequent Sunni powers, including the Zengids, Ayyubids, Mamluks, and Ottomans. The Shiite populations of Tunisia, Egypt, the Hijaz Arabia, such parts of Syria as the city of Aleppo, and parts of northern Iraq either converted or migrated to other areas.

Twelver Shiism, the largest Shiite sect, represents the overwhelming majority in Iran and a slim majority in Iraq, Lebanon, and Bahrain. Significant Twelver Shii minorities are found in Syria, Kuwait, eastern Saudi Arabia, Afghanistan, Pakistan, Azerbaijan, and both northern and southern India. Zaydi Shiis, important in Iraq and northern Iran in the ninth to the eleventh centuries, have for long been confined to Yemen and Yemeni diaspora communities. Ismaili Shiis, who controlled Egypt and much of the eastern Mediterranean between the tenth and twelfth centuries, dispersed after the fall of the Fatimid caliphate in 1171, establishing strongholds in Iran and Syria, and became famous as the Assassins during the Crusades. Their reign of terror ended with conquests by the Mongols and the Mamluks. Although small communities remain in Syria and Iran, the bulk of Ismailis ended up in Bombay and Gujarat in India, with smaller communities in Pakistan, Tajikistan, Yemen, and diaspora communities in Africa, Europe, Canada, and elsewhere.

Shiism as a movement bursts into full view with the assassination of 'Uthman and the ensuing civil war. In 656 'Uthman was assassinated in Medina by Muslims angered by his open nepotism in making appointments to lucrative governorships in the newly conquered provinces. At this point, 'Ali was chosen as caliph, but soon met opposition from the Umayyah clan, the Prophet's widow 'A'isha, and others, who accused him of complicity in 'Uthman's assassination. War ensued, pitting 'Ali's supporters, centered in Kufa in Iraq, against forces in Basra and Syria. In 656, 'Ali's forces met those of 'A'isha, Talha, and al-Zubayr just outside Basra in the "Battle of the Camel," so called because 'A'isha joined the fray in an

armored palanquin mounted on her camel 'Askar. 'Ali's forces killed Talhah and al-Zubayr, captured 'A'isha, and returned her to Medina in humiliation. The following year, 'Ali lost the battle of Siffin in the Syrian desert after his deputy bungled arbitration with the agent of Mu'awiya, the governor of Damascus. A large group of 'Ali's supporters, angered that he had submitted to arbitration, left him at this point. Known as the Kharijis (or Kharijites, "deserters"), they became 'Ali's bitter enemies. 'Ali retreated to Kufa and defeated a Kharijites army at Nahrawan in 658. In 661, he was assassinated by the Khariji ibn Muljam in Kufa. His supporters recognized his eldest son Hasan as their leader, but Hasan soon entered into a truce with Mu'awiya, renouncing his claim to the caliphate, and the war ended. The Muslim community was reunited under one regime; Mu'awiya became caliph of the entire community by default; the capital was moved to Damascus; and, when Mu'awiya designated his son Yazid as his heir, the Umayyad dynasty (661–750) was established. Doctrinally, however, the Muslim community would remain divided into three main groups, 'Ali's supporters (the Shia), enemies of 'Ali who had originally supported him but renounced their allegiance at Siffin (the Kharijis), and the main body of his opponents, the Umayyads and their supporters.

Throughout Umayyad rule, the Shia engaged in periodic uprisings against the illegitimate caliphs, rebelling in the name of various members of *ahl al-bayt*. The most famous of these incidents is the revolt of Husayn, 'Ali's second son, on the death of Mu'awiya and the accession of his son Yazid in 680. Husayn was summoned to Kufa to lead the revolt. He set out from Medina with a small contingent, but Umayyad forces halted him in the Iraqi desert, preventing him from reaching his supporters in Kufa. Rather than surrender, Husayn and his followers fought; most were slaughtered, and Husayn's head was delivered to Yazid in Damascus. The martyrdom of Husayn and his followers is retold and reenacted by the Shia on 'Ashura, the tenth day of Muharram, the first month of the Islamic calendar. Four years later, Kufan Shia known as al-Tawwabun ("the Penitents") led a revolt, reflecting their dedication to the cause of Husayn and their regret that they had had not come to his aid. In 686, Mukhtar al-Thaqafi led an initially successful revolt in the name of Muhammad b. al-Hanafiyya, another son of 'Ali, holding Kufa in 686–687. In 740, Zayd, a grandson of Husayn, led a revolt in southern Iraq and was defeated and killed. 'Abd Allah b. Mu'awiya, a great-grandson of Muhammad's cousin Ja'far, led yet another insurrection (744–747).

The Abbasid revolution that toppled the Umayyads in 750 began in part as a Shii movement, adopting the slogan *al-rida min al al-bayt*, "the acceptable candidate from the family of the Prophet." Upon victory, a descendant of the Prophet's uncle 'Abbas assumed rule as caliph. In a clear pro-Shii move, the new dynasty established its capital in Iraq, first at Wasit, then at Baghdad, founded in 761. The Abbasids, however, soon turned on their Shii allies and eventually took over the Umayyads' role as illegitimate rulers and the nemesis of Shii aspirations. Muhammad al-Nafs al-Zakiyya ("the Pure Soul") led a Shiite revolt against the Abbasids in 762. The Abbasid period would witness countless more revolts in the name of

'Alid leaders. Attempts at reconciliation, the most notable being al-Ma'mun's appointment of 'Ali al-Rida, the eighth imam of the Twelver Shii line, as his successor in 816, were short-lived.

Conflict over leadership of the community and over succession among rival Shii claimants to the imamate gave rise to theological doctrines and concepts that would remain important throughout Islamic history. In the course of the eighth century the Shia developed the doctrines of the imam's *'isma* ("infallibility" or "divine protection from sin"), and *nass,* the theory that the imam must be explicitly designated by his predecessor, with divine sanction. The *ghulat* ("extremists") developed beliefs that the imam did not die but went into occultation (*ghayba*) or that he would return (*raj'a*) as a messianic figure (*mahdi*) before the apocalypse. Others claimed that the imam shared in prophetic authority, had status equal to that of the Prophet, possessed divine qualities, or manifested divinity through divine infusion (*hulul*). Some "extreme" concepts, particularly occultation, would become standard doctrine in the main divisions of the Shia in later centuries. A second set of issues had to do with the status of the Prophet's Companions. To bolster the legitimacy of 'Ali, the Shiites used hadith reports and historical accounts concerning the first three caliphs, 'A'isha, and many other Companions to impugn their characters, casting them as sinners, incompetent leaders, or outright unbelievers. The Sunnis, on the other hand, adopted a compromise position, using similar accounts to uphold the view that the Companions, both those who had supported 'Ali and those who were opposed to him, were all exemplary. The Shiite position, while certainly exaggerated over time, readily admits the seriousness of the conflicts that wracked the early Muslim community, whereas Sunni historiography has often endeavored to cover them up or explain them away.

Shiites share with Sunnis the main holy days of the Islamic calendar: 'Id al-Adha ("the Feast of the Sacrifice") on the tenth of the twelfth month, Dhu al-Hijja, coinciding with the culmination of the annual pilgrimage rites in Mecca, the fast of Ramadan, the ninth month of the calendar, together with the ensuing 'Id al-Fitr ("Breaking the Fast"), and the birthday of the Prophet Muhammad. Distinctly Shiite holy days include Ashura, the tenth of Muharram, the first month of the calendar, which commemorates Husayn's martyrdom. Ceremonies performed on this day and during the ten days leading up to it include emotional readings of the story of Husayn's martyrdom, processions in which the participants chant slogans, rhythmically beat their chests, flagellate their backs, and on occasion lacerate their backs or foreheads, and *ta'ziyah* passion plays, reenactments of the Battle of Karbala', often in great detail. This is followed on Safar 20 by the *arba'in,* the forty-day mourning ceremony for Husayn's death, the most important date of the year for pilgrimage (*ziyarah*) to Karbala'. 'Id al-Ghadir, on the 18th of Dhu al-Hijja, commemorates the speech Prophet Muhammad made at Ghadir Khumm on the return trip from the Farewell Pilgrimage to Medina in which he designated 'Ali his heir as leader of the Muslim community. In addition, the Shiite calendar includes birthday celebrations for the imams, the most important of which are 'Ali's birthday and the birthday of the Twelfth Imam. Pilgrimages

to the imams' tombs and to the tombs of their descendants are an important feature of Shiite ritual life.

A number of significant differences exist between Sunni and Twelver Shiite law and ritual practices. Shiites often add to the *shahadah* or fundamental Islamic creed, "There is no god but God, and Muhammad is God's Messenger" a third clause, *'Aliyyun waliyyu Llah* ("'Ali is God's ward/ally/supporter"). They include in the call to the dawn prayer the phrase *hayya 'ala khayral-'amal* ("Come to the best of works") in place of the phrase *as-salatu khayrun min al-nawm* ("Prayer is better than sleep") used in Sunni tradition. In questions of ritual purity, the Shiites hold that one may wipe one's inner shoes (*khuffayn* meaning "socks" or "slippers") rather than washing one's feet, when they have not been soiled since last washed. In prayer, Shiite men generally hold their hands down at their sides when in standing position, rather than clasping them in front of the chest or belly, as Sunnis do. They commonly join the noon and afternoon prayers in one session and the sunset and evening prayers in one session, praying daily in three sessions rather than in five. Many Shiites set a *muhr* ("seal"), a baked clay tablet made of earth from Karbala', before them when praying, touching their foreheads to it when they prostrate. They consider the tarawih, extra prayers by Sunnis at night during the month of Ramadan, as a heretical innovation. Shiite dietary law is a bit more strict than that of the Sunnis. They do not allow the believer to eat meat slaughtered by Jews and Christians and agree with Jewish dietary law in prohibiting shellfish (any seafood without scales) and rabbit. Shiites have some stricter requirements for the pronouncement of unilateral divorce by the husband—there must be two male witnesses for it to be valid. They also allow *mut'ah,* a type of marriage that is undertaken for a fixed duration stipulated in the contract and that Sunnis consider forbidden. Finally, Shiite inheritance law differs substantially from Sunni inheritance law in that it negates the rights of the *'asabah* or agnate relatives (the deceased's brothers, paternal uncles, and cousins) to receive any surplus left over after dividing the set shares of the inheritance, favoring the nuclear family and, significantly, daughters instead. The *khums,* or fifth, that must be paid according to Sunni law on war booty and the product of mines is generalized to a type of income tax payable to the imam or his representative, meaning, for many centuries now, one of the top Shiite legal authorities. The *khums* funds are divided into six shares, of which three go to support the descendants of the Prophet, who cannot receive ordinary alms, and three go to support religious education and the poor and afflicted in general.

In theology, the Twelver and Zaydi Shiites have largely adopted Mu'tazili doctrines; this sets them apart from the Sunnis, who have generally adopted Ash'ari and Hanbali doctrines on such questions as God's justice. The Shiites hold that God is obligated to act justly, conforming to the definition of good and evil arrived at through rational inquiry. Sunni theology generally sees this as limiting God's power and presuming to dictate to God something that cannot be known with certainty and remains inscrutable to humans.

The question of the imamate was early subsumed under the purview of theology, as were questions of the status of the

Prophet's Companions and other prominent figures in early Islamic history. This has been historically the biggest bone of contention between the Shiis, who deplore the actions of certain Companions, including the first three caliphs—Abu Bakr, 'Umar, and 'Uthman—and some of the Prophet's own wives, including 'A'isha and Hafsah; other Companions, such as Talhah and al-Zubayr; and Mu'awiyah for usurping the position of leadership of the Community, which rightly belonged to 'Ali, or for opposing 'Ali, his allies, or the later imams. The Sunni position is one of compromise. All early figures are praised, despite the conflicts that definitely occurred, and the first four caliphs are all accepted as the best of the Companions, in descending order of excellence. For this reason Shiites are continually accused in the medieval sources of *rafd* and *sabb*, meaning rejection of the Companions' exalted status, blasphemy against them, and vituperation or cursing of them. On the Shiite side there developed an extensive literature on the foibles and defects of 'Ali's enemies among the Companions as well as of the injustices they perpetrated. Some of these undoubtedly preserve kernels of authentic material, but many may derive from later exaggeration, including stories designed to prove the extreme cowardice and conniving of Abu Bakr and 'Umar as opposed to 'Ali's outlandish feats of bravery, or suggestions that 'Umar prevented the dying Prophet Muhammad from dictating his will and testament.

By the eleventh century, Twelver Shii jurists made strong claims that, during the prolonged occultation, certain roles of the imams naturally devolved on them. Much later, in the sixteenth century, this idea would be justified by the claim that the jurists as a group, and, more specifically, the leading jurist(s) of the age, were in effect the "general deputy" (*al-na'ib al-'amm*) of the occulted imam. Although they had not developed this theory of the general deputyship, Twelver jurists of earlier centuries, such as al-Shaykh al-Mufid (d. 1025), al-Sharif al-Murtada (d. 1044), and al-Shaykh al-Tusi (d. 1067), argued that duties of judging between litigants, the holding of Friday prayer, collection of *khums* funds, and so on, could indeed be held in the absence of the imam by virtue of the jurists' authority. Al-Karajaki (d. 1057) goes so far as to term Twelver scholars "intermediaries" between the imam and Shii laypeople.

In the seventeenth and eighteenth centuries, there was a significant challenge to the authority of Twelver scholars qua jurists by the Akhbari movement, which denied that expertise in legal interpretation, with rational and extra-scriptural bases, could justify religious authority. The Akhbari movement met resounding defeat by the end of the eighteenth century, and in the process their opponents, the Usulis, made very strong arguments for the jurists' authority, stressing their ability to perform *ijtihad* (independent investigation of the law) and stressing their exclusive authority. One may see the development in the nineteenth and twentieth centuries of the concept of *wilayat al-faqih*, or the comprehensive authority of the jurist, as an extension of this move to bolster the jurists' authority. Khomeini, the most outspoken proponent of this doctrine, and author of a work by that title based on his 1971 lectures, held that the leading Twelver jurist was, as the general deputy of the imam, entitled not only to take over some

of the "religious" prerogatives of the imam, such as the collection of *khums,* but also to take over political rule itself. This radical extension of Twelver doctrine later became the basis for the constitution of the Islamic Republic of Iran, which designated the office of rahbar, or leader, to be held by the leading Twelver jurist of the age and concentrated in that figure tremendous political powers, including command of the armed forces and the right to appoint the members of the Shura Council.

*See also* **Islam: Sunni; Religion: Middle East.**

### BIBLIOGRAPHY

Amir-Moezzi, M. A. *The Divine Guide in Early Shi'ism: The Sources of Esotericism in Islam.* Translated by David Streight. Albany: State University of New York Press, 1994.

Arjomand, S. A. *The Shadow of God and the Hidden Imam.* Chicago: University of Chicago Press, 1984.

Bill, J. A., and J. A. Williams. *Roman Catholics and Shi'i Muslims: Prayer, Passion, and Politics.* Chapel Hill: University of North Carolina Press, 2002.

Crone P., and M. Hinds. *God's Caliph: Religious Authority in the First Centuries of Islam.* New York: Cambridge University Press, 1986.

Daftary, F. *The Isma'ilis: Their History and Doctrines.* New York: Cambridge University Press, 1990.

Donaldson, D. M. *The Shi'ite Religion.* London: Luzac, 1933.

Goldziher, I. *An Introduction to Islamic Theology and Law.* Translated by Andras and Ruth Hamori. Princeton, N.J.: Princeton University Press, 1981.

Halm, H. *Shiism,* Edinburgh: Edinburgh University Press, 1991.

Kohlberg, E. *A Medieval Muslim Scholar at Work, Ibn Tawus and His Library.* New York: E. J. Brill, 1992.

Madelung, W. *The Succession to Muhammad: A Study of the Early Caliphate.* New York: Cambridge University Press, 1997.

McDermott, M. J. *The Theology of al-Shaikh al-Mufid.* Beirut: Dar el-Machreq, 1978.

Modarressi Tabata'i, H. *An Introduction to Shi'i Law: A Bibliographical Study.* London: Ithaca Press, 1984.

Moddarressi, H. *Crisis and Consolidation in the Formative Period of Shi'ite Islam.* Princeton, N.J.: Darwin Press, 1993.

Momen, M. *An Introduction to Shi'i Islam: The History and Doctrines of Twelver Shi'ism.* New Haven, Conn.: Yale University Press, 1985.

Moussavi, A. K. *Religious Authority in Shi'ite Islam: From the Office of Mufti to the Institution of Marja'.* Kuala Lumpur: International Institute of Islamic Thought and Civilization, 1996.

Newman, A. J. *The Formative Period of Twelver Shi'ism: Hadith as Discourse Between Qum and Baghdad.* Richmond, Surrey, U.K.: Curzon, 2000.

Richard, Y. *Shi'ite Islam: Polity, Ideology, and Creed.* Translated by Antonia Nevill. Cambridge, U.K.: Blackwell, 1995.

Sachedina, A. A. *Islamic Messianism: The Idea of the Mahdi in Twelver Shi'ism.* Albany: State University of New York Press, 1981.

Stewart, D. J. *Islamic Legal Orthodoxy: Twelver Shiite Responses to the Sunni Legal System.* Salt Lake City: University of Utah Press, 1998.

Watt, W. M. *The Formative Period of Islamic Thought.* Edinburgh: Edinburgh University Press, 1973.

*D. J. Stewart*

## SOUTHEAST ASIA

The Muslim population of Southeast Asia is in excess of 250 million. It is the religion of the majority in Indonesia and Malaysia, with significant minorities in Singapore, Thailand, and the Philippines.

Islam has a five-hundred-year history in this region. Importantly, it was not imposed by conquest but freely adopted, initially by royal and upper classes and then percolating down to the masses. Of course its progress has been uneven, despite organized missionary efforts that began in the seventeenth century and continue into the early twenty-first century. However, the result has been that Islam in Southeast Asia is expressed in local idioms reflecting local cultural norms. These variations do not mean that the basics of revelation are or have been abandoned but that localized expressions incorporating indigenous philosophies are primary. To "know Islam" is thus to know the local forms.

### Literature and Philosophy

The tradition of writing on these subjects dates from the seventeenth century. It is firmly within the Islamic tradition and consists of translation and commentary on the fundamentals of doctrine, accounts of the life of the Prophet, and, most important, speculative work on the outer limits of the permissible in doctrine—sometimes subsumed under the rubric of "Sufi" texts. This speculative work is the major distinctive feature of Southeast Asian Islam and is often explained as a reaction to or accommodation with preexisting Hindu or Buddhist religious philosophies. Whatever the reason, this way of thinking about religion has persisted into the twenty-first century. The Arabic texts are mediated through the languages of the area (Malay, Indonesian, and cognates) and have become intensely localized.

One example of this distinctive development of Islam is the idea of gnosis originally expressed by Hamzah Fansuri, who taught in the seventeenth century that the believer could be one with God. That idea resonates in the early twenty-first century in Aceh in Sumatra (as well as other places), where something like 15 to 20 percent of state fatwas concern "heresy," in this case gnosis. This is an incredibly high figure, and the texts involved take us back to the seventeenth century. But a reaction to this idea began in the 1850s and continues in the twenty-first century; "purity" of doctrine has become a priority, inspiring a return to the uncontaminated sources, the Koran and the sunna. The literature and philosophy deriving from these sources, especially since the 1920s and 1930s, is minimalist or, some would say, "scripturalist." Its main characteristic is rejection of cultural complexity combined with a (perhaps) excessive respect for literal translations from the original Arabic. While this may be conducive to "purity," it is also impractical in daily life. The tension between culture and purity is ongoing and, at the beginning of the twenty-first century, largely unmediated. Increasingly the proponents from each side are becoming disengaged from each other; there is little communication, let alone attempts at mutual understanding. Each side produces its own literature and each claims its own authenticity.

### Law

Before the establishment of Dutch and British rule (from about 1800), the Muslims of Southeast Asia had sophisticated polities based on Muslim state practice in the Middle East. From thence were derived theories and practices of sovereignty, legitimacy of rule, public order and duty, and the distribution and exercise of power. However, the European powers replaced this tradition with colonial ("Western") principles, chief among which was the conviction that God was not necessary to validate government. Islam, and Islamic law and government, was reduced in status. From being the foundation of the state it became just a religion like any other. It had no public presence.

The Dutch in the Netherlands East Indies (now Indonesia) saw Islam as a political and military threat. Their solution was to deny the religion any credible public presence, and an important aspect of this effort was to deny *shari'a* (Islamic law) by subordinating it to custom (*adat*), thus reducing its status to just a personal law. In time, however, the *shari'a* did receive limited recognition, which it retains in contemporary Indonesia. It is now a state-sponsored Compilation of Islamic Law (1991) administered through religious courts. Together these changes have successfully secularized the classical *shari'a*, which is now in a form unrecognizable to a classical scholar.

The same result has been achieved in Malaysia (formally British Malaya). Here a few selected rules of family law and trusts have been incorporated into English law precedents and statutes. These are a direct colonial legacy, and in contemporary Malaysia they are the *shari'a* that is administered in religious courts of restricted jurisdiction. Because Malaysia is a federation, each state has its own legislation, and thus *shari'a* varies from place to place, but the variations are not major. The main point to understand is that anyone trained in Anglo-American law can read and understand the *shari'a* in this form, whereas a classically trained *qadi* (judge) would be completely at a loss.

In short, for Southeast Asia, the *shari'a* has been redefined in secular terms, for administration by the state. It is not now necessary to know Arabic or the classical texts.

### Islam and the State

With the ending of colonial repression in the 1950s, it became possible once more for Islam to have a public face in Indonesia and Malaysia. As well as establishing the religious courts and statutes of *shari'a*, both states introduced ministries or departments of religion and councils of muftis or ulema (authorities in Islamic law) and, most importantly, permitted political parties that promoted Islam as an ideology suitable for the nation-state. Religion became and remains an alternative to secular constitutionalism, although it has never been clear what an "Islamic state" would be, except that God's revealed truth would be fundamental. Neither Indonesia nor Malaysia describes itself as "Islamic" but rather as states populated by "a Muslim majority."

The Malaysian constitution says that "Islam is the religion of the Federation" (Article 3), but it also establishes freedom of religious belief and observance (Article 11). In practice there is no compulsion in religion. At the same time, a significant Islamic political party, the Pan-Malaysian Islamic Party, centered in the northeastern Malay Peninsula, a quite poor area, has been locally successful in elections. It appeals to "Islam," but this is not defined; the reason for the party's success is a justifiable resentment against lack of development. The religious card is hence quite potent for a Muslim audience, though it can be overplayed. For example, draft Islamic criminal law bills have been produced in the provinces of Kelantan and Trengganu that seek to introduce the seventh-century Arabian punishments (amputations, stoning) into modern Malaysia. They are unconstitutional, and they represent a definition of Islam that, as the 2004 elections showed, is soundly rejected. The present and future of Islam does not lie in these barbarisms, but such theologically illiterate interpretations remain potent justifications of extremism.

In Indonesia, Islam has no place as such in the constitution but is subsumed into the "belief in one God" principle, which encompasses all religions. The years since independence have seen debate between secular and religious interests regarding the status of Islam, and it remains unresolved. However, unlike Malaysia, Indonesia does have many (over eighty) mass movement organizations founded on Islam. The largest, the Nahdlatul Ulama, based in East and Central Java, represents a "traditionalist" (Arabic-based) interpretation of religion. The smaller Muhammadiyah promotes a "modernistic" agenda through which the individual, by an effort of rational thought, can find the true meaning of religion. Neither of these movements, founded in the early twentieth century, is directly affiliated with any political party, but both are immensely influential because they own and run kindergartens, schools, universities, hospitals and clinics, and a wide variety of social outreach programs. There are other, smaller groups that perform similar functions.

Both Malaysia and Indonesia have a huge publishing industry devoted to Islam. Quality is highly variable and ranges from short, simple texts (mostly addressed to women on religious duty to husband and family) to complex expositions of law, philosophy, and the relation between Islam and the state. Books on the latter topic have increased greatly in number since the mid-1990s. The important point is that this vibrant literature has come to form a new, local "Southeast Asian Islam." It is written by locals for a local audience and both reflects and adds to an Islam that is distinct in its politics, laws, and social and literary expressions.

Muslim societies in Southeast Asia are agrarian, rapidly modernizing, and engaging in democratic forms of government. Huge social and intellectual tensions are widespread in the twenty-first century, and Islam is at the heart of these tensions in all of Southeast Asia. As a consequence, one must be time- and place-specific in defining Islam; there is no simplistic monolith to be accepted or rejected.

*See also* **Law, Islamic; Mysticism: Islamic Mysticism in Asia; Religion: East and Southeast Asia; Sufism; Westernization: Southeast Asia.**

BIBLIOGRAPHY

Hefner, Robert. W., and Patricia Horvatich, eds. *Islam in an Era of Nation-States.* Honolulu: University of Hawaii Press, 1997.

Hooker, M. B. *Indonesian Islam: Social Change through Contemporary Fatawa.* Sydney, Australia: Allen and Unwin, 2003.

Hooker, M. B., ed. *Islam in South-East Asia.* Leiden, Netherlands: Brill, 1983.

*M. B. Hooker*

## SUNNI

The term *Sunni* is an adjective formed from the noun *sunna* (plural *sunan*), an ancient Arabic word meaning "customary practice." Although in the pre-Islamic world of tribal Arabia the word *sunna* referred generally to the time-tested and widely accepted customs of a tribe, in the Islamic period the term came to refer specifically to the customary practices or "way" of the prophet Muhammad and the first generation of pious Muslims. Eventually the adjective *Sunni* came to describe the largest of the three primary sectarian divisions among Muslims: Sunnis, Shiites, and Kharijites.

Accounting for nearly 90 percent of the world's Muslims, Sunnis emphasize their commitment to both the precedents established by the Prophet and the unity of the historic community (referred to in Arabic as either the *umma* or the *jama'a*). The term *Sunni* is actually an abbreviation of the fuller expression *ahl al-sunna wa-l-jama'a,* "the people of the [Prophet's] way and the community." Of course nothing in this self-description by the majority of Muslims should convey that either Shiites or Kharijites see themselves as any less committed or faithful to the Prophet's way.

### Early History

In the mold of great Hebrew prophets, Muhammad combined both political and religious authority as the leader of the early Islamic community (*umma*). On his death in 632 the Prophet left no clear message as to how leadership of the Muslim community should devolve after him. Initially, therefore, divisions among Muslims were prompted by disputes over succession to the leadership of the community, rather than by doctrinal differences. The first five successors to the Prophet were, in fact, elevated in different ways to leadership of the community, reflecting the ambiguity among early Muslims about the Prophet's intentions regarding succession.

The majority position, which eventually appropriated the appellation *Sunni* to describe itself, held that in the absence of a clear message detailing an alternative arrangement, the Prophet intended for the Muslim community to proceed in selecting its leaders according to ancient Arab tribal custom. Traditionally, tribal leaders were selected from a relatively small pool of respected senior figures within the tribe. Once consensus on a new leader was achieved through deliberations of the tribal council, the choice of a new leader was confirmed by the public offering of an oath of allegiance, known as the *bay'a,* to the new leader by senior clan leaders within the tribe.

The earliest accounts suggest that following the Prophet's death, the early Muslim community in Medina was initially thrown into confusion even about whether or not the Prophet intended the Muslim community to remain unified under a single leader, combining both political and religious authority, or whether each tribe was expected to revert to selecting its own tribal chief. The matter was temporarily, though not decisively, resolved when 'Umar ibn al-Khattab, a highly respected figure among the Prophet's inner circle, offered the public *bay'a* to Abu Bakr, the Prophet's oldest and closest friend. This dramatic gesture convinced other leading figures to quickly follow suit in offering the *bay'a* to Abu Bakr. However, during his two-year reign Abu Bakr was engaged in re-extending authority over various tribes throughout Arabia that believed their submission to the Muslim state ended with Muhammad's death.

There was no doubt among the early Muslims that although the Prophet's successors would continue his function as political and religious leader of the *umma,* they would not continue his prophetic role. The Arabic term used among Sunnis to designate the successors of the Prophet is *khalifat rasul al-lah* (deputy of the Prophet of God), from which the English term *caliph* is derived. Sunnis recognize four legitimate caliphal successors to Muhammad: Abu Bakr (r. 632–634), 'Umar (r. 634–644), 'Uthman ibn 'Affan (r. 644–656), and 'Ali ibn Abi Talib (r. 656–661), who are collectively referred to among Sunnis as the "Rightly Guided Caliphs" (*al-khulafa' al rashidun*). Following the assassination of the last of these four caliphs in 661, the governor of Syria, Mu'awiya (r. 661–680), was successful in establishing the Umayyad dynasty, which ruled over the early Islamic empire for nearly a century. Although the Umayyads, like many dynasties that succeeded them, also claimed the title of caliph, subsequent Muslim historiography tended to refer to the Umayyad rulers as *muluk* (kings) to indicate that the political authority they exercised lacked the legitimacy of religious leadership over the *umma,* which the first four caliphs enjoyed.

Exact details of the succession disputes that established the three main divisions among Muslims are now clouded by centuries of partisan accounts, but the broad outlines are clear. During the first two decades after the Prophet's death, probably about the time of the accession of the third caliph, 'Uthman, in 644, a minority party among Muhammad's companions began to champion the cause of 'Ali ibn Abi Talib as the rightful successor to the Prophet. 'Ali was the first cousin and later son-in-law of Muhammad. He was also the son of Abu Talib, in whose house the Prophet had been raised after he was orphaned at age six. 'Ali clearly enjoyed a very close personal relationship to Muhammad, probably analogous to a devoted younger brother, and he is reported to have been the first male convert to Islam. Although 'Ali did not contest the elevation of the first three caliphs before him, the early histories make clear that 'Ali and his supporters resented his being passed over in favor of 'Uthman in 644. Devoted support to the cause of 'Ali survived his own assassination in 661 and was transferred to his two sons through the Prophet's daughter Fatima: al-Hasan (c. 625–669) and al-Husayn (c. 626–680).

The supporters of 'Ali and his heirs became known as *shi'at 'Ali,* "the party of 'Ali," from which the abbreviated *shia*

(Shiite) comes. Over time the Shiites developed an elaborate doctrine rejecting the Sunni claim that the Prophet had left no clear message about succession after his death. Based on their own interpretation of a widely accepted statement made by the Prophet during his farewell pilgrimage to Mecca, the early Shiites asserted that Muhammad in fact left a very clear message that succession to the combined political and religious leadership of the Muslim community rightfully lay with 'Ali and his two sons through the Prophet's daughter Fatima. Shiites, therefore, rejected the first three caliphs, on whose memory they are known to invoke curses, in favor of 'Ali ibn Abi Talib and his descendents, whom they refer to as imams, rather than caliphs. In the early twenty-first century Shiites account for nearly 10 percent of the world's Muslims.

Kharijites, the smallest of the three major divisions among Muslims (currently less than 1 percent), also arose out of these early succession struggles. When 'Ali was elevated to the caliphate following the assassination of the third caliph, 'Uthman, in 656, the new caliph faced several challenges to his authority. The most serious opposition came from the governor of Syria, Mu'awiya, a cousin of the murdered third caliph, who suspected 'Ali of complicity in the death of his kinsman. Mu'awiya refused to give the *bay'a* (oath of allegiance) to 'Ali, which quickly led to battle between 'Ali's forces and the Syrian garrison. When stalemate was reached between the two sides, 'Ali reluctantly agreed to a call for arbitration in hopes of ending bloodshed between Muslims. Although the arbitration process ultimately proved futile, the very fact that 'Ali had accepted arbitration, rather than allow God to decide matters on the battlefield, prompted a group of 'Ali's own supporters to withdraw from among his ranks. Forced to make an example of these deserters, 'Ali's forces engaged and massacred them at the Nahrawan canal in Iraq in 658. Among Sunnis this group of deserters became known pejoratively as Khawarij, meaning "those who go out." In revenge for the massacre at the Nahrawan canal, 'Ali was himself assassinated by a Kharijite in 661. Like the Shiites and the Sunnis, the Kharijites eventually developed their own elaborate doctrine of the caliphate and their own legal schools. Essentially, the Kharijites held a radically egalitarian view of who was qualified to serve as caliph. They also came to hold an extreme view that any caliph who failed to apply or abide by the holy law of Islam forfeited both his office and his life—an idea that has inspired many modern Islamic political extremists.

The evolution and elaboration of each of these three major sectarian divisions among Muslims occurred slowly over time and did not spring wholly formed from these early disputes over succession. Each sect would also eventually generate numerous of their own subsects and divisions, which underscores the frequently unappreciated historical fact that the formation of Islam as a whole unfolded over centuries, not decades. Furthermore, the critical geographical location where the formation of Islam occurred between the mid-seventh and the mid-tenth centuries was not Arabia, but rather Syria and Iraq. The primitive form of Islam that came out of Arabia with the early Muslim conquests of the mid-seventh century, therefore, possessed very little of the sophisticated theological or legal superstructure recognized as so central to the tradition today. The fact that Islam came fully into formation in Iraq and Syria is significant because this area had long served as the frontier between the two great Mediterranean civilizations of late antiquity, Rome and Persia. As the new Islamic order began to take shape in this dynamic region between great empires, it drew important inspiration from both of the great civilizations that had previously dominated the Mediterranean world.

Unlike the earlier Christian experience, where slow conversion over nearly three centuries preceded the exercise of political power beginning in the reign of Constantine (r. 306–337), the early Islamic state came to dominate a vast empire in a remarkably short period. Within a century of the Prophet's death, Muslim armies had reached southern France in the west and northern India in the east. The rapidity of the early Muslim conquests, combined with the fact that Islam and the civilization that it inspired were still in formation, presented the Umayyad rulers of the first unified Muslim empire with enormous challenges. Faced with the task of administering a vast empire before the superstructure of Islamic law, institutions, political thought, and theology was yet in place, the Umayyads were compelled to make a variety of pragmatic administrative decisions that were effective but hardly uniform in character. Essentially, the Umayyads tended to confirm prevailing practice, whatever that might be, in the eclectic and far-flung empire they ruled from their capital in Damascus.

Unfortunately for the Umayyads, much of what eventually became accepted Sunni theory and practice of law, government, and administration was defined in opposition to whatever exigency-driven expediencies the Umayyads felt compelled to employ in ruling their empire. Not only does this circumstance explain the generally unfavorable evaluation of the Umayyads in subsequent Muslim historiography, but it also contributed greatly to the coalescence of opposition to the Umayyad dynasty, which resulted in their overthrow and replacement by the Abbasids in 750.

Under the Abbasids (750–1258), especially during the first three centuries of their rule, classical Islamic civilization reached fruition. Their new capital of Baghdad was by all accounts not only a fabulous city in its own right, but it was also a great magnet for artists, belletrists, craftsmen, and thinkers from throughout the Islamic world. It was thus during this golden age of early Abbasid rule that the distinctive and characteristic forms of classical Islamic thought and institutions took definitive shape.

By the mid-ninth century the political fragmentation of the universal empire was too advanced for the Abbasids to check. From this point forward, the political unity of the Islamic *umma* would remain an ideal for Muslims but not a practical reality as a host of local powers and regional empires asserted themselves. By this point, however, the basic outlines of classical Islamic thought and institutions were well enough established that they flourished even without the benefit of political unity that the universal empire had once afforded. This was a remarkably vibrant and highly cosmopolitan civilization of great cities, closely linked by shared religion and language, as well as by extensive crisscrossing trade networks and frequent

artistic and intellectual exchange. Rival courts competed with each other in patronizing philosophers, scholars, theologians, jurists, physicians, craftsmen, writers, master builders, and poets, all of whose creativity and genius reflected positively on their benefactors. In this sense the political fragmentation of the universal empire from the mid-ninth century onward probably contributed greatly to the diverse and vibrant creativity of this period by ensuring multiple sources of patronage in all fields of learning and creative production. The economic vitality of Islamic civilization, with its vast and ever-expanding trade networks stretching from East Asia to the Atlantic and from sub-Saharan Africa to Central Asia, ensured an unparalleled level of wealth and further expanded the patronage base well beyond royal courts.

### Principal Doctrines and Ritual Practice

Islam falls squarely within the tradition of Abrahamic monotheism and shares certain parallels with both Judaism and Christianity. As explained above, the three major sectarian divisions among Muslims did not originate in doctrinal disagreements. Although certain doctrinal differences among them developed over time, these do not affect essential core beliefs, which are shared universally by Muslims.

At the heart of Islamic theology lies an uncompromising and absolute belief in the unity of God, whom Muslim and Christian speakers of Arabic alike refer to as Allah. The Islamic doctrine of the oneness of God, referred to as *tawhid* in Arabic, forms the first half of the Muslim profession of faith: "There is no god, but God." The Koran is quite specific in its rejection of the Christian doctrine of the Incarnation, and Muslim theologians have traditionally shared the skepticism of their Jewish colleagues about the genuineness of Christian monotheism.

To associate anything else with God, or to submit to anything other than God, is *shirk* (polytheism), the one sin that God does not forgive. Idolatry in the Muslim understanding involves far more than worshiping pagan deities, and *shirk* occurs whenever people place their own personal desires above the will of God.

The God of Koranic revelation is, like the God of the Hebrew Bible, both the creator of the universe and the ultimate judge before whom all people will eventually be called to account at the end of time. These dual qualities of creator and judge help to explain why the Koran stresses both God's mercy and wrath.

Muslim theologians distinguish between the transcendent essence of divinity, which is unknowable, and the attributes of God, which are manifest in the cosmos. In discussing these divine attributes, classical Muslim theologians usually referred to the "Beautiful Names of God." Although the attributes, or names, of God are frequently paired in contrasting qualities (e.g., "He who gives life" and "He who brings death"), the "names of mercy" are said to dominate the contradictory "names of wrath."

Having created the universe, God ordains an order or law according to which all things rightfully submit. Submission to the will of God, in fact, is central to veneration of the divine—in which the entire created cosmos is properly engaged. Ironically, humanity, which stands at the apex of the created universe, is almost uniquely endowed with the capacity to something less than full submission to God's will. Like Jews and Christians, Muslims believe that humanity comprises a very special part of creation, being created in the image or "form" of God. This unique attribute of human beings affords humanity the possibility of realizing its noble calling—serving as God's deputies on earth (*khalifat allah fi'l-ard*). Because human beings possess the ability throughout their lives to submit to things other than God, it is on the sincere extent of his submission that each person will be judged by God at the end of days. The awesome and inescapable reality of Judgment itself is dealt with in great detail in the Koran, as are the alternative destinations of paradise and hell to which the judged are ultimately consigned.

The ultimate sign of God's mercy is the fact of divine guidance, which has come to humanity through the agency of prophets (*anbiya'*, singular *nabi*). Beginning with the first man, Adam, and concluding with Muhammad, God has sent prophets bearing revelation outlining the divine will for mankind. Unfortunately, the human capacity for ignoring and twisting the revelations of God is limitless, which necessitates God's correcting and restating revelation by sending subsequent prophets. With Muhammad and the Koran, however, Muslims believe, humanity has the corrected and most complete version of God's revealed word. And assertion of the prophetic role of Muhammad forms the second half of the Muslim profession of faith. The Koran reflects God's considerable impatience with the human capacity to corrupt the divine message, which is underscored by warnings that God's patience in this regard is at an end, and hence there will be no further divine revelation. Muhammad, therefore, is understood as the "seal of the prophets."

The Koran, as the complete and perfected word of God, made manifest in the world through the prophetic agency of Muhammad, is the earthly version of a heavenly archetype existing eternally with God. It must be emphasized here that Muslims understand the Koran not as the word of Muhammad, somehow inspired by God, but as the absolute word of God himself. In this sense, Muslims see Islam as "the religion of the Book." They likewise regard Jews and Christians as "people of the Book," because they are believed to have also received genuine, though incomplete, divine revelation. The actual content of both the Hebrew Bible and the Christian New Testament, however, have historically held very little interest for Muslims because not only are they incomplete, but Muslims believe that Jews and Christians either willfully or carelessly corrupted the content of the divine scripture they received.

The fact that Christians and Jews were recipients of genuine revelation, however, has historically implied for Muslims that neither Jews nor Christians could be forcibly converted to Islam. This same prohibition against forcible conversion was later applied to various other religious communities that Muslims identified as genuinely monotheistic. Polytheists,

however, did not fare so well, and were forcibly converted, on pain of death or enslavement, particularly in the early Islamic period.

Although Christians, Jews, and other monotheists, referred to collectively as *dhimmis,* or "protected peoples," were not routinely compelled to convert to Islam, they were frequently subjected to various disabilities, such as the payment of a special tax known as the *jizya,* and indignities, such as sumptuary laws, designed to encourage their conversion to Islam. Although this limited tolerance that medieval Muslim societies traditionally afforded other monotheistic faiths would not satisfy contemporary sensibilities, by comparison with such institutions as the Inquisition in Christian Europe, Islamic tolerance of other monotheistic faiths was indeed remarkable.

The refusal of Christians and Jews to recognize the prophecy of Muhammad was viewed by Muslims as willful disobedience of God, which should not be ignored but actively challenged. This sense of responsibility for the fate of the souls of others was very much part of a larger understanding Muslims traditionally had, that they were specifically commanded by God to "command what is good, and forbid what is evil" in the world. Muslims in the classical period suffered no doubts about the answer to Cain's rhetorical question in the Book of Genesis: they clearly understood that they were indeed their brother's keeper.

The word *Islam* itself in Arabic conveys a notion of inner peace that humans can only achieve through sincere submission to the will of God. The most obvious demonstration of this submission to God is expressed in what are frequently referred to as the five pillars of Islamic faith: devout and public profession of faith (*shihada*), the ritual performance of worshipful prayer (*salat*) at five appointed times each day, the annual giving of alms to the poor (*zakat*), annual fasting (*sawm*) from before sunrise until sunset throughout the Islamic month of Ramadan, and the performance of a pilgrimage (*hajj*) to Mecca at least once during one's life, assuming health and finances permit. It must be stressed, however, that these ritual obligations only demarcate the most basic outlines of submission to God's will. Devout Muslims see themselves as engaged in a profound struggle to submit their own wills to God's law in every aspect of life. In fact, they frequently refer to this inner struggle as the greater jihad.

## Practice, Law, and Authority

The scope of God's law, the *shari'a,* is as expansive and as comprehensive in Islam as is halakah in Judaism. In fact, all human actions and interactions fall into and are analyzed by Muslim jurists in one of five categories: (1) actions that God specifically commands (such as fasting and five daily performances of prayer); (2) actions that God encourages but does not insist upon (such as charity beyond what the *zakat* requires); (3) neutral actions about which God is indifferent; (4) discouraged but not prohibited actions (such as divorce); and finally (5) forbidden actions (such as murder and drinking alcohol). In very much the same manner as rabbinic law, Islamic jurists submit all actions to careful analysis in an effort to determine the will of God. Ultimately, submission to God lies in the considerable effort that devout believers invest in ensuring that all of their actions are measured in the light of and conform to the *shari'a*. This emphasis on the correctness of action among the faithful in both Judaism and Islam distinguishes these traditions as orthopractic and sets them both apart from Christianity, with its historic emphasis on orthodoxy, the correctness of doctrine, among believers.

Although Muslims, like Jews, historically focused primarily on faithful adherence to God's law, it is important to note that the *shari'a* is not in any sense a uniform legal code. Rather it is a legal framework within which considerable disputation occurs. Basing their analysis primarily on the Koran and extensive collections of reports, known as *hadith*, about what the Prophet did and said, as well as several subsidiary sources of divine law, Muslim jurists generated an immense body of jurisprudence over the centuries in their efforts to discern and apply the specific content of divine law.

Because Sunnis, unlike Shiites, never developed a clerical order or hierarchy, there was no body or institution in Sunni Islam charged with establishing definitively which legal opinions were authoritative and which were not. Again, very similar to the rabbinic system, jurisprudence in Sunni Islam is remarkably decentralized. The opinions of certain jurists gain authority over time as they are cited positively by subsequent jurists in their own legal opinions. Legal reasoning among Sunnis divided itself into a number of "schools" of jurisprudence known as *madhahib* in Arabic, of which four survive: Hanafi, Shaf'i, Hanbali, and Maliki. Although both the approach to legal reasoning and the specific content of law in each school do not vary greatly, there are some important differences among them. As a general rule these legal schools predominate regionally (for example, Malikis in North Africa and Hanbalis in northern and central Arabia). Shiites and Kharijites developed their own legal schools.

The decentralized character of authority in Sunni jurisprudence extends more broadly to the entire field of religious knowledge. Because there is neither a formal clergy nor any ordination process among Sunni religious scholars, referred to collectively in Arabic as the *'ulama'* (Anglicized as *ulema*), the educational process through which individuals gained admission to the class of religious scholars traditionally tended to be highly personal. Again, much like the rabbinic system, promising students sought and were granted permission to study under recognized authorities. Upon the completion of their studies they received a certificate from the master certifying their competence in whatever field of religious science they had studied with him.

Like Judaism and Christianity before it, Islam was profoundly affected by its encounter with Hellenistic thought. By the early Abbasid period, speculative theology among Sunnis was dominated by a series of competing schools that emerged in response to various major doctrinal debates among the ulema over such issues as predestination versus free will, whether the Koran was created or coexistent with God, and the extent to which the Koran should be interpreted literally or metaphorically. The assistance of politically powerful patrons was frequently sought by partisans in these contentious

debates among the ulema to ensure the persecution of their opponents.

Islamic mysticism, usually referred to as Sufism, like law, theology, and philosophy, also played a major role in shaping Sunni spirituality from an early date. In Sufism authority also tended to be both highly diffuse and personal in character. By the mid-thirteenth century an elaborate series of mystical brotherhoods, known as *tariqas*, emerged and replaced an earlier, more informal collection of individual mystics surrounded by their disciples. Under the *tariqa* system, with each brotherhood having its master and established rule of esoteric development, a greater measure of conformity to normative Sunni doctrine among mystics was finally achieved—to the great relief of mainstream Sunni ulema, who were frequently troubled by the more exuberant and ecstatic expressions of mystical gnosis among the Sufis.

The great mystical brotherhoods of the later Middle Ages also attracted large followings among all sectors of the population. Many people were especially attracted by the public veneration of great mystical saints, known in Arabic as *awliya'* (singular *wali*), "the friends of God," especially at the site of their tombs. In a religious system where prophetic revelation ended decisively with Muhammad's death in 632, *wilaya*, or sainthood, offered an important opportunity for mediation with God. Although many Sunni jurists opposed the cult of the saints, others found ways to accommodate this highly popular practice within the framework of normative Sunni practice.

Despite the fact that political and religious authority were theoretically unified for Sunnis in the office of caliph, as a practical matter, after the breakdown of centralized power in the Abbasid period, effective political power passed to and was monopolized by various regional dynasties and other secular political forces, which, nonetheless, frequently maintained the fiction that they were ruling in the name of the caliph. Philosophers, such as Abu Nasr al-Farabi (c. 878–c. 950), articulated elaborate theories of the caliphate and its qualifications long after caliphs ceased wielding effective political power. Thus the office of caliph continued to symbolize the ideal unity of the Muslim *umma* for Sunnis in a reality characterized by political fragmentation. Although the ulema class frequently decried the failure of secular political authorities to rule in accordance with the *shari'a*, the religious establishment came to see their primary role as guardians of the *shari'a* in a world without effective caliphs. Whenever possible they sought to pressure political authorities to adhere more closely to the *shari'a*, but the ulema effectively recognized a de facto division between political and religious authority from the Abbasid period onward.

*See also* **Death and Afterlife, Islamic Understanding of; Jihad; Law, Islamic; Mysticism: Islamic Mysticism; Philosophies: Islamic; Religion: Middle East; Religion and the State: Middle East; Sufism.**

**BIBLIOGRAPHY**
Berkey, Jonathan P. *The Formation of Islam: Religion and Society in the Near East, 600–1800.* Cambridge, U.K.: Cambridge University Press, 2003.

Cook, Michael. *Commanding Right and Forbidding Wrong in Islamic Thought*. Cambridge, U.K.: Cambridge University Press, 2000.

———. *Early Muslim Dogma*. Cambridge, U.K.: Cambridge University Press, 1981.

Donner, Fred M. *The Early Islamic Conquests*. Princeton, N.J.: Princeton University Press, 1981.

Ernst, Carl W. *Sufism: An Essential Introduction to the Philosophy and Practice of the Mystical Tradition of Islam*. Boston: Shambhala, 1997.

Hallaq, Wael B. *A History of Islamic Legal Theories*. Cambridge, U.K.: Cambridge University Press, 1997.

Hawting, G. R. *The First Dynasty of Islam: The Umayyad Caliphate AD 661–750*. London: Croom Helm, 1986.

Hodgson, Marshall G. S. *The Venture of Islam: Conscience and History in a World Civilization*. 3 vols. Chicago: University of Chicago Press, 1974.

Lapidus, Ira M. *A History of Islamic Societies*. 2nd ed. Cambridge, U.K.: Cambridge University Press, 1988.

Madelung, Wilferd. *Religious Trends in Early Islamic Iran*. Albany, N.Y.: Bibliotheca Persia, 1988.

———. *The Succession to Muhammad: A Study of the Early Caliphate*. Cambridge, U.K.: Cambridge University Press, 1997.

Morony, Michael G. *Iraq After the Muslim Conquest*. Princeton, N.J.: Princeton University Press, 1984.

Murata, Sachiko, and William C. Chittick. *Vision of Islam*. New York: Paragon House, 1994.

Renard, John. *Seven Doors to Islam: Spirituality and the Religious Life of Muslims*. Berkeley: University of California Press, 1996.

Taylor, Christopher S. *In the Vicinity of the Righteous: Ziyara and the Veneration of Muslim Saints in Medieval Egypt*. Leiden, Netherlands: Brill, 1999.

Watt, W. Montgomery. *The Formative Period of Islamic Thought*. Oxford: Oneworld, 1998.

*Christopher S. Taylor*

# ISLAMIC SCIENCE.

History of science in non-Western societies is often either disregarded—because it is not linked with that in Western societies—or disfigured into a member of a chain of transmission that links antiquity with Latin Christendom. Rather than attempt to fit Islamic science into the history or notions of Western science, this essay examines the relationships between various scientific disciplines in Islamic societies and other intellectual, cultural, and social fields in these societies. The word *science/s* is used as a rendition of the Arabic plural *'ulum* of *'ilm* because in many historical sources this plural designates a group of scholarly disciplines (religious, philological, philosophical, mathematical). The singular alone often stands for religious knowledge. In combination with a qualifier, for instance *hisab* (calculation) or *nujum* (stars), it names particular scholarly disciplines—for example, arithmetic or astronomy. The survey is divided into three parts that demarcate important shifts and changes in the history of science in Islamic societies: the mid-eighth to the eleventh centuries; the twelfth to the mid-fifteenth centuries; and the mid-fifteenth to the nineteenth centuries.

## Mid-Eighth to the Eleventh Centuries

Healers with some kind of hospital training and adepts of alchemy were already active in the time of the Prophet and under the Umayyad dynasty (661–750) of Damascus. The earliest preserved fragments of and references to Arabic astronomical and astrological texts are from 679 and 735. Historians of science, medicine, and philosophy, however, disagree as to whether all writings ascribed to the alchemist and Sufi Jabir ibn Hayyan (c. 721–c. 815) were indeed his own or rather composed by later authors.

***Translation movement.*** The major breakthrough as far as philosophy and the ancient sciences are concerned occurred from the mid-eighth to the first third of the ninth centuries under the Abbasid dynasty (750–1258). During these decades, the extraordinary "translation movement" started and gained solid footing. The movement covered different kinds of scholarly heritage (Iranian, Indian, Byzantine, Hellenistic, Hellenic) whose transfer into Arabic flourished over different periods.

Translations were a major aspect of scholarly culture in several Islamic societies until the early eleventh century. Previous scholarship saw the reasons for this movement primarily in practical needs of physicians, astrologers, and patrons as well as in an intellectual superiority of the non-Muslim communities that persuaded the Muslims to acquire their knowledge and standards of debate. Dmitri Gutas proposes a different view in *Greek Thought, Arabic Culture* (1998). He points to the suppression of intellectual activities in the centers of the Byzantine Empire after the sixth century and the preservation of the heritage among persecuted and marginalized Christian minorities, whose status and liberty of movement changed drastically after the conquest of their lands by Arab Muslim armies. The second factor Gutas emphasizes is the need for legitimacy-creating measures by Abbasid caliphs at two points of their dynastic history (after 750 when they had successfully conquered the Umayyad empire and after 819 when al-Ma'mun decided to return to Baghdad after his successful overthrow of his brother, the caliph al-Amin in 813). In both instances, Gutas believes, the two caliphs, al-Mansur (r. 754–775) and al-Ma'mun (r. 813–833), chose to implement a cultural politics that favored translations of foreign knowledge. In the case of al-Mansur the emphasis was on Persian knowledge, although the caliph had already commissioned the acquisition of Greek scientific manuscripts, while in the case of al-Ma'mun the translation of Greek texts was primary. The purpose of this politics was to lend al-Mansur the legitimizing aura of Sassanian royalty and to bind his Persian allies more closely to his rule. Al-Ma'mun, on the other hand, strove to foster the alliances he deemed necessary by means of devaluating the reputation of the only surviving pre-Islamic enemy of substantial power, Byzantium, and hence this enemy's right to claim imperial rule in the Mediterranean world.

***Astrologers and physicians.*** The first known scholars of the Abbasid court were astrologers and physicians, mostly from western Persia. They lent their expertise for determining the auspicious day for building Baghdad in 762 and for treating sick caliphs and their wives. They calculated horoscopes and composed astrological histories. They were the first translators mostly of Pahlavi (a group of Iranian languages and dialects used from 300 B.C.E. and 900 C.E.) but also of some Greek and Syriac texts on astrology, logic, medicine, astronomy, mathematics, ethics, and wisdom sayings.

Descendants of Byzantine nobles, clergymen of various Orthodox churches in Mesopotamia (present-day Iraq) and Syria, and members of the Sabian communities of northern Mesopotamia began to participate in these translations during the later decades of the eighth century. Until the end of the ninth century, many books were translated twice, or even three times, because of conflicting approaches to what constituted a good translation and what or who mattered more—language or scientific content, the author or the translator. These translations were executed and interpreted within the set of ideas and practices that developed during the eighth and the early ninth centuries. An example is Qusta ibn Luqaal-Ba'labakki's (fl. 860–900) rendering of Diophantes' number theory in the technical language of algebra found in the book of Abu Ja'far Muhammad ibn Musa Al-Khwarizmi (fl. c. 780–840). On the other hand, the translations were a major component of a process that transformed the set of earlier ideas and practices into new, often hybrid forms. An example is the combination of Indian and Ptolemaic concepts, methods, and parameters in astronomical handbooks of the so-called Sindhind tradition— that is, the tradition based indirectly on the *Brahma-sphuta-siddhanta* (628) by Brahmagupta (598–c. 665).

*Science at court.* From the ninth to the eleventh centuries, most students of the ancient sciences earned their living as scholars at courts, as itinerant scholars, and as merchants, or they lived from their family fortunes. Mathematicians were often either astrologers or physicians. Occasionally they also served as secretaries and historians. The social and cultural acceptance of the ancient sciences is expressed by the high ranks given to several leading scholars at various courts in the center of the Abbasid empire and its provinces. They acted as teachers of princes, table companions of caliphs and viziers, courtly ambassadors, and heads of delegations of city notables charged to negotiate credits, war, and peace with their feuding sovereigns. In the ninth century, they presented their scientific results as letters to princely students and viziers, as answers to friends and critics, as interpolations to and comments on translated pre-Islamic books, and as treatises that focused on a particular set of research questions. Cross-confessional cooperation was another major feature of scholarly life and applied to both scholars and patrons.

Beginning in the second half of the tenth century, new Islamic dynasties evolved inside and outside the Abbasid empire. This political, religious, and cultural diversification produced more possibilities for patronage and scholarship. Scientists introduced new forms of communication, such as the exchange of letters between scholars in far away towns through riding messengers. Long-distance cooperation also included shared research activities, such as observations of eclipses. The mobility of scientists increased too. They wandered between regions as far away as modern Uzbekistan and Syria and worked at several courts and for different patrons.

The new forms of scholarly life spread the sciences over the large territories of the Islamic world and enabled other dynasties to formulate their own cultural politics. In al-Andalus on the Iberian Peninsula, for instance, the heirs of the only Umayyad prince who had survived the Abbasid massacre of his family supported scientific activities as part of their anti-Abbasid foreign politics. At their court, the relationship between the newly arriving sciences and the previously established Maliki branch of Sunni jurisprudence was tense. Since the early ninth century, poets, sponsored by the emirs, had espoused astrology disapproved by Maliki scholars. As Mònica Rius has shown, the conflicts between poets and jurists were not motivated solely by legal concepts of right and wrong but included power struggles, issues of reputation, and courtly politics. She believes that despite Maliki condemnations, astrology became an obligatory element in the courtly educational canon.

In the late tenth and early eleventh centuries, a new type of scholar emerged in Andalusia who taught parts of Maliki law together with number theory. Maslama ibn Ahmad al-Majriti (d. 1008) is the first known scholar of this group. He and his students recalculated, edited, modified, and criticized astronomical tables devised in Baghdad, in particular those by al-Khwarizmi and al-Battani (c. 858–929). Their successors, such as the judge Sa'id al-Andalusi (1029–1070) and his collaborator al-Zarqallu (c. 1030–1099), compiled and calculated new astronomical handbooks such as the Toledan Tables, the Alphonsine Tables, and many others. One of the multiple changes that these Andalusian scientists introduced was a new longitude of Cordoba, which shortened the Ptolemaic length of the Mediterranean Sea almost to its correct size. Other changes included theoretical and conceptual innovations such as cycles that regulate the obliquity of the ecliptic or a corrected Ptolemaic lunar model.

*Fine arts.* The ancient sciences and their proponents in Islamic societies also stimulated the fine arts. Illuminated Byzantine manuscripts on pharmacy, medicine, and mechanics as well as illustrated Sassanian historical books inspired the art of the book in Islamic societies. The first preserved illuminated Arabic manuscripts on medicine, pharmacology, astrology, astronomy, and natural history are from the twelfth and early thirteenth centuries. But astrologers of previous centuries, such as 'Abd al-Jalil al-Sijzi (c. 950–c. 1025) or 'Abd al-Rahman al-Sufi (903–998), already had persuaded central Asian and Persian princes to sponsor the scientific treatises and occasionally also their illumination.

*Philosophers and mathematicians.* The relationship between philosophers and mathematicians was rather strained during the ninth century, mainly due to the conflicts that raged between the philosopher al-Kindi (d. c. 870) and the three Banu Musa: Muhammad, Ahmad, and al-Hasan. The conflicts concerned questions of content and style as much as they revolved around issues of patronage, courtly power, and cultural superiority. Notwithstanding, a few mathematicians of the ninth century, such as Thabit ibn Qurrah (d. 901), wrote about philosophical subjects. Al-Kindi, as did philosophers in antiquity, applied Aristotelian notions to his discussions of mathematics. Other, anonymous writers strove to harmonize Euclid's (fl. c. 300 B.C.E.) geometry with Nicomachus of Gerasa's (fl. c. 100 C.E.) number theoretical philosophy by reinterpreting book 2 of the *Elements* as dealing with mixed arithmetical-geometrical objects (bricks) rather than lines and surfaces, which were in this view objects of a lower ontological status.

In the second half of the tenth and early eleventh centuries, things started to change. The Persian mathematician and astronomer Abu al-Wafa' al-Buzajani (940–998) lent his support to the secretary and philosopher Abu Hayyan al-Tawhidi (d. 1023) at the Buyid court in Baghdad. Ibn al-Haytham (965–1042) in Basra and Cairo and Omar Khayyám (1048–1131) in Balkh, Bukhara, and Samarkand engaged in serious philosophical study and writing.

*Science and religion.* The relationship between the ancient sciences and religious disciplines covered conceptual as well as practical aspects. In the eighth century, a newly emerging faction among the religious scholars, the Mu'tazilites, began to use mathematical and philosophical arguments in discussions of matter and movement. Representatives of Ash'ari kalam, founded against Mu'tazili doctrines in the early tenth century, participated in debates about number theory, physics, astronomy, and astrology and wrote about such themes. Mathematicians in the ninth century such as al-Khwarizmi tried to relate their fields of knowledge to religion. Opening his book on algebra by advertising the new discipline as an appropriate tool for merchants, he ended it with an exposé of algebraic solutions for legal problems. While this is usually seen as a further aspect of applied mathematics, it also reflects the mathematician's participation in the not-yet-finished process of codifying Abu Hanifa's (699–767) school of law. Anonymous readers of Euclid's *Elements* added to the definition of a solid in book 11 that "it is all that has a corpse" (*kull ma lahu juththa*), alluding to discussions of whether God was or had a body.

The cornerstone of the efforts to apply mathematics and astronomy to Muslim religious practice was to find the *qibla,* the direction toward Mecca, and to determine the prayer times. Ahmad b. 'Abdallah al-Marwazi called Habash al-Hasib (c. 770–c. 870), Abu l-'Abbas al-Fadl al-Nayrizi (d. c. 922), and al-Battani (c. 850–929) used methods such as the analemma of Hellenistic geometry to find exact solutions or spherical triangles and the Indian sine function to find approximate solutions. The visibility of the new moon and possibly the issue of the beginning of the world also belong in this context. Ibn al-Nadim ascribed a lost treatise touching on the latter question to Muhammad (d. 872), the eldest of the Banu Musa.

*Mathematicians, astronomers, and astrologers.* Mathematicians, astronomers, and astrologers held different views about what was important, valuable, and feasible in their disciplines. Thabit ibn Qurrah interpreted al-Khwarizmi's algebra in terms of book 2 of Euclid's *Elements* on particular geometrical constructions. Al-Karaji (d. c. 1030), like Thabit ibn Qurrah, placed geometry over algebra because he regarded it as the science that guaranteed certain knowledge. Al-Hasan ibn Musa (d. after 870) was accused of inventing solutions to mathematical problems without having done what was proper—reading all books of the *Elements.* Ibrahim b. Sinan (908–946, a grandson of Thabit ibn Qurrah), Abu Sahl al-Kuhi (tenth–eleventh centuries), al-Sijzi, Abu l-Jud b. al-Layth (tenth–eleventh centuries), al-Biruni (973–1048), and others struggled with one another about the appropriate methods for

solving difficult mathematical problems and the deficiencies of certain forms of analysis and synthesis, two major geometrical methods since antiquity.

The sharp debates that surrounded the twin disciplines of astronomy and astrology ranged from the two standard challenges of lacking reliability and religious heterodoxy to the kinds of philosophical foundations necessary for a well-functioning astrology, the appropriate demonstrative methods, and the relationship to astronomy. George Saliba argues that these debates motivated astronomers in the ninth century to set up a new kind of astronomy or mathematical cosmography, *'ilm al-hay'a,* that aimed at drawing clear fences between a mathematically sound discipline of the heavens and astrology (2002). Similarly, F. Jamil Ragep, who thinks that two different kinds of *'ilm al-hay'a* emerged, sees the more general type aiming at setting a mathematical science of the heavens apart from ancient *astronomia* or *'ilm al-nujum* (science of the stars) that included astrology. The other, more restricted project of *'ilm al-hay'a* evolved as a specific genre that strove to harmonize physical, that is, philosophical, principles and mathematical models of planetary movements and included the mathematical description of the earth (1993). As the works of Thabit ibn Qurrah and al-Hasan al-Nawbakht (d. c. 920) illustrate, a third realm of debate focused on Ptolemy's (second century C.E.) work and the various new astronomical tables, in particular the *Zij al-Mumtahan* (The corrected tables). These and other tables were calculated by al-Ma'mun's court astronomers Yahya b. Abi Mansur (d. c. 830), Khalid b. 'Abd al-Malik al-Marwarrudhi (first half of the ninth century), al-'Abbas al-Jawhari (first half of the ninth century), Habash al-Hasib, and others on the basis of astronomical observations. While Thabit ibn Qurrah explained and propagated specific theories and methods from Ptolemy's *Almagest,* he apparently held the "Corrected Tables" in less esteem.

David A. King, Julio Samsó, and B.R. Goldstein believe that the debates that surrounded and permeated the new tables caused the gradual elimination of Persian and Indian elements from Islamic astronomy in favor of Ptolemaic theory. The debates also led to the replacement of some Ptolemaic parameters such as the obliquity of the ecliptic by new observational results and to the abandonment of certain Ptolemaic beliefs, such as the immobility of the solar apogee or the impossibility of annular solar eclipses. Al-Hasan al-Nabawkht, in contrast, wrote a disputation against Ptolemy's planetary models as well as against the Platonic stance that the cosmos was a living, rational being. His rejection of Ptolemy and Plato may have been linked to his political-religious preference of the quietist Shia in opposition to the Shii revolutionary wing of the period, the Batiniyya.

*Major themes and achievements.* Major mathematical, astronomical, mechanical, and optical themes and achievements of these four centuries concern the gradual emergence of a new, distinctly Islamic trigonometry; the use of analysis and synthesis; the construction of the side of a regular heptagon; the study of conic sections; efforts to solve specific problems of number theory such as the so-called theorem of Fermat; the creation of a geometrical as well as a numerical theory of cubic equations; the determination of centers of gravity as well as of specific weights; the study of the law of the lever and the construction of balances; the introduction of a new theory of seeing, reflection, and refraction; the interpretation of the moon's light; the construction of burning mirrors; and the physical foundation of mathematical astronomy. This vibrant pursuit of theoretical themes fostered an atmosphere in which claims to invention, innovation, and novelty thrived. Experimentation was regarded as a means to achieve new insights and build new theories. Ibn al-Haytham carried out experiments for solving optical questions, for deciding between alternative explanatory approaches, and for modeling astronomical processes. Abu Sahl al-Kuhi used thought experiments for finding new results for geometrical questions related to mechanics. Criticizing predecessors and compatriots was a favored stylistic means to establish credibility and claims to priority and to propagate new results.

Parallel to the attention directed toward theoretical aspects of science, much work went into practical fields such as calculating calendars and horoscopes; determining geographical coordinates; teaching the basics for calculating exchange rates, wages, business transactions, and the hire of labor; surveying fields and properties; and determining surfaces and volumes used in architecture and for ornamental decorations. Leading mathematicians such as Abu al-Wafa and Ibn al-Haytham wrote about these practical subjects, as did a number of religious scholars, such as the founder of the Ash'ari kalam, Abu al-Hasan 'Ali al-Ash'ari (873 or 874–935 or 936) and his eminent follower 'Abd al-Qahir al-Baghdadi (d. 1038). The two mathematicians also contributed to the new field of magic squares—that is, squares filled with numbers in a way that the sum of each column equals the sum of each row as well as each diagonal. Abu l-Wafa', Ibn al-Haytham, and later writers created methods for constructing pair and impair magic squares of higher order, partitioned magic squares, or bordered magic squares. Over the centuries, magic squares attracted the attention of scholars who were interested in mathematics as well as that of writers, mystics, artisans, sultans, military leaders, and ordinary people who applied magic squares—from the most elementary to the very large and fairly complex—to protect themselves from all sorts of misfortunes.

### Twelfth to Mid-Fifteenth Centuries

Substantial changes in the context of the sciences took place between the twelfth and the mid-fifteenth centuries. They resulted from the adoption of the *madrasa* (Muslim institution for higher education) as an appropriate means for achieving cultural, religious, legal, and social purposes by the Sunni Turkish and Kurdish dynasties of the Saljuqs, Zangids, Artuqids, and Ayyubids since the second half of the eleventh and during the twelfth century. Scholarly opinions about the place of the sciences and philosophy in this institution vary profoundly. Some such as George Makdisi argue that they were denied access to institutionalized teaching and could be at best taught privately, occasionally having even to go into hiding. Others, for example Seyyed Hossein Nasr, point to the integration of logic, philosophy, astronomy, arithmetic, and geometry into the Persian *madrasas*. They see this process as limited

to Persia. J. Lennart Berggren takes a middle position by stressing that certain parts of the mathematical sciences, such as elementary arithmetic and algebra, became fully integrated into the legal teaching. Several others have shown that in contrast to the belief in a religiously motivated marginalization of the sciences, new professional and disciplinary settings emerged that led to a flourishing high theory (planetary models), the invention and construction of new scientific instruments (new types of astrolabes, quadrants, and compounds with compasses), and a vigorous practice of solving astronomical problems central for Muslim religious ritual.

The new profession of the *muwaqqit* (timekeeper) focused on the mathematical and astronomical treatment of problems of religious ritual and on instruments. The *muwaqqits* were attached to mosques and *madrasas* mainly in Syria, Egypt, the Maghrib, Andalusia, and under the Ottomans also in Anatolia and the Balkans. The new disciplinary realm, that of the rational sciences, combined certain religious studies with some of the ancient sciences. In a gradual process, parts of logic, epistemology, metaphysics, physics, astronomy, and geometry were assimilated to kalam (rational theology), *usul al-din* (the fundaments of religion), and to a lesser extent to *usul al-fiqh* (the fundaments of law). The assimilation took place either by integrating these elements into the religious disciplines themselves or by teaching them together by the same professor to the same group of students.

The search for new planetary models that superseded those of Ptolemy and were the basis for the work of Nicolaus Copernicus (1473–1543) was almost exclusively sponsored through princely patronage until the thirteenth and early fourteenth centuries, when it experienced a new period of innovation through the works of Mu'ayyad al-Din al-'Urdi (d. 1260), Muhyi l-Din al-Maghribi (d. c. 1290), Nasir al-Din al-Tusi (1201–1274), and Qutb al-Din al-Shirazi (1236–1311). The Mongol adaptation of the *madrasa* to the needs of an itinerant court and the spreading inclination among religious scholars of southern Mesopotamia and western Persia to include in their education the study of philosophy and the mathematical sciences apparently led to the later integration of planetary models in the courses taught at Persian *madrasas* and in textbooks on kalam. As a result, major religious scholars from the fourteenth century onward also wrote on *'ilm al-hay'a* and contributed to improving the models.

As in the case of the *muwaqqit*, the discussions on astronomical theory did not spread over the entire Islamic world. They took place mainly in Persia between the thirteenth and the early sixteenth centuries with some extension to Anatolia, Syria, central Asia, and India, where it lasted occasionally until the eighteenth century. But parts of this theory, for instance the so-called Tusi-couple, spread to Byzantium and Andalusia, and among Jewish circles of southern France and Italy. The submission of large parts of Asia under Mongol rule in the second half of the thirteenth and the first third of the fourteenth century ensured a vivacious exchange of scientific texts, instruments, and methods between the Islamic east and China. Texts on medicine, agriculture, and astronomy were translated either into Persian or into Chinese and commented on in

Uighur and Tibetan. Chinese tables based on Islamic ancestors were discussed and modified in Korea.

## Mid-Fifteenth to Nineteenth Centuries

Between the late fourteenth and the early sixteenth centuries, the geographical, political, ethnic, religious, and cultural properties of the Islamic world underwent new, profound changes. Andalusia was gradually lost to invading Christian forces. New, powerful dynasties rose in central Asia (Timurids), Anatolia, Greece, and the Balkans (Ottomans), Persia (Safavids), and north and central India (Mughals). Merchants carried Islam farther east to Sumatra, Java, Bali, and the Philippines. The new imperial dynasties and several smaller Muslim Indian dynasties built their own intellectual landscapes by translating Arabic scientific, geographical, philosophical, historical, literary, and religious texts into Persian and Turkish, Persian texts into Turkish and Sanskrit, and Sanskrit texts into Persian. They sponsored new artistic programs of illuminated works on natural history, astrology, astronomy, geography, history, and literature. Their scholars integrated in these emerging canons written, pictorial, and oral elements of the new sciences that evolved in the Renaissance and during the seventeenth century in Catholic and Protestant Europe. These cultural activities were linked with a conscious religious politics that often took recourse to philosophical concepts and debates. Parallel therewith, various efforts aimed to reform military and educational institutions, to introduce new technologies from Catholic and Protestant Europe, and to apply newly invented methods of observation and measurement to well-known disciplines such as geography and cartography.

Over several centuries, the processes of exchange went in multiple directions, linking the various Islamic societies with one another and with several countries in Christian Europe. Alliances between Christian and Muslim rulers against their immediate enemies, whether Christian or Muslim, were the norm rather than the exception, as was the hiring of scholars, mostly physicians, of different religious creed at the courts in Fez, Istanbul, Agra, or Hyderabad. Colonial expansion of Portugal, Great Britain, the United Provinces of the Netherlands, France, and Russia at different moments in time determined the form and the content of the alliances, not only with respect to weapons, fortress building, military strategy and tactic, and trade but also with regard to scholarly travel, cartographic measurements, astronomical observations, hiring of foreign professors, founding of new teaching institutions—meant first to complement the older educational system and later to replace it—and the creation of botanical gardens. British, French, and Russian colonial supremacy in the nineteenth century, while pursuing different objectives and politics, finally led to the abolishment of Islamic scholarly institutions and knowledge in most of India, central Asia, and northern Africa and to its replacement by those of the colonizers.

*See also* **Communication of Ideas: Middle East and Abroad; Education: Islamic Education; Islam; Mathematics; Religion: Middle East; Religion and Science; Science.**

## BIBLIOGRAPHY

Berggren, J. Lennart. "Islamic Acquisition of Foreign Sciences: A Cultural Perspective." In *Tradition, Transmission, Transformation: Proceedings of Two Conferences on Pre-Modern Science Held at the University of Oklahoma*, edited by F. Jamil Ragep and Sally P. Ragep with Steven Livesey, 263–284. Leiden, Netherlands, and New York: Brill, 1996.

Brentjes, Sonja. "On the Location of the Ancient or 'Rational' Sciences in Muslim Educational Landscapes (AH 500–1100)." *Bulletin of the Royal Institute for Inter-Faith Studies* 4, no. 1 (2002): 47–72.

Dhanani, Alnoor. *The Physical Theory of Kalām: Atoms, Space, and Void in Basrian Mu'tazili Cosmology.* Leiden, Netherlands, and New York: Brill, 1994.

Gutas, Dimitri. *Greek Thought, Arabic Culture: The Graeco-Arabic Translation Movement in Baghdad and Early 'Abbasid Society (2nd–4th/8th–10th centuries).* London and New York: Routledge, 1998.

Haq, Nomanul. *Names, Natures and Things: The Alchemist Jābir ibn Hayyān and his Kitāb al-Ahjār* (Book of stones). Dordrecht Netherlands, and Boston: Kluwer 1994.

King, David A. *In Synchrony with the Heavens: Studies in Astronomical Timekeeping and Instrumentation in Medieval Islamic Civilization.* Vol. 1, *The Call of the Muezzin.* Leiden, Netherlands, and Boston: Brill, 2004.

———. "On the Role of the Muezzin and the *Muwaqqit* in Medieval Islamic Society." In *Tradition, Transmission, Transformation: Proceedings of Two Conferences on Pre-Modern Science Held at the University of Oklahoma*, edited by F. Jamil Ragep and Sally P. Ragep with Steven Livesey, 285–346. Leiden, Netherlands, and New York: Brill, 1996.

King, David A., Julio Samsó, and B. R. Goldstein. "Astronomical Handbooks and Tables from the Islamic World (750–1900): An Interim Report." *Suhayl, Journal for the History of the Exact and Natural Sciences in Islamic Civilisation* 2 (2001): 9–105.

Langermann, Y. Tzvi. "Medieval Hebrew Texts on the Quadrature of the Lune." *Historia Mathematica* 23 (1966): 31–53.

Makdisi, George. *The Rise of Colleges: Institutions of Learning in Islam and the West.* Edinburgh: Edinburgh University Press, 1981.

Nasr, Seyyed Hossein, and Oliver Leaman, eds. *History of Islamic Philosophy.* London and New York: Routledge, 1996.

Ragep, F. Jamil. "Freeing Astronomy from Philosophy: An Aspect of Islamic Influence on Science." *Osiris* 16 (2001): 49–71.

Ragep, F. Jamil, ed. "Nasīr al-Dīn al-Tūsī's Memoir on Astronomy (al-Tadhkira fī 'ilm al-hay')." In *Sources in the History of Mathematics and Physical Sciences* 12, edited by G. J. Toomer. 2 vols. New York: Springer-Verlag, 1993.

Sabra, Abd al-Hamid I. "The Appropriation and Subsequent Naturalization of Greek Science in Medieval Islam: A Preliminary Report." *History of Science* 25 (1987): 223–243. Reprinted in *Tradition, Transmission, Transformation: Proceedings of Two Conferences on Pre-Modern Science Held at the University of Oklahoma*, edited by F. Jamil Ragep and Sally P. Ragep with Steven Livesey, 3–27. Leiden, Netherlands, and New York: Brill, 1996.

———. "Science and Philosophy in Medieval Islamic Philosophy: The Evidence of the Fourteenth Century." *Zeitschrift für Geschichte der arabisch-islamischen Wissenschaften* 9 (1994): 1–42.

Saliba, George. *A History of Arabic Astronomy: Planetary Theories during the Golden Age of Islam.* New York: New York University Press, 1994.

———. "Islamic Astronomy in Context: Attacks on Astrology and the Rise of the *Hay'a* Tradition." *Bulletin of the Royal Institute for Inter-Faith Studies* 4, no.1 (2002): 25–46.

van Dalen, Benno. "Islamic Science and Chinese Astronomy under the Mongols: A Little-Known Case of Transmission." In *From China to Paris: 2000 Years Transmission of Mathematical Ideas,* edited by Yvonne Dold Samplonious, Joseph W. Dauben, Menso Folkerts, and Benno van Dalen, 327–356. Stuttgart, Germany: Frans Steiner Verlag, 2002.

*Sonja Brentjes*

# J

**JAINISM.** Famous for its promotion of nonviolence and often paired with Buddhism as one of ancient India's two greatest dissenting religions, Jainism is currently professed by roughly 0.4 percent of the population of India. Its adherents are prominent in business, and some of modern India's wealthiest and most powerful families are Jains. Jain communities are divided between a majority of lay men and women and a much smaller mendicant elite of peripatetic monks and nuns. The mendicants are a source of teaching and blessings for the laity, who in turn supply them with food and other forms of support. A disagreement over monastic discipline underlies the division between Jainism's two main sects: the *Shvetambaras* (white-clad), whose monks and nuns wear white garments, and the *Digambaras* (space-clad), whose monks wear no clothing.

## Origin

Jainism first emerged into historical visibility in the sixth century B.C.E. when it was one among many religious movements of the period that stressed world renunciation and rejected the religious culture and ritualism of the Brahman priestly class. Western scholars often single out Mahavira (who lived, according to *Shvetambara* tradition, from c. 599–527 B.C.E.) as Jainism's founder. The Jains, however, maintain that Jainism's teachings are eternal and uncreated, and consider Mahavira to have been only the most recent of an infinite series of great Jain teachers. In fact, although Jainism's roots predate Mahavira, he played a key role in defining doctrines and practices that became central to Jainism as it evolved. Viable monastic communities with lay followings formed and grew after Mahavira's death. Patronized mainly by newly emerging urban classes (especially merchants) Jainism spread in two directions from its region of origin in the Ganges River basin: down India's eastern coast into the south and westward in the direction of Mathura. The division between the *Svetambaras* and *Digambaras* crystallized in the fifth century C.E. The south ultimately became the heartland of the *Digambaras;* there they flourished and found royal patronage, especially in Karnataka. The *Shvetambaras* became prominent in the west, especially in what is now Gujarat and Rajasthan.

## Canonical Texts

Although their soteriological beliefs are basically the same, the *Shvetambaras* and *Digambaras* possess separate bodies of scripture. All Jains believe that their most ancient scriptures, known as the *Purvas,* have been lost, and that existing texts represent only a remnant of Mahavira's actual teachings. The *Shvetambara* canon, usually said to consist of forty-five texts, probably assumed its present form in the fifth century C.E. Its most important texts are the twelve *Angas* (or limbs, one of which has been lost) and twelve *Upangas* (subsidiary limbs); they deal with a vast range of subjects, including doctrine, monastic discipline, duties of the laity, cosmography, and much else. The *Digambaras* reject the *Shvetambara* canon as inauthentic. Their most important texts, each containing material on the soul and the nature of its bondage, are two: the *Shatkhandagam* (Scripture in Six Parts), dating from the second century C.E., and a slightly later work entitled *Kasayaprabhata* (Treatise on the Passions).

## Doctrine

The term Jain (in Sanskrit, *Jaina*) means someone who venerates the *jinas. Jina* (conqueror) in this context refers to one who, by conquering desires and aversions, achieves liberation from the bondage of worldly existence. Achieving such liberation is the object of Jain belief and practice.

Jains believe that the cosmos contains an infinite number of immaterial and indestructible souls (*jivas*). In common with other Indic traditions, the Jains also believe that each soul is reborn after death, and that the type of body it inhabits depends on the moral character of its deeds in past lives. According to Jainism, souls exist in every cranny of the cosmos: they inhabit the bodies of deities, humans, the inhabitants of hell, and plants and animals, and are also present in earth, water, fire, and air. Because the cosmos was never created, each soul has been wandering from one embodied state to another from beginningless time, and will continue to do so for infinite time to come unless it achieves liberation.

The cause of the soul's bondage is karma (action), which in other Indic religious traditions refers to the process by which one's good or bad acts give rise to consequences to be experienced in one's present or subsequent lives. The Jains, however, maintain that karma is an actual material substance (often likened to a kind of dust) that pervades the cosmos; it adheres to the soul, and the encumbrance of accumulated karmic matter is responsible for the soul's continuing rebirth. Karmic matter is drawn toward the soul by volitional actions, and its adhesion to the soul is a consequence of the emotional state of the actor. The passions, especially those of desire and aversion, create a moisture-like stickiness that causes karmic matter to build up on the soul.

To achieve liberation, therefore, one must avoid attracting more karmic matter and shed one's already existing accumulations. This is a complex and arduous process that begins with the awakening of faith in Jain teachings and ends with the removal of the last vestiges of the soul's burden of karmic matter. The liberated soul then rises to the abode of liberated souls at the top of the cosmos, where it will exist for all of endless time to come in a condition of omniscient bliss.

Avoiding violence is essential to one's progress toward liberation. Because violent actions are associated with the passions that contribute to the influx and adhesion of karmic matter, Jains are strongly committed to nonviolence (*ahimsa*). At a minimum, Jains should be vegetarian. Observant Jains avoid even vegetarian foods deemed to involve excessive violence in their acquisition or preparation. Root vegetables such as potatoes are proscribed because they are believed to contain multiple souls. Such restrictions are most onerous for monks and nuns who are debarred from activities that run the risk of harming even the humblest and most microscopic of living things. Lay Jains have been attracted to business precisely because buying, selling, and banking are activities that do not involve physical violence.

Ascetic practice is also essential to the attainment of liberation. Often likened to a fire that burns away karmic matter, ascetic practice subdues harmful passions that bring about the influx and adhesion of karmic matter and removes already existing karmic accumulations. Jain mendicants are renowned for the severity of their asceticism, and even lay Jains are expected to engage in periodic fasts and other ascetic practices.

The Jains maintain that the truth of their beliefs is guaranteed by the omniscience of their teachers. Known as *tirthankaras* ("ford-makers") or *jinas,* they are human beings who attained omniscience by their own efforts and without the guidance of other teachers, and who, before becoming fully liberated, imparted liberating knowledge to others. The Jains maintain that our section of the cosmos is subject to an eternally repeating cycle of world improvement and decline. Each ascent and descent is immensely long, and in each cycle exactly twenty-four *tirthankaras* successively appear. We are currently nearing the end of a descending era, and Mahavira was the twenty-fourth and hence the final *tirthankara* of our era and part of the cosmos. No new *tirthankaras* will appear until the next ascending period.

The concept of omniscience, seen as a natural quality of the soul when unoccluded by karmic matter, underlies Jainism's celebrated doctrine of epistemological relativity. Known as *syadvad* (the doctrine of "may be"), it holds that in contrast with omniscient knowledge, which incorporates all points of view simultaneously, ordinary knowledge discloses only partial glimpses of reality.

## Contemporary Jainism

Although it was once a proselytizing religion and continues vigorously to promote vegetarianism and animal welfare, Jainism has become a religion into which one is born by virtue of birth in a particular family, lineage, or caste. The castes to which Jains belong are typically merchant castes, although there are many Jains in other occupations, including agriculture. The Jains cannot be said to constitute a single community. Even in situations where they live in close proximity,

relations between *Shvetambaras* and *Digambaras* are usually minimal because they belong to different castes, and are frequently adversarial, especially because of disputes over control of sacred sites claimed by both sects.

A major recent development in Jainism is the emergence of a diaspora-based religious subculture. The spread of Jainism beyond the subcontinent has been inhibited historically by the requirement that monks and nuns travel only on foot, but in recent times the number of Jains living outside India has risen to around 100,000, most of whom live in North America, Great Britain, and Africa. The difficulty of practicing Jainism in the traditional way abroad has led to a weakening of sectarian differences. It has also given rise to a tendency to stress the contemporary relevance of Jainism by downplaying traditional soteriology and capitalizing on Jainism's emphasis on nonviolence and vegetarianism by recasting the tradition in an eco-religious and environmentalist mold.

*See also* **Asceticism: Hindu and Buddhist Asceticism; Buddhism; Heaven and Hell (Asian Focus); Hinduism; Immortality and the Afterlife; Nonviolence.**

**BIBLIOGRAPHY**

Babb, Lawrence A. *Absent Lord: Ascetics and Kings in a Jain Ritual Culture.* Berkeley: University of California Press, 1996.

Banks, Marcus. *Organizing Jainism in India and England.* Oxford: Clarendon, 1992.

Carrithers, Michael, and Caroline Humphrey, eds. *The Assembly of Listeners: Jains in Society.* Cambridge, U.K.: Cambridge University Press, 1991.

Cort, John E. *Jains in the World: Religious Values and Ideology in India.* New York: Oxford University Press, 2001.

Dundas, Paul. *The Jains.* 2nd ed. London: Routledge, 2002. A comprehensive overview of Jainism and an excellent introduction to the subject.

Jaini, Padmanabh S. *The Jaina Path of Purification.* Berkeley: University of California Press, 1979. The standard general study of Jainism.

Laidlaw, James. *Riches and Renunciation: Religion, Economy, and Society among the Jains.* Oxford: Oxford University Press, 1995.

*Lawrence A. Babb*

# JAPANESE PHILOSOPHY, JAPANESE THOUGHT.

To write about Japanese intellectual history is to take part in the lasting Japanese scholarly tradition of recalling the past in order to make sense out of the present, that is, the writing of Japanese history. These histories, official or nonofficial, are structured around key ideas reflecting the intellectual life of a particular period. Constituting a rational effort at legitimizing the power of the elites, these histories also have a more reflective and critical dimension offering insights about the social, political, and religious dimensions of a particular period. What becomes clear through these histories is that Japanese identity is rooted in the construction of a virtual "other" source of fear and admiration. That "other," whether it is China, the West, or the United States, serves as an incentive to the construction of a Japanese "self." The Japanese "self" is not the result of an imitation or a reproduction of an exterior model, but the result of a long and painful interior process of realizing that what is idealized in the "other" is in fact the essence of Japanese culture. For example, the *Kojiki* (712 C.E.; Record of ancient matters) and the more voluminous *Nihon shoki* (720 C.E.; Chronicles of Japan), expose the prestigious genealogy of the leaders of the Japanese kingdom. These historical records were created after encountering Chinese culture and are meaningful as long as they can be contrasted with Chinese historical records. The sense of excellence and uniqueness emphasized by these histories is not exclusivist or isolationist but relational and agonistic. When later on during the twentieth century the "other" became the "West," historians forged the image of a Japanese "self" as a model of Asian civilization, rivaling the Western one.

From the short-term horizon of the Heisei era (the name *Heisei,* meaning "peace everywhere," was introduced in 1989 by the emperor Akihito after the death of his father, the emperor Showa [Hirohito]), the other is still the West and more precisely the West as an idealized United States. However, a strong conviction that it is time for Japan to establish a new order has surfaced in the early twenty-first century through the traditional and symbolic call for reformation (Jap. *kaizo* or *kaikaku*).

All levels of twenty-first-century Japanese society are affected by a confused but real desire for reform. Still, one has difficulties in grasping what precisely are the key ideas that would guide the effort toward the building of a new Japanese identity. The Heisei era is one of paradoxes and uncertainties generated by a long-lasting economic crisis, a lack of leadership, a sense of insecurity, a loss of moral and religious incentives, and above all a younger generation that values impermanence (*mujo*). In that context, education and new means of communication are calling back to memory aspects of the Japanese past. Under the initiative of the Ministry of Education, new history textbooks have been written, but they are the object of continuing controversies. Replacing the traditional *monogatari* (romantic tales), novels, comic books, and movies nourish a popular taste for what is exotic and perceived as unique in the Japanese past, that is, geomancy (*onmyodo*), romantic tales, and biographies of religious leaders. The weakening of political, academic, and scientific authority as well as the discrediting of leftist revolutionary ideals have reopened the debate on Japanese culture. The Japan of the Heisei era is experiencing a postcolonial, postwar, post-Marxist, postmodern phase. After the aborted attempts to restore the intellectual tendencies characterized by the theorization on "Japaneseness" (*Nihonjin ron*), the intellectual discourse has shifted to the notion of "belonging": how does one belong to Japan? What has probably been underestimated about twenty-first-century Japanese thought is the effect the new concept of globalization has had on the Japanese imagination. This concept is in fact very disorienting because it radically transforms the perception of space and renews the reflection on belonging. Globalization does not seem to be compatible with the establishment of a virtual other, reopening the questioning about what makes one Japanese.

## The Production of Thought: Writing as Philosophy

When the Silk Road and other trade roads were flourishing, when the Han Empire and the Korean kingdoms entertained relations with the emerging Yamato kingdom, not only goods and ideas, but also a new means of communication—the Chinese writing system—reached the Japanese islands. The mastering of reading and writing Chinese characters gave to the populations living on the Japanese islands a new conception of space and time: educated Japanese could now belong to the vast thinking network that had brought together Indian, Chinese, and many other inspiring cultural centers. A few hundred years later, the *Utsuho monogatari* (976–983) mentions for the first time the word *kana* (provisional names) to speak about a writing system derived from *mana* (perfected names), that is, the original Chinese characters. The invention of the kana writing system was interpreted during the Edo era (1600–1867) and up to twenty-first-century Japan as a symbol of Japanese cultural unity, independence, and superiority. Some twenty-first-century scholarship has criticized such an approach and offers new readings of Heian creativity. These new studies tend to emphasize hybridity and hierarchy as the key factors involved in the formation of the classical Japanese community. The kana system has never been a mere tool to transcribe phonemes and was never really thought of as independent from the *mana* system. These studies underline the importance of looking at the Japanese writing system as a whole entity ensuring the intelligibility of inscription. In brief, a study of Japanese thought requires an in-depth study of the working out of "philosophies of writing" shared by cultures using Chinese characters. From the Heian period (794–1185) up to contemporary Japan, Japanese have been using an ever-increasing variety of writing systems in order to preserve the intelligibility (not to be confused with clarity or efficiency) of written communication. The combination of Chinese characters, kana scripts, Sanskrit syllabary, and, later, the Western alphabet in the Japanese writing system is a constant reminder of the importance of inscription as a symbol of the complex correspondence between the social, political, and cosmological orders.

At the time of the formation of the Japanese writing system, the power and authority received through the mastering of the art of calligraphy gave to Heian scholars the possibility of uniting the social order of the kingdom with the cosmological order found in Buddhist texts. Furthermore, the reading of written works gave to Japanese scholars the sense that texts written in the past were the ultimate source of authority and perfection from which the present derived its legitimacy. Finally, written works gave access to Buddhist teachings, adding new figures such as Sanskrit letters to symbolize new types of associations.

## The Capital City as the Space of Thought Production

Originality, clarity, or imitation cannot serve as guiding ideas for studying Japanese thought in the first centuries of the Heian era. Japanese scholars are part of a network in which intellectuals of the past and present influence one another. Thinking insightfully is bound to a space of rivalry. This is why, very early on, the Japanese court organized carefully planned contests between its best intellectuals (Buddhists, Confucians, Nativists) for the production of an insightful intellectual space. Thus, from a Western perspective the modes of production of ideas in Japan are quite original. After the encounter with Chinese literature, one of the favored means of conceptualization became poetry. Even in the most philosophical commentaries on Buddhist teachings, poems appear in the text as unique and powerful modes of conceptualization. Later on, other written works combine poetry and prose and develop in the forms of popular tales. All these written works share in common an appeal to the senses of the readers. Ideas have to be embodied in order to be understood and to influence modes of life.

The production of ideas requires a space and that space is symbolized by the "capital city" (*miyako*). Protected from evil forces, that sacred and pure space allows the formation of the quintessence of Japanese thought. This is why a study of Japanese thought is bound to be a study of the representations of the city in general and of the capital city in particular. Heijo, Heian, Kamakura, Edo, Tokyo are not just names of capital cities but emblems of unique symbolic structures allowing the production of thought.

### Time as a Gift of Nature

Another important factor in the production of ideas in Japan is an element of stability assuring the basic structure of the understanding of time. The temperate climate of the islands with their five seasons (autumn, winter, spring, rainy, summer) generates a cyclical notion of time. Japanese poetry and literature created a rich set of symbols characterizing each one of the five seasons. The description of the passing of seasons and their return is associated with the Japanese landscape. Mountains, plains, and rivers change according to seasons and offer the senses a unique experience of time. Historical figures like the Buddha or Christ, the founding of the Japanese kingdom at a particular point in time, or important historical events have never structured the basic experience of time shared by the Japanese. Among the many symbols that are used to represent their experience of time, rice is definitely the most important. Rice appears as the symbol of an enduring identity, a "Japaneseness" that is not so much handmade but given by natural forces, that must be offered, eaten, or drunk in order to assure the communion among Japanese, including the sharing of thoughts.

### Periodization of Japanese Intellectual History

Japanese intellectual history can be roughly divided into four periods, Buddhism, Confucianism, the Western Canon, and the Heisei era. Each period is characterized by the production of a "virtual other" and a "canon."

*China and the Buddhist canon.* The Japanese inherited from the kingdoms of Korea and China a great variety of texts belonging to different traditions, namely, Confucian, Buddhist, and Daoist. However, during the first period of Japan's intellectual history, literati chose the sacred texts of Buddhism as the most authoritative. During that period the major centers of learning were Buddhist monasteries and the most influential thinkers were Buddhist monks. Buddhist teachings rely on

a common set of sutras that are used by all Mahayana traditions, the most important sutras being the Flower Garland (*Kegon*) and the Lotus (*Hoke*). The teaching of Buddhism also relied on a variety of Chinese commentaries, mainly those of late Mahayana (Mahyamika and Yogacara). One of the characteristics of Japanese Buddhism is that, while it is highly intellectual, it is also down to earth and often very practical, thus appealing not only to the literati but also to ordinary Japanese. Buddhist teachings are not confined to the highly sophisticated treatises produced by Kukai (774–835), who transmitted the Shingon tradition to the Japanese, or by the monks of the Tendai tradition. Works such as the *Nihonryoiki,* written by the Nara monk Kyokai in the early Heian period, spread Buddhist principles to ordinary Japanese. Contrary to what is often said, Buddhism did not wait until the Kamakura period (1185–1336) to become popular. Sophisticated and popular Buddhist works contributed to the harmonization of religious teachings and practices by incorporating former Japanese beliefs (*honjisuijakusetsu* and *ryobushinto*). Through the deeds and stories of the monks, Japanese as a whole took Buddhist cosmology—the theory of karma, the theory of the six worlds (*rokudo*), Buddhist piety, Buddhist architecture, and Buddhist rituals—as their norm. The study of the *Genji monogatari* (early 1000s C.E.; *Tale of Genji*), as well as other *monogatari* of the Heian period also show that Japanese writers used the concept of impermanence and instability (*mujo*) to characterize their perception of nature and society.

During the twelfth century, dissonant voices began to disturb the harmony of Heian society. The military were opposed to the rich and grandiose capital city of Kyoto and preferred the modest and rustic "tent government" (*bakufu*) of Kamakura. To the hierarchical distribution of the Heian system, a new age favoring the nonhierarchical and the provisional had succeeded. On the Buddhist side, dissident monks, most of them trained in the Tendai tradition, abandoned the traditional Buddhist centers to experiment with new forms of practices. Among many other Buddhist monks, Kakuban (1095–1143), Jien (1155–1225), Myoe (1173–1232), Honen (1133–1212), Shinran (1173–1262), Eisai (1141–1215), Dogen (1200–1253), and Nichiren (1222–1282) addressed—each one in a very creative way—the new concern that Buddhist teachings might have entered a period of decay (*mappo*). The rich debates affecting all the Buddhist traditions had remarkable effects on Japanese Buddhism. However, the Buddhist traditions were now offering such a variety of cosmologies, visions of the perfect society and understandings of the human, that Buddhist texts could no longer be the authoritative canon. After a short encounter with Western thought that accompanied the arrival of Jesuit missionaries, the Japanese literati constructed a new authoritative canon.

### China and Confucianism: Tokugawa Japan

Years of war and social chaos ended in the year 1600 at the battle of Sekigahara. The return of peace under the Tokugawa leadership opened a new era of intellectual creativity on the Japanese islands. The predominant concern of the Tokugawa elite was the maintenance of a peaceful and harmonious society; they emphasized human responsibility in the formation and maintenance of such a society. In order to achieve that goal, the intellectual discourse had to be rational, pragmatic, humanistic, and focused on social concerns. During the first Tokugawa century, the official discourse found inspiration in three intellectual traditions: Nativism (Shinto), Buddhism, and Confucianism. The new order drew its legitimization using insights from these three traditions, combining them in a very creative way. At the beginning of the Tokugawa era, a ruling class did not yet exist. Intellectuals were to create that virtuous ruling class of warriors, invent its new symbols, and sacralize the new order. While Buddhism and Shinto played an important role in creating a new "common sense" among peasants, craftsmen, and merchants for the legitimization of the warrior class hegemony, Confucianism produced a great variety of concepts to nourish the intellectual discourse of the elites. The genius of the Tokugawa leaders was to never name their organic intellectuals but use for their own advantage the insights of competing intellectual traditions in search of official recognition.

One of the characteristics of the new intellectual setting of the Tokugawa era was new developments in Confucian studies. Fujiwara Seika (1561–1619) and Hayashi Razan (1583–1657) were among the first Japanese intellectuals who presented Confucianism as a useful philosophical instrument for justifying the new Tokugawa policies. Over the centuries, the Japanese had received from China and Korea a variety of Confucian teachings. Japanese intellectuals of the early Tokugawa period began a process of critical analysis of the Confucian intellectual tradition. Through a process of selection and creation, they developed original types of teachings adapted to their cultural and social environment. Some of these Confucian scholars focused on human relationships of loyalty, cooperation, and obedience to superiors. Others offered the ethical incentives for the class of loyal and unselfish civil servants of the new era. Emphases on education, ceremonial, and tradition became a trademark of Confucian scholarship. Furthermore, the development of Confucian teachings included a severe criticism of Buddhism and Daoism as being too otherworldly, irrational, and opposed to Japanese tradition. Thus, Confucian scholars played an important role in the revival of Nativist or Shinto teachings. Other Confucian scholars like Nakae Toju (1608–1648) and Yamazaki Ansai (1618–1682) renewed Confucian teachings by emphasizing the importance of practicing Confucian virtues based on the notion of an "innate moral intuition" culminating in unique interpretations about the meaning of sincerity (*makoto*). The appropriate pedagogy for teaching Confucian moral virtues thus became an important theme of debate. Meanwhile, other intellectuals such as Yamaga Soko (1622–1685) defended the importance of Shinto as the only way for Japanese to put into practice the virtues that were so important to maintain the unity and peace of the kingdom. At the end of the seventeenth century, literati like Ogyu Sorai (1666–1728) criticized neo-Confucian interpretations. This marked a return to original Confucian teachings and offered the possibility to renew the reflection on virtues by abandoning relativist positions and by opening the search for eternal and natural virtues.

The critical analysis of Confucian canonical texts and the realization that the latest development in Confucian thinking might not be the most insightful, generated a movement of return to original texts that affected the entire intellectual landscape at the end of the seventeenth century. The School of Ancient Meaning (*Kogaku*) started by Ito Jinsai (1627–1705) focused on the direct study of the Confucian classics starting with the Analects. In parallel, the National Learning movement (*Kokugaku*), which specialized in the search for purely Japanese sources, unspoiled by Chinese influence, was inaugurated by Motoori Norinaga (1730–1801). This also opened a new reflection on Japaneseness around the key notions of human emotions: love, sorrow, longing, and regret. Motoori saw the superiority of Japanese thinking in the proper usage of emotions and sensibility.

In the eighteenth century, the debates between Confucian, Shinto, and Buddhist scholars were slowly corroded by the encounter with Western scholarship and the development of Dutch or Western learning (*Rangaku*). The growing awareness among many scholars of the suffering and poverty of ordinary people in Japan, the lack of medical progress, and the need for technical improvements, encouraged scholars to study what was seen at the time as the extraordinary achievement of Western scholarship. The growing skepticism toward the importance of Chinese learning came paradoxically from the reading of the Chinese translations of major Western authors and gave Japanese scholars their first incentive toward "modernization." These Chinese translations also exposed Japanese literati to Western philosophy.

## The West and the Western Canon: Meiji, Taisho, and Early Showa

During the nineteenth century, interest in Western rational discoveries and scientific and technological advances increased. The industrial revolution, which had led to radical political transformations and the formation of powerful and growing empires, became a source of inspiration for renewing Japanese institutions. Japan entered a phase of intense reflection on its own identity that served as the foundation for its modern intellectual history. This period is characterized by a tension between the "traditional" and the "modern" leading to the new beginnings of the Meiji era. Notions like civilization, enlightenment, progress, and success captured the imagination of a new generation of intellectuals. Western learning was no longer encountered through Chinese translations. The encounter was now without any intermediary, through attending classes taught by foreign scholars or by being sent to foreign universities. However, Japanese intellectuals found themselves in a paradoxical situation. On the one hand, they understood that without acquiring Western science and technology, Japan would become a colony of Europe the way China had become one. On the other hand, they wanted to protect Japanese identity and proclaim Japanese uniqueness and superiority. Debates about abandoning the Chinese script, about adopting one European language as the national one, and about making Christianity the national religion of a modern Japan, show how much the creative imagination of Japanese literati was again at work. With the Meiji era a turn to European philosophy began and the word *tetsugaku* was finally forged to mark the Japanese interest in that new discipline. The main centers for philosophical studies were the University of Tokyo and Kyoto University. Included among the most famous philosophers of the time were Kitaro Nishida (1870–1945), Hajime Tanabe (1885–1962), Keiji Nishitani (1900–1990), and Tetsuro Watsuji (1889–1960). The Japanese literati looked at Western philosophy as part of a larger whole including religion, science, and literature. For these four philosophers and also for most Japanese intellectuals, there was no antagonism between philosophy, religion, and Japanese culture. One of their important contributions is their reflection on the inner self. During the post–World War II period, questions about the involvement of Japanese thinkers in the support of imperialistic ideology shadowed the philosophical contributions of these philosophers. It is only very recently that intellectuals have shown a new interest in the first Japanese contributions to world philosophy. During the same period, in Buddhist circles, the philosophy of Georg Wilhelm Friedrich Hegel was actively studied in order to defend the position that Mahayana Buddhism, especially Kegon and Tendai, could serve as a bridge between Western and Eastern thought.

The defeat and the occupation of Japan by foreign troops inaugurated a new period of reflection, this time centered on repentance. In philosophical circles, thinkers like Hajime Tanabe reflected on collective responsibility, repentance, and the new opportunities the defeat was giving to the Japanese people. However, in the fall of 1945, a new Japan was just a potentiality, and fierce debates about what that new Japan should consist of centered on the notion of democracy. Most intellectuals turned to Marxism or Christianity in order to think about that new Japan, and they developed philosophies of action. The most fascinating contribution of the period is on "subjectivity" (*shutaisei*). The Korean War and later the Vietnam War gave a second occasion for Japanese intellectuals to clarify their position about war, violence, and peace. At the end of the 1950s, an awareness that Japan had been able to modernize its economy and society in a matter of a few decades and had entered a phase of Westernization was felt by many intellectuals. The following decades were characterized by a turn to economy. After a period of social conflict and agitation in the universities, Japan emerged as a model of economic success. Democratic Japan had become one of the strongest economies in the world and Japanese society was the focus of the attention of Western and other Asian countries. However, many intellectuals expressed their doubts that the economic miracle has been matched with a parallel cultural development. Japan had become rich and powerful but with what kind of soul?

**Toward a Post–U.S. and Postnormative Canon: The Heisei Era**

The Japan of the Heisei era has undergone a new period of inquiry in order to express what Japaneseness is about. The fact that many Japanese live a good part of their lives in foreign countries, that there are a growing number of Japanese children with a parent who does not have Japanese nationality, and the growing awareness that some parts of the non-Japanese population have lived in Japan for generations, are among the factors that generate some uneasiness when one attempts to define Japaneseness. Japan may have reached a period in its history where there is no longer the possibility of defining the self through an other such as China or the West. Japan may have entered a period that requires the creation of a "mythic Japan" as another source of creativity for constructing the Japanese self. In many ways, Japan has become foreign to itself, thus allowing the possibility for a completely new Japanese identity to emerge.

*See also* **Confucianism; Daoism; Education: Japan; Religion: East and Southeast Asia; Shinto.**

**BIBLIOGRAPHY**
Abe, Masao. *A Study of Dōgen: His Philosophy and Religion.* Edited by Steven Heine. Albany: State University of New York Press, 1992.
Bolcker, H. Gene, and Christopher I. Starling. *Japanese Philosophy.* Albany: State University of New York Press, 2001.
Breen, John, and Teeuwen Mark, eds. *Shinto in History: Ways of Kami.* Honolulu: University of Hawai'i Press, 2000.
Hakeda, Yoshito S., trans. *Kūkai: Major Works* New York: Columbia University Press, 1972.
Heisig, James W. *Philosophers of Nothingness: An Essay on the Kyoto School.* Honolulu: University of Hawai'i Press, 2001.
Inagaki, Hisao. *The Three Pure Land Sutras.* Kyoto: Nagata Bunshodo, 1994.
Jansen, Marius B. *The Making of Modern Japan.* Cambridge, Mass., and London: Harvard University Press, 2000.
Kasulis, Thomas P. *Intimacy or Integrity: Philosophy and Cultural Difference.* Honolulu: University of Hawai'i Press, 2002.
LaFleur, William R. *The Karma of Words: Buddhism and the Literary Arts in Medieval Japan.* Berkeley and London: University of California Press, 1983.
Lamarre, Thomas. *Uncovering Heian Japan: An Archaeology of Sensation and Inscription.* Durham, N.C., and London: Duke University Press, 2000.
Nelson, John K. *Enduring Identities: The Guise of Shinto in Contemporary Japan.* Honolulu: University of Hawai'i Press, 2000.
Nosco, Peter, ed. *Confucianism and Tokugawa Culture.* Princeton, N.J.: Princeton University Press, 1984.
Ohnuki-Tierney, Emiko. *Rice as Self: Japanese Identities Through Time.* Princeton, N.J.: Princeton University Press, 1993.
Payne, Richard K., ed. *Re-Visioning "Kamakura" Buddhism.* Honolulu: University of Hawai'i Press, 1998.
Tanabe, George J. *Myōe the Dreamkeeper: Fantasy and Knowledge in Early Kamakura Buddhism.* Cambridge, Mass.: Harvard University Press, 1992.
Tanabe, George J., Jr., and Willa Jane Tanabe, eds. *The Lotus Sutra in Japanese Culture.* Honolulu: University of Hawai'i Press, 1989.
Wakabayashi, Bob Tadashi, ed. *Modern Japanese Thought.* Cambridge, U.K.: Cambridge University Press, 1998.

*Thierry Jean Robouam*

**JIHAD.** *Jihad,* in Islam, is an idea of action. The Arabic word literally means "striving." When followed by the modifying phrase *fisabil Allah,* "in the path of God," or when this phrase is absent but assumed to be in force, *jihad* has the specific sense of fighting for the sake of God and religion. Other Arabic words are closely related in meaning and usage, including *ribat,* which also refers to a kind of building associated with ascetic and mystical gatherings.

Jihad refers first to a body of legal doctrine. The manuals of Islamic law all contain a section called "Book of Jihad" or something similar. Here is something like what Western jurisprudence calls *ius in bello,* law governing the conduct of war—declaration and cessation of hostilities, treatment of nonbelligerents, division of spoils, and so on. One also finds something like *ius ad bellum,* the right to enter a state of war. At the same time, however, jihad is more than a set of juridical principles. Historians must take it into account when they consider political mobilization and contested authority within many Islamic societies. Above all, jihad has never ceased changing, right down to our own day.

Jihad has both an external and an internal aspect. The external jihad is physical combat against real enemies. The internal or "greater" jihad is a struggle against the self in which one suppresses one's base desires and then, perhaps, rises to contemplation of higher truth. Most modern Western writing on the jihad considers the spiritualized combat of the internal jihad as secondary and derivative, despite all the importance it eventually acquired in Muslim thought and society. However, much of Muslim opinion in our day favors the opposite view.

## The Koran

Considered to be literally the word of God as conveyed to the world through the Prophet Muhammad (570?–632 C.E.), the Koran is the single most important source for the doctrine and practice of jihad. However, when one puts together the relevant passages of the Koran, one finds apparent contradictions or, at any rate, differences in emphasis. The many themes relating to fighting and jihad in the Koran include calls for self-restraint and patience in propagating the faith (16:125–128); permission to engage in defensive war (22:39–41); permission to wage in offensive war within certain traditional limits, including those of the ancient Arabian "holy months," during which fighting was suspended (2:194, 217); calling on the believers to "slay the idolaters wherever you find them," unless they "repent and perform the prayer and pay the alms," as in the famous "sword verse" (Koran 9:5; translation per Arberry 1:207); the requirement to subdue the "people of the Book," that is, Jews and Christians (Koran 9:29); evidence of internal tension and reluctance to fight (Koran 2:216; "Fighting has been prescribed for you, though you dislike it").

These themes are commonly related to a chronological narrative about the life of Muhammad and the earliest Islamic community. For many Islamic jurists, the principles that prevail are the ones associated with the later parts of this narrative. For example, at some point in the narrative God permits warfare, but only in limited circumstances. Afterward, when conditions have changed, God provides a new ruling that allows the conduct of warfare with fewer restrictions. In juridical terms, the later ruling abrogates or supersedes the earlier one. From the point of view of literary narrative, however, such chronological schemes encounter difficulties in the details of the Koranic text.

## Narratives

One finds sustained, connected narratives about the earliest Islam in Arabic books on Muhammad's life (called *sira,* "the way") and on the early community and its wars (called *maghazi,* "raids") as well as in works of Koranic exegesis and in the *hadith,* which one may define as reports of authoritative sayings and deeds attributed to the Prophet or to those around him. In the form in which they exist, these works date from the ninth century C.E. or later. Here one finds that the last part of Muhammad's life, after the Emigration (*Hijra*) from Mecca to Medina in 622, was devoted largely, though not entirely, to the conduct of war.

In year 2 of the Hijra (624), at a place called Badr, a raiding expedition turned into a full confrontation with Muhammad's kin and adversaries, the Quraysh of Mecca. Divine intervention came in the form of angels fighting on the Muslim side—this is how the *maghazi* narratives interpret several passages in the Koran regarding Badr, the first full battle of Islam and a great victory. Once Muhammad achieved final victory in his war against Mecca, he sent expeditions against Byzantine frontier defenses in the north, and he may have been planning an extensive campaign against Palestine and Syria. However, he died (in 632) before this campaign could get under way. The works of *sira* and *maghazi* place these narratives squarely in the foreground, providing a kind of salvation history (*Heilsgeschichte*). The *hadith,* by contrast, directs all eyes toward the Prophet, who, with epigrammatic precision, dictates the Example (*Sunna*) through his actions and words. Here one finds the doctrine of the jihad enunciated clearly, together with eloquent exhortations to perform jihad.

## Early Conquests

In the decades following Muhammad's death, the Arab Muslims conquered Arabia, Syria, Palestine, Iraq, Egypt, and Iran; Central Asia, North Africa, Spain, and other regions came soon afterward. Among the explanations for these successful conquests, an important point of difference involves the jihad. Were these conquests "Islamic" or "Arab"? According to the "Islamic" view, the Muslims fought because God commanded them to do so. They were motivated by neither fear nor greed but by a desire to propagate the faith. "Arab" explanations, on the other hand, which prevailed among Western specialists until fairly recently, looked at conditions in ancient Arabia. By the seventh century, it was thought, desiccation and desertification had reduced many of Arabia's centers of civilization to ruins; meanwhile the peninsula suffered from overpopulation. Inevitably the Arabs felt pressure to migrate, raid, or conquer. More recently others have emphasized the political aspects of the conquests. It is increasingly clear, however, that religion and jihad did take a major role.

## Martyrdom

Non-Muslim observers attributed the zeal of the Muslim fighters to the promise of heaven that the new religion made to those who died in battle. In the Koran those who die in combat in the path of God are "alive with God," enjoying the delights of paradise, which include marriage to dark-eyed maidens. The *hadith* and Islamic law declare that these dead warriors are martyrs. As in Christianity, the word *martyr* originally meant "witness" (Greek *martys,* Arabic *shahid*). However, there are differences. The Jewish and Christian martyr was passive and refused to employ violence. In Islam the martyr is one who takes up arms. Islamic law also recognized non-combatant types of martyrs. For Shii Islam, martyrdom is associated with the revered descendants of the Prophet through his daughter Fatima and his cousin and son-in-law 'Ali, many of whom died at the hands of oppressive (Muslim) rulers. For the Sunni majority, however, armed struggle has most often been at the heart of the concept of martyrdom.

## Treatment of Non-Muslims

Arabic sources for the early conquests report agreements between conquerors and conquered, including the famous "Pact of 'Umar." The "people of the Book" (who were eventually considered to include Zoroastrians in addition to Jews and Christians) are granted protection of their persons and property and are allowed to practice their religion with certain constraints. They must pay *jizya,* which at first meant a collective tribute but which soon referred to a poll tax levied on individuals and households, derived from Koran 9:29 ("Fight those who believe not in God and the Last Day and [who] do not forbid what God and His Messenger have forbidden—such men as practice not the religion of truth, being of those who have been given the Book—until they pay the tribute [*jizya*] out of hand and have been humbled") (translated by Arberry, 1:207).

Here are the foundations of the *dhimma,* the "protection" of non-Muslims who live under the rule of Islam. People living under this protection could not be enslaved and were free to pursue whatever professions they liked. However, non-Muslims living outside the lands of Islam could be and often were captured and enslaved. Forced conversion was not allowed, following a clear Koranic principle (2:256) and in fact happened only in exceptional instances. Islamic jurists represented the world as divided between an Abode of Islam (*Dar al-Islam*) and an Abode of War (*Dar al-Harb*). Since the only legitimate sovereign is God and the only legitimate form of rule is Islam, the rulers of the Abode of War are mere tyrants, and the normal state of affairs between the two abodes is war. The Muslim state—in classical theory its leader, the imam—may conclude a truce with those rulers for a maximum of ten years but not a permanent peace. Some jurists added an intermediate Abode of Truce, but this did not alter the territorial character of the doctrine of jihad. This doctrine does not aim at the immediate conversion of populations or individuals but rather at the extension of God's rule over all the world, until "the religion is God's entirely" (Koran 8:39).

## The Obligation of Jihad

Warfare and territorial expansion were a priority for the rulers of the early Islamic state. Soon, however, jurists raised the question of individual participation. Is jihad an obligation that each must perform to the best of his or her ability, like pilgrimage and daily prayer? There was broad consensus that volunteering for the armies was a meritorious act. From a practical, military point of view, however, these undisciplined volunteers could create more problems than they solved. In Islamic law

the problem was resolved in the doctrine of "obligation according to sufficiency," associated with the great jurist al-Shafi'i (767–820). This doctrine declares that the obligation of jihad may be considered fulfilled so long as a sufficient number of volunteers perform it. However, if a military emergency occurs and the enemy threatens the lands of Islam, then the obligation falls upon each individual.

Many people sought to participate in the jihad through residence in frontier regions and in fortified strongholds (often called ribats), whether for a limited period or for a lifetime. These included jurists, ascetics, mystics, and others in search of religious merit and knowledge, in addition to people seeking simply to fight the enemy. It is here, along Islam's many frontiers, that the jihad acquired its social expression. In many cases it is not known whether people were engaged in devotional practices, the transmission of learning, or combat or guard duty against the enemy. For many of them, jihad consisted precisely in the combination of all these. "Internal" and "external" jihad were thus always present. In this way the jihad was a basic element—social and political as well as rhetorical—in the rise and success of a long series of Islamic dynasties and states, including that of the Almoravids in Morocco and Spain in the eleventh and twelfth centuries, the Ottomans from the fourteenth century until the twentieth, and many more.

## Resistance and Reform

When the European colonial powers arrived in several Islamic countries in the nineteenth century, resistance against them involved the jihad and usually failed. When successful resistance eventually emerged, it was through secular, nationalist ideologies. Meanwhile Muslim thinkers in several countries took a new look at the jihad, seeking to make it compatible with what they saw as progress and modernity. A new body of juridical work defined the jihad as defensive warfare, while an "Islamic law of nations" presented the eighth-century al-Shaybani (750–803 or 805), an Islamic jurist who wrote a book of the law of war, on a par with the seventeenth-century Grotius. In this way the relations of Islamic and non-Islamic states became placed firmly on a basis of peace.

## Islamism and Fundamentalism

This recognition of the modern state infuriated certain other thinkers who declared their own societies to be Islamic in name only; in reality, they said, these societies lived in *jahiliyya,* coarse ignorance, the condition of ancient Arabia before the coming of Islam. They summoned all Muslims to the jihad, calling this an individual (not a collective) obligation because of the gravity of the situation. Unlike the modernist reformers, they had no qualms about "offensive" jihad, which one of their books, by Muhammad 'Abd al-Salam Farag, called "the neglected duty." However, they concentrated their fury against the modern Middle Eastern state rather than non-Muslim powers. After the assassination of President Anwar Sadat in October 1981, radicals were driven abroad or deep underground in Egypt and other countries.

The 1990s brought a new, international turn. Osama bin Laden's fatwas of 1996 and 1998 call upon Muslims to set aside the war against the corrupt regimes in their own countries to fight the common enemy. Like other radical Islamists of modern decades, bin Laden identified the enemy as a "Crusader–Zionist" alliance, but he singled out the leader of the alliance, the United States, for special attention. This new, global jihad has vague, grandiose political projects that it postpones until some remote future time. Its real concern is to attract attention and arouse passions through spectacular acts of terrorism. The practitioners of this new jihad often begin with little knowledge of their own religion and its texts and are drawn by a desire for violence, destruction, and revenge. This desire coincides with one of the most shocking aspects of the new jihad, its promotion of suicide and the indiscriminate killing of noncombatants, including women and children, actions that the classical doctrine generally condemns and that have appeared in Islamic history only in marginal episodes.

As fundamentalists, these practitioners of the new jihad have little interest in what has happened since the mid–seventh century; when they look to the past, it is mostly to the Prophet's Medina and the earliest Islam. For these and other reasons, while it is certainly useful for us to know about the classical doctrine and about the long, complex history of the jihad within Islamic societies, one must not think that such knowledge will on its own lead to an understanding of the circumstances and conditions of the new, global jihad. These must be sought first of all in the world of the twenty-first century.

*See also* **Anti-Semitism: Islamic Anti-Semitism; Ethnicity and Race: Islamic Views; Fundamentalism; Islam; Law, Islamic; Sacred Texts: Koran.**

BIBLIOGRAPHY

Arberry, A. J. *The Koran Interpreted.* New York: Macmillan, 1955.

Bonner, Michael. *Les origines du jihad.* Paris: Editions du Téraèdre, forthcoming. English-language version also forthcoming.

Donner, Fred McGraw. *The Early Islamic Conquests.* Princeton, N.J.: Princeton University Press, 1981.

Firestone, Reuven. *Jihad: The Origin of Holy War in Islam.* New York: Oxford University Press, 1999.

Kepel, Gilles. *Muslim Extremism in Egypt: The Prophet and Pharaoh.* Translated by Jon Rothschild. Berkeley and Los Angeles: University of California Press, 1986.

Kohlberg, Etan. "Medieval Muslim Views on Martyrdom." *Mededeelingen der Koninklijke Akademie van Wetenschappen* 60, no. 7 (1997): 279–307.

Morabia, Alfred. *Le Ǧihâd dans l'Islam médiéval: Le "combat sacré" des origines au XII siècle.* Paris: Albin Michel, 1993.

Peters, Rudolph. *Islam and Colonialism: The Doctrine of Jihad in Modern History.* The Hague and New York: Mouton, 1979.

Roy, Olivier. *L'Islam mondialisé.* Paris: Editions du Seuil, 2002. To appear in English as *Global Islam.* New York: Columbia University Press, forthcoming.

*Michael Bonner*

**JOUISSANCE.** French psychoanalyst Jacques Lacan's (1901–1981) use of the term *jouissance,* like most other Lacanian concepts, shifts over the years and can be difficult to pin down. Translating from the French, *jouissance* can be rendered literally as "enjoyment," "both in the sense of deriving pleasure from something, and in the legal sense of exercising property rights" (Evans, p. 1). The term has sexual connotations as well, also meaning orgasm in French.

**Lacan's Early Work: *Jouissance* as Pleasure**

Lacan's first use of the term *jouissance* can be found in the seminar of 1953–1954, where it appears just twice (1998, pp. 205 and 223) and is used only in relation to Hegel's dialectic of the master and the slave. Here Lacan equates *jouissance* with pleasure, noting the "relation between pleasure [*jouissance*] and labour" and notes that "a law is imposed upon the slave, that he should satisfy the desire and pleasure [*jouissance*] of the other" (1998, p. 223). Until Seminar IV (1956–1957), *jouissance* as simply "pleasure" is Lacan's only and infrequent use of the term.

In his early work, Lacan's notion of *jouissance,* although not a Freudian term, has parallels to Freud's concept of the drive. After 1957, the sexual connotations of the word move to the forefront, and in 1958 he first uses *jouissance* to refer explicitly to orgasm. Thus, in 1958, Lacan speaks of "masturbatory *jouissance,*" which he attributes to the phallic stage and the "imaginary dominance of the phallic attribute" (1977, p. 282).

**Lacan's Work of the Late 1950s and 1960s: *Jouissance* Versus Pleasure**

After 1958, Lacan begins to distinguish between *jouissance* and pleasure. This can be found in Seminar VII (1960–1961), where Lacan discusses *jouissance* as an ethical stance in relation to Kant and Sade. In this phase of his work, *jouissance* comes to figure as that which Freud referred to as "beyond" the pleasure principle or, as Lacan puts it, "*jouissance* . . . is suffering" (1992, p. 184). In relation to Kant's example of the man who refuses a night of pleasure with a woman if the price to be paid is death, Lacan remarks that, although that may be true for the man in pursuit of pleasure, the man in pursuit of *jouissance* (as the figures of de Sade's are) will accept death as the price to be paid for *jouissance*: "one only has to make a conceptual shift and move the night spent with the lady from the category of pleasure to that of *jouissance* . . . for the example to be ruined" (1992, p. 189). In the acceptance of death as the price, the subject experiences *jouissance,* in which "pleasure *and* pain are presented as a single packet to take or leave" (1992, p. 189).

Despite these earlier references, it is not until 1960 that Lacan gives his first structural account of *jouissance*. In "Subversion of the Subject," he posits pleasure as that which "sets the limits on *jouissance*" (1977, p. 319). The sacrificing of *jouissance* also becomes here, for the first time, a necessary condition for subjectivity—the subject, by submitting him- or herself to the symbolic order must sacrifice some *jouissance,* since "*jouissance* is forbidden to him who speaks" (1977, p. 319). In this Lacan rewrites Freud's theory of the castration complex: "Castration means that *jouissance* must be refused" (1977, p. 324). The sacrificed (or "alienated") *jouissance* becomes the object, that which is the cause of desire but never attainable.

## Lacan in the 1970s: Masculine and Feminine *Jouissances*

Finally, in the 1970s, especially in Seminar XX (1972–1973), Lacan brings to the forefront his distinction between masculine and feminine *jouissance*. Although he had discussed *jouissance* in conjunction with femininity as early as 1958, it is only in *Encore* that Lacan first comes to speak of a qualitatively different type of feminine *jouissance*. He posits feminine *jouissance* against that of the phallic, termed the "*jouissance* of the Idiot" (1998, p, 81). In *Encore*, Lacan defines phallic *jouissance* (which he sometimes refers to as sexual *jouissance*) as that which "is marked and dominated by the impossibility of establishing as such . . . the One of the relation 'sexual relationship'" (1998, p. 6–7). Lacan's use of the term *One* refers to mathematical logic (Frege), to the Platonic myth of the lovers' unity in the *Symposium*, and to the (presumed) unity of the (male) subject in a philosophical sense. Phallic *jouissance* is thus seen as a barrier to these forms of unity. Or, to put it another way, "[P]hallic jouissance is the obstacle owing to which man does not come . . . to enjoy woman's body, precisely because what he enjoys is the jouissance of the organ. . . . Jouissance, qua sexual, is phallic—in other words, it is not related to the Other as such" (1998, pp. 7 and 9). The term *Other* here refers both to the linguistic Other and to the Other sex—woman. It is precisely man's experience of phallic or sexual *jouissance* that "covers or poses an obstacle to the supposed sexual relationship" (1998, p. 9).

Although women have, according to Lacan, access to a *jouissance* that is beyond the phallus, men, by virtue of the fact that it is "through the phallic function that man as whole acquires his inscription" (1998, p. 79), have to make do with inadequate phallic or sexual *jouissance*, one that causes him to be unable to "attain his sexual partner . . . except inasmuch as his partner is the cause of his desire" (1998, p. 80). A further cause of the inadequacy of phallic *jouissance* is its incompatibility with feminine *jouissance*, thus posing an obstacle to the sexual relationship.

Feminine *jouissance* differs from masculine or phallic *jouissance* through its relation to the Other, especially the Other sex, which for Lacan means woman. Although in his earlier work, Lacan attributed to women a *jouissance* associated with the phallic stage and the clitoris (1977, p. 282), his work of the 1970s moved away from that position. In particular, Lacan posits for women a specifically feminine *jouissance* that is "beyond the phallus" (1998, p. 74). Women have access *both* to phallic, or sexual, *jouissance*, and to a supplementary form of *jouissance* by virtue of being not wholly subsumed by the phallic function as men are: "being not-whole, she has a supplementary *jouissance* compared to what the phallic function designates by way of *jouissance*" (1998, p. 73). It is, however, impossible to know anything about this other *jouissance* other than that some women (and men) experience it. Lacan's paradigmatic example of feminine *jouissance* is that of mystics such as Hadewijch d'Anvers, Saint John of the Cross, and Saint Teresa, thus relating feminine *jouissance* to God. As he asks in relation to mysticism, "Doesn't this *jouissance* that one experiences and knows nothing about put us on the path of existence? And why not interpret one face of the Other, the God face, as based on feminine *jouissance*?" (1998, p. 77).

In his later uses of the term *jouissance*, one can see just where Lacan parts ways with Freud. First, in his claim that "there is no sexual relationship," Lacan asserts the inherent failure of genital sexuality, which Freud did not do. Finally, through his description of a specifically feminine *jouissance*, one that implies a different type of sexual satisfaction for women, Lacan's later work does away with Freud's notion of libido's being only masculine.

## Feminist and Political Applications of *Jouissance*

Feminists and cultural critics have appropriated Lacan's term and refined it for their own purposes. Among feminists, *jouissance* is most often used by French feminists. The two most prominent are Julia Kristeva and Luce Irigaray. Similarly to Lacan, both also discuss a specifically feminine *jouissance*, related to the mother and woman's body. Kristeva views *jouissance* as bound up with the maternal and the semiotic *chora* and views art as "the flow of *jouissance* into language" (p. 79). Irigaray, in a manner almost as cryptic as Lacan's, also claims that women experience two types of *jouissance*: a phallic one and one "more in keeping with their bodies and their sex" (p. 45).

In terms of the political, theorists such as Slavoj Žižek and Tim Dean have picked up on Lacan's remarks in *Television* regarding racism, the melting pot, and the *jouissance* of the Other to view social problems such as ethnic hatred or homophobia as motivated by resentment of the (ethnically or sexually) Other's *jouissance*.

*See also* **Body, The; Other, The, European Views of; Sexuality.**

### BIBLIOGRAPHY

PRIMARY SOURCES

Irigaray, Luce. "The Bodily Encounter with the Mother." Translated by David Macey. In *The Irigaray Reader*, edited by Margaret Whitford, 34–46. Cambridge, Mass.: Blackwell, 1991.

Kristeva, Julia. *Revolution in Poetic Language*. Translated by Margaret Waller. New York: Columbia University Press, 1984.

Lacan, Jacques. *Écrits: A Selection*. Translated by Alan Sheridan. New York: W. W. Norton, 1977.

———. *The Seminar of Jacques Lacan. Book I: Freud's Papers on Technique 1953-54*. Edited by Jacques-Alain Miller. Translation and notes by John Forrester. New York: W. W. Norton, 1988.

———. *The Seminar of Jacques Lacan. Book VII: The Ethics of Psychoanalysis 1956-1960*. Edited by Jacques-Alain Miller. Translation and notes by Dennis Porter. New York: W. W. Norton, 1992.

———. *The Seminar of Jacques Lacan. Book XX: Encore. On Feminine Sexuality: The Limits of Love and Knowledge 1972–73*. Edited by Jacques-Alain Miller. Translation and notes by Bruce Fink. New York: W. W. Norton, 1998.

———. *Television: A Challenge to the Psychoanalytic Establishment*. Edited by Joan Copjec. Translated by Denis Hollier, Rosalind Krauss, Annette Michelson, and Jeffrey Melhman. New York: W. W. Norton, 1990.

SECONDARY SOURCES

Dean, Tim. *Beyond Sexuality.* Chicago: University of Chicago Press, 2000.

Evans, Dylan. "From Kantian Ethics to Mystical Experience: An Exploration of Jouissance." In *Key Concepts of Lacanian Psychoanalysis,* edited by Dany Nobus, 1–28. New York: Other Press, 1998.

Žižek, Slavoj. *For They Know Not What They Do: Enjoyment as a Political Factor.* New York: Verso, 1991.

———. *Looking Awry: An Introduction to Jacques Lacan Through Popular Culture.* Cambridge, Mass.: MIT Press, 1991.

*Brenda L. Bethman*

# JUDAISM.

This entry includes two subentries:

*Judaism to 1800*
*Modern Judaism*

## JUDAISM TO 1800

As a religion developing over three millennia, Judaism changed, diversified, and acculturated to many cultural and spiritual environments, while maintaining at the same time some basic characteristics. In the following, an attempt is made to describe both the continuities and the variations characteristic of the various forms of Judaism up to 1800.

Four main concepts organize the majority of the developments in this period: memory, corporate personality, performance, and order. A traditional form of mentality, Jewish culture has been oriented toward an accumulative understanding of the development of literature and has preserved much of the earlier forms of literature, though strongly reinterpreted, as part of homogenizing enterprises in search of cohesion.

Beginning in the Middle Ages, Judaism developed into a complex ray of processes that combine biblical, rabbinic, and speculative trends in different ways and proportions. The biblical trend is represented by materials that constitute the biblical literature of the first millennium B.C.E. and is concerned basically with what happened in history and what is the best religious behavior, understood as the commandments of God.

The rabbinic trend deals with literatures, primarily interpretive narratives that began to appear in the first millennium C.E., that aim to explicate the biblical materials: the Mishnah (compiled c. 200 C.E..) and the Talmuds (Palestinian, c. 400, and Babylonian, c. 500) deal with the codification of the biblical commandments, and with detailed explanations of how to perform them, while most of the Midrashic literatures interpret the historical parts of the Bible, that is, what happened and how, and what is missing in the elliptic biblical style.

During the second millennium C.E., philosophical and mystical forms of Judaism emerged. These can be described as speculative, since they put a stronger emphasis on the question *why* than did the biblical and rabbinic writings. Drawing from

a variety of Greek, Hellenistic, Arabic, and Christian sources, and sometimes even from Hindu ones, more comprehensive accounts of the meaning of Judaism, including new theologies and anthropologies, were articulated by Jewish thinkers.

### Forms of Memory

Identity is a matter of memory. Selective as both individual and collective memory is, it moves to the center those events and acts that are conceived of as most important. Naturally these change with time. For example, in biblical Judaism the remembrance that the Israelites belong to God, who saved them from Egypt, was a major religious concern. Rituals that celebrate this belonging, like the donning of the phylacteries, the special garments known as tallith, the mezuzah, and circumcision—what I call the "envelope of reminders"—were emphasized and remained part and parcel of later forms of Judaism. Rabbinic literature, however, conceived of the will of God as embedded in the Torah, or inlibrated in the way H. A. Wolfson understood this term, and the memorization of the Torah moved to the center of rabbinic spirituality. To be sure, the biblical ideals did not disappear, but the structures of remembrance and reminders in rabbinic literature became more complex.

These two forms of Judaism envisioned the approach to the divine as involving the entire human personality. The anthropology that inspires these literatures is more integrative, meaning that they take into consideration the importance of both bodily and psychological aspects of man. In medieval forms of Judaism, a third form of memory becomes important, in which remembrance was less mediated by concrete activities—related to the "envelope of reminders" or the study of the canonical book—but was related to thinking and concentrating on God as an intellectual concept, on nature as the manifestation of his attributes, and on God's names.

The biblical, rabbinic, and contemplative/mystical (or speculative) stages of Judaism convey quite a similar picture: remembrance and forgetting represent the two poles of the positive and negative evaluations, which are applied to those values that organize the different types of Judaism surveyed above. In the Hebrew Bible, the will of God is the central religious factor, and it informs the course of history, especially the Jewish one. Therefore, the Israelites see in history, though not in it alone, a manifestation of the divine will; and the remembrance of this will and its linkage to the fate of the Jewish nation is crucial. The change in history, in the form of the liberation of the Israelites from Egypt, constitutes a formative moment that should be remembered in order to make the linkage with the redeeming God. Most of the literature created in the biblical period is concerned solely with a sacred history, while the more general events that took place after the destruction of the Second Temple were conceived of as peripheral from the religious point of view, a view shared by rabbinical, philosophical, and kabbalistic authors. Historical writings are scant and played a marginal role in the general economy of Judaism.

### Concepts of Corporate Personality

Biblical forms of Judaism share a concept of a unified mythical body of the people of Israel, made up of the individual

Israelites. Identity is attained by participation in the broader group, which is the main bearer of identity. In the pseudepigraphic intertestamental texts, and in many Hebrew discussions from late antiquity and the Middle Ages, Israel is sometimes described as an angel appointed over the nation. In rabbinic literature, this corporate personality was sometimes called *Knesset Yisrael,* the assembly of Israel, a concept close to the contemporaneous *Ecclesia,* and *Kelal Yisrael,* the entire people of Israel, was described by dicta like "All the [individuals belonging to] Israel are friends" or alternatively, "are warrant of each other." One of the main assumptions in this layer of thought is the common experience shared at the Sinaitic revelation, on the one hand, and the concept of an elect people on the other hand. This corporate personality is understood both as an organic internal cohesion and as separated from all the other nations. In some kabbalistic forms of Judaism since the Middle Ages, this cohesion is portrayed as depending on a union between Israel, God, and the Torah. Some more philosophically oriented forms of Judaism conceived of man as essentially the intellect and, consequently, of Israel as an intellectual attainment.

The destiny of this corporate personality is imagined to be a central issue of human history in general, and the vicissitudes of the Jews are related to their disobedience of the divine imperatives, which attracts divine intervention in the course of history and nature. Thus matters related to exile and redemption, including the various concepts of *Messiah,* are related to the centrality of corporate personality. According to some rabbinic views, the exile is not only a matter of the Jewish people, but God too—or sometimes his presence, the *Shekhinah*—participates in it. The historical vicissitudes are seen not as accidents, unrelated or meaningless events, but as part of a broader story that gravitates around the ritual order, namely the fulfillment of the divine will by a very definite national entity, whose emergence and continuity is one of the main concerns of these literatures

## The Centrality of Ritual Performance

In most of its historical forms up to 1800, Judaism was a halakocentric religion. The main religious activity was the performance of the 613 commandments, addressed to the God of Israel. Halakah, a central concept in traditional Judaism, stands for the regulations of the details of religious behavior. Made up of interpretations of biblical and then rabbinical discussions, halakah represents the most vast and influential literature in Jewish culture. However, while addressing the concrete aspects of performance, it rarely addresses the religious goals of this behavior—these questions are discussed in the speculative literatures. Until modern Judaism, halakic behavior was the basic skeleton of Jewish life, though the details—the customs and much more their meaning—changed over centuries.

The two main religious rituals performed in public, prayer and reading of the Torah, are paramountly vocal. The halakic regulation to recite them is an essential part of their performance. (Anthropologically speaking, any thick description of Judaism should pay close attention to the role played by the voice in the communal rites.) However, as far as the vast majority of members of communities are concerned, there is no

reason to assume that an awareness of any of the above three models was instrumental in significantly shaping religious experience. What is described in the literature deals primarily with conceptualizations and experiences of small elites, rather than with widespread understandings of Jewish practices. Indeed, according to some few examples, in which the vocal aspects of prayer were conceived of as secondary, preference was given to the mental aspects of prayer, as implied for example by Moses ben Maimon (Maimonides; 1135–1204) and his followers. Adding important forms of spiritualized versions of Judaism, this Neoaristotelian thinker—and before him the eleventh-century Bahya ibn Paqudah—had a strong impact on some aspects of the internalization of religious life in Judaism.

Nevertheless, the more common experiences, based on vocal religious activities, created communities that were characterized, at least for those periods in which the rites were performed, by a shared sonorous ambiance. More than the praying, Jews were united by their sharing the same semantic world—they became a group by experiencing a rhythm of life punctuated by the same sounds. Eminent representatives of more intellectually inclined versions of Kabbalah and Hasidism even attributed a surplus role to loud recitation, rather than a mere compliance with a halakic regulation. This means that, despite the acceptance of axiologies, which elevated mental processes to a very high status, even outstanding representatives of elite Jewish mysticism (though not all of them) maintained the importance of vocal activities rather than devalue them, as some philosophers did. More interesting than this apotheosis of the loud study of the Talmud and the mouthing of the Torah, which continued classical rabbinic regulations, is the ascent of the loud study of kabbalistic books. For example, evidence has emerged regarding the loud study of the book of the *Zohar* in northern Africa beginning in the late sixteenth century.

Though there can be no doubt that loud study and prayer were intended to improve the memorization of the studied text—unlike the halakic reading of the Torah and prayer—the result was the same: sounds became an integral part of ritual in rabbinic academies as they were in synagogues. The active participation in the formation of a sonorous ambiance that encompasses the entire community with an actualization of canonical texts may be considered a formative experience for the group. The sonority created during these Jewish rituals distinguishes them from the greater solemnity that is characteristic of many rituals related to reading of sacred texts. The sonority is not a unison of coordinated voices that are consonant to each other. Musically speaking, it more often resembles cacophony than symphony. Indeed, the traditional study of the Torah or prayer, and even the ritualistic loud reading of the Torah, often took place in an ambiance dominated by discordant voices. This participation in very loosely coordinated vocal activity is characteristic of a community that cooperates in a major project, but allows, or at least bears, the individuals that study and pray in their own rhythms.

## Different Forms of Order in Judaism

In the context of Judaism, *order* refers to a sequel of homogenous signs, events, or actions whose knowledge and enactments have meanings beyond their immanent one.

***Biblical and rabbinic literatures.*** In the biblical and rabbinic literatures, three types of order are discernible: the ritual, the literary, and the historical. The ritual order, which is the most important, is shared by the two bodies of literatures. The assumption is not only that the Jewish rites are quintessential from the religious point of view, but also that their performance has wider implications, like the descent of rains, according to the biblical view, or the enhancement of the divine power according to the rabbinic view. However, it is not clear how precisely the affinities between performance and wider effects are related. The absence of detailed and systematic explanatory discussions is characteristic of the apodictic propensity of rabbinic writings.

The literary order—which refers to the intense and repeated study of the Hebrew Bible, the Mishnah, and the Talmud—became a central preoccupation among Jews, and even God was imagined to participate in it. Torah, the Hebrew language, and divine names were conceived as perfect beings that were used in order to create reality and that might also be used by man in order to impact reality. Though the biblical texts and, later on, the rabbinic ones embody both ritual and literary order, the literary order has a specific dimension, that of dense textuality. This means that not only the messages but also the precise details of the document that conveys them, are of paramount importance.

The common denominator of these types of order is the centrality of human action and fate in the universe, that is, the historical order. Objective structures that are not primarily oriented toward the well-being of man—like the invisible Platonic Ideas or the Aristotelian God as intellect—cannot be considered quintessential from the religious point of view. Furthermore, while the Greek conceptions of the cosmos were basically static, gravitating around concepts of perfections, the Jewish orders, which have human fate as the main topic, are much more dynamic.

***Speculative literatures.*** The nature of intermediary structures—like divine attributes, known as *middot,* the divine Glory, decadic structures, or angelic structures—and their specific orders play only secondary roles in the biblical and rabbinic literatures, but they are manifest in literatures that were, for the rabbinic authors, secondary, like the *Heikhalot* literature, or some forms of Jewish magic from late antiquity, like *Sefer ha-Razim* (Book of the mysteries). These forms of order are basically nonconstellated, that is, they operate without substantial speculative superstructures or orders.

Most of the Kabbalists were religious figures whose conservative propensities were amply testified in their literary activity and sometimes in the records of their lives. They contributed to the emergence of types of ontological concatenations (linkages or chains) between various aspects of reality in manners unknown to or marginal to rabbinic Judaism. The concatenation of supernal orders and rites created structures similar to myth-and-ritual views, although the supernal orders do not uniformly assume the form of mythical narrative.

Jewish speculative literatures that emerged in the Middle Ages, including works on Hebrew grammar and on poetics, and first accounts of scientific thought in Judaism, were in a constant search for comprehensive forms of order. This was also true of philosophical works, including the first systematic descriptions of the divine realm, of human psychology, and of the concept of nature. Attempting to organize the various views on some of those topics found in early Jewish literatures, medieval Jewish thinkers used categories previously absent from Judaism. Words for *theology, metaphysics, psychology, nature,* and *science,* did not exist in the Hebrew and Aramaic of biblical and rabbinic literatures, so the use of these categories of thought necessitated linguistic innovation. Some Jewish thinkers had to attenuate the more personalistic, voluntaristic forms of order. Different as the various forms of Jewish philosophy, grammar, science, or kabbalistic literatures are, they share nevertheless a pathos for stable forms of order operating not only in the realm of objective nature, but also in the structure of language and of the human psyche, and in the realm of religious activities.

The idea of sympathetic affinities between the different levels of order created modes of integration that were new to Judaism. Not only was the world conceived of as an organized universe, a cosmos, but also even God was attracted within this integrated system and was conceived of as a part of it. This was already obvious in the Greek systems in which God or gods were not only generative but also paradigmatic concepts: Aristotle's metaphysics, which describes God as an intellect, created an axiology in which the human act of intellection becomes paramount. Sympathetic magic of Neoplatonic and Hermetic extraction, which relates human acts to astral processes, is another example of an integrated system. Both modes of integrated thought were adopted in some forms of medieval Judaism, including by different forms of Kabbalah.

The pathos for integrated orders also generated more specifically Jewish expressions. The most widespread is the assumption, found in the theosophical-theurgical school of Kabbalah, that human actions, the commandments or the *mitzvot,* correspond to the divine structure, designated as a system of ten *sefirot* (or creative forces). This dynamic correlation presupposes the possibility of the impact of human acts in the lower realm on the higher entities, that is, a theurgical impact. In another example, each of the supernal divine attributes was conceived of as governing a corresponding celestial sphere, a theory I call *theo-astrology.*

The Kabbalists thought they possessed knowledge of forms of order unknown to, or hidden from the eyes of, other Jewish masters, and that this knowledge, and the use of it were part of their superiority as religious persons. Unlike the rabbinic treatment of the *mitzvot* as basically nonconstellated by metaphysical structures, most Kabbalists subordinated them to supernal entities and processes, thus creating more comprehensive frames. This tendency to create hierarchies and ontological chains of being by connecting in an active manner between analogical levels of reality is especially evident in the philosophical and kabbalistic resort to the concept of *hishtalshelut,* or *shalshelet,* terms pointing to intradivine chains of emanation. Many of the Kabbalists created an *imaginaire* of the universe permeated by many concatenations, analogies, occult affinities, detailed sympathies, intricate subordinations, and hierarchies, most of which are absent from the rabbinic literatures. What is characteristic of many of these emanational chains is their flexibility—that is, their dependence on human religious acts below—and thus their vulnerability. Unlike the idea of the great chain of being (described in Arthur Lovejoy's classic study), which is characterized by its static nature—that is, its total independence of human acts—many of the kabbalistic descriptions assume mutual influence between the performance of the ritual and the supernal constellations that govern that performance.

The transition between the biblical and rabbinic literatures and the medieval speculative literatures, thus, is characterized by the transformation from a nonconstellated to a constellated approach. The different speculative constellations constitute different forms of attributing meaning to modes of religiosity that were more concerned with shaping a religious modus operandi than with establishing systematic worldviews. These creations of meaning were attained by constructing narratives that confer on ritualistic acts and on mystical techniques the possibility of transcending the situation of relative disorder in the external world, in the human psyche, or within divinity, thus attaining a superior order. Far from avoiding the strictures of the rabbinic life, most Kabbalists actually added customs and demanded a more intense performance of all the religious precepts understood as being fraught with special mystical valences. This effort of attributing special import to human religious deeds has much to do with the process of creating new systems of affinities evident in the voluminous kabbalistic literature dealing with the rationales of the commandments.

*See also* **Dialogue and Dialectics: Talmudic; Judaism: Modern Judaism; Mysticism: Kabbalah.**

BIBLIOGRAPHY

Idel, Moshe. *Kabbalah: New Perspectives.* New Haven, Conn.: Yale University Press, 1988/

Idel, Moshe, and Mortimer Ostow. *Jewish Mystical Leaders and Leadership in the Thirteenth Century.* Northvale, N.J.: Aronson, 1998.

Kraemer, David Charles. *The Jewish Family: Metaphor and Memory.* New York: Oxford University Press, 1989.

Myers, David N., and David B. Ruderman. *The Jewish Past Revisited: Reflections on Modern Jewish Historians.* New Haven, Conn.: Yale University Press, 1998.

Ruderman, David B. *Jewish Thought and Scientific Discovery in Early Modern Europe.* Detroit: Wayne State University Press, 2001.

Zolty, Shoshana. *And All Your Children Shall Be Learned: Women and the Study of Torah in Jewish Law and History.* Northvale N.J.: Aronson, 1993.

*Moshe Idel*

## MODERN JUDAISM

Judaism has never been monolithically uniform. Made irreducibly complex by 3,500 years of turbulent history, it resists simplification. Its data refuse to be straitjacketed or handled dispassionately. Impartial attempts to understand it are easily spoiled by the partisan sympathies and deeply held antagonisms it activates in observers. Consider a mere sampling of the evidence. Its implications startle. In 1920, the American automotive industrialist Henry Ford articulated a widely held opinion that was infected by virulent strains of secular anti-Semitism without which the Holocaust would have been impossible: "Poor in his masses, [the Jew] yet controls the world's finances. . . . The single description which will include a larger percentage of the Jews than members of any other race is this: he is in business . . . the Jew is gifted for business" (Mendes-Flohr, p. 513). Vast numbers of Jews, however, were politically active in the labor union movement and on the Left. Four years earlier, Rosa Luxemburg, born to a Jewish family in Poland, an ardent socialist and leader of the Communist Party in Germany, acknowledged "that I have no separate corner in my heart for the ghetto: I feel at home in the entire world wherever there are clouds and birds and human tears" (Mendes-Flohr, p. 262). In 1930, Bertha Pappenheim, a religiously observant German-Jewish woman, a pioneering feminist and energetic social worker, explained that "women [in contrast to men] showed a ready understanding to relate the command to love your neighbor to modern times. . . . Out of a new congruence of German cultural elements and Jewish civilization grew a spiritual substance of greatest importance . . . These women who did not know how Jewish they were through their inherited spirituality became strong pillars of the feminist movement" (quoted in Mendes-Flohr, p. 288).

Similar divergence over other fundamental issues abounds. In 1885, a Conference of Reform Rabbis gathered in Pittsburgh. Echoing the rationalist ideals of the Enlightenment, they declared that "we consider ourselves no longer a nation but a religious community . . . ever striving to be in accord with the postulates of reason" (Mendes-Flohr, p. 468). In 1917, Ozjasz Thon, a Polish Zionist from Kraków, broadcasting the zeal that ultimately led to the establishment of the State of Israel in 1948, announced that "the Jews are a nation, not a religious sect" (Mendelsohn, p. 17). Further complicating the challenge of defining Judaism, in 1966, in the refuge of Belgium, Jean Amery, a survivor of the Nazi death camps in Auschwitz, the son of a Catholic mother and a Jewish father, wrote: "The necessity and impossibility of being a Jew, that is what causes me indistinct pain" (Mendes-Flohr, p. 292). In 1913, Gustav Landauer, a German-Jewish intellectual, echoing the ideals of romanticism embraced by countless Jews, proclaimed that "I feel my Judaism in the expressions of my face, in my gait, in my facial features, and all these signs assure me that Judaism is alive in everything that I am and do" (Mendes-Flohr, p. 276). In 1926, Sigmund Freud, the founder of psychoanalysis, confessed that "what bound me to Jewry was (I am ashamed to say) neither faith nor national pride, for I have always been an unbeliever and was brought up without any religion. . . . But plenty of other things remained to make the attraction of Jewry and Jews irresistible—many obscure emotional forces . . . as well as a clear consciousness of inner identity, the safe intimacy of a common mental construction" (Mendes-Flohr, p. 278). The juxtaposition of these divergent, contradictory voices is cautionary and instructive. Judaism is elusive.

Lexicons reflect this reality. Meticulously preserving popular usage and conventional wisdom, they report that Judaism signifies a religion, faith, set of theological beliefs and ceremonial practices, culture, nation, race, people, polity, tradition, heritage, or ethnic identity. The long string of terms is baffling. It fails to note whether the terms are neutrally descriptive or ideologically prescriptive. This failure wreaks conceptual havoc. Many of the string's terms are ambiguous; others are anachronistic. In combination, several of the terms are logically incoherent or mutually exclusive. The search for clarity seems doomed.

For scholarly purposes, Judaism may nevertheless be characterized as the sum total of symbiotic interactions between the Jews and their diverse geographical, sociopolitical environments. Perceived in this strictly descriptive, all-inclusive light, Judaism appears to have completed three phases of premodern development: ancient Near Eastern; Greco-Roman; and medieval, both Christian and Islamic. Currently, Judaism is undergoing its latest phase, the modern. As the contradictory voices cited above suggest, the modern phase may be the most tumultuous, fragmented, and poignant of all.

Like Judaism, modernity is irreducibly complex. Scene of utopian achievement and apocalyptic terror, modernity resists simplification. It swarms with counterpoint and paradox: unprecedented prosperity and abject deprivation, revolutionary reform and conservative reaction, egalitarian liberation and fascist brutality. Modernity simultaneously produces satisfied customers and frustrated discontents. Its beneficiaries and victims offer radically different assessments of its character. Jews have been both beneficiary and victim; they bear witness of a different kind. Historians nevertheless tend to agree that modernity is coterminous with the emergence of the bourgeoisie, the rise of the centralized nation-state, and the subsequent establishment of global hegemony in the West, in places such as Europe and North America.

Modernity may be said to have originated with the French, American, and Russian revolutions. Acting on the belief that "all men are created equal," the revolutions reordered society. They outlawed the denial of citizenship, special taxes, demeaning sumptuary regulations, and physical ghettos that had segregated Jews from society for centuries. The revolutions abolished the privileges of the agrarian-based aristocracy. They retrenched or eliminated the direct influence of clergy on public governance. Modernity may also be said to owe its temper to capitalism and its muscle to ongoing revolutions in science, technology, and industrialized productivity. These revolutions have transformed all aspects of life, especially the spheres of labor, communication, medicine, and warfare. In turn, the opportunistic combination of capitalism, nation-state, and technology spawned diverse modes of thinking: secularism, naturalism, materialism, and cultural relativism together with their dialectical counterparts, religious fundamentalisms, and variously insatiable appetites for the certainty of metaphysical absolutes.

## Dynamics of Westernization

In North Africa and the Middle East, for example, where vast populations of Jews had lived for centuries in premodernity as *dhimmis,* one of several protected minorities, modernity witnessed the dismemberment and balkanization of the Islamic Ottoman Empire, establishment of European colonies, Westernization of the local cultures, subsequent wars of liberation, and eventual establishment of newly formed, autonomous states. The process was well under way in the 1820s when Georg Wilhelm Friedrich Hegel lectured on the philosophy of history. His words reek with Eurocentric propaganda. Hegel declared that Islam had surpassed Judaism's ethnic particularism by embracing universalistic ideals. He then acknowledged medieval European debts to Islamic "science and knowledge, especially that of philosophy." He also noted Europe's contemporary appreciation of Islamic "noble poetry and free imagination." Capping the argument, Hegel reversed directions. Performing feats of imperious Orientalism, he lambasted the "East" and triumphantly erased Islam from the later stages of history: "But the East itself. . . . sank into the grossest vice. The most hideous passions became dominant . . . At present, driven back into its Asiatic and African quarters . . . Islam has long vanished from the stage of history at large, and has retreated into Oriental ease and repose" (Hegel, p. 360).

As with Islam, so too with Judaism. Hegel's remarks expose the underlying pressures that have shaped and reconfigured Judaism for the past three hundred years. Dangling numerous incentives, the West circulated an interlocking set of guidelines: To reap the benefits of unprecedented prosperity after earning and being granted legal emancipation, the Jews would have to eliminate the "Oriental" habits that Westerners find odious. The Jews must modernize, accommodate, secularize, adapt, acculturate, integrate, and assimilate. Convert to Christianity, if they will. Remain Jewish, if they must, but let them heed the counsel offered in 1866 by Judah Leib Gordon, the Russian Hebrew poet, who wrote: "Be a man abroad and a Jew [in the privacy of] your tent, A brother to your [European] countryman and a servant to your [European] king" (Mendes-Flohr, p. 384). Be universalistic in outlook and education. Let the Jews preserve and continue to nurture only those elements of their premodern, rabbinic culture that conform to European tastes in science, philosophy, and the arts of "noble poetry and free imagination." Jews must dismantle traditional communal structures that privilege aristocratic leadership. Jews must retrench or eliminate the direct influence of the rabbinate on public governance. If it pleases, let them reenter "history at large" by wholeheartedly joining the contemporary nation-states of the West. Failing that, either for lack of interest in capitalism and global hegemony or because of virulent anti-Semitic backlash, let them re-enter "history at large" by creating an autonomous Jewish nation-state based on Western models.

Like all the other premodern societies that have encountered the hegemonic West in recent times, the Jews adhered to these guidelines, with varying degrees of resistance and success. Like all these others and the West itself, Judaism became a perpetual site of cultural demolition, construction, and renovation. Like them all, like memory itself, Judaism became a tangled work in progress where nostalgia for the past and hope for the future jostled for attention.

The pace, extent, and contour of modernization differed from one geographical location to another. Jews living in the heartland of the West—in France, North America, England, and Germany—were the first to be legally emancipated, culturally integrated, and professionally diversified. Pioneers, they underwent the crisis of transformation and adjustment long before their kin living in East Europe. In turn, the Jews of Europe became the beneficiaries of modernity earlier than their kin living in the peripheries of modernity situated in colonial North Africa and the Middle East. Alas, between 1933 and 1945, the Jews of Europe also suffered the worst of modernity's evils. The Jews fell victim to the dialectical waste products of liberal attempts to reform society: xenophobia and racism leading to bureaucratically managed and technologically enabled mass murder, genocide, the Holocaust.

Wherever they resided, the Jews were buffeted by an array of centrifugal and centripetal forces compelling them to formulate a livable equation that balanced loyalty to the past with openness to the present. The proportion of continuity and discontinuity with premodern Judaism differed in each of the equations. No single equation enjoyed universal consent. As the juxtaposition of contradictory voices cited above suggests, the equations provoked controversy. Among the Jews who preferred life in the Diaspora and identified Judaism primarily with religion, the spectrum of opinion and practice included Reform, Reconstructionist, Conservative, Orthodox, ultra-Orthodox, and Hasidic varieties. Among the Jews who identified Judaism primarily with nationalism, the spectrum of opinion and practice included political, cultural, Socialist, Marxist, utopian, and religious Zionists of every stripe imaginable. Among the Jews, like Freud, who identified Judaism primarily with a cultural heritage or a set of ethical ideals, the spectrum of opinions and practices defies description.

In the traumatic midst of adjusting to Westernization, the Jews availed themselves of every tool available to make sense of their predicament and to stabilize their fluctuating fortunes. In the realms of philosophy and theology, the Jews flocked to rationality and romanticism, pragmatic naturalism and religious existentialism, sober positivism and exuberant mysticism, taking freely and modifying extensively what they needed from the resources of premodern Jewish tradition as well as from Immanuel Kant, Friedrich W. Schelling, Hegel, Karl Marx, Friedrich Nietzsche, Martin Heidegger, Ludwig Wittgenstein, John Dewey, Jacques Derrida, and the entire host of speculative virtuosi. In the realms of literature, music, and art, they participated fully in both the avant-garde and in the popular rear. In their ranks stand Heinrich Heine, Shmuel Yosef Agnon, Sholem Aleichem, Franz Kafka, Marc Chagall, and Arnold Schoenberg. Composing in every language, they uncovered the depths of humanity and mapped the enigmas of Jewish selfhood. In the realms of scholarship, other Jewish intellectuals invented the strictly academic, scientific study of Judaism. In all these realms, as in the realms of innovative political organization and religious experimentation, the unsettling and creative traces of modernity are unmistakable.

See also **Diasporas: Jewish Diaspora; Genocide; Ghetto; Identity, Multiple: Jewish Multiple Identity; Judaism:** *Judaism to 1800; Orientalism; Religion; Religion and the State.*

**BIBLIOGRAPHY**

PRIMARY SOURCES

Hegel, Georg W. F. *The Philosophy of History.* Translated by J. Sibree. Amherst, N.Y.: Prometheus Books, 1991.

Hertzberg, Arthur, ed. *The Zionist Idea: A Historical Analysis and Reader.* New York: Atheneum, 1984.

Mendes-Flohr, Paul, and Jehuda Reinharz, eds. *The Jew in the Modern World: A Documentary History.* New York: Oxford University Press, 1995.

SECONDARY SOURCES

Alter, Robert. *After the Tradition: Essays on Modern Jewish Writing.* New York: Dutton, 1969.

Ezrahi, Sidra Dekoven. *Booking Passage: Exile and Homecoming in the Modern Jewish Imagination.* Berkeley: University of California Press, 2000.

Guttman, Julius. *Philosophies of Judaism: A History of Jewish Philosophy from Biblical Times to Franz Rosenzweig.* Translated by David W. Silverman. New York: Schocken Books, 1973.

Hodgson, Marshall G. S. *The Gunpowder Empires and Modern Times.* Vol. 3 of *The Venture of Islam: Conscience and History in a World Civilization.* Chicago: University of Chicago Press, 1974.

Mendelsohn, Ezra. *On Modern Jewish Politics.* New York: Oxford University Press, 1993.

Meyer, Michael. *The Origins of the Modern Jew: Jewish Identity and European Culture, 1749–1824.* Detroit: Wayne State University Press, 1967.

Peskowitz, Miriam, and Laura Levitt, eds. *Judaism since Gender.* New York: Routledge, 1997.

*Kalman P. Bland*

# JUSTICE.

This entry includes three subentries:

*Overview*
*Justice in American Thought*
*Justice in East Asian Thought*

## OVERVIEW

Virtually everyone becomes involved in disputes about justice at some point. Sometimes our involvement in such disputes is rooted in the fact that we believe ourselves to be victims of some form of injustice, such as job discrimination; sometimes our involvement is rooted in the fact that others believe us to be the perpetrators or at least the beneficiaries of some form of injustice affecting them, such as unfair taxing policies. Elimination of the injustice may require drastic reform, or even revolutionary change in the political system, such as took place in the Soviet Union, Eastern Europe, and South Africa. In other cases, redress of the injustice may require only some electoral pressure or administrative decision, such as that required to end a war, for example, the Vietnam War. Whatever the origin and whatever the practical effect, disputes about justice are difficult to avoid, especially when dealing with issues that have widespread social effects like access to employment opportunities, distribution of income, structure of political institutions, and use of the war-making capabilities of a nation.

Reasonable resolutions of such disputes require critical evaluation of the alternative conceptions of justice available to us. Philosophical debate at the beginning of the twenty-first century supports five major conceptions of justice: (1) a libertarian conception, which takes liberty to be the ultimate political ideal; (2) a socialist conception, which takes equality to be the ultimate political ideal; (3) a welfare liberal conception which takes contractual fairness or maximal utility to be the ultimate political ideal; (4) a communitarian conception, which takes the common good to be the ultimate political ideal; and (5) a feminist conception, which takes a gender-free society to be the ultimate political ideal.

All of these conceptions of justice have features in common. Each has requirements that belong to the domain of obligation rather than to the domain of charity; differences arise as to where the line between these domains should be drawn. Each is concerned with giving people what they deserve or should rightfully possess; disagreements exist about what those things are. Each is secular rather than religious in character because for justice to be enforceable it must be accessible to all who apply for it; only a conception of justice that is based on secular reason rather than on religious faith could have that accessibility. Each is thought to apply cross-culturally in virtue of its being accessible to everyone on the basis of reason alone. These common features constitute a generally accepted core definition of justice. What we need to do, however, is examine that part of each of these conceptions of justice over which there is serious disagreement in order to determine which, if any, is most defensible.

## Libertarian Justice

Libertarians frequently cite the work of F. A. Hayek (1899–1992), particularly his *Constitution of Liberty* (1960), as an intellectual source of their view. Hayek argues that the libertarian ideal of liberty requires "equality before the law" and "reward according to market value" but not "substantial equality" or "reward according to merit." Hayek further argues that the inequalities due to upbringing, inheritance, and education that are permitted by an ideal of liberty actually tend to benefit society as a whole. In basic accord with Hayek, early-twenty-first-century libertarians define "liberty" as "the state of being unconstrained by other persons from doing what one wants." This definition limits the scope of liberty in two ways. First not all constraints, whatever the source, count as restrictions on liberty; the constraints must come from other persons. For example, people who are constrained by natural forces from getting to the top of Mount Everest have not been deprived of liberty in this regard. Second the constraints must run counter to people's wants. Thus people who do not want to hear Beethoven's Fifth Symphony do not have their liberty restricted when other people forbid its performance, even though the proscription does in fact constrain what the former are able to do.

Given this definition of liberty, libertarians go on to characterize their moral and political ideal as requiring that each person should have the greatest amount of liberty commensurate with the same liberty for all. From this ideal, libertarians claim that a number of more specific requirements, in particular a right to life, a right to freedom of speech, press, and assembly, and a right to property, can be derived.

The libertarian's right to life is not a right to receive from others the goods and resources necessary for preserving one's life; it is simply a right not to be killed. So understood, the right to life is not a right to receive welfare. In fact there are no welfare rights in the libertarian view. Accordingly the libertarian's understanding of the right to property is not a right to receive from others the goods and resources necessary for one's welfare, but rather a right to acquire goods and resources either by initial acquisition or by voluntary agreement.

By defending rights such as these, libertarians can support only a limited role for government. That role is simply to prevent and punish initial acts of coercion—the only wrongful actions in the libertarian view.

Libertarians do not deny that having sufficient goods and resources to meet basic nutritional needs and basic heath care needs is a good thing, but they do not believe that government has a duty to provide such goods and resources. Libertarians claim that some good things, such as the provision of welfare and health care to the needy, are requirements of charity rather than justice. Accordingly failure to make such provisions is neither blameworthy nor punishable.

A basic objection to the libertarian conception of justice is its claim that rights to life and property, as the libertarian understands these rights, derive from an ideal of liberty. Why should we think that an ideal of liberty requires a right to life and a right to property that excludes a right to welfare? A libertarian understanding of a right to property might well justify a rich person depriving a poor person of the liberty to acquire the goods and resources necessary for meeting the latter's basic nutritional needs. How then could we appeal to an ideal of liberty to justify such a deprivation of liberty? Surely we could not claim that such a deprivation is justified for the sake of preserving a rich person's freedom to use the goods and resources he or she possesses to meet luxury needs. By any neutral assessment, the liberty of the deserving poor not to be interfered with when taking from the surplus possessions of the rich what they require to meet their basic needs should have priority over the liberty of the rich not to be interfered with when using their surplus possessions to meet their luxury needs. But if this is the case, then a right to welfare, and possibly a right to equal opportunity as well, would be grounded in the libertarian ideal of liberty.

## Socialist Justice

In contrast with libertarians, socialists take equality to be the ultimate political ideal. In the *Communist Manifesto* (1848), Karl Marx (1818–1883) and Friedrich Engels (1820–1895) maintain that the abolition of bourgeois property and bourgeois family structure is a necessary first requirement for building a society that accords with the political ideal of equality. In the *Critique of the Gotha Program* (1891), Marx provides a much more positive account of what is required to build a society based upon the political ideal of equality. Marx claims that the distribution of social goods must conform, at least initially, to the principle from each according to his/her ability, to each according to his/her contribution. But when the highest stage of communist society has been reached, Marx adds, distribution will conform to the principle from each according to his/her ability, to each according to his/her need.

At first this conception might sound ridiculous to someone brought up in a capitalist society. How can people be asked to contribute according to their ability if income is distributed on the basis of their needs and not on the basis of their contributions?

The answer, according to a socialist conception of justice, is to make the work itself as enjoyable as possible. As a result, people will want to do the work they are capable of doing because they find it intrinsically rewarding. For a start, socialists might try to get people to accept existing, inherently rewarding jobs at lower salaries—top executives, for example, would work for $300,000, rather than the much higher salaries they can actually command. Ultimately socialists hope to make all jobs as intrinsically rewarding as possible, so that when people are no longer working primarily for external rewards and are making their best contributions to society, distribution can proceed on the basis of need.

Socialists propose to implement their ideal of equality by giving workers democratic control over the workplace. They believe that if workers have more to say about how they do their work, they will find their work intrinsically more rewarding. As a consequence, workers will be more motivated to work because the work itself will be meeting their needs. Socialists believe that extending democracy to the workplace will necessarily lead to socialization of the means of production and the end of private property. Socialists, of course, do not deny that civil disobedience or even revolutionary action may be needed to overcome opposition to extending democracy to the workplace.

Even with democratic control of the workplace, some jobs, such as collecting garbage or changing bedpans, probably cannot be made intrinsically rewarding. Socialists propose to divide up such jobs in an equitable manner. Some people might, for example, collect garbage one day a week, and then work at intrinsically rewarding jobs for the rest of the week. Others would change bedpans or do some other unfulfilling job one day a week, and then work at an inherently rewarding job on the other days. By making jobs as intrinsically rewarding as possible, in part through democratic control of the workplace and an equitable assignment of unrewarding tasks, socialists believe people will contribute according to their ability even when distribution proceeds according to need.

Another difficulty raised concerning the socialist conception of justice involves the proclaimed necessity of abolishing private property and socializing the means of production. It seems perfectly possible to give workers more control over their workplace while the means of production remain privately owned. Of course private ownership would have a somewhat different character in a society with democratic control of the workplace, but it need not cease to be private ownership.

After all, private ownership would also have a somewhat different character in a society where private holdings, and hence bargaining power, were distributed more equally than they are in most capitalist societies, yet it would not cease to be private ownership. Accordingly we could imagine a society where the means of production are privately owned but where—because ownership is so widely dispersed throughout the society and because of the degree of democratic control of the workplace—many of the criticisms socialists make of existing capitalist societies would no longer apply.

## Welfare Liberal Justice: The Contractarian Perspective

Finding merit in both the libertarian ideal of liberty and the socialist ideal of equality, welfare liberals attempt to combine both liberty and equality into one political ideal that can be characterized as contractual fairness or maximal utility.

A classical example of the contractual approach to welfare liberal justice is found in the political works of Immanuel Kant (1724–1804). Kant claims that a civil state ought to be founded on an original contract satisfying the requirements of freedom (the freedom to seek happiness in whatever way one sees fit as long as one does not infringe upon the freedom of others to pursue a similar end), equality (the equal right of each person to restrict others from using his or her freedom in ways that deny equal freedom to all), and independence (the independence of each person that is necessarily presupposed by the free agreement of the original contract).

According to Kant, the original contract, which ought to be the foundation of every civil state, does not have to "actually exist as a fact." It suffices that the laws of a civil state are such that people would agree to them under conditions in which the requirements of freedom, equality, and independence obtain. Laws that accord with this original contract would then, Kant claims, give all members of society the right to reach any degree of rank that they could earn through their labor, industry, and good fortune. Thus the equality demanded by the original contract would not, in Kant's view, exclude a considerable amount of economic liberty.

The Kantian ideal of a hypothetical contract as the moral foundation for a welfare liberal conception of justice was further developed by John Rawls (1921–2002) in *A Theory of Justice* (1971) and in *Justice as Fairness: A Restatement* (2001). Rawls, like Kant, argues that principles of justice are those principles that free and rational persons who are concerned to advance their own interests would accept in an initial position of equality. Yet Rawls goes beyond Kant by interpreting the conditions of his "original position" to explicitly require a "veil of ignorance." This veil of ignorance, Rawls claims, has the effect of depriving persons in the original position of the knowledge they would need to advance their own interests in ways that are morally arbitrary.

According to Rawls, the principles of justice that would be derived in the original position are the following:

1. Each person has the same indefeasible claim to a fully adequate scheme of equal basic liberties, which scheme is compatible with the same scheme of liberties for all; and

2. Social and economic inequalities are to satisfy two conditions: First they are to be attached to offices and positions open to all under conditions of fair equality of opportunity; second, they are to be to the greatest benefit of the least advantaged members of society (the difference principle).

Rawls holds that these principles of justice would be chosen in the original position because persons so situated would find it reasonable to follow the conservative dictates of the "maximin strategy" and *maxi*mize the *min*imum, thereby securing for themselves the highest minimum payoff and because these principles express an ideal of reciprocity.

Rawls's defense of a welfare liberal conception of justice has been challenged in a variety of ways. Some critics endorse his contractual approach while disagreeing with him over what principles of justice would be derived from it. These critics usually attempt to undermine the use of a maximin strategy in the original position. Other critics, however, have found fault with the contractual approach itself. Libertarians, for example, challenge the moral adequacy of the very ideal of contractual fairness because it conflicts with their ideal of liberty.

This second challenge to the ideal of contractual fairness is potentially more damaging because, if valid, would force its supporters to embrace some other political ideal. The challenge, however, would fail if the libertarian ideal of liberty, when correctly interpreted, can be shown to lead to much the same practical requirements as are usually associated with the welfare liberal ideal of contractual fairness.

### Welfare Liberal Justice: The Utilitarian Perspective

One way to avoid the challenges directed at a contractarian defense of welfare liberal justice is to find some alternative way of defending it. Historically utilitarianism has been thought to provide such an alternative defense. Under a utilitarian view, the requirements of a welfare liberal conception of justice can be derived from considerations of utility in such a way that following these requirements will result in the maximization of total happiness or satisfaction in society. The best-known classical defense of this utilitarian approach is that presented by John Stuart Mill (1806–1873) in *Utilitarianism* (1863).

In chapter 5 of this work, Mill surveys various types of actions and situations that are ordinarily described as just or unjust, and concludes that justice simply denotes a certain class of fundamental rules, the adherence to which is essential for maximizing social utility. Thus Mill rejects the idea that justice and social utility are ultimately distinct ideals, maintaining instead that justice is in fact derivable from the ideal of social utility.

Nevertheless a serious problem remains for the utilitarian defense of welfare liberal justice. There would appear to be ways of maximizing social utility overall that do an injustice to particular individuals. Think of the Roman practice of throwing people to the lions for the enjoyment of all those in the Colosseum. This unjust practice arguably maximized social utility overall.

Rawls makes the same point somewhat differently. Since utilitarianism sees society as a whole as if it were just one person, it treats the desires and satisfactions of separate persons as if they were the desires and satisfactions of just one person. Thus, according to Rawls, utilitarianism fails to preserve the distinction between persons.

But is Rawls right? Suppose we were to interpret utilitarianism to be constrained by the "ought" implies "can" principle, according to which people are not morally required to do what they lack the power to do or what would involve so great a sacrifice that it would be unreasonable to ask, and/or in cases of severe conflict of interest, unreasonable to require them to abide by. So constrained, utilitarianism would not impose unreasonable sacrifices on individuals, and so would not then have the consequences to which Rawls objects.

### Communitarian Justice

Another prominent political ideal defended by contemporary philosophers is the communitarian ideal of the common good. As one might expect, many contemporary defenders regard the communitarian conception of justice as rooted in Aristotelian moral theory. In the *Nicomachean Ethics* (c. 335–322 B.C.E.), Aristotle (384–322 B.C.E.) distinguishes between different varieties of justice. He first distinguishes between justice as the whole of virtue and justice as a particular part of virtue. In the former sense, justice is understood as what is lawful, and the just person is equivalent to the moral person. In the latter sense, justice is understood as what is fair or equal, and the just person is one who takes only a proper share. Aristotle focuses his discussion on justice as a part of virtue, which further divides into distributive justice, corrective justice, and justice in exchange. Each of these varieties of justice can be understood to be concerned with achieving equality. For distributive justice it is equality between equals; for corrective justice it is equality between punishment and the crime; and for justice in exchange it is equality between whatever goods are exchanged. Aristotle also claims that justice has both its natural and conventional aspects: This twofold character of justice seems to be behind Aristotle's discussion of equity, in which equity, which is a natural standard, is described as a corrective to legal justice, which is a conventional standard.

Note that few of the distinctions Aristotle makes seem tied to the acceptance of any particular conception of justice. One could, for example, accept the view that justice requires formal equality, but then specify the equality that is required in different ways. Even the ideal of justice as giving people what they deserve, which has its roots in Aristotle's account of distributive justice, is subject to various interpretations. An analysis of the concept of desert would show that there is no conceptual difficulty with claiming, for example, that everyone's needs should be satisfied or that everyone deserves an equal share of the goods distributed by society. Consequently Aristotle's argument is primarily helpful in clarifying the distinctions that can be made within the concept of justice without committing oneself to any particular conception of justice.

Rather than discussing the particular requirements of communitarian justice, proponents have frequently chosen to defend it by attacking other concepts. They have focused their criticism on the welfare liberal conception of justice.

Alasdair MacIntyre, for example, argues, in "The Privatization of the Good" (1990), that virtually all forms of liberalism attempt to separate rules defining right action from conceptions of the human good. MacIntyre contends that these forms of liberalism not only fail but have to fail because the rules defining right action cannot be adequately grounded apart from a conception of the good. For this reason, MacIntyre claims, only some version of a communitarian theory of justice that grounds rules supporting right action in a complete conception of the good can ever hope to be adequate.

But why not view most forms of liberalism as attempts to ground moral rules on part of a conception of the good—specifically, that part of a conception of the good that is more easily recognized, and should be publicly recognized, as good? For Rawls, for example, this partial conception of the good is a conception of contractual fairness, according to which no one deserves his or her native abilities or his or her initial starting place in society. If this way of interpreting liberalism is correct, then, in order to evaluate welfare liberal and communitarian conceptions of justice properly, we would need to do a comparative analysis of their conceptions of the good and their practical requirements. Moreover there is reason to think that once the practical requirements of both liberal and communitarian conceptions of justice are set out, they will be quite similar.

## Feminist Justice

Defenders of a feminist conception of justice present a distinctive challenging critique to defenders of other conceptions of justice. In his *The Subjection of Women* (1869) Mill, one of the earliest male defenders of women's liberation, argues that the subjection of women was never justified but was imposed upon women because they were physically weaker than men; later this subjection was confirmed by law. Mill argues that society must remove the legal restrictions that deny women the same opportunities enjoyed by men. However Mill does not consider whether because of past discrimination against women it may be necessary to do more than simply remove legal restrictions: He does not consider whether positive assistance may also be required.

Usually it is not enough simply to remove unequal restrictions to make a competition fair. Positive assistance to those who have been disadvantaged in the past may also be required, as would be the case in which some competitors were unfairly impeded by having to carry ten-pound weights for part of a race. To render the outcome of such a race fair, it may be necessary to transfer the weights to other runners, and thereby advantage the previously disadvantaged runners for an equal period of time. Similarly positive assistance, such as affirmative action programs, may be necessary to enable women who have been disadvantaged in the past to compete fairly with men.

In *Justice, Gender, and the Family* (1989), Susan Okin argues for the feminist ideal of a gender-free society. A gender-free society is a society where basic rights and duties are not assigned on the basis of a person's biological sex. Since a conception of justice is usually thought to provide the ultimate grounds for the assignment of rights and duties, we can refer to this ideal of a gender-free society as feminist justice.

Okin goes on to consider whether Rawls's welfare liberal conception of justice can support the ideal of a gender-free society. Noting Rawls's failure to apply his original position-type thinking to family structures, Okin is skeptical about the possibility of using a welfare liberal ideal to support feminist justice. She contends that in a gender-structured society, male philosophers cannot achieve the sympathetic imagination required to see things from the standpoint of women. According to Okin, original position-type thinking can only really be achieved in a gender-free society.

Yet while Okin despairs of doing original position-type thinking in a gender-structured society, she herself does a considerable amount of just that type of thinking. For example, she claims that Rawls's principles of justice "would seem to require a radical rethinking not only of the division of labor within families but also of all the nonfamily institutions that assume it" (p. 104). She also argues that "the abolition of gender seems essential for the fulfillment of Rawls's criterion of political justice" (p. 104). Okin's own work indicates that people can engage in original position-type thinking and her reasons for arguing otherwise are not persuasive. It is not necessary that all people have the capacity to put themselves imaginatively in the position of others, just that some have the ability to do so. Some people may not be able to do original position-type thinking because they have been deprived of a proper moral education. Others may be able to do original position-type thinking only after they have been forced to mend their ways and live morally for a period of time.

Even among those in our gendered society who are, generally, capable of a sense of justice, some may not be able to do original position-type thinking with respect to the proper relationships between men and women and may acquire the ability only after laws and social practices shift significantly toward a more gender-free society. Others may have the ability to think in this in this way, having effectively used the opportunities for moral development available to them to achieve the necessary sympathetic imagination.

## Conclusions

What conclusions should we draw from this discussion of libertarian, socialist, welfare liberal, communitarian, and feminist conceptions of justice? Is MacIntyre's opinion, described in *After Virtue* (1981), that such conceptions of justice are incommensurable and, hence, there is no rational way of deciding between them correct? Many philosophers have challenged this view, and even MacIntyre, in *Three Rival Versions of Moral Enquiry* (1990), has significantly qualified it, contending that it is possible to argue across conceptions of justice.

One could also conclude that *if* the ideal of liberty of libertarian justice can be shown to require the same rights to welfare and equal opportunity that are required by the welfare liberal conception of justice, and *if* the communitarian critique of welfare liberalism can be rebutted, that it may then be possible to reconcile, at a practical level, the differences between welfare liberal justice, socialist justice, and feminist justice. To reasonably resolve our disputes about justice, we then need only understand the shared practical requirements of these conceptions of justice and simply act upon them.

It can be argued, however, that even if these conceptions of justice can be reconciled in practice, such reconciliation would not have cross-cultural validity because the discussion derives primarily from Western philosophical traditions. While this objection cannot be fully addressed in the absence of a detailed examination of non-Western conceptions of justice and morality, there is good reason to think that, like the results of a well-reasoned discussion of mathematics derived from Western sources, this discussion of conceptions of justice also has cross-cultural validity. The conceptions of justice considered here arguably run the full gamut from least demanding (libertarian justice) to most demanding (socialist justice). Egoism is less demanding than libertarian justice, but it is a not a moral view because egoism entails a rejection of morality. Pure altruism is more demanding than socialist justice, but no conception of justice could require us to sacrifice ourselves to the degree that pure altruism does; pure altruism goes beyond the requirements of justice and morality. If libertarian justice and socialist justice, and those conceptions that purportedly fall in between, can all be practically reconciled in the way suggested, there is good reason to think that the argument is valid not only for Western philosophical traditions but cross-culturally as well.

*See also* **Liberalism; Marxism; Virtue Ethics.**

**BIBLIOGRAPHY**
Aristotle. *Nicomachean Ethics.* Bk. 5. Translated by Martin Ostwald. Indianapolis: Bobbs-Merrill, 1962.
Hayek, Friedrich. A. *The Constitution of Liberty.* Chicago: University of Chicago Press, 1960.
Jaggar, Alison M. *Feminist Politics and Human Nature.* Totowa, N.J.: Rowman and Allenheld, 1983.
Machan, Tibor. *The Passion for Liberty.* Lanham, Md.: Rowman and Littlefield, 2003.
MacIntyre, Alasdair. *After Virtue.* Notre Dame, Ind.: University of Notre Dame Press,1981.
———. "The Privatization of the Good." *Review of Politics* 52 (1990): 1–20.
———. *Three Rival Versions of Moral Enquiry.* Notre Dame, Ind.: University of Notre Dame Press, 1990.
Marx, Karl, and Engels, Friedrich. *The Communist Manifesto.* n.p., 1848. First published in English by Friedrich Engels in 1888.
Mill, John Stuart. *The Subjection of Women.* Indianapolis: Hackett. 1988.
———. Chapter 5 in his *Utilitarianism.* Indianapolis: Hackett, 2001.
Nielson, Kai. *Liberty and Equality.* Totowa, N.J.: Rowman and Allanheld, 1985.
Nozick, Robert. *Anarchy, State and Utopia.* New York: Basic Books, 1974.
Okin, Susan. *Justice, Gender, and the Family.* New York: Basic Books, 1989.
Rawls, John. *Justice as Fairness: A Restatement.* Cambridge, Mass.: Harvard University Press, 2001.
———. *A Theory of Justice.* Cambridge, Mass.: Harvard University Press, 1971.
Sommers, Christina. *Who Stole Feminism?* New York: Simon and Schuster, 1994.
Sterba, James P. *Justice for Here and Now.* New York: Cambridge University Press, 1998.

*James P. Sterba*

## JUSTICE IN AMERICAN THOUGHT

Justice appears as a paradoxical concept in the history of the United States. On the one hand, it has been absent as a rallying cry in the major struggles that have shaped, and continue to shape, the plurality of identities of the American nation. The concept "justice" is not prominent in the Declaration of Independence or in the Constitution. It was not the cornerstone of the abolitionist movement, the Civil War, the women's suffrage movement, or the civil rights movement. It did not surface in the demands of Native Americans against the encroaching and overwhelming force of local states and the federal government. Nor does it carry major weight in the pro-statehood movement that is still hoping to move Puerto Rico away from its colonial status and to see the island as a state of the American union. In contrast to the Platonic Republic, in which justice is viewed as the central virtue of an ideal society, justice seems to appear as an afterthought, as in the last sentence in the pledge of allegiance.

On the other hand, justice has infused the political ideas and practices that define the American society, and it should not be confined exclusively to the arena of legal procedures. Rather, justice has been refracted through the ideas of rights, liberty, equality, democracy, state institutions, and other concepts that have dominated the moral language of American citizens or the people who wanted to become, or were forced into the framework of, American citizenship. The absence of clear definitions of justice guiding public discussions since the arrival of the Puritans takes a different meaning when the theoretical inquiry focuses on the multiplicity of dimensions entwined with justice.

These dimensions include: a providential understanding of a communal identity; the conception of individuality; the relationship between individuals and the government; the view of political power and the proper nature of the state; the protections and bulwarks in the judicial sphere; and justice as the first principle that ought to guide both the individual's life and governmental policies. All these dimensions place a high premium on rights, but the relationship between rights and justice is clarified by looking at the link between liberty and justice. This link presupposes that people must be free to choose rules of justice, but then justice is understood as the principle that delineates the scope of liberty, which means that justice defines the boundaries of rights. The refracted and yet ubiquitous presence of justice in American thought helps to explain why John Rawls's philosophy, which dominated American liberalism in the last three decades of the twentieth century, portrayed justice as the standard by which to measure both a well-ordered society and a just citizen.

### Puritan Conceptions of Justice
Though the Mayflower Compact (1620) stresses the importance of "just and equal Laws," John Winthrop's sermon "A

Modell of Christian Charity" (1630) is a reasonable point of departure in examining justice in the American context. This sermon is important not only for the location where it was delivered—on the ship *Arabella* en route to a new continent—but also for the distinction between mercy and justice as well as for its emphasis on an ordered and tightly knit community predicated on mutual assistance. According to the principle of mercy, Christians must help their brothers and sisters beyond their ability in order to fulfill the gospel. But in lending means of subsistence and forgiving debts, justice intervenes. If a Christian brother, for instance, possesses the resources to repay a debt, "thou art to looke at him, not as an Act of mercy, but by way of Commerce, wherein thou arte to walke by the rule of Justice . . . ." (p. 32). When the probability of a debt being re-payed is null, Christians ought to lend according to the rule of mercy, which expects nothing. Along similar lines, whether the loan was an act of mercy or of justice, when the borrower has nothing to pay back, "thou must forgive him (except in cause where thou hast a surety or a lawful pleadge)" (p. 33). In this way, if there is a "lawful pleadge," justice overrules mercy.

The association of justice, commerce, and a lawful pledge delimits justice to the sphere of agreements and contracts sanctioned by the law. Though this view seems to narrow significantly the scope of justice, the refraction principle shows itself when the text is examined in more detail. At the end of his sermon, Winthrop presents the well-known analogy of the pilgrims as a "city upon a Hill." But it must be emphasized that the city upon a hill does not refer to the original biblical reference found in the Gospel according to Matthew. In Winthrop's reasoning, the context of the phrase is provided by the Israelites on their journey to the promised land. As in the Israelites' case, Winthrop's arguments center upon a covenant between God and the Christian community, and God will expect a strict compliance with the "Articles contained in it . . . ," for otherwise "wee shall surely perishe out of the good Land whether wee passe over this vast Sea to possesse it. . . ." (p. 43). In other words, the relationship between God and Winthrop's fellow travelers is one ruled by justice in the form of a covenant, and an intrinsic part of this justice was the possession of the land where they would live.

Seen from this perspective, justice is no longer limited to contractual relations between persons. Rather, the boundaries encompassing justice widen substantially. At the same time, a covenant that carries the high penalty of divine wrath is ominous for all people who are outside the particular community Winthrop is addressing. Justice thus straddled two conflicting points of departure. The city upon the hill echoes the love Winthrop found in the gospel, while the covenant belonged to the Hebrew warriors who were to possess a land already inhabited. The New Testament "law of grace" and the Old Testament justice were inseparable. The mention of the city upon a hill is preceded by an explicit reference to God's command to Saul to destroy Amalek. In other words, the textual transplantation preceded the cultural transplantation. Justice, then, had two dimensions: a secular one defined by legal contracts among individuals as well as a providential dimension manifested in a covenant between God and a community bonded by shared beliefs.

The double character of Winthrop's conception of justice insisted on the individual's obligation to comply with his or her contracts and gave the community a privileged position in its dealings with non-Christians and even with Christians who did not share the same doctrinal tenets. Unity and fragmentation emerged as two central components that would be present in the understanding and application of justice. Winthrop's view of love anticipated this conclusion. Love stems from the fact that people see in others what they see and cherish in themselves. In this way, the root of otherness, as a standpoint that demands the conversion and "civilization" of non-Christians, or as the establishment of boundaries to keep outsiders at bay, was thus inscribed in the view of justice sketched in Winthrop's famous sermon. The "Dedham Covenant" (1636), a document specifying the form of government in the town of Dedham, Massachusetts, was more eloquent in describing the quest of unity and how exclusion was part of this quest. In section two, the limits of admittance into the community were specified: "That we shall by all means labor to keep off from us all such as are contrary minded, and receive only such unto us as may be probably of one heart with us . . . ." (p. 68).

Several years earlier, Virginia had already put into place a system of legal clauses that contained both a mix of exclusion and a call for fairness. The "Articles, Laws, and Orders, Divine, Politic, and Martial for the Colony in Virginia" (1610–1611) stipulated that no man "of what condition so-ever shall barter, trucke, or trade with the Indians, except he be thereunto appointed by lawful authority upon paine of death." (Article 15, p. 319). In the following article, the colonists were forbidden from despoiling any "Indian" who would come to trade, and the punishment would also be death (Article 16). By 1619, freemen were allowed to trade with the Indians, but offensive or defensive weapons could not be part of these commercial transactions.

The twofold nature of unity and exclusion should not obfuscate other features that would have a deep influence in the evolution and conceptualizations of the idea of justice. The "Plymouth Oath of Allegiance and Fidelity" (1625) contained an oath given to the governor and members of the council in which they would swear to administer justice "equally & indifrently without respect of persons." (p. 34) The same principle of impartiality is present in the "Pilgrim Code of Law" (15 November 1636) and runs consistently in the founding documents of the early settlements. The historical evidence thus shows that the English philosopher John Locke's (1632–1704) arguments about consent and impartial laws as the cornerstones of a political and just society were already present in the ideas animating the Puritans of the early colonies, the same ideas that permeated their providential and secular understanding of justice.

During King Philip's War (1674–1677), between the New England colonists and the Indian tribes in the region, the providential character of justice showed the consequences of its privileged standpoint. Increase Mather would remind his listeners that their unfaithfulness was the cause of the violent upheaval that threatened them. But he saw the destruction of the heathens as an act that abided with the justice expected from a people ruled by a providential design. For the war was just, and the army was executing "the vengeance of the Lord upon the perfidious and bloudy Heathen" (p. 107).

## Providential View of Justice

The same providential view of justice that erected boundaries against outsiders and allowed Mather to justify the obliteration of a community of Native Americans also called for universal descriptions that would later haunt institutions tethered to partiality and particularity. That is to say, it was contradictory to use a universal language of justice to justify political institutions and then attempt to circumvent and ignore the consequences of this language. The phrase "all men are created equal," a phrase that belongs to the domain of justice, could not be used to justify slavery. In his 1858 debates with Stephen Douglas, Abraham Lincoln could confidently use the Declaration of Independence and the Constitution to oppose the extension of slavery. This task was fraught with obstacles, though. The universality of categories pertaining to justice transformed the American Constitution into a battleground of competing conceptions of morality and conflicting views of the relationship between individuals and the government. For William Lloyd Garrison, the Constitution was a covenant with hell that vitiated its potentiality for individual liberty. Frederick Douglass followed, at first, the Garrisonian view, but he concluded that the founders had bestowed enough room to challenge the institution of slavery. In his speech of May 28, 1856, addressing the radical abolition party convention in New York, Douglass said: "This Constitution sets forth several propositions, which, if carried out, would abolish slavery. What are they? The Constitution declares its object to be 'to form a more perfect union.' How can you form a more perfect union with slavery? . . . The Constitution is declared to be established for the people, and who are the people? The men and women of the country. We are part of the people" (pp. 389–390).

While Douglass found refuge in the universal goals that the Constitution clearly pursued, Ralph Waldo Emerson and Henry David Thoreau invoked transcendental categories that were congenial to the providential view of justice. In his opposition to slavery, Emerson saw the universe, nature, power, justice, and the moral order as transcendental realities of a divine unity. The universe, Emerson wrote in 1845, "is not bankrupt: still stands the old heart firm in its seat, and knows that, come what will, the right is and shall be. Justice is for ever and ever" (p. 36). The planter's predicament is always unsafe, no matter how powerful he might appear to be. Nature fights against him, and "as power is always stealing from the idle to the busy hand, it seems inevitable that a revolution is preparing at no distant day to set these disjointed matters right" (p. 37). In the twentieth century, Martin Luther King, Jr., followed Douglass's footsteps and resorted to the universality embedded in the American conception of justice to challenge civil inequalities, and to fulfill Emerson's hope of setting right matters that were still "disjointed."

The providential covenant as a central component of the American conception of justice has shown a remarkable resistance to the passing of time. In 1795, Bishop James Madison painted the providential character in a language that was more emphatic than Winthrop's. God had thrown a veil upon the American continent in order "to conceal it from the nations of the east," thus saving America from the ravages of tyranny and inequality that went untrammeled in the European nations. The veil would not be lifted until the emergence of "a new race of men" that would be responsible for the redemption of humankind. "It is in America," Bishop Madison declared, "that the germs of the universal redemption of the human race from domination and oppression have already begun to be developed" (p. 1312). In 1820, Daniel Webster echoed similar themes in his "Plymouth Oration," and in 1900, Albert Beveridge, the Republican senator from Indiana, portrayed the divine plan that was in the offing.

In addressing the question of acquiring and administering territories whose population, he opined, was not yet ready for self-government, Beveridge asserted that God "has marked the American people as His chosen nation to finally lead in the regeneration of the world" (p. 704). "[O]ur place, therefore, is at the head of the constructing and redeeming nations of the earth" (p. 712).

It is worth noticing that the emphasis on redemption, covenant, natural rights, and government evinced a duty to carry out the designs of divine justice refracted through human institutions. The secular and providential notions of justice thus complemented one another. While the emphasis on legal contracts might have led individuals to seek their own interests, the providential covenant would bring them back to their public duty. It is in this providential notion that one finds the centrality of a legitimate government anchored upon the principle of consent.

## The Individual and the State

Another sphere of justice revolves around the proper role of state power and the relationship between individuals and their government. The Federalists bestowed on the American intellectual landscape the best articulation of justice in connection with social order and public institutions. The Federalist view made clear that the institutional framework ought to exist to protect the basic rights of citizens, and property stood out as one of the most important personal rights. Clearly, the root of the centrality of property was derived from Locke's reasoning in the *Second Treatise of Government* (1690), which postulates a civil or political society founded on just laws, which are not available in a state of nature, no matter how rational men could be or how harmoniously they might work together. Even in this scenario, common rules of justice, accepted as part of a free compact, were necessary to avoid the vagaries of the individual's judgment. As already indicated, in the first half of the seventeenth century, the Pilgrims anticipated Locke's reasoning. In "Federalist Paper number 10," however, James Madison was more explicit than Locke. Justice, according to Madison, was needed to regulate the potentially lethal conflicts arising from disagreements on property. This regulation envisaged the rise of factions as inevitable, but sought to contain its effects by dispersing those factions through the whole society.

It might appear that Madison's vision of a society fragmented into different factions would be a denial of Winthrop's concern for a strong community. But this is not the case. Winthrop's community was one among many others and, in this sense, it might be seen as a faction in Madison's use of the term. In a nutshell, Madison argues that the diversity of factions would be the warranty against the prospect of a tyrannical majority. In a fragmented milieu, this majority would lack the means to arise, let alone to succeed. Hence the Lockean need of a central government that was conceived as the embodiment of a just social order seeking to regulate the disparity of interests. The anti-federalists consistently applied the logic of fragmentation. Just as a fragmented society was a guardrail against a tyrannical majority, so also a fragmented legislature would cancel the proclivity to factionalism. Hence a government in which all the classes of society should be represented as both the Federal Farmer and Brutus, two of the leading voices in the anti-federalist cause, insisted.

The slavery question that led to the Civil War (1861–1865) was the lightning bolt that limned the fissures underlying the moral and political landscape of the American society. Even when Lincoln's paramount concern was the preservation of the Union, and both the thirteenth and fourteenth amendment sought to create a new juridical reality for all people born under the jurisdiction of the United States, justice, understood as a set of principles and regulations serving as the moral compass of both individuals and public institutions, became more fragile and malleable. Neither women nor Native Americans were part of the notion of citizenship implicit in the post-civil war constitutional amendments. And in a series of decisions, the Federal Supreme Court reinstated inequalities and legal boundaries that the fourteenth amendment wanted to remove.

In the *Slaughterhouse Cases* (1873), the Supreme Court established a distinction between citizens of the United States and citizens of particular states, and concluded that Congress lacked power to regulate state actions in matters of local government, property, and civil rights. In other words, the court reasserted the "disjointed matters" that Emerson had mentioned in 1845. According to the legal doctrine of the *Slaughterhouse Cases*, the states, not the federal government, would be final arbiters in controversies pertaining to the same issues that had led to the Civil War. It would not take long to show how the purview of the state would perform when dealing with the rights of black citizens. In *United States* v. *Cruickshank* (1876), a case involving the murder of African-American citizens in Colfax, Louisiana, the sane court struck down the conviction of three white men. Writing for the majority, Chief Justice Morrison R. Waite found that the right of the victims to "peaceably assemble," as well as their right not to be deprived of life and liberty without due process, had not been violated. Furthermore, Waite argued that the power to initiate prosecution for murder belonged, exclusively, to the states. This was another way of saying that the dominant beliefs of particular states would prevail. If the states decided not to act, there would be no crime. In the *Civil Right Cases* (1883), the Supreme Court upheld racial segregation in public places, and in *Plessy* v. *Ferguson* (1895), put the seal of legality not only on segregation, but also on the social inequalities that the fourteenth amendment intended to overcome.

These cases show that the providential view of justice of the puritans was superseded by all the ramifications embedded in the very first phrase of the preamble to the Constitution: "We the people . . ." It was a phrase that departed from the self-evident truths so prominent in the Declaration of Independence. And this phrase carried a foreboding about the unstable and precarious role of natural law arguments in the American conception of justice. More than a democratic sentiment, "We the people . . ." expressed the design of a secular order without any transcendental anchors. Since the phrase, along with the whole constitutional text, would receive its authoritative interpretation from a political institution presiding over a society that blurred the line between diversity (in which there are some common links) and fragmentation (in which common links are absent), the outcome would be far too evident. It is ironic that Representative John A. Bingham, Republican from Ohio, referred to the universal and "higher laws" principles that he saw inscribed in the Declaration of Independence when he argued for the need of the Fourteenth Amendment, while the Supreme Court would resort to the particular beliefs of the states when eroding the clear meaning of this amendment.

The fractures of a social order continued unabated in the early twentieth century, especially with the territorial expansion of the American empire. The newly acquired territories after the Hispano-American War (1898) would be excluded from the constitutional protections available to white citizens.

In the *Cherokee Nation* v. *Georgia* (1831), the Supreme Court abandoned the providential view of justice, and upheld rights emanating from an idea of cultural superiority; namely, upheld rights stemming from the power to define and impose a definition of a superior culture. In the *Plessy* case the Supreme Court mangled the constitutional meaning in order to demarcate a new reality that justified segregation and inferior citizenship. Thus, the trajectory of the United States Supreme Court clearly suggests that the idea of justice as a dimension of natural law has stood on precarious grounds and not played any significant role in legal controversies concerning minority groups. Natural law served neither Native Americans nor African-Americans. Natural law presupposes an agreement on universal principles of morality, an agreement that, in a context of moral and cultural fragmentation, was nowhere to be found. Native Americans had to be civilized. A civil war was needed to alter the juridical classification of African-Americans. Yet, natural law arguments continue to lurk in judicial decisions addressing private conduct or decisions. The right of privacy seems to be the closest area whose underpinning insinuates natural law principles.

## John Rawls

As Gordon Wood argues, the pluralism so dear to the anti-federalists triumphed in the short run and became the dominant conception of politics in the American society. It was in the context of this pluralism that John Rawls developed and polished what turned out to be the most influential theory of justice in the intellectual vistas of American society during the last three decades of the twentieth century.

With the publication of *A Theory of Justice* (1971), John Rawls set out to establish the institutional framework and the moral principles of a well-ordered society conceived in perpetuity. He did this by constructing an imaginary scenario that he called the "original position" and designing the parties who were to deliberate about the agreement that would rule their society. The arguments were then premised on the social-contract tradition to the extent that the end of deliberation was to reach a binding agreement for present and future generations. In the first version of his theory, Rawls saw the agreement on justice as a paradigm that would apply to all societies. In the original position, "a veil of ignorance" covers the parties, which means that they lack knowledge about their gender, race, social status, philosophical beliefs, and religious beliefs. In other words, they are selves that, placed in a context of fairness, would arrive at a fair agreement. This is why Rawls calls his theory "justice as fairness." The assumption is that the lack of knowledge about personal and social features would lead the parties to advocate an institutional arrangement that would benefit all of them. The original position brings forth a basic agreement on two principles of justice: the principle of equal liberties and the difference principle. In *Justice as Fairness. A Restatement* (2001), Rawls offers his last articulation of these principles:

a. Each person has the same indefeasible claim to a fully adequate scheme of equal basic liberties, which scheme is compatible with the same scheme of liberties for all; and

b. Social and economic inequalities are to satisfy two conditions: first, they are to be attached to offices and positions open to all under conditions of fair equality of opportunity; and second, they are to be to the greatest benefit of the least-advantaged members of society (the difference principle). (pp. 42–43)

The principle of equal liberties protects constitutional essentials that will be settled once and for all. There is no need to deliberate about them. The difference principle sets a goal, which is to maximize the long-term expectations of the least advantaged members of society over the long run. This maximization, Rawls believes, is achieved by providing a social minimum to the disadvantaged. It is worth mentioning that the right of property does not count as one of the constitutional essentials. Rawls even defends the creation of a distributive branch with the responsibility of watching over society to rein in excessive inequalities, though what counts as excessive is not specified.

In a second version of his theory, Rawls abandoned the quest of universality and declared that the parties were representatives of democratic citizens; namely, historical members of a particular society. His theory depended not on a metaphysical view of persons as empty shadows but on the political culture of the United States. In *Justice as Fairness: A Restatement*, Rawls says that his theory takes into account three kinds of contingencies: social class, "native endowments," and "good or ill fortune." In light of this political culture, Rawls believes, there are two intuitive ideas that will justify the choice of his two principles of justice. The first idea stands for the moral equality of all citizens, while the second defends a system of fair cooperation. Bound together, these two intuitive ideas are seen as already embedded in the political vocabulary and practices of a constitutional democracy. More importantly, they are completely free of what Rawls calls "comprehensive moral doctrines," which are doctrines that seek to provide all or partially encompassing answers to the deepest questions surrounding the meaning, if any, of life and the human good.

In the three decades after the publication of *Theory,* Rawls expanded and modified his arguments in several areas, while leaving intact its basic tenets. The most important upshot of his reflections was the articulation of what he called "political liberalism," a liberalism that is bereft of questions of truth, the human good, and any transcendental realm; that is, it eschews any form of comprehensive doctrines. These doctrines are seen as belonging to the private sphere, and citizens should not use them in deliberations about justice. Furthermore, justice is expected to supersede the injunctions of comprehensive doctrines even in the private domain.

Under the aegis of political liberalism, the emphasis is not so much on distributive justice as it is on the quest of an overlapping consensus embracing all reasonable doctrines that may flourish in a constitutional democracy. Political liberalism is deeply aware of the fact of pluralism in modern times and the impossibility of having a universal agreement on a single conception of the human good. Hence the need of fair principles of justice to achieve the overlapping consensus Rawls seeks to undergird stability. Rawls assumes that "justice as fairness" is capable of commanding the kind of support a theory of justice needs to provide stability. He further assumes that, in a well-ordered society, citizens see themselves as fully cooperating members of society over their whole life. The terms "reasonable" and "fully cooperating" mean that people will see the two principles of justice as moral principles, abide by their outcomes, and use them in choosing and revising their conceptions of the human good.

Rawls's theory is vulnerable to a question that "justice as fairness" leaves unanswered: how could the second principle maximize people's long-term expectations when all Rawls expects from the state is the allocation of a social minimum? This question leads to a problem that haunted the Rawlsian view. In both *Theory* and *Political Liberalism* Rawls accepts that his well-ordered society is compatible with the existence of large economic inequalities. As long as the constitutional essentials are preserved and the difference principle is in operation, these inequalities will not tarnish the moral character of a Rawlsian society. Though the issue of large inequalities is present in *Justice as Fairness: A Restatement*, Rawls introduces the following modification. Instead of writing about maximizing the long-term expectations of the least advantaged over the long run, he writes about "an appropriate interval of time" in which the expectations mentioned above should be maximized.

*Other theories of justice.* Though John Rawls's theory of justice set the context for discussions of justice in the last three decades of the twentieth century, it was not the only theory advanced. Ronald Dworkin developed his own theory that he calls "Equality of Resources." This theory insists that, without the need of resorting to an original position, people ought to be aware of the true cost of their life-plans for other people, and to be willing to redesign these life-plans when they go beyond the fair share of resources available to all citizens. Unfortunately, Dworkin is not clear about the criteria and the institutions that will decide what a "fair share" of resources is and when the individual is taking more than what this "fair share" demands. Iris Marion Young brought to the fore an alternative conception of justice that relies not on an abstract equality but on the recognition that different groups have different needs and, accordingly, may require unequal allocations of public resources. At first sight, this view seems to reject the universal understanding of justice that imbued the Rawlsian philosophy, but, ultimately, Young advocates general rules of justice to regulate the competing interests of a group-based politics.

## Communitarianism and Liberalism

During the 1980s, the American conception of justice revolved around the conflicting arguments of liberalism and communitarianism. The ensuing debates had at their core the role of visions of the human good and the question of how the individual's identity is formed, and not issues of distributive justice. Michael Walzer, Michael Sandel, and Alasdair MacIntyre stood out as thinkers who challenged the Rawlsian view and its design of a situation in which selves who are bereft of any contingent traits are expected to arrive at a universally binding agreement on justice. On this issue, the communitarian side won the day. Rawls admitted that the parties to the original position are representatives of democratic citizens, thus introducing a substantial element of contingency into his assumptions. On the further issue of the need of shared values to sustain a just order, the communitarian standpoint also prevailed. Rawlsian justice obtains guidance and derives its principles from the common values that distinguish the constitutional democracy of the United States.

But for all its insistence on how conceptions of the human good ought to guide visions of justice, communitarianism did not muster enough theoretical resources to deal with the fact that, in contemporary societies, multiple and opposing views of the human good are fated either to accept one another or to compete for supremacy via state power. This is not to say that the different versions of political liberalism articulated, among others, by John Rawls and Charles Larmore, fared better. In Rawls's and Larmore's theories, the agreement on principles of justice has an important rider. The agreement is only concerned with people who may hold reasonable conceptions of the human good. And a reasonable conception is one that accepts the principles of justice. Communitarianism excludes conceptions of the human good at variance with the dominant views of a particular society, and contemporary liberalism excludes comprehensive doctrines that justice has not certified as reasonable. Yet, the liberal argument that, in a context

ridden by conflictive ideas, an agreement on principles of justice is more feasible than one on a conception of the human good, remains unassailable.

The end result is circularity, which according to Richard Rorty is the most that can be expected in a world devoid of ultimate foundations. Individuals ought to justify their principles, Rorty argues, not by invoking a transcendental realm or a universal or true morality, but by referring to those principles and institutions that have proven, so far, to provide stability and respect for people. A conception of justice should be described by making reference to its outcomes, and these outcomes ought to be described by referring back to the principles of justice.

Michael Walzer was the only philosopher who put forward a communitarian version of justice. Walzer's theory distances itself from the Rawlsian paradigm by positing a diversity of social goods that obtain their meaning from their society and inhabit different social spheres. These spheres are not meant to cross their boundaries. The sphere of need is not the sphere of desert and, accordingly, they should not be judged according to a single criterion. Similarly, a social good in one sphere should not carry any import in another or, in Walzer's words, should not be "convertible." Wealth in the economic sphere should not be translated into more political power or access to better health care. He calls his theory "complex equality" as a contradistinction to "simple equality," which is the term he uses to describe Rawlsian justice. In simple equality, the state needs to intervene frequently to curtail any hindrances that may undermine the difference principle. In complex equality, "the autonomy of distributive spheres" is vindicated, and individuals, not the state, would have "local monopolies," but social conflicts would be diffused across the social and political spectrum. Local monopolies refer to the goods some people may control. Physicians, through their education, experience, and talents, control their areas of expertise. But it does not follow that this monopoly entails power to determine people's needs. These needs ought to be defined by the community. "Equality," Walzer writes, "is a complex relation of persons, mediated by the goods we make, share, and divide among ourselves; it is not an identity of possessions. It requires then, a diversity of distributive criteria that mirrors the diversity of social goods" (p. 18). The demarcation of the spheres of justice will depend on the dominant morality of a particular society. While Rawls argues that his arguments belong in the realm of ideal theory, Walzer goes into historical examples to buttress his theoretical reflections.

## Moral Context of Justice

The last word on the moral context of justice in American thought might belong to William Connolly and Alasdair MacIntyre. Connolly defends an agonistic ethos in which a person's identity, the same identity that the Puritans saw as fixed by God's grace, could recognize its contingent character. In this recognition, Connolly sees a conversation in which cherished assumptions about the individual's character and the United States' foundations would be open to redefinitions and negotiations. MacIntyre did not feel at home in this conversation, which in his view is sequestered by a liberal marketplace of ideas regulated by justice. In his discussion of virtue, he envisages a rather dark horizon for the American intellectual landscape. Current times, he argues, are analogous to the era when the Roman Republic dwindled and finally fell. As in those times, citizens should retreat from the public sphere and move to small communities that may share the same conception of the human good. This, again, is the fragmentation that has been a constitutive element of the American landscape. Rawls himself is not free from the suspicion that his theory, though envisioning a stable interplay between a multiplicity of social unions, is ridden, too, by a fragmented ethos.

Indeed, Rawls's theory treads its way along two paths that are prone to deny one another. There is a strong sense of community to the extent that members of particular groups see their worth as being determined by the appreciation they receive from others. For self-esteem, in Rawls's view, does not depend on the individual's convictions, but on the external approval of his or her peers. This is similar to Winthrop's understanding of love, which is an "apprehension of some resemblance in the things loved to that which affectes it . . . soe a mother loves her childe, because shee throughly conceives a resemblance of herself in it" (p. 37). As in the Puritan context, the Rawlsian sense of community requires clear delimitations. Since a Rawlsian society may have large inequalities that, through envy, may bring havoc to stability, the plurality of associations comes to the rescue. These associations tend "to reduce the visibility, or at least the painful visibility, of variations in men's prospects. . . . The various associations in society tend to divide it into so many noncomparing groups, the discrepancies between these divisions not attracting the kind of attention which unsettles the lives of those less well placed" (Rawls 1971, p. 537).

From John Winthrop's message that the rich and the poor ought to accept their place as part of a divine order, to the Federalist recognition of the unavoidability of factions, the anti-federalist advocacy of a fragmented legislature, and John Rawls's call to avoid the "painful visibility" of "variations in men's prospects" by dividing society into "noncomparing groups" that would not intersect in their respective paths, unity and fragmentation stand as consistent strands in the way justice has been woven into the inner fabric of American thought. In this consistency, "justice as fairness" appears as a dim echo of the arguments John Winthrop put forward aboard the *Arabella*.

*See also* **Abolitionism; Philosophies, American; Philosophy, Moral: Modern; Pluralism; Populism; Pragmatism.**

**BIBLIOGRAPHY**
Beveridge, Albert J. "In Support of an American Empire." U.S. Senate. 56 Cong. 1 sess., 704–712.
Connolly, William. *Identity/Difference: Democratic Negotiations of Political Paradox.* Ithaca: Cornell University Press, 1991.
Douglass, Frederick. *The Life and Writings of Frederick Douglass: Supplementary Volume.* Vol. 5: 1844–1860. Edited by Philip S. Foner. New York: International Publishers, 1975.
Dworkin, Ronald. "What Is Equality? Part 2: Equality of Resources." *Philosophy and Public Affairs* 10, no. 4 (fall 1981): 283–345.
———. "What Is Equality? Part 3: The Place of Liberty." *Iowa Law Review* 73, no. 1 (October 1987): 24–50.
Larmore, Charles. *Patterns of Moral Complexity.* Cambridge, U.K: Cambridge University Press, 1987.
"Letters I, III–IV." In Alexander Hamilton, James Madison, and James Jay, *The Federalist: With Letters of Brutus,* edited by Terence Ball, 453–465. Cambridge, U.K.: Cambridge University Press, 2003.
"Letters II, V." In *The Complete Anti-Federalist: Writings by the Opponents of the Constitution,* edited by Herbert J. Storing, selected by Murray Dry, 60–65. Chicago: Chicago University Press, 1981.
Locke, John. *A Second Treatise of Government.* Edited by C. B. Macpherson. Indianapolis: Hackett, 1980.
Lutz, Donald S., ed. *Colonial Origins of the American Constitution: A Documentary History.* Indianapolis: Liberty Fund, 1998. See especially: "Articles, Laws, and Orders, Divine, Politic, and Martial for the Colony in Virginia. 1610–1611," pp. 314–326; "Laws Enacted by the First General Assembly of Virginia, August 2–4, 1619," pp. 327–335; "[Agreement Between the Settlers of New Plymouth] (The Mayflower Compact). November 11, 1620," pp. 31–32; "Plymouth Oath of Allegiance and Fidelity (1625)," pp. 33–34; "Pilgrim Code of Law, November 15, 1636," pp. 61–67; "Dedham Covenant. 1636," pp. 68–69.
MacIntyre, Alasdair. *After Virtue.* 2nd ed. Notre Dame: University of Notre Dame Press, 1984.
Madison, James. "Federalist Paper No. 10." In Hamilton, Madison, and Jay, *The Federalist: With Letters of Brutus,* edited by Terence Ball, 40–46. Cambridge, U.K.: Cambridge University Press, 2003.
Madison, James (Bishop). "Manifestations of the Beneficence of Divine Providence towards America." In *Political Sermons of the American Founding Era, 1730–1805,* edited by Ellis Sandoz, 1305–1320. Indianapolis: Liberty, 1991.
Mather, Increase. "A Brief History of the War with the Indians in New England." In *So Dreadfull a Judgment: Puritan Responses to King Philip's War, 1676–1677,* edited by Richard Slotkin and James K. Folsom, 81–163. Middletown, Conn.: Wesleyan University Press, 1978.
Rawls, John. *Justice as Fairness: A Restatement.* Edited by Erin Kelly. Cambridge, Mass.: Harvard University Press, 2001.
———. *Political Liberalism.* New York: Columbia University Press, 1993.
———. *A Theory of Justice.* Cambridge, Mass.: Harvard University Press, 1971.
Rorty, Richard. *Contingency, Irony, and Solidarity.* Cambridge, U.K.: Cambridge University Press, 1989.
Sandel, Michael. *Liberalism and the Limits of Justice.* Cambridge, U.K.: Cambridge University Press, 1982.
Walzer, Michael. *Spheres of Justice: A Defense of Pluralism and Equality.* New York: Basic Books, 1983.
Winthrop, John. "A Modell of Christian Charity." In *American Sermons. The Pilgrims to Martin Luther King Jr.,* 28–43. New York: The Library of America, 1999.
Wood, Gordon S. "Interests and Disinterestedness in the Making of the Constitution." In *Beyond Confederation,* edited by Richard Beeman, Stephen Botein, and Edward C. Carter II, 69–107. Chapel Hill: University of North Carolina Press, 1987.
Young, Iris Marion. *Justice and the Politics of Difference.* Princeton, N.J.: Princeton University Press, 1990.

*Roberto Alejandro*

### JUSTICE IN EAST ASIAN THOUGHT

East Asian thought should include a wide range of Japanese, Korean, and Chinese concerns covering more than twenty-five hundred years of history. This article is limited to the Chinese sphere, and its primary focus is on the preimperial period (before 221 B.C.E.).

How issues related to justice have appeared in the preimperial Confucian ("Ruist") and Daoist traditions involves both historical and philosophical investigation. While penal codes ("corrective justice") were enforced even by the ancient sage, Confucius (Master Kong; 551 B.C.E.–479 B.C.E.), the political emphasis of Confucian scholars in general was to support an elitist system where humane forms of fairness provided flexible standards for determining the appropriate distribution of opportunities and goods ("distributive justice") and so sought to lessen the need for corrective justice. Early Daoist philosophical texts advocated an alternative way, something like a benign form of anarchism. Their rulers would be compassionate, frugal, and unobtrusive, allowing every person within the kingdom to follow the Way (*Dao*) in a spontaneous and uncontrived manner.

In what follows, central themes and institutions related to justice that appeared within Confucian and Daoist teachings in preimperial China will be explained and evaluated, followed by brief comments about later developments.

### Preimperial Confucianism

Three persons stand out as fulcrum figures in preimperial Confucian developments: the pioneer sage, Confucius; the apologist, Mencius (Master Meng; c. 371 B.C.E.–c. 289 B.C.E.); and the secular rationalist, Master Xun (Xunzi; active c. 298 B.C.E.–c. 230 B.C.E.). While the influence of Confucius's life and teachings overshadows the other two, the latter pair produced more systematic worldviews, including questions related to justice that continue to have historical significance.

***Confucius, or "Master Kong."*** Records about political policies and concepts in ancient China began at least five hundred years before Confucius, but his teachings provided the first philosophical basis for its ideological and institutional development. His political vision rested on these earlier sagely antecedents but sought to provide moral and political justifications for reestablishing the monarchical form during his own instable age. Conceiving of a ritually articulate group of intellectuals who could balance the interests of smaller political states and establish a larger and harmonious kingdom, Confucius promoted cultivated humaneness (*ren*) as the necessary cultural foundation for the king, government ministers, and his people. Any person who achieved this exemplary status knew how to properly subdue selfish interests in order to perform ritually appropriate services according to their given roles and duties (*Analects* 12:2). All these ritual actions (*li*)—whether among humans or toward spirits including a supreme deity known as "Heaven"—were consequently conditioned upon a sense of rightness (*yi*). Propriety between humans should always seek an appropriateness intuited through analogical projection (*shu*) and faithful consistency (*zhong*). Embodied in these two methods was a generalized sense of

> Tzu-lu said, "If the Lord of Wei left the administration of his state to you, what would you put first?" The Master said, "If something has to be put first, it is, perhaps, the rectification of names. . . . When names are not correct, what is said will not sound reasonable; when what is said does not sound reasonable, affairs will not culminate in success; when affairs do not culminate in success, rites and music will not flourish; when rites and music do not flourish, punishments will not fit the crimes; when punishments do not fit the crimes, the common people will not know where to put hand and foot."
>
> SOURCE: Confucius, *Analects* 13:3, translated by D. C. Lau (Harmondsworth, U.K.: Penguin, 1979).

personhood, though ancient traditions indicate how Confucius recognized limitations in their application to women, slaves, and angry persons (*Analects* 14:34, 17:25).

Some scholars feel that this account of ritual-based personhood offers a generalizable humane alternative to modern human-rights-based litigation. So, for example, while Confucius did mediate in litigations (*song*), he sought to create social conditions where they would not be needed (*Analects* 12:13). In defining the roles of rulers and ministers, he deemphasized punishments (*xing*), seeking that they humanely fit the crimes rather than produce fear of authority (*Analects* 2:3; 4:11; 13:3). Nevertheless, later Confucian teachings in the *Book of Rites* advocated moral justifications for blood-revenge as a putative principle supported by Confucius, illustrating limits to this elitist form of fairness in later imperial history.

***Mencius, or "Master Meng."*** Political justifications for humane government were explored at greater length in the *Mengzi*, a work named after Mencius. Cultivated humaneness and rightness became twin virtues grounding all moral and political life, nurtured initially in familial relationships and extendable into other appropriate social ties. Both virtues were intended to be augmented by wise elaborations, ritual articulateness, and harmonious music (*Mengzi* 1A:7; 4A:27). Significantly, a society dominated by a humanely cultivated lifestyle would entail in Mencius's philosophy various claims and liabilities within relationships, even to the extent that a tyrannical ruler could be resisted and justifiably deposed (*Mengzi* 1B:1, 3). Maintaining rightness (*yi*) was more important than life itself, whenever dilemmas forced a choice between them (*Mengzi* 6A:10). In this emphasis there are tendencies toward asserting a humanely inspired form of social justice, based on a positive account of human nature.

According to Mencius, all persons are defined as humans because they possess four basic moral sensitivities without which they could not appropriately participate in human society: compassion, shame, respect or yielding, and discerning between right and wrong (*Mengzi* 2A:6; 6A:6). When these inward sensitivities are nurtured into full-fledged virtues (humane cultivation, rightness, propriety, and wisdom), any willing person becomes exemplary and may attain sagely status. Once these virtues are embodied in exemplary persons and leaders, social obligations are fulfilled and beneficent forms of government can be realized and sustained. The crucial social transformations they would inspire would be nurtured by worthy officers and cultivated scholars. This would result in a harmonious society expressing just and accountable relationships.

Mencius also offered details about how this elitist form of social justice would operate. He envisioned opportunities for fair treatment by providing public education and coordinating publicly and privately owned farming, so that government institutions were sustained by appropriately cultivated personnel and sufficient material resources, and no one family was overburdened by taxes. While there is no indication that these institutions were ever realized in his own time, they do reveal how Mencius's philosophy could bear a populist flair. Never democratic in polity, his political philosophy manifested demophilic (*mínben*) principles of regal concern for commoners, and so set limits to any ruler's authority by arguing for these moral restraints within a kingdom.

These early Confucian scholars promoted justice as arising from virtues cultivated among a chosen elite, in some ways like Plato's conception of a righteous city-state in his *Republic*. Aristotle's support for limited democracy also suggests that justice should produce harmony between different classes within society, but these early Confucian philosophers preferred monarchy, and their vision of social harmony was not worked out in detail. Both early Confucian and Greek visions of social justice rely on rational criticisms and selective adoptions of received traditions, but the former relies more heavily on sagely precedents, while the latter promoted rational development through education and practices leading to ethical competence. Clearly, the predominance of a rational method and rationalized ideal of human nature in Plato's discussion is qualified by the early Confucians' multidimensional account of human nature based on a harmony of emotive and rational constituents. Here Aristotle and these early Confucians have much in common, but Aristotle retains a preference for rationalized understandings of ethics and social justice, while the Confucians placed more emphasis on basic emotional sensitivities. All of them nevertheless agreed that the best form of society would be achieved through the guidance of cultivated rulers imbued with the virtues they promoted.

***Master Xun.*** Unlike previous Confucian philosophers, Master Xun conceived of ritual and role attunements as a result of teaching rather than of internal personal cultivation, so that sociocultural values were inculcated rather than nurtured from within. Believing that human beings were naturally bad, Master Xun highlighted the roles of cultural change agents—sages, teachers, good friends—in educating willing persons. He explained

differences in cultivated attainments and social roles as a result of different intellectual capabilities and various degrees of courage (*Xunzi* 23). Consequently, his account of *yi* aligns well with Platonic understandings of justice: an enlightened ruler (*ming jun*) must clearly distinguish class divisions and their appropriate roles, supporting them by ritual principles, righteous laws, and uniform administrative policies (*Xunzi* 10). Standards of distributive justice, while providing certain privileges to the elite leadership class, operate generally under utilitarian conditions: the whole society (*qun*) is always more important than the ruler or any other member or clique within it. Consequently, what is good is "correct, in accord with natural principles, peaceful, and well-ordered"; what is bad is "wrong through partiality, wickedly contravenes natural principles, [is] perverse, and rebellious" (*Xunzi* 23). These standards are also applied economically in considering distribution of limited resources, fully recognizing that the ruler and the people will either thrive or devolve together because, even in spite of their class differences, each one constitutes only a part of the social whole.

Master Xun manifestly employs a more rationalized methodology in accounting for varieties in human personalities, social classes, and roles, as well as the methods for attaining and maintaining social order. In spite of his utilitarian standards for administrating distributive justice, his use of criminal justice is still inspired by a humanely cultivated ideal, that all persons can ultimately be transformed and become sagely. In this way he balances punitive and distributive justice by means of a rational appeal to a more secularized, but still firmly ritually oriented, form of harmonious society.

Given the importance of ritual orientations for Confucian society, women and slaves seem clearly to have been relegated to subservient roles in many settings. Ritual formalization became complete in the imperial period, greatly influenced (somewhat paradoxically) by the female politician Ban Zhao (c. 48–c. 120). These restrictive rites and their attendant values set the stage for later nonegalitarian developments.

### Preimperial Daoism

Both the historical identification of Old Master (Laozi) and the nature of the famous Daoist text normally associated with him, *Dao de jing,* have become controversial topics of debate. Rather than some ancient text scripted by a mysterious pioneering recluse, the book of *Laozi* is now generally associated with the same period as the *Zhuangzi,* appearing during the fourth century B.C.E. Nevertheless, political themes are a major aspect of the eighty-one chapters of this Daoist scripture, whether in its standard or earlier forms. In the case of the *Zhuangzi,* it is the first seven chapters of the book that are considered most representative of the historical person, Master Zhuang (c. 369 B.C.E.–286 B.C.E.). These early Daoists' views of society have been put into sharper contrast by developments within the so-called Huang-Lao school occurring in the fourth and third centuries B.C.E., which provided mediating and positive social doctrines carrying much influence during the early imperial period.

**Dao de jing *and the* Zhuangzi.** The form of social justice found in the *Dao de jing* has been described as a benevolent anarchism, but in fact it does speak of sagely rulers and supports some overriding moral and political values within Dao-centered communities. Taking spontaneity and noninterference as major principles of communal life, the text vigorously opposes artificial impositions of Confucian elitist values (such as sageliness, wisdom, humaneness, rightness) or other utilitarian interests (such as military aggressiveness or social benefits), since all of these are considered to be contrived restraints that harm the people (ch. 19). Instead it urges all, including the ruler, to have "little thought of self and as few desires as possible." Under these conditions, people will be able to lead Dao-centered lives without interference, being naturally kind and faithful, and so will become self-transformed. Whether a large or small political state, each takes a "lower position" (ch. 61) and so they become harmonized through mutual responsiveness rather than aggressiveness. Images of an ideal state suggested that the people would live simply, being contented with what they have, and so may even live and die in a place without ever leaving it (ch. 80). This is because a Daoist ruler would be exemplary in embodying "three treasures": compassion, frugality, and "not daring to take the lead" in the community (ch. 67). So unobtrusive is this way of ruling that people would feel all things move naturally, and would only know the fact that the ruler is there. Any other form or ruling (whether by charisma, fear, or rules) could not achieve the personal peace and social harmony that the Daoist ruler attains by unobtrusive and spontaneous action (wu wei). Daoist justice of this sort is therefore manifest in stoic-like naturalness, for the Way will be followed by avoiding extremities and learning the paradox that greater and lasting strength lies in what is putatively weak. Guided by sympathetic and frugal leadership, people living within Dao-centered communities would be unconcerned about any rationalized worldview and its attendant values, such as penal codes and rules regarding possessions. Among other values promoted by Daoists, feminine qualities were raised to a new height, defining the fecundity of the Dao in maternal terms. As a consequence, roles for women and feminine values in general were enhanced within early Daoist circles, but this would change later when Daoist religious ethics gradually adjusted to Confucian precedents.

In the Zhuangzi there is a vigorous skepticism at work, challenging any attempt to go beyond the principle of noninterference. Expressing sarcastic opposition toward government and other social institutions, the "Inner Chapters" (the first seven chapters) view these matters regularly from a transcendent perspective. Narrow pettiness and self-inflicted harm are the regular results of government policies. This is a Rousseau-like vision: humans who follow the Way can be free and creative, but society has imposed institutional shackles that make this impossible. As a consequence, Master Zhuang supports a more anarchistic vision of a simple life expressed in radical egalitarianism, letting everyone live by means of the Way according to their own inclinations and without external restrictions.

***The Huang-Lao school.*** Archeological discoveries in the 1970s stimulated further consideration of another facet of Daoist reflection, one that developed more positive doctrines of governance and rightness. Living about the time of Masters Zhuang and Xun, intellectuals from the state of Qi developed a mediating approach to earlier Daoist doctrines. They understood the secret of life and governance by responsiveness to proper timing, and so sages and institutions must be responsive to the natural changes that occur over time. Consequently, institutions that are outdated (such as Confucian rites) should be reformed to become suitable. Their worldview included the idea that laws and institutions could emerge from an understanding of the Way, and would necessarily reflect the needs of people as well as historical change in society. Political life continued to assert that the ruler be spontaneous and unobtrusive, but this was because appropriate institutions and laws were in place, and ministers were taking care of the administrative details associated with them. In this way, the Huang-Lao tradition advocated a version of justice closer to the position of Master Xun, but without its rationalized and utilitarian emphases.

## Subsequent Developments

Once the Qin dynasty was established and a greatly enlarged Chinese imperial state was brought into being (221 B.C.E.), standards of ethical and political life shifted gradually from legalistic and Huang-Lao forms of life to a dominant Confucian cultural standard. For most of the 2,200-year-long imperial period, Confucian advocates dominated the political arena. Nevertheless, the Huang-Lao school did have a revival and development during the third and fourth centuries, especially as seen among the writings of "neo-Daoists" or advocates of Abstruse Learning (Xuánxué). They envisioned the "lone transformation" (duhua) of all persons, developing a theme advocated by Master Zhuang. This included a radical form of egalitarianism, but also advocated a reformist vision of changing institutions according to the times and conditions of life.

The most outstanding contributions to Confucian traditions came during the Song dynasty (ninth to twelfth centuries). Confucian scholars then promoted a form of political justification that based all social values on heavenly patterns (tianli), resembling many aspects of a natural-law system of ethics and governance. Justice was then determined by alignment with patterns of heavenly harmony and was rationalized in a rigorous manner by Zhu Xi (1130–1200), whose interpretive precedents became the standard Confucian teachings for much of the subsequent seven hundred years. Under these more expansive cosmological influences, the roles of women became framed within a set of more subordinate conditions associated with universal symbols systematically denoting the passiveness and receptivity of earth, flexibility, coolness, fecundity, and hiddenness. Family rituals were established by Zhu Xi that formalized these relationships in a manner that reflected patriarchal values and that had been less systematic during earlier centuries. Though mothers in particular were highly honored within systems of filial allegiance, their own roles within the family were largely restricted. This became all the more entrenched in general society during the Ming and Quin dynasties (fourteenth to early twentieth centuries).

Alternative Confucian visions included remarkably advanced democratic ideals opposing imperial policies in Huang

Zongxi's (1610–1695) writings—ideals that were never realized and became justifications for revolution in 1911—and the utopian egalitarian vision of a great commonwealth (*datong*) advocated by the influential reformer, Kang Youwei (1858–1927). This latter vision was unusual in both its pseudoscientific idealism, promoting government-sponsored eugenic reconstructions of human societies, and its advocacy of a radical egalitarian worldview based on a relatively hedonistic ethic, thus offering much more freedom to women than had been previously considered proper or feasible.

## Law and Justice during the Ming and Quing Dynasties

Legal codes during the last two dynasties of imperial China were framed under values undergirding patrifamilial order and class differences. In principle, lands belonged to a family in perpetuity, but when faced with the need for survival many commoners sold these lands under leases that often brought privilege and power to the already wealthy. Courts did uphold reclaiming these properties, as a form of traditional justice, when the previously needy families had overcome their difficulties, but otherwise debts were in principle to be paid. Only in the case of economic desperation, hinging on basic survival, were compromises reached, mostly outside of court. These compromising tendencies, however, led to situations in which women could be sold as daughters, wives, or widows in order to raise adequate funds to meet basic needs. Though a woman might be able to return to her natal home if other needs were demonstrated, she was seen always as a passive agent in a social context where men's choices dominated. So, for example, a married woman could be expelled from marriage and sent to her natal home for seven basic reasons under these patrifamilial assumptions: barrenness (especially, bearing no male child), licenciousness, negligence in the care of her parents-in-law, talkativeness, theft, jealousy, and chronic illness. Though female virtues could also be employed legally to protect a woman's dignity, such an endeavor regularly required extensive evidence, and the burden of proof was often costly in both social and personal terms. In this regard, traditions generally supported patrifamilial structure, so that women were disadvantaged in inheritance, personal choices, and political options. Major legal changes in these areas began to take place only after 1911 with the advent of republican China.

*See also* **Confucianism; Daoism; Law; Legalism, Ancient China.**

### BIBLIOGRAPHY

PRIMARY SOURCES

Legge, James. *The Chinese Classics.* Oxford: Clarendon, 1893–1895. A standard rendering and authoritative interpretation of the *Four Books* and three ancient Confucian canonical scriptures by this famous Scottish missionary-scholar.

———. *The Sacred Books of China.* Oxford: Clarendon, 1879–1891. Six volumes in the *Sacred Books of the East,* edited by F. Max Müller. Vols. 3, 16, 27, 28, 39, 40. Revised and new translations of Confucian and Daoist canonical scriptures.

SECONDARY SOURCES

Bontekoe, Ron, and Marietta Stepaniants, eds. *Justice and Democracy: Cross-Cultural Perspectives.* Honolulu: University of Hawai'i Press, 1997. Includes helpful articles on Asian and comparative perspectives.

Cheng, Chung-ying, et al. Special Issue on Rawlsian and Confucian Justice. *Journal of Chinese Philosophy* 24, no. 4 (December 1997). Consists of six separate articles addressing different aspects of this comparison.

Feng, Youlan. *A History of Chinese Philosophy by Fung Yu-lan.* 2 vols. Translated by Derk Bodde. Princeton, N.J.: Princeton University Press, 1952–1953.

Huang, Philip C. C. *Code, Custom, and Legal Practice in China: The Qing and the Republic Compared.* Stanford, Calif.: Stanford University Press, 2001. Describes actual cases, including accounts about land ownership, handling of debts, old age provisions, and dynamic and oppressive elements in stipulations related to women in general society.

Lee, Lily Xiao Hong. *The Virtue of Yin: Studies on Chinese Women.* Broadway, Australia: Wild Peony, 1994. Poignant stories about Chinese women, including an essay on Ban Zhao.

Lee, Seung-Hwan. "Was There a Concept of Rights in Confucian Virtue-Based Morality?" *Journal of Chinese Philosophy* 19 (1992): 241–261. Seminal article claiming that rights-like concepts did exist in ancient Confucian texts and were norms for practice in ancient Chinese societies.

Liú Zéhuá, ed. *Zhōngguó Zhèngzhì Sīxiang Shi.* Hangzhou, China: Zhejiang People's Press, 1996. 3 vols. A thorough study covering twenty-five hundred years of Chinese political thought, including Confucian, Daoist, and Buddhist contributions.

Peerenboom, Randall P. "Confucian Justice: Achieving a Humane Society." *International Philosophical Quarterly* 30 (1990): 17–32. A comparative philosophical analysis of a secularized version of justice from a Confucian-inspired vision of humane society.

Pfister, Lauren F. "A Study in Comparative Utopias—K'ang Yuwei and Plato." *Journal of Chinese Philosophy* 16, no.1 (1989): 59–117. Showing points of comparison between Plato and certain Confucian themes embodied in an unusual work by this nineteenth-century Chinese intellectual and reformer.

Sim, May. "Aristotle in the Reconstruction of Confucian Ethics." *International Philosophical Quarterly* 41, no. 4 (2001): 453–468. Showing points of comparison between Aristotle and early Confucian traditions.

Wood, Alan T. *Limits to Autocracy: From Sung Neo-Confucianism to a Doctrine of Political Rights.* Honolulu: University of Hawai'i Press, 1995. Provides constructive comparisions between European medieval natural rights ideologies and Song dynasty (tenth to twelfth centuries) principle-centered Confucian political ideology.

*Lauren F. Pfister*
*Fèi Lèrén*

# K

## KANTIANISM.
The philosophy of Immanuel Kant (1724–1804) radically transformed the rationalism and empiricism of the seventeenth and eighteenth centuries and has set many of the problems for epistemology, metaphysics, and philosophy of science, moral and political philosophy, aesthetics, philosophy of history, and philosophy of religion ever since. Almost all philosophy after Kant could be divided into either "Kantianism" or "anti-Kantianism," but it is natural to reserve the term *Kantianism* to designate the philosophy of Kant himself, his immediate followers, and a variety of movements in the late nineteenth century and the twentieth century that have explicitly identified themselves with Kant.

### Immanuel Kant
Kant developed his philosophy after thirty years of reflection on foundational problems in contemporary natural science; on the rationalism of René Descartes (1596–1650), Gottfried Wilhelm Leibniz (1646–1716), and Christian Wolff (1679–1754); on the critique of rationalism by Christian August Crusius (c. 1715–1775) and David Hume (1711–1776); and on the political and educational views of Jean-Jacques Rousseau (1712–1778). Kant presented his mature views in the *Critique of Pure Reason* (1781, substantially revised in 1787), the *Critique of Practical Reason* (1788), and the *Critique of the Power of Judgment* (1790); in the *Prolegomena to Any Future Metaphysics* (1783) and *Groundwork of the Metaphysics of Morals* (1785); in two detailed works applying his general principles, the *Metaphysical Foundations of Natural Science* (1786) and the *Metaphysics of Morals* (1797), comprising a "Doctrine of Right" and a "Doctrine of Virtue"; and in polemical works such as *Religion within the Boundaries of Mere Reason* (1793), a bold argument that the central concepts of Christianity can have only symbolic value for pure reason, and *The Conflict of the Faculties* (1798), an argument for the freedom of philosophical thought.

In these works, Kant argued that both ordinary experience and natural science rest on informative but certain principles, or "synthetic a priori cognitions," such as that every event we can place at a determinate position in time must be linked to antecedent events by causal laws, which we can explain only by supposing that they reflect the forms of our own thought, in particular the spatial and temporal forms of our intuitions or perceptions and the logical categories of our understanding that we impose on our experience. But by the same token, these forms of intuition and thought can determine only how things appear to us, not how they are in themselves (Kant called this doctrine "transcendental idealism"). Kant then ar-

gued that when we conceive of the soul, the world as a complete whole, or God, we overstep the limits of our sensory perception and can have no genuine knowledge of such things.

However, the gap between appearance and things in themselves that explains the certainty of the application of the fundamental principles of our knowledge to the former also makes it at least possible for us to conceive of, if not know, the latter, particularly to conceive of ourselves as being free to make moral choices that may seem inconsistent with the determinism of our actions in the empirical world and of a God who is the author of laws of nature that are ultimately consistent with the laws of morality. Kant argued that the latter are given by our own pure practical rather than theoretical reason and that we can know them without any appeal to God; the laws of morality are discerned by pure reason as necessary to achieve autonomy, the independence of our actions from determination by the mere inclinations of ourselves or others.

Kant then argued that the fundamental principle of justice is that each person must be allowed the maximal freedom of action consistent with a like allowance for all others and that we have ethical duties to promote the free and effective use of our capacities to set and pursue our own ends and those of others, which cannot be coercively enforced within the political sphere. Finally, Kant argued that our pleasures in the beautiful and the sublime are experiences of the disinterested freedom of the imagination from constraint by the direct demands of science and morality, but also that as an experience of freedom of the imagination, aesthetic experience is indirectly conducive to moral and political development. He also argued that a teleological view of nature as a purposive system, while of merely heuristic value for the pursuit of natural science, is also a morally valuable perspective on the world and our place within it.

### First Response
Kant's work immediately produced both acclaim and hostility. It was first popularized by the 1786 *Letters on the Kantian Philosophy* by Karl Leonhard Reinhold (1757–1823), but by 1789 Reinhold had turned against Kant's dualisms—his distinctions between sensibility and understanding, between appearances and things in themselves, and between theoretical cognition and practical reason—and initiated the attempts to derive all of philosophy from a single principle that would be taken up in the "absolute idealism" of Johann Gottlieb Fichte (1762–1814), Friedrich Wilhelm Joseph Schelling (1775–1854), and Georg Wilhelm Friedrich Hegel (1770–1831). Other thinkers remained closer to Kant, especially the poet

and historian Friedrich Schiller (1759–1805), who, in "On Grace and Dignity" (1793) and the *Letters on the Aesthetic Education of Mankind* (1795), argued for a greater confluence between our inclinations and our moral principles than Kant thought possible without being tempted by the monism of the absolute idealists. Johann Wolfgang von Goethe (1749–1832) was also deeply affected by Kant's third critique in the development of his own conception of nature.

## Neo-Kantianism

Hegel's dominance of German philosophy in the 1820s through the 1840s ended the first wave of Kantianism, but the version of Kantianism propounded by Arthur Schopenhauer (1788–1860) in the *Fourfold Root of the Principle of Sufficient Reason* (1813) and *The World as Will and Representation* (1818) became influential after 1848 and prepared the way for a tremendous resurgence in the influence of Kant in German philosophy beginning in the 1860s. The "neo-Kantian" movement begun at that time dominated German philosophy until the 1920s. This movement took many forms. The scientist Hermann Helmholtz (1821–1894) gave a psychological interpretation of Kant's conception that the mind brings its own innate structure to perception, which influenced research into perception well into the twentieth century. But within academic philosophy, the two main forms of neo-Kantianism were the Marburg and Heidelberg schools.

The main representatives of the Marburg school were Hermann Cohen (1842–1918), Paul Natorp (1854–1924), and Ernst Cassirer (1874–1945). Cohen made his reputation with a series of commentaries on Kant's three critiques, published between 1871 and 1889, and then with his own system of philosophy, published between 1902 and 1912. He also published *The Religion of Reason out of the Sources of Judaism* (1919), an influential work on Judaism modeled on Kant's *Religion*. Cassirer's main work was the three-volume *Philosophy of Symbolic Forms* (1923–1929; trans. 1953–1957 with a fourth volume posthumously published in 1996). The Marburg school developed Kant's idea that we bring to both ordinary experience and more formalized science presuppositions reflecting the structure of our own thought; but especially by the time of Cassirer the school also recognized that we bring a multiplicity of such principles to our experience and that they may change over time. Cassirer's views were to some extent paralleled by those developed by the British philosopher Robin George Collingwood (1889–1943) in his *Essay on Philosophical Method* (1933) and *Essay on Metaphysics* (1940), although Collingwood did not call himself a neo-Kantian.

The chief representatives of Heidelberg neo-Kantianism were Wilhelm Windelband (1848–1915) and Heinrich Rickert (1863–1936). They stressed Kant's distinction between the principles of theoretical and practical reason and focused attention on our projections of values as well as knowledge into our experiences. Rickert developed the philosophical views of the school in *The Limits of Concept Formation in Natural Science* (1896–1902; trans. 1986) and *Science and History* (1899; trans. 1962). Both Windelband and Rickert also stressed the difference between the methods of natural science and history and thereby greatly influenced the methodological thought of

the sociologist Max Weber (1864–1920), especially his theory of "ideal types" and his distinction between fact and value in the practice of social science.

## Kant in the Later Twentieth Century

Kantianism in the early twentieth century was not limited to the self-designated neo-Kantian schools, however. The 1928 *Logical Structure of the World* (trans. 1967) by Rudolf Carnap (1891–1970) was clearly a modernization of Kant's theory of our application of the forms of logic to the raw data of our experience, as was the nearly contemporaneous *Mind and World Order* (1929) by the American Clarence Irving Lewis (1883–1964), who was himself influenced by the many Kantian elements in the works of Charles Sanders Peirce (1839–1914). The main revival of interest in Kant in the Anglo-American world came after World War II, however. In Britain, a great revival of Kantian philosophy was stimulated by two books by Sir Peter Strawson (1919– ), *Individuals: An Essay on Descriptive Metaphysics* (1959) and *The Bounds of Sense: An Essay on Kant's Critique of Pure Reason* (1966). Strawson based his appropriation of Kant on a theory of meaning, arguing that a subject can apply the concept of his own self only in contrast to a concept of an objective world, while Jonathan Bennett (1930– ) stayed closer to Kant in his *Kant's Analytic* (also 1966), arguing that it is our judgments about our own experience that can be confirmed only within a structure of judgments about the external world.

The work of Strawson and Bennett initiated a major debate about "transcendental arguments" in the United States as well as Britain that continued into the twenty-first century. Meanwhile, in the United States interest in Kant was independently inspired by the work of Wilfrid Sellars (1912–1989), whose famous attack upon the "myth of the given" in his "Empiricism and the Philosophy of Mind" (1956) was clearly intended as an alternative to C. I. Lewis's version of Kant and whose *Science and Metaphysics: Variations on Kantian Themes* (1968) presented a Peircian version of Kant using the resources of contemporary philosophy of language.

The strongest influence of Kant on contemporary philosophy, however, was mediated by the political philosopher John Rawls (1921–2002), whose *A Theory of Justice* (1971) was Kantian in both method and substance. Rawls argued that principles of distributive justice should be chosen in an "original position" of impartiality that models Kant's conception of universality and that the principles that would be so chosen would prioritize equal liberty over other forms of equality, reflecting Kant's emphasis on autonomy as the fundamental moral and political value. Rawls's work has inspired a great deal of further work on Kantian moral and political philosophy in Britain and the United States and has also been influential in Germany, although there an independent version of Kantianism, the theory of Jürgen Habermas (1929– ) that political principles should be chosen in an "ideal communicative situation" has also been widely influential.

*See also* **Continental Philosophy; Idealism; Metaphysics; Philosophy.**

**BIBLIOGRAPHY**

Beiser, Frederick C. *The Fate of Reason: German Philosophy from Kant to Fichte.* Cambridge, Mass.: Harvard University Press, 1987.

———. *German Idealism: The Struggle against Subjectivism, 1781–1801.* Cambridge, Mass.: Harvard University Press, 2002.

Bennett, Jonathan. *Kant's Analytic.* Cambridge, U.K.: Cambridge University Press, 1966.

———. *Kant's Dialectic.* London and New York: Cambridge University Press, 1974.

Carnap, Rudolf. *The Logical Structure of the World: Pseudoproblems in Philosophy.* Translated by Rolf A. George. Berkeley: University of California Press, 1967.

Cassirer, Ernst. *An Essay on Man: An Introduction to the Philosophy of Human Culture.* New Haven, Conn.: Yale University Press, 1944.

———. *The Philosophy of Symbolic Forms.* Vols. 1–3 translated by Ralph Manheim. Vol. 4 edited by J. M. Krois and D. P. Verene. New Haven, Conn.: Yale University Press, 1953–1956 and 1996.

———. *Substance and Function; and, Einstein's Theory of Relativity.* Translated by William Curtis Swabey and Marie Collins Swabey. Mineola, N.Y.: Dover Publications, 2003.

Cohen, Hermann. *Religion of Reason: Out of the Sources of Judaism.* Translated with an introduction by Simon Kaplan. Introductory essay by Leo Strauss. New York: Frederick Unger, 1972.

Guyer, Paul, ed. *The Cambridge Companion to Kant.* Cambridge, U.K., and New York: Cambridge University Press, 1992. A multiauthored introduction to main themes in Kant's philosophy with an extensive bibliography.

Habermas, Jürgen. *Knowledge and Human Interests.* Translated by Jeremy J. Shapiro. Boston: Beacon Press, 1971.

———. *Moral Consciousness and Communicative Action.* Translated by Christian Lenhardt and Shierry Weber Nicholsen. Introduction by Thomas McCarthy. Cambridge, Mass.: MIT Press, 1990.

———. *The Theory of Communicative Action.* Translated by Thomas McCarthy. Boston: Beacon Press, 1984–1987.

Herman, Barbara. *The Practice of Moral Judgment.* Cambridge, Mass.: Harvard University Press, 1993.

Hill, Thomas E., Jr. *Dignity and Practical Reason in Kant's Moral Theory.* Ithaca, N.Y.: Cornell University Press, 1992.

———. *Human Welfare and Moral Worth: Kantian Perspectives.* Oxford and New York: Oxford University Press, 2002.

———. *Respect, Pluralism, and Justice: Kantian Perspectives.* Oxford and New York: Oxford University Press, 2000.

Kant, Immanuel. *The Cambridge Edition of the Works of Immanuel Kant.* Edited by Paul Guyer and Allen W. Wood. 16 vols., 12 published as of 2004. Cambridge, U.K.: Cambridge University Press, 1992– . The standard English translation of all of Kant's published works as well as extensive selections from his lectures, correspondence, and posthumous material.

———. *Kants gesammelte Schriften.* Edited by the Royal Prussian, subsequently German, then Berlin-Brandenburg Academy of Sciences. 29 vols., 28 published as of 2004. Berlin: Georg Reimer, subsequently Walter de Gruyter and Co.: 1900– . The standard German edition of Kant's writings.

Köhnke, Klaus Christian. *Entstehung und Aufstieg der Neukantianismus: Die deutsche Universitätsphilosophie zwischen Idealismus und Positivismus.* Frankfurt am Main, Germany: Suhrkamp, 1986. Translated without endnotes as *The Rise of Neo-Kantianism: German Academic Philosophy between Idealism and Positivism.* Translated by R. J. Hollingdale. Cambridge, U.K., and New York: Cambridge University Press, 1991.

Korsgaard, Christine M. *Creating the Kingdom of Ends.* Cambridge, U.K., and New York: Cambridge University Press, 1996.

Lewis, Clarence Irving. *Mind and the World-Order: Outline of a Theory of Knowledge.* New York: Dover, 1956.

Nell (O'Neill), Onora. *Acting on Principle: An Essay on Kantian Ethics.* New York: Columbia University Press, 1975.

O'Neill, Onora. *Constructions of Reason: Explorations of Kant's Practical Philosophy.* Cambridge, U.K., and New York: Cambridge University Press, 1989.

Pinkard, Terry. *German Philosophy 1760–1860: The Legacy of Idealism.* Cambridge, U.K., and New York: Cambridge University Press, 2002.

Rawls, John. *A Theory of Justice.* Rev. ed. Cambridge, Mass.: Harvard University Press, 1999.

———. "Kantian Constructivism in Moral Theory." In his *Collected Papers,* edited by Samuel Freeman. Cambridge, Mass.: Harvard University Press, 1999.

Rickert, Heinrich. *The Limits of Concept Formation in Natural Science: A Logical Introduction to the Historical Sciences.* Edited and translated by Guy Oakes. Abridged ed. Cambridge, U.K., and New York: Cambridge University Press, 1986.

———. *Science and History: A Critique of Positivist Epistemology.* Translated by George Reisman. Princeton, N.J.: Van Nostrand, 1962.

Sellars, Wilfrid. *Science and Metaphysics: Variations on Kantian Themes.* London: Routledge and Kegan Paul, 1968.

Strawson, P. F. *The Bounds of Sense: An Essay on Kant's "Critique of Pure Reason."* London: Methuen, 1966.

Strawson, P. F. *Individuals: An Essay in Descriptive Metaphysics.* London: Methuen, 1959.

Willey, Thomas E. *Back to Kant: The Revival of Kantianism in German Social and Historical Thought, 1860–1914.* Detroit: Wayne State University Press, 1978.

Wood, Allen W. *Kant.* Malden, Mass.: Blackwell, 2005. An excellent short introduction to Kant's philosophy.

*Paul Guyer*

**KINGSHIP.** *See* **Monarchy.**

**KINSHIP.** Kinship—which can be initially described as the study of the links between people established on the basis of descent, marriage, or adoption—has been a defining domain of anthropological investigation since the inception of this discipline in the last twenty years of the nineteenth century. The detailed description of the complexities of kinship systems was for many decades considered essential to the understanding of non-Western societies. This field went through an intense phase of restructuring from the end of the 1970s to the late 1990s as a result of major paradigmatic shifts within the discipline of anthropology, such as the cultural turn, feminism, and political economy. In the early twenty-first century kinship studies, profoundly redefined, have experienced a revival, also in light of tremendous technological changes, such as the emergence of new reproductive technologies, the development of genetics, new family forms, the gay and lesbian movement, immigration, globalization and such correlated phenomena as transnational adoption that have opened new frontiers to anthropological investigation.

The publication of *Systems of Consanguinity and Affinity* (1870) and *Ancient Society* (1877) by Lewis Henry Morgan have traditionally been recognized as steppingstones in the history of anthropological kinship. In line with his evolutionary thinking, Morgan saw kinship as a social institution identifying the earlier steps of societal organization. In other words, kinship was presented as the epicenter of so-called primitive societies' social organization. According to this line of reasoning, kinship was less central in modern societies. Territoriality, the social contract, and the state dominated modern society. As a result, politics and the economy, as distinct fields of social action, regulated important aspects of modern women's and men's lives. Morgan's work is representative of a certain understanding of what were then called primitive societies. He saw them as societies based on blood (kinship), a view that dominated anthropology until the early 1970s. Morgan also established the approach that would characterize anthropological studies of kinship for several decades; that is, the emphasis on kinship terminology and the partition of kinship as a field in a number of constitutive "blocks"—that is, descent, marriage, postmarital residence, inheritance, and so on.

Kinship maintained its centrality in the history of the discipline until the cultural turn in anthropology in the 1970s. Kinship was indeed a central theme of investigation within functionalist and structuralist paradigms. Kinship allowed scholars to answer some fundamental sociological questions. It offered a plausible explanation of the problem of the maintenance of social order in the absence of state-based organizations. Indeed, anthropological knowledge came to question a well-established tradition of Western political thought that had identified in the state the only viable solution for the maintenance of social order and discipline.

One major systematic trend within the traditions of kinship studies is represented by descent theory, the dominant paradigm until the mid-1960s (Kuper, 1982). Classic examples of this approach are *African Political Systems, The Nuer,* and *The Political System of the Anuak.* Proponents of descent theory presented non-Western societies as based on their kinship organization. According to this view, a person's place in society was largely determined by his or her position within the kinship system. Crucial was the determination of an individual's position within the line of filiation privileged by a given society (descent). Anthropologists singled out various principles of descent—unilineal with its patrilineal (through the father's line) and matrilineal (through the mother's line) variants and double (through both lines of descent). Non-Western societies were seen as emphasizing one particular line of descent whose analysis was believed to unpack their social mechanisms and account for the maintenance/reproduction of the social order. Thus in the classic studies of the Tallensi (e.g., Fortes, 1949) or the Nuer (Evans-Pritchard, *The Nuer,* 1940), the modalities of kinship organization and the functioning of descent as a structuring principle were presented as central to understanding these societies, their boundaries, and their internal equilibrium.

Key within functionalist and structural-functionalist approaches was the distinction between de facto descent (biological descent) and de jure descent (the lines of descent a society effectively recognized). In other words, anthropologists distinguished between facts of nature and the selection or play with natural facts of which each kinship system was the recognized expression. Each society was seen as characterized by an emphasis on certain genealogical links and a disregard for others. Thus in a matrilineal society a father's position was generally perceived as marginal. Meanwhile a mother and her relatives, in particular the mother's brother, were seen as the center of a child's social life and largely determine his or her future prospects.

Many functionalists and structural-functionalists claimed to investigate the domain of the social as separate from other domains of social analysis, namely the biological and the psychological. Building on the work of French sociologist Émile Durkheim, they were concerned with the delimitation of objects and methods of enquiry exclusive to the social sciences (with some notable exceptions, of course, such as Bronislaw Malinowski and his theory of needs and corresponding cultural institutions). Despite their intentions, later research has demonstrated that they were often unaware of the biologism that tainted some of their own theoretical constructions. As David Schneider and other anthropologists after him have highlighted, the realm of nature (natural kinship) was left out from traditional anthropological accounts. Yet each kinship system, with varying degrees of adherence, was seen as reflecting certain aspects of the natural order, but the latter was taken as a given and thus unquestioned realm. However, conceptions of nature and its relations to culture vary and change over time, across and within societies. An important contribution in this direction was constituted by the publication of *Nature, Culture, and Gender* by Carol MacCormack and Marilyn Strathern in 1980, which showed the inapplicability of Western dichotomies between culture and nature, men and women cross-culturally, and the historical variation of such constructs within the West.

As Janet Carsten (2004) has highlighted, anthropologists' study of kinship did not entail an interest in domestic life or other forms of connectedness aside from genealogical links, thus excluding the study of women, children, alternative forms of solidarity, or the more intimate aspects of sexuality from anthropological accounts. This gap can also partly be explained by the belief that non-Western people were deemed not to have an individualized Western sense of self but were seen as identifying with the collectivities they belonged to (read descent groups), with the latter seen as corporate entities (which found collective expression in their male elders). In addition, only the more public aspects of kinship (the so-called politico-jural aspects) were of privileged interests to anthropologists. Within kin-based societies, kinship defined people's economic, religious, and political rights and obligations.

Claude Lévi-Strauss, the leading proponent of the structuralist turn in French anthropology and beyond, introduced in the 1960s a conflicting paradigm known as alliance theory. Influenced by structural linguistics, Lévi-Strauss turned his attention not to descent but to marriage, the latter interpreted as a system of exchange and communication. In his theoretical constructs marriage is presented as the matrix of the kinship social order. Marriage produces at once two fundamental classes of kin, consanguineal kin (blood relatives) and affinal kin (in-laws). In the course of marriage transactions, women "serve" as the vectors via which social alliances are established (a perspective whose androcentric bias feminist anthropologists will readily point out). By renouncing to marry their own sisters (via the imposition of the incest rule) and by agreeing to marry other men's sisters outside of their own biological family, men establish the foundations of human society.

According to Lévi-Strauss, kinship marks the overcoming of the state of nature (determined by the rule of the biological) and the imposition of the cultural order by humans. In this sense kinship is a cultural universal—that is, something shared by all societies—although its content varies across cultures. By unpacking the systems of marriage and unveiling their deeper logic, Lévi-Strauss came to complement British anthropologists' privileged attention on descent. However, his reliance on linguistic structuralism enabled him to further capture the symbolic quality of human life and distance himself further from the biologism of functionalist and structural–functionalist accounts.

An important turn in kinship studies was marked by the publication of David Schneider's work. In *American Kinship: A Cultural Account* (1968) and *A Critique of the Study of Kinship* (1984), Schneider developed an important critique of the study of kinship, one that ultimately laid the foundations for contemporary approaches to the study of kinship. According to Schneider, kinship studies were mostly the expression of anthropologists' ethnocentric biases and disciplinary preoccupations. The centrality of biological reproduction was indeed a character identifying Western perspectives on kinship. Indeed, within a number of other societies, such as the Yap of the West Caroline Islands, it is "hard work" that cements what we would call kinship ties, not biology. It followed that kinship as a field of study was the outcome of the biases of Western scientists who once carved out a predefined interpretive scheme based on their own experience of kinship and then proceeded to investigate other societies, thus missing local understandings of kinship and the relationship between social and natural aspects of kinship (as well as the usefulness of such categories in the analysis of a specific society/culture).

A number of lines of research emerged from this initially seemingly devastating critique. This of course happened after a critical reassessment of Schneider's symbolic theory. Indeed, several aspects of this have been questioned by successive generations of anthropologists. Schneider's view of culture as an integrated whole and his exclusive focus on symbols are now seen as too schematic and limited (Stone, 2004). Twenty-first

century anthropologists typically share a more complex and less bounded understanding of culture, an attention to practice and processes in addition to meanings, and a keen interest in the social construction of science (a topic left unresolved in Schneider's writings as Carsten [2000] clarifies). Post-Schneiderian kinship is characterized by the inclusion of the study of Western kinship systems. This is partly due to the realization that an increased understanding of a researcher's own cultural assumptions and social practices is a powerful strategy to come to terms with researchers' biases, as well as changes in the object and methods of anthropological studies. In addition, nature is no longer taken for granted. Indeed, changing conceptions of nature and the varying relationships between culture and nature are regarded as central topics in order to understand kinship within Western and non-Western societies.

Post-Schneiderian kinship studies are often characterized by the insertion of kinship into a wider analytic field. Indeed, kinship studies have benefited from the insights of feminist anthropology, historical anthropology, and postmodern anthropology.

The feminist turn in anthropology in the mid-1970s (that is, the study of the much-neglected study of gender in a cross-cultural perspective) brought new life to anthropology as a discipline and to kinship studies in particular. The relationship between gender and kinship was the topic of Jane Collier and Sylvia Yanagisako's edited collection *Gender and Kinship: Essays Towards a Unified Analysis* (1987). These authors argued for a unified theory of gender and kinship. Indeed, they suggested that gender relations and gender asymmetries are central to the understanding of kinship systems cross-culturally (see also Yanagisako and Delaney). For instance, how would one understand, within the patrilineal Bamana families of Mali, women's differential positions and their limits and possibilities as mothers, daughters, and sisters if gender and kinship are not taken into consideration. The coupling of studies of gender, kinship, power, and inequality has contributed much to a renewed interest in anthropology. These studies also reflect the decline of the traditional separation between social studies and social activism, disclosing indeed a well-formulated agenda for the expansion of human rights. (See, for instance, the 2004 statement by the American Anthropological Association in support of gay and lesbian marriage at http://www.aaanet.org/press/ma_stmt_marriage.htm.)

Particularly rich is the study of new reproductive technology (NRT) (Strathern, *After Nature*, 1992 and *Reproducing the Future*, 1992; Ginsburg and Rapp; Ragone and Winddance Twine). The study of NRT has led people in Western societies to begin to deconstruct traditional distinctions between nature and culture/choice, given that NRTs have widened human possibilities of intervention and modification of what were once believed unchangeable biological phenomena. Similarly, the growing body of literature on gays and lesbians cross-culturally has led to a more complex understanding of the complexity of gender, which once were viewed more simplistically (see, for instance, Weston). It has also promoted new understanding of people's mediations with Western dictates of kinship.

Political economy and later developments (for example, historical anthropology) have added an important dimension to the study of kinship. From the path-breaking work by Jack Goody (1958) that included attention to the temporal dimension in the study of kinship, as well as the work of Esther Goody on marriage as a process (1962), the work of Claude Meillassoux on kinship and the formation of social inequalities (1981) to more recent accounts of political and economic processes that look for more satisfactory mediations between neo-Marxist and interpretive analyses (for example, work by McClintock; Cooper and Stoler), that kinship phenomena do not stand in a vacuum; instead they simultaneously reflect and affect wider societal trends. Kinship is indeed a privileged site for societal reproduction and the construction of local, ethnic, and national identities. (See, for instance, Kahn on NRT in Israel or De Jorio on kinship and politics in postcolonial Mali.)

In sum, early-twenty-first-century studies highlight the importance of local conception of kinship and the impact of such constructs on people's identity formation. Some anthropologists look at kinship as conceived in the West as a specific network of relatedness whose generality and interest should be ascertained in the course of open-ended fieldwork. Other trends also consist of broader approaches to the study of kinship (e.g., in the context of larger paradigms such as political economy), the inclusion of relatively recent developments (NRT), or traditionally excluded phenomena such as sexuality and third genders, thus contributing to new understandings of different lifestyles and cultural traditions.

*See also* **Anthropology; Family; Gender Studies: Anthropology.**

BIBLIOGRAPHY

Broch-Due, Vigdis, Ingrid Rudie, and Tony Bleie, eds. *Carved Flesh/Cast Selves: Gendered Symbols and Social Practices.* Oxford: BERG, 1993.

Butler, Judith. *Bodies that Matter: On the Discursive Limits of "Sex."* New York: Routledge, 1993.

———. *Gender Trouble. Feminism and the Subversion of Identity.* New York: Routledge. 1990.

Carsten, Janet. *After Kinship.* New York: Cambridge University Press, 2004.

———. *Cultures of Relatedness.* New York: Cambridge University Press, 2000.

Carsten, Janet, and Stephen Hugh-Jones, eds. *About the House: Lévi-Strauss and Beyond.* New York: Cambridge University Press, 1995.

Collier, Jane F., and Sylvia J. Yanagisako, eds. *Gender and Kinship: Essays Towards a Unified Analysis.* Stanford, Calif.: Stanford University Press, 1987.

Comaroff, John L. *The Meaning of Marriage Payments.* New York: Academic, 1980.

Cooper, Frederick, and Ann Laura Stoler, eds. *Tensions of Empire: Colonial Cultures in a Bourgeois World.* Berkeley: University of California Press, 1997.

De Jorio, Rosa. "Women's Organizations, the Ideology of Kinship, and the State in Postindependence Mali." In *New Directions in Anthropological Kinship,* edited by Linda Stone. Lanham, Md.: Rowman and Littlefield, 2001.

Evans-Pritchard, Edward E. *The Nuer: A Description of the Modes of Livelihood and Political Institutions of a Nilotic People.* Oxford: Clarendon, 1940.

———. *The Political System of the Anuak of the Anglo-Egyptian Sudan.* London: Lund, 1940.

Feinberg, Richard, and Martin Ottenheimer. *The Cultural Analysis of Kinship: The Legacy of David M. Schneider.* Urbana: University of Illinois Press, 2001.

Franklin, Sarah, and Susan McKinnon, eds. *Relative Values: Reconfiguring Kinship Studies.* Durham, N.C.: Duke University Press, 2001.

Fortes, Meyer. *The Web of Kinship among the Tallensi.* London: Oxford University Press, 1949.

———, ed. *Marriage in Tribal Societies.* Cambridge, U.K.: Cambridge University Press, 1962.

Fortes, Meyer, and E. E. Evans-Pritchard, eds. *African Political Systems.* London: Oxford University Press, 1940.

Fox, Robert. *Kinship and Marriage: An Anthropological Perspective.* Baltimore: Penguin, 1967.

Foucault, Michel. *The History of Sexuality.* New York: Pantheon, 1978.

Ginsburg, Faye D., and Rayna Rapp, eds. *Conceiving the New World Order: The Global Politics of Reproduction.* Berkeley: University of California Press, 1995.

Goody, Esther. "Conjugal Separation and Divorce Among the Gonja of Northern Ghana." In *Marriage in Tribal Societies,* edited by Meyer Fortes. Cambridge, U.K.: Cambridge University Press, 1962.

Goody, Jack. *The Development of the Family and Marriage in Europe.* Cambridge, U.K.: Cambridge University Press, 1983.

———. *The Oriental, the Ancient, and the Primitive: Systems of Marriage and the Family in the Pre-Industrial Societies of Eurasia.* New York: Cambridge University Press, 1990.

———, ed. *The Developmental Cycle in Domestic Groups.* Cambridge, U.K.: Cambridge University Press, 1958.

Gottlieb, Alma. *The Afterlife Is Where We Come from: The Culture of Infancy in West Africa.* Chicago: University of Chicago Press, 2004.

Haraway, Donna. *Primate Visions: Gender, Race, and Nature in the World of Modern Science.* New York: Routledge, 1989.

———. *Simians, Cyborgs, and Women: The Reinvention of Nature.* New York: Routledge, 1991.

Hutchinson, Sharon Elaine. "Identity and Substance: The Broadening Base of Relatedness Among the Nuer of Southern Sudan." In *Cultures of Relatedness,* edited by Janet Carsten. Cambridge, U.K.: Cambridge University Press, 2000.

Kahn, Susan Martha. *Reproducing Jews: A Cultural Account of Assisted Conception in Israel.* Durham, N.C.: Duke University Press, 2000.

Kelly, Raymond. *Constructing Inequality: The Fabrication of a Hierarchy of Virtue Among the Etoro.* Ann Arbor: University of Michigan Press, 1993.

Kuper, Adam. *The Invention of Primitive Society: Transformation of an Illusion.* London: Routledge, 1988.

———. "Lineage Theory: A Critical Retrospect." *Annual Review of Anthropology* 11 (1982): 71–95.

Lévi-Strauss, Claude. *The Elementary Structures of Kinship.* Translated from the French by James Harle Bell, John Richard von Sturmer, and Rodney Needham, editor. Boston: Beacon Press, 1969.

McClintock, Anne. "No Longer in a Future Heaven." In her *Imperial Leather: Race, Gender, and Sexuality in the Colonial Con-*

*text.* New York: Routledge, 1995.

MacCormack, Carol, and Marilyn Strathern, eds. *Nature, Culture, and Gender.* Cambridge: Cambridge University Press, 1980.

Martin, Emily. *The Woman in the Body: A Cultural Analysis of Reproduction.* Boston: Beacon, 1987.

Meillassoux, Claude. *Maidens, Meal, and Money: Capitalism and the Domestic Community.* New York: Cambridge University Press, 1981.

Morgan, Lewis Henry. *Systems of Consanguinity and Affinity of the Human Family.* Washington, D.C.: Smithsonian Institution, 1870.

Needham, Rodney. *Rethinking Kinship and Marriage.* New York: Tavistock, 1971.

Ortner, Sherry. *Making Gender: The Politics and Erotics of Gender.* Boston: Beacon Press, 1996.

———. "Is Female to Male as Nature Is to Culture." In *Woman, Culture, and Society,* edited by Michelle Rosaldo and Louise Lamphere. Stanford, Calif.: Stanford University Press, 1974.

Peletz, Michael. "Kinship Studies in Late Twentieth-Century Anthropology." *Annual Review of Anthropology* 24 (1995): 343–72.

Ragone, Helena, and France Winddance Twine, eds. *Ideologies and Technologies of Motherhood: Race, Class, Sexuality, Nationalism.* New York: Routledge, 2000.

Rosaldo, Michelle, and Louise Lamphere, eds. *Woman, Culture, and Society.* Stanford, Calif.: Stanford University Press, 1974.

Schneider, David. *American Kinship: A Cultural Account.* Englewood Cliffs, N.J.: Prentice-Hall, 1968.

———. *A Critique of the Study of Kinship.* Ann Arbor: University of Michigan Press, 1984.

Stack, Carol. *All Our Kin: Strategies for Survival in a Black Community.* New York: Harper and Row, 1975.

Stone, Linda. "Contemporary Directions in Kinship." In *Kinship and Family: An Anthropological Reader,* edited by Robert Parkin and Linda Stone. Malden, Mass.: Blackwell, 2004.

———. ed. *New Directions in Anthropological Kinship.* Lanham, Md.: Rowman and Littlefield, 2001.

Strathern, Marilyn. *After Nature: English Kinship in the Late Twentieth Century.* Cambridge: Cambridge University Press, 1992.

———. *Reproducing the Future: Essays on Anthropology, Kinship, and the New Reproductive Technologies.* New York: Routledge, 1992.

Weston, Kath. *Families We Choose: Lesbians, Gays, Kinship.* New York: Columbia University Press, 1991.

Yanagisako, Sylvia J., and Carol Delaney, eds. *Naturalizing Power: Essays in Feminist Cultural Analysis.* New York: Routledge, 1995.

*Rosa De Jorio*

**KNOWLEDGE.** Four words of ancient Greek are important to the first philosophical discussions of knowledge in the Western tradition. In a given context any of them might be translated with the word "knowledge": *epistēmē, technē, mētis,* and *gnōsis.*

*Epistēmē* names the most philosophical idea of knowledge: contemplative, disinterested, logical knowledge of truth and reality. Such knowledge is not merely true; it is self-certifying, indubitable, a rock-solid foundation on which to build scientific understanding. That was important. Philosophical thinking begins with the idea that belief or opinion (*doxa*) is not knowledge even if it happens to be true. *Doxa* is changeable, especially in a city, where people may be swayed by sophists and demagogues. Through its root (*histēmi,* "to stand firm, to set up"), *epistēmē* evokes ideas of firmness and stability. That is what the philosophers sought in the best and highest knowledge: an immovable point no persuasive speech can overturn.

Stoic philosophers defined *epistēmē*-knowledge as "apprehension (*katalepsis*) that is safe and unchangeable by argument," according to the *Florilegium* (extracts from Greek authors compiled by Joannes Stobaeus in the late fifth century). About two generations earlier, Plato (c. 428–348 or 347 B.C.E.) had put forward his highly influential vision of philosophical progress from *doxa,* the opinions of the crowd, to the correct opinion (*orthodoxos*) of specialists, and finally the summit, *epistēmē,* the best and highest knowledge. In the *Theaetetus,* what sets *epistēmē* apart from true opinion is called an *aitias logismos,* a reasoned account, explaining why the knowledge is and must be true. In the *Republic,* however, what sets *epistēmē*-knowledge apart from *doxa* is the object that it apprehends—a Form or Idea. Opinion cannot turn into knowledge because the "objects" of opinion are ultimately incoherent particulars for which no reasoned account is possible. Plato also explains how the Form of the Good is the cause of things being knowable at all. It is not the presence of a Form as such that makes *epistēmē*-knowledge possible; rather, it is the Form's place in the cosmic system. Form becomes logical and Ideas intelligible only when grasped in the light of the whole (the Good).

The philosophers did not invariably construe *epistēmē* as disinterested. The ordinary sense of the word is simply to have a good understanding of a thing, anything, archery, for instance. Aristotle (384–322 B.C.E.) divided *epistēmē* into three parts: theoretical (science and philosophy), practical (ethics, economics, politics), and productive, an *epistēmē* he called *technē. Technē* (from which *technology, technique,* and so on) refers to the knowledge of a recognized expert, like a physician, musician, or carpenter. Such knowledge is skillful, artful, reliable, specialized, and usually organized in professional associations. Plato explored the comparison of *epistēmē* and *technē,* using the words interchangeably in some dialogues. Could the best and highest knowing be some kind of art? One difficulty is that *technē*-knowledge aims at something concrete—a ship, a healthy human, a drama. The objects of philosophical *epistēmē,* however, are not these mundane artifacts, but the eternal Forms in which particulars merely participate. A further difficulty is that *technē*-knowledge can be used for good or ill alike. Such knowledge is instrumental, serving other ends, and the effectiveness of technique is no guarantee that the ends are good, whereas *epistēmē* is knowing in the light of the Good itself. This intrinsic value for knowledge of truth became traditional in Western thought, seldom questioned until Friedrich Wilhelm Nietzsche (1844–1900) at the end of the nineteenth century.

*Mētis* is cunning, clever, effective knowledge, as exemplified by the mythical figures of Odysseus and Daedalus. This knowledge combines flair and wisdom, subtlety and deception,

By A.D. 600 each inhabitable island of the south and central Pacific had been discovered and settled. . . . Magellan [1480–1521] traversed the whole Pacific from the tip of South America; he never sighted any land until he reached the Marianas, just east of the Philippines. Not only had Pacific islanders discovered and settled all the suitable islands of the Pacific, but there is solid linguistic, ethnobotanical, and archaeological evidence that they made two-way voyages among them. They sailed, for example, between Tahiti and Hawaii and back again, a distance over three thousand miles of open sea. All this was done by stone age people without writing, charts, or navigational instruments of any kind. In spite of a long series of fanciful theories of lost continents, primitive navigational instincts, and accidental drift voyages, we now know the secret of what made Pacific Island voyaging possible. *The secret was knowledge.* The navigational abilities of Pacific Islanders depended on a profound general knowledge of the sea, the sky and the wind; on a superb understanding of the principles of boat-building and sailing; and on cognitive devices—all in the head—for recording and processing vast quantities of ever changing information.

SOURCE: C. O. Frake, "Dials: A Study in the Physical Representation of Cognitive Systems." In *The Ancient Mind: Elements of Cognitive Archaeology,* edited by Colin Renfrew and E. B. W. Zubrow, pp. 123–124. Cambridge, U.K.: Cambridge University Press, 1994. (Emphasis added).

resourcefulness and mastery of many skills. Far from disinterested or contemplative, it proves its value most concretely, especially in situations that are shifting or ambiguous, where art outweighs the force of violence. The philosophers either pass over the qualities of *mētis*-knowledge or mention them with hostile irony. Plato (in *Gorgias* and *Philebus*) condemns the inexactitude, oblique procedures, cunning, and guesswork. Everything about *mētis*-knowledge confirms its limitation to the shadow theater Plato famously depicted our life as being. The philosopher seeks to penetrate those shadows to an immortal knowledge of the changeless Source of change.

*Gnōsis* usually has the sense of an intelligent grasp of a thing or situation. In the common account of Heracleitus (c. 540–c. 480 B.C.E.), Parmenides (515 B.C.E), and Plato, only one who fully *knows* (*gignōskein*) can be sure to have grasped a thing as it veritably is. All that is required to transform this *gnosis* into the lauded philosophical *epistēmē* is the rational account by which we understand things in the light of the Good and the Whole. The so-called *Gnostics* were heretical sects of the early common era. They conceived of knowing as an immersion into the divine energy, to be possessed and transformed by it. The *gnōsis* sought by the Gnostics is an *epignōsis,* or knowledge of the self, its origin and destiny, a supernatural superknowledge that is supposed to save our lives.

The European Middle Ages divide into two parts, before and after about 1200. The thought of the first period is broadly Platonic, a legacy of St. Augustine (354–430). Later medieval thought benefited from the recovery of the works of Aristotle and the Islamic commentators. Augustine's outlook is notably Plato's: the senses depreciated in favor of immutable truths directly intuited, and a grudging admission of practical knowledge (*technē*) as a lower use of reason directed not toward wisdom but practical necessity. Human knowledge is possible because God illumines our minds, showing us the divine ideas, the archetypes of phenomena.

The most original, if not influential, medieval philosopher of knowledge is Rogen Bacon (c. 1214–c. 1292). Interested in problems that would occupy Galileo three hundred years later (especially falling bodies and optics), he anticipated the Italian astronomer's conviction that the solutions to these and other scientific problems lies in mathematics: "He who is ignorant of mathematics cannot know the other sciences nor the affairs of the world" (*Opus majus* 4.1). Even more against the scholastic grain was his enthusiasm for experiments: "He who wishes to rejoice without doubt in regard to the truths underlying phenomena must know how to devote himself to experiment" (*Opus majus* 4.1).

Thomas Aquinas (1225–1274) dominates the later period. He was the greatest of medieval Aristoteleans. Aristotle had argued that the object of the *epistēmē*-knowledge (*scientia* for Thomas) is immutable and necessary, incapable of being otherwise. Such knowledge is true and certain, being deduced from first principles. A thing is known when we learn its cause, and it is not known without the certainty of deduction from principles, confirming that the thing could not possibly be any other way. As John Buridan (c. 1300–1358) explains, "Science differs from opinion because . . . opinion does not judge with certainty but with fear and science judges with certainty and without fear" (*Questions on the Nicomachean Ethics of Aristotle*). This remains the view of practically all the European philosophers down to René Descartes and John Locke.

## Modernity

The early modern philosophers of the seventeenth century accepted most of ancient thought about knowledge. The clear and distinct ideas that alone count as knowledge for René Descartes (1596–1650) are not notably different from the reasonable account that is Plato's criterion of *epistēmē*-knowledge. Even supposedly "empirical" philosophers like John Locke (1632–1704) assume that there is a strict and proper sense of knowledge that requires nothing less than rational certainty.

The break with tradition came from outside philosophical epistemology, in the new experimental natural philosophy of Galileo Galilei (1564–1642), Robert Boyle (1627–1691), Isaac Newton (1642–1727), and others. The first attempt to describe the experimental method was by Francis Bacon (1561–1626). The most influential account, however, is in Immanuel Kant's *Critique of Pure Reason* (1781). Kant famously explains how concepts are empty without a content they acquire from experience, and how sensations are chaotic noise without a priori concepts we bring to the process of understanding. In this account, empirical knowledge is a synthesis, a mental construction, combining what the senses offer with concepts that, in their broadest features, are a priori forms of human understanding.

Conceiving of knowledge as something put together in the service of understanding suggests that the control of experience may be a more important cognitive goal than the fidelity (or "correspondence") of a disinterested representation. This idea was explored in the nineteenth century by Arthur Schopenhauer (1788–1860) and Nietzsche. Further reflection on scientific experiments confirmed a similar view. What we learn from experiments is how to produce highly controlled effects, not how things are "in themselves," apart from the experimental intervention. This idea of knowledge as an external force of control was taken up by the Vienna positivists, including Ernst Mach (1838–1916), and the American Pragmatists—Charles Sanders Peirce (1838–1914), William James (1842–1910), and John Dewey (1859–1952), who reached conclusions not dissimilar to those of Nietzsche.

*Sociology of knowledge.* Twentieth-century thinkers influenced by Auguste Comte (1798–1857) and Karl Marx (1818–1883) proposed a sociological theory of knowledge. The first premise of these theories is that no knowledge is entirely autonomous in structure or development from the group that produces it. How one looks at data, how one construes given facts, what one takes seriously, depend on social position. Karl Mannheim's seminal *Ideologie und Utopie* (1929; translated as *Ideology and Utopia*, 1936) argued that social circumstances determine both what we seek to know and the validity of knowledge attained. Later accounts abandon

the idea of *validity*, rejecting the philosophical distinction between knowledge and *doxa*, an ideal subject matter for sociology.

*Skepticism.* For much of the twentieth century, philosophical discussion of knowledge was preoccupied with the problem of skepticism. Originally, *skeptikos* meant an inquirer, and later came to refer to followers of the Greek philosopher Pyrrho of Elis (c. 360–c. 272 B.C.E). Their school flourished in the classical world between 100 B.C.E and 200 C.E. These Skeptics taught the radical suspension of judgment, liberating the self of dogmatic convictions (and all convictions are dogmatic), as the way to mental tranquility (*ataraxia*). The point of skeptical arguments is to instill doubt about the most obvious matters, to show that belief is futile. Nothing can be proved because anything can be proved. There is no argument so convincing that an equally convincing argument for the opposite cannot be constructed. Mental peace lies in getting over the vanity of knowledge.

Skepticism fell into decline after Roman times. By the Middle Ages the school and its arguments were forgotten. This situation changed abruptly in the latter sixteenth century, when long-lost texts of ancient skepticism were republished. From then on skepticism played a role in early modern thought, especially in the work of Michel de Montaigne (1533–1592), Descartes, Pierre Bayle (1647–1706), and David Hume (1711–1776). Yet Kant and Georg Wilhelm Friedrich Hegel (1770–1831) both suppose they have overcome skepticism or shown it to involve a mistake, and for most of the nineteenth century skeptical problems were not much discussed in Euro-American philosophy.

In the twentieth century the so-called Analytic philosophers rediscovered skeptical problems as ideal for their methods of precise, rigorous, often logically formalized argumentation. Their problem is to prove the objectivity of knowledge, which usually means refuting the skeptic, who asks how you know that you are not dreaming, or are not a brain in a vat, or that the universe did not come into existence a minute earlier, complete with your faulty memories. The presumption is that unless we can prove *that* we can prove nothing, and unless something is *proved* there is no objective knowledge. Over a period of two thousand years, then, skepticism changed from being a way of life, as it was for Pyrrhonians, to a mood and method of self-knowledge in Montaigne and Descartes, to a technical problem for the most formidably technical work since high-Medieval scholasticism.

## The Linguistic Turn

The linguistic turn in twentieth-century philosophy refers to the rising influence of logical positivism (especially the work of Rudolf Carnap [1891–1970]), as well as positivism's discontents (Willard Van Orman Quine [1908–2000]), heretics (Ludwig Wittgenstein [1889–1951]), and satellites (Bertrand Russell [1872–1970], Karl Popper [1902–1994]). The movement began in German-speaking countries in the 1930s but rose to predominance in English-language philosophy after World War II. It mingled with an independently evolved linguistic analysis and so-called ordinary-language philosophy, as in the work of George Edward Moore (1873–1958), J. L. Austin (1911–1960), and Gilbert Ryle (1900–1976). For all these thinkers, everything in philosophy is a matter of language. The problem of knowledge is a problem of semantic analysis: how is the word used? What is the language game, the logic of the concept?

*Gettierology.*   In a widely discussed article, "Is Justified True Belief Knowledge?" (1963), Edmund Gettier claimed to prove that knowledge is not conceptually equivalent to justified true belief. Gettier's paper shows the style of the then-new analytic approach, using contrived scenarios as logical counterexamples to the definition of *knowledge* as justified true belief. The counterexamples usually work by drawing a reasonable inference from a justified though false belief, inferring something true by accident. Suppose I believe that a neighbor, Jones, owns a Ferrari. I have evidence: it is parked by his house, I see him in it, and so on. Because I believe Jones owns a Ferrari, and because Jones is my neighbor, I infer that *a neighbor* owns a Ferrari. Jones, however, does not own the car, which is owned by my neighbor on the other side, who, unknown to me, works with Jones. Still, it is true that *a neighbor* owns a Ferrari, and I believe that truth on good evidence. I have a justified true belief, but do I know that a neighbor owns a Ferrari? To most people it seems wrong to say so, especially since the neighbor I am thinking of is not the neighbor who owns the automobile. Apparently, then, knowledge is not justified true belief.

Gettier's argument spurred an academic industry. The problem was to render the justified-true-belief formula invulnerable to Gettier-type cases, or replace this "classical" definition of knowledge with something equally plausible and immune to counterexample. Nothing memorable came of it. And contrary to what is often said, the definition of knowledge as justified true belief is not in any sense "classical." It has never been widely accepted and first entered philosophical discussion (in Plato's *Theaetetus*) as a *refuted* theory.

Between Gettier-inspired concerns about the analysis of knowledge and the project of refuting the skeptic, epistemologists fell into two broad camps, depending on whether they considered knowledge to require an element of justification or understanding, or whether, contrary to tradition, true belief might be enough. The idea that knowledge requires only true belief, provided the cause of the belief is appropriate or reliable, is known as *externalism.* Such theories reject the traditional assumption that knowledge requires the knower to understand the reason why a belief is true. They thereby finesse both the Gettier problem and the problem of skepticism. If knowing does not require understanding, then neither must a person who knows be able to refute the skeptic. And if knowledge does require that the cause of belief be reliable, even if the reasons for trust are unknown to the knower, then Gettier-scenario counterexamples fail due to an unreliable source for the (accidentally) true belief.

The heyday of linguistic philosophy had passed by 1980. The movement had led to little in the theory of knowledge. Pure conceptual or semantic analysis was largely abandoned. Exchanging those discredited methods for the richer data of the sciences, Quine called for a "naturalized epistemology." The idea was to reframe the theory of knowledge in terms of empirical hypotheses about the neurological, cognitive, and evolutionary matrix of human knowledge. Quine's project attracted many followers, and Analytic philosophers formed new and often quite deep alignments with scientific research in these areas.

A second trend in post-linguistic-analysis philosophy is a movement of internal critique, a deconstructive diagnosis of epistemology as a pseudoproblem. Wittgenstein inspired this turning of philosophy upon itself, claiming to find conceptual confusion and intellectual neurosis everywhere. The autocritique of epistemology was led by Richard Rorty's *Philosophy and the Mirror of Nature* (1979). Rorty finds the very idea of a "theory of knowledge" premised on an untenable concept of mental representation as a kind of "correspondence" or "isomorphism" with things in themselves.

*Evolutionary epistemology.*   The word *cognition* relates to the ways in which people (and other species) draw information from the world, combine and interpret it, and make decisions about the information. Identifying this cognitive, information-processing function with *knowledge* seemed to open the way to a biological, evolutionary theory of knowledge, as by Konrad Lorenz (1903–1989). Later evolutionary accounts usually make two claims. The first is that human knowledge is an evolved adaptation, an outcome of natural selection. The second is that *any* adaptation of *any* species is a kind of knowledge, that evolutionary adaptation is the *primary* way of knowing the world. In these accounts an insect's camouflage coloration is knowledge of its environment; the fleshy water-conserving cactus stem "knows" that water is locally scarce; the shape of the hummingbird beak expresses knowledge of the structure of the flowers it lives on. Human knowledge is a special case of this primary and ubiquitous biological knowledge of adaptation.

*Feminism.*   By the latter twentieth century feminism had established a presence in the academy, criticizing and developing theories in several areas of philosophical research, including the theory of knowledge. Most feminists have nothing good to say about what has been done in epistemology. Presuming to speak in a universal voice, philosophical theories of knowledge are gendered and do not know it. Feminists challenge epistemology's concept of knowledge (as objective, transcendent, disinterested) and its conception of the knower (as autonomous, self-interested, isolated). They deepen the discontent of the postpositivist philosophy of science and urge points similar to the sociologists of knowledge. Distinctive is the attention to early experience, emotion, racism, class, and, above all, gender as vectors of knowledge repressed from a sexist epistemology.

## Continental Philosophy

For much of the latter twentieth century philosophy in the Western countries was divided into two camps, usually called Analytic and Continental. The division is not a happy one for many reasons, not least because the idea of dividing philosophy this way is an invention of the positivists, foisted upon an otherwise heterogeneous selection of mostly French and German thinkers who often had little in common. Continental research did not pursue the theory of knowledge with anything like the industry of the Analysts. Many agreed with Hegel's assessment that the whole idea of a theory of knowledge (which would presumably itself be knowledge) is naive and superfluous.

**Habermas.** Three European thinkers are exceptions to the tendency to dismiss the theory of knowledge. One is German social philosopher Jürgen Habermas (b. 1929) and his work *Knowledge and Human Interests* (1968). By "human interests" Habermas means orientations of thought and action rooted in the fundamental evolutionary conditions of our species, which he reduces to the interests of work, social interaction, and emancipation. He describes three categories of possible knowledge corresponding to these interests: (1) instrumental, technical knowledge, expanding our power of control; (2) knowledge of language or, more broadly, of language games and cultural traditions, which orient people in common action; and (3) critical-social knowledge about political legitimacy and subordination. The conditions of objectivity differ in each case. When we are interested in a device that works, objectivity has one meaning; when interested in a social interaction, for instance a negotiation, objectivity requires different criteria. And when our interest is in emancipation, we require knowledge of the real conditions of social power in a given society. Social-scientific methods should take their objectivity from this emancipatory interest and not imitate the differently funded objectivity of the natural and technological sciences.

**Lyotard and Foucault.** Jean-François Lyotard's widely read *The Postmodern Condition* (1979) was subtitled *A Report on Knowledge*. Under the conditions of what he calls postmodernity, knowledge has become discontinuous, catastrophic, nonrectifiable, and paradoxical. Getting used to knowledge in such a condition should refine our sensitivity to differences and reinforce our ability to tolerate incommensurables. Another French thinker contributing influential ideas about knowledge is Michel Foucault (1926–1984). The point of his neologism "power/knowledge" is to indicate a reciprocity linking the production and circulation of knowledge with the political economy of government. Power and knowledge flourish together, confirming each other, reproducing each other's authority. Power so entrained with knowledge need not falsify or repress any truth that may be discovered, nor must research sacrifice scientific credibility merely because it owes a debt to coercive social power. To reach these conclusions, however, Foucault had to reduce knowledge to socially prestigious discourse, the arbitrary output of an institutional "discursive apparatus," generating statements its authorities take seriously. There is in this account no more to "knowing" than who gets to say what and say it impressively enough to leave a trace, to have an effect, to make a legible difference in the archive.

## Knowledge and Truth

That knowledge must be true is a longstanding presupposition of Western thought. Yet there are many instances of knowledge that cannot be called true. These include knowledge expressed in technological objects like a bridge or satellite, or in works of art and the imagination. A technological artifact or a work of art is not true (or false) in the way a proposition is. In the face of this discontinuity between knowledge and truth, one may question whether truth properly has the value for knowledge philosophers tend to suppose, or one may make subtle distinctions, dividing knowledge so as to preserve the necessary truth of its best and highest instances. Unsurprisingly, philosophers prefer to distinguish and preserve. Where ancient philosophy distinguished a scientific *epistēmē* from the *technē* of art and craft, twentieth-century analysts discovered a "semantic" or "conceptual" distinction between *knowing how* and *knowing that*.

This distinction is not a neutral analysis. It may be no more than a linguistic rationalization for the assumption that knowledge must divide along lines of intrinsic truth and mere instruments. Western thought consistently ignores, misdescribes, and underappreciates the knowledge involved in art and technology. The philosophers seldom have a good word for artisanal *technē*-knowledge, or the ingenuity and cunning (*mētis*) of the architect or hunter. Although these other knowledges are indispensable to human existence, that very thing has seemed to make them base, materialistic, unsuited to higher minds. To the philosophers, how-to (or *technē*) knowledge is routine, mechanical, and thoughtless, while knowledge of truth is a disinterested grasp of nature and reality.

Philosophers even preferred to invent new concepts of truth rather than reconsider whether the best and most important knowledge has to be true. Kant's theory suggested (though not to Kant) that truth may not be a matter of "correspondence" between thought and reality but merely a coherence of experience. The pragmatists took experimental knowledge as exemplary and promptly introduced a new theory of truth, defining it in terms of "working." It would be equally logical, however, to simply *drop* the condition of truth on the best sort of knowledge.

Certainly there is *some* difference between knowing that the earth rotates around the sun (a true proposition) and knowing how to play the flute (a skill or art). But is the difference one in kinds of knowledge? What is obviously different about them is how the knowledge is expressed. In one case by producing a proposition, in the other by a musical performance. But that is a difference in the artifacts that express knowledge, and does not prove a difference in what makes these examples of knowledge at all. In both cases the knowledge concerns artifacts, constructions of ours, whether propositions or musical performances. And in both cases these artifacts must rate as notable accomplishments. Not just any true proposition expresses knowledge; it has to be informative, important, an insight or discovery. And not just any playing constitutes knowledge (mastery) of the flute.

Heliocentric astronomy and musical artistry are therefore not so different *as knowledge*. Whether we speak of *knowing that* (such and such is true) or *knowing how*, we are qualifying capacities for performance at a certain high level with artifacts of some kind. As examples of knowledge, a surgical operation or a bridge may serve as well as any scientific truth.

**New Dictionary of the History of Ideas**

Their quality as knowledge depends not on their truth but on other, equally rare qualities of artifactual construction. Knowledge has much less to do with theory and truth than philosophers assume. What makes knowledge desirable and worth cultivating is the enhancement it brings to the effectiveness with which we operate in an artifactual environment. *Knowing how* and *knowing that* are not different kinds of knowledge. They are different kinds of use for different artifacts, all expressing the only kind of knowledge there is: a human capacity for superlative artifactual performance.

*See also* **Learning and Memory, Contemporary Views; Logic; Mind; Philosophy.**

**BIBLIOGRAPHY**

Allen, Barry. *Knowledge and Civilization.* Boulder, Colo.: Westview, 2004. Develops account of knowledge as superlative artifactual performance.

———. *Truth in Philosophy.* Cambridge, Mass.: Harvard University Press, 1993. Discusses ideas of truth in Nietzsche, Heidegger, and other Continental philosophers.

Elias, Norbert. *Norbert Elias on Civilization, Power, and Knowledge: Selected Writings.* Edited and with an introduction by Stephen Mennell and John Goudsblom. Chicago: University of Chicago Press, 1998.

Everson, Stephen, ed. *Companions to Ancient Thought.* Vol. 1, *Epistemology.* Cambridge, U.K.: Cambridge University Press, 1990.

Feenberg, Andrew, and Alastair Hannay, eds. *Technology and the Politics of Knowledge.* Bloomington: Indiana University Press, 1995.

Harding, Sandra, and Jean F. O'Barr, eds. *Sex and Scientific Inquiry.* Chicago: University of Chicago Press, 1987.

Laudan, Rachel, ed. *The Nature of Technological Knowledge: Are Models of Scientific Change Significant?* Dordrecht, Netherlands: Reidel, 1984.

Machlup, Fritz. *Knowledge: Its Creation, Distribution, and Economic Significance.* 3 vols. Princeton, N.J.: Princeton University Press, 1980–1984.

Marglin, Frédérique Apffel, and Steven A. Marglin, eds. *Decolonizing Knowledge: From Development to Dialogue.* Oxford: Oxford University Press, 1996.

———. *Dominating Knowledge: Development, Culture, and Resistance.* Oxford: Oxford University Press, 1990.

McCarthy, E. Doyle. *Knowledge As Culture: The New Sociology of Knowledge.* New York: Routledge, 1996.

Mignolo, Walter D. *Local Histories / Global Designs: Coloniality, Subaltern Knowledges, and Border Thinking.* Princeton, N.J.: Princeton University Press, 2000. A contribution from postcolonial cultural studies.

Moser, Paul K., ed. *Oxford Handbook of Epistemology.* Oxford: Oxford University Press, 2002.

Renfrew, Colin, and E. B. W. Zubrow, eds. *The Ancient Mind: Elements of Cognitive Archaeology.* Cambridge, U.K.: Cambridge University Press, 1994.

Tanesini, Alessandra. *An Introduction to Feminist Epistemologies.* Malden, Mass.: Blackwell, 1999.

Wuketits, Franz M. *Evolutionary Epistemology and Its Implications for Humankind.* Albany: State University of New York Press, 1990.

*Barry Allen*

# L

**LANDSCAPE IN THE ARTS.** The *Oxford English Dictionary* defines landscape as both a verb and a noun, signifying not simply its multiple references in vernacular and specialized parlance or its active and passive modes but more importantly the varying perceptions of landscape as an artistic, cultural, and religious entity. Among the definitions of landscape as a noun, the *OED* proffers first "A picture representing natural inland scenery, as distinguished from a sea picture, a portrait, etc." Further definitions include "The background of scenery in a portrait or figure-painting," "A distant prospect: a vista," and significantly, "The object of one's gaze." While as a transitive verb, landscape proposes "to represent as a landscape; to picture, depict." This verbal form further connotes "to lay out (a garden, etc.)" as a landscape. Western art history classifies landscape as both iconography and theme; that is, as a series of signs and symbols that form the visual

vocabulary that is encoded with specific meanings, such as the metaphor of the "errand into the wilderness," or the Garden of Eden. As a topic, landscape is either the subject matter of a painting or a series of prominent elements in a painting that coordinate the diversity of public understanding of the idea of "landscape." The early nineteenth-century transformation of landscape into an acceptable category of painting by the academy equal to history and portraiture signaled a shift in Western cultural and religious values.

Traditionally landscape is designated by such explanatory signifiers as pastoral, ideal, naturalism, and picturesque. Further, landscape is discussed as a background, a symbolic element, a historical setting, and a motif, so that the visual diversity of the paintings that form this visual essay are all appropriately identified as landscape paintings. The journey in the history

**Overwhelmed by the natural world.** *Monk by the Sea* (1809) by Caspar David Friedrich. Oil on canvas. PHOTO CREDIT: BILDARCHIV PREUSSISCHER KULTURBESITZ/ART RESOURCE, NY

of the idea of landscape—from the symbolic stylization found in classical Egyptian frescoes and early Christian mosaics to the awesome sublimity of Caspar David Friedrich's *Monk by the Sea* (1809–1810; Schloss Charlottenberg, Berlin) and Georgia O'Keeffe's *Red Hills, Lake George* (1927; Phillips Collection, Washington, D.C.)—are interwoven with artistic, cultural, economic, political, and religious influences. Perhaps the most significant issue to be considered is whether or not any discussion of landscape painting is privileged as Western in orientation and classifications, especially following the attitudinal metamorphosis toward landscape shaped first by Edmund Burke's eighteenth-century treatise on the sublime and reaffirmed by Immanuel Kant's discussion of the sublime in his *Critique of Judgment* (1790). Essentially Kant argued that the sublime was premised upon the immeasurable extent and stunning intensity of nature and the sense of awe that these expressions of *dynamis* effect in humanity. The amalgamation of terror and delight educed simultaneously from the sight of such phenomena as fulminating cataracts and colossal mountains, thunder and lightning, volcanoes and hurricanes, elicits both a fascination with and a distrust of nature.

*The Dictionary of Art* (1986) has a major entry of nearly one hundred pages under the rubric of "landscape painting" that details the history and variations of landscape painting in the West and references descriptions of landscape as either a motif or a category in discrete entries dedicated to the world beyond the West, for example, China. This is not to suggest that landscape painting in the West is not a significant or an enormous entry topic in its own right but rather to recognize that the universality of landscape as a visual recording of human attitudes and perceptions of the natural world has been abbreviated. Therefore the tradition of defining and describing landscape requires reformulation of it as a pandemic idea. With that in mind, this essay will discuss origins and modern examples of landscape in Europe and the United States as well as in Japan and China. Whether rendered as ideal or real, harmonious or discordant, bucolic or refined, the landscape communicates solace, spiritual grandeur, and space for solitude.

Panoramic depictions of the subtle but expansive beauty of nature are incorporated into the landscape designs and themes found on Japanese screens. Sequential visual episodes are depicted upon individual panels, which when encountered as a unity create an effective visualization of the natural order, with its coordination of foreground, sky, middle ground, and flora and fauna. As a public or private form of display, these Japanese screens may be unfolded either in full or in segments, providing an ever-renewing composition of natural elements. Varying in size from personalized miniature screens to public monumental exhibition screens, the visual image extends from right to left in a horizontal flow of natural symbols ranging from cherry blossoms to gnarled branches to recognizable species of birds. As in Chinese landscape paintings, the most distinctive element of the Japanese landscape screen is the void or empty space for "no-thing-ness," which offers a spatial threshold for contemplation and quietude, for refreshment and solace.

The dramatically unique depiction of a diminutive, almost miniature, human figure in solitary contemplation of the limitless and enveloping expanse of sky, sea, and sand in Friedrich's *Monk by the Sea* stunned its original Western viewers. The minimizing of the natural elements to a state of abstracted essences transformed the conventional relationship between humanity and nature as the monk stands silently, almost belittled before the void. The traditional Western presentation of human dominion over nature had been reversed so that nature overpowers this "everyman," who is confronted by the enormity of the emptiness before him. Hypothesizing that Friedrich, who never ventured out of his native country, would not have seen or been influenced by the Eastern religio-aesthetic that informs the Japanese landscape, it is necessary to consider the cultural and artistic route to this singular yet artistically significant presentation of communion with nature by a Western painter. Even without any contact with the Eastern idea of landscape, Friedrich's new vision transformed the Western visual tradition of depictions of saints seated as the prominent subject in size, scale, and placement within a canvas. The normative pattern both of design and iconography was to site a large—usually out-of-proportion figure in comparison to the landscape imagery—human form in such a position as to garner the viewer's immediate attention thereby reaffirming human dominion over nature. Friedrich, on the other hand, eliminates all elaborate details and symbols within the frame of this painting; thereby, he creates and controls the visual emphasis on the atmospheric conditions and the immensity of nature. The miniaturized rendering of the monk required the viewer's complete attention to be located, perceived, and introduced almost to the shock of the viewer. The subject is no longer that of attesting to the human dominion over nature but rather that of the power of nature.

An atmosphere of mystery. *La Tempesta* (*The Tempest;* 1507–1508) by Giorgione. Oil on canvas. GALLERIA DELL ACCADEMIA, VENICE, ITALY. © THE ART ARCHIVE/DAGLI ORTI

A dual interpretation of landscape. *Sacred and Profane Love* (c. 1515) by Titian. Oil on canvas.

## The Path toward Landscape

Throughout the course of Western history, the concept of landscape and the technique of painting changed, interchanged, and exchanged with social, political, and religious modifications. Classical Egyptian art privileges depictions of the human figure and human activities over the landscape, which is more often than not included to provide a background or setting for an event or activity. The classical Greeks were biased toward humanism, human values, and, thereby, the human figure, so that feelings or artistic expressions of nature were as a background or historical setting. Although disputed among scholars, the connections between Hellenistic poetry and art may signal the origin of both landscape painting and of the concept of *amoenus,* or the "lovely place," a term thought to have been introduced by Theocritus (c. 310–250 B.C.E.). The Romans, however, who might be aptly defined as hesitant in their depictions of nude human figures, greatly admired nature and the landscape. Roman poets sang of the delights and beauty of the countryside and natural realm, and writers including Horace, Pliny the Elder, Ovid, Vitruvius, and Virgil discussed the mutualities between the image and the poetry of landscape, with Virgil identified as the originator of the concept of the Georgic landscape. The finest examples of the visualizing of the Roman idea of the landscape are found in the decorative walls covered with illusionistic landscape that redefined the size and borders of individual rooms. During the early Christian and Byzantine periods, presentations of the landscape were related in terms of decorative designs and symbols. These were bifurcated: paradisal gardens or the wilderness exile were rendered through a symbolic vocabulary of flora and fauna, topographical elements, and human presence.

While the Middle Ages saw a retrieval of classical naturalism in presentations of the landscape, symbolic codings of nature, especially in the metaphorical paradise garden, continued. Medieval attention to the landscape involved the introduction of meteorological properties. Renaissance attitudes toward the landscape were divided between idealization and visual poetry, with an artistic concern for the interplay of light and spatial relations. With the religious and cultural revolution known as the Reformation and its southern European correlative, the Counter-Reformation, landscape painting began its journey toward an independent genre, as evidenced by Albrecht Dürer's employment of the term *landschaft* and the contemporary appearance of the *paese* in the Italian center for landscape painting, Venice. The secularization of the arts in the Reformed countries emphasized the turn to history, portraiture, still-life, and genre themes, which included landscape. Dutch landscape painting in particular experimented with effective displays of light and weather and was fostered by the Calvinist dictum that God's largesse is manifested in the natural world. The economic prosperity of the rising middle class created a new audience and patronage for landscape paintings in northern Europe. The next major shift in the idea of landscape came in the eighteenth century with the delicate pastoral formulated by Jean-Antoine Watteau. In the nineteenth century the famed Kantian turn to the subject and his discussion of the sublime conjoined with a

**Human as subordinate to nature.** *Harvesters* (1565) by Pieter Brueghel the Elder. Oil on panel. THE GRANGER COLLECTION, NEW YORK

variety of technological advances in painting, the economic and societal ramifications of the Industrial Revolution, and the political modifications of revolution and democratic governance to support first the development of romantic landscape, then realist and impressionist landscape by midcentury, and expressionist and abstract landscapes at the end of the century. The twentieth century, with its cultural and religious pluralism, provided new lenses affected by science, technology, and societal revolutions through which the landscape could be interpreted no longer as a major artistic topic but as a nostalgic vision of spiritual values. Landscapes of the late twentieth and early twenty-first centuries were affected by ecological concerns, computer technology, and the development of specialized movements such as land art. From the middle of the nineteenth century to the present, Western art was first challenged and then influenced by the development of photography; similarly the technological advances of moving pictures, television, and computer art have re-formed the modes through which landscape is perceived and imaged.

Despite the variations in attitudes, interpretations, and perceptions of the landscape in Western painting, there are two consistent and fundamental modes of artistic representation employed by Western artists: classic and romantic. Essentially the classic type reorders and enhances nature in an expression of emotion tempered by technical perfectionism evidenced by smooth surface, measured if not invisible individual brush strokes, and careful delineation between colors, forms, and figures often identified as painting with a hard line. The romantic landscape is characterized by its visioning of the undisciplined and savage dimensions of nature as connotative of the sacred mysteries of the divine, signified by textural variations in the layering of and brushwork for paint and the indecipherable borders between colors, forms, and figures identified as painting with a soft line. The art historian Joshua C. Taylor counseled that what is here identified as the classic has prevailed during periods of economic, political, and social unrest whereas the romantic style has been favored during times of economic, political, and social stability.

Two works from the Renaissance era provide an important series of visual comparisons that can be "read" to clarify the classic and romantic modes: Giorgione's *La Tempesta* (*The Tempest;* 1507–1508; Galleria dell Accademia, Venezia) and Titian's *Sacred and Profane Love* (c. 1515; Galleria Borghese, Rome). Neither of these two paintings is a dedicated landscape painting; rather, they incorporate nature into the background, Giorgione more speculatively than Titian. The theme and subject of Giorgione's mysterious *La Tempesta* remains an encoded secret, as it appears to be without a narrative, historical, mythic,

**A pastoral landscape with figures.** *Departure from the Island of Cythera* (1717) by Jean-Antoine Watteau. Oil on canvas. THE ART ARCHIVE/MUSÉE DU LOUVRE PARIS/DAGLI ORTI (A)

religious, or cultural referent. Such a task of aesthetic discernment should reveal the meaning of this painting and the relationships among the three human figures and between the human elements and nature. The juxtaposition of an undressed nursing mother holding her suckling child at her right breast with a standing, fully dressed male pilgrim may signify everything and nothing. The mysterious positioning of the indecipherable human figures and their story (stories) within the boundaries of this canvas are secondary to the physical presentation that Kenneth Clark identifies as "the quintessence of poetic landscape." The creation of space within Giorgione's canvas is enhanced by a series of triangular intersections of topographical and architectural elements that lead the viewer's eye into the center space, which then evaporates into the wafting storm clouds. This mixture of hard- and soft-line effects evokes an atmospheric aura of ambiguity and heightened emotion as the storm either approaches or passes over.

Titian's equally difficult-to-interpret canvas is visually divided between the characteristics of sacred and profane love represented anthropomorphically by the two female figures, one dressed, the other nude. This same dialectic is signified in the two attitudes toward landscape, as untouched natural vegetation flourishes behind the elegant figure of sacred love while an idyllic pastoral vista proffers its mannered display behind

the classical figure of profane love. Titian's ability to present both approaches to the landscape connotes his artistic recognition of the symbolic values attributed to nature.

The visual transition evident from Pieter Brueghel's *Harvesters* (1565; The Granger Collection, New York) to Jean-Antoine Watteau's *Departure from the Island of Cythera* (1717; Musée du Louvre, Paris) to John Constable's *Salisbury Cathedral from the Bishop's Grounds* (1825; Metropolitan Museum of Art, New York) provides a progression toward the idea of pure landscape in Western painting. Paralleling this evolution in attitudes to the landscape are the economic and social influences of the move from an agrarian to a mercantile to an industrialized society. Brueghel's harvest scene follows the medieval tradition of the "labors of the month" first captured in cathedral carvings and adapted later in the fourteenth century into richly elaborate paintings. Brueghel's harvesters incorporate those currently at work and those at rest. The canvas is bifurcated by a diagonal path that separates the reapers who are integrated into the tall hay on the left side of the canvas from those who rest under the shade of a single tall tree in the right foreground. The right-hand side of Brueghel's canvas displays the cut hay either onto rectangular or tentlike forms. The distant background is also divided into a mannered mountain vista on the left and a verdant wilderness on the right. Although premised, one could

**New Dictionary of the History of Ideas**

**Awesomeness of nature.** *Salisbury Cathedral from the Bishop's Grounds* (c. 1825) by John Constable. © GEOFFREY CLEMENTS/CORBIS

argue, upon scriptural passages related to the Fall, *Harvesters* is devoid of mythological, political, or literary referent, and yet the familiarity of the theme makes commentary unnecessary and its appeal immediate and widespread. Brueghel has moved the viewer beyond the landscape as symbolic setting or backdrop for a painting to the landscape as subject, with its allusions to the eternal passing of the seasons and the vastness of space. The abundance of nature herein affirms the transition to a situation in which the human is subject to nature.

On the other hand, Watteau's ethereal re-visioning of the pastoral landscape emphasizes soft colors and lines as the large group of revelers crosses the undulating horizon line. This famed rendering of a romantic idyll incorporates handsome couples who apparently will attend the *fête galante*. The freshness and informality of the artist's vision is highlighted by his development of a new genre painting of a pastoral landscape with figures. Demonstrating his debt to Giorgione and the evocation of a poetic mood, Watteau positions his strolling lovers in a garden setting in which the division between foreground and background is a semicircular arrangement of figures over a gentle central knoll. The background vista, like that of

Giorgione, is softer in line and color as the floating wispy clouds fuse with the lofty trees and airy mountains. The idyllic garden then becomes simultaneously a setting for an event and the event itself as the poetic tranquility, fluidity, and atmosphere create an aura of intimacy and magic much like the enchanted gardens of classical and medieval landscape painting.

Constable's sunlit pastoral landscape is one of his many simple and quiet scenes anchored in his childhood memories of life in Suffolk. In this version of Salisbury Cathedral, he divides the canvas both horizontally and vertically to highlight the painting's centerpiece—the cathedral building itself. On the narrow pathway on the left side of the canvas are diminutive male and female figures walking together away from the viewer, while two rows of grazing cows are located on the right-hand side in parallel relationship to the strolling couple. The association between humanity and nature veers toward a recognition of the awesomeness and mystery of the romantic landscape. Constable's use of sunlight predetermines his disposition toward the heightened color of fresh greens, bold brushwork, and the meteorological modulations between stability and

**Humanity's spiritual relationship to the natural world.** *Two Men in Contemplation of the Moon* (1819–1820) by Caspar David Friedrich. Oil on canvas. PHOTO CREDIT: ERICH LESSING / ART RESOURCE, NY

change. Like his contemporaries, this British artist was torn between science as a mode of observation of nature and religion as the center of values. As this painting demonstrates, however, restitution of a moral high ground was his clear choice. Nature, thereby the landscape, is the direct messenger of God's divine providence, and landscape painting conveys moral ideas and values.

This transformation from Brueghel's agrarian landscape with its overt partnership between humanity and nature to Watteau's ethereal enclosed garden in which humanity continued in a major role and finally to Constable's resplendent pastoral in which the human figure is so diminished as to be noticeably absent is signified by the transition from populated to nonpopulated. The journey toward landscape, then, is a process of both definition and liberation.

### Landscape East and West

Expanding the art historian Benjamin Rowland's now classic comparative discussions of *Art in East and West* (1954), we recognize that landscape is not simply a Western idea or artistic theme. Indeed, for Chinese, Korean, and Japanese artists, landscape was a primary artistic motif centuries earlier than in the West, and their religious and cultural attitudes interpreted nature and thereby landscape as an independent topos at least from the early tenth century. Perhaps best represented by the Chinese name, *shanshui*, or "mountains and water," this Eastern esteem for landscape was predicated upon more than an appreciation or respect for nature, its awesome wonders, and its universal processes; there was also a recognition of the place of humanity within the natural world. It was believed that a retreat or temporary withdrawal from society or "the modern" into a situation permitting contemplation of nature—countryside, mountains, or desert—facilitated a revelation of the ever-present pervasive spirit of the universe. Thus the idea of the landscape was as a retreat for renewal of an individual's mind and refreshment of the spirit. However, this landscape, which had its own life force, was not to be depicted as an illustration, that is line for line, form for form; rather, the real essence of the landscape was to be captured in a style prophetic of "the romantic." The distinction is simply understood if the Greek signifies the West and the Chinese the East. Where the

**A visual harmony of tones and forms.** *Old Battersea Bridge* (1872–1875) by James Abbott McNeill Whistler. Oil on canvas. TATE GALLERY, LONDON. © THE ART ARCHIVE

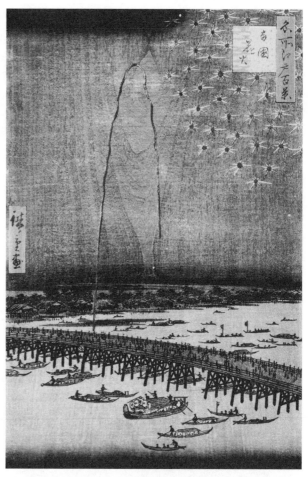

**Flatness of landscape, figures, and fireworks.** *Fireworks at Ryōgoku Bridge* (mid-nineteenth century) by Hiroshige. © CHRISTIE'S IMAGES/CORBIS

Greek sought the personification (or anthropomorphization) of a grove or a tree, the Chinese saw a manifestation of the divine through the labors of the universal spirit.

Consider, for example, the renowned Chinese *shanshui* of *Sage Contemplating the Moon* by Ma Yüan (1200; Kuroda Collection, Tokyo), in which the economy of line and classic asymmetrical composition extends an invitation to the viewer to participate in the quietude and meditation of the reclining sage entranced within his contemplation of the vast emptiness before him and the singular present of the full moon. A potential Western conversation partner is Caspar David Friedrich's romantic vision of *Two Men Contemplating the Moon* (c. 1830; Metropolitan Museum of Art, New York). As beautiful a visual recording of this mysterious partnership between the two men and nature is, and as carefully as the viewer is invited through the painterly convention of interlocuter figures to participate in this experience, the visual differences between the Eastern and Western images are telling and help the viewer to recognize the cultural distinctions in the idea of landscape. Both paintings express the emotive power of the human connection with nature and the spirituality of this relationship. Both paintings could be classified within the Western category of romantic, with their soft edged forms, artistic focus on the evocation of mood, and presentation of nature mysticism.

However, Friedrich designed a series of internal spatial connectives between the mountainous foreground, the evergreen and gnarled empty trees, the distant mountainscape, and the two men that so clutter the canvas as to obscure the focus on the moon and thereby of the spiritual potential of nature. Further, his inclusion of two men who appear almost as partners in physical stature and social position suggests a common search for, and thereby discussion and explication of, the meaning of this encounter. Alternatively, Ma Yüan offers a simpler, more restrained vision of a mountainous landscape that includes a distorted gnarled tree and two men. However, these two men are separated not simply by the internal topographical barrier of a small mountain but also by their own physical size and social status. There is no internal conspiracy between them; rather, the sage and the boatman contemplate, each in his own way, the mystery and spiritual power of nature—the sage by concentrating on the moon, the boatman on the mountain. The large internal space given over by the artist to the void provides a sense of both the monumental vastness of the night sky and the place of the human within the context of the natural world. Further, this void provides a space in which the viewer, like the contemplative sage, can write her own story. One additional

Mountains surreal, yet geologically precise. *The Virgin of the Rocks* (c. 1483) by Leonardo da Vinci. Oil on wood. © NATIONAL GALLERY COLLECTION. REPRODUCED BY KIND PERMISSION OF THE TRUSTEES OF THE NATIONAL GALLERY, LONDON/CORBIS

An interplay of vertical and horizontal forms. *Mont Sainte-Victoire* (1902–1904) by Paul Cézanne. Oil on canvas. PUSHKIN MUSEUM, MOSCOW, RUSSIA. © ALEXANDER BURKATOWSKI/ CORBIS

and perhaps ironic difference to note is that Friedrich employs a horizontal canvas and Ma Yüan a vertical one. Normally the former would be described as accessing the aesthetics of immanence and the latter the aesthetics of transcendence. However, this is open to debate, as these two paintings create internal attitudes toward the relationships of humanity with nature and of the human with the spirit.

Reversing the horizontal and vertical references is another comparison of Eastern and Western romantic views of landscape in James Abbott McNeill Whistler's *Old Battersea Bridge* (1872–1875; Tate Gallery, London) and Hiroshige's *Fireworks at Ryūgoku Bridge* (1858; Fogg Art Museum, Cambridge, Mass.). Perhaps this visual consideration of the universal elements of landscape is enhanced by the fact that the American expatriate painter had seen, owned, and was influenced by Japanese woodblock prints such as Hiroshige's prior to his painting of the *Old Battersea Bridge*. *Japonisme* swept through Paris, especially among the artistic circles Whistler frequented, beginning in the late 1850s and reaching a fervor in the

mid-1860s. *Japonisme* was a major influence on the development of both Impressionism and the art for art's sake movement. Whistler, foremost among all his Impressionist, symbolist, and art for art's sake colleagues, was affected by the visual principles and religio-aesthetics of Japan. Although much of the Japanese woodblock art and pottery that entered the European and American markets was made for export, thereby not necessarily within the proper boundaries of theme, design, and execution for a Japanese audience, Whistler had a discerning eye, and his own approach to painting was transformed by the finest among such objects.

Hiroshige's depiction of a summer fireworks display is visualized at early evening when the bridge is covered with diminutive figures who stand above the water and mountains almost like birds looking down on the natural environment. The foreground and background of the print is divided by the vertical lines forming the Ryūgoku Bridge, with the fireworks boats and the boats with passengers viewing the display, almost obliterating the river waters. The bridge also partially obscures a series of mountains and beaches in the background. The falling lights of the fireworks are condensed into a small segment of the night sky, yet again diffused by the bridge. The internal tonal arrangement of soft, neutral colors works in tandem with the complex patterning of lines and curves to create on first glance an abstract pattern distinguished by the character of "flatness." The details of the fireworks, the varied audiences, and even parts of the natural environment became homologous elements in the visual pattern of colors and forms. A work such as Hiroshige's requires careful looking, as the first glance suggests an unpopulated landscape.

Whistler's painting is even more abstract in its presentation of form and figure. He sought to create a visual harmony of tones and forms that create a mood similar to that evoked in a listener by music, even unto his minimizing of titles to musical parallels: *Old Battersea Bridge* is among his "Nocturnes."

**The enchanted garden.** *Humay and Humayun in a Garden* (c. 1430). Manuscript illumination. PHOTO CREDIT: GIRAUDON/ART RE-SOURCE, NY

To attain this effect he minimized the details, colors, forms, and lighting in paintings such as this, which he also distanced from a narrative. Through his presentation of the atmospheric relations of water, earth, and sky in a moment of poetic enchantment, Whistler invites the viewer to contemplation of the spirituality of landscape. However, what Whistler has also created here is a new vision, or perhaps a retrieval, of the classic mode, of the landscape of symbolic potential.

One of the major distinctions between Eastern and Western presentations of the landscape is the void. In the Chinese *shanshui* (landscape painting) the visual emphasis is as much upon the void as it is upon the sparsity of detailed renderings of botanical and topographical forms. Despite the economy of line, these paintings project the visual effect of nature. The placement of the majority of pictorial imagery left of center balances the void right of center to comprise the traditional asymmetrical composition favored by Chinese, Korean, and Japanese artists. However, the void has multiple roles, including a spiritual threshold for preparation to encounter the universal spirit and an aesthetic invitation to participate in this image of contemplation by painting or writing the viewer's own story in this otherwise empty space. The important sociopolitical function is clarified when a landscape with an empty poetry hall is contrasted to a landscape with the poetry hall filled in. The texts written into the poetry hall record the thinking of those who have contemplated the image with great care and, when the calligraphy includes seals, those of rank who saw the image in situ. The verses provide the viewer with a recognition of what others have experienced in front of this painting, perhaps as a spiritual guide or entry point for viewers who find images disturbing but words comfortable. Neither of these *shanshui* is a precise transcription of what this natural vista looks like; each depicts the spirit or essence of this landscape episode in the world of nature.

When these *shanshui* are compared with Western paintings in which the mountains perform a central, if not dominant, role, it becomes apparent that the fundamental distinction between East and West is in the spiritual and symbolic significance of the idea of landscape. The mountain connotes a variety of Western symbolic references, ranging from the classical Mediterranean "home of the gods" to the Hebraic monumental setting for conversations with Yahweh to the Christian site of transfiguration. The Chinese attitude toward the mountain is also multivalent and ranges from a site for celestial activity to a symbol of permanence and immensity. Shrouded in mist, clouds, or shadows, the mountains dissolve into a delicately splendid form that speaks to the senses rather than the intellect as the essence of the landscape.

Consider, for example, the surrealistic mountain formations found in the art of Leonardo da Vinci, which provide both a form of geological precision and an aura of mystery. His investigations of nature, and thereby his depictions of the landscape, were premised upon careful observation of the natural world and the anatomy of vision. Leonardo captured the rhythm and quiet energy of plants, water, and light. His passion for scientific investigation may have led him to the prominent inclusion of atmospheric blues in his renderings of the landscape, as in *The Virgin of the Rocks* (c. 1483; The National Gallery, London). The surreal shapes of the background mountains and

**After the Fall: the earth as a place of exile.** *October,* calendar miniature from *Les Très Riches Heures de le Duc de Berri* (1413–16) by the Limbourg Brothers. PHOTO CREDIT: RÉUNION DES MUSÉES NATIONAUX/ART RESOURCE, NY

surrounding rock distinguish this as a Western landscape premised upon the Greek principle of the personification: visual parallels between the rocks and human figures are evident in the gesturing hands and fingers and other extremities. By contrast, the Chinese strove to present the living spirit that vitalized the mountain in a painterly vision of mystical and lyrical aestheticism.

Paul Cézanne's *Mont Sainte-Victoire* (1902–1904; Pushkin Museum, Moscow) provides a Western approach to imaging the harmony of and within nature. A technical exercise in the interplay between vertical and horizontal forms, Cézanne's painting is divided into the traditional tripartite foreground, middle ground, and background. However, he creates a new way of understanding this perspectival relationship as his use of line and color moves the viewer's eye back and up toward Mont Sainte-Victoire, which is the object of his gaze. His experiments with brushwork provided him with the skill to create a rapid, loose brush stroke that results in an internal interplay between surface and depth, so that the viewer experiences a sense of perspective, depth, mass, and volume when there isn't any.

**New Dictionary of the History of Ideas**

**America as the "new Eden."** *The Oxbow: The Connecticut River Near Northampton* (1836) by Thomas Cole. Oil on canvas. METRO-POLITAN MUSEUM OF ART, NEW YORK CITY. GIFT OF MRS. RUSSELL SAGE. © FRANCIS G. MAYER/CORBIS

Nonetheless, his explorations of the vista and monumentality of Mont Sainte-Victoire resulted in a series of regulated and erudite renderings of the landscape far removed from the spiritual attachment to nature fundamental to *shanshui.*

**Attitudes toward the Landscape**

A series of universal attitudes toward the idea of landscape in painting can be found in Eastern and Western cultures through the centuries. These are identified through the motifs of garden/paradise, space/place, awesomeness/sublimity, and form/formlessness. These attitudes relate to developments in religious values, philosophy, economics, and politics as well as to technological and stylistic changes in the arts.

*Garden/paradise.* Traditionally understood to be derived from the Persian for "a walled enclosure," the paradise, particularly the paradise garden, is a widespread visual motif among world cultures and mythologies. Oftentimes synonymous with the enchanted garden, the paradise garden signifies first and foremost a place of safety where love and friendship can thrive. The glorious details of its flowery meadows, sweet aromas, shade-giving trees, and gentle animals are important, especially in its connotation as a metaphor of the heavenly paradise. The motif of the garden denotes both a space of beauty and vegetation and, in a number of religions, the site of the origins of humanity. A major metaphor for the earthly paradise,

the Garden of Eden was first the home of Adam and then of Eve, in which all the terrestrial gifts of the creation were abundant until the primordial couple fell from God's favor and was expelled from the garden.

Early Christianity reformulated the classical perception of the natural world as a place of delight into a metaphor for our exile from the garden. Thus early Christian artists formulated an image of landscape as a symbolic paradise, as seen in the glistening apse mosaic featuring heaven and earth in the *Transfiguration* (c. 548; San Apollinaris in Classe, Ravenna, Italy). The highly stylized trees and plants are in keeping with the early Christian concern with flatness as an attribute distinguishing image from idol. The decorative glorification of the natural world denotes what Kenneth Clark identified as the "landscape of symbols" present in this Ravenna mosaic alluding to the lost but not forgotten garden. The garden motif was regularly contrasted to the desert and/or the wilderness in early Western monotheism; the "land of milk and honey" was the earthly locale providing a foretaste of the heavenly paradise.

During the twelfth century, the enchanted garden motif was reformed and aligned with the Christian *hortus conclusus* (enclosed garden) and the Islamic enclosed garden, as exemplified by the Master of the Upper Rhine's *Paradise Garden* (1410; Städelesches Kunstinstitut, Frankfurt) and the manuscript illumination of *Humay and Humayun in a Garden* (c. 1430; Musée des Arts Décoratif, Paris). In the former, the normative medieval elements of a garden are fused with the Hellenistic poetic *amoenus,* or "lovely place," as the delicate sights and smells of flowers—including the singular form of thornless rose that medieval Christianity reserved as the sign of the Virgin's

**A modernist approach to landscape.** *Red Hills, Lake George* (1927) by Georgia O'Keefe. Oil on canvas. THE PHILLIPS COLLECTION, WASHINGTON, D.C. © 2004 THE GEORGIA O'KEEFFE FOUNDATION/ARTISTS RIGHTS SOCIETY (ARS), NEW YORK

"enclosed garden"—and other flourishing vegetation create a visual delight. The Christ Child merrily plays music as his mother reads peacefully in this place of love, comfort, and safety. Similarly the earthly Humay and Humayan find happiness in both their pronouncements of love and in the enchanting setting for their rendezvous. This flower-filled garden is surrounded by a series of appropriately decorated screens that extend the floral and arboreal patterns against a romantic night sky. The presumably perfumed atmosphere, tender bird songs, shade-giving trees, and cool water of these enclosed gardens continue their visual analogies to the lost paradise of Adam and Eve.

The earth as a place of exile is fundamental to the medieval motif of the "labors of the months," which eventually was transformed into the fifteenth-century illuminations in books of hours, in particular, those of the Limbourg Brothers such as *October* from *Trés Riches Heures de le Duc de Berry* (1413; Musée Condé, Chantilly). The Limbourg Brothers here combine the "lost garden" motif with the result of the Fall, that is, that humans must toil in the fields. So as one man rides a horse to till the earth and another sows the winter seed in front of the then Palais du Louvre, the viewer experiences the sensation of the enclosed garden, because the wall in the background can be interpreted as a closing off of the farmed lands from the world of aristocratic and political activity. The passing of the seasons is highlighted by the astrological calendar that frames the top of this illuminated page. Further, the Limbourg Brothers connect the natural with the spiritual in their concern for the meteorological effects of the changing

**A merging of the awesome and the sublime.** *Icebergs (The North)* (1860) by Frederic Edwin Church. Oil on canvas. PHOTO CREDIT: ART RESOURCE, NY

**Chaos of nature meets the constancy of the natural world.** *Under the Wave off Kanagawa* from *Thirty-six Views of Mount Fuji* (1830–1835) by Katsushika Hokusai. © HISTORICAL PICTURE ARCHIVE/CORBIS

> We are surrounded with things which we have not made and which have a life and structure different from our own: trees, flowers, grasses, rivers, hills, clouds. For centuries they have inspired us with curiosity and awe. They have been objects of delight. We have come to think of them as contributing to an idea which we have called nature. Landscape painting marks the stages of our conception of nature.
>
> SOURCE: Kenneth Clark, *Landscape into Art* (1979 [1946]), p. 1.

seasons, evidenced by the costuming and postures of the farmers as well as by the landscape. That which had been the happy home of the primordial couple has become the site of exile for their descendants, who must contend with the challenges of nature's bounty and powers.

***Space/place.*** The notion of space in landscape is twofold, that is, it occurs both inside and outside the frame. Further, there is a philosophic if not psychological reality to the transformation of space into place. This idea of land as space and place is promoted in the work of the geographer Yi-Fu Tuan. The activity of transforming space into place encompasses the acts of identification, naming, possession, and privileging. Perhaps, as in the journey toward landscape, the path toward place is a metaphor for the process of individuation. Further, the spatial relationships within and without the frame have implications beyond the vista of a landscape.

Thomas Cole's now classic rendering of *The Oxbow: The Connecticut River near Northampton* (1836; Metropolitan Museum of Art, New York) is a multivalent reading of the idea of landscape in nineteenth-century American art. A diagonal line runs from the painting's lower right corner upward toward the swirling storm clouds in the upper left corner. To the left of this diagonal line Cole's landscape is a classic display of the wilderness: untamed and unmannered, with lushly green vegetation, decaying broken trees, and a storm-filled sky signaling the tempestuous conditions of nature. Correspondingly the landscape to the right of the diagonal is basked in sunlight, carefully managed and arranged, implicitly under human dominion and exuding a sense of serenity and silence. The founder of the Hudson River School of painters and later also of writers, Cole is further identified as the first American landscape painter. A devout Christian, Cole used his renditions of the landscape as a visual mode of moral and spiritual reflection. Knowing the date of this

**A passionate vision of landscape.** *The Starry Night* (1889) by Vincent van Gogh. Oil on canvas. MUSEUM OF MODERN ART, NEW YORK CITY. LILLIE P. BLISS BEQUEST. © THE ART ARCHIVE/ALBUM/JOSEPH MARTIN

painting, it becomes necessary to consider the effect of the economic disasters of 1835 and the then-common reading of this painting as an omen of future disasters, most notably the Civil War. *The Oxbow* is also a depiction by Cole of America as the "new Eden," an artistic and literary motif popular in the early period of American landscape painting that both offered a connection to the European tradition of landscape painting and served as a vehicle for an American "Christian" art.

However, it is Cole's development and evolution of the intersecting concepts of space and spatial relations into "a place" that characterizes this idea of landscape in America. As a horizontal canvas, *The Oxbow* offers its viewers a peripheral range of vision as well as the traditional foreground, middle ground, and background. The meteorological effects of the stormy and thunderous clouds on the left of the center diagonal, and of the available sunlight with a series of soft clouds on the right, reflect a modernizing of the Limbourg Brothers' point of correspondence. Providing his viewer with a horizon line through which one can enter into this wilderness and pastoral landscape, Cole did not forget that Western characteristic

necessity of the presence of the human. Toward the lower right-hand corner, as the wild vegetation begins to soften into the mannered presentation of the river and the farmed pastures, the disciplined viewer espies a white and red umbrella slanting away from the now decipherable diminutive portrait of the artist.

The twentieth-century painter Georgia O'Keeffe dedicated the last years of her life to the depiction of the landscape in the American Southwest. However, earlier in life she painted landscapes reflecting the places where she lived, including Texas, New York City, and Lake George. Influenced by the modernist ethos that incorporates Oriental (as in Chinese and Japanese) art and philosophy, her paintings such as *Red Hills, Lake George* (1927; The Phillips Collection, Washington, D.C.) are minimized presentations of economical delineations of forms that express the ideas and evoke the emotions that characterize the artist's theme. Like Cole, she leaves an empty space in the upper sky that can be correlated to the void in Chinese and Japanese landscapes. Further, her use of hot- and cool-toned colors, in coordination with the simplicity of her forms, leads us to experience the essence of her idea of the landscape.

**New Dictionary of the History of Ideas**

**The essence of landscape through formlessness.** *Utsunoyama: The Pass through the Mountains* (Edo period, 1699–1757) by Fukaye Roshu. Six-fold screen: opaque color on gold ground. FUKAYE ROSHU, JAPANESE, 1699–1757, EDO PERIOD. *IVY LANE*, C. 1700. SIX-FOLD SCREEN, INK AND COLOR ON GILDED PAPER, 132.5 X 267.2 CM. © THE CLEVELAND MUSEUM OF ART, 2002. JOHN L. SEVERANCE FUND, 1954.127

Physically small in scale and squarer in shape than *The Oxbow,* O'Keeffe's painting creates the visual sensation of a wide-open space with the intersecting "v" formations of mountains. The viewer is without an entry point but comes to the recognition that this is a new way of seeing and expressing the idea of the landscape: the viewer is standing within the frame.

*Awesomeness/sublimity.* The expression of energy and power found in the landscape is delineated by the categories of the awesome and the sublime. Depictions of extraordinary meteorological events, natural disasters, and spiritual intensity in landscape capture the essence of these categories. The nineteenth-century American painter Frederic Edwin Church created an image merging the awesome and the sublime in *The Icebergs (The North)* (1861; Dallas Museum of Art). Overcast by an aura of solitude and silence, *The Icebergs* draws viewers into the eerie blue-green water, the reflected colored lights on the other icebergs, and the almost surreal iceberg formations reminiscent of Leonardo's rock. One may not even initially see the broken, half-sunk ship frozen in the wintry waters of the north, the only sign of human presence.

Katsushika Hokusai's *Mount Fuji Seen below a Wave at Kanagawa* from his *Thirty-six Views of Mount Fuji* (Tokugawa period, 1830–1835; Museum of Fine Arts, Boston) communicates a moment of simultaneous awe and terror. The dramatic energy of the inland sea is seen in the large, threatening waves, most significantly in the tallest ocean wave, which curls over with such intensity that it froths with foam and dwarfs Mount Fuji, which is visible in the background. The frothing waves extend talons of water and foam that reach out to overturn the boats cascading over the curvilinear water slides. Despite all these raging waters and potentially overturned boats, Mount

Fuji, the sacred mountain, stands calmly, majestically, and re-assuringly in the distant background. The awesome and the sublime fuse into an image that at once captures nature's swirling energies and its stability.

Vincent van Gogh's *The Starry Night* (1889; Museum of Modern Art, New York) coordinates warm and cool colors with an intensity of line to express a passionate vision of the landscape. The undulating swirls electrify the night sky, enhancing the white, blue-white, and yellow circles of "fire" that traverse the upper realm of this canvas. The large yellow crescent moon in the upper right corner is balanced by the flamelike vertical cypress trees in the lower left corner. The country village unfolding beyond these two reference points is accentuated by the church that stands almost at the center of the frame. The rhythm of the internal forms creates an atmosphere of spiritual intensity and reawakens the primordial awe at the vast magnificence and limitless powers of the natural world.

*Form/formlessness.* The common perception is that natural objects such as trees, mountains, and flowers should be depicted accurately in Western painting. Representational forms, that is, those recognizable through their resemblance to what is seen in everyday life, are the most comfortable to the human eye and the least threatening to the human psyche. However, abstracting forms in order to artistically distill the essence of the thing or idea became an artistic convention in Western landscape most prominently with the influence of *Japonisme* in the 1860s. Thus a formless style of characterization became a visual mode for evoking emotion and response from viewers. Although a new practice among Western landscape painters, this "formlessness," or abstraction, had been common to Eastern artists almost from the inception of interest in nature as an

**Merging form with formlessness.** *The Day of the God (Mahana no Atua)* (1894) by Paul Gauguin. Oil on canvas. PAUL GAUGUIN, FRENCH, 1848–1903, *DAY OF THE GODS (MAHANA NO ATUA)*, 1894, OIL ON CANVAS, 68.3 X 91.5 CM. HELEN BIRCH-BARTLETT MEMORIAL COLLECTION, 1926.198. REPRODUCTION, THE ART INSTITUTE OF CHICAGO

universal reflection of spiritual values. Fuyake Roshu's *Utsunoyama: The Pass through the Mountains* (Edo period, 1699–1757; Cleveland Museum of Art) incorporates highly stylized but nonrepresentational forms for his mountains, vegetation, and river. This patterning of undulating masses, curvilinear flattened forms, and decorative vegetal shapes present the essence of landscape in a dynamic yet challenging mode.

Translated into Western art first by Whistler and then by the Impressionists, this artistic interest in formlessness, or "formless form," reached new heights in the late nineteenth century with paintings such as Paul Gauguin's *The Day of the God (Manaha no Atua)* (1894; Art Institute of Chicago). In this work, one of the paintings influenced by his Tahitian sojourn, the exotic is referenced not simply by title or attitude toward the human figure but also the expressive quality of Gauguin's colors. In this canvas he clearly merges form with formlessness in the abstractions of landscape in the foreground, where the discarded garments of the ritual celebrants are almost indistinguishable from the topography and the pool of water.

Pursuing the idea of landscape as a merger of form and formlessness one step further, Salvador Dalí painted images

such as *The Persistence of Memory* (1931; Museum of Modern Art, New York) in which the viewer's normal concept of proportion is also skewed, as for example in the larger-than-life-size limp watch that hangs over a bare branch of a diminutive tree. Objects fuse with anthropomorphic elements in this landscape of dreams, as the formless foreground is absorbed into the recognizable forms of the lake and mountainside by Dalí's home in Port Lligat, Spain. In this way he coordinates the known with the unknown, dream with reality, and form with formlessness within the idea of landscape.

## Scholarship on the Landscape

Formal discussions of the idea of landscape date, as mentioned earlier, to the philosophic and poetic texts from the classical era of Greece and Rome. In the early Christian era, however, beyond scriptural and patristic references to landscape as the garden, the wilderness, the land of milk and honey, or the desert, little attention was given to either landscape as an art form or as nature until the time of Francis of Assisi (1181 or 1182–1226), who retrieved and reshaped the pre-Christian understanding of the beauty of the natural order as a reflection of God.

**New Dictionary of the History of Ideas**

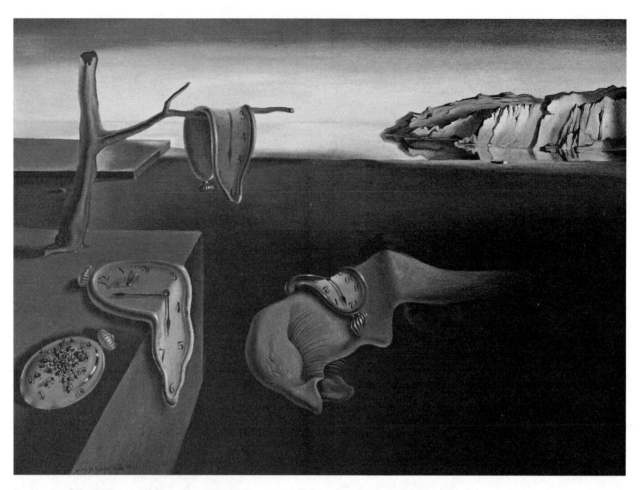

**A merger of the known and the unknown.** *The Persistence of Memory* (1931) by Salvador Dali. Oil on canvas. DIGITAL IMAGE ©
THE MUSEUM OF MODERN ART/LICENSED BY SCALA/ART RESOURCE, NY. © 2004 SALVADOR DALI, GALA-SALVADOR DALI FOUN-
DATION/ARTIST RIGHTS SOCIETY (ARS), NEW YORK

Giovanni Paolo Lomazzo (1538–1600) is recognized as the
first author to discuss formally an aesthetics of landscape
through his distinction of "privileged places" and "places of
delight" in his *Trattato dell'arte della pittura, Libro VI* (1584).
Seventeenth-century commentaries by Roger de Plies, André
Félibien, and Samuel van Hoggstraten, among others, continued to define, classify, and elevate the idea of landscape in art.
The eighteenth century produced significant philosophic reflections on the idea of landscape, particularly with relation to
the sublime, by Edmund Burke, William Gilpin, Uvedale
Price, and Immanuel Kant. Curiously, nineteenth-century
painters wrote more influential texts on landscape than philosophers or theologians, including Caspar David Friedrich, John
Constable, and Thomas Cole, although the writings of John
Ruskin and Ralph Waldo Emerson would be formative on later
aesthetics of landscape. With the advent of the twentieth century, critical assessments of the idea of landscape, particularly
in painting, began to appear; however, most were limited to
studies of "modern" attitudes toward landscape.

There is no single classic study of the theme of the idea of
landscape either in the arts or more specifically in painting
throughout the history of either Eastern or Western culture.

However, classic studies such as Michael Sullivan's *The Birth
of Landscape Painting in China* (1962) and Barbara Novak's
*Nature and Culture* (1980) consider the development of landscape painting in relation to a specific geographic location or
chronological period. Kenneth Clark's singular *Landscape into
Art* (1946) is an observant analysis of the cultural concepts of
landscape in Western culture with a subthesis that the artistic
move to landscape as a recognized category of "high art" corresponds to the secularization of Western culture and values.

A variety of intriguing texts including Leo Marx's now classic *The Machine in the Garden: Technology and the Pastoral Ideal
in America* (1964) and Yi-Fu Tuan's *Space and Place: The Perspective of Experience* (1977) provide lenses through which to
expand the boundaries of art-history-based analyses of landscape. Similarly Robert Rosenblum's *Modern Painting and the
Northern Romantic Tradition: From Friedrich to Rothko* (1975),
Denis E. Cosgrove and Stephen Daniels's edited volume *The
Iconography of Landscape: Essays on the Symbolic Representation,
Design, and Use of Past Environments* (1988), and any of Barbara
Novak's texts provide specialized studies integrating theologi-
cal, cultural, scientific, and philosophic influences on the mean-
ing and presentation of landscape in painting.

> Why does a virtuous man take delight in landscapes? It is for these reasons: that in a rustic retreat he may nourish his nature; that amid the carefree play of streams and rocks, he may take delight; that he may constantly meet in the country fishermen, woodcutters, and hermits, and see the soaring of the cranes, and hear the crying of the monkeys. The din of the dusty world and the locked-in-ness of human habitations are what human nature habitually abhors; while, on the contrary, haze, mist, and the haunting spirits of the mountains are what human nature seeks, and yet can rarely find.
>
> SOURCE: Kuo His, *An Essay on Landscape Painting*, trans. Shio Sakanishi (1936), p. 30.

The reality of both the interdisciplinary motif and methodology for the study of this theme, that is, the idea of landscape (through painting), has been emphasized by Western scholars within the categories of Western art and cultural studies. The most creative work being done appears to come from the research and curatorial presentation for special exhibitions. For example, the reader should consult *The Natural Paradise: Painting in America, 1800–1950* (1976), edited by Kynaston McShine; *American Light: The Luminist Movement, 1850–1875* (1980), edited by John Wilmerding; and *American Sublime: Landscape Painting in the United States, 1820–1880* (2002), edited by Andrew Wilton and T. J. Barringer.

*See also* **Arts: Overview; Chinese Thought; Classicism; Creativity in the Arts and Sciences; Gender in Art; Humanity in the Arts; Iconography; Japanese Philosophy, Japanese Thought.**

**BIBLIOGRAPHY**

Apostolos-Cappadona, Diane. *The Spirit and the Vision: The Influence of Christian Romanticism on the Development of 19th-Century American Art.* Atlanta, Ga.: Scholars Press, 1995.

Appleton, Jay. *The Symbolism of Habitat: An Interpretation of Landscape in the Arts.* Seattle: University of Washington Press, 1990.

Cafritz, Robert C., Lawrence Gowing, and David Rosand. *Places of Delight: The Pastoral Landscape.* Washington, D.C.: Phillips Collection in association with the National Gallery of Art, 1988. Exhibition catalog.

Clark, Kenneth. 1946. *Landscape into Art.* New York: Harper and Row, 1979.

Cosgrove, Denis E., and Stephen Daniels, eds. *The Iconography of Landscape: Essays on the Symbolic Representation, Design, and Use of Past Environments.* Cambridge, U.K., and New York: Cambridge University Press, 1988.

Hawes, Louis. *Presences of Nature: British Landscape, 1780–1930.* New Haven, Conn.: Yale Center for British Art, 1982. Exhibition catalog.

Kemal, Salim, and Ivan Gaskell, eds. *Landscape, Natural Beauty, and the Arts.* Cambridge, U.K.: Cambridge University Press, 1993.

Langmuir, Erika. *Landscape.* London: National Gallery, 1997.

Lee, Sherman E. *Chinese Landscape Painting.* 2nd ed. Cleveland: Cleveland Museum of Art, 1962.

Marx, Leo. 1964. *The Machine in the Garden: Technology and the Pastoral Ideal in America.* New York: Oxford University Press, 2000.

McShine, Kynaston, ed. *The Natural Paradise. Painting in America, 1800–1950.* New York: Museum of Modern Art, 1976. Exhibition catalog.

Nasgaard, Roald. *The Mystic North: Symbolist Landscape Painting in Northern Europe and North America, 1890–1940.* Toronto: Art Gallery of Ottawa in association with University of Toronto Press, 1984. Exhibition catalog.

Novak, Barbara. "Defining Luminism." In *American Light: The Luminist Movement, 1850–1875,* edited by John Wilmerding, 23–29. Washington, D.C.: National Gallery of Art, 1980. Exhibition catalog.

——. *Nature and Culture: American Landscape and Painting, 1825–1875.* New York: Oxford University Press, 1980.

Nygren, Edward J., Bruce Robertson, and Amy R. Meyers. *Views and Visions: American Landscape before 1830.* Washington, D.C.: Corcoran Gallery of Art, 1986. Exhibition catalog.

Redford, Scott. *Landscape and the State in Medieval Anatolia: Seljuk Gardens and Pavilions of Alanya, Turkey.* Oxford: Archaeopress, 2000.

Rosenblum, Robert. *Modern Painting and the Northern Romantic Tradition: Friedrich to Rothko.* New York: Harper and Row, 1975.

Sullivan, Michael. *The Birth of Landscape Painting in China.* London: Routledge and Kegan Paul, 1962.

Sutton, Peter C., and Albert Blankert. *Masters of Seventeenth-Century Dutch Landscape Painting.* Boston: Museum of Fine Arts, 1987. Exhibition catalog.

Tuan, Yi-Fu. *Space and Place: The Perspective of Experience.* Minneapolis: University of Minnesota Press, 1977.

Turner, A. Richard. *The Vision of Landscape in Renaissance Italy.* Princeton, N.J.: Princeton University Press, 1966.

*Visions of America: Landscapes as Metaphor in the late Twentieth Century.* Denver: Denver Art Museum, 1994.

Warnke, Martin. *Political Landscape: The Art History of Nature.* Cambridge, Mass.: Harvard University Press, 1995.

Wilton, Andrew, and T. J. Barringer. *American Sublime: Landscape Painting in the United States 1820–1880.* Princeton, N.J.: Princeton University Press, 2002.

*Diane Apostolos-Cappadona*

**LANGUAGE AND LINGUISTICS.** Estimates of the number of languages spoken on earth at the turn of the twenty-first century range between four and six thousand. Considering that this number has been rapidly declining for the last couple of centuries, there must at one time have been many more languages, perhaps upwards of ten thousand. Of the languages spoken in the twenty-first century, a few have tens or hundreds of millions of speakers spread over enormous stretches of land, while most languages have severely restricted population distribution. No matter exactly how many different languages there are or how many speakers each of them has, the multiplicity of human speech patterns is staggering, and any attempt to reduce this overwhelming plethora of sounds, meanings, and structures to a finite set of rules and procedures is both daunting and humbling. Yet that is precisely the charge that linguists take as their solemn duty. No wonder that linguistics is probably the most contentious of all academic disciplines; there is no easy, transparent mechanism for bringing order to the wild proliferation of human speech (not to mention writing).

The varieties of linguistic experience are so profuse as to defy accurate enumeration: grammar, syntax, etymology, phonology, phonetics, morphology, psycholinguistics, anthropological linguistics, sociolinguistics, educational linguistics, taxonomy, philology, historical linguistics, lexicography, and so on. It would be futile to attempt any sort of exhaustiveness with regard to the branches and sub-branches of this protean discipline. What is more, each division and subdivision of linguistics has its own generation after generation of leading lights. Thousands of linguists have left their imprint on the field, but here it will be possible to mention only a few of those who represent major trends, particularly in the realm of thought (both about the discipline itself and about human beings and their world).

## Philosophers, Grammarians, and Neogrammarians

Throughout most of human history, the study of language has been subsumed under philosophy. The distinction between philosophical linguistics and linguistic philosophy is subtle but telling: Is the driving concern language or philosophy?

The Austrian-born English philosopher Ludwig Wittgenstein (1889–1951) was instrumental in bringing language-related questions to the fore for those who were not professional linguists. He accomplished this in two respects: (1) discussions on the philosophy of language, and (2) elaboration of logical theories. Wittgenstein was a protégé of Bertrand Russell (1872–1970), absorbing features of the analytic philosophy of Russell and Gottlob Frege (1848–1925), but fundamentally posing a whole series of innovative questions of his own devising. Wittgenstein's genius is enshrined in his *Logisch-philosophische Abhandlung* (*Tractatus Logico-Philosophicus,* 1922), a brilliant work that is only about seventy-five pages in length. Despite its extreme brevity, the *Tractatus* manages to raise provocative questions concerning the nature of language, logic, ethics, death, and other, often disturbing, topics. How is language possible? How does a sequence of words come to mean something? How can it be understood? For Wittgenstein, a sentence is a depiction of reality, thus he presents what might be called a picture theory of language. The *Tractatus* deals, above all, with the limits of language: "What can be said can only be said by means of a proposition, and so nothing that is necessary for the understanding of *all* propositions can be said." (In such statements by Wittgenstein, "said" means "represented.") The limits of language correspond to the limits of thought, hence there are certain things that cannot be thought, which accounts for the famous last sentence of the book: "Whereof one cannot speak, thereof one must be silent."

In *Tractatus,* Wittgenstein expressed the idea that there was a unifying essence beneath the diversity of language, and that the philosopher strives to discern this essence. In his posthumously published *Philosophische Untersuchungen* (Philosophical investigations, 1953), he had come to the conclusion that this supposed underlying essence was illusory. Rather, one demolishes obsessive concern with such perplexing questions as knowledge, intuition, and assertion by simply describing what one experiences in the daily use of language. In short, throughout his philosophical studies, Wittgenstein was perpetually in quest for *das erlösende Wort* ("the redemptive word").

Another important British thinker who followed the later Wittgenstein in pursuing philosophical analysis through detailed study of mundane language was John Langshaw Austin (1911–1960). Austin maintained that linguistic analysis can solve philosophical problems, but was opposed to the language of formal logic as contrived and incomplete. According to Austin, daily language is actually more subtle and complex than formal logic, and hence better able to get at the crux of critical issues. His approach helped to underscore the significance of language for philosophy.

One tradition of thought in which philosophy and concern with language are given almost equal weight is semiotics. Simply stated, semiotics (or semiology) is the study of signs and their diverse applications. The notion of *sign* is fundamental to the study of language, but its protean ubiquity (including for nonlinguistic purposes) makes it extraordinarily difficult to define. One of the earliest sign theories is that of St. Augustine of Hippo (354–430) as enunciated in *De Doctrina Christiana*: "A sign is a thing that causes us to think of something beyond the impression the thing itself makes upon the senses." The semiotic frame of reference is vast, being designed to encompass all other types of inquiry, but it became an independent mode of investigation with the American philosopher Charles S. Peirce (1839–1914). Originally a logician, Peirce did not offer a systematic presentation of his major principles and frequently changed his doctrines. He basically contended that all human experience could be organized at three levels that, roughly stated, are felt qualities, experiential effect, and signs, the latter being the abstract class of all sensorially perceived "signals" that refer to the same object or phenomena.

The German mathematician, logician, and philosopher Gottlob Frege contributed to the early development of semiotics by adding, among other things, the crucial distinction between *Sinn* ("sense") and *Bedeutung* ("meaning"). Frege enunciated the principle of *compositionality* whereby a sentence can be described according to the functional interdependence of the meanings of its appropriately formed elements.

In his *Foundations of the Theory of Signs* (1938), another American philosopher, Charles W. Morris (1901–1979), offered a tripartite organizational scheme for semiotics: syntax (the interrelations among signs), semantics (the relation between signs and the objects they designate), and pragmatics (the relationship between the sign system and the user). Morris collaborated with the German scholar Rudolf Carnap (1891–1970), who developed an ideal language that became a model for semioticians. A major figure in the development of symbolic logic was the Polish-American scholar Alfred Tarski (1902–1983), who is well known for his concept of truth in formalized languages.

Semiotics was further developed in the monumental work of another German thinker, Ernst Cassirer (1874–1945), entitled *Philosophie der symbolischen Formen* (The Philosophy of symbolic forms, 1923–1929). Cassirer recognizes the vital role of language in articulating and conceptualizing a preexisting reality, but his project is primarily philosophical. He emphasizes that human beings are *animal symbolicum* ("the symbol-creating animal"), not merely because of their ability to manipulate verbal language itself, but also because of their creation of other symbolic spheres: art, myth, religion, science, history, and so on.

Semiotics and grammar converged in the synthesis of the American logician Richard Montague (1930–1971), who followed in the path of Frege, Tarski, and Carnap. Based upon the semantics of formal languages, Montague grammar puts forward the premise that there is no theoretically relevant difference between artificial (formal) and natural (human) languages. Therefore, the logical structure of natural languages may be described through universal algebra.

Having pursued the philosophical path thus far, this article now follows the grammatical thread. Classical grammarians were concerned with prescriptive principles. This suited the sharply defined structure of Indo-European languages. It is one of the perennial questions of linguistics, however, whether such principles apply equally well (or at all) to non-Indo-European languages. China had its own sort of language studies, known as *xiaoxue* ("minor learning," in contrast to *daxue* ["major learning"], which signified ethics), for at least two millennia. An early philosopher named Xun Zi (c. 310–210 B.C.E.), moreover, had elaborated a doctrine of "names" that bore striking similarity to doctrines about language expressed by Plato (c. 428–348 or 347 B.C.E.) in his "Cratylus." But it was not until the end of the nineteenth century that Literary Sinitic (Classical Chinese) was forced into a Latin grammatical mold—and it fit very badly. This question of the appropriateness of classical Western grammar for non-Indo-European languages shall return below (both directly and under the guise of universal grammar). For the moment, however, the focus will be on Western grammars for Indo-European languages.

The Modistae (also known as Modists and speculative grammarians), who flourished around Paris from about 1260 to 1310, wrote medieval treatises on the *modi significandi* ("modes of signifying," the semantic and deictic functions of words and word classes). They were generally Aristotelian in their aim to explain language, not simply to describe it, and had a large impact on the terminology and systematicity of later grammarians.

After having investigated grammars for various specific languages (Greek, Latin, Hebrew, Spanish, etc.), Claude Lancelot (1615?–1695), professor at the Petites Écoles de Port-Royal des Champs, in collaboration with Antoine Arnauld (1612–1694) wrote the *Grammaire générale et raisonée* (1660), often referred to as *Grammaire de Port-Royal*. This is a general grammar that enunciates certain principles that presumably govern all languages and are meant to define language in general, while individual languages are thought to be particular cases of the universal model. By and large, eighteenth-century grammarians followed in the footsteps of their Port Royal predecessors. Lancelot and Arnauld imply, and later grammarians (for example N. Beauzée) specify, that communication of thought by means of speech demands that the latter be a sort of "picture" or "imitation" of thought (cf. Wittgenstein). That is to say, the function of language is to be a representation of thought. Already in the seventeenth century, Gottfried Wilhelm von Leibniz (1646–1716) and other thinkers subscribed to the belief in the imitative value of language sounds. This leads to the consideration of the place of phonology in the history of linguistics.

In comparing Old Norse, Greek, and Latin, the Danish linguist Rasmus Rask (1787–1832) had discovered regular sound differences. In 1822, the German philologist and folklorist Jacob Grimm (1785–1863) construed these differences as systematic sound changes that had led to the development of Germanic as a separate branch of Indo-European. This recognition became enshrined as Grimm's Law (also referred to as the Germanic sound shift) and was a major milestone in the evolution of linguistics as a rigorously scientific discipline.

The neogrammarians (*Junggrammatiker* in German, also known as the Leipzig School), subscribed to positivistic atomism. During the 1870s, they arose in staunch opposition to the metaphysical and biological approaches to language then current. Their name was actually a pejorative term applied to them by the older generation of traditionalists in language studies. The school is said to have its inception from the publication of Karl Verner's (1846–1896) celebrated explanation of apparent exceptions to Grimm's Law in 1877, of August Leskien's (1840–1916) postulation of the inviolability of sound laws in relation to declension in 1876, of Karl Brugmann's (1849–1919) studies on the morphology of Indo-European, and of Hermann Paul's (1846–1921) *Prinzipien der Sprachgeschichte* (Principles of the history of language) in 1880. They insisted upon the absolute autonomy of phonology from syntax and semantics, with phonology having the most important position. Their main aim was to describe historical change, plus they had an overriding interest in diachronic aspects of language and the development of precise methods of reconstruction. The structuralists and transformationalists of the twentieth century criticized virtually all of the basic premises of the neogrammarians, yet the neogrammarians arguably did more to establish linguistics as an independent science (in the strictest sense of the term) than any other school.

### The Structuralist Era

The father of structuralism (and many would say of the modern science of linguistics) was the Swiss linguist Ferdinand de Saussure (1857–1913). But Saussure was a reluctant father whose seminal *Cours de linguistique générale* (Course in General Linguistics, 1916) was edited and posthumously published by two colleagues and a student who assiduously took notes at his lectures. The peculiar nature of its composition has resulted in a work that is fraught with contradictions and puzzling self-doubts cheek by jowl with superbly confident, dogmatic assertions. Despite all the vagaries of its composition, *Cours de linguistique générale* is a hugely influential work and has probably done more to establish linguistics as an independent discipline than any other single book.

Although Saussure had a background in the historical study of language and had made significant advances in the understanding of the Indo-European vowel system, he was unusually critical of neogrammarian philology, which he accused of being overly absorbed in diachrony (that is, issues of the evolution of languages). Saussure also criticized traditional grammarians for neglecting entire aspects of language and for lacking overall perspective, but allowed that their method was fundamentally correct and that they properly emphasized synchrony. Hence, whereas the discipline of historical linguistics that grew up in the nineteenth century was almost wholly diachronic in its orientation, linguistics in the first half of the twentieth century—following the lead of Saussure—became a largely synchronic enterprise. It was not long before European structuralism crossed the Atlantic to become the predominant methodology of American linguistics.

The German-born American anthropologist Edward Sapir (1884–1939) was responsible for many enduring concepts in linguistic research. Author of the landmark volume *Language* (1921), Sapir emphasizes that language is tightly linked to culture. For Sapir, language is an acquired function of culture rather than being biologically determined. This view is diametrically opposed to that of the transformationalists (see below), who believe (but have not proved) that human beings possess a genetically determined predisposition for language—including many of its most specific and distinguishing features—that is already present at the moment of birth. Sapir is undoubtedly correct when he points out that, sans society, an individual will never learn to talk in meaningful terms—that is, to communicate ideas to other persons within a given community. This can easily be demonstrated by observation of feral or mentally abused children and in children suffering from autism or other psychological disorders that affect the acquisition and manipulation of language. Similarly, infants who are born into one linguistic environment but are adopted into a completely different linguistic environment will obviously not grow up speaking the language of their biological parents. If there is any "hardwiring" of linguistic abilities, it occurs around puberty, after which time it becomes increasingly difficult to attain full fluency in a second language or to lose all ability in one's mother tongue. Sapir, of course, could not have foreseen the degree to which the transformationalists would divorce language from its social and cultural matrix, but he would undoubtedly have been horrified by this turn of events and would have regarded it as a fallacious approach to language. While Sapir may not be around to point out the speciousness of the transformationalists' so-called LAD (Language Acquisition Device, also styled the "language module," "language instinct," and so forth), which stipulates hardwired language ability at birth, that has been done ably by Jerome Bruner (b. 1915) with his cognitive learning theory that builds on the cultural-cognitive developmental model of the Russian psychologist Lev Vygotsky (1896–1934).

Although Leonard Bloomfield (1887–1949) was a contemporary and colleague of Sapir, and the two are widely regarded as the founders of American structuralism, they were quite dissimilar in temperament and outlook. Whereas Sapir was more dramatic and imaginative, Bloomfield tended to be methodical and preferred as much as possible to rely strictly upon evidence in formulating his positions. In 1914 he wrote *Introduction to the Study of Language,* which in later editions was called simply *Language* (1933). Bloomfield was responsible for an enormously influential synthesis that brought together three earlier traditions of language study (historical, philological, and practical), and forged them into a coherent whole. He was fiercely determined to establish linguistics as a science. In particular, he wished to distinguish linguistics from the speculative philosophers who assumed that the structure of their own language embodied universal forms of human thought or even the cosmic order. In addition to the speculative philosophers, Bloomfield censured the grammarians of the old school tradition who strove to apply logical standards to language, ignoring actual usage in favor of prescriptive rules. Bloomfield was especially critical of those who took the features of Latin as the normative form of human speech. He was much more favorably disposed toward the grammatical studies of the ancient Indians because the latter were themselves excellent phoneticians who had also developed an intelligent systematization of grammar and lexicon.

In Europe, structuralism did not remain a monolithic linguistic monopoly. The Prague School (which grew out of the Prague Linguistic Circle) is a branch of structuralism, but with a difference. The members of this school hold language to be a system of functionally related units and focus on the observation of linguistic realia at discrete moments. They are interested in language change, not in maintaining a strict dichotomy of *langue* and *parole* (linguistic system versus linguistic utterance)—a key tenet of Saussure—or of synchrony and diachrony. The starting point of the Prague School is to clarify the function of the various elements of actual utterances. The Prague School has made a lasting impact upon many areas of modern linguistics, particularly with regard to the analysis of the sounds of language and their effect in literature.

Another noteworthy structuralist school is the Copenhagen Linguistic Circle. One of its leading theoreticians was Louis Hjelmslev (1899–1965), whose *Prologomena* (1943; English edition 1953) is intended as a series of preliminary statements essential for the formulation of any theory of language. Laying down the most basic ground rules for linguistics, Hjelmslev faults the humanities for being overly descriptive and insufficiently systematizing. He is opposed to the confusion of philosophy of language with theories of language. Hjelmslev views language as a self-sufficient totality of its own. He foresees the emergence of an "algebra of language," which he calls "glossematics." This novel linguistic approach, which strongly emphasizes form, is intentionally designed to distinguish the ideas of the Copenhagen School from more traditional forms of structural linguistics, such as those of the Prague School. Hjelmslev does adhere to Saussure's basic principles of structuralism, but attempts to make his theory more axiomatic, having been influenced by the logical empiricism of Alfred North

Whitehead (1861–1947), Russell, and Carnap. With the ostensible goal of eliminating confusion between the object (language) being studied and the methodology used to describe it, Hjelmslev tries to create noncontradictory descriptive terminology by employing carefully crafted abstractions and mathematical logic.

Around the middle of the twentieth century, Morris Swadesh (1909–1967), a student of Sapir, devised a statistical method for determining the family relationships of languages and the probable dates of their separation from a common parent. This technique, which is called lexico-statistics or glottochronology, is premised upon the idea that the vocabulary of a language is replaced at a constant rate, much like the steady radioactive decay of carbon-14 that is used to date organic remains. The Swadesh lists select a core vocabulary of one hundred or two hundred words consisting of body part terms, lower numerals, pronouns, primary kinship terms, common flora and fauna, words for ordinary topographical features, and so forth. Widely used in the 1960s and 1970s, glottochronology provoked an emotional debate, with all manner of objections being raised against it: the rate of decay is not universal, cognates may be partial and may or may not be recognizable, even core terms may be borrowed, and so forth. Despite the outcry, glottochronology is still employed, but in mathematically increasingly complex and conceptually more sophisticated models. For example, a geographical dimension may be incorporated into the tree, and more careful attention is paid to historical reconstruction.

Another controversial legacy of structuralism that continues to attract attention is the Sapir-Whorf hypothesis concerning the relationship among language, thought, and culture developed by Benjamin Lee Whorf (1897–1941), who was also a student of Sapir and who based his hypothesis on the approach of his mentor. The Sapir-Whorf hypothesis has two main facets: (1) linguistic determinism (the language one uses conditions the way one thinks), (2) linguistic relativity (the complex of distinctions made in a given language are unique and not to be found in any other language). Both of these facets are somewhat at odds with the Bloomfieldian notion (broadly ascribed to by modern linguists) that all languages—like all people—are equal in their ability to express whatever thoughts their speakers need or want to convey. Whorf did intensive work on North American indigenous languages that have dramatically different grammatical and lexical properties from Indo-European languages, so it is altogether comprehensible that his intimate familiarity with their distinctive outlooks would lead him to develop the hypothesis that he did. While the two main facets of the hypothesis would appear to be innocuous, commonsense propositions, they are anathema to certain sectors of the modern political spectrum. Furthermore, continuing the tinctorial theme, the strong form of the Sapir-Whorf hypothesis (that a given language determines the thought and perception of its speakers) is seen by many to have been refuted by the study of Brent Berlin and Paul Kay on basic color terms and their supposed universality (1969). The conclusions of Berlin and Kay, however, have not gone unchallenged: John A. Lucy and Richard Shweder have demonstrated significant behavioral differences in regard to color

perception on the part of speakers of different languages. In any event, the Sapir-Whorf hypothesis should be easily testable by extensive investigation of the thought patterns of individuals who are thoroughly bilingual (or multilingual) in markedly dissimilar languages. Simply asking such individuals whether it is easier to think certain thoughts in a given language than in another language, or whether it is impossible to think the thoughts of one language in another language, should go far toward determining the validity of the Sapir-Whorf hypothesis.

## The Transformational Generative Insurrection

Few would disagree that Noam Chomsky (b. 1928) was the dominant figure in linguistics from the late 1950s through the 1970s. Two early works, *Syntactic Structures* (1957) and *Aspects of the Theory of Syntax* (1965), laid the foundations and set the tone for Chomsky's linguistic project that has lasted (albeit in increasingly attenuated versions) into the twenty-first century. From the very beginning of his career, Chomsky adopted a highly combative stance against his intellectual and ideological opponents. Since Chomsky is a clever debater, he usually wins his arguments, and this has been one of the main factors in his meteoric rise. Chomsky's highly polemical orientation spills over into many nonlinguistic fields. Although he has been remarkably prolific writing about language-related matters, Chomsky's publications on a wide range of politically sensitive topics would appear to be still more numerous.

In general, Chomsky is favorably disposed to traditional grammar but is hostile to structural linguistics. His hostility to the structuralists seems to stem from their emphasis on anthropologically grounded fieldwork and formal description of numerous languages, which is in stark contrast to his own psycho-philosophical orientation and nearly exclusive attention to English. Chomsky is opposed to reliance on what he calls "discovery procedures" and "objective methods," opining that linguists are simply awash in the particularities of data unless they possess profound notions of linguistic theory to guide them. For Chomsky, theory is clearly more important than data, intuition more desirable than induction. Chomsky is an introspective mentalist who believes that the methodological purity and attention to minutiae of the structuralists and behaviorists prevents them from asking the big questions about language that really count.

Chomsky posits a perfectly competent, ideal speaker-hearer whose actual linguistic performance may display deviations from rules but who is capable of correctly analyzing the underlying processes of language. This accounts for his well-known concept of generative grammar, a synonym for transformational grammar, which is made up of formal operations that are said to mediate between the deep structure underlying linguistic utterances and the surface structure of the sentences that are actually produced by a speaker. Transformational-generative grammar (hereafter TGG) is asserted to be a universal grammar that is supposedly innate in all human beings.

As a complement (or rather supplement) parallel to the mastery of internalized generative grammar of the individual, Chomsky posits an externalized universal grammar that possesses profound regularities. Although he is strongly in favor of determining linguistic universals, Chomsky is vague about how this is to be accomplished. Chomskyan linguistics also touches upon other areas, such as Cartesian rationalism (to reinforce his faith in innateness), and has evolved into other forms, most notably government and binding theory, which focuses on modularity of syntax. Yet all of the elaborations and refinements of the 1970s and 1980s only serve to underscore the concerns that Chomsky had already embraced in the 1950s and 1960s. By the 1990s, while still residually influential, Chomsky's linguistics program had essentially run its course and was badly fragmented in its second generation. A few younger disciples, such as Steven Pinker, however, still carry the torch.

The last main restatement of Chomsky's theories was his minimalist program that followed government-binding theory and principles and parameters theory. This final designation gives the distinct impression that the Chomskyan insurrection has at last imploded, ending with a whimper, not with a bang.

Chomsky claims that one of the chief inspirations for his generative grammar was the concept of language as "activity" (Greek *energeia*) rather than as a "(static) entity" (Greek *ergon*) waiting to be surveyed in its entirety. This view of the dynamic, "continuously self-generating" processes inherent in language is attributed to Wilhelm von Humboldt (1767–1835) and has become a linchpin of what is now called ethnolinguistics.

Chomsky was a student of Zellig Harris (1909–1992) and borrowed extensively from the analytical procedures that the latter devised. To be sure, it was Harris who had developed the concept of linguistic transformation, which he borrowed from mathematics, and this was the crux of the entire Chomskyan enterprise. The distinction was that Harris worked within the structuralist paradigm, whereas Chomsky rejected it. Chomsky began by giving the impression that he was following Harris's still fundamentally Bloomfieldian approach, but soon made clear that it was his intention to extend it. Not long thereafter, he launched attacks against all of the main pillars of American structuralism: positivism, behaviorism, and descriptivism.

The most vulnerable was behaviorism, which maintains that psychology should be based solely on observable, measurable phenomena. Bloomfield applied these guidelines to linguistics, holding that language researchers should concentrate on observable, precisely describable verbal behavior and refrain from unnecessary theorizing. In 1957, the Harvard psychologist B. F. Skinner (1904–1990) published *Verbal Behavior,* which attempted to interpret language in strictly behaviorist terms. In that same year, Chomsky penned a harsh denunciation of Skinner's book, with the result that many young linguists were persuaded to embark upon theorizing as a safer path than that of mere observation, description, and measurement.

But all was not peace and calm within Chomsky's own camp, which we may refer to as transformational-generative linguistics (TGL). Disputes had begun to erupt within TGL already during the 1960s and 1970s, some of them quite nasty. There is no point in chronicling the vitriolic arguments that took place during this period. Suffice it to say that, at base,

many of them had to do with how to handle linguistic structures that were larger and more complicated than the phrase.

The most productive departure from the TGL camp is that of George Lakoff, who, together with Mark Johnson and his collaborators, has led the development of conceptual metaphor and cognitive linguistics. Lakoff was one of the early generative semanticists who questioned the validity of syntactic deep structure. This led him to formulate metaphor as a schema in the Kantian sense. One of the most fascinating aspects of cognitive linguistics and conceptual metaphor theory is that it is data-driven, not theory-driven. That is to say, it has to be (empirically) responsible to meaning making as it occurs in human communication, which is why meaning exists in the first place. Consequently, grammar cannot be conceived of as an algorithmic process that proceeds regardless of the constituent meanings. Furthermore, if human meaning making uses the same elements and principles (namely, conceptual metaphor and blending), then all aspects of human creation—literature, religion, history, philosophy, art, music, science, even mathematics—are constituted by these elements and principles, and subject to analysis through them. Cognitive linguistics, conceptual metaphor, and conceptual blending have been adopted by a second generation of students who are every bit as enthusiastic about it as were the second generation of adherents to TGG back in the 1960s and 1970s. They believe that this new, interdisciplinary approach to language will revolutionize our understanding of ourselves and our world. The fact that their numbers are growing impressively indicates that, to a certain extent, they may well be right.

## Other Voices

Although structuralism and TGL were respectively paramount in the first and second halves of the twentieth century, this is by no means to say that competing approaches were lacking. During the period when structuralism dominated linguistics, other interesting approaches to language proliferated. One that caught the popular imagination was that of general semantics, a philosophical movement originated by the Polish-American philosopher and mathematician Alfred Korzybski (1879–1950). Korzybski, who once famously declared that "The map is not the territory," called for a heightened awareness of the conventional relationship between words and the things to which they refer. It was his intention to promote clear thought (to free human beings from the "tyranny of words," as enunciated by one enthusiast) and thereby to improve systems of communication. That is to say, it should be recognized that language does not directly reflect reality. Indeed, the structure of language may be said to distort our perception of reality. This deficiency can be remedied by insight into the nature of mundane language and, further, by the creation of more refined language that is structured in the same way reality is. Korzybski's fundamental ideas are spelled out in *Science and Sanity: An Introduction to Non-Aristotelian Systems and General Semantics* (1933). General semantics was further popularized by S. I. Hayakawa (1906–1992), whose *Language in Thought and Action* (1938) has been a bestseller for decades. After serving in the United States Senate from 1977 to 1983, Hayakawa founded U.S. English, Inc., which is dedicated to making English the official language of the United States.

Also showing how politics and linguistics can become tightly intertwined is a nonstructuralist school of a very different sort. Marrism, founded in the 1920s by the Soviet archeologist and linguist Nikolai Y. Marr (1865–1934), was quintessentially Marxist in holding that all linguistic phenomena are purely a reflection of economic functions and social forces (superstructure). Marr considered Caucasian as the proto-language of Europe (the so-called Japhetic theory), which oddly coincided with German racialist theories of Johann Friedrich Blumenbach (1752–1840). Joseph Stalin (1879–1953) (who, incidentally, had much to say about language), however, put an end to Marr's influence on Soviet linguistics when in 1950 he refuted the superstructure theory of language, declaring that it was independent of human productivity.

Politics aside, there were plenty of other nonaligned linguistic practitioners during this period, both in Europe and in America. Bringing together the philological exactitude of Antoine Meillet (1866–1936) with the conceptual grandeur of Georges Dumézil (1898–1986), the French scholar Émile Benveniste (1902–1976) was the author of the redoubtable *Le vocabulaire des institutions indo-européennes* (1969; English trans. *Indo-European Language and Society,* 1973). In it, employing what has been referred to as ethnosemantics (or ethnographic semantics), he strove to "elucidate the genesis" of the vocabulary of Indo-European institutions in six fundamental realms: economy, kinship, society (status), authority (especially royalty and its prerogatives), law, and religion. Benveniste was particularly interested in the religious doctrines of the Indo-Europeans.

J. R. Firth (1890–1960) was one of the chief founders of linguistics in Great Britain. He held the first chair in general linguistics in England, which was established at the School of Oriental and African Studies of the University of London in 1944. Firth is noted for his development of prosodic phonology, and insisted on analyzing both sound and meaning in context. Furthermore, Firth held that no single system of analytical principles and categorization could adequately account for language; different systems are required for different situations. Unlike most theorists, but very much like Benveniste, Firth recognized the importance of religion for the history of linguistics. Himself an Orientalist, Firth acknowledged the great merit of early Indian grammars (the first in the world) and the tremendous significance of Sanskrit for understanding the development of Indo-European. At the same time, he admits that the classical grammarians (Panini for Sanskrit, Dionysius for Greek, Priscian for Latin) were not concerned with the vernacular. Firth is thus also one of the few major linguistic theoreticians who is aware of the great gulf between classical and vernacular languages, a subject that awaits future research.

One of Firth's outstanding students, M. A. K. Halliday (b. 1925), countered Chomsky on many points, including the central concept of competence, against which Halliday adduces the notion of "meaning potential." This is defined in terms of culture, to which Halliday is unusually sensitive, not mind. He possesses a keen sense of the social functions of language and its existential acquisition during childhood. Halliday developed a grammatical theory according to which language is

viewed as an intersecting set of categories and scales operating at different levels. He is also responsible for creating systemic functional grammar, which is particularly well adapted to non-Indo-European languages.

In the United States, one of the most estimable twentieth-century linguists whose work lay outside of both structuralism and TGL is Kenneth Lee Pike (1912–2000). His *Language in Relation to a Unified Theory of the Structure of Human Behavior* (1967) is a massive, ambitious tome. In keeping with the combative atmosphere pervading the discipline, Pike speaks of the "battle ground" of language study and his determined efforts to promote thoroughgoing changes in language theory. Pike's theoretical work (he is also celebrated for his achievements in applied linguistics) derives from an attempt to describe empirical data drawn from a literally worldwide range of languages in the absence of a satisfactory grounding in contemporary linguistic theory. It was due to his search for a theoretical basis that would permit him to analyze and make sense of a vast amount of empirical data that he developed his brand of tagmemics. (A tagmeme is normally defined as the smallest functional grammatical element of a language. It is parallel in usage to the morpheme [the smallest functional lexical unit of a language] and the phoneme [the smallest functional phonological unit of a language].)

Pike's tagmemic approach differs from mainstream American linguistics in various technical respects, but above all in its complexity. A key feature of Pike's thinking about language is that he abandons the Saussurian distinction between *langue* and *parole*. His reason for doing so was because the large amounts of materials that he and his collaborators collected showed that speech itself was highly standard, an analytical characteristic that was normally reserved for formal, written language according to the mainstream view. As elaborated by Pike, tagmemics remained an important branch of American structuralism, but he distanced himself from other leading linguists of his day in striving to describe linguistic regularities in accord with sociocultural behavior instead of abstract models. Part of the methodology of tagmemics was determined by the sheer necessity of the chief task that its practitioners faced: translating the Bible into previously unwritten, unresearched, "esoteric" languages. Pike goes further in combining tagmemes to form syntagmemes, thus enabling him to engage in advanced syntactical analysis. Pike's most profound and far-reaching contribution to the history of ideas, however, is his application of etic and emic analysis to linguistic research. This distinction between the material and functional study of language had an enormous impact upon anthropology and other fields, albeit often in poorly understood and badly distorted guises.

After a couple of decades in which theoretical research reigned supreme, the restoration of empirical studies of language was furthered in the 1970s and 1980s with the inauguration of discourse studies. A landmark in this development is *Strategies of Discourse Comprehension* (1983), co-authored by Teun van Dijk, a linguist, and Walter Kintsch, a psychologist. A salient feature of their work is its interdisciplinary quality, requiring linguistic and computer analysis of texts, experiments in psychology laboratories, sociological field studies, and so forth. They also relied on literary scholarship, classical poetics and rhetoric, Russian formalism, and Czech structuralism, as well as sociolinguistics, ethnography, and folklore studies. All of these approaches were integrated under the umbrella of "the wide new field of cognitive science."

A linguistic loner who has had a remarkable impact on the classification of languages is Joseph H. Greenberg (1915–2001). Greenberg started out as a language typologist. Language typology identifies ideal types (for example, agglutinative, [in]flectional, isolating, etc., but there are, of course, many other characteristics that must be taken into account) and proceeds to group individual languages under these categories. Greenberg's fame rests in part on his seminal contributions to synchronic linguistics and his indefatigable quest to identify language universals. His typological approach contrasts with that of genetic classification, which is premised on delineating the development of languages from older precursors. Greenberg was always collecting data, which he copied down in countless notebooks. Known as a "lumper" (as opposed to a "splitter") par excellence, in 1955 Greenberg reduced more than 1,500 African languages to just four supergroups. Later he would ascribe all of the indigenous languages of the Americas to just three main waves of migrants, whereas they had formerly been grouped into hundreds of families. Greenberg achieved these nearly miraculous feats through the application of what he styled mass lexical comparison or multilateral comparison. Mainstream linguists were outraged, with one of the most distinguished among them publicly calling for Greenberg to be "shouted down." At stake were sacrosanct issues of methodology relating to phonology, etymology, and other vital components of linguistics. Undaunted, Greenberg dedicated the last years of his life to the study of Eurasiatic, which brought together all of the languages of Europe and Asia (and then some—except isolates) and was similar to earlier proposals for Nostratic, minus certain African languages.

In linguistics and language studies, writing is often overlooked. When attention is devoted to writing, it is usually minimized as secondary to speech. The Akkadian specialist I. J. Gelb (1907–1985) aimed to lay the foundations for a new science of writing that he called grammatology. This approach would not be merely descriptive, as were earlier histories of writing. In his classic work, entitled humbly and plainly *A Study of Writing* (1952), Gelb attempted to establish general principles governing the use and evolution of written forms of language through comparative and typological analysis. His is the first, and still the only, work to present a universal theory of all known writing systems. Gelb was able to achieve this considerable synthesis by distinguishing clearly between forerunners of writing and writing proper, and by distinguishing further between word-syllabic systems, syllabaries, and alphabets.

In the opinion of those who are involved in computational linguistics, the most important development since the 1980s has been to resurrect the use of statistical methods for analyzing distributional evidence. This general approach was pioneered by Zellig Harris in the early 1950s, but starting around 1955, his student Chomsky simultaneously cast doubt on the viability of such methods and presented a different vision of

how to proceed, employing a more axiomatic approach based on explorations in formal language theory. The "cybernetic underground" began skirmishes in the engineering hinterlands during the 1980s and took over computational linguistics entirely by the 1990s. By the early twenty-first century, psycholinguistics had largely succumbed, though there are pockets of resistance. Plain or unhyphenated linguistics is increasingly influenced by statistical methods, both in methodology and in terms of the empirical techniques that are used.

The phonetician Mark Liberman is responsible for building gigantic corpora of data that are used to solve both theoretical issues and practical problems of great merit (such as voice recognition by cybernetic-electronic devices). Many of the brightest minds in linguistics are now laboring quietly at the task of figuring out how to enable human beings and machines to talk to each other. One of the leading theoreticians engaged in this area of research is Roland Hausser, whose *Foundations of Computational Linguistics: Man-Machine Communication in Natural Language* (1999) offers a prescient look at what the future holds in store with regard to the human-machine interface.

One of the most exciting new realms of investigation in historical linguistics is the application of genetics. According to Luigi Luca Cavalli-Sforza, one of the leading researchers in this field, the genes of modern populations contain a record of the human species stretching back 100,000 years. What is more, conclusions drawn from the study of modern genetic material are now being corroborated by direct recourse to ancient DNA. It is striking that genetic and linguistic trees match each other closely, and archeological data provide further confirmation of the movements and intricate interrelationships of ancient peoples.

## Conclusion

Although human beings have for millennia taken an intense interest in the languages they speak, modern linguistics has gradually developed as an independent discipline (some would be willing to call it a science) only during the past few centuries. Hundreds of major figures have contributed to this development, and thousands of others have had a significant impact upon linguistics and its host of subfields. It has been possible here only to introduce briefly some of the main ideas of several of the individuals who have been instrumental in making language study what it is at the beginning of the twenty-first century. In many cases, it has been possible to do little more than mention some of their names and their areas of expertise to signal to the interested reader the necessity of investigating further the full range of their work. Scores of other truly outstanding linguists have not even been mentioned at all.

Linguistics is a vibrant, unsettled field, one in which passions run high. In the end, as with so much else pertaining to the intellectual pursuits of humankind, it is evident that a goodly portion of the contradictions and energy that suffuse linguistics can be attributed to the perennial dichotomy between the Aristotelian and the Platonic, between unity and infinity, between the fox and the hedgehog.

*See also* **Language, Linguistics, and Literacy; Language, Philosophy of.**

**BIBLIOGRAPHY**

Aronoff, Mark, and Janie Rees-Miller, eds. *The Handbook of Linguistics*. Malden, Mass.: Blackwell, 2001.

Beaugrande, Robert de. *Linguistic Theory: The Discourse of Fundamental Works*. London: Longman, 1991.

Bloomfield, Leonard. *Language*. New York: Henry Holt, 1933.

Bright, William, ed. *International Encyclopedia of Linguistics*. 4 vols. Oxford: Oxford University Press, 1992.

Bussmann, Hadumod. *Routledge Dictionary of Language and Linguistics*. Translated and edited by Gregory P. Trauth and Kertin Kazzazi. London: Routledge, 1996.

Cavalli-Sforza, Luigi-Luca. *Genes, Peoples, and Languages*. Translated by Mark Seielstad. New York: North Point, 2000.

Chomsky, Noam. *Aspects of the Theory of Syntax*. Cambridge, Mass.: MIT Press, 1965.

———. *Syntactic Structures*. The Hague: Mouton, 1957.

Comrie, Bernard. *Language Universals and Linguistic Typology: Syntax and Morphology*. 2nd ed. Chicago: University of Chicago Press, 1989.

Crystal, David. *The Cambridge Encyclopedia of Language*. Cambridge, UK: Cambridge University Press, 1987.

DeFrancis, John. *Visible Speech: The Diverse Oneness of Writing Systems*. Honolulu: University of Hawaii Press, 1989.

Dixon, R. M. W. *The Rise and Fall of Languages*. Cambridge, U.K.: Cambridge University Press, 1997.

Fauconnier, Gilles, and Mark Turner. *The Way We Think: Conceptual Blending and the Mind's Hidden Complexities*. New York: Basic Books, 2002.

Gelb, Ignace J. *A Study of Writing: The Foundations of Grammatology*. Rev. ed. Chicago: University of Chicago Press, 1963.

Givón, Talmy. *On Understanding Grammar*. New York: Academic Press, 1979.

Goody, Jack. *The Logic of Writing and the Organization of Society*. Cambridge, U.K.: Cambridge University Press, 1986.

Greenberg, Joseph H. *Language Typology: A Historical and Analytical Overview*. The Hague: Mouton, 1974.

Harris, Zellig S. *Methods in Structural Linguistics*. Chicago: University of Chicago Press, 1951.

Hausser, Roland R. *Foundations of Computational Linguistics: Man-Machine Communication in Natural Language*. Berlin: Springer, 1999.

Johnson, Mark. *The Body in the Mind: The Bodily Basis of Meaning, Imagination, and Reason*. Chicago: University of Chicago Press, 1987.

Koerner, E. F. K., and R. E. Asher, eds. *Concise History of the Language Sciences: From the Sumerians to the Cognitivists*. New York: Pergamon, 1995.

Labov, William. *Sociolinguistic Patterns*. Philadelphia: University of Pennsylvania Press, 1972.

Lakoff, George. *Women, Fire, and Dangerous Things: What Categories Reveal about the Mind*. Chicago: University of Chicago Press, 1987.

Lakoff, George, and Mark Johnson. *Metaphors We Live By*. Chicago: University of Chicago Press, 1980.

———. *Philosophy in the Flesh: The Embodied Mind and Its Challenge to Western Thought*. New York: Basic Books, 1999.

Langacker, Ronald. *Foundations of Cognitive Grammar*. 2 vols. Stanford, Calif.: Stanford University Press, 1987–1991.

Lapschy, Giulio, ed. *History of Linguistics*. 4 vols. London: Longman, 1994.

Mair, Victor H. "Ma Jianzhong and the Invention of Chinese Grammar." In *Studies on the History of Chinese Syntax*, edited by Chaofen Sun. *Journal of Chinese Linguistics* Monograph Series 10 (1997): 5–26.

Malmkjaer, Kirsten, ed. *The Linguistics Encyclopedia*. London: Routledge, 1991.

Ong, Walter J. *Orality and Literacy: The Technologizing of the Word*. London: Methuen, 1982.

Pinker, Steven. *The Language Instinct*. New York: Morrow, 1994.

Robins, R. H. *A Short History of Linguistics*. 4th ed. London: Longman, 1997.

Sapir, Edward. *Language: An Introduction to the Study of Speech*. New York: Harcourt, Brace, 1921.

Saussure, Ferdinand de. *Cours de linguistique générale*. 4th ed, Edited by Charles Bally and Albert Sechehaye with the collaboration of Albert Reidlinger. Paris: Payot, 1949.

Steiner, George. *After Babel: Aspects of Language and Translation*. Oxford: Oxford University Press, 1975.

*Victor H. Mair*

# LANGUAGE, LINGUISTICS, AND LITERACY.

Language and writing are not the same (although people now confuse them), and the former is far older than the latter. Human spoken language developed late in the Paleolithic, probably 100,000–120,000 years ago, whereas true writing—the representation of language, element by element, in a permanent medium—was not invented until about 5,200 years ago.

## Language

Our current estimate of when language itself evolved is based on skeletal evidence for a swift evolutionary push toward the modern human vocal tract during the Upper Paleolithic. These changes—away from the throat, tongue, and mouth configuration typical of other primates—made rapid spoken speech possible while making it easier to die of obstructed air passages (choking, etc.). Such difficulties for the individual must have been well offset for the species by the survival benefits of rapid, voluntary, and abstract communication, one of humankind's most powerful "ideas." Indeed, language's most important design characteristics are that it is:

1. voluntary (unlike the call systems of other primates, speech is initiated from the voluntary part of the motor cortex);

2. arbitrary (we can talk even about things that do not exist, allowing us to solve hypothetical problems and form abstractions; language is not tied to immediate reality);

3. productive (we can use already known vocabulary and syntactic patterns to generate an infinite supply of new messages, not to mention new vocabulary and patterns);

4. largely linear (messages unfold rapidly through time, a choice that places major constraints on the details of language design); and

5. two-way (individuals can both produce and understand messages).

As a result of being arbitrary, languages must be learned. Only the propensity to learn language is instinctive, not the individual languages themselves. Hence, babies must have a long period of apprenticeship to learn to communicate linguistically, a fact equally true of spoken tongues and visual languages like American Sign Language (ASL). (ASL has all the structural features and design complexities of a spoken language, only in a different—and equally evanescent—medium.) Research shows that children deprived of early exposure to linguistic communication (which happens sometimes with deaf babies) do not develop the neurological structures in the brain necessary for handling the complexities of language later.

Because languages are arbitrary, they change constantly, adapting easily to the changing world of things to talk about and social messages to send. As a result of this constant change, speakers of a single language who move away from each other will change their systems differently, a process that may continue until we perceive them as speaking different dialects or even (after many centuries) different languages. This process is called *language divergence* and leads to what linguists call *language families*.

The members of a language family are simply changed later forms of what was once one language. For example, the speakers of Latin fanned out across the Roman Empire 2,000 years ago, but after the breakup of the empire, when travel became dangerously difficult, the local versions of Latin began to diverge, producing the so-called Romance language family, consisting notably of Italian, French, Spanish, Portuguese, and

Romanian (along with several other dialects and languages, less well known because they have fewer speakers). But Latin itself was a changed later form of yet older languages, going back to something we call proto-Italic (for lack of knowing what its speakers called it), and even further back to one we call proto-Indo-European.

## Linguistics

Modern linguistics—the scientific study of language in all its aspects—began in the eighteenth and nineteenth centuries with the investigation of just such historical questions. The 2,500 years of continuous written records of Latin and the Romance languages provided one useful "laboratory" in which language change could be observed. The brothers Grimm (Jacob Grimm [1785–1863] and Wilhelm Grimm [1786–1859]), in recording verbatim their famous collection of German folktales, accidentally created another linguistic data set in which they kept noticing interesting relations among the Germanic dialects of the crones who recounted the tales. Elsewhere, other scholars were noting the more distant relations among Greek, Latin, Sanskrit, and other languages we now recognize as Indo-European.

Eventually linguists realized that the relationships between languages within a family were in certain ways regular (if complex), especially in how their sounds changed. This fact allowed scholars to begin to reconstruct forms of the ancestor languages, even when those forms were not attested in writing. To facilitate this linguistic reconstruction, they needed to

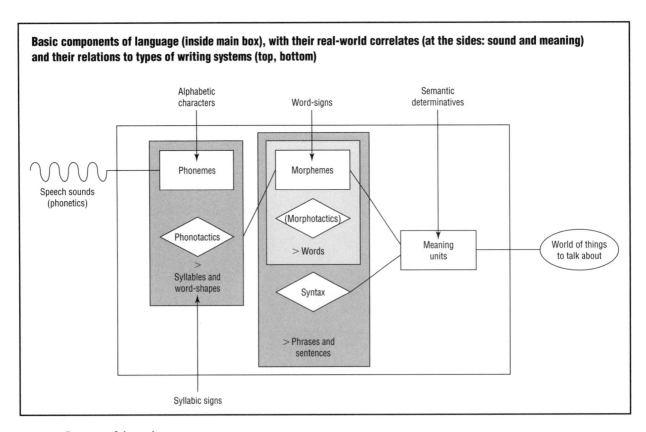

**Basic components of language (inside main box), with their real-world correlates (at the sides: sound and meaning) and their relations to types of writing systems (top, bottom)**

SOURCE: Courtesy of the author

study the structural properties of each language, since, before they could compare thoroughly, they had to know in detail what they were comparing. In this way, the systematic study of the synchronic (as opposed to historical) features of languages was added to the field of linguistics around 1900.

The most basic components of a spoken language, all needing study, are the speech sounds themselves (*phonetics*), the system of using certain sounds to tell words apart in a given language (traditionally called *phonemics,* although other approaches to sound contrast are sometimes used), the forms of words (*morphology*), the structures by which words are combined into phrases and sentences (*syntax*), and the meaning components (*semantics*). In the mid-twentieth century, linguists began to explore beyond the sentence level to analyze the structure of discourse, poetry, formulaic speech, and other large units.

Nineteenth-century European scholars were not the first people, of course, to inquire about language history or structure. (For example, around the fifth or fourth century B.C.E., the Indian scholar Panini compiled a thorough grammar of Sanskrit, including what amounts to an excellent structural analysis of its sounds.) But it is their work on which modern linguistic science is principally based. They, in turn, were continually spurred on by the masses of inscriptions that archaeologists were turning up, many in unknown and unreadable scripts.

## Writing
The most important scripts deciphered in the nineteenth century were Mesopotamian cuneiform and Egyptian hieroglyphics. Their importance came from the fact that they belonged to the two oldest traditions of true writing: the representation of connected linguistic structures rather than only single concepts or situations.

Jean François Champollion (1790–1832) deciphered Egyptian hieroglyphics in the 1820s. Using the Rosetta Stone discovered in 1799, he recognized that the hieroglyphic pictures represented the successive elements of a normal language (some phonological, some semantic) and not some sort of lost religious magic, since the Rosetta Stone clearly had the same message in Egyptian hieroglyphics, Demotic (everyday Egyptian script), and Greek. Champollion's progress was greatly speeded when he recognized that the language in question was the immediate ancestor of Coptic, the still-used religious language of a Christian sect in Egypt and, therefore, a version of a known language.

Cuneiform required more of a team effort, in part because "it" turned out to be more than one script, and because even the mainstream version had serviced several languages over nearly 3,000 years and had evolved considerably in form during that time. *Cuneiform* means "wedge-shaped" and refers to a whole family of scripts written by impressing wedge-shaped marks into clay with a stylus. The first breakthroughs occurred in the 1840s, and scholars gradually disentangled the various scripts and languages, from later to earlier (although some, like Elamite, remain undeciphered because we do not know enough about the language family represented). Most of the languages written in cuneiform belonged to the Semitic language family, although at least one (Hittite) was Indo-European and several belonged to still other families.

**Ancient cuneiform engraved into stone.** Cuneiform writing was utilized for thousands of years by the purveyors of many varied languages, making it difficult to decipher. Progress was achieved in the mid-nineteenth century thanks to the work of several different scholars. © DIEGO LEZAMA OREZZOLI/CORBIS

In fact, the very first language written in cuneiform was not Semitic, it was Sumerian, a language that we still cannot relate conclusively to any other known language or family. Sumerian cuneiform writing first appeared in the early cities of Mesopotamia (Iraq) late in the fourth millennium B.C.E.

## Origin of Writing
Although many nations have claimed to have invented writing from scratch, only one culture in the Eastern Hemisphere, Mesopotamia, can show in its archaeological record the long series of steps needed to develop this significant invention. It is easy to invent a writing *system* once someone points out that language can be represented in a permanent form by making visible squiggles, each standing for a word or sound. But the notion that *one can write at all* is far more difficult to conceive the first time, truly one of the world's great ideas. Evidence shows that such an abstraction did not come easily. To trace its origin in the Near East, we must go back another 5,000 years to 8000 B.C.E., to early Neolithic sites in Syria and Iraq.

The Neolithic, or New Stone Age, differs from the Paleolithic, or Old Stone Age, in that people now had domestic plants and animals, permanent open-air settlements, and stone tools ground to a fine edge instead of merely chipped. At a number of Neolithic Near Eastern sites, along with evidence for early experiments in architecture and weaving, we find experiments with clay: hundreds of tiny balls, cones, disks, and other simple geometric shapes, which archaeologists at first took for children's game pieces. We now know they were used for keeping accounts of livestock, grain, and other possessions, each shape denoting a different commodity and each animal or unit of goods tallied by a separate piece of clay. Thus, five disks with crosses might correspond to five sheep, and three balls to three measures of grain.

The developmental history of this accounting system (which soon spread across the Near East and into southeast Europe), together with linguistic reconstructions indicating the lack of abstract number words (for example, *six, seven, eight*) in any language prior to 3000 B.C.E., indicate that Stone Age peoples did not have an abstract notion of number yet. Lacking number words, they counted simply by matching the animals or jars in question to an equal number of concrete tokens. (Such systems continue to be used in a few societies.) With a simple Neolithic economy, this was sufficient for keeping track of things, although, apparently for security against swindlers, the Mesopotamians added the habit of sealing the little clay tokens of a transaction into a clay ball onto which each token had been impressed once. (This enabled everyone to see what the account was, but no one could snitch or add tokens.) But when, in fourth-millennium Mesopotamia, people began gathering in huge cities and needed to redistribute goods for labor in complex ways, they were forced to devise a more powerful and more flexible system.

The later history of writing systems shows that each new idea for restructuring writing to make it more efficient (such as moving from word writing to syllabic writing, or from syllabic to alphabetic) came from a new group learning the old way of doing things and saying, in effect, "There's got to be a better way." Just as each new generation of children restructures slightly the language data learned from its elders, so systems of writing and notation have been restructured by those with a fresh view. The same presumably happened here.

About 3100 B.C.E., in the Mesopotamian city of Uruk, we suddenly see a new "take" on the meaning of the impressions on the clay envelopes holding tokens. Before, the impression of a small cone meant a small measure of grain and that of a big cone meant a larger measure of grain (which happened to equal sixty of the little measures, just as a gallon happens to equal sixteen cups in our system). But now the small cone was reinterpreted as meaning "1" and the big cone as "60," and another measure in-between (similar to our quart) was reinterpreted as "10" (since it was equal in volume to ten of the smallest unit). With these impressed shapes reinterpreted as designating the *number* intended, however, the scribe now had to specify separately the *object* being counted. At that moment, the system developed into two types of signs: one kind for abstract numbers, the other for names of objects. The latter corresponded to the vocabulary words of language. Thus, if we want to speak of four rings, we don't say "ring ring ring ring" (or write "oooo," which is how the Neolithic scribes did it); we use only two words, one for the number (*four*) and another for the object (*rings*). To write this as "4 o" would then correspond unit-for-unit to the words we speak.

The only problem with this system was that words for abstract numbers did not exist. Because we see such words hastily cobbled into being at just this time, we know that they must have been forced into existence by the reinterpretation of the impressed tokens. Now humans had two new ideas to expand upon: the notion of abstract numbers (numbers independent of any particular thing being counted), and the notion that the impressed patterns could correspond to the successive words in a spoken phrase or sentence (*four rings*).

Drawing little pictures to denote words like *ring* or *tree* (pictograms) was fine, but what do you do with grammatical words and other unpicturables like *the* and *or*? The easiest way was to use sound-alikes (homonyms or near homonyms), as in the modern game of charades. Thus, if one did this in English, *or*

**Sumerian clay tablet showing livestock tally.** Sumerian was the first language represented in cuneiform script. In Mesopotamia, around 3100 B.C.E., a new system evolved in cuneiform wherein some shapes represented numbers and others represented objects. © GIANNI DAGLI ORTI/CORBIS

could be denoted by a picture of an oar, and so on. (This game, called *rebus writing*, was easier to play in Sumerian than in English because most Sumerian words were only one syllable long.) To tell which word with that sound was meant, scribes began adding extra signs to give clues to the semantic realm. Thus the "oar" pictogram might have a schematic tree beside it when it meant "oar," warning the reader to pick the word sounding that way that denoted something wooden (eliminating *or* and *ore*). In this way the script gradually became adequate for representing anything in the language, although it was centuries before grammatical words were consistently written along with the "content" (lexical) words. As this writing system became more adequate, it also became more unwieldy, requiring the student to learn hundreds of signs.

## Spread of Writing and Literacy

Other early scripts were equally large and unwieldy, and their structures give some clues to their origins. The Egyptians appear to have gotten the idea that *one could write with pictograms and rebuses* from the Mesopotamians around 3100 B.C.E., almost as soon as the Mesopotamians invented true writing, and then made up their script themselves, basing some signs on traditional proprietary marks and drawing pictures for others. So far we lack evidence showing the Egyptians working up step by step to the abstract notion of writing, and we know they borrowed a number of other cultural ideas from Mesopotamia at exactly this period, so this hypothesis of borrowing is the best one we have to date. The Egyptian push to write, unlike that in Mesopotamia, seems to have been chiefly religious rather than economic, especially the desire to preserve personal names for an eternal afterlife. The very earliest

Egyptian inscriptions that have come down to us are names of kings and pharaohs.

Egyptian writing maintained its predominantly religious character to the very end, even though faster cursive forms of the script were eventually devised for writing mundane secular documents. But the Egyptian script never became simpler, retaining its many hundreds of signs until it fell out of use in Roman times.

The Chinese script, which began to blossom during the first great dynasty of China, the Shang (1500–1100 B.C.E.), appears so much later than cuneiform or Egyptian hieroglyphics, in a period when Chinese already contained loan words from Iranian and possibly other Indo-European languages from the West, that probably the script was jumpstarted like Egyptian, by diffusion of at least the idea that one could write. The signs themselves seem to have been created indigenously, but the writing system closely resembles the Near Eastern scripts in being composed of several hundred pictograms, rebuses, and semantic determinatives. On the other hand, archaic Chinese (like Sumerian) contained mostly words of one syllable, so the Chinese were in a convenient position to (re)invent for themselves the notion of rebuses.

When a script contains hundreds of signs and considerable ambiguity, an individual must devote enormous time and energy to becoming literate. In early societies this had two major consequences: (1) scribes/writers were specialists (fully supported by the rest of society with food, etc.), and (2) there were very few of them. In other words, literacy was not something that many could attain, and, with so few writers, only the most important things got written down. For the Mesopotamians the important topic initially was economic transactions, for the Egyptians, religious matters pertaining to eternity, and, for the Chinese, oracles about future events. Gradually other matters—both religious and secular—came to be recorded, but the cost of educating scribes was always a bottleneck, while the past investment by each of these cultures in their systems made throwing them out unthinkable.

Such was not the case for neighboring cultures. Over and over neighbors restructured these systems as they borrowed them, usually recasting them in such a way as to make the writing more efficient. Living with the Sumerians in Mesopotamia were speakers of various Semitic dialects, such as Akkadian. When Sargon of Akkad took over Mesopotamia soon after 2400 B.C.E., his scribes took the Sumerian pictograms at their *phonetic value alone* (no meaning whatsoever implied) in order to spell out their native Akkadian syllable by syllable (syllabic signs). Conceptually, this was a big step forward because there are so few sounds in a language compared to the huge number of words. Unfortunately, the scribes only went halfway, retaining many Sumerian pictograms as a shorthand for Akkadian words, since a Sumerian word required only one sign, in general, whereas Akkadian words, which typically contained two to five syllables, required many more. So, although the Semitic scribes had made a major conceptual breakthrough (one that the Chinese never made), it remained for others to benefit from this simplification.

**Hieroglyphs from the *Book of the Dead,* in the Tomb of Ramses VI, Valley of the Kings, Thebes, Egypt.** First deciphered by Jean François Champollion in 1822, hieroglyphs represent one of the earliest types of true linguistically structured forms of writing. Hieroglyphs are descended from Coptic, an ancient religious language. © GIANNI DAGLI ORTI/CORBIS

The Hittites, an Indo-European group in Anatolia (modern Turkey), attempted to simplify the Sumerian system. When they borrowed cuneiform they dropped most of the duplicate ways of writing a given syllable, whittling down the syllabary to just over one hundred basic signs. But these scribes, too, found it handy to keep the Sumerian pictograms as shorthand for many of their vocabulary words, which on average were even longer than Akkadian words. (If you had to write out absolutely everything by hand, with no word processor, photocopier, or even typewriter, you, too, would look for *faster* ways to write, even if the *system* ended up more complex.)

The people of the Aegean, however, when they borrowed the idea that one could write, eliminated everything except the notion of signs for syllables, creating their own sign-shapes from scratch. They also simplified the notion of "syllable" from the four sorts used in cuneiform (V, CV, VC, CVC, where V = vowel, C = consonant) to two (V, CV), which meant they could manage with a mere eighty or so signs. (Well, almost: for economic accounts, they also used a roster of single signs—pictograms or ideograms—for each different commodity, but these signs were not mixed together with syllabic signs to form a sentence.) This sort of system took much less time to learn and made it possible, at least theoretically, for more people to become literate in their spare time. The people of Minoan Crete, who used this system for a short time in the mid-second millennium B.C.E., left us elegant inscriptions on jewelry and stone, economic accounts on clay, and graffiti on walls and pottery, suggesting widespread literacy. Unfortunately, they wrote most of their texts on perishable materials that have not survived.

A similar reinterpretation, leading to an even more radical simplification, occurred in the Sinai peninsula, around 1900 B.C.E., where Semites from the north encountered Egyptians from the south at the local copper and turquoise mines. The Semites apparently saw the Egyptian writing system and learned something of its structure, but concluded, "There must be a simpler way." The Egyptian script, unlike cuneiform, did not specify the vowel that a syllabic sign was to convey, only the consonant(s). So when the Semites, like the Minoans, pared away all the duplicate ways of writing syllables, they found themselves with a mere twenty-some signs, specifying that many different consonants.

This new script, the so-called Sinitic consonantal syllabary, was clearly based on Egyptian sign-shapes at first, and it had a tremendous advantage: anyone could learn this tiny number of signs in a few hours. Spelling consisted simply of sounding out the words as one wrote, so spelling did not need to be learned as such. The drawback, of course, was the ambiguity for readers. The writer knew what spoken vowels were intended, but *th rdr hd t gss thm,* leaving much potential ambiguity, unless writers wrote only for their own use. This may have been the dominant use, however, because variants of this simple script quickly spread up the coast all the way to Syria. Along the way it generated what became the Hebrew, Phoenician, Ugaritic, Aramaic, and Arabic scripts (and more), all of which are/were consonantal syllabaries, and generated a much wider range of uses, implying wider literacy.

We know all these scripts are related because they all use(d) the same canonical order of signs for teaching the script, an order ancestral to our modern alphabetical order. One clear and early document of this sort is a tablet from a schoolroom in the city of Ugarit, on the coast of Syria, in which the signs have been modeled for the pupil in this standard order. Because Syria was heavily influenced by Mesopotamian culture, the letters are written with wedge-shapes on clay, but those shapes have nothing to do with the shapes of signs in mainstream cuneiform. Only the cheap clay medium was borrowed.

The final step in developing the most efficient possible writing system was to add separate signs for vowels, eliminating the guesswork without adding many more signs. Remarkably, this step was first taken around 1400 B.C.E. in Ugarit, six centuries before the Greeks produced their alphabet. The structure of Hamito-Semitic languages is such that vowels are not so important for determining the basic semantic contents of a message as they are in virtually all other languages. (It is surely no accident, therefore, that it was Semites who made the big step in simplification to the consonantal syllabary.) But Ugarit had two main linguistic populations: Western Semites and Hurrians. The Hurrian language belonged to yet another family, centered in the Caucasus to the north. The Hurrian

merchants, searching for a better way, reused a sign here and added a sign there to obtain the vowel signs they needed to write their language readably.

As they did so, however, the system cracked into two entirely new types of signs—signs for single vowels and signs for single consonants—such that the latter were no longer signs for entire syllables (of a consonant plus an implied vowel). Each sound in the language now had a sign of its own, and each sign represented a single sound (the definition of a true alphabet). Now readers could read unambiguously what the writer wrote, and for only the cost of learning a couple of dozen symbols.

Unfortunately, this brilliant idea was almost immediately lost in the massive destructions curtailing the Bronze Age (1200 B.C.E.), and it remained for the Greeks to reinvent the same step around 800 B.C.E. as they pondered the ambiguous consonantal syllabary still used by Phoenician traders. The canonical order of the Sinitic script thus passed to the Greeks and is still visible despite the reuse of some unneeded consonantal signs as vowels, the addition of a few letters, and the retention of some unnecessary signs. The Greeks passed one version of their alphabet to the Etruscans, who passed it to the Romans—each time with minor modifications. With a few more changes in medieval times, it came down to us today as the "Roman" alphabet. (The Cyrillic alphabet used in Eastern

**Greek funerary stele. Limestone, fourth–third century** B.C.E. The Roman alphabet used in North and South American countries and those of Western Europe is based on one version of an ancient Greek alphabet that was passed through the Etruscans to the Romans. © ARCHIVO ICONOGRAFICO, S.A./CORBIS

Europe branched off in medieval times directly from the Greek alphabet.)

## Alphabetic Literacy

The simplicity of the alphabet should have meant that now everyone would learn to read and write. Yet the evidence tells a somewhat different story: everyone *could* learn to write, but for centuries few did. Early Greek inscriptions are few, mostly labels and short dedications. The first person we know who used writing systematically to record everything he wanted to "make note of" was the great Athenian statesman Solon, living around 600 B.C.E., who apparently kept personal notes of what he learned abroad and what he thought about political matters. This is a use of writing not seen before, but soon to become commonplace. (The fragmentary nature of our evidence may, of course, have hidden some other earlier examples in other scripts—one might suspect the Third Dynasty Egyptian genius Imhotep (fl. c. 2650 B.C.E.) of similar practices—but clearly such a use was not common elsewhere.) When Solon had something he thought important for his countrymen to remember, he habitually put it into verse so they could memorize it easily, a fact indicating that most of the population was *not* literate.

By 500 B.C.E., however, citizens of Athens (that is, those inhabitants who were free and male) were expected to know how to read the public notices and write their own ballots, although anecdotes show that not all could. And throughout the fifth century—the Golden Age of Athens—literature was still primarily oral, still experienced communally in the theater, as the great dramas of Aeschylus (c. 525–456 B.C.E.), Sophocles (495–406 B.C.E.), Euripides (484?–406 B.C.E.), and Aristophanes (c. 448–385 B.C.E.) attest. Written copies of the plays were, however, increasingly available. Our first reference to a new form of literacy, reading to oneself for one's own idle pleasure, occurs in Aristophanes's *The Frogs,* written in 405 B.C.E., in which a not very bright Athenian citizen says he was sitting around on shipboard between practice maneuvers reading one of Euripides's tragedies to himself. In fact, at this time both Aristophanes and Socrates (469–399 B.C.E.) voiced concern over the rise of mass literacy, worrying that a flood of written information would cause people to forget the important things of life.

Then the flood hit: from then on great drama on the stage was replaced in Greek society by great books to be read—the philosophical works of Plato (427–347 B.C.E.) and his successors (which start, interestingly, as "oral" dialogues in form, although too deep to be fully appreciated in one hearing). And there were new types of lesser works, such as novels to be read purely for fun. A major watershed had been crossed.

The new literacy entailed new problems. How could so many literate people obtain the works they wanted to read? Copying by hand was very slow, so the idea of libraries, where numerous readers could share copies, was conceived. The famous library at Alexandria (destroyed in the mid-seventh century C.E.), although the largest, was only one of many. But with increasing amounts to read, people wanted to be able to read faster, so in Roman times letter shapes became simpler and more regular, allowing the eye to take in and distinguish the letters more rapidly.

In the West, most of this progress was lost with the destruction of the Roman Empire around 400 B.C.E. by illiterate hordes. Literacy retreated to the monasteries, where the storing, copying, and reading of books became sacred tasks. Letter shapes ceased to be clean and simple, since now the criteria were different. The desire to shorten the task of copying (rather than speed the reading) led to complex ligatures and other methods of abbreviation, while seriphs, curlicues, and other scriptal flourishes embellished the page even as they impeded easy recognition.

Books had been printed in China since at least 868 B.C.E. (and probably earlier), using carved wooden blocks, but Johannes Gutenberg's (c. 1397–1468) idea of printing with movable type, in the mid-1400s, changed all that. His first printed books are very difficult to read, but simplicity of letter design returned quickly as easier access to books fostered greater literacy, and greater literacy, together with the possibility of multiple copies, fostered more new texts to read. The Renaissance of learning, already started among the rich merchants of southern Europe, could now blossom fully.

But there was a new bottleneck: the high cost of a printing medium. Vellum and parchment were very expensive and paper a little-explored craft (although invented long ago by the ancient Egyptians and Chinese). With the invention of pulp paper late in the eighteenth century, however, books could be printed so cheaply that even lower-class workers could afford them, carrying in their pockets not just novels but printed manuals for the increasingly complex machines they had to operate. In a sense, it was manuals printed on pulp paper that fueled the Industrial Revolution. In the twentieth century, people were so inundated with printed materials that computers were invented to manage the glut, and those computers are inevitably changing patterns of literacy once again.

*See also* **Communication of Ideas: Orality and the Advent of Writing; Diffusion, Cultural; Language and Linguistics; Prehistory, Rise of; Reading.**

### BIBLIOGRAPHY

Barber, E. J. W. *Archaeological Decipherment: A Handbook.* Princeton, N.J.: Princeton University Press, 1974. Discusses history, theory, and methods of archaeological decipherment.

———. *The Mummies of Ürümchi.* New York: Norton, 1999. Discusses literature on early Chinese loans from Iranians and other evidence for early trans-Eurasian contact.

Daniels, Peter, and William Bright. *The World's Writing Systems.* Oxford: Oxford University Press, 1996. An encyclopedia of all known writing systems.

Deacon, Terrence W. *The Symbolic Species: The Co-Evolution of Language and the Brain.* New York: Norton, 1997. Physical evidence for human development toward language, including evidence from brain studies for change to voluntary speech centers.

de Saussure, Ferdinand. *Cours de linguistique générale.* Paris: Payot (1964 reprint of 1915 original). First major treatise on descriptive linguistics; early analysis of language as arbitrary and linear.

Friedrich, Johannes. *Extinct Languages.* Translated by F. Gaynor. New York: Philosophical Library, 1957. Story of all the major decipherments (including Egyptian and cuneiform), written by one of the decipherers of Hittite.

Gelb, Ignace J. *A Story of Writing.* 2nd ed. Chicago: University of Chicago Press, 1963. Analytical history of the development of scripts.

Hockett, Charles. *A Course in Modern Linguistics.* New York: Macmillan, 1958. Chapter 64 contains an important discussion of arbitrary and productive properties of language.

Justus, Carol. "Indo-European Numerals Since Szemerenyi." In *The Emergence of the Modern Language Sciences,* Vol. 2: *Methodological Perspectives and Applications,* edited by S. Embleton, J.E. Joseph, H.-J. Niederehe, 131–152. Philadelphia and Amsterdam: John Benjamins, 1999. Discussion of lack of number words in early languages and the process of their introduction.

Lieberman, Philip. *Uniquely Human: The Evolution of Speech, Thought, and Selfless Behavior.* Cambridge, Mass.: Harvard University Press, 1991. Discusses evidence for the rapid push toward a vocal tract usable for speech.

Pedersen, Holger. *The Discovery of Language: Linguistic Science in the Nineteenth Century.* Translated by J. W. Spargo. Bloomington: Indiana University Press, 1959. Development of historical linguistics, with discussion of key discoveries of scripts and texts, and the basic theories generated about the language families of much of the world.

Schmandt-Besserat, Denise. *Before Writing,* Vol. I: *From Counting to Cuneiform.* Austin: University of Texas Press, 1992. Development of the Near Eastern token system into writing and numbers.

*E. J. W. Barber*

# LANGUAGE, PHILOSOPHY OF.

This entry includes two subentries:

*Ancient and Medieval*
*Modern*

## ANCIENT AND MEDIEVAL

Only in recent times has philosophy of language been considered a distinct branch of philosophy. But ancient and medieval philosophers had different, sophisticated theories about the relation between language—both individual words and whole sentences—and reality, and the thirteenth century saw one of the most thorough attempts ever to give an abstract, analytical account of the grammar of a natural language.

### Words and Things: Plato and Aristotle

In the *Cratylus,* the one dialogue he devoted exclusively to questions about language, Plato (c. 428–348 or 347 B.C.E.) contrasts two ways of explaining how words link with things. Is it purely a matter of "convention and agreement," so that "whatever name you give to something is the right one"? Or are some words naturally suited to stand for certain given things? Superficially, Plato certainly seems to lend support to the latter, naturalist answer, exploring through usually fanciful etymology how words can be analyzed into significant elements (for instance, *psuchos*—soul—"derives" from *echei*—has/

holds—and *phusin*—nature), and even attributing aspects of meaning to the sounds of individual letters. Yet Plato also points, by irony and more directly, to the inadequacies of such naturalism. Other philosophical schools, such as the Stoics and Epicureans, held to a naturalist view without such reservations.

But not Aristotle (384–322 B.C.E.). He was clearly a conventionalist: a name is "a spoken sound significant by convention." But how do such spoken sounds link with the world? In *On Interpretation* (16a), Aristotle writes that

> Spoken sounds are symbols of affections in the soul, and written marks symbols of spoken sounds. But what these are in the first place signs of—affections of the soul—are the same for all; and what these affections are likenesses of—actual things—are also the same.

Aristotle's semantic scheme, in which things are signified by words only through the intermediary of thoughts or mental images ("affections of the soul"), is underwritten by his psychology and metaphysics. Human beings know about the world through being affected by the forms that account for things being as they are: the heat of a hot stone, for instance, or the humanity that makes someone a human. Aristotle is therefore justified, to his own way of thinking, in supposing that although words vary from language to language, the mental signs they stand for are the same for all people and can correspond directly with the objects themselves.

### Sentences and Facts: Aristotle and the Stoics

Aristotle's aim in thinking about language was not merely to look at the relation of naming-words to things, but to explain how words combine to form assertoric sentences, which can be true or false. *On Interpretation* studies the functions of nouns and verbs and the mechanism of predication in some detail, but Aristotle remains rather vague about how sentences as a whole link up with reality. In the *Categories* (14b) he talks of what makes a sentence true (what we might call a state-of-affairs) as a *pragma*—a vague word, meaning act, thing, or matter.

In the following centuries, it was the Stoics who gave deeper consideration to the semantics of sentences. They distinguished between signifiers (words and groups of words as utterances: for instance *Dion*), name-bearers (for instance, Dion himself), and significations. They called these significations *lekta* ("sayables") and understood by them the states-of-affairs revealed by utterances (for instance, Dion's standing, the *lekton* of "Dion stands"). From this description, it sounds as if the Stoics had an ontology that included both things and states-of-affairs, and the latter were called *lekta* because they neatly filled the role of being what assertoric sentences signify. The concept of *lekta* may well have originated in this way, but there are two important qualifications to consider. First, the Stoics held that not only complete assertoric sentences, but also other types of sentences, such as commands and questions, have their *lekta*; and also that, in addition to these complete *lekta,* there are incomplete *lekta,* which are the meanings of predicates (for instance, standing, the *lekton* of "stands"). Second, the Stoics were materialists, and they considered *lekta* to be not merely incorporeal but not even to exist.

## Abelard and the Early Middle Ages

Early medieval philosophers were deeply influenced by the semantic scheme of *On Interpretation.* The way in which Boethius (c. 480–c. 524) discussed it in his commentaries (early sixth century) linked with ideas they found in the writings of St. Augustine of Hippo (354–430) to suggest the following, widely accepted basic scheme: written language signifies spoken languages, which in turn signify a mental language common to all humans, and the terms of this mental language signify things in the world. In medieval texts signification is usually therefore a causal, psychological relation: *w* signifies a thing *x* if and only if *w* causes a thought of *x* in the mind of a competent speaker of the language. There were, however, other influences, especially the grammatical writings of Priscian (fl. 500 C.E.), who was heavily influenced by Stoic theories.

By the eleventh century, there was already a strong philosophical interest in questions about language. For example, St. Anselm of Canterbury (1033 or 1034–1109) wrote a dialogue about the problems caused by a word such as *grammaticus,* which means "grammarian" but also has the adjectival sense of "grammatical": is *grammaticus* a substance, then, or a quality? In Peter Abelard's (1079–?1144) logical writings (c. 1115–1125) the semantics of both words and sentences receive careful and searching attention. Abelard accepts the usual psychologico-causal understanding of signification, but his nominalism—the view that nothing except particulars exists—made it problematic. He accepts that predicates signify universals, and then (in accord with his theory) goes on to identify these universals with what are not things—mental images or, in the latest version of his theory, a thought-content. Abelard also developed an account of the semantics of sentences. Assertoric sentences signify what he calls *dicta* (literally, "things said")—by which he means states of affairs or (on some occasions, something nearer to) propositions. *Dicta,* however, are not things; they are, literally, nothing. The parallel with the Stoics' *lekta* is striking, although direct influence does not seem possible. Thirteenth-century thinkers talked of sentences signifying *enuntiabilia* (things able to be said), and some fourteenth-century thinkers use the term *complexe significabilia* (complexly signifiables)—in both cases bringing themselves even closer to the meaning of the Stoics' term.

### Speculative grammar.

Speculative grammar was a striking, though short-lived, episode in medieval thinking about grammar. Its outstanding exponents, Boethius and Martin of Dacia, and Radulphus Brito, were arts masters at the University of Paris in the period from approximately 1250 to 1300. They aspired to give grammar the universality demanded of an Aristotelian science and, although they worked entirely with Latin, they believed that the underlying structure they were uncovering was that of any language, although each language represented it using different combinations of sounds.

At the basis of speculative grammar is the Aristotelian semantics, which aligns things in the world, thoughts, and words. The speculative grammarians held that there are modes of being (properties of things, such as being singular or plural, active or passive) and, parallel to these, modes of thinking (as when the intellect thinks of a thing as being singular or plural,

and so on). The modes of signifying (*modi significandi*—from whence the term *modistic grammarians* or *modists*) parallel these modes of being and of thinking. So, a first imposition links a sound with a certain sort of thing, and this root becomes a part of speech by being given *modi significandi* that first of all make it into one of the parts of speech (noun, verb, and so on) and then add features such as case and number (for nouns) or tense and person (for verbs). The modists' assumption is that the Latin grammatical categories are precisely molded to the general structure of reality, which is captured accurately in thought.

### The terminists and Ockham.

A little earlier in the thirteenth century, logicians at Paris and Oxford were busy developing a different approach to the relation between words and things, the theory of the properties of terms, which was given its most popular exposition in the *Tractatus* (the so-called *Summulae logicales*) of Peter of Spain (Pope John XXI; d. 1277). The theory of the properties of terms concerns the way in which nouns refer in the context of a sentence. One distinction (in the terminology of the English logician William of Sherwood) is between material supposition, where a word refers to itself ("Man has three letters")—a medieval equivalent of quotation marks—and formal supposition, where it refers to something in the world. Formal supposition can be either simple or personal: in simple supposition, a word refers to a universal ("Man is a *species*"), whereas in personal supposition it refers to particulars in various different ways, which the terminists further distinguished. The theory provided for the (personal) supposition of a word to be "ampliated" or "restricted" by its context. By adding *white* to *man,* one restricts the supposition of *man* to just those men who are white; by making it the subject of a future-tense verb, one will restrict the supposition of the noun to men in the future. Expressions like "think of" and "it is possible that" ampliate the reference of nouns in their scope to include all thinkable or possible such individuals.

Terminism did not fit the interests of mid- and late-thirteenth-century thinkers, but it was revived again in the fourteenth century. William of Ockham (c. 1285–?1349) uses it, in an adapted form, in setting out one of the most elaborate medieval theories about mental language. William is so fully committed to the idea of our thoughts being naturally structured in a language-like (indeed, Latin-like) way, that he breaks the Aristotelian mold and holds that, rather than words signifying thoughts, both words (natural language) and thoughts (mental language) signify reality in much the same way. Since Ockham—like Abelard before him—was a nominalist, he could not accept the usual idea that simple supposition is of universals: according to him, a word has simple supposition when it supposits for a mental term, but does not signify it.

## Linguistic Diversity: Dante and the Arabs

The mainstream Western medieval tradition of thought about language concentrated on a single language, Latin. By doing so, it gained the advantage of allowing philosophers to see more clearly the large, abstract questions that concern the relation of any language to the mind and to reality. It also suffered, because scholars (as appears strikingly in the case of the speculative grammarians) simply assumed that features in fact special to the structure of Latin were universal to every language. By

**New Dictionary of the History of Ideas**

the later Middle Ages, however, there was at least some analytical investigation of the facts of linguistic diversity. The great poet Dante Alighieri (1265–1321), writing his *On Eloquence in the Vernacular* in Latin to defend writing in Italian, tried to explain how all languages derive from the original tongue spoken by Adam, and how they have changed and developed.

Things were very different in the Arabic tradition. During the eighth and ninth centuries, a great quantity of Greek scientific and philosophical work was translated into Arabic. In the earliest period, at least, those thinkers in Islam who thought of themselves as followers of the Greek philosophers tended to play down the value of grammatical study. Their attitude led to a famous confrontation in 932 between the grammarian Abu Sa'id al-Sirafi and the philosopher Abu Bishr Matta. While Matta held that logic provided a universal key to thinking, al-Sirafi's contention was that Greek logic is based on the Greek language: writers in Arabic need, rather, to study their own language. The contrast with thirteenth-century Latin thought is piquant. There, grammar was made into a sort of universal linguistic logic; here logic itself is argued to be as particular as the grammars of different languages.

*See also* **Language and Linguistics; Language, Linguistics, and Literacy; Philosophy: Historical Overview and Recent Developments.**

BIBLIOGRAPHY

PRIMARY SOURCES

Aristotle. *'Categories' and 'De interpretatione.'* Translated by J. L. Ackrill. Oxford: Oxford University Press, 1974.

Long, A. A., and D. N. Sedley. *The Hellenistic Philosophers.* 2 vols. Cambridge, U.K.: Cambridge University Press, 1987.

Peter of Spain. *Language in Dispute: An English Translation of Peter of Spain's* Tractatus. . . . Translated by Francis P. Dinneen. Amsterdam and Philadelphia, Benjamins, 1990.

SECONDARY SOURCES

Abed, S. B. "Language." In *History of Islamic Philosophy,* edited by Seyyed Hossein Nasr and Oliver Leaman, vol. 2, 898–925. London and New York: Routledge, 1996.

Barnes, J., and D. Schenkeveld. "Linguistics: 'Part II, 6.1'" In *The Cambridge History of Hellenistic Philosophy,* edited by Keimpe Algra et al., 177–216. Cambridge, U.K.: Cambridge University Press, 1999.

Ebbesen, S. "Language, Medieval Theories of." In *Routledge Encylopedia of Philosophy,* 10 vols, edited by Edward Craig, 389–404. New York: Routledge, 1998.

Everson, Stephen, ed. *Language.* Cambridge, U.K.: Cambridge University Press, 1994.

Rosier, Irène. *La grammaire spéculative des modistes.* Lille, France: Presses universitaires de Lille, 1983.

*John Marenbon*

## MODERN

Although discussions of language in seventeenth- and eighteenth-century philosophy foreshadowed many issues that came to full bloom in the twentieth century, before the twentieth century language was thought to have a secondary role in understanding the special place human beings have in the world. The fundamental concern was the problem of knowledge. How is it possible for human beings to have knowledge of the world? The solution for both rationalists and empiricists was to be found in the nature of mind since, as was universally held, all we can know directly are the ideas of our own minds. To solve this problem of knowledge, philosophers had to account for how we grasp generalities (and not just particulars) and how we determine which of our ideas represent the world truly.

Language was seen as the public conventional medium for communicating private thought. A simple denotational theory of meaning predominated. The meanings of words are their denotations, the objects that the words stand for or denote, or the ideas of particular objects. Proper names, like "Silver," denote particular objects. There was great controversy over what general terms, like "horse," denote. Three major positions emerged: (1) realism or Platonism, the view that general terms name real abstract objects (horsiness); (2) conceptualism, the view that terms stand for abstract ideas or concepts (the concept of horsiness); and (3) nominalism, the view that a term is general if it denotes more than one particular object. The important problem concerned the nature of abstract ideas. The solution to the problem of general words would follow from this.

### Founders of the Twentieth-Century "Linguistic Turn"
In the twentieth century, Anglo-American philosophy took "the linguistic turn." Instead of seeking solutions to problems of knowledge and thought in an examination of the nature of our ideas, philosophers looked to the nature of language. This great shift began with Gottlob Frege's foundational work in mathematical logic.

### Logical Syntax and Semantics
Well into the nineteenth century, Aristotelian logic dominated. Logic was seen as the study of thought itself. Gottlob Frege (1848–1925) revolutionized our conception of logic and its relation to thought and language. Frege's key insight was to see that formal arithmetic modeling can be used to display the structure of language. Just as "$x + y = z$" expresses the form of all instances of addition through the use of variables ($x$, $y$, $z$) and a special sign for the addition function ($+$), so language can be modeled. "Horses are mammals" can be written in a special concept-script (*Begriffsschrift*) that displays the different roles that the constituent words play in the sentence, "$(x)(Hx \rightarrow Mx)$." This is done in a way that abstracts from the meaning of any particular sentence. The new logic, thus, distinguishes the formal features of language from meaning, laying the groundwork for the tripartite distinction between syntax, semantics, and pragmatics.

*Syntax* concerns the rules for combining expressions into well-formed sentences within the language while *semantics* gives us a theory of the meanings of words and sentences. On this view, language is a formal object that consists of a finite interpreted lexicon and a finite set of recursive rules for combining lexical items. Recursive rules are rules that can be applied repeatedly. This permits the construction of any of an infinite array of possible sentences. The lexicon consists of several kinds of terms—proper names, predicates, and relations, each distinguished by its distinctive role within a sentence. This conception of language, which continues to dominate discussion, is a *representational theory of language,* for it treats the essence of language as the representation of possible states of the world using finite resources. *Pragmatics* studies whatever practical and contextual aspects of language use are left.

***Frege's semantic theory.*** In trying to apply the traditional denotational theory of meaning to language, Frege identified a number of problems. One of the most important arises with "contingent identity" statements. The sentences "The Morning Star is the Morning Star" and "The Morning Star is the Evening Star" have different "cognitive values." If meaning is just a matter of denotation, then it is hard to see how this could be so. Frege's theory distinguishes two kinds of meaning: *reference* (what the term denotes) and *sense* (the mode of presenting the denoted object). Each meaningful expression must have both a sense and a referent. Names ("Walter Scott") and definite descriptions ("the author of *Waverley*") denote particular objects by way of their mode of presenting the object. The sense of a predicate expression is the mode of presenting a concept, the referent of the expression. Questions about the nature of, and relation between, sense and reference have been at the center of philosophy of language ever since.

***Logical analysis.*** Frege came to logic and the philosophy of language through concerns with the foundations of mathematics. Bertrand Russell (1872–1970) and Ludwig Wittgenstein (1889–1951) shared this concern but saw the new logic as the key to philosophy in general. Both held that the new logic would enable philosophy to break with its metaphysical tradition, by showing that metaphysics had resulted from mistakes and confusions rooted in a failure to understand language properly. One must distinguish between the surface grammar of ordinary sentences and the underlying logical form of these sentences. The new logic is the means for characterizing this deep structure (or logical form), a structure hidden by surface grammatical form. Logical form is reached through a process of *logical analysis.*

Russell's classic example of an analysis that removed puzzlement was his treatment of definite descriptions. It was thought that definite descriptions ("the author of *Waverley*") should be treated like proper names; to be meaningful they must refer to some particular. But this creates a problem for non-referring definite descriptions like "the present king of France." This is a meaningful phrase and yet there is no individual answering to this description. Russell's solution was to argue that the underlying logical form of the expression is quite different from what it appears to be on the surface. Analysis reveals that the sentence "the present king of France is bald" has the logical form of "There is one and only one person such that that person is now king of France and is bald." Russell's analysis eliminates the apparently referring expression "the present king of France." Correctly analyzed, this puzzling sentence turns out to be merely false.

Wittgenstein took this idea even further. In his first work, *Tractatus Logico-Philosophicus* (1922), Wittgenstein argued that all sentences (in any language whatsoever) have a *determinate* meaning. A sentence says that things are thus-and-so. Wittgenstein took this to imply that any sentence must be analyzable into a set of "elementary" sentences composed of constituent words that denote simple objects. Complex sentences are just functions of combinations of elementary sentences. Strings of words that look like sentences, but resist analysis, are not really sentences at all. They are nonsense. Only the sentences of ordinary factual talk and the natural sciences are meaningful. Ethical, aesthetic, and religious statements, though important to our lives, are strictly meaningless. Most (if not all) traditional philosophy is nonsensical on this view.

## Logical Positivism and Its Challengers

The next important step was taken by a number of leading physicists, mathematicians, and philosophers who formed a group in Vienna known as the Vienna Circle. The Vienna Circle was committed to a repudiation of metaphysics in favor of science, and they saw in the ideas of Frege, Russell, and Wittgenstein the philosophical foundation for their movement. They embraced a philosophy of "logical positivism." At the heart of this movement was the thesis, known as the *principle of verification,* that only sentences making empirically confirmable claims are meaningful at all. Unverifiable sentences are nonsense. In the 1930s, many positivists had to flee Austria and Germany. As émigrés, they exercised a profound influence on philosophy in the English-speaking world.

***Challenges to the positivist conception of language.*** The 1950s and 1960s saw a reaction against the positivist theory of language. The challenge had two sources: the ordinary language movement of Oxford University and a powerful critique of the very idea of meaning by the American philosopher W. V. O. Quine of Harvard.

***Ordinary language movement.*** Wittgenstein's *Philosophical Investigations* (1953) and J. L. Austin's writings were the mainsprings of the ordinary language movement. These philosophers retained the positivist suspicion of metaphysics as confused theorizing, but they rejected the celebration of science at the expense of all other forms of understanding and its theory of language. Wittgenstein and Austin, in their different ways, argued that the theories of language represented by Frege, the *Tractatus,* and the positivist movement are themselves as confused as the metaphysical theories they deride. One of the striking consequences of the verificationist theory of meaning is that ordinary objects, from pigs to chairs to electrons, are logical constructions out of our sensory experiences, a view called "phenomenalism." Phenomenalism is the theory that all empirical sentences are analyzable into sets of sentences about actual and possible observations that would confirm (or disconfirm) the truth of the sentence. Meaning is ultimately rooted in sensory experience. "This is a penny" is thus analyzable into a set of experiential sentences: "this is copper-colored, round, hard and cool; or this is copper-colored, elliptically shaped, hard and cool; or . . . " The full analysis would consist of a potentially infinite disjunction of experiential sentences, one for each possible experience of a penny.

Critics argued that the positivist theory is belied by the realities of ordinary language. They used nuanced descriptions of our actual uses of language to challenge the claims both that language has an underlying logical form revealed through analysis and that referential theories of meaning, and phenomenalism in particular, are correct. Early referential theories state that the semantic relation between words and the world is fixed by ostensive definitions, that is, by naming an object. But ostensive definition cannot fix meaning since any object has many distinct properties, which the ostensive definition in itself does not distinguish. Defining "horse" by pointing to Silver does not show whether the expression is intended to be a proper name or to pick out Silver's horsiness or his being four-legged or white. So, it is concluded, reference cannot explain meaning, but presupposes it.

Meaning seems better explained in terms of how words are used in connection with our actions and interactions with the world and each other. Meaning is not the denoted object, but the use to which the word is put in practice. This idea of meaning as use brings with it a *holistic* conception of meaning rather than the *atomistic* conception of referential theories of meaning. A number of different positions developed within this movement: (1) Some advocate a use theory of meaning, which replaces the idea of language as a single systematic totality with that of an array of overlapping ways of using language. It replaces the search for necessary and sufficient experiential conditions for the applicability of an expression in favor of criterial grounds, where *criteria* constitute necessarily good evidence for the presence of some object while nonetheless falling short of entailment of the presence of that object. (2) J. L. Austin and others introduced the speech act theory of language, according to which the act of utterance and the context within which it occurs is the starting point for a theory of meaning. This too leads to a holistic conception of meaning and blurs the distinction between what belongs to semantics (the meanings of our words) and what belongs to pragmatics (the background and contextual considerations that inform actual speech). (3) Lastly, there are those who see in the ordinary language critique of the representational picture a rejection of the possibility of theorizing about language at all. There can only be the diagnosis of error in any such attempt.

### Quine's philosophy of language.
The second great challenge to the dominant picture of language comes from W. V. O. Quine (1908–2000) with his critique of the distinction between *analytic* and *synthetic* truth ("Two Dogmas of Empiricism," 1951) and his more general attack on the very idea of meaning (*Word and Object,* 1960). Sentences that are analytically true are true solely in virtue of the meanings of the constituent words. The truth of synthetic sentences, on the other hand, is a function both of the meanings of the words and of the nature of the world. It is the difference between "Bachelors are unmarried" and "Sam is a bachelor." Quine argues that the sentences we accept as true hang together holistically in a "web of belief" that can be adjusted at any point. He concludes that there is no point in classifying some sentences as true by meaning and some as empirical.

In *Word and Object,* Quine introduces what proves to be the greatest challenge to the dominant view. With "the museum myth of meanings" (words as labels for objects) fully discredited, we must look at language in a new way. The way to understand meaning is to ask what translation preserves. Much translation is customary, so we should look at *radical translation.* The situation of radical translation is one in which the linguist seeks to translate a language that is wholly alien to him. We find that there is no uniquely correct way to specify the translations of the unknown language into the known language ("the indeterminacy of translation") and no way to specify determinately what objects or properties the terms refer to ("the inscrutability of reference"). Further Quine attacks the idea that language has a logical form that is captured by formal logic. He argues that such an ideal is at best the regimentation of a part of our language. Quine's challenge set the agenda for the 1960s and 1970s.

### Philosophy of Language since Quine
Donald Davidson (1926–2003) builds on Quine's project, developing his own interpretationist theory of language. Davidson argues that truth is the fundamental semantic notion and that meaning is given by specifying the truth conditions for a sentence. This specification can only be achieved by a method of radical interpretation, which requires treating the speaker as holding mostly true beliefs. This approach differs from the representationalist picture in the following ways: Reference is not the fundamental semantic relation between language and the world, but a derivative relation; meaning and belief are interdependent—there is no way to separate them in a principled fashion; the method of radical interpretation requires, as a normative constraint, that the speaker be rational.

The 1990s brought a defense of inferentialist theories of meaning against representationalist theories. On an inferentialist view, the meaning of a sentence is a matter of the inferential relations that acceptance incurs. Instead of thinking of a sentence as representing a state of affairs, we should think of the sentence as entitling and committing the utterer to say and believe other things. To assert "Horses are mammals" is thereby to be committed to holding true "Horses are warm-blooded" and to rejecting as false "Horses lay eggs."

### New theories of reference.
The second reaction to Quine was the construction of new theories of reference that are held to avoid the problems of the simple denotational theory. These are causal theories of reference and "direct reference" theories. Causal theories of reference identify the reference relation between words and properties with causal relations. Direct reference theories state that the object or property referred to just is the meaning of the expression; the reference relation is not explained by way of ostensive definition or some special causal chain. Both approaches free the notion of reference from necessarily involving some kind of mental act. Saul Kripke introduced key elements of both theories in his highly influential book *Naming and Necessity* (1972). There he maintains that referring terms "rigidly designate" their objects. Once an object has been baptized, that name denotes its object in any possible world in which the object (is specified to) occur(s). What secures the link for those who have no direct relation to the object is the socially transmitted causal chain that extends from the baptism to subsequent uses of the name. Kripke extended

his theory of rigid designation and socially sustained causal chains to natural kinds as well as individuals.

***Realism vs. Anti-Realism.*** This debate concerning the nature of reference and whether it can explain the meaningfulness of language is at the heart of a philosophical debate that dominated the 1980s and continues to be felt. In the 1980s, the great metaphysical debate between realism and idealism was recast in terms of the relation between language and the world. This debate concerns both how reference and truth should be understood and whether the correct theory of meaning for language is a *truth-conditional theory* or an *assertability conditional theory.* A truth-conditional theory holds that the meaning of a sentence just is the truth condition for that sentence. An assertability conditional theory of meaning states that the meaning of a sentence is given by its assertability conditions, namely, the conditions by which one can recognize the statement is true. These are distinct versions of the representationalist picture of language. This debate became focused on vying theories of truth. Michael Dummett, the leading defender of the assertability conditional account, characterized the difference between realist and antirealist positions in terms of whether a statement could be meaningful and yet transcend any possible evidence for its truth or falsity.

This interest in truth as a semantic value has generated a lively debate. Both the realist and the antirealist hold substantive theories of truth. The realist identifies the truth of a sentence with its corresponding to the facts. The antirealist assesses truth in terms of coherence with other sentences and our recognitional capacities. Challenging both of these positions are "deflationary" theories of truth. Such theories deny that truth has a substantive nature (whether correspondence or coherence). The truth predicate is a device for semantic ascent, for moving from the sentence "snow is white" to the sentence "the sentence 'snow is white' is true." There are things that one can say by talking about sentences that are not easily said in other ways.

***Other issues.*** The 1990s saw a number of developments. Most important was the debate between inferentialist theories of language and representationalist theories. Other important issues concerned the nature of "vague" predicates like "bald" that have fuzzy borders (is the "fuzziness" a feature of the property itself or our ignorance?), the compositionality of meaning (is it essential to the explanation of meaning?), innate rules of grammar, and the infinite reach of language. Many of these issues have become highly technical and specialized, but they are all in the service of the great debates about the general character of language and meaning.

*See also* **Language and Linguistics; Language, Philosophy of: Ancient and Medieval; Linguistic Turn.**

BIBLIOGRAPHY

Austin, J. L. *How to Do Things With Words.* Edited by J. O. Urmson. Oxford, U.K.: Clarendon Press, 1962.
———. *Philosophical Papers.* Edited by J. O. Urmson and G. J. Warnock. Oxford, U.K.: Clarendon Press, 1961.
Ayer, A. J. *Language, Truth, and Logic.* 2nd ed. New York: Dover Publications, 1946.

Brandom, Robert. *Making It Explicit: Reasoning, Representing, and Discursive Commitment.* Cambridge, Mass.: Harvard University Press, 1994.
Davidson, Donald. *Inquiries into Truth and Interpretation.* Oxford, U.K.: Clarendon Press, 2001.
Dummett, Michael. "What Is a Theory of Meaning? I and II." In his *The Seas of Language.* Oxford, U.K.: Clarendon Press, 1993.
Frege, Gottlob. "Begriffsschrift" and "On Sense and Reference." In *Philosophical Writings of Gottlob Frege,* edited by Peter Geach and Max Black. Oxford, U.K.: Blackwell, 1969.
Kripke, Saul A. *Naming and Necessity.* Cambridge, Mass.: Harvard University Press, 1972.
Quine, W.V.O. "Two Dogmas of Empiricism." In his *From a Logical Point of View: 9 Logico-Philosophical Essays.* New York: Harper & Row, 1961.
———. *Word and Object.* Cambridge, Mass.: MIT Press, 1960.
Russell, Bertrand. "Lectures on Logical Atomism." In *Logic and Knowledge,* edited by Robert Charles Marsh. London: George Allen and Unwin, 1956.
———. "On Denoting." In *Logic and Knowledge: Essays, 1901–1950,* edited by Robert Charles Marsh. London: George Allen and Unwin, 1956.
Wittgenstein, Ludwig. *Philosophical Investigations.* Translated by G. E. M. Anscombe. New York: Macmillan, 1953.
———. *Tractatus Logico-Philosophicus.* Translated by D. F. Pears and B. F. McGuinness. London: Routledge and Kegan Paul, 1975.

*Meredith Williams*

# LAW

**LAW.** The development of law and jurisprudential ideas since the 1970s represents a significant change from the conventional models that had earlier dominated the province of legal theory in the history of ideas. This entry focuses on two salient theoretical emphases that have continued to influence developments of conventional legal theory and postmodern paradigms of legal thought: the analytical tradition, and the jurisprudence inspired by the revolt against formalism, or legal realism.

## Twentieth-Century Schools

Within the received tradition, the rules-based model (which regards law as a pure science), identified with Herbert Lionel Adolphus (H. L. A.) Hart (1907–1992) and the Oxford school of analytical positivism, was subjected to both strong internal critique and important development by such figures as Ronald Dworkin, a Yale law professor who later became professor of jurisprudence in Oxford. Dworkin's redevelopment of the analytical model focused centrally on the development of a powerful rights-based theory of law. The approach moved the consideration of conventional legal theory strongly in the direction of the moral foundations of political community. This created an awkward fit for analytical positivism, which traditionally strove to separate law from moral discourse, that is, to radically distinguish the law that *is* from the law that *ought* to be. Dworkin's work led him to stress the principle that the foundations of a rights-based approach to law are indeed rooted in the values of equal respect and dignity, the core moral precepts in a political community committed to taking rights seriously.

***Responses to legal realism.*** In the United States the dominant version of legal realism (an intellectual movement that advocates policy-oriented jurisprudence informed by developments in social and behavioral sciences, such as psychology and anthropology), which had reached its apex in American legal culture prior to World War II, also remained influential. The general criticism leveled at legal realism argued that an approach to adjudication that is result-selective and that only makes sense from an external observer's point of view is flawed. It compromises the conventional view of law and in particular undermines its special juridical character rooted in the ubiquity and special characteristics of rules governing social and legal relations. This criticism reflects the idea—implicit in pragmatic approaches to philosophy—that law, like all human relations, should be conceived in terms of process.

Three distinctive responses to legal realism developed in the United States. The first was an acceptance of a rules-rights–based approach to law from an internal point of view, with the corresponding conclusion that the foundations of any legal theory from an external point of view (an about-law point of view) was simply incompatible with a professional internal perspective of law based on rules. This critique gave analytical jurisprudence an important place not only in developments in the United States, but more broadly in the general development of legal theory.

The second response, associated primarily with the Harvard Law School, is known as the legal-process school. At Harvard, Henry M. Hart Jr. (1904–1969) and Albert M. Sacks (1920–1991) focused attention on the nature of adjudication from the point of view of a principle of institutional competence. Instead of asking the classical questions of analytical jurisprudence: "What is a valid law?" and "By what criteria might we objectively determine what a valid law is?," they asked a different question, namely, "What is a legal question?" They were particularly interested in the objective indices used to distinguish administrative, executive, legislative, or indeed more broadly, political questions from those distinctively legal. This approach provided more flexibility and focused, so to speak, on law as a process requiring a continuing definition and redefinition of legal/professional roles, distinguishing these roles from other roles in the broader processes of settling community disputes. A central feature was the principle that one could still use an objective standard to interpret either what the law is or what falls within the scope of judicial competence. In this sense, analytical jurisprudence and the legal-process school shared a deep commitment to the role of objectivity in law.

Doubtless, ideology could influence the nature of the indicators used to either broaden or narrow the scope of what an appropriate judicial role is or should be. It cannot, therefore, be said that the legal-process approach settled deep ideological differences about the role of law in governing human relations. Rather, it provided a framework that justified greater flexibility in managing the tasks of judicially settling disputes while maintaining fidelity to the importance of objectivity in law.

Morton J. Horwitz summarizes the essential challenge to which the legal-process school responded as follows:

> The legal process school sought to absorb and temper the insights of Legal Realism after the triumph of the New Deal. Its most important concession to Realism was in its recognition that doctrinal formalism was incapable of eliminating discretion in the law. The task was instead to harness and channel that discretion through institutional arrangements.

The third response, generally associated with the Yale Law School, is known as "Law Science and Policy." It was identified with the political scientist Harold D. Lasswell (1902–1978) and the international lawyer Myres S. McDougal (1906–1998). These scholars were deeply influenced by legal realism, but were dissatisfied with the implication that at the end of the day legal realism might lead to legal nihilism. Their initial collaboration, which came during World War II, resulted in the 1943 publication of "Legal Education and Public Policy: Professional Training in the Public Interest." In this article, they raise the broad question of what the purpose of professional training is and, indeed, how professional training relates to the public interest. In this view, the professions are not neutral, but rather have a great deal to do with the nature and quality of the system of public order a society promotes and defends. From this article, they developed a system of jurisprudential thought for a free society and developed a wide range of specific applications of their theory to international law. Their work in international law became identified with the so-called New Haven School of International Law.

Jurisprudence in this view had a radically different, but distinctively scientific orientation. Jurisprudence was to be a theory for inquiry about law. The theory had a deliberate focus on policy- and decision-making. Indeed, law would now be defined as a process of authoritative and controlling decision-making wherein members of the community seek to clarify and implement their common interests. The approach would be radically context-sensitive, it would be problem-oriented, goal-guided, multidisciplinary, and solution-oriented. Among the central elements of this jurisprudential emphasis was the meaning it gave to the task of problem definition. Law, in this view, is not about the scope of different rules created by current or past elites, or about how to interpret or reconcile contradictory rules created by the same legal sources. A problem is to be observed from the perspective of the subjectivities of individuals involved in social interaction in society itself. In short, human beings in society are making subjective demands for value allocations, and these demands often reproduce social conflict for which the community provides institutional mechanisms specialized with whatever degree of efficacy for responding to them. Thus, law is one of the specialized mechanisms in social organization that responds to the raw, subjective claims of individuals in the larger social process.

By focusing the lens of legal inquiry on individual subjectivities, that is to say perspectives, for example, of identity, demand, and expectation, the Law Science and Policy approach radically changed the starting point of the central ideas required for legal inquiry. This had large-scale impacts on the development of ideas within the framework of legal culture. Lasswell's work in the social sciences and his collaboration with McDougal also anticipated the later development of postmodernism in the social sciences and its particular application to law, influenced by such theorists as Michel Foucault (1926–1984), Jacques Derrida (b. 1930), Jacques Lacan (1901–1981), and Jürgen Habermas (b. 1929).

Since human subjectivities are the central raw materials from which human problems evolve, and if law is a response to these problems, then human subjectivities are a critical element in a realistic and comprehensive understanding of jurisprudence and law. When, for example, human beings make distinctively economic demands, we bring in the relevance of microeconomic theory. When we consider that the rules and doctrines of the past in virtually all legal cultures have been largely made by men, we see that we must account for women's perspectives in law, which leads to the development of feminist conceptions of jurisprudence. Critical conceptions of jurisprudence, such as critical legal studies and critical race theory, as well as Lat/Crit theory (a branch of critical race theory), such as it is, have entered the discourse about legal culture as a result of the breach in the edifice of legal objectivism identified with conventional legal theory, as well as the legal process perspective.

The Law Science and Policy approach is a theory *about* and not *of* law. The insistence on a theory about law was a cardinal tenet of legal realism and was central to unpacking confusions of vantage point generated by both participants (decision-makers and claimants) and observers who represent a degree of scientific detachment required for the scientific study of law. However, the most direct influence of the McDougal-Lasswell school was in the area of international law, which they styled the public order of the world community. It is, of course, not the case that all of international law reflects their basic tenets; however, their work has had substantial influence on how international law is conceived and on the salience and importance of many of its important doctrines.

## International Law

McDougal, Lasswell, and W. Michael Reisman sought to apply jurisprudential insights and ideas directly to the study of international law. Apart from the relevance of context, the problem orientation, and the salience of multiple methods of inquiry about law, their approach stressed the importance of specific intellectual criteria for the study of jurisprudence in international law. These criteria included goal-thinking, trend-thinking, scientific-thinking, predictive-thinking, and alternative-thinking. The approach was also explicit in articulating the standards by which one could compare and evaluate all systems of legal thought. These criteria included the procedures used to maintain and establish a clear observational vantage point, the critical importance of focusing both comprehensively and specifically on the actual processes of policy and decision, the development and use of critical intellectual tasks, and the importance of the provisional postulation of fundamental public-order goals. These criteria could be applied in the study of a national system or the entire global system.

The central feature of the New Haven School of International Law was its insistence on universality and comprehensiveness. This approach coincided with the creation of new states out of the debris of colonial rule. The new states were not always new. They were often old and dependent. In order to stake a claim for statehood, doctrines had to be invented and supported by contemporaneous developments in international law and jurisprudence. Nationalist elites seeking freedom from colonial rule would stake a claim to self-determination and independence. This claim of course would be an attack on sovereignty, or at least the colonial version of it. American idealism in the form of Wilsonian internationalism succeeded after World War II in making German colonies a sacred trust of civilization while at the same time paying service to colonial hegemony. Thus, for example, German South West Africa, which was conquered by South Africa in 1917, was given to South Africa to administer as a special international mandate. The precedent created here was that colonial rule was not altogether to be insulated from international responsibility, in particular the sacred trust for the well-being of the inhabitants. After World War II, the dominant victorious allies, namely the United States and the Soviet Union, shared a common objective, supported for radically different reasons, that colonialism become obsolete. The United Nations was created, and a part of its growing mandate was to facilitate decolonization, self-determination, and independence.

The paradox of claims to resist colonial rule was that they were also claims to weaken the sovereignty idea in international law. If self-determination and independence were supported by international legal precepts, then international support for the integrity of sovereignty would be constrained by these competing claims. In short, sovereignty admits limitation, particularly limitations based on international obligations. Thus, the sovereignty idea began to evolve within the framework of a global constitutive process, as expressed in the theories of the New Haven School.

## Problems of Sovereignty

The model for expanding the community of nation-states became the model of a sovereignty-dominated world order, which included the new Afro-Asian sovereigns. This model was largely Eurocentric, and its juridical roots are often identified with the Peace of Westphalia (1648). The claims about sovereignty now represented a paradox. Colonial sovereignty was to be seen as weaker and permeable: "soft sovereignty," as it were. However, the new sovereigns were based on political foundations that were both internally and externally vulnerable. The same elites who demanded a weak version of sovereignty to justify decolonization were now demanding something akin to an absolutist version for national survival. In short, they were frequently demanding a form of sovereignty identified with the international legal culture prior to World War II, a version largely unconstrained by respect for international obligations (hard or thick sovereignty).

The problems of weakening sovereigns coincided with the Cold War, and the hegemons could find surrogates to spearhead strategic interventions intended to weaken sovereigns ostensibly identified with one superpower or another. The normative status of sovereignty thus generated two powerful contradictory trends. The first trend was the high priority given to principles of sovereign equality and nonintervention. The second was the high priority given to the imperatives of international legal obligation and the competence to intervene when fundamental international values, such as peace, security, and humanitarian values, are compromised.

Thus, while the nation-state system was still expanding in the early 2000s—with approximately 192 sovereigns—sovereignty, in fact, was changing, as nations found that in giving up some sovereignty, they, in effect, *strengthen* their sovereignty. The expansion of NATO (North Atlantic Treaty Organization) is an illustration of this phenomenon; the development in the direction of the European Constitution is a further example; and the development of the African Union Constitution is a major doctrinal shift in the dynamic of sovereignty. This suggests that the political and juridical conceptions of sovereignty had the possibility of embracing theoretical reification and practical obsolescence, or becoming more refined, flexible, fluid, and relevant to the practicalities of governance.

The importance of understanding the context in which sovereigns are created, maintained, and possibly changed is a reflection of the insistence in legal theory that international sovereignty itself is the outcome of problems of power in the international system. What is apparent in the complex global network of institutions and participant actors is that there are many active participants in this process, such as international, continental, and regional organizations, and private-sector institutions of business, capital, and labor, as well as the vast organization and partial structure of nongovernmental operators and individuals who constitute national and global civil society. Therefore, it will be seen that the meaning of sovereignty itself derives not so much from state absolutism, but from the ways in which global society constructs and orders political identity and participation through sovereigns and other institutions of global salience.

*Statehood.* The concept of sovereignty in the twenty-first century is, of course, tied to the concept of statehood. For a state to be recognized in international law, the state must meet certain practical and normative requirements. The first set of criteria relates to practical matters of power and control. The state must have control over territory, people, and institutions of governance, and must be competent to handle the international environment.

These matters are often collapsed into what is sometimes known as the declaratory theory of recognition. In order to become a member of the United Nations, a state must not only meet these criteria, but it must also meet certain normative standards. It must indicate a willingness to respect and honor the principles on which the United Nations is founded, including respect for peace and security, the rule of law, human rights, and more. In practice, governments have—from time to time—unilaterally indicated that certain states do not maintain standards of behavior consistent with the concept of international obligation. Thus, the United States has a list of states it regards as "terrorist," and has expanded this notion to include what it calls "rogue states." This indicates the beginning

of a discourse that is more substantive with regard to the nature of the state itself and therefore the nature of sovereignty. Thus, the notion emerges of the abuse of sovereignty, and some writers have suggested that descriptive typologies of states could include such descriptions as failed states, anarchic states, genocidal states, homicidal states, rogue states, drug-influenced states, organized-crime-influenced states, kleptocratic states, terrorist states, authoritarian states, garrison or national security states, totalitarian states, and democratic rule of law states. Behind this discourse is the evolving notion of sovereignty itself. The older idea of sovereignty was identified with state absolutism. Among the elements of the new concept are the ideas and ideals of transparency, responsibility, and accountability in the analysis of both sovereignty and the state.

### Sovereignty and the International Order

Sovereignty is ambiguously defined in the Charter of the United Nations. The first principle holds that the charter derives its legitimacy from the people of the earth-space community, but the constitutional scheme is weighted heavily in favor of the state-sovereignty paradigm, and limits, in some significant measure, the role of nongovernmental participation. Membership is open to sovereign states only. However, the basis of sovereignty is further clarified in the International Covenant on Civil and Political Rights. Individuals who constitute the "people" according to Article 16 "shall have the right to recognition everywhere as a person before the law." Article 18 specifies the people's right to freedom of thought; Article 19 stresses the people's "right to hold opinions without interference" and that the people "shall have the freedom of expression;" and Article 25 puts stress on the right to participate in the political welfare of the State, and the universal rights to vote and to participate in public service.

Thus, a significant change created by the UN Charter (along with subsequent practice) is that the conceptual basis of sovereignty is rooted not only in the monopoly of effective power, but also is predicated on authority and legitimacy, which are rooted in the expectations of people. The Declaration on the "Guidelines on the Recognition of New States in Eastern Europe and in the Soviet Union" made recognition and sovereign acceptance into the European community of states, subject to strong normative standards of international justice. The Guidelines include "respect for the provisions of the Charter of the UN and the commitments subscribed to in the Final Act of Helsinki and in the Charter of Paris, especially with regard to the rule of law, democracy and human rights." The Summit of the Americas Declaration of Principles and Plan of Action articulated that democracy is the sole political system that guarantees respect for human rights and the rule of law. The 1990 Charter of Paris is another important expectation-creating instrument wherein sovereignty is predicated in the will of the people. Participating states affirmed their respect for human rights protections and fundamental freedoms as "essential safeguards against an over-mighty State." Democracy is "based on the will of the people" and is the "foundation of human respect" (pp. 193–194).

These examples illustrate that fundamental expectations of the nature of the state, including its sovereignty and governance, are being conditioned by what scholars call a right to democratic governance. The idea is that the formal historic requirements for the de facto recognition of a state have been enhanced by the normative constraints and demands of critical symbols of authority associated or identified with the human right to democratic governance. These demands include transparency, responsibility, accountability, and a commitment that the rule of law must be an intrinsic component of the nature, scope, and practical functions of sovereignty.

The newer meaning of sovereignty, which ties control to authority and to decision-making, also raises the question about how power and authority (i.e., governance) and decision-making are constituted in the global environment. For example, there are nation-states with constitutions in Africa. There is also the Constitution of the African Union, which is a form of constitutionalism with linkages to the constitutions of African member states. In Europe, nation-states are tied together in an economic and political union. Each nation-state has its own constitution, which is an overt indicator of how governance is constituted in the state, but the continental linkages of these states are to a larger political and economic community, and a draft constitution has been formulated that will obviously have linkages to the constitutional scheme within each state.

At a more inclusive level, all of these developments (national and continental) have evolved complex constitutional orders, which fall under the umbrella of the global constitution: the Charter of the United Nations. It will be very obvious that sovereignty now involves complex clusters of competence; some competences are shared, and smaller states (pooling their economic and political capital) might now have a larger say in the important decisions affecting them in the larger international environment than would be the case if they were acting as individual, isolated sovereigns. However, collected powers also require submission to the rules of the game. In short, in the early twentieth century, sovereignty can be described as a strengthened expression of its former self to some degree, but it is nevertheless much changed.

### Sovereignty and the International Community
The conceptual positioning of national sovereignty within the framework of constituting authority and control permits us now to see the importance of the fact that there are many other participants in the global community, power, and constitutive process. As a technical matter, the question of whether an international organization, such as the United Nations, could have an international legal personality for the purpose of suing another state at the international level was decided by the World Court in a case called *The Reparations Case*. In this case, the World Court recognized that even though the United Nations was not a state, it was nonetheless an organization with an international legal personality and the right to sue or otherwise act in the international environment within the framework of its constituted competence.

It was the Nuremberg Tribunal that, in fact, opened the breach to the possibility that individuals might have some sovereignty in the international legal environment. The Nuremberg defendants were made directly accountable for war crimes and crimes against humanity under international law. But these defendants were also given the right to a fair trial under international law. They not only had duties under international law, but they could also exercise rights. Thus the narrow principle was established that individuals could have rights directly under international law; for some purposes, the individual could exercise these rights and, thus, rights and duties in international law were not confined to formal sovereign entities. Two important developments were born of these events. The first was the development of the human-rights provisions in the UN Charter through the Universal Declaration of Human Rights (UNDHR) and the extensive treaty-based regime for the protection of global and regional human rights. The preamble of the UNDHR states that member states recognize:

> [T]he inherent dignity and . . . the equal and inalienable rights of all members of the human family is the foundation of freedom, justice and peace in the world . . . [and] disregard and contempt for human rights have resulted in barbarous acts which have outraged the conscience of mankind, and the advent of a world in which human beings shall enjoy freedom of speech and belief and freedom from fear and want has been proclaimed as the highest aspiration of the common people . . . [and that] it is essential, if man is not to be compelled to have recourse, as a last resort, to rebellion against tyranny and oppression, that human rights should be protected by the rule of law.

The second development was that in the aftermath of the Cold War, two ad hoc tribunals were established to try governmental officials and others for humanitarian and grave human-rights violations. The relative successes of the International Criminal Tribunal for the Former Yugoslavia (ICTY; 1993) and the International Criminal Tribunal for Rwanda (ICTR; 1994) provided a renewed impetus for the creation of an International Criminal Court (1998), which was indeed established. It is therefore critical that we see the development of international legal order since the 1970s as having finally been able to capitalize on the revolutionary breakthrough established at Nuremberg, where it was determined that individuals could not hide behind the veil of the state when they committed horrendous crimes against the peace and against humanity. For example, Article 7 of the Statute of the International Tribunal for the Former Yugoslavia and Article 6 of the Statute of the International Tribunal for Rwanda harmonize on the issue of individual criminal responsibility. Both state that:

1. A person who planned, instigated, ordered, committed or otherwise aided and abetted in the planning, preparation or execution of a crime referred to in articles 2 to 5 of the present Statute, shall be individually responsible for the crime.

2. The official position of any accused person, whether as Head of State or Government or as a responsible Government official, shall not relieve

such person of criminal responsibility nor mitigate punishment.

3. The fact that any of the acts referred to in articles 2 to 5 of the present Statute was committed by a subordinate does not relieve his superior of criminal responsibility if he knew or had reason to know that the subordinate was about to commit such acts or had done so and the superior failed to take the necessary and reasonable measures to prevent such acts or to punish the perpetrators thereof.

4. The fact that an accused person acted pursuant to an order of a Government or of a superior shall not relieve him of criminal responsibility, but may be considered in mitigation of punishment if the International Tribunal determines that justice so requires.

With regard to Yugoslavia, the former president of that country was tried in The Hague in the early 2000s, and in Rwanda, high governmental officials had already been convicted. The question is, what do these events mean for the history of ideas?

These ideas establish the revolutionary principle that, both politically and juridically, the international community may directly hold governmental officials to account (in certain circumstances) and punish them accordingly. It also establishes that the conditions of governance, such as transparency, responsibility, and accountability, are integral features of the authority foundations of the state, and therefore the normative foundations of the state itself have changed on a continuum that moves from state absolutism to rooting governance and constitutionalism in the foundations of authority. What is even more critical as a complement to these developments is the growth not simply of human-rights law, but of human rights as an integral part of governance and constitutionalism and as a deeply rooted expectation in the political and legal culture of the global community. What is important in these developments is that the human-rights culture finds strong intellectual roots in the development of rights-based jurisprudence, as well as in the jurisprudence that roots law in fundamental policy. The rights-based approach seeks to ensure that individual rights are taken seriously. The policy-based approach insists that law be responsive to the claim, the identity, and the fundamental expectation of the individual participation in the international legal and political environment. Central to each concept is the idea of fundamental respect, which is seen as the heart of responsible constitutionalism and accountable sovereignty, and which is fundamental to all human rights.

## Human Dignity

Central problems emerged—at least in theory—with regard to how to justify the principle of respect as the cornerstone of the principle of human dignity. It is unclear whether the concept of human dignity can itself be objectively justified, and indeed modern philosophers have even suggested that at a fundamental level, human values about dignity may be

incommensurable. Apparently conflicting values might have to be contextualized (or more deeply analyzed) in light of broader, more abstract formulations of value judgment. Thus, values including power, respect, rectitude, affection, enlightenment, well-being, skill, and wealth must be construed in terms of their enhancement of a more abstract human-dignity postulation. The policy-maker seeking the development of universal dignity must develop technical methods of decision-making, including sophisticated standards of construction and interpretation. Perhaps at this operational level, practical lawyers, social scientists, and real-world policy-makers must render decisions regarding how to integrate what are often regarded to be ostensibly conflicting values and norms in order to genuinely enhance the universal ethic of human dignity.

The South African Constitutional Court, for example, dealt in 1998 with a political party's claim regarding the "Truth and Reconciliation" statute that provided individuals who would otherwise have been prosecuted for human-rights violations with amnesty; essentially, this party contested the constitutionality of the statute and regarded it as a grave violation of international law. The Constitutional Court was confronted with a mechanism to explore truth and guide reconciliation that comprised a critical foundation for the internal peace and security of the entire Republic of South Africa, as well as of the effort to afford each South African political freedom. This statute, however, was in ostensible conflict with universally accepted tenets of international law, which do not accept excuses to mitigate the commission of grave crimes against humanity. It is possible to argue that the ethic of universal respect and human dignity demands universal compliance, but at what cost?

To ensure that respect, humanitarian law, and democratic entitlement are continuously adhered to and honored demands in-depth analysis and delicacy with regard to the process of decisional interventions. Rules of construction and interpretation painstakingly pieced together articulate, for example, that even if a peremptory norm of international law comprises an *erga omnes* obligation, it should be appraised and applied to enhance similar rights, which might also have to be accommodated. The currency underlying the ethic of human dignity is that it affords practical decision makers standards and goals that permit the transformation of regional, continental, and international law into a greater approximation of the standards and goals embodied in the United Nations Charter.

***Principle of equality.*** A central element in the development of the respect–human dignity precept is that it is rooted in the principle of equality. The principle of equality has a longstanding normative basis in the rule of law. For example, rule-governed behavior works on the principle of equality, namely, that rules cover like cases, regardless of identity, status, or personality. The more normative expression of the equality principle is established in the idea that all participants are formally equal before the law. Practical experience suggests, however, that even if formal equality is embraced it too often entrenches hierarchy, a lack of equity, and a depreciation of substantial justice. The specific way in which the international legal system approached the equality principle was a clear-cut recognition that the business of why World War II was fought was, in part, rooted in the racialism and Herrenvolkism of the Nazis. It would therefore be no surprise that both the preamble and the purposes of the UN Charter would codify not simply the importance of human rights, but would establish that racial and gender equality were crucial to a meaningful expression of the human-rights principle. Two of the most important covenants that reflect the specific development of the equality principle are the 1965 International Convention on the Elimination of All Forms of Racial Discrimination (ICERD) and the 1980 Convention on the Elimination of All Forms of Discrimination Against Women (CEDAW).

International human-rights law has also made criminal the practice of seeking to destroy groups of human beings in whole or in part based on race, nationality, ethnicity, and religion as labels of identity. Thus, the very first human-rights treaty following World War II made genocide a human-rights crime. The full development of the equality principle in international law has also permitted regional developments and has deeply influenced constitutional development on the principle of equality. The race relations convention, for example, goes further than the idea of formal equality in race relations. It specifically holds that affirmative action to achieve substantive equality is not unfair or prohibited discrimination. It cannot be said that the public order of the world community has achieved a community in which both substantive and formal equality are, in fact, realized. However, enormous developments have been stimulated by the development of the equality principle at the international level through the prism of universal human rights. This rise has served as a base of power for important levels of social activism within the framework of civil society to improve the condition of women discriminated against because of sex, as well as minorities discriminated against because of race.

## Globalization

One of the most important factors influencing international society in the early 2000s is the principle of globalism. The impact of globalism on sovereignty is fueled by the vast growth in the flow of goods, services, capital, and labor across state and national lines. This process has been dramatically accelerated by the communications revolution, and the impact on state sovereignty suggests that these global forces have seriously weakened the territorial boundaries of states. This intense flow of values across state and national lines also invited instant comparison and appraisal. As barriers to human interaction have been liberalized, what has been the social benefit and the social cost? There is no clear answer to this question. We know, for example, that without the communications revolution, it is possible that the global HIV/AIDS pandemic might have been containable. Thus, following the SARS (Severe Acute Respiratory Syndrome) outbreak of 2003, dramatic limitations were placed on communication to prevent the disease from spreading globally.

If nation-state barriers are not as salient, other barriers in the global age challenge the concept of global equity and fairness. While the world has generated more wealth than mankind has ever before achieved, the conditions of impoverishment throughout huge sections of the planet suggest a global

economic apartheid rather than a global vista of improved and shared equity. It is widely recognized that a planet that is radically divided between the haves and the have-nots, in which there is an acceleration of short-term gains for the haves and an acceleration of poverty and deprivation for the have-nots, will ultimately result in the depreciation of all. In short, underdeveloped as the concept of global equity is, it may be the cornerstone upon which the improvement of the global condition of deprivation is built, not because this is necessarily a spiritually beneficial thing, but because the long-term prosperity—and possibly the survival—of the human race may depend on it. The history of ideas in the future will therefore be challenged by the ideological and jurisprudential relevance of the concept of equity and whether equity can be the critical lever that provides us with universal concepts of respect and freedom in a global commonwealth of dignity.

*See also* **Authority; Critical Race Theory; International Order; Justice; Sovereignty; State, The.**

### BIBLIOGRAPHY

Charter of Paris for A New Europe, 21 November 1990. In *International Legal Materials* 30 (1991): 190 ff. Also available at www.ejil.org.

Convention on the Elimination of All Forms of Discrimination against Women, *opened for signature* Mar. 1, 1980, G.A. Res. 34/180, U.N. GAOR, 34th Sess., Supp. No. 46, at 193, U.N. Doc. A/34/46 (1979), 1249 U.N.T.S. 13, *reprinted in* 19 I.L.M. 33 (1980) (entered into force on Sept. 3, 1981). One hundred sixty-three states are party to the treaty. Also available at www.un.org.

Dworkin, Ronald. *Taking Rights Seriously.* Cambridge, Mass.: Harvard University Press, 1977.

———. "'Natural' Law Revisited." *University of Florida Law Review* 34 (1982): 165–188.

Finnis, John. *Natural Law and Natural Rights.* New York: Oxford University Press, 1980.

Hart, H. L. A. *The Concept of Law.* Oxford: Clarendon, 1961.

Hart, Henry M. Jr., and Albert M. Sacks. *The Legal Process: Basic Problems in the Making and Application of Law.* Prepared from the 1958 tentative edition by and containing an introductory essay by William N. Eskridge Jr. and Philip P. Frickey. Westbury, N.Y.: Foundation, 1994.

Horwitz, Morton J. *The Transformation of American Law, 1870–1960: The Crisis of Legal Orthodoxy.* New York: Oxford University Press, 1992.

International Convention on the Elimination of All Forms of Racial Discrimination, Dec. 21, 1965, 660 U.N.T.S. 195 (entered into force on Jan. 4, 1969; and for the United States on Nov. 20, 1994). One hundred fifty-two states are party to the treaty. See U.S. Department of State, Treaties In Force 427 (1997). Also available at www.unhchr.ch.

International Covenant on Civil and Political Rights, U.N.G.A. Res. 2200 A (xxi), 999 U.N.T.S. (Dec. 16, 1966); *International Legal Materials* 6 (1967): 368 ff. Also available at www.unhchr.ch.

Lasswell, Harold D. *Politics: Who Gets What, When, How.* New York: McGraw-Hill, 1936.

Lasswell Harold D., and Myres S. McDougal. *Jurisprudence for a Free Society: Studies in Law, Science, and Policy.* Boston: Nijhoff, 1991.

————. "Legal Education and Public Policy: Professional Training in the Public Interest." *Yale Law Journal* 52 (1943): 203 ff.

Marmor, A. "An Essay on the Objectivity of Law." In *Analyzing Law: New Essays in Legal Theory,* edited by Brian Bix. Oxford: Clarendon, 1998.

McDougal, Myres S. "The Comparative Study of Law for Policy Purposes: Value Clarification As an Instrument of Democratic World Order." *Yale Law Journal* 61 (1952): 915 ff.

McDougal, Myres S., Harold D. Lasswell, and W. Michael Reisman. "Theories about International Law: Prologue to a Configurative Jurisprudence." *Virginia Journal of International Law* 8 (1968): 188 ff.

————. "The World Constitutive Process of Authoritative Decision." In *The Future of the International Legal Order.* Edited by Richard A. Falk and Cyril E. Black. Princeton, N.J.: Princeton University Press, 1969.

Nagan, Winston P. "Conflicts Theory in Conflict: A Systematic Appraisal of Traditional and Contemporary Theory." *New York Law School Journal of International and Comparative Law* 3 (1982): 343 ff.

————. "Dunwody Commentaries: Not Just a Descending Trail: Traversing Holmes' Many Paths of the Law." *Florida Law Review* 49 (1997): 463 ff.

Rawls, John. *A Theory of Justice.* Cambridge, Mass.: Harvard University Press, 1971.

Statute of the International Tribunal for the Former Yugoslavia, adopted at New York, May 25, 1993, S.C. Res. 827, U.N. SCOR, 48th Sess., 3217th mtg., at 1–2, U.N. Doc. S/RES/827 (1993), reprinted in *International Legal Materials* 32 (1993): 1159 ff. Also available at www.un.org.

Statute of the International Tribunal for Rwanda, adopted at New York, Nov. 8, 1994, S.C. Res. 955, U.N.SCOR, 49th Sess., 3453d mtg., U.N. Doc. S/RES/955 (1994). Reprinted in *International Legal Materials* 33 (1994): 1598 ff. Also available at www.ictr.org.

Stacy, Helen M. *Postmodernism and Law: Jurisprudence in a Fragmenting World.* Burlington, Vt.: Dartmouth, 2001.

*Winston P. Nagan*

## LAW, ISLAMIC.

Islam, like Judaism and unlike Christianity, is a nomocracy, a religion of the law as opposed to theology. It is evident from the Koranic text that sacred law is a crucial feature of the covenants that God establishes, through prophets, with the various nations of mankind. Prophets are united by their main directive, to worship God alone, by their moral exhortations, and by accompanying miracles proving that their messages are of divine and not human origin. Some prophets also bring with them a Scripture: the Koran mentions the *Scrolls* of Abraham, the *Torah* of Moses, the *Psalms* of David, and the *Gospel* of Jesus. Some prophets also bring with them a new sacred law. In the Koran, the term that corresponds to this sacred law is *din,* now the ordinary term for "religion" in Arabic, and individual fundamental laws are termed *hudud Allah* ("God's limits"). However, the term for the sacred law that gained general acceptance from early Islamic history on is the *shari'a* ("the way, or path"), parallel to the Jewish term for the sacred law, *halacha* (also "the way, or path"). The *shari'a* is Islamic sacred law taken in toto: the

idealized system of all religious obligations God has imposed on believers.

Muslim scholars of the sacred law devote themselves to discovering the rulings of the *shari'a,* in effect seeking to determine God's intentions concerning the specific obligations of believers on the basis of available evidence. Law as a branch of academic study or as a product of human discourse is termed *fiqh* (literally, "understanding"). A jurist or specialist in law is termed *faqih* ("one who understands, is perspicacious.") The goal of the jurist is to determine reliably, given a set of circumstances—including time, place, identity of the legal agent, and so on—the legal status of particular possible acts. There are five main categories for the legal assessment of acts: forbidden (*haram*; e.g., marrying one's aunt); disfavored but allowed (*makruh*; e.g., a husband's repudiation of his wife without cause); indifferent (*mubah*; e.g., eating raisins); recommended but not obligatory (*mustahabb*; e.g., a man's marrying as soon as he can afford to do so); and obligatory (*wajib*; e.g., supporting one's elderly parents, fasting during the day in Ramadan). Other legal assessments, such as valid (*sahih*) and invalid (*batil*), do not apply to acts, but to contracts of sale or marriage contracts, for example. Islamic law is also a moral system; it is intended to preserve morality and not simply mete out justice. It does so by maintaining a stable social order, whereby the five cardinal values of religion, life, offspring, property, and rationality are conserved.

By the late eighth and early ninth centuries C.E., from which date the earliest extant compendia of the points of law, such as the *Kitab al-umm* of Muhammad b. Idris al-Shafi'i (d. 820), Islamic law was already a sophisticated science with a substantial tradition behind it. In such works, the law was organized into chapters in a more or less standard order, falling into three main sections: *'ibadat* ("devotions"), including ritual purity, prayer, almsgiving, fasting, the pilgrimage, and related topics; *mu'amalat* ("transactions, contracts"), including sales, debt, rental, pawning and mortgage, partnership, loans, inheritance, marriage, divorce, slavery, gifts, endowments, etc.; and *ahkam* ("verdicts"), including payment of indemnity for injuries, criminal punishments, and court procedure. Obviously, the law includes not only topics directly related to religious devotions and rituals but also general topics of family, commercial, and criminal law. Not all legal issues were addressed by the jurists in their theoretical writings, and even some that were rarely enforced by them. For example, Islamic penal law only prescribes punishments for six specific crimes: adultery or fornication, false accusation of adultery or fornication, robbery, drinking intoxicants, and banditry. Other offenses, except injury and murder, which are covered by *lex talionis,* or the payment of indemnity, are subject to discretionary punishments that may be determined by the ruler or the judges he has appointed. For this reason, large bodies of extra-religious law were created by various dynasties, the most developed example being that of the *qanun* of the Ottoman Empire, which covered many areas of public, fiscal, administrative, and criminal law. Islamic jurisprudence recognizes that not all areas are covered by the scriptural law, and it is generally held that *'urf,* or the custom of a particular locale, may serve as the basis of law as long as it does not contradict other legal principles. Custom has played a particularly important role in commercial arrangements, which varied widely from one area of the Muslim world to another.

As in Rabbinic Judaism, in Islam it was primarily expertise in the law that endowed one with religious authority. Although legislative authority, the right to set the law itself, theoretically belongs to God alone, interpretive or declarative authority belongs to the jurists, on the grounds that their interpretations represent the closest possible assessment of God's will with regard to legal questions. Other groups have claimed religious authority in the course of Islamic history, including theologians, mystics, and charismatic leaders, but the jurists have succeeded in establishing and justifying their authority as a group more than any other ever since the tenth century C.E. Nevertheless, the jurists regularly assumed the existence of an Islamic polity under a Muslim sovereign with absolute political authority. In a historical compromise, the jurists carefully delimited the sphere within which the sovereign could exercise his authority, granting him a great deal of latitude in public law, such as taxation and public safety, while endeavoring to maintain the jurists' own control over private law, including marriage, divorce, sales, and so on. There therefore exists something akin to a split between church and state, but it is between private and public law, and both the jurists and the rulers justify their position on claims to religious authority and divine sanction.

Islamic law differs from the common law in some important respects. In the Islamic judiciary system, there are no lawyers (i.e., advocates for the plaintiff or defendant), nor is there a jury. Trials are conducted by the judge, and the plaintiff and defendant represent themselves. They may call witnesses or produce evidence as needed. The decision is up to the judge alone, though he may consult other jurists, experts, and so on. Attached to the judge's court were one or more notary-witnesses (*shahid*) and a document clerk. Their function was to serve as character witnesses for the people of their district, draw up and execute legal documents, record the court proceedings, and certify the judge's verdicts and other documents. However, court decisions or judges' verdicts do not have law value; they do not set precedent, as in the common law system. Law value resides in the jurists' theoretical elaboration of the law, found in *fatwa*s ("consultative legal opinions" or "answers to legal questions"). The *fatwa* is a responsum to a legal question posed by a lay petitioner (*mustafti*) to a legal expert or issuer of legal opinions (*mufti*). The problem may be potential or actual, but the answer is not binding on the petitioner, in contrast with a judge's verdict, which must be carried out. It is this process of legal consultation and response, followed by the open debate of disputed questions among the available authorities, that creates new law. Nor were there traditionally any codes in Islamic law, in contrast with the Napoleonic legal system, and, surprisingly, with Rabbinic law since the sixteenth century, which has treated the *Shulchan Aruch* by Joseph Karo more or less as a code. All later development of the law is presented in the form of commentaries on that law. Scholarship to date has emphasized that Islamic law is a jurists' law, developed by the jurists themselves without governmental interference. It was therefore relatively uninfluenced by rulers' edicts and decrees. It was, however, shaped by two crucial institutions that have lasted from the tenth and eleventh centuries until the modern period: the *madhhab*,

which one may render variously as "legal school," "jurists' guild," or "tradition of legal study," and the *madrasa*, or college of law.

## Legal Literature and Institutions

The origins of Islamic law are obscure, mostly because many seminal works have been lost. As mentioned earlier, the oldest extant legal compendia show that the study of the law was already quite sophisticated; there are indications that its systematic formulation dates back to the first half of the eighth century. It is likely that it was significantly influenced in its early stages by Roman provincial, Byzantine, Sassanian, and Rabbinic law. A few specific instances of influence have been suggested, such as P. Crone's study on the law of the patronate, but scholarship in this field is still in its infancy. The theoretical development of the law seems to have taken off in Iraq under the Abbasid caliphate (750–1258 C.E.). By 900 C.E., all the main genres of legal literature had been established, including extensive legal compendia (*mabsut*), epitomes of the points of law (*mukhtasar*), collections of model legal documents (*shurut, watha'iq*), collections of model court records (*mahadir, sijillat*), manuals for judges (*adab al-qadi, adab al-qada'*), collections of responsa (*fatawa, masa'il*), and manuals of jurisprudence or legal method and interpretation (*usul al-fiqh*).

In the course of the ninth and tenth centuries, the *madhhab*s, or schools of law, were formed, in an attempt, it has been claimed, to maintain autonomy from the caliph and exclude the dogmatic theologians and sectarian groups from religious authority. They had no charters, patents, or membership lists; their organization was informal. Nevertheless, by the mid-tenth century, it became impossible to study and teach Islamic law without belonging to one of the established schools. Six legal *madhhab*s, each named after a famous jurist of the past, gained recognition in Sunni Islam: the Hanafi *madhhab*, named after Abu Hanifah (d. 767); the Maliki *madhhab*, named after Malik b. Anas (d. 795); the Shafi'i *madhhab*, named after Muhammad b. Idris al-Shafi'i (d. 820); the Hanbali *madhhab*, named after Ahmad b. Hanbal (d. 855); the Dawudi or Zahiri *madhhab*, named after Dawud b. Khalaf al-Isbahani (d. 884); and the Jariri *madhhab*, named after Muhammad b. Jarir al-Tabari (d. 923). The projection of the institution back to the time of these jurists is anachronistic except in the case of al-Tabari, and perhaps Dawud b. Khalaf. The Dawudi and Jariri *madhhab*s, although important in the tenth century, dwindled and died out in the eleventh; the four remaining *madhhab*s survived until modern times. In general, the jurists of the *madhhab*s recognized each other's traditions as legitimate and their opinions on disputed legal questions as equally valid. Together, the four surviving legal *madhhab*s have represented Sunni legal orthodoxy, an idea confirmed by such historical developments as the establishment of four chief judgeships, one for each *madhhab*, under the Mamluks (1250–1517) in Egypt and Syria. They played the crucial role in shaping legal interpretation and the transmission of legal knowledge, and at the same time provided a strong element of continuity and homogeneity in Islamic society over space and time.

Closely related to the *madhhab* was the institution of the *madrasa*, or college of law, which began in the eleventh century in Baghdad with the founding of the Nizamiyya in 1067 and subsequently spread throughout the Muslim world. The

**New Dictionary of the History of Ideas**

*madrasa* was usually a building that provided space for teaching large classes as well as lodging for students, often on an upper story. It was supported by a perpetual endowment (*waqf*) that generated income from the produce of agricultural land or the rent from a row of shops, for example. These funds paid the salaries of the overseer of the endowment (*nazir, mutawalli*), the professor of law (*mudarris*), the repetitor (*mùid*), and other staff, as well as student stipends, repairs, and other expenses. Generally, the *madrasa* was devoted in the endowment deed (*waqfiyya*) to the law of one of the four *madhhab*s and had one professor who taught the law of that *madhhab*. Stipends were also provided for students who studied the law of that particular *madhhab*. *Madrasa*s soon became the most important institutions of learning in the Muslim world. They tended to exclude the teaching of the Greek sciences, including philosophy, medicine, astronomy, and so on, relegating their teaching to private settings, and to accept the teaching of other religious sciences, such as Arabic grammar, rhetoric, hadith, scriptural commentary, and so on, but as ancillary to the study of the law. The system of legal education that developed in conjunction with the *madhhab* and the *madrasa* involved three main levels: ancillary studies in Arabic grammar, rhetoric, and related fields; intermediate study of the legal tradition of the *madhhab*; and advanced study on the disputed questions of the law (*khilaf*). Disputation and dialectic (*jadal*) were major foci of the advanced law student's training; they played an important role in the elaboration of the law. Certainly by the thirteenth century, but possibly earlier, the completion of legal study was recognized by the conferral of a diploma termed the *ijazat il-ifta' wa'l-tadris* ("authorization to grant legal responsa and teach law"), granted by a master jurist to his student.

## Jurisprudence: The "Sources" of the Law

Overall, the main focus of Muslim jurists has been the interpretation of scripture. Classical Sunni Islamic jurisprudence has at its heart a theory of four "roots," or bases, of the law, generally listed as (1) the Koran, (2) the *Sunna* of the Prophet Muhammad, (3) consensus (*ijma'*), and (4) legal analogy (*qiyas*). The Koran is granted pride of place as a legal source, yet many do not realize how little of the law is based on the text of the Koran itself. Muslim jurists reckoned that only five hundred verses of the Koran, about one-thirteenth of the entire text, have legal content. A genre of legal literature styled *Ayat al-ahkam* ("The Verses of Legal Rulings") developed that was a commentary on these verses in particular, extracting the legal content. Of these verses, many are not very specific, such as the many commands to hold prayer and give alms that do not specify how, when, and where to perform these actions.

In addition to the Koran, early jurisprudence relied on *Sunna*, which seems to have originally meant the general or time-honored usage of the community, and *ra'y*, which at this stage meant "sound opinion" or "considered opinion." With the work of al-Shafi'i, and generally for Sunnis in the course of the ninth century, it became standard theory that there was not one scripture in Islam, but actually two. The definition of *Sunna* narrowed to refer to the usage of the Prophet, and then further narrowed to mean "the usage of the Prophet as established

by *hadith*," oral reports concerning the Prophet's statements and behavior transmitted from the Companions, early Muslims who were eyewitnesses of the Prophet's mission. These reports were gathered and published in collections arranged according to the Companion transmitters (*musnad*), or in collections arranged for easy reference by jurists according to the standard chapters of the law (*sunan*). Six collections, dating from the middle to late ninth century, came to be recognized as more or less canonical by Sunni Muslims of all *madhhab*s: the *Sahih*s of al-Bukhari (d. 870), Muslim (d. 875), and al-Tirmidhi (d. 892), and the *Sunan* of Ibn Majah (d. 886), Abu Dawud (d. 888), and al-Nasa'i (d. 915). In the ninth and tenth centuries, the relative importance of hadith as a body of scripture was highly contested. Some rationalist jurists threw it out completely; most rationalists restricted the use of individual reports severely, setting very stringent requirements for establishing its authenticity. Many traditionalists, on the other hand, based their understanding of the law almost entirely on hadith reports and sought thereby to emulate the Prophet's *sunna*, or exemplary behavior, as closely as possible, even in everyday matters such as trimming one's mustache and letting one's beard grow long, or using a *miswak* twig as a sort of toothbrush. They set out to avoid all innovations, *bid'a* in opposition to *sunna*, which could lead one into error. Even these traditionalist scholars realized that many hadith reports were forged: some hadiths spoke for and against sectarian and other theological positions that had only arisen generations after the Prophet. Others contained translations of Bible verses or other Jewish or Christian lore. They devised criteria for establishing the authenticity of hadith reports, but most of these were formal, probabilistic criteria, based on examination of the authorities in the chain of transmission (*isnad*) of the hadith report. If they were all known to be reliable and each could have met the preceding person in the chain, then the report was considered formally reliable, even if the text itself was recognized to be odd.

In the genre of *usul al-fiqh*, Islamic jurisprudence developed sophisticated scriptural hermeneutics, focusing on the interpretation of God's address (*khitab Allah*) to mankind, in which He conveyed the law. Particular attention was paid to commands (*awamir*) and prohibitions (*nawahi*) in the text, for they establish obligations and set up legal boundaries. Several concepts were developed to cope with apparent contradictions in the text, including abrogation, according to which a later prooftext canceled out the legal effect of an earlier prooftext, the distinction between general and particular prooftexts, which allowed jurists to distinguish the intended audience or set of legal agents to which a particular command was addressed. Over the centuries, the discussions of these topics grew more and more elaborate and linguistically sophisticated, anticipating a number of theories of modern linguistics and philosophy by many centuries.

The third "source" of the law according to classical Sunni jurisprudence was consensus, usually defined as "the unanimous agreement of legal authorities of a given generation on a particular legal." This has often been confused with popular opinion, but is in essence the agreement of the community of interpretation constituted by qualified master jurists, after debate has subsided. The existence of consensus is established through the absence of dissent. The legal questions subject to consensus, together with the disputed questions, on which a number of authoritative variant opinions are held, form the range of orthodox opinion.

The fourth "source" of the law has been variously designated as *qiyas* ("legal analogy") or *ijtihad* ("exhaustive investigation"). They both came about in an attempt to eschew *ra'y* ("considered opinion") as a source of the law and to tie elaboration of the law more closely to scripture. By the tenth century, and particularly in traditionalist circles, *ra'y* came to take on the pejorative meaning "completely unfounded or idiosyncratic opinion," as opposed to its early usage. All four Sunni *madhhab*s eventually renounced *ra'y* and accepted *qiyas*. *Qiyas*, in its simplest form, is an analogy tying the ruling of Y to the ruling of X based on a crucial similarity, termed the *'illa* ("cause") of the ruling. For example, it is established from the Koranic text that drinking alcoholic beverages is forbidden, but there are no scriptural texts that apply to other drugs, such as hashish or opium. If jurists could show (1) that God declared drinking alcoholic beverages forbidden specifically because they intoxicate and (2) that hashish and opium intoxicate in a manner similar to alcohol, then the consumption of hashish or opium should also be forbidden. The jurists of the short-lived Zahiri *madhhab* rejected *qiyas* altogether, arguing that it is impossible for humans to assign a cause to God's legal declarations without explicit designation in scripture. To do so is to usurp God's legislative power. *Qiyas* also came to serve as a general rubric encompassing a number of logical arguments, many of which were not actually based on analogy, including *reductio ad absurdum, a fortiori,* and other logical arguments.

*Ijtihad* (literally, "effort") is the term used to describe the process of legal interpretation undertaken by a qualified expert in jurisprudence. Such an expert is termed a *mujtahid* and is forbidden from adopting the opinions of other experts on authority (*taqlid*). Only a layman, or a jurist who is not fully qualified, is permitted to perform *taqlid*. A great deal of controversy surrounds the term *ijtihad;* it was until recently commonplace to claim that "the gate of *ijtihad*" was closed long ago, as early as the ninth or tenth century, and that from that time forward, "independent" interpretation was forbidden. This is not true. Those who claimed that the gate of *ijtihad* was closed meant that it was forbidden or impossible to establish a new legal *madhhab,* not that there was a moratorium on independent thought. Manuals of jurisprudence throughout the middle ages and up until the present have stressed the necessity of performing *ijtihad* on the part of the qualified jurist, and Muslim jurists have been addressing novel issues in the law and coming up with new interpretations throughout history. Nevertheless, it is true that many jurists felt that their interpretative leeway had narrowed considerably by the late middle ages and that they were constrained by the tradition of their own *madhhab* in ways that earlier jurists had not been.

By the eleventh and twelfth centuries, Sunni jurists had come to accept the role of probability in legal interpretation. In the absence of clear scriptural prooftexts, the individual jurist, after exhaustive investigation of a legal question, professed that answer that was preponderant in his mind. This opinion did not rest on certitude (*yaqin*) but on strong presumption (*ghalabat al-zann*). Although it was not guaranteed to be correct, the *mujtahid* was not held to have sinned for coming up with the wrong answer as long as he had investigated the topic exhaustively, and the lay petitioner was permitted to perform his religious obligations according to this opinion. Probable answers to legal questions acquired authority in the absence of a certain answer.

## The Modern Period

In the modern era, traditional Islamic law and its institutions have been eclipsed by secular law and institutions at the hands of the colonial powers and modern nation-states. In most Muslim nations, the endowment properties that supported legal education have been confiscated by the government and put under the control of a government ministry. The professors and others who teach and work in these institutions have become government employees. Secular education has radically reduced the importance of the *madrasa*s in the contemporary world. There has been a widespread application of Western legal codes, whether the Napoleonic code or the related Swiss code, on the law of modern nation-states in the Muslim world, especially in the areas of commercial and criminal law. The only areas that have remained under the purview of Islamic law in most countries are family law, including marriage, divorce, inheritance, and related topics. In these areas, the flexibility of the law has been radically reduced by attempts to establish a standard code. In British India, for example, the *Hidaya* by al-Marghinani (d. 1196), *Minhaj al-talibin* by al-Nawawi (d. 1277), and *Shara'i' al-Islam* by al-Muhaqqiq al-Hilli (d. 1276) were chosen to serve as the law codes for Hanafi Sunnis, Shafi'i Sunnis, and Twelver Shiis, respectively.

At the same time, beginning in the nineteenth century, Muslim reformers such as Muhammad 'Abduh, Rashid Rida, and others attempted to reform Islamic law from within. Approaches have varied widely. Some thinkers have criticized the insularity of the individual *madhhab*s, arguing for a sustained study of comparative law (*fiqh muqaran*) within traditional institutions. Other methods include choosing freely (*takhayyur*) among the opinions of past authorities, or combining the legal doctrines of various *madhhab*s to come up with an appropriate solution, a process termed *talfiq* ("patching, piecing together"). These last methods have been used in many actual reforms of Islamic family law, such as the well-known reform of Anglo-Muhammadan law that drew on the Maliki tradition to alter Hanafi marriage law so as to facilitate access to divorce for women in bad marriages. Other, more radical thinkers have argued that the law of the *madhhab*s should be jettisoned altogether and that a new Islamic law should be derived directly from the scripture, from the Koran alone, or from that portion of the Koran that was revealed at Mecca. These radical reforms have met with little success, as most movement in the Muslim world today seems to be in the opposite direction. In Saudi Arabia, Iran under the Islamic Republic, Afghanistan under the Taliban, and Sudan, various forms of Islamic law have been applied. In addition, Islamist political groups throughout the Muslim world are clamoring for application of the *shari'a* in an attempt to fend off Western cultural influence, fight corruption, and engender public morality and social

# LEADERSHIP

justice. The classical legal system has not lost its vitality, and, given the centrality of a divinely ordained law to Islam, it cannot easily be replaced or substituted.

*See also* **Islam; Law; Sacred Texts: Koran.**

BIBLIOGRAPHY

Anderson, J. N. D. *Law Reform in the Muslim World.* London: Athlone Press, 1976.

Coulson, Noel J. *A History of Islamic Law.* Edinburgh: Edinburgh University Press, 1964.

Crone, Patricia. *Roman, Provincial, and Islamic Law: The Origin of the Islamic Patronate.* Cambridge, U.K.: Cambridge University Press, 1987.

Hallaq, Wael B. *A History of Islamic Legal Theories: An Introduction to Sunni Usul al-Fiqh.* Cambridge, U.K.: Cambridge University Press, 1997.

Johansen, Baber. *Contingency in a Sacred Law: Legal and Ethical Norms in the Muslim Fiqh.* Boston: Brill, 1999.

Kamali, Mohammad H. *Principles of Islamic Jurisprudence.* Cambridge, U.K.: Islamic Texts Society, 1991.

Makdisi, George. *The Rise of Colleges: Institutions of Learning in Islam and the West.* Edinburgh: Edinburgh University Press, 1981.

Melchert, Christopher. *The Formation of the Sunni Schools of Law, 9th–10th Centuries C.E.* Boston: Brill, 1997.

Reinhart, A Kevin. *Before Revelation: The Boundaries of Muslim Moral Thought.* Albany: State University of New York Press, 1995.

as-Sadr, Muhammad Baqir. *Lessons in Islamic Jurisprudence.* Translated by Roy Parviz Mottahedeh. Oxford: Oneworld Press, 2003.

Schacht, Joseph. *Introduction to Islamic Law.* Oxford: Clarendon, 1964.

———. *The Origins of Muhammadan Jurisprudence.* Oxford: Clarendon, 1950.

Weiss, Bernard. *The Search for God's Law: Islamic Jurisprudence in the Writings of Sayf al-Din al-Amidi.* Salt Lake City: University of Utah Press, 1992.

———. *The Spirit of Islamic Law.* Athens: University of Georgia Press, 1998.

*D. J. Stewart*

**LEADERSHIP.** Although there are seemingly as many descriptions of leadership as there are men and women who fill leadership roles, most meaningful definitions echo the one commonly ascribed to former U.S. president Harry S. Truman: leadership is the ability to get others to willingly move in a new direction in which they are not naturally inclined to move on their own. While the related but distinct concept of *authority* has since antiquity been a subject for scholarly analysis, the field of *leadership theory and development* has emerged more recently. It is primarily an American phenomenon, although its influence has quickly spread across continents.

## Leadership in Historical Context

Of the myriad forms of human and social capital, leadership may be the most rare and precious. One can point to hundreds of companies that were collapsing despite legions of consultants and new plans and policies, until finally its chief executive officer was removed, a new head was brought in, and the company turned around as though by magic. History abounds with similar examples among armies, universities, churches, and nations.

Conversely, the untimely loss of a talented and effective leader can prove disastrous for the organization she was leading. Try as they may, a succession of new leaders cannot stem the inexorable decline of the very same organization that a few months or years before was at the peak of health and vitality.

Moreover, sometimes whole societies lose their ability to produce great leaders. There are numerous cases of societies that lost their earlier, highly developed culture and retrogressed to a more primitive way of life. In some of these cases, external factors such as invasion or drought played a role, but in many cases it would seem that the retrogression was due to a failure of will and a lack of leadership.

### History's Slaves or History's Masters?
A striking contrast in worldviews about leadership can be found in the writings of Leo Tolstoy, who believed that history shapes and determines leaders, versus those of Thomas Carlyle, who believed that leaders shape and determine history. In his epilogue to *War and Peace,* Tolstoy contended that kings and generals are history's slaves. Tolstoy believed that leaders merely ride the crests of historical waves that have been set in motion by myriad forces beyond these leaders' control or comprehension. "Every act of theirs, which appears to them an act of their own free will," wrote Tolstoy, "is in an historical sense involuntary and is related to the whole cause of history and predestined from eternity."

On the other side is Carlyle, the nineteenth-century British historian and essayist, who was convinced that "history is the biography of great men," the greatest of them being kings. The very word *king,* Carlyle contended, derives from the ancient word *Can-ning,* which means "Able-man" (although his etymology can be disputed). In Carlyle's view, the Ablemen (and Ablewomen) of the human species direct the course of history and determine humanity's destiny.

### Leadership as a Skill
Learned examinations of the lives of great leaders abound, among them Arrian's *History of Alexander* and Plutarch's *Parallel Lives,* bona fide leadership manuals have been relatively rare; only a few have survived the centuries, among them Niccolò Machiavelli's *The Prince* and Sun Tzu's *The Art of War.* Most such works were military in nature, where meritocracies tended to flourish.

Popular opinion through the ages has typically held that leadership flows from the throne of the gods to a privileged few, as evidenced by most societies' willing subjection to and adulation for inherited royalty. In the biblical account contained in the first book of Samuel, the Israelites beg Yahweh to abandon his plans for a pure theocracy, asking in exchange not for democracy but for "a king to lead us." The equation began to change at the end of the global tendency toward dynastic succession and the advent of republican government and other broad meritocracies.

Currently, in an era that can be considered far more Carlylean than Tolstoyan in its worldview, the analysis of living and dead authorities has given way to a dramatic development: the belief that leaders can and should be trained. The worldwide explosion of leadership study and leadership development is an even more recent phenomenon, launched primarily at American universities. Beginning in the 1960s, the most informed academic opinions held that leadership could be taught effectively if prevalent past assumptions about human nature could be overcome. The concept grew in popularity through the 1970s and 1980s, and the result by the turn of the twenty-first century was a $250 billion industry—the amount spent annually on management training and executive education around the world.

Leadership theory and development was to a degree an offshoot of inquiry into organizational life, as industry and government bureaucracies evolved rapidly, with figures such as Vienna-born economist and management editor Peter Drucker forging roles as key commentators. Theories of organizational life gradually gave way to theories of leadership as an exalted vocation.

Once scholars began not only to assess the impact of leaders but to dissect the traits that fueled their success, a legion of authors and consultants rose up to offer seven habits, ten techniques, or twenty secrets of top leaders. Eventually American corporations, universities, and even secondary schools began setting aside funds for leadership development programs.

## The Rise of Contemporary Leadership Theory

Theories of leadership in any period are driven by a set of convictions and hopes on the part of the theorist. One conviction is that rapid societal evolution makes it imperative to keep one's pulse on social changes and their implications for how groups of human beings can best be led, an inherent assumption in the writings of leadership theorist Rosabeth Moss Kanter and numerous other scholars. A competing view is that human nature is static and unchanging and that the lasting lessons of history provide surer instruction in leadership than do the passing ripples of modernity. Ironically, the exemplars of this view are relatively ancient figures such as Lao Tzu and Machiavelli.

A core Western assumption about leadership is that leaders who succeed have "vision," a tangible end goal toward which they and their followers can strive. But countless Eastern leaders have been more influenced by the worldview of Lao Tzu, who observed, "A good traveler has no fixed plans and is not intent upon arriving. . . . Let go of fixed plans and concepts, and the world will govern itself" (Lao Tzu, chapters 27 and 57).

In a related manner, some maintain that the leader must be an idealist set on speaking to that which is highest, while others hold that a leader must be a realist who is aware of human limitations. Plato contended in *The Republic* that:

> until philosophers are kings, or the kings and princes of this world have the spirit and power of philosophy, and political greatness and wisdom meet in one, and those

commoner natures who pursue either to the exclusion of the other are compelled to stand aside, cities will never have rest from their evils.

Yet as though he were responding directly to Plato, Machiavelli soberly observed in *The Prince* almost two thousand years later:

> Many have imagined republics and principalities which have never been seen or known to exist in reality; for how we live is so far removed from how we ought to live, that he who abandons what is done for what ought to be done will rather bring about his own ruin than his preservation; for a man who strives after goodness in all his acts is sure to come to ruin, since there are so many who are not good. Hence it is necessary that a prince who is interested in his survival learn to be other than good, making use of this capacity or refraining from it according to the need.

The collective tendency has tilted toward idealism in recent decades. This shift is not a current echo of Plato's philosopher-king. It is, rather, an expression of *democratic* ideals, positing an assumption that intrinsic in human nature is a capacity to lead that only need be unearthed and cultivated in order to flourish.

The participative management and leadership style ascendant in the late twentieth century was exemplified by the work of Douglas McGregor of the Massachusetts Institute of Technology (MIT). In his landmark work, *The Human Side of Enterprise* (1960), McGregor distinguished between a traditional Theory X, which fundamentally viewed humanity in a negative light (the view classically ascribed to Machiavelli), and a newly emerging Theory Y, which viewed human beings in a more positive light. Given Theory X's assumption that human beings are essentially flawed and resistant to work, a successful leader presumably needed to manage them in an authoritarian manner, with rigorous controls.

McGregor heralded his new Theory Y, which demonstrated that human beings are far more willing to invest themselves in their work if it bears personal meaning. If they can escape the suffocation of being overmanaged and begin to make a collaborative investment through their labor, they will bring untapped new fountains of creativity and energy to an organization or cause. The democratic model of organizational leadership began to develop, with its flattened organizational pyramids and concepts such as empowerment and shared vision.

Unlike the so-called hard sciences, the tenets of the social sciences cannot readily be subjected to the test of falsification, and, as a consequence, are often viewed with suspicion. Nevertheless, since the mid-1950s, the social sciences produced a large number of attractive theories of leadership. Management expert Tom Peters noted that Warren Bennis's work at MIT during the 1960s "foreshadowed—and helped bring about—the early twenty-first century's headlong plunge into less hierarchical, more democratic and adaptive institutions, both public and private." Bennis, a protégé of McGregor, found

LEADERSHIP

among other things that hierarchical and autocratic approaches were the best way for teams to carry out simple tasks, while democratic and collaborative approaches were the best way for teams to carry out complex tasks. In such cases, all team members experienced a high average level of contentment in their work, unlike in hierarchical arrangements, where the top person enjoyed maximum contentment and the others experienced minimum contentment.

American corporations were shaped most dramatically by such new models. The gradually increasing tendency toward participative management received a kick-start in the 1980s, when American and European business executives came to admire their Japanese counterparts. Japanese industry was remarkable for its emphasis on the group rather than the individual, and for team processes and a participative work style. Not out of idealism but out of pure self-interest, Western managers began to adopt similar practices. Within a few years, programs for and courses in leadership theory and development were more often housed in American universities' business schools than in departments of political science, psychology, history, or social science. For many years this resulted in an amoral emphasis on technique rather than ethics—in other words, democratic leadership was good for the bottom line as opposed to being intrinsically right—although some business-school-based experts such as Bennis and James O'Toole championed a more deontological approach.

By the last decade of the twentieth century, few successful American leaders in any profit-seeking or not-for-profit organization had avoided participating in at least one seminar, visioning session, or strategic-planning task force built on democratic management principles. However, the good intentions of democratically inclined managers and consultants collided with the limitations of human nature—and a wave of satire (as evidenced in the "Dilbert" comic strip) and public cynicism followed. This cynicism, or frustrated idealism, offers a study in contrasts with Machiavelli's brutal unsentimentality, which had seemingly been discredited by modern practitioners of democratic management and leadership. Machiavelli was above all a coolly detached student of human nature. His repeated advice to leaders was to believe in the *reality* of human nature, as opposed to what they *wished* it were.

Quoted again more widely in an era of renewed global realpolitik, Machiavelli has proved to be neither inerrant nor irrelevant. He illustrated sides of human nature that must be closely examined by every leader, painful though that process may be. The good news for leaders is that there are nobler facets of human nature that have just as great a chance of asserting themselves as those identified by Machiavelli. As such, his greatest legacy may be his ability to help leaders develop a more integrated understanding of human nature and leadership.

**Theories in Flux**

Just as popular and scholastic leadership theory has been shaped and reshaped by the epochs of industrialization, bureaucratization, the communications revolution, and the widespread entry of women into management, leadership theory will continue to undergo changes, determined in part by prevailing societal values such as idealism or realism.

Through it all, a middle ground appears to exist between Tolstoy's persuasive fatalism and Carlyle's enthusiastic activism. It may well be that this world is largely Tolstoyan, subject to historical forces that no man or woman can fully measure and analyze and the consequences of which no person can fully predict. To that extent, leaders are in fact history's slaves. However, Carlyle's Ablemen (and Ablewomen) have still made an impact on the course of human events; their decisions have had a lasting influence on the world, so that historical determinism has never quite had the final word.

Finally, leadership tends to be remarkably situational and contingent: what works for one person at one point in time will not necessarily work for everyone else or even for that person at a different time. Thus, in a very real sense, leadership is an art, not a science. Effective management may be a science (though that too is questionable), but effective leadership is most certainly an art. In this sense, leadership is more akin to music, painting, and poetry than it is to more routinized endeavors. And just as there is no comprehensive theory of art, there is no comprehensive theory of leadership.

Every leader is therefore locked in a moment-to-moment struggle with the context and circumstances of his own place and time. This excruciating yet exhilarating aspect of leadership is what makes the study of great historical figures so timelessly appealing—and, in this democratic age, makes millions of would-be leaders such eager students of this peculiar calling.

*See also* **Authority; Machiavellism; Power.**

BIBLIOGRAPHY

PRIMARY SOURCES

Arrian. *The Campaigns of Alexander.* London: Penguin, 1976.
Bible, The. The life of David, in I and II Samuel; Jesus, in Matthew; and Paul, in Acts. Various editions, including the Revised Standard Edition.
Confucius. *The Analects.* Translated by Arthur Waley. New York: Vintage, 1989.
Dante. *The Divine Comedy.* Translated by John Ciardi. New York: Norton, 1977. Significant for its portrayal of the full range of human triumphs and foibles.
Lao Tzu. *The Tao Te Ching.* Translated by Stephen Mitchell. New York: Perennial, 1992.
Machiavelli, Niccolò. *The Prince.* Translated by George Bull. New York: Bantam, 1984. One of the most enduring and significant leadership manuals, with some fifty editions currently in print.
Plato. *The Republic.* New York: Oxford University Press, 1951.
Shakespeare, William. *Hamlet.* New York: Oxford University Press, 1998. Shakespeare's plays offer insight into the human condition and human motivations, a deep understanding of which is required for leadership. *Hamlet,* in particular, gives humanity a terrifying look inside itself.
———. *Othello.* New York: Oxford University Press, 2002. Offers a view of how a leader is undone by an evil lieutenant.
Sophocles. *Antigone.* Translated by Richard Emil Braun. New York: Oxford University Press, 1990. Notable for its display of the pitfalls of rigidity in a leader.

Sun Tzu. *The Art of War*. Translated by Ralph D. Sawyer. Boulder, Colo.: Westview Press, 1994.

SECONDARY SOURCES

Bennis, Warren. *On Becoming a Leader*. Reading, Mass.: Addison Wesley, 1989.

Carlyle, Thomas. *On Heroes, Hero Worship, and the Heroic in History*. New York: Ginn and Co., 1902. Notable for its theory of leadership in contrast to that of Tolstoy.

Drucker, Peter. *The Essential Drucker: Selections from the Management Works of Peter F. Drucker*. New York: HarperBusiness, 2001. A significant modern leadership book.

Kanter, Rosabeth Moss. *The Change Masters: Innovations for Productivity in the American Corporation*. New York: Simon and Schuster, 1983.

———. *When Giants Learn to Dance: Mastering the Challenge of Strategy, Management, and Careers in the 1990s*. New York: Simon and Schuster, 1989.

McGregor, Douglas. *The Human Side of Enterprise*. New York: McGraw-Hill, 1960.

O'Toole, James. *Leading Change: The Argument for Values-Based Leadership*. New York: Ballantine, 1996.

Tolstoy, Leo. *War and Peace*. Translated by Louise and Aylmer Maude. New York: Oxford University Press, 1931. Of interest for its theory of leadership, in contrast to that of Carlyle.

*Steven B. Sample*

# LEARNING AND MEMORY, CONTEMPORARY VIEWS.

People have long wondered how best to characterize learning and memory. Most people typically conceive of memory as a place in which information is stored. As Henry Roediger has noted, this spatial metaphor has dominated the study of memory: "We speak of storing memories, of searching for and locating them. We organize our thoughts; we look for memories that have been lost, and if we are fortunate, we find them" (1980, p. 232). Aristotle compared memory to a wax tablet, Plato invoked the image of an aviary, and St. Augustine of Hippo suggested similarities to a cave. Increasingly, the metaphors involved the most recent or most impressive technological accomplishment, as with René Descartes and his analogy to the water-powered automata in the French royal gardens and later by comparisons to the gramophone (an updating of the wax-tablet metaphor) and then a telephone exchange.

The so-called "cognitive revolution" that began in the mid-1950s ushered in the information-processing approach to the study of learning and memory. The main metaphor became the computer; people were seen as general-purpose processors of information capable of manipulating internal representations. As with computers, there was an emphasis on the interaction between hardware and software, usually relabeled structure and process, respectively. By the end of the 1960s, the standard view of memory was the modal model (after the statistical term *mode*) with its set of stores, registers, and buffers. Structuralist views continue to use the spatial metaphor and emphasize a memory system in which information is stored. According to these accounts, the store in which a memory resides determines the mnemonic properties.

An alternative to the structural approach is the proceduralist approach, which views memory not so much as a thing that is stored but rather as the result of a process. As David Wechsler put it, "Memories are not like filed letters stored in cabinets. . . . Rather, they are like melodies realized by striking the keys on a piano" (p. 151). The melodies are a by-product of pressing keys just as memory is a by-product of processing information. According to this account, the processing performed at encoding and retrieval determines the mnemonic properties.

Consider the essential difference between these two accounts. Within the modal model of the 1960s and early 1970s there were three memory structures: a sensory register, short-term memory (STM), and long-term memory (LTM). Information is first briefly registered in the appropriate sensory buffer, visual information in iconic memory, auditory information in echoic memory, and so on. These buffers hold raw physical information in an unanalyzed form for a very short period of time, perhaps 250 milliseconds. Additional processing is required to convert the information from its sensory form to a more durable representation that is held by short-term memory. Short-term memory serves mainly as a buffer in which information can be temporarily stored and has a limited capacity, usually given as 7 plus or minus 2 items. Items in short-term memory decay over time unless rehearsed; rehearsal is also the way in which information gets copied into long-term memory. Long-term memory is the main memory system and stores all knowledge. It has no known capacity limitations. Whereas information loss from short-term memory is thought to be permanent, it is unclear whether there is permanent loss from LTM.

Table 1 summarizes the essential points from the structuralist point of view. When an item is in STM, it will be stored using an acoustic code (how the word sounds), the capacity will be limited to 7 plus or minus 2 items, and the items will decay within about twenty seconds. In contrast, when an item is in LTM, it will be stored using a semantic code (what the word means), the capacity will be (almost) unlimited, and the item may very well never be forgotten.

A proceduralist would agree with almost everything the structuralist has proposed, except that the proceduralist would ask the following question: What does the top row in the table add to our understanding? In other words, we could delete the top row and still have a complete and accurate description of memory. When words are processed based on how they sound, there will be a very small capacity and the information will not be available for very long. When words are processed based on what they mean, however, there will be an enormous capacity, and the information will be available for a long time.

The divergence between the structuralist and proceduralist approaches has grown since the 1970s. One current debate concerns whether memory is best characterized as a set of

| | STM | LTM |
|---|---|---|
| **Format** | Acoustic | Semantic |
| **Capacity** | 7 ± 2 | Infinite (?) |
| **Duration** | 20 s | Infinite (?) |

independent systems—a continuation of the spatial metaphor—or as a set of interrelated processes (see, for example, Foster and Jelicic). This more modern structuralist approach has greatly changed the modal model and generally names five different memory systems. The proceduralist approach has refined the idea of memory as a by-product of processing to focus on the relationship between the processing performed at encoding and the processing performed at retrieval.

## The Structuralist Approach

Typically, structuralists are concerned not only with delineating the number of memory systems but also in locating them within the brain. Advocates of the systems approach identify five major memory systems: working memory, semantic memory, episodic memory, the perceptual representation system, and procedural memory.

Working memory is a system for the temporary maintenance and storage of internal information and can be thought of as the place where cognitive "work" is performed. It has multiple subsystems, most notably one for the processing of verbal or speech-like stimuli and another for the processing of visual-spatial information. Each features a store (the phonological store and the visual-spatial sketchpad) and a maintenance process that offsets decay (articulatory control process and the visual scribe). Unlike short-term memory, the capacity limit is based on a trade-off between the rehearsal process and decay.

Semantic memory refers to memory for general knowledge and includes facts, concepts, and vocabulary. The term is somewhat misleading, however, as it implies storage of only semantic information, which is not the case. Rather, the distinguishing feature of this system is the lack of conscious awareness of the learning episode. In contrast, episodic memory is the system that does provide this awareness of the learning episode and thus enables the individual to "travel back" mentally into his or her personal past, to use Endel Tulving's term. As an example of the difference, consider the fact—picked hopefully for its obscurity—that Samuel Beckett is the only first-class cricket player to win a Nobel Prize (he played for Dublin University and won the 1969 Nobel Prize for Literature). Imagine that two weeks from now you happen to participate in a conversation about Nobel Prizes, and you recall the above information about Samuel Beckett. If you remember reading the information in this book, where you were, whether it was hot or cold, or anything else about the episode other than the mere facts, then the information is said to be in episodic memory. If you remember only the fact itself, then the information is said to be in semantic memory.

All three of these systems are part of declarative memory, which is contrasted with procedural memory, the fourth proposed major memory system. Declarative memory is concerned with knowing "that" rather than with knowing "how." For example, if you know that two plus two equals four, the information is said to be in declarative memory. By contrast, if you know how to ride a bicycle, that information is said to be in procedural memory. One distinction is that you can usefully communicate declarative information but not procedural information: simply telling someone how to ride a bicycle (explaining balance, pedaling, and steering) does not work.

Finally, the perceptual representation system is a collection of non-declarative domain-specific modules that operate on perceptual information about the form and structure of words and objects. Although currently the dominant approach, the structuralist conception of memory is not without its problems.

First, there is little agreement on what the criteria should be for a memory system, let alone agreement on the number of systems. In particular, there are no criteria that result in producing just the five systems named above. The most well-specified criteria for determining whether two systems are separate were proposed by David Sherry and Daniel Schacter in 1987: (1) functional dissociations: an independent variable that has one effect on a task thought to tap system A either has no effect or a different effect on a task thought to tap system B; (2) different neural substrates: system A must depend on different brain regions than system B; (3) stochastic independence: performance on a task that taps system A should be uncorrelated with performance on a task that taps system B; and (4) functional incompatibility: a function carried out by system A cannot be performed by system B.

Henry Roediger, Randy Buckner, and Kathleen McDermott have shown how recall and recognition meet the first three of these criteria: the variable word frequency produces functional dissociations (high-frequency words are recalled better than low, but low-frequency words are recognized more accurately than high); neuropsychological dissociations between recall and recognition are observable in amnesiac subjects; and numerous studies have found essentially no correlation between performance on the two tests. A thought experiment suggests that recall and recognition might also demonstrate functional incompatibility: memory for odors is a function that is well supported by recognition (consider the case of Marcel Proust) but not very well supported by recall.

Second, the proposed systems have not yet been anatomically isolated (although it remains an empirical question whether they will be), and even when isolation is found, the results are often equivocal. For example, many studies show that retrieval in episodic tasks involves right prefrontal activation, whereas retrieval of semantic information involves left prefrontal activation. This neuropsychological distinction, however, reverses when the two tasks are equated for difficulty: retrieval of semantic information now produces larger amounts of right frontal activation than the episodic task.

Third, this view does not account for the general pattern of decline seen when normally healthy people get older. One would expect a systematic relationship between tasks that shows a decrement in performance and the underlying system. For example, one might expect that episodic memory might deteriorate faster than semantic memory. In fact one finds no such relationship. Performance on some episodic tasks is unaffected, whereas performance on some semantic tasks is quite impaired. Rather, the pattern of performance loss is better described based on the processes, especially those at retrieval.

## The Proceduralist Approach

The modern incarnation of the proceduralist approach began with the levels of processing framework of Fergus Craik and Robert Lockhart. Rather than viewing memory as something that is stored in a system, they viewed memory as the by-product of performing processing. Because the emphasis is on processing rather than on structure, Craik and Lockhart argued that the most informative research will occur when the experimenter has control over the processing and that therefore researchers should use an incidental learning procedure. The experimenter might ask the subject to judge whether two words rhyme or to judge which of two words has the most pleasant associations. The learning is "incidental" in that the subject is unaware that the material being processed will be tested later on and so is not intentionally trying to remember the information. The type of processing performed at retrieval can also be manipulated.

The basic premise of the transfer-appropriate processing account of memory is that memory will be best when the processing performed at encoding is appropriate given the processing demands required at test. For example, if you processed how an item sounds at encoding but the test emphasizes the meaning of the item, performance will be worse than if your processing focused on how the item sounds at both encoding and retrieval or than if your processing focused on the meaning of the item at both encoding and retrieval. This view offers an explanation for why intent to learn is not an important factor in subsequent tests of learning and memory: if a person uses an inappropriate process, performance will be poor regardless of the intent to learn.

This idea applies very generally. For example, context-dependent memory refers to the observation that memory can be worse when tested in a new or different context relative to performance in a condition in which the context remains the same at both encoding and retrieval. Context can refer to mood (such as happiness at both encoding and retrieval, sadness at both encoding and retrieval, or a mismatch) or to physical location (for example, underwater at both encoding and retrieval, on land at both encoding and retrieval, or a mismatch). One practical implication for divers is that if they memorize decompression tables on land, they may not remember them very well when needed, underwater. The idea is that if you are happy, you are likely to have quite different processing than if you are sad. Neither mood is inherently better (from a memory perspective); the point is that the results of processing while in a sad mood are different from the results of processing while in a happy mood.

One problem with the transfer-appropriate processing view is determining exactly which processes are being used. Larry Jacoby introduced the process dissociation technique, in which a subject is asked to perform two tasks. The experiment is set up so that on one task, two processes can contribute to memory performance, but on a second task, the processes work in opposition. Using this procedure, one can estimate the relative contribution of each process. It remains an empirical question whether this will result in a sufficiently detailed description of the various processes that can be used.

## Dynamic Memory

In addition to the divergence between the structuralist and the proceduralist views, another major difference between memory research now and memory research in the 1960s and 1970s is the emphasis on the dynamic, reconstructive nature of memory. Long gone is the library metaphor in which memory was like a book in a library that just sat on a shelf. Instead, memories are seen as being dynamically constructed and changed according to the current available information. It is now well documented that people can even remember things that never happened.

Memory is now viewed as inherently reconstructive. This term emphasizes that at the first retrieval attempt, one constructs a memory from all available information. At the second retrieval attempt, the memory is constructed again. Consider what happens when an event is retrieved and then retrieved a second time. At the first retrieval attempt, you will have two sources of information: memory of the event itself and general knowledge. At the second retrieval attempt, you have three sources of information: memory of the event itself, general knowledge, and memory of your first retrieval.

This process is nicely illustrated from experiments that intentionally try to implant a memory of an event that did not happen. For example, Ira Hyman and F. James Billings asked their subjects, college students, to recall as much information as they could about events from their early childhood. Each subject was asked about two to four events that actually occurred (according to the subject's parents) and one event that did not occur. This event supposedly happened when the subject was five years old and concerned going to a wedding and knocking over the punch bowl, spilling some punch on the bride's parents. Originally only 3 percent recalled the wedding episode, as it had not occurred. Two days later the subjects were again asked to recall as much as they could, and this time 27 percent indicated remembering the event. Subjects were also asked to rate their confidence in the accuracy of their memory. There was no difference in the confidence ratings for real or made-up events.

This is not an isolated finding. People who read a story and were then told that the main character of a story was Helen Keller were likely to remember reading the sentence, "She was deaf, dumb, and blind," even though that sentence was not presented. A student in one of my memory classes had a memory of a favorite pet golden retriever. After hearing my lecture on this topic, she checked with her parents: the dog had died two years before she was born. Apparently she had heard stories about the dog and had seen slides featuring the dog and was attributing memory of these as memory of real events.

Studies from the eyewitness memory literature show that eyewitnesses readily incorporate information from questions into their recollections of events. Unless there is objective evidence available, there is no way of assessing the accuracy of recollection of an eyewitness: they may be very accurate, very inaccurate, or somewhere in the middle. Among the many factors that do not predict subsequent accuracy are the duration of the event; the emotional intensity of the event; the unusualness of the event; the number of details that can be recalled;

the confidence expressed about the memory; and the delay between the event and the subsequent questioning.

Memory then is fundamentally active, dynamic, and reconstructive. Like other cognitive processes, memory processes recruit information from a variety of sources, including from memory of the event itself as well as from generic knowledge, memory of past recollections of the event, and even inferences, with the goal of constructing a sensible, coherent memory.

*See also* **Computer Science; Language and Linguistics; Psychology and Psychiatry.**

BIBLIOGRAPHY

Baddeley, Alan D. *Working Memory.* New York: Oxford University Press, 1986.

Craig, Fergus, and Robert Lockhart. "Levels of Processing: A Framework for Memory Research." *Journal of Verbal Learning and Verbal Behavior* 11 (1972): 671–684.

Foster, Jonathan K., and Marko Jelicic, eds. *Memory: Systems, Process, or Function?* New York: Oxford University Press, 1999.

Hyman, Ira E., and F. James Billings. "Individual Differences and the Creation of False Childhood Memories." *Memory* 6 (1998): 1–20.

Jacoby, Larry. "A Process Dissociation Framework: Separating Automatic from Intentional Uses of Memory." *Journal of Memory and Language* 30 (1991): 513–541.

Neath, Ian, and Aimée M. Surprenant. *Human Memory: An Introduction to Research, Data, and Theory.* 2nd ed. Belmont, Calif.: Thomson/Wadsworth, 2003.

Parkin, Alan J. "Component Processes versus Systems: Is There Really an Important Difference?" In *Memory: Systems, Process, or Function?* edited by Jonathan K. Foster and Marko Jelicic, 273–287. Oxford: Oxford University Press, 1999.

Roediger, Henry L. "Memory Metaphors in Cognitive Psychology." *Memory and Cognition* 8 (1980): 231–246.

Roediger, Henry L., Randy L. Buckner, and Kathleen B. McDermott. "Components of Processing." In *Memory: Systems, Process, or Function?* edited by Jonathan K. Foster and Marko Jelicic, 32–65. New York: Oxford University Press, 1999.

Schacter, Daniel L., Anthony D. Wagner, and Randy L. Buckner. "Memory Systems of 1999." In *The Oxford Handbook of Memory,* edited by Endel Tulving and Fergus I. M. Craik, 627–643. New York: Oxford University Press, 2000.

Sherry, David F., and Daniel L. Schacter. "The Evolution of Multiple Memory Systems." *Psychological Review* 94 (1987): 439–454.

Tulving, Endel. *Elements of Episodic Memory.* New York: Oxford University Press, 1983.

Wechsler, David B. "Engrams, Memory Storage, and Mnemonic Coding." *American Psychologist* 18 (1963): 149–153.

*Ian Neath*

# LEGALISM, ANCIENT CHINA.

Legalism (*fa jia*) is a label applied since the second century B.C.E. to a group of Chinese thinkers of the Warring States period (453–221 B.C.E.). The label is doubly misleading: first, because the thinkers concerned did not necessarily consider themselves members of a unified intellectual current, much less a common school of

thought; and second, because the notion of law (*fa*), albeit important, is by no means central in the thought of all these thinkers. Legalism is thus not a scientific category but rather a scholarly convention.

Major sources for Legalist thought are the works attributed to the leading Legalist thinkers, Shang Yang (d. 338 B.C.E.), Shen Buhai (d. 337 B.C.E.), Shen Dao (fl. late fourth century B.C.E.), and Han Feizi (d. 233 B.C.E.), as well as portions of the Warring States collectanea, the *Guanzi* and *Lüshi chunqiu.* Of these only the first has undisputed Legalist credentials, while the intellectual affiliation of the others is constantly questioned. These disputes notwithstanding, we may discern several major approaches that characterize these thinkers and texts and distinguish them from contemporary intellectual currents. First, all of them sought to strengthen the state versus society through the perfection of a centralized bureaucratic mechanism. Second, Legalists adopted a ruler-centered perspective, which held that reinforcing the ruler's authority was crucial for social stability and that this authority should be absolute and limitless. Third, the Legalists rejected the authority of the past and favored institutional and intellectual innovations to match rapid changes in the sociopolitical situation. Fourth, they rejected the priority of moral values over practical considerations advocated by most of their rivals and adopted a pragmatic and often cynical stand toward political issues. Finally, since major Legalist thinkers had rich experience as administrators, military advisers, and diplomats, their writings are often dominated by practical issues to the extent that some modern critics question their philosophical credentials altogether. Paraphrasing Marx, it may be said that while other philosophers often sought to explain the world, the Legalists did their best to change it—and indeed achieved remarkable results.

## Shang Yang

Shang Yang is the major Legalist thinker and statesman. As a chancellor of Lord Xiao of Qin (r. 361–338 B.C.E.), he initiated a series of profound reforms that turned the relatively weak and peripheral state of Qin into the strongest power and the eventual conqueror and unifier of the Chinese world. Shang Yang's views are presented in the *Shang jun shu* (Book of Lord Shang); although parts of the book were composed after his death, the text reflects to a significant extent Shang Yang's legacy.

Shang Yang aimed to turn Qin into a powerful state through two parallel and interconnected processes: encouraging agricultural production and strengthening military prowess. To achieve these goals he advocated a clear system of rewards and punishments, according to which aristocratic ranks would be granted for high grain yields and for military merits, while high taxation would be applied against merchants and other "parasites," and harsh penalties would be imposed on those who fled the battlefield and on their relatives. He claimed that rational management of state funds and allocating more resources for reclaiming the wastelands would promote agricultural production, while military achievements would be attained through abandoning any pretension of moral behavior on the battlefield: "When you undertake whatever the enemy is ashamed to do, you will benefit."

Shang Yang's major concern was to assist the ruler to subdue and overcome his people. The people are inherently selfish and stupid, and they do not know how to attain prosperity and peace. Hence a uniform legal system of rewards and punishments is needed to bring order. The punishments should be severe: imposing harsh penalties for the slightest violations of the law can prevent the appearance of capital offences. Only by frightening the people, establishing a system of collective responsibility and mutual surveillance, can the ruler eliminate crimes and achieve peace for the citizens. This ultimately moral goal should be attained therefore through overtly immoral means.

Shang Yang ridiculed traditional culture, moral values, and beliefs in harmonic relations between the ruler and his subjects. All these are bygone ways, appropriate perhaps in the remote past but meaningless in the current age of constant warfare and internal struggles. The only meaningful lesson from the past is that wise rulers changed their laws and regulations to accord with changing circumstances. Shang Yang constructed an evolutionary model of social development, from a kin-based order toward a legal-based one; later Legalist thinkers adopted and further modified this model.

Shang Yang succeeded in creating a harsh and intrusive state that deeply penetrated society and eliminated or weakened previously autonomous social units, such as lineage and the agricultural commune. His success, admitted even by his rivals, explains his appeal, despite his overt attacks against the intellectuals, whom he called parasites and whose moral and intellectual credentials he constantly sought to undermine. In the long run, however, these anti-intellectual philippics backfired against Shang Yang and his followers, turning Legalism into an overtly negative label among the members of educated elite.

## Shen Buhai

Shen Buhai, Shang Yang's contemporary, was a chancellor in the state of Han. Reportedly his administrative reforms restored stability in this state and made it a model of efficiency for the rest of the Chinese world. Indeed where Shang Yang is associated with the law (*fa*), Shen Buhai's hallmark was the development of technique of rule (*shu*). Shen Buhai's book was lost and partly reconstructed from remaining quotations in the nineteenth century.

Shen ridiculed the traditional emphasis on harmonious relations within the ruling apparatus and warned the ruler that his worst enemy would not "batter in barred doors and gates" but would rather be one of the ministers "who by limiting what the ruler sees and restricting what the ruler hears, seizes his government and monopolizes his commands, possesses his people and takes his state." Rather than trusting his deceitful aides, the ruler should establish a strict system of surveillance over his ministers. He should divide the tasks between the officials, inspect their performance, and prevent a horizontal flow of information between them. To maximize his power, the sovereign must strictly preserve his prerogatives as a chief decision maker but should never interfere in the everyday administrative routine that is the task of the ruled. Shen's system, perfected and modified by others, contributed greatly toward the establishment of an efficient bureaucracy on Chinese soil.

## Han Feizi

Han Feizi, the last and most sophisticated of the Warring States' Legalist thinkers, is credited with synthesizing Shang Yang's and Shen Buhai's achievements. He furthermore based his philosophy of law on solid metaphysical foundations, borrowing ideas from the Daoist classic the *Laozi* (or *Dao de jing*). The monistic transcendent power of Dao ("Tao," the Way) is embodied in the ruler, whose authority is hence limitless and unquestionable. The principles (*li*) of Dao are manifested in the law, which thus becomes the constant and unshakable foundation of human society. Social hierarchy also reflects cosmic principles and so is similarly unassailable.

Philosophical sophistication notwithstanding, Han Feizi's fame derives from his astute and cynical analyses of political and social laws and practices. Politics are a battlefield in which deceit and treachery are common, and mutual trust and morality are an anomaly. The ruler should trust neither the people nor his aides, neither his kin nor his closest friends. This candor is revealing because, being a minister himself, Han Feizi actually claimed that he also cannot be trusted. This contradiction between Han Feizi's ideas and his personal aspirations ultimately led to a personal tragedy: after he arrived at the state of Qin, Han Feizi was imprisoned and executed as a potential spy for his Han homeland. Later the king of Qin reportedly admired Han Feizi's teachings and regretted his decision. Han Feizi thus did not witness the ultimate triumph of his ideology, which came shortly after his death with the imperial unification of 221 B.C.E.

## Later Legalism

The triumph of Legalism in the Qin empire (221–207 B.C.E.) was to a certain extent a Pyrrhic victory. Qin's harsh treatment of independent thinkers, which culminated in the burning of privately held book collections, backfired against the Legalist ideology, which lost its popularity among the educated elite. Although Legalist methods and ideas remained influential throughout the imperial millennia, the rulers overtly rejected Legalists' cynicism and anti-intellectualism and their emphasis on constant innovation. In the twentieth century the Legalists' ideas of the powerful state strongly appealed to modern intellectuals, and the school's fame reached its peak during the pro-Legalist campaign in the People's Republic of China in the early to mid-1970s. After Mao Zedong's death in 1976, however, the tide reversed again, and the Legalist contribution to traditional China's polity was again deemphasized.

*See also* **Chinese Thought; Confucianism; Machiavellism; Mohism.**

### BIBLIOGRAPHY

Creel, Herrlee G. *Shen Pu-hai: A Chinese Political Philosopher of the Fourth Century B.C.* Chicago: University of Chicago Press, 1974.

Fu, Zhengyuan. *China's Legalists: The Earliest Totalitarians and Their Art of Ruling.* Armonk, N.Y.: Sharpe, 1996.

*Han Feizi jijie.* Compiled by Wang Xianshen. Beijing: Zhonghua shuju, 1998. Collected commentaries on Han Feizi.

*Han Fei-tzu: Basic Writings.* Translated by Burton Watson. New York: Columbia University Press, 2003.

*Shang jun shu zhui zhi.* Edited by Jiang Lihong. Beijing: Zhonghua shu ju, 1986.

Wang, Hsiao-po, and Leo S. Chang. *The Philosophical Foundations of Han Fei's Political Theory.* Monograph no. 7 of the Society for Asian and Comparative Philosophy. Honolulu: University of Hawai'i Press, 1986.

Zheng, Liangshu. *Shang Yang ji qi xuepai.* Shanghai: Gu ji chu ban she, 1989.

*Yuri Pines*

**LEISURE.** *See* **Wealth.**

**LESBIAN STUDIES.** *See* **Gay Studies; Queer Theory.**

**LIBERALISM.** It is widely agreed that fundamental to liberalism is a concern to protect and promote individual liberty. This means that individuals can decide for themselves what to do or believe with respect to particular areas of human activity such as religion or economics. The contrast is with a society in which the society decides what the individual is to do or believe. In those areas of a society in which individual liberty prevails, social outcomes will be the result of a myriad of individual decisions taken by individuals for themselves or in voluntary cooperation with some others.

Liberalism in the political sphere cannot be a simple application of individual liberty, because decisions have to be taken collectively and are binding on all. Political liberalism means, first, that individual citizens are free to vote for representatives of their choice and to form voluntary associations to promote their ideas and interests in the realm of collective decision-making. Second, it means the adoption of constitutional procedures for limiting government power and making it accountable to the citizens.

### Liberal Practice

In discussing liberalism, it is important to distinguish between liberal practices and liberal theories. Liberal practices are those institutional and customary arrangements that support individual liberty. Of prime importance are individual legal rights to engage in certain activities such as to practice the religion of one's choice, to use one's property and labor as one pleases, and to enjoy freedom of opinion, expression, association, and movement. Political rights and constitutional procedures designed to put limits on government power, such as the independence of the judiciary, the separation of legislative and executive power, freedom of the press, and electoral accountability, are liberal practices insofar as they are designed to protect or express individual liberty.

Individual nonpolitical rights are necessarily limited by the equal rights of others. A religion or other association, or a use of property, that violates the rights of others, cannot be protected. Individual rights may also be limited by consideration of the public good, such as limits on public meetings that will produce disorder. A liberal account of such public-good constraints must limit them to whatever arrangements are necessary to protect a liberal society.

In talking about individual rights, it is essential to note, in order to understand liberalism, that the liberal individual is a human being not otherwise differentiated by status, class, race, religion, or gender. This formulation describes an ideal—implicit in liberalism and eventually standardly affirmed—rather than the actual practice of liberalism as it originally developed. With respect to the latter, many individual rights were variously restricted in different countries: universally at first to men, in America to white men. Nevertheless, the standard justifications for the exclusions were the incapacity of the excluded class of human beings to make effective use of the liberal freedoms or their existence as a threat to the established liberal order. In this way, it was still possible to say that all human beings capable of freedom and not threatening public order were entitled to rights.

As the practice of particular societies, liberal individual rights, although proclaimed as the rights of human beings, would be restricted to members of that society and to resident aliens only under the developing provisions of international law. The standard justification for such limitations was that the rights could be given practical effectiveness only through the legal and political systems of particular states. Liberal practices emerged in the states of northern Europe and North America in the course of the seventeenth and eighteenth centuries and contributed substantially to their dynamic international power through the early twenty-first century despite the life-threatening challenges to them in the twentieth century by the fascist and communist powers. The liberal societies of the West, above all the United States, have given liberalism as a practice and a theory a dominant status in the contemporary world.

While the aforementioned legal and institutional arrangements are important for the constitution of a liberal society, they are not enough. A fully liberal society requires a tolerant public opinion as well. This is one of the main points of John Stuart Mill's famous essay *On Liberty* (1859), in which he seeks to defend individuality and difference from the coercive pressure of public opinion.

Liberalism as a social practice is a matter of degree along three dimensions. First, a society may be more or less liberal according to how many aspects of its life are governed by the principle of individual liberty. A society may be very liberal in matters of belief but illiberal in the economic and/or the political sphere or conversely. It may be liberal in all these areas but illiberal with regard to sexual conduct. Second, a society may be more or less liberal with regard to each of these spheres. It may allow only a limited degree of economic freedom or a limited degree of freedom of belief. Finally, a society may be more or less inclusive of its adult population in the scope of the liberal freedoms.

### Liberal Theories

Liberal theories are theories designed to show that the liberal organization of society is the best for human beings with regard to their fundamental nature and interests. The Western intellectual tradition includes several discourses of major importance that have this aim. It is widely held that the principles of liberalism can be traced back to the seventeenth-century natural rights and social contract theorists who attach primary significance in just interaction between persons to an equal individual liberty and who derive the constraints of organized society from an agreement by individuals to submit to such constraints for the sake of the protection of their liberty and other natural rights.

A radically different type of liberal theory, which was very scornful of the idea of natural rights, was the utilitarian one. This flourished in the nineteenth century, particularly in Great Britain, and remains influential in English-speaking countries. This theory holds that the best organization of society is the one that produces the greatest amount of utility or happiness, taking equally into account every individual's utility. Such a theory is liberal only insofar as it argues, as the classic British utilitarians did, that the liberal order of society would best satisfy the utilitarian principle.

The theory that has been most influential in liberal thought on the continent of Europe and also on contemporary thought in English-speaking countries is that of Immanuel Kant (1724–1804) and German idealism. This theory seeks to provide a rational deduction of the natural rights principle of equal individual liberty from human beings' capacity for autonomy, which is understood as a capacity to govern one's conduct by laws or principles that one freely imposes on oneself.

Modern Western political theory from the seventeenth century is largely dominated by liberal ideas. Even thinkers who have been thought to be fundamentally illiberal, such as Thomas Hobbes (1588–1679), Jean-Jacques Rousseau (1712–1778), Edmund Burke (1729–1797), and Georg Wilhelm Friedrich Hegel (1770–1831) are really illiberal, if at all, only in regard to the state and not in regard to society. A liberal society may, thus, be supported on very different theoretical bases within Western thought, including religious ones. Indeed, the dominant status of liberalism in the contemporary world, together with the high importance attached to recognizing the equal worth of non-Western cultures, has led to many attempts to construct support for liberal practices from within religious systems of belief. Thus, there exist forms of liberalism that can be called Confucian, Islamic, and Buddhist.

## The Historical Development of the Liberal Idea

From the discussion of liberalism above, one might assume that the term itself came into use in seventeenth-century northern Europe. In fact the term *liberal* was first used in connection with politics in Spain in the early nineteenth century to describe a political movement whose object was to establish constitutional constraints on government power. The term rapidly came to be applied to movements and ideas aimed at promoting individual liberty of choice, and it is now generally considered reasonable to use the term retrospectively to describe thinkers such as John Locke (1632–1704), Adam Smith (1723–1790), and many others whose thought exhibited this character.

*Natural rights theories.* As claimed earlier, liberalism was nurtured in the natural rights doctrines of the seventeenth century. The Dutch scholar Hugo Grotius (1583–1645) is widely held to be the main innovator of the modern doctrine, and his mode of theorizing, involving the idea of a prepolitical state of nature and a social contract as the ground for political society, was taken up and given major formulations by Hobbes and Locke in England and Benedictus de Spinoza (1632–1677) and Samuel von Pufendorf (1632–1694) on the European continent. The reason for holding these theories to be the ground in which liberalism grew is that they start with a presumption in favor of individual liberty and limit liberty only to protect the equal rights of others or to provide the public order considered necessary to secure everyone's liberty to the greatest extent. These theorists refer to other natural rights besides liberty, as in Locke's classic formulation of rights to life, liberty, health, and possessions. All these rights, however, are to be understood as negative in character. The rights to life and health are rights not to be deprived of one's life or health by the actions of others and are thus rights to go about one's business as one thinks fit without being killed or injured. The right to possessions is again a negative right not to be hindered in the exercise of one's liberty to acquire possessions in order to preserve and enhance one's life. Furthermore, all individuals are held to have the natural right to govern themselves in accordance with their own judgment of their entitlements under natural law.

All these theorists recognize that constraints on individual liberty are necessary if people are to enjoy the maximum of equal liberty in a peaceful society, so it is rational for them to agree to establish a political society on the basis of their natural interests in liberty. This is a new and essentially liberal mode of thinking about a just society, because the aim is to leave people as free as possible to form their own lives as they think fit compatibly with a peaceful and orderly society. The contrast is with conceptions of just order that are based on a substantive conception of the good. In the latter view, one starts with a conception of how human beings should live in order to achieve the good life, such as that of Plato, and then organizes society politically to enable its members to realize this end. Individual liberty, in such a view, is only what is left over after the structure of the good life is in place.

The natural rights theorists explicitly adopted the primacy of liberty conception because they were especially impressed by the quarrelsome nature of human beings and by the devastating consequences of the contemporary disputes over religion involving Protestants and Catholics and the skepticism about the good that could thereby be engendered. These theorists' aim, therefore, was to construct a minimal social ethics that all could agree on while leaving as much room as possible for each to decide for him- or herself what to believe and how to live. Of course, it is always possible to say that the liberal view of just interaction still involves a conception of the good life, namely one of maximum equal liberty. But this is a very thin conception of the good that leaves people as free as possible to make their own choices.

The natural rights theorists developed the central ideas of a liberal *society*. Their politics, however, was in many cases far from being liberal. Despite the grounding of political society in a social contract and thus apparently basing it on the consent of all, Grotius, Hobbes, and Pufendorf defended absolute monarchy, while Locke and Spinoza restricted political rights to property owners. A crucial argument of the absolutists was that, although the ruler's authority was based on a contract, the contract necessarily involved the surrender by the contractors of their natural right to interpret the natural law for themselves to the sovereign whose judgment could not subsequently be questioned without undermining political society itself and returning everyone to a lawless state of nature. It is for this reason that Hobbes, and later the conservative thinker Burke, can appear to be so illiberal. Although they do not deny that human beings have natural interests in an equal liberty and that sovereigns are well advised to respect that liberty, sovereigns cannot be held to account for not respecting it. Hence, their subjects' enjoyment of their liberties can only be at the discretion of the ruler or the political traditions of the society.

The partial political liberalism of Locke is presented as an attack on the absolutists and consists of making the government responsible to the property owners who are taxed to support it and who are held to be the more rational members of society; and additionally an embryonic version of the idea of the separation of government powers in different hands. Nevertheless, absolute sovereignty still lurks in Locke's theory insofar as citizens who are aggrieved at the actions of a legitimately constituted government have to appeal to the members of political society as a whole whose decision, in principle by majority will, is presented as necessarily binding. Thus, Locke's political theory contains an unelaborated majoritarian democratic principle that could be and was seized on by more radical thinkers and movements concerned to develop the egalitarian implications of liberal rights to promote political democracy.

Rousseau can be understood as one of these radical egalitarian Lockean thinkers in some respects, and his theory was very influential in inspiring the French revolutionaries of the late eighteenth century. But Rousseau is rarely regarded as a liberal. This is largely because his theory of the general will and his belief in direct rather than representative democracy were seen, especially in the light of the actions of the French revolutionaries and through the criticism of the early-nineteenth-century French liberal thinker Benjamin Constant, as wholly antipathetic to individual liberty. He is said to identify liberty with participation in collective decision-making rather than individual choice. However, this is to misunderstand the general will. The general will is supposed to be aimed inherently at securing laws that equally protect the individual liberty of all. Insofar as it is a collective will through participation in which all persons equally impose general laws with a liberal character on themselves and others, its collective nature and positive conception of freedom is merely the necessary political element in a self-governing liberal society.

Rousseau does depart radically from the economic liberalism implicit or explicit in most natural rights theorists of the seventeenth and eighteenth centuries. For Rousseau the equality element in the doctrine of equal rights requires a rough equality of all as property owners and an opposition to capitalist ownership and market society. Because the foundational liberal principle affirms both the equality and liberty of all, Rousseau's interpretation of it would seem to be a possible one while its egalitarian commitments have become more and more influential.

Other notable figures in the democratic development natural rights theory are Thomas Paine (1743–1809) and the Marquis of Condorcet (1743–1794). They played noteworthy parts in the political revolutions that transformed America and France at the end of the eighteenth century and produced important theoretical works justifying a liberal-democratic order.

***Utility-based liberalism.*** Rights-based liberalism has two apparent weaknesses: It is not clear where the natural rights come from, and no principled account of conflicts involving rights is given or seems to be possible. Utilitarian-based liberalism offers a single solution to both. The principle of utility, which tells moral agents to do those acts that will produce the greatest amount of utility, is interpreted by the great liberal utilitarians to mean that one should act to bring about a society in which individuals enjoy the standard liberal rights enumerated earlier in this entry. At the same time what to do when rights conflict is to be settled by appeal to the principle of utility, which establishes a suitable hierarchy of rights in such cases.

The most important liberal utilitarians are Jeremy Bentham (1748–1832) and Mill. To get a defense of liberalism from the principle of utility, Bentham adopts a number of secondary principles reflecting the fundamental interests of individuals. One of these is that individuals are the best judges of their own interests. So, there must be a presumption on the part of government that social outcomes will be better if individuals are left as free as possible to decide for themselves what to believe and do. His other secondary principles were those of security (or liberty), subsistence, abundance, and equality. Security of person and property involves the protection of people's liberty while ensuring that both subsistence and the possibility of abundance are best accomplished by leaving people free economically. Equality, arising from the fact that in the utilitarian calculus each is to count for one and no one for more than one, might suggest redistribution from rich to poor were that not to conflict in an unacceptable way with the operation of the other secondary principles and so is outweighed by them.

Unlike most of his contemporary rights-based liberals, Bentham believed that the only way of ensuring that governments followed policies that best promoted the general utility rather than their own interest was to establish a representative democracy. He thought that the great majority would see that their interests lay in the institution of a liberal society and polity, a view repudiated by those partially political liberals who doubted that non–property owners could be trusted to support liberty because they lacked the necessary independence and rationality.

Mill introduced significant modifications to the liberal theory he inherited from Bentham. One of these is his extension of the liberty principle, which requires persons to be allowed to pursue their own good in their own way so long as they do not harm others, to cover the coercive pressure of public opinion mentioned earlier. Furthermore, the area of conduct falling within this principle includes what Mill calls experiments in living. People should be encouraged to experiment (so long as they do not harm others) in order to promote the long-term utility of the human race. Underlying these views is a belief in the fundamental importance of individuality to a person's happiness. This is the capacity to make choices for one's life that express one's own individual nature. A liberal society will be one that promotes the development in its members of this capacity. Adult human beings and whole societies will not necessarily manifest it and can benefit up to a point from the tutelage of others.

***Kant and post-Kantian liberal idealism.*** Kant, the deeply anti-utilitarian and still very influential German philosopher, identifies human beings' capacity for autonomy as the grounds for claiming the existence of a natural right to an equal liberty. Autonomy is the capacity to govern oneself by freely imposing rational laws on the operation of one's natural inclinations. In following one's inclinations even through rational calculation, one is bound by causal laws operating independently of one's will. One is free and self-determining only insofar as one's end is rational and self-imposed. One achieves this in willing principles that are universal and apply to everyone. In subjecting one's natural self-interested maxims of conduct to the requirement of a universal legislation for its own sake and not for any advantage, one is treating rational being in oneself and others as an end in itself and of absolute worth. The laws one wills from that perspective will be ones that could be willed by every rational human being, who is not only a rational being but also a natural one. One will then be participating as an equal colegislator in willing rational laws to govern the pursuit by each of his or her natural ends.

Among the fundamental laws such beings will legislate is one bestowing the universal right to an equal liberty. Human beings as rational beings embodied in a particular natural being are ends in themselves, and this means that their will insofar as it is rational and thereby conforms to rational universal law must not be coerced but must be left free to pursue its natural ends as it chooses. To the extent that a person's will violates the equal freedom of another, however, that will itself may be coerced, and in order to ensure the precision and effectiveness of this fundamental law, human beings must rationally will their entry into political society and their formation of a public order and sovereign will.

Kant's significance lies not so much in his working out the implications of the principle of equal liberty but in his invention of a new rational ground in autonomy for it. Contemporary liberals who still seek to provide justifications for preferring liberalism to other social and political schemes are largely either Kantians or utilitarians, with Kantians for the moment predominating.

Post-Kantian idealism, most elaborately developed by Hegel in Germany but also influential in Britain in the second half of the nineteenth century through the writings of Thomas Hill Green, Francis Herbert Bradley, and Bernard Bosanquet, historicizes and socializes the Kantian scheme. The general idea is that historical forms of society and the reflective philosophies that arise in them are the result of the struggle of human beings to grasp and actualize the free will inherent in their nature as rational beings. This struggle culminates in the development of a liberal civil society and a partially liberal state. A liberal self-organizing civil society in which all persons are responsible for their own life economically and socially is necessary to develop in all the idea and partial actualization of their autonomy. This society, however, can exist only within the framework of a system of legislation that is the ultimate locus of the self-determining free will of human beings through their participation in and identification with the general will of the state. This theory socializes the individualist character of the liberal philosophy, because although individuals are the beings within which free will is realized, this is achieved only through their development in and membership of liberal social forms.

***Twentieth-century liberalism and the influence of Rawls.*** A striking characteristic of twentieth-century political theory is its loss of belief in the possibility of finding rational foundations for moral and political prescriptions. Adherence to liberal or antiliberal principles became a matter of espousing an ideology.

Liberal practices were, nevertheless, deeply embedded in English-speaking societies but, as it turned out, less so in the societies of Continental Europe, above all Germany and Russia. In those nations, in the chaos of the aftermath of World War I and the economic misfortunes of the 1920s and 1930s, the powerful antiliberal political movements of fascism and communism seized power, destroyed the forms of liberal society, and threatened the very survival of liberalism in the Western world. The victory of the liberal states (together with the Soviet Union) in World War II led to their strong reaffirmation of the individualist values of liberalism. This was least marked in the economic sphere, where the apparent industrial success of Stalinist Russia encouraged many Western and developing states to adopt extensive policies of economic socialism in the form of the nationalization of major industries. The postwar liberal states also for the most part greatly expanded the provision of state welfare to their subjects. While such policies were contrary to the principles of classical liberalism, they were perfectly justifiable under the revision of liberal theory that took place in the second half of the nineteenth century.

Political and moral theory remained marooned in the swamp of ideological contestation largely between liberalism and communism until the publication of John Rawls's *A Theory of Justice* in 1971 and the collapse of the other great antiliberal power in the 1980s (that is, the Soviet Union). The former generated an extraordinary revival of political theory based on the belief that Rawls had invented a new rational justification of liberalism. Rawls supposes that persons engaged in social interaction have the need and the desire to justify their actions to those affected by them and that this justification must take the form of everyone agreeing from an initially fair position to a set of cooperative principles that will then be seen to be fair. The initially fair position is one in which the contractors are understood to be free and equal persons—free because they have the capacity to form conceptions of the good and govern themselves by these conceptions, and equal because no one has any more power than another to secure favorable terms for him- or herself. The contractors would choose two principles. The first is a principle of equal liberty by which each is to have as much liberty as is compatible with a like liberty for all. This principle takes priority over the second principle, which is concerned with fair equality of opportunity and the distribution of income and wealth. With regard to the latter Rawls holds that the contractors would choose that distribution that maximizes the long-run position of the worst-off group in society. These principles are commonly taken to justify a liberal welfare state with a leaning toward egalitarian outcomes.

One of Rawls's main claims about liberalism is that it is a method of political cooperation that is neutral between different conceptions of the good. Rawls believes, as did the original natural rights theorists, that human beings differ and tend to quarrel disastrously about the good. Any attempt to establish a coercive state on the basis of a particular conception is bound to generate conflict and be unfair to those holding different conceptions because there is no way of conclusively establishing the truth of any one conception. Liberalism, as Rawls understands it, and as presented in this entry, is a way of achieving peaceful social cooperation on the basis of agreement on principles that leave people as free as is compatible with allowing a like freedom to others.

In *A Theory of Justice,* however, Rawls claims that the ultimate ground for accepting his liberalism is that it expresses the Kantian idea of free and equal autonomous persons cooperating together in a social order. Rawls later came to accept the criticism that to base the theory on a Kantian conception of autonomy, which some persons could reasonably reject, violated the neutrality of the scheme. So in *Political Liberalism* (1993) he holds that the burdens of judgment regarding the good are such that it is unreasonable to seek to impose one's own conception on others by making it the basis of the state's order. But this claim raises the question of whether the unreasonableness of imposing one's conception of the good is solely pragmatic or whether it is based on principle, and, if the latter, what that principle is if it is not the Kantian one. Taking the former view would force one to abandon the belief that Rawls has effectively countered the general twentieth-century skepticism regarding foundations.

## Some Issues in Liberal Theory and Practice

Liberalism has deep internal tensions primarily between the claims of equality and those of liberty arising from its equal commitment to both these principles. The tensions are held by some thinkers who are not well-disposed towards liberalism to be contradictions that prevent liberalism from living up to its own principles. Some of these issues are discussed briefly below together with some important distinctions between types of liberalism.

***Liberalism and cultural difference.*** Liberalism prides itself on its toleration of cultural and other differences. Some cultural groups, however, are internally illiberal. They do not treat their members as free and equal autonomous individuals with rights but as having identities defined by their membership in and place within the group, and by relation to the group's values. They are communal selves rather than individual ones. People so identifying themselves cannot easily flourish in liberal society by taking advantage of its freedoms. Hence, it is said that liberalism cannot treat such minority cultures fairly in accordance with its own principles.

Liberalism can tolerate such groups provided that they do not harm others and provided that their members are free to leave without suffering unjust discrimination. The problem is whether persons formed in such groups are really free to leave unless they have had a liberal education that enables them to think of themselves as individuals with the power and right of choice. But if they do think of themselves in this way, they will no longer be the communal selves they were. The liberal education of its members would undermine the group's illiberal identity and force it to reconstitute itself in liberal terms. It is clear also that illiberal groups could not be specially represented in the political realm without turning that realm from a principled association into what would be at best a pragmatic compromise between conflicting groups. There is no reasonable compromise between liberalism and illiberalism. In the end one must seek to show the superiority of a liberal society by appealing to some foundational principle and by reiterating that there is no possible social scheme compatible with a principled order that is more tolerant of difference than liberalism.

A more modest claim for the special recognition of cultural difference would be that of cultural minorities whose values are not incompatible with liberalism but whose members are disadvantaged relative to the majority in terms of their ability to compete on fair terms to obtain the benefits of liberal society. The demand would be in part for the preferential treatment of the members of such groups so that they could enjoy fair equality of opportunity. But this would not be to give special recognition to the culture as such but to its members as disadvantaged individuals. Some cultural minorities might also reasonably claim to be given symbolic public recognition as distinct and loyal members of the polity in public ceremonies celebrating the history of the nation and the contributions of its various citizens.

***Liberalism and women's difference.*** In the beginning, feminism was just the application of liberal principles to women. Women were conceived as having fundamentally the same nature and interests as men and thereby entitled to the same rights.

Radical feminists from the 1970s, however, opposed the liberal assimilation of women's claims on the grounds that the liberal conception of the person did not reflect women's nature. This nature had been obscured by millennia of patriarchal rule and needed liberation from patriarchal society before its true content could be revealed. But whatever it turned out to be, the radical feminists were certain that it would not be a liberal individual. They held that whereas the liberal individual was based on impersonal rationality and abstraction, women's ethical life was rooted in her body and its emotions.

Insofar as women's difference amounts to an illiberal nature opposed to liberal man, the same issues are raised as those that occur in the cultural case, although compounded by the fact that men and women would seem to have to live together in the private realm if the race is to be satisfactorily continued. Women cannot be treated as a self-reproducing cultural group. Nevertheless, illiberal women could be specially represented in the public sphere. Yet, this would turn it once again into a reasonable compromise between the representatives of conflicting values.

Women could, of course, be seen as a disadvantaged group whose members need preferential treatment in order to achieve fair equality of opportunity. But this is not incompatible with liberalism. Some contemporary women writers claim that it is incompatible on the grounds that if women are given special treatment because of their difference, for example, their maternal being, then liberalism's claim to treat all persons equally without respect for gender will be breached. Nevertheless, because the ground for special treatment is to achieve fair equality of opportunity for different individuals in regard to their different circumstances, this argument seems invalid.

The radical feminists belief in a special women's nature was subverted by the postmodernist feminists, who reject the idea of essential selves. Identities are socially produced and always subject to challenge and change. This view would seem to make it impossible to claim that women as such are oppressed in patriarchal or liberal society because there is no such thing as women as such. Nevertheless, postmodern feminists believe that it is still possible within particular discourses to resist established conventions and develop alternative discourses regarding women. But to what end is unclear.

***Economic liberalism.*** Economic liberalism is the view that the best economic order is a free market. This view may be justified by utilitarian considerations, as in those of Bentham, or by a combination of natural rights and utilitarian consequences, as in the theory of Adam Smith.

Fundamental to Smith's view is the idea of a natural order. This is the social order that develops when individuals are allowed to pursue their interests through specialization and exchange of goods and services. It is an expression of human beings' natural right to liberty. But it is also the best way for a society to promote the accumulation of wealth and national power.

Individuals are motivated in the natural order by the desire to improve their material condition, and given a suitable economic environment competition among them will normally produce beneficial consequences. Such an environment requires the free movement of labor, capital, and goods; many buyers and sellers; sound information among buyers and sellers; security of person and property; and the abolition of monopolies, tariffs, and government regulation of production and consumption. Yet Smith acknowledges that there exists a class of public goods that it is the function of government to provide, including the administration of justice, defense, and education.

Smith is not blind to the defects of the liberal economic individual and society but thinks liberal society is still preferable to aristocratic society. In particular, he deplores the condition of the poor but believes that their only hope lies in the accumulation of wealth. Furthermore, he distrusts the capacity and interests of the poor to make political decisions in the general interest, which he identifies with the system of liberal liberty. So, like many other early liberals, he wants a liberal polity to be restricted to property owners.

Smith is the founder of classical economics, which is committed to free markets and hence economic liberalism. Another major figure in this school is David Ricardo (1772–1823), whose *Principles of Political Economy and Taxation* dominated the subject until the end of the nineteenth century. However, in Ricardo the subject becomes more technical and abstract and less concerned with its connections with liberal values more generally.

Economic liberalism of the Smithian kind is commonly thought to have been practiced by the British government during the nineteenth century and to a lesser extent by others. But this is far from being unqualifiedly true. The British government interfered in market outcomes during this period by regulating working conditions, trade unions, and the rates of utility companies, and by imposing an income tax and maintaining a monopoly of the money supply. The general spirit of economic liberalism is better described as a strong presumption in favor of laissez faire unless it was clear that intervention was to the general benefit.

***Classical and revisionist liberalism.*** Classical liberalism is the liberalism that prevailed mainly in northern Europe and North America up to the second half of the nineteenth century. It consisted of minimal government intervention in economy and society. But it was by no means politically democratic, especially in Europe where liberals were for the most part and for a long time strongly resistant to the inclusion of the propertyless in the benefits and burdens of a liberal polity. Its principles received notable political expression in the declarations of the rights of man and the citizen of the American and French Revolutions at the end of the eighteenth century, while the extremes of the latter revolution confirmed many middle-class liberals in their hostility to democracy. Because of its economic and political association with the middle classes, classical liberalism can easily be represented as the ideology of the capitalist class, a position taken by Karl Marx (1818–1883) and other socialists. As presented in this entry, however, the fundamental tenets of classical liberalism go far wider and deeper than that claim implies. This is shown by the way the application of its principles was revised in the course of the nineteenth century to accommodate what most liberals came to accept as inevitable, namely the arrival of democracy.

The revision in practice took the form of increasing government intervention in the economy to protect the interests and promote the welfare of workers. Government resources, obtained through general taxation, are used to provide for the basic needs of the population. The revision in liberal theory that justified the change to big government involved a shift from the belief of the classical liberals that normal adult human beings would automatically have developed the capacity to exercise their freedom in their own interests to the view that this capacity needed suitable economic, educational, and social conditions for its development—a belief found in the works of Mill and especially the nineteenth-century idealists. If individuals cannot provide these conditions for themselves, then fellow citizens must do so through state action. In general the move is to a greater emphasis on the equality aspect of equal liberty, as exemplified in Rousseau's thought, a change requiring more protection for workers and the poor.

Rather than as an abrupt and radical break, this revision of classical liberalism should be considered a movement along a continuum of possible social forms, all based on the liberal principle of equal liberty. At one extreme of this continuum is libertarian anarchy with no government at all, which is followed by the minimal state as described above in Smith's theory, and increasing levels of government intervention all the way to the government ownership of the means of production at the other extreme. The latter can still be called liberal provided that individual freedom prevails in all but the economic realm and that economic socialism is understood as the best means of assuring an equal liberty. Classical liberalism shares with revisionist liberalism the belief that government intervention can be justified if it works out to the general advantage.

***Liberalism and nationalism.*** Liberalism and a weak form of nationalism developed together. Liberalism was a way of organizing society for the benefit of its members in a manner that promoted, better than any alternative, the society's harmony, prosperity, and power in a world of independent states. The nation here is just the collection of people organized in a state and thereby sharing common interests in their peace, prosperity, and power.

A strong form of nationalism holds that a nation is an ethnocultural group sharing a common ancestry, history, and culture and that membership in such a group is fundamental to the identity and value of the individual. Nationalism in this sense is totally antithetical to liberalism, for which individual identity is deeper than national identity.

A form of nationalism intermediate between the two is to be found in Mill and the contemporary thinker David Miller. According to this view a democratic liberal state will work better—be more harmonious and just—if the great majority share a nationality in the ethnocultural sense.

Liberalism has also been allied with imperialism. The argument here is that the rule of a liberal state over other peoples, such as the rule of Britain over India, may be justified if it serves to develop the subject peoples' capacity to become self-governing individuals and a self-governing people—in other words to develop in them the culture of liberalism. It is held by some that cultural imperialism of this kind, if not political imperialism, has been pursued by the Western powers after World War II through the United Nations program on Human Rights. Ultimately, the only justification for pursuing a liberal program domestically or internationally is that liberalism describes a better way for human beings to live together than any alternative because it better expresses and actualizes their fundamental nature and interests.

*See also* **Conservatism; Constitutionalism; Democracy; Enlightenment; Utilitarianism.**

## BIBLIOGRAPHY

### PRIMARY SOURCES

Bentham, Jeremy. *The Works of Jeremy Bentham.* Vol. 1. Edited by John Bowring. 1838–1843. Reprint, New York: Russell and Russell, 1962.

Condorcet, Marie Jean Antoine Nicolas Caritat, Marquis de. *Sketch of a Historical Picture of the Progress of the Human Mind.* Translated by June Barraclough with an introduction by Stuart Hampshire. New York: Noonday Press, 1955.

Constant, Benjamin. "The Liberty of the Ancients Compared with That of the Moderns." 1819. In *Political Writings,* edited and translated by Biancamaria Fontana. Cambridge, U.K.: Cambridge University Press, 1988.

Grotius, Hugo. *The Law of War and Peace.* 1625. Translated by Francis W. Kelsey. Indianapolis: Bobbs-Merrill, 1962.

Hegel, Georg Wilhelm Friedrich. *Elements of the Philosophy of Right.* 1821. Edited by Allen W. Wood and translated by H. B. Nisbet. Cambridge, U.K.: Cambridge University Press, 1991.

Hobbes, Thomas. *Leviathan.* 1651. Reprint, edited by Richard Tuck, Cambridge, U.K.: Cambridge University Press, 1996.

Kant, Immanuel. *The Groundwork for the Metaphysics of Morals.* 1785. Edited by Thomas E. Hill Jr. and Arnulf Zweig and translated by Arnulf Zweig. Oxford: Oxford University Press, 2002.

———. *The Metaphysical Elements of Justice.* 1797. Translated by John Ladd. Indianapolis, Ind.: Bobbs-Merrill, 1965.

Locke, John. "A Letter concerning Toleration." 1689. Reprint, in *John Locke: "A Letter concerning Toleration," in Focus,* edited by John Horton and Susan Mendus. London: Routledge, 1991.

———. *Two Treatises of Government.* 1690. Reprint, edited with an introduction and notes by Peter Laslett, Cambridge, U.K.: Cambridge University Press, 1988.

Mill, John Stuart. *On Liberty.* 1859. Reprint, edited by Gertrude Himmelfarb, New York: Penguin, 1982.

Paine, Thomas. *The Rights of Man, Common Sense and Other Political Writings,* edited with an introduction and notes by Mark Philp. Oxford: Oxford University Press, 1998.

Pufendorf, Samuel. *On the Duty of Man and Citizen According to Natural Law.* 1673 Edited by James Tully and translated by Michael Silverthorne. Cambridge, U.K.: Cambridge University Press, 1991.

Rawls, John. *Political Liberalism.* New York: Columbia University Press, 1993.

———. *A Theory of Justice.* Cambridge, Mass.: Harvard University Press, Belknap Press, 1971.

Ricardo, David. *The Principles of Political Economy and Taxation,* with an introduction by Donald Winch. London: Dent, 1973.

Rousseau, Jean-Jacques. *"The Social Contract" and Other Later Political Writings.* Edited and translated by Victor Gourevitch. Cambridge, U.K.: Cambridge University Press, 1997.

Smith, Adam. *An Inquiry into the Nature and Causes of the Wealth of Nations.* 1776. Reprint, edited by R. H. Campbell, A. S. Skinner, and W. B. Todd, Oxford: Clarendon Press, 1976.

Spinoza, Benedictus de. *Tractatus theologico-politicus.* 1670. In *The Political Works,* edited and translated by A. G. Wernham. Reprint, Oxford: Clarendon Press, 1958.

### SECONDARY SOURCES

Arblaster, Anthony. *The Rise and Decline of Western Liberalism.* Oxford: Basil Blackwell, 1984.

Barry, Brian. *Culture and Equality: An Egalitarian Critique of Multiculturalism.* Cambridge, U.K.: Polity Press, 2001.

de Ruggiero, Guido. *The History of European Liberalism.* Translated by R. G. Collingwood. 1927. Reprint, Gloucester, Mass.: Peter Smith, 1981.

Freeden, Michael. *The New Liberalism: An Ideology of Social Reform.* Oxford: Clarendon, 1978.

Girvetz, Harry K. *The Evolution of Liberalism.* New York: Collier, 1963.

Grampp, William D. *Economic Liberalism.* New York: Random House, 1965.

Gray, John. *Liberalism.* 2nd ed. Minneapolis: University of Minnesota Press, 1995.

Hobhouse, L. T. *"Liberalism" and Other Writings.* Edited by James Meadowcroft. Cambridge, U.K.: Cambridge University Press, 1994.

Kymlicka, Will, ed. *The Rights of Minority Cultures.* Oxford: Oxford University Press, 1995.

Laski, Harold J. *The Rise of European Liberalism.* 1936. Reprint, with a new introduction by John Stanley. New Brunswick, N.J.: Transaction Publishers, 1997.

Miller, David. *On Nationality.* Oxford: Oxford University Press, 1995.

Phillips, Anne, ed. *Feminism and Politics.* Oxford: Oxford University Press, 1998.

Tamir, Yael. *Liberal Nationalism.* Princeton, N.J.: Princeton University Press, 1993.

Weedon, Chris. *Feminism, Theory, and the Politics of Difference.* Oxford: Blackwell, 1999.

*John Charvet*

# LIBERATION THEOLOGY.

The broad definition of liberation theology stresses the interrelatedness of differing structures of oppression and domination. Liberation from oppressive structures necessarily involves political, economic, social, racial, ethnic, and sexual aspects. As a paradigm, liberation theology today places explicit emphasis on assessing different forms of human oppression and suffering, and liberation from them, as layers in a complicated process.

Liberation theology is one of the most significant currents in modern theology. Because of its multidisciplinarity and its emphasis on social, political, and ecclesial praxis, it has come to have importance far beyond academic theology or institutional churches. Liberation theology can be defined either narrowly or broadly. In the former sense, it is limited to Latin American liberation theology (*teología de la liberación, teologia da libertação*), born of a specifically Latin American context in the late 1960s. In the broader sense, liberation theology also includes other theological currents, most importantly black theology (mostly in the United States and South Africa), feminist theology, and variations of Asian and African liberation theologies. In the latter sense, it would be even more accurate to speak of theologies of liberation in the plural. Among different liberation theologians, this understanding of liberation theology as plural, heterogeneous, and global (with multifaceted local expressions) is common. There are also non-Christian theologies of liberation, even if the term sometimes is not fully accurate in all contexts. However, there has also been dialogue between Christian and Jewish, Muslim, and Hindu theologians of liberation. This article will concentrate on Christian liberation theologies in the broader, global meaning.

It is often wrongly assumed that liberation theology first appeared in Latin America and then spread to other continents and contexts. Some classical works on black theology (for example, James Cone's *A Black Theology of Liberation,* 1970) and feminist liberation theology (Rosemary Ruether's *Liberation Theology,* 1972) were published at about the same time as the first major works of Latin American liberation theology, such as Gustavo Gutiérrez's *Teología de la liberación* (1972). It is more accurate to say that the term *liberation theology* arose simultaneously in different contexts. The different theologies within the liberation theology movement have had some dialogue with each other, most importantly in the context of the Ecumenical Association of Third World Theologians (EATWOT), founded in 1976. Counted among "Third World theologies" are liberation theologies inside the First World, especially the United States. Liberation theologians have learned from each other through critical dialogue: for example, the critique of the meagerness of the analysis of racism and sexism and the emphasis on economic and class issues at the cost of cultural elements in Latin American liberation theology; or for a feminist theology from industrialized countries that has been slow to admit that white, educated, and affluent women are a small minority.

Each liberation theology, whether black, feminist, or Latin American, is characterized by its distinctive viewpoint, but what they all share is a commitment to social justice. To some extent, all liberation theologies are situated in contemporary political struggles and movements (such as different human rights movements against Latin American dictatorships, the U.S. civil rights movement, and feminist movements in different countries and regions). Liberation theologians usually refer to this as praxis, not only as their aim or objective, but also as their point of departure.

Liberation theology stems from the conviction that giving priority to the poor and the oppressed in theology and in the church, and the concrete defense of their rights in different societies, is a central, if not the most central, element of the Christian faith. Christian liberation theologies aim their critical analysis not only at society but at the church and theology as well in order to judge to what extent they are accomplices in maintaining structures of domination.

Liberation theologies understand theology as critical reflection on the presence of the divine within different liberation struggles. This reflection is accomplished with the help of both sacred scriptures and tenets of the faith tradition, as well as other disciplines, in order to understand the root causes (and ways of eradication) of phenomena such as poverty and racism.

The concept *contextual theology* has been used interchangeably with liberation theology. It has been claimed that because all human activity, including the study of theology, is born in a particular context, all human activity is contextual. However, contextual theology has been used mainly to designate the changing character of Christianity as it took root outside the Western world. In this sense, contextual theology would be a wider term than liberation theology, Latin American liberation theology, for example, being just one form of contextualized theology from a particular colonialized and Christianized part of the world. In the sense that the term contextual theology refers to a local political, social, and religious context—for example, Ghana or the Philippines—it is a narrower term than liberation theology, which stresses a global struggle against different systems of domination.

No single article can do justice to the contemporary richness of different liberation theologies, such as Dalit theology (India), gay and lesbian liberation theologies, *minjung* theology (Korea), indigenous peoples' theologies and spiritualities of liberation all over the globe, and the Palestinian theology of liberation, among others. In the remainder of this essay, to the discussion will be limited to Latin American liberation theology, black theology, and feminist theology.

## Latin American Liberation Theology

The Catholic Church was, for centuries, one of the pillars of Spanish power in Latin America, which was Christianized more than five hundred years ago, unlike other areas later colonized by European countries. The circumstances that made liberation theology possible have deep historical roots; however, there are some more immediate causes, both secular and ecclesial.

The generally conflictive atmosphere, and the rise of authoritarian military dictatorships all over Latin America in the 1960s and 1970s, created the conditions in which the Roman Catholic Church had to take a political stance regarding growing violations of human rights, deepening poverty, and organized, armed guerrilla struggle, culminating in some cases in a successful popular revolution (Cuba in 1959 and Nicaragua in 1979). An influential idea behind early liberation theology was the dependency theory, according to which the main reason for the poverty and underdevelopment of the Third World was its dependency on industrialized countries, which were largely developed through the use of, and profit from, dependent regions. Theologically, liberation theology was a radicalization and contextualization of the influence from European political theology and, certainly, in a tradition as long as Christianity itself, of prophetic denunciation of injustice and oppression and declaration of freedom and liberation to those suffering from them.

The Second Vatican Council (1962–1965) of the Roman Catholic Church established a global opening of the church to society and had an extremely important influence especially on Catholic churches in North America and Latin America. Ecumenically, the World Council of Churches took steps that encouraged Protestant churches to commit themselves to issues of social justice, especially the eradication of poverty. In Latin America, the Latin American Catholic Bishops' Conference (CELAM, *Consejo Episcopal Latinoamericano*) met in Medellín, Colombia, in 1968, a meeting often interpreted as a critical point in the departure of the Catholic Church (as an institution) from its five-hundred-year-old relationship to the state. The church formally made "a preferential option for the poor" and aspired to become "a church of the poor." Some of the first important Catholic liberation theologians were Gustavo Gutiérrez, Leonardo Boff, Juan Luis Segundo, Hugo

Assmann, Jon Sobrino, and Pablo Richard; on the Protestant side were theologians such as Rubem Alves, José Míguez Bonino, and Elsa Tamez.

At the grassroots level, priests, pastors, nuns, and laypeople started to work with the rural and urban poor, forming ecclesial base communities, or *comunidades eclesiales de base* (CEBs), in which people learned to interpret their everyday realities in the light of their Christian identity and faith. In some countries, such as Nicaragua and Brazil, the local CEBs played an important sociopolitical role.

According to Gutiérrez, liberation theology is "a critical reflection on praxis in the light of the Word of God." While there is a clear Marxist influence in liberation theologians' use of the concept of praxis, the Vatican's claim that liberation theology is camouflaged Marxism is exaggerated. Liberation theologians interpreted both Christianity and the Latin American situation from a new perspective, that of the colonized "Christian South," in which the majority of people lived in widespread poverty under extremely repressive governments. The method of liberation theology—to give primacy to praxis over theological speculations—has influenced nearly all contemporary theology.

In the 1990s, the influence of both liberation theology and the CEBs has diminished, partly due to the growing presence of Pentecostalism and the rise in Protestant churches in Latin America. Also, the Catholic Church has become much more conservative during the papacy of John Paul II, leaving very few liberation-theological bishops, such as Helder Camara of Brazil and Oscar Romero of El Salvador in the 1970s and 1980s, in the Latin American Catholic Church. At the same time, ever-deepening poverty and the globalization of market economies, issues of sexism and racism, and ecological concerns raise both old and new questions for liberation theologians. An analysis of idolatry as well as of the common roots of Western theology and economy (for example, the sacrificial elements in both) has led to some of the new developments that have deepened the original insights of liberation theology. Capitalism as religion and the "necessary" production of victims as a basically theological belief have been theorized by Franz Hinkelammert and Hugo Assmann. Christianity should always side with the victims and defend their lives, which is why liberation theology is also called the theology of life, *teología de la vida*, reflecting on the meaning of the God of life, *el Dios de la vida*.

Liberation theology today might best be seen as forming part of the so-called globalization critique, which, along with theories and practices of alternative globalization, tend to bring together actors and theories from both the First and Third Worlds in order to create alternatives to contemporary economic policies. A lack of democratic control of economic policies, poverty, ecological disasters, the concentrated control of natural resources, and the concomitant issues of sexism and racism, remain as issues.

## Black Theology

Black theology in the United States arose out of the civil rights and black power movements of the 1950s and 1960s.

However, its historical roots go back to the beginning of African slavery in the United States and the founding of black independent Baptist and Methodist churches in the late eighteenth and early nineteenth centuries. Important contributors to this literature are James H. Cone, J. Deotis Roberts, and Gayraud S. Wilmore. "In a racist society, God is not color blind," says James Cone. Also, if all humans were created in the image of God, it must not only mean that black people are created in God's image, as are whites, but also that "God is black." In a related sense, "blackness" is a category in black theology similar to that of "poverty" in Latin American liberation theology. To be black, or poor, is to be conscious both of one's oppression and of one's authentic humanity.

As in other liberation theologies, black women's voices, and their critique, have been central for the later development of black theology. In the United States, African-American feminist theologians prefer to call their work *womanist theology,* after a term borrowed from the African-American writer Alice Walker. Important Christian womanist theologians are Delores Williams, Jacquelyn Grant, and Katie G. Cannon. Most U.S. black and womanist theologians are Protestant. In a racist and sexist society, black women cannot prefer one identity at the cost of the other: they are marginalized both as women and as a racial minority.

As in the United States, the struggle against institutionalized racism, often legitimized by religious beliefs, has been the source of black theology in Africa, especially South Africa. Reformed Christianity in South Africa has been one of the ideological pillars of apartheid, the repressive political system of that country for decades, which is why black theology in the South African context has been different from that in the United States. Important black South African theologians such as Desmond Tutu, Allan Boesak, and Manas Buthelezi have often also been leaders in the churches and in movements against apartheid. A black theology of liberation, *la teología negra de la liberación,* including a feminist version, is also being developed in the Latin American and Caribbean context.

## Feminist Theologies

By virtue of its large and varied racial and ethnic minorities, the United States has produced the largest variety of feminist theologies. At the same time, theologies from the United States are not only not applicable in other parts of the world but also often reflect the specific historical and cultural circumstances of that country. Thus, Latina feminist theology (exemplified by María Pilar Aquino from the Catholic tradition and Daisy Machadofrom the Protestant), womanist theology, *mujerista* theology (including Latina female theologians such as Ada María Isazi-Díaz and Yolanda Tarango), Native American, and Asian-American feminist theologies (for example, Kwok Puilan and Chung Hyun Kyung), have been influenced by feminist thinking from other contexts and countries, but also reflect the situation of women from ethnic and racial minorities in the United States. It is sometimes difficult to draw a clear line between Latin American and U.S. Latino or Asian and Asian-American theological production because individual theologians often have spent parts of their lives in both their countries of origin and in the United States.

Some important white North American feminist theologians who have done groundbreaking work are Elizabeth Schüssler Fiorenza and Rosemary Radford Ruether (Catholic), Mary Daly (post-Christian), Judith Plaskow (Jewish), and Letty M. Russell (Protestant). Schüssler Fiorenza and Ruether also explicitly define themselves as liberation theologians.

In Europe, scholars such as Catharina J. M. Halkes, Elisabeth Moltmann-Wendel, and Mary Grey identify themselves as feminist liberation theologians. The European Society for Women in Theological Research has been an important forum for the development of European feminist theologies. Both in Europe and the United States, there are also feminist theologians (after *thea,* Greek for "goddess") who depart from the Judeo-Christian tradition by reclaiming different goddess traditions. Many feminist theologians in different parts of the world include eco-feminist and ecological concerns in their work.

All feminist theologies share the importance of the analysis of sexism in different religious traditions, women's exclusion from both theology and positions of power in religious institutions, and the often explicitly religious legitimization of the subordination of women. Many burning ethical issues, such as abortion and violence against women, cannot be adequately assessed without a critical feminist theological analysis of the religious underpinnings of ethical thinking; and dialogue with feminist theories from other fields is also important.

*See also* **Authoritarianism: Latin America; Christianity; Feminism; Human Rights; Marxism: Latin America; Poverty; Religion: Latin America; Religion and the State: Latin America; Womanism.**

**BIBLIOGRAPHY**

Boff, Leonardo. *Igreja, carisma e poder.* Petrópolis, Brazil: Vozes, 1981.
Cone, James H. *A Black Theology of Liberation.* Maryknoll, N.Y.: Orbis, 1990.
Cone, James H., and Gayraud S. Wilmore, eds. *Black Theology: A Documentary History.* 2 vols. 2nd rev. ed. Maryknoll, N.Y.: Orbis, 1993.
Ellacuría, Ignacio, and Jon Sobrino, eds. *Mysterium Liberationis: Conceptos fundamentales de la teología de la liberación.* 2 vols. San Salvador: UCA Editores, 1991.
Fabella, Virginia, and R. S. Sugirtharajah, eds. *Dictionary of Third World Theologies.* Maryknoll, N.Y.: Orbis, 2000.
Gibellini, Rosino, ed. *Paths of African Theology.* Maryknoll, N.Y.: Orbis, 1994.
Gutiérrez, Gustavo. *Teología de la liberación: Perspectivas.* Salamanca: Sígueme, 1972.
Isasi-Díaz, Ada María, and Fernando F. Segovia, eds. *Hispanic/Latino Theology: Challenge and Promise.* Minneapolis: Fortress, 1996.
King, Ursula, ed. *Feminist Theology from the Third World: A Reader.* Maryknoll, N.Y.: Orbis, 1994.
Pieris, Aloysius. *An Asian Theology of Liberation.* Maryknoll, N.Y.: Orbis, 1988.
Ruether, Rosemary R. *Liberation Theology: Human Hope Confronts Christian History and American Power.* New York: Paulist Press, 1972.
———. *Sexism and God-talk: Toward a Feminist Theology.* Boston: Beacon, 1983.

Schüssler Fiorenza, Elisabeth. *In Memory of Her: A Feminist Theological Reconstruction of Christian Origins.* New York: Crossroad, 1983.

Thistlethwaite, Susan B., and Mary P. Engel, eds. *Lift Every Voice: Constructing Christian Theologies from the Underside.* San Francisco: Harper and Row, 1990.

*Elina Vuola*

**LIBERTY.** Liberty is an integral concept in Western political and social thought. Liberty as an inalienable social and political attribute of individuals emerged in the formation of the modern political discourse in the West. Since Georg Wilhelm Friedrich Hegel (1770–1831) the concept has often been categorized in a threefold manner: moral liberties (freedom of moral choice, such as freedom of conscience), civil liberties (freedom of individuals as constituting members of a civil society, such as freedom of speech) and political liberties (freedom of individuals in relation to the state, such as freedom of political association), all being attributes of individuals. Premodern Europe, by contrast, did not necessarily attribute liberties to individuals but to social relations and communities. Non-Western worlds did not produce an idea equivalent to liberty in their own intellectual traditions. Around the nineteenth century, however, they assimilated the Occidental idea of liberty primarily as a concept denoting the independence of the nation state rather than the liberties of individual human beings. In what follows we shall survey Western conceptions of liberty chronologically, and discuss the Islamic, Indian, Chinese, and Japanese variations of it.

### Ancient Conceptions

Liberty or freedom (*eleutheria*) in ancient Greece denoted the status of the free man and woman as opposed to that of the slave. The division between free persons and slaves was deemed to be a social and natural institution. Free status was identified by a set of various rights and privileges. Hence, liberty was exclusive and could not be shared by every individual. Indeed, one of the rights of free individuals was to own other individuals as slaves. Similarly, the political freedom of a community also denoted the subjugation of other communities under its control. The preservation of an individual's liberty was not considered to be inconsistent with the depravation of another's, and this was also the case with a political community. In addition, the Greek (especially Athenian) concept of liberty entailed equality of political rights and freedom of male political participation in the public sphere.

In his philosophical framework, Plato (c. 428–348 or 347 B.C.E.) left little room for liberty or freedom. Liberty was not a constituent element of human dignity, and freedom of thought was nothing other than the freedom to be incorrect, that is, a greater chance to deviate from the objective truths. Aristotle's (384–322 B.C.E.) definition of liberty resembles the contemporary notion; for him, the general essence of freedom is being one's own person for one's own sake rather than belonging to another. What discriminates the slave from the free man, then, is not that he is restricted in his actions and subject to coercion but that everything he does is done to serve the interest of someone else. Whether Aristotle enshrined individual freedom in the sense of personal autonomy is a contentious issue. The place of autonomous practical rationality in his ethics becomes problematic when set against his claim of the individual's subordination to the state (*polis*). Aristotle's alleged dearth of interest in personal autonomy would be consistent with the reduction of the individual to a mere part of the state, while the recognition of personal autonomy in the Aristotelian ethical system would not.

The Roman idea of liberty (*libertas*) was a civic right acquired under positive law; namely, it was a constituent of the membership of the civic body (citizenship). Roman civil law was applicable to citizens of Rome only; noncitizens were ruled by the law of nations. Roman liberty was by definition a positive right that was guaranteed (but could also be withdrawn) by the law. Law-abiding citizens enjoyed the liberty of a Roman citizen and, before the law, all the citizens were equal. The slave was legally defined as a thing (*res*)—rather than person (*persona*)—and was subject to the mastery of another person.

In the final days of Roman republicanism, Cicero (106–43 B.C.E.) significantly related forms of government with the idea of liberty. He drew on the Polybian discourse on the change of constitutions and characterized each form of polity according to the degree of liberty attributed to it. Cicero's notion of liberty was equality of juridical rights, not equality before the law. He considered that democracy was marked by the excess of liberty granted to the ruled, and he recommended a just equality proportionate to *dignitas* (reputation or merit).

Early Christian ideas of liberty concerned interior disposition, which contrasted sharply with Greek and Roman ideas of liberty. St. Augustine of Hippo's (354–430 C.E.) discourse on freedom revolved around the idea of free will. Just as God is by definition unwilling and incapable of sin, so Adam, before the Fall, knew the distinction between good and evil and had the God-given power to choose the good alone. After the Fall, however, Adam and his descendents were motivated to choose evil. At the heart of Augustine's conception of liberty was the incapability of sin. From this perspective, individuals, who are "free" in the this-worldly sense are no more free than slaves. In terms of sinful humanity, neither "free" persons nor slaves have the right to be free in this world: the liberty of humans can only be achieved eschatologically.

### Medieval Conceptions

Medieval Europe, it is often argued, is an insignificant period in the history of liberty. And yet "liberty" (*libertas* or *franchise*) is a word that can be found in a wide range of medieval documents: charters, plea rolls, theological treatises, and polemical writings. Liberty was, in medieval Europe, widely and primarily grasped as territorial immunity from seigneurial justice. The exclusion of public judges from an individual's land was the privilege attached to and exercised in the landlord's territory, and it could only be granted by a higher authority that acknowledged the capacity to act as a holder of a court or to be a judge.

The *libertas* and franchise, however, were privileges, and their recipients were often communities. They were not the rights of individual citizens. Indeed, medieval European society has been described as consisting of tightly bound corporate groups, in which individuals were absorbed, and liberty was often attributed to such groups rather than individuals. Should "liberty" be supposed to be an attribute of individuals, it might appear difficult to narrate a medieval history of liberty. But the "discovery of the individual" is now traced back to the world of intellectuals, higher clergy, and aristocracy in the twelfth century. Accordingly, recent research has denied that liberty as an attribute to individuals was not known in medieval Europe. Liberties as individual rights were also known in terms of personal freedom from, say, arbitrary imprisonment and extortion of money for release. This idea of individual liberties can be found in the record of royal justices and parliaments. Article 39 of the Magna Carta (1215) stipulated that "no free man should be captured and imprisoned or disseized or outlawed or exiled or in any way harmed except by a lawful tribunal of his peers and by the law of the land." King John (r. 1199–1216) was compelled to concede to the requests of the rebellious barons and accepted that royal legislative and judicial authority was limited not only by the divine and natural law but also by his need to obtain counsel and consent of his subjects. In the fourteenth century, the privilege was not limited to the aristocracy as "free men" but to all: no men of whatever estate or condition he may be was to be captured and imprisoned unlawfully. Historians are divided over the significance of the charters of liberties. While the charters appear to offer new liberties, some scholars argue that they merely acknowledged freedoms that had already been enjoyed de facto by individuals as well as communities.

Similar conceptual change took place in the sphere of political and legal theory. It is well known that Henry de Bracton (d. 1268) noted the concept of liberty in Roman law as "the natural power of every man to do what he pleases, unless forbidden by law or force." Thomas Aquinas (c. 1224–1274) maintained that by nature all human beings were both free and equal. Aquinas's concept of liberty denotes the individual's capacity for free choice, in which one is master of oneself, as opposed to servitude, a markedly Aristotelian conception. The English philosopher William of Ockham (c. 1285–?1347) was perhaps the greatest champion of individual liberty before the Renaissance and the Reformation. His ecclesiastical protest against the heretical doctrine of papal absolutism culminated in his assertion of the liberty of evangelical law, which may be grasped as volitional freedom of moral choice. Also Ockham's "nominalist" outlook rejected the quintessentially medieval idea of corporation, thus attributing what he called "right and liberties granted by God and nature" to all individual humans rather than any fictitious groups. His discourse on natural rights and individual liberty has long been considered as the "semantic revolution" of the medieval language of rights. His intrinsically destructive anarchism, it was argued, anticipated the collapse of medieval Latin Christendom followed by the Reformation. Recent research, however, has shown that Ockham's notion of right as the subjective power of an individual's volition originates in the writings of canon lawyers in the twelfth century, such as Uguccione da Pisa (d. 1210), who held that human rationality included a capacity for moral discernment.

## Modern Conceptions

Niccolò Machiavelli (1469–1527) has often been considered as a theorist of political leadership, a founder of modern political science, or a preacher of amoral power politics. Recent scholarship, however, has increasingly paid attention to his republicanism, describing him as a theorist of political liberty. His *Discorsi sopra la prima deca di Tito Livio* (1535; trans. *Discourses on the First Ten Books of Livy*) discussed why the city of Rome attained supreme greatness, and liberty was considered as a means to such greatness. The work, filled with references to Roman writers such as Livy, Cicero, and Sallust, is interpreted as an assertion of republican liberty. Machiavelli grasped liberty as the counter-concept of slavery, which parallels his contrast between the free way of life and tyranny. According to him, the preservation of liberty is closely related to the maintenance of a particular form of polity because the enslavement of a political community will inevitably jeopardize individual freedom. The liberty of individual citizens can only be secured if the political community is maintained in a state of liberty. In this sense, coercion to a specific type of polity does not obstruct but rather warrants freedom, and coercion and the Machiavellian concept of liberty are not mutually exclusive. This maintenance of a free commonwealth in turn requires the individual citizen's service to the common good, which can be motivated through the cultivation of civic virtues. This republican idea of liberty was influential among the English Puritan writers in the seventeenth century including James Harrington (1611–1677) and John Milton (1608–1674), and America's Federalists in the eighteenth century.

Thomas Hobbes (1588–1679) has been regarded as no more a defender of liberty than Machiavelli, and yet his conception of liberty, in sharp contrast to Machiavelli's, was no less important in the history of the concept. Hobbes's notion of human freedom was characterized by the absence of external impediments: he discerned when an individual is not hindered to do whatever he has the will, desire, or inclination to do. Hobbes rejected freedom of the will; for him, to say that the will is free is nothing other than to say that a form of internal motion is not constrained from moving by something external, and this was absurd. According to him, liberty "properly called" is what he called "natural liberty," that is, under the "natural" condition, humans have no legal obligations; they are capable of exercising powers without being physically prevented or compelled. In the Hobbesian world of nature, then, one can maximize the enjoyment of liberty when one is alone: a radical and extreme departure from the ancient conception that is embedded in a political and social context. The "artificial" condition of humans, under which people give up their natural liberties and live under human law is in sharp contrast to the natural condition. Liberty we can enjoy under the artificial condition was called the "liberty of subjects," which is identified with the absence of legal prescriptions; hence, "artificial" liberties. Unlike Machiavelli, Hobbes dismissed the idea that the preservation of individual liberty requires the maintenance of a particular type of regime. There is no such thing as a "free" commonwealth because all the commonwealths have laws. To enter subjection to civil rule, however, did not require the complete

*Liberty Leading the People* (1830) **by Eugène Delacroix. Oil on canvas.** After the Enlightenment, many authors began to focus on the constraints that society often placed on freedom. Prior to this, freedom was viewed more as the purview of communities as a whole rather than that of individual citizens. LOUVRE, PARIS, FRANCE. © THE ART ARCHIVE/DAGLI ORTI

renunciation of natural liberty; indeed, natural liberties, for instance, to preserve oneself, were inalienable natural rights.

It has been argued that liberty as a universal God-given attribute rather than a privilege determined by political and social institutions is a distinctively "modern" notion. Indeed, the ancient concept of liberty was inconceivable apart from the political and social context, while the modern one was free from such contexts and was rather linked to metaphysical views about the nature of humans. In such modern views, liberty is prior to any political or social arrangements. However, recent research has traced its origin back into medieval Scholastic discourse; hence, the distinction between "modern" and "premodern" concepts of liberty is increasingly blurred and contentious. Seen in this light, Sir Robert Filmer's (d. 1653) attack on the "modern" idea of natural liberty by asserting the naturalness of subjection to an absolute monarch was a radical break with the long-established tradition. Filmer derived his vision of patriarchal monarchy from Adam's unlimited dominion over his spouse

and offspring. The traditional theory of natural liberty, for Filmer, identifies liberty with license and would allow the members of society to withdraw their obedience as it pleased them, thereby making social order unstable. John Locke (1632–1704) defended the older idea of natural liberty against Filmer's criticism by demonstrating the rationality of liberty. Liberty was the will or power to do or not to do what was willed and it gains a moral dimension when it is exercised through identifying the will with the dictates of the reason or intellect that discovers objective good in the natural law. According to Locke, law and freedom are not mutually exclusive; unlike Hobbes, following the law constitutes the fulfillment of liberty. Locke thus restored the nexus between liberty and moral order that was severed by Hobbes. In contrast to Hobbes and Filmer, moreover, Locke attributed to the state the function of assuring the protection of its citizen's "property" including civil and religious liberty.

In criticizing the malaise of inequality in the despotism of the *ancien régime,* Jean-Jacques Rousseau (1712–1778) was perhaps the most eloquent proponent of the idea of liberty in modern Europe. Rousseau considered that human beings enjoyed freedom in the "natural" state where social and political customs and institutions were nonexistent. The emergence and development of society, however, created moral and political inequality and undermined human beings' "natural" virtue, freedom and equality, which, in his view, culminated in the France of his day. Rousseau thus reclaimed human freedom by asserting popular sovereignty. In participating in the making of the law, men would obey themselves through obeying the law. The kernel of Rousseau's idea of liberty was thus self-mastery, namely every individual's unlimited sovereignty. This conception of liberty transformed the function of the state. In contrast to Locke, who separated religion and morality from politics, Rousseau held that the state might become the constitutive element of the intellectual and moral development of man. This doctrine of liberty influenced Immanuel Kant's (1724–1804) idea of freedom. In their passionate celebration of liberty commentators like Benjamin Constant (1845–1902) discerned the potential danger of legitimating totalitarian tyranny or charismatic dictatorship exemplified by the experience of Jacobinism.

Before the Enlightenment the idea of liberty revolved around its relationship to the moral order on the one hand and the relationship between state and individuals or society on the other. After the time of the revolutions at the turn of eighteenth and nineteenth centuries, however, a new perspective was introduced in the discourse on liberty. The pre-Enlightenment perspective overlooked the fact that individual freedom could be constrained and even undermined by power of society, as opposed to the external constraints represented by the state. This problem, which Jeremy Bentham (1748–1832) first highlighted in his defense of homosexuality and Alexis de Tocqueville (1805–1859) discussed in his *Democracy in America* (1835, 1840), was the main subject of John Stuart Mill's (1806–1873) incisive and extensive criticism in *On Liberty* (1859). Mill's work was primarily written in protest against the coercive force of moralism that pervaded Victorian society. What Mill called the "tyranny of the majority" captured and criticized the coercive reality of public opinion that was intolerant of any dissidence, eccentricity, and difference. Hence, he limited the authority of society over individuals from his utilitarian perspective; interference with other individual's activities is permitted only if they are likely to cause definite harm to some other persons, thereby violating their social rights. The flip side of this idea was the assertion of the freedom of thought. "If all mankind minus one, were of one opinion, and only one person were of the contrary opinion, mankind would be no more justified in silencing that one person, than he, if he had the power, would be justified in silencing mankind." This defense of freedom of thought and speech was rooted in his emphasis on individuality and self-development, which formed an antithesis to the Protestant ethic of self-restraint. Mill's criticism of the "tyrannical" force of social custom also crystallized in his assertion that the women should be liberated from the "subjection" to the men.

## Contemporary Conceptions

Modern liberalism regarded liberty as a property of each individual, thereby conceptualizing it as free from politics. Hannah Arendt (1906–1975) criticized this "anti-political" conception of liberty and preached a return to the ancient political notion. For Arendt, freedom was something "disclosed" in the collective action of individuals toward a shared goal; freedom and the act of exercising power are synonymous, not mutually exclusive. Arendt's celebration of political practice in the polis of ancient Greece resulted in an assertion of republican freedom.

Although Arendt's conception increasingly received serious attention, what has determined the paradigm of the discourse on liberty since the middle of the twentieth century was Isaiah Berlin's (1909–1997) 1958 lecture "Two Concepts of Liberty," which was later published in *Four Essays on Liberty* (1969). Its basic framework is easy to draw: Berlin distinguished between positive and negative liberty. Positive liberty denotes rational self-determination or autonomy, while negative liberty denotes the absence of constraints imposed by others. Despite its simplicity, however, Berlin's conceptualization was controversial and required further clarification. In 1969 he reformulated the concept by introducing two questions. Negative freedom can be determined by answering the question: "How much am I governed?" By contrast, the positive concept can be determined by the answer to the question: "By whom am I governed?" Thus Berlin offered a revised definition of negative liberty: "not simply the absence of frustration (which may be obtained by killing desires), but the absence of obstacles to possible choices and activities." Berlin's negative freedom concerns "opportunity for action rather than action itself," which was labeled later by Charles Taylor (b. 1931) as an "opportunity-concept."

Berlin acknowledged positive freedom as "a valid, universal goal," and yet his goal was to suggest the potential danger that positive liberty could readily be turned into the principle that legitimizes oppression, thereby demonstrating why negative liberty was preferable. Positive freedom as self-mastery, according to him, generates a metaphysical fission of the self into a "higher," "real," or "ideal" self and a "lower," "empirical," or "psychological" self. When the "higher" self is identified with institutions, churches, nations, races, and so forth, the doctrine of positive freedom turns into a doctrine of authority, or at times, of oppression. Berlin's discourse forms an intriguing parallel to Benjamin Constant's dual concept of liberty. Constant made a distinction between ancient and modern notions of freedom. He argued that liberty for the ancients was the freedom to participate collectively in the exercise of sovereignty, while liberty for the moderns was the freedom from interference by the community. Constant criticized Rousseau's unlimited notion of sovereignty—he read Rousseau's texts as supporting despotism. The resemblance between Constant's criticism of modern liberty and Berlin's caution about "positive" freedom is striking, and yet they differed significantly. Constant grasped modern liberty as the inalienable right of individuals, while Berlin's positive freedom is "choice among alternatives or options that is unimpeded by others" (John Gray). Constant's modern freedom and despotism are mutually exclusive, while Berlin's freedom and despotism can coexist.

Berlin's negative liberty was underpinned by his commitment to pluralism. For Berlin, the absence of constraint covers a diverse and conflicting range of values from good to evil. Berlin never tried to reconcile colliding and incommensurable values and rejected any principle that claims to resolve the conflicts. This position forms an intriguing contrast with that of Joseph Raz, who defended negative freedom, by anchoring the moral basis of freedom in autonomy. For Raz, the value of free choice-making is determined by its contribution to the positive freedom of autonomy, which is the intrinsic value. Berlin refuses to give negative freedom such an instrumental status; namely, he celebrates negative freedom as the intrinsic value.

The criticism against the negative concept of liberty highlights the notion's indifference to opportunities or choices. Charles Taylor argues that freedom is important to us because we are purposive beings; hence, we discriminate external obstacles (and, therefore, opportunities available to us as the result of the absence of the external obstacles) according to their significance. The restrictions of religious practice, for instance, may be deemed a serious obstacle and hence a significant threat to liberty, while more traffic lights may not be perceived as serious blow to our freedom. Furthermore, obstacles are not necessarily external; we may be fettered by feelings such as shame or fear or by two conflicting desires (for instance the choice between career and marriage), and we have to discriminate between our motives. Actions arising out of irrational fear or spite cannot be said to be free. Thus Taylor suggests that the negative notion as an "opportunity-concept" is seriously flawed, and abandons one of the important elements of liberalism, that is "self-realization."

Berlin's negative concept of liberty did not only attract criticisms but also found a loyal heir in John Rawls; he understood liberty as freedom from interference. Rawls did not offer an explicit general definition of liberty, but his attribution of the exalted status of liberty, which constituted one of the two principles of justice, is noteworthy. According to the first principle, "Each person is to have an equal right to most extensive scheme of equal basic liberties compatible with a similar system of liberty for others." Rawls was very specific about "basic liberties," which included "political liberty (the right to vote and to be eligible for public office) together with freedom of speech and assembly, liberty of conscience and freedom of thought, freedom of the person along with the right to hold (personal) property, and freedom from arbitrary arrest and seizure as defined by the rule of law." The priority of these liberties does not allow any of them to be sacrificed except for the sake of liberty.

In addition to the arguments surrounding Berlin's thesis, a "third" concept of liberty has emerged. Intellectual historians, including J. G. A. Pocock and Quentin Skinner, have explored the republican (or "neo-Roman") concept of liberty in early modern republican discourses, and the political philosopher Philip Pettit has theorized republicanism with a focus on the new notion of liberty as nondomination. Hannah Arendt's republican ideals were inspired by political practice in ancient Greece and the American Revolution, while this "third" concept of liberty does not originate in Arendt's vision but rather derives from sixteenth-century Italian humanism and seventeenth-century English republicanism.

Domination, according to Pettit, is exemplified by the relationship of master to slave or master to servant. The "third" concept of liberty proposed by Pettit is neither "non-interference" nor "self-mastery" but "non-domination" that requires that no one has the capacity to interfere on an arbitrary basis in the choices of the free person. Liberty as nondomination differs from the positive notion in that the former emphasizes avoiding interference rather than achieving participation. Yet, republican liberty also differs from the negative concept. Domination occurs without actual interference; and republican liberty would repudiate the presence of a master who did not actually interfere, while the negative concept of liberty would not. Republican liberty rejects arbitrary interference, and what is required for non-arbitrariness in the exercise of power is not consent to the power, as is often claimed by the contractarian theorists, but "the permanent possibility of effectively contesting it." Institutionalized contestability, Pettit argues, would promote "the absence of uncertainty, the absence of a need to defer strategically to the powerful, and the absence of a social subordination to others."

Quentin Skinner participates in the debate from an entirely different angle: he has revised the history of the concept, thereby offering a third concept of liberty that contemporary political philosophers have overlooked. Skinner's case studies of the history of the concept of republican liberty range from Machiavelli to seventeenth-century republican writers including John Milton. Skinner's notion of neo-Roman liberty underlines that it opposes dependence or slavery rather than coercion, on the one hand, and that it requires a specific institutional arrangement, namely the "free state," on the other. The former point represents an antithesis to the Rawlsian narrower notion of liberty as natural rights, and coercion as the antonym of liberty, while, as for the latter, Skinner departed from Berlin who asserted that liberty is independent of the forms of polity.

In the early 1990s Francis Fukuyama proclaimed the "end of history," in a work by the same title, marked by the victory of liberal democracy and market capitalism. Although the number of "liberal democracies" is steadily increasing worldwide, one can hardly say that the notion of liberty is universally shared. Indeed, the civilizations outside the Occidental world did not embrace liberty as a social and political concept until the encounter with Western ideas, especially in the middle of the nineteenth century. The reception of these ideas was, largely speaking, lukewarm at best and, more often, hostile. In addition, those who favored the Western idea confronted the following two problems: one was doctrinal—how to relate a foreign idea to the their own intellectual traditions—and the other was semantic—how to translate the word "liberty" into their own language.

## Islamic World

The Arabic word for liberty or freedom is *hurriyya*, stemming from *hurr*, meaning "free." "Free" as a legal term signified the opposite of "slave," while it denoted, as an ethical term, "noble" character and behavior. The legal concept of freedom, which was already known to the pre-Islamic world, continued to be used in Muslim jurisprudence. *Hurriyya* occupied an important place also in metaphysics: one of the significant repercussions of Sufism on political thought was the retreat from politics. The Sufist doctrine of renunciation maintained that poverty, self-humiliation and complete surrender of personality was the highest value of life, which underpinned the apolitical character of the doctrine. Accordingly, a Sufi mystic philosopher, Ibn al-Arabi (1165–1240), defined *hurriyya* as "slavery to God," namely freedom from everything but God. Personal freedom was valued within the religious, moral, and customary sphere determined by the *umma* (Islamic community of believers), yet it was never considered to be an absolute moral value. Thus *hurriyya* never enjoyed exalted status as a fundamental political value.

It was Ottoman Turkey in the eighteenth century that introduced the Western ideas of liberty to Islam. The treaty of Kücük Kaynarch in 1774 between Russia and Turkey established the free and independent status of the Crimean Tatars from the two countries. The Turkish term first used for liberty, however, was not *hürriyet,* derived from the Arabic *hurriyya,* but *serbestiyet. Serbest* is a Persian word, meaning "exempt," "untrammeled," and "unrestricted"; accordingly, *serbestiyet* denotes the absence of limitations or restrictions. This negative concept of liberty does not convey such meanings as citizenship or participation to government. The use of *serbestiyet* in a political context dates from the early fourteenth century and was a commonplace in political discourse by the late eighteenth century. Celebrated Ottoman ambassadors, such as Azmi Efendi and Morali Esseyid Ali Efendi, used *serbestiyet* in terms of political liberty in their memoranda.

*Hurriyya* entered the Islamic political lexicon in 1798 when Napoléon Bonaparte arrived in Egypt and addressed the Egyptians in Arabic on behalf of the French Republic "founded on the basis of freedom and equality," and the term *hurriyya* was chosen for the translation of "freedom." Again, the Ottomans made a significant contribution to the widespread political use of the term. Sadik Rifat Pasa (1807–1856) was one such writer. He observed that European prosperity derived from political conditions such as security of life and property and freedom. Rifat's *Concerning the Condition of Europe,* which was written during his sojourn in Vienna, represents the early Ottoman reception of the Western idea of political liberty. But his understanding of liberty was limited to the security of subjects from arbitrary coercion by the government, not the right to participate in it. Rifat also introduced the new language of rights into his largely traditional framework of Islamic political thought.

The Ottoman assimilation of the concept of political liberty was accelerated by the rise of a new Turkish literary movement led by the Young Ottomans including Ibrahim Sinasi (1826–1871), Ziya Pasa (1825–1880), and Namik Kemal (1840–1888). Their popular weekly journal *Hürriyet* was launched in 1868. Perhaps Namik Kemal is the most systematic of these thinkers; he was the first to correlate the ideas of human right and parliamentary government so as to achieve a new vision of freedom and self-government. Heavily influenced by the writings of Montesquieu and Rousseau as well as the practice of the French Third Republic and the British

parliamentary system, Kemal attempted to marry the language of modern liberal-parliamentary democracy to Islamic political language. For the first time in the history of Islamic political thought, popular sovereignty was based on the liberty of the individual. However, the tyranny of Abdülhamīd II (1842–1918) stifled the Ottoman pursuit of liberty.

Egypt under British rule assimilated liberal political thought quite independent of the Turkish experience. Ahmad Lutfi al-Sayyid (1872–1963) was probably the most systematic exponent of Islamic liberalism. Under the influence of Mill, Lutfi al-Sayyid squarely situated freedom at the center of this thought. For him, freedom meant absence of unnecessary control by the state: a negative concept of liberty. Freedom was "the necessary food for our life," the human's inalienable natural right: it was a necessary condition for humans to be human in the fullest sense. Hence, Lutfi al-Sayyid celebrated limited government: political and legal arrangements and institutions that safeguard liberty were the "natural" and "true" form of government. An opponent of pan-Islamism and Arab nationalism, Lutfi al-Saiyyd was also concerned with the freedom of the nation. He argued for the liberation of Egypt from foreign rule. In this context, liberty and independence were considered almost synonymous.

## India

Liberty in the sense of spiritual liberation from the cycle of birth and death was a key idea in Indian thought. The liberty of the individual in civil or political society was foreign to classical Indian political thought. The equivalent to the idea of civil rights can be found in the ancient literature of Smritis, but it differed significantly from the Western idea in that the former was considered to belong exclusively to the upper classes (especially the order of the Brahmanas).

The idea of liberty came to the fore of Indian political thinking with the encounter with the modern West, epitomized by the intellectual contributions of Mahatma Gandhi (1869–1948) and Manabandra Nath Roy (1887–1954). Gandhi's idea of liberty was framed in the idea of *swaraj,* a multifaced concept of the utmost importance in his thought. *Swaraj,* literally meaning "self-rule," was also used by Gandhi to signify national independence and the political, economic and spiritual freedom of the individual. As was the case with the "modern" Islam, national independence was closely related to the idea of liberty, meaning collective freedom from alien rule. Gandhi, however, did not conceptualize it negatively. National independence, framed in the idea of *swaraj,* was not merely freedom from foreign rule but also self-government. Gandhi's commitment to political freedom turned him into a defender of rights, and yet he refused to base the peace and security of collective life on rights. He always placed individual duty (dharma) and social and moral interdependence above rights because, for him, rights were the consequence of the fulfillment of duties. Gandhi considered his celebrated *satyagraha* (passive resistance) as the performance of his duties and hence also as a method of securing rights by personal suffering. Gandhi's conception of liberty also entailed an economic dimension: it denoted freedom from poverty. He attacked the contemporary reality of poverty by practicing voluntary poverty in order to demonstrate solidarity with the poor, while he criticized technology-oriented industrialization for its imperialistic exploitation of the masses. Although Gandhi located liberty in a political and economic context, his notion of liberty was also spiritual: self-rule through the practice of virtues toward self-realization. Gandhi's novelty lies in the fact that to the notion of spiritual freedom, which was derived from the classical Indian tradition, he added political, economic, and social dimensions. This perspective derived from Gandhi's internal dialogue between the Western Utopian thought represented by Henry David Thoreau (1817–1862), John Ruskin (1819–1920), Ralph Waldo Emerson (1803–1882), and Leo Tolstoy (1828–1910) and the classical Indian thought manifested in the Hindu devotional work the *Bhagavad Gita.*

Whereas Gandhi's leadership of the Hindu masses was enormously influential and successful, Manabendra Nath Roy's gained no popular appeal. Roy's political position changed over time from nationalism, then to communism, and finally to radical humanism. His colorful but unsuccessful commitment to the Indian freedom movement, however, was guided consistently by an ardent desire for individual freedom. The intellectual context of Roy's political and literary activity was, unlike that of Gandhi, distinctively Westernized, markedly severed from the Indian traditions. Roy defined freedom as the "progressive disappearance of all restrictions on the unfolding of the potentialities of individuals," and anchored the desire for freedom in biological nature. His conception of liberty was radically negative to the extent that individual freedom and social responsibility were mutually exclusive. Roy considered liberty to be dependent upon the mind of the individual rather than external conditions, and yet his belief in popular sovereignty as an inalienable right determined his preference for people's direct political participation in parliamentary democracy.

## China

The Chinese language did not know a word for "liberty" before the nineteenth century. The modern translation of "liberty," *ziyou* (meaning, literally, self-determination), had to be coined in response to the reception of Western ideas. The closest classical term, *ziran* (meaning, literally, "the natural"), denoted a Taoist sense of harmony with nature. This is not to say that the idea of personal freedom was totally foreign to classical Chinese philosophy. Confucian belief in human perfectibility, however, concerned interior spiritual freedom, differing from the Western political and social concept. Likewise, freedom as a right was not conceptualized until the nineteenth century. Kang Youmai (1858–1927) was one of the first Chinese intellectuals who introduced the Protestant idea of free will. His *Complete Book of Substantial Principles and General Laws* (written between 1885 and 1887) described human beings as owners of the "right of autonomy" (*zizhu zhi quan*), thereby adopting the language of rights.

The Chinese encounter with the Western idea of liberty may well be illustrated by the translation of the works of nineteenth-century English intellectuals by Yan Fu (1854–1921). He became widely known for his translation of T. H. Huxley's *Evolution and Ethics,* which introduced evolution theory to the Chinese intellectual world at the turn of nineteenth and twentieth centuries. Deeply inspired by Herbert Spencer's (1820–1903) concept of social organism, Yan Fu maintained that the individual's pursuit of self-interest would generate a Darwinian struggle for survival that should result in the evolution of a more harmonious society. Yan Fu claimed to have derived from Spencer his own notion of human freedom denoting the release of an individual's "energy." His Spencerian liberalism was a radical departure from the orthodox Confucian ethic that regarded the pursuit of self-interest as the source of evil, while his translations also distorted the original meaning of other writings from the West. One such case is his translation of Mill's *On Liberty.* Yan Fu bent Mill's original conception of liberty to meet his own political purposes. Mill considered liberty of the individual as an end in itself. However, Yan Fu's Spencerian outlook produced a distorted understanding of Mill's concept as a means to the advancement of the people's virtue and intellect, ultimately to achieve the freedom of the state.

One of the powerful promoters of individual liberties (*ziyou*) and rights (*quanli*) in the Late Qing China was Liang Qichao (1873–1929). He absorbed a wide range of Western philosophy and social sciences through Japanese translations, but he endeavored to anchor the ideas of liberty and rights in the Confucian intellectual heritage. It has been debated how the Chinese reception of social and political concepts and discourses from the modern West relates to classical Chinese traditions. For instance, freedom of thought is at the heart of contemporary Western liberal democracy, while "harmony and unity of thought" (*tongyi sixiang*) is celebrated in post-socialist China. This contrasting attitude toward freedom of thought has received scholarly attention in connection with the lingering Confucian tradition.

## Japan

In modern Japanese, "liberty" is normally translated *jiyu*. The Japanese first encountered the idea of liberty in Dutch, *vrijheid,* and the translator could not find any proper translation, leaving it untranslated. Indeed, when Western scholarship flooded into the Japanese intellectual scene through the translation of works such as Samuel Smiles's *Self Help* (1859) and Mill's *On Liberty,* "liberty" was commonly recognized as a difficult word to translate. After a variety of translations were attempted, *jiyu* survived as the only term widely used today. Unlike the case in China, *jiyu* had already existed in the Japanese vocabulary before Japan's exposure to the Western idea of liberty; however, the first Japanese translators of "liberty" were not entirely convinced with their choice of the term. Fukuzawa Yukichi (1834–1901) is arguably responsible for the proliferation of the word, and yet he noted that *jiyu* (and any other Japanese word) failed to capture the precise meaning of liberty. According to the contemporary usage, *jiyu* signified "selfishness," "arbitrariness," and "emancipation of human desire"—in a word "license." The moral connotation of *jiyu* was rather negative. Some maintain that the notion of *jiyu* is rooted in the Taoist idea of formless but freely moving spirit, while others see its affinity to the National Learning (*kokugaku*) emphasis on human desire, as the novelist and poet Ihara Saikaku (1642–1693) once wrote: "Humans are the desires with four limbs." The first translators' concern with possible misunderstanding and misconceptions soon became real: although *jiyu* became a buzz word in the 1880s when the Freedom and People's Rights Movement (*jiyu minken undo*) reached its height, the majority of intellectuals and political leaders who supported the movement grasped *jiyu* in terms of "license." Consequently liberalism was considered to be a licentious ideology.

The leaders of the Japanese Enlightenment often understood the concept of *jiyu* in connection with the independence of their country as a nation state. The liberty and independence of the state were the focus of debate, whereas civil liberties often escaped the attention of intellectuals. The indifference to civil liberties forms the background to the state's oppression of free speech and academic enquiry. In 1919, Morito Tatsuo (1888–1984), of the Faculty of Economics in Tokyo Imperial University, published an article on the social thought of the anarchist Pyotr Kropotkin (1842–1921), and the authorities filed charges against him and the editor of the journal that published the paper. Morito was expelled from the university and imprisoned. Minobe Tatsukichi (1873–1948) of the Faculty of Law at Tokyo Imperial University was known for his view that the emperor was an organ of the state. In 1935, his "organ theory," which had gained wide support in the academic community, suddenly became the object of public condemnation. Minobe was compelled to resign from the Membership of the House of Peers, and his books were banned and burned. These incidents did not merely represent the state's oppression of intellectual freedom, but also reflected the public's skepticism toward the mistranslated "liberty." The widespread confusion of *jiyu* with license had prevented the Japanese from appreciating the value of civil liberties, and heavily discredited liberalism until Japan's disastrous defeat in 1945.

*See also* **Autonomy; Enlightenment; Equality; Human Rights; Liberalism; Sovereignty; State, The.**

BIBLIOGRAPHY

Angle, Stephen C. *Human Rights and Chinese Thought: A Cross-Cultural Inquiry.* Cambridge, U.K.: Cambridge University Press, 2002.

Berlin, Isaiah. *Four Essays on Liberty.* Oxford: Oxford University Press, 1969.

Bhattacharjee, G. P. *Evolution of Political Philosophy of M. N. Roy.* Calcutta: Minerva Associates, 1971.

Black, Antony. *The History of Islamic Political Thought from the Prophet to the Present.* Edinburgh: Edinburgh University Press, 2001.

Coleman, Janet. *A History of Political Thought from Ancient Greece to Early Christianity.* Oxford: Blackwell, 2000.

———. *A History of Political Thought from the Middle Ages to the Renaissance.* Oxford: Blackwell, 2000.

Constant, Benjamin. *Political Writings.* Translated by Biancamaria Fontana. Cambridge, U.K., and New York: Cambridge University Press, 1988.

de Bary, Wm. Theodore, and Weiming Tu, eds. *Confucianism and Human Rights.* New York: Columbia University Press, 1998.

Ghoshal, U. N. *A History of Indian Political Ideas: The Ancient Period and the Period of Transition to the Middle Ages.* Oxford: Oxford University Press, 1966.

Gray, John. *Isaiah Berlin.* London: HarperCollins, 1994.

Harding, Alan. "Political Liberty in the Middle Ages." *Speculum* 55 (1980): 423–443.

Hourani, Albert. *Arabic Thought in the Liberal Age, 1798–1939.* Cambridge, U.K., and New York: Cambridge University Press, 1983.

Howland, Douglas. *Translating the West: Language and Political Reason in Nineteenth-Century Japan.* Honolulu: University of Hawai'i Press, 2002.

Lewis, Bernard. *The Emergence of Modern Turkey.* 3rd ed. Oxford: Oxford University Press, 2002.

———. *The Political Language of Islam.* Chicago: University of Chicago Press, 1988.

Mill, John Stuart. *On Liberty, with The Subjection of Women, and Chapters on Socialism.* Edited by Stefan Collini. Cambridge, U.K.: Cambridge University Press, 1989.

Miller, James. *Rousseau: Dreamer of Democracy.* New Haven: Yale University Press, 1984.

Parel, Anthony J., ed. *Gandhi, Freedom and Self-Rule.* Lanham, Md.: Lexington Books, 2000.

Pelczynski, Zbigniew, and John Gray, eds., *Conceptions of Liberty in Political Philosophy.* London: Athrone Press, 1984.

Pettit, Philip. *Republicanism: A Theory of Freedom and Government.* Oxford: Clarendon Press, 1997.

Rawls, John. *A Theory of Justice.* Cambridge Mass.: Belknap Press, 1971.

Raz, Joseph. *The Morality of Freedom.* Oxford: Clarendon Press, 1986.

Schwartz, Benjamin. *In Search of Wealth and Power: Yen Fu and the West.* Cambridge, Mass.: Belknap Press, 1964.

Skinner, Quentin. *Visions of Politics.* 3 vols. Cambridge, U.K., and New York: Cambridge University Press, 2002.

Taylor, Charles. "What's Wrong with Negative Liberty?" In *Philosophical Papers 2: Philosophy and the Human Sciences.* Cambridge, U.K.: Cambridge University Press, 1985.

Tierney, Brian. *The Idea of Natural Rights: Studies on Natural Rights, Natural Law, and Church Law, 1150–1650.* Atlanta: Scholars Press, 1997.

Tully, James. *An Approach to Political Philosophy: Locke in Contexts.* Cambridge, U.K.: Cambridge University Press, 1993.

Wakabayashi, Bob Tadashi, ed. *Modern Japanese Thought.* Cambridge, U.K.: Cambridge University Press, 1998.

Wood, Neal. *Cicero's Social and Political Thought.* Berkeley and Los Angeles: University of California Press, 1988.

*Takashi Shogimen*

**LIFE.**　Throughout recorded history human beings have recognized the qualitative difference between the living and nonliving worlds, the animate and inanimate. Placing that recognition on solid, rational footing or giving it a quantitative basis has remained a major challenge, however. What exactly makes a living being so different from one that is nonliving? Living organisms carry out oxidation, for example, but so does a candle when it burns; living organisms grow from some sort of seedlike beginning to a larger form, but so does a crystal in a supersaturated solution; some organisms move, but others, like plants, do not; organisms reproduce (that is, make copies of themselves), but so do some molecules in the chemical process known as autocatalysis; viruses, probably the most confusing of all forms of matter in this regard, can enter living cells, reproduce themselves, break out of the cell, and infect other cells, yet they can also be crystallized and placed on a shelf for decades, only to become reactivated when placed in a solution in contact with host cells. In short, no single criterion or set of behaviors can unequivocally be said to distinguish living from nonliving matter. Yet there is also little doubt in most cases when we encounter a living organism. Life is characterized by a whole set of activities or functions, no one of which is unique but which collectively set living organisms apart from other physical entities.

In the history of Western thought, attempts to define life have been characterized by a series of alternative or dialectically opposed approaches that have reflected changing philosophical, cultural, and economic conditions. These alternative approaches will be described briefly and then applied to various aspects of the characterization of life.

### Idealist versus Materialist Conceptions of Life

One of the oldest debates about the nature of life centered on whether living organisms functioned by means of a nonphysical process that lay outside material nature and therefore could not be fully understood by rational investigation or whether they could be understood in terms of everyday natural processes. The view that dominated the ancient and medieval worlds, known philosophically as idealism, claimed that living beings were qualitatively different from nonliving, representing a special set of categories whose "essence" existed only in the mind of the Creator. Associated particularly with the philosophy of Plato (c. 428–348 or 347 B.C.E.), this idealistic perspective claims that rational understanding of the essence of life is philosophically impossible, since by definition the categories of each unique species exist not in the material world but only in the nonmaterial, essentialist categories conceived by the Creator. Idealists did not deny the material reality of living organisms but only claimed that the essence of living organisms could never be understood by human investigation. Most idealists saw life as originating from a special, supernatural process of creation by a nonmaterial being.

The diversity of living organisms observed in the world was always viewed as a product of the creation of separate essences known as species, which were absolute and immutable. The biologist's role was to try to understand the essence as much as possible by examining individual representatives of the species and determining their common or essential features. Variation among individual members of a species was recognized of course but was viewed as natural deviations from the "essence" in the same way that any given piece of pottery can be viewed as a deviation from the potter's mold. The Platonic tradition thus became the basis for the Western idealistic view of "life" in the biological sense, informing questions not only about the functionality of organisms but also about their origin.

Idealism continued to form a backdrop to discussions of the nature and origin of species in the eighteenth and nineteenth centuries in the works of the taxonomist Carolus Linnaeus (Carl von Linné; the so-called "father" of taxonomy), the anatomist and paleontologist Georges Cuvier, and others who continued to see species as fixed entities formed by special creation. The

"scientific creation" movement in the United States in the 1970s and 1980s and "intelligent design" arguments in the early twenty-first century are yet more manifestations of idealistic thinking, because they are based on the claim that creation by supernatural (nonmaterial) processes has occurred and is as theoretically valid as theories of descent with modification by material processes, such as gene mutation, selective agents of the environment, and differential fertility. "Intelligent design" is idealistic in that it postulates a supernatural, nonmaterial "designer" to explain the structure, function (adaptation), and diversity of organisms.

A second approach to understanding life, known as materialism, denies that living organisms have any special status in the physical world, maintaining that they are material beings, more complex than other entities in the universe but not immune to rational study. To materialists, all aspects of living organisms can potentially be understood by the same processes—known at present or knowable in the future—that govern all physical systems. Materialists have generally rejected all accounts of the origin of life by supernatural processes or nonmaterial "Creators." Historically the study of living systems has been characterized by the gradual retreat of idealistic in favor of materialistic approaches to understanding the nature of life.

*Mechanistic materialism.* A long-standing debate among materialists has concerned whether and to what degree it is possible to treat organisms as simply special, complex kinds of machines or whether they are qualitatively different from machines, due to characteristics such as the ability to self-replicate or repair themselves, control their internal environment by self-regulating feedback loops, and so on. Mechanists argue that the basic principles on which machines function—matter in motion, transformation of energy, chemical reactions—are also at work in living organisms and provide a way of understanding life in accordance with the same laws of physics that govern nonliving systems.

Proponents of mechanistic thinking advocate the idea that complex entities are composed of separate, dissociable parts; that each part has its own characteristics that can only be investigated separately from other parts; that the functioning of the whole organism or machine is a result of the sum of its interacting parts and nothing more; and finally, that changes in the state of a machine or organism are the result of factors impinging on it from the outside (for example, machines and organisms decline in function due to physical wear and tear over time).

With the advent of the scientific revolution in the sixteenth and seventeenth centuries, living organisms came to be seen for the first time as truly mechanical entities functioning physically like machines and chemically like alchemical retorts. The "mechanical philosophy," as it was called, was a version of mechanistic materialism, describing organisms in terms of levers, pulleys, and chemical combustions. William Harvey (1578–1657) compared the animal heart to a pump, with valves to insure one-way flow; Giovanni Borelli (1608–1679) described flight in birds as the compression of a "wedge" of air between the wings as they moved upward; and René Descartes (1596–1650) described the contraction of muscles as due to a hydraulic flow of "nervous fluid" down the nerves into the muscle tissue. This view persisted through the Enlightenment, which made the mechanical analogy explicit in its obsession with "automata," models of birds, insects, and humans that moved by a series of windup gears and levers, drank from dishes of water, flapped their wings, or crowed.

In the nineteenth and twentieth centuries mechanistic views again gained considerable support with the school of Berlin medical materialists, spearheaded by the physicist Hermann von Helmholtz (1821–1894). In a famous manifesto of 1847, Helmholtz and his colleagues Ernst Brücke and Emil Du Bois-Reymond stated emphatically that living organisms have no special "vital force," and thus research on organisms should be based only on the known laws of physics and chemistry. Life was, to the medical materialists, a manifestation of matter in motion. Their successor in the next generation, the German-born physiologist Jacques Loeb, after moving to the United States published a new version of the materialists' manifesto as the widely read book *The Mechanistic Conception of Life* (1912). With a blatant mechanistic, materialist bias, Loeb declared that organisms moving unconsciously toward a light source were "photochemical machines enslaved to the light" and that life could ultimately be explained in terms of the physical chemistry of colloidal compounds. Though somewhat extreme, such claims emphasized that the biologist needed to probe "life" with the tools of physics and chemistry, not abstract or metaphysical conceptions.

*Holistic materialism.* Opposed to the mechanistic view is a philosophy known as holism. While some forms of holism, especially in the early twentieth century, had a mystical, idealistic quality about them (associated in particular with Ludwig von Bertalanffy [1901–1971] and Jakob von Uexküll [1864–1944] in Germany and Pierre Teilhard de Chardin in France), holistic views within a materialist framework have become more and more common since the 1960s. The holistic materialist view maintains that while organisms (or any complex systems, for that matter) are indeed only material entities, they acquire special properties by virtue of their multiple levels of organization (from the atomic and molecular to the organismic and populational) and through the interactions of their parts.

What is missing from the mechanistic view, to holistic thinkers, is the description of each component of a system in terms not only of its isolated properties but also of its interactions with others. The characteristics derived from such interactions are known as "emergent properties" and function at a higher level of organization (including the parts and their interactions) than the individual parts alone. A cell can carry out certain functions in isolation (in a culture dish), but the many different functions it carries out as part of a tissue (a group of like cells) represent a higher level of organization. Individual nerve cells, for example, can depolarize when stimulated and release neurotransmitters at their terminal ends, thus acting like neurons; but when integrated into a nerve network, they function to stimulate a whole set of other neurons that can lead to complex outcomes, such as coordinated muscle contraction or thought, which would be emergent properties of the complex, integrated system. Holistic materialists do not admit supernatural or metaphysical explanations, only the

insistence that complex systems are more than the sum of their individual parts.

*Dialectical materialism.* A particular version of holistic materialism known as dialectical materialism emerged in the later nineteenth century in the work of Karl Marx (1818–1883) and Friedrich Engels (1820–1895) and was further developed in the twentieth century by Karl Kautsky (1854–1938) and Gyorgy Plekhanov (1856–1918) in the Soviet Union and J. B. S. Haldane (1892–1964) and others in Britain and subsequently by Richard Lewontin and Richard Levins (*The Dialectical Biologist;* 1985) in the United States. Dialectical materialists maintain not only that the whole is greater than the sum of its parts and that complex systems have various levels of organization, each with its own emergent properties, but also that such systems are always in flux, changing dynamically due to the interaction of opposing forces within them. Thus organisms move developmentally through their life cycle in a constant struggle between the opposing forces of anabolism (building up of molecules, tissues) and catabolism (the breaking down of molecules and tissues). Ultimately the forces of catabolism win out, and death follows. Similarly evolution can be seen as change in a species over time due to the interaction of the opposing forces of heredity (faithful replication) and variation (unfaithful replication). Constant temperature in homoeothermic organisms is maintained by the interaction of heat-generating and heat-dissipating processes. A dialectical materialist view of life particularly emphasizes the dynamic, ever-changing nature of living systems.

Holistic approaches to "life"—dialectical or otherwise—have become increasingly prominent in certain areas of the life sciences since the 1980s, for example, in physiology (especially the study of homeostatic feedback systems), in neurobiology (brain and behavior in particular), and in population biology and ecosystems work, where any useful understanding of the system must take into account numerous variables and their interactions. The advent of the computer in the study of such systems has aided greatly in providing ways of handling the immense amount of data that such investigations must utilize. Growing out of this revived holistic movement is an increasingly prominent field known as "systems science" or in some quarters as "the study of complexity."

## Methodological Debates about the Study of Life
A corollary of the philosophical contrast between mechanistic and holistic materialist conceptions of life is the distinction between reductionist and integrative methodologies. Reductionism, closely allied to mechanistic materialism, is the view that the proper way to study organisms is to take them apart and examine and characterize their individual components in isolation under strictly controlled external conditions. For example, to study the way in which the heart functions, a reductionist would remove the organ from the body and place it in a chamber where temperature, pH, and concentration of other ions could be held constant. Integrative biologists argue that the reductionist approach is a necessary if insufficient approach to understanding complex systems. The heart in the intact animal, they point out, is connected to nerves, blood vessels, and other organs and thus is subject to neural and

hormonal influences that cannot be understood from investigation of the heart in an isolated chamber. According to proponents of holism, it is necessary to devise methods for studying component parts in the living state, in the context of the whole organism of which they are a part (in vivo), as opposed to studying them only as isolated entities (in vitro).

A component of the methodological debate between reductionism and holism is the debate between the strictly observational and the experimental approach to living systems. Proponents of strictly observational studies, such as the Austrian animal behaviorist Konrad Lorenz (1903–1989) from the 1930s to the 1960s, argue that living systems must be studied in their natural context and that when experimenters bring organisms into the laboratory under highly artificial (controlled) conditions, they create an environment so foreign to the organisms that the information obtained is an artifact and of limited use. In contrast, proponents of experimentation, such as the behaviorist Daniel Lehrman, point out that restricting investigations to only what can be observed under "natural" conditions limits the kinds of questions the investigator can ask and the kinds of information that he or she can obtain. Such debates have surfaced in fields such as ecology, evolution, and animal behavior, where field investigators have often claimed that laboratory conditions are so different from those the organisms experience in the wild that the information obtained can have little relevance to how the organism functions in its natural habitat. Experimentalists argue that those who limit their work strictly to field observation have no ways to test their theories and consequently can never develop a rigorous, scientific explanation. Of course as many scientists and philosophers have pointed out, the approaches, like those of reductionism and holism, are actually complementary. Nonetheless, debates on reductionism and holism, observation and experimentation, have continued to resurface and influence the development of biology down to the twenty-first century.

## Unity and Diversity in Living Organisms

Another important aspect of life is its vast diversity built on a base of underlying unity. For example, organisms as outwardly dissimilar as a bacterium, a human, and an oak tree are all composed of the same basic structural element, the cell, which in turn have many similar subcellular and molecular components. All eukaryotic cells (those cells of higher organisms that have a membrane-bound nucleus) contain mitochondria (organelles that carry out oxidation and thus provide energy), Golgi apparatus (a membrane system involved in packaging newly synthesized proteins), endoplasmic reticulum (a complex system of internal membranes), and ribosomes (small structures that form the site of protein synthesis). Simpler cells known as prokaryotes (bacteria, blue-green algae, and so forth), while lacking mitochondria and other organelles, contain ribosomes and share all the basic molecular infrastructure with eukaryotes. For example, both prokaryotes and eukaryotes have their hereditary information encoded in the molecule of deoxyribonucleic acid (DNA), transcribe that message into messenger RNA (mRNA), and translate that message into proteins in exactly the same ways. Furthermore the language in which the DNA code is written is the same in all organisms: as a triplet in which specific sequences of three out of four possible bases (adenine, thymine, guanine, and cytosine) specify

each of the twenty amino acids that make up all proteins in the living world. Thus beneath apparent diversity lies a major infrastructure of unity. How to interpret this obvious contradiction has motivated a wide variety of views of the nature of life since at least the early twentieth century.

## The Molecular and Biochemical View of Life

Deriving from the reductionism-holism debate, an important issue from the 1930s onward has been the extent to which living systems are ultimately reducible to molecules and chemical reactions. Biochemical definitions of life surfaced in the late nineteenth century with the discovery of enzymes as "living ferments" and became particularly prominent during the heyday of biochemical work (in England and Germany from 1920 to 1939) on enzyme-catalyzed pathways for synthesizing or degrading the major molecules in living systems. Many biochemists, flushed with success in elucidating the multistep pathways for fermentation or oxidation, attempted to define life in terms of enzyme catalysis. They held that what differentiated living from nonliving systems was the rapidity with which enzyme-catalyzed reactions and energy conversions could take place and the precision with which they could be controlled. The cell, one biochemist argued, is nothing more than a bag of enzymes. The biochemical view of life paid little if any attention to cell structure and organization, focusing almost exclusively on metabolic pathways, their interconnections, reaction kinetics, and energetics.

In the decades following the working out of the double helical structure of DNA by James D. Watson and Francis Crick in 1953, the biochemical definition of life was replaced by, or encompassed within, what came to be called the molecular view of life. The molecular view was more comprehensive than the biochemical, including the study of the three-dimensional structure of molecules, such as hemoglobin and myoglobin, and attention to cell structure and its relation to function, using techniques such as electron microscopy, ultracentrifugation, electrophoresis, fluorescence dyeing, and later confocal microscopy. Paradigmatic along these lines were detailed investigation of the structure of hemoglobin, the oxygen-carrying molecule in animal blood, and the discovery of its allosteric changes (positional shifts) in structure as it alternately bonds to and releases oxygen. The molecular and biochemical views of life tended to be highly reductionist, seeing life as merely a manifestation of molecular structure. Nonetheless, the molecular view did emphasize the importance of understanding life in terms of molecular configurations and the ways various molecules interacted chemically in such living processes as respiration, photosynthesis, protein synthesis, cell-to-cell communication, and signal transduction (the way a cell responds internally to receiving a specific message from the outside).

A particularly prominent aspect of the biochemical and molecular views of life has been the field of abiogenesis or the origin of life. Beginning with the work of the Russian biochemist A. I. Oparin (1894–1980) in the 1930s through that of Sidney Fox (1912–2001) from the 1950s to the 1990s, Stanley Miller in the 1950s, and Cyril Ponnamperuma in the 1970s, investigations as to how living systems might have originated on the primitive earth (or other extraterrestrial bodies) have gained considerable attention. Oparin showed that simple globular formulations that he called coacervates (formed from gum arabic and other organic substances in an aqueous medium) could perform simple functions analogous to living cells (movement, fission). Miller's experiments in the early 1950s demonstrated that basic amino acids, sugars, and other organic compounds (formic acid, urea) could be produced from components of what was hypothesized to have been the earth's early atmosphere (ammonia, carbon dioxide, water vapor, and hydrogen), thus giving credence to the view that life could indeed have originated on earth by simple biochemical processes. Later work of Fox and others on how the basic building blocks of organic matter (amino acids, simple sugars, nucleotides, and glycerides) could have become organized into macromolecules and basic cell structures showed that the origin of the next level of organization up from the molecule, the cell and its components, could be studied by experimental means. These investigations gave considerable support to the view that life is truly an expression, though an emergent one, of the basic properties of all matter, as understood through the analysis of atomic and molecular structure.

See also **Behaviorism; Biology; Creationism; Determinism; Development; Ecology; Evolution; Historical and Dialectical Materialism; Life Cycle; Materialism in Eighteenth-Century European Thought; Natural History; Nature; Naturphilosophie; Organicism; Science, History of; Sexuality; Suicide.**

BIBLIOGRAPHY

Allen, Garland E. "Dialectical Materialism in Modern Biology." *Science and Nature* 3 (1980): 43–57.

———. *Life Science in the Twentieth Century.* New York: Wiley, 1975.

Bertalanffy, Ludwig von. *Problems of Life.* New York: Harper, 1960. Translation of vol. 1 of *Das Biologische Weltbild* (1949).

Coleman, William. *Biology in the Nineteenth Century: Problems of Form, Function, and Transformation.* New York: Wiley, 1971.

Fruton, Joseph S. *Proteins, Enzymes, Genes: The Interplay of Chemistry and Biology.* New Haven, Conn.: Yale University Press, 1999.

Hall, Thomas S. *Ideas of Life and Matter.* 2 vols. Chicago: University of Chicago Press, 1969.

Harrington, Anne. *Reenchanted Science.* Princeton, N.J.: Princeton University Press, 1996.

Lenoir, Timothy. *The Strategy of Life: Teleology and Mechanism in Nineteenth-Century German Biology.* Dordrecht, Netherlands: Reidel, 1982.

Mayr, Ernst. *The Growth of Biological Thought.* Cambridge, Mass.: Belknap Press, 1982.

Oparin, A. I. *Life: Its Nature, Origin, and Development.* Translated by Ann Synge. New York: Academic Press, 1961.

*Garland E. Allen*

# LIFE CYCLE.

This entry includes three subentries:

*Overview*
*Adolescence*
*Elders/Old Age*

## OVERVIEW

The Sphinx, according to an ancient Greek tale, was a monster with the face of a woman, the body of a lion, and gigantic wings. Sent by the goddess Hera to punish the city of Thebes, she sat on a hilltop and stopped passersby, posing them a riddle: "What has one voice, and is four-footed, two-footed, and three-footed?" Every time the Thebans gave a wrong answer, she devoured one of them—including Haemon, the king's son. Only Oedipus, a stranger traveling through town, was able to give the correct answer: "Man."

The riddle makes allusion to the life-cycle: man travels "four-footed" (i.e., on hands and knees) as an infant, on two feet as an adult, and "three-footed" (with the aid of a cane) in old age. To solve it, it is necessary to think of a man both as a singular individual—with "one voice"—and as a being who changes form over time. Apparently the puzzle was widely known in the ancient Mediterranean, a bit of folk wisdom that gradually made its way into Oedipus's tale. (It is not to be found in written versions before 600 B.C.E., including that of Hesiod [fl. c. 700 B.C.E.].) Its depiction of a normative life course casts an oblique shadow over Oedipus's own, for by solving the puzzle and reclaiming the king's prize—his own mother as a bride—he twists the normal sequence of the generations into grotesque and tragic form.

The notion of the life cycle, then—that there are stages in life through which every individual must pass—is old and widespread. And, as in this tale, it is both descriptive and prescriptive: It describes inevitable physiological changes that are readily observable in humans as in all living things, but it also suggests that one ought to move through life in a certain prescribed manner. This dual meaning can be found in examples far removed in time and space from Oedipus, as for example in two of the greatest examples of early American literature: *Primeros Memoriales,* written in Nahuatl in Mexico by Bernardino de Sahagún (1499–1590) between 1558 and 1561, and *Nueva corónica y buen gobierno,* completed by Felipe Guaman Poma de Ayala (1538?–1620?) in Peru in 1615 and likewise primarily written in a Native American language, Quechua. Each of these books is an act of cultural translation that presents an imperial society of the Americas—Aztec and Inca, respectively—as their authors wish Spanish readers to see them. In each of them, we find detailed, carefully illustrated presentations of the stages of human life. Guaman Poma depicts first ten stages of a man's life, then ten stages of a woman's; curiously, he begins each with the adult in his or her prime, which he calls the "first road"; he then progresses through to old age, then lists in reverse order the four stages of youth, ending with infancy. Sahagún likewise depicts women and men in separate but equivalent sequences; and his Nahuatl informants, like Guaman Poma, emphasize productive labor more than simple physiological change. At each point except for the very beginning and the very end, women and men are shown performing the work appropriate to their time of life. For women in both empires, these stages are defined in terms of textile production, with adult women weaving at looms, while youngsters and the elderly spin. This emphasis upon work—possibly intended to show the contributions that citizens were expected to make to the state—underlines the normative quality of the concept of the life cycle; Sahagún's artists and writers also passed judgment on leisure activities, indicating that while drunkenness and idleness were acceptable in the old, they were to be condemned in the young. In European art, the moralizing version of the life cycle can be seen in the series of engravings by William Hogarth (1697–1764), "The Harlot's Progress" (1732) and "The Rake's Progress" (1735)—humorous visions of the life sequence gone awry.

But of course, the life cycle can also be seen not as a set of expectations, but as an inevitable and even a tragic fate. This vision of the life course often emphasizes the notion of the life course as a cycle: that is, as occurring within a circular, natural form of time rather than the linear historical time invented by humans. As such, it often calls upon metaphors from nature, such as the seasons of the year; and in turn, it becomes a metaphor for the life of a society or an empire, which like the human body may be born, grow, mature, sicken, and die. Although it employs few metaphors from nature, a classic evocation of the life cycle as a circle is to be found in *As You Like It* by William Shakespeare (1564–1616), first performed in 1599 and first published in 1623. The famous soliloquy spoken by Jaques that begins "All the world's a stage" presents seven stages in the life of man, with the end marking a return to the beginning:

> All the world's a stage,
> And all the men and women merely players:
> They have their exits and their entrances;
> And one man in his time plays many parts,
> His acts being seven ages. At first, the infant,
> Mewling and puking in the nurse's arms.
> And then the whining schoolboy, with his satchel
> And shining morning face, creeping like a snail
> Unwillingly to school. And then the lover,
> Sighing like a furnace, with a woeful ballad
> Made to his mistress' eyebrow. Then a soldier,
> Full of strange oaths and bearded like the pard,
> Jealous in honour, sudden and quick in quarrel,
> Seeking the bubble reputation
> Even in the cannon's mouth. And then the justice,
> In fair round belly with good capon lined,
> With eyes severe and beard of formal cut,
> Full of wise saws and modern instances;
> And so he plays his part. The sixth age shifts
> Into the lean and slipper'd pantaloon,
> With spectacles on nose and pouch on side,
> His youthful hose, well saved, a world too wide
> For his shrunk shank; and his big manly voice,
> Turning again toward childish treble, pipes
> And whistles in his sound. Last scene of all,
> That ends this strange eventful history,
> Is second childishness and mere oblivion,
> Sans teeth, sans eyes, sans taste, sans everything. (2.7.139)

In art, literature, and mythology, then, the life cycle is a powerful theme, played both for comedy and tragedy. With the modern emergence of the social sciences, this concept has continued to fascinate and trouble scholars because of its dual grounding in nature and culture. On the one hand, childhood,

maturity, and old age are physiological processes that most humans will experience; on the other hand, cultural norms and expectations about what these phases mean and how they should be lived—and even whether the stages of childhood and adolescence are distinct from adulthood—vary tremendously across time and space. Each of these periods, childhood, adolescence, and old age, has given rise to its own social science literature. Within each, debates about what, if anything, is transhistorical and what must be seen only within its own cultural context have provided lively and stimulating conversations, as exemplified by the tremendous public attention accorded to Margaret Mead's *Coming of Age in Samoa* (1928) and Philippe Ariès' *Centuries of Childhood: A Social History of Family Life* (1962), two of the best-known examples of works that challenged prevailing conceptions about our experience of the life cycle.

*See also* **Cycles; Life Cycle: Adolescence; Life Cycle: Elders/ Old Age.**

BIBLIOGRAPHY

Ariès, Philippe. *Centuries of Childhood: A Social History of Family Life*. Translated by Robert Baldick. New York: Knopf, 1962.

Guaman Poma de Ayala, Felipe. *Nueva corónica y buen gobierno*. Caracas, Venezuela: Biblioteca Ayacucho, 1980.

Mead, Margaret. *Coming of Age in Samoa*. New York: Morrow, 1928.

Sahagún, Bernardino de. *Primeros Memoriales*. Norman: University of Oklahoma Press, 1993.

*Mary J. Weismantel*

## ADOLESCENCE

Many social historians have argued that *adolescence* emerged as a distinct life stage only with the advent of industrialization. Using case studies from regions where the historical record is plentiful, such as France, England, and the United States, scholars contend that prior to the industrial revolution, the physical processes of maturity did not necessarily signal a change in life status for the individual. Rather, adolescence as a distinctive stage in the life course emerges only in societies where certain social characteristics are present. While the processes are complex, in general the characteristics include the formation of an indeterminate period of "dependence" on parents that occurred most often in urbanizing areas where old rules about land inheritance and marriage were obsolete, child labor was unnecessary or of questionable value, and where investing in children's education became profitable. Noting that prior to the mid-nineteenth century there was no word for "adolescence," historians point out that words such as "child" might be used to encompass children as young as eight or as old as nineteen or, in the transition stages prior to industrialization, the word *youth* often referred to semi-independent unmarried children who were often removed from their parents' homes to work on large estates. While the concept of adolescence first emerged among the middle classes (those who could afford to send children to school and not to the sweatshop), by the end of the nineteenth century, adolescence had become "democratized" (Gillis) in western societies, and teenagers of all social classes were experiencing this life stage.

## Conceptualizing Adolescence

While the necessary link between industrialization and a life stage of adolescence is debatable (see Schlegel below) what is clear is that by the twentieth century the term *adolescence* and the understanding that it represents a life stage that is distinct from both childhood and adulthood was thoroughly embedded in European and North American thinking. Usually linked to the years just after puberty and before marriage, adolescence was not only seen as a unique and distinctive life stage but it was identified as one that posed particular problems and concerns. In 1904 the psychologist G. Stanley Hall published a two-volume set succinctly titled *Adolescence* that attempted to set forth current theories about this "vast and complex theme" (Hall, p. xix). While Hall's work on adolescence was nothing if not prodigious, his most controversial claim was essentially that "ontogeny recapitulates phylogeny" or, in other words, that the psychic development of each individual mirrors and re-creates the evolutionary stages of the species. If this is true, then the behaviors associated with adolescence, which at the time were often referred to as filled with "storm and stress," were rooted in nature and therefore were assumed to be universal. Hall's theories on adolescence, and in particular his concern for describing it as a universal stage of human development, were inspired in part by popular theories of the age concerning both physical and social evolution. Indeed, Hall claims in the concluding chapter of his second volume that "savages" "in most respects are children, or, because of sexual maturity, more properly, adolescents of adult size" (Hall, vol. 2, p. 649).

For several decades before and after the publication of Hall's *Adolescence,* social theorists were interested in developing ways to incorporate evolution as a conceptual tool for understanding human behavior and cultural difference. Most of their arguments centered on two interconnecting themes: how cultural and social differences could be explained through an evolutionary model; and how much of human behavior could be explained by evolutionary inheritance, or biology. Both of these themes easily qualify as "racist" by twenty-first-century standards, with their emphasis on white, Western civilization (and behaviors) as the apex of social evolution, while "primitive" societies or "races" were held to represent "earlier" stages along the evolutionary trajectory.

By the early decades of the twentieth century, evolutionary theories dominated the social sciences and influenced social policies through ideas such as eugenics. In anthropology, human societies were described as following "natural" laws and many believed that the "history of mankind is the history of nature" (Stocking, 1968, p. 116). A leading theorist of the time, E. B. Tyler, argued both for delineating how different societies could be understood as models of the different stages of a unilinear evolutionary process, and for the concept of the "psychic unity of mankind" (p. 115), which claimed that humans share an evolutionary history and therefore a uniform "nature." Human nature, therefore, was inextricably linked to biology.

## Anthropological Critique

The most important anthropological critique of the social evolutionary model came from Franz Boas, who published *The Mind of Primitive Man* in 1911. Boas used extensive ethnographic data to make an argument for the separation of culture from biological determinism and the importance of diffusion, rather than evolution, in the formation of cultural traits. Boas became best known for the concept of "cultural relativism," which argues against judging a culture by outside standards. As he states in the conclusion of *The Mind of Primitive Man,* "Then we shall treasure and cultivate the variety of forms that human thought and activity has taken, and abhor, as leading to complete stagnation, all attempts to impress one pattern of thought upon whole nations or even upon the whole world" (1932 ed., p. 272). Over time, Boas attracted a wide range of students who studied with him at Columbia University and by the 1920s his theory that culture is historically created, not evolutionarily structured, became the dominant paradigm in American anthropology.

By 1924 Boas had successfully argued for the importance of cultural diffusion—the sharing of ideas between cultures—as an important mechanism of culture change, but he was still looking for ethnographic data to demonstrate how culture specifically influences the psychological development of individuals and creates distinctive patterns of behavior. In particular, Boas decided that a study of adolescence would be a useful way to demonstrate how culture, not nature, patterns human behavior. He chose one of his young graduate students, twenty-three-year-old Margaret Mead, to conduct a study in Samoa; her assignment was to determine whether adolescence was filled with the same troubles in the South Seas as it was in America. Mead was trained in psychology and she knew Hall's work well. As she explains in her book *Coming of Age in Samoa* (1928), she embarked on that research to answer the question: "Are the disturbances which vex our adolescents due to the nature of adolescence itself or to civilization?" In other words, what takes primacy? Nature or nurture?

While Mead did not overly concern herself with defining "adolescence," it is clear from many of her conclusions that she closely associates adolescence with the years directly surrounding puberty; nevertheless, her conclusion that "there are no great differences" between girls in adolescence and those about to enter it or who have just left it, downplays its significance as a Samoan life stage. Noting the general "casual" nature of Samoan society, Mead argued that adolescence is not filled with "storm and stress" but rather this was a period of orderly maturing interests and activities (1961 ed., p. 157). Maturing girls in Samoa had few restrictions placed on their sexual encounters, few judgments passed on the behaviors, and negligent pressure to prepare for an unseen future. This, she argued, created an adolescence that was peaceful and enjoyable. Comparing the United States to Samoa, Mead noted that American youths "grow up in a world of dazzling choices" and that all choices are "the half-ripened fruit of compromise" (p. 205). Addressing educators directly, Mead used her Samoan research to call for changes in the expectations and pressures put on American adolescents.

Mead's book, which was intentionally written for the "educated layman," became a best-seller and positioned Mead to become one of the most important and influential voices in

American anthropology, and in American society, for the next five decades. Among Mead's most noteworthy contributions were her works on childhood (*Growing Up in New Guinea,* 1930) and gender roles (*Sex and Temperament in Three Primitive Societies,* 1935) both of which continued the argument that cultures create patterns of behaviors in consistent and holistic ways.

Mead's conclusions about the role that culture plays in shaping the experience of adolescence were never seriously challenged until 1983 when Derek Freeman, an Australian anthropologist, wrote *Margaret Mead and Samoa: The Making and Unmaking of an Anthropological Myth.* Freeman, who studied Samoa, albeit several decades after Mead, argued that Mead was a "cultural determinist," who ignored any ethnographic evidence that did not support her contention that culture (not biology) is primarily responsible for human behavior. Freeman argued that adolescence was in fact stressful in Samoa and defended an "interactionist" perspective that interpreted behavior as a result of the intersection of biology and culture. Freeman's book sparked controversy both in anthropology and outside because it directly attacked Mead's evidence but also because it attempted to reinvigorate the nature/nurture debates that had remained relatively sidelined in cultural anthropology. Mead was dead by the time Freeman's book was published so could not defend her own work. However, her reputation, which was only partially constructed from her early work, was never seriously in jeopardy.

By 2000 the dust had settled, with no one on either side effectively convincing the other of the truth of their sides' claims. Given the importance, or at the very least, the prominence of Margaret Mead in the development of American anthropology, it is paradoxical that the study of adolescence in anthropology did not flourish at all in the second half of the twentieth century. In fact, it stagnated. While the study of childhood was continued in a limited but impressive fashion (most notably at Harvard), and gender studies blossomed after the 1970s, the systematic study of adolescence all but disappeared in anthropology until the 1990s. While mention might be made of youths or adolescents in longer ethnographic studies, there were no titles in anthropology focusing exclusively on adolescents for several decades. Indeed, even Freeman's attack on Mead was directed toward her conclusions about the primacy of culture in human development, and was never intended as a serious contribution to the study of adolescence. The study of adolescents did not disappear from academia, but was continued by psychologists, child development specialists, historians, and sociologists. Two important sociological studies about teens in America that furthered Mead's general sociocultural orientation were Hollingshead's *Elmtown Youth,* which focused on teenagers in 1942 and 1943, and *Growing Up in River City,* a longitudinal study of teens in the postwar boom.

## Contemporary Perspectives

While the approaches to certain questions had been significantly refined by the 1980s and 1990s when anthropologists once again began to study adolescence, these studies can still generally be separated into those that seek to find some universals across cultures in the adolescent experience, and those studies that attempt to provide in-depth context for "youth" culture in specific places. In the first case, biology or evolution (understood broadly) is assumed to play some role in the experience of adolescence, while in the other, situating cultural contexts is of exclusive concern.

The two dominant voices for the first perspective are Alice Schlegel and Herbert Barry III. Schlegel (an anthropologist) and Barry (a psychologist) published *Adolescence: An Anthropological Inquiry* in 1991. Arguing for an ethological perspective, in their case reflecting upon observations of primate groups to inform questions and buttress conclusions, Schlegel and Barry assume that adolescent behaviors are both "antecedent," that is, linked to earlier socialization and development and "situational"—influenced by the particular conditions of adolescence. Moreover, Schlegel and Barry argue that reproduction, in particular the (often extended) gap between sexual maturity and social adulthood, is a "key issue" in understanding how adolescence is managed and understood cross-culturally. In this view, biology (in the form of sexual maturity and the necessities of reproduction) and culture (which rarely allows for the full assumption of adult roles at puberty) intersect, literally creating this life stage. In their thinking, neither biology nor culture should be given explanatory primacy.

Schlegel and Barry's methodology consists primarily of reviewing existing cross-cultural ethnographic works that discuss adolescence—if only briefly—and coding for a select number of variables. Their statistical analysis of 173 societies for boys and 175 for girls points to both regularities and differences in adolescence across cultures. For example, the authors argue for the universality of the life stage of adolescence and refute the contention that it is linked exclusively to industrialization. They also point out the ways in which adolescence differs for boys and girls within a culture, and the variable degrees of discord in the adolescent period that can exist between them.

The 1990s also saw the emergence of a number of journal articles, edited volumes, and book length ethnographies that focused on adolescence, or "youth culture." The shift in terminology from *adolescence* to *youth culture* is not arbitrary but reflects the growing emphasis on seeing adolescents as producers of culture, not just as individuals awkwardly situated between culturally sanctioned life stages. The term *youth culture* itself is not new and comes from the sociologist Talcott Parsons who argued in 1942 that middle-class American teens lived in a distinctive cultural world. In today's usage, youth culture has come to mean that teens are viewed as social agents who impact their cultures in meaningful ways (Wulff).

Studies of youth culture are diverse and cover a wide range of topics, but they reflect some of the larger concerns of late twentieth and early twenty-first century anthropology. First, they reflect the shift away from viewing culture as holistic and consistent as described by Mead and others, toward an understanding of culture as "contested" and represented by multiple perspectives and voices. Women, minorities, and even youths are fully part of cultures, yet they may have distinctive interpretations and perspectives on that culture, and act upon that culture accordingly. Second, studies of youth culture reflect a concern for the ways power impacts social organization and cultural expression. Youth are not only influenced by larger societal power structures such as race, class, or gender; they produce, respond to, and manipulate power in different ways (Caputo; Sharp). Finally, youth culture studies are also influenced by anthropology's increasing interests in the processes of globalization and transnationalism (see Kathleen Hall). Teens are often the first to embrace media and technology, they may be the only ones in their migrant families to speak the dominant language or, because of transnational migration, they may find a stunning disjuncture between their experiences as adolescents and the experiences of their parents. "Youth culture" is now seen as responsive and dynamic and worthy of study in its own right.

The study of adolescence in anthropology has been one in which the disciplinary debates between nature and nurture have played out with intense fervor, but also one that represents the fruit of disciplinary cross-fertilization. From the outset, anthropological studies of adolescence have built upon and contributed to debates in multiple disciplines, most especially sociology, psychology, history, and more recently cultural studies. Beginning with Mead, some anthropological work has contributed to public policy debates, most especially in education. While the study of adolescence lay relatively dormant in anthropology for many decades, the resurgence of studies on adolescence such as Schlegel and Barry's signal an attempt to unite divergent perspectives while those on "youth culture" seek to bring the study of young people back to the center of anthropological theorizing.

*See also* **Diffusion, Cultural; Evolution; Gender.**

**BIBLIOGRAPHY**

Boas, Franz. *The Mind of Primitive Man.* Reprint. New York: Free Press, 1938. Originally published in 1911.

Caputo, Virginia. "Anthropology's Silent 'Others': A Consideration of Some Conceptual and Methodological Issues for the Study of Youth and Children's Culture." In *Youth Cultures: A Cross-Cultural Perspective,* edited by Vered Amit-Talai and Helena Wulff. London and New York: Routledge, 1995.

Côté, James E. *Adolescent Storm and Stress: An Evaluation of the Mead-Freeman Controversy.* Hillsdale, N.J.: L. Earlbaum, 1994.

Freeman, Derek. *Margaret Mead and Samoa: The Making and Unmaking of an Anthropological Myth.* Cambridge, Mass.: Harvard University Press, 1983.

Gillis, John R. *Youth and History: Tradition and Change in European Age Relations, 1770–Present.* New York: Academic Press, 1981.

Hall, G. Stanley. *Adolescence.* 2 vols. New York: D. Appleton and Company, 1904.

Hall, Kathleen D. *Lives in Translation: Sikh Youth as British Citizens.* Philadelphia: University of Pennsylvania Press, 2002.

Havighurst, Robert J., et al. *Growing Up in River City.* New York: Wiley, 1962.

Hollingshead, August De Belmont. *Elmtown's Youth: The Impact of Social Classes on Adolescents.* New York: Wiley, 1949.

Mead, Margaret. *Coming of Age in Samoa: A Psychological Study of Primitive Youth for Western Civilization.* Foreword by Franz Boas. Reprint. Morrow, 1961. Originally published in 1928.

Schlegel, Alice, and Herbert Barry III. *Adolescence: An Anthropological Inquiry.* New York: Free Press, 1991.

Sharp, Lesley A. *The Sacrificed Generation: Youth, History and the Colonized Mind in Madagascar.* Berkeley: University of California Press, 2002.

Stocking, George W. Jr. *Race, Culture and Evolution: Essays in the History of Anthropology.* New York: Free Press, 1968.

———, ed. *The Shaping of American Anthropology, 1883–1911: A Franz Boas Reader.* New York: Basic Books, 1974.

Wulff, Helena. "Introducing Youth Culture in its Own Right: The State of the Art and New Possibilities." In *Youth Cultures: A Cross-Cultural Perspective,* edited by Vered Amit-Talai and Helena Wulff. London and New York: Routledge, 1995.

*Ann Miles*

## ELDERS/OLD AGE

The study of the human life cycle is primarily a study of the aging process. The question of why humans age has long intrigued social and biological scientists. While a fountain of youth has yet to be discovered, public health and hygiene interventions have lengthened the human life expectancy greatly over the course of the past hundred years. And yet life expectancy varies greatly within and between societies, relating to their relative socioeconomic status, gender, reproductive history, and environment, among other factors. Biologists have estimated the human life span to be approximately 120 years; however, there are no well-documented lives of this length. This discrepancy between life expectancy and life span raises the important and complex relationship between biological and cultural determinants of aging. In effect, an understanding of the life cycle and human aging is predicated upon exploring these determinants of physical, cognitive, and social decline in later life.

All societies possess some mechanism by which to denote or mark stages in the life cycle—in particular, the transition from youth to adult and from adult to elder. Anthropologists have enumerated many formal age classification systems. Age classification systems such as age sets—groups of persons born within a set number of years and considered to be the same age—are more rigid and formalized among horticulturist and pastoralist societies; industrialized societies tend to have less formalized mechanisms to denote elder status and often rely upon physical and chronological markers of aging. Gerontologists also conceptualize age in terms of age grades, cohorts, and social age. Age grades are status differences predicated on culturally defined social ages. Cohorts are generations of people who experience similar historically defining moments that shape their experience. Social age is a way of grouping elders based on particular cultural experience, such as retirement, widowhood, or grandparenthood.

### Social Theories of Aging

Leo Simmons's is the first major work to explore the relationship between culture and the experience of old age. Using existing ethnographic works, Simmons evaluated the effects of selected societal traits on the social roles, treatment, and status of the aged across seventy-one globally distributed tribal groups. This work set the stage for further investigation into the sources of cross-cultural variation in the status of older people. In part drawing upon Simmons's work, Donald Cowgill and Lowell

Holmes formulated one of the first substantive theories on variation in the life cycle and aging processes. This collection drew upon ethnographic examples from both tribal- and state-level societies and theorized that modernization was the driving force behind the wide range in elder treatment. As societies become increasingly drawn toward modernization, the productive and social roles available to older adults concomitantly grow fewer and less prestigious. With modernization, the status of elders decreases, the proportion of elders within society increases, and the responsibility for elder care is transformed from a domestic to a public sphere; cross-culturally, all elders are channeled into less physically demanding roles, and all cultures place a high value on a good and long life. Critics of modernization theory point to the ethnocentric bias inherent in modernization's naturalization of Western social structure.

The differentiation between what is biological and what is cultural in the aging process continues to drive research into the experience of aging as well as social theories of the aging process. Older adults' disengagement from social and economic life was first understood as a natural process predicated upon decreasing physical and mental capacities; later theories emphasized the importance of reciprocal relationships in determining an elder's likelihood of social withdrawal. Marxist approaches postulated that elders' circumscribed relationship to the means of exchange was the underlying cause of their social alienation. Carroll Estes's groundbreaking work on the "aging enterprise" introduced and explicated the political economic production of elders' relative disadvantage. The aging enterprise is the invention of new needs for the elder population, which are provided by new technologies, services, medications, and goods. This process exploits elders' economic and political power and works to isolate them further from the rest of society.

The 1980s brought a new direction in life-cycle research, one that focused less upon macrosocial functionalism and the ways in which elders as a group function within society and instead directed attention toward the effects of lifelong experiences and social locations on the status and experience of older age. The double-jeopardy hypothesis proposes that elders are first disadvantaged by age and that this disadvantage is intensified by other layers of their identity, such as ethnicity, gender, or sexual preference. In contrast, the life-course perspective seeks to understand elders' status as a product of their lifelong interaction with systems of discrimination and privilege as well as their individual personal experiences. The experience of older age is often positively affected by elders' social support system or their social networks. Social support networks can be characterized by the amount of reciprocity among members, the intensity of exchange, the complexity or number of activities performed by members, or the level of interconnectedness among different members of the network. Elders who possess intense, complex, reciprocal, and dense social networks experience greater social integration and may have greater relative status within the elder population.

Elders' relative status in society may often be predicated upon the various roles they fulfill. Some roles, such as grandparent, provide a high status, while other roles available to elders, such as the sick role, connote low status. All societies possess some

unwritten rules for which roles are accessible to older adults. These age norms, while generally not formalized, can serve as a form of social control to discourage older adults from engaging in activities deemed unfit for their age. Another term used to describe this phenomena is "social clock," the culturally defined time of life for particular social activities to be performed. Marriage, employment, childbirth, grandparenthood, and death are just a few of the human activities governed by social clocks.

**Aging as Stigma**

While the status of older adults varies cross-culturally, in the United States and other industrialized nations, elders are ascribed low status. This low status may be attributed to the cultural associations of elders with disease, disability, death, and dying. In the United States, the emphasis on independence, autonomy, and bodily integrity casts persons who deviate from the norm as morally and socially suspect. The sick, disabled, dying, and elderly are often stigmatized and socially isolated. Undoubtedly elders experience these negatively valued states more often than any other age group; however, the cultural value of any one of these experiences depends upon a particular sociohistorical and cultural context. For instance, immigrant and minority subcultures in the United States may accord far greater prestige and importance to elders than is found in the dominant culture.

Many social scientists in aging studies have examined how to forestall or decrease disability and disease among older adults in order to improve their quality of life and ensure prolonged social integration. Activity theory was one of the first approaches to understanding elders' social experience. Activity theory asserts that older adults have better lives if they maintain a high level of varied activities. Somewhat commonsensical, activity theory does not address the underlying reasons for relinquishment of activities. This shortcoming may open the possibility of "blaming the victim"—if elders have a poor quality of life, it is because they chose to disengage from their social roles and activities.

Disengagement theory is a response to activity theory and seeks to remove the blame for relinquishment of activities from individual elders and instead houses responsibility within human biological change. It proposes that the biological changes accompanying the aging process naturally disincline elders toward continued participation in the productive spheres. However, disengagement theory has the potential to conflate aging with senescence and works to naturalize the segregation of older adults within society. Continuity theory might be conceived as a middle-of-the-road approach. It explains the circumscribed social experience of older adults as a product of role continuity. The roles one acquires as an adult do not change, and as elders age and relinquish physically or mentally demanding spheres, the remaining roles available to them become more rigidly claimed and new roles are not sought after. Continuity theory does not explain why some elders continue to seek new experiences and skills.

**Critical and Constructionist Perspectives on Aging**

The work that Estes began with *The Aging Enterprise* experienced a resurgence of activity in the later 1990s and the early twenty-first century. Critical gerontology aims to examine the sociopolitical processes and policies that conspire to disadvantage certain classes of people disproportionately. As a group, elders are often economically and socially disadvantaged, but critical theorists deepen the investigation of disadvantage by pointing to the heterogeneities within the elder population. Hence critical perspectives are often feminist ones, theories that investigate the ways in which women are systematically denied access to avenues of privilege. Critical theorists also explore the ways in which other markers of identity—race, ethnicity, native language, sexuality, disability, HIV status, educational attainment, employment history, or social class— intersect with age to exacerbate age-related disadvantage. Feminist gerontologists have been particularly vocal within critical gerontology in the study of gender bias in state-sponsored pension systems, health insurance programs, biomedical research, and paid and unpaid caregiving.

The constructionist perspective also gained steam from the late 1980s onward. Constructionists step back from an attempt to explain the totality of the aging experience and instead examine specific facets of experience in an effort to understand the roots of social problems or cultural beliefs. Constructionists differ from critical scholars (though they are in no way exclusionary of the others) in that their focus is on the cultural determinants of disadvantage rather than sociopolitical or economic systems. Many scholars within this vein turn toward narrative analysis to help explain the experiences of elders. Elders' narratives allow for an individual level of analysis as well as providing a means by which elders can be conceptualized as active agents in the creation of meaning and value in their lives rather than as products of political economic systems.

## Geroanthropology: A Cross-Cultural and Holistic Inquiry

Jennie Keith characterizes geroanthropology as a tripartite endeavor consisting of the anthropology of old age, old age within anthropology, and the anthropology of age. Early and contemporary ethnographic works that did not focus on the experience of elders but rather referred to the knowledge and wisdom of elders as repositories and keepers of cultural traditions comprise "old age in anthropology." The anthropology of old age is represented by texts that seek to explore the experience of older adults across cultural or national boundaries. Works by Jay Sokolovsky and Margaret Lock represent just a few of the recent texts in this genre. The anthropology of age seeks to understand aging as a social and biological process and does not focus entirely on the end product of aging per se but looks to elders as active participants and creators of the meaning and experience of later life. All three of these endeavors have been dramatically influenced by three widespread processes: the demographic transition, globalization, and the medicalization of aging.

The world's population is aging, but demographic profiles differ widely among nations. The populations of the United States, Canada, and Western Europe are widely known to be "graying," yet the proportions of the populations that are grandparents in nations such as China, Kenya, or Mexico pose entirely different social and economic questions. Industrialized

nations view their "aging problem" to be primarily one of social services, health care, and cost containment, whereas nations within sub-Saharan Africa struggle with ways to support elders who are caring for orphans of the HIV pandemic. China, the nation with the largest population in the world, will be facing a caregiver shortage of huge proportions due to shrinking family size and because its elders are concentrated in rural areas with fewer young adults to provide, informally or formally, caregiving support. The demographic transition is often thought to be of concern only to industrialized nations that have the longest life expectancies; however, elders in many nations are suffering the effect of low status and lack of support.

Globalization is often bandied about as a ubiquitous covering term referring to the confluence of goods, labor, and information traveling across national borders, but it is not often considered particularly germane to gerontological research. In fact, however, increased economic globalization since the mid-1980s has had an enormous impact on the status and quality of life of the world's elders. Among other things, globalization has decreased job security, decreased employment-related health and retirement benefits, increased the seasonal migration of low-paid workers, upset local economies, and increased international disease transmission. These changes have forced low-income workers to remain in the workforce longer in order to provide economic support for their households, have raided the retirement funds of those middle-income families who had planned for retirement, and have often increased the cost of prescription drugs and other health care products vital to elders. Globalization is often conceived as an economic boon to national economies and a harbinger of prosperity, but it has also worked to exacerbate the existing systems of relative disadvantage for elders.

Estes was one of the first scholars to point out the trend toward the medicalization of aging. Medicalization, broadly defined, is the transformation of behaviors, bodily states, or bodily functions from a state of naturalness or idiosyncratic or cultural behavior to disease states that can be defined, diagnosed, and perhaps treated. It has been characterized as a form of social control and a tool for the expansion of cultural hegemony. Medicalization affects health insurance policies, the quality of life of those living or working in long-term care facilities, the economic security of unpaid caregivers, notions of self and identity, and access to choice of healing modality. It is an interactional process that occurs between social structures, patients, health care providers, or medical technologies. However, medicalization is steeped in the legitimacy and authority accorded biomedicine. The authority and dominance of the biomedical model in the United States limits the range of appropriate responses to disease. Once medicalized, a disease is appropriately treated as a medical, physical (or psychiatric) problem. Further, medicalization does not necessarily imply an opportunity for efficacious treatment or health improvement. Alzheimer's disease, for example, could be considered a newly medicalized interpretation of senility in older adults. Those who are diagnosed with Alzheimer's are given the stigma and gravity of the diagnosis but are then offered limited caregiver support, pharmacological treatment, or long-term care assistance.

Geroanthropology has been profoundly changed by demographic transition, globalization, and medicalization. The demographic transition forces gerontologists to examine elders' status and quality of life cross-culturally while questioning ethnocentric ideas regarding the definition of old age, retirement, caregiving, and grandparenthood. Globalization has complicated cross-cultural research as national and cultural boundaries are increasingly understood as dynamic and historically contingent products of competing international political and cultural forces. Cultural ideas and beliefs are shared via electronic media at an unprecedented rate, and the values associated with specific cultural groups become taxed under new forms of economic exploitation or pressure. Medicalization has substantively changed the scope of geroanthropology. It has also compelled social-scientific researchers to couch their projects in terms of biomedical categories, contributing to an increasing emphasis upon short-term, problem-, or crisis-oriented research rather than longitudinal or prospective studies. This may have the unintended effect of further stigmatizing diagnosed persons as being artificially divorced from society.

These processes have encouraged gerontological research to work toward problem-solving rather than theory-building and ironically may have compartmentalized the experiences of elders while working toward their increased status and social integration. Research with or of the aged or about the aging process itself must remain as holistic as possible in order to encapsulate the complexity of social and physical experience at the end of life. The status of elders varies within and across cultural groups. The current study of cross-cultural variation tends not to focus on documenting these differences but instead looks at the effects of privilege and disadvantage on particular classes of elders in specific situations or alternatively examines meanings and values elders create as active participants in society.

*See also* **Cycles; Family; Generation; Life Cycle: Overview; Life Cycle: Adolescence; Wisdom, Human.**

**BIBLIOGRAPHY**

Amoss, Pamela T., and Stevan Harrell, eds. *Other Ways of Growing Old: Anthropological Perspectives.* Stanford, Calif.: Stanford University Press, 1981.
Bengston, Vern L., and K. Warner Schaie, eds. *Handbook of Theories of Aging.* New York: Springer, 1999.
Browne, Colette V. *Women, Feminism, and Aging.* New York: Springer, 1998.
Cohen, Lawrence. "Old Age: Cultural and Critical Perspectives." *Annual Reviews of Anthropology* 23 (1994): 137–158.
Cowgill, Donald O., and Lowell D. Holmes. *Aging and Modernization.* New York: Appleton-Century-Crofts, 1972.
Estes, Carroll L. *The Aging Enterprise.* With contributions by Philip R. Lee, Lenore Gerard, and Maureen Noble. San Francisco: Jossey-Bass, 1979.
Fry, Christine L., ed. *Aging in Culture and Society: Comparative Viewpoints and Strategies.* New York: Praeger, 1980.
Keith, Jennie. "'The Best Is Yet To Be': Toward an Anthropology of Age." *Annual Reviews of Anthropology* 9 (1980): 339–364.
Kertzer, David I., and Jennie Keith, eds. *Age and Anthropological Theory.* Foreword by Matilda White Riley. Ithaca, N.Y.: Cornell University Press, 1984.
Lock, Margaret. *Encounters with Aging: Mythologies of Menopause in Japan and North America.* Berkeley: University of California Press, 1993.
Simmons, Leo W. *The Role of the Aged in Primitive Society.* Hamden, Conn.: Archon Books, 1970.
Sokolovsky, Jay, ed. *The Cultural Context of Aging: Worldwide Perspectives.* 2nd ed. Westport, Conn.: Bergin and Garvey, 1997.

*Samantha Solimeo*

**LINGUISTICS.** *See* **Language and Linguistics.**

**LINGUISTIC TURN.** "Where word breaks off no thing may be": this is the line from a poem by Stefan George repeatedly cited by Martin Heidegger to indicate his version of the linguistic turn, which affected many philosophers in the early twentieth century—literary scholars already having made the turn, whether consciously or not (Heidegger, p. 60). The phrase "linguistic turn" is actually Gustav Bergman's, given new currency by Richard Rorty, but the phenomenon is far from unprecedented. Friedrich Nietzsche's idea of "the infinite interpretability of all things" is an analogy drawn from language, and a century earlier there was what H. G. Gadamer called "Herder's ill-fated criticism of the Kantian transcendental turn"—that is, his "metacriticism" of Immanuel Kant, which Jacques Derrida likewise recalled. Renaissance humanism, too, was in part a linguistic—a philological, a rhetorical, and a literary—protest against the excessive abstraction of Scholasticism, following the lead of the ancient Sophists and orators.

The "linguistic turn" has been made by many philosophical movements by now, even analytical and Marxist philosophy, and as usual this has been done in the search for foundations and a universal standpoint from which to pass judgments on the human condition. Linguistic criticism certainly undercuts the spiritual world of ideas; but "language," when divorced from the particularities of different linguistic traditions, can also be "reified" and made into a philosophical fetish. Martin Heidegger speaks of language but in practice regards German and Greek (rather than, say, Sanskrit or Chinese) as closer to Being than any other. His former pupil Gadamer, while regarding hermeneutics as universal, is more self-critical, speaking of "trying to draw out of one's mother tongue new ways of thinking." The implication is that there is not only no *Ding an sich* (thing in itself) but also no *Geist as sich* (spirit) and moreover that "there is no meaning where expression fails." Language is the ocean in which we all swim—and whatever our dreams of rigorous science, we are fishes before we can become oceanographers.

**Literary Aspects**

The linguistic turn was apparent in other connections, one the "new rhetoric" of the past generation, which draws attention to the habits and conventions of language, like Michel Foucault calling into question the control of speakers and writers over their own discourse. The arts of speaking and writing are both based on conscious imitation, but every literate person is moving in linguistic channels carved by predecessors, deposited in the memory, and repeated in different contexts. Particular languages produce semantic fields that make possible communication and dialogue; and linguistic usage—particular topoi, copulas, and word combinations—has its own inertial force that acquires meaning apart from the intentions of users. This is one reason for being wary of the "intentional fallacy" in interpreting texts.

One of the most impressive vistas opened up by the linguistic turn is the modern philosophy of hermeneutics in the form given by Gadamer, who, following Heidegger, extended the line of thought in the direction suggested not by Friedrich Nietzsche (as did Heidegger and Derrida) but rather by Wilhelm Dilthey. Rejecting revolutionary ruptures as a condition of understanding, Gadamer preserved belief in a kind of continuity making communication and "dialogue" possible not only between speakers but also over time. There are no absolute beginnings, no understanding without prejudice, without "forestructures of understanding" provided by language and the "life-world." Pursuing Friedrich Schleiermacher's old quest for "the I in the Thou," Gadamer accepts the horizon-structure of experience but doubles it to accommodate the contexts of the past as well as the inquiring present. Language is a continuum making interpretation possible, but it does not permit the sort of retrospective mind reading assumed by the "empathy" of Romantic hermeneutics. That meaning must always be constructed in the present is the hermeneutical condition of Gadamer's kind of historicism. To understand, in short, is always to understand differently.

An important offshoot of hermeneutics is reception theory, or reception history (*Rezeptionsgeschichte*), which follows Gadamer's line by shifting attention from writing to reading. In fact intellectual history is more concerned with the original intention of authors and meaning of their texts than with their "fortune" in later contexts. What Paul Ricoeur calls the "semantic autonomy" of texts is the condition of the interpretations and misinterpretations that accompany the reception of writings. For Ricoeur the poles of interpretation are the hermeneutics of tradition and the hermeneutics of suspicion, the first locating the position of Gadamer (and of Arthur Lovejoy), who seeks an experience of tradition, the second that of Foucault, who is devoted to the critique of ideology. For Gadamer "tradition" and continuity make possible the common ground of understanding and communication that, via ideas, connects present and past (the Western past); for Foucault they mean entrapment in or complicity with ideology and a denial of the ruptures between the successive epistemes that represent decipherable codes (critically fabricated *Weltanschauungen*) of culture and patterns of underlying power relations.

## Textualism

The linguistic turn prompted another and more severe tactic, which was the textualist turn. In this literary/philosophical game of one-upmanship Derrida substituted the transcendent phenomenon of language by the visible presence of "writing," through which—or rather through the hyper-textualist device

of "traces"—he attempts not only to operate in the "margins" of texts but also speak in the realm of the unspeakable and in effect to "get behind the back of language" (in Gadamer's terms) and of philosophical discourse. Taking writing as the condition of knowledge is itself a traditional move, as illustrated in the Renaissance preoccupation with *littera* (*letteratura*) and *scriptura* and, more conspicuously, in the tradition of rabbinical (but also of Protestant) scholarship.

In this and other metalinguistic maneuvers of deconstruction, Derrida surpasses even Heidegger in claiming to be a "beginning thinker"—in the goal of transcending criticism or even, as in the notorious (non-)confrontation with Gadamer, dialogue. The very idea of situating Derrida's own writing in the history of philosophical thought, declares one devotee, "would amount to defusing its alterity and explosive potential." To be effective, it seems, cultural criticism, like philosophy, must be beyond the horizons of historical inquiry. Breaking with tradition is itself traditional in philosophical thought, as this Derridean adds, though without suggesting that the break and the "alterity" occur in the medium of rhetoric, or writing, rather than a transcendent tradition of thinking (in Derridean terms a transcendental state of "*différance, née différence*")—or an antitradition of deconstruction—that is itself set beyond language, criticism, and perhaps even history.

Foucault, too, sought to transcend language and "the history of historians," hoping, with the help of his episteme, to uncover the structures of society and relations of power underlying social practice and discourse, but historians have questioned the methods and especially his attitude toward historical evidence. For Foucault learning does not enjoy high priority; and whether or not he himself was, by intention or vocation, a historian, his opinion was that history was too important to leave to such. Foucault had more important things on his agenda. Criticisms of the concept of episteme (and of "practice" and "discourse") must be of the same order as criticisms of other such collective abstractions as spirit (*Welt-* or *Volksgeist*), *Weltanschauung, mentalité,* and other shorthand devices for grouping apparent homologies in various areas of behavior within a particular cultural horizon. Like Marxism, Freudianism, and Critical Theory, including the work of Jürgen Habermas, it is another effort of getting "behind the back of language," which had for centuries been the dream of "philosophy as a rigorous science."

## Intellectual History

This is also to some extent the noble dream of the German approach to intellectual history that succeeded old-fashioned *Geistesgeschichte* or *Ideengeschichte* (history of thought, history of ideas). Like the French *mentalités*, German "history of concepts" (*Begriffsgeschichte*) is an effort to reconstruct an intellectual field through the history of terms and families of terms like the English study of "keywords." In fact *Begriffsgeschichte* is a species of cultural history focusing on semantic change and the social and political context of ideas, and its program depends on metahistorical considerations to determine the meanings behind the keywords being analyzed. This enterprise began in the early 1970s, before databases like Proteus and ARTFL made possible a much more extensive searching of semantic fields, but it has nonetheless greatly enriched the practices of intellectual and social history.

The linguistic turn in women's studies allowed for the awareness of gender constructs throughout historical records as well as in the limited questions of historians. Words such as *masculinity, femininity,* and *androgyny* became keywords as gender studies scholars began new inquiries into the history of ideas. A last new frontier of intellectual history at the end of the twentieth century is the effort to understand cultures not only past but also alien. Philosophy has not been much concerned with alterity, what Michel de Certeau calls "heterology," which has been faced by historians, anthropologists, archaeologists, mythographers, and other outward- and backward-looking scholars. "The course of history does not show us the Becoming of things foreign to us," argued Georg Wilhelm Friedrich Hegel, "but the Becoming of ourselves and of our knowledge." But the hermeneutical philosophy of his contemporary Schleiermacher sought the *thou* as well as the *I*—the Other as well as the We—and this aim has been carried on and intensified by more recent followers. It is here that the methods of "anthropology," which had been found suspect by Immanuel Kant and Foucault alike, again become relevant, especially the interpretive anthropology of Clifford Geertz, which depends on a language model rather than a natural science model of understanding and that has made its way also into historical studies. Language is the "house of being," in Heidegger's famous aphorism, and the history of ideas, too, has taken up residence here.

*See also* **Language and Linguistics; Language, Linguistics, and Literacy; Language, Philosophy of.**

**BIBLIOGRAPHY**
Gadamer, H.-G. "Die Begriffsgeschichte und die Sprache der Philosophie," *Arbeitsgemeinschaft für Forschung des Landes Nordheim-Westfalen* 170 (1971).
Heidegger, Martin. *On the Way to Language.* Translated by Peter D. Hertz. San Francisco: Harper and Row, 1982.
Jay, Martin. "Should Intellectual History Take a Linguistic Turn?" In *Modern Euopean Intellectual History: Reppraisals and New Perspectives,* edited by Dominick LaCapra and Steven L. Kaplan. Ithaca, N.Y.: Cornell University Press, 1982.
Koselleck, Reinhard. *Futures Past: On the Semantics of Historical Time.* Translated by Keith Tribe. Cambridge, Mass.: MIT Press, 1985.
Nelson, John S., Allan Megill, and Donald N. McCloskey, eds. *The Rhetoric of the Human Sciences: Language and Argument in Scholarship and Public Affairs.* Madison: University of Wisconsin Press, 1987.
Richter, Melvin. *The History of Political and Social Concepts: A Critical Introduction.* New York and Oxford: Oxford University Press, 1995.
Ricoeur, Paul. *Interpretation Theory: Discourse and the Surplus of Meaning.* Fort Worth: Texas Christian University Press, 1976.
Rorty, Richard, ed. *The Linguistic Turn: Recent Essays in Philosophical Method.* Chicago: University of Chicago Press, 1967.
Schrift, Alan D. *Nietzsche and the Question of Interpretation: Between Hermeneutics and Deconstruction.* New York: Routledge, 1990.
Scott, Joan Wallach. "Gender: A Useful Category of Historical Analysis." In her *Gender and the Politics of History.* Rev. ed. New York: Columbia University Press, 1999.
Smith, Bonnie G. *The Gender of History: Men, Women, and Historical Practice.* Cambridge, Mass.: Harvard University Press, 1998.
Williams, Raymond. *Keywords: A Vocabulary of Culture and Society.* London: Fontana, 1976.

*Donald R. Kelley*

**LITERARY CRITICISM.** When the definitive account of post-1960s intellectual technologies is written, the history of literary movements will constitute a key chapter. Perhaps paradigmatic of the closing decades of the twentieth century in its dramatic shifts and realignments, literary criticism at the opening of the twenty-first century shows all the earmarks of specialized knowledge, professionalization, and market maneuvering that have successfully permeated the precincts of human activity in advanced industrial society since the end of World War II. Virginia Woolf's "common reader," for all intents and purposes, has disappeared, replaced by professional practitioners trained in the efficacies of "close reading" and highly conscious of a critical landscape represented by "schools" of criticism, from mythic to Marxist, from structuralist to feminist, from psychoanalytic to poststructuralist. Deconstruction and postcolonial critiques have joined a range of cultural studies that encompass race, gender, and sexual orientation. With allied movements in linguistic, rhetorical, narrative, and semiotic theory, criticism at the turn of the twenty-first century accommodates the study of ethics regarding nonhuman species as well as conduct toward the environment. English and American literature at the university level cut across interdisciplinary formations; thus, the English department, situated in the humanities, could as easily play host to the analysis of legal documents, congressional legislation, aspects of the medical archives, and the fashion modes of hairdressers, as to the recurrence of images of senescence in William Shakespeare's sonnets, or the irreality of closure in Toni Morrison's novels, or the rhythm of repetition in William Faulkner's fiction. The field of literary criticism is a growth industry, its latest paradigm shift related to global transformations brought on by the terrorist attacks of 11 September 2001. Regarding its susceptibility to change, then, the critical field offers a good example of centrifugal movement.

Literary criticism had rather complicated beginnings, apparently unrelated to the project of literary study. Richard Ohmann argues in *English in America: A Radical View of the Profession* that the "technology of the Industrial Revolution gave *knowledge* a new and central place in the business of making a living" (p. 264; emphasis added). The modern American university is dynamically linked to the centrality of knowledge, "the regularizing of technical innovation, and the bending of knowledge to profit" (p. 266). An older technological model, with industries localized in the domestic sphere and skills transmitted from generation to generation, through hands-on experience, was displaced onto the site of the factory, which brought the worker together with the organizational talent of the manager and the stochastic innovations of the entrepreneur. As Ohmann explains, this new model required "a high concentration of special and theoretical knowledge, of the capacity to create more knowledge as needed, and of the managerial skill to bring this about." If these changes necessitated the systematization of knowledge, as well as its spread across "a large and diverse corps of people whose main work is generating, communicating, and developing ideas" (p. 271), then the modern university of the late nineteenth century would become fully complicit with the new social order and its growing market demands. The university would answer both the will and the imperative to knowledge and the demand for skills in an increasingly national population.

According to Ohmann, then, the humanistic project and its situation in the modern university springs from *material* grounds. Ohmann's work is subtitled "a radical view," playfully reinforced by the book's original cover collage, which superimposes the facial images of Edgar Allan Poe and Karl Marx. The graphic conveys the interarticulations of the aesthetic and materialist realms, and poses the conditions by which it is possible to understand not only the role of the university and the ascent of ideas in a market economy, but also the specific performances of criticism and theory. Not at all an oppositional movement to a "business civilization," the view usually taken by humanists, the "business" of the English department, for Ohmann, is compatible with the rationalizations of the "technostructure" and owes its prosperity to that structure's interventions.

Terry Eagleton pursues the provenance of literary criticism and theory back to the "rise of English" and the modern sense of literature that emerged with the English Romantics of the nineteenth century. A counterweight to the alienation of workers bred by the ravages of the industrial revolution, the literature of the Romantics "appears as one of the enclaves in which the creative values expunged from the face of English society by industrial capitalism can be celebrated and affirmed" (p. 19). The Romantics' "creative imagination" was enlisted on the side of the "intuitive, transcendental scope of the poetic mind" (p. 19) and marshaled in the interest of a "living criticism of those rationalist or empiricist ideologies enslaved to 'fact'"(p. 19). The literary work as a "mysterious organic unity" was opposed "to the fragmented individualism of the capitalist marketplace," and whereas the latter yields rational calculation, the former offers spontaneity. In time, the literary artifact would emerge "as an ideal model of human society itself" (p. 22).

Under the impact of scientific development and the related decline of religious sentiment, literature became in this context a decisive moral and aesthetic regimen: according to one of Eagleton's sources, English literature would in time be solicited "'to save our souls and heal the State'" (p. 23). From Matthew Arnold on, "English," in a period of religious decline, "is constructed as a subject to carry the ideological freight of social cohesion" (p. 24). The "poor man's Classics," English literature marked the route to a liberal, humanizing education, first institutionalized as an academic course of study in unexpected venues—not in England's great universities, Eagleton contends, but in the "Mechanics' Institutes, working men's colleges and extension lecturing circuits" (p. 27). Installed in the British curriculum during the final quarter of the nineteenth

century, English literary studies commenced as a "subject fit for women, workers, [and, given England's colonial project] those wishing to impress the natives" (p. 29).

Though Eagleton's and Ohmann's respective accounts of the development of English critical studies are contrastive, what they have in common is the attempt to put in perspective the relationship between manifestations of the creative and imaginative impulses as curricular objects and the material and political bases on which the former are predicated. Not some glorious abstraction, English, which will become the place of habitation of literary criticism and theory, belongs, one way or another, to the industrial phase of capital. Either as a preserve of creative values or as an elaboration of a radically transformed scene of labor, English in the twentieth century would supersede the old, time-honored trivium of the curricula of the Middle Ages—grammar, logic, and rhetoric.

## The New Criticism

In 1930 Harper and Brothers published *I'll Take My Stand: The South and the Agrarian Tradition, by Twelve Southerners,* which might be considered the central doctrinal statement of the Fugitives literary circle and advanced the names of some of the founding personalities of what became the New Criticism in the United States. John Crowe Ransom, whose *New Criticism* (1941) named the movement, the poet Allen Tate, the fiction writer Andrew Nelson Lytle, and the critic and fiction writer Robert Penn Warren, among others, contributed essays to this collection, and there is a good deal of justification to support the view that the New Criticism, running conceptually parallel to Russian formalism, did not exhaust itself for decades to come; if one concludes that "close reading," or concentration on the text of a literary work, constitutes a minimal condition for the performance or practice of literary criticism, then its strategies would be adaptable to all the "schools" of criticism. In other words what began as a value peculiar to a certain social formulation was transformed into standard operating procedure: the practitioner is no longer focused on "close reading," but does it automatically. Close reading is considered so "natural" a posture to the work of the critic that whatever else he or she might do with a conceptual object or "hermeneutic demand" is predicated on its facilities. Terry Eagleton argues that close reading involves both a "limiting" and a "focusing of concern"—both because it excises superfluities—considerations such as the length of Tennyson's beard, for example—and because it enforces, among other things, "the illusion that any piece of language . . . can be adequately studied or even understood in isolation" (p. 44). In any case, for some critics, close reading is an act of reification, or the treatment of the literary work "as an object in itself" (p. 44).

M. H. Abrams describes the autonomous object as a "heterocosm," or "second nature": it is "an end in itself, without reference to its possible effects on the thought, feeling, or conduct of its readers" (pp. 35, 327). If, as Eagleton suggests, the poetic object for the New Critics "became a spatial figure rather than a temporal process" (p. 48), then the texts that one associates with the heterocosm, "chartered" by the Coleridgean imagination, makes the critical process itself as demanding as the thing it is interpreting: irony, ambiguity, paradox, and ambivalence are highly valued poetic practices for the New Critics and will yield, in turn, an appreciation for textual "density" and "complexity" as the watchword of value. The idea is that the poem, in rendering disparate things to harmony, in Shelley's formulation, achieves a dynamic stillness among competing linguistic and imagistic elements.

That a poem could be imagined to body forth such a beautifully orchestrated outcome makes it the model of a perfected world, well out of reach then and now. But *I'll Take My Stand* sketches the social and political presuppositions against which some of the early New Critics were operating and how poetic perfection might have provided them with a strategy of retreat from the realm of realpolitik in an era of global depression. These southern intellectuals were on the cultural defensive, given the South's defeat in the Civil War; General Robert E. Lee's surrender at Appomattox had occurred in 1865, only sixty-five years before the appearance of the manifesto. It is not difficult to imagine that the "political unconscious" of the "twelve southerners" could engage with, up close and personal, their own historical memory: Robert Penn Warren's contribution to the volume, "The Briar Patch," bristles with all the energy of revelation, illuminating Penn Warren's great anxiety—the industrial/technological transformations homing in on the South: "The chief problem for all alike [the Negro and the white] is the restoration of society at large to a balance and security which the industrial regime is far from promising to achieve" (p. 264). Although what appears to be nostalgia for the full range of social relations imagined as complementary to the "agrarian tradition" runs through the entire volume, the unsigned "statement of principles" (the introduction) could easily be read in concert with "The Briar Patch," or even anticipatory of it. Written in opposition to the "American industrial ideal," *I'll Take My Stand* argues boldly in its introduction that the "capitalization of the applied sciences has now become extravagant and uncritical; it has enslaved our human energies to a degree now clearly felt to be burdensome" (p. xi). Labor relations in this new order also fall under the microscope, as do the new means of production: "The act of labor as one of the happy functions of human life has been in effect abandoned, and is practiced solely for its rewards" (p. xiii). Just so, the apologists for industrialism "have been obliged to admit that some economic evils follow in the wake of the machines," yet the remedies that they propose "are always homeopathic," insofar as they "expect the evils to disappear when we have bigger and better machines, and more of them" (p. xiii).

A series of consequences follow from the new relations, and a crucial number of them point toward the cultural indices: "We receive the illusion of having power over nature, and lose the sense of nature as something mysterious and contingent" (p. xiv). If the delicate balance between humans and nature has been upset by the "machine in the garden," then it follows that for the Fugitives, art, as well as religion, is dependent on "a right attitude to nature" (p. xv). "Neither the creation nor the understanding of works of art is possible in an industrial age except by some local and unlikely suspension of the industrial drive" (p. xv). "Under the curse of a strictly-business or industrial civilization," life's amenities "suffer." Furthermore, a community must find a way to extricate itself from

the toils of industrialism, the "evil dispensation," as the failure to do so is not only the mark of pusillanimity, but the loss of political genius and the embrace of impotence (p. xx). Despite themselves, context insistently bore down on the New Critics, although, surprisingly, some of them would be keenly attuned to it: "We cannot recover our native humanism by adopting some standard of taste that is critical enough to question the contemporary arts but not critical enough to question the social and economic life which is their ground" (p. xvi).

Bill Readings argues that F. R. Leavis in England and the New Critics in the United States would have "an enormous impact on the educational system" transatlantically (p. 84). According to Readings, the radical claim "for the benefits of literary scholarship was accompanied by a massive attention to the training of secondary school teachers who went out from the University entrusted with a sense of their mission to uphold literary culture" (p. 84). The impact of the new literary scholarship was hardly limited to teacher training, but profoundly altered the exercise of reading by removing the tasks of evaluation and canon-making from the precincts of common sense; in other words, pronouncements on the modern text—the poetry of T. S. Eliot and Ezra Pound, the fiction of James Joyce, for example—would become the vocation of the professional critic, who would read literary passages not only against the context of the text in which it was embedded, but with attention to the "total context provided by the [author's] work" (Brooks and Warren, p. 1616). Because criticism would become the province of the professionally trained, canonicity and how to determine the canonical would take on capital significance for American criticism. Readings contends that the New Criticism generated disagreement about the canon precisely because the latter was, in fact, "the surreptitious smuggling of *historical* continuity into the study of supposedly discrete and autonomous artworks" (p. 84; emphasis added). The New Criticism brought to fruition a development that quite probably began with the proliferation of "little magazines"—Harriet Monroe's *Poetry*, which Venture launched in 1912, became a promoter of modern poetry—and the culture of literary salons on both sides of the Atlantic, flourishing as early as the 1910s. The artistic entrepreneurial spirit of Bloomsbury, the London intellectual circle dominated by Leonard and Virginia Woolf, as well as the intense collaborative energy central to some literary masterworks, such as Eliot's *Waste Land* (1922), strongly shaped by Pound, prepared the basis of reception for the very notion of the art work as autonomous. In fact, the stirrings across the range of the "seven arts"—in literature, painting, music, modern dance, drama and the stage, photography, and the new kid on the block, cinema, all heralded the heady transformation and new persuasions at work. For poetry and literary criticism, the New Critics would give the impulse a name: modernism.

***Formalism and Beyond.*** It might come as a matter of surprise for some readers that according to Lee Lemon and Marion J. Reis, "During the 1920s a group of Russian critics urged the separation of literature and politics [which] challenges our popular clichés about Soviet control of literary theory" (p. ix). In their succinct account of Russian formalist criticism, Lemon and Reis go on to observe that the early work of the Russian formalists and the America New Critics demonstrated certain concepts and strategies in common, among them: (1) "an attack against traditional academic scholarship"; (2) a critical theory that drives a corridor between literature and other disciplines of the human sciences, such as history, philosophy, and sociology; and (3) a strategy of literary investigation that would advance the "analysis of structure" in the place of discourse about "background, social usefulness, or intellectual content" (p. x). Literary critical performance would later annul the breach with related disciplines, not so much by "going over" to them, but by "translating" their content, in effect, into literary values and analogues, as is the case with poststructuralism, which gained ground from the 1970s on. But the isolation of structure, beginning with the formalists and the New Critics, enables the emergence of a conceptual object that gains a precision of focus comparable to the scientific object.

The wedding of formalism and the New Criticism, never officially pronounced as such, provided a merger called "formalism" that dominated literary study on both sides of the Atlantic from the 1930s through the late 1960s. The aims of this prolific period of theorization are perhaps most poignantly captured in the titles of certain works that attempt to configure literary study as a "system"—René Wellek and Austin Warren's *Theory of Literature* (1942) and Northrop Frye's *Anatomy of Criticism* (1957), for example. More pointed investigations in genre theory—the meaning of poetry, the development of the novel and short story, studies in allegorical, symbolic, and mythic modes, as well as inquiries into the "grammar of motives," the "rhetoric of motives," and the "philosophy" of literary form—all mark this period as one of the most distinct and distinguished chapters in the history of the modern humanities, but they also help to establish the foundations of what was referred to earlier as a centrifugal movement in literary study. In other words, formalism brings about the *institutionalization* of the study of literature and language, both in the academy and in the marketplace of ideas. But it also opens onto the possibilities of a broader application of literary method across the universe of signs. The not entirely playful or lighthearted complaint from scholars outside the field that personnel in English believe that they can "read" anything is not exactly misplaced; there is an ascendant logic operative here that grants primacy to the word/words. If the Russian formalists, as early as the period of the Russian Revolution, had been influenced by the enormous impact of the science of modern linguistics— primarily by way of Roman Jakobson—then the "structuralist turn," via Parisian intellectual circles, would integrate linguistic method and ideas into new systems of thought.

It would appear to the graduate student in English in 1968 that something quite astonishing was happening on the ground. Change was in the air and coming from a number of different directions, not the least of them political. The ramifications of those changes—the presence of larger numbers of minorities and women, on faculties and in student bodies, at American colleges and universities, as well as the commencement of "multiculturalism" as a mode of scholarly study and address—would reverberate right through the contemporary period. The year 1968 might be regarded as a time of rupture, on the one hand, brought on by the transatlantic youth movement (in the United States, the Vietnam War protest movement ran parallel to the

black nationalist movement and the continuation of the civil rights struggle, while in Europe, particularly in the big cities, students, demanding transformation in the educational system and allied with Labor, especially in the French instance, threatened political order). On the other hand, the literary object, destabilized by a reinvigorated debate on the canon, would seem to displace continuity with formalist and neoformalist persuasions onto questions that had not been asked before, such as How does one read as a woman, or a black person, or a postcolonial subject? Though it appears from the vantage of the early twenty-first century that these transformations occurred all at once, it is fair to say that they systematically unfolded over the last three decades of the twentieth century, falling out in a kind of domino pattern. As new legislation had been required to reinforce equal protection for minorities in public accommodations and at the ballot box, rights initially secured by the "citizenship" amendments (the Fourteenth, Fifteenth, and Sixteenth Amendments) to the U.S. Constitution, gender equality in access to higher education followed by legislative mandate. The entire panoply of multicultural occasions swam in its wake. While it would be appropriate to regard the 1960s protest movements in light of global development subsequent to the end of World War II, the isolation of intellectual currents in this sea of change is instructive.

Just as John Crowe Ransom's *New Criticism* in 1941 heralded a paradigm shift that had been well under way for at least two decades, Richard Macksey and Eugenio Donato's *The Languages of Criticism and the Sciences of Man: The Structuralist Controversy* (1971), which introduced to an English-speaking scholarly audience many of the themes that would come to dominate critical inquiry for the next few decades, pointed to a radical shift in the humanities repertoire. Macksey and Donato's table of contents contains the names of many of the major continental thinkers whose projects would model the new scholarship, from René Girard, Georges Poulet, and Lucien Goldmann to Roland Barthes, Tzvetan Todorov, Jacques Lacan, and Jacques Derrida. Though the volume was not published, originally, until 1971, the event that engendered it had taken place during the fall of 1966 at the Humanities Center of the Johns Hopkins University. Supported by a grant from the Ford Foundation, this international symposium brought together more than one hundred humanists and social scientists from the United States and eight other nations. According to Macksey and Donato, the symposium initiated "a two-year program of seminars and colloquia which sought to explore the impact of contemporary 'structuralist' thought on critical methods in humanistic and social studies" (p. xv). The purpose of the symposium was not to consolidate an orthodox view on structuralist method and thinking, but, rather, "to bring into an active and not uncritical contact leading European proponents of structural studies in a variety of disciplines with a wide spectrum of American scholars" (p. xv). The 1966 convocation marked a turning point in the way that literary studies would be configured, and it also enabled the interdisciplinary extension of the latter in the direction of "cultural studies."

Perhaps the single most radical mark of the "structuralist turn" is the "death" of the subject, which opened the way to critical practices, deconstruction prominent among them, in the contemporary era. But the fate of the subject might be thought of as the consequences, or end results, of a series of premises that begin with the concept of "system," which Culler describes as "behind the event, the constitutive conventions behind any individual act" (1975, p. 30). If the prestige and success of the science of linguistics had had an enormous impact on literary study, then it would find application to other cultural and material phenomena on two fundamental grounds: First, cultural phenomena are constituted of objects and events that are riddled with meaning. Such events are, therefore, signs, and signs, as Ferdinand de Saussure (one of the preeminent founders of modern linguistics) contended, are made up of *signifiers* (auditory images that match a concept) and *signifieds* (strings of signifiers that yield meaning). Because cultural phenomena behave like language in yielding meaning, one can, then, in Culler's words, "investigate the system of relations that enables meaning to be produced" (p. 4). The science of signs, or semiology, was therefore enabled by the insights of linguistics. Second, the event in question is not only rule bound, but its rules cohere in an entire ensemble of relations: According to Culler, "Rules . . . do not regulate behavior so much as create the possibility of particular forms of behavior" (p. 5). The best example, interestingly enough, comes out of lived experience: the English speaker has unconsciously mastered a host of complex operations called language competence; but the utterances that she will speak over a lifetime do not exhaust the *possibilities* of sentence formation in the English language (or any other), nor do such utterances even use up the *potential* formations that this individual speaker could generate. Following on the distinction between *la langue* ("a system, an institution, a set of interpersonal rules and norms") and *la parole* ("the actual manifestations of the system in speech and writing"), structuralism was able to posit *systematicity* across the universe of signs, from fashion modes and food consumption to the conduct of poems, novels, and films (Culler, 1975, p. 8). By investigating the rules behind material manifestations and events and what ensemble of relations they were configured in, the structuralist, at least in theory, could reconstruct how things come *to mean.*

When the French theorist Michel Foucault argued the "death" of "Man," or his "end," he was not talking about a nuclear holocaust, but, rather, the displacement of an anthropomorphic centrality onto theories of the constructed character of human and social events; in other words, the human subject, though events pass through him and have meaning for him by way of institutional and conventional practices, is not the autonomous being that Hegelian metaphysics had posited; he is instead the *outcome* of cultural forces and processes not only beyond his control, but beyond his knowledge. The radical nature of this proposition is perhaps most poignantly demonstrable in language itself: As Culler attests, "Individuals choose when to speak and what to say . . . but these acts are made possible by a series of systems which the subject does not control" (1975, p. 29). Therefore, "I" do not speak so much as "I" am "spoken," or enter into a system of human and social relations on which the individual "I" is entirely dependent. When these influences are juxtaposed with the innovations of Sigmund Freud and psychoanalytic practice and theorization

in the wake of Freud's *Interpretation of Dreams* (1900) and its revelation of the *symptom* in dreams and the neurosis, then we reach the Lacanian synthesis of psychoanalysis, heavily influenced by structuralist thought. In the *Four Fundamental Concepts of Psycho-analysis,* Jacques Lacan would assert that the unconscious (the privileged site of the Freudian mental theater) is "structured like a language" (p. 20). Moreover, even "before strictly human relations are established, certain relations have already been determined" (p. 20). Lacan calls these preestablished or prior relations "supports," offered by nature and "arranged in themes of opposition."

## Deconstruction and Beyond

It would be difficult to overstate the implications of (1) the recession of the subject of the humanities, (2) the emphasis on systematicity and process, and (3) the flattening out of the literary object in a vast sea of textual properties and equalities; in the aftermath of structuralism, between the mid-1960s and the mid-1970s, "literary criticism" would become one of a number of critical foci that joined a textualized universe wholly explicable by a generous term called "theory." Texts of philosophy, history, anthropology, and psychoanalytic practice, among other writings deemed to have powerful explanatory value, mixed and mingled in the corridors of criticism with uncustomary abandon, "guests," as it were, of the English department and the departments of comparative literature and modern languages. Bridges between these allied disciplines were supplied by a widespread importation of the writings of continental thinkers, particularly the French contingent. Of prime importance to these developments were the philosophy and methodology of deconstruction, articulated through a critique of modern philosophy by Jacques Derrida, in his *De la Grammatologie* (1967; *Of Grammatology*), a work that was enormously influential to the development of theory in the poststructuralist period.

Deconstruction casts its gaze at the dominant trend lines of metaphysical philosophies that posit the centrality of the *logos* (the word) and the presence of speech/voice; through a "double gesture," as Jonathan Culler explains it, the deconstructionist project seeks to *reverse* the classical oppositions of philosophical writings at the same time that it exploits or uses them. By way of such reversals, deconstruction effects a displacement of the philosophical system. Deconstruction is carried out primarily as paradoxical procedure because it undermines "the hierarchical oppositions on which it relies" (1982, p. 86). One might think of deconstruction, then, as "the story of reading" writing (1982, p. 35), insofar as it ultimately holds that writing is a "writing-in-general," an "archi-écriture," or a "protowriting which is the condition of both speech and writing in the narrow sense" (1982, p. 102). It seems that the key displacement executed by deconstruction is that of the "origin," or "beginnings"; as origin recedes, "transcendence" follows in its wake. If the "origin" of the "word" is taken as leading figures of thought to be displaced in the classical schemata, then a universe of oppositions opens up, splitting off positives and negatives, truth and falsity, presence and absence, good and bad, superior and inferior. The negatives can be lined up under one rubric and the positives under another, or the degraded class of objects over and against the transcending ones. By contending that these punctualities are the result of the manipulations of language, or the effects of the play of signification, rather than the hallmarks of truth, deconstruction posits *différance* (a French neologism) as the condition of meaning—an interminable interpretation and analysis, or in Culler's words, an "act of differing which produces differences" (p. 97). *Différance,* as a paronomastic device, contains deferral (or cancellation of closure), as well as difference, in the sense of *differing from.* From Sausserian linguistics, the deconstructionalist reinforces the notion that *meaning* works by *signification,* but the latter is driven not by the meeting of opposites, but by the annulment of the latter. In other words, we can only account for the bombardment of differing elements. For example, a "tree," the sign vehicle, is a "tree" because something else is "not-tree," and so on, ad infinitum.

Interestingly, some of the best examples of the play of difference are presented in the "Sense-Certainty" segment of Georg Wilhelm Friedrich Hegel's *Phenomenology of Mind* (1807), and in the vertiginous exceptions of Plato's *Parmenides.* The "now" that Hegel turns over, for instance, is not something under the thumb and pinpointed, since it is a continuity that "grows" into the present, ever passing into the "not-now," both the future and the has-been (p. 152). That simple "now," according to Hegel, is "therefore not something immediate, but something mediated." It might appear that this tedious activity of discrimination would sustain only esoteric appeal, but in truth, it seems convertible into a powerful heuristic tool or "speculative instrument," insofar as it also calls into question the entire repertoire of the mundane, of the domination and dogma of "common sense," "reality," "what we all know and believe," and the limitless orthodoxy of "*what is*"—"that which everywhere, that which always, that which by all." Furthermore, if truth no longer has a guarantor in an undivided origin, then we are doomed to, or liberated from, *essences*—or the gold buried beneath the dross, as the philosopher Louis Althusser would have it—to the entanglements of *existence.*

The contemporary women's movement or the critique of knowledge undertaken by the black studies project, and deconstruction, are not customarily spoken of in the same breath, but if the latter is thought of as the inscription of an *attitude* toward the symbolic enterprise, then it might be seen as the perfect context for a radically altered humanities academy. If origin is questionable, then it follows that canons will be, as well, and once canons are toppled, then an entire ensemble of hierarchical operations (one gender over another, one dominant race and its "others") might be rendered moribund, or at least brought down to size.

The curricular objects of women's studies and African American, Marxist, and postcolonial critiques are the newest epistemologies of the humanities academy, both enabled by poststructuralist methodologies and going well beyond them. The repertory of critical inquiries on sexuality, the New Historicism, and a range of cultural studies constitute the most exciting developments in a field generally known in the opening years of the twenty-first century simply as "theory." From Chicago to China, one of the languages that speaks across the cultures is that of "theory," now a global language of scholars in the humanities.

*See also* **Continental Philosophy; Formalism; Literary History; New Criticism; Postmodernism; Psychoanalysis.**

**BIBLIOGRAPHY**

Abrams, M. H. *The Mirror and the Lamp: Romantic Theory and the Critical Tradition.* Oxford and New York: Oxford University Press, 1953.

Adams, Hazard, ed. *Critical Theory Since Plato.* New York: Harcourt Brace Jovanovich, 1971.

Althusser, Louis, and Étienne Balibar. *Reading Capital.* Translated by Ben Brewster. London: Verso, 1979.

Ashcroft, Bill, Gareth Griffiths, and Helen Tiffin, eds. *The Postcolonial Studies Reader.* London and New York: Routledge, 1995.

Baker, Houston A., Jr. *Blues, Ideology, and Afro-American Literature: A Vernacular Theory.* Chicago: University of Chicago Press, 1984.

Barthes, Roland. *Mythologies.* Selected and translated by Annette Lavers. New York: Hill and Wang, 1972.

———. *S/Z: An Essay.* Translated by Richard Miller. Preface by Richard Howard. New York: Hill and Wang, 1974.

Brooks, Cleanth, and Robert Penn Warren. "The Reading of Modern Poetry." In *American Poetry and Prose,* edited by Norman Foerster. 4th ed. Boston: Houghton Mifflin, 1957.

Burke, Kenneth. *A Grammar of Motives.* New York: Prentice-Hall, 1945.

———. *The Philosophy of Literary Form: Studies in Symbolic Action.* 3rd ed. Berkeley: University of California Press, 1974.

———. *A Rhetoric of Motives.* New York: Prentice-Hall, 1950.

Culler, Jonathan. *Structuralist Poetics: Structuralism, Linguistics, and the Study of Literature.* Ithaca, N.Y.: Cornell University Press, 1975.

———. *On Deconstruction: Theory and Criticism after Structuralism.* Ithaca, New York: Cornell University Press, 1982.

De Man, Paul. *Allegories of Reading: Figural Language in Rousseau, Nietzsche, Rilke, and Proust.* New Haven, Conn.: Yale University Press, 1979.

———. *Blindness and Insight: Essays in the Rhetoric of Contemporary Criticism.* 2nd rev. ed. Minneapolis: University of Minnesota Press, 1983.

Derrida, Jacques. *Of Grammatology.* Translated by Gayatri Chakravorty Spivak. Baltimore: Johns Hopkins University Press, 1976.

Drake, William, ed. *The First Wave: Women Poets in America 1915–1945.* New York: Macmillan, 1987.

Eagleton, Terry. *Literary Theory: An Introduction.* Minneapolis: University of Minnesota Press, 1983.

Empson, William. *Seven Types of Ambiguity.* 2nd ed. London: Chatto and Windus, 1947.

———. *Some Versions of Pastoral.* New York: New Directions, 1974.

Feldstein, Richard, and Judith Roof, eds. *Feminism and Psychoanalysis.* Ithaca, N.Y.: Cornell University Press, 1989.

Fletcher, Angus. *Allegory: The Theory of a Symbolic Mode.* Ithaca, N.Y.: Cornell University Press, 1964.

Foucault, Michel. *The Archaeology of Knowledge.* Translated by A. M. Sheridan Smith. New York: Pantheon, 1972.

———. *The Order of Things: An Archaeology of the Human Sciences.* New York: Vintage, 1973.

Frye, Northrop. *Anatomy of Criticism: Four Essays.* Princeton, N.J.: Princeton University Press, 1957.

**New Dictionary of the History of Ideas**

Gasché, Rodolphe. *The Tain of the Mirror: Derrida and the Philosophy of Reflection.* Cambridge, Mass.: Harvard University Press, 1986.

Gates, Henry Louis, Jr. *The Signifying Monkey: A Theory of Afro-American Literary Criticism.* New York: Oxford University Press, 1988.

Goldberg, David Theo, ed. *Multiculturalism: A Critical Reader.* Oxford, U.K., and Cambridge, Mass.: Blackwell, 1994.

Grossberg, Lawrence, Cary Nelson, and Paula A. Treichler, eds. *Cultural Studies.* New York: Routledge, 1992.

Guha, Ranajit, ed. *A Subaltern Studies Reader, 1986–1995.* Minneapolis: University of Minnesota Press, 1997.

Hegel, G. W. F. *The Phenomenology of Mind.* Translated by J. B. Baillie. 2nd ed. London: Allen and Unwin; New York: Macmillan, 1931.

Hirsch, Marianne, and Evelyn Fox Keller. *Conflicts in Feminism.* New York: Routledge, 1990.

*I'll Take My Stand: The South and the Agrarian Tradition, by Twelve Southerners.* New York and London: Harper and Brothers, 1930.

Jakobson, Roman, and Morris Halle. *Fundamentals of Language.* 2nd rev. ed. The Hague: Mouton, 1971.

Jameson, Fredric. *The Political Unconscious: Narrative as a Socially Symbolic Act.* Ithaca, N.Y.: Cornell University Press, 1981.

———. *Postmodernism; or, The Cultural Logic of Late Capitalism.* Durham, N.C.: Duke University Press, 1991.

Kester-Shelton, Pamela, ed. *Feminist Writers.* Detroit: St. James Press, 1996.

Lacan, Jacques. *The Four Fundamental Concepts of Psycho-analysis.* Edited by Jacques-Alain Miller. Translated by Alan Sheridan. New York: Norton, 1978.

Lemon, Lee T., and Marion J. Reis, trans. *Russian Formalist Criticism: Four Essays.* Lincoln: University of Nebraska Press, 1965.

Macksey, Richard, and Eugenio Donato, eds. *The Languages of Criticism and the Sciences of Man: The Structuralist Controversy.* Baltimore: Johns Hopkins University Press, 1971.

Napier, Winston, ed. *African-American Literary Theory: A Reader.* New York: New York University Press, 2000.

Nicholson, Linda J., ed. *Feminism/Postmodernism.* New York: Routledge, 1990.

Ohmann, Richard. *English in America: A Radical View of the Profession.* New York: Oxford University Press, 1976.

Readings, Bill. *The University in Ruins.* Cambridge, Mass.: Harvard University Press, 1996.

Richards, I. A. *Speculative Instruments.* Chicago: University of Chicago Press, 1955.

Said, Edward W. *Orientalism.* New York: Vintage, 1979.

Saussure, Ferdinand de. *Course in General Linguistics.* Edited by Charles Bally and Albert Reidlinger. Translated by Wade Baskin. New York: Philosophical Library, 1959.

Spillers, Hortense J. *Black, White, and in Color: Essays on American Literature and Culture.* Chicago: University of Chicago Press, 2003.

Wall, Cheryl A. *Changing Our Own Words: Essays on Criticism, Theory, and Writing by Black Women.* New Brunswick, N.J.: Rutgers University Press, 1991.

Warren, Robert Penn. "The Briar Patch." In his *I'll Take My Stand: The South and the Agrarian Tradition, by Twelve Southerners.* New York and London: Harper and Brothers, 1930.

Wellek, René, and Austin Warren. *Theory of Literature.* 3rd ed. New York: Harcourt, Brace, 1956.

Wheelwright, Philip. *The Burning Fountain: A Study in the Language of Symbolism.* Rev. ed. Bloomington: Indiana University Press, 1968.

Wimsatt, W. K., Jr. *The Verbal Icon: Studies in the Meaning of Poetry.* Lexington: University of Kentucky Press, 1954.

*Hortense J. Spillers*

**LITERARY HISTORY.** History traces the passage of men and women through time. Literary history charts their developments and experiments in writing in the hope that global discourse will be stimulated and cultures come to understand one another. It relates, compares, and categorizes the poetry, prose, drama, and reportage of authors at various periods. The process started when the artistic deployment of language (poetry, polemic, drama, and stories) began to inspire a significant following. There arose a "culture of response" or a body of people—priests, scholars, educators, and fellow writers—who extolled select works and ensured their preservation in archives and public buildings. In this manner a "canon" or corpus of writing was put together that was deemed significant in relation to the culture because it reflected nationalistic bias, religious, political, or aesthetic partiality. The "models" or frameworks of admission altered as knowledge progressed, printing became widespread, and attitudes and styles of writing changed. Around the world separate cultures evolved their own criteria, forms, and traditions, ranging from doctrinal works such as Buddhist sutras and Vedic hymns to Japanese dance-drama (the Noh plays) and Chinese operatic drama or chuanqui. Within such works were found ideas that had a lasting effect.

In the Western model, for instance, Plato (c. 428–348 or 347 B.C.E.) believed poetry was merely imitative, but Aristotle (384–322 B.C.E.) praised its imaginative truth, while Homer thought his inspiration "God given"—standpoints that were echoed and debated down the centuries. After the Greeks and Romans, many critical ideologies emerged in Europe, invoking morality, passion, and truth to life and authorial intention, but it was not until the twentieth century that the sound of theories clashing drowned the traditional debate between critic and author (a debate that did not much affect the public who continued to read books for pleasure). Ironically the shift of spotlight from creator to commentator climaxed in a critical task force that sought to detonate its own foundations or "deconstruct" the very language of its discourse. Ostensibly radical, this was no more than a revival of an ancient revolt. For language from the start had always sought to analyze or "argue" the authority of its being, just as man had always sought to challenge the authority of God. From the beginning, literary history tended to be presented as a sequential progression—a dialogue or "confrontation" between successive ages and schools of writing, one "great book" or "genius" spurring another, starting with texts concerned with man's status in the universe, specifically his mortal limitations as opposed to the immortal gods.

Early interest focused on myth, out of which emerged the hero who stood taller than the rest, loyal, brave, and fabulously resilient. The Sumerian *Epic of Gilgamesh* tells of a swaggering young prince who defies the gods, bonds with another warrior-hero, and meets the fate that such a rebellion inevitably courts. It ends with a massively moving death lament. Gilgamesh *has* to die in order that he retain his humanity. If he did not, he would be a god and forfeit that essential *realism,* or truth to the mutable world, that is the hallmark of great literature.

The Greeks showed a similar preoccupation with gods and heroes. If their analysis went deeper, they too held by laws in which the overreacher—the man who commits an irreversible act against nature—is abandoned to the Furies (primitive avenging spirits), who demand he be sacrificed in order to maintain the status quo. This is notable in Greek tragedies, especially Sophocles' *Oedipus Rex,* whose harsh, unrelenting climax is often viewed as pitiless. With respect to such forms, Aristotle introduced an ethical dimension when he analyzed the rhetorical devices and idioms of the fourth century B.C.E. in his *Poetics,* a foundation-stone for students of literature (as well as Hollywood scriptwriters), for it launched the notion of plot or *mythos* as a device conveying unity of theme and action. Crucially, the concepts *mimesis* and *catharsis* were defined, the first positing language as imitation and the second dealing with the emotional purgation—a mix of horror and pity—arising in the spectator of a powerful tragedy. Aristotle's compatriot, Plato, denied the highest truth to literary art, seeing literature as too attractively persuasive. As for the Greek myths, with their stunning organic imagery and metamorphoses, they inspired every age of literature, perpetually updated and adapted as novels, operas, and plays.

## The Religious Imperative

Equally far-reaching, in Europe, was the impact of Christianity. With its volatile mix of stories, poems, and sacred and prophetic texts, the Bible provided a moral groundwork that formed the basis for hagiographies, sermons, and devotional verses. The book of Genesis unlocked "Logos," the divine word or sacred seal of inspiration: thus, being literally "God given," language was able to transcend the clasp of mortality and enshrine the numinous. Literature was annexed for the promulgation of doctrine. A library was an institution that preserved sacred texts rather than a place where a commoner might go and acquire knowledge. The one great rebel was Satan, who, having been expelled from Heaven, pursued his counteroffensive among the fallen and fallible of the world.

With the spread of monotheism, the relationship of man to God dominated prose and poetry. In the early medieval period, fables, histories, and courtly tales of love and chivalry predominated. Stories were promoted as exempla, designating a suitable way to behave in order to draw down grace or, alternatively, court damnation. However, in the *Phaedrus,* Plato had placed art a rung below "truth," being a product of materiality rather than spirit. Hence it could never be wholly trusted.

So that the Bible should hold absolute authority, this doctrine was modified by the Scholastics (c. 800–1400), whose era of crippling, devotional studiousness was shattered by the

Renaissance of the fifteenth and sixteenth centuries—an amazing upsurge in learning that held fast to classical models (Plato, Aristotle, and Cicero's rules of rhetoric) yet managed to accommodate a vast influx of new ideas—from science, natural history, philosophy, theology, botany, mechanics, anatomy, and engineering. Literary art promoted a worldview with God and his angels at the top, a spiritual cartography that found its acme in Dante's *Divine Comedy,* in which love was the redeeming force and every station of saint and sinner had their precise place and part.

Naturally a great deal of literature was the preserve of monks and scholars who tended to propagate heroes of a devotional bent. By the time of the Reformation (1517), this mold showed signs of cracking. Eventually it was superseded by a new type of psychological truth, typified in England by the dramas of an emergent laity that included men such as Shakespeare, Christopher Marlowe, and Ben Jonson, writers who portrayed characters—villains, nobles, and commoners—bursting with painful, turbulent contradictions hinting at the inadequacy of religion in engaging human dilemmas.

## Enlightenment and Romanticism

The Enlightenment of the seventeenth and eighteenth centuries is often vaunted as the age of reason. But it was also an age of passion, profound thinking, and revolutionary zeal, allied to a robust practicality, Aristotelian in outlook. John Locke (1632–1704) evolved a theory of the personality and a farsighted, liberal political philosophy. Less idealistic, Thomas Hobbes wrote *Leviathan* (1651), a masterly analysis of man's place with regard to nature and society. Religion remained institutionally entrenched (if a little shriveled by the skepticism of David Hume) and the dominant literary mode, classic in character and reformist in outlook, found its outlet in urbane, sometimes sardonic stylists like Voltaire (1694–1778) and Diderot (1713–1784) in France. Equally puncturing of pretensions were the heroic couplets of Alexander Pope and John Dryden in England and novelists like Samuel Richardson and Henry Fielding, portraying social rather than God-seeking characters engaging in intrigues and amours.

The French Revolution brought republicanism, in which commoners replaced kings, and taxes were more evenly distributed. But military aspirations rampaged across Europe and Russia until the defeat of Napoléon Bonaparte. The Romantics of the late eighteenth and early nineteenth centuries were caught up in this spirit of rebellion. *Liberty* was the shibboleth of the poets William Wordsworth, Lord Byron, and Percy Bysshe Shelley—a word hoarding spiritual and political connotations. Language no longer favored the noble above the plain, for it was thought that the artist's intention elevated the subject matter. German Romanticism followed in the wake of the English initiative and, like its forerunner, throbbed with nature, passion, and intrigue but with an added spicing of wit and sexuality.

Where the Romantics had shown a preoccupation with themes like murder, intrigue, and incest, the nineteenth century developed the skills of everyday observation. Above all, it was the age of realism in the novel, embodied in the psychological narratives of Leo Tolstoy, Fyodor Dostoyevsky, Charles Dickens, and George Eliot: multilayered fictions set in worlds so convincingly realized that they seemed to reflect life as *experienced* rather than imagined. It was also a time of the professional man of letters who, at intervals, appraised the state of culture, typical English examples being Matthew Arnold and John Ruskin, the first a poet of distinction and the second a social critic and art historian. Victorian poetry was marked by a facile, routine romanticism that finally darkened and putrefied: hence the morbidity of content, the gothic shadow falling over some of the works of Robert Browning (1812–1889), Alfred, Lord Tennyson (1809–1892), and Edgar Allan Poe (1809–1849).

The final decade of the nineteenth century was enlivened by the walk-on of the decadents, who started in France but quickly spread over the English Channel, espousing a doctrine similar to the symbolists: that art was free to treat whatever subject it saw fit, whether pernicious or virtuous. Art for art's sake (a slogan translated from the French of the philosopher Victor Cousin) was the byword, emancipating the creator—if he or she so wished—from conscience or morality. The decadents liked to celebrate small, exquisite instants in small, exquisite poems, sipping at life as if it were a rare wine.

**From Masterpiece to Text**
With the advent of the twentieth century came a shift from elitism to inclusivism. Despite the elite radicalism of factions such as the modernist who sought to break with the past and incorporate in their projects the staggering breakthroughs in science, anthropology, medicine, and psychology, the citadel of high culture was opening its gates. In the same way that the people of various countries were demanding a government in which their opinions could play a central role, literature became more democratic, spawning free libraries, open scholarships, and popular editions. Eventually there spread an awareness that all facets of culture, oral or written, constitute a "text," and the traditional fixation on a corpus of "masterpieces" was a blinkered way of evaluating culture.

A noted leveler was the psychologist Sigmund Freud (1856–1939), who showed how people tend to think and act the same—that all are dominated by hidden urges. Each man and woman has a subconscious in which sexual desires bubble and fume and are liable to spill over in erratic or outrageous behavior—ideas that opened the floodgates of creativity and literary experiment, unleashing the "stream of consciousness" technique, in which a rush of unpunctuated, sometimes loosely associated words are made to stand for dreaming or thought-play, notable exponents of the latter being James Joyce, Virginia Woolf, and William Faulkner.

As experiment brewed in artistic circles, elsewhere the dream of freedom was degenerating into tyranny and nightmare. In the Soviet Union, Joseph Stalin wrested power in 1924, followed by Adolf Hitler in Germany in 1933. Both the Communist and Nazi regimes banned free speech. In Russia, novelists were condemned as "insufficiently ideological" or as putting self before state, and in Germany the works of select writers were ritually burned as "Jewish" or "decadent." Literature was promoted as an extension of a cause, much as it had

been during the Middle Ages. Whereas Nazism had effectively died out after World War II, the Communist dream persisted through the writings of Karl Marx (1818–1883), whose ideas pioneered an influential school of literary criticism.

Marx's thesis was that the worker, alienated from his product by contractual enslavement, had no status and was there solely to serve his master. And, of course, to him the master was equally remote, unsolid, and this notion of invisibility or "nonpresence" takes us to the core of modern literary theory: the author as anonymous ghost haunting the boundaries of his or her text.

For just as science at the turn of the century was breaking matter into tinier and tinier particles, literary criticism was separating the finer elements of language, analyzing units of sound and syntax. The theories of Ferdinand de Saussure (1857–1913) identified sequences of self-contained signs whose parts could be isolated into vocal utterances (*parole*) and the abstract structure that organized them (*langue*). Saussure was a major influence on the Russian formalist movement, which had its inception in 1914 at Saint Petersburg, headed by the critic Viktor Shklovsky (1893–1984), who fused symbolist ideas with his own manifesto, demanding autonomy for the text, discarding any social role for literature, and cultivating metaphor, mystery, and radical perception.

This propensity to focus on language, its emotional and figurative charge, was also a precept of the New Criticism that developed in England and the United States after World War I. Treating a poem or novel as a self-contained artifact, this approach took the text apart in a precise, clinical manner, paying attention to aesthetic balance, the interplay and opposition of imagery, excluding social and biographical factors that existed beyond the page. The overall unity of the work—how parts were orchestrated to harmonize or counterpoint one another—was considered as indicative of its quality in the "Western tradition," which held by formal standards of excellence.

With emphasis on the autonomy of texts, words drifted from their anchorage in the physical. Signifiers were seen as signaling to each other rather than the reader. This reached its apotheosis in the writings of Jacques Derrida (b. 1930), who subverted the notion of a single meaning. The author was not a spider presiding over a web of words. No, he was a fly trapped in it—unaware that his work held messages at odds with the stance he thought he had taken. What critics of the past had done was "privilege" various angles and themes, taking in current thought and social mores, but their readings were more acts of faith than rational appraisals. Derrida drastically hinted that the totalitarianization of meaning—the obsession with a single clear authorial intention—found a counterpart in the inflexible rationalism of the Nazi death camps.

Such theories began to infuse the novel, which started to question its own fictive illusion, just as had the German playwright Bertolt Brecht (1898–1956) when he sought to separate the political message from the drama by exaggerating the elements of artifice and so creating a sense of "alienation." So-called metafictions were produced that ridiculed the procedures of novel writing and, in one instance (B. S. Johnson's

1964 novel *Albert Angelo*), had the angry author breaking through the page shouting, "O fuck all this lying!" At last, Narcissus had smashed the mirror.

## Guilt and Contrition

Aside from innovation, propaganda, and linguistic debate, the twentieth century was an age of guilt and contrition. The guilt was based on a dawning awareness of the elitism of Western culture. Contrition took the form of an eagerness to make good the oversight by broadening the definition of literature and including in its field hitherto silent minorities whose voices initially took the form of protest, their cultures having been so long patronized that the "imaginative" content needed longer to emerge. In 1925 the educator and critic Alain Locke (1885–1954) issued a manifesto to young black American artists, challenging them to draw upon the power of African art as avant-garde artists in Europe had done. However, many of those to whom he appealed had not even been to Africa, and to them it was as much a place of fantasy as it was to the white men. Africa was grasped in terms of distance, vastness, and a savage sensuality—qualities that writers like D. H. Lawrence (1885–1930) had strained to capture. Negritude had its origin in the Caribbean and was defined by poets like Léopold Sédar Senghor, who conveyed a sense of anger and injustice in torn, surreal images.

Another minority impacting on current thought were women writers who mobilized to form a cultural force after World War II, key texts being Simone de Beauvoir's *The Second Sex* (1949) and Kate Millet's *Sexual Politics* (1970). The matter had earlier been raised in Virginia Woolf's *A Room of One's Own* (1929), but the tone was now combative, attacking the patriarchal roots of the Western canon and drawing attention to female writers whose stature had been overlooked or denied. Such efforts stimulated a massive wave of gender-based critiques—gynocriticism—that analyzed and tried to reshape the culture that, as they saw it, was based on male bias and partiality.

With the interest in hitherto marginalized groups and communities came an increased recognition of the political and economic factors that permeate culture and leave their impress. Insights like these gave rise to the New Historicism, a mainly American school of criticism, Marxist in flavor, that used texts to pinpoint the political and social conditions, the ideologies and judgments that, inevitably, color and bias writing—in opposition to the Romantic view of the author being a wellspring of unpolluted inspiration. The critic analyzes oddments, small, previously ignored details and facts, typical yet eloquent, exposing literature as a tool of history.

## Contemporary Dilemma

By the twenty-first century, the Western model of literary history had been dramatically extended, taking in Asia, Africa, Australia, South America, the South Pacific, and the Arab world. Its approach had been criticized as a series of "generalizations" working through contrasts and continuities—an "institutionalized subjectivity," as the French critic Roland Barthes would have it. (And yet, many believed, such a summary or "distortion" is inevitable if information is to be condensed

within a certain remit.) It infers an almost kinetic impact between literary movements, whereas a scientist might argue this is not *how things happen,* merely a habit of human perception. Is the model then valid? Or is it a piece of illusionism, a series of traditionally accepted linkages? This is the type of question literary history had begun to ask of itself. Having broadened its scope to encompass the world, it was almost the history of everything ("everything" and therefore "nothing," some critics might say).

Thus previous classifications were being reexamined and fresh approaches made, considering not just the text but, for example, the prevalent institution, the critical orthodoxy or heterodoxy, in which it was first received. Threads of movements such as classicism, romanticism, and naturalism, together with critical theory, were being redefined within a pattern that, inevitably, will grow more intricate and extensive as the field of study reaches out to the vernacular, cinematic, and oral, where previously it had focused on the canonical. The new methodology will go far beyond the aesthetic, developing an increasingly comparative methodology, moving between past and present, drawing on disciplines like sociology, economics, and politics.

This epic inclusiveness generates anxiety as well as excitement among its practitioners, who must trace vibrations from reader to society, from society to politics, from politics to the world. Keeping literary history up to date is like being both cannibal and victim, devouring past texts in the hope of completion, only to be swallowed in turn by the recorders of futurity.

*See also* **Literary Criticism; Literature.**

**BIBLIOGRAPHY**

Aristotle. *Poetics.* Translated by Malcolm Heath. London and New York: Penguin, 1996. A friendly, accessible rendering that reads well.

Auerbach, Erich. *Mimesis: The Representation of Reality in Western Literature.* Translated by Willard R. Trask. Princeton, N.J.: Princeton University Press, 1953. Analytical classic demonstrating how great works of literature stand in relation to their times.

Blake, N. F. *An Introduction to the Language of Literature.* New York: St. Martin's, 1990. Aims to define what sets "literature" apart.

*The Cambridge History of Literary Criticism.* 9 vols. Cambridge, U.K., and New York: Cambridge University Press, 1989–2001. Authoritative reference series.

Derrida, Jacques. *Writing and Difference.* Translated by Alan Bass. Chicago: University of Chicago Press, 1978. Key text of deconstructionism.

Lodge, David, ed. *Modern Criticism and Theory: A Reader.* London and New York: Longman, 1988. Both this book and the one below contain useful introductions and selections of source material.

———. *Twentieth Century Literary Criticism: A Reader.* London and New York: Longman, 1972.

Norris, Christopher. *The Truth about Postmodernism.* Oxford and Cambridge, Mass.: Blackwell, 1993. A counteroffensive to the "heresies" of postmodern culture.

Saussure, Ferdinand de. *Course in General Linguistics.* Edited by Charles Bally and Albert Reidlinger. Translated by Wade Baskin. New York: Philosophical Library, 1959. Foundation stone of linguistics.

*Paul Newman*

# LITERATURE.

This entry includes two subentries:

*Overview*
*African Literature*

## OVERVIEW

Almost all senses of the English word *literature* and its cognates in other Indo-European languages can eventually be traced back to the act of scratching (on a piece of leather or on clay, stone, wood, wax, pottery, lead, or papyrus). But this primitive act very quickly became associated with superior development: civilization.

### The Appearance of Literacy

The word goes back first to the Latin *litteratura* (writing, grammar) and *litteratus,* which denote learnedness derived from writing, or literacy, and then to *littera,* or letter. (The French *littérature* has the same roots.) It is conjectured that the Greek root of the Latin *littera* is *diphthera,* meaning a leather hide prepared for inscription. In his *Institutio oratoria,* Quintilian (c. 35–c. 100 C.E.) uses the word *litteratura* as a translation of the Greek *grammatikē* (Wellek). As such, it represents the art of the letter (*gramma*), which would denote the ability to read and write and hence the rules or "grammar" governing this ability. But the Greek word for writing, *grammata,* also means "scratchings"—its Indo-European root, *gerebh-,* means "to scratch." The English verb *to write* derives from the Germanic *wrītan,* also meaning "to scratch." The English word *Scripture,* like the German *Schrift* (a *Schriftsteller* is a literary person), can be traced back to the Latin verb *scribere,* "to write," and then to the Indo-European root *skeri-,* from which come a host of words having to do with cutting. The Indo-European *skeri-* has a variant form *krei-,* denoting separation, sifting, and discrimination, from which comes the Greek *krinein,* meaning "to judge," and later English words such as *critic* and *criterion.* One of the meanings of *sker-* is excrement, hence something worth knowing how to avoid. One can discover in literature's philological beginnings nascent forms of nearly the entire family of ideas that would come to be associated with the word *literature*: letters, writing, literacy, learnedness, discrimination, distinction, criticism, and judgment. Because, almost everywhere, writing and reading—unlike speech, acquired in infancy—were skills that demanded time and effort to acquire, literature, more or less by its nature, had its beginnings among groups that not only were socially empowered to make distinctions (priests, scribes, bards, chiefs) but also were socially distinguished by the very fact of being literate.

As Barry Powell observes, it has long been a puzzle why the narratives generally considered the oldest examples of Western literature, Homer's *Iliad* and *Odyssey,* have all the structural characteristics of advanced, literate societies yet contain no mention of writing itself. The one reference to "baneful signs"—not yet *grammata,* or writing—in the story of Bellerophon (*Iliad* 6.157–211) came to Homer from the Levantine East, as did many other elements of the Homeric epics, and it may suggest that the poet whose version of the *Iliad* was finally written down did not yet understand what writing was. Literature in any guise came late to the West: the written forms of the Homeric epics date from around the time of the invention of the Greek alphabet, c. 800 B.C.E., while reference to written documents appear regularly in much older narratives from Egypt and the Near East, c. 1800 B.C.E.

The oxymoron *oral literature* has been used to describe unwritten compositions in story, poetry, or song, transmitted with many variations over time, though the rubric remains mired in much dispute (Lord). People have most likely told stories about themselves, their gods, their heroes, and the creatures, both real and imagined, surrounding them from the beginnings of language, and such storytelling is still an integral part of what is meant by the term literature. But the process by which supposedly oral compositions like Homeric epic poetry came to be written down is unknown. Similarly, while the extant Bible is largely a mix of documents assembled piecemeal from preexisting (and now lost) documents, oral accounts must have been part of many biblical stories. Abraham may have existed as early as 2000 B.C.E., Moses around 1200 B.C.E., but no written account of them survives from before the sixth century B.C.E. Well before the Latin word *litteratura* existed, Homer's epics and Hesiod's *Theogony* already included what is now recognized as a wide range of genres or modes of writing, from the skillfully entertaining to the legal, philosophical, historical, and religious. If oral traditions that survived into the modern period are any guide, oral performances designed for entertainment employed a range of structural devices and tropes that helped define what came to be called "literary" language. A general consensus arose in the late twentieth century that alphabetic writing made possible whole ways of thinking not available to nonliterate societies (for different approaches, see Ong and Goody). Certainly literacy seems to have facilitated military conquest and administrative authority. But it is hard to know precisely how the psychological or cultural consequences of alphabetic writing in the West, beginning in Mesopotamia, differed from those of writing in China, which had a quite distinct history; or how much of what is called the "literariness" of novels, poems, and plays ultimately derives from preliterate oral performance or perhaps from the innate structure of human consciousness.

In Sumeria and Egypt and in China written documents and ways of talking about writing appear earlier. Writing first appears in Sumer c. 3400 B.C.E. with the inscription of shapes into clay for the purpose of counting objects, though the use of smaller objects themselves as tokens is much older. At a certain point, perhaps first via pictures (pictograms) and then via increasingly abstract symbols, phonetic units came to be linked to written ones, and writing came to be considered the legible form of speech. It can be said that the earliest (cuneiform, logographic) literary texts could not actually be "read," since one still needed aural instruction to be able to pronounce the radically incomplete sequence of signs. The epic story of Gilgamesh survives in several different language families (Sumerian, Semitic, and Indo-European) and scripts (cuneiform and Luwian), the longest version from the seventh century B.C.E., the earliest from perhaps the fourteenth century; the hero-king himself seems to have existed in the third millennium. Chinese script may be even older than the Sumerian and certainly dates from at least the second millennium. In Chinese, unlike the phonetic writing that developed in Sumeria and then in the Greek and Latin alphabet, one finds in the same sign a phonetic element and a nonphonetic element, or semantic "radical."

## Literature in the Early West

The Hellenistic Greeks had a robust sense of the different kinds of writing within the idea of *grammata*. In book 10 of the *Republic,* Plato distinguished sharply, for example, between philosophy (dialectic), which he championed, and poetry, which he wanted to ban because of its propensity to settle for superficial views of things and to stir the emotions unnecessarily. Aristotle's treatises *Interpretation* (comprising grammar and logic), *Rhetoric,* and *Poetics* are some of the earliest examples of criticism. His *Poetics* is generally considered the founding text of literary interpretation in the West, though the term explicated by Aristotle is not *grammata* but *poiēsis,* which means "making" or "creating" as well as "poetry" and "poem." Nevertheless, the treatise clearly sets out a theory of literary genres and thoroughly anatomizes one of them—tragic drama—to demonstrate its essential structure; its psychological effects on its audience; its bases in Greek culture and myth; its distinctness from history and philosophy as well as from other types of poetry, such as epic and lyric; its ability to give pleasure and to reveal truth; and its relation to fate and the gods. Aristotle's ideas have remained touchstones throughout the history of literature in the West, and it would be fair to say that the academic study of literature would not be the same without them. They were revived in a dogmatic form by the French in the seventeenth century and are still routinely taught in the twenty-first century.

Romans such as Cicero used the term *litteratura* to mean both writing itself and learning. It was the early church fathers of the second century, such as Tertullian in *De spectaculis,* who distinguished between sacred and profane writing—*scriptura* versus *litteratura*—within the Christian tradition and who elevated the former above the latter for several centuries. During this period, the profane term *literature* and its cognates appear to have had little currency. In the British Isles there is a small canon of Anglo-Saxon poetry beginning in the late sixth century. With the exception of *Beowulf,* a narrative poem assembled from earlier sources in the seventh or eighth century, the development of a major classical genre, such as epic, seems to have been hindered for a time by the dominance of Christianity. In France literacy and learning were revived by the court of Charlemagne (742–814), king of the Franks from 768 until his death and Holy Roman emperor (from 800), but the legend of Charlemagne is handed down in various forms before the epic *La chanson de Roland* appears in early twelfth-century medieval France. The twelfth-century *Poema del Cid,* perhaps the most important of early Spanish epics, embellishes

in courtly, Christian terms the deeds of a noble, eleventh-century Castilian soldier of fortune.

The patristic Scripture-literature hierarchy was vigorously challenged by Dante Alighieri (1265–1321) in *De vulgari eloquentia* (1304–1309), a treatise defending "eloquence in the vernacular," albeit written in Latin and perhaps with Quintilian as a model. Dante argued, first, that profane literature could be read with the same seriousness and interpreted along the same lines as Scripture, and second, that morally serious profane literature could be written not only in Latin, which was then the language of statecraft and high culture throughout Europe, but also in the vernacular, that is, in the commonly spoken regional languages. Such regional languages were assumed at the time not to be governed by the rules of grammar and hence not to be suitable for important matters. Although Dante's ideas had a negligible influence in his day, his vision of vernacular literature would be realized in the subsequent rise of distinct national cultures following the fragmentation of Roman Catholic hegemony in Europe. Martin Luther's early sixteenth-century Reformation and perhaps more important, the translation of the Bible into modern languages prepared the ground for the later idea that literature, whether historical, philosophical, or imaginative, embodied distinct national spirits. Still, the study of vernacular literatures would not occur in most European academies until the nineteenth century.

In a fourteenth-century Scottish version of the lives of the saints, the word *lateratour* is used to mean essentially what its Latin root had meant for Quintilian and Cicero: familiarity with books, including the polite learning and elite cultural status associated with literacy. In 1513 Henry Bradshaw wrote in verse of "the comyn people symple and neclygent, / Whiche without lytterature and good informacyon / Ben lyke to Brute beestes" (vol. 2, p. 4). Something of Bradshaw's "good informacyon" persists in one of the secondary modern meanings of the term literature, which allows the term to denote the totality of written material on a given subject, as when one speaks of the literature on a particular medical treatment, or the literature on child development. In the part of the sixteenth-century school curriculum called the trivium, designed to teach both spoken and written Latin, grammar was intimately related to rhetoric and logic: to have "literature" was to write both persuasively and rationally. This academic synthesis, based on the study of Latin and Greek, persisted into the nineteenth century and also governed the early study of vernacular languages. Theater, both in the Elizabethan London of Shakespeare and in the fashionable seventeenth-century Paris of Corneille and Racine, supplied early intimations of the idea of literature in its primary modern sense: imaginative writing pursued as a vocation and for profit. It is in this context that in 1635 Cardinal Richelieu founded the Académie Français, an essentially literary academy, for which Charles Perrault proposed in 1666 a section devoted to "belles lettres," to include grammar, eloquence, and taste. By 1710 the phrase "belles lettres" is used by Jonathan Swift in an issue of the *Tatler* magazine to denote a profession on a par with history and politics. On the whole, literature bears its traditional, inclusive meaning through most of the eighteenth century, as exemplified by Voltaire's definition of *littérature* in his

## By Way of Comparison: *Literature* in Chinese

The word for literature in Chinese (*wenxue*) is an ancient term revived for twentieth- and twenty-first-century needs. In a Chinese schoolroom or bookstore, *wenxue* designates a familiar activity: the reading of poetry, plays, and novels augmented by criticism and the study of some historical and philosophical works for pleasure and instruction. The properties of *wenxue* map precisely onto those of European literature. This is not a coincidence or an astonishing parallel between diverse cultures but rather a case of influence, the contagion of modernity: the categories of thought that have framed the institutions of literature in the West since about 1800 also contributed toward reforming and refounding modern East Asian cultures.

Confucius (551–479 B.C.E.) described two of his students as *wenxue*. *Wen* means "writing," "documents," or "culture" in an extended sense, including customs and ritual; *xue* means "learning." Hence Confucius has always been understood as saying that the strong point of these two disciples was in documentary knowledge, as opposed to others who specialized in policy or argumentation. *Wenxue* has been used as a metonym for scholars or schoolmasters as well as for the activities they engage in, primarily the preservation, interpretation, and transmission of written records. The vast and meticulously administered empire of China had a constant need for such literate men. Periodic examinations held at local, provincial, and imperial levels qualified and requalified candidates for office. The subjects covered in these examinations varied from reign to reign, but policy essays and poetic composition were prominent during most of the fifteen hundred–year history of the examination system.

It was not until the seventeenth century that *wenxue* began to be used, but only rarely, as a catchall term for polite or imaginative letters, as opposed to other kinds of writing. It seems that the impetus for the specialization of the term was given by foreign missionaries who wrote, both in the reports they sent home and in their Chinese evangelical texts, that the Chinese Empire was unique in selecting its high officials on the basis of literary attainment. From an internal Chinese point of view, the world of letters was multifarious, including every kind of verbal artistry and application, but not divided into the subspecies of verbal art and instrumental communication. That distinction came to be canonical for external reasons.

In the late nineteenth century, as the Meiji Restoration set Japan on a course of determined centralization and westernization, new Japanese educational institutions redistributed the many fields of letters to include foreign languages but to exclude most practical or scientific subjects. The term adopted for the faculty of humanities was *bungaku*—the Japanese pronunciation of the Chinese characters for *wenxue*. Within the humanities, *bungaku* specifically referred to literary disciplines, as distinguished from philosophical or historical studies. On the Asian mainland, as the Qing dynasty gave way to the People's Republic of China in 1911 the original Chinese term made a triumphal return—probably on the lips of Chinese revolutionaries who had studied in Japan—as an object of knowledge, a species of publication, a career path, and a division of learning. The definition and reform of this emergent field was a particular concern of the intellectuals associated with the May Fourth (1919) Movement, whose vision of a "Chinese Renaissance" implied a democratic political order, a scientific epistemology, and a national literature written in the vernacular. The imperial order of letters, in which elegance of expression was—without explicit differentiation—a resource to be wielded in the exercise of power as well as a social mark of distinction and a private amusement, had vanished. As in Europe, the new divisions of learning heralded a new society populated by a new kind of person.

*Haun Saussy*

## BY WAY OF COMPARISON: *LITERATURE* IN ARABIC

The semantic range of the Arabic word *adab*, which in modern usage designates literature in the specialized sense of artistic writing, has shifted considerably over time. As an intellectual standard of cultivation, the notion of *adab* came into being after the emergence of poetry, the cardinal genre of Arabic literature, called "the register of the Arabs" (Allen, p. 104). The Arabic ode in the pre-Islamic era, originating in oral forms and possibly in song, followed an aesthetic that appealed primarily to the listener and had tightly codified tropes. The figure of the poet was associated with "divine inspiration"; the poet was seen as the tribal spokesperson, one who praised the tribe's illustrious past and hurled invective at its enemies. The connection between poetry and patronage, which predates Islam, grew after the establishment of the new religion: the shift to urban life and the espousal of eulogistic poetry by rulers and the administrative aristocracy as an enhancement of their prestige and power modified without at first annulling the role of the tribal poet. This new poet was the client of a given court, and poetry began to address new themes. It is speculated that etymologically *adab* referred to standards of conduct, to customs, and to enrichment. But the word "came to mean 'high quality of soul, good upbringing, urbanity, courtesy' . . . corresponding to the refining of bedouin ethics and customs as a result of Islam," as well as urbanization, the emergence of a city-bred elite and administrative class, and contact with other cultures (Gabrieli, p. 175). The term gradually acquired an additional "intellectual meaning" and "came to imply the sum of knowledge which makes a man courteous and 'urbane'" (Gabrieli, p. 175). Such "profane culture" was "at first strictly national" and later, through contact with other cultures, developed from "Arab humanitas, into humanitas without qualification" (Gabrieli, p. 175). Although its primary significance is now homologous with the modern idea of literature in English—that is, imaginative writing—*adab* can

still also be used to denote "good manners" and "refinement."

Derived from early prose antecedents, such as the compilations of the Prophet Muhammad's biography and of traditions associated with the premodern corpus, *adab* (the tradition of belles lettres written in classical Arabic) includes poetics, biography, historical and geographical writings, travelogues, rhetoric, compilations of entertaining anecdotes, and monographs. Debate about the origin of the modern Arabic novel has hinged on whether it is an imported genre or one that draws on indigenous antecedents, especially elite ones, such as the *maqamah* ("assembly," a form of fictional narrative in rhyming prose; also poetry and quotations from poetry). Scholarly discussions have tended to overlook popular antecedents such as *The Thousand and One Nights*, a collection of Arabian tales of unknown origin probably collected in Egypt in the fourteenth to sixteenth centuries with a Persian frame narrative that is first mentioned in the tenth century C.E. In his study of the origins of modern Arabic *narrative discourse* (a term he uses to cover the short story, novel, and drama), Sabry Hafez approaches the issue through "intertextuality" rather than "genealogy." Tracing the "cultural revival" in modern Egypt and the Levant back to the eighteenth century, before Napoléon's occupation of Egypt, Hafez demonstrates that these new genres emerged through a complex and dynamic process based in socioeconomic and cultural changes. These included increasing urbanization, improved means of transport, the printing press, and education as well as "the rise of national and political consciousness, journalism and the contact with European culture and thought," largely through translation (Hafez, p. 64). The result was a new reading public with a different worldview and a demand for narrative texts. Such conditions encouraged writing that drew on a wide range of codes and literatures, writing that would eventually lead to the emergence of modern narrative forms.

*Hala Halim*

*Dictionnaire philosophique* (1764–1772)—"a knowledge of the works of taste, a smattering of history, poetry, eloquence, and criticism"—though by this time one can sense the semantic gravitation of the word toward its emerging and narrower modern meaning (Wellek). Not until the late eighteenth century, however, was the word *literature* actually used more narrowly to designate imaginative writing per se, that is, the genres of poetry, fictional narrative, and drama.

## The Modern Idea of Literature

In 1777 Samuel Johnson (1709–1784) was invited to compose critical essays for an edition of English poets, beginning with Geoffrey Chaucer (c. 1342–1400), then being prepared by London booksellers. Once the anthology—which was shortened to begin with the early seventeenth-century poet Abraham Cowley—was complete, Johnson's fifty-two introductions were published separately as *Lives of the English Poets* (1779–1781). In his portrait of John Milton, Johnson still used literature in the classical sense of learning or erudition, observing that the great poet "had probably more than common literature, as his son addresses him in one of his most elaborate Latin poems" (vol. 1, p. 85). But when introducing Cowley, Johnson gave the term a significance that would become central by the early twentieth century. Johnson described Thomas Sprat, Cowley's biographer, as "an author whose pregnancy of imagination and elegance of language have deservedly set him high in the ranks of literature" (vol. 1, p. 1). By the early nineteenth century, a period marked by the prominence of the entrepreneurial author-publisher Sir Walter Scott (1771–1832), the idea that literature refers primarily to a particular *kind* of writing—imaginative—also meant that the word could signify a particular professional occupation. Isaac Disraeli (1766–1848), father of Benjamin Disraeli, used the word in this new, narrower sense when he wrote in 1823, "Literature, with us, exists independent of patronage or association" (vol. 2, p. 407). The primary modern meaning of literature—autonomous, professional, imaginative writing designed for a market economy—had emerged.

At almost the same time that literature was beginning to signify primarily the imaginative genres of poetry, fiction, and drama, two complementary semantic changes were occurring. The first is that the word was being used to designate the total body of writing defined by national (or at least linguistic) origin. Thus Johann Gottfried von Herder (1744–1803) published a book called *Über die neuere deutsche Litteratur* (On the more recent German literature) in 1767, and L'abbé Antoine Sabatier de Castres published a book called *Les trois siècles de notre littérature* (Three centuries of our literature) in 1772, which became *Les trois siècles de la littérature française* (Three centuries of French literature) in subsequent editions. In 1836 Robert Chambers (1802–1871) produced *A History of English Language and Literature*. Such texts both contributed and responded to a political sensibility in the eighteenth and nineteenth centuries that had begun to categorize cultural artifacts in national terms. By the late nineteenth century this way of looking at literature, and especially imaginative literature, would be normalized. The study of modern literature (as opposed to Greek and Latin) came to be used in the schools to standardize linguistic usage; to elevate the culture of populations with little access to classical learning; to produce social integration across the divisions of economic class; and to provide a basis for a national collective consciousness (Weber).

The second semantic change in the word literature is a reflection of the idea of "aesthetics" in the eighteenth century. Since antiquity, claims had been made that the arts, including poetry and drama, were rational and rule governed, quite despite their aura of divine inspiration. Both Aristotle and Horace, in different ways, made these claims. On the whole, so did neoclassical French critics of the seventeenth century such as Nicolas Boileau. With the third earl of Shaftesbury, and especially the version of his ideas found in Francis Hutcheson's *Inquiry into the Origin of Our Ideas of Beauty and Virtue* (1726), English moral philosophy based on the sentiments began to translate the older idea of "good taste" in terms of a specific, subjective "aesthetic intuition" present in both the "genius" of artistic creation and the perception of beauty. For Shaftesbury and Hutcheson, the sensation of the beautiful became nothing less than the path by which all the traditional antinomies of philosophy—subject versus object, innate ideas versus empirical learning, necessity versus contingency, reason versus passion—can be overcome. In Germany, with Alexander Baumgarten (1714–1762) and especially Immanuel Kant (1724–1804) and his *Critique of Judgment,* the project emerges of a specific science or philosophy of beauty that emphasizes the disinterested and universal nature of the human response to beauty (Cassirer, pp. 275–360). The Greek word *aesthēsis,* which had covered a range of meanings, including sensation, perception, feeling, knowledge, and consciousness, came to be *aesthetics,* used exclusively to refer to our response to beauty. In the 1790s Friedrich Schiller (1759–1805) wrote his *Letters on the Aesthetic Education of Man,* which outlines a project for making the education of the aesthetic sensibility the central component of a wholesale moral and political reform of humanity. Along with the other arts, literature became a part of that project, though often the term *poetry* or *poetics* (as in Aristotle's treatise) was still used to denote the artfulness of literature. For Georg Wilhelm Friedrich Hegel (1770–1831), lecturing on aesthetics in the 1820s, art evolves in human history from more material to less material forms, from architecture to sculpture to poetry, as it approaches the ideal of reason. But this means that poetry becomes the most elevated Romantic art form only by virtue of becoming pure sound: poetry is the least burdened by matter, that is, by written *letters.* It is as if the putative oral basis of literary art had for Hegel returned to become its highest form.

Along with the nationalizing of imaginative literature in the nineteenth century—a development that was the dominant institutional form of literary studies in the twentieth-century academy—two complementary ideas arose. The first is the idea of *Weltliteratur* (world literature) used by Johann Wolfgang von Goethe (1749–1832) when commenting in 1827 on his translation of Torquato Tasso (1544–1595). It is a vague but visionary term suggested by the ideal of universal humanity promulgated during the French Revolution and embodied more ambiguously by Napoléon's subsequent attempt to "liberate" Europe, Asia, and the Middle East by force. The second is the notion of "comparative literature," which began to be used in the early nineteenth century, perhaps in imitation of concurrent scholarly movements, such as "comparative anatomy," "comparative philology," and other comparative enterprises in history, philosophy, and anthropology. Abel-François Villemain gave a course of lectures at the Sorbonne in the 1820s in which he used the term *littérature comparée,* and two German journals appeared later. *Zeitschrift für vergleichende Literatur* (Journal of comparative literature), edited by Hugo von Meltzl de Lomnitz, was published between 1877 and 1888, and *Zeitschrift für vergleichende Literaturgeschichte* (Journal of comparative literary history), founded in 1866 by Max Koch, was published until 1910.

## Contemporary Developments

In some ways, "world" literature predates the nationalizing of literary traditions, since the classical and medieval period is quite polyglot and multicultural. But world literature and comparative literature were given new life in the late twentieth century by the awareness of the historical power of European imperialism and the rise of postcolonial literatures in India, Africa, South America, Asia, and the Middle East and later by the emphasis on globalization as a cultural phenomenon. The fate of specifically *national* imaginative literatures hangs in the balance. At the same time, two other critical perspectives on literature served to challenge once again what the term means. On the one hand, the Romantic idea of literature as the vehicle of aesthetic sensibility was called into question to emphasize the political function of the literary text, especially in terms of class, gender, and race. On the other hand, the idea that imaginative literature represents a kind of writing qualitatively distinct from philosophical writing or historical writing was also radically questioned. The paradoxical result is that the word *literature* at the beginning of the twenty-first century in many ways has begun to recover some of the inclusive significance that was lost when it was narrowed to fit nationalist and aesthetic sensibilities during the Enlightenment. Literature once again refuses to be confined to national borders or to be defined by the imaginative and the aesthetic. With the arrival in the 1990s of electronic literature, produced and consumed with the help of computers, the traditional medium of literature in print or manuscript—the book—acquired a potentially powerful rival. The root idea of literature as writing, that is, the scratching (or printing or typing) of marks into an impressionable material, may well be superseded by the flash of digital impulses across video screens.

*See also* **Aesthetics; Autobiography; Biography; Genre; Language and Linguistics; Language, Linguistics, and Literacy; Narrative; Oral Traditions.**

### BIBLIOGRAPHY

Allen, Roger. *The Arabic Literary Heritage: The Development of Its Genres and Criticism.* Cambridge, U.K.: Cambridge University Press, 1998.

Beeston, A. F. L., et al., eds. *Arabic Literature to the End of the Umayyad Period.* Cambridge, U.K.: Cambridge University Press, 1983.

Bradshaw, Henry. *The Life of Saint Werburge of Chester.* Edited by Carl Horstmann. Millwood, N.Y.: Krauss Reprint Co., 1975.

Cassirer, Ernst. *The Philosophy of the Enlightenment.* Translated by Fritz C. A. Koelln and James P. Pettegrove. Princeton, N.J.: Princeton University Press, 1951.

Damrosch, David. *What Is World Literature?* Princeton, N.J.: Princeton University Press, 2003.

Disraeli, Isaac. *Curiosities of Literature.* 3 vols. London: G. Routledge and Co., 1858–1859.

Elman, Benjamin A. *A Cultural History of Civil Examinations in Late Imperial China.* Berkeley: University of California Press, 2000.

Gabrieli, F. "Adab." *The Encyclopaedia of Islam: New Edition.* Vol. 1. Edited by H. A. R. Gibb et al., 175–176. Leiden, Netherlands: Brill, 1960.

Goody, Jack. *The Logic of Writing and the Organization of Society.* Cambridge, U.K.: Cambridge University Press, 1986.

Hafez, Sabry. *The Genesis of Arabic Narrative Discourse: A Study in the Sociology of Modern Arabic Literature.* London: Saqi Books, 1993.

Johnson, Samuel. *Lives of the English Poets.* 3 vols. Edited by George Birkbeck Hill. Oxford: Clarendon, 1905.

Liu, Lydia H. *Translingual Practice: Literature, National Culture, and Translated Modernity, China, 1900–1937.* Stanford, Calif.: Stanford University Press, 1995.

Lord, Albert Bates. *The Singer of Tales.* Cambridge, Mass.: Harvard University Press, 1960.

Ong, Walter. *Orality and Literacy: The Technologizing of the Word.* New York: Methuen, 1982.

Powell, Barry B.. *Writing and the Origins of Greek Literature.* Cambridge, U.K.: Cambridge University Press, 2002.

Saussy, Haun. *Great Walls of Discourse and Other Adventures in Cultural China.* Cambridge, Mass.: Harvard University Asia Center, 2001.

Voltaire. *Dictionnaire philosophique.* Introduction, notes, and annexes by Béatrice Didier. Paris: Impr. Nationale Editions, 1994.

Weber, Eugen. *Peasants into Frenchmen: The Modernization of Rural France, 1870–1914.* Stanford, Calif.: Stanford University Press, 1976.

Wellek, René. "Literature." In *Dictionary of the History of Ideas,* edited by Philip P. Weiner. New York: Scribners, 1973–1974.

*Vincent P. Pecora*

### AFRICAN LITERATURE

African literature is best understood within the context of Ali Mazrui's categorization of African historical experience as a "triple heritage": Africa as a space produced by endogenous historical traditions, Arab/Islamic influences, and Western Judeo-Christian influences. This triple heritage has produced a literature characterized by a tripodal identity, based on its relationship to each element. Africa's indigenous heritage is of its rich oral traditions. The Arab/Islamic heritage is associated with the written literatures of North Africa and parts of East and West Africa. The Arabic and Western aspects of Africa's triple heritage reflect the continent's experience with the historical trauma of conquest, evidenced by such events as the Arab invasion of North Africa and West Africa, the trans-Atlantic slave trade, and colonialism. The Western/Judeo-Christian heritage has shaped the literature written in English, French, and Portuguese.

## Oral Tradition

Oral tradition comprises the specialized verbal art forms—proverbs, riddles, chants, lyric poetry, tales, myths, legends, and epics—through which African societies have ensured cultural continuity. It is the repository of a community's core values, philosophies, mysteries, rituals, and, most importantly, memory. It survives by virtue of transmission from one generation to another by word of mouth. Performance is its most important distinguishing feature. It exists only in its moment of actuation, when performer and audience come together in a quasi-spiritual engagement. The performer draws his or her materials from the collective ancestral lore familiar to the audience; distinctiveness comes with innovation and inventiveness, delivery, and command of language.

Ruth Finnegan sparked the most significant controversy on the status of oral tradition when she concluded, in her influential *Oral Literature in Africa* (1970), that Africa had no epic. Isidore Okepwho's *The Epic in Africa* (1979) and *Myth in Africa* (1983) became crucial to the institutional and conceptual legitimization of those genres against the backdrop of the Finnegan controversy. Allied to the development of a robust critical apparatus on African oral tradition was the process of recording the various oral genres—folktales, proverbs, riddles, myths, praise poetry, epics, and sagas—for posterity. Birago Diop's (1906–1989) *Les contes d'Amadou Koumba* (1947; Tales of Amadou Koumba) and *Les nouveaux contes d'Amadou Koumba* (1958; New tales of Amadou Koumba) and Bernard Dadié's (b. 1916) *Le pagne noir* (1955; The black cloth) have become classics of the folktale genre. The Sundiata, Mwindo, Ibonia epics and the Ozzidi saga are also extant in significant textual versions.

## Written Literature

Africa's written literature could easily span close to five thousand years, depending on the persuasion of various commentators. Thinkers in the Afrocentric tradition trace the antecedents of African written literature to such touchstones as the scribal tradition of ancient Egypt, the Arabic poetic tradition, which began roughly with the Arab conquest of Egypt in the seventh century C.E., the spread of that tradition to the Maghreb and West Africa from the ninth century C.E., which culminated in the development of Hausa Islamic/Arabic verse from the seventeenth century on.

The twentieth century witnessed the blossoming of a generation of North African writers whose craft combined centuries of Arab narratological conventions and Western influences. These writers either write in Arabic and have influential translations of their works in English and French, or they write directly in the two European languages. Of those whose works attained international recognition in English are the Egyptians Naguib Mahfouz and Nawal El Saadawi. Mahfouz's deft handling of historical realism, his inimitable depiction of quotidian life in Cairo turned his fiction into an important opus of Arab imagination and earned him the Nobel prize for literature in 1988, while Saadawi's transgressive novels have become some of the most important feminist works in the twentieth century.

The modern novel in French came much later in the Maghreb. The Algerian, Kateb Yacine's *Nedjma* (1956), is usually considered the first significant work of the fiction from the Francophone Maghreb, even though the Moroccan, Driss Chraibi had published a novel, *Le passé simple* (The simple past), two years earlier. North Africa fiction in French soon blossomed with internationally acclaimed writers such as Tahar Ben Jelloun, Abdelhak Serhane, Abdelkébir Khatibi, and Assia Djebar. Djebar's expansive fictional opus, which explores wide-ranging themes such as the trauma of French colonization of Algeria, the brutal war of liberation, and the condition of women in the context of religion and tradition, has become the quintessence of North African literature in French.

With regard to subsaharan Africa, discussions of written literatures tend to take the late nineteenth century as a rough starting point. Indigenous language literatures evolved as a consequence of missionary activity during this period. Missionaries established churches and schools and introduced forms of orthography into local languages to facilitate translations of religious literature. As a result, indigenous language literatures blossomed in western, central, eastern, and southern Africa in the nineteenth and the first half of the twentieth centuries. The Yoruba fiction of Nigeria's D. O. Fagunwa (1903–1963) and the Sotho fiction of Lesotho's Thomas Mofolo (1876–1948) are notable examples.

European language literature, usually referred to as modern African literature, is the dominant African literature. Although the violence of colonialism and the attendant sociopolitical ruptures it occasioned in Africa constitute the background of modern African literature, texts have evolved over several decades and across numerous genres in a manner that allows for the identification of divergent thematic and ideological clusters, all of which underscore modern African literature's investment in the representation of the African experience.

Negritude poetry was the medium through which modern African literature came to international attention in the twentieth century. The Negritude movement grew out of the encounter of young African intellectuals and their black Caribbean counterparts in Paris in the 1920s and 1930s. The Senegalese Léopold Sédar Senghor (1906–2001), the Martinican Aimé Césaire (b. 1913), and the Guyanese Léon-Gontran Damas (1912–1978) were the avant garde of the movement. Negritude philosophy involved a coming into consciousness of the condition of one's blackness in the racist European context of the time and the validation of Africa as the matrix of a proud black race after centuries of European misrepresentation. Damas's *Pigments* (1937) was the first volume of poetry to properly signal the birth of the Negritude movement, but Césaire's *Cahier d'un retour au pays natal* (1939; Notebook of a return to the native land) became its bible. Senghor's *Chants d'ombre* (1945; Shadow songs) and *Hosties noires* (1948; Black hosts) transformed the movement into a full-blown aesthetic phenomenon. However, the full dimensions of Negritude angst were not recorded until the publication of David Diop's (1927–1960) *Coups de pilon* (1956; Pounding).

Poetry comparable in stature with Negritude poetry did not come out of Anglophone and Lusophone (Portguese-speaking) Africa until the period of the 1960s–1980s. Wole Soyinka (b. 1934), Christopher Okigbo (1932–1967), Gabriel Okara

(b. 1921), John Pepper Clark (b. 1935), Kofi Awoonor (b. 1935), Lenrie Peters (b. 1932), Taban Lo Liyong (b. 1938), Okot P'Bitek (1931–1982), Kwesi Brew (b. 1928), Dennis Brutus (b. 1924), Agostino Neto (d.1979), and Antonio Jacinto (1925–1991) were the leading lights of Anglophone and Lusophone African poetry. Okigbo's collection, *Limits* (1964), is representative of this phase of African poetry.

The African novel also developed within the ambit of historical revaluation, cultural nationalism, political contestation, and anticolonial protest. Although modern African fiction started with the publication of the Ghanaian Joseph Casely-Hayford's (1866–1930) *Ethiopia Unbound* (1911), it was not until Amos Tutuola's (1920–1997) *The Palm Wine Drunkard* appeared in 1952 that Anglophone West African fiction attained international recognition. Francophone Africa's first novel, René Maran's (d. 1960) *Batouala*, was published to considerable acclaim in 1921 and went on to win the prestigious prix Goncourt. *Batouala* owed its fame to Maran's vivid portrayal of the effects of French colonial rule in Africa as well as his evocative and humanizing descriptions of African life and its environment.

The novel came of age in Francophone Africa from the 1950s onward when writers such as Camara Laye (1928–1980), Seydou Badian (b. 1928), Mongo Beti (1932–2001), Ferdinand Oyono (b. 1929), Sembene Ousmane (b. 1923), Cheikh Hamidou Kane (b. 1928), Ahmadou Kourouma (1927–2003), Williams Sassine (b. 1944), Sony Labou Tansi (1947–1995), Henri Lopès (b. 1937), Alioum Fantouré (b. 1938), and Tierno Monenembo (b. 1947) arrived on the scene. The thematic spectrum of these writers is broad and their range reveals the shifts that occurred in the sociopolitical dynamics of their informing contexts, particularly the tragedy of one-party states and military dictatorships that became the rule in postcolonial Francophone Africa. For instance, Laye's *L'enfant noir* (1953; The African child) is a powerful bildungsroman that explores the growing up of an African child who loses the values of his traditional society in a world permeated by European values. In *Le pauvre Christ de Bomba* (The poor Christ of Bomba) and *Une vie de boy* (Houseboy), both published in 1956, Beti and Oyono, respectively, deploy critical satire to expose the hypocrisies of the colonial situation. Ousmane brings class analysis to the crisis of colonialism in *Les bouts de bois de dieu* (1960; God's bits of wood).

However, it was Chinua Achebe's (b. 1930) *Things Fall Apart* (1958) that placed African fiction in the ranks of twentieth-century greats. In *Things Fall Apart,* the epic dimension of Africa's contact with the West, a preoccupation of much of modern African literature, reaches its philosophical and aesthetic peak. Much of Anglophone West African fiction explores versions of Achebe's themes either as collective sociopolitical fissures in a changing world or as individual dramas of alienation. Cyprian Ekwensi (b. 1921), T. M. Aluko (b. 1918), Elechi Amadi (b. 1934), Onuora Nzekwu (b. 1928), John Munonye (b. 1929), Wole Soyinka, Kofi Awoonor, Ayi Kwei Armah (b. 1939), Ngugi wa Thiong'o (b. 1938), Kole Omotoso (b. 1943), and Festus Iyayi (b. 1947) all became major Anglophone West African novelists in the period from the 1960s through the 1980s. While Armah adds a humanist/universal dimension to the drama of man's alienation from his

environment in *The Beautyful Ones Are Not Yet Born* (1968), Ngugi offers a Marxist exploration of the African experience of colonialism and neo-colonialism in *A Grain of Wheat* (1967) and *Petals of Blood* (1977).

Apartheid and race relations are the background of Southern African fiction. Peter Abrahams (b. 1919), Richard Rive (1931–1989), Es'kia Mphahlele (b. 1919), Lewis Nkosi (b. 1936), Alex La Guma (1925–1985), and the Afrikaner novelists, J. M. Coetzee (b. 1940) and André Brink (b. 1935), all produced novels emblematic of the South African situation. Abraham's *Mine Boy* (1946), Rive's *Emergency* (1964), Alex la Guma's *A Walk in the Night* (1962), and J. M. Coetzee's *Waiting for the Barbarians* (1980) document the scale of the human tragedy created by apartheid in South Africa.

African drama is perhaps the genre that has explored the resources of oral tradition most effectively as a result of the ontological linkages between the two: African religious ceremonies—rituals, sacrifices, festivals, funerals, christenings—are forms of drama and the roots of that modern African genre. Wole Soyinka, Wale Ogunyemi (1939–2001), Ola Rotimi (1938–2000), Femi Osofisan (b. 1946), Bode Sowande (b. 1948), and Olu Obafemi (b. 1950) have all written plays exploring the full range of human experience within the cosmic order and within the material contexts of colonialism, neo-colonialism, and the self-imposed tragedies of the African postcolonial order. Soyinka's plays, the most notable of which are *A Dance of the Forest* (1963) and *Death and the King's Horseman* (1975), explore the entire range of these thematic preoccupations. In South Africa, drama proved to be one of the most versatile cultural instruments in the antiapartheid struggle because of its immediate accessibility to a large audience. The South African dramaturgy of Athol Fugard (b. 1932) comes closest to Soyinka's in terms of artistic accomplishment and thematic range.

## Women's Writing

African women arrived on the literary scene much later than their male counterparts. Cultural impediments to the education of women, coupled with the Western sexism of the colonial system, kept girls out of the earliest missionary schools. Flora Nwapa's (1931–1993) *Efuru* (1967) was Anglophone Africa's first female novel. Other Anglophone female novelists include Buchi Emecheta (b. 1944), Ama Ata Aidoo (b. 1942), Ifeoma Okoye Zaynab Alkali (b. 1955), Nadine Gordimer (b. 1923), Maryam Tlali (b. 1933), Bessie Head (1937–1986), and Grace Ogot (b. 1930). Some women also became accomplished playwrights, Efua Sutherland (b. 1924), Zulu Sofola (b. 1938), and Tess Onwueme (b. 1955) being the most famous. Thérèse Kuoh-Moukoury's (b. 1938) *Rencontres essentielles* (2002; Essential encounters) is the first novel to be published by a Francophone woman. But women's fiction from that part of Africa did not fully take off until the 1970s when two Senegalese women, Aminata Sow Fall (b. 1941) and Mariama Bâ (1929–1981), arrived on the scene.

Because women's writing arose out of the desire to introduce a female perspective to the sociopolitical vision of Africa portrayed by male writers and to address issues relative to female subjectivity in order to expose the cultural impediments to female agency, African women writers have treated a wide range of themes. The position and role of women as mothers and daughters within the institution of marriage, especially polygamy, the encumbrances attendant on societal/traditional role prescriptions for women, female circumcision, and gender inequality are all themes explored in such classics as Emecheta's *The Joys of Motherhood* (1979), Aidoo's *Our Sister Killjoy* (1966), and Bâ's two novels, *Une si longue lettre* (1979; So long a letter) and *Un chant écarlate* (1981; Scarlet song).

## Children of the Postcolony

A new generation of writers attained international recognition beginning in the mid-1980s. The most important factor that distinguishes them from earlier generations is that most of them, but for a few born in the late 1950s, were born after 1960, the year that African nations began to achieve independence. The political reality of these writers is that of the failed African postcolony, something that prompted the Francophone novelist, Abdourahman Waberi (b. 1965), himself a new writer, to describe them as "les enfants de la postcolonie" (children of the postcolony). Difficult socioeconomic conditions in the continent have forced most of the new writers to relocate to the West. Exile, migration, deracination, home, and diasporic identity issues are the major themes of the displaced. Female writers have been very visible in this group: Tsitsi Dangarembga (b. 1959), Yvonne Vera (b. 1964), Ammah Darko (b. 1956), and Chimamanda Adichie (b. 1977) have all achieved international recognition. Their male counterparts, Helon Habila (b. 1967), Chris Abani (b. 1967), Moses Isegawa (b. 1963), Ike Oguine, and Okey Ndibe (b. 1960) have all published internationally acclaimed novels as well. The Cameroonian, Calixthe Beyala (b. 1961), is the most successful of the Francophone authors in this generation. Other notable Francophone writers include Sami Tchak (b. 1960), Daniel Biyaoula (b. 1957), Alain Patrice Nganang (b. 1970), Alain Mabanckou (b. 1966), and Fatou Diome (b. 1968).

## Debates and Critical Engagements

A rich critical tradition developed early around modern African writing. Francophone Africa had journals such as *Présence Africaine* (African presence), *Peuples noirs, peuples africains* (Black peoples, African peoples), *Abbia,* and *L'Afrique littéraire et artistique* (Literary and artistic Africa). Anglophone Africa had a wider array of early journals: *Black Orpheus, The Conch, The Horn, The Muse, Drum, Okike, Transition, Ba Shiru,* and *African Literature Today.* While most of these journals no longer publish, *Notre Librairie* (Our bookstore) and *Research in African Literatures* remain the most important. Furthermore, writers became implicated in the early process of elaborating a critical tradition by engaging critics or one another in debates ranging from the question of critical standards to the role of the writer in society. Chinua Achebe's *Morning Yet on Creation Day* (1975), Wole Soyinka's *Myth, Literature, and the African World* (1976), and Ngugi wa Thiong'o's *Decolonising the Mind* (1986) are some of the most important contributions to African literary criticism.

One of the earliest debates concerned the definition of African literature. The writers and critics who gathered in Uganda in 1963 faced the fundamental question of determining who qualified as an African writer and what qualified as African writing. The high point of the ensuing debate was the famous essay by Obi Wali, "The Dead End of African Literature" (1963), in which he declared that the literature written in European languages did not qualify as African literature. This was the beginning of the ongoing atavistic language debate. Although Achebe countered Wali's position, Ngugi embraced it, transforming the call for a return to African languages into a critical crusade that has lasted for more than three decades.

Another important debate concerned the issue of who was better qualified to critique African literature: the Western or the African critic. The high point of this debate occurred in *African Literature Today* between the American, Bernth Lindfors, and the Nigerian, Ernest Emenyonu. Lindfors had written an unflattering essay on the fiction of the Cyprian Ekwensi. Emenyonu wrote a fiery rejoinder, questioning the aptitude of Lindfors as a Western critic. The next big debate occurred in 1980, when the troika of Chinweizu, Onwucheka Jemie, and Ihechukwu Madubuike published their famous book, *Toward the Decolonisation of African Literature,* condemning the overwhelming recourse to Western literary models and forms by writers such as Soyinka and urging a return to African traditions. With the explosion of postcolonial and postmodernist theories in the West at the end of the twentieth century, African critics became engaged in debating the appropriateness of applying those theories to African literature.

*See also* **Communication of Ideas: Africa and Its Influence; Negritude; Postcolonial Theory and Literature; Third World Literature.**

**BIBLIOGRAPHY**

Almeida, Irène Assiba d'. *Francophone African Women Writers: Destroying the Emptiness of Silence.* Gainesville: University Press of Florida, 1994.

Beier, Ulli, ed. *Introduction to African Literature: An Anthology of Critical Writing from Black Orpheus.* London: Longmans, 1967.

Cazenave, Odile. *Femmes rebelles: naissance d'un nouveau roman africain au féminin.* Paris: L'Harmattan, 1996.

Chevrier, Jacques. *Littérature nègre.* Paris: Armand Colin, 1974.

Dathorne, O. R. *African Literature in the Twentieth Century.* London: Heinemann, 1975.

Gikandi, Simon, ed. *Encyclopedia of African Literature.* London: Routledge, 2003.

Irele, Abiola. *The African Experience in Literature and Ideology.* London: Heinemann, 1981.

———. *The African Imagination: Literature in Africa and the Black Diaspora.* Oxford: Oxford University Press, 2001.

Jahn, Jaheinz. *A History of Neo-African Literature: Writing in Two Continents.* Translated by Oliver Coburn and Ursula Lehrburger. New York: Grove, 1969.

Kesteloot, Lilyan. *Les écrivains noirs de langue française: naissance d'une littérature.* Brussels, Belgium: Université Libre de Bruxelles, 1965.

Larson, Charles R. *The Ordeal of the African Writer.* London: Zed, 2001.

Mazrui, Ali. *Africans: A Triple Heritage.* Boston: Little, Brown, 1986.

Miller, Christopher. *Nationalists and Nomads: Essays on Fran-cophone African Literature and Culture.* Chicago: University of Chicago Press, 1998.

Moore, Gerald. *Seven African Writers.* London: Oxford University Press, 1962.

Mphahlele, Ezekiel. *The African Image.* London: Faber, 1962.

Oyěwùmí, Oyèrónké, ed. *African Women and Feminism: Reflecting on the Politics of Sisterhood.* Trenton, N.J.: Africa World Press, 2003.

Pieterse, Cosmo, and Donald Munro, eds. *Protest and Conflict in African Literature.* London: Heinemann, 1969.

Wauthier, Claude. *The Literature and Thought of Modern Africa.* Translated by Shirley Kay. London: Pall Mall, 1966.

*Pius Adesanmi*

# LOGIC.

Logic is the study of correct reasoning. A host of philosophical themes have clustered around this central concern: the nature of truth and validity, of possibility and necessity; the semantics of words, sentences, and arguments; and even questions about substances and accidents, free will and determinism.

## Aristotle

Aristotle (384–322 B.C.E.) was the first person to formulate an explicit theory of correct reasoning, as he himself claimed in *Sophistical Refutations.* He owed a good deal to the exploration into forms of argument carried out in the course of argument contests, such as those illustrated by Plato in some of his Socratic dialogues. Book 8 of his own *Topics* reads like a handbook for contestants, and the *Topics* as a whole is designed to teach its readers how to construct "dialectical" arguments: arguments that, in keeping with the idea of a real contest, use generally accepted premises that will be granted by the interlocutor. In an argument, says Aristotle, "when certain things have been laid down, something other than what has been laid down necessarily results from them." This definition captures the idea of logical consequence, and in his *Prior Analytics* Aristotle develops his "syllogistic," a formal theory of logical consequence, which he applies to "demonstrations," arguments in which the premises must not be merely accepted, but true.

Syllogisms (in the narrow sense considered in the *Prior Analytics*) consist of three assertoric sentences, two of them premises, from which the third, the conclusion, follows. In an assertoric sentence, something is "predicated" of a subject, and a predicate can stand in one of just five relations to a subject: it may be its definition, its genus ("Man is an animal"), its differentia (the element of the definition that differentiates things of one species from another: "Man is rational"), an accident (a characteristic the particular thing happens to have: "Socrates is curly-haired"), or its characteristic property (a feature that all and only things of the subject's species have, but is not part of its definition: "Man is able to laugh").

The two premises of a syllogism share a common ("middle") term, and they have "quantity" (universal/particular) and "quality" (affirmative/negative). They may be, then, universal affirmative (A-sentences: "Y belongs to every X"), universal negative (E-sentences: "Y belongs to no X"), particular affirmative (I-sentences: "Y belongs to some X"), or particular negative (O-sentences: "Y does not belong to some X"). Depending on the position of the middle term—predicate of both premises ("third figure"), subject of both premises ("second figure"), or subject of the first, predicate of the second ("first figure")—from some combinations of two A, E, I, and O sentences as premises, there follows an A, E, I, or O sentence as a conclusion—and this conclusion follows purely in virtue of the form of the argument. (Although ancient logicians rarely used false premises as their examples, they too made their conclusions follow logically.) So, for example, in the first figure, the patterns AAA, EAE, AII, and EIO are valid arguments. First-figure syllogisms were held by Aristotle to be self-evident: for example, Mortal belongs to every man (every man is mortal); man belongs to every philosopher; thus mortal belongs to every philosopher. Aristotle also shows how second- and third-figure syllogisms can be reduced to first-figure ones, using a set of conversion rules.

Aristotle's other logical works both fill in the discussions in the *Topics* and the *Prior Analytics* and introduce new philosophical dimensions. *On Interpretation* discusses assertoric statements and their relations (such as contradiction and contrariety). It also proposes a basic semantics, in which sentences are signs for thoughts, and thoughts for things, and it ventures into difficult questions of possibility and necessity. If it is true that there will be a sea battle tomorrow, then how can we avoid the unpalatable conclusion that it is a matter of necessity that the battle will take place tomorrow? The *Posterior Analytics* uses the theory of demonstration as a basis for a theory of scientific knowledge. The *Sophistical Refutations* explore fallacious but apparently valid arguments. The *Categories* has, in part, the aspect of a preface to the *Topics,* but it is in part a work of metaphysics—a forerunner of Aristotle's treatise of that name.

## The Stoics

The Stoics developed a logic different from Aristotle's, and to a large extent independently from him. Their greatest logician, Chrysippus, lived from about 280 to 206 B.C.E. and, as with most of the Stoics, his thought has mostly to be reconstructed from reports and fragments in later writers. Whereas Aristotelian syllogistic is a term-logic, Stoic logic was propositional: it explored the relations between what they called "assertibles"—that is to say, sentences that can be used to make assertions. Assertibles can be simple ("It is day") or complex ("If it is day, it is light"/ "It is day or it is not light"). The argument forms classified by the Stoics involve one complex and one simple assertible: for example, "If it is day, it is light. It is day. So, it is light." This is the first of five "indemonstrables"—basic argument forms—distinguished by Chrysippus. The Stoics had a schematic way of representing the indemonstrables—what they called their "modes"—using ordinal numbers. The four remaining modes of the five indemonstrables are (2) If the first, then the second; not the second; so not the first; (3) Not both the first and the second; the first; so not the second; (4) Either the first or the second; the first; so not the second; (5) Either the first or the second; not the first; so the second. Since the assertibles could be either negative or positive, and the complex assertible could itself include complex assertibles ("If both the first and the second, then the third"), there was quite a wide range of indemonstrable argument schemes. But Stoic logic was not limited to them. Nonindemonstrable forms of argument could be valid, and the Stoics had a theory of "analysis" in which, using certain basic rules (*themata*) and, if wanted, additional theorems, the nonindemonstrable arguments were shown to be made up of demonstrable ones or of conversions of them.

Stoic logicians also explored modal concepts. One of their main starting points was provided by the fourth-century B.C.E. Megaric logician Diodorus Cronus, who formulated a "Master Argument," the subject of many attempts at reconstruction by modern historians, which attempts to show that, from the premises that true past propositions are necessary, and that an impossibility never follows from what is possible, it follows that nothing is possible except what is or will be true. The Stoic logicians rejected the argument by querying one or other of its premises, and Chrysippus developed his own understanding of possibility and necessity.

## The Neoplatonists

Although Aristotle's pupil and successor, Theophrastus (c. 372–c. 287 B.C.E.), wrote extensively on logic, and Alexander of Aphrodisias (fl. c. 200 C.E.) cultivated Aristotelian logic, the most important enthusiasts of Aristotelian logic were, surprisingly, the Neoplatonists, from Porphyry (c. 234–c. 305) onward. Porphyry wrote an introduction (*Eisagoge*) to the *Categories*, which itself became for later students a part of the Aristotelian logical corpus (known as the *Organon*), and he wrote extensive commentaries on Aristotle's logical works. Despite his Platonic metaphysics, Porphyry believed that logic, which is concerned with the world of appearances that is the subject of normal discourse, should be studied in strictly Aristotelian terms. Although later Neoplatonic commentators, following the lead of Iamblichus, tended more to introduce their characteristic metaphysical ideas into discussions of logic, Porphyry's approach was transmitted to the medieval Latin West by Boethius (c. 480–c. 524), who translated into Latin most of the *Organon* and wrote commentaries on some of it and logical textbooks on topical argument (the late ancient development of the *Topics*), division, and on syllogisms.

## The Medieval Latin West, 790–1200

The study of logic was revived in the Latin West at the court of Charlemagne; his adviser, Alcuin, wrote the first medieval logical textbook (*On Dialectic*) in about 790. Logic was central to the intellectual life of medieval Europe in a way that it had not been in antiquity, and has not been since the Renaissance. Yet, until the 1130s, medieval logicians made do with what became known as the *logica vetus* ("old logic"): just Porphyry's *Eisagoge*, Aristotle's *Categories* and *On Interpretation,* and Boethius's commentaries and textbooks. They had only the most limited access to the Stoic tradition, through mentions by Boethius and the *On Interpretation* of Apuleius (second century C.E.). Ninth-century authors, such as John Scotus Erigena, were interested especially in the *Categories*—its metaphysical aspects and the question, raised by Augustine

and by Boethius, of whether any of the ten categories distinguished by Aristotle apply to God. Anselm of Canterbury (1033 or 1034–1109) was a gifted logician who explored and questioned the Aristotelian doctrine of the *Categories* and made imaginative use of the ideas on possibility and necessity in *On Interpretation.*

In the twelfth century, the *logica vetus* was the central concern of the flourishing Paris schools. Peter Abelard (1079–1142), the greatest logician of the time, developed a nominalist metaphysics on its basis and elaborated a semantics to explain how sentences that use universal words (such as "Socrates is a man") are meaningful although there are no universal things, only particulars. Abelard also excelled in more purely logical matters. Starting from the hints and misunderstandings he found in Boethius, he rediscovered propositional logic and, in his *Dialectica* (c. 1116), he explored in great depth the truth conditions for conditional ("if . . . then . . .") sentences. Abelard was thus able to pioneer the analysis of sentences that are of ambiguous interpretation in terms of propositional logic, an aspect of logic that became especially popular from the 1130s onward, when *On Sophistical Refutations* and then the rest of Aristotle's logic (the *logica nova*—"new logic") became available. And he is one of the few logicians ever to have examined the logic of impersonal sentences, such as "It is good that he came today."

## The Medieval Latin West, 1200–1500

From the middle of the twelfth century, logicians developed various branches of their subject, known as the *logica modernorum* ("contemporary logic"), that had not been treated specially, or at all, in antiquity. Peter of Spain's widely read *Tractatus* (often called *Summulae logicales*) illustrates how parts of the *logica modernorum* had developed up until about the 1230s. There was a lull in interest and innovation in logic for nearly a century, but in the first half of the fourteenth century writers at Oxford, such as Walter Burley (d. 1344/45), William of Ockham (d. ?1349), Thomas Bradwardine (d. 1349), and William of Heytesbury (d. 1372/23), and, in Paris, John Buridan (d. after 1358) revived the branches of the *logica modernorum* and brought them to new levels of sophistication. The *Logica magna* (Great logic) of Paul of Venice (d. 1429) is a vast record of these achievements.

Some branches of the *logica modernorum* grew directly from the mid-twelfth-century interest in fallacies. For example, *sophismata* were a sort of disputation, involving a master and his pupils, built around sentences that either are apparently false but can be interpreted so as to make them true (e.g., "The whole Socrates is less than Socrates") or at least are open to different interpretations (e.g., "Every man is"). The ambiguities usually centered around the use of what were called "syncategorematic" words—words other than ordinary nouns, adjectives, and verbs with their own referential content: for instance, "only," "except," "all," "begins," "ceases"—and specialized treatises were devoted to studying these syncategoremata. Another type of disputation, "obligations," involved trying to force an opponent who has agreed to defend a particular statement into a self-contradiction, while following a very strict set of rules for what statements may be accepted or must be rejected. Liar paradoxes ("What I am now saying is false")—"insolubles"—formed another branch of study. In the theory of the "properties of terms" a highly elaborate theory was developed about the reference of words depending on their function within a sentence. Propositional logic was elaborated in treatises on what were called "consequences" (*consequentiae*), although it remains questionable how far the approach was purely propositional.

Aristotle's texts and methods were not, however, forgotten in the later Middle Ages. Aristotelian syllogistic, studied earlier through Boethius's textbooks, could now be learned directly from the *Prior Analytics*. It was a basic tool for almost every medieval philosopher or theologian, and a set of mnemonics ("bArbArA," "cElArEnt," etc.) were devised to enable students to remember the valid patterns. *On Interpretation* continued to be central to discussions about possibility, necessity, and divine prescience, and the *Posterior Analytics* provided the criteria for organizing branches of knowledge as diverse as grammar and theology.

## Medieval Islam

Logic was no less important for Islamic than for Christian philosophers and theologians. By the time of al-Farabi (c. 878–950), the first important Islamic logician, the whole of Aristotle's logical *Organon* was available in Arabic—far more material, then, than in the Latin West at this period, especially since the Arabic logicians tended to follow the habit of late antiquity in regarding the *Rhetoric* and the *Poetics* as parts of the *Organon* and assigning to them their own characteristic modes of argument, to contrast with demonstrative argument as taught in the *Analytics* and dialectical argument in the *Topics*.

Al-Farabi, who worked in Baghdad, Damascus, and elsewhere, saw his task as a logician to represent Aristotle faithfully, although this task involved him in a number of interpretations that went beyond the letter of the text. He was also concerned to vindicate logic in face of the grammarians, who doubted the need for this additional discipline; earlier in the tenth century, there had been a famous debate between the grammarian Abu Sa'id as-Sirafi and the logician Abu Bisr Matta, in which Abu Sa'id seems to have had the upper hand.

The great Persian philosopher Avicenna (Ibn Sina; 980–1037) respected al-Farabi and was also an ardent Aristotelian, but his approach to logic differed. In semantics, he rejected al-Farabi's theory that logic is concerned with expressions insofar as they signify meanings. Rather, he claimed, logic deals with meanings that classify meanings—so-called "second intentions." In his approach to syllogistic, Avicenna was far more inclined than al-Farabi had been to pursue his own train of analysis and accommodate Aristotle to it. For example, in modal logic he proposed a number of different readings of modal sentences: they could be taken absolutely (as in "God exists") or according to a condition—for example, "while something exists as a substance" (as in "man is necessarily a rational body") or "while something is described in the way it is" (as in "all mobile things are changing").

Logic continued to be studied in Islam because it was accepted by theologians as useful to their discipline rather than—as they often thought with regard to other areas of Aristotelian

philosophy—a dangerous rival to it. Particularly important was the endorsement of al-Ghazali (1058–1111): whereas he wrote a work specifically designed to attack other areas of Aristotelian philosophy, he was himself the author of two short logical works, based on Avicenna. In the next century, Averroës (Ibn Rushd), who worked in Muslim Spain, followed al-Farabi (and the general direction of all his own work as the commentator par excellence on Aristotle) in seeking a greater fidelity to Aristotle, but it was Avicenna who remained the dominant influence on later Islamic logic.

*See also* **Aristotelianism; Neoplatonism; Philosophy; Philosophy, History of; Scholasticism; Stoicism.**

### BIBLIOGRAPHY

PRIMARY SOURCES

Aristotle. *The Complete Works of Aristotle.* Edited by Jonathan Barnes. Vol. 1. Princeton, N.J.: Princeton University Press, 1984.

———. *Prior Analytics.* Translated by Robin Smith. Indianapolis: Hackett, 1989.

Kretzmann, Norman, and Eleonore Stump, eds. *Logic and the Philosophy of Language.* Vol. 1 of *The Cambridge Translations of Medieval Philosophical Texts.* Cambridge, U.K.: Cambridge University Press, 1988.

Peter of Spain. *Summulae logicales.* Translated by Francis P. Dinneen. Amsterdam and Philadelphia: Benjamins, 1990.

SECONDARY SOURCES

Barnes, Jonathan, Suzanne Bobzien, Mario Mignucci, and Dink M. Schenkeveld. "Part 2: Logic and Language." In *The Cambridge History of Hellenistic Philosophy,* edited by Keimpe Algra et al. Cambridge, U.K.: Cambridge University Press, 1999. Excellent, up-to-date survey.

Kretzmann, Norman, Anthony Kenny, and Jan Pinborg, eds. *Cambridge History of Later Medieval Philosophy.* Cambridge, U.K.: Cambridge University Press, 1982. Pages 101–381 contain the most complete available account of medieval logic in the Latin West.

Marenbon, John. *Boethius.* New York: Oxford University Press, 2003. See pages 17–65. Includes bibliography for Greek Neoplatonic tradition.

Martin, C. J. "Embarrassing Arguments and Surprising Conclusions in the Development of Theories of the Conditional in the Twelfth Century." In *Gilbert de Poitiers et ses contemporains,* edited by Jean Jolivet and Alain De Libera. Naples: Bibliopolis, 1987. Discusses Abelard and the twelfth-century rediscovery of propositional logic.

Smith, Robin. "Logic." In *The Cambridge Companion to Aristotle,* edited by Jonathan Barnes. Cambridge, U.K.: Cambridge University Press, 1995. Excellent bibliography on pp. 308–324.

*John Marenbon*

## LOGIC AND PHILOSOPHY OF MATHEMATICS, MODERN.

This article surveys many of the main positions that have been held in the logic and philosophy of mathematics from around 1800 up to recent times. Most attention

> Axiomatized logics are far removed from the normal use of logic. In teaching and practice "natural deduction" has recently gained much popularity: state the "local" premises, and deduce conclusions from them using rules for introducing and eliminating connectives. The name was introduced in the 1930s by Hilbert's follower Gerhard Gentzen.

is given to symbolic logics of some kind. No position has been definitive; indeed, especially over the last seventy years the variety has continually increased. To compensate for this article's lack of exhaustiveness, the bibliography is wide-ranging.

## The Revival of Logic from the 1820s, and Its Algebraic Flourishing

Some major philosophers gave logic a high status in the seventeenth and early eighteenth centuries; in particular, Gottfried Wilhelm von Leibniz advocated it as a *lingua characteristica*, with an attendant *calculus ratiocinator*, while John Locke took it as a case of *semeiotiké*, the theory of signs. The subject did not flourish, however; thus, while René Descartes stressed rules for correct thinking and deduction, and Immanuel Kant viewed logic as analytic knowledge (with mathematics as synthetically a priori), neither philosopher gave logic itself much attention. Most figures in all disciplines were content to appeal to Aristotelian syllogistic logic, while mathematicians normally saw the *Elements* of Euclid as the apotheosis of rigor.

The revival in logic came from an unexpected quarter: the *Elements of Logic* (1826) by the English theologian Richard Whately. Within a decade four more editions of this treatise had appeared, and various contemporaries commented at length. The strength of the reception is puzzling, for Whately did not advocate any radical new stances; nevertheless, interest in logic increased considerably and some notable advances occurred, especially the quantification of the predicate (1827) of George Bentham, in which Aristotle's modes were greatly extended by admitting forms such as *all As are some Bs.*

These advances attracted the mathematician Augustus De Morgan, who from the 1840s symbolized in an algebraic manner the forms of syllogistic modes and the relationships between them. He also studied the logical form of the proofs in Euclid, and came away rather perplexed; for the flow of argument in Euclid involved far more than logical deductions. A more sweeping change to logic was effected by George Boole, who started out from a new algebraic principle. Take a "universe of discourse" (his phrase) *1* of, say, boxes, and divide it into the class *x* of black ones and the complementary class (*1−x*) of nonblack ones. Then lay down the basic laws obeyed by *x*, including the novelty that *x* together with *x* is the same as *x*. Make deductions by formulating algebraically relationships between classes *x, y, . . .* and using the laws and attendant theorems to find as a

deduction the relationships between say, *y* and the other classes. Boole elaborated his method especially in *The Laws of Thought* (1854), where syllogisms occupied only the last chapter on logic. Finally, in 1860 De Morgan enriched syllogistics with a logic of (two-place) relations: at last the failure properly to handle, for example, *John is older than Jack* had been recognized.

The contributions of these two English algebraists were distinct: the American logician Charles S. Peirce conjoined them from the 1870s. One of his major insights, arrived at with his student O. H. Mitchell, was to individuate the "quantifier," both the existential *there is an X such that . . .* and the universal *for all X . . .* , and to stress the importance of watching quantifier order. Continuing the algebraic style, Peirce and Mitchell regarded these quantifiers as generalizations of logical disjunctions and conjunctions respectively. The interpretation of quantifiers was to be an enduring theme in the philosophy of logic. Their logic was extended, especially as an algebra, by the German Ernst Schröder in his vast *Vorlesungen über die Algebra der Logik* (1890–1905).

Many others wrote upon logic, especially in Britain; I note three figures. John Stuart Mill's *System of Logic* (1843, and many later editions), while not tied to syllogistics, relied much on it for an analysis of reasoning and deduction; mathematicization was absent, but in Mill's account of "induction," which we would regard as philosophy of science, he touched upon probability theory. Mill was broadly aligned to British empiricism: by great contrast, an influential "neo-Hegelianism" later became popular in academic circles. Francis H. Bradley's *Principles of Logic* (1883), its landmark, is an idealistic meditation upon the basic laws of logic (such as that of the excluded middle), judgments, and the reconciliation of thesis and antithesis in synthesis. Finally, Lewis Carroll produced some rather dull books on logic (1886; 1896); but in his *Alice* books (1865; 1871) he had brilliantly anticipated several concerns of those logicians of the next century who were to launch a new tradition that came to eclipse the algebraic logicians.

## Set Theory and the Rise of Mathematical Logic

Especially from the 1820s with the Frenchman Augustin Louis Cauchy, mathematicians had become more sensitive to the need for rigor in proofs, carefully stating assumptions and definitions and formulating theorems in conditional form. Cauchy's approach was refined from the 1860s by the lectures at Berlin University of Karl Weierstrass. The main context was the calculus and its extension into mathematical analysis. Two consequences are of special import.

First, in the early 1870s the German Georg Cantor began to develop set theory, initially treating points and numbers but later as a general treatment of collections of things; he even claimed that sets enabled him to define the natural numbers, and by implication to reduce mathematics to sets. His theory differed from the traditional part-whole theory that dates back to the Greeks and that was used by, for example, the algebraic logicians; for Cantor distinguished membership of objects in a set from the inclusion of subsets of objects within it. More controversially, he also incorporated a mathematical theory of the "actual infinite," showing that infinities came in different sizes.

Second, from the 1880s the Italian mathematician Giuseppe Peano began to symbolize as much as possible not only the notions of mathematical analysis (including set theory) but also the logical connectives and predicates with quantification. Thereby he launched "mathematical logic" (his name, in the sense usually adopted today). With an impressive school of followers he came to handle a wide range of mathematical theories this way, and enchanted the young Englishman Bertrand Russell, who came across him in 1900. Russell quickly added a logic of relations to mathematical logic, and converted Cantor's claim that set theory could ground mathematics into the "logicist" thesis (a name provided later by Rudolf Carnap) that mathematical logic could ground sets and thereby (much) mathematics. Russell also found that the German Gottlob Frege had already asserted this thesis for arithmetic and some parts of mathematical analysis, though in a Platonist spirit very different from his own empiricism.

So much for the good news. The bad arrived soon afterwards, in the form of a paradox now named after Russell: a certain set was a member of itself if and only if it was not. Paradoxes are at least a nuisance in mathematical theories: when the theory in question encompasses logic itself, their presence is a disaster. Eventually Russell produced an articulation of logicism in *Principia Mathematica* (1910–1913), written with Alfred North Whitehead; but his and other paradoxes were avoided rather than solved, and by an unwieldy and epistemologically questionable "theory of types": the ensemble of objects was divided into individuals, sets of individuals, sets of sets of individuals, . . . , ordered pairs of individuals, . . . , and so on, and membership was severely restricted.

## Axiomatics and the Rise of Proof and Model Theories

Meanwhile, contentment with Euclidian rigor was dissolving. From the 1860s non-Euclidean geometries had been accepted as legitimate theories, especially due to the insights of Bernhard Riemann. In addition, various mathematicians, including Peano, had noticed that Euclidian geometry itself needed several more axioms than Euclid had stated.

These developments made mathematicians still more aware of finding and expressing the assumptions involved in a theory. Another stimulus was the rise in importance of algebras (for example, among several, Boole's), each with its own basic laws. David Hilbert, the leading mathematician of his generation, studied geometries and algebras intensively, and was led around 1900 to seek for a mathematical means of studying axiom systems. He found it in "metamathematics" (his later name for it), in which a system was examined to establish its completeness, consistency, and independence.

One of Hilbert's axioms for geometry was a meta-assumption that the other axioms supplied all the objects required. This soon led the young American mathematician Oswald Veblen to consider two different sets of objects satisfying an axiom system; if the members of each could be put in one-one correspondence, then the system was "categorical." The study of (non-)categoricity enriched model theory considerably.

Set theory itself was influenced by these developments, for in 1908 Hilbert's follower Ernst Zermelo axiomatized it. His

With the re-creation of their country after World War I, the Poles produced a remarkable cohort of logicians, with Jan Łukasiewicz and Stanisłav Leśniewski as leaders, Luand Tarski perhaps the most dominant figure. While Hitler saw to its demise, several members emigrated; for example, Tarski was a major figure later in the development of model theory.

system included his own discovery, the "axiom of choice," a nonconstructive assumption that some colleagues found doubtful. A strong debate broke out; most participants agreed that the axiom was unavoidable. However, it was unacceptable for "constructivist" mathematicians, who admitted only procedures that built up mathematical objects in explicit stages: for them the axiom was outlawed, along with some standard proof methods such as by contradiction (to prove theorem *T*, assume *not-T* and get into a logical mess). The most prominent figure in this tradition was the Dutch mathematician L. E. J. Brouwer, who elaborated his alternative "intuitionistic" mathematics especially in the 1920s. At that time Hilbert's metamathematical program was in its definitive phase; but in 1927 Brouwer derided it as "formalism," a misleading name that Hilbert himself never used but that has regrettably become standard.

## Gödel, Tarski, and the Individuation of Metatheory

More bad news for Hilbert arrived in 1931, when the young Austrian Kurt Gödel proved that his metamathematical program could not be achieved for arithmetic with quantification over integers, and thus a fortiori for almost all acclimatized mathematical theories *T*; for Gödel showed that, in order to prove the consistency of *T*, its metamathematics had to be richer in assumptions than *T* itself rather than poorer, as Hilbert had hoped. This theorem was a corollary of another one, which torpedoed logicism by showing that there was a proposition *M* statable within *T* but neither provable nor disprovable; thus *T*, assumed to be consistent, was undecidable.

In addition, Gödel's proof-method soon led to a focus on recursion and to computability as conceived by the Englishman Alan Turing, thus launching a link between logic and computing. Finally, for Gödel's proofs to work the distinction between *T* and its metatheory had to be observed rigidly, as a central feature of both metamathematics and metalogic. The Polish logician Alfred Tarski also stressed this distinction around this time, for formal systems in general; his motive was treating as metatheoretic the (meta-)proposition that a proposition was true if it corresponded to the facts.

## Logics and Pluralism from the 1940s

The consequences of Gödel's theorems were profound. For example, logicism was replaced, especially by the American W. V. Quine, by elaborate systems of set theory and logic such as those developed in Quine's *Mathematical Logic* (1940); however, Russellian reductions of the former to the latter were not claimed.

Quine adhered to classical logic, with its two truth-values. But nonclassical logics gained adherents from the 1930s. The American C. I. Lewis had been a pioneer already in the 1910s, when he advocated "modal logics," where necessity and possibility were adjoined in various ways to truth and falsehood, as a means of clarifying the undoubtedly messy treatment of implication in *Principia Mathematica*. But from the 1930s these logics were viewed as viable alternatives to classicism in their own right. Another notable adherent was Gödel's friend Carnap, especially with his *Meaning and Necessity* (1947).

Since then logics classical and nonclassical have proliferated enormously, with their metalogics; many connections have been forged with computer science and aspects of semantics and linguistics. Notable among many cases are deontic logic, with its focus on sentences using "ought" and applications to law; temporal logics, seeking means to formulate deductions such as *John eats; thus John will have eaten;* many-valued logics, allowing for values other than true and false; non-monotonic logic or defeasible reasoning, defined by the property (in the simplest case) of propositions *A, B,* and *C* that given *A ∴ C,* then *A and B ∴ C* does not hold; paraconsistent logics, where various heresies are entertained, such as paradoxical propositions being both true and false; and fuzzy logic and set theory, where the vagueness of *John is very tall* is itself studied mathematically, initially by engineers rather than professional logicians.

This last topic bears upon control theory, which became associated with the discipline of cybernetics during the 1950s; logics of some kind were used in areas such as machine learning and brain modeling. Such concerns then developed further within the field of artificial intelligence, and were involved also in topics such as the representation of knowledge, automated theorem proving, and the relationship between complexity and recursion. These and very many more topics are now also linked to theoretical computer science, where many (meta)logics are used, with further connections to programming, formal and natural languages, and linguistics.

Partly due to these connections a renaissance of interest has occurred in higher-order logic, where quantification is executed over predicates as well as individuals. This revises a practice followed freely by Frege and by Russell and Whitehead. Theories of types have also been revived, appearing in several of the above contexts.

## Philosophies of Mathematics

Especially since World War II, new philosophies have emerged separate from logicism, formalism, and intuitionism. One kind is called naturalism, in which mathematical objects are said to be accessible to ordinary sense perception. Forms of Platonism are advocated, partly inspired by the enthusiasm of Gödel. Disaffection from concerns with mathematical truth has stimulated conventionalism; Henri Poincaré was an eminent early advocate. Versions of constructivist mathematics have been developed, broadly following the same prohibitions as Brouwer's but avoiding his peculiar philosophy; Erret Bishop was a notable

figure. Structuralism emphasizes the ubiquity of structures, perhaps to excess; mathematics has them rather than *is* them.

Most of this philosophy is by and for philosophers; the mathematical content is usually limited to set theory and/or arithmetic, even among empiricists who claim to attend to mathematical practice. In particular, little is said about the creation and development of mathematical theories in the first place. Here the eminent Hungarian Georg Polya was an important contributor, with books such as *Mathematics and Plausible Reasoning* (1954) discussing themes such as proofs themselves modifying old theorems and motivating new ones. A rather neglected area is the philosophy of mechanics and (classical) mathematical physics, despite the attraction of physical interpretation as well as rigor and proof.

By contrast, quantum mechanics has gained much attention, partly in connection with the philosophy of probability, which has a rather separate history. What kind of knowledge is expressed by *the probability that the next throw of the die will be 5 is 1/6*? Influential answers include the logical (it is a deduction from axioms), propensity (it is an assertion about the die and also its environment), subjective or Bayesian (it is a rational belief, drawing upon prior performance), and frequency (it is the limiting case of evidence drawn from long runs of throws).

## Concluding Remark

Whately would be astonished at the current range and variety of logics. However, there is often still a considerable professional distance between logicians and both mathematicians and philosophers; in the mid-1930s an Association of Symbolic Logic was created to provide a venue and a journal for those active in the field. Now perhaps too many logical and philosophical flowers are blooming, and many may wither for want of genuine need. One area of exploration is metametalogic and metametaphilosophy of mathematics, which have been largely ignored so far.

*See also* **Logic; Quantum.**

**BIBLIOGRAPHY**

Abramsky, S., Dov Gabbay, and T. S. E. Maibaum, eds. *Handbook of Logic in Computer Science.* 5 vols. Oxford and New York: Oxford University Press, 1992–2000.

Aspray, William, and Philip Kitcher, eds. *History and Philosophy of Modern Mathematics.* Minneapolis: University of Minnesota Press, 1988.

Barwise, Jon, ed. *Handbook of Mathematical Logic.* Amsterdam and New York: North-Holland, 1977.

Benacerraf, Paul, and Hilary Putnam, eds. *Philosophy of Mathematics: Selected Readings.* 2nd ed., Cambridge, U.K., and New York: Cambridge University Press, 1983.

Fraenkel, Abraham. *Abstract Set Theory.* Amsterdam: North-Holland, 1953. Outstanding bibliography.

Gabbay, Dov, and F. Guenthner, eds. *Handbook of Philosophical Logic.* 1st ed. 4 vols. Dordrecht and Boston: Reidel, 1983–1987. 2nd ed., much expanded, in progress. Dordrecht: Kluwer, 2000–.

Grattan-Guinness, Ivor. *The Search for Mathematical Roots, 1870–1940: Logics, Set Theories, and the Foundations of Mathematics from Cantor through Russell to Gödel.* Princeton: Princeton University Press, 2000.

Grattan-Guinness, Ivor, ed. *Companion Encyclopedia of the History and Philosophy of the Mathematical Sciences.* 2 vols. London: Routledge, 1994. Reprint, Baltimore: Johns Hopkins University Press, 2003. See especially Part 6.

Haack, Susan. *Philosophy of Logics.* Cambridge, U.K.: Cambridge University Press, 1978.

Jacquette, Dale, ed. *Philosophy of Mathematics: An Anthology.* Oxford and Malden, Mass.: Blackwell, 2002.

Kitcher, Philip. *The Nature of Mathematical Knowledge.* New York: Oxford University Press, 1983.

Kneale, William, and Martha Kneale. *The Development of Logic.* Oxford: Clarendon, 1962.

Krüger, Lorenz et al., eds. *The Probabilistic Revolution.* 2 vols. Cambridge, Mass.: MIT Press, 1987.

Priest, Graham. *Beyond the Limits of Thought.* Cambridge, U.K.: Cambridge University Press, 1995.

Shapiro, Stewart, ed. *The Limits of Logic.* Aldershot, U.K.: Dartmouth, 1996. Source book, mainly oriented around model theory and higher-order logics.

van Heijenoort, Jean, ed. *From Frege to Gödel: A Source Book in Mathematical Logic, 1879–1931.* Cambridge, Mass.: Harvard University Press, 1967.

*I. Grattan-Guinness*

## LOVE, WESTERN NOTIONS OF.

In the West, probably more has been written about love than any other topic except the nature of God. There is, however, no consensus on what the word *love* or *amor, agape, Liebe, eros,* or hundreds of other terms signifies. It is clear, however, that it is more than a simple animal urge to procreate. Harry Harlow, for example, demonstrated that mother love was essential to the normal development of infant monkeys, and that infants deprived of love and nurturance became disturbed, unhappy adults, unfit for monkey society. But love is much more than the feelings of a mother for a child, although mother love has usually been regarded as much more intense than that of a father. Among other things the term *love* has been used to describe the feelings of a child toward a parent, one's feelings for friends and comrades, a religious yearning for transcendence, an entirely materialistic desire for physical sexual gratification, and the list could go on.

### Love in Western History

One kind of love that might best be called romantic love has been the gift or curse to the world of Western culture. This is a phenomenon that at its simplest might be described as the practice of choosing one's mate based on personal preference, rather than societal obligations. Such a concept emerged in the Middle Ages, and the true lover as described by Andreas Capellanus in his twelfth century *De Amore* is continually and without interruption obsessed by the image of his beloved. Capellanus also wrote that love was an inborn suffering that proceeded from the sight of, and excessive thought on, the form of the opposite sex.

This was a different view of love than had existed previously in Western culture, although there are hints of it in earlier societies and cultures. In Judaism the closest approach to erotic love appears in the Song of Solomon:

I am my beloved's, and my beloved is mine. . . . (6:3)
Many waters cannot quench love, neither can the floods drown it. . . . (8:7)

Greek myths include scenes of passionate sexual attraction but for the most part, after the successful sexual liaison, the male god goes on to seek other candidates. The tale of Eurydice and Orpheus emphasizes, however, that love in the Greek world was far more complex than simple sexual conquest. The deeper meanings of love appear in discussion by the eighth-century B.C.E. Greek writer Hesiod, who held *eros* or love to be the essential creative urge that brought the universe into being. A somewhat different view is put forth in the fourth century B.C.E. by Plato, who has Socrates explain in the *Symposium* that the lover is attracted to his beloved because he sees reflected there the higher realm of eternal truth. Love in this case is the bridge between the mundane and the transcendental, the wellspring from whence all meaningful human values derive. In the same dialogue, Plato has Aristophanes explain that the search for a lover is driven by a search to find part of oneself. This is because people were originally androgynes who were split apart because of their rebellion against the Olympian gods. Thus finding one's love was no less than the recovery of an original unity of souls.

The object of this original form of Platonic love could be of the same or different sex, although Plato makes a clear distinction between the love of youths and the love of women, with the former being held much higher than the latter kind. In fact Greek literature from the poets to the playwrights was essentially misogynistic with much of the erotic literature male focused.

In Roman society, where women had a higher standing than in Greece, the general conclusion of the first century B.C.E. lyric poets Catullus, Tibullus, and Propertius was that love (and women) inevitably brought misery to man. Lucretius, a contemporary of the poets, agreed that love made one miserable, and his solution was to eradicate love. He admitted that while a particular mistress might be faultless, a man could still free himself from the pangs of love by reflecting that in her physical nature his love object was no different from all other women. Ovid, another contemporary, built up the charms of sexual love in his *Ars amoris* (*Art of Love*) but in its sequel, *Remedia Amoris,* he shows how to counteract the attractions of a mistress and solve the problems of love. Both the Romans and the Greeks tended to separate love from marriage.

While Christianity emphasized love, it was love of humanity or or god (*agape*), not eros or sexual love. Such a love appeared in the Song of Solomon, and it is a strong theme in early Christian literature (see Bynum, 1982) and later in the surviving letters and prayers of St. Catherine of Sienna (1347?–1380), who portrayed the crucified Jesus as the supreme sign and pledge of divine love and as motive for ours. As Christianity became institutionalized, sexuality, one of the base points of love in the Greek and Roman classics, was downplayed. It certainly was not necessarily involved in marriage, which was a pragmatic affair that united scions of two families and their possessions. As Caroline Walker Bynum notes in her *Holy Feast, Holy Fast,* medieval female saints before the twelfth century tended to be charity-giving queens who obediently married and used their influence and wealth to perform good deeds, often ending up in the cloisters. This began to change in the twelfth century with the development of what might be called romantic love, and it is this concept that came to dominate Western notions of love.

## Romantic Love

Scholars have spent a good deal of time and energy in trying to trace the source of romantic love to Islamic lyric poetry, to Greek Platonism, to Ovid, to heretical Christian Cathars—apparently all contributing factors—but extremely influential in the period was the rise of the female patron of literature and arts. Literature is molded by the type of audience it has. In much of the past the audience that counted most was male. It was the men who had the money to hire poets to sing their praises and to recount the epic stories of war as well as the successful conquests of females. When prose developed it was men who were usually literate since so many obstacles were put into the path of women who wanted to be educated. During the Middle Ages, when the most literate group was the clergy, women and love had very little place in their literature. Nonetheless, women could be patrons of literature and it was this patronage that some, including the present authors, believe was a major factor in the development of romantic love.

Sidney Painter speculated in the 1940s upon a scenario in which a hungry minstrel who was wandering about the duchy of Aquitaine came to a castle where he hoped that his tales of battles and his tumbling tricks would earn him a good dinner. The lord of the castle, however, was absent, and the lady who acted as his hostess found his endless stories of battles rather tiring and boring and his tumbling unattractive. It somehow occurred to the poet that his stay in the castle would not be very long nor would his meals be particularly enjoyable unless he managed to gain her attention. Being very inventive he composed a song in praise of the lady's beauty and virtue and described their effect on him in rather glowing terms. This pleased the lady, who rewarded him with a better bed and more ample food. He and others got the message.

On this scene came William IX (1071–1127), count of Poitou and duke of Aquitaine, who thought such romantic songs might prove a pleasant accompaniment to his numerous triumphs over feminine virtue. The duke's accounts of his amorous adventures proved as interesting to his friends as his stories of battle, and with the example of a powerful prince who ruled one-third of France to spur it on, the fashion grew and expanded. One of the great patrons of chivalric love literature was Eleanor of Aquitaine (1122–1204), the granddaughter and heir of the duke and later the queen of England. Her role of patroness was continued by her daughters, Marie, countess of Champagne, and Alix, countess of Blois, as well as other women. A few women contributed to the love literature on their own, as did Heloise in her love letters to Abelard in the twelfth century. Marie de France wrote more traditional chivalric love literature

in the late twelfth century, but she did not differ significantly from her male poets in their description. The love literature penned by Christine de Pizan (c. 1365–c. 1430), on the other hand, has led to her being described as an early feminist.

Romantic love was originally associated with knighthood and chivalry, and in poems and stories love was pictured as a despairing and tragic emotion that drove the lover to accomplish great deeds of daring to perform for his beloved as well as for the Christian God. In theory true love was unattainable love, that is, it was not to be consummated by sexual intercourse; in fact, the female object of the love was usually married to a man other than her beloved, and the theory reflected the real situation of the noble ladies who acted as patrons. Adultery probably occurred in some cases, but unattainable love was the dominant theme. The medieval romantic love espoused by the French poets spread and was profoundly embraced throughout Europe in a way that reached directly into daily life. The concept erected impassable barriers between us and the classical past or the Oriental present.

As the theme of romantic love developed, modifications in the ideal took place, and sexual intercourse and ultimately marriage became an integral and sometimes necessary part of the conception of love. How often either took place in the past is debatable. Clearly until recently romantic love remained separate from marriage. Marriage was a contractual obligation while love was entirely voluntary. True love might well become adulterous but it need not end up that way. Romantic love, however, became an ideal and it became a major theme of song, poetry, and literature of Western culture.

Protestantism with its emphasis on marriage and hostility to celibacy gave companionate marriage a theological stamp of approval. Henry Smith, an English Puritan preacher, wrote in his 1591 *Preparative to Marriage*: "the mate must be fit: it is not enough to be virtuous, but to be suitable . . . So shall the man be pleased which finds a wife according to his own heart, whether he be rich or poor . . . like a pair of glove, or a pair of hose are like; so man and wife should be like, because they are a pair of friends."

Catholicism, even though it placed renewed emphasis on abstinence and celibacy, never quite lost the idea of romantic love embedded in the literary tradition. Both Catholic and Protestant countries saw an increase of love literature, especially of references to romantic love in guides to proper manners and mores, magazines and newspapers, often accompanied by warnings to young women not to be persuaded into giving up their virtue to sweet-tongued suitors.

The eighteenth century saw the popularization of love with a steady increase of love literature in the New World and the Old. Even in an arranged marriage such as that in Oliver Goldsmith's 1773 play, *She Stoops to Conquer,* a parental choice in mates is sold to the daughter, Kate Hardcastle, in romantic terms. By the nineteenth century in England and America, romantic writers, according to Peter Gay, saw it as their historic mission to re-enchant the world with love. Love was not only a reinvigoration of ancient and medieval traditions but the triumph of impulse over pragmatism. The Romantics, such as Percy Bysshe

Shelley (1792–1822) and Lord Byron (1788–1824), lived as they wrote. By reunifying physical and spiritual love, they believed they established a harmony between the body and mind.

As arranged marriages declined, and the ability of individuals able to make their own decisions concerning a marriage partner increased, romantic love was increasingly seen as the basis for marriage. The work of English novelists such as John Galsworthy (1867–1933) and the real-life experience of George Eliot (Mary Ann Evans; 1819–1880) demonstrated that despite romantic love's strong pull, reality often intervened. Still, the ideal persisted. With the twentieth century, and the world of new inventions and institutions such as the automobile, motion pictures, and public coeducational high schools, romantic love received renewed vigor. If Clara Bow could go from being a Brooklyn waif to a Hollywood starlet, and if she could play a department store clerk who marries a millionaire in the movies, then young women everywhere wanted to emulate her. Romantic love had crossed all class barriers.

Inhibiting full-blown romantic love, however, were always the consequences, namely the fear of pregnancy. With the development of the birth control pill and the widespread dissemination of contraceptive information, romantic passion could be verified or rejected by sexual experience with few qualms. Was romantic love different from simple sexual impulse? After centuries of literary and philosophical explanations, love became a major research field for the emerging social sciences.

## "Scientific" Analysis of Love

In a sense Sigmund Freud (1856–1939) had begun this investigation. He had challenged the Christian-philosophical ideal of transcendental, universal love. For him, the urge to love came from the self, born out of base instinct. Freud's id was, in many ways, a revival of the Greek idea of love as an unreasoning furor. While his ideas were soon challenged, Freud was important for placing love more or less on the dissecting table, a subject for research and discussion. Others such as Havelock Ellis had joined the efforts to reexamine love and sex. Psychologists entered the field in the 1960s through efforts to distinguish different types of love. Elaine Hatfield, one of the pioneers, argued that people themselves distinguished several types of love and might do so at different times in their life cycle. Passion, she said, is pleasurable but the strong emotion involved creates the potential for relationship instability. Lovers want stability and often desire friendship as well as passion. Romantic love in effect remained complicated by reality.

Another psychologist, R. J. Sternberg, put forth a triangular theory of love involving intimacy, passion, and commitment, but also recognized that this did not describe all cases and that a sudden burst of passion and commitment could appear at a first meeting. Others, such as John Bowlby, developed an elaborate theory of human infant attachment as the precursor of and foundation for human love.

Not surprisingly, some researchers have found that men and women differ somewhat in their descriptions of love. They note a tendency for men to describe themselves as more involved in game-playing while women describe themselves as more friendship-oriented, practical, yet dependent. Men idealize an altruistic love more than women do, while women are more realistic. Both, however, emphasize the importance of passionate love. This phenomenon is no longer, if it ever was, confined to the Western world. According to W. R. Jankowiak and others, romantic love is everywhere.

The actual physiology of love has also been investigated. Intense love physiologically has been found to be distinct from sexual arousal, something that was often assumed in the past but is now demonstrated. Love, it now seems, evolved in tandem with two other primary neural systems: the sex drive and adult male-female attachment. The sex drive, according to this theory, evolved to motivate individuals to seek sexual union with appropriate mating partners, while the romantic attraction evolved to enable individuals to prefer and pursue a specific partner, whether male or female, since the same reaction is noted in homosexual and heterosexual individuals. In fact, as the literature of the past is reprinted without the censorship of earlier generations, homosexual love has come to play a significant role in the romantic literature of love as well. Lillian Faderman's 1981 study *Surpassing the Love of Men* broadly traces the literary history of romantic friendship and love between women from the Renaissance to the present. As the debate over gay and lesbian marriages in the first decade of the twentieth century would indicate, homosexual and heterosexual love are driven by the same forces.

Though love in popular fiction and accounts seem to belong to the young, love spans all of human life. Most studies have shown that friendship and passionate love are positive predictors of marital satisfaction across the life span. Love, in fact, has come to be regarded by most researchers as fundamentally important to humanity. It has a strong biological basis that is undoubtedly influenced by cultural developments. Love, it seems, is in a sense what makes the world go round.

*See also* **Emotions; Friendship; Marriage and Fertility, European Views; Sexuality.**

**BIBLIOGRAPHY**

Bowlby, John. *Attachment and Loss.* Vol. 1. New York: Basic Books, 1969.

Bullough, Vern L., and Bonnie Bullough. *The Subordinate Sex.* Champagne: University of Illinois Press, 1973.

Bynum, Carolyn Walker. *Holy Feast and Holy Fast: The Religious Significance of Food to Medieval Women.* Berkeley: University of California Press, 1987.

———. *Jesus as Mother: Studies in the Spirituality of the High Middle Ages.* Berkeley: University of California Press, 1982.

Capellanus, Andreas. *The Art of Courtly Love,* translated and edited by John Jay Parry. New York: Columbia University Press, 1941.

De Rougement, Denis. *Love in the Western World,* translated by Montgomery Belgion. New York: Harcourt Brace, 1940.

Faderman, Lillian. *Surpassing the Love of Men.* New York: Morrow, 1981.

Gay, Peter. *The Naked Heart.* New York: Norton, 1995.

———. *The Tender Passion.* New York: Oxford University Press, 1986.

Harlow, Harry F. *Learning to Love.* New York: Jason Aronson, 1974.

Hatfield, Elaine. "Passionate and Companionate Love." In *Psychology of Love,* edited by Robert J. Sternberg and Michael L. Barnes. New Haven: Yale University Press, 1988.

Hatfield, Elaine, and Richard L. Rapson. *Love and Sex: Cross Cultural Perspectives.* Boston: Allyn and Bacon, 1996.

Hopkins, Andrea. *The Book of Courtly Love: The Passionate Code of the Troubadours.* San Francisco: Harper, 1994.

Jankowiak, William, ed. *Romantic Passion: A Universal Experience?* New York: Columbia University Press, 1995.

Jankowiak, W. R., and E. F. Fischer. "A Cross-Cultural Perspective on Romantic Love." *Ethnology* 31 (1992): 149–155.

Lewis, C. S. *The Allegory of Love: A Study in Medieval Tradition.* New York: Oxford University Press, 1958.

Lucretius. *De Rerum Natura,* edited and translated by W. H. D. Rouse. London: Heinemann, 1924.

Montgomery, Marilyn, and G. T. Sorell. "Differences in Love Attitudes Across Family Life States." *Family Relationships* 46 (1997): 55–63.

Murstein, Bernard L. *Love, Sex and Marriage through the Ages.* New York: Springer 1974.

Ovid. *Ars Amoris,* edited and translated by J. H. Mogley. London: Heinemann, 1962.

Painter, Sidney. *French Chivalry.* Baltimore: Johns Hopkins Press, 1947.

Sternberg, R. J. "A Triangular Theory of Love." *Psychological Review* 93 (1986): 119–135.

*Vern L. Bullough*
*Kenneth Mondschein*

# LOYALTIES, DUAL.

Loyalty is devotion to a cause and is marked by faithfulness, a sense of just purpose, and a willingness to serve in spite of any suffering that may result from service. Dual loyalty involves simultaneous obligations, express or implied, to two parties, with the second party typically constituting a state. Multiple loyalties can threaten the security and survival of a state. Nationality may affect political allegiance by prompting immigrants to place the interests of their country of origin over the welfare of their adopted home. Religion may influence loyalty when those people holding minority religious views feel a loyalty to their faith that is greater than the duty owed to their country. Soldiers fight and citizens pay taxes out of loyalty, a fact that has led many states to link dual loyalties with treason.

## Ancient World
The question of loyalty is an age-old one. In ancient Greece, Socrates (c. 470–399 B.C.E.) remained loyal to the laws of the state even though they were unjust and resulted in his death. Plato (c. 428–348 or 347 B.C.E.), identifying internal political conflict as a far stronger test of loyalty than a foreign war, demanded the death penalty for any citizen who turned against the gods or the state. Aristotle (384–322 B.C.E.) argued that loyalty based upon usefulness or pleasure, such as that accorded a tyrant or corrupt politician, disappeared as soon as the motives vanished. None of these ancient philosophers addressed the question of dual allegiance except in the form of conflict between loyalty to the state and loyalty to family members or friends.

As long as the people of a state shared the same religion, loyalty involved allegiance to rulers or forms of government. The rise of Christianity threatened this type of loyalty by presenting a strong competing claim for allegiance. In the Bible, early Christians are recorded as asking Jesus Christ for guidance on dual loyalties. They were advised that no compromise was possible where spiritual matters were involved. Duty to God involved obedience to all of the commandments with any act of disloyalty categorized as sinful.

## The Christian Era
After the ascendancy of Christianity to a position of worldly power, the issue of loyalty to God became entangled with the problems of loyalty to the church as an institution with influence in the world. The theologian Saint Augustine (354–430) believed that the church should be the supreme ruler of all Christian nations. Underpinning Saint Augustine's idea of the unity of Christendom was the notion that secular kings owed loyalty to the pope, the earthly leader of Christianity. This idea of rule by the church did not appeal to the secular world, and history records a divergence of views about the proper role of the church. Saint Thomas Aquinas (1225–1274), the most prominent of the dissenters, made a sharp distinction between a person's loyalty to God and to an earthly superior by declaring a right to resist tyranny.

The Renaissance and Reformation witnessed the emergence of dual loyalties as the hold of the Catholic Church weakened and power concentrated in the hands of European monarchs. The Italian political theorist Niccolò Machiavelli (1469–1527) did not rely upon religion to justify loyalty but instead advised rulers to use cruelty to keep subjects united and faithful. The first loyalty tests grew out of the development of a new religious-political system during this time. When in the 1530s Henry VIII split with the Catholic Church and elevated Protestantism in England, he needed to identify and intimidate his opponents to maintain power. Loyalty tests weakened domestic enemies by forcing them to publicly declare allegiance to the English monarchy. As late as the seventeenth century, they would be required of Catholics settling on English land in the New World.

## Enlightenment and Revolution
The idea that the divine right of kings mandated loyalty began to die in the seventeenth century. Thomas Hobbes (1588–1679) tied loyalty to passion and self-interest by arguing that the power of a state derived from fear of disorder. He saw no personal loyalty to a monarch, only allegiance to the person providing peace and security. John Locke (1632–1704), perhaps the most widely read political philosopher of the eighteenth century, built upon Hobbes's idea of a contract. Locke stated that the right to govern derived from the consent of the governed. People gave loyalty to a government that governed justly, protected property, and ensured certain liberties. If a government violated the natural rights of the individual, it reneged on its contract and forfeited the loyalty of its subjects.

In proclaiming the Declaration of Independence in 1776, the founding fathers of the United States relied upon the ideas of Locke. The British government had violated its contract with the American people, thereby forfeiting any right to allegiance. The American stance on loyalty would be duplicated throughout the world as newly liberated peoples used the Declaration as a model for their own definitions of loyalty. Allegiance would be not to a king or a section of land but to the purpose of protecting citizens against the exercise of abusive power by government officials.

Various political regimes, such as that of Henry VII (r. 1485–1509) and the new American state, have demanded tests for allegiance, typically during wartime. Whenever a political culture or institution is firmly established and feels no threat to itself from any quarter, the question of loyalty is pushed to the background. All kinds of doctrines that are hostile to the culture may be tolerated. However, if the culture feels its existence is threatened, there may be vigorous attempts to gain complete political conformity. Requirements and loyalty tests are instituted.

Loyalty played a primary role in structuring the American Revolution in the form of tests that became widespread throughout the many years of political upheaval. With the population evenly divided between supporters of the king, supporters of liberty, and those committed to neutrality, a means had to be devised to create unity. These loyalty tests, often just a public voicing of support for the revolutionaries, helped spur the creation of an American patriotism and accelerated the development of a decade of discontent by placing Americans in increasingly extreme stances regarding allegiance to the British crown. Such positioning finally made independence inevitable by creating an American identity. Both John Adams (1735–1826) and George Washington (1732–1799) viewed such statements of faithfulness as the cornerstone of discipline for troops and the source of national spirit for civilians.

## Modern Era

Dual loyalty has formed a political threat in the modern era because difference is only acceptable between national identities and not within them. The modern state sought to instill political loyalties in order to maintain territorial concentrations of power. In doing so, it came into competition with communal centers of loyalty. These ethnic, religious, and regional ties resisted the state's declaration of power and rights as seen among the Aborigines of Australia, the Jews of the diaspora, and the Kurds of southwest Asia. Such expressions of dual loyalty threatened national unity by presenting the image of a divided community.

While many political regimes retain a fear of multiculturalism and attack dual loyalty, this concept of allegiance is becoming superseded by the idea of shared loyalties. The twentieth-century transportation and communication revolutions enabled immigrants to maintain close ties with their countries of origin and maintain multiple cultural identities. The many countries granting dual citizenship recognize the shared loyalties of these immigrants. The challenge for governments is to be able to distinguish between those immigrants who are benign and those who pose a security threat.

*See also* **Americanization, U.S.; Assimilation; Identity, Multiple; State, The.**

BIBLIOGRAPHY

Cecil, Andrew R. *Equality, Tolerance, and Loyalty: Virtues Serving the Common Purpose of Democracy.* Dallas: University of Texas, 1990.

Hyman, Harold M. *To Try Men's Souls: Loyalty Tests in American History.* Berkeley: University of California Press, 1959.

Shain, Yossi. *The Frontier of Loyalty: Political Exiles in the Age of the Nation-State.* Middletown, Conn.: Wesleyan University Press, 1989.

Waller, Michael, and Andrew Linklater, eds. *Political Loyalty and the Nation-State.* London: Routledge, 2003.

Yuh, Ji-Yeon. *Beyond the Shadow of Camptown: Korean Military Brides in America.* New York: New York University Press, 2002.

*Caryn E. Neumann*

**LYSENKOISM.** *Lysenkoism* is a censorious name for a movement that demands either censure or faith in *agrobiology,* as Soviet agronomist Trofim Denisovich Lysenko (1898–1976) called his aggressive creation. He also named it *Michurinism,* in tribute to the plant breeder Ivan V. Michurin, who won fame with claims of improving fruit while scorning genetics. *Obscurantist* (*mrakobes*), the word a geneticist flung at Lysenko in 1935, recurs even when scholars bend over backward to avoid censure. Lysenkoism defies efforts to disentangle claims of scientific knowledge from assertions of practical authority and from the use of state power to achieve progress.

## The Rise of Lysenkoism

The movement emerged as Joseph Stalin's "revolution from above" (1928–1932) forced peasants into collective farms, where the dream of a leap to scientific agriculture suffered practical failure. Lysenko saved the dream with a string of recipes for quick solutions of long-standing problems. He was a poorly trained agronomist with great talent for snap judgments, grand claims, and celebrity. "Vernalization," his breakthrough to fame, began as a scheme to moisten and chill seeds for protection against drought and freezing, with tests on a few plots, crude theorizing about stages in plant development and about heredity, testimonials by some agricultural officials, a rush to mass use on collective farms, journalistic hype—and telltale silence on long-term results. Yet the movement thrived until the 1950s.

Farm bosses quietly discarded Lysenko's recipes, but he had new ones, with crude theorizing pitted against standard science to justify mass campaigns for rapid triumphs that could not otherwise be won. Lysenko argued that the Soviet Union could not afford to lose time conducting preliminary small-scale testing, but had to keep moving forward, applying theories to the masses while still working out the methods in the laboratory. His view of theory and practice fit in with Stalin's "great break," a leap from reasoned arguments over planning to furious drives toward blue-sky goals, most famously summed up in Stalin's 1931 speech to business managers: "We are fifty or a hundred years behind the advanced countries. We must race through that distance in ten years. Either we do it, or they will crush us." In 1941 Nazi armies that had subdued Western Europe struck the Soviet Union, winning a victory that proved the wisdom of berserk modernization. Pragmatists who would dispute that logic must confront tyrannical pragmatism in a context of backwardness: willful drive combined with brush-off or jail (or death) for specialists offering reasoned warning. That is how farming by fiat gained the reassurance of science in Lysenkoism, until long-term self-defeat grew obvious to political bosses, who rehabilitated standard science and its specialists, posthumously in some cases.

By 1939 Lysenkoists ruled many institutes of biological science; universal rule was decreed in 1948, at a highly publicized conference where Lysenko announced that the Communist Party's Central Committee endorsed his speech. Stalin himself had edited the speech, but Lysenko was not allowed to boast of that. Long after, when the system fell apart and archives opened, a historian found Lysenko's draft with red lines and marginal notes by Stalin. Stalin deleted, with sarcasm, a claim that science, like ideology, is divided into bourgeois and proletarian camps. In 1950 he published that rule: science is *not* divided by class conflict. He ignored his own much-publicized urging of practical men to tolerate no caution from specialists, to "smash" what is "old and dying in science." Such zigzags between willfulness and restraint are blips on a Communist trajectory through faith in swift modernization and social justice to frustration and apostasy.

## Criticism
The highest leaders started to back away from Lysenkoism in the 1950s, when a recipe for tree planting failed Stalin's "Great Plan for the Transformation of Nature." Saplings in clusters did not thin themselves for the greater good of shelter belts, as Lysenko's "Soviet Darwinism" had predicted. Massive die-off occurred, a practical fiasco that was only hinted at in public, lest faith in authority be shaken. But biologists were allowed to revive their dispute with Lysenko's denial of competition within species. They could even hope for larger freedom implied by Stalin's startling decree of separation between science and ideology.

Stalin published that criticism of his own system in 1950, challenging specialists to make tests of free thought within their fields, though power remained centralized and violent. The hazards of such boldness within a despotic system kept most specialists quiet and still hinder historians' recognition that Communist bosses learned by bossing, with enormous waste and cruelty. Stalin's efforts to avert self-defeat by calling for criticism from below foreshadowed greater efforts of that sort by his successor, Nikita Khrushchev, and eventually by Mikhail Gorbachev, who pushed criticism of the old system to the limit in the 1980s. The death of Stalin in 1953 set his lieutenants into retreat from mass terror and worship of a "chief" (*vozhd'*) as methods of rule and into easing of thought control, with growing confusion over such willful practicality as Lysenko boasted of. Khrushchev helped revive genetics, ordered farm specialists to tell him when he was wrong, and scolded those who criticized his campaign for planting maize all over the country. He had grown it at his dacha. He also rebuked ministers of agriculture for ignoring Lysenko's final recipes: training cows to increase butterfat and composting earth with fertilizer before spreading. "Harebrained scheming" was the laconic explanation that the Central Committee gave out in 1964 for the abrupt dismissal of Khrushchev. Genetics was

fully reestablished in research and education, but an exposé of its repression was stifled. A meeting of experts demolished Lysenko's butter and earth schemes, ignoring his angry reminders of past testimonials by practical bosses. He was retired to one farm. Without power, his movement melted away.

## Lysenkoism and Human Evolution
Issues of human heredity entered the furor over Lysenkoism in the late 1930s, when the ideological bureaucracy condemned any interest in the topic as racism, if not Nazism. Even medical genetics fell under the ban until the 1960s, when the field revived in defiance of Lysenko's dismissal of genes. The closest Lysenko himself ever came to issues of human heredity was to brush aside the whole topic: "Man, thanks to his mind, ceased long ago to be an animal." That statement was a caricature of the rule that the emergence of Homo sapiens marks a transition from biological to sociocultural evolution. Major issues in biology and historical sociology are entangled in that rule, as Soviet Marxists discovered in the 1920s. In the 1930s ideological bureaucrats stifled further thought about human evolution and about ideas of progress; lifeless scholasticism served a faith that was withering away.

In any case the common tendency of Marxists, East and West, has been to separate social from biological evolution. The human breed is declared equally gifted in all its races and classes, which need only a suitable environment to show the common potential. A contrary faith ascribes social ranking to inherited experience of rule and submission. But an upperclass master-race bias can also make use of arguments denying that acquired characters are inherited; one need only assume that genes determine place in the social hierarchy. Any way one turns it, ideology shapes beliefs and reasoning about winners and losers.

Genetics actually supports apologists of no nation, race, or class. Precise science favors a vague egalitarianism: individual differences in hereditary capacities are far greater than average group differences may prove to be. Lysenkoism had nothing to say on such issues; it simply ignored them. But ideas of progress drove its claim of practicality, its support by Soviet men of power, and their disillusion and return to faith in world science as worked out by autonomous specialists. The presumptive utility of such science, a major reason for its flourishing, involves a dogma of universality, a belief that claims of knowledge which win out in developed contexts are practically useful everywhere. That dogma is weakly challenged by talk of "ethnoscience" or "indigenous knowledge" as anthropologists try to be respectful in studying, say, rain dancing and belief in its influence on weather. The challenge by Lysenkoism was strong, for proponents seized on its boast of superseding the science of advanced countries.

*See also* **Biology; Eugenics; Evolution; Genetics; Science, History of; Social Darwinism; Totalitarianism.**

**BIBLIOGRAPHY**
Hudson, P. S., and R. H. Richens. *The New Genetics in the Soviet Union.* Cambridge, U.K.: English School of Agriculture, 1946.

Joravsky, David. *The Lysenko Affair.* Cambridge, Mass.: Harvard University Press, 1970.

Lysenko, Trofim D. *Agrobiology.* Moscow: Foreign Language Publishing House, 1954.

Medvedev, Zhores A. *The Rise and Fall of T. D. Lysenko.* Translated by I. Michael Lerner. New York: Columbia University Press, 1969.

Rossiianov, Kirill O. "Editing Nature: Joseph Stalin and the 'New' Soviet Biology." *Isis* 84 (1993): 728–745.

Soyfer, Valery N. *Lysenko and the Tragedy of Soviet Science.* Translated by Leo Gruliow and Rebecca Gruliow. New Brunswick, N.J.: Rutgers University Press, 1994.

Steele, Edward J., Robyn A. Lindley, and Robert V. Blanden. *Lamarck's Signature: How Retrogenes Are Changing Darwin's Natural Selection Paradigm.* Reading, Mass.: Perseus, 1998.

*David Joravsky*

GERMANNA COMM COLLEGE LOCUST GROVE VA

3 7218 000 174 875

Ref
CB
9
.N4
200
v.3

# For Reference

**Not to be taken from this room**

**GERMANNA COMMUNITY COLLEGE**
GERMANNA CENTER FOR ADVANCED TECHNOLOGY
18121 TECHNOLOGY DRIVE
CULPEPER, VA 22701